Sources of Chinese Tradition

SECOND EDITION

VOLUME I

INTRODUCTION TO ASIAN CIVILIZATIONS

Introduction to Asian Civilizations

WM. THEODORE DE BARY, GENERAL EDITOR

Sources of Japanese Tradition
(1958)

Sources of Chinese Tradition
(1960, rev. 1999)

Sources of Indian Tradition
(1958, rev. 1988)

Sources of Korean Tradition
(1997)

Sources of Chinese Tradition

SECOND EDITION

VOLUME I

FROM EARLIEST TIMES TO 1600

Compiled by Wm. Theodore de Bary and Irene Bloom

WITH THE COLLABORATION OF
Wing-tsit Chan, Ron Guey Chu, John Dardess, Edward Farmer, Leon Hurvitz,
David N. Keightley, Richard John Lynn, David S. Nivison, Sarah Queen,
Harold Roth, Conrad Schirokauer, Nathan Sivin, Daniel Stevenson,
Franciscus Verellen, Burton Watson, Philip B. Yampolsky, Chün-fang Yü

and contributions by
Joseph Adler, Martin Amster, Carl Bielefeldt, Anne Birdwhistell, Bettine Birge,
Hok-lam Chan, Julia Ching, T'ung-tsu Ch'ü, Albert Dien, Patricia B. Ebrey,
T. Griffith Foulk, J. Mason Gentzler, Marie Guarino, Charles Hartman,
Robert Hymes, Wallace Johnson, Theresa Kelleher, Daniel W. Y. Kwok,
Thomas H. C. Lee, Liu Shu-hsien, John T. Meskill, Charles D. Orzech,
Stephen Owen, Kristofer Schipper, Joanna Handlin Smith, Kidder Smith,
George Tanabe, Hoyt Tillman, Tsai Heng-ting, and Tu Weiming

COLUMBIA UNIVERSITY PRESS

NEW YORK

Columbia University Press
Publishers Since 1893
New York   Chichester, West Sussex

Library of Congress Cataloging-in-Publication Data
de Bary, William Theodore, 1919–
    Sources of Chinese tradition : from earliest times to 1600, vol. 1 / compiled by
Wm. Theodore de Bary and Irene Bloom ; with the collaboration of
Wing-tsit Chan . . . [et al.]. — 2d ed.
      p.   cm. — (Introduction to Asian civilizations)
    Includes bibliographical references and index.
    ISBN 0–231–10938–5 (cloth) — 0–231–10939–3 (pbk.)
     1. China — Civilization — Sources.   I. Bloom, Irene.   II. Chan, Wing-tsit,
1901–1994.   III. Title.   IV. Series.
DS721.D37   1999
951 — dc21   98–21762
♾

To Harry James Carman,
dean of Columbia College, 1943–1950,
who foresaw the need to include Asia in the core curriculum
and helped to initiate this series of *Sources*

and to Millicent Carey McIntosh,
dean of Barnard College, 1947–1952,
president, 1952–1962,
who helped in the coordination of these efforts at Barnard

CONTENTS

6. The Evolution of the Confucian Tradition in Antiquity 112

7. Legalists and Militarists 190

EXPLANATORY NOTE

The sources of translations given at the end of each selection are rendered as concisely as possible; full bibliographical data can be obtained from the list of sources at the end of the book. Unless otherwise indicated, the author of the text is the writer whose name precedes the selection; the initials following each selection are those of the translator, as indicated in the table of contents. Excerpts that have been taken from existing translations have sometimes been adapted or edited in the interests of uniformity with the book as a whole.

In translating Chinese terms it is rarely possible to find an exact or full equivalent in Western languages. In view of this difficulty, some scholars consider the path of strict virtue to lie in reproducing the romanized form of the word rather than some mere approximation of it. This may do for those already familiar with the original language but not for readers who have difficulty coping with many foreign names and terms all at once, especially if they are encountering for the first time several Asian traditions in succession and several different (and often confusing) romanization systems. Consequently, we have felt obliged to give a rendering in English wherever possible, and some explanation where it is not possible. Although this policy may not satisfy the purist (for whom only a reading of the text in the original would really suffice), it does face, directly if not perfectly, what these terms can mean in another language instead of leaving the meaning altogether obscure behind the veil of romanization.

Given the need to translate, we have tried to be consistent, but often it is not possible to provide a single rendering of terms so broad in meaning as to function in different senses in different contexts. Therefore, at the point of first appearance we insert the romanized Chinese word in parentheses following the translation, and if another rendering has to be given later for the same word in Chinese, we insert the romanized form again. At the end of the book is a glossary of key terms listed in romanized Chinese (*pinyin* and Wade-Giles), with alternate renderings in English; from this the reader can approximate the range of meanings that cluster around such pivotal terms.

Chinese words and names are rendered according to the *pinyin* system of romanization. For readers unfamiliar with *pinyin*, it is useful to know that the consonants *q* and *x* are to be read as *ch* and *hs*, respectively. The Wade-Giles romanization is also given for names and terms already well known in that form, as are the renderings preferred by important modern figures and in common use (such as Sun Yatsen). A comparative table of *pinyin* and Wade-Giles romanizations may be found at the end of the book. Indic words appearing in the chapters on Buddhism as technical terms or titles in italics follow the standard systems of transliteration.

Chinese names are rendered in their Chinese order, with the family name first and the personal name last. Chinese names are romanized in the *pinyin* system, except for persons known to have preferred Wade-Giles or an alternative spelling, in which case that preference is honored both in the text and in the bibliography. Dates given after personal names are those of birth and death; in the case of rulers, their reign dates are preceded by "r." An approximation of the active lifespan of persons whose exact dates of birth and death are not known is indicated by "fl." (*floruit*).Generally the name by which a person was most commonly known in Chinese tradition is the one used in the text. Since this book is intended for the general reader rather than the specialist, we have not burdened the text with a list of the alternate names or titles that usually accompany biographical reference to a scholar in Chinese or Japanese historical works.

PREFACE

When this book was first compiled in the 1950s, its aim, and that of the accompanying volumes on other Asian civilizations, was to provide a counterpart to the source readings used in the Columbia College course "Contemporary Civilization in the West." As such, it was to be centrally concerned with the problems of civilized life — not those of the whole of human culture by any means, but that of how civilization could be sustained in the twentieth century. *Civilization* in that case referred primarily to human society in urban settings, conducting its affairs through literate, civil discourse. In this volume, too, we have attempted to reproduce something of that continuing discourse in China, as nearly as possible in its own terms. *Chinese tradition* in this sense, as open, articulate discourse (and not simply as unspoken custom), has survived all the attempts in revolutionary China to eradicate it, and instead of being swept into the dustbin of history or confined to the museum, it is showing signs of new life.

The initial focus of the parent Western course, inaugurated in the aftermath of World War I, was on war and peace issues — pressing contemporary problems the roots of which were seen to lie deep in Western history and thought. These issues could best be addressed, it was thought, and personally engaged by students, through examination of original documents revealing the practical choices and value judgments made at key turning points in the development of Western civilization. Similar considerations have guided our selection of source readings for the study of Asian civilizations.

A different approach was taken in Columbia's core courses in the humanities, which dealt with products of literature and the arts — with classic works that, though products of given social and cultural settings, spoke directly to the human imagination in terms not limited to the circumstances of their creation. To serve this latter purpose, single whole works have been translated in the series "Translations from the Asian Classics." Here, although some selections are included from the same works and there is thus a degree of overlap between the two series, the excerpts chosen relate more directly to society, civility, and practical affairs (especially education) than to philosophy, religion, literature, and aesthetics as such.

For this second edition there has been a considerable expansion to include important documents dealing with historical issues, while some of the more theoretical and doctrinal texts have been abridged. A second principal change has been to conclude volume 1 at the end of the Ming (1644) and start volume 2 in the mid-seventeenth century. The breaking point between "traditional" and "modern" is arbitrary in any case, since so many features of modern states appear early in Chinese history and persist into the present, but we have felt it of some advantage to begin volume 2 with the retrospective, critical assessment by seventeenth-century Chinese writers themselves of the key elements in traditional civilization — both values to be preserved and weaknesses to be remedied — rather than leaving this judgment to be made solely in relation to the highly conflicted encounter with the West.

Since the original edition of *Sources of Chinese Tradition* was prepared in the 1950s, more than forty years ago, many aspects of Chinese studies have undergone substantial development, and even though we have had to be most selective in adapting new researches to the needs of introductory courses, we have tried to draw on new studies wherever possible. Hence the list of contributors has expanded greatly, and the principal compilers have become indebted to many distinguished colleagues for their cooperation in this project. In the table of contents, the names of contributors are given with the sections for which they have been mainly responsible, and at the end of each translated excerpt, the initials of the translator are given along with the source citation. The compilers, however, take responsibility for the contents as presented here.

The original volumes took almost ten years to complete; that the present ones have taken a little less time, despite the extensive revision undertaken, is attributable to the help of many collaborators, among whom we are especially grateful to Ron Guey Chu, David N. Keightley, Thomas H. C. Lee, Conrad Schirokauer, Nathan Sivin, and the late Philip B. Yampolsky for guidance and help going well beyond their individual contributions to this volume. Martin Amster provided invaluable research support that could have been offered only by someone highly knowledgeable in Chinese history, deeply devoted to the project, and impressively grounded in Chinese sources and reference materials. Marianna Stiles coordinated the production of the typescript, carrying out innumerable tasks, demonstrating remarkable technical skill, and displaying an energy, grace, humor, and dedication that were truly sustaining. Aihe Wang and Moss Roberts were exceptionally generous in responding to requests for expert advice in their respective fields. David Branner brought to the project a finely honed linguistic expertise and a deep scholarly and personal understanding of Chinese culture; his careful scrutiny of the volume in its final stages of preparation was invaluable. We wish also to thank our colleagues and coworkers Arthur Tiedemann, Pei-yi Wu, and Miwa Kai for help of diverse kinds and to express our warm appreciation to Jennifer Crewe, publisher for the humanities at Columbia University Press, for her sustained interest in and informed support of this project. Anne McCoy, Jan McInroy, and Leslie Kriesel provided meticulous and thoughtful editorial assistance. Linda Secondari was patient and accommodating as well as highly gifted in her handling of the book's design. Our sincere thanks to all of them. We are most grateful as well for the help of the National Endowment for the Humanities and the Chiang Ching-kuo Foundation, both of which have made major contributions to the development of Chinese studies; their support for this undertaking was instrumental to the completion of the present work.

The Chinese Tradition in Antiquity

Prehistory and Early History
(Pre–Zhou dates and entries are traditional; modern dating in parentheses)

B.C.E.	Dynasty	
2852		Fu Xi, inventor of writing, nets and snares, hunting and fishing
2737	Culture heroes	Shen Nong, inventor of agriculture, commerce
2697		Yellow Emperor
2357	Sage kings	Yao Shun Yu, virtuous founder of dynasty
1818	Hsia	Jie, degenerate terminator of dynasty
1766	Shang or Yin	King Tang, virtuous founder of dynasty
[c. 1300]		[Beginning of archaeological evidence]
1154		Zhou, degenerate terminator of dynasty
Three Dynasties	Zhou	King Wen, virtuous founder of dynasty
1122 (1045/1040?)		King Wu, virtuous founder of dynasty King Cheng, virtuous founder of dynasty
	Western Zhou	
771		
	Eastern Zhou	
722–479		Spring and Autumn period
551–479		Confucius
479–221		Warring States period (479–221)
6th to 3d centuries		Period of the "hundred schools" of thought: Confucius, Mozi, Mencius, Laozi (?), Zhuangzi, Terminologists, Shang Yang, Xunzi, Sunzi, Han Fei
4th to 3d centuries		Extensive wall–building and waterworks by Qin and other states
249		Lü Buwei, prime minister of Qin
221–207	Qin	The First Emperor; Li Si, prime minister
214		The Great Wall "completed"

PART 2

The Making of a Classical Culture

B.C.E.

221–207	Qin dynasty
202–9 C.E.	Former Han dynasty
202–195	Reign of Han Gaozu
170	Lu Jia (?–170), advisor to Han Gaozu
188–180	Reign of Empress Lü
180–157	Reign of Emperor Wen
201–168?	Jia Yi, poet, essayist, and advisor to Emperor Wen
178	Memorial on encouragement of agriculture by Chao Cuo
141–87	Reign of Emperor Wu
136	Doctors for the Five Classics appointed
124	Increased use of examinations in recruitment of officials
122	Death of Liu An, patron of compilers of *Huainanzi*
c. 120	Employment of Legalist–minded officials to manage fiscal operations of the state. State monopoly of production of iron and salt; debased coinage and commercial taxes; expansion of empire
115	Campaigns into western regions
195?–105?	Dong Zhongshu, leading Confucian philosopher and advisor to Emperor Wu
108	Chinese administration in north Korea
101	Conquest of states of Tarim basin
145?–86?	Sima Qian, author of *Records of the Grand Historian*
81	Debates on Salt and Iron

C.E.

1	Wang Mang regent
9–23	Xin dynasty, established by usurper Wang Mang
25–220	Latter Han dynasty
32–92	Ban Gu, principal compiler of the *History of the Former Han*
79	Collation of the Five Classics by Confucians in White Tiger Hall
105	Invention of paper recorded
175	The Five Classics and the *Analects* engraved in stone
182	Yellow Turban uprising
220	Han emperor deposed

PART 3

Later Daoism and Mahāyāna Buddhism in China

814	Baizhang Huaihai (720–824), reputed author of first Chan monastic rules
845	Official repression of Buddhism
867	Linji Yixuan (d. 867), founder of Linji school of Chan Buddhism
869	Dongshan Liangjie (807–869), founder of Caodong sect of Chan Buddhism
901	Caoshan Benji (840–901), follower of Liangjie in the Caodong tradition
907–960	Five Dynasties period: disunion after fall of Tang
933	Du Guangting (850–933), scholar and court Daoist
960–1279	Song dynasty
972	Printing of Buddhist canon begun
1063–1135	Yuanwu Keqin, Chan master whose lectures are collected in the *Blue Cliff Records (Biyanlu)* of 1128.
1112–1170	Wang Zhe, founder of the Quanzhen tradition of Daoism

PART 4

The Confucian Revival and Neo-Confucianism

1567	Chen Jian (1497–1567), scholar and historian, critic of Wang Yangming school
1583	Wang Ji (1498–1583); follower of Wang Yangming; believed human mind to be beyond good and evil; faith in innate knowledge
1602	Matteo Ricci established in Peking
1602	Li Zhi (1527–1602); individualism, subjectivism, non-conformism
1604	Neo–orthodox Donglin Academy founded, Gu Xiancheng (1550–1612) principal founder; criticism of corruption at Ming court
1618	Lü Kun (1536–1618); compassion for common people; dedication to humanitarian service
1644	Fall of the Ming to internal revolt and invading Manchu forces
1645	Suicide of Liu Zongzhou (1578–1645)

Sources of Chinese Tradition

SECOND EDITION

VOLUME I

PART 1

The Chinese Tradition in Antiquity

Chapter 1

THE ORACLE-BONE INSCRIPTIONS OF THE
LATE SHANG DYNASTY

THE SHANG DYNASTY

Traditional accounts of early China present the Shang as the second historical dynasty (ca. 1554–1045/1040 B.C.E.),[1] succeeding to the Xia and succeeded by the Zhou (1045/1040–256 B.C.E.). Because no written records of the Xia have yet been discovered, the Shang, with its inscriptions on oracle bones and bronze vessels, may currently be regarded as China's first historical dynasty. Archaeology now reveals that other incipient Bronze Age states were emerging from the chiefdom stage toward the end of the second millennium B.C.E. It was the Shang, however, that literati of the Zhou and Han (206 B.C.E.–220 C.E.) came to regard as one of the dynastic models upon which later versions of the Chinese polity were founded. Modern research generally confirms that judgment. The oracle-bone inscriptions indicate the degree to which the Late Shang kings and

---

1. The traditional dating of the Shang and Zhou dynasties has been revised in recent years on the basis of modern studies of archaeological and astronomical evidence. Chinese historians once dated the Shang dynasty from the eighteenth century to the late twelfth century B.C.E.; the revised dating places Shang rule slightly later on the time line, from the sixteenth century to the middle of the eleventh century B.C.E. Experts still disagree about the precise dating of the Zhou conquest, some favoring 1045 and others 1040 B.C.E.

their diviners articulated many of the concerns that were to be central to the classical Chinese tradition. In many cases they appear to have provided solutions that proved seminal.

Approximately 150,000 fragments of inscribed Shang oracle bones have now been recovered from near Anyang, in the northern Henan panhandle. This was evidently the site of a major cult center where the Late Shang (ca. 1200–1045 B.C.E.) worshiped their ancestors and buried their last nine kings in large cruciform pit burials in the royal cemetery situated at Xibeigang. The inscriptions, written in an early Chinese script that scholars have been laboring to decipher since the importance of the oracle bones was first recognized a century ago, reveal the existence of an incipient state whose elites dominated a highly stratified society and whose king was able to exercise sovereignty as he issued orders to the officers and populations of various territories under his control. Benefiting from highly developed craft specialization and relying upon an administrative hierarchy, the king and his supporters extracted the agricultural surplus from the dependent peasants and mobilized them for large public works and for warfare.

The dynasty was centered on the royal lineage in which the title of king (*wang*; the graph — i.e., Chinese character — represented the frontal view of a "big man") was often passed from brother to brother before descending to the next generation, though increasingly toward the end of the dynasty, it was passed directly from father to son. Various other powerful groups were attached to this lineage by ties of kinship, real or fictive, and by political interest. Assisted by a core of officers at the capital, the king was able to mobilize his laborers and foot soldiers in groups of thousands, direct them in the construction of royal tombs, send his armies into battle against numerous regional powers on the periphery of the Shang homeland, and, like the rest of the Shang elite, enjoy the products of a sophisticated bronze-casting industry of almost industrial proportions, whose most important products were thousands of glistening ritual bronze vessels. The living used these bronzes in their sacrifices to the ancestors and then placed them in burials, evidently in the belief that the dead could thereby continue to perform cultic practices in the next world, still participating in what may be regarded as "a great chain of ancestral being."

The cult offerings to the ancestors involved the shedding of much blood — of both animal victims and human captives. That a Shang king, when he died, was buried with numerous retainers from all levels of society who accompanied him in death indicates the degree to which the fate of the living was tied to that of their rulers and the degree to which status in this life was continued into the next. Such ties of hierarchical dependency — sanctified by religious belief and reinforced by, as they reinforced, political linkages — were among the great emotional resources of the evolving state, in which religion and kin were inseparable from secular and political activities.

THE ORACLE-BONE INSCRIPTIONS

Although archaeological discoveries are now suggesting the existence of written characters scratched on Neolithic pots as early as 3000 B.C.E., the earliest corpus of Chinese writing consists of the oracle-bone inscriptions of the Late Shang. These inscriptions record the pyromantic divinations performed at the court of the last nine Shang kings. In this kind of divination, the king or his diviners would address an oral "charge," such as "We will receive millet harvest,"[2] to a specially prepared turtle plastron or cattle scapula while applying a hot poker or brand to produce a series of heat cracks in the shell or bone. They then interpreted these cracks as auspicious or inauspicious, and the king would deliver a prognostication, such as "Auspicious. We will receive harvest."[3] After the divination had taken place, engravers carved the subject of the charge, and (sometimes) the king's forecast, and (less frequently) the result, into the surface of the shell or bone — hence the modern Chinese term *jiaguwen*, "writings on shell and bone." The diviners themselves — whose names, like Chu, Gu, Bin, Que, and Xing, appear in the inscriptions translated below — were apparently members of groups capable of casting their own ritual bronzes, groups whose social and political power was at the service of the king.

Because the twenty-first Shang king, Wu Ding (fl. 1200–1181 B.C.E.), in particular, divined about a wide range of matters — including sacrifices and rituals, divine assistance or approval, requests to ancestral or Nature Powers, sickness, childbirth, the good fortune of the night, the day, or the coming ten-day week, disaster, distress, trouble, dreams, troop mobilizations, military campaigns, meteorological and celestial phenomena, agriculture, settlement building, administrative orders, hunting expeditions and excursions — the inscriptions, carved on bones that the king himself must frequently have seen and handled, provide us with a direct and vivid sense of his daily activities and his religious beliefs.

Many of the divination charges were about what the king should do; he sought the guidance of the cracks in making up his mind. In other cases, the king informed the bone or shell of his intended plans, seeking spiritual reassurance and validation. Many of these charges may be regarded as wishful predictions, demonstrating that Shang divination served as a form of royal prayer, conjuration, and legitimation. In yet other cases the king sought to discover the symbolic, spiritual meaning of events — such as crop failures, illnesses, and dreams — that had already happened. In all these instances, the Shang diviners were searching for hidden meanings — in the cracks themselves

---

2. *HJ* 9950 front. *HJ* is an abbreviation for the standard collection of oracle-bone rubbings; Guo and Hu, *Jiaguwen heji* (hereafter *HJ*).

3. *HJ* 9950 back.

and also in the mundane but spiritually charged phenomena of their daily lives. Because the inscriptions document the king's continual attempts to contact the spiritual Powers that shaped his universe, they throw much light on the concerns of the Shang elite at a time when the earliest Chinese state was being created. The sample inscriptions translated below will indicate how the Shang diviners worked.[4]

SHANG CONCEPTIONS OF TIME

To the Shang diviner, who meticulously dated the great majority of his divination charges, time was as portentous as place and direction. Observed, shaped, and regulated, it, like space, was an indispensable dimension of religious cosmology, an integral part of all religious observance and divinatory prognostication. Human time — concerned with the hours of the day, the agricultural cycles of the year, the birth of royal sons, the timing of royal hunts, the mobilization of conscripts for fighting, agriculture, or other public work — was inextricably mixed with and conceived in terms of religious time — concerned with the schedule of rituals and sacrifices, the luck of a particular day or week, the portentous significance of particular events.

The days and the nights, moreover, together with the ten-day week (as in inscription 35 below), were the primary units in which both humans and the Powers were thought to act:

1. Crack-making on *bingxu* (day 23), (we) divined: "Today it will not rain."[5]
2. Crack-making on *renwu* (day 19), Chu (the diviner) divined: "Today there will not be the coming of bad news from the border regions."[6]
3. Crack-making on *yichou* (day 2): "Today, *yichou*, we offer one penned sheep to Ancestor Xin, promise five cattle."[7]

The constantly repeated and rigid cycle of the sixty day names was formed by what in later times became known as the ten "heavenly stems" (*tiangan*) — *jia, yi, bing, ding,* etc. — combined with the twelve "earthly branches" (*dizhi*) — *zi, chou, yin, mao,* etc. This sixty-day sequence — *jiazi* (day 1), *yichou* (day 2), *bingyan* (day 3), and so on[8] — was important in practical terms because it was the only firm calendrical frame the

---

4. As with all texts, the meaning of particular divinations needs to be considered in context; other inscriptions on the same bone or shell or about the same topic on another bone or shell, for example, may sometimes provide more information than the brief presentation of one divination by itself can do.

5. *HJ* 24146.

6. *HJ* 24149.

7. *HJ* 1732.

8. See ch. 10, pp. 351–52.

Shang possessed. In religious terms, the temple name of an ancestor or ancestress (like Ancestor Yi, Father Jia, or Mother Bing), conferred after death, employed the "heavenly stem" of the day on which he or she received cult or ritual attention. Thus every ancestor and ancestress was associated with one of the ten suns that rose in turn over the course of the ritual ten-day week.[9] The identity between day name and ancestral cult would have given a strongly religious, ancestral overtone to all activities scheduled for these days, just as a still active cult to the Norse Woden, occurring every Wednesday, might remind us of his existence and power at every mention of his day name.

DIVINATION AND ADMINISTRATION

Some of the Shang divinations involved routine administrative choices, as in:

4A. Crack-making on *gengzi* (day 37): "(We) order Fu to inspect Lin."[10]

4B. "It should be Qin whom we order to inspect Lin."

4C. "It should be Bing whom we order to inspect Lin."[11]

Other divinations involved choices about ritual activity, involving the number and type of victims to be offered, the timing or desirability of the offering, or the recipient of the cult:

5A. Divined: "On the next day, *jiawu* (day 31), (we) should not make offering to Ancestor [Yi] (the twelfth king)."

5B. Divined: "On the next day, *jiawu*, (we) should make offering to Ancestor Yi."[12]

The king also divined about his own participation in matters both secular and ritual:

6. On *dingmao* (day 4) divined: "If the king joins with Zhi [Guo] (an important Shang general) to attack the Shaofang, he will receive [assistance]." Cracked in the temple of Ancestor Yi (the twelfth king). Fifth moon.[13]

7A. Divined: "If the king dances (for rain), there will be approval."

---

9. See the inscriptions numbered below as 31A–B to 35.

10. The designations 4A, 4B, and so on mean that inscriptions A and B are found on the same bone.

11. *HJ* 33237.

12. *HJ* 6167.

13. *Tunnan* 81. *Tunnan* is an abbreviation for Zhongguo shehui kexueyuan kaogu yanjiusuo, *Xiaotun nandi jiagu.*

7B.   Divined: "The king should not dance (for rain, for if he does, there will not be approval)."[14]

THE POWER OF THE DEAD

The Shang oracle-bone inscriptions document the fear and respect that the living king showed his dead ascendants. This might manifest itself in general concerns about nonspecific harm:

8.   Crack-making on *yiwei* (day 32), Gu divined: "Father Yi (the twentieth Shang king, Xiao Yi, the father of Wu Ding) is harming the king."[15]

9A.   Divined: "Grandfather Ding (the fifteenth king, father of Xiao Yi) is harming the king."

9B.   Divined: "It is not Grandfather Ding who is harming the king."[16]

Many of these divinations involved the king's health, as in:

10.   Divined: "There is a sick tooth; it is not Father Yi (= Xiao Yi, as above) who is harming (it/him)."[17]

In addition to their ability to harm the king personally, the senior ancestors, like some of the Nature Powers, had the ability to influence both the weather and the harvests upon which the fate of the dynasty as a whole depended:

11.   Crack-making on *dingchou* (day 14), Bin divined: "In praying for harvest to Shang Jia (the predynastic founder of the royal lineage) we offer in holocaust three small penned lambs and split open three cattle."[18]

12A.   "It is Shang Jia who is harming the rain."

12B.   "It is not Shang Jia who is harming the rain."[19]

One of the ways by which the king showed his concern for his people, in fact, was expressed in his divinatory prayers for harvest in his domains, as in the late inscription:

13A.   On *jisi* (day 6), the king cracked and divined: "[This] season, Shang will receive [harvest]." The king read the cracks and said: "Auspicious."

13B.   "The Eastern Lands will receive harvest."

---

14. *HJ* 11006 front.
15. *HJ* 2231.
16. *HJ* 1901 front.
17. *HJ* 13636 front.
18. *HJ* 10109.
19. *HJ* 12648.

13C.   "The Southern Lands will receive harvest." (The king read the cracks and said:) "Auspicious."

13D.   "The Western Lands will receive harvest." (The king read the cracks and said:) "Auspicious."

13E.   "The Northern Lands will receive harvest." (The king read the cracks and said:) "Auspicious."[20]

Ancestresses were less powerful than ancestors but appear to have had special jurisdiction in matters of childbearing:

14.   On *xinsi* (day 18) divined: "(We) will pray for a child to Mother Geng and Mother Bing and offer a bull, a ram, and a white boar."[21]

The great importance that the Shang kings attached to male progeny is well revealed by the following charge, prognostication, and verification:

15A.   Crack-making on *jiashen* (day 21), Que divined: "Lady Hao's (a consort of Wu Ding's) childbearing will be good." (Prognostication:) The king read the cracks and said: "If it be on a *ding*-day that she give birth, there will be prolonged luck." (Verification:) (After) thirty-one days, on *jiayin* (day 51), she gave birth; it was not good; it was a girl.[22]

15B.   (Prognostication:) The king read the cracks and said: "If it be a *ding*-(day) childbearing, it will be good; if (it be) a *geng*-day (childbearing), there will be prolonged luck; if it be a *renxu* (day 59) (childbearing), it will not be lucky."[23]

Ancestresses played at least one other important role: they served to identify, by their presence in the cult of the five-ritual cycle, those kings who were subsequently treated by the Han historian Sima Qian (145? B.C.E.–86? B.C.E.) as members of the main line of descent, the *dazong* or "great lineage." This designation was reserved for kings who were both the sons and the fathers of other kings. The consorts of none of the collateral kings received such cultic attention; only the consorts of the main-line kings were so honored:

16.   Crack-making on *renyin* (day 39), Xing divined: "The king hosts Da Geng's (the fifth king's) consort, Mother Ren, and performs the *xie*-ritual; there will be no trouble."[24]

---

20. *HJ* 36975.

21. *HJ* 34082.

22. *HJ* 14002 front.

23. *HJ* 14002 back.

24. *HJ* 23314.

17. Crack-making on *xinsi* (day 18), divined: "The king hosts Wu Ding's (the twenty-first king's) consort, Mother Xin, and performs the *zai*-ritual; there will be no trouble."[25]

The ancestors apparently served as mediators with Di, God — occasionally referred to as Shangdi, the High God. Just as the Shang kings frequently divined about hosting (*bin*) their ancestors with ritual and cult, so too did the kings divine, although less frequently, to determine which of the ancestors would be hosted by increasingly senior ancestors who, in turn, would be hosted by, and thus be in communication with, the High God, Di, as the following inscriptions selected from a large turtle plastron reveal:

18A. Divined: "Cheng (= Da Yi, the first king) will be hosted by Di."
18B. Divined: "Cheng will not be hosted by Di."
18C. Divined: "Da Jia (the third king) will be hosted by Cheng."
18D. Divined: "Da Jia will not be hosted by Cheng."
18E. Divined: "Da [Jia] will be hosted by Di."
18F. Divined: "Da Jia will not be hosted by Di."[26]

THE HIGH GOD (DI) AND OTHER POWERS

The Shang kings lived in a world that was dominated by a complex pantheon of Powers that included: Di, the High God; Nature Powers, like the (Yellow) River, the Mountain, and Ri, the Sun; Former Lords, like Wang Hai, who were apparently ex-humans whom the cultists now associated with the dynasty; predynastic ancestors, like Shang Jia; dynastic ancestors, whose cult started with Da Yi and ended with the deceased father of the reigning king; and the dynastic ancestresses, the consorts of those kings on the main line of descent, who likewise received cult in the order of their husbands' accession. The worship of the nondynastic Powers, whether natural or human (a distinction that was not sharp), strengthened the king's position by enlarging the scope of his influence in the spiritual world. Such worship may be regarded as a form of "spiritual imperialism" in which the powers worshiped by local populations were co-opted into the Shang pantheon, frequently being placed in the shadowy, and relatively "empty," predynastic space in the ritual genealogy before the time of Da Yi, the founder. The jurisdictional distinctions within the pantheon, particularly those between the Nature Powers, Former Lords, and Predynastic Ancestors at the head of the hierarchy, were by no means rigid; the Shang ritualists conceived of these Powers as sharing many essential features, applying names like High Ancestor to some of them.

---

25. *HJ* 36268.
26. *HJ* 1402 front.

The original meaning of the word *di*, the name or title by which the Shang kings addressed their High God and, occasionally, their royal ancestors, remains hard to determine. It is equally hard to determine if the Shang kings regarded Di as their distant ancestor, but the lack of cult addressed to Di suggests that the ancestral tie, if it ever existed, had been greatly muted. If Di had once been an ancestor, the Late Shang kings treated him with uncharacteristic parsimony. The contrast with the generous way in which the kings treated their ancestors is so notable that it implies a difference in kind.

Di's jurisdictions were not always exclusive. The ancestors and Nature Powers could, like Di, also affect harvest, weather, campaigns, and the king's health.[27] It is clear, however, that Di stood at the peak of the ultra-human, ultra-natural hierarchy, giving orders, which no ancestor could do, to the various natural phenomena and responding to the intercessions of the Shang ancestors who were acting on behalf of their living descendants below. That Di was virtually the only Power who could directly order (*ling*) rain or thunder, as well as the only Power who had the winds under his control, sets him apart from all the other Powers, natural, predynastic, or ancestral. His ability to act in this commanding way helps to establish his unique role as the sky god of the Shang pantheon, foreshadowing the role of Heaven in the Zhou period that followed.

Although Di's wishes were not easy to divine, his approval was important to the Shang:

19A. Crack-making on *renzi* (day 49), Zheng divined: "If we build a settlement, Di will not obstruct (but) approve." Third moon.
19B. Crack-making on *guichou* (day 50), Zheng divined: "If we do not build a settlement, Di will approve."[28]
20A. Crack-making on *xinchou* (day 38), Que divined: "Di approves the king (doing something?)."
20B. Divined: "Di does not approve the king (doing something?)."[29]

Di was also a provider of rain. The king evidently took pride in his ability to forecast Di's meteorological intentions:

21A. Crack-making on *wuzi* (day 25). Que divined: "Di, when it comes to the fourth moon, will order the rain."
21B. Divined: "Di will not, when it comes to the present fourth moon, order the rain."
21C. (Prognostication:) The king read the cracks and said: "On the *ding*-day

---

27. As, for example, in 11, 12A–B, 26A–B, 29, and 30.
28. *HJ* 14206.
29. *HJ* 14198.

(e.g., *dingyou* [day 34]) it will rain; if not, it will be a *xin*-day (e.g., *xinchou* [day 38] (that it rains)."

21D. (Verification:) "(After) ten days, on *dingyou* (day 34), it really did rain."[30]

And, like the ancestors, Di was also capable of causing harm to the Shang:

22A. Divined: "It is Di who is harming our harvest." Second moon.
22B. Divined: "It is not Di who is harming our harvest."[31]

Di's role as a sender of difficulties, moreover, was not limited to the floods, droughts, and crop failures of the natural world; he could also, on occasion, stimulate an enemy attack:

23.   [Divined:] "The Fang (enemy) are harming and attacking (us); it is Di who orders (them) to make disaster for us." Third moon.[32]
24A. Divined: "(Because) the Fang are harming and attacking (us, we) will raise men."
24B. Divined: "It is not Di who orders (the Fang) to make disaster for us."[33]

Di was in part a god of battle. Some twenty divinations end with the incantatory formula "Di will confer assistance on us," and, when the context was specified, Di's assistance always involved warfare, as in:

25.   Crack-making on *jiachen* (day 41), Zheng divined: "If we attack the Ma-fang (another enemy group), Di will confer assistance on us." First moon.[34]

Di's great distance from the Shang, evident in the lack of cult and in his readiness to order enemy attacks (as in 23 and 24A–B) suggests that Di was accessible to various groups, Shang and non-Shang, and probably enigmatic to all. Di at best was an uncertain ally. The Shang prayed for his assistance (as in 25) but divined no ritual or sacrificial procedures for obtaining it in a routine, institutionalized way. After the reign of Wu Ding, in fact, they ceased to divine about Di's assistance at all. Di, in short, does not appear to have been a Jehovah-like figure, watching over his chosen Shang people. That the divination inscriptions record virtually no cult to Di was perhaps because his allegiance was so uncertain that no attempt to influence his intentions

---

30. *HJ* 14138.
31. *HJ* 10124 front.
32. *HJ* 39912.
33. *HJ* 6746.
34. *HJ* 6664 front.

was worth pursuing or, at least, divining. The Shang placated their ancestors through the offering of cult; it was evidently the ancestors who were expected to intercede with Di, as suggested by 18A–F.

Harm might also come from the Nature Powers.

26A. Crack-making on *bingwu* (day 43) divined: "It is the Mountain Power that is harming the rain."
26B. "It is the (Yellow) River Power that is harming the rain."[35]

One of the most common of all Shang divinations, in fact, involved the apotropaic conjuration, divined on the last day of the Shang week, that "in the next ten days (i.e., the next week), there will be no disasters" (as in 35). It was the king's constant concern to forestall harm and disasters of various types by identifying and mollifying the Powers that might be causing them. The king was particularly exposed to harm (frequently conceived in terms of bad weather) when he left the confines of the cult center on campaign or hunt, as the following conjurations suggest:

27. "On the present *xin*-day, if the king hunts, the whole day (he) will have no disasters and it will not rain."[36]
28. "If the king goes to hunt, the whole day he will not encounter the Great Winds."[37]

Other inscriptions reveal that the Winds were not simply meteorological phenomena but were conceived as Powers of great spiritual significance. It is evident, indeed, that the Shang kings lived in and traveled through a landscape that was pregnant with spiritual meaning. They offered cult and prayer to a variety of these non-Shang Powers:

29. Crack-making on *renwu* (day 19): "To the (Yellow) River Power (we) pray for rain and offer a holocaust."[38]
30. Crack-making on *xinwei* (day 8): "To the Mountain Power, (we) pray for rain."[39]

The considerable overlap in the jurisdictions of the ancestors and other Powers where the weather and harvests were concerned suggests, in fact, that the Shang had not yet developed orderly and consistent religious explanations for such large and strategically capricious phenomena.

---

35. *Tunnan* 2438.
36. *HJ* 29093.
37. *HJ* 29234.
38. *HJ* 12853.
39. *HJ* 34916.

REGULARITY OF THE ANCESTRAL CULT

The Shang treated their ancestors with the kind of ritual regularity and order that they were unable to apply either to the Nature Powers or to Di himself. As ex-humans, the ancestors were approachable and comprehensible in ways that the other Powers were not. This regularity is seen most clearly in the use of the temple names that the Shang ritualists assigned to their dead kings, offering them cult or pyromantic attention on the days whose names they bore. One sees this strict ritual regularity, which became increasingly the rule after the reign of Wu Ding, in the following inscriptions, in which the day of cult matches the temple name of the cult recipient:

31A.   Crack-making on *jiawu* (day 31), Que divined: "On the next day, *yiwei* (day 32), (we) should make offering to Ancestor Yi (the twelfth king)."

31B.   "On the next day, *yiwei*, (we) [should not] make offering to Ancestor Yi."[40]

32A.   Crack-making on *guiwei* (day 20), Que divined: "On the next day, *jiashen* (day 21), the king should host Shang Jia (the predynastic founder) and offer the (*jia-*) day cult." (Prognostication:) The king read the cracks and said: "Auspicious. We should host (Shang Jia)." (Verification:) "(We) really did host (Shang Jia)."

32B.   Divined: "On the next day, *jiashen*, the king should not host Shang Jia and offer the (*jia-*) day cult."[41]

Thus in 31A–B the diviner contemplated offering cult to Ancestor Yi on an *yi*-day; in 32A–B, the cult was to be offered to Shang Jia on a *jia*-day. During the reign of Wu Ding, however, the identity of day name and temple name was still a topic for divination, as these two pairs of inscriptions indicate; similar uncertainty is shown in 5AB, where *jia*-day cult was being proposed for an Yi ancestor. During and after the reign of Ancestor Jia, the twenty-third king, however, such matching of cult name and cult day was rigorously observed:

33.   Crack-making on *yihai* (day 12), Xing divined: "The king hosts Xiao Yi (the twentieth king) and performs the *xie*-ritual; he will have no fault." Eleventh moon.[42]

34.   Crack-making on *dingsi* (day 54), divined: "The king hosts the fourth Ancestor Ding (the fifteenth king) and performs the *xie*-day ritual; he will have no fault."[43]

---

40. *HJ* 9504 front.
41. *HJ* 1248 front.
42. *HJ* 23120.
43. *HJ* 35713.

In these cases the divinations and the cult to the Yi- and Ding-named ancestors were both performed on the *yi*- and *ding*-days, respectively. The regularity of the ritual schedule was so marked, in fact, that by the end of the dynasty, the rituals themselves were being employed to fix particular divinations in the calendar of royal cult. Divinatory time was frequently cultic time, as the following postface indicates:

35. On *guiwei* (day 20) the king made cracks in the Hui encampment and divined: "In the (next) ten days, there will be no disasters." (Prognostication:) The king read the cracks and said: "Auspicious." (Postface:) It was in the fifth moon, (for the week starting on the) *jiashen* (day 21) (on which we) offered the *ji*-ritual to Ancestor Jia (the twenty-third king) and the *xie*-day ritual to Xiang Jia (the seventeenth king).[44]

Although the king, the diviner of record in this case, was traveling, he evidently kept track of the *ji*- and *xie*-day rituals, which he used to situate the divination in the ritual calendar. The king may even have offered the *ji*- and *xie*-rituals while on the road. It is a striking fact, however, that the king never divined about performing such rituals or about hosting his ancestors when he was traveling; the ancestors, whose "hosting" was contemplated in numerous inscriptions like 32A–B, 33, and 34, could evidently not be contacted when the king put a distance between himself and the ancestral temples and royal burial grounds of the cult center at Anyang.

That the consorts of the main-line kings received cult on their own name days rather than those of their husbands — as in 16 and 17 — indicates that these royal women preserved their own ritual identity after death. Indeed, the distribution of the temple names, in which the kings tended to be awarded names that fell during the first half of the week (*jia, ding, yi, geng*) and the consorts tended to be awarded names that fell during the second half of the week (*wu, ji, xin, gui*), indicates the degree to which kings and consorts were part of separate yet related ritual systems.

DIVINATION AND THE ANCESTORS

A number of divinations were actually performed in the ancestral temple, as in 6 and 36:

36. On *dingwei* (day 44) divined: "It should be tonight that (we) perform the *you*-cutting sacrifice and perform an exorcism." Cracked in the temple of Father Ding (i.e., Wu Ding).[45]

---

44. *HJ* 35886.
45. *HJ* 32330.

This suggests that the Powers to whom many of the divination charges were addressed may well have been the ancestors who, through the cracks, were speaking to their royal descendant, known in the bones as "I, the one man" (*yu yi ren*), at least partly because of his unique ability to communicate with his ascendants in this way. Other divinations specifically invoke an ancestor as the object of the prayer being divined:

37. Divined: "(We) pray for Lady Hao (one of Wu Ding's consorts) to Father Yi (the twentieth king and Wu Ding's father)."[46]

38. Crack-making on *guiyou* (day 10): "To Father Jia (the seventeenth king), we pray for (good) hunting."[47]

In such cases, the Powers who were responding through the bone cracks were, in all likelihood, the ancestors, like Father Yi and Father Jia, to whom the prayers were explicitly directed.

Many Shang divinations, however, appear to have involved general prayers for assistance that did not specify the particular Power whose blessings were being invoked. Whether the record was simply abbreviated in such cases or the Shang diviners themselves were being deliberately vague about the "divinee" is hard to tell.

DIVINATION AND LEGITIMATION

The power of the Shang elites depended, in part, upon their control of superior armaments like bronze dagger-axes and horse-and-chariot teams, but the true authority of the dynasty — like that of the Neolithic chieftains who had preceded them — was psychological. Their material power had to be sanctified and legitimated. Much of the elites' legitimacy derived from their ability — through divination — to define, explain, and control reality, a reality that, in a Bronze Age theocracy, was primarily conceived in religious and familial terms.

The virtual absence of divinatory records that clearly contradict the king's forecasts suggests that the process of divination and record-keeping was generally designed to validate the king's powers as a seer or spiritual intermediary who could forecast and perhaps influence the future, as in:

39A. Crack-making on *jimao* (day 16), Que divined: "It will not rain."

39B. Crack-making on *jimao*, Que divined: "It will rain." (Prognostication:) The king read the cracks (and said): "If it rains, it will be on a *ren*-day." (Verification:) On *renwu* (day 19), it really did rain.[48]

---

46. *HJ* 2634 front.

47. *HJ* 28278.

48. *HJ* 902 front.

In this case, the king had forecast rain on a *ren*-day, and the record proved that he had been right. Verifications, in fact, frequently confirmed royal prognostications where divinations about the weather were concerned, as already seen in 21C–D.

Wu Ding, moreover, appears to have validated his role as prognosticator and king by anticipating impending trouble:

40. Crack-making on *guisi* (day 30), Que divined: "In the (next) ten days there will be no disasters." (Prognostication:) The king read the cracks and said: "There will be calamities; there will be (someone) bringing alarming news." (Verification:) When it came to the fifth day, *dingyou* (day 34), there really was (someone) bringing alarming news from the west. Zhi Guo reported and said: "The Tufang have attacked in our eastern borders and have seized two settlements. The Gongfang likewise invaded the fields of our western borders."[49]

The king's forecast of calamities had been confirmed by events. This inscription, furthermore, like many others from the reign of Wu Ding, has certain striking features — the large, bold calligraphy, the use of red pigment to beautify the inscribed characters, and the inscribing of the charge, prognostication, and verification as a single continuous unit — which suggest that such validating records had been made for display. Perhaps they were intended to impress the king's supporters.

By the end of the dynasty, divinations about hunting were also increasingly represented as records of successful prognostication:

41. On *renzi* (day 49), (the king) made cracks and divined: "(We) will hunt at Wu; going and coming back there will be no disasters." (Prognostication:) The king read the cracks and said: "Auspicious." This was used. (Verification:) (We) caught one wild buffalo; one tiger; seven foxes.[50]

THE ORIGINS OF HISTORICAL RECTITUDE: FALLIBILITY AND ACCURACY IN THE SHANG DIVINATION RECORDS

Given the validating role that divination played in the court's general activities, the king, one may suppose, would not have been likely to employ engravers who recorded on scapula or plastron what could be regarded as royal forecasts that had failed. This would explain why, as in 39A–B and 40, the vast majority

---

49. *HJ* 6057 front.
50. *HJ* 37363.

of the verifications confirm the king's forecasts. It may also help explain why, in many other cases, forecasts and results were not recorded at all.

Shang verifications, however, particularly during the reign of Wu Ding, were not simply royal propaganda that recorded the king's divinatory successes. A small number of them reveal, on the part of the king's servitors, a pre-Zhou commitment to truthful record-keeping; they betray the possible existence of early tensions between the king, on the one hand, anxious to maintain his prestige, and his record keepers, on the other, anxious to record the truth.

Most of the cases that lead to this conclusion involve scenarios in which the king's forecast was not confirmed by the results recorded. One of the most typical involved the king's forecasts about childbirth, as in 15A–B. In that case, the king forecast that Lady Hao's childbearing would be auspicious if it occurred on a *ding*-day or a *geng*-day. In fact, she gave birth on a *jia*-day and, since she gave birth to a girl, the birth was "not good" — a verification recorded in 15A. The king's accuracy as a forecaster was not, strictly speaking, invalidated by the inauspiciousness of the result, for the actual birth occurred on neither of the two days for which he had made auspicious forecast. In effect, the king had said, "I can only tell you about births on two days, *ding* and *geng*; I have no information about the other eight days (of the ten-day week)." In the event, the results took place on one of those eight days. Such forecasts seem to have been modest in their expectations, and, in fact, such disjunctions between the forecast and the verification were relatively common. That the engravers recorded that the king had "missed" the day indicates the degree to which these inscriptions were kept not merely for propaganda purposes.

Forecasts in which the king "missed" the day were not limited to divinations about birth. One set of rainfall inscriptions, in which forecast and verification did not match, implies more clearly than any other case a royal divinatory "failure." These verifications, once again, neither confirmed nor contradicted the forecast, but the detailed record suggests a sustained (and eventually unsuccessful) effort to escape the wrongness of the king's prognostication.

42A.   Crack-making on *guisi* (day 30), Zheng divined: "In the present first moon, it will rain." (Prognostication:) The king read the cracks and said: ". . . on the *bing*-day it will rain."

42B.   Crack-making on *guisi*, Zheng divined: "In the present first moon, it will not rain."

42C.   (Verification:) "In the (next) ten-day week, on *renyin* (day 39), it rained; on *jiachen* (day 41), it also rained."[51]

---

51. *HJ* 12487 front.

42D. (Verification:) "On *jiyou* (day 46), it rained; on *xinhai* (day 48), it also rained."[52]

In divination 42A the king forecast on day 30 that it would rain on a *bing*-day (i.e., days 33, 43, 53, and so on); the two verifications — 42C on the front of the plastron and 42D on the back — record that it rained on four other days — days 39, 41, 46, and 48. There is no record, however, that rain fell on the *bing*-day as forecast.

For the diviners of 42A–D to have recorded rainfall in this way over an eighteen-day period is unusual, particularly during the first moon, a month when little if any rain falls today in North China. (The existence of such inscriptions, incidentally, is one indication that the Late Shang climate was warmer and wetter, and the growing season longer, than it is today.) It seems likely that in 42C–D the verification process was being "kept open" — even to the extent of continuing to record the verifications on the back of the plastron in 42D in hopes that rain would eventually fall on a *bing*-day, as forecast in 42A. Having waited in vain through at least two full ten-day weeks, the diviners finally closed the case.

Such a record, once again, did not entirely delegitimate the king. Rain, after all, did fall on four separate occasions, thus confirming that the king, as the general tester of the spiritual "climate," had been sufficiently right in this case — a lot of rain fell — even though he had been wrong about the precise day. "Well, it did rain a lot" might have sufficed to save some royal face. In no other Shang oracle-bone inscription, however, does the verification so nearly give the lie to the king's forecast as in the 42A–D inscriptions.

DIVINATORY "FAILURE" AND THE ORIGINS OF HISTORY

This discussion of forecasts and verifications suggests two conclusions. First, the king himself made no exaggerated claims to infallibility; many of his recorded forecasts specified a number of possible days, as in 15A–B and 21C, rather than a single one; he was frequently not specific about what would (as opposed to what would not) happen; he did not, for example, claim to have forecast lunar eclipses in advance, and so on. Second, Wu Ding's staff of pyromantic experts did infrequently incise records that revealed, obliquely to be sure, the king's limitations as seer and, by implication, the limitations of the entire pyromantic process. In these cases, the king had not been formally wrong, but he certainly had not been right.

That Wu Ding and his diviners did not adopt the simplest expedient for dealing with oracular failure — that of dispensing with recorded forecasts and verifications entirely — testifies to the commitment that must have existed in his

---

52. *HJ* 12487 back.

reign to both genuine divinatory acts and genuine historical records. Certain potentially delegitimating divinations were incised into the bones and shells. These were delegitimating to the king, but they served to legitimate the process of divination itself by stressing, even at some cost to the ruler, the importance of recording the divinations accurately. And it was, of course, precisely the belief in the authenticity of royal divination that made it such a valuable institution for legitimating royal power. The frequent balancing of positive and negative charges, placed in matching opposition on the bone itself,[53] reflected the workings of a world whose metaphysical balances were changeable and uncertain. So long as the divinatory record showed a strong balance of successful forecasts, so long as it demonstrated a continual and realistic attempt to understand and shape spiritual and mundane realities, then the king was fulfilling his role as "I, the one man" who, better than others, could foresee and influence what was likely to happen.

THE ROLE OF THE KING

The king played a central role in Shang divination. Many of the charges were about his plans, his activities, and his health. Many involved his choice of officers. He was virtually the only human who could read the cracks and make forecasts. By the end of the dynasty, moreover, the king had become virtually the sole diviner of record. That the king also participated directly in the royal cult is further evidence of the great value that religious activities of this sort played in the functioning of the Shang state; there can, indeed, have been little distinction between cult and divination, between prayer and administration. The king presided over a theocratic,[54] patrimonial state; as the living head of the royal lineage who had the sole ability to communicate with the dead ancestors upon whose blessings the continued success of the dynasty depended, the king focused religious, political, and social power in his royal person.

THE EVOLUTION OF SHANG DIVINATION

Finally, it must be stressed that the form and content of Shang divination were continually evolving. By the reigns of the last two Shang kings, Di Yi and Di Xin (first half of the eleventh century B.C.E.), recorded prognostications were

---

53. As in 5A–B; 7A–B; 9A–B; 12A–B; 18A–B, C–D, E–F; 19A–B; 20A–B; 21A–B; 22A–B; 31A–B; and so on.

54. In describing Shang political culture, *theocratic* refers to the rule of a king whose undifferentiated political and religious authority derived from his status as the descendant and representative of his ancestors, the spiritual powers most directly concerned with the fortunes of their royal descendant and his lineage state.

always auspicious, and they tended to be clustered on particular oracle bones. Moreover, by contrast with the frequently elaborate prognostications of Wu Ding's period,[55] those of the last two rulers, Di Yi and Di Xin,[56] were invariably brief and nonspecific. Similarly, the verifications of the closing reigns were far terser than those of Wu Ding's time and were generally limited to divinations about averting disasters, about the weather, and about the hunt.

When considered in the light of other changes involving the reduced scope of the divination charges, the disappearance of the complementary, positive-negative charge pairs, and the markedly reduced size of the late-period callig-raphy, it is clear that the vital divinatory scenarios of Wu Ding, in which the king submitted virtually all aspects of his life to the pyromantic shell or bone for spiritual guidance, had become a thing of the past. Since the Shang diviners sometimes consulted clumps of numerals, piled on top of one another and carved into the oracle bones, that can be converted into trigrams and hexagrams like those used in the *Classic of Changes (Yijing)*,[57] it is possible that the Late Shang diviners employed both *Yijing*-like achillomancy (which involved the manipulation of milfoil stalks or counting rods) and pyromancy in conjunction and that the diminished scope of the pyromantic record may have been due in part to the growing popularity of the alternative system. That system has left few Shang records of its use, but the combination of pyromancy and achillo-mancy was certainly routine in the ensuing Zhou period.

THE LEGACY OF SHANG

There can be little doubt that the cultural assumptions of the Late Shang pre-pared the way for many of the more elaborate articulations of Zhou and later times. The divinatory impulse itself, for example, which sought to uncover the hidden meanings of events, may be regarded as ancestral to the "new text" *(jinwen)* interpretations of the Han,[58] whose political history, like that of the Zhou, was marked by an enduring concern with divination and portents. The concern with timeliness and good order that was so central to Shang divination[59] was also to prove central to many of the schools of Eastern Zhou (771–256 B.C.E.) thought; the Shang would have fully appreciated, for example, the un-derlying assumptions of the "Monthly Ordinances" of the *Record of Rites (Liji)*.[60] The hierarchical conception of the Shang ancestors, in which the more

---

55. Represented by 15A–B, 21C, 39B, and 40.
56. Represented by 13A–E, 35, and 41.
57. See ch. 2 and ch. 10, pp. 318–25.
58. See ch. 10, pp. 314–16.
59. Such as those about cult, for example, in 5A–B, 31A–B, 32A–B, 33, 34.
60. See ch. 10, pp. 329–44.

senior ancestors appear to have grown more powerful as they moved up the genealogical ladder with the passage of time, must also have provided a strong emotional basis for, as it may have been reinforced by, similar hierarchies of organization and ritual among the living. The rigid scheduling of the cult to the ancestors, the use of a limited number of day-name categories to classify them, and the willingness to give them ordinal temple names, such as "fourth Ancestor Ding," all indicate a preference in the religious world for the kind of orderly and impersonal arrangements that can be associated with the development of the imperial bureaucracy in Zhou and Han. That kin connections were frequently to play a key role in the operations of that bureaucracy only confirms the closeness of the link to the earlier ancestral cult. The historians' commitment to keeping a true record of what the ruler did and said also appears to have its roots in Shang divinatory record-keeping.[61]

The Shang king's concern for good harvests and rainfall[62] was also continued in a variety of Zhou and Han rituals, such as the ploughing of the sacred field at the start of the agricultural year (referred to in the *Classic of Odes* and the *Record of Rites*), all of which assumed the ruler's responsibility for encouraging Heaven's benevolence toward the state and its people. The general assumption that the ancestors, when properly treated, continued to smile on their living descendants is again central to much of the religion of Zhou and Han. The preference for male children — so marked in later Chinese culture and entirely comprehensible in a dynastic system in which descent passed through the male line — was already present in the Shang divinatory record. The central value of *xiao* or "filiality" must surely have had its origins in the great reverence that the Shang paid to their ancestors — in divinatory inquiry, in cultic offerings, and in the rich furnishing of their graves.

And, not least, the Zhou conception of a supreme being, *Tian* (Heaven), presiding over the universe,[63] was analogous to the Shang conception of Di, who not only stood above the ancestors[64] and Nature Powers but might on occasion command other groups to attack the Shang[65] in a way that appears, at least in its mechanism, to have anticipated the Zhou "Mandate of Heaven." Unlike *Tian*, however, Di as he is recorded in the oracle-bone inscriptions seems not to have been a force for moral good; he was evidently inscrutable in his actions, an impartial and mysterious figure whose existence may have been invoked to explain the Shang ancestors' inability to answer their descendants' prayers. The Zhou claim that Di (or *Tian*) had ordered the Zhou rulers to conquer the Shang would thus have been not a new invention of Zhou political

---

61. See the discussion above of 15A–B and 42A–D.
62. As in 7A–B, 12A–B, 13A–E.
63. See ch. 2.
64. As in 18A–F.
65. As in 24B; see also 21A–B for another instance in which Di issues commands.

theory but a logical extension from the religious belief of Shang times. The readiness with which the Shang are said to have accepted their conquerors' explanation for the Zhou victory lends some support to the view that a "Mandate of Di" was part of Late Shang political culture.

The intensely religious nature of Shang political culture — in which virtually all aspects of the king's activities were subject to the approval and scrutiny of the Powers — suggests the considerable humanization that the philosophers of the Eastern Zhou, most notably Confucius (551–479 B.C.E.),[66] were to undertake in articulating their concerns. Ancestor worship, by its very interest in honoring and replicating the deeds and beliefs of the ancestors, is bound to be a powerful force for conservatism in any theocratic political culture. That the magico-religious assumptions of Shang divinatory culture still played a large role in the elite culture of Zhou and Han further suggests the degree to which these assumptions must have satisfied social and psychological needs. Whether or not the Shang diviners forecast or shaped the future with notable accuracy — and it is worth reflecting on the record of modern economic forecasters before reaching too harsh a judgment — Shang divination worked so well to satisfy the cultural demands of those who used it that many of its underlying assumptions were to endure for a millennium and more.

[— DNK]

---

66. See ch. 3.

Chapter 2

CLASSICAL SOURCES OF CHINESE TRADITION

The classics of almost every major tradition have at some point in their history invited close scrutiny and intense debate, with those who have valued them disagreeing over such issues as dating, authenticity, authorship, and stratification (the layers of the text as it was built up over time). This has been particularly true of the most ancient Chinese texts — and not only in the light of modern critical scholarship. From early times to the present day, the Chinese classics have been carefully studied, deeply mined, and extensively compared — testimony, no doubt, to the importance the Chinese have assigned to the art of history and perhaps also to their understanding of these texts as human achievements rather than as the products of divine revelation. While interpretations have differed, there remains the larger question of how these texts were understood and appropriated within the mainstream of Chinese culture, became standard reference points for later writers, and formed the basis of a continuing traditional discourse. It is true of almost any major tradition that its foundational texts exhibit a powerful mythic quality and, regardless of their exact provenance or historicity, prove no less formative of tradition and axial to a civilization for partaking of this transhistorical, mythic quality. Indeed, this seems true even of Confucian legends that pertain to the human world rather than to some extraterrestrial realm and of texts understood to derive from human experience rather than from some extrahuman origin.

We turn then to a body of literature traditionally accepted by the Chinese as a heritage of these ancient times, the Confucian classics. According to the order in which they are customarily discussed in later times, the first of these is the *Classic of Changes (Yijing)*. As we have seen, the people of the Shang dynasty had practiced divination by means of cattle scapulas and turtle plastrons. Toward the end of the Shang another method of divination was coming into use based on sixty-four hexagrams (six-line symbolic diagrams) that were consulted through the casting of milfoil stalks. The *Classic of Changes* consists of a short text giving clues to the interpretation of the results of this type of divination, followed by a number of appendices or "wings," which elaborate upon the metaphysical significance of the interpretations. The basic text is attributed to very ancient times, while Confucius was traditionally supposed to have provided the "wings." Because the *Classic of Changes* came into existence over time and was later compiled and assumed its special importance in the tradition during the Former Han period (second and first centuries B.C.E.), it is discussed in chapter 10.

The second classic is the *Classic of Documents* or *Classic of History (Shujing,* also known as the *Shangshu*). This work consists of announcements, counsels, speeches, or similar oral reports said to have been made by various rulers and their ministers from the times of the sage rulers Yao and Shun down to the early Zhou period. Several hundred years ago, scholars in China established that many parts of the *Shujing* (though not the parts represented here) were later forgeries, probably of the fourth century C.E. Still, most Chinese have until recent times accepted this classic as providing accurate descriptions of the people and society of ancient China. Moreover, the collection of texts was traditionally believed to have been edited by Confucius, who was thought to have written a short introduction to each document explaining the circumstances of its composition.

The third classic is the *Classic of Odes* or *Classic of Poetry (Shijing)*, an anthology of some three hundred poems dating mostly from early Zhou times. Some of these are folk songs from the various feudal states, while others are songs used by the aristocracy in their sacrificial ceremonies or at banquets and other functions. One section doubtfully purports to include ceremonial songs of the earlier Shang period. Confucius is supposed to have selected and edited these poems from a larger body of material, and, though this tradition is open to question, there seems no reason to doubt the authenticity of the songs themselves.

The fourth classic, the *Rites*, is actually a collection of texts, the most famous of which is the *Record of Rites (Liji)*. These texts cover a vast range of subjects from the broadest philosophical pronouncements to the most minute rules for the conduct of everyday life. It is uncertain when the collections assumed their present form, though the texts themselves appear to date from middle or late Zhou times down to early Han. Again, Confucius is often credited with having been the compiler and editor of some of these texts.

The fifth of the classics, the *Spring and Autumn Annals* (*Chunqiu*), is a laconic chronicle of events in or affecting the state of Lu in the years from 722 to 481 B.C.E. Lu was the native state of Confucius, and it has been asserted that Confucius himself compiled the *Annals* from earlier records existing in the archives of Lu. Because the text of the *Annals* is so spare, a number of commentaries have been appended to explain the background and significance of the events referred to in the basic text. Of these, the most important are the *Zuo Commentary* (*Zuozhuan*), the *Gongyang*, and the *Guliang* commentaries. The exact dating of these commentaries is still a matter of controversy, though they were all apparently in existence by early Han times. It is in the light of these three commentaries that the *Spring and Autumn Annals* has traditionally been read and interpreted.

These works make up the Five Confucian Classics. A sixth, the "Music," is often mentioned in early writing. Whether there was ever a separate text on music we do not know. No such separate work exists today, though an essay on music is found in the *Record of Rites*.

All of these texts, with the exception of the *Record of Rites* and the *Spring and Autumn Annals*, with its three commentaries, purport to date from pre-Confucian times and to represent the earliest literature of the Chinese people, although modern scholarship in some cases denies such claims. In every case Confucius himself is assigned a personal role as transmitter, editor, and even commentator. It is true that other schools of thought also studied and made use of these early texts, or even put forward texts of their own for which they claimed equal authority and age. But the Confucian school always viewed itself as the guardian and transmitter of the old literature, and from the time in the first century B.C.E. when Confucianism gained general acceptance, the Five Classics became for the educated class the chief object of study; they were regarded by many not only as the final authority on questions of ancient history and practice but also as the embodiment of the moral law of Confucius and his predecessors and the source of all wisdom and right knowledge. The *Classic of Changes*, interpreted in the light of its "wings," was taken as a description of the metaphysical structure and Way of the universe. The speeches of the *Classic of Documents* were regarded as records of the government and institutions of the ancient sage kings and as models for all later rulers. The folk songs and ceremonial hymns of the *Classic of Odes* were interpreted as praises by the people or by the officials for good government or satires against misrule. The ritual texts were the final authority on questions of procedure and etiquette. Finally, it was asserted that Confucius had compiled the *Spring and Autumn Annals* not as an impartial record of historical fact but as a vehicle to convey his personal judgments on the human beings and events of the past and thereby to suggest certain moral laws and principles that would provide guidance in the management of human affairs. These moral lessons, however, are by no means apparent in the brief text of the *Annals*; one would have to turn to the commentaries and ponder each subtle variation in word choice in order to grasp the true significance of what Confucius was trying to say.

Let us note now a few of the terms and concepts that seem to be of greatest importance in this body of ancient literature. As we have seen in the discussion of the religious culture of the Shang, the inscriptions on the oracle bones and shells contain frequent references to a deity called Di — God — or, much more rarely, Shangdi — the High God. There are many references also to Ancestral Powers and Nature Powers, such as the Yellow River, other rivers and streams, and sacred mountains. The practice of sacrifice to ancestors, especially on the part of the Shang king, was central to religious life and, as we shall see, was to remain an important part of the political and religious culture of the Zhou.

At some point, certainly no later than the early Zhou period, a second concept, that of *Tian* — Heaven or Nature — began to appear alongside that of Di — or God. Moreover, Di is often referred to in Zhou sources as Shangdi — the High God. Just how the three terms were understood in the early Zhou is less than clear, but it appears that, over time, the term *di* would come to be used increasingly to refer not to a supreme deity, as in the Shang, but to the supreme ruler of human society, the emperor, while the word *tian*, or "Heaven," would more often be employed to denote the power that governed all creation. As the term is used in Zhou texts, *Heaven* seems to represent a more universalized concept — a cosmic moral order, and a being or power, possessing intelligence and will, that impartially guided the destinies of human beings.

After the leaders of the Zhou lineage had overthrown the Shang dynasty and set up their own rule, around 1045/1040 B.C.E., they issued a number of proclamations, preserved in the *Classic of Documents*, explaining to the defeated Shang people why they should submit to their conquerors. In their arguments the Zhou rulers appealed to a concept called *tianming*, or the Mandate of Heaven. Heaven, they said, charged certain good men with rulership over the lineages of the world, and the heirs of these men might continue to exercise the Heaven-sanctioned power for as long as they carried out their religious and administrative duties with piety, rightness, and wisdom. But if the worth of the ruling family declined, if the rulers turned their backs upon the spirits and abandoned the virtuous ways that had originally marked them as worthy of the mandate to rule, then Heaven might discard them and elect a new family or lineage to be the destined rulers of the world. The Shang kings, it was argued, had once been wise and benevolent rulers, enjoying the full blessing and sanction of Heaven. But in later days they had grown cruel and degenerate, so that Heaven had called upon the Zhou chieftains to overthrow the Shang rulers, punish their evil ways, and institute a new dynasty.

As one of the sacrificial songs of the *Classic of Odes* expresses this idea: "Zhou is an old people, but its charge is new." Since the Zhou had received this new charge from Heaven to rule the world, it was useless and perverse for the Shang people to continue to resist its officers. Thus the Zhou rulers explained the change of dynasties not as an action by which a strong state overthrew a weak one but as a Heaven-directed process by which a new group of wise and virtuous leaders was commissioned to take up the moral mandate forfeited by an older group whose wickedness and corruption had disqualified them as rulers. To reinforce this view, the Zhou leaders advised the people of Shang to look back to their own history. This same process had taken place when King Tang, the virtuous founder of the Shang dynasty, had been directed by Heaven to overthrow the degenerate ruler of the old Xia dynasty and institute a new rule.

From Zhou times down to the present day, this description of the dynastic cycle and the Mandate of Heaven has been accepted by nearly all Chinese. Chinese historians have been fully aware of the various power factors that contribute to the weakening and downfall of one dynasty and the rise of another. Yet they have held to the idea that behind these factors and underlying them is a deeper problem of the moral qualification of an individual or a family to rule. A ruler may, like the last king of the Shang, be powerful and astute, but if he is selfish and cruel and oppresses his people, Heaven will cease to aid and protect him or sanction his rule and he will fail. On the other hand, a state may be comparatively weak and insignificant, as the early leaders of the Zhou are traditionally pictured to have been, but if rulers are wise and humane in their administration and care for their people, all men will flock to their rule and Heaven will aid them to rise to the highest position. Such is the power and gravity of the Mandate of Heaven and the moral obligation that it implies.

The following, then, are among the basic beliefs that emerge in the Chinese literature of the Zhou period: a belief in a supreme deity or moral force that ruled the world and took an interest in the affairs of mankind; a belief in the existence and power of ancestral spirits who had to be served and placated with sacrifices; and a belief in the celestial sanction of the political order and the grave responsibility of the ruler to fulfill his moral duties to Heaven and to his people. The more purely religious belief in the existence and power of intervention of the spirits is probably older, going back at least to the Shang, and continued to be of importance in Chinese religious life, while reverence for the spirits of ancestors also continued to be a vital factor in the Chinese family system. But the concept of the moral responsibilities of the ruler, and the way in which the ruler should discharge these responsibilities so as not to lose the favor and protection of Heaven, became a major concern of Chinese thinkers. Indeed, so important did this problem seem to Confucius (551–479 B.C.E.) and his followers that they were led to reinterpret the whole body of ancient literature — the texts of divination, the speeches and pronouncements, the folk songs, the rules of ritual and etiquette, the chronicles of the feudal states — in search of a solution.[1] It is largely because of them that these ancient texts have been preserved and that the ancient concepts and terms, altered though they were by later interpretations, have remained alive and vital in Chinese thought and life.

The Classic of Documents

THE "CANON OF YAO" AND THE "CANON OF SHUN"

These texts, which appear at the beginning of this classic, purport to relate the events and pronouncements of the sage kings Yao and Shun, said to have reigned around the twenty-second century, who stand as the founding fathers and exemplars of Chinese civilization. Originally one and divided into two from the Latter Han period, these texts fill a kind of mythic function in the Chinese tradition by establishing benevolent patriarchal rule as the constitutional basis of a vast family system.

In this ideal conception, with the ruler personifying civil and familial virtue rather than military domination, his gentle charisma radiates out to successive degrees of kinship, so that all humankind is harmonized in one loving family. The core value here — that of personal virtue — is underscored by Yao's passing over his own son to find a successor in Shun, himself the embodiment of modesty and filial duty. In this process, the idea of rule by virtue and personal merit is no doubt put forward as an implicit critique of forceful rule, inherited by dynastic succession. Thus, while family values are assumed into the person of the ruler, the family itself is subsumed into the larger human family.

Examining into antiquity, we find that the Emperor Yao was called Fangxun. He was reverent, intelligent, accomplished, sincere, and mild. He was sincerely respectful and capable of modesty. His light covered the four extremities of the empire and extended to Heaven above and the Earth below. He was able to make bright his great virtue and bring affection to the nine branches of the family. When the nine branches of the family had become harmonious, he distinguished and honored the hundred clans. When the hundred clans had become illustrious, he harmonized the myriad states. The numerous people were amply nourished and prosperous and became harmonious. Then he

---

1. The term *feudal* can be applied to China of the Zhou dynasty only on the understanding that no exact correspondence to Western feudalism is implied. It serves here, and hereafter in these pages, to differentiate, as traditional Chinese historians did, between the Zhou and the relatively more centralized and bureaucratic regimes of the imperial dynasties beginning with the Qin (221–207 B.C.E.). However, some of the basic features associated with these later regimes had already made their appearance in Zhou society, distinguishing it markedly from the institutional patterns of feudal Europe.

charged Xi and He with reverence to follow August Heaven and calculate and delineate the sun, the moon, and the other heavenly bodies, and respectfully to give the people the seasons. . . . The emperor said, "Ah, you Xi and He, the year has three hundred and sixty-six days, and by means of an intercalary month you must fix the four seasons and complete the year. If you earnestly regulate all the functionaries, the achievements will all be glorious." The emperor said, "Who will carefully attend to this? I will raise him up and employ him." Fang Qi said, "Your heir-son Zhu is enlightened." The emperor said, "Alas, he is deceitful and quarrelsome; will he do?" . . . The emperor said, "Oh, you Chief of the Four Mountains, I have been on the throne for seventy years. If you can carry out the Mandate, I shall resign my position to you." The Chief of the Four Mountains said, "I have not the virtue. I would only disgrace the high position." The emperor said, "Promote someone who is already illustrious, or raise up someone who is humble and of low status." They all said to the emperor, "There is an unmarried man in a low position called Shun of Yu." The emperor said, "Yes, I have heard of him. What is he like?" The Chief said, "He is the son of a blind man. His father is stupid, his mother is deceitful, his half brother Xiang is arrogant. Yet he has been able to live in harmony with them and to be splendidly filial. He has controlled himself and has not come to wickedness." The emperor said, "I will try him; I will wive him and observe his behavior toward my two daughters." He gave orders and sent down his two daughters to the bend of the Gui River to be wives in the House of Yu. The emperor said, "Be reverent!"

The emperor said, "Come, you Shun, in the affairs on which you have been consulted, I have examined your words; your words have been accomplished and capable of yielding fine results for three years; do you ascend to the imperial throne." Shun considered himself inferior in virtue and was not pleased. But in the first month, the first day, he accepted the abdication of Yao in the Temple of the Accomplished Ancestor. . . . Then he made *lei* sacrifice to the Lord-on-High; he made *yin* sacrifice to the six venerable ones; he made *wang* sacrifice to mountains and rivers, and he made comprehensive sacrifices to all the spirits. . . . In the second month of the year he went around the east to the fiefs and came to the Venerable Dai Mountain, where he made burnt offering; he made *wang* sacrifice successively to mountains and rivers, and he gave audience to the eastern princes. He put into accord the seasons, the months, and the proper days. He made uniform the pitch pipes, the measures of length, the measures of capacity, and the weights. . . . He delimited the twelve provinces and raised altars on twelve mountains, and he deepened the rivers.

["Yaodian," "Shundian," *Shujing* —BW]

THE GRAND MODEL

Chapter 24 in the *Classic of Documents*, "The Grand Model" (*Hongfan*), purports to be a plan offered by the viscount of Ji, who had served the Shang dynasty, to King Wu of Zhou. Though the viscount had been imprisoned by Di Xin, the last ruler of the Shang, and released by King Wu of Zhou, he nonetheless refused to serve the Zhou and made known his plan to flee to Korea. Admiring his fidelity to the Shang, King Wu is supposed to have announced his intention to enfeoff the viscount in Korea. The model for good government associated with the sage king Yu, founder of the Xia dynasty, was believed to have been presented by the viscount when he appeared at the Zhou court. Reformers of later dynasties often cited "The Grand Model" as the classic basis for their radical reform plans. Here the translation is abridged.

In the thirteenth year, the king went to inquire of the Viscount of Ji and said to him, "Ah. Viscount of Ji, Heaven, unseen, has given to humankind their constitution, aiding the harmonious development of it in their various conditions. I do not know how their proper virtues in their various relations should be brought forth in due order."

The Viscount of Ji thereupon replied, "I have heard that of old Gun dammed up the inundating waters and thereby threw into disorder the arrangement of the Five Phases.[2] God (Di) was thereby roused to anger and did not give him the 'Grand Model with its Nine Divisions,' whereupon the proper virtues of the five relations were left to go to ruin. Gun was then kept a prisoner until his death, and Yu rose up to continue his undertaking. To him Heaven gave 'The Grand Model with its Nine Divisions,' and thereby the proper virtues of the various relations were brought forth in their order."

Of the Nine Divisions, only a portion of the fifth and the ninth are reproduced here. The first deals with the Five Phases (or Agents); the second with moral conduct and intellectual virtues; the third with branches of administration; the fourth with the calendar; the fifth with rulership, as follows:

"Fifth, of royal perfection: the sovereign, having established his highest point of excellence, concentrates in himself the five happinesses and then diffuses them so as to give them to his people. Then on their part the multitudes of the people, resting in your perfection, will give you the preservation of it. . . . When men have ability and administrative power, cause them still more to cultivate

---

2. The Five Phases are water, fire, wood, metal, and earth. (See ch. 10, pp. 347–49.) Gun, the father of the sage king Yu, dammed up the waters instead of creating an outlet for them; he was therefore punished. The work was then taken up by Yu, who employed a different strategy and obtained a different result.

their conduct, and the prosperity of the country will be promoted. All right men, having a competency, will go on to be good.

"If you cannot cause men to have what they love in their families, they will only proceed to be guilty of crime. As to those who do not love virtue, though you may confer favor on them, they will only involve you in the guilt of employing the evil.

> "Without deflection, without unevenness,
> Pursue royal rightness;
> Without any selfish likings,
> Pursue the royal way;
> Without any selfish dislikings,
> Pursue the royal path;
> Without partiality, without deflection,
> The royal path is level and easy;
> Without perversity, without onesidedness,
> The royal path is right and straight.
> Seeing this royal excellence,
> Turn to this perfect excellence."

He went on to say, "This amplification of the royal perfection contains the unchanging [rule] and is the [great] lesson. It is the lesson from God (Di). All the multitudes, instructed in this amplification of the perfect excellence, and carrying it into practice, will approximate to the glory of the Son of Heaven and say, 'The Son of Heaven is the parent of the people, and so becomes the sovereign of the empire.'"

The sixth division deals with questions of governance, adapted to different people and times; the seventh is concerned with the examination of doubts and the investigation of dubious matters in consultation with the nobles, officers, and masses of the people, and through divination by the turtle and milfoil. The eighth deals with confirmation from seasonable weather, and the ninth with the resultant five happinesses.

"Ninth, of the five happinesses: the first is long life; the second is riches; the third is soundness of body and serenity of mind; the fourth is the love of virtue; the fifth is an end crowning one's life."

["Hongfan," *Shujing* — trans. adapted from Legge, *Shoo king*, pp. 320–343]

THE METAL-BOUND COFFER

This document, while perhaps dating from as late as the fifth or fourth century B.C.E., purports to celebrate events that occurred at a critical juncture at the inception of the Zhou dynasty and affords insight into Zhou attitudes toward the religious authority on which the rule of the Zhou house was based. As the story opens, King Wu, the first of the Zhou sovereigns actually to rule, is ill and believed to be near death. One of his younger brothers, Dan, known as the Duke of Zhou, appeals through prayer to the spirits of his forebears to accept him as a sacrifice in the place of King Wu. He divines and receives in response an auspicious sign. The king improves. Later, after the king dies, rumors are spread casting doubt on the fidelity of the Duke of Zhou to King Cheng, his young nephew who has succeeded King Wu. Note here the invocation of the idea of the Mandate of Heaven and the way in which Heaven is understood to intervene in the human sphere.

It must be acknowledged that there remain differences among scholars about the interpretation of this fascinating text, and the translation offered here is an innovative one. One of the most interesting departures from earlier interpretations comes at the point in the text immediately following the divination by the Duke of Zhou with three turtle shells; here we find a prognostication that our translator believes is meant to represent the Duke of Zhou speaking *in the voice of the king*, or in the king's role. In other words, while the gravely ill King Wu is not present here, the duke is seen to be ritually representing him — a reflection, perhaps, of the fact that it would always have been the king who, in the earlier divinatory tradition, uttered the prognostication.

However that may be, the underlying implication of the story is an ideal virtually eternal in China, and the celebration of the Duke of Zhou merely exemplifies and dramatizes it: a ruler rules by his "virtue." Virtue requires of the king restraint, humility, and willingness to listen to advice. In principle this does not limit royal authority but rather demands its exercise — and virtue is not limited to kings. If a king acquires virtue by his action and an attitude that can be seen as self-sacrificial or self-denying, this will also be true of others, notably the king's ministers. So, paradoxically, it is precisely by a minister's self-denial — his renunciation of any interest of his own, in a complete demonstration of loyalty, to the death, if need be — that he gains and establishes the authority that effectively requires his king to heed him. In this story, the duke's demonstration of selflessness is made complete by his swearing the witnesses to silence, setting up the situation that *requires* Heaven's intervention. This is the deeper meaning of the myth celebrated in "The Metal-Bound Coffer."

Two years after the conquest of the Shang dynasty, the king caught a fever and was quite ill. The Two Dukes said, "Let us reverently consult the turtle concerning the king." But the Duke of Zhou said, "You may not so distress our former kings."

He then took the business on himself and made three altars of earth on the same cleared space; and having made another altar on the south, facing north, he there took his own position. He placed the jade *bi*-discs [on the three altars], while he himself held his jade *gui*-mace.[3] He then addressed King Tai, King Ji, and King Wen.

---

3. A jade tablet or mace conferred by kings on feudal lords as a symbol of rank.

The recorder accordingly wrote [the duke's] prayer on a tablet:

"N., your chief descendant,[4] is suffering from an epidemic disease and is violently ill. If you Three Kings are obligated to Heaven for a great son, let me Dan be a substitute for his person. I am graceful and accommodating, clever and able. I am possessed of many abilities and arts which fit me to serve spiritual beings. Your chief descendant, on the other hand, has not so many abilities and arts as I and is not so capable of serving spiritual beings. Moreover, he was appointed in the hall of Di to extend his dominion to the four quarters [of the world], so that he might establish your descendants in the lands below [Heaven] and so that none of the peoples of the four quarters would fail to be in awe and fear. Oh! Do not let that precious Heaven-conferred Mandate fall to the ground; then [all] our former kings will also ever have security and resort.

"Now I accordingly make this charge to the great turtle. If you grant what I request, I will take these discs and this mace and will go back and await your command [i.e., my death]. If you do not grant it, I will put the discs and mace away."

[The duke] then divined with three turtle [shells], and all alike were favorable. He opened the tubes and read the [oracle] texts, and these too were favorable.

The duke [speaking in the king's role] said, "Let there be no harm [to the duke]. I, humble prince, have a renewed mandate from the three kings. It is a lasting future that [I] may expect. Then what [we] 'await' [is not the duke's death, but] is that they will have concern for me, the One Man."

The duke went back and then placed the tablet [with the charge] in a metal-bound coffer. On the next day the king recovered.

After King Wu died, [other sons of King Wen,] Guan Shu and his brothers spread talk around the country, saying, "The duke will do no good to the [king's] young son."[5] The Duke of Zhou accordingly declared to the Two Dukes, "If we do not punish them, we will be unable to report to the royal ancestors [that we have done our duty]." The Duke of Zhou spent two years in the east, whereupon the guilty men were apprehended. Afterward the duke made a poem and presented it to the king, calling it "The Owl." The king on his part did not dare to blame the duke [for thus punishing King Cheng's uncles].

In the autumn there was a great [impending] harvest that had not yet been reaped; Heaven then sent a great storm of thunder and lightning, with wind. The grain was all beaten down and great trees were ripped up. The people of

---

4. "N" (i.e., "N[ame]") renders a Chinese word (*mou*, "so-and-so") conventionally used in order to avoid actually writing down the name of a person who must be accorded great respect. Though the custom arose in the Zhou period of avoiding naming a king directly, it is possible that the duke would actually have referred to his brother, King Wu, by name and that this circumlocution was introduced by a later speaker or recorder.

5. King Wu's successor was King Cheng, whom the Duke of Zhou was to serve as a regent.

the land were all terrified. The king and his great officers thereupon all put on their caps of state and opened the metal-bound coffer [and examined the] writings in it, and thus obtained the account of the Duke of Zhou taking it upon himself to be a substitute for King Wu. The Two Dukes and the king then questioned the recorder and all the other officers about the matter. They replied, "It was truly so. But, ah, the duke ordered us not to dare to speak about it."

The king held the writing and wept, saying, "Let us not reverently divine [for the truth is plain]. Formerly the duke had an earnest concern for the royal house, but I, only a child, was not able to know about it. Now Heaven has moved its terrors to display the virtue (*de*) of the Duke of Zhou. I, princeling, will greet him in person. The rites of our country indeed make this right."

The king went forth to the suburbs [to meet the duke]; Heaven then sent down rain, and a contrary wind, so that the grain all stood up. The Two Dukes gave orders to the people of the land to take up all the great trees that had been blown down and replant them. The year then turned out very fruitful.

["Jinteng," *Shujing* — DSN]

SHAO ANNOUNCEMENT

The "Shao Announcement" (*Shaogao*) purports to record the occasion of the founding of a new Zhou capital near the Luo River, an event that occurred during the reign of King Cheng, whom we encountered above in "The Metal-Bound Coffer." King Cheng was at this time still young, and his uncles, the Duke of Shao and the Duke of Zhou, served as his chief advisers. At this point the Duke of Zhou, also familiar from "The Metal-Bound Coffer," was in the seventh and last year of his regency.

The text opens with an account of the preparations made by the Duke of Shao and the Duke of Zhou for the building of the new city — taking oracles about the site and offering sacrifices before putting the Yin (i.e., Shang) people to work on its construction. Our selection begins with the main narrative: a declaration by one of the dukes about the background of the Zhou accession to power and the nature of the political order that the Zhou must maintain. While modern scholars differ as to whether this declaration was made by the Duke of Shao or the Duke of Zhou, the present translation is based on the view that the principal speaker is the latter. Whatever the attribution, the interest of the declaration lies in its powerful articulation of the concept of the Mandate of Heaven (*tianming*) as a doctrine of political legitimization and its assertion of a concomitant responsibility on the part of the ruler to listen to wise counsel and to benefit the people.

He [the Duke of Zhou] said,

"I salute with joined hands and bow my head to the ground, in respect for you, king-favored duke. And in a [formal] announcement I declare [this] to [you] Yin peoples and to your managers of affairs.

"Ah! August Heaven, High God, has changed his principal son and has revoked the Mandate of this great state of Yin. When a king receives the Mandate, without limit is the grace thereof, but also without limit is the anxiety of it. Ah! How can he fail to be reverently careful!

"Heaven has rejected and ended the Mandate of this great state of Yin. Thus, although Yin has many former wise kings in Heaven, when their successor kings and successor people undertook their Mandate, in the end wise and good men lived in misery. Knowing that they must care for and sustain their wives and children, they then called out in anguish to Heaven and fled to places where they could not be caught. Ah! Heaven too grieved for the people of all the lands, wanting, with affection, in giving its Mandate to employ those who are deeply committed. The king should have reverent care for his virtue.

"Look at the former peoples of ancient times, the Xia. Heaven guided, indulged, and cherished them, so that they would strive to understand what Heaven favors, but by this time they have let their Mandate fall to the ground. Now look at the Yin; Heaven guided them, stayed near them, nourished them, so that they would strive to comprehend what Heaven favors; but now they have let their Mandate fall to the ground.

"Now a young son succeeds to the throne; let him not, then, neglect the aged and experienced. Not only do they comprehend the virtue of our men of old — nay, more, they are sometimes able to comprehend counsels that come from Heaven.

"Ah! Even though it be that the king is young, he is [Heaven's] principal son. Let him be grandly able to be in harmony with the little people. In the present time of grace, the king must not dare to be slow, but should be prudently apprehensive about what the people say.

"The king will come representing the High God and himself undertake [the government here] in the midst of the lands. I, Dan, say, 'Let a great city be made here; may he from this place function as the mate of August Heaven, reverently sacrificing to the higher and lower spirits. May he from this place centrally govern. When the king has a fully effective mandate, his governing of the people will then enjoy [Heaven's] grace.

"Undertaking [the administration of] the Yin managers of affairs, the king should first associate them with our Zhou's managers of affairs, so as to discipline their natures, and they will day by day advance.

"Let the king reverently function in his position; he cannot but be reverently careful of his virtue. We cannot fail to mirror ourselves in the Xia; also we cannot fail to mirror ourselves in the Yin. We must not presume to suppose that the Xia received the Mandate of Heaven for a fixed period of years; we must not presume to suppose that it was not going to continue. It was because they did not reverently care for their virtue that they early let their Mandate fall. We must not presume to suppose that the Yin received the Mandate of Heaven for a fixed period of years; we must not presume to suppose that it was not going to continue. It was because they did not reverently care for their virtue that they early let their Mandate fall. Now the king has succeeded them in receiving their Mandate; let us also, in regard to the mandate of these two states, continue it with like achievements; [if we do,] then the king will [truly] now begin to undertake the mandate.

"Ah! It is like bearing a child: all depends on what happens when it is first born; one gives it oneself its allotment of [future] wisdom. Now as to whether Heaven is going to give an endowment of wisdom, of good fortune or bad, or an endowment of so-and-so many years, we [just] know that now we begin the undertaking of the Mandate.

"Dwelling in this new city, now let the king just earnestly have reverent care for his virtue. If it is virtue that the king uses, he may pray Heaven for an enduring Mandate. As he functions as king, let him not, because the common people stray and do what is wrong, then presume to govern them by harsh capital punishments; in this way he will achieve much. In being king, let him take his position in the primacy of virtue. The little people will then pattern themselves on him throughout the world; the king will then become illustrious.

"Those above and below being zealous and careful, let them say, 'As we receive Heaven's Mandate, let it grandly be like the long years enjoyed by the Xia, and not fail of the years enjoyed by the Yin' — in order that [as one would wish] the king, through the little people, may receive Heaven's enduring Mandate."

[Response:] He [the Duke of Shao, replying] saluted with joined hands, touching his head to the ground, and said, "I, your humble servant, together with the grandees of the king's vanquished peoples, and with the allied peoples, presume to receive and cherish the king's dread command and bright virtue, so that the king will finally [as you have said] have a fully effective Mandate, and the king will also be illustrious. We do not presume to encouragement; we just respectfully offer [these] gifts, so as to supply the king with the means to pray for Heaven's enduring Mandate."

[From "Shaogao," *Shujing* — DSN]

The Classic of Odes

FROM THE *GREATER ODES* AND *SACRIFICIAL ODES OF ZHOU*

These odes celebrate the virtues of King Wen, founder of the Zhou, as successor to the Shang rulers who failed to fulfill their moral responsibility. Heaven's Mandate or charge is no less real and compelling for being intangible (i.e., spiritual, moral values not reducible to words), and his successors can take King Wen as an example to live up to.

King Wen (Ode 235)

1

King Wen is on high,
Oh, he shines in Heaven!
Zhou is an old people,
but its Mandate is new.
The leaders of Zhou became illustrious,
was not God's Mandate timely given?
King Wen ascends and descends
on the left and right of God.

4

August was King Wen,
continuously bright and reverent.
Great, indeed, was the Mandate of Heaven.
There were Shang's grandsons and sons,
Shang's grandsons and sons.
Was their number not a hundred thousand?
But the High God gave his Mandate,
and they bowed down to Zhou.

7

The Mandate is not easy to keep;
may it not end in your persons.
Display and make bright your good fame,
and consider what Yin had received from Heaven.
The doings of high Heaven
have no sound, no smell.
Make King Wen your pattern,
and all the states will trust in you.

[From "Wenwang" *Da ya, Shijing* — BW]

Rich Year (Ode 279)

Rich is the year with much millet and rice;
and we have tall granaries
with hundreds and thousands and millions of sheaves.

We make wine and sweet spirits
To offer to ancestor and ancestress,
thus to fulfill the hundred rites
and bring down blessings in abundance.

[From "Fengnian," *Zhou song, Shijing* — BW]

AIRS FROM THE STATES

The *Airs* are folk songs from the various feudal states of early Zhou times telling of the joys and sorrows of the common people in their daily lives. Some of them are love songs, while others lament the hardships of war or complain about the ills of government. Of the two selections given here, "Big Rat" is clearly such a complaint, about high taxes and corrupt officials. The other is probably a song of love, but it is worth noting that from very early times it has been given a strictly political interpretation by the Confucian school. Thus under Confucian influence even the old folk songs were turned into lessons on political morality.

Big Rat (Ode 113)

The farmers of Wei complain of the tax officials.

1

Big rat, big rat,
don't eat my millet!
Three years I've served you
but you won't care for me.
I'm going to leave you
and go to that happy land,
happy land, happy land
where I'll find my place.

3

Big rat, big rat,
don't eat my sprouts!
Three years I've served you
but you give me no comfort.
I'm going to leave you
and go to those happy fields,
happy fields, happy fields,
who will moan there for long?

[From "Shishu," *Wei feng, Shijing* — BW]

The North Wind (Ode 41)

This is probably a love song, but it has traditionally been interpreted as the song of the peasants of Bei, who, oppressed by a cruel and corrupt government (the cold wind of the song), urge each other to flee to another state. Thus political relations were subsumed under the category of affective human relations.

1

Cold is the north wind,
the snow falls thick.
If you are kind and love me
take my hand and we'll go together.
You are modest, you are slow,
but oh, we must hurry!

2

Fierce is the north wind,
the snow falls fast.
If you are kind and love me,
take my hand and we'll go home together.
You are modest, you are slow,
but oh, we must hurry!

3

Nothing redder than the fox,
nothing blacker than the crow.
If you are kind and love me,
take my hand and we'll ride together.
You are modest, you are slow,
but oh, we must hurry!

[From "Beifeng," *Beifeng, Shijing* — BW]

Chapter 3

CONFUCIUS AND THE ANALECTS

Kong Qiu (551–479 B.C.E.) was known among his contemporaries as Kongzi or Master Kong. Among some later followers he was honored as Kong Fuzi — "our Master Kong," which became the basis for "Confucius," the Latinized form that has been widely used in the West. It is also common in the West to acknowledge the importance of Confucius in the later history of China and of East Asia by designating the tradition of thought and practice with which he was associated as Confucian*ism*. In the languages of East Asia, however, this tradition has been identified instead with a scholarly group known as *ru*. *Ru* means "soft," "gentle," "enduring," and, sometimes, "weak." Very likely the term *ru* — evoking a commitment to learning, refinement, cultural accomplishments, and the practice of rites and music — came to be applied to persons whose notion of virtue had more to do with decorous conduct than with martial prowess. Confucius did not think of himself as the founder of this tradition but as one who hoped to keep it alive in the world. His followers were, from early times, identified as *ru*.

Early sources suggest that Confucius was born in the feudal state of Lu in eastern China into a family of the lower ranks of the nobility, one that was probably in straitened circumstances. It is clear that by the middle of the sixth century the Zhou dynasty, whose founders he honored, was in an advanced state of decline, having lost much of its real power and authority some two centuries earlier. Warfare was endemic, as the rulers of contending states vied for territory and power. Uncertainty surrounded the future of those states, and, in the eyes of many, shrouded the fate of civilization itself. Confucius emerged as one of a number of scholars who responded to an apparent crisis of civilization. He traveled from one feudal state to another, seeking an audience with various rulers and hoping to be employed by one capable of sharing his vision. He put forward the perspective of the *ru* — his purpose having been to promote the style and manners of the noble person (*junzi*) and the efficacy of moral force or virtue (*de*), rather than violence and coercion, as a strategy for rulers. Toward the end of his life, disappointed but evidently unembittered by his failure to gain an influential political office, he continued in the role of a teacher to promote these same causes. Not immediately, but over a period of centuries, the significance of Confucius as a teacher would become apparent, and within a century or so he would acquire the reputation of a sage. In subsequent centuries his example would be woven into the fabric of an entire culture as perhaps its most persistent pattern.

The *Analects* is the single most important source for understanding the thought of Confucius and the traditions to which he subscribed. It is clearly, however, not a work that he himself wrote. The English word *analects* (from the Greek *analekta*) means "a selection," while the Chinese title *Lunyu* may be translated as "conversations." This selection of conversations was compiled by later followers, themselves apparently representing different points of view. Some evidently contributed to the written record a century or more after Confucius's lifetime. The twenty short chapters or books of the *Analects* contain, among other things, recollections of conversations that transpired among Confucius and his disciples or between Confucius and rulers of several of the feudal states that he visited during the peripatetic phase of his teaching career. There are also descriptions of the man, brief but often telling vignettes of the way he appeared to those most intimately acquainted with him.

Most of the conversations recollected in the *Analects* focus on the practicalities of interpersonal relationships, personal cultivation in the context of those relationships, and the relationship of personal cultivation on the part of rulers and ministers to the conduct of government. In many exchanges Confucius speaks about the conduct and the dispositions of the *junzi* — a term commonly translated as "gentleman," "superior man," or "noble man." Originally, the meaning of the term *junzi* was "son of a lord," but the descriptions of the *junzi* found in the *Analects* suggest something different. Here the *junzi* is less the noble man whose nobility derives from inherited *social* nobility than the noble person whose nobility derives from personal commitment and a developed *moral* power (*de*). Still, a careful reader of the *Analects* may discover a kind of tension in the text's references to the *junzi*. On the one hand, the term seems to have a far more egalitarian implication than it could have had in earlier usage, since in the Confucian perspective anyone could become a *junzi*. On the other hand, it is clear that one who aspired to become a *junzi* faced stringent moral requirements that applied no less to attitude and motivation than to behavior. The term *de*, which in earlier sources conveyed a sense of charismatic power or force, almost magical in character, here takes on the meaning of "virtue," though without necessarily shedding its former associations.

Among the kinds of conduct that Confucius associated with moral nobility, and evidently expected of the *junzi*, perhaps the three most important were filial devotion (*xiao*), humaneness (*ren*), and ritual decorum (*li*). The moral vocabulary of Confucius is by no means exhausted in these three, but these are central, expressing in three distinct modes the Confucian awareness of and concern with human interrelatedness. Close attention to each of them as they occur in the selections that follow should make clear that what Western readers may be inclined to encounter as ideas are, from the perspective of Confucius and his followers, also feelings and practices — understood to have a bearing on what a human being will be like as a person, within as well as without. Embedded in these thoughts are not simply behavioral rules or standards but expectations about what the practitioner of these virtues should be like as a cultivated human being.

Each of these three practices — filiality, humaneness, and ritual decorum — figures into Confucius's views on government as well. Inasmuch as he sees governance as modeled on the family, he understands the practice of filial devotion to have a bearing on the stability of society as a whole. He is convinced that filial devotion practiced within one's family has ramifications in a far wider sphere. Humaneness, associated with fellow feeling,[1] is bound up with reciprocity. From a Confucian perspective, perhaps the most important capacity that a ruler can have is the capacity for recognizing that he must treat the people as he himself would want to be treated in their position.[2] Ritual, which affords an ideal means for ordering one's personal life, also represents the ideal mode of governance because the rites are the vehicle through which the ruler expresses his own virtue or moral power and also encourages a sense of dignity and responsiveness among the people.

The concept of the Mandate of Heaven (or "what Heaven ordains," *tianming*) that had emerged in the early Zhou period, with a largely political significance,[3] finds its way into his reflections on his own life, suggesting that the ordered process that prevails in the wider world is found to operate in an individual life as well (*Analects* 2:4). And while it appears to be just that — an order, rather than a deity — it is a beneficent presence, to which Confucius feels

---

1. In other translations *ren* is rendered as "Goodness," "benevolence," "kindness," "supreme virtue," and so on, but the graph for *ren* refers to humankind, not abstract ideas of "Goodness" (Waley) or benevolence (literally, "goodwill").

2. See, for example, 12:2 and 12:22.

3. See ch. 2.

personally responsible, as well as a source of life, support, and even a certain austere comfort. He recognizes that it will not always be given to human beings to understand Heaven's functioning, an insight that shows up in his conversations and observations in a distinctive and often poignant interplay of confidence and resignation. There can be no expectation that the reward for right conduct or punishment for its opposite will be immediately apparent within the lifetime of particular individuals: Heaven's ordinations are apparently expressed within a longer and larger frame. Still, he seems to believe that human beings have a home in the natural order and some assurance of the ultimate significance, and even resonance, of moral action. There is something remarkably subtle about this view and something immensely powerful as well, a subtlety and a power that seem to have inhered as much in the personality as in the ideas of this very worldly teacher.

Selections from the Analects

There are enough differences in the way Confucius' teaching is described in the twenty chapters of the received text of the Analects to suggest that there must have been multiple recorders or compilers, and it seems clear that these chapters must have been incorporated into the text at different times. Without attempting to reconstruct the historical strata of the work, we offer the following selections in an order that follows the arrangement of the received text as it has been known over the course of centuries to readers in China and in East Asia as a whole. For a cogent attempt to reconstruct the text chronologically, see Brooks and Brooks, The Original Analects. For those who prefer a topical arrangement, the following numbered items in our text may serve as a guide to some of the major themes. (The numbering of passages follows James Legge.)

Learning: 1:1, 1:6, 1:7, 1:8, 1:14, 2:4, 2:15, 5:27, 6:2, 7:2, 7:3, 8:13, 11:6, 14:25, 14:37, 15:3, 15:30, 16:9, 19:6
The noble person (junzi): 1:1, 1:2, 1:8, 1:14, 2:12, 2:14, 4:5, 4:16, 6:16, 9:13, 12:5, 13:3, 13:23, 14:7, 14:29, 14:45, 15:1, 15:18, 16:8, 17:21, 20:3
Filial devotion (xiao): 1:2, 1:6, 1:7, 1:11, 2:5, 2:6, 2:7, 2:21, 4:20, 13:18, 17:9
Humaneness (ren): 1:2, 1:3, 1:6, 3:3, 4:2, 4:5, 4:6, 5:7, 6:5, 6:20, 6:21, 6:28, 7:29, 8:7, 9:1, 9:28, 12:1, 12:2, 12:3, 12:22, 13:19, 14:2, 14:18, 15:8, 15:32, 15:35, 17:6, 19:6
Wealth and poverty, economy, material possessions: 1:5, 1:14, 1:15, 2:7, 4:5, 6:9, 7:15, 8:21, 12:5, 12:7, 13:9, 14:1, 15:1, 16:1
Virtue or moral force (de): 2:1, 2:3, 4:24, 7:3, 7:22, 9:17, 12:19, 14:36, 15:3, 16:1; 17:13
Rites and sacrifices: 2:3, 2:5, 3:3, 3:4, 3:11, 3:12, 3:15, 3:18, 3:19, 4:13, 9:10, 11:25, 12:1, 12:2, 12:5, 13:3, 14:13, 15:1 17:21, 20:3
Laws and punishments: 2:3, 13:3
Government: 1:5, 2:1, 2:19, 2:21, 3:19, 4:13, 8:18, 11:25, 12:7, 12:11, 12:19, 12:22, 13:3, 13:16, 13:17, 15:4, 15:10, 15:32, 16:1

Heaven, Mandate of Heaven (or Heaven's ordinances): 2:4, 7:22, 8:19, 11:8, 12:5, 14:37, 16:8, 17:19

Friends, friendship: 1:1, 1:4, 1:7, 1:8, 2:21

Reverence: 1:5, 2:7, 13:19, 14:45, 19:1

Rightness, righteousness (yi): 4:16, 7:3, 14:13, 19:1

Culture or refinement (wen): 1:6, 3:14, 6:16, 7:24, 8:19, 9:5, 9:10, 16:1

The Way (Dao): 1:2, 1:14, 1:15, 4:5, 4:15, 6:10, 8:13, 11:23, 12:19, 14:1, 15:28, 18:6

Destiny, fate, allotted span (ming): 6:2, 9:1, 11:6, 11:25, 12:2, 12:5, 14:29, 20:3

Words, rectification of names: 1:3, 1:7, 13:3, 16:8, 17:9, 20:3

1:1 The Master said, "To learn, and at due times to practice what one has learned, is that not also a pleasure? To have friends come from afar, is that not also a joy? To go unrecognized, yet without being embittered, is that not also to be a noble person?"

1:2 Master You [You Ruo] said, "Among those who are filial toward their parents and fraternal toward their brothers, those who are inclined to offend against their superiors are few indeed. Among those who are disinclined to offend against their superiors, there have never been any who are yet inclined to create disorder. The noble person concerns himself with the root; when the root is established, the Way is born. Being filial and fraternal — is this not the root of humaneness?"

1:3 The Master said, "Those who are clever in their words and pretentious in their appearance, yet are humane, are few indeed."

1:4 Zengzi[4] said, "Each day I examine myself on three things: In planning on behalf of others, have I failed to be loyal? When dealing with friends, have I failed to be trustworthy? On receiving what has been transmitted, have I failed to practice it?"

1:5 The Master said, "In ruling a state of a thousand chariots, one is reverent in the handling of affairs and shows himself to be trustworthy. One is economical in expenditures, loves the people, and uses them only at the proper season."

1:6 The Master said, "A young man is to be filial within his family and respectful outside it. He is to be earnest and faithful, overflowing in his love for living beings and intimate with those who are humane. If after such practice he has strength to spare, he may use it in the study of culture."

1:7 Zixia said, "One who esteems the worthy and has little regard for sexual attraction, who in serving his parents is able to summon up his entire strength, who in serving his ruler is able to exert himself with utmost devotion, who in

---

4. Zengzi was one of the most important of Confucius' followers. He is quoted numerous times in the *Analects* and is Confucius' sole interlocutor in the *Classic of Filial Piety* (see ch. 10).

interacting with friends shows himself trustworthy in his words — though it may be said of him that he has not studied, I would definitely call him learned."

1:8 The Master said, "If the noble person is not serious,[5] he will not inspire awe, nor will his learning be sound. One should abide in loyalty and trustworthiness and should have no friends who are not his equal.[6] If one has faults, one should not be afraid to change."

1:11 The Master said, "When a person's father is alive, observe his intentions. After his father is no more, observe his actions. If for three years he does not change his father's ways, he is worthy to be called filial."

1:14 The Master said, "The noble person who seeks neither satiety in his food nor comfort in his dwelling, who is diligent in his undertakings and careful in his speech, who goes together with those who possess the Way in order to be corrected by them — he is worthy to be called a lover of learning."

1:15 Zigong said, "'Poor yet free from flattery; rich yet free from pride.' How would that be?" The Master said, "That would do, but is not as good as 'poor yet finding joy in the Way, rich yet loving the rites.'"

Zigong said, "The Ode says, 'As with something cut, something filed, something carved, something polished.'[7] Does this resemble what you were saying?"

The Master said, "With Si [Zigong] one can begin to talk about poetry. Being told what is past, he knows what is to come."

1:16 The Master said, "One should not grieve that one is unrecognized by others; rather, one should grieve that one fails to recognize others."

2:1 The Master said, "One who governs through virtue may be compared to the polestar, which occupies its place while the host of other stars pay homage to it."

2:3 The Master said, "Lead them by means of regulations and keep order among them through punishments, and the people will evade them and will lack any sense of shame.[8] Lead them through moral force (de) and keep order among them through rites (li), and they will have a sense of shame and will also correct themselves."

The following passage might be described as the world's shortest autobiography, in which Confucius describes, with exquisite brevity, his maturation throughout the course of his life.

2:4 The Master said, "At fifteen, my heart was set upon learning; at thirty, I had become established; at forty, I was no longer perplexed; at fifty, I knew

---

5. Literally, "heavy" or "weighty."
6. I.e., in moral terms.
7. Quoting Ode 55, which describes a refined and elegant gentleman.
8. Or, as Arthur Waley interprets it, "self-respect."

what is ordained by Heaven;[9] at sixty, I obeyed; at seventy, I could follow my heart's desires without transgressing the line."

2:5 Meng Yi Zi asked about being filial. The Master said, "Let there be no discord." When Fan Chi was driving him, the Master told him, "Mengsun asked me about being filial and I said, 'Let there be no discord.'" Fan Chi said, "What did you mean by that?" The Master said, "When one's parents are alive, one serves them in accordance with the rites; when they are dead, one buries them in accordance with the rites and sacrifices to them in accordance with the rites."

2:6 Meng Wu Bo asked about being filial. The Master said, "One's parents' only concern should be lest one become ill."

2:7 Ziyou asked about filial devotion. The Master said, "Nowadays filial devotion means being able to provide nourishment. But dogs and horses too can provide nourishment. Unless one is reverent, where is the difference?"

2:9 The Master said, "I talk with [Yan] Hui for a whole day, and he does not oppose me. It is as if he were stupid. But when I look into what he does in private after he has withdrawn, he can be considered exemplary. Hui is not stupid."

2:11 The Master said, "One who reanimates the old so as to understand the new may become a teacher."

2:12 The Master said, "The noble person is not a tool."[10]

2:14 The Master said, "The noble person is inclusive, not exclusive; the small person is exclusive, not inclusive."

2:15 The Master said, "To learn without thinking is unavailing; to think without learning is dangerous."

2:17 The Master said, "You,[11] shall I teach you what knowledge is? When you know something, to know that you know it. When you do not know, to know that you do not know it. This is knowledge."

2:19 Duke Ai[12] asked, "What must be done so as to cause the people to submit?" The Master replied, "Raise up the upright; put them over the crooked: the people will submit. Raise up the crooked; put them over the upright: the people will not submit." [See 12:22]

2:21 Someone said to Confucius, "Why does the Master not take part in government?" The Master said, "What do the *Documents* say about being filial? 'Be filial. Just being filial and friendly toward one's brothers has its effect on government.'[13] Why should one have to take part in government?"

---

9. In Chinese, *tianming*, also translated in other contexts as the Mandate of Heaven. See pp. 35–37 (*Classic of Documents*).

10. Unlike a tool, a noble person is thought neither to have just one particular function nor to be merely a tool of others.

11. Zhong You, also known as Zilu, was known especially for his impetuousness.

12. Ruler of the state of Lu, 494–468 B.C.E.

13. *Classic of Documents*, "Jun Chen." Legge, *The Chinese Classics* 3:535.

3:3 The Master said, "If one is human yet not humane — what can one have to do with rites? If one is human yet not humane — what can one have to do with music?"

3:4 Lin Fang asked about what is fundamental in rites. The Master said, "This is indeed a great question. In rites, it is better to be sparing than to be excessive. In mourning, it is better to express grief than to emphasize formalities."

3:11 Someone asked for an explanation of the *di* sacrifice. The Master said, "I do not know. If I knew the explanation it would be as if all-under-Heaven were displayed right here." He pointed to the palm of his hand.

3:12 "Sacrifice as if they were present" means to sacrifice to the spirits as if they were present. The Master said, "If I am not present at the sacrifice, it is as if there were no sacrifice."

3:14 The Master said, "The Zhou surveyed the two dynasties [Xia and Shang]. How refined is its culture! I follow the Zhou."

3:15 When the Master entered the great temple he asked about everything. Someone said, "Who will say that this son of the man of Zou[14] knows about ritual? When he enters the great temple, he asks about everything." The Master heard of it and said, "This is the ritual."

3:18 The Master said, "Serving one's ruler according to the fullness of ritual — people would consider this flattery."

3:19 Duke Ding asked how a ruler should employ his ministers and how ministers should serve their ruler. Confucius replied, "The ruler should employ the ministers according to ritual; the ministers should serve the ruler with loyalty."

4:1 It is humaneness that brings beauty to one's surroundings. Should one not make the choice to abide in humaneness, how could one become known?

4:2 The Master said, "One who is not humane is able neither to abide for long in hardship nor to abide for long in joy. The humane find peace in humaneness; the knowing derive profit from humaneness."

4:5 The Master said, "Wealth and honor are what people desire, but one should not abide in them if it cannot be done in accordance with the Way. Poverty and lowliness are what people dislike, but one should not avoid them if it cannot be done in accordance with the Way. If the noble person rejects humaneness, how can he fulfill that name? The noble person does not abandon humaneness for so much as the space of a meal. Even when hard-pressed he is bound to it, bound to it even in time of danger."

4:6 The Master said, "I have not seen one who loved humaneness, nor one

---

14. Confucius's father, having served as an official in Zou, was "the man of Zou," making this an indirect and deprecatory reference to Confucius.

who hated inhumanity. One who loved humaneness would value nothing more highly. One who hated inhumanity would be humane so as not to allow inhumanity to affect his person. Is there someone whose strength has for the space of a single day been devoted to humaneness? I have not seen one whose strength was insufficient. It may have happened, but I have not seen it."

4:13 The Master said, "If one can govern a state through rites and yielding, what difficulty is there in this? If one cannot govern through rites and yielding, of what use are the rites?"

4:14 The Master said, "One is not anxious about having no office but is anxious about having the wherewithal to hold office. One is not anxious about not being recognized by others but is anxious about being worthy of recognition."

4:15 The Master said, "Shen! In my Way there is one thing that runs throughout." Zengzi said, "Yes." When the Master had gone out the disciples asked, "What did he mean?" Zengzi said, "The Master's Way is loyalty and reciprocity, that is all."

4:16 The Master said, "The noble person is concerned with rightness; the small person is concerned with profit."

4:20 The Master said, "If for three years one does not alter the ways of one's [deceased] father, one may be called filial."

4:25 The Master said, "Moral force is not solitary; it *will* have neighbors."

5:7 Meng Wu Bo asked whether Zilu was humane. The Master said, "I do not know." He asked again. The Master said, "As for You, he might be employed to manage the military levies in a state of a thousand chariots, but whether he is humane, I do not know." "What about Qiu?" The Master said, "In a town of a thousand households or a family of a hundred chariots, he could be employed as a governor, but whether he is humane I do not know." "What about Chi?" The Master said, "As for Chi, when he puts on his sash and takes his place in court, he might be engaged in conversation with the guests, but whether he is humane I do not know."

5:11 Zigong said, "What I do not want others to do to me, I also want to refrain from doing to others." The Master said, "Zi, this is not something to which you have attained."

5:19 Ji Wenzi thought three times before acting. The Master heard of it and said, "Twice might be enough."

5:27 The Master said, "In a town of ten households, there must certainly be those as loyal and trustworthy as I,[15] but none who care as much about learning as I do."

---

15. Confucius actually does not use the first-person pronoun but refers to himself by his given name, Qiu.

6:2 Duke Ai asked who among the disciples loved learning. Confucius replied, "There was Yan Hui. He loved learning. He did not transfer his anger, nor did he repeat a mistake. Unfortunately, his allotted span was short, and he died. Now that he is gone I have not heard of one who loves learning."

6:5 The Master said, "As for Hui, he went for three months without his mind's departing from humaneness. As for the others, they might persist for a day or a month, but that is all."

6:9 The Master said, "How excellent was Hui! Having just a single bowl of food and a single ladle of drink, and living in a narrow lane — others could not have endured such hardship, while Hui's joy was unaltered. How excellent was Hui!"

6:10 Ran Qiu said, "It is not that I do not delight in the Master's Way, but my strength is insufficient." The Master said, "Those whose strength is insufficient drop out midway, but now you are setting limits."

6:16 The Master said, "Where substance prevails over refinement, there is the savage; where refinement prevails over substance, there is the scribe; where refinement and substance are symmetrically ordered, there is the noble person."

6:18 The Master said, "Knowing it does not compare with loving it; loving it does not compare with delighting in it."

6:20 Fan Chi asked about wisdom. The Master said, "Devote yourself to what must rightly be done for the people; respect spiritual beings, while keeping at a distance from them. This may be called wisdom." He asked about humaneness. The Master said, "One who is humane first does what is difficult and only thereafter concerns himself with success. This may be called humaneness."

6:21 The Master said, "The wise take joy in water; the humane take joy in mountains. The wise are active; the humane are tranquil. The wise enjoy; the humane endure." [See 9:28]

6:28 Zigong said, "What would you say of someone who broadly benefited the people and was able to help everyone? Could he be called humane?" The Master said, "How would this be a matter of humaneness? Surely he would have to be a sage? Even Yao and Shun were concerned about such things. As for humaneness — you want to establish yourself; then help others to establish themselves. You want to develop yourself; then help others to develop themselves. Being able to recognize oneself in others, one is on the way to being humane."[16]

7:1 The Master said, "I transmit but do not create. In believing in and loving the ancients, I dare to compare myself with our old Peng."[17]

---

16. Literally, "The ability to take what is near and grasp the analogy may be called the direction of humaneness."

17. The identity of "our old Peng" is unclear, but he is usually taken to be the Chinese counterpart to Methuselah.

7:2 The Master said, "Knowing it in silence, learning without tiring, instructing others without weariness — which of these may be found in me?"[18]

7:3 The Master said, "Virtue (*de*) not being cultivated, learning not being discussed, hearing of rightness without being able to follow it, or of what is not good without being able to change it — these are my sorrows."

7:5 The Master said, "How extreme is my decline! It has been so long since I have dreamed I saw the Duke of Zhou."

7:7 The Master said, "From one who brought only a bundle of dried meat[19] on up, I have never declined to give instruction to anyone."

7:8 The Master said, "To one who is not eager I do not reveal anything, nor do I explain anything to one who is not communicative. If I raise one corner for someone and he cannot come back with the other three, I do not go on."

7:15 The Master said, "Having coarse rice to eat, water to drink, a bent arm for a pillow — joy lies in the midst of this as well. Wealth and honor that are not rightfully gained are to me as floating clouds."

7:18 The Duke of She asked Zilu about Confucius, and Zilu did not answer him. The Master said, "Why did you not simply say, 'This is the sort of person he is: so stirred with devotion that he forgets to eat, so full of joy that he forgets to grieve, unconscious even of the approach of old age'?"

7:19 The Master said, "I am not one who was born with knowledge; I am one who loves the past and is diligent in seeking it."

7:20 These things the Master did not speak about: anomalies, prodigies, disorder, spirits.

7:21 The Master said, "Walking along with three people, my teacher is sure to be among them. I choose what is good in them and follow it and what is not good and change it."

7:22 The Master said, "Heaven has given birth to the virtue (*de*) that is in me. What can Huan Tui[20] do to me?"

7:23 The Master said, "You two or three, do you suppose there is something I conceal from you? I have nothing that I conceal, and nothing I do that is not done together with you two or three. This is Qiu."[21]

7:24 There were four things the Master taught: culture, conduct, loyalty, and trustworthiness.[22]

---

18. Interpretations of this passage vary. Confucius is generally understood to be suggesting his strengths, but in a spirit of deep humility.

19. Dried meat, or other food, was offered as a present for teachers. Here it suggests the least one might offer.

20. Confucius, traveling through the feudal state of Song, was set upon by Huan Tui, one of that state's ministers. Though his life was apparently in danger, he allayed the fears of his followers through this affirmation of confidence in the power of Heaven.

21. Referring to himself by his given name.

22. Compare with the list of things the Master reputedly did *not* speak about in 7:20 above.

7:29 The Master said, "Is humaneness far away? If I want to be humane, then humaneness is here."

7:37 The Master was mild and yet strict, dignified and yet not severe, courteous and yet at ease.

8:7 Zengzi said, "The man of service[23] cannot but be broad and resolute. His burden is heavy, and his way is long. Humaneness is the burden that he takes upon himself. Is it not heavy? Only in death does his way come to an end. Is it not long?"

8:13 The Master said, "Earnest and faithful, he loves learning and clings unto death to the good Way. He neither enters a state that is in peril nor dwells in a state that is in disorder. When the Way is present in the world, he appears; when the Way is absent, he hides. When the Way prevails in a state, to be poor and lowly is cause for shame. When the Way is absent in a state, to be rich and honored is cause for shame."[24]

8:18 The Master said, "Sublime, sublime — Shun and Yu possessing all-under-Heaven as if it were nothing to them."

8:19 The Master said, "Great was Yao as a ruler! How sublime! Heaven alone is great, and Yao alone took it as a model. How boundless! The people could find no name for it. How sublime in the success of his achievements! How brilliant in the signs of his culture and discourse (wenzhang)!"

8:21 The Master said, "In Yu I can find no fault. Abstemious in his food and drink, he yet displayed the utmost filial devotion toward spiritual beings. Poorly clad, he yet showed the utmost elegance in his sacrificial robe and headdress. Living in a humble dwelling, he yet exerted all of his strength on the ditches and water channels. In Yu I can find no fault."

There has been much discussion about why, in the following passage, Confucius is said to have spoken "little" about topics on which there are many recorded pronouncements. This is especially true in the case of humaneness, which is discussed at many points in the Analects. *While there is no fully convincing answer to this, one possibility is that in many instances when Confucius discusses humaneness, he seems to have been responding to questions from disciples, and then guardedly, preferring to leave the question and its answer open-ended. For him humaneness knew no limit and could not be explicitly defined.*

9:1 The Master seldom spoke about profit (li) and destiny (ming) and humaneness (ren).

---

23. Or officer.
24. Compare with 4:5 above.

9:4 Four things the Master eschewed: he had no preconceptions, no prejudices, no obduracy, and no egotism.

9:5 The Master, being imperiled in Kuang,[25] said, "Now that King Wen is no more, does the culture not reside here?[26] If Heaven had intended to destroy this culture, later mortals would not have been able to share in it. And if Heaven is not going to destroy this culture, what can the people of Kuang do to me?"

9:7 The Master said, "Have I knowledge? I have *no* knowledge. But if an ordinary fellow asks me a question — as if empty, empty — [27]I knock it about from both ends until everything is yielded up."

9:10 Yan Yuan, sighing deeply, said, "I look up to it and it is higher still; I delve into it and it is harder yet. I look for it in front, and suddenly it is behind. The Master skillfully leads a person step by step. He has broadened me with culture and restrained me with ritual. When I wish to give it up, I cannot do so. Having exerted all my ability, it is as if there were something standing up right before me, and though I want to follow it, there is no way to do so."

9:13 The Master wanted to go and live among the Nine Yi.[28] Someone said, "They are rude. How can you do that?" The Master said, "Where a noble person dwells, what rudeness can there be?"

9:16 Standing by a stream, the Master said, "Passing on like this, it never ceases, night or day."

9:17 The Master said, "I have never seen anyone who loved virtue (*de*) as much as he loved beauty (*se*)."

9:25 The Master said, "The Three Armies can be deprived of their commander, but even a common person cannot be deprived of his will."

9:28 The Master said, "The wise have no doubts; the humane have no sorrows; the courageous have no fears."

11:3 The Master said, "[Yan] Hui was of no help to me. Nothing I said failed to delight him."

11:6 Ji Kang Zi asked which of the disciples loved to learn. Confucius replied, "There was Yan Hui. He loved to learn, but unfortunately his allotted span (*ming*) was short, and he died. Now there is no one."[29]

11:8 When Yan Yuan died, the Master said, "Alas, Heaven is destroying me! Heaven is destroying me!"

---

25. The most frequently encountered explanation is that Kuang was a border town variously controlled by several feudal states. There Confucius was mistaken for someone who had previously made trouble in the town and was attacked in a case of mistaken identity.

26. That is, in himself.

27. It is unclear whether the description "as if empty, empty" refers to the person who asks the question or the one who answers it.

28. The Nine were tribes living in the east.

29. Compare with 6:2 above.

11:11 Jilu asked about serving spiritual beings. The Master said, "Before you have learned to serve human beings, how can you serve spirits?" "I venture to ask about death." "When you do not yet know life, how can you know about death?"

11:23 Ji Ziran asked whether Zhong You [Zilu] and Ran Qiu could be called great ministers. The Master said, "I thought you were going to ask a different question, but you ask about You and Qiu. One who is called a great minister serves his ruler according to the Way. When he cannot do so, he quits. Now You and Qiu may be called ordinary ministers." "Then this means that they will always follow him?" The Master said, "If it were a matter of slaying father or ruler, they would not follow."

11:25 Zilu, Zeng Xi, Ran You, and Gongxi Hua were seated in attendance. The Master said, "Never mind that I am a day older than you.[30] Often you say, 'I am not recognized.' If you were to be recognized, what would you do?" Zilu hastily replied, "In a state of a thousand chariots, hemmed in by great states, beset by invading armies, and afflicted by famine — You,[31] if allowed to govern for the space of three years, could cause the people to have courage and to know their direction." The Master smiled.

"Qiu, what about you?" He replied, "In a state of sixty or seventy li[32] square, or even fifty or sixty — Qiu,[33] if allowed to govern for three years, could enable the people to have a sufficient livelihood. As for ritual and music, however, I should have to wait for a noble person."

"Chi,[34] what about you?" He replied, "I do not say that I am capable of this, yet I should like to learn it. At ceremonies in the ancestral temple and at the audiences of the lords at court, I should like, dressed in the dark robe and black cap, to serve as a minor assistant."

"Dian,[35] what about you?" As he paused in his playing the qin[36] and put the instrument aside, he replied, "My wish differs from what these three have chosen." The Master said, "What harm is there in that? Each may speak his wish." He said, "At the end of spring, when the spring clothes have been made, I should like to go with five or six youths who have assumed the cap, and with six or seven young boys, to bathe in the River Yi, to enjoy the breeze among the rain altars, and to return home singing." The Master sighed deeply and said, "I am with Dian."

---

30. Confucius, while acknowledging indirectly that his disciples respect him in part because of his age, tries to ease their sense of restraint and to encourage them to speak openly.

31. Referring to himself.

32. A li is equal to about one-third of a mile.

33. Referring to himself.

34. Referring to Gongxi Hua.

35. Referring to Zeng Xi or Zeng Dian.

36. A five-stringed musical instrument, such as a zither.

When the other three went out Zeng Xi remained behind and said, "What did you think of the words of the others?" The Master said, "Each one spoke his wish, that is all." "Why did the Master smile at You?" "One governs a state through ritual, and his words reflected no sense of yielding. This is why I smiled." "Was it not a state that Qiu wanted for himself?" "Yes, could one ever see a territory of sixty or seventy *li*, or of fifty or sixty *li*, that was not a state?" "And was it not a state that Chi wanted for himself?" "Yes, is there anyone besides the lords who frequent the ancestral temple and the audiences at court? If Chi were to play a minor role, who would play a major one?"

12:1 Yan Yuan asked about humaneness. The Master said, "Through mastering oneself and returning to ritual one becomes humane. If for a single day one can master oneself and return to ritual, the whole world will return to humaneness. Does the practice of humaneness come from oneself or from others?" Yan Yuan said, "May I ask about the specifics of this?" The Master said, "Look at nothing contrary to ritual; listen to nothing contrary to ritual; say nothing contrary to ritual; do nothing contrary to ritual." Yan Yuan said, "Though unintelligent, Hui[37] requests leave to put these words into practice."

12:2 Zhonggong [Ran Yong] asked about humaneness. The Master said, "When going abroad, treat everyone as if you were receiving a great guest; when employing the people, do so as if assisting in a great sacrifice. What you do not want for yourself, do not do to others. There should be no resentment in the state, and no resentment in the family." Zhonggong said, "Though unintelligent, Yong requests leave to put these words into practice."

12:3 Sima Niu asked about humaneness. The Master said, "The humane person is cautious in his speech."[38] Sima Niu said, "Cautious of speech! Is this what you mean by humaneness?" The Master said, "When doing it is so difficult, how can one be without caution in speaking about it?"

12:5 Sima Niu, grievingly, said, "Other men all have brothers; I alone have none."[39] Zixia said, "Shang[40] has heard this: Death and life are ordained; wealth and honor depend on Heaven. If the noble person is reverent, unfailingly courteous toward others, and observant of the rites, then all within the four seas are his brothers. Why should he be distressed at having no brothers?"

12:7 Zigong asked about government. The Master said, "Sufficient food, sufficient military force, the confidence of the people." Zigong said, "If one had, unavoidably, to dispense with one of these three, which of them should

---

37. Referring to himself.

38. There is a pun here, humaneness (*ren*) being a homophone of "cautious" (*ren*). The two are written with different Chinese characters.

39. It was not that he actually had no brothers but that he was worried about his elder brother, Huan Tui, who was an enemy of Confucius. See 7:22 above.

40. Referring to himself.

go first?" The Master said, "Get rid of the military." Zigong said, "If one had, unavoidably, to dispense with one of the remaining two, which should go first?" The Master said, "Dispense with the food. Since ancient times there has always been death, but without confidence a people cannot stand."

12:11 Duke Jing of Qi asked Confucius about government. Confucius replied, "Let the ruler be a ruler; the minister, a minister; the father, a father; the son, a son." "Excellent," said the duke. "Truly, if the ruler is not a ruler, the subject is not a subject, the father is not a father, and the son is not a son, though I have grain, will I get to eat it?"

12:19 Ji Kang Zi asked Confucius about government, saying, "How would it be if one killed those who do not possess the Way in order to benefit those who do possess it?" Confucius replied, "Sir, in conducting your government, why use killing? If you, sir, want goodness, the people will be good. The virtue of the noble person is like the wind, and the virtue of small people is like grass. When the wind blows over the grass, the grass must bend."

12:22 Fan Chi asked about humaneness. The Master said, "It is loving people." He asked about wisdom. The Master said, "It is knowing people." When Fan Chi did not understand, the Master said, "Raise up the upright, put them over the crooked, and you should be able to cause the crooked to become upright."

After Fan Chi had withdrawn, he saw Zixia and said, "A while ago I went to see the Master and asked him about wisdom. The Master said, 'Raise up the upright, put them over the crooked, and you should be able to cause the crooked to become upright.' What did he mean?" Zixia said, "How rich this saying is! When Shun possessed all-under-Heaven, he selected from among the people as a whole and employed Gao Yao, which caused all who were not humane to go far away. When Tang possessed all-under-Heaven, he selected from among the people as a whole and employed Yi Yin, which caused all who were not humane to go far away."

13:3 Zilu said, "The ruler of Wei has been waiting for the Master to administer his government. What should come first?" The Master said, "What is necessary is the rectification of names." Zilu said, "Could this be so? The Master is wide of the mark. Why should there be this rectification?" The Master said, "How uncultivated, You! In regard to what he does not know, the noble person is cautiously reserved. If names are not rectified, then language will not be appropriate, and if language is not appropriate, affairs will not be successfully carried out. If affairs are not successfully carried out, rites and music will not flourish, and if rites and music do not flourish, punishments will not hit the mark. If punishments do not hit the mark, the people will have nowhere to put hand or foot. Therefore the names used by the noble person must be appropriate for speech, and his speech must be appropriate for action. In regard to language, the noble person allows no carelessness, that is all."

13:6 The Master said, "If one is correct in one's person, things will be accomplished without one's issuing orders. If one is not correct in one's person, although one gives orders, they will not be followed."

13:9 When the Master went to Wei, Ran You served as his driver. The Master said, "How numerous the people are!" Ran You said, "Since they are already numerous, what more should be done for them?" He said, "Enrich them." Ran You said, "And when they have been enriched, what more can be done for them?" He replied, "Teach them."

13:16 The Duke of She asked about government. The Master said, "Those who are nearby should be pleased, and those who are far off should be attracted."

13:17 Having become prefect of Qufu, Zixia inquired about government. The Master said, "Do not desire quick results, nor look for small advantages. If one desires quick results, one will not succeed, and if one looks for small advantages, great affairs will not be brought to completion."

13:18 The Duke of She told Confucius, "In our part of the country there is one Upright Gong. His father stole a sheep, and the son bore witness against him." Confucius said, "In our part of the country, the upright are different from that. A father is sheltered by his son, and a son is sheltered by his father. Uprightness lies in this."

13:19 Fan Chi asked about humaneness. The Master said, "In private life, courtesy; in the conduct of affairs, reverence; in relations with others, loyalty. Even if one is among the Yi and the Di this should not be set aside."

13:21 The Master said, "Since I cannot get those who follow the middle way to associate with, I must accept the madly ardent and the cautiously restrained. The madly ardent go forward and seize their opportunities, while the cautiously restrained have things that they will not do."

13:23 The Master said, "The noble person is conciliatory but not conformist; the small person is conformist but not conciliatory."

13:29 The Master said, "When a good man has taught the common people for seven years, they should be ready to be employed in war."

13:30 The Master said, "To lead the people to war without having taught them is to throw them away."

14:1 [Yuan] Xian asked about shame. The Master said, "When the Way exists in a state, to be thinking mainly of one's salary; when the Way does not exist in a state, to be thinking mainly of one's salary — this is shameful."

14:2 "Relinquishing arrogance, boasting, resentment, and covetousness may be considered to be humaneness."[41] The Master said, "This may be considered doing what is difficult, but whether it can be considered humaneness, I do not know."

---

41. Presumably a statement by Yuan Xian, the questioner in the preceding paragraph.

14:7 The Master said, "It may happen that the noble person is not humane, but never that the small person is humane."

14:13 Zilu inquired about the complete man. The Master said, "Were one as knowledgeable as Zang Wuzhong, as free from desire as Gongchuo, as courageous as Zhuang Zi of Bian, as accomplished as Ran Qiu, and also refined through rites and music, he could indeed be called a complete man." Then he said, "In the present day what need is there for a complete man to be like this? If, seeing the prospect of gain, he thinks of rightness; confronting danger, he is prepared to sacrifice his life; faced with an old agreement, he does not forget what he always said — he too can be considered a complete man."

14:18 Zigong said, "Surely Guan Zhong[42] was not humane?" When Duke Huan killed his brother, Jiu, Guan Zhong was unable to die with Jiu and even became prime minister to Duke Huan." The Master said, "Guan Zhong became prime minister to Duke Huan and made him hegemon among the lords, uniting and reforming all-under-Heaven. Down to the present day the common people continue to receive benefits from this. Had it not been for Guan Zhong we would be wearing our hair unbound and folding our robes to the left.[43] How can this be compared to the ordinary fidelity of the common man and woman who might commit suicide in a ditch without anyone's knowing of it?"

14:23 Zilu asked how to serve a ruler. The Master said, "You may not deceive him, but you may stand up to him."

14:25 The Master said, "In ancient times learning was for the sake of oneself, whereas now learning is for the sake of others."[44]

14:29 The noble person is ashamed if his words exceed his actions.

14:36 Someone said, "What do you think of the saying, 'Respond to injury with virtue (de)'?" The Master said, "How then will you respond to virtue? Respond to injury with uprightness and to virtue with virtue."

14:37 The Master said, "There is no one who knows me." Zigong said, "How could it be that no one knows you?" The Master said, "I bear neither a grievance against Heaven nor a grudge against men. And as learning here below penetrates to what is above, it must be Heaven that knows me!"

14:41 Zilu was lodging for the night at the Stone Gate. The gatekeeper asked where he came from. Zilu said, "From the Kong family." The gatekeeper said, "Isn't that the one who, although knowing it's no use, keeps working anyway?"

14:45 Zilu asked about the noble person. The Master said, "He cultivates

---

42. Guan Zhong was a Legalist minister famous for his service to the hegemon, Duke Huan of Qi. Some of the statements attributed to Confucius in the *Analects* are critical of Guan Zhong, and others, like the one that follows here, are laudatory, perhaps suggesting different views among the compilers of the text.

43. In the style common among the non-Chinese tribes.

44. I.e., in order to gain their approval rather than for the full development of the self.

himself with reverence." "Is that all there is to it?" "He cultivates himself in order to bring peace to others." "Is that all there is to it?" The Master said, "He cultivates himself so as to give peace to all the people. Cultivating oneself so as to give peace to all the people — Yao and Shun were also anxious about this."

15:1 Duke Ling of Wei asked Confucius about tactics. Confucius replied, "I have heard about sacrificial vessels but have learned nothing about the deployment of troops." The next day he made his departure.

When he was in Chen, the provisions ran out and his followers were sick, so that none were able to rise. Zilu, appearing aggrieved, said, "Does the noble person also suffer such poverty?" The Master said, "The noble person indeed suffers poverty, but when it afflicts the small man he is swept away."

15:2 The Master said, "Zi, do you think of me as one who learns many things and remembers them all?" He replied, "Yes. But perhaps this is not so?" The Master said, "It is not. With me there is the one that runs throughout it all."[45]

15:3 The Master said, "You, those who understand virtue (*de*) are few indeed."

15:4 The Master said, "As for governing through nonassertion (*wu-wei*), was not Shun an example of this? What did he do? All he did was make himself reverent and face south[46] in a correct posture, that is all."

15:8 The Master said, "It does not happen that the dedicated officer and the humane person seek life if it means harming their humaneness. It does happen that they sacrifice their lives so as to complete their humaneness."

15:10 Yan Yuan asked about governing a state. The Master said, "Follow the calendar of the Xia, ride in the carriage of the Yin, wear the ceremonial cap of the Zhou. As for music, let it be the *shao* and the *wu*.[47] Banish the Zheng songs; stay away from artful talkers. The Zheng songs are licentious; artful talkers are dangerous."

15:11 The Master said, "A person who has no regard for what is distant will surely encounter sorrow close by."

15:18 The Master said, "The noble person is anxious about his own lack of ability, not about the failure of others to recognize him."

15:23 Zigong asked, "Is there one word that one can act upon throughout

---

45. This is sometimes translated as "With me, there is one thread that runs right through it." The image conveyed by the verb *guan* is that of cowrie shells threaded on a single string.

46. The position of the ruler is to face south.

47. The *shao* music is associated with the sage king Shun, who, having been selected by Yao as his successor, came to rule upon Yao's abdication. The *wu* music is associated with King Wu, who, completing the conquest begun by his father, King Wen, came to rule through military force. In *Analects* 3:25 Confucius is quoted as saying that the *shao* music is perfectly beautiful and perfectly good, while the *wu* music is perfectly beautiful but not perfectly good.

the course of one's life?" The Master said, "Reciprocity (*shu*) — what you would not want for yourself, do not do to others."

15:27 The Master said, "When all of the people dislike a man, it is necessary to investigate the situation; when all of the people like a man, it is necessary to investigate the situation."

15:28 The Master said, "A human being can enlarge the Way, but the Way cannot enlarge a human being."

15:30 The Master said, "I have spent an entire day without eating, and an entire night without sleeping, so as to think. It was of no use. It is better to learn."

15:32 The Master said, "When a person's knowledge is sufficient to attain it, but his humaneness does not allow him to hold on to it, he may get it but will inevitably lose it again. When his knowledge is sufficient to attain it, and his humaneness allows him to hold on to it, but yet he cannot govern with dignity, the people will not respect him. If his knowledge is sufficient to attain, and his humaneness allows him to hold on to it, and he governs with dignity yet does not act in accordance with the rites, it will still not be good."

15:35 The Master said, "In the matter of humaneness, one should not defer even to one's teacher."

15:38 The Master said, "In education there should be no class distinctions."

16:1 The head of the Ji family was about to attack Zhuanyu.[48] Ran You and Jilu[49] saw Confucius and said, "The Ji family is about to become involved[50] with Zhuanyu." Confucius said, "Qiu [Ran You], are you not at fault here? Now Zhuanyu was made by the former kings[51] to preside over eastern Meng mountain. Moreover, it is within the state [of Lu], and its ruler is minister to the altars of land and grain. How can it be attacked?"

Ran You said, "Our master wants it. Neither of us two ministers wants it." Confucius said, "Qiu, Zhou Ren had a saying, 'When one has strength to display, let him join the ranks; when he is unable to do so, let him quit.' Of what use are those assistants who do not sustain one when he is in peril nor support him when he falls? Besides, what you have said is wrong. If the tiger or the rhinoceros escapes from its cage, or a piece of tortoiseshell or jade is damaged in its box, whose fault is that?"

Ran You said, "But now Zhuanyu is strong, and close to Bi, and if it is not taken now, it is sure to become a source of trouble for his sons and grandsons

---

48. Zhuanyu was a small "attached" state or dependency within the state of Lu that had been assigned by the Zhou house the responsibility of sacrificing to the eastern Meng mountain. It was about to be attacked by the head of the Ji family, one of the ruling families of Lu.

49. Also known as Zilu.

50. Here, a euphemism for an attack.

51. Referring to the Zhou rulers.

in later generations." Confucius said, "Qiu, the noble person is offended when someone denies that he wants something but yet insists on making a case for it.[52] Qiu[53] has heard that the rulers of states and the heads of families 'worry not that the population is sparse but that it is unevenly distributed; worry not that the people are poor but that they are not at peace.' For when there is even distribution, there will be no poverty; when there is harmony, there will be no sparseness of population; when there is peace, there will be no upheaval. Thus it is. Therefore when those who are far off do not submit, one cultivates one's culture and virtue so as to attract them, and when they have been attracted, one brings them peace. Now You and Qiu are assisting a ruler who finds that the people who are far off are not submissive, nor is he able to attract them. His own territory is divided and disintegrating, disunited and disrupted. He cannot preserve it, yet he is planning to wield shield and dagger axe within the state. I fear that the trouble of the Jisun lies not in Zhuanyu but within the screen of their own court."

16:8 Confucius said, "The noble person has three objects of awe: he is in awe of the ordinances of Heaven (*tianming*);[54] he is in awe of the great man; and he is in awe of the words of the sage. The small man, not knowing the ordinances of Heaven, is not in awe of them; he is disrespectful toward great men; and he ridicules the words of the sages."

16:9 Confucius said, "Those who are born knowing it are of the highest kind; the next are those who come to know it through study; and then those who learn through painful exertion. Finally there are those who, despite painful exertion, do not learn; these are the lowest among the people."

17:2 The Master said, "By nature close together; through practice set apart."[55]

17:3 The Master said, "It is only those whose knowledge places them in the highest category or whose ignorance places them in the lowest category who do not change."

17:6 Zizhang asked Confucius about humaneness. Confucius said, "One who could carry out the five everywhere under Heaven would be humane." "I beg to ask what they are." "Respect, liberality, trustworthiness, earnestness, and kindness. If you are respectful, you will have no regret; if you are liberal, you will win the multitude; if you are trustworthy, you will be trusted; if you are

---

52. The suggestion seems to be that Ran You and Zilu actually support the war policy, at least tacitly, while claiming that the responsibility lies with the ruler whom they serve.

53. The Chinese character is different; here Confucius is referring to himself.

54. Also translated as the "Mandate of Heaven."

55. This simple observation attributed to Confucius was agreed upon as the essential truth with regard to human nature and racial difference by a group of international experts in the UNESCO "Statement on Race" published in July 1950.

earnest, you will be effective; if you are kind, you will be able to influence others."

17:9 The Master said, "Little ones, why does none of you study the Odes? The Odes may be used for stimulation, for contemplation, and for sociability. Through them you are able to express your grievances. At home they may be used to serve your parents and, abroad, to serve your ruler. Through them you may gain broad acquaintance with the names of birds and animals, plants and trees."

17:13 The Master said, "The village paragon is the thief of virtue."

17:19 The Master said, "I would prefer not to speak." Zigong said, "If the Master did not speak, then what would we disciples have to record?" The Master said, "Does Heaven speak? The four seasons follow their course, and the hundred creatures are born. What speaking does Heaven do?"

17:21 Zai Wo inquired about the three years of mourning,[56] saying that one year was quite long enough. "If for three years the noble person does not perform the rites, the rites must fall into neglect. If for three years he does not perform music, music will fall into ruin. The old grain will have been exhausted; the new grain will have sprung up. Fresh drilling will have brought into being new fire. A year is enough." The Master said, "If you were to eat good food and wear fine clothing, would you feel at ease?" "I would feel at ease." "If you would be at ease, then do it. But the noble person, throughout the period of mourning, derives no pleasure from the food that he eats, no joy from the music that he hears, and no comfort from his dwelling. Thus he does not do it. But now you would feel at ease, and so you may do it." After Wo went out the Master said, "How inhuman[57] Yu [Zai Wo] is! Only when a child is three years old does it leave its parents' arms. The three years' mourning is the universal mourning everywhere under Heaven. And Yu — was he not the darling of his father and mother for three years?"

17:25 Women and servants are most difficult to nurture. If one is close to them, they lose their reserve, while if one is distant, they feel resentful.

18:6 Chang Ju and Jie Ni were working together tilling the fields. Confucius passed by them and sent Zilu to inquire about the ford. Chang Ju said, "Who is it who is holding the reins in the carriage?" Zilu said, "It is Kong Qiu." "Would that be Kong Qiu of Lu?" "It would." "In that case he already knows where the ford is."

Zilu then inquired of Jie Ni. Jie Ni said, "Who are you, sir?" "Zhong You." "The follower of Kong Qiu of Lu?" "Yes." "A rushing torrent — such is the world.

---

56. This passage implies that the ritual prescription for mourning for parents specified a period of three years, or, more precisely, twenty-five months — one month into the third year.

57. Literally, "not humane."

And who can change it? Rather than follow a scholar who withdraws from particular men, would it not be better to follow one who withdraws from the world?" He went on covering seed without stopping.

Zilu went and told the Master, who sighed and said, "I cannot herd together with the birds and beasts. If I do not walk together with other human beings, with whom shall I associate? If the Way prevailed in the world, [I] Qiu would not be trying to change it."

19:1 Zizhang said, "The scholar who, perceiving danger, is prepared to sacrifice his life;[58] who, seeing the possibility for gain, thinks of rightness; who, in sacrificing, thinks of reverence; who, in mourning, thinks of grief; is worthy of approval."

19:6 Zixia said, "In broadly learning, in being genuinely dedicated, in earnestly inquiring, in reflecting on things at hand — humaneness lies right here."

20:3 The Master said, "Without knowing what is ordained [by Heaven], one has no way to become a noble person. Without knowing the rites, one has no way to take one's stand. Without knowing words, one has no way to know other people."

[— IB]

---

58. Literally, "to fulfill the ordinance (of Heaven)."

Chapter 4

MOZI: UTILITY, UNIFORMITY, AND UNIVERSAL LOVE

The Warring States period (479–221 B.C.E.) in ancient China witnessed a remarkable proliferation of philosophical schools — often referred to as the "hundred schools of thought." Among the "hundred philosophers" of ancient China, Mozi had a place of special importance. When Mencius, the first great follower of Confucius, felt called upon to defend and revitalize Confucianism in the fourth century B.C.E., he singled out the philosophy of Mozi as being among its most dangerous rivals. Although Mohism did not hold this strong position for long, its founder and his teachings were extremely influential in later Chinese thought. Today they serve as a reminder that the eventual supremacy of Confucian ideas and values was not achieved simply by default or intellectual inertia but was won in a difficult struggle with worthy opponents.

Mo Di, who became known as Mozi, or Master Mo, apparently lived during the period of about a century between the death of Confucius and the birth of Mencius. The name Mo was in all likelihood not a surname: it has been thought by some to have denoted a form of punishment, indicating that the man known as Mo Di may have come from a class of prisoners or slaves. However that may be, the Mohist school came to be associated with the interests and energies of artisans, merchants, and small-property owners, and the text attributed to Mozi often characterizes the Confucians as pretentious aristocrats who stand very much on their own dignity and on ceremony, suggesting perhaps a degree of plebeian hostility on the part of Mozi's followers. Mozi was, however, well educated in the classics and may even have followed the Confucian school himself until he took up a position of strong opposition on certain fundamental points. Thus he condemned what he viewed as the skepticism of many Confucians in regard to Heaven and spiritual beings, their tendency toward fatalism, and their preoccupation with ritual. These criticisms may perhaps be understood as testimony to the direction in which Confucius's thought was being taken by his immediate followers.

Some of Mozi's most striking arguments are political in nature and reveal a characteristic blend of populism and authoritarianism. To illustrate this blend, we offer excerpts from one of a set of three chapters of the *Mozi*, "Honoring of the Worthy" — in which Mozi argues that government positions should be filled by the most qualified individuals — and two of a set of three chapters, "Identifying with the Superior" — in which he insists on the need for uniformity of thought, based on an elaborate form of thought control, to achieve social order.

Mozi's most characteristic doctrine comes close to asserting that "all human beings are equal before God." Believing in Heaven as an active power manifesting love for all, he urged that all people follow Heaven in this by practicing universal love. But this has nothing to do with love between persons or human affectivity. His standard of action is strictly based on utility: love for all human beings is demonstrated by satisfying their immediate material needs and by abandoning all forms of activity and expense that do not contribute to the feeding, clothing, and housing of the people. For this reason Mozi condemned ritual and music, extravagant entertainment, and, above all, offensive warfare. Moreover, to concentrate human energies on the achievement of social goals, Mozi believed, unity of thought and action was necessary, with the people obeying their leaders and the leaders following the will of Heaven.

What we know of Mozi's career shows him to be a rigorist who set the most exacting standards for himself and his followers. In trying to gain acceptance for his principles, he drove himself tirelessly and unmercifully. Unlike the Confucians, who offered advice only when treated respectfully by a ruler and assured of his honorable intentions, Mozi was ready to preach his gospel to anyone who would listen. At times, upon hearing of the plans of a state to make war, he would hasten to dissuade the ruler from perpetrating such an outrage. On one of these peace missions, it is said, he walked ten days and ten nights, tearing off pieces of his garments to bind up his sore feet as he went. Often Mozi and his followers, failing in their efforts at conciliation, would rush to aid in the defense of the state attacked, gaining a reputation for their skill in siege operations. In this way they became a tightly knit and highly disciplined group, leading an ascetic life and, even after Mozi's death, obediently following the directions of their "elders."

Some of the chapters of the *Mozi* are believed to represent the views of his later followers, whose utilitarian aims inevitably led them into the study of more basic questions of both a philosophical and a technical character. Thus, for instance, their evangelistic approach and readiness to discuss or debate with anyone may explain why the later Mohist canon is so much concerned with logic and dialectics. Yet even in the portions believed to represent Mozi's original teaching, there is a laborious, even tedious attention to step-by-step argumentation. For this reason, perhaps, Mozi has been much less admired for his literary style, or even for his ideas, than for the nobility of spirit that he revealed in his life of service to others.

Selections from the Mozi

SECTION 9: HONORING THE WORTHY (PART 2)

Mozi said, "In caring for the people, presiding over the altars of the soil and grain, and ordering the state, the ruler and high officials these days strive for stability and seek to avoid any error. But why do they fail to perceive that honoring the worthy is the foundation of government? . . .

"The sage kings of ancient times took great pains to honor the worthy and employ the capable, showing no special consideration for their own kin, no partiality for the eminent and rich, no favoritism for the good-looking and attractive. They promoted the worthy to high places, enriched and honored them, and made them heads of government; the unworthy they demoted and rejected, reduced to poverty and humble station, and condemned to penal servitude. Thus the people, encouraged by the hope of reward and awed by the fear of punishment, led each other on to become worthy, so that worthy persons increased in number and the unworthy became few. This is what is called advancing the worthy. And when this had been done, the sage kings listened to the words of the worthy, watched their actions, observed their abilities, and on this basis carefully assigned them to office. This is called employing the capable. . . .

"When a worthy man is given the task of ordering the state, he appears at court early and retires late, listens to lawsuits, and attends to the affairs of government. As a result, the state is well ordered and the laws and punishments are justly administered. When a worthy man heads a government bureau, he goes to bed late and gets up early, collecting taxes on the barriers and markets and on the resources of the hills, forests, lakes, and fish weirs, so that the treasury will be full. As a result the treasury is full and no source of revenue is neglected. When a worthy man governs an outlying district, he leaves his house early and returns late, plowing and sowing seed, planting trees, and gathering vegetables and grain. As a result there will be plenty of vegetables and grain and the people will have enough to eat. When the state is well ordered, the laws and punishments will be justly administered, and when the treasury is full, the people will be well off. The rulers will thus be supplied with wine and millet to use in their sacrifices to Heaven and the spirits, with hides and currency to use in their intercourse with the feudal lords of neighboring states, and with the means to feed the hungry and give rest to the weary within their realm, to nourish their subjects, and to attract virtuous persons from all over the world. Then Heaven and the spirits will send down riches, the other feudal lords will become their allies, the people of their own realm will feel affection for them, and the worthy will come forward to serve them. Thus all that they plan for they will achieve, and all that they undertake will be brought to a successful conclusion. If they stay within their realm, their position will be secure, and if they venture forth to punish an enemy, they will be victorious. . . .

"But if one knows only the policy to be adopted, but does not know what means to use in carrying it out, then he cannot be sure of success in government. Therefore three principles should be established. What are the three principles? They are that if the titles and positions of worthy men are not exalted enough, then the people will not respect such men; if their stipends are not generous, then the people will not have confidence in them; and if their orders are not enforced, then the people will not stand in awe of them. Therefore the sage kings of antiquity honored the worthy with titles, treated them to generous stipends, entrusted them with important affairs, and empowered them to see that their orders were carried out. . . .

"If the worthy do not come to the side of the ruler and his officers, it will be the unworthy who will wait at their left and right. . . . It was for this reason alone that the evil kings of the Three Dynasties — Jie, Zhou, You, and Li — lost their kingdoms and brought destruction to their altars of soil and grain.[1]

"All of this comes about as a result of understanding petty affairs but failing to understand important ones. Now the rulers and high officials know that if they cannot cut a suit of clothes for themselves, they must employ the services of a skilled tailor, and if they cannot slaughter an ox or a sheep for themselves, they must employ the services of a skilled butcher. In these two instances the rulers are perfectly aware of the need to honor the worthy and employ the capable to get things done. And yet when they see the state in confusion and their altars of soil and grain in danger, they do not know enough to employ capable men to correct the situation. Instead they employ their relatives, or men who happen to be rich and eminent or pleasant-featured and attractive. But just because a man happens to be rich and eminent or pleasant-featured and attractive, he will not necessarily turn out to be wise and alert when placed in office. If men such as these are given the task of ordering the state, then this is simply to entrust the state to men who are neither wise nor intelligent, and anyone knows that this will lead to ruin."

[*Mozi jicheng* 2:5a–6b, 8a–9b
— adapted from Watson, *Mo Tzu*, pp. 22–24, 26–28]

---

1. Jie was the last ruler of the Xia dynasty, Zhou the last ruler of the Shang, and You and Li two rulers of the Zhou dynasty in the ninth and eighth centuries B.C.E. All four are symbols of evil and incompetent rulers.

SECTION 11: IDENTIFYING WITH THE SUPERIOR (PART 1)

Mozi said, "In ancient times, when humankind was first born and before there were any laws or government, it may be said that each person's view of things was different. One person had one view, two persons had two views, ten persons had ten views — the more persons, the more views. Moreover, each person believed that his own views were correct and disapproved of those of others, so that people spent their time condemning one another. Within the family fathers and sons, older and younger brothers grew to hate each other and the family split up, unable to live in harmony, while throughout the world people all resorted to water, fire, and poison in an effort to do each other injury. Those with strength to spare refused to help out others, those with surplus wealth would let it rot before they would share it, and those with beneficial doctrines to teach would keep them secret and refuse to impart them. The world was as chaotic as if it were inhabited by birds and beasts alone.

"To anyone who examined the cause, it was obvious that this chaos came about because of the absence of rulers and leaders. Therefore the most worthy and able man in the world was selected and set up as the Son of Heaven.[2] After the Son of Heaven had been set up, because his strength alone was insufficient, other worthy and able men were selected from throughout the world and installed as his three high ministers. After the Son of Heaven and the three high ministers had been set up, because the world was so broad, and because it was not always possible for the ruler and his ministers alone to judge accurately what would be right and profitable for people living in distant countries and strange lands, the world was divided up into countless states, and feudal lords and chiefs were set up to administer them. After the feudal lords and chiefs had been set up and because their strength alone was insufficient, worthy and able men were chosen from the various states to act as their officials.

"When all these officials had been installed, the Son of Heaven proclaimed the principle of his rule to the people of the world, saying, 'Upon hearing of good or evil, one shall report it to one's superior. What the superior considers right all shall consider right; what the superior considers wrong all shall consider wrong. If the superior commits any fault, his subordinates shall remonstrate with him; if his subordinates do good, the superior shall recommend them. To identify oneself with one's superior and not to form cliques on the lower levels — such conduct as this shall be rewarded by those above and praised by those below. If, upon hearing of good or evil, one fails to report it to one's

---

2. It is not clear who does the selecting. In the original, the sentence is in the active mood but with no subject expressed, a construction that is perfectly permissible in Chinese but that must be rendered into English in the passive unless the translator chooses to supply a subject. If pressed, Mozi, like the Confucians, would no doubt say that Heaven, expressing its will through some human or natural agency, did in fact select the Son of Heaven.

superior; if what the superior considers right is not accepted as right and what the superior considers wrong is not accepted as wrong; if his subordinates fail to remonstrate with the superior when he commits a fault, or if the superior fails to recommend his subordinates when they do good; if the subordinates make common cause among themselves and fail to identify themselves with their superiors — if there is such conduct as this, it shall be punished by those above and condemned by the people at large.' The rulers meted out their rewards and punishments on this basis, examining with the greatest care to be sure such rewards and punishments were just.

"The head of each local community was the most humane man in the community, and when he took office, he proclaimed to the people of the community the principle of his rule, saying, 'Upon hearing of good or evil, you shall report it to the town head. What the town head considers to be right all shall consider right; what the town head considers wrong all shall consider wrong. Leave your evil words and imitate the good words of the town head; leave your evil actions and imitate the good actions of the town head!' As long as this command was heeded, how could there be any disorder in the township? . . ."

The argument is then built up in successive stages: from the level of the community, Mozi proceeds to the level of the township, the region, and, ultimately, the world. At each level, the people are to identify with the appropriate authority — the town head, the lord of the region, and the Son of Heaven — in recognition of an ever-ascending hierarchy of command. In closing, Mozi makes the point that the people must ultimately identify with Heaven itself, though how they are to do this is not specified.

"If we examine the reason why the world was well ordered, we find that it was simply that the Son of Heaven was able to unify the standards of judgment throughout the world, and this resulted in order. . . .

"But although all the people in the world may identify themselves with the Son of Heaven, if they do not also identify themselves with Heaven itself, then calamities will never cease. The violent winds and bitter rains that sweep the world in such profusion these days — these are simply the punishments of Heaven sent down upon the people because they fail to identify themselves with Heaven."

[*Mozi jicheng* 3:1a–2b, 3a — adapted from Watson, *Mo Tzu*, pp. 34–36, 37]

SECTION 16: UNIVERSAL LOVE (PART 3)

Mozi said, "It is the business of the humane person to try to promote what is beneficial to the world and to eliminate what is harmful. Now at the present time, what brings the greatest harm to the world? Great states attacking small ones, great families overthrowing small ones, the strong oppressing the weak, the many harrying the few, the cunning deceiving the stupid, the eminent lording it over the humble — these are harmful to the world. So too are rulers who are not generous, ministers who are not loyal, fathers who are without kindness, and sons who are unfilial, as well as those mean men who, with weapons and knives, poison, fire, and water, seek to injure and undo each other.

When we inquire into the cause of these various harms, what do we find has produced them? Do they come about from loving others and trying to benefit them? Surely not! They come rather from hating others and trying to injure them. And when we set out to classify and describe those who hate and injure others, shall we say that their actions are motivated by universality or partiality? Surely we must answer, by partiality, and it is this partiality in their dealings with one another that gives rise to all the great harms in the world. Therefore we know that partiality is wrong. . . ."

Mozi said, "Partiality should be replaced by universality. But how can partiality be replaced by universality? If men were to regard the states of others as they regard their own, then who would raise up his state to attack the state of another? It would be like attacking his own. If men were to regard the cities of others as they regard their own, then who would raise up his city to attack the city of another? It would be like attacking his own. If men were to regard the families of others as they regard their own, then who would raise up his family to overthrow that of another? It would be like overthrowing his own. Now when states and cities do not attack and make war on each other and families and individuals do not overthrow or injure one another — is this a harm or a benefit to the world? Surely it is a benefit. . . .

"When we set out to classify and describe those persons who love others and benefit others, shall we say that their actions are motivated by partiality or by universality? Surely we must answer, by universality, and it is this universality in their dealings with one another that gives rise to all the great benefits in the world. Therefore Mozi has said that universality is right. . . .

"Yet the men of the world continue to criticize it, saying, 'It may be a good thing, but how can it be put to use?' "

Mozi said, "If it cannot be put to use, even I would criticize it. But how can there be a good thing that still cannot be put to use? Let us try considering both sides of the question. Suppose there are two men, one of them holding to partiality, the other to universality. The believer in partiality says, 'How could I possibly regard my friend the same as myself, or my friend's father the same as my own?' Because he views his friend in this way, he will not feed him when he is hungry, clothe him when he is cold, nourish him when he is sick, or bury him when he dies. Such are the words of the partial man, and such his actions. But the words and actions of the universal-minded man are not like these. He will say, 'I have heard that the truly superior man of the world regards his friend the same as himself, and his friend's father the same as his own. Only if he does this can he be considered a truly superior man.' Because he views his friend in this way, he will feed him when he is hungry, clothe him when he is cold, nourish him when he is sick, and bury him when he dies. Such are the words and actions of the universal-minded man.

"So the words of these two men disagree, and their actions are diametrically opposed. Yet let us suppose that both of them are determined to carry out their words in action, so that word and deed agree like the two parts of a tally, and nothing they say is not put into action. Then let us venture to inquire further. Suppose that here is a broad plain, a vast wilderness, and a man is buckling on his armor and donning his helmet to set out for the field of battle, where the fortunes of life and death are unknown; or he is setting out in his lord's name upon a distant mission to Ba or Yue, Qi or Jing, and his return is uncertain. Now let us ask, to whom would he entrust the support of his parents and the care of his wife and children? Would it be to the universal-minded man, or to the partial man? It seems to me, on occasions like these, there are no fools in the world. Though one may disapprove of universality himself, he would surely think it best to entrust his family to the universal-minded man. Thus people condemn universality in words but adopt it in practice, and word and deed belie each other. I cannot understand how the men of the world can hear about this doctrine of universality and still criticize it!" . . .

At this point, Mozi extends the argument to apply to rulers, setting up a hypothetical case of two rulers, one partial and the other universal-minded. The partial ruler adopts an attitude toward his subjects that is similar to that of the partial and uncaring friend, while the universal-minded ruler thinks of his subjects first and himself last. The conclusion is clear: there being "no fools in the world," everyone will favor the universal-minded ruler. They will favor universality in practice even if they criticize it in words.

"And yet the men of the world continue to criticize, saying, 'This doctrine of universality is humane and right. And yet how can it be carried out? As we see it, one can no more put it into practice than one can pick up Mount Tai and leap over a river with it! Thus universality is only something to be longed for, not something that can be put into practice.'"

Mozi said, "As for picking up Mount Tai and leaping over rivers with it, no one from ancient times to the present, from the beginning of humankind to now, has ever succeeded in doing that! But universal love and mutual aid were actually practiced by four sage kings of antiquity. How do we know that they practiced these?"

Mozi said, "I did not live at the same time as they did, nor have I in person heard their voices or seen their faces. Yet I know of it because of what is written on bamboo and silk that has been handed down to posterity, what is engraved on metal and stone, and what is inscribed on bowls and basins. . . ."

Mozi here offers a number of historical examples, drawn from the Classic of Documents *and the* Classic of Odes, *to establish the success with which the sage kings of antiquity translated their universal-mindedness into effective action.*

"And yet the men of the world continue to criticize, saying, 'If one takes no thought for what is beneficial or harmful to one's parents, how can this be called filial?'"

Mozi said, "Let us examine for a moment the way in which a filial son plans for the welfare of his parents. When a filial son plans for his parents, does he wish others to love and benefit them, or does he wish others to hate and injure them? It stands to reason that he wishes others to love and benefit his parents. Now if I am a filial son, how do I go about accomplishing this? Do I first make it a point to love and benefit other men's parents, so that they in return will love and benefit my parents? Or do I first make it a point to hate and injure other men's parents, so that they in return will love and benefit my parents? Obviously, I must first make it a point to love and benefit other men's parents, so that they in return will love and benefit my parents. So if all of us are to be filial sons, can we set about it in any other way than by first making a point of loving and benefiting other men's parents? And are we to suppose that the filial sons of the world are too stupid to be capable of doing what is right? . . .

"Now universal love and mutual benefit are both profitable and easy beyond all measure. The only trouble, as I see it, is that no ruler takes any delight in them. If the rulers really delighted in them, promoted them with rewards and praise, and prevented neglect of them by punishments, then I believe that people would turn to universal love and mutual benefit as naturally as fire turns upward or water turns downward, and nothing in the world could stop them."

[*Mozi jicheng* 4:10b–11b, 12b–14a, 15a–b, 18a–b, 20a
— adapted from Watson, *Mo Tzu*, pp. 39–42, 44, 46–47, 49]

SECTION 26: THE WILL OF HEAVEN (PART 1)

Mozi said, "The gentlemen of the world today understand small matters but not large ones. How do we know this? We know it from the way they conduct themselves at home. If at home a man commits some offense against the head of the family, he may still run away and hide at a neighbor's house. And yet his parents, brothers, and friends will all join in warning and admonishing him, saying, 'You must be more cautious! You must be more circumspect! When you are living at home, how can it be right for you to offend the head of the family?'

"This is true not only of a man who lives at home but of a man who lives in a state as well. If a man living in a state commits some offense against the ruler of the state, he may still run away and hide in a neighboring state. And yet his parents, brothers, and friends will all join in warning and admonishing him, saying, 'You must be more cautious! You must be more circumspect! How can you live in a state and still consider it right to offend the ruler of the state?'

"If people warn and admonish a man this sternly when he still has someplace to run away and hide, how much more sternly should they feel obliged to warn and admonish him if there is no place for him to run away and hide! There is a saying that goes, 'If you commit a crime here in the broad daylight, where will you run and hide?' There is no place to run and hide, for Heaven will spy you out clearly even in the forest, the valley, or the dark and distant place where no one lives! And yet with regard to Heaven the gentlemen of the world for some reason do not know enough to warn and admonish each other. Thus I know that the gentlemen of the world understand small matters but not large ones.

"Now what does Heaven desire and what does it hate? Heaven desires rightness and hates what is not right. Thus if I lead the people of the world to devote themselves to rightness, then I am doing what Heaven desires. If I do what Heaven desires, then Heaven will do what I desire. Now what do I desire and what do I hate? I desire good fortune and prosperity and hate misfortune and calamity. If I do not do what Heaven desires and instead do what Heaven does not desire, then I will be leading the people of the world to devote themselves to what will bring misfortune and calamity.

"How do I know that Heaven desires rightness and hates what is not right? In the world, where there is rightness there is life; where there is no rightness there is death. Where there is rightness there is wealth; where there is no rightness there is poverty. Where there is rightness there is order; where there is no rightness there is disorder. Now Heaven desires life and hates death, desires wealth and hates poverty, desires order and hates disorder. So I know that Heaven desires rightness and hates what is not right.

Moreover, rightness is what is right. Subordinates do not decide what is right for their superiors; it is the superiors who decide what is right for their subordinates. Therefore the common people devote their strength to carrying out their tasks, but they cannot decide for themselves what is right. There are gentlemen to do that for them. The gentlemen devote their strength to carrying out their tasks, but they cannot decide for themselves what is right. There are ministers and officials to do that for them. The ministers and officials devote their strength to carrying out their tasks, but they cannot decide for themselves what is right. There are the three high ministers and the feudal lords to do that for them. The three high ministers and the feudal lords devote their strength to managing the affairs of government, but they cannot decide for themselves what is right. There is the Son of Heaven to do that for them. But the Son of Heaven cannot decide for himself what is right. There is Heaven to decide that for him. The gentlemen of the world have no difficulty in perceiving that the Son of Heaven decides what is right for the three high ministers, the feudal lords, the gentlemen, and the common people. But the people of the world are unable to perceive that Heaven decides what is right for the Son of Heaven. . . .

"How do we know that Heaven loves the people of the world? Because it enlightens them universally. How do we know that it enlightens them universally? Because it possesses them universally. How do we know that it possesses them universally? Because it accepts sacrifices from them universally. Because within the four seas, among all the people who live on grain,[3] there are none who do not feed their sacrificial oxen and sheep, fatten their dogs and pigs, prepare clean offerings of millet and wine, and sacrifice to the Lord-on-High and the spirits. Since Heaven possesses all the cities and people, how could it fail to love them?

"Moreover, I say that he who kills one innocent person will invariably suffer one misfortune. Who is it that kills the innocent person? It is man. And who is it that sends down the misfortune? It is Heaven. If Heaven did not love the people of the world, then why would it send down misfortune simply because one man kills another? Thus I know that Heaven loves the people of the world. . . ."

Mozi said, "The intent of Heaven is to me like a compass to a wheelwright or a square to a carpenter. The wheelwright and the carpenter use their compass and square to measure what is round or square for the world, saying, 'What fits these measurements is right; what does not fit them is wrong.' Now the books of the gentlemen of the world are too numerous to be listed, and their sayings too many to be examined in full. In the higher circles the gentlemen lecture to the feudal lords, and in lower circles they expound to men of honor. And yet on matters of humaneness and rightness they are far apart. How do I know? Because I measure them by the clearest standard in the world [i.e., the intent of Heaven]."

[*Mozi jicheng* 7:1a–3a, 4a–b, 5a — adapted from Watson, *Mo Tzu*, pp. 78–80, 81–83]

SECTION 27: THE WILL OF HEAVEN (PART 2)

Mozi said, "The intent of Heaven does not desire that large states attack small ones, that large families overthrow small ones, that the strong oppress the weak, the cunning deceive the stupid, or the eminent lord it over the humble. This is what Heaven does *not* desire. But this is not all. It desires that among men those who have strength will work for others, those who understand the Way will teach others, and those who possess wealth will share it with others. It also desires that those above will diligently attend to matters of government, and those below will diligently carry out their tasks. If those above diligently attend to matters of government, then the state will be well ordered. If those below diligently carry out their tasks, then there will be enough wealth and goods."

[*Mozi jicheng* 7:6b — adapted from Watson, *Mo Tzu*, pp. 85–86]

---

3. I.e., the Chinese, as opposed to the nomadic tribes surrounding China.

SECTION 39: AGAINST CONFUCIANS (PART 2)[4]

"The Confucians say, 'There are degrees to be observed in treating relatives as relatives, and gradations to be observed in honoring the worthy.'[5] They prescribe differences to be observed between close and distant relatives and between the honored and the humble. Their code of rites says, 'Mourning for a father or mother should last three years; for a wife or eldest son, three years; for a paternal uncle, brother, or younger son, one year; and for other close relatives, five months.' Now if the length of the mourning period is determined by the degree of kinship, then close relatives should be mourned for a long period and distant relatives for a short one. Yet the Confucians mourn the same length of time for a wife or eldest son as for a father or mother. And if the length of the mourning period is determined by the degree of honor due, then this means that the wife and eldest son are honored the same as the father and mother, while the paternal uncles and brothers are placed on the same level as younger sons! What could be more perverse than this?[6] . . .

"When a Confucian takes a wife, he goes to fetch her in person. Wearing a formal black robe, he acts as his own coachman, holding the reins and handing her the cord by which to pull herself up into the carriage, as though he were escorting an honored parent. The wedding ceremonies are conducted with as much solemnity as the sacrifices to the ancestors. High and low are turned upside down, and parents are disregarded and scorned. Parents are brought down to the level of the wife, and the wife is exalted at the expense of service to the parents. How can such conduct be called filial? . . .

"In addition, the Confucians believe firmly in the existence of fate and propound their doctrine, saying, 'Long life or early death, wealth or poverty, safety or danger, order or disorder are all decreed by the ordinance of Heaven[7] and cannot be modified. Failure and success, rewards and punishments, good fortune and bad, are all fixed. Human wisdom and strength can do nothing.' If the various officials believe such ideas, they will be lax in their duties; and if the common people believe them, they will neglect their tasks. . . .

---

4. This chapter, while numbered part 2 in the *Mozi* text, is actually the only surviving chapter of this pair, part 1 having been lost.

5. The *Mean*, a section of the Confucian *Record of Rites*, contains a passage much like this: "Humaneness is what it means to be human, and being affectionate toward one's kin is the greatest part of it. Rightness is doing what is right, and honoring the worthy is the greatest part of it. The diminishing degree of affection due to one's kin and the different gradations of honor owed to the worthy are born of ritual" (*Zhong yong* 20:5). See ch. 10, pp. 333–39.

6. Mozi is assuming that there is a closer relationship between a man and his parents than between a man and his wife and children and that he owes greater respect to his parents and elder relatives than to his younger ones. The Confucians agreed in principle with these assumptions but, as we may see from their rules for mourning, modified them somewhat in practice.

7. The Chinese term is *tianming*, elsewhere translated as the "Mandate of Heaven."

"Moreover, the Confucians corrupt men with their elaborate and showy rites and music and deceive parents with lengthy mournings and hypocritical grief. They propound fatalism, ignore poverty, and behave with the greatest arrogance. . . .

"The Confucians say, 'The noble person must use ancient speech and wear ancient dress before he can be considered humane.' But we answer, 'The so-called ancient speech and dress were all modern once, and if at that time the men of antiquity used such speech and wore such dress, then they must not have been noble persons. Must we then wear the dress of those who were not noble persons and use their speech before we can be considered humane?'"

[*Mozi jicheng* 9:16a–18b, 19b–20a — adapted from Watson, *Mo Tzu*, pp. 124–28]

Chapter 5

THE WAY OF LAOZI AND ZHUANGZI

Next to Confucianism, the most important and influential native philosophy of the Chinese has undoubtedly been Daoism. In many ways the doctrines of Confucianism and Daoism complement each other, running side by side like two powerful streams through all later Chinese thought and literature. To the solemn gravity and burden of social responsibility of Confucianism, Daoism opposes a flight from respectability and the conventional duties of society; in place of the Confucian concern for things worldly and human, it holds out a vision of other, transcendental worlds of the spirit. As the two streams of thought developed in later times, Confucianism has often been understood to represent the mind of the Chinese scholar in his office or study, concerned with matters of family and society, while Daoism represents the same individual in a private chamber or mountain retreat, often seeking surcease from the cares of official life.

METAPHYSICS AND GOVERNMENT IN THE *LAOZI*

The term *Daoist* — the school or family of the Dao — did not enter the Chinese vocabulary until the Han dynasty, around the second century B.C.E. In earlier periods this current of thought was referred to as "the teachings of the Yellow

Emperor and Laozi" (Huang-Lao, in Chinese) and, later, of "the teachings of Laozi and Zhuangzi." Though the Yellow Emperor is a legendary figure, we do possess two books attributed to Laozi and Zhuangzi.

The name Laozi simply means "the old master." Who the philosopher known as Laozi was, when he lived, and what his connection was with the text that has come down to us, are questions that have been debated for centuries. There have also been lively controversies about when the text was compiled and whether it actually appeared any earlier than the third century B.C.E. Contemporary scholars are generally inclined to agree that the book known as the *Laozi* or *Daodejing* was likely the work of more than one author, writing over a period of time, and that it contains different textual strata. Still, the compiler or compilers of the work seem to have had a rather consistent integrative vision, and despite — or perhaps because of — its brevity the document that has come down to us is one of the most provocative and inspired works in all Chinese literature.

In a sense the *Laozi*, like so many of the works of this period of political chaos and intellectual ferment, proposes a philosophy of government and a way of life for the ruling class, probably the only people who were capable of reading it. Yet its point of view and approach to the problems of government are vastly broader than this statement might suggest. The teaching of the *Laozi* is based on a great underlying principle, the Way, or Dao (from which the later name of the school derives), which is the source of all being, the governor of all life, human and natural, and the basic, undivided unity in which all the contradictions and distinctions of existence are ultimately resolved. Much of the book deals with the nature and workings of this first principle, while admitting that it must remain essentially indescribable and can be known only through a kind of mysterious intuition. The way of life that accords with this basic Dao is marked by an impulse toward acceptance and yielding, an absence of strife and coercion, and a manner of action that is completely spontaneous, effortless, and inexhaustible. This approach to action is often expressed in terms of "doing nothing" — or doing nothing that is unnatural or out of keeping with the Way (*wuwei*).

In the human sphere the *Laozi* describes the perfect individual, the sage, who comprehends the Dao and whose life and actions are ordered in accordance with it. It is clear that the sage is conceived of as the ideal ruler, for the *Laozi* gives definite instructions as to how the sage's government is to be conducted. The sage is to refrain from meddling in the lives of the people, give up warfare and luxurious living, and guide the people back to a state of innocence, simplicity, and harmony with the Dao. This is a state thought to have existed in the most ancient times, before civilization appeared to arouse the material desires of the people and impel them to strife and warfare, and before morality was invented to divert their minds from simple goodness and to beguile them with vain distinctions.

But such is the vagueness and ambiguity of the *Laozi* text and the subtlety of its thought that it may yield different interpretations and be approached on very different levels. At times in Chinese history, notably at the beginning of the Han dynasty, a political interpretation of the text has been highlighted and attempts have been made to translate the doctrines of the *Laozi* into action through government policies embodying an extreme laissez-faire attitude. But the teachings of the *Laozi* may also be understood as the philosophy of the recluse, the person of superior wisdom and insight who, instead of taking part in society, chooses to retire from public life to perfect a personal purity and intelligence and to seek harmony with the world of nature. It is this interpretation of the *Laozi* that has often prevailed in later Chinese thought.

The style of the *Laozi* is quite unlike that of the works of other schools. The text appears to be a combination of very old adages or cryptic sayings, often in rhyme, extended passages of poetry, and sections of prose interpretation and commentary. There is extensive use of parallel construction and balanced phrases; the statements are laconic and often paradoxical, intended not to convince the mind by reasoning but to startle and capture it through poetic vision. Among the prominent images are those of water — symbol of a humble, self-effacing force that is in the end all-powerful — and the female and the mother — symbol of passivity and creativity. This symbolism — and the paradoxical and poetic view of life that it suggests — have won for the work a popularity and influence that have endured through the centuries. These same appealing qualities have made it the Chinese work most often translated into foreign languages.

The selection that follows includes slightly less than half of the original work, which is divided into eighty-one brief chapters or sections. The translation owes much to that of the late Wing-tsit Chan. Like the Chan translation, it is based on several different Chinese texts of the *Laozi*, but it also takes into account two texts that were not available to Professor Chan at the time his translation was made — the silk manuscripts found in 1973 in an archaeological discovery at Mawangdui in Hunan province. These two closely related versions, the oldest texts of the *Laozi* to have been discovered thus far, have become known as *Dedaojing* because the eighty-one sections appear in a different order from that found in the previously known texts. The order in these newly discovered but very ancient texts has been taken by some to lend further weight to the argument that, whatever the impulses toward transcendence revealed in the work, the political significance of the *Laozi* must be recognized as profound.

FROM THE *DAODEJING*

1

The Way that can be spoken of is not the constant Way;
The name that can be named is not the constant name.
The nameless is the beginning of Heaven and Earth;

The named is the mother of all things.
Thus be constantly without desire,
so as to observe its subtlety,
And constantly have desire,
so as to observe its outcome.
These two have the same origin,
But are named differently.
Both may be called mysterious.
Mysterious and still more mysterious,
The gateway of all subtleties!

2

When everyone in the world knows beauty as beauty,
ugliness appears.
When everyone knows good as good,
not-good arrives.
Therefore being and non-being give birth to one another;
Difficult and easy give completion to one another;
Long and short form[1] one another;
High and low fill[2] one another;
Sound and voice harmonize with one another;
Ahead and behind follow after one another.
Therefore the sage accomplishes things by doing nothing (*wuwei*),
Furthering a teaching that is without words.
All things arise, and he does not leave them.
He gives them life but without possessing them.
He acts but without relying on his own ability.
He succeeds but without dwelling on his success.
And because he does not dwell on it, it does not leave him.

3

Do not exalt the worthy,
and the people will not compete.
Do not value goods that are hard to come by,
and the people will not steal.

---

1. Reading *xing* with the Mawangdui texts rather than *qiao* with the text of the third-century commentator, Wang Bi.
2. Reading *ying* with the Mawangdui texts rather than *qing* with the Wang Bi text.

Do not display objects of desire,
and the people's minds will not be disturbed.
Therefore the ordering of the sage
empties their minds,
fills their bellies,
weakens their ambitions,
strengthens their bones.
He always causes the people to be without knowledge,
without desire,
And causes the wise ones not to dare to act.
He does nothing (*wuwei*), and there is nothing that is
not brought to order.

4

The Way is empty.
It may be used without ever being exhausted.
Fathomless, it seems to be the ancestor of all things.
Blunting the sharpness,
Untying the tangles,
Subduing the light.
Merging with the dust.
Profound, it appears to exist forever.
Whose child it is I do not know.
It seems to have existed before the Lord.

5

Heaven and Earth are not humane,
Regarding all things as straw dogs.[3]
The sage is not humane,
Regarding the people as straw dogs.
Between Heaven and Earth — how like a bellows!
Vacuous but inexhaustible,
Moving and producing ever more.
An excess of words ends in impoverishment.
It is better to hold to the center.

---

3. Straw dogs were used for sacrifices in ancient China. After they had been used, they were thrown away and there was no sentimental attachment to them.

6

The spirit of the valley does not die.
It is called the mysterious female.
The gate of the mysterious female
Is called the root of Heaven and Earth.
Being continuous, it is as if it existed always.
Being used, it is still not exhausted.

9

To hold it upright and fill it
Is not as good as stopping in time.
To sharpen it to its sharpest,
Means it cannot last for long.[4]
When gold and jade fill your hall,
You will not be able to keep them.
When honor and wealth make you proud,
You bring disaster upon yourself.
When your work is done, then withdraw:
This is Heaven's Way.

10

In preserving the soul and embracing the One,
can you avoid departing from them?
In concentrating your qi[5] and arriving at utmost weakness,
can you be like an infant?
In cleansing and purifying your profound insight,
can you be without fault?
In loving the people and governing the state,
can you be without knowledge?
In the opening and closing of the gates of Heaven,
can you play the role of the female?
In understanding all within the four reaches,
can you do nothing (*wuwei*)?

---

4. Implicit in these first four lines are the image of a cup or a bowl and the image of a sword, respectively.

5. *Qi* is a fundamental concept in Chinese thought. Its sense depends on the context, but among the most frequently encountered translations are "vital energy," "vital force," "material-force," and "breath."

Give life to things, rear them,
Give them life but without possessing them,
Act but without relying on your own ability,
Lead them but without ruling them —
This is called profound virtue.

11

Thirty spokes conjoin in one hub;
there being nothing in between,
the cart is useful.
Clay is molded to form a vessel;
there being nothing inside,
the vessel is useful.
Doors and windows are carved out to make a room:
there being nothing within,
the room is useful.
Thus, with something one gets advantage,
While with nothing one gets usefulness.

12

The five colors cause a person's eyes to go blind,
The five tones cause a person's ears to go deaf.
The five flavors cause a person's palate to be spoiled.
Racing and hunting cause a person's mind to run wild.
Goods that are hard to come by impede a person's actions.
This is why the sage concerns himself with the belly,
not the eye.
And why he rejects the one and chooses the other.

13

Favor and disgrace are like a warning,
And honor is a great affliction, like one's body.
What does it mean to say favor and disgrace are like a warning?
For favor to be bestowed is like a warning,
For favor to be withdrawn is like a warning.
This is what is meant by favor and disgrace being like a warning.
What does it mean to say honor is great affliction, like one's self?
The reason there is great affliction is that I have a self.

If I had no self, what affliction would I have?
Therefore to one who honors the world as one's self
The world may be entrusted,
And to one who loves the world as one's self
The world may be consigned.

17

The highest is one whose existence no one knows,
The next is one who is loved and admired,
The next, one who is feared,
And the next, one who is hated.
When his faith in them is not sufficient,
They will have no faith in him.
Anxiously, he values his words,
Fulfills his tasks, completes his work.
The people all say,
"And with us, it happened naturally."

18

When the great Way declined,
There were humaneness and rightness.
When intelligence and wisdom emerged,
There was great artifice.
When the six relations[6] were no longer harmonious,
There were filial children.
When the realm fell into disorder,
There were loyal ministers.

19

Do away with sageliness, discard knowledge,
And the people will benefit a hundredfold.
Do away with humaneness, discard rightness,
And the people will once more be filial and loving,
Dispense with cleverness, discard profit,

---

6. The six relations are those between parent and child, older and younger brother, husband and wife.

And there will be no more bandits and thieves.
These three, to be regarded as ornaments, are insufficient.
Therefore let the people have something to cling to:
Manifest plainness,
Embrace uncarved wood,
Diminish selfishness,
Reduce desires.

22

Be bent so as to become whole,
Be crooked so as to become straight,
Be empty so as to become full,
Be worn so as to become new.
Possess little so as to acquire;
To possess much is to be perplexed.
Therefore the sage, by embracing the One,
Becomes a model for the world.
By not showing himself,
He becomes illustrious.
By not being self-important,
He becomes prominent.
By not being given to self-praise,
He is given credit.
By not promoting himself,
He endures for long.
Because he does not contend,
There is no one in the world who can contend with him.
When the ancients said, "Be bent so as to become whole,"
Could these have been empty words?
In truly becoming whole, one returns to it.

28

Knowing the male, but keeping to the female,
One may become a ravine to the world.
Becoming a ravine to the world,
The constant virtue does not depart;
One returns to the state of infancy.
Knowing the white, but keeping to the black,
One may become a model for the world.

Becoming a model for the world,
The constant virtue does not deviate;
One returns to the limitless (*wuji*).
Knowing honor but keeping to lowliness,
One may become a valley to the world.
Becoming a valley to the world,
The constant virtue will be sufficient;
One returns to uncarved wood.
When the uncarved wood is broken up, it becomes vessels.
The sage, using them, becomes head of the officials.
Great carving does not rend asunder.

29

If one desires to take the empire and act on it,
I see that he will not succeed.
The empire is a sacred vessel,
That cannot be acted upon.
In being acted upon, it is harmed;
And in being grasped, it is lost.
For among living things some move ahead and others follow,
Some breathe easily and others hard,
Some are strong and others are weak,
Some rise up and others are brought low.
Thus the sage rejects the excessive, the extravagant, the extreme.

36

If you would shrink it,
You must first cause it to be expanded.
If you would weaken it,
You must first cause it to be strengthened.
If you would destroy it,
You must first cause it to flourish.
If you would take from it,
You must first give to it.
This is called the subtly illumined.
The soft and the weak overcome the hard and the strong.
The fish should not be removed from the deep;
The state's sharp weapons should be revealed to no one.

37

The Way is constant: by doing nothing,
nothing is left undone.
If lords and kings can hold to it, all things will,
of themselves, be transformed.
If, as they are transformed, desires arise,
I suppress them by means of the nameless uncarved wood.
From the nameless uncarved wood comes absence of desire,
Through not desiring one becomes tranquil,
And the empire, of itself, becomes settled.

38

One of superior virtue is not virtuous
and therefore has virtue;
One of inferior virtue never loses virtue
and therefore lacks virtue.
One of superior virtue does nothing,
and has no motive to do anything;
One of inferior virtue does things,
and has a motive for doing them.
One of superior humaneness does things,
but has no motive for doing them;
One of superior rightness does things,
and has a motive for doing them;
One of superior propriety takes action,
and when no one responds,
stretches his arms and resorts to force.
Therefore after the Way was lost there was virtue,
After virtue was lost there was humaneness,
After humaneness was lost there was rightness,
And after rightness was lost there was ritual propriety.
Now ritual is the wearing thin of fidelity and trustworthiness
and the beginning of chaos.
Those who are the first to know
have the flowers of the Way
and the beginning of ignorance.
Therefore the great man abides in the thick
and does not dwell in the thin,
Abides in the substance

and does not dwell in the flower.
Therefore he rejects the one and chooses the other.

39

Of old, among those that attained the One:
Heaven attained the One and thereby became clear.
Earth attained the One and thereby became quiet.
Spirits attained the One and thereby became numinous.
Valleys attained the One and thereby became full,
All beings attained the One and thereby they live.
Lords and kings attained the One and thereby became
the upright ones of the empire.
This came about through the One.
Without what allows it to be clear,
Heaven might have been sundered.
Without what allows it to be settled,
Earth might have been shaken.
Without what causes them to be numinous,
spirits might have ceased.
Without what allows them to be full,
the valleys might have been depleted.
Without what allows them to live,
all beings might have perished.
Without what allows them to be honorable and exalted,
lords and kings might have fallen.
Therefore what is honored is rooted in the humble;
And what is exalted is founded in the lowly.
This is why lords and kings refer to themselves
as the orphaned, the lonely ones, the unfortunate.
Is this not taking humility as the root? Is it not?
Therefore if you approach a chariot and enumerate its parts,
you still have no chariot.
Seek neither to be rare like jade nor common like stone.[7]

---

7. Controversy surrounds the final line of this section — does it mean to prefer stone, which is common, to jade, which is rare? Or to strike a middle way between the two? The interpretation adopted above seems to be supported by both the Wang Bi and the Heshang Gong commentaries.

42

The Way gives birth to the One;
The One gives birth to two;
Two give birth to three;
And three give birth to all things.
All beings support the yin and embrace the yang;
And through the blending of qi[8] they create harmony.
What people hate is to be orphaned, lonely, unfortunate,
Yet kings and lords call themselves by these names.[9]
Therefore things may gain by losing, and lose by gaining.
What others teach, I also teach:
The violent do not attain a natural death.
This I take as the father of my teaching.

43

What is softest in the world
Overcomes what is hardest in the world.
No-thing penetrates where there is no space.
Thus I know that in doing nothing there is advantage.
The wordless teaching and the advantage of doing nothing —
there are few in the world who understand them.

47

Without passing through the door one may know
all-under-Heaven;
Without looking out the window one may observe
the Way of Heaven.
The further one goes, the less one knows.
This is why the sage knows without moving,
understands without seeing,
succeeds without doing.

48

Devotion to learning means increasing day by day;
Devotion to the Way means decreasing day by day.

---

8. Vital energy, vital force, material-force, breath. See note 5, above.
9. See sec. 39.

Decreasing, and decreasing still more, one arrives at
doing nothing,
And in doing nothing, nothing remains undone.
If one would take control of all-under-Heaven one should always refrain from
     activity;
One who is engaged in activity is unworthy to control all-under-Heaven.

56

Those who know do not speak;
Those who speak do not know.
Close the openings;
Shut the gates.
Untie the tangles;
Subdue the light.
Merge with the dust:
This is called the mysterious merging.
Therefore intimacy cannot be gained nor remoteness achieved;
Benefit cannot be conferred nor harm inflicted;
Honor cannot be bestowed nor dishonor imposed;
This is why it is honored by the world.

57

Govern the state by correctness;
Deploy the army by deception;
Acquire the empire by taking no action (*wushi*).
How do I know this is so?
By this.[10]
The more prohibitions there are in the world,
The poorer are the people.
The more sharp weapons the people have,
The more disorder is fomented in the family and state.
The more adroit and clever men are,
The more deceptive things are brought forth.
The more laws and ordinances are promulgated,
The more thieves and robbers there are.
Therefore the sage says:
I do nothing (*wuwei*),
And the people are transformed by themselves.

---

10. Through looking within oneself.

I value tranquillity,
And the people become correct by themselves.
I take no action (*wushi*),
And the people become prosperous by themselves.
I have no desires,
And the people of themselves become like uncarved wood.

60

Governing a large state is like cooking a small fish.
By using the Way to manage the empire,
Spiritual forces lose their potency.
Not that they lose their potency,
But that their potency does not harm people,
Not only does their potency not harm people,
But the sage also does not harm people.
The two do not harm one other,
So that virtue accumulates in both and returns [to the people].[11]

61

A large state is the effluence of a river,
Confluence of the world,
Female of the world.
Through stillness the female always overcomes the male.
Through stillness she submits.
Thus, by submitting, a large state wins a small one,
And a small state, by submitting to a large state,
wins the large state.
Thus one submits in order to win,
The other submits in order to be won.
The large state only wants to nourish the people as a whole.
The small state only wants to enter the service of others.
Each getting what it wants, it is right to submit.

65

Of old, those who were good at practicing the Way
Sought not to illuminate the people but to keep them ignorant.

---

11. Based on the reading of Wing-tsit Chan, which is in turn based on the reading in *Han Feizi, juan* 20.

The people become difficult to govern
as their knowledge increases.
Therefore one who governs a state through wisdom
is the robber of the state.
One who does not govern the state through wisdom
is the blessing of the state.
Knowing these two things one is also a standard and a guide;
Always knowing the standard and the guide is called
mysterious virtue.
Mysterious virtue is deep and far-reaching:
With it, all things revert [to their true reality],[12]
And then reach great harmony.

66

What enables the great rivers and seas to be king
over all the valley streams
Is that they are good at staying below them,
And thus can be kings over the valley streams.
Therefore if one wants to be above the people,
One must, in using words, remain below them.
If one wants to be ahead of the people,
One must, in using one's person, remain behind them.
Therefore when the sage places himself above,
The people do not find it a burden.
When he places himself ahead,
The people are not hurt.
Therefore the world finds joy in praising him, without wearying of it,
And because he contends with no one,
No one can contend with him.

67

All the world says that my Way is great,
And appears not to resemble anything.
It is because it is great that it appears
not to resemble anything.
Were it to resemble something,
It would long ago have become slight.

---

12. Following the interpretation of Wang Bi.

I have three treasures to hold and to keep:
The first is compassion.
The second is frugality.
The third is not daring to be first in the world.
Being compassionate, one is able to be courageous.
Being frugal, one is able to be broad-minded.
Not daring to be first in the world,
one is able to become its leader.
Now if one abandons compassion so as to be courageous,
If one abandons frugality so as to be broad-minded,
If one abandons being last so as to be first,
This is death.
Compassion helps one to overcome in battle,
And to be secure in defense.
Whom Heaven would save, it protects with compassion.

70

My words are very easy to understand,
And very easy to practice,
Yet none in the world are able to understand them,
And none are able to practice them.
My words have a master; my deeds have a lord.
Because people do not know this they do not know me.
Because there are few who know me, I am highly valued.
Therefore the sage wears a coarse cloth without,
and carries a fine jade within.

74

The people are not afraid of death.
So why use death to threaten them?
Suppose that the people were always afraid of death,
And that we could seize and kill the deviant among them.
Who would dare to do it?
There is always the master of killing[13] who kills.
Now to kill on behalf of the master of killing
Is known as hewing wood on behalf of the great carpenter.
Among those who hew wood on behalf of the great carpenter
Few avoid hurting their hands.

---

13. I.e., Heaven.

80

Let the state be small and the people be few.
There may be ten or even a hundred times as many implements,
But they should not be used.
Let the people, regarding death as a weighty matter,
not travel far.
Though they have boats and carriages, none shall ride in them.
Though they have armor and weapons, none shall display them.
Let the people return once more to the use of knotted ropes.[14]
Let them savor their food and find beauty in their clothing,
peace in their dwellings, and joy in their customs.
Though neighboring states are within sight of one another,
And the sound of cocks and dogs is audible
from one to the other,
People will reach old age and death
and yet not visit one another.[15]

81

True words are not beautiful,
Beautiful words are not true.
Those who are good do not argue,
Those who argue are not good.
Those who know have no wide learning,
Those with wide learning do not know.
The sage does not hoard,
The more he uses on behalf of others,
The more he has himself.
And the more he gives to others,
The more comes back to him.
The Way of Heaven is to bring benefit and not to harm.
The Way of the sage is to do things without contending.

[*Laozi* (*SBBY*) —IB]

14. Tradition has it that knotted ropes were used for record-keeping before the invention of writing.

15. According to the commentary by Wang Bi, this is because there is nothing they want to acquire.

TRANSFORMATION AND TRANSCENDENCE IN THE *ZHUANGZI*

In Zhuang Zhou — or Zhuangzi — we encounter a true intellectual and spiritual genius, one of the most philosophically challenging and verbally adept contributors to the early Chinese tradition and also one of its wittiest and most intriguing personalities. Zhuangzi probes philosophical depths in ways that are often unsettling and even unnerving; simultaneously he achieves literary heights that are literally breathtaking. While the *Daodejing* offers its sententious wisdom in the form of a kind of gnomic poetry, the text that bears Zhuangzi's name is a linguistically flamboyant tour de force, opening with a dazzling flight of the spirit and closing, thirty-three chapters later, with a comprehensive and remarkably sober survey of the world of thought in the late Warring States period. In between there are conversations, often highly fanciful, between real or, more often, imaginary people, along with anecdotes, parables, meditations, and poems. The characters that inhabit the pages of the *Zhuangzi* include craftsmen, cripples, a slyly reconstructed Confucius, and a talking tree — among a host of others.

While it is now generally accepted that the author and teacher known as Laozi, "the old master," was not actually a single person, Zhuang Zhou, though biographical detail concerning his life is scant, has been recognized as a distinct individual. The Han dynasty historian Sima Qian (145?–86? B.C.E.) records that he was a native of a place called Meng, where he once served as "an official in the lacquer garden," and that he lived during the times of King Hui of Liang (370–319 B.C.E.) and King Xuan of Qi (319–301 B.C.E.). The location of Meng is still uncertain, but it may well have been in the feudal state of Song, where hundreds of years earlier the vestiges of the Shang royal family had been enfeoffed. The years of Zhuang Zhou's life are also not reliably known, but if Sima Qian's chronology is even approximately correct, Zhuang Zhou would have been a contemporary of Mencius.

Following the fourth-century commentator Guo Xiang (d. 312 C.E.), scholars generally attribute to this presumably historical Zhuang Zhou the first seven chapters of the *Zhuangzi*, which have become known as the Inner Chapters. All of the selections that follow below derive from these seven chapters. The rest of the *Zhuangzi* was divided into fifteen Outer Chapters and eleven Miscellaneous Chapters, which are generally acknowledged to have been the work of other, later hands.[16]

Given the subtlety and ambiguity of the thought encountered in the Inner Chapters of the *Zhuangzi*, it is difficult to characterize it in broad strokes,

---

16. Selections from these later chapters may be found in ch. 9, pp. 263–68.

though it is possible to highlight Zhuangzi's most prominent concerns. One of these is the issue of universality and particularity, the *Zhuangzi* being memorable for its meditation on the diversity of the human world as well as the world of nature as a whole, its reflection on how, amid the diversity of life, the universality of the Way may be perceived. Zhuangzi is also concerned with the nature of knowledge, the possibilities and limitations of language, the metaphysical implications of moral values, and the understanding of the self. For him, self-understanding is gained through an awareness that life involves both infinite variety and inexorable change and that death is both inevitable and unfathomable. Like Laozi, Zhuangzi is concerned also with transcendence, to be found here in the realization that life and death alike are simply two aspects of the great process of transformation.

The *Zhuangzi* has always been a challenge for translators, in part because it is so difficult to capture both its philosophical depth and its literary brilliance — the deep places and dark shadows within which Zhuangzi often works and the high humor and bright light with which he manages to illumine the darkness. Fortunately, readers of English have benefited from the fact that in recent years the text has been translated by two of the greatest Sinologists and translators of the twentieth century — Burton Watson and Angus Graham. Both of these masterful translations are represented in the selections that follow, Watson's in chapters 1 and 3–7, Graham's in chapter 2.

FROM CHAPTER 1, "FREE AND EASY WANDERING"

In the northern darkness there is a fish and his name is Kun.[17] The Kun is so huge I don't know how many thousand *li* he measures. He changes and becomes a bird whose name is Peng. The back of the Peng measures I don't know how many thousand *li* across and, when he rises up and flies off, his wings are like clouds all over the sky. When the sea begins to move,[18] this bird sets out for the southern darkness, which is the Lake of Heaven.

The *Universal Harmony*[19] records various wonders, and it says: "When the Peng journeys to the southern darkness, the waters are roiled for three thousand *li*. He beats the whirlwind and rises ninety thousand *li*, setting off on the sixth-month gale." Wavering heat, bits of dust, living things blowing each other

---

17. *Kun* means "fish roe." So *Zhuangzi* begins with a paradox — the tiniest fish imaginable is also the largest fish imaginable.

18. Probably a reference to some seasonal shift in the tides or currents.

19. Identified variously as the name of a man or the name of a book. Probably Zhuangzi intended it as the latter and is poking fun at the philosophers of other schools who cite ancient texts to prove their assertions.

about — the sky looks very blue. Is that its real color, or is it because it is so far away and has no end? When the bird looks down, all he sees is blue too.

If water is not piled up deep enough, it won't have the strength to bear up a big boat. Pour a cup of water into a hollow in the floor and bits of trash will sail on it like boats. But set the cup there and it will stick fast, for the water is too shallow and the boat too large. If wind is not piled up deep enough, it won't have the strength to bear up great wings. Therefore when the Peng rises ninety thousand *li*, he must have the wind under him like that. Only then can he mount on the back of the wind, shoulder the blue sky, and nothing can hinder or block him. Only then can he set his eyes to the south.

The cicada and the little dove laugh at this, saying, "When we make an effort and fly up, we can get as far as the elm or the sapanwood tree, but sometimes we don't make it and just fall down on the ground. Now how is anyone going to go ninety thousand *li* to the south!"

If you go off to the green woods nearby, you can take along food for three meals and come back with your stomach as full as ever. If you are going a hundred *li*, you must grind your grain the night before; and if you are going a thousand *li*, you must start getting the provisions together three months in advance. What do these two creatures understand? Little understanding cannot come up to great understanding; the short-lived cannot come up to the long-lived.

How do I know this is so? The morning mushroom knows nothing of twilight and dawn; the summer cicada knows nothing of spring and autumn. They are the short-lived. South of Chu there is a caterpillar that counts five hundred years as one spring and five hundred years as one autumn. Long, long ago there was a great rose of Sharon that counted eight thousand years as one spring and eight thousand years as one autumn. They are the long-lived. Yet Pengzu alone is famous today for having lived a long time, and everybody tries to ape him. Isn't it pitiful! . . .

In the bald and barren north, there is a dark sea, the Lake of Heaven. In it is a fish that is several thousand *li* across, and no one knows how long. His name is Kun. There is also a bird there, named Peng, with a back like Mount Tai and wings like clouds filling the sky. He beats the whirlwind, leaps into the air, and rises up ninety thousand *li*, cutting through the clouds and mist, shouldering the blue sky, and then he turns his eyes south and prepares to journey to the southern darkness.

The little quail laughs at him, saying, "Where does he think *he's* going? I give a great leap and fly up, but I never get more than ten or twelve yards before I come down fluttering among the weeds and brambles. And that's the best kind of flying anyway! Where does he think *he's* going?" Such is the difference between big and little.

Therefore a man who has wisdom enough to fill one office effectively, good conduct enough to impress one community, virtue enough to please one ruler, or talent enough to be called into service in one state, has the same kind of self-pride as these little creatures. Song Rongzi[20] would certainly burst out laughing at such a man. The whole world could praise Song Rongzi and it wouldn't make him exert himself; the whole world could condemn him and it wouldn't make him mope. He drew a clear line between the internal and the external, and recognized the boundaries of true glory and disgrace. But that was all. As far as the world went, he didn't fret and worry, but there was still ground he left unturned.

Liezi[21] could ride the wind and go soaring around with cool and breezy skill, but after fifteen days he came back to earth. As far as the search for good fortune went, he didn't fret and worry. He escaped the trouble of walking, but he still had to depend on something to get around. If he had only mounted on the truth of Heaven and Earth, ridden the changes of the six breaths, and thus wandered through the boundless, then what would he have had to depend on?

Therefore I say, the Perfect Man has no self; the Holy Man has no merit; the Sage has no fame. [pp. 29–32]

Huizi said to Zhuangzi, "I have a big tree of the kind men call *shu*. Its trunk is too gnarled and bumpy to apply a measuring line to, its branches too bent and twisty to match up to a compass or a square. You could stand it by the road and no carpenter would look at it twice. Your words, too, are big and useless, and so everyone alike spurns them!"

Zhuangzi said, "Maybe you've never seen a wildcat or a weasel. It crouches down and hides, watching for something to come along. It leaps and races east and west, not hesitating to go high or low — until it falls into the trap and dies in the net. Then again there's the yak, big as a cloud covering the sky. It certainly knows how to be big, but it doesn't know how to catch rats. Now you have this big tree and you're distressed because it's useless. Why don't you plant it in Not-Even-Anything Village, or the field of Broad-and-Boundless, relax and do nothing by its side, or lie down for free and easy sleep under it? Axes will never shorten its life, nothing can ever harm it. If there's no use for it, how can it come to grief or pain?" [p. 35]

[*Zhuangzi* (SBBY) 1:1a–5b, 9a–b
— adapted from Watson, *Chuang Tzu*, pp. 29–32, 35]

---

20. Referred to elsewhere in the literature of the period as Song Jian or Song Keng. According to chapter 33 of the *Zhuangzi*, he taught a doctrine of social harmony, frugality, pacifism, and the rejection of conventional standards of honor and disgrace.

21. Lie Yukou, a Taoist sage frequently mentioned in the *Zhuangzi*. The *Liezi*, a work attributed to him, is of uncertain date and did not reach its present form until the second or third century C.E.

FROM CHAPTER 2, "THE SORTING WHICH EVENS THINGS OUT"

This chapter is considered the most philosophically significant in the *Zhuangzi*, dealing as it does with matters of knowledge and language, life and death, dream and reality. In the following passage Zhuangzi starts from a quotation or provisional formulation of his own. His theme is the mind or heart, the organ of thought. Should it be allowed to take charge of our lives? Isn't it merely one of many organs, each with its own functions within an order that comes from beyond us, from the Way?

"Without an Other there is no Self, without Self no choosing one thing rather than another."

This is somewhere near it, but we do not know in whose service they are being employed. It seems that there is something genuinely in command, and that the only trouble is we cannot find a sign of it. That as "Way" it can be walked is true enough, but we do not see its shape; it has identity but no shape. Of the hundred joints, nine openings, six viscera all present and complete, which should I recognize as more kin to me than another? Are you people pleased with them all? Rather, you have a favorite organ among them. On your assumption, does it have the rest of them as its vassals and concubines? Are its vassals and concubines inadequate to rule each other? Isn't it rather that they take turns as each other's lord and vassals? Or rather than that, they have a genuine lord present in them. If we seek without success to grasp what its identity might be, that never either adds to nor detracts from its genuineness. [p. 51]

Once we have received the completed body we are aware of it all the time we await extinction. Is it not sad how we and other things go on stroking or jostling each other, in a race ahead like a gallop which nothing can stop? How can we fail to regret that we labor all our lives without seeing success, wear ourselves out with toil in ignorance of where we shall end? What use is it for man to say that he will not die, since when the body dissolves the heart dissolves with it? How can we not call this our supreme regret? Is man's life really as stupid as this? Or is it that I am the only stupid one, and there are others not so stupid? But if you go by the completed heart and take it as your authority, who is without such an authority? Why should it be only the man who knows how things alternate and whose heart approves his own judgments who has such an authority? The fool has one just as he has. For there to be "That's it, that's not" before they are formed in the heart would be to "go to Yue today and have arrived yesterday."[22] This would be crediting with existence what has

---

22. "I go to Yue today but came yesterday" was a paradox of the Sophist Hui Shi, with whom Zhuangzi argued, here mentioned only for its absurdity. Yue was an area far to the east populated by non-Chinese.

no existence; and if you do that even the daemonic Yu could not understand you, and how can you expect to be understood by me? [p. 52]

The following passage refers to conventions of disputation or argument that were current in Zhuangzi's time. In disputation, if an object fits the name "ox," one affirms with the demonstrative word shi "[That] is it"; if it is something other than an ox one denies with a fei "[That] is not." Here Zhuangzi tries to discredit disputation by the objection that at any moment of change both alternatives will be admissible. He appeals to a paradox of Hui Shi, "The sun is simultaneously at noon and declining, a thing is simultaneously alive and dead," and generalizes to the conclusion that any statement will remain inadmissible at the very moment when it has just become admissible. It was also recognized in current disputation (as practiced by followers of Mozi) that one can say both "Y is long" (in relation to X) and "Y is short" (in relation to Z) and that even with words such as black and white, which are not comparative, one has to decide whether to "go by" (yin) the black parts or the white when deeming someone a "black man." Zhuangzi sees it as the lesson of disputation that one is entitled to affirm or deny anything of anything. He thinks of Confucians and Mohists who stick rigidly to their affirmations and denials as lighting up little areas of life and leaving the rest in darkness; the illumination of the sage is a vision that brings everything to light.

Saying is not blowing breath, saying says something; the only trouble is that what it says is never fixed. Do we really say something? Or have we never said anything? If you think it different from the twitter of fledglings, is there proof of the distinction? Or isn't there any proof? By what is the Way hidden, that there should be a genuine or a false? By what is saying darkened, that sometimes "That's it" and sometimes "That's not"? Wherever we walk, how can the Way be absent? Whatever the standpoint, how can saying be unallowable? The Way is hidden by formation of the lesser, saying is darkened by its foliage and flowers. And so we have the "That's it, that's not" of Confucians and Mohists, by which what is *it* for one of them for the other is not, what is *not* for one of them for the other is. If you wish to affirm what they deny and deny what they affirm, the best means is Illumination.

No thing is not "other," no thing is not "it." If you treat yourself too as "other," they do not appear; if you know of yourself you know of them. Hence it is said:

> "Other" comes out from "it," "it" likewise goes by "other,"

the opinion that "it" and "other" are born simultaneously. However,

> "Simultaneously with being alive one dies,"

and simultaneously with dying one is alive; simultaneously with being allowable something becomes unallowable and simultaneously with being unallowable it becomes allowable. If going by circumstance that's it, then going by circumstance that's not; if going by circumstance that's not, then going by circumstance that's it. This is why the sage does not take this course, but opens things up to the light of Heaven; his too is a "That's it" which goes by circumstance. [p. 52]

In the following exchange Gaptooth is pressing for an admission that there must be something that is knowable. Wang Ni denies it, perhaps because there could be no independent viewpoint from which to judge a universally shared opinion. Then at least one knows what one does not know. But that is another contradiction, or so Zhuangzi thinks. Then one knows that no one knows anything — another contradiction.

Gaptooth put a question to Wang Ni.
  "Would you *know* something of which all things agreed 'That's it'?"
  "How would I know that?"
  "Would you know what you did not know?"
  "How would I know that?"
  "Then does no thing know anything?"
  "How would I know that? However, let me try to say it — 'How do I know that what I call knowing is not ignorance? How do I know that what I call ignorance is not knowing?'
  "Moreover, let me try a question on you. When a human sleeps in the damp his waist hurts and he gets stiff in the joints; is that so of the loach? When he sits in a tree he shivers and shakes; is that so of the ape? Which of these three knows the right place to live? Humans eat the flesh of hay-fed and grain-fed beasts, deer eat the grass, centipedes relish snakes, owls and crows crave mice; which of the four has a proper sense of taste? Gibbons are sought by baboons as mates, elaphures like the company of deer, loaches play with fish. Maoqiang and Lady Li were beautiful in the eyes of men; but when the fish saw them they plunged deep, when the birds saw them they flew high, when the deer saw them they broke into a run. Which of these four knows what is truly beautiful in the world? In my judgment the principles of humaneness and rightness, the paths of 'That's it, that's not,' are inextricably confused; how could I know how to discriminate between them?"
  [Gaptooth said,] "If you do not know benefit from harm, would you deny that the utmost man knows benefit from harm?"
  [Wang Ni replied,] "The utmost man is daemonic.[23] When the wide woodlands blaze, they cannot sear him, when the Yellow River and the Han freeze they cannot chill him, when swift thunderbolts smash the mountains and whirlwinds shake the seas they cannot startle him. A man like that yokes the clouds

---

23. Or spiritual, *shen*.

to his chariot, rides the sun and the moon, and roams beyond the four seas; death and life alter nothing in himself, still less the principles of benefit and harm!" [p. 58]

Ququezi asked Changwuzi, "I heard this from the Master,[24] 'The sage does not work for any goal, does not lean toward benefit or shun harm, does not delight in seeking, does not fix a route by a Way, in saying nothing says something and in saying something says nothing, and roams beyond the dust and grime.' The Master thought of the saying as a flight of fancy, but to me it seemed the walking of the most esoteric Way. How does it seem to you?"

"This is a saying that would have puzzled the Yellow Emperor, and what would old Confucius know about it? Moreover, you for your part are counting your winnings much too soon; at the sight of the egg you expect the cock-crow, at the sight of the bow you expect a roasted owl. Suppose I put it to you in abandoned words, and you listen with the same abandon:

> "Go side by side with the sun and moon,
> Do the rounds of Space and Time.
> Act out their neat conjunctions,
> Stay aloof from their convulsions.
> Dependents each on each, let us honor one another.
> Common people fuss and fret.
> The sage is a dullard and a sluggard.
> Be aligned along a myriad years, in oneness, wholeness, simplicity.
> All the myriad things are as they are,
> And as what they are make up totality.

"How do I know that to take pleasure in life is not a delusion? How do I know that we who hate death are not exiles since childhood who have forgotten the way home? Lady Li was the daughter of a frontier guard at Ai. When the kingdom of Jin first took her the tears stained her dress; only when she came to the palace and shared the king's square couch and ate the flesh of hay-fed and grain-fed beasts did she begin to regret her tears. How do I know that the dead do not regret that ever they had an urge to life? Who banquets in a dream, at dawn wails and weeps; who wails and weeps in a dream, at dawn goes out to hunt. While we dream we do not know that we are dreaming, and in the middle of a dream interpret a dream within it; not until we wake do we know that we were dreaming. Only at the ultimate awakening shall we know that this is the ultimate dream. Yet fools think they are awake, so confident that they know what they are, princes, herdsmen, incorrigible! You and Confucius are both

---

24. I.e., Confucius.

dreams, and I who call you a dream am also a dream. This saying of his, the name for it is 'a flight into the extraordinary'; if it happens once in ten thousand ages that a great sage knows its explanation it will have happened as though between morning and evening." [pp. 59–60]

[*Zhuangzi* (SBBY) 1:10a–15a, 15b–17b, 20a–23b
— adapted from Graham, *Chuang-tzu*, pp. 51–53, 58–60]

Once Zhuang Zhou dreamed he was a butterfly. A butterfly fluttering happily around — was he revealing what he himself meant to be? He knew nothing of Zhou. All at once awakening, there suddenly he was — Zhou. But he didn't know if he was Zhou having dreamed he was a butterfly or a butterfly dreaming he was Zhou. Between Zhou and the butterfly there must surely be some distinction. This is known as the transformation of things.

[*Zhuangzi* (SBBY) 1:25b — IB]

FROM CHAPTER 3, "THE SECRET OF CARING FOR LIFE"

Your life has a limit but knowledge has none. If you use what is limited to pursue what has no limit, you will be in danger. If you understand this and still strive for knowledge, you will be in danger for certain! If you do good, stay away from fame. If you do evil, stay away from punishments. Follow the middle, go by what is constant, and you can stay in one piece, keep yourself alive, look after your parents, and live out your years.

Cook Ding was cutting up an ox for Lord Wenhui. At every touch of his hand, every heave of his shoulder, every move of his feet, every thrust of his knee — zip, zoop! He slithered the knife along with a zing, and all was in perfect rhythm, as though he were performing the dance of the Mulberry Grove or keeping time to the Jingshou music.[25]

"Ah, this is marvelous!" said Lord Wenhui. "Imagine skill reaching such heights!"

Cook Ding laid down his knife and replied, "What I care about is the Way, which goes beyond skill. When I first began cutting up oxen, all I could see was the ox itself. After three years I no longer saw the whole ox. And now — now I go at it by spirit and don't look with my eyes. Perception and understanding have come to a stop and spirit moves where it wants. I go along with the natural makeup, strike in the big hollows, guide the knife through the big openings, and follow things as they are. So I never touch the smallest ligament or tendon, much less a main joint.

---

25. The Mulberry Grove is identified as a rain dance from the time of King Tang of the Shang dynasty, and the Jingshou music as part of a longer composition from the time of Yao.

"A good cook changes his knife once a year—because he cuts. A mediocre cook changes his knife once a month—because he hacks. I've had this knife of mine for nineteen years and I've cut up thousands of oxen with it, and yet the blade is as good as though it had just come from the grindstone. There are spaces between the joints, and the blade of the knife has really no thickness. If you insert what has no thickness into such spaces, then there's plenty of room—more than enough for the blade to play about it. That's why after nineteen years the blade of my knife is still as good as when it first came from the grindstone.

"However, whenever I come to a complicated place, I size up the difficulties, tell myself to watch out and be careful, keep my eyes on what I'm doing, work very slowly, and move the knife with the greatest subtlety, until—flop! the whole thing comes apart like a clod of earth crumbling to the ground. I stand there holding the knife and look all around me, completely satisfied and reluctant to move on, and then I wipe off the knife and put it away."

"Excellent!" said Lord Wenhui. "I have heard the words of Cook Ding and learned how to care for life!" . . . [pp. 50–51]

When Lao Dan[26] died, Qin Shi went to mourn for him; but after giving three cries, he left the room.

"Weren't you a friend of the Master?" asked Laozi's disciples.

"Yes."

"And you think it's all right to mourn him this way?"

"Yes," said Qin Shi. "At first I took him for a real man, but now I know he wasn't. A little while ago, when I went in to mourn, I found old men weeping for him as though they were weeping for a son, and young men weeping for him as though they were weeping for a mother. To have gathered a group like *that*, he must have done something to make them talk about him, though he didn't ask them to talk, or make them weep for him, though he didn't ask them to weep. This is to hide from Heaven, turn your back on the true state of affairs, and forget what you were born with. In the old days, this was called the crime of hiding from Heaven. Your master happened to come because it was his time, and he happened to leave because things follow along. If you are content with the time and willing to follow along, then grief and joy have no way to enter in. In the old days, this was called being freed from the bonds of Di.

"Though the grease burns out of the torch, the fire passes on, and no one knows where it ends." [pp. 52–53]

> [*Zhuangzi* (SBBY) 2:1a–4a —Watson; *Chuang Tzu*, pp. 50–53]

---

26. Laozi, the reputed author of the *Daodejing*.

FROM CHAPTER 4, "IN THE WORLD OF MEN"

This chapter of the *Zhuangzi* opens with an exchange between Confucius and his favorite disciple, Yan Hui — an exchange concocted, of course, by Zhuangzi. Zhuangzi imagines Yan Hui requesting permission to journey to the state of Wei and contemplating what he might do to exert a positive influence over the young ruler of that state. Confucius is skeptical about Yan Hui's chances for success and points out that rulers motivated by concerns for fame or gain are likely to be intractable. After repeatedly cautioning Yan Hui, he asks to hear the disciple's plan.

Yan Hui said, "If I am grave and empty-hearted, diligent and of one mind, won't that do?"

"Goodness, how could *that* do? You may put on a fine outward show and seem very impressive, but you can't avoid having an uncertain look on your face, any more than an ordinary man can. And then you try to gauge this man's feelings and seek to influence his mind. But with him, what is called "the virtue that advances a little each day" would not succeed, much less a great display of virtue! He will stick fast to his position and never be converted. Though he may make outward signs of agreement, inwardly he will not give it a thought! How could such an approach succeed?"

"Well, then, suppose I am inwardly direct, outwardly compliant, and do my work through the examples of antiquity? By being inwardly direct, I can be the companion of Heaven. Being a companion of Heaven, I know that the Son of Heaven and I are equally the sons of Heaven. Then why would I use my words to try to get men to praise me, or try to get them not to praise me? A man like this, people call The Child. This is what I mean by being a companion of Heaven.

"By being outwardly compliant, I can be a companion of men. Lifting up the tablet, kneeling, bowing, crouching down — this is the etiquette of a minister. Everybody does it, so why shouldn't I? If I do what other people do, they can hardly criticize me. This is what I mean by being a companion of men.

"By doing my work through the examples of antiquity, I can be the companion of ancient times. Though my words may in fact be lessons and reproaches, they belong to ancient times and not to me. In this way, though I may be blunt, I cannot be blamed. This is what I mean by being a companion of antiquity. If I go about it in this way, will it do?"

Confucius said, "Goodness, how could *that* do? You have too many policies and plans and you haven't seen what is needed. You will probably get off without incurring any blame, yes. But that will be as far as it goes. How do you think you can actually convert him? You are still making the mind[27] your teacher."

---

27. Not the natural or "given" mind but the mind that makes artificial distinctions.

Yan Hui said, "I have nothing more to offer. May I ask the proper way?"

"You must fast!" said Confucius. "I will tell you what that means. Do you think that it is easy to do anything while you have [a mind]? If you do, Bright Heaven will not sanction you."

Yan Hui said, "My family is poor. I haven't drunk wine or eaten any strong foods for several months. So can I be considered as having fasted?"

"That is the fasting one does before a sacrifice, not the fasting of the mind."

"May I ask what the fasting of the mind is?"

Confucius said, "Make your will one! Don't listen with your ears, listen with your mind. No, don't listen with your mind, listen with your spirit.[28] Listening stops with the ears, the mind stops with recognition, but spirit is empty and waits on all things. The Way gathers in emptiness alone. Emptiness is the fasting of the mind."

Yan Hui said, "Before I heard this, I was certain that I was Hui. But now that I have heard it, there is no more Hui. Can this be called emptiness?"

"That's all there is to it," said Confucius. "Now I will tell you. You may go and play in his bird cage, but never be moved by fame. If he listens, then sing; if not, keep still. Have no gate, no opening, but make oneness your house, and live with what cannot be avoided. Then you will be close to success.

"It is easy to keep from walking; the hard thing is to walk without touching the ground. It is easy to cheat when you work for men, but hard to cheat when you work for Heaven. You have heard of flying with wings, but you have never heard of flying without wings. You have heard of the knowledge that knows, but you have never heard of the knowledge that does not know. Look into that closed room, the empty chamber where Brightness is born! Fortune and blessing gather where there is stillness. But if you do not keep still — this is what is called sitting but racing around. Let your ears and eyes communicate with what is inside, and put mind and knowledge on the outside. Then even gods and spirits will come to dwell, not to speak of men! This is the changing of the ten thousand things, the bond of Yu and Shun, the constant practice of Fu Xi and Ji Qu.[29] How much more should it be a rule for lesser men!" . . . [pp. 56–58]

Carpenter Shi went to Qi, and when he got to Crooked Shaft, he saw a serrate oak standing by the village shrine. It was broad enough to shelter several thousand oxen and measured a hundred spans around, towering above the hills. The lowest branches were eighty feet from the ground, and a dozen or so of them could be made into boats. There were so many sightseers that the place looked like a fair, but the carpenter didn't even glance around and went on his way without stopping. His apprentice stood staring for a long time and then ran

---

28. Literally, with your *qi*, material-force or vital energy.
29. Mythical sage rulers.

after Carpenter Shi and said, "Since I first took up my ax and followed you, Master, I have never seen timber as beautiful as this. But you don't even bother to look, and go right on without stopping. Why is that?"

"Forget it — say no more!" said the carpenter. "It's a worthless tree! Make boats out of it and they'd sink; make coffins out of it and they'd rot in no time; make vessels and they'd break at once. Use it for doors and it would sweat sap like pine; use it for posts and the worms would eat them up. It's not a timber tree — there's nothing it can be used for. That's how it got to be that old!"

After Carpenter Shi returned home, the oak tree appeared to him in a dream and said, "What are you comparing me with? Are you comparing me with those useful trees? The cherry apple, the pear, the orange, the citron, the rest of those fructiferous trees and shrubs — as soon as their fruit is ripe, they are torn apart and subjected to abuse. Their big limbs are broken off, their little limbs are yanked around. Their utility makes life miserable for them, and so they don't get to finish out the years Heaven gave them, but are cut off in mid-journey. They bring it on themselves — the pulling and tearing of the common mob. And it is the same way with all other things.

"As for me, I've been trying a long time to be of no use, and though I almost died, I've finally got it. This is of great use to me. If I had been of some use, would I ever have grown this large? Moreover, you and I are both of us things. What's the point of this — things condemning things? You, a worthless man about to die — how do you know I'm a worthless tree?"

When Carpenter Shi woke up, he reported his dream. His apprentice said, "If it's so intent on being of no use, what's it doing there at the village shrine?"[30]

"Shhh! Say no more! It is only *resting* there. If we carp and criticize, it will only conclude that we don't understand it. Even if it weren't at the shrine, do you suppose it would be cut down? It protects itself in a different way from ordinary people. If you try to judge it by conventional standards, you'll be way off!" [pp. 63–65]

> [*Zhuangzi (SBBY)* 2:6a–8a, 12a–13a
> — adapted from Watson, *Chuang Tzu*, pp. 56–58, 63–65]

FROM CHAPTER 5, "THE SIGN OF VIRTUE COMPLETE"

Huizi said to Zhuangzi, "Can a man really be without feelings?"
Zhuangzi: "Yes."
Huizi: "But a man who has no feelings — how can you call him a man?"

---

30. The shrine, or altar of the soil, was always situated in a grove of beautiful trees. So the oak was serving a purpose by lending an air of sanctity to the spot.

Zhuangzi: "The Way gave him a face; Heaven gave him a form — why can't you call him a man?"

Huizi: "But if you've already called him a man, how can he be without feelings?"

Zhuangzi: "That's not what I mean by feelings. When I talk about having no feelings, I mean that a man doesn't allow likes or dislikes to get in and do him harm. He just lets things be the way they are and doesn't try to help life along."

Huizi: "If he doesn't try to help life along, then how can he keep himself alive?"

Zhuangzi: "The Way gave him a face; Heaven gave him a form. He doesn't let likes and dislikes get in and do him harm. You, now — you treat your spirit like an outsider. You wear out your energy, leaning on a tree and moaning, slumping at your desk and dozing — Heaven picked out a body for you and you use it to gibber about 'hard' and 'white'!"[31]

[*Zhuangzi* (SBBY) 2:15b–17b, 23a–b
— adapted from Watson, *Chuang Tzu*, pp. 75–76]

FROM CHAPTER 6, "THE GREAT AND VENERABLE TEACHER"

Nanbo Zikui said to the Woman Crookback, "You are old in years and yet your complexion is that of a child. Why is this?"

"I have heard the Way!"

"Can the Way be learned?" asked Nanbo Zikui.

"Goodness, how could that be? Anyway, you aren't the man to do it. Now there's Buliang Yi — he has the talent of a sage but not the Way of a sage, whereas I have the Way of a sage but not the talent of a sage. I thought I would try to reach him and see if I could get anywhere near to making him a sage. It's easier to explain the Way of a sage to someone who has the talent of a sage, you know. So I began explaining and kept at him for three days, and after that he was able to put the world outside himself. When he had put the world outside himself, I kept at him for seven days more, and after that he was able to put things outside himself. When he had put things outside himself, I kept at him for nine days more, and after that he was able to put life outside himself. After he had put life outside himself, he was able to achieve the brightness of dawn, and when he had achieved the brightness of dawn, he could see his own aloneness. After he had managed to see his own aloneness, he could do away with

---

31. Huizi and Gongsun Long, often identified as representatives of the School of Names (*mingjia*), were known for spending much time discussing the relationship between attributes such as "hard" and "white" and the things to which they pertain.

past and present, and after he had done away with past and present, he was able to enter where there is no life and death. That which kills life does not die; that which gives life to life does not live.[32] This is the kind of thing it is: there's nothing it doesn't send off, nothing it doesn't welcome, nothing it doesn't destroy, nothing it doesn't complete. It's name is Peace-in-Strife. After the strife, it attains completion. . . ." [pp. 82–83]

Master Si, Master Yu, Master Li, and Master Lai were all four talking together. "Who can look upon nonbeing as his head, on life as his back, and on death as his rump?" they said. "Who knows that life and death, existence and annihilation, are all a single body? I will be his friend!"

The four men looked at each other and smiled. There was no disagreement in their hearts and so the four of them became friends.

All at once Master Yu fell ill. Master Si went to ask how he was. "Amazing!" said Master Yu. "The Creator is making me all crookedy like this! My back sticks up like a hunchback, and my vital organs are on top of me. My chin is hidden in my navel, my shoulders are up above my head, and my pigtail points at the sky. It must be some dislocation of the yin and yang!"[33]

Yet he seemed calm at heart and unconcerned. Dragging himself haltingly to the well, he looked at his reflection and said, "My, my! So the Creator is making me all crookedy like this!"

"Do you resent it?" asked Master Si.

"Why, no, what would I resent? If the process continues, perhaps in time he'll transform my left arm into a rooster. In that case I'll keep watch on the night. Or perhaps in time he'll transform my right arm into a crossbow pellet and I'll shoot down an owl for roasting. Or perhaps in time he'll transform my buttocks into cartwheels. Then, with my spirit for a horse, I'll climb up and go for a ride. What need will I ever have for a carriage again?

"I received life because the time had come; I will lose it because the order of things passes on. Be content with this time and dwell in this order and then neither sorrow nor joy can touch you. In ancient times this was called the 'freeing of the bound.' There are those who cannot free themselves, because they are bound by things. But nothing can ever win against Heaven — that's the way it's always been. What would I have to resent?"

Suddenly Master Lai grew ill. Gasping and wheezing, he lay at the point of death. His wife and children gathered round in a circle and began to cry. Master Li, who had come to ask how he was, said, "Shoo! Get back! Don't disturb the process of change!"

---

32. I.e., that which transcends the categories of life and death can never be said to have lived or died; only that which recognizes the existence of such categories is subject to them.

33. Yin and yang are complementary energies associated with dark and light, cold and heat, female and male, Earth and Heaven, etc.

Then he leaned against the doorway and talked to Master Lai. "How marvelous the Creator is! What is he going to make of you next? Where is he going to send you? Will be make you into a rat's liver? Will he make you into a bug's arm?"

Master Lai said, "A child, obeying his father and mother, goes wherever he is told, east or west, south or north. And the yin and yang—how much more are they to a man than father or mother! Now that they have brought me to the verge of death, if I should refuse to obey them, how perverse I would be! What fault is it of theirs? The Great Clod burdens me with form, labors me with life, eases me in old age, and rests me in death. So if I think well of my life, for the same reason I must think well of my death. When a skilled smith is casting metal, if the metal should leap up and say, 'I insist upon being made into a Moyeh!'[34] he would surely regard it as very inauspicious metal indeed. Now, having had the audacity to take on human form once, if I should say, 'I don't want to be anything but a man! Nothing but a man!' the Creator would surely regard me as a most inauspicious sort of person. So now I think of Heaven and Earth as a great furnace, and the Creator as a skilled smith. Where could he send me that would not be all right? I will go off to sleep peacefully, and then with a start I will wake up." . . . [pp. 83–85]

Yan Hui said, "I'm improving!"

Confucius said, "What do you mean by that?"

"I've forgotten humaneness and rightness."

"That's good. But you still haven't got it."

Another day, the two met again, and Yan Hui said, "I'm improving!"

"What do you mean by that?"

"I've forgotten rites and music."

"That's good. But you still haven't got it."

Another day, the two met again, and Yan Hui said, "I'm improving!"

"What do you mean by that?"

"I can sit down and forget everything."

Confucius looked very startled and said, "What do you mean, sit down and forget everything?"

Yan Hui said, "I smash up my limbs and body, drive out perception and intellect, cast off form, do away with understanding, and make myself identical with the Great Thoroughfare. This is what I mean by sitting down and forgetting everything."

Confucius said, "If you're identical with it, you must have no more likes! If you've been transformed, you must have no more constancy! So you really are

---

34. A famous sword of King Helü of Wu.

a worthy man after all![35] With your permission, I'd like to become your follower." [pp. 90–91]

[*Zhuangzi* (SBBY) 3:7a–10a, 14a–b — Watson, *Chuang Tzu*, pp. 82–85, 90–91]

FROM CHAPTER 7, "FIT FOR EMPERORS AND KINGS"

The sovereign of the Southern Sea is called Impatient; the sovereign of the Northern Sea is called Impulsive; the sovereign of the center of the world is called the Primal Whole (*hundun*). Impatient and Impulsive met from time to time in the territory of the Primal Whole, and the latter treated them well. Impatient and Impulsive discussed together how they could repay his kindness. They said, "All men have seven holes in their bodies for seeing, hearing, eating, and breathing. Our friend here has none of these, Let us try to bore some holes for him." Each day they bored one hole. On the seventh day the Primal Whole died.

[*Zhuangzi* (SBBY) 3:19a–b — deB]

---

35. Zhuangzi may have intended a humorous reference to the words of Confucius in *Analects* 6:9: "The Master said, 'What a worthy man was Hui!'"

Chapter 6

THE EVOLUTION OF THE CONFUCIAN
TRADITION IN ANTIQUITY

In the two and a half centuries following the death of Confucius, the Chinese world changed enormously. During the lifetime of Confucius, China was still nominally ruled by the Zhou dynasty, though in fact the Zhou had lost virtually all of its actual power some three hundred years earlier, with real, if always uncertain, power having passed by the eighth century B.C.E. into the hands of the wayward rulers of contending feudal states. A certain tension seems to come through at various points in the Confucian *Analects* surrounding the status and prerogatives of the feudal lords who exercised power within the states but were nonetheless judged by Confucius to be deficient when it came to their claims to legitimacy. Several statements attributed to Confucius seem to imply that the prerogatives of the Zhou house should not have been usurped. Nonetheless, Confucius's recorders seem to have sensed in him — or attributed to him — an uncertainty about the future political order and, with it, a tendency to think of the Zhou more in terms of the nobility of its ancient culture than in terms of any possible restoration of its power.

Mencius (385?–312? B.C.E.), the first great successor to Confucius, held out even less hope for the future of the House of Zhou, or such is the implication of questions that are raised repeatedly, if often indirectly, in the Mencian conversations: who might be capable of uniting "all under Heaven," and by what means? The same questions occupied Xunzi (310?–219? B.C.E.), the third major figure in the early Confucian tradition, who returns to them repeatedly in his own reflections on government. By the closing years of Xunzi's lifetime, these questions would be at least partially resolved. When in 221 B.C.E. the feudal state of Qin conquered the last of the remaining feudal states, uniting China for the first time under a single ruler, the feudal order would finally be destroyed, and in its place a new empire would be established. That the empire would be founded on force was apparent; that the empire could be maintained and stabilized through force was not. Some of the long-standing questions about governance would persist and become ever more closely intertwined with questions about culture and history.

In fact, long before the Qin conquest and the founding of the empire, questions had begun to arise about the nature and the hold of the past — how it should be understood and in what respects it should be honored in changing circumstances. These may, in fact, have been the most persistent and pervasive questions to be pondered and debated at the time, not only among Confucians but among other thinkers of the Warring States period (479–221 B.C.E.) as well. For Confucians, the most urgent questions focused on the survival of moral attitudes and ritual forms that had been associated with the older feudal order. What was the role of courtesy and ritual, honor and fidelity, in a world marked by increasing social mobility, ever greater uncertainty about established social relationships, and escalating violence?

It was typical of Confucians to recognize civilization as both an ongoing process and an inheritance from the past, but was the cumulative achievement of "the ancients" to be preserved in the fullness of its form and detail or was their record of accomplishment to be treasured more for the noble and inspiring personal models that they provided for later generations following in a common cause? In either case, how much was to be preserved in the name of civilization as a legacy from the past, and how much was susceptible to change in defense of larger human purposes?

In this chapter we present excerpts from three of the most important texts of the Confucian tradition in ancient China. Each of them addressed these questions, though in different ways. The *Mencius* and the *Xunzi* may be described as philosophical works — quite different from each other in both form and content, yet similar in the sense that they reflect on matters of governance and personal cultivation and, like virtually all Confucian works, assume a direct relationship between the two. The *Zuozhuan* — or *Zuo's Commentary* — is China's oldest narrative history. It is not, perhaps, a Confucian work in the same sense that the *Mencius* and the *Xunzi* are, but at many points it vividly illustrates a similar alertness to the connection between the moral dispositions of individuals and the dynamics of their lives and political careers. Moreover, from very early times the *Zuozhuan*, traditionally believed to be a commentary on the classic known as the *Spring and Autumn Annals*, was itself accorded the status of a Confucian classic, whereas the *Mencius* was so honored only much later, in the twelfth century, and the *Xunzi*, for complex reasons, not at all.

Each of these texts provides a fascinating perspective on changes in values in the time of Confucius and in the subsequent Warring States period, while together they suggest the variety and complexity to be found within the Confucian tradition as it evolved in ancient China.

MENCIUS

Meng Ke — or Mencius, as he is known to readers of English translations — lived in the fourth century B.C.E., more than a century after the time of Confucius. Confucius, who in his own lifetime had enjoyed only the most qualified success, had by Mencius's time acquired the reputation of a sage. Mencius acknowledged him as such and seems to have shared his most cherished values, though not without transforming many of them. The Warring States period witnessed a process of consolidation in which larger and more powerful feudal states swallowed up smaller and weaker ones. A concomitant of this development was a change in the character of warfare, which now became more brutal, with large conscript armies pitted against each other in battles that typically took a terrible toll in human lives. During these uncertain times Mencius traveled from one feudal state to another, speaking to rulers about government, deploring the effects of warfare on the people, and pleading the case for the practicality of humaneness. His response to the political situation was determined, yet subtle: he reaffirmed a profound Confucian confidence in the efficacy of morality but was resigned to the possibility that he himself might not figure into, or even personally witness, the restoration of a moral order.

The *Mencius* is a record of conversations between Mencius and rulers of the contending feudal states, disciples, and philosophical adversaries. It also includes pronouncements by Mencius on a variety of subjects, especially government and human nature. We find in it not an authorial presence providing form, structure, and coherence to the work but rather a more disparate, even fragmented collection of exchanges that occurred at various times and places and were recorded after the fact. Many of these exchanges take the form of arguments. While maintaining that he was disinclined to argument, he insists that his career as a controversialist has been forced upon him — that he is compelled to dispute with rulers and scholars who fail to understand the legacy of civilization and, underlying it, the human potential for goodness.

In the selections that follow, some of the most prominent Mencian attitudes and themes emerge. A recurrent theme — one that echoes and reechoes in virtually all later Confucian discourse — is the idea that what ultimately matters in human interactions is the motivation of the actors and their capacity for mutual respect and regard based on recognition of a common humanity. Mencius both recalls and enlarges the Confucian idea of *ren*, or humaneness. Alongside it he places the complementary principle of *yi*, or rightness, a complex idea of what is right in particular situations as individuals perform their distinct roles and confront the different circumstances of their lives.

Mencius appeals to rulers to draw on humaneness in their conduct of affairs of state rather than doubting their own capacity for compassion and to recognize the claims of rightness rather than succumbing to the expedient. He is direct to the point of acerbity in criticizing rulers for their role in instigating warfare, devout in deploring war's pernicious effects on the lives of the common people. Perhaps influenced by his adversaries, the Mohists and the Legalists, he displays a keen awareness that human beings have certain basic needs — food, clothing, shelter, and education — and that these must be met if their very existence as human beings is to be possible. War inevitably interferes with the satisfaction of these basic human needs, he observes, as does overindulgence on the part of rulers.

Mencius's discussions of matters of state draw on historical memory — or re-creations of history. He seems to reclaim, in memory, the moral aura of a time before the beginning of the dynastic system, when rulers were selected on the morally compelling basis of merit rather than the less reliable basis of heredity. Much that he has to say about the ancient sage kings Yao, Shun, and Yu has to do with the moral authority that they wielded by virtue of their having gained the empire through the will of Heaven as signaled in the willingness of the people. Mindful of the potent idea of the Mandate of Heaven that he believed derived from the early Zhou, Mencius maintains that Heaven oversees a kind of overarching moral order in which it is given to rulers to rule for the sake of the common people, with the object of achieving their well-being and prosperity.

At many points in these conversations the reader will find evidence of Mencius's psychologically rich conception of human moral potential. One notable instance may be found in his discussion of the varieties of courage and of the cultivation of the "vast, flowing *qi*" — a psychophysical energy or vitality within the individual that he seems to find directly related to moral effort. Most famous are his discussions of the "four beginnings" — natural tendencies within all human beings that, he believes, can be cultivated and developed into the capacities for humaneness, rightness, propriety, and wisdom. This idea of a natural human tendency toward sympathetic responsiveness to others is, in fact, one of Mencius's most important contributions to the later history of Chinese thought.

It is clear from Mencius's arguments that many in his own time held different views of human nature, discounting his optimism, questioning his confidence in a moral potential inherent in each person, doubting his affirmation of the human capacity for perfectibility through self-cultivation. Some who followed Mencius, including such eminent Confucians as Xunzi, also challenged his views. Still, a survey of the long history of Confucian thought confirms that

Mencius was the single most influential contributor to a view of human nature that would ultimately become dominant, not only in China but also in the rest of Confucianized East Asia, and not only in the thought of an intellectual and social elite but in the value system of an entire culture.

The following numbered items may serve as a guide to some of the major themes of the text:

Humaneness (ren): 1A:1, 1A:5, 1A:7, 2A:6, 3A:3, 3B:9, 4A:1–4, 4A:10, 4A:14, 4A:20, 4B:5, 4B:19, 4B:28, 6A:1, 6A:4, 6A:6, 6A:11, 6A:16–19, 7A:4, 7A:15, 7A:45, 7B:13

Rightness (yi): 1A:1, 1A:7, 1B:8, 2A:2, 2A:6, 3A:4, 3B:9, 4A:1, 4A:10, 4B:5–6, 4B:19, 6A:1, 6A:5–7, 6A:10, 6A:16, 7A:15, 7B:37

Rites, ritual propriety (li): 1A:7, 2A:6, 4A:1, 4A:10, 4A:20, 4B:6, 6A:6–7, 6A:10, 7B:33

Serving parents: 1A:5, 2A:6, 4A:12, 4A:19, 4A:26–27, 5A:2

Government: 1A:1–7, 1B:6, 1B:8, 1B:11, 2A:5, 3A:3–4, 3B:9, 4A:1–5, 4A:12, 4A:14, 4A:20, 4B:1, 4B:3–5, 5A:5, 5A:7, 5B:2, 5B:9, 6A:6, 7B:13–14

Economic livelihood: 1A:2–3, 1A:7, 3A:3–4

Well-field system: 3A:3

Regicide, deposing a ruler: 1B:6, 1B:8, 3B:9, 5B:9

War, violence: 1A:2, 1A:5–6, 1B:11, 2A:3, 3B:9, 4A:14

The noble person (junzi): 1A:7, 4A:26, 4B:14, 4B:19, 4B:22, 4B:28, 5A:2, 7A:40–41, 7A:45, 7B:33, 7B:37

Sages: 2A:2, 3A:4, 3B:9, 4A:1–2, 4A:26, 4B:1, 4B:19, 4B:28, 4B:32, 5A:2, 5A:5, 5A:7, 6A:6–7, 6B:2, 6B:15, 7A:38, 7B:33, 7B:37–38

The nature, human nature: 2A:6, 6A:1–6, 7A:1, 7A:38

Qi (energy, material force): 2A:2, 6A:8

Mind: 1A:7, 2A:2, 2A:6, 3A:3–4, 4B:12, 4B:28, 6A:7–11, 6A:15, 6A:17, 6B:15, 7A:1, 7B:35

Heaven: 3A:4, 5A:5, 6A:6–7, 6A:15–16, 6B:15, 7A:1, 7A:38, 7A:41, 7B:14

Destiny, the mandate: 4A:4, 7A:1–2

Nobility: 5B:2, 6A:16

Selections from the Mencius

1A:1 Mencius saw King Hui of Liang.

The king said, "So venerable an elder, having come a thousand *li*, and not considering that too far, must surely have some means to profit our state?"

Mencius replied, "Why must the king speak of profit? There are humaneness and rightness, that is all. If the king says, 'How can I profit my state?' the officers will say, 'How can I profit my house?' and the gentlemen and the common people will say, 'How can I profit my person?' Those above and those below will be competing with one another for profit, and the state will be imperiled. One who would murder the ruler of a state with ten thousand chariots would have to be from a house of a thousand chariots; one who would murder the ruler of a state of a thousand chariots would have to be from a house of a hundred chariots. A share of a thousand out of ten thousand or a hundred out of a thousand is hardly negligible; yet when rightness is subordinated to profit the urge to lay claim to more becomes irresistible. It has never happened that one given to humaneness abandons his parents, or that one given to rightness subordinates the interests of his lord. The king should speak of humaneness and rightness. Why is it necessary to speak of profit?"

1A:2 Mencius saw King Hui of Liang. As he stood overlooking a pond, watching the geese and the deer, the king asked, "Do the worthy also enjoy such things?"

Mencius replied, "Being worthy, they enjoy these things. Were they not worthy, although they might have such things, they would find no enjoyment in them. The Ode says,

> He began by measuring the spirit tower,
> He measured it and planned it.
> The common people worked on it,
> Finishing before a day was out.
> In beginning to measure he urged against haste,
> Yet the people came as if they were his children.
> The king was in the spirit park,
> The doe lying down,
> The doe glistening,
> The white bird glittering.
> The king was by his spirit pond,
> How full it was with dancing fish![1]

"King Wen used the strength of the people to build his tower and his pond, and the people found their delight and their joy in it. They called his tower the spirit tower and his pond the spirit pond and found joy in his having deer, and birds, and turtles. The ancients shared their joys with the people and it was this that enabled them to feel joy.

"The 'Declaration of Tang' says,

> O sun, when will you perish?
> We will die along with you.[2]

---

1. Ode 242.

2. *Classic of Documents*, in Legge, *The Chinese Classics*, 3:175. The people were so eager for the death of Jie, the "bad last ruler" of the Xia, that they were willing to die themselves to ensure that end.

"If the people wished to die along with him, although he had a tower and pond, how could he enjoy them alone?"

1A:3 King Hui of Liang said, "As regards the state, this solitary man[3] devotes his entire mind to it — when the year is bad within the river, transferring people to the east of the river and transferring grain to the area within the river, and when the year is bad to the east of the river, again, acting accordingly. Look into the governments of neighboring states: there is no one as mindful as this solitary man, and yet people in the neighboring states do not decrease, nor do the people of this solitary man increase. Why should this be?"

Mencius said, "The king is fond of war; so please allow an analogy that derives from war. Drums rumbling, the soldiers having crossed weapons, some then flee, abandoning their armor and trailing their weapons behind them. Some stop after a hundred paces and some after fifty paces. How would it be if those who ran only fifty paces were to laugh at those who ran a hundred paces?"

The king said, "That should not be. It was only that they did not run a hundred paces, that is all. But they also ran."

Mencius said, "If the king understands this, there is no reason to expect the people to be more numerous than they are in neighboring states. If the agricultural seasons are not interfered with, there will be more grain than can be eaten. If close-meshed nets are not allowed in the pools and ponds, there will be more fish and turtles than can be eaten. And if axes are allowed in the mountains and forests only in the appropriate seasons, there will be more timber than can be used. When grain, fish, and turtles are more than can be eaten, and timber is more than can be used, this will mean that the people can nourish life, bury their dead, and be without rancor. Allowing them to nourish life, bury their dead, and be without rancor is the beginning of kingly government.

"Let mulberry trees be planted around households of five *mu*, and people of fifty will be able to be clothed in silk. In the raising of chickens, pigs, dogs, and swine, do not neglect the appropriate breeding times, and people of seventy will be able to eat meat. With fields of a hundred *mu*, do not interfere with the appropriate seasons of cultivation, and families with several mouths to feed will be able to avoid hunger. Attend carefully to the education provided in the schools,[4] which should include instruction in the duty of filial and fraternal devotion, and gray-haired people will not be seen carrying burdens on the roads.

---

3. The Chinese term *guaren*, literally, "lonely or friendless person," was one used by rulers to speak of themselves. It implies a sense (or a pretense) of self-depreciation.

4. Mencius here mentions two kinds of schools, the *xiang* and the *xu*. In 3A:10 he refers to these and several more, explaining that *xiang* was a Zhou term, while *xu* was a term used in the Shang dynasty.

It has never happened that people of seventy have worn silk and eaten meat, and the black-haired people been neither hungry nor cold, without the ruler having been a true king.

"The king's dogs and pigs eat food intended for human beings, and he does not know enough to prohibit this. On the roads there are people dying of starvation, and he does not know enough to distribute food. People die, and he says, 'It was not I; it was the year.' How is this different from killing a person by stabbing him and then saying, 'It was not I; it was the weapon'? When the king ceases to place the blame on the year, then the people of the world will come to him."

1A:5 King Hui of Liang said, "No state in the empire was stronger than Jin [or Liang], as the venerable elder is aware. But when it came to this solitary man, we were defeated by Qi in the east, and my eldest son died there. In the west seven hundred *li* were lost to Qin, while in the south we were humiliated by Chu. This solitary man is ashamed of this and wishes, before he dies, to expunge it. How may this be done?"

Mencius replied, "With a territory of so much as one hundred *li*, one can become a king. If the king bestows humane government on the people, reduces punishments, and lightens taxes, causing the plowing to be deep and the weeding thorough, the strong will be able to use their leisure time to cultivate filiality and brotherliness. Within the home they will serve their fathers and brothers, and outside they will serve their elders and superiors. They can then be made to take up sticks and overcome the strong armor and the sharp weapons of Qin and Chu.

"Those other rulers lay claim to the time of their people, so that they are unable to plow or to weed and thus to nourish their parents. Their parents then suffer from cold and hunger; elder and younger brothers are parted; wives and children are separated. These rulers bury their people and drown them. If the king will go and punish them, who would there be to stand as an enemy to him? Therefore it may be said that the humane man has no enemy. May it please the king to have no doubt about this."

1A:6 Mencius saw King Xiang of Liang. On emerging he said to someone, "Seeing him from a distance, he does not appear to be a ruler of men; approaching him, one sees nothing imposing about him. He abruptly asked, 'How can the empire be settled?'

"I replied, 'It can be settled through unity.'

"'Who is able to unite it?'

"I replied, 'One who is not fond of killing people can unite it.'

"'Who can give it to him?'

"I replied, 'There is no one in the empire who will deny it to him. Does the king know the way of seedlings? If there is drought in the seventh or eighth month, the seedlings dry out. But when dense clouds gather in the sky, and the rain falls in torrents, the plants spring up and are revived. When this happens, who can stop it? Now among the herders of men in the empire there is none who is not fond of killing people. If there were one who was not fond of killing people, the people of the empire would crane their necks to look for him. Were this truly to happen, the people would return to him like water flowing downward, torrentially — and who could stop it?'"

1A:7 King Xuan of Qi asked, "Would it be possible to hear about the affairs of Huan of Qi and Wen of Jin?"[5]

Mencius replied, "The followers of Confucius would not speak of the affairs of Huan and Wen, and thus nothing about them has been transmitted to later generations. Not having heard, and having nothing to say on that matter, how would it be if the minister were to speak of kingship?"

The king said, "What must one's virtue be like in order to become a king?"

Mencius said, "One who protects the people becomes a king, and no one is able to stop him."

"Could someone like this solitary man protect the people?"

"He could."

"How do you know that I could?"

"The minister heard Hu He say that, while the king was seated in the upper part of the hall, someone led an ox through the lower part. Upon seeing this, the king asked where the ox was going and was told that it was being taken to serve as a blood sacrifice in the consecration of a bell. The king said, 'Spare it. I cannot bear its trembling, like one who, though blameless, is being led to the execution ground.' Asked whether in that case the consecration of the bell should be dispensed with, the king said, 'How can it be dispensed with? Substitute a sheep instead.' Did this actually happen?"

"It did."

Mencius said, "With such a mind one has enough to become a king. Though the people all thought that it was because the king grudged the ox, the minister certainly knows that it was because the king could not bear to see its suffering."

---

5. Duke Huan of Qi (r. 685–643 B.C.E.), one of the most powerful feudal lords of the seventh century, was considered the first of the "Five Hegemons," and Duke Wen of Jin (r. 636–628 B.C.E.) was considered the second. Mencius's statement in the ensuing passage that he has "heard nothing about" these hegemons is not to be taken literally. The reputation of neither ruler was entirely negative, but Mencius is making the point here that he prefers to talk about morally legitimate kings (*wang*) rather than "hegemons" (*ba*), whose claim to rule was believed by most Confucians to be more ambiguous, morally speaking.

The king said, "That is so. The people must truly have thought this, but, although the state of Qi is small and narrow, how could I grudge a single ox? It was because I could not bear its trembling, like one who, though blameless, was being led to the execution ground, that I had a sheep substituted instead."

Mencius said, "The king should not think it strange that the people assumed that he grudged the ox. How could they know why he substituted the smaller thing for the larger one? Had the king been grieving over its being led, blameless, to the execution ground, then what was there to choose between an ox and a sheep?"

The king smiled and said, "What kind of mind was this, after all? It was not that I grudged the expense, and yet I did exchange the ox for a sheep. No wonder the people said that I grudged it."

Mencius said, "There is no harm in this. This was after all the working of humaneness — a matter of having seen the ox but not the sheep. This is the way of the noble person in regard to animals: if he sees them alive, then he cannot bear to see them die, and if he hears their cries, then he cannot bear to eat their flesh. And so the noble person stays far away from the kitchen."

The king was pleased and said, "When the Ode says, 'What other people have in their minds, I measure by reflection,'[6] it is speaking about the Master. When I tried it, going back and seeking my motive, I was unable to grasp my own mind. Yet when the Master spoke of it, my mind experienced a kind of stirring. How is it that this mind of mine accords with that of a king?"

Mencius replied, "Suppose someone were to report to the king, saying, 'My strength, while sufficient to lift a hundred *jun*, is not sufficient to lift a feather. My sight, while sufficient to scrutinize the tip of an autumn hair, is not sufficient to see a cartload of firewood.' Would the king accept this?"

"No," he said.

"Then what is there so different about the case of kindness sufficient to extend to animals yet without its benefits reaching the people? Not lifting a feather is the result of not exerting one's strength to do so; not seeing a cartload of firewood is the result of not employing his eyesight on it. That the people are not protected is because one does not exercise kindness toward them. Therefore, that the king is not kingly is because he does not do it; it is not because he is unable to do it."

The king asked, "How can one distinguish between 'not doing something' and 'being unable to do it'?"

Mencius said, "If it were a matter of taking Mount Tai under your arm and jumping over the North Sea with it, and one were to tell people, 'I am unable to do it,' this would truly be a case of being unable to do it. If it is a matter of breaking off a branch of a tree at the request of an elder, and one tells people,

---

6. Ode 198. Translation adapted from Legge, *The Chinese Classics*, 4:342.

'I am unable to do it,' this is a case of not doing it rather than a case of being unable to do it. And so the king's failure to be a king is not in the category of taking Mount Tai under one's arm and jumping over the North Sea with it; his failure to be a king is in the category of not breaking off a branch for an elder. By treating the elders in one's own family as elders should be treated and extending this to the elders of other families, and by treating the young of one's own family as the young ought to be treated and extending this to the young of other people's families, the empire can be turned around on the palm of one's hand. The Ode says,

> He set an example for his wife;
> It extended to his brothers,
> And from there to the family of the state.[7]

"This speaks of taking this mind and extending it to others, that is all. Thus if one extends his kindness it will be enough to protect all within the four seas, whereas if one fails to extend it, he will have no way to protect his wife and children. The fact that the ancients so greatly surpassed others was nothing other than this: that they were good at extending what they did. Now what is there so different in the case of kindness that is sufficient to extend to the animals without the benefits reaching the people?

"It is by weighing that we know which things are light and which are heavy, and by measuring that we know which are long and which are short. This is true of all things, and especially so with regard to the mind. May it please the king to measure his mind. When the king raises arms, endangers his subjects, and excites the enmity of the other feudal lords — does this perhaps bring pleasure to his mind?"

The king replied, "No. How could I take pleasure from this? It is just that I seek to realize that which I greatly desire."

"May I hear about what it is that the king greatly desires?"

The king smiled and did not speak.

Mencius said, "Is it that the king does not have enough rich and sweet foods to satisfy his mouth? Or enough light and warm clothing for his body? Or enough beautiful colors for his eyes to gaze upon, or enough sounds for his ears to listen to? Is it that he does not have servants enough to come before him and receive orders? The king's ministers are sufficient to provide for all of this. How could the king's desire be for any of these?"

He said, "No, it is none of these."

Mencius said, "Then what the king greatly desires can be known. His desire is to expand his territory, to bring Qin and Chu into his court, to rule the

---

7. Ode 240.

Middle Kingdom, and to pacify the four Yi [non-Chinese peoples]. But to pursue such a desire by such an action is like climbing a tree to look for fish."

The king said, "Is it as bad as that?"

"It is even worse than that. When one climbs a tree to seek for fish, though one gets no fish, no disaster will ensue. But if one does what you are doing in pursuit of what you desire, and devotes the full strength of his mind to it, disaster is bound to ensue."

"May I hear about this?"

"If the people of Zou go to war with the people of Chu, who, in the king's opinion, will win?"

"The people of Chu will win."

"Thus the small definitely cannot contend with the large, the few definitely cannot contend with the many, and the weak definitely cannot contend with the strong. Within the seas, there are nine territories of a thousand leagues square, and Qi is only one of them. What difference is there between one part attacking the other eight and Zou contending with Chu? Why not rather return to the root of the matter? If the king were to institute a government that dispensed humaneness, he would make all the officers in the world wish to stand in his court, all of the tillers wish to till his fields, all merchants wish to entrust their goods to his marketplaces, and all travelers wish to go forth on his roads. All those in the world who have grievances to express against their rulers would wish to lay their complaints before him, and this being the case, who would be able to stop it?"

The king said, "I am unintelligent and have been unable to progress this far. I should like the Master to assist my will and be clear in giving me instruction, so that, while I am not clever, I may endeavor to carry it out."

"It is only a gentleman who will be able to have a constant mind despite being without a constant means of livelihood. The people, lacking a constant means of livelihood, will lack constant minds, and when they lack constant minds there is no dissoluteness, depravity, deviance, or excess to which they will not succumb. If, once they have sunk into crime, one responds by subjecting them to punishment — this is to entrap the people. With a person of humanity in a position of authority, how could the entrapment of the people be allowed to occur? Therefore an enlightened ruler will regulate the people's livelihood so as to ensure that, above, they have enough to serve their parents and, below, they have enough to support their wives and children. In years of prosperity they always have enough to eat; in years of dearth they are able to escape starvation. Only then does he urge the people toward goodness; accordingly, they find it easy to comply.

"At present, the regulation of the people's livelihood is such that, above, they do not have enough to serve their parents and, below, they do not have enough to support wives and children. Even in years of prosperity their lives are bitter, while in years of dearth they are unable to escape starvation. Under these circumstances they only try to save themselves from death, fearful that they will not succeed. How could they spare the time for the practice of rites and rightness?

"If the king wishes to put this into practice, he should return to the root of the matter. Let mulberry trees be planted around households of five *mu*, and people of fifty will be able to be clothed in silk. In the raising of chickens, pigs, dogs, and swine, do not neglect the appropriate breeding times, and people of seventy will be able to eat meat. With fields of a hundred *mu*, do not interfere with the appropriate seasons of cultivation, and families with eight mouths to feed will be able to avoid hunger. Attend carefully to the education provided in the schools, which should include instruction in the duty of filial and fraternal devotion, and gray-haired people will not be seen carrying burdens on the roads. It has never happened that people of seventy have worn silk and eaten meat, and the black-haired people have been neither hungry nor cold, without the ruler having been a true king."[8]

THE DUTY OF MINISTERS TO REPROVE A RULER

In the following exchanges Mencius goes so far as to remind King Xuan of Qi that a ruler risks being deposed for crimes against humanity. This very forceful assertion, sometimes understood in our own time as implying a "right of revolution," actually involves no notion of either "rights" or "revolution" per se, having been advanced by Mencius centuries before the idea of rights was conceived anywhere in the world. In another conversation with King Xuan (translated in 5B:9) Mencius says that before the situation in a state reaches the point at which the ruler must be deposed, his ministers should remonstrate with him, quit his court if not listened to, and then have ministers of the royal blood depose him as a last resort. Thus Mencius's main emphasis is on the need for remonstrance and reproof, lest the situation in a state come to violence.

1B:6 Mencius said to King Xuan of Qi, "Suppose that one of the king's subjects entrusted his wife and children to his friend and journeyed to Chu. On returning he found that he had allowed his wife and children to be hungry and cold. What should he do?"

The king said, "Renounce him."

"Suppose the chief criminal judge could not control the officers. What should he do?"

The king said, "Get rid of him."

---

8. What Mencius describes here as a return to what is fundamental repeats almost exactly what he has told King Hui of Liang in 1A:3.

"Suppose that within the four borders of the state there is no proper government?"

The king looked left and right and spoke of other things.

1B:8 King Xuan of Qi asked, "Is it true that Tang banished Jie and King Wu assaulted Zhou?"[9]

Mencius replied, "This is contained in the records."[10]

"For a minister to slay his ruler — can this be countenanced?"

"One who despoils humaneness is called a thief; one who despoils rightness is called a robber. Someone who is a robber and a thief is called a mere fellow. I have heard of the punishment of the fellow Zhou but never of the slaying of a ruler."

1B:11 The people of Qi having attacked Yan and taken possession of it, the several lords were making plans to rescue Yan. King Xuan said, "Many of the lords are making plans to attack this solitary man. How shall I prepare for them?"

Mencius replied, "Your minister has heard that there was one who with seventy *li* extended his government to the entire realm: this was Tang. I have not heard of one with a thousand leagues who feared others. The *Classic of Documents* says,

When Tang undertook the work of punishment he began with Ge.[11] The whole world trusted him. When he pursued the work of punishment in the east, the Yi in the west felt aggrieved; when he pursued the work of punishment in the south, the Di in the north felt aggrieved, saying, "Why does he leave us until last?"[12]

"The people looked to him as to clouds and rainbows in a time of great drought. Those going to market had no need to stop; those tilling the fields were unimpeded. He punished the rulers but comforted the people. He was like timely rain descending, and the people were greatly delighted. The *Classic of Documents* says,

---

9. According to tradition, Tang, as the first ruler of the Shang dynasty, was responsible for ousting the depraved Jie, the last ruler of the Xia dynasty. King Wu, as one of the founders of the Zhou dynasty, is credited with deposing the wicked Zhou, the last ruler of the Shang.

10. Tang's ousting of Jie is recorded in the *Classic of Documents*, "The Announcement of Zhonghui" and "The Announcement of Tang," and King Wu's removal of Zhou in the *Classic of Documents*, "The Great Declaration" and "The Successful Completion of the War."

11. This quotation, while not exact, is close to the language of "The Announcement of Zhonghui" in the *Classic of Documents*. See Legge, *The Chinese Classics*, 3:180.

12. Again, though the wording is slightly different, this quotation is close to the language of "The Announcement of Zhonghui" in the *Classic of Documents*. See ibid., pp. 180–181.

"'We await our ruler; when he comes we will be revived.'[13]

"Now Yan oppressed its people, and the king went and punished it. The people believed he was going to deliver them from out of water and fire and, bringing baskets of rice and pitchers of drink, they welcomed the king's army. Then to have slain their fathers and elder brothers, bound their sons and younger brothers, destroyed their ancestral temple and carried off their treasured vessels — how can this be condoned? Certainly the world fears the might of Qi. Now the king has doubled his territory but has not practiced humane government: it is this that is setting the troops of the realm in motion. If the king will immediately issue orders to return the captives and stop the removal of the precious vessels, and if he will consult with the people of Yan about withdrawing once a ruler has been installed for them, he may still be able to stop an attack."

2A:2 Gongsun Chou asked, "If the Master were appointed to be a high officer and prime minister of Qi, and were able to put the Way into practice, it would hardly be surprising if the ruler were to become leader of the feudal lords or even king. Were this to occur, would your mind be moved or not?"

Mencius said, "No, since I was forty my mind has been unmoved."

"In that case the Master far surpasses Meng Bin."

"This is not difficult. Gaozi attained an unmoved mind before I did."

"Is there a way to attain an unmoved mind?"

"There is. Bogong Yu's way of nourishing his valor was neither to shrink from blows nor to avert his gaze. He thought that merely to be jostled by someone was like being flogged in the marketplace. What he would not accept from a poor fellow in coarse clothing he would not accept from a lord with ten thousand chariots, and he would cut down the lord with ten thousand chariots as soon as he would the poor man, coarsely clad. He was unawed by any of the several lords, and if an insult came his way he would invariably return it.

"Meng Shishe's way of nourishing his valor is expressed in his saying, 'I regard defeat just as I do victory. To advance only after having assessed the strength of the enemy, to engage only after having calculated the prospects for victory — this is to be intimidated by the opposing force. How can I be certain of victory? I can only be fearless, that is all.'

"Meng Shishe resembled Zengzi, while Bogong Yu resembled Zixia. I do not know which kind of valor should be considered superior, but Meng Shishe kept hold of what is essential. Formerly, Zengzi said to Zixiang, 'Does the Master[14] love valor? I once heard this account of great valor from the Master:[15]

---

13. The language closely resembles "The Announcement of Zhonghui." See ibid., p. 181.

14. That is, Zixiang.

15. That is, Confucius.

"If, on examining myself, I find that I am not upright, I must be in fear of even a poor fellow in coarse clothing. If, on examining myself, I find that I am upright, I may proceed against thousands and tens of thousands."' So Meng Shishe's keeping hold of his *qi* was, after all, not comparable to Zengzi's keeping hold of what is essential."

"I venture to ask you, Master, about your unmoved mind compared to Gaozi's unmoved mind."

"Gaozi said, 'What you do not get in words, do not seek in the mind; what you do not get in the mind, do not seek in the *qi*.'[16] It may be acceptable to say that what one does not get in the mind should not be sought in the *qi*. But it is unacceptable to say that what one does not get in words should not be sought in the mind. The will is the leader of the *qi*, and it is *qi* that fills the body. When the will goes forward the *qi* follows it. Therefore I say, maintain the will and do no violence to the *qi*."

"Since you say, 'When the will goes forward the *qi* follows it,' why is it that you also say, 'Maintain the will and do no violence to the *qi*'?"

"If the will is unified it moves the *qi*, whereas if the *qi* is unified it moves the will. Now when a person stumbles or runs, it is the *qi* that acts, but it also moves the mind."

"May I presume to ask the Master in what he excels?"

"I understand words. I am good at nourishing my vast, flowing *qi*."

"May I presume to ask what is meant by 'vast, flowing *qi*'?"

"It is difficult to speak of it. This is *qi*: it is consummately great and consummately strong. If one nourishes it with uprightness and does not injure it, it will fill the space between Heaven and Earth. This is *qi*: it is the companion of rightness and the Way, in the absence of which it starves. It is born from an accumulation of rightness rather than appropriated through an isolated display. If one's actions cause the mind to be disquieted, it starves. I therefore said that Gaozi did not understand rightness because he regarded it as external.

"Always be doing something, but without fixation, with a mind inclined neither to forget nor to help things grow. One should not be like the man of Song. There was a man of Song who, worried that his seedlings were not growing, pulled them up. Having done so, he returned home wearily, telling people, 'I am tired today—I have been helping the seedlings to grow.' When his sons rushed out to have a look, they found the seedlings were all withered. There are few in the world who do not try to help the seedlings to grow. Those who believe that there is no benefit in it neglect them and do not weed the seedlings. Those bent on helping them grow pull them up, which is not only of no benefit, but, on the contrary, causes them injury."

---

16. The meaning of Gaozi's statement has been subject to a variety of interpretations, but since Mencius provided almost no context for it, it remains difficult to know exactly what he intended. What is clear from Mencius's disagreement with Gaozi is that Mencius himself believed that language, the mind (or will), and physical energy are all closely interrelated.

"What is meant by 'understanding words'?"

"From distorted words, one knows the obscuration; from licentious words, one knows the corruption; from deviant words, one knows the waywardness; from evasive words, one knows the desperation. What is born in the mind does damage to government, and what arises in government does damage to the conduct of affairs. Were a sage to arise again, he would certainly follow my words. . . ."

2A:3 Mencius said, "One who, supported by force, fakes being humane is a hegemon, and a hegemon has to have a large state. One who out of virtue practices humaneness is a king, and a king does not need anything large. Tang did it with only seventy *li*, and King Wen did it with a hundred.

"When one uses force to make people submit, they do not submit in their hearts but only because their strength is insufficient. When one uses virtue to make people submit, they are pleased to the depths of their hearts, and they sincerely submit. So it was with the seventy disciples who submitted to Confucius. The Ode says,

> From the west, and from the east,
> From the south and from the north,
> No one thought of not submitting.[17]

This is what was meant."

2A:5 Mencius said, "When a ruler honors those who are exemplary and employs those who are capable, so that outstanding persons hold positions of authority, all of the world's scholars will be pleased and will want to stand in his court. When in his marketplace he levies a ground-rent, but without levying a tax on goods, or else enforces the regulations but without levying any ground-rent, all of the world's merchants will be pleased and will want to store their goods in his marketplace. When at his frontier passes there is an inspection but no tax is levied, all of the world's travelers will be pleased and will want to travel on his roads. When tillers are required to render their assistance[18] but are not taxed, then all of the world's farmers will be pleased and will want to till his fields. When individuals are not fined and no levy of cloth is exacted,[19] then all the world's people will be pleased and will want to people his state. If one is truly able to do these five things, the people of neighboring states will look to him like a father and mother and follow him like his children. Never since

---

17. Ode 244.

18. This appears to be a reference to the mutual assistance owed under the well-field system, discussed in 3A:3.

19. The meaning of this passage is unclear. Some commentators refer to the *Zhouli* (*Rites of Zhou*), which indicates fines were imposed on those who did not do sufficient work, as well as a tax, levied in cloth, on families that failed to plant a requisite number of mulberry trees.

the birth of humankind has anyone ever succeeded in causing people to attack their parents. So the ruler will have no enemies in the world, and one who has no enemies in the world is the agent of Heaven. Could he then fail to be a king?"

2A:6 "All human beings have a mind that cannot bear to see the sufferings of others. The ancient kings had a commiserating mind and, accordingly, a commiserating government. Having a commiserating mind, a commiserating government, governing the world was like turning something around on the palm of the hand.

"Here is why I say that all human beings have a mind that commiserates with others. Now,[20] if anyone were suddenly to see a child about to fall into a well, his mind would always be filled with alarm, distress, pity, and compassion. That he would react accordingly is not because he would use the opportunity to ingratiate himself with the child's parents, nor because he would seek commendation from neighbors and friends, nor because he would hate the adverse reputation. From this it may be seen that one who lacks a mind that feels pity and compassion would not be human; one who lacks a mind that feels shame and aversion would not be human; one who lacks a mind that feels modesty and compliance would not be human; and one who lacks a mind that knows right and wrong would not be human.

"The mind's feeling of pity and compassion is the beginning of humaneness (*ren*); the mind's feeling of shame and aversion is the beginning of rightness (*yi*); the mind's feeling of modesty and compliance is the beginning of propriety; and the mind's sense of right and wrong is the beginning of wisdom.

"Human beings have these four beginnings just as they have four limbs. For one to have these four beginnings and yet to say of oneself that one is unable to fulfill them is to injure oneself, while to say that one's ruler is unable to fulfill them is to injure one's ruler. When we know how to enlarge and bring to fulfillment these four beginnings that are within us, it will be like a fire beginning to burn or a spring finding an outlet. If one is able to bring them to fulfillment, they will be sufficient to enable him to protect 'all within the four seas'; if one is not, they will be insufficient even to enable him to serve his parents."

THE WELL-FIELD SYSTEM OF LANDHOLDING

The following conversation between Mencius, a ruler, and one of his ministers offers another illustration of Mencius's concern for the responsibility of the state to help the people meet their basic needs for material livelihood. It also illustrates a typically

---

20. At the beginning of the passage Mencius recalls that the ancient kings had this "mind that cannot bear to see the sufferings of others." Here he affirms that people of the present also have it.

Confucian style of argument. In his discussion of the well-field system Mencius harks back to a time in the past when, according to tradition, landholding among the common people had been generally equal and village life had been cooperative. Whether the well-field system actually pertained in the past, as Mencius claims, or represented an idealization that gained reality through a process of re-creation of the historical past, his recalling it suggests that equality of landholding and mutual cooperation among the people represented themes of considerable antiquity and moral resonance. Many later Confucians would follow Mencius in identifying with these themes. Their defense against recurring charges of impracticality rested in the claim that the principles and measures they advocated had been implemented by sage rulers in the historical past and had formed the basis for civilized life.

3A:3 Duke Wen of Teng asked about governing the state. Mencius replied, "The people's business may not be delayed. The Ode says,

> In the morning gather the grasses,
> In the evening twist the ropes;
> Be quick to climb to the housetop,
> Begin to sow the hundred grains.[21]

"The Way of the people is this: that when they have a constant livelihood, they will have constant minds, but when they lack a constant livelihood, they will lack constant minds. When they lack constant minds there is no dissoluteness, depravity, deviance, or excess to which they will not succumb. If, once they have sunk into crime, one responds by subjecting them to punishment — this is to entrap the people. When a humane man is in authority, how could the entrapment of the people be allowed to occur? Therefore an exemplary ruler must be respectful, frugal, and reverent toward his subjects, and must take from the people only in accordance with the regulations. . . ."

The duke sent Bi Zhan to inquire about the well-field system. Mencius said, "Since the Master's lord intends to practice humane government, and the Master has been selected by him for employment, he must put forth great effort. Now humane government must begin with the setting of boundaries. If the boundaries are not set correctly, the division of the land into well-fields will not be equal and the grain allowances for official emoluments will not be equitable. This is why harsh rulers and corrupt officials are prone to neglect the setting of boundaries. Once the boundaries have been set correctly, the division of the fields and the determination of emoluments may be settled while sitting down.[22] Now while the territory of Teng is narrow and small, it has both noblemen and

---

21. Ode 154.

22. That is, while effort is required to set boundaries, once the boundaries have been properly set, the rest of the work of government can be done effortlessly.

country people. Without noblemen, there would be no one to rule the country people, and without the country people there would be no one to feed the noblemen. Please allow that in the countryside one square of land out of nine should be used for mutual aid. In the capital the people should assess themselves with a tax amounting to one part in ten. From the highest officers on down everyone must have a *gui* field,[23] and that *gui* field should be fifty *mu*. Remaining males should have twenty-five *mu*. Neither at the occasion of a death nor of a change of residence should people leave the village. When those in a village who hold land in the same well-field befriend one another in their going out and their coming in, assist one another in their protection and defense, and sustain one another through illness and distress, the hundred surnames will live together in affection and harmony. A square *li* constitutes a well-field, and the well-field contains 900 *mu*. The central plot among them is a public field, and eight families each have private holdings of a hundred *mu*. Together they cultivate the public field, and only when the public work is done do they dare attend to their private work, this being what distinguishes the country people. This is the general outline; the elaboration of it will be up to the ruler and to the Master."

3A:4 Xu Xing, who espoused the views of Shennong [the agriculturist], came from Chu to Teng. Going directly to the gate, he announced to Duke Wen, "A man from distant parts, having heard that the lord practices humane government, wishes to receive land to live on so as to become a subject." Duke Wen gave him a place to live. Xu Xing's followers, numbering several tens, all wore clothing of unwoven hemp, made sandals, and wove mats for a living.

Chen Liang's follower, Chen Xiang, along with his brother Xin, came with their ploughs on their backs from Song to Teng. They said, "Having heard that the lord practices sagely government, and is also a sage, we wish to become the sage's subjects."

When Chen Xiang met Xu Xing he was extremely pleased and, completely abandoning what he had learned before, became his disciple. When Chen Xiang met Mencius, he recounted the words of Xu Xing, saying, "The lord of Teng is truly an exemplary ruler; however, he has not yet heard the Way. The exemplary man works alongside the people and eats what they eat. He prepares his own meals, morning and evening, while at the same time he governs. Now Teng has granaries and treasuries. This is for the ruler to burden the people in order to nourish himself. How can he be called an exemplary man?"

Mencius said, "Master Xu must only eat the grain that he has planted himself?"

"Yes."

---

23. Officials received a *gui* field, the income from which was to be used to support the conduct of sacrifices.

"And Master Xu must wear only cloth that he has woven himself?"

"No, Master Xu wears unwoven hemp."

"Does Master Xu wear a cap?"

"He wears a cap."

"What kind of cap?"

"His cap is plain."

"Does he weave it himself?"

"No, he exchanges grain for it."

"Why does Master Xu not weave it himself?"

"That would interfere with his tilling the soil."

"Does Master Xu use an iron cauldron and an earthenware pot to cook his food, and does he till his fields with iron implements?"

"Yes."

"Does he make them himself?"

"No, he exchanges grain for them."

"To exchange grain for these various implements and utensils is not to burden the potter or the founder, nor could the potter and the founder, in exchanging their implements and utensils for grain, be burdening the agriculturalist. Then why doesn't Master Xu become a potter and a founder so that he can obtain everything he uses from his own household? Why does he go about this way and that trading and exchanging with the various craftsmen? Why does Master Xu not spare himself the trouble?"

"The work of the craftsman definitely cannot be carried on simultaneously with the work of tilling the soil."

"Then is governing the world unique in that this alone can be carried out simultaneously with the work of tilling the soil? There are the affairs of the great man, and the affairs of the small man. In the case of any individual person, the things that the craftsmen make are available to him; if each person had to make everything he needed for his own use, the world would be full of people chasing after one other on the roads. Therefore it is said, 'Some labor with their minds, while others labor with their strength. Those who labor with their minds govern others, while those who labor with their strength are governed by others. Those who are governed by others support them; those who govern others are supported by them.' The rightness of this is universally acknowledged in the world.

"In the time of Yao the world was not yet settled. The waters of the deluge overran their channels, and the world was inundated. Grasses and trees were luxuriant; birds and beasts proliferated. The five grains could not be grown. Birds and beasts crowded in on people, and the prints of the beasts and the tracks of the birds crisscrossed each other throughout the Middle Kingdom. Yao alone grieved anxiously over this. He elevated Shun to institute the regulations of government, and Shun employed Yi to manage fire. Yi set fire to the mountains and marshes and burned them, and the birds and beasts escaped into hiding. Yu dredged out the nine rivers. He cleared the courses of the Qi and the Ta, leading them to flow to the sea, opened the way for the Ru and the Han, and guided the courses of the Huai and the Si, leading them to flow to the Yangtze.[24] Only then could the Middle Kingdom get to [cultivate the land and] eat. During that time Yu was abroad in the land for eight years. Three times he passed his own door but did not enter. Although he may have wanted to cultivate the fields, could he have done so?

"Hou Ji taught the people to sow and to reap and to cultivate the five grains. When the grains ripened, the people had their nourishment. It is the way of human beings that when they have sufficient food, warm clothing, and comfortable dwellings, they will, without education, come close to the birds and beasts. It was the part of the sage to grieve anxiously over this. He caused Xie to be Minister of Education and to teach people about human relations: that between parents and children there is affection; between ruler and minister, rightness; between husband and wife, separate functions; between elder and younger, proper order; and between friends, faithfulness. Fangxun[25] said,

> Encourage them, lead them,
> Reform them, correct them,
> Assist them, give them wings,[26]
> Let them "get it for themselves."[27]
> Then follow by inspiring them to virtue.

"How could the sages, who were so anxious about the people, have the leisure to till the soil? What caused anxiety for Yao was the thought of not getting Shun [as his successor]; what caused anxiety for Shun was the thought of not getting Yu and Gao Yao. The one whose anxiety is caused by a plot of one hundred *mu* not being properly cultivated is a farmer.

"To share one's wealth with others is called kindness. To teach others to be good is called loyalty. To find the right man for the empire is called humaneness. Thus to give the empire to someone is easy, whereas to find the right man

---

24. The twelfth-century scholar Zhu Xi and, following him, James Legge, have pointed out that there are problems with the geography here. Zhu Xi explains this as an error on the part of the recorder of Mencius's words. See Zhu Xi, *Sishu jizhu*, commentary on *Mencius* 3A:4, and Legge, *The Chinese Classics*, 2:251.

25. I.e., Yao, who is referred to by this term in the *Classic of Documents*. Legge has doubts that this refers to Yao, though Zhu Xi, whose interpretation Legge usually follows, apparently has none.

26. This translation follows Legge, who, in turn, seems to follow the spirit of Zhu Xi's commentary. An alternative translation would be "shelter them," but the sense of enabling the people to become moral agents on their own fits in better with the last two lines of the quotation.

27. Cf. *Mencius* 4B:14.

for the empire is difficult. Confucius said, 'Great indeed was Yao as a ruler. Only Heaven is great, and yet Yao patterned himself after Heaven. How vast, how magnificent! The people could find no name for it. What a ruler was Shun! How lofty, how majestic! He possessed the empire as if it were nothing to him.' As Yao and Shun ruled the empire, it could not have been done without their fully devoting their minds to it, but they did not devote themselves to tilling the fields.". . .

Chen Xiang said, "If Master Xu's way were followed, there would not be two prices in the marketplace, nor would there be any duplicity in the state. If even a small boy were sent to the market, no one would deceive him. Equal lengths of cloth would be sold for a comparable price, as would equal weights of hemp and silk, and equal quantities of the five grains. This would be true as well of shoes of the same size."

Mencius said, "For things to be unequal is the natural tendency of things. Some are worth twice, some five times, or ten, or a hundred, or a thousand, or ten thousand times more than others. For the master to try to make them the same would bring chaos to the world. If large shoes were the same price as small shoes, who would make them? To follow the way of Master Xu would be to lead people to practice duplicity. How could one govern a state this way?"

MENCIUS' ARGUMENTS WITH YANG ZHU AND MOZI

Philosophically speaking, Mencius identifies as his primary antagonists the adherents of the schools of Yang Zhu and Mozi. Yang Zhu, sometimes characterized as an individualist, evidently defended the individual's withdrawal from public life or from official service in the interests of self-preservation. Mozi, as we have seen, espoused a morality predicated on the idea that a very practical sort of wisdom based on a self-regarding calculation of personal advantage should prompt everyone to adopt the imperative of universal love, or love without discrimination. Such love, which was to be extended to everyone equally and to be received from everyone equally, without regard to the primacy of family bonds, put morality at a remove from the familial context that Mencius recognized as its natural source and matrix. For him, Yang Zhu's idea entailed the denial of one's ruler and Mozi's, denial of one's parents. His own morality, by contrast, was based on a conception of the subtlety and richness of the human moral sense, with its roots in the deepest dimensions of biological and psychic life and its ramifications in the whole of human experience.

3B:9 Gongduzi said, "Outsiders all say that the Master is fond of argument. I venture to ask why?"

Mencius said, "How should I be fond of argument? I am compelled to do it. A long time has passed since the world was born, and periods of order have alternated with periods of chaos. In the time of Yao the waters overflowed their channels, inundating the Middle Kingdom; snakes and dragons dwelled in it, depriving the people of a settled life. Those who lived in low-lying places made nests, while those who lived on higher ground made caves. The *Classic of Documents* says,

> The overflowing waters were a warning to us.[28]

" 'The overflowing waters' refers to the waters of the deluge. Shun caused Yu to control them, and Yu dug out the earth so that the water would flow to the sea. He drove the snakes and dragons into the marshes. The waters flowed through the channels, and so it was with the Yangtze, the Huai, the Yellow, and the Han rivers. Once the dangers had been removed, and the birds and beasts that had injured people had disappeared, the people got the level ground and could dwell in it.

"Once Yao and Shun were no more, the Way of the sages declined, and oppressive rulers arose one after another. They destroyed houses and dwellings in order to make pools and ponds, and the people had no peaceful refuge. They caused fields to be abandoned to make parks and gardens, and the people could not get clothing and food. As deviant speech and oppressive actions became more prevalent, and as pools and ponds, thickets and marshes proliferated, wild animals returned. When it came down to the time of the tyrant Zhou, the world was once again in great chaos. The Duke of Zhou assisted King Wu and destroyed Zhou. He attacked Yan and after three years put its ruler to death. He drove Feilian[29] to a corner by the sea and annihilated him. The kingdoms he destroyed were fifty. He drove away tigers, leopards, rhinoceroses, and elephants, and the people of the world were greatly delighted. The *Classic of Documents* says,

> How great and splendid were the plans of King Wen,
> How greatly realized through the energies of King Wu!
> They are for the help and guidance of us, their descendants,
> Correct in everything, deficient in nothing.[30]

"Again the world declined, and the Way was concealed. Deviant speech and oppressive actions again became prevalent. There were cases of ministers murdering their rulers, of sons murdering their parents. Confucius was afraid, and

---

28. The phrase quoted by Mencius is a slight variant of a statement by the sage king Shun in the "Counsels of the Great Yu" of the *Classic of Documents*. See Legge, *The Chinese Classics*, 3:60.

29. Nefarious minister of the tyrant Zhou.

30. From the "Junya" section of the *Classic of Documents*. Translation adapted from Legge, *The Chinese Classics*, 3:581.

he made the *Spring and Autumn Annals*. The *Spring and Autumn* is concerned with the affairs of the Son of Heaven, and thus Confucius said, 'It is by the *Spring and Autumn* alone that I will be known, and for it alone that I will be condemned.'

"Once again sages and kings do not appear, the lords become arbitrary and intemperate, and unemployed scholars indulge in uninhibited discussion. The words of Yang Zhu and Mo Di overflow the world; the world's words all go back if not to Yang then to Mo. Yang holds for egoism, which involves denial of one's sovereign; Mo holds for universal love, which entails denial of one's parents. To deny one's parents or to deny one's sovereign is to be an animal. Gongming Yi said, 'In their kitchens there is fat meat. In their stables there are fat horses. The people have a hungry look, and in the wilds there are those who have died of starvation. This is leading beasts to eat people.' If the way of Yang and Mo is not stopped, and the way of Confucius is not made known, the people will be deceived by these deviant views, and the path of humaneness and rightness will be blocked. When the path of humaneness and rightness is blocked, animals are led to eat humans, and then humans come to eat one another. I am fearful about this and defend the way of the former sage by resisting Yang and Mo and banishing their licentious words. Those who espouse deviant views must be prevented from putting them into effect, for what is effected in the mind causes harm in affairs, and what is effected in affairs causes harm to government. If a sage should arise again, he would not change my words.

"In former times Yu controlled the waters of the deluge, and the world was at peace. The Duke of Zhou controlled the Yi and the Di and drove away the wild animals, and the people enjoyed repose. Confucius made the *Spring and Autumn*, and rebellious ministers and violent sons were struck with terror. The Ode says,

> The Rong and the Di, he strikes,
> Jing and Shu, he punishes;
> So that none of them will dare to withstand us.[31]

"As the Duke of Zhou would have chastised those who denied fathers and rulers, I too want to correct people's minds, to stop deviant speech, to resist distorted actions, to banish licentious words, and so to carry on the work of the three Sages. In what way am I fond of argument? I am compelled to do it. Whoever can resist Yang and Mo with words is a follower of the sage."

4A:1 Mencius said, "If one had the clarity of Li Lou and the skill of Gong-shuzi, but lacked the compass and square, one would not be able to form

---

31. Ode 300. Translation adapted from Legge, *The Chinese Classics*, 4:626.

squares and circles. If one had the keen ear of Music Master Kuang, but lacked the six pitch pipes, one would not be able to adjust the five notes correctly. If one had the Way of Yao and Shun, but lacked humane government, one would not be able to rule the world. Though he may have a humane heart and a reputation for humaneness, one from whom the people receive no benefits will not serve as a model for later generations because he does not practice the Way of the former kings. Therefore it is said, 'Goodness alone does not suffice for the conduct of government; Laws alone do not implement themselves.' The Ode says,

> Not transgressing, not forgetting,
> But following the statutes of old.[32]

"No one has ever erred by following the laws of the former kings.

. . . .

"The Ode says,

> When Heaven is about to move,
> Do not be indifferent.[33]

"To be indifferent is to be remiss. Serving the ruler without rightness, advancing and withdrawing without regard to rites, and maligning the Way through one's words — this is like being remiss. Therefore it is said, 'Charging one's ruler with what is difficult is called showing respect for him. Exposing goodness while foreclosing on evil is called being reverent toward him. Saying that he is "unable to do it" is called stealing from him.'"[34]

4A:2 Mencius said, "From the compass and the square comes the ultimate standard for circles and squares, and from the sage comes the ultimate standard in human relations. The desire to be a ruler requires that one fully develop the Way of the ruler; the desire to be a minister requires that one fully develop the Way of the minister. In both cases all that is necessary is to take Yao and Shun as the model. Not to serve one's ruler as Shun served Yao is not to respect one's ruler; not to rule the people as Yao ruled them is to act as a thief to the people. Confucius said, 'There are just two ways: being humane and being inhumane.' One whose oppression of his people is extreme will himself be killed and his state will be lost. One who is less extreme will place himself in danger and weaken his state. He will be called You ('the Dark') or Li ('the Tyrannical'),

---

32. Ode 249.
33. Ode 254.
34. See 1A:7, where Mencius makes the distinction between "not doing" something and "being unable" to do it. See also 2A:6.

and though he may have filial sons and devoted grandsons, they will be unable in a hundred generations to change those names. The Ode says,

> The mirror of the Yin is not far off,
> It is found in the time of the last of the Xia.[35]

This is what was meant."

4A:3 Mencius said, "The way the three dynasties gained the empire was through humaneness, and the way they lost it was through not being humane. So too it is in the flourishing or decline of states, and in their preservation or loss. If the Son of Heaven is not humane, he will be unable to protect all within the four seas. If a feudal lord is not humane, he will be unable to protect the altars of the soil and grain. If a high officer is not humane, he will be unable to protect the ancestral temple. And if an ordinary person is not humane, he will be unable to protect his four limbs. Now to dislike death and ruin and yet to take pleasure in not being humane is like disliking drunkenness and yet forcing oneself to drink to excess."

4A:4 Mencius said, "If one loves others yet they are not affectionate, he should turn within and examine his own humaneness; if one rules others yet they are not well governed he should examine his own wisdom; if one behaves decorously toward others yet they do not respond, he should examine his own reverence. Whenever one acts to no avail one should turn within and examine oneself. When one has made one's own person correct, the rest of the world will follow. The Ode says,

> Long may you be worthy of the Mandate,
> And seek for yourself many blessings."[36]

4A:5 Mencius said, "Among the people there is the common saying, 'The empire, the state, the family.' The empire has its basis in the state; the state has its basis in the family, and the family has its basis in oneself."

4A:10 Mencius said, "With those who do violence to themselves, one cannot speak, nor can one interact with those who throw themselves away. To deny decorum and rightness in one's speech is what is called 'doing violence to oneself.' To say, 'I am unable to abide in humaneness or follow rightness' is

---

35. Ode 255, which suggests that the experience of the tyrant Jie, the last ruler of the Xia dynasty, should be taken as an example by later rulers. The Xia (traditional dates, 1818–1766 B.C.E.) was supposed to have been the first dynasty. In its decadence, it succumbed to attack by the Shang.

36. Ode 235.

what is called 'throwing oneself away.' For human beings, humaneness is the peaceful dwelling, and rightness is the correct path. To abandon the peaceful dwelling and not abide in it and to reject the right road and not follow it — how lamentable!"

4A:12 Mencius said, "When those occupying positions below do not gain the respect of those above, they cannot succeed in governing the people. There is a way to gain the respect of those above: one who does not inspire the confidence of friends will not have the respect of those above. There is a way to gain the respect of friends: one who does not serve his parents so as to please them will not inspire the confidence of friends. There is a way to please one's parents: one who turns within and finds himself not to be sincere does not please his parents. There is a way to be sincere within oneself: if one is not clear about what is good, one will not be sincere within oneself. Therefore to be sincere is the Way of Heaven, and to think about sincerity is the human Way. It has never happened that one who is sincere fails to move others, or that one who is not sincere is able to move others."

4A:14 Mencius said, "When Ran Qiu served as chief officer of the Ji clan, he was unable to reform their character, and yet he doubled the tax in grain over what the people had previously paid. Confucius said, 'Qiu is no follower of mine. Little ones, you may beat the drums and attack him.'

"From this it can be seen that one who enriched a ruler who was not given to the practice of humane government was cast off by Confucius. How much more would this be true in the case of one bent on making war? In wars that arise from territorial contests, they kill people until the fields are filled; in wars that arise from contests over cities, they kill people until the cities are filled. This is what is called leading the earth to devour human flesh. Death is not an adequate punishment for such a crime. Therefore those who are skilled in fighting should suffer the highest punishment, followed by those who are responsible for bringing about alliances among the feudal lords, and then by those who open up uncultivated lands and oblige the people to cultivate them."

4A:19 Mencius said, "Of all forms of service, which is the greatest? It is serving one's parents. Of all kinds of vigilance, which is the greatest? It is vigilance over one's own person. I have heard of those who by not losing their own persons have been able to serve their parents, but I have not heard of those who, having lost their own persons, have been able to serve their parents. There are many services one must perform, but the serving of one's parents is the root of all of them. There are many kinds of vigilance that one must exercise, but vigilance over one's own person is the root of all of them. When Zengzi was nurturing Zeng Xi he always provided wine and meat, and when the meal was being cleared, he always asked to whom the remaining food should be given. If his father asked whether there was food remaining, he always replied that there was. When Zeng Xi died, and Zeng Yuan was nurturing Zengzi, he always provided wine and meat, but when the meal was being cleared, he did not ask to whom the remaining food should be given, and if his father asked if there was food remaining, he said that it had been finished because he intended to serve it again. This is what is called 'nourishing the mouth and body,' whereas doing it in the way Zengzi did can be called 'nourishing the intentions.' In serving one's parents, the way Zengzi did it is correct."

4A:20 Mencius said, "It is not enough to censure a ruler over those who have been appointed to office, nor is it enough to criticize the policies of his government. Only a great man can correct what is wrong in a ruler's mind. If the ruler is humane, everyone will be humane. If the ruler does what is right, everyone will do what is right. If the ruler is correct, everyone will be correct. Once the ruler has been rectified, the state will be settled."

4A:26 Mencius said, "There are three things that are unfilial, and the greatest of them is to have no posterity. The reason that Shun married without informing his parents was out of concern that he might have no posterity. The noble person considers that it was as if he had informed them."

4A:27 Mencius said, "The reality of humaneness is serving one's parents; the reality of rightness is following one's elder brother; the reality of wisdom is knowing these two things and not departing from them; the reality of ritual propriety is regulating and adorning these two; the reality of music is in taking joy in these two. When there is joy, they grow; when they grow, how can they be stopped? When they come to the point where they cannot be stopped, then, without one's realizing it, the feet begin to dance and the hands to move."

4B:1 Mencius said, "Shun was born in Zhufeng, moved to Fuxia, and died in Mingtiao — a man of the Eastern Yi. King Wen was born at Mount Qi in Zhou and died at Biying — a man of the Western Yi. In terms of place, they were separated from one another by more than a thousand *li*, and in terms of time, by more than a thousand years. But when they realized their intentions and effected them in the Middle Kingdom it was like uniting the two halves of a tally: the sage who came earlier and the sage who came later were one in their dispositions."

4B:3 Mencius said to King Xuan of Qi, "When the ruler regards his ministers as his hands and feet, the ministers regard the ruler as their stomachs and hearts. When the ruler regards his ministers as dogs and horses, the ministers regard the ruler as just another person. When the ruler regards his ministers as dirt and grass, the ministers regard the ruler as a bandit and an enemy."

The king said, "According to ritual, a minister wears mourning for a ruler he has once served. How must one behave in order for this practice to be followed?"

Mencius said, "When a minister whose admonitions have been followed and whose advice has been heeded, with the result that benefits have extended down to the common people, has reason to depart the state, the ruler sends an escort to conduct him beyond its borders. He also prepares the way for him at his destination. Only after he has been gone for three years without returning does the ruler repossess his land and residence. This is called the threefold courtesy. When a ruler acts in such a way, the minister will wear mourning for him. Now, however, a minister's admonitions are not followed and his advice is not heeded, with the result that benefits do not extend down to the common people. When he has reason to depart, the ruler tries to seize and detain him and even tries to place him in extreme jeopardy at his destination. He repossesses his land and residence on the day of his departure. This is known as being a bandit and an enemy. What mourning should there be for a bandit and an enemy?"

4B:4 Mencius said, "When scholars are put to death though they are guilty of no crime, the great officers may leave; when the people are slaughtered though they are guilty of no crime, the scholars may depart."

4B:5 Mencius said, "If the ruler is humane, everyone will be humane. If the ruler keeps to rightness, everyone will keep to rightness."

4B:6 Mencius said, "A ritual that is not a true ritual, rightness that is not truly right — the great person does not practice them."

4B:7 Mencius said, "Those who keep to the Mean nurture those who do not; those who have talent nurture those who have not. Therefore people take pleasure in having exemplary fathers and elder brothers. If those who keep to the Mean were to cast aside those who do not, and if those who have talent were to cast aside those who have not, then the space between the exemplary and those found wanting would narrow to less than an inch."

4B:8 Mencius said, "Only when a person has some actions that he will not take is he able to take action."

4B:12 Mencius said, "The great person is one who does not lose the child's mind."

4B:14 Mencius said, "The noble person delves into it deeply according to the Way, wishing to get it for himself. As he gets it for himself, he abides in it calmly; abiding in it calmly, he trusts in it deeply; trusting in it deeply, he draws on its source, which he finds both at his left and at his right. This is why the noble person wishes to get it for himself."

4B:19 Mencius said, "That wherein human beings differ from the birds and animals is but slight. The multitude of people relinquish it, while the noble person retains it. Shun was clear about the multitude of things and observant of human relationships. Humaneness and rightness were the source of his actions; he did not just perform acts of humaneness and rightness."

4B:22 Mencius said, "The influence of a noble person ends with the fifth generation, and the influence of a lesser person also ends with the fifth generation. Although I was not able to be a follower of Confucius, I have cultivated myself through others."

4B:28 Mencius said, "That whereby the noble person differs from others is that he preserves his mind. The noble person preserves his mind through humaneness, preserves his mind through courtesy. One who is humane loves other people; one who possesses courtesy respects other people. One who loves other people is always loved by them; one who respects other people is always respected by them. Here is a man who treats me with malice. The noble person must turn within: 'I must not have been humane; I must have been lacking in courtesy, or how could such a thing have happened to me?' If on turning within, one finds oneself to be humane, if on turning within one finds oneself to be courteous, and yet the maliciousness continues, the noble person must *again* turn within: 'I must not have shown good faith.' If, on turning within, one finds good faith in oneself, and still the maliciousness continues, the noble person will say, 'This is a wild man. Since he is like this, how then can one choose between him and the animals? Why should I contend with an animal?'

"Therefore the noble person has anxiety that lasts a lifetime rather than troubles that occupy a morning. And indeed the anxiety has a cause: 'Shun was a human being; I too am a human being. Shun was a model for the world, one that could be transmitted to later generations. If I am nothing more than a villager, this is something to be anxious about.' And what kind of anxiety is it? To be like Shun, nothing more. There is nothing that troubles the noble person. Taking no action that is not humane and engaging in no practice that is not courteous, the noble person, in case of a morning's troubles, would not be troubled."

4B:32 Chuzi said, "The king sent someone to spy on the Master[37] to see whether he was different from other people." Mencius said, "How should I be different from other people? Yao and Shun were the same as other people."

5A:2 Wan Zhang asked, "The Ode says,

> To marry a wife, what should one do?
> He must inform his parents.[38]

"If it were truly as it says here, no one should have known it better than Shun. Why did Shun marry without informing them?"

Mencius said, "If he had informed them, they would not have allowed him to marry. For a man and a woman to live together is the greatest of human relationships. To have informed his parents, and then to have had to forgo this

---

37. I.e., Mencius.
38. Ode 101.

greatest of human relationships, would have resulted in antagonism between him and his parents. This is why he did not inform them."

Wan Zhang said, "The reason why Shun married without telling his parents has now become apparent to me. But how was it that the Emperor gave his daughters to Shun in marriage without having informed his parents?"

"The Emperor, too, knew that if he informed them he could not have given his daughters to him in marriage."

Wan Zhang said, "Shun's parents sent him to repair a granary, and having removed the ladder, the Blind Man[39] set the granary ablaze. They sent him to dig a well and, having followed him out, they then covered it over. Xiang[40] said, 'Credit for the plan to immolate this lord-who-creates-capitals[41] rests solely with me. Let his oxen and sheep go to my parents, and also his storehouses and granaries. His spear will be mine, his lute will be mine, and his bow will be mine. My two sisters-in-law shall be put in charge of my women's quarters.' Xiang went to Shun's palace, and there was Shun on his couch, playing the lute. Xiang said, 'I have been concerned only for you, my lord.' He was embarrassed. Shun said, 'My sole concern has been for my subjects. You should govern them on my behalf.' Could it have been that Shun did not know that Xiang had tried to kill him?"

Mencius said, "How could he not have known? When Xiang was anxious, he too was anxious, and when Xiang was glad, he too was glad."

"Then was Shun pretending to be glad?"

"No. Once someone gave a live fish to Zichan of Zheng. Zichan had his pondkeeper put it into a fishpond, but the pondkeeper cooked it. Going back to report, he said, 'When I first released it, it still seemed trapped, but after a little while it came into its own and joyfully swam away.' Zichan said, 'It came into its element! It came into its element!' The pondkeeper went out and said, 'Who says that Zichan is wise? I cooked and ate the fish, and he said, "It came into its element! It came into its element!"'

"Thus a noble man may be taken in by what is right, but he cannot be misled by what is contrary to the Way. Xiang came in the way that brotherly love should have impelled him to do, and therefore Shun believed him and was glad. In what way was he pretending?"

5A:5 Wan Zhang said, "Was it the case that Yao gave the realm to Shun?"
Mencius said, "No. The Son of Heaven cannot give the realm to someone."
"But Shun did possess the realm. Who gave it to him?"

---

39. Shun's father.

40. Shun's brother.

41. A commentary by Zhu Xi (1130–1200 C.E.) explains that wherever Shun lived for three years became a capital, which accounts for Xiang's sarcastic description of him.

"Heaven gave it to him."

"When Heaven gave it to him, did it ordain this through repeated instructions?"

"No. Heaven does not speak. This was manifested simply through his actions and his conduct of affairs."

"In what way was this manifested through his actions and his conduct of affairs?"

"The Son of Heaven can present a man to Heaven, but he cannot cause Heaven to give him the realm. The feudal lords can present a man to the Son of Heaven, but they cannot cause the Son of Heaven to make him a feudal lord. A great officer can present a man to the feudal lords, but he cannot cause the feudal lords to make him a great officer. Yao presented Shun to Heaven, and it was Heaven that accepted him. He displayed him to the people, and the people accepted him. This is why I said that, 'Heaven does not speak.' This was manifested simply through his actions and his conduct of affairs."

"I venture to ask how it was that Yao presented him to Heaven and Heaven accepted him, and he showed him to the people and the people accepted him?"

"He caused him to preside over the sacrifices, and the hundred spirits enjoyed them. This shows that Heaven accepted him. He put him in charge of affairs, affairs were well ordered, and the hundred surnames were at peace. This shows that the people accepted him. Heaven gave it to him, the people gave it to him — this is why I said that, 'The Son of Heaven cannot give the realm to someone.' Shun assisted Yao for twenty-eight years. This is not something that could have been brought about by a human being. It was Heaven. After Yao died, and the three-years mourning was completed, Shun withdrew from Yao's son and went to the south of the South River. But the feudal lords of the realm, when they went to court, went not to Yao's son but to Shun. Litigants went not to Yao's son but to Shun. Singers sang not of Yao's son but of Shun. This is why I said, 'It was Heaven.' It was after all of this that he went to the Middle Kingdom and ascended to the position of the Son of Heaven. If he had just taken up residence in Yao's palace and ousted his son, this would have been usurpation and not Heaven's gift. The 'Great Declaration' says,

> Heaven sees as my people see,
> Heaven hears as my people hear.[42]

"This is what was meant."

5A:7 Wan Zhang asked, "People say that Yi Yin sought the attention of Tang[43] through his cooking. Was this so?"

---

42. See the "Taishi" in the *Classic of History*. Legge, *The Chinese Classics*, 3:292.

43. First the tutor and later a minister to Tang the Accomplished, the first ruler of the Shang dynasty, Yi Yin is regarded as one of the exemplary ministers of Chinese history.

Mencius said, "No, it was not so. Yi Yin farmed in the lands of the ruler of Xin, and there he delighted in the Way of Yao and Shun. Had it involved anything contrary to rightness or to the Way, though he were offered the ruler-ship of the empire, he would not have considered it, and though a thousand teams of horses were yoked for him, he would not have given them a glance. Had it involved anything contrary to rightness or to the Way, he would neither have given the smallest trifle to anyone nor accepted the smallest trifle from anyone. Tang sent a messenger with presents by way of entreaty, and, with utter indifference, he said, 'What could I do with Tang's presents? Wouldn't it be better to be amidst these fields, delighting in the Way of Yao and Shun?'

"After Tang sent messengers three times to entreat him he changed and, with altered countenance, said, 'Were I allowed to remain amidst these fields, I might delight in the Way of Yao and Shun. But might it not be better if I caused this ruler to become a Yao or a Shun? Might it not be better if I caused this people to become the people of Yao and Shun? Might it not be better if I saw these things for myself in my own person? Heaven in giving birth to this people causes those who are first to know to awaken those who are later to know; and causes those who are first awakened to awaken those who are later to be awakened. I am one of those of Heaven's people who has awakened first; I must take this Way in order to awaken this people. If I do not awaken them, who will do so?'

"He thought that if, among the people in the world, there was any ordinary man or woman who did not enjoy the benefits of Yao and Shun, it was as if he himself had pushed them into a ditch. So it was that he took as his own re-sponsibility the heavy weight of the whole world. Therefore he went to Tang and spoke with him about attacking the Xia and saving the people.

"I have not heard of one who bent himself and in so doing straightened others, how much less could one disgrace himself and in so doing correct the world! The sages have differed in their actions. Some have kept their distance; others have approached. Some have departed; others have not. The point of convergence has been in keeping their persons pure, that is all. I have heard of seeking the attention of Tang through the Way of Yao and Shun; I have not heard of doing so through cooking. . . ."

5B:2 Bogong Qi asked, "How were the ranks of nobility and the emoluments arranged by the house of Zhou?"

Mencius said, "The details of it cannot be heard, as the several lords, dislik-ing them as having been damaging to themselves, did away entirely with the records. Yet the essentials of it I have heard. The Son of Heaven represented one rank; the dukes one rank; the marquises, one rank; the earls, one rank; the viscounts and the barons shared one rank. Altogether there were five levels. The ruler represented one rank; the chief ministers, one rank; the great officers, one rank; the scholars of the highest grade, one rank; the scholars of the middle grade, one rank; the scholars of the lower grade, one rank. Altogether there were six levels. The land allotted to the Son of Heaven was a thousand *li* square; the land allotted to the dukes and marquises was in all cases a hundred *li*; to the earls and viscounts, seventy *li*; to the barons, fifty *li*. Altogether there were four levels. One who could not have fifty *li* could not have access to the Son of Heaven but, being attached to one of the marquises, was called a 'dependent.'

"The chief ministers of the Son of Heaven received land equivalent to that of the marquises; the great officers received land equivalent to that of the earls; a scholar of the first rank received land equivalent to that of a viscount or a baron. In a great state in which the territory was a hundred *li* square, the ruler had an emolument ten times that of the chief minister; the chief minister, an emolument four times that of the great officers; a great officer, twice that of a scholar of the highest grade; a scholar of the highest grade, twice that of a scholar of the middle grade; a scholar of the middle grade, twice that of a scholar of the lower grade; a scholar of the lower grade, the same emolument as an ordinary person serving in an official position, an emolument sufficient to compensate for what would have been earned tilling the fields.

"In a state of the next size, with a territory equal to seventy *li*, the ruler would have ten times the emolument of the chief minister; a chief minister three times that of a great officer; a great officer, twice that of a scholar of the highest grade; a scholar of the highest grade, twice that of a scholar of the middle grade; a scholar of the middle grade, twice that of a scholar of the lower grade; a scholar of the lower grade, the same emolument as an ordinary person serving in an official position, an emolument sufficient to compensate for what would have been earned tilling the fields.

"In a small state, with a territory equal to fifty *li*, the ruler would have an emolument ten times that of the chief minister; a chief minister, twice that of a great officer; a great officer, twice that of a scholar of the highest rank; a scholar of the highest rank, twice that of a scholar of the middle rank; a scholar of the middle rank, twice that of a scholar of the lower rank; a scholar of the lower grade, the same emolument as an ordinary person serving in an official position, an emolument sufficient to compensate for what he would have earned tilling the fields.

"As to the tillers of the fields, each received a hundred *mu*. With an allotment of a hundred *mu*, the most capable tillers could feed nine people; the next level, eight; the next level, seven; the next level, six; and the lowest level, five. The emoluments of ordinary people serving in office were adjusted according to this."

5B:9 King Xuan of Qi asked about high ministers.
Mencius said, "Which high ministers is the king asking about?"
The king said, "Are the ministers not the same?"

"They are not the same. There are ministers who are from the royal line and ministers who are of other surnames."

The king said, "May I inquire about those who are of the royal line?"

"If the ruler has great faults, they should remonstrate with him. If, after they have done so repeatedly, he does not listen, they should depose him."

The king suddenly changed countenance.

"The king should not misunderstand. He inquired of his minister, and his minister dares not respond except truthfully."

The king's countenance became composed once again, and he then inquired about high ministers of a different surname.

"If the ruler has faults, they should remonstrate with him. If they do so repeatedly, and he does not listen, they should leave."

6A:1 Gaozi said, "The nature is like willow wood; rightness is like cups and bowls. To make humaneness and rightness out of human nature is like making cups and bowls out of the willow wood."

Mencius said, "Are you able to make cups and bowls while following the nature of the willow wood? You must do violence to the willow wood before you can make cups and bowls. If you must do violence to the willow wood in order to make cups and bowls, must you also do violence to a human being in order to make humaneness and rightness? The effect of your words will be to cause everyone in the world to think of humaneness and rightness as misfortunes."

6A:2 Gaozi said, "The nature is like swirling water. Open a passage for it in the east, and it will flow east; open a passage for it in the west, and it will flow west. Human nature does not distinguish between good and not-good any more than water distinguishes between east and west."

Mencius said, "It is true that water does not distinguish between east and west, but does it fail to distinguish between up and down? The goodness of human nature is like the downward course of water. There is no human being lacking in the tendency to do good, just as there is no water lacking in the tendency to flow downward. Now by striking water and splashing it, you may cause it to go over your head, and by damming and channeling it, you can force it to flow uphill. But is this the nature of water? It is the force that makes this happen. While people can be made to do what is not good, what happens to their nature is like this."

6A:3 Gaozi said, "Being alive is what is called the nature."

Mencius said, "When you say that 'being alive is called the nature,' is it like saying that 'white is what is called white'?"

"Yes."

"Is the whiteness of a white feather like the whiteness of snow, and the whiteness of snow like the whiteness of white jade?"

"Yes."

"Then is the nature of a dog like the nature of an ox, and the nature of an ox like the nature of a human being?"

6A:4 Gaozi said, "The appetite for food and sex is the nature. Humaneness is internal rather than external; rightness is external rather than internal."

Mencius said, "Why do you say that humaneness is internal while rightness is external?"

Gaozi said, "One who is older than I, I treat as an elder. This is not because there is in me some sense of respect due to elders. It is like his being white and my recognizing him as white, responding to the whiteness that is external. Therefore I call it external."

Mencius said, "There is no difference between the whiteness of a white horse and the whiteness of a white man. But is there no difference between the age of an old horse and the age of an old man? What is it that we speak of as rightness — the man's being old or my regarding him with the respect due to one who is old?"

Gaozi said, "Here is my younger brother; I love him. There is the younger brother of a man from Qin; him I do not love. The feeling derives from me, and therefore I describe it as internal. I treat an elder from Chu as old, just as I treat our own elders as old. The feeling derives from their age, and therefore I call it external."

Mencius said, "Our fondness for the roast meat provided by a man of Qin is no different from our fondness for the roast meat provided by one of our own people. Since this is also the case with a material thing, will you say that our fondness for roast meat is external as well?"

6A:5 Meng Jizi asked Gongduzi, "Why do you say that rightness is internal?"

Gongduzi said, "We are enacting our respect, and therefore it is internal."

"Suppose there were a villager who was one year older than your elder brother — for whom would you show respect?"

"I would respect my elder brother."

"For whom would you pour wine first when serving at a feast?"

"I would pour it first for the villager."

"You feel respect for the one, but it is the other whom you treat as the elder. So in the end rightness is external and not internal."

Gongduzi, being unable to reply, told Mencius about it. Mencius said, "Ask him for whom he shows greater respect, his uncle or his younger brother? He will say that he respects his uncle. You then ask him, if his younger brother were impersonating the deceased at a sacrifice, for whom he would then show greater respect? He will say that he would show respect for his younger brother. Then ask where is the respect due to an uncle? He will say that it is because of his younger brother's position that he shows him greater respect. Then you may also say that it is because of the position of the villager that you show him respect. While ordinarily the respect belongs to your brother, on occasion the respect belongs to the villager."

Meng Ji heard this and said, "When respect is due to my uncle, I show him respect; when respect is due to my brother I show the respect to him. So respect is after all determined by externals and is not internally motivated."

Gongduzi said, "In the winter we drink hot water, while in the summer we drink cold water. Does this mean that drinking and eating too are externally determined?"

6A:6 Gongduzi said, "Gaozi says that the nature is neither good nor not-good. Others say that the nature can be made to be good or not-good, which is why during the reigns of Kings Wen and Wu the people were inclined to goodness, whereas under the reigns of You and Li, the people were inclined to violence. Still others say that the natures of some are good and the natures of others are not-good, which is why when Yao was the ruler there could be Xiang,[44] while with a father like Gusou there could be Shun,[45] and with Zhou[46] as the son of their elder brother as well as their ruler there could be Qi, the Viscount of Wei, and Prince Bigan. Now you say that the nature is good. Does this mean that these others are all wrong?"

Mencius said, "As far as the natural tendencies are concerned, it is possible for one to do good; this is what I mean by being good. If one does what is not good, that is not the fault of one's capacities. The mind of pity and commiseration is possessed by all human beings; the mind of shame and aversion is possessed by all human beings; the mind of respectfulness and reverence is possessed by all human beings; and the mind that knows right and wrong is possessed by all human beings. The mind of pity and commiseration is humaneness; the mind of shame and dislike is rightness; the mind of reverence and respect is decorum; and the mind that knows right and wrong is wisdom. Humaneness, rightness, decorum, and wisdom are not infused into us from without. We definitely possess them. It is just that we do not think about it, that is all. Therefore it is said, 'Seek and you will get it; let go and you will lose it.'[47] That some differ from others by as much as twice, or five times, or an incalculable order of magnitude, is because there are those who are unable fully to develop their capacities. The Ode says,

---

44. According to this view of human nature, which is obviously not that of Mencius, the fact that a violent man like Xiang could have lived during the reign of the sage king Yao is evidence that people differ widely in their natures. Xiang was the depraved brother of Yao's exemplary successor, Shun. See 5A:2.

45. Gusou, also known as the blind man, was the paradigm of the cruel father, to whom Shun remained nonetheless filial and devoted.

46. Zhou was universally believed to have been a monstrous tyrant. His elder brother, Qi, and his uncle, Bigan, attempted, with notable lack of success, to counsel him.

47. See also the statement attributed to Confucius at the end of *Mencius* 6A:8.

> Heaven in giving birth to humankind,
> Created for each thing its own rule.
> The people's common disposition
> Is to love this admirable virtue.[48]

"Confucius said, 'How well the one who made this Ode knew the Way!' Therefore for each thing there must be a rule, and people's common disposition is therefore to love this admirable virtue."

6A:7 Mencius said, "In years of abundance, most of the young people have the wherewithal to be good, while in years of adversity, most of them become violent. This is not a matter of a difference in the capacities sent down by Heaven, but rather of what overwhelms their minds.

"Now let barley be sown and covered with earth. The ground being the same, and the time of planting also the same, it grows rapidly, and in due course of time it all ripens. Though there may be differences in the yield, this is because the fertility of the soil, the nourishment of the rain and the dew, and the human effort invested have been incommensurate.

"Things of the same kind are thus like to one another. Why is it that we should doubt this only when it comes to human beings? The sage and we are the same in kind. So Master Long said, 'If someone makes shoes without knowing the size of a person's feet, I know that he will not make baskets.' That shoes are similar is because everyone in the world has feet that are alike. And when it comes to taste, all mouths are alike in their preferences. Yi Ya was first to apprehend what all mouths prefer. If, with regard to the way mouths are disposed to tastes, the nature differed from person to person, as is the case with dogs and horses that differ from us in kind, why should it be that everyone in the world follows Yi Ya in matters of taste? The fact that everyone in the world takes Yi Ya as the standard in matters of taste is because we all have mouths that are similar. It is likewise with our ears: when it comes to sounds, everyone in the world takes Music Master Kuang as the standard because the ears of everyone in the world are similar. And so likewise with our eyes: when it comes to Zidu, there is no one in the world who fails to recognize his beauty because one who failed to recognize the beauty of Zidu would have to be without eyes. Therefore I say mouths prefer the same tastes; ears hear the same sounds; eyes perceive the same beauty. When it comes to our minds, could they alone have nothing in common? And what is it that our minds have in common? It is principle and rightness. The sage is just the first to apprehend what our minds have in common. Therefore principle and rightness please our minds in the same way that viands please our mouths."

---

48. Ode 260.

6A:8 Mencius said, "The trees on Ox Mountain were once beautiful. But being situated on the outskirts of a large state, the trees are hewn down by axes. Could they remain beautiful? Given the air of the day and the night, and the moisture of the rain and the dew, they do not fail to put forth new buds and shoots, but then cattle and sheep also come to graze. This accounts for the barren appearance of the mountain. Seeing this barrenness, people suppose that the mountain was never wooded. But how could this be the nature of the mountain? So it is also with what is preserved in a human being: could it be that anyone should lack the mind of humaneness and rightness? If one lets go of the innate good mind, this is like taking an axe to a tree; being hewn down day after day, can it remain beautiful? Given the rest that one gets in the day and the night, and the effect of the calm morning *qi*, one's likes and dislikes will still resemble those of other people, but barely so. One becomes fettered and destroyed by what one does during the day, and if this fettering occurs repeatedly, the effect of the night *qi* will no longer be enough to allow him to preserve his mind, and he will be at scant remove from the animals. Seeing this, one might suppose that he never had the capacity for goodness. But can this be a human being's natural tendency? Thus, given nourishment, there is nothing that will not grow; lacking nourishment, there is nothing that will not be destroyed. Confucius said, 'Hold on and you preserve it; let go and you lose it. There is no appointed time for its going out and coming in, and no one knows its direction.' In saying this, was he not speaking of the mind?"

6A:9 Mencius said, "The king's lack of wisdom is hardly surprising. Take something that is the easiest thing in the world to grow. Expose it to the heat for a day, and then expose it to cold for ten days, and it will not be able to grow. I see the king but seldom, and when I withdraw, the agents of cold arrive. Even if I have caused some buds to appear, what good does it do?

"Now chess is one of the minor arts, but without concentrating one's mind and applying one's will, one cannot succeed in it. Chess Qiu is the finest chess player anywhere in the state; suppose that Chess Qiu is teaching two people to play chess. One of them concentrates his mind and applies his will, listening only to Chess Qiu. The other, while listening to him, is actually occupying his whole mind with a swan that he believes is approaching. He thinks about bending his bow, fitting his arrow, and shooting the swan. While he is learning alongside the other man, he does not compare with him. Is this because his intelligence is not comparable? I would say that this is *not* so."

6A:10 Mencius said, "I desire fish, and I also desire bear's paws. If I cannot have both of them, I will give up fish and take bear's paws. I desire life, and I also desire rightness. If I cannot have both of them, I will give up life and take rightness. It is true that I desire life, but there is something I desire more than life, and therefore I will not do something dishonorable in order to hold on to it. I detest death, but there is something I detest more than death, and therefore there are some dangers I may not avoid. If among a person's desires there were none greater than life, then why should he not do anything necessary in order to cling to life? If among the things he detested there were none greater than death, why should he not do whatever he had to in order to avoid danger? There is a means by which one may preserve life, and yet he does not employ it; there is a means by which one may avoid danger, and yet he does not adopt it.

"Thus there are things that we desire more than life, and things that we detest more than death. It is not only exemplary persons who have this mind; all human beings have it. It is only that the exemplary ones are able to avoid losing it, that is all.

"Suppose there are a basketful of rice and a bowlful of soup. If I get them I may remain alive; if I do not get them I must die. If they are offered contemptuously, a wayfarer would decline to accept them; if they are offered after having been trampled upon, a beggar would not demean himself by taking them. And yet when it comes to ten thousand bushels I accept them without regard for decorum and rightness. What do the ten thousand bushels add to me? Is it for the sake of beautiful dwellings that I take them, or for the service of wives and concubines, or for the recognition of those afflicted by poverty? What formerly I would not accept even if it meant my death, I now accept for the sake of beautiful houses. What formerly I would not accept even if it meant my death, I now accept for the service of wives and concubines. What formerly I would not accept even if it meant my death, I now accept for the recognition of those afflicted by poverty. Could this not have been declined as well? This is what is called 'losing one's original mind.'"

6A:11 Mencius said, "Humaneness is the human mind. Rightness is the human path. To quit the path and not follow it, to abandon this mind and not know enough to seek it, is indeed lamentable. If a man has chickens and dogs, and they are lost, he knows enough to seek them. But when he has lost his mind, he does not know enough to seek it. The way of learning is none other than this: to seek for the lost mind."

6A:12 Mencius said, "Now suppose there is a person whose fourth finger is bent so that it cannot be straightened. This may be neither painful nor incapacitating, and yet if there is someone who is able to straighten it, he will not consider the road from Qin to Chu too far to go because his finger is not like other people's. When one's finger is unlike the fingers of others, one knows enough to hate it, but when one's mind is not like the minds of others, one does not know enough to hate it. This is what is called a failure to understand distinctions."

6A:13 Mencius said, "Anyone who wants to grow a *tong* tree, or a catalpa, which can be grasped with the hands, will know how to nourish it. But when it comes to one's person, one does not know how to nourish it. Could it be that one's love for one's own person is not comparable to one's love for the *tong* or the catalpa? What a failure to think!"

6A:14 Mencius said, "Human beings love all parts of themselves equally, and, loving all parts equally, nurture all parts equally. There being not an inch of flesh that one does not love, there is not an inch of flesh one does not nurture. In examining whether one is good at it or not, the only way is to observe what one chooses in oneself.

"Some parts of the body are superior and others inferior; some are small and others are great. One should not harm the great for the sake of the small, nor should one harm the superior for the sake of the inferior. One who nurtures the smaller part of himself becomes a small person, while one who nurtures the greater part of himself becomes a great person. Here is a master gardener who neglects his *wu* and *jia* trees while nurturing thorns and brambles: he is an inferior gardener. Here is a person who, unknowingly, nurtures a single finger while neglecting his back and shoulders: he is a hurried wolf. A person given to drinking and eating is considered by others to be inferior because he nourishes what is small in himself while neglecting what is great. Would a person who, while drinking and eating, was not neglectful, regard his mouth and stomach as just an inch of flesh?"

6A:15 Gongduzi asked, "All are equally persons, and yet some are great persons and others are small persons — why is this?"

Mencius said, "Those who follow the part of themselves that is great become great persons, while those who follow the part of themselves that is small become small persons."

[Gongduzi] said, "Since all are equally persons, why is it that some follow the part of themselves that is great, while others follow the part of themselves that is small?"

Mencius said, "The faculties of seeing and hearing do not think and are obscured by things. When one thing comes into contact with another, they are led away. The faculty of the mind is to think. By thinking, one gets it; by not thinking, one fails to get it. This is what Heaven has given to us. When we first establish the greater part of ourselves, then the smaller part is unable to steal it away. It is simply this that makes the great person."

6A:16 Mencius said, "There is the nobility of Heaven and the nobility of man. Humaneness, rightness, loyalty, and truthfulness — and taking pleasure in doing good, without ever wearying of it — this is the nobility of Heaven. The ranks of duke, minister, or high official — this is the nobility of man. Men of antiquity cultivated the nobility of Heaven and the nobility of man followed after it. Men of the present day cultivate Heavenly nobility out of a desire for the nobility of man, and, once having obtained the nobility of man, they cast away the nobility of Heaven. Their delusion is extreme, and, in the end, they must lose everything."

6A:17 Mencius said, "In their desire to be honored, all human minds are of like mind. And all human beings have within themselves what is honorable. It is only that they do not think about it, that is all. The honor that derives from men is not the original, good honor. Whom Zhao Meng honors, Zhao Meng can also debase. The *Classic of Odes* says,

> We have been plied with wine,
> And satisfied with virtue.[49]

"To 'satisfy with virtue' means that one is satisfied with humaneness and rightness and therefore does not crave the flavors of the meat and grain served by men, and when a good reputation and widespread esteem accrue to one's person, one does not crave the elegant embroidered garments worn by men."

6A:18 Mencius said, "Humaneness overcomes inhumaneness just as water overcomes fire. Those today who practice humaneness do it as if they were using a cup of water to put out the fire consuming a cartload of firewood, and then, when the flames are not extinguished, they say that water does not overcome fire. This is to make an enormous concession to what is not humane, and in the end it must inevitably result in the destruction of humaneness."

6A:19 Mencius said, "The five kinds of grain are the finest of all seeds. But if they are not mature, they are not even as good as the tares or weeds. With humaneness too, ripeness is everything."

6A:20 Mencius said, "When Yi taught people archery he was always determined to draw the bow to the full, and the students necessarily did the same. When the master carpenter instructs others, he always uses the compass and the square, and the students necessarily use the compass and the square as well."

6B:2 Cao Jiao asked, "Is it true that all human beings are capable of becoming a Yao or a Shun?"

Mencius said, "It is true."

"I have heard that King Wen was ten feet tall, while Tang was nine feet tall. I am nine feet four inches tall,[50] and yet all I can do is eat millet. What shall I do to become a Yao or a Shun?"

"What is there to do but just to do it? Here we have a man who is not strong enough to lift a chicken; he is a man who lacks strength. If he now says that he

---

49. Ode 247.
50. Obviously, the Chinese foot was considerably shorter than the Western measurement.

can lift a hundred *jun*, he is a man of strength, for by lifting Wu Huo's burden one becomes Wu Huo. Why should a person make a calamity of what he has not yet mastered? It is just that he has not done it. To walk slowly behind an elder brother is called fraternal; to walk quickly ahead of an elder brother is called unfraternal. Is there anyone who is unable to walk slowly? It is just that he does not do it. The Way of Yao and Shun was that of filial and fraternal duty, that is all. By wearing the clothes of Yao, speaking the words of Yao, and performing the actions of Yao, you become Yao. By wearing the clothes of Jie, speaking the words of Jie, and performing the actions of Jie, you become Jie."

Jiao said, "If I can get to see the ruler of Zou I may be able to ask him for a house where I may live. I should like to stay here to receive instruction at your gate."

"The Way is like a great road. It is not difficult to know it. The failing people have is simply that they do not seek it. If you, sir, will go back and seek it, you will have more than enough teachers."

6B:15 Mencius said, "Shun emerged from the fields; Fu Yue was elevated from among the boards and earthworks; Jiao Ge from the fish and salt; Guan Yiwu from the hands of the jailer; Sunshu Ao from the seacoast; and Boli Xi from the marketplace. When Heaven intends to confer on a person a great responsibility it first visits his mind and will with suffering, toils his sinews and bones, subjects his body to hunger, exposes him to poverty, and confounds his projects. Through this, his mind is stimulated, his nature strengthened, and his inadequacies repaired. People commonly err, but later they are able to reform; their minds are troubled and their thoughts perplexed, but then they become capable of acting. This becomes evident in their expressions, emerges in their voices, and, finally, they understand.

"Thus in the absence of law-abiding families and worthy counselors within and hostile states and external challenges without, a state will often perish. From this we may know that out of sorrow and calamity life is born, while from comfort and joy comes death."

7A:1 Mencius said, "One who has fully developed his mind knows his nature. Knowing his nature, he knows Heaven. By preserving one's mind and nourishing one's nature one has the means to serve Heaven. When neither the brevity nor the length of a lifespan engenders doubts, and one cultivates one's person in an attitude of expectancy, one has the means to establish one's destiny."

7A:2 Mencius said, "There is, for everything, a destiny. One should follow and accept what is proper for oneself. Therefore one who knows destiny does not stand under a wall in danger of collapsing. To die in the course of fulfilling the Way is a proper destiny, while dying in manacles and fetters is not a proper destiny."

7A:4 Mencius said, "All the ten thousand things are complete in me. To turn within to examine oneself and find that one is sincere — there is no greater joy than this. To dedicate oneself in all earnestness to reciprocity — there can be no closer approach to humaneness."

7A:5 Mencius said, "To carry it out without reflecting on it; to practice it without inquiring into it; to follow it over the course of a lifetime but not recognize it as the Way — this is the way with most people."

7A:6 Mencius said, "A person may not be without shame. Shamelessness is the shame of being without shame."

7A:15 Mencius said, "What people are able to do without having learned it is original, good ability. What they know without having to think about it is original, good knowledge. There are no young children who do not know to love their parents, and there are none who, as they grow older, do not know to respect their older brothers. To be affectionate toward those close to one — this is humaneness. To have respect for elders — this is rightness. It is just this that is shared by everyone in the world."

7A:38 Mencius said, "Physical form and expressions belong to the nature endowed by Heaven. Only the sage is able to follow his physical form."

7A:40 Mencius said, "There are five ways in which the noble person teaches others. One is by exerting a transforming influence, like a timely rain. One is by causing their virtue to be fulfilled; one is by furthering their talents; one is by answering questions; another is by enabling them to cultivate and correct themselves on their own. These five are the ways in which the noble person teaches."

7A:41 Gongsun Chou said, "How lofty the Way is, and how beautiful! Indeed it is like ascending to Heaven — so attainable does it seem. Why not make it something that others might expect to attain in order to encourage them to make daily effort?"

Mencius said, "The great artisan does not change or dispense with the marking line for the sake of an unskilled craftsman, nor did Yi change his rule for drawing the bow for the sake of an inept archer. The noble person, having drawn the bow but not yet released the arrow, as if by a leap, positions himself at the center of the Way. Those who are able to do so will follow him."

7A:45 Mencius said, "The noble person loves creatures but is not humane toward them. With the people he is humane but not affectionate. He is affectionate toward his parents, humane toward the people, and loving toward creatures."

7B:13 Mencius said, "It has happened that one who is not humane has gained control of a state but not that one who is not humane has gained control of the empire as a whole."

7B:14 Mencius said, "The people are of greatest importance, the altars of the soil are next, and the ruler is of least importance. This is why one who gains the allegiance of the peasants will become the Son of Heaven, and one who gains the allegiance of the Son of Heaven will become one of the several lords, and one who gains the allegiance of the several lords will become a great officer. When one of the lords endangers the altars of the soil and grain, he is replaced. When the sacrificial animals have been perfect, the sacrificial vessels of millet have been pure, and the sacrifices have been timely, yet droughts or floods occur, then the altars should be replaced."

7B:33 Mencius said, "Yao and Shun had it as their nature; Tang and Wu returned to it. When every expression of one's countenance and every movement of one's body is exactly in conformity with ritual, this is the ultimate in flourishing virtue. Weeping for the dead should be out of grief and not for the sake of the living. Following the path of virtue without deviation is not for the sake of an emolument. Speech must be trustworthy and not for the sake of acting correctly. The noble person carries out the law and awaits his destiny, that is all."

7B:35 Mencius said, "To nourish the mind, there is nothing better than making the desires few. Here is a man whose desires are few; although there may be certain instances in which he is unable to preserve his mind, they will be few. Here is a man whose desires are many; although there may be instances in which he is able to preserve his mind, they will be few."

7B:37 Wan Zhang asked, "When Confucius was in Chen he said, 'Would it not be better to return home? The scholars of my school are madly ardent and impetuous. Intent on going forward and seizing their opportunity, they do not forget their origins.'[51] Since Confucius was in Chen, why should he have been thinking about the mad scholars of Lu?"

Mencius said, "Since Confucius did not get those who followed the middle way, he had to accept the madly ardent and the cautiously restrained.[52] The ardent go forward and seize their opportunities; the restrained have things that they will not do. Confucius would have preferred those who followed the middle way but, since he could not be sure of getting them, he thought in terms of the next best."

"I venture to ask what they were like — those who were called the 'madly ardent'?"

"Those whom Confucius called 'madly ardent' were such persons as Qin Zhang, Zeng Xi, and Mu Pi."

"Why were they called 'madly ardent'?"

"Their resolution led them to ostentatious invocations of 'The ancients! The ancients!' But, impartially assessed, their actions did not measure up to their words. When even the 'madly ardent' could not be found, Confucius wanted

---

51. Cf. *Analects* 5:21.
52. Cf. *Analects* 13:21.

to get scholars who would not deign to involve themselves with anything impure. These were the cautiously restrained, and they were his next choice."

"Confucius said, 'When people pass my door without entering my house, it is only in the case of the village paragon that I feel no regret. The village paragon is the thief of virtue.' What sort of person was this that he could refer to as a 'village paragon'?"

"He is the sort of person who might say, 'Why are you so ostentatious? Your words are not supported by your actions, nor are your actions supported by your words, yet you invoke "the ancients! the ancients!" Why are you so self-possessed, so cold? We are born into this world and must be of this world. It is quite enough simply to be good.' Eunuch-like, he ingratiates himself with a whole generation — such is the village paragon."

Wan Zhang said, "An entire village will praise this paragon; he is a paragon in everything he does. Why did Confucius consider him a thief of virtue?"

"Blame him — you find nothing blameworthy. Reprove him — there is nothing to reprove. He conforms to prevailing customs; he harmonizes with an impure world. In his commitments he seems loyal and trustworthy; in his actions he seems incorruptible and untainted. The crowd is pleased with him, and he considers himself to be right. It is not possible to enter the Way of Yao and Shun together with him, and he was therefore called the 'thief of virtue.'

"Confucius said, 'I dislike something that appears to be what in reality it is not; I dislike the weed for fear it will be confused with the grain; I dislike flattery for fear it may be confused with rightness; I dislike verbal facility for fear it may be confused with faithfulness; I dislike the music of Zheng for fear it be confused with authentic music; I dislike violet for fear it may be confused with vermilion; I dislike the village paragon lest his qualities be confused for virtue.'

"The noble person turns back to an invariable regularity, that is all. The invariable regularity being correct, the multitudes will then be aroused, and when the multitudes are aroused there will no longer be deviance and iniquity."

7B:38 Mencius said, "From Yao and Shun down to Tang was more than five hundred years. Yu and Gao Yao had seen Yao and Shun and knew them personally, while Tang had heard about them and knew them by reputation. From Tang down to King Wen was more than five hundred years. Yi Yin and Lai Zhu saw Tang and knew him personally, while King Wen had heard of him and knew him by reputation. From King Wen down to Confucius was more than five hundred years. Taigong Wang and Sanyi Sheng had seen King Wen and knew him personally, while Confucius had heard of him and knew him by reputation. From Confucius down to the present day there have intervened more than a hundred years. We are so little removed from the time of the sage, and so close to the place where he dwelled. Is there then no one? Is there no one?"

[Mencius, in Shisanjing zhushu — IB]

XUNZI

Xun Kuang or Xun Qing, better known as Xunzi, or Master Xun, was born about 310 B.C.E. He lived a very long life, during which he may have witnessed the final demise of the Zhou dynasty, which Mencius had anticipated but had not lived to see. In all probability, he was still alive in 219 B.C.E., and perhaps for several years thereafter, which would mean that he endured through not only the final conquest in 221 B.C.E. by the state of Qin of all of the surviving feudal states but also through at least the initial stages of the formation under the Qin dynasty (221–207 B.C.E.) of the first unified empire. The wars leading up to this conquest in the late third century were almost indescribably brutal, and the intrigues surrounding them often intensely bitter. Xunzi was not only aware of many of these events but personally involved in some of them. It is hardly surprising, then, that he held views of society, government, education, and especially of human nature that contrasted with those of Mencius. His view of the world was darker than that of Mencius, and the remedies he advocated for its troubles were more cautious and complex.

The differences between Mencius and Xunzi have often been explained in terms of these momentous changes that were under way in the Chinese world between the fourth and third centuries. Still, Xunzi's thought cannot be reduced to an inevitable or predictable reaction to the troubling political situation in the waning years of the Zhou, nor can it be understood simply as a repudiation of a lofty and expansive Mencian optimism in favor of a cramped and pervasive pessimism. Xunzi was sober, even somber, when it came to his assessment of the basic nature of human beings — their original disposition — and he explicitly challenged Mencius's positive conception of human nature as fundamentally good. At the same time he reaffirmed certain shared and enduring Confucian values, above all the devotion to learning, culture, and the possibility of human perfectibility — all the more remarkable an affirmation in light of his personal experience of what must sometimes have seemed an almost limitless human capacity for violence, treachery, and self-aggrandizement.

The aspects of the Confucian inheritance that Xunzi was apparently inclined, both by personal temperament and intellectual disposition, to emphasize were the commitment to order and hierarchy and the highly formalistic mode of personal cultivation and community organization associated with ritual. In these commitments he was firmly grounded in the earlier tradition associated with the *ru* or ritualists, in ideas and values that were, in a sense, Confucian bedrock. At the same time he involved himself with great intellectual fervor and, evidently without temperamental reluctance, in contemporary intellectual debates. Many of his most distinctive ideas, particularly those having to do with government, education, and the relation of the human world to Heaven or the natural order, seem to have been articulated in the course of these debates, not only with Mohists and Daoists, but also with adherents of the school that later became known as Legalism, or the School of Law.

Xunzi began his scholarly career at the Jixia Academy in the feudal state of Qi, an academy long famous as a gathering place for scholars of virtually every school or filiation of thought current at the time. In a time marked by contention among the so-called hundred schools of thought and in a place where lively and serious controversies among scholars were actively encouraged, Xunzi seems to have encountered and become engaged with some of the outstanding thinkers and most of the leading ideas and teachings of his day. After Qi became engulfed in political crisis around 284 B.C.E., Xunzi departed for the state of Chu, only to return some years later to Qi and to a restored Jixia Academy, apparently becoming its leading figure. But though he spent altogether well over twenty years of his life in the role of an academician, Xunzi was by no means cut off from the major political events of the third century. In the mid-260s he traveled to the state of Qin, where he had the opportunity to observe firsthand its highly authoritarian form of government and its relentless rise to military prominence. Later, during a stay in his native state of Zhao, then menaced by Qin, he had further occasion to reflect on the implications of Qin's Legalist policies and offensive strategies and on the prospect of its conquest of the empire. The closing years of Xunzi's life were spent in Lanling, in southern Shandong, where he was employed for several extended periods as a magistrate, yet always simultaneously engaged as a teacher. His students included Han Fei and Li Si, who would become leading figures in the Legalist school and in the state of Qin, as well as several Confucian scholars who would assume an extremely influential role in the intellectual life of the ensuing Han dynasty.

The work that bears Xunzi's name, having been compiled and edited more than a century after his time, has not come down to us in its original form. Whatever the interventions of the first-century compiler of the text may have entailed, however, the basic form of the work was probably not significantly altered. As the selections that follow will indicate, Xunzi's work is distinguished from the *Analects* and the *Mencius* by the fact that it is not a record of conversations but a work composed primarily of essays. Unlike the relatively fragmentary form of the Confucian or Mencian conversations, reconstructed after the fact, these essays by Xunzi seem to involve his sustained reflections on topics of particular concern to him — including learning, self-cultivation, government, military affairs, Heaven or Nature, ritual, language, and human nature. In the selections presented here we encounter a powerful intellect arguing, often eloquently and always strenuously, for values and views that, for him, were essential to the cultivation of the individual as well as the preservation of civilization in a world where its survival must have seemed by no means assured.

Selections from the Xunzi

CHAPTER 1: ENCOURAGING LEARNING

Xunzi is known as a scholar of highly refined intelligence and powerful intellect. Though Mencius personally valued and publicly promoted learning, one does not find in his conversations and pronouncements the self-conscious sense of intellectuality that is everywhere present in the writing of Xunzi. It is noteworthy, however, that in this opening chapter of his work Xunzi, deeply concerned with finding accessible models and promoting learning that is relevant to the present, makes a strong case for the value of *personal* association with a teacher and of *personal* involvement in ritual practice as against a bookish or antiquarian absorption in the past.

The noble person says: Learning must never cease. Blue comes from the indigo plant, yet it is bluer than indigo. Ice is made from water, yet it is colder than water. Wood as straight as a plumb line may be bent into a wheel that is as round as if it were drawn with a compass, and, even after the wood has dried, it will not straighten out again because this is the way it has been bent. Thus wood marked by the plumb line will become straight, and metal that is put to the whetstone will become sharp. The noble person who studies widely and examines himself each day will become clear in his knowing and faultless in his conduct.

Therefore if you do not climb a high mountain, you will not know the height of Heaven; if you do not look down into a deep valley, you will not know the depth of the earth; and if you do not hear the words handed down from the ancient kings, you will not know the greatness of learning and inquiry. The children of Han and Yue and of the Yi and the Mo[53] all make the same sounds at birth, but as they grow up they have different customs because this is the way they have been educated. The Ode says,

> O you noble men,
> Do not be constantly at ease and at rest.
> Be thoughtful in your official positions.
> Love those who are upright and correct.
> And the spirits will heed you,
> And will increase your blessings.[54]

Of spirits there is none greater than being transformed through the Way; of blessings there is none more lasting than being without misfortune.

---

53. Han and Yue were ancient Chinese states; the Yi and the Mo were non-Chinese tribes.
54. Ode 207.

Once I spent an entire day in thought, but it was not as good as a moment of study. Once I stood on tiptoe to gaze into the distance, but it was not as good as climbing to a high place to get a broad view. Climbing to a high place and waving will not make your arm any longer, but you can be seen from farther away. Shouting down the wind will give your voice no added urgency, but you can be heard more distinctly. By borrowing a horse and carriage you will not improve your feet, but you can cover a thousand *li*. By borrowing a boat and paddles you will not improve your ability in water, but you can cross rivers and seas. The noble person is by birth no different from others, but he is good at borrowing from external things.

In the southern regions there is a bird called the *meng* dove. It makes its nest out of feathers woven together with hair and suspends it from the tips of the reeds. When the wind comes, the reeds break, the eggs are smashed, and the young are killed. This is not because the nest is wanting but, rather, because of the way it is attached. In the west there is a tree called the *yegan*. Its trunk is four inches tall, and it grows on top of high mountains, looking down into chasms a hundred fathoms deep. This is not because the tree's trunk is able to grow but, rather, because of the place where it stands. If raspberry vines grow in the midst of hemp, they will stand up straight without being staked; if white sand is mixed with mud, it too will turn black. If the root of the orchid and the rhizome of the valerian are soaked in the water used to wash rice,[55] the noble person will not go near them, and the commoner will not wear them — not because their substance is not beautiful but because of what they have been soaked in. Therefore the noble person will choose with care the place where he will reside, and will be accompanied by scholars when he travels. In this way he avoids depravity and meanness and approaches centrality and correctness.

Accumulate earth to make a mountain, and wind and rain will flourish there. Accumulate water to make a deep pool, and dragons will be born from it. Accumulate goodness to create virtue, and spiritual clarity will naturally be acquired; there the mind of the sage will be fully realized. Thus if you do not accumulate little steps, you will not have the means to journey a thousand *li*, and if you do not pile up small streams, you will have no way to fill a river or a sea. Though a thoroughbred like Qiji cannot cover ten paces in one leap, the sorriest nag can do it in ten yokings. Achievement consists of never giving up.

If you start carving, and then give up, you cannot even cut through a piece of rotten wood; but if you persist without stopping, you can carve and inlay metal or stone. Earthworms lack the power of sharp claws or teeth, or strong muscles or bones, yet above ground they feast on the mud, and below they drink

---

55. Following the reconstruction proposed by John Knoblock in *Xunzi — A Translation and Study of the Complete Works*, vol. 1, pp. 137, 268–69.

at the yellow springs. This is because they keep their minds on one thing. Crabs have six legs and two pincers, but unless they can find an empty hole dug by a snake or a water serpent, they have no place to lodge. This is because they allow their minds to go off in all directions. Thus if there is no dark and dogged will, there will be no bright and shining clarity; if there is no dull and determined effort, there will be no brilliant and glorious achievement. One who travels two roads at once will arrive nowhere; one who serves two masters will please neither. . . .

The learning of the noble person enters his ear, is stored in his mind, spreads through his four limbs, and is made visible in his activity and his tranquillity. In his smallest word, in his slightest movement, in everything, he may be taken as a model and a standard. The learning of the lesser man enters his ear and comes out his mouth. With only four inches between ear and mouth, how can he possess it long enough to beautify a seven-foot body? In antiquity learning was carried on for the sake of one's self; today learning is carried on for the sake of others.[56] The learning of the noble person is for the sake of beautifying himself; the learning of the lesser man is offering bird and beast [to win attention from others]. Thus to proffer information when you have not been asked for it is called officiousness; to proffer information on two questions when you have only been asked about one is garrulity. Officiousness is to be condemned, so too is garrulity. The noble person is like an echo.

In learning nothing works so well as to be near a person of learning. The *Rites* and the "Music" provide models but no explanations. The *Odes* and the *Documents* are devoted to antiquity and lack immediacy. The *Spring and Autumn Annals* is laconic and not readily accessible. But following alongside a person of learning and repeating the explanations of the noble person bring one honor everywhere and allow one comprehensive knowledge of the world. Therefore it is said that "In learning nothing works so well as to be near a person of learning."

In the course of learning there is nothing more expedient than to devote yourself to a person of learning, and next to this is to pay homage to the rites. If you can neither devote yourself to a person of learning nor pay homage to the rites, how will you do anything more than learn randomly or passively follow the *Odes* and the *Documents*? In this case you will never to the end of your days escape from being merely a vulgar scholar. If you would take the ancient kings as your source and humaneness and rightness as your foundation, then rites are the means of correctly ordering warp and woof, pathways and byways. . . .

One who misses one shot in a hundred does not deserve to be called a good

---

56. Quoting *Analects* 14:25. A similar idea is found in *Mencius* 4B:14. The idea is that learning is properly dedicated to self-improvement but often distorted in the interests of impressing others.

archer; one who does not take the last half step in a journey of a thousand *li* does not deserve to be called a good carriage driver; one who does not comprehend moral relationships and categories and does not become one with humaneness and rightness does not deserve to be called good in learning. Surely learning is learning to unify oneself. Someone who on departing does one thing and on entering does another is a person of the roads and alleys; one who does a small amount of good and much that is not good is a Jie or Zhou or Robber Zhi. Complete it, realize it to the fullest — only then will you be learned.

The noble person knows that what is not complete or what is not pure is unworthy to be called beautiful. Therefore he recites and reiterates so as to integrate it, reflects and ponders so as to comprehend it, determines his associations so that he may dwell in it, and eliminates what is harmful in order to preserve and nourish it. He causes his eyes to be devoid of any desire to see what is not right, his ears to be devoid of any desire to hear what is not right, his mouth to be devoid of any desire to say what is not right, and his mind to be devoid of any desire to think what is not right. Having arrived at this, he takes utmost pleasure in it. His eyes will take greater pleasure in it than in the five colors; his ears will take greater pleasure in it than in the five sounds; his mouth will take greater pleasure in it than in the five flavors; and his mind will benefit more from it than from possession of the world.[57] Therefore he cannot be subverted by power or profit, nor swayed by the masses and multitudes, nor unsettled by the whole world. He follows this in life; he follows it in death — this is what is called holding firm to inner power. He who holds firm to inner power is able to order himself; being able to order himself, he can then respond to others. He who is able to order himself and respond to others is called the complete man. Heaven manifests itself in its brightness; earth manifests itself in its breadth; the noble person values his completeness.

["Quanxue," *Xunzi yinde*, 1–2 — IB]

CHAPTER 2: CULTIVATING ONESELF

Much of early Chinese thought focused on finding the most appropriate method of personal cultivation, and differences concerning the practice as well as the ultimate purpose of self-cultivation became a focus of controversy among contending schools of thought. In this chapter Xunzi dwells on the contrast between the openness and seriousness of the noble person and the shallowness and defensiveness of the inferior person, emphasizing the need to be receptive to constructive criticism. Self-cultivation, for him, is part of a social process, something one works on in the course of interaction with others. He makes a similar point in the passages in which he defends the impor-

---

57. John Knoblock reads this, alternatively, to mean, "his mind benefits from possessing all that is in the world" (*Xunzi*, vol. 1, p. 142).

tance of following the guidance of a teacher and remaining committed to the practice of ritual. In this, Xunzi places himself at a considerable remove from the Daoists. Whereas Mencius spoke of cultivating his "vast, flowing *qi*," and connected this with "accumulated acts of rightness" through which the individual was to become connected with Heaven and Earth, Xunzi, more explicit in his psychology, offers detailed suggestions about ways to "regulate the *qi* and cultivate the mind" in order to achieve a balanced and harmonious personality.

Seeing what is good and cultivating it, one is sure to preserve it within oneself. Seeing what is not good and sorrowing over it, one is sure to search within oneself. Finding good within one's own person and devoting oneself to it, one is sure to love it within oneself; finding what is not good in one's person and despising it, one is sure to hate it within oneself. Therefore those who have good reason to find fault with me are my teachers; those who have good reason to find me praiseworthy are my friends; and those who flatter me do me injury.[58]

Therefore the noble person honors his teachers, feels affection for his friends, but hates those who do him injury. Being untiring in his love of the good, he accepts criticism and is able to take warning from it. Even if he were not prompted by the desire to advance, how could he do otherwise?

The lesser man is just the opposite. He is utterly chaotic, yet hates others to find him in the wrong; he is altogether worthless, yet desires others to find him worthy. With a heart like that of tigers and wolves and conduct like that of birds and beasts, he nonetheless hates those who do him injury. He is affectionate toward flatterers but aloof from those who would admonish and reprove him. He finds cultivating uprightness to be laughable and the utmost loyalty to be injurious. Although he may desire to avoid ruin and destruction, how can he do so? . . .

The proper way to regulate the *qi* and cultivate the mind: With a temperament that is too strong and vigorous, soften it with balance and harmony. With an intellect that is too penetrating and deep, unify it with mildness and geniality. Given courage and daring that are too violent and fierce, be guided by obedience to the Way. Given a mind that is too quick and speech that is too glib, regulate them through activity and repose. What has become narrow and constrained, broaden with liberality and magnanimity. What has become base and low due to greed for gain, raise up with high resolve. What has become ordinary, common, enervated, and unfocused, relieve with the help of teachers and friends. Respond to negligence, lassitude, levity, and heedlessness with the prospect of imminent disaster. Complement simpleminded loyalty and sober correctness with rites and music. . . . Of all the ways to regulate the *qi* and cultivate the mind, none is more direct than to follow ritual, none more essential than

---

58. Literally, "play the thief toward me." Mencius uses the same image; see *Mencius* 2A:6, 4A:1, 6A:1, etc.

to find a teacher, none more spiritual than to love one thing alone. This is what is called the method of regulating the *qi* and cultivating the mind.

If one's will and intentions are cultivated, one may feel pride before wealth and eminence; if one has respect for the Way and rightness, one may have small regard for kings and dukes. Search within yourself, and you may look lightly on external things. A tradition has it, "The noble person uses things; the lesser man is used by things." Though it means labor for the body, if the mind finds peace in it, do it. Though the profit in it may be small, if there is much rightness in it, do it. Finding success in the service of a chaotic ruler is not as good as following the right in the service of an impoverished one. Therefore a good farmer does not stop plowing because of flood or drought; a good merchant does not give up going to market because of occasional losses; the scholar and the noble person do not neglect the Way because of hardship and poverty. . . .

Ritual is the means by which one's person is rectified; the teacher is the means by which ritual is rectified. Without ritual, how can you rectify yourself? Without a teacher, how can you know which ritual is correct? By behaving according to ritual, your emotions will find peace in ritual. By speaking as your teacher speaks, your understanding becomes like that of your teacher. When your emotions find peace in ritual and your understanding is like that of your teacher, then you have become a sage. Therefore, to reject ritual is to be without a guide, and to renounce one's teacher is to be without a teacher. Not to approve of a teacher and a guide, preferring to do everything your own way, is like relying on a blind man trying to distinguish colors or a deaf man, tones. There is no way to put aside chaos and confusion. Therefore learning means regarding ritual as your guide. The teacher takes his own person as the standard of proper conduct and values that in himself which is at peace.

["Xiushen," *Xunzi yinde*, 3–5 — IB]

CHAPTER 9: THE REGULATIONS OF THE KING

The following selection reveals several of the characteristic features of Xunzi's political thought, including his concern with ranks and social distinctions and with what in modern parlance might be called the management of human resources. In a sense he may be described as a realist in politics. Whereas Mencius refused to talk about a lord-protector or hegemon, being willing only to talk about the ideal way of a true king, Xunzi undertakes to describe the different styles of government suitable to a "man who understands force," a lord-protector, and a true king. At the same time it is clear that he, no less than Mencius, believes that the humaneness and rightness of the true king give him an unassailable authority and an ability to compel the allegiance of others. In the final passage in this selection Xunzi speaks of the noble person "providing the patterns for Heaven and Earth" and "forming a triad with Heaven and Earth," a theme he takes up again in his chapter "A Discussion of Heaven."

Someone inquired about the conduct of government. I replied: In the case of the worthy and capable, promote them without regard to the established order. In the case of the inept and incompetent, dismiss them without hesitation. In the case of the fundamentally evil, punish them without trying to instruct them.[59] In the case of ordinary people, transform them without waiting to rectify them.

Even before social distinctions have been fixed, there will still be [such basic distinctions as] the one between the left and the right ancestors in the mortuary temple.[60] Although they may be descendants of kings, dukes, men of service, or grand officers, if they are unable to adhere to the rites and to moral principles, they should be consigned to the ranks of the commoners. Although they may be the descendants of commoners, if they have acquired culture and learning, are upright in their personal conduct, and are able to adhere to the rites and moral principles, they should be assigned to the ranks of prime minister, men of service, or high court officials. Therefore, with those whose words are wanton, whose theories are wanton, or whose undertakings are wanton, and whose talents are wanton, with people given to avoidance and evasion, employ them and teach them. Wait for a while, encouraging them with rewards and disciplining them with punishments. If they perform their work with ease, then accept them as subjects; if they do not perform their work with ease, cast them out. In the case of those who have one of the Five Defects,[61] raise them up, gather them together, nurture them, and give them work according to their capacities. Employ them, provide them with clothing and food, and take care to see that none are left out. If anyone is found acting or using his talents to work against the good of the time, condemn him to death without mercy. This is what is called the power of Heaven and the government of a king. . . .

Where ranks in society are equal, there will not be proper distinctions; where power is equally distributed, there will be no unity; when the masses are on the

---

59. There has been discussion of whether Xunzi is actually referring here to incorrigible evil. As Burton Watson observes, this "seems to contradict the rest of Xunzi's philosophy and is rare in early Confucian thought as a whole" (*Hsün Tzu: Basic Writings*, p. 33). Still, as Watson notes, Xunzi does refer to this elsewhere, as in section 18 ("Rectifying Theses"), "where he argues that the existence of a very few such perverse and unteachable men even in the time of a sage ruler is not to be taken as evidence that the ruler himself is at fault."

60. The mortuary temple of the founder of a noble family occupied the central position, with the temples of his descendants in the second, fourth, and sixth generations arranged to the left and called *zhao*, and those of descendants in the third, fifth, and seventh generations arranged to the right and called *mu*. Here Xunzi refers to the kind of distinction that, to him, seems prior to other social arrangements.

61. The category is defined differently by different commentators. One list includes those who are mute, deaf, crippled, missing an arm or leg, or dwarfed. Another includes the blind rather than the mute.

same level, it will be impossible to employ them. That there is Heaven and there is Earth shows that there are differences of higher and lower, but it is only after an enlightened king is established that the state is managed on the basis of regulations. Two men of equal eminence cannot serve one other; two men of equally humble station cannot employ one other. This is the rule of Heaven. When power and position are equally distributed, likes and dislikes are the same, and there are not enough goods to allow satisfaction, there will inevitably be contention. Contention must lead to chaos, and chaos to impoverishment. The former kings abhorred chaos, and therefore they established rites and morality so as to bring about ranks. They created sufficient distinctions between rich and poor, eminent and humble, such that it was possible to bring people together and supervise them. This is the basis on which the people of the world are nourished. It says in the *Classic of Documents*, "There can be equality only where there is inequality."....[62]

One who understands the way to use force does not rely upon force. Rather, he considers how to utilize the king's mandate in order to perfect his strength and consolidate his inner power. When his strength is perfected, the several lords cannot weaken him; with his inner power consolidated, the lords cannot remove him. If there should be no true king or lord-protector in the world, he will always be victorious. This is the way of one who understands the way to use force.

The lord-protector is not like this. He opens up wilderness lands for cultivation, fills the granaries and storehouses, and makes provision for necessities. He is careful in recruiting and selecting officials, employing scholars of talent and ability and thereafter gradually bestowing rewards and commendation in order to encourage them or strictly applying penalties and punishments in order to correct them. He preserves those faced with destruction and sustains those threatened with extinction; he protects the weak and prohibits aggression. If he is not minded to annex the territories of his neighbors, then the several lords will draw close to him. If he follows a way of treating them as friends and equals and is respectful in his dealings with them, the lords will be pleased with him. He becomes intimate with them by not attempting to annex their territory, but if he shows any inclination to annex their territory, they will turn away from him. He causes them to be pleased by treating them as friends and equals, but if he should treat them as subjects, they will depart from him. Therefore he makes clear through his actions that he does not intend to annex their territories, and he inspires confidence in them through his way of treating them as friends

---

62. Xunzi's intent here is not entirely clear; however, it does seem to differ from the purport of his source, the *Lüxing* or "The Code of Marquis Lü," in the *Classic of Documents*, where the phrase has a quite different meaning.

and equals. If there is no true king in the world, he will always be victorious. This is the way of one who understands how to be a lord-protector. . . .

A true king is not like this. His humaneness is the loftiest in the world, his rightness is the loftiest in the world, and his authority is the loftiest in the world. Since his humaneness is the loftiest in the world, there is no one in the world who does not draw close to him. Since his rightness is the loftiest in the world, there is no one who does not respect him. Since his authority is the loftiest in the world, there is no one who dares to oppose him. With an authority that cannot be opposed and a way that compels the allegiance of others, he gains victory without battle and attains his objectives without attack. Without his wearing out his arms and men, the whole world submits to him. This is the way of one who understands how to be a king. One who understands all three of these ways may, if he wishes to be a king, become a king; if he wishes to be a lord-protector, become a lord-protector; or, if he wishes to be a man of force, become a man of force. . . .

On the model of a king: He fixes the several rates of taxation, regulates affairs, and utilizes the myriad things in order to nourish the myriad people. From the product of the fields, the tax rate is one part in ten. At the barriers and in the marketplaces, goods are inspected, but no tax is imposed. The mountains and forests, marshes and weirs, are closed or opened according to the season, but taxes are not levied. Land is inspected for its quality, and taxes are differentially assessed. The distance over which goods must be transported is taken into account in fixing tribute payments. The circulation of resources and grain is unimpeded, allowing them to be offered and exchanged so that "all within the four seas are like one family." Therefore those who are close do not hide their abilities, and those who are distant do not resent their labors. Nowhere in the state, in however secluded or remote a place, are there any who do not hasten to serve him or who do not find peace and joy in him. This is called being a leader of the people. This is the model of a king. . . .

From general categories one moves to the particular; from unity one moves to multiplicity. In beginnings there are endings; in endings there are beginnings; it is like a circle with no starting point. Lose hold of this, and the empire will fall into decline. Heaven and Earth are the beginning of life; rites and rightness are the beginning of order; and the noble person is the beginning of rites and rightness. Enacting them, practicing them, accumulating them, and loving them more than anything else — this is the beginning of the noble person. Therefore Heaven and Earth produce the noble person, and the noble person provides the patterns for Heaven and Earth. The noble person forms a triad with Heaven and Earth: he is the agent of the myriad things, father and mother of the people. Without the noble person, there would be no patterns in Heaven and Earth, no continuity in the rites and rightness, no ruler or leader above, no father or son below. This is what is called utmost chaos.

The relationships between ruler and subject, father and son, elder and younger brother, and husband and wife begin and are carried through to the end; in ending they begin again. They share the same pattern as Heaven and Earth and endure in the same way for ten thousand generations. This is what is called the great basis.

["Wangzhi," *Xunzi yinde*, 25–28 — IB]

CHAPTER 17: A DISCUSSION OF HEAVEN

In translating this selection we have in most instances retained the translation "Heaven" for the Chinese word *tian*, even while recognizing that at many points we would come much closer to Xunzi's understanding of the concept were we to render it as "Nature." Actually neither "Heaven" nor "Nature" fully expresses the meaning of *tian*, which has a variety of senses, including the sky, weather, the natural order, and also a moral order. Uses of the word also varied over time and among different filiations or schools of thought. From at least as far back as the early Zhou period, when the idea of the Mandate of Heaven assumed such powerful political and moral significance, the relation of the human world to Heaven or the natural order was a central concern of Chinese thought. Over the course of centuries a number of crucial issues arose, including how *tian* should be conceptualized, how it might intervene in human affairs, and how its imperative or will might be discovered.

Here Xunzi represents *tian* as a natural order, operating according to unchanging principles, not intervening in extraordinary ways in human affairs but, rather, providing the context within which all living things exist. Against those, like Zhuangzi, who seemed to overemphasize the natural order and deemphasize the role of the human, Xunzi reverses the argument: Heaven, Earth, and human beings exist in a relationship of complementarity; human beings should neither encroach on the work of Heaven nor neglect their own. Against believers in a variety of superstitions that depicted unusual events as signs or portents indicating intervention by Heaven in the human sphere, he makes a similar point: human beings must recognize that they themselves are in control of their own affairs. Heaven's ways, being constant, do not vary in accordance with changes in human government, so that what matters in ensuring human prosperity and well-being is human effort. Xunzi's assertion that in recognizing the complementary relationship among the three spheres human beings are able to "form a triad with Heaven and Earth" became one of the seminal ideas in Confucian cosmological and ethical thought.

The processes of Heaven are constant, neither prevailing because of Yao nor perishing because of Jie. Respond to them with order, and good fortune will result; respond to them with chaos, and misfortune will result. If you strengthen what is basic and are frugal in your expenditures, then Heaven cannot make you poor. If you nourish and provide for the people, acting in accordance with the seasons, then Heaven cannot cause you to be ill. If you practice the Way and are not of two minds, then Heaven cannot visit calamities on you. Thus flood or drought cannot bring about starvation, heat or cold cannot produce illness, and strange or preternatural events cannot result in misfortune. But if you neglect the basis and are extravagant in your expenditures, then Heaven cannot make you rich. If you are deficient in nourishing and dilatory in your actions, then Heaven cannot make you whole. If you turn your back on the Way and behave recklessly, then Heaven cannot bestow good fortune on you. Thus even before floods or droughts have arrived you starve; even before heat or cold has set in, you grow ill; even when no strange or preternatural events have occurred, you suffer misfortune. The seasons come just as they do in a well-ordered age, but the disasters and calamities that occur show the difference between a well-ordered age and this one. You should not blame Heaven; it is a matter of the way you have followed. Therefore if you can distinguish between the natural and the human you deserve to be called a perfect man.

To bring to completion without acting, to obtain without seeking — this is called the working of Heaven. Thus, although one is profound, he does not contemplate it; although great, he adds nothing to its ability; although clever, he does not attempt to search it out. Hence it is said that he does not contend with Heaven for its work. Heaven has its seasons; Earth has its resources; man has his government. For this reason it is said that they may form a triad. If one abandons that which allows him to form a triad, yet longs for the triad, he is deluded.

The constellations revolve in an orderly procession, the sun and the moon shine by turns, the four seasons succeed each other, the yin and the yang enact the great transformations, the wind and the rain pass over everything. It is through attaining harmony with Heaven that each of the myriad living things grows, and through obtaining its nourishment that each one comes to completion. Not seeing its operations, yet seeing their result, we call it "spiritual." Everyone realizes how completion has come about, yet no one understands its formlessness, and so we call it "natural" (or "heavenly"). Only the sage acts without seeking to understand Heaven.

When the work of Heaven has been established and the achievements of Heaven brought to completion, the form is made whole, and the spirit is born. The love and hate, delight and anger, sorrow and joy that are stored there are called Heaven-endowed (or natural) feelings. Ears, eyes, nose, mouth, and body each have perceptions that do not share the same competencies, and these are called Heaven-endowed (or natural) faculties. The mind-and-heart dwells in the vacuity at the center and governs the five faculties, and thus it is called the Heavenly (or natural) lord. Material resources that are not of the same species are used to nourish the [human] species, and these are called Heaven's nourishment. Acting in accord with what is proper to the species is called felicitous, while acting in defiance of what is proper to the species is called calamitous, and this is called Heaven's rule. To darken the Heavenly lord, disorder the Heavenly faculties, abandon Heaven's nourishment, contravene Heaven's rule, repudiate the Heavenly feelings, and thereby destroy Heaven's accomplishments is called great misfortune. The sage, by purifying the Heavenly lord, rectifying the Heavenly faculties, cherishing Heaven's nourishment, acting in accord with Heaven's rule, and nourishing the Heavenly feelings, perfects the accomplishments of Heaven. In this way he understands what is to be done and what is not to be done, so that Heaven and the Earth hold office and all things are made to serve him. His actions are wholly ordered; his nourishing is wholly appropriate; his life is free from injury. This is called understanding Heaven. Thus the greatest skill lies in what is not done, the greatest wisdom in what is not pondered.

In regard to Heaven, his thoughts are fixed solely on what the images he has perceived enable him to anticipate. In regard to Earth, his thoughts are fixed solely on what the rightness he has recognized allows him to utilize. In regard to the four seasons, his thoughts are fixed solely on how the measurements he has made enable him to carry out his undertakings. In regard to yin and yang, his thoughts are fixed solely on how what he has understood permits him to bring about order. The experts concern themselves with Heaven; he concerns himself with the Way.

Are order and chaos determined by Heaven? I say, the sun and moon, the stars and constellations revolved in the same way in the time of Yu and in the time of Jie. Yu achieved order thereby; Jie brought disorder. Order and chaos are not determined by Heaven. Are they determined by the seasons? I reply, the crops sprout and grow in spring and summer and are harvested and stored away in autumn and winter. This was also the same under both Yu and Jie. Yu achieved order thereby; Jie brought disorder. Order and disorder are not determined by the seasons. Are they determined by the land? I reply, by acquiring land, one lives; in losing it, one dies. This was the same in the time of Yu and in the time of Jie. Yu achieved order thereby; Jie brought disorder. Order and disorder are not due to the land. This is what the Ode means when it says:

> Heaven made a high mountain
> King Tai opened it up.
> He began the work.
> King Wen dwelt there in peace.[63]

Heaven does not revoke the winter because people dislike cold; the earth does not reduce its expanse because people dislike great distances; the noble person does not refrain from acting because lesser persons create clamor and

---

63. Ode 270. The point here is that it is human effort, and not the intervention of Heaven, that has made the difference.

tumult. Heaven has its constant Way; Earth has its constant measurements; the noble person has his constant substance. The noble person follows what is constant; the petty person calculates his achievements. . . .

The king of Chu has a retinue of a thousand chariots, but this is not because he is wise. The noble person eats pulse and drinks water, but this is not because he is foolish. Both are due to the rhythms of circumstance.[64] To be refined in purpose, rich in virtuous action, and clear in understanding; to live in the present and be intent on the past — these are the things that are within my power. Therefore the noble person cherishes what is within his competence and does not long for what is within the competence of Heaven alone. The lesser person neglects what is within his competence and longs for what is within the competence of Heaven. Because the noble person cherishes what is within his competence and does not long for what is within the competence of Heaven, he goes forward day by day. Because the lesser person sets aside what is within his competence and longs for what is within the competence of Heaven, he goes backward day by day. Therefore what causes the noble person to go forward day by day and the lesser person to go backward is the same; what sets the two apart lies in this alone.

When stars fall or trees groan, all the people in the state are frightened and ask, What does this mean? I reply, There is no meaning. It is just that, with the changes in Heaven and Earth and the transformations of yin and yang, such things occur from time to time. While it is all right to wonder about them, it is wrong to be frightened by them. Eclipses of the sun or the moon, the untimely coming of wind or rain, the appearance of strange stars — there has never been an age when such events have not occurred. If the one above is enlightened, and his government is just, then even if such events occur simultaneously, no harm will come of it. If the ruler is benighted and his government is reckless, then even if no such event occurs, no good will come of it. Now stars falling and trees groaning are the changes of Heaven and Earth and the transformations of yin and yang. Such things occur from time to time. While it is all right to wonder about them, it is wrong to be frightened of them.

When such events do occur, the ones to be feared are human portents. When the plowing is poorly done so that the crops suffer, when the weeding is badly done so that the harvest fails; when the government is reckless and the people are lost; when the fields are neglected and the crops badly tended; when grain is sold dear and the people are starving; when there are people dying on the roads — these are what is called human portents. When the orders of the government are unenlightened, when population levies are undertaken at the wrong season, and the basic matter[65] is not properly ordered — these are called

---

64. Following the reading of Robert Eno in *The Confucian Creation of Heaven*, p. 167.
65. I.e., agriculture.

human portents. When ritual and rightness are not cultivated, private and public affairs are not properly distinguished, and men and women mingle wantonly, so that fathers and sons doubt each other; when superior and inferior are opposed, and bandits and thieves arrive at once — these are called human portents. Portents such as these are born from chaos, and if all three types occur at once the state will know no peace. The explanation for their occurrence may be found close by; the injury they cause is most grievous. . . .

If you perform the sacrifice for rain, and it rains, what does that mean? I reply, there is no meaning. It is as though the sacrifice for rain had not been performed and yet it rained anyway. The sun or the moon is eclipsed, and one "saves" it; a drought occurs, and the rain sacrifice is performed; only after divination has been carried out is a decision taken on a matter of great consequence. These actions are performed not as a means of achieving some result but as a means of ornament. Therefore the noble person regards them as ornaments, while the common people regard them as supernatural. To consider them as ornaments is fortunate; to consider them as supernatural is unfortunate. . . .

> Exalt Heaven and contemplate it?
> Better to nourish its creatures and regulate them.
> Follow Heaven and sing hymns to it?
> Better to determine Heaven's mandate and utilize it.
> Look forward to the seasons and attend them?
> Better to respond to the seasons and employ them.
> Follow along with things and cause them to multiply?
> Better to quicken their capacities and transform them.
> Contemplate things but regard them as external to you?
> Better to provide a pattern for things and not lose them.
> Long for the source from which things are born?
> Better to have the means to bring them to completion.

Therefore if you set aside what belongs to the human and contemplate what belongs to Heaven, you miss the genuine realities of all things.

["Luntian, *Xunzi yinde*, 62–64 — IB]

CHAPTER 19: A DISCUSSION OF RITES

Ritual is at the heart of Xunzi's version of Confucian thought. The following selection affords an illustration of how his highly practical orientation and his aesthetic concerns are blended.

What is the origin of rites? I reply, human beings are born with desires, and when they do not achieve their desires, they cannot but seek the means to do so. If their seeking knows no limit or degree, they cannot but contend with one another. With contention comes chaos, and with chaos comes exhaustion. The ancient kings hated chaos and therefore established rites and rightness in order to limit it, to nurture people's desires, and to give them a means of satisfaction. They saw to it that desires did not exhaust material things and that material things did not fall short of desires. Thus both desires and things were supported and satisfied, and this was the origin of rites. . . .

Rites have three roots. Heaven and Earth are the root of life, the ancestors are the root of the human species, and rulers and teachers are the root of order. If there were no Heaven and Earth, how could there be life? If there were no ancestors, how could there be begetting? If there were no rulers and teachers, how could there be order? If even one of these were lacking, human beings would have no peace. Thus rites serve Heaven above and Earth below; they honor ancestors; they exalt rulers and teachers. These are the three roots of rites. . . .

Rites always begin in coarseness, are completed in forms, and end in joy. Thus in their most perfected state both emotion and the forms are fully realized; in the next state, emotions and forms prevail by turns; and in the lowest state, everything returns to emotion and reverts to a great unity.

> Heaven and Earth find harmony,
> The sun and moon become bright,
> The four seasons follow in order,
> The stars and constellations move,
> The rivers and streams flow,
> And all things flourish.
> Likes and dislikes are regulated;
> Joys and hates are made appropriate.

Those below are compliant; those above are enlightened; the myriad things change but do not become chaotic. One who turns his back upon rites will be lost. Are rites not perfect? When they have been properly established and brought to the ultimate point, no one in the world can add to or subtract from them. Root and branch are put in proper order; beginning and end are correlated; distinctions are expressed through the most elegant forms; explanations derive from the utmost discernment. Those in the world who follow the rites will be orderly; those who do not follow them will be chaotic. Those who follow them will be at peace; those who do not follow them will be in danger. Those who follow them will be preserved; those who turn against them will perish. This is something that the lesser person cannot comprehend.

The principle of the rites is truly deep. Discriminations of hard and white, same and different,[66] enter there and drown. The principle of the rites is truly

---

66. Referring to the Mohist logicians and to the dialecticians such as Hui Shi and Gongsun Long.

great. Crass and vulgar theories on wielding authority and exerting control enter there and perish. The principle of the rites is truly lofty. Contumelious arrogance, haughty disdain, and the contempt for common customs that presumes one's own superiority to ordinary people[67] enter there and are brought low. . . .

Rites are most strict in the ordering of birth and death. Birth is the beginning of a human being; death is his end. When both beginning and end are good, the human way is complete. Therefore the noble person is reverential toward the beginning and watchful over the end, so that beginning and end are as one. This is the way of the noble person; this is the refinement of rites and rightness. To be generous in the treatment of the living but miserly in the treatment of the dead is to show reverence for a being who has consciousness and contempt for one who lacks consciousness. This is the way of an evil person and an offense against the heart. The noble person would be ashamed to treat a bondservant in a way that offends the heart; how much more ashamed would he be to treat those whom he honors and loves in such a way!

Because the rites of the dead can be performed only once for each individual, and never again, they provide the final occasion at which the subject may express the utmost respect for his ruler, and the son may express the utmost respect for his parents. Therefore to serve the living without loyalty and generosity, or without reverence and good form, is called rudeness, and to send off the dead without loyalty and generosity, or without reverence and good form, is called miserliness. The noble person disdains rudeness and is ashamed of miserliness. . . .

Rites contract what is too long and expand what is too short, reducing excesses and repairing deficiencies, pervading the forms of love and reverence and enlivening the beauties of right conduct. Therefore, while refined beauty and coarse ugliness, joyful music and mournful weeping, calm contentment and anxious grief are opposites, rites bring them together and make use of them, eliciting and employing each in due course. Therefore, refined beauty, joyful music, and calm contentment serve to induce an attitude of tranquillity and are employed on auspicious occasions. Coarse ugliness, mournful weeping, and anxious grief induce an attitude of inquietude and are employed on inauspicious occasions. Therefore when refined beauty is utilized, it should never reach the point of shallowness or sensuality, and when coarse ugliness is utilized, it should never lead to the point of starvation or self-abandonment. When joyful music and calm contentment are utilized, they should never lead to profligacy or indolence, and though mournful weeping and anxious grief are utilized, they should never lead to faintheartedness or injury to life. If this is done, then rites will achieve the middle state. . . .

---

67. Possibly referring to the followers of Prince Mou of Wei, a contemporary of Xunzi's known for his hedonism.

It is always true that rites, when they serve the living, are an adornment to joy, and when they serve the dead, an adornment to grief. In sacrifices they are an adornment to reverence, and in military affairs, an adornment to authority. This was the same for the rites of the hundred kings; it is what unites antiquity and the present. The source for this we do not know. . . .

Sacrificial rites give expression to the feelings of remembrance and longing for the dead. There inevitably come times when one is overwhelmed by emotions of grief and loss, and a loyal minister or a filial son finds that, even while others are given to the enjoyment of congenial company, these sorrowful emotions arrive. If when they come to him, and he is greatly moved, he nonetheless represses them, his feelings of remembrance and longing will be thwarted and unfulfilled, and his ritual practice will be deficient and incomplete. Therefore the ancient kings established certain forms so that the duty of honoring those who deserve honor and demonstrating affection for those who deserve affection might be fulfilled. Therefore I say that the sacrificial rites give expression to the feelings of remembrance and longing. They are the perfection of loyalty, good faith, love, and reverence, and the flourishing of ritual deportment and refined demeanor. Only the sage can understand them. The sage understands them clearly; the man of service and the noble person are content to carry them out; the officials are careful to maintain them; and the hundred names accept them as established custom. The noble person understands them as the human way; the hundred names think of them as matters having to do with spirits.

["Lilun," *Xunzi yinde*, 70–75 – IB]

CHAPTER 21: DISPELLING OBSCURATION

The following selection illustrates the thorough integration — or perhaps more aptly, the nonseparation — of psychological, ethical, spiritual, and political elements in Xunzi's thought.

A common human defect is to be in the dark about great principles because one's mind is obscured by a single detail. If one can control this, one can return to correct standards, but if one continues to be of two minds, one will become deluded. There are no two Ways in the world, nor is the sage of two minds.

At present the several lords have different theories of government and the hundred schools of thought have different doctrines. Inevitably some will be right and others, wrong; some will be conducive to order and others, to chaos. Even the ruler of a chaotic state or the follower of a chaotic school is bound with a sincere mind to seek what is proper and to try to better his condition. But he is jealous and misguided about the Way and deflected from his course by other people. He is partial to his own familiar ways and only fears to hear some ill spoken of them; he relies on what is familiar to him, and when he encounters a different theory, he only fears to hear it praised. This is how he moves further away from an ordered state, without ceasing to think that he is in the right. Isn't this what it means to be blinded by a partial truth and to fail in the search for what is right? . . .

What are the causes of obscuration? Desires may cause obscuration; so too may hates. Obscuration may be brought about by the beginnings of things or by the ends, by those far away or by those close by, by breadth or by shallowness, by the past or by the present. Whenever one dwells on the differences among the myriad things, all such differences become causes of obscuration. This is a common failing in the exercise of the mind. . . .

How does one understand the Way? I reply, through the mind. And how can the mind understand it? I reply, because it is empty, unified, and still. The mind is always storing things, and yet it is said to be empty. The mind is always marked by diversity, and yet it is said to be unified. The mind is always moving, and yet it is said to be still. Human beings are born with awareness, and when there is awareness there is memory. To remember is to store, and yet the mind is said to be empty because what has already been stored in it does not impede what is about to be received. From birth the mind has awareness, and where there is awareness there is consciousness of differences. Consciousness of differences means that one is aware of different things simultaneously, and when one is aware of different things simultaneously, there is duality. Yet the mind is said to be unified. Because it does not allow one thing to interfere with another it is said to be unified. When the mind is asleep, one dreams; when it is unoccupied, it moves on its own and, if one allows it to do so, it will make plans. Thus the mind is constantly moving, and yet it is said to be still because it does not allow these dreams and imaginings to disorder its understanding. Therefore it is said to be still. . . . Being empty, unified, and still is called great and pure enlightenment.

Of the myriad beings, there are none that have form and yet are not seen, none that are seen and yet are not understood, none that are understood and yet not accorded their proper place. One may sit in a room and see everything within the four seas; one may dwell in the present and discuss the most remote ages. One has a trenchant view of the myriad beings and knows their genuine tendencies; one inquires into the phenomena of order and disorder and has insight into the rules that govern them. One perceives the warp and woof of Heaven and Earth, exerts mastery and authority over the myriad things, regulates and controls the great principle and all that is in the universe. Broad, vast — who knows his limits? Expansive, magnanimous — who knows his inner power? Permutable and prolific — who knows his form? His brightness matches the sun and moon; his greatness fills the eight directions. He is called the great person. How could he have any obscuration?

The mind is the ruler of the body and the master of its spiritual intelligence. It gives commands, but does not receive them. Of itself it prevents or enables, seizes or selects, moves or stops. Thus the mouth can be compelled to be silent or to speak; the body can be compelled to contract or to extend itself, but the mind cannot be made to change its intentions. What it considers right it will accept; what it considers wrong it will reject. Therefore we say of the mind that its choices are subject to no prohibitions. And though, inevitably, the things it sees for itself are numerous and diverse, the feelings that come to it will not be divided. . . .

Something of a given category can admit no duality. Thus the wise person chooses one thing and finds unity in it. The farmer is skilled in the work of the fields, but he cannot become a director of agriculture. The merchant is skilled in the ways of the market, but he cannot become a director of commerce. The artisan is skilled in the use of tools, but he cannot become a director of crafts. There are those who are able to do none of these three things, yet they may control these three offices. Therefore one says that they are skilled in the Way. He who is skilled with things will treat each thing as a particular thing. He who is skilled in the Way will consider things together. Therefore the noble person, having found unity in the Way, examines things and compares them. Through having found unity in the Way, he becomes correct. Through examining things and comparing them, he becomes clear. Through carrying out investigations based upon correct intentions, he is able to be the director of all things. In ancient times when Shun governed the world he did not issue proclamations concerning each matter, and yet all things were brought to completion. He dwelt in a single attitude of fearful caution, and his glory became complete. He nourished an attitude of subtle watchfulness and achieved a glory that was not understood. Hence the *Classic of the Way*[68] says, "The human mind is fearful; the mind of Dao is subtle." Only a noble person possessed of enlightenment can know the hidden power of fearfulness and subtlety.

["Jiebi," *Xunzi yinde*, 78, 80–81 — IB]

CHAPTER 23: HUMAN NATURE IS EVIL

Human nature is evil; its goodness derives from conscious activity. Now it is human nature to be born with a fondness for profit. Indulging this leads to contention and strife, and the sense of modesty and yielding with which one was born disappears. One is born with feelings of envy and hate, and, by indulging these, one is led into banditry and theft, so that the sense of loyalty and good faith with which he was born disappears. One is born with the desires of the ears and eyes and with a fondness for beautiful sights and sounds, and, by indulging these, one is led to licentiousness and chaos, so that the sense of

---

68. This work is unknown. A similar phrase is found in the "Plan of the Great Yu" in the *Classic of Documents*.

ritual, rightness, refinement, and principle with which one was born is lost. Hence, following human nature and indulging human emotions will inevitably lead to contention and strife, causing one to rebel against one's proper duty, reduce principle to chaos, and revert to violence. Therefore one must be transformed by the example of a teacher and guided by the way of ritual and rightness before one will attain modesty and yielding, accord with refinement and ritual, and return to order. From this perspective it is apparent that human nature is evil and that its goodness is the result of conscious activity.

Thus warped wood must be laid against a straightening board, steamed, and bent into shape before it can become straight; blunt metal must be ground on a whetstone before it can become sharp. And in that human nature is evil, it must wait for the example of a teacher before it can become upright, and for ritual and rightness before it can become orderly. Now, if people lack the example of teachers they will be partial and narrow rather than upright; if they lack ritual and rightness they will be rebellious and chaotic rather than orderly. In ancient times the sage kings, recognizing that the nature of human beings is evil — that they incline toward evil and are not upright, that they are disposed toward chaos and are not orderly — created ritual and rightness and established models and limits in order to reform and improve the human emotional nature and make it upright, in order to train and transform the human emotional nature and provide it with a guide. They caused them to attain order and to conform to the Way. And so today a person who is transformed by the instructions of a teacher, devotes himself to study, and abides by ritual and rightness may become a noble person, while one who follows his nature and emotions, is content to give free play to his passions, and abandons ritual and rightness is a lesser person. It is obvious from this, therefore, that human nature is evil, and that its goodness results from conscious activity.

Mencius said, The fact that human beings learn shows that their nature is good. I say this is not so; this comes of his having neither understood human nature nor perceived the distinction between the nature and conscious activity. The nature is what is given by Heaven: one cannot learn it; one cannot acquire it by effort. Ritual and rightness are created by sages: people learn them and are capable, through effort, of bringing them to completion. What cannot be learned or acquired by effort but is within us is called the nature. What can be learned and, through effort, brought to completion is called conscious activity. This is the distinction between the nature and conscious activity. That the eyes can see and the ears can hear is human nature. But the faculty of clear sight does not exist apart from the eye, nor does the faculty of keen hearing exist apart from the ear. It is apparent that the eye's clear vision and the ear's acute hearing cannot be learned.

Mencius said, Now, human nature is good, and [when it is not] this is always a result of having lost or destroyed one's nature. I say that he was mistaken to take such a view. Now, it is human nature that, as soon as a person is born, he departs from his original substance[69] and from his natural disposition, so that he must inevitably lose and destroy them. Seen in this way, it is apparent that human nature is evil. Those who say that the nature is good find beauty in what does not depart from the original substance and value in what does not diverge from the natural disposition. They consider that the beauty of the natural disposition and the original substance and the goodness of the mind's intentions are [inseparable from the nature] in the same way that clear sight is inseparable from the eye and keen hearing is inseparable from the ear. Hence they maintain that [the nature possesses goodness] in the same way that the eye possesses clear vision or the ear possesses keenness of hearing.

Now, it is human nature that when one is hungry he will desire satisfaction, when he is cold he will desire warmth, and when he is weary he will desire rest. This is the emotional nature of human beings. Yet, even if a person is hungry, he will not dare to be the first to eat if he is in the presence of his elders because he knows that he should yield to them. Although he is weary, he will not dare to seek rest because he knows that he should work on behalf of others. For a son to yield to his father and a younger brother to yield to his elder brother, or for a son to work on behalf of his father and a younger brother to work on behalf of his elder brother — these two acts are contrary to the nature and counter to the emotions, and yet they represent the way of filial devotion and the refinement and principle that are associated with ritual and rightness. Hence, to follow the emotional nature would mean that there would be no courtesy or humility; courtesy and humility run counter to the emotional nature. From this perspective it is apparent that human nature is evil, and that goodness is the result of conscious activity. A questioner asks: If human nature is evil, then where do ritual and rightness come from? I reply: ritual and rightness are always created by the conscious activity of the sages; essentially they are not created by human nature. Thus a potter molds clay and makes a vessel, but the vessel is created by the conscious activity of the potter and is not created by his human nature. In the same way a carpenter carves a piece of wood and makes a utensil, but the utensil is created through the conscious activity of the carpenter and is not created by his human nature. A sage gathers his thoughts and reflections, engages in conscious activity, and thus creates ritual and rightness and produces models and regulations. Hence ritual, rightness, models, and limits are created by the conscious activity of the sage and not by his human nature. . . .

When a person desires to do good he always does so because his nature is evil. A person who is shallow aspires to depth; one who is ugly aspires to beauty; one who is narrow aspires to breadth; one who is poor aspires to wealth; one who is humble aspires to esteem. Whatever one lacks in oneself he must seek

---

69. The word Xunzi uses here is *pu*, a term that occurs frequently in the *Daodejing* and is often translated in that context as "the uncarved block."

outside. Therefore if a person is rich, he will not aspire to wealth, and if he is esteemed, he will not long for power. What a person possesses in himself he need not seek outside. One can see from this that the reason human beings desire to do good is that their nature is evil. Now human nature is definitely devoid of ritual and rightness. Therefore, they compel themselves to study and to seek to possess them. The nature knows nothing of ritual and rightness, and therefore they reflect and ponder and seek to understand them. Thus the nature is inborn, that is all, and human beings neither possess ritual and rightness, nor do they understand them. . . .

If human nature were good, we could dispense with the sage kings and desist from the practice of ritual and rightness. Since human nature is evil, we must elevate the sages and esteem ritual and rightness. Therefore the straightening board was created because of warped wood, and the plumb line came into being because of things that are not straight. Rulers are established and ritual and rightness are illuminated because the nature is evil. From this perspective it is clear that human nature is evil and that goodness is the result of conscious activity. Wood that is straight need not wait for the straightening board to become straight; it is straight by nature. But a warped piece of wood must be laid against a straightening board, steamed, and bent into shape before it can become straight because its nature is not straight. Now since human nature is evil, people must await ordering by the sage kings and transformation through ritual and rightness, and only then do they attain order and accord with goodness. From this perspective, it is clear that human nature is evil and that goodness is the result of conscious activity. . . .

Someone may ask whether ritual and rightness and sustained conscious activity are not themselves human nature, which would explain why the sage is able to create them. I reply that this is not the case. A potter may mold clay and produce an earthen pot, but how could molding pots out of clay be the potter's nature? A carpenter may carve wood and produce utensils, but how could carving utensils out of wood be the carpenter's nature? The sage stands in the same relation to ritual and rightness as the potter to the things he molds and produces. How then could ritual and rightness and sustained conscious activity be the original human nature?

In their human nature, Yao and Shun were one with Jie and Zhi, just as the noble person and the lesser person are, by nature, one. How could it be that ritual and rightness and sustained conscious activity are human nature? If this were the case, what reason would there be to honor Yao or Yu or to honor the noble person? People honor Yao, Yu, and the noble person because of their ability to transform their nature, to generate conscious activity, and, through this conscious activity, to create ritual and rightness. Thus the sage necessarily stands in the same relation to ritual and rightness and conscious activity as does the potter to the things he molds and produces. From this perspective, how could it be that ritual and rightness and sustained conscious activity are human nature? The reason people despise Jie, or the lesser person, is that they follow their nature, indulge their emotions, and are content to give free rein to their passions, so that their conduct is marked by greed and contentiousness. Therefore it is clear that human nature is evil and that goodness is the result of conscious activity. . . .

"The man in the street can become a Yu."[70] What does this mean? I reply, What made the sage emperor Yu a Yu was the fact that he practiced humaneness and rightness and took uprightness as his standard. This being so, humaneness, rightness, and proper standards must be based upon principles that can be known and practiced. Any man in the street has the natural endowment needed to understand humaneness, rightness, proper standards, and uprightness and the ability to practice humaneness, rightness, proper standards, and uprightness. Therefore it is clear that he can become a Yu.

Is one to suppose that humaneness, rightness, proper standards, and uprightness are not based upon principles that can be known and practiced? If that were so, then even a Yu could not have understood and practiced them. Is one to suppose that the man in the street does not have the natural endowment needed to understand them or the ability to put them into practice? If that were so, then the man in the street, within his family, could not understand the rightness that pertains between father and son and, without, could not comprehend the correctness that pertains between ruler and subject. But this is not the case. The man in the street, within, can understand the rightness that pertains between father and son and, without, can understand the correctness between ruler and subject. Thus it is clear that he has in him the natural endowment needed to understand and the talent to put them into practice. Now if the man in the street takes this endowment that enables him to know and this talent that enables him to act and applies them to the principles of humaneness and rightness, which are knowable, and the practice of humaneness and rightness, which is practicable, then it is clear that he can become a Yu. If the man in the street applies himself to training and study, concentrates his mind, unifies his will, and pondering and examining things carefully, continues his efforts over a long period of time, accumulating good acts without stop, then he can penetrate to a spiritual understanding and form a triad with Heaven and Earth. The sage is a person who has arrived where he has through the accumulation of good acts.

["Xing'e," *Xunzi yinde*, 86–89 — IB]

THE ZUOZHUAN

There are many mysteries surrounding the text of the *Zuozhuan*, including its authorship and its original form. *Zuozhuan* or *Zuoshi zhuan* means "The Commentary

---

70. This was apparently an old saying. Cf. *Mencius* 6B:2: "Cao Jiao asked, 'Is it true that all human beings are capable of becoming a Yao or a Shun?' Mencius said, 'It is true.'"

of Mr. Zuo," and this Mr. Zuo has often been identified as Zuo Qiuming or Zuoqiu Ming, allegedly a contemporary of Confucius. Actually, however, the identity of the author is unknown. A traditional view of the *Zuozhuan* is that it was written as a commentary on the *Spring and Autumn Annals (Qunqiu)*. As we have seen in chapter 2, the *Annals* was a record of events in various feudal states during the period 722–481 B.C.E. that many Chinese scholars believed to have been edited by Confucius[71] and to contain, in somewhat cryptic form, his profound moral judgments on the events of the past as well as those of his own day and on the relation of human events to those in the natural order. In this view the *Zuozhuan* was like the *Gongyang Commentary* and the *Guliang Commentary*, two other important commentaries on the *Spring and Autumn Annals*, in having been written to clarify — or almost to decode — Confucius's ideas and intentions. While this is possible, it seems more likely in the case of the *Zuozhuan* that it was originally an independent work that was later broken up and attached to the text of the *Annals*. However the work came into being, it has become part of the Confucian canon and has survived as a masterpiece of Chinese prose and one of the most important historical works in a tradition in which the art of history would assume central and abiding importance.

SELECTIONS FROM THE *ZUOZHUAN*

In the following passage Duke Dao of Jin discusses with Shi Kuang, or Music Master Kuang, the forced abdication of Duke Xian, ruler of the neighboring state of Wei. Duke Xian had been driven out of his domain in 559 B.C.E. as a result of his own misrule. Shi Kuang uses the opportunity to speak of the love and concern of Heaven for the common people and to underscore the responsibility of a ruler to devote himself to their well-being and, especially, to heed the remonstrations of his ministers. In this case, however, all levels of society, down to the very lowest, are seen as participating in the process of admonition. Particularly striking is the inclusion of artisans, blind musicians, merchants, and commoners in this picture of a participatory process that does not restrict the counseling function only to the elite.

Duke Xiang, 14th year (559 B.C.E.)

Shi Kuang was attending the ruler of Jin. The latter said, "The people of Wei have driven out their ruler — what a terrible thing!"

Shi Kuang replied, "Perhaps it was the ruler himself who did terrible things. When a good ruler goes about rewarding good and punishing excess, he nourishes his people as if they were his children, shelters them like Heaven, accommodates them like the earth. And when the people serve their ruler, they love him as they do their parents, look up to him like the sun and moon, revere him like the all-seeing spirits, fear him like thunder. How could they drive him out?

---

71. This, at least, was the view of Mencius (see *Mencius* 3B:9) and many later writers.

"The ruler is host to the spirits and the hope of the people. But if he exhausts the people's livelihood, deprives the spirits, skimps in the sacrifices to them, and betrays the hopes of the populace, then he ceases to be the host of the nation's altars of the soil and grain, and what use is he? What can one do but expel him?

"Heaven gave birth to the people and set up rulers to superintend and shepherd them and see to it that they do not lose their true nature as human beings. And because there are rulers, it provided helpers for them who would teach and protect them and see that they do not overstep the bounds. Hence the Son of Heaven has his chief officers, the feudal lords have their ministers, the ministers set up their collateral houses, gentlemen have their friends and companions, and the commoners, artisans, merchants, lackeys, shepherds, and grooms all have their relatives and close associates who help and assist them. If one does good they praise him, if he errs they correct him, if he is in distress they rescue him, if he is lost they restore him.

"Thus from the sovereign on down, each has his father or elder brother, his son or younger brother to assist and scrutinize his ways of management. The historians compile their documents, the blind musicians compose poems, the musicians chant admonitions and remonstrances, the high officials deliver words of correction, the gentlemen pass along remarks, the commoners criticize, the merchants voice their opinions in the market, and the hundred artisans contribute through their skills.

"Hence the 'Documents of Xia' says: 'The herald with his wooden-clappered bell goes about the roads saying, "Let the officials and teachers correct the ruler, let the artisans pursue their skills and thereby offer remonstrance." ' [72] In the first month, the beginning month of spring, this was done so that people might remonstrate against departures from the norm.

"Heaven's love for the people is very great. Would it then allow one man to preside over them in an arrogant and willful manner, indulging his excesses and casting aside the nature Heaven and Earth allotted them? Surely it would not!"

[Adapted from Watson, *The Tso chuan*, pp. xv–xvi]

Duke Xiang, 25th year (548 B.C.E.)

The chief actors in this episode are Duke Zhuang of Qi (r. 553–548 B.C.E.) and his high minister, Cui Shu, neither of them attractive figures. Duke Zhuang by his stu-

---

72. The quotation is from an unknown work purporting to describe the government of the Xia dynasty in high antiquity. It was later incorporated into the short text titled "Yin zheng," one of the spurious sections of the *Classic of Documents* that were put together in the third century C.E.

pidity and immoral behavior courts the fate that overtakes him, while Cui Shu is an example of the scheming head of a powerful ministerial family who betrays his duty to the ruling house. But the interest in the passage lies not so much in the sordid actions of the principals as in the opportunities that the flow of events affords to lesser personages in the narrative to demonstrate their dedication to higher ideals. The episode is famous for the example of the dauntless historians who choose to die rather than falsify the record, an example that no doubt served as a source of inspiration to later historians of China.

The wife of the lord of Tang in Qi was an older sister of Dongguo Yan, a retainer of Cui Shu. When the lord of Tang died, Dongguo Yan drove Cui Shu to the lord's residence so he could offer condolences. Cui Shu observed the lord's wife, Lady Jiang, and admired her beauty. He instructed Dongguo Yan to arrange a marriage.

Dongguo Yan said, "Man and wife must be of different surnames. But you, my lord, are descended from Duke Ding of Qi, and I am descended from Duke Huan. It is out of the question!"

Cui Shu divined by the milfoil stalks and arrived at the hexagram *kun* or "adversity," which changed into the hexagram *daguo* or "excess."[73]

The historians who conducted the divination all declared the response to be auspicious.[74] But when Cui Shu showed the results to the Qi minister Chen Wenzi, he said, "Husband gives way to wind, wind blows the wife away. Such a match will never do! Moreover, the interpretation reads, 'Troubled by rocks, thorns and briers to rest on, the man enters his house but does not see his wife — misfortune!' 'Troubled by rocks' means he cannot cross over. 'Thorns and briers to rest on' means that what he leans on injures him. 'He enters his house but does not see his wife — misfortune!' means he has no place to turn to."

Cui Shu said, "She's a widow, so what does that all matter? Her former husband has already suffered the misfortune!" Thus in the end he married Lady Jiang.

Duke Zhuang of Qi carried on an adulterous affair with Lady Jiang, paying frequent visits to Cui Shu's house. At one time he took Cui Shu's hat and presented it to someone else. His attendant said, "That will not do!" But the duke replied, "Is Cui the only person who deserves a hat?"

For these reasons, Cui came to hate the duke. Also, when Duke Zhuang took advantage of the trouble in Jin to launch an attack on that state, Cui said, "Jin is certain to pay us back for this!" He therefore resolved to assassinate the

---

73. Cui Shu divines according to the *Classic of Changes*, and in the ensuing passage Chen Wenzi offers an interpretation of the meaning of the hexagrams at which Cui has arrived. For the *Classic of Changes*, see ch. 10.

74. Presumably the historians who declare the result to be auspicious are merely toadying to Cui Shu, in contrast to the principled historians who appear at the close of the passage.

duke in order to ingratiate himself with Jin, but could find no opportunity to do so. However, the duke thrashed one of his attendants, named Jia Ju, and then later allowed the man to wait on him again. The man spied on the duke for Cui Shu.

In the summer, the fifth month, the ruler of the state of Ju came to pay a court visit to Qi because of the military action carried out by Ju at Juyu.[75]

On the day *jiaxu* a banquet was held for the ruler of Ju at the northern outer wall of the capital. Cui Shu, pleading illness, played no part in the affair.

On the day *yihai* Duke Zhuang went to Cui Shu's house to inquire how he was. While there, he sought out Cui Shu's wife, Lady Jiang. She led him into a chamber, but then she and Cui Shu slipped out by a side door. The duke began rapping on a pillar and singing.

Meanwhile, the duke's attendant Jia Ju instructed the party of men who had accompanied the duke to remain outside while he went in the house. Then he shut the gate on them. At that point Cui Shu's soldiers made their appearance.

The duke clambered up to the upper terrace, where he begged to be allowed to go free. His request was refused. He begged to be allowed to conclude an alliance with Cui Shu, but his request was refused. He begged to be allowed to take his own life in the ancestral temple, but his request was refused.

The soldiers all said, "The ruler's minister Cui Shu is sick and cannot inquire of the ruler's orders. Since this house is close to the ducal palace, we retainers of the Cui family have been assigned to patrol the area at night. If there are trespassers, the only orders we have are to attack!"[76]

The duke tried to climb over the wall, whereupon someone shot at him with an arrow and hit him in the thigh. He fell backward from the wall, and in this way was finally assassinated.

Jia Ju, Zhou Chuo, Bing Shi, the ducal son Ao, Feng Ju, Duo Fu, Xiang Yi, and Lü Yin all died in the fighting.

The invocator Tuofu had been conducting sacrifices at Gaotang. When he returned to the capital to report on his mission, he was killed by the Cui forces before he could even remove his hat.

Shen Kuai, who was serving as supervisor of fisheries, withdrew from court and said to his house steward, "You take your family and flee. I intend to die here!" The steward replied, "If I were to flee, I would be going against the rightness of your decision!" So they all of them died together.

The Cui family forces killed Zong Mie at Pingyin.

---

75. In 550, when Duke Zhuang was on his way back from his attack on Jin, he attacked the state of Ju, situated just southeast of Qi. He was wounded in an attempt to storm the city gate at Juyu, and his attack ended in failure. But because Ju was a small and relatively powerless state, it was forced to sue for peace with Qi.

76. The soldiers are pretending they do not know the identity of the man they are pursuing.

The Qi official Yan Pingzhong stood outside the gate of the Cui family mansion. His followers said, "Do you intend to die?"

"Was he *my* ruler only? Why should I die for him?"

"Will you go abroad?"

"What crime have I committed? Why should I flee?"

"Will you go home then?"

"My ruler is dead! How can I go home like this? Nevertheless, when one acts as ruler of the people, how is it right to abuse the people? He should conduct himself as master of the altars of the soil and grain. And one who acts as a minister to a ruler, how can he think only of his emoluments? He should help to sustain the altars of the soil and grain. Therefore if a ruler dies for the sake of the altars of the soil and grain, then one should die with him. If he flees for the sake of the altars of the soil and grain, one should flee with him. But if he dies for personal reasons, or flees for personal reasons, then unless one is among his intimates or particular favorites, who would presume to share his fate?

"Moreover, just because a man has risen up against his ruler and assassinated him, why should that oblige me to die for the ruler, or why should it oblige me to flee for him? And yet how could I simply return home like this?"

When the gates were opened, Yan Pingzhong entered the house, pillowed the body of the duke on his lap, and wept over it. Then he stood up, performed three ritual leaps, and departed.[77]

Someone told Cui Shu that Yan Pingzhong should by all means be killed. But Cui Shu said, "The people look up to him. By sparing him I can gain the support of the people.". . .

When Shusun Qiaoru was in Qi, Shusun Huan arranged for Shusun Qiaoru's daughter to enter the household of Duke Ling of Qi. She gained favor with the duke and bore him a son who later became Duke Jing.

On the day *dingchou* Cui Shu set up this son, Duke Jing, as ruler of Qi, with himself as prime minister. Qing Feng was appointed prime minister of the left. They swore an oath with the people of the state in the ancestral temple of the founder. The words of the oath began, "Should anyone fail to ally himself with the Cui and Jing families. . . ." Yan Pingzhong raised his eyes to Heaven and said with a sigh, "Should I fail to ally myself with those who are loyal to the ruler alone and who work to benefit the altars of soil and grain, may the High God witness it!" Only then would he smear his lips with the blood of the sacrifice.

---

77. Yan performs the ritual of lamentation out of respect for his dead lord, though this act might well have cost him his life. But, as he has already made clear, he will take no steps to avenge the murder.

On the day *xinsi* the new duke and his high officers concluded an alliance with the ruler of Ju.

The grand historian wrote in his records: "Cui Shu assassinated his ruler." Cui Shu had him killed. The historian's younger brother succeeded to the post and wrote the same thing. He too was killed, as was another brother. When a fourth brother came forward to write, Cui Shu finally desisted.

Meanwhile, when the assistant historian living south of the city heard that the grand historians had been killed, he took up his bamboo tablets and set out for the court. Only when he learned that the fact had been recorded did he turn back.

[Adapted from Watson, *The Tso chuan*, pp. 143–147]

Duke Wen, 13th Year (614 B.C.E.)

This final selection from the *Zuozhuan* provides insight into the potent concept of *ming* (fate or destiny), which may refer either to one's mission in life or to one's allotted life span.

Duke Wen of Zhu divined by the turtle shell to determine if he should move his capital to the city of Yi. The historian who conducted the divination replied, "The move will benefit the people but not their ruler."

The ruler of Zhu said, "If it benefits the people, it benefits me. Heaven gave birth to the people and set up a ruler in order to benefit them. If the people enjoy the benefit, I am bound to share in it."

Those around the ruler said, "If by taking warning from the divination you can prolong your destiny, why not do so?"

The ruler replied, "My destiny lies in nourishing the people. Whether death comes to me early or late is merely a matter of time. If the people will benefit thereby, then nothing could be more auspicious than to move the capital."

In the end he moved the capital to Yi. In the fifth month Duke Wen of Zhu died.

The noble person remarks: He understood the meaning of destiny.

[Adapted from Watson, *The Tso chuan*, p. 210]

Chapter 7

LEGALISTS AND MILITARISTS

"Legalism" (*fajia*) is a name that came to be applied to a set of ideas and practices associated with the rise of the Chinese imperial bureaucratic state in the third and second centuries B.C.E. The key term in this name, *fa*, refers to several ways in which state power could be organized and exercised: through laws and punishments, administrative and military systems, policy planning, statecraft, or methods of personnel management. Although comparatively late in developing a systematic doctrine, the Legalists — as they would become known — while not actually a formal school, had unquestionably the greatest influence of any upon the political life of the time. Typically proponents of these ideas were practicing statesmen more concerned with immediate problems and specific mechanisms of control than with theories of government. Indeed, some of them were strongly anti-intellectual and evidenced a special hostility toward the "vain" talk of philosophers.

In its earliest form, "Legalism" was probably the outgrowth of a need for more rational organization of society and resources so as to strengthen a state against its rivals. This was to be accomplished by concentrating power in the hands of a single ruler and by adopting governmental institutions that afforded greater centralized control. Guan Zhong in the seventh century, for example, worked to make Qi the strongest state of his time by increasing the power of the ruler, but at the same time he upheld many of the traditional moral virtues and accepted the old enfeoffment system.

As the struggle among the Warring States became more intense, however, technicians of power came forward who put the state and its interests ahead of all human and moral concerns — who, in fact, glorified power for its own sake and looked upon human beings as having no worth apart from their possible use to the state. Men like Shang Yang (d. 338 B.C.E.) completely rejected the traditional virtues of humanity and rightness that the Confucians had urged upon rulers, denying that such lofty ideas had any practical relationship to the harsh realities of political life. They openly advocated war as a means of strengthening the power of the ruler, expanding the state, and making the people strong, disciplined, and submissive. They conceived of a political order in which all old feudal divisions of power would be swept away and all authority would reside in one central administration headed by an absolute monarch. The state would be ordered by a set of laws that would be administered with complete regularity and impartiality. Severe punishments would restrain any violations, while generous rewards would encourage what was beneficial to the strength and well-being of the state. Agriculture, as the basis of the economy, would be promoted intensively, while commerce and intellectual endeavor, regarded as nonessential and diversionary, were to be severely restricted. The people would live frugal and obedient lives devoted to the interests of the state in peace and war. These ideas were put into actual practice by the rulers of the state of Qin.

In their complete rejection of traditional ethical values, in their emphasis upon government by law rather than by personal example, and in their scorn for the ideals drawn from the past, the Legalists represent the antithesis of Confucian thinking. On the other hand, the Legalists obviously learned something from both the Mohists and the Daoists. Mozi's stress on uniform standards and on the mobilization of society for the achievement of utilitarian ends is strongly echoed in the totalitarian aims of the Legalists, although they obviously had no use for his doctrine of universal love or his condemnation of offensive warfare. Laozi's idea of nonassertion (*wuwei*) as a way of government is applied to the Legalists' own conception of the ideal ruler, who takes no direct part in the government but simply presides as a semi-divine figurehead while the elaborate legal machinery of government functions of its own accord, obviating the need for the ruler's direct intervention. Having so regulated the lives of his people that there is no longer any possibility of disorder or need for improvement or guidance, the ruler may retire to dwell, as Han Fei (d. 233 B.C.E.) says, "in the midst of his deep palace," far removed from the eyes of the populace, enjoying the luxuries and sensual delights appropriate to his exalted position.

One may imagine the horror and revulsion that such a doctrine aroused among the Confucians, who attached such importance to personal relations and human values. Their horror grew as they saw that the policies of the Legalist statesmen succeeded greatly in strengthening the state of Qin, whose campaign of conquest moved inexorably onward while the older states decayed and fell victim to its expansions. With the final unification of China by the First Emperor of the Qin, it looked as if the harsh policies of Shang Yang and Han Fei had won out over the other schools of political thought. The proponents of "Legalism" were now in a position of power from which, by repressive measures, they could at last deal the death blow to their rivals.

THE GUANZI

The text titled *Guanzi* (Master Guan), attributed to the seventh-century statesman Guan Zhong, but actually of much later date, contains an unsystematic mix of pronouncements concerning governmental administration, political economy, and public morality. Much of it is Confucian in tone, but more attention is given to practical, organizational matters and economic problems of the kind with which the Legalists were identified. Thus, out of its heterogeneous contents, the *Guanzi* often served as the earliest reference to such recurring issues and practices as collective responsibility for law and order in the local community, the analysis of supply and demand in the market, the use of "Ever-Normal Granaries" to maintain food stocks and price stability, and so on. Such systems became perennial features of Chinese government in later times. The following passage illustrates how traditional virtues (usually thought to be Confucian) were to be promoted and enforced by local systems of collective responsibility. This general model was adopted, in variant forms and with somewhat different degrees of social pressure and legal enforcement, in most imperial dynasties. The statesman Shang Yang (represented in the second selection in these readings) was also closely identified with this system.

All special cases of filial piety and respect for elders, loyalty and faithfulness, worthiness and goodness, or refinement and talent on the part of the sons, younger brothers, male or female slaves, and retainers or guests of the head of a household shall be reported accordingly by the leaders of the groups of ten or five [families] to the clan elder of the circuit. The clan elder shall report them to the village commandant, who in turn shall report them to the subdistrict prefect. He shall summarize them for the district governor, who will record them for the chief justice.

In all cases where the participants in a crime are members of a household, collective responsibility shall extend to the head of the household. If the participants include the heads of households, collective responsibility shall extend to the leaders of the groups of ten and five. If the participants include these leaders, collective responsibility shall extend to the clan elder of the circuit. If the participants include clan elders, collective responsibility shall extend to the village commandant. If the participants include village commandants, collective responsibility shall extend to the subdistrict prefect. If the participants include subdistrict prefects, collective responsibility shall extend to the district governor. If the participants include district governors, collective responsibility extends to the chief justice.

Reports shall be made once every three months, summaries once every six, and permanent records once every twelve. Whenever the worthy are promoted, they shall not be allowed to exceed their proper rank. When the able are employed, they shall not be allowed to hold more than one office at a time. When punishments are imposed, they shall not be applied to the guilty person alone. When rewards are granted, they shall not be bestowed merely on the person credited with the achievement.

[*Guanzi* (GXJC), p. 13; trans. adapted from Rickett, *Guanzi*, pp. 104–105]

THE *BOOK OF LORD SHANG*

Credit for the rise to power of the state of Qin in the fourth century B.C.E. is usually assigned to the innovative methods of Gongsun Yang or Shang Yang (d. 338 B.C.E.), who was prime minister of Qin in the middle of the fourth century. The *Book of Lord Shang* (*Shangjun shu*), though of later date and uncertain provenance, contains a variety of materials representative of the ideas and policies for which he became well known, especially the need for strong and decisive leadership, state domination over the people, and reliance on strict laws, including generous rewards and harsh punishments rather than on traditional fiduciary relations and family ethics. Shang Yang also advocated concentration of the people's energies on agriculture and war and suppression of political parties, particularly targeting Confucian scholars who raised troublesome political issues.

Reform of the Law

Duke Xiao [of Qin] discussed his policy. The three Great Officers, Gongsun Yang (Shang Yang), Gan Long, and Du Zhi, were in attendance on the ruler. Their thoughts dwelt on the vicissitudes of the world's affairs; they discussed the principles of rectifying the law, and they sought for the way of directing the people. The ruler said, "Not to forget, at his succession, the tutelary spirits of the soil and of grain, is the way of a ruler; to shape the laws and to see to it that an intelligent ruler reigns are the tasks of a minister. I intend, now, to alter the laws, so as to obtain orderly government, and to reform the rites, so as to teach the people, but I am afraid that all-under-Heaven will criticize me."

Gongsun Yang said, "I have heard it said, that he who hesitates in action does not accomplish anything, and that he who hesitates in affairs gains no merit. Let your highness settle your thoughts quickly about altering the laws and perhaps not heed the criticism of all-under-Heaven. Moreover, he who surpasses others is, as a matter of course, disapproved of by the world; he who has thoughts of independent knowledge is certainly despised by the world. The saying runs, 'The stupid do not even understand an affair when it has been completed, but the wise see it even before it has sprouted.' . . . [pp. 167–169]

Ordinary people abide by old practices, and scholars are immersed in the study of what is reported from antiquity. These two kinds of men are all right for filling offices and for maintaining the law, but they are not the kind who can take part in a discussion that goes beyond the law. The Three Dynasties have attained supremacy by different rites, and the five Lords Protector have attained their protectorships by different laws. Therefore, a wise man creates laws, but a foolish man is controlled by them; a man of talent reforms rites, but a worthless man is enslaved by them. . . . [p. 171]

Agriculture and War

The means whereby a ruler of men encourages the people are office and rank; the means whereby a country is made prosperous are agriculture and war. Now those who seek office and rank do not do so by means of agriculture and war but by artful words and empty doctrines. That is called "wearying the people." The country of those who weary their people will certainly have no strength, and the state of those who have no strength will certainly be dismembered. Those who are capable in organizing a state teach the people that office and rank can only be acquired through one opening, and, thus, there being no rank without office, the state will do away with fine speaking, with the result that the people will be simple; being simple, they will not be licentious. . . . [p. 185]

The way to organize a state well is, even though the granaries are filled, not to be negligent in agriculture, and even though the state is large and its population numerous, to have no license of speech. [This being so,] the people will be simple and have concentration. . . . But now people within the territory and those who hold office and rank see that it is possible to obtain office and rank from the court by means of artful speech and sophistry . . . with the result that, at court, they deceive their ruler and, retiring from court, they think of nothing but of how to realize their selfish interests. . . . [pp. 186–187]

The way to administer a state well is for the laws regulating officials to be clear; one does not rely on men to be intelligent and thoughtful. The ruler makes the people single-minded so they will not scheme for selfish profit. Then the strength of the state will be consolidated, and a state whose strength has been consolidated is powerful, but a country that loves talking is dismembered. . . .

The state depends on agriculture and war for its peace, and likewise the ruler, for his honor. Indeed, if the people are not engaged in agriculture and war, it means that the ruler loves words and that the officials have lost consistency of conduct. If there is consistency of conduct in officials, the state is well governed, and if single-mindedness is strived for, the country is rich. To have the state both rich and well governed is the way to attain supremacy. . . . [pp. 188–189]

The people will love their ruler and obey his commandments, even to death, if they are engaged in farming morning and evening; but they will be of no use if they see that glib-tongued, itinerant scholars succeed in being honored in serving the prince, that merchants succeed in enriching their families, and that artisans have plenty to live upon. If the people see both the comfort and the advantage of these three walks of life, then they will indubitably shun agriculture; shunning agriculture, they will care little for their homes; caring little for their homes, they will certainly not fight and defend them for the ruler's sake. . . . [pp. 192–193]

When a ruler loves their sophistry and does not seek for their practical value, then the professional talkers have it all their own way, expound their crooked sophistries in the streets; their various groups become great crowds, and the people, seeing that they succeed in captivating kings, dukes, and great men, all imitate them. Now, if men form parties, the arguments and discussions in the state will be confusing in their diversity; the lower classes will be amused, and the great men will enjoy it, with the result that among such a people farmers will be few and those who, in idleness, live on others will be many. . . . [p. 195]

The Elimination of Strength

A strong state knows thirteen figures: the number of granaries within its borders, the number of able-bodied men and women, the number of old and weak people, the number of officials and officers, the number of those making a livelihood by talking, the number of useful people, the number of horses and oxen, the quantity of fodder and of straw. If one who wishes to make his state strong does not know these thirteen figures, though his geographical position may be favorable and the population numerous, his state will become weaker and weaker until it is dismembered. . . . [p. 205]

Discussing the People

In this passage, the disparagement of "virtue" refers to the traditional Confucian family ethic, seen here as prejudicial to the workings of an impersonal bureaucratic rationality. The virtue that Shang Yang favors, as in the final paragraph, is directed toward service of the state.

Sophistry and cleverness are an aid to lawlessness; rites and music are symptoms of dissipation and license; kindness and humaneness are the mother of transgressions; employment and promotion are opportunities for the rapacity of the wicked. If lawlessness is aided, it becomes current; if there are symptoms of dissipation and license, they will become the practice; if there is a foster mother for transgressions, they will arise; if there are opportunities for the rapacity of the wicked, they will never cease. If these eight things come together, the people will be stronger than the government; but if these eight things are nonexistent in a state, the government will be stronger than the people. . . . [pp. 206–207]

If virtuous officials are employed, the people will love their own relatives, but if wicked officials are employed, the people will love the statutes. To agree with and to respond to others is what the virtuous do; to differ from and to spy upon others is what the wicked do. If the virtuous are placed in prominent positions, transgressions will remain hidden; but if the wicked are employed, crimes will be punished. In the former case the people will be stronger than the law; in the latter, the law will be stronger than the people. . . . [p. 207]

It is the nature of the people to be orderly, but it is circumstances that cause disorder. Therefore in the application of punishments, light offenses should be regarded as serious; if light offenses do not occur, serious ones have no chance of coming. This is said to be "ruling the people while in a state of law and order."

If in the application of punishments, serious offenses are regarded as serious, and light offenses as light, light offenses will not cease, and, in consequence, there will be no means of stopping the serious ones. This is said to be "ruling the people while in a state of lawlessness." So if light offenses are regarded as serious, punishments will be abolished, affairs will succeed, and the state will be strong; but if serious offenses are regarded as serious and light ones as light, then punishments will appear; moreover, trouble will arise and the state will be dismembered. . . . [p. 209]

If the people are poor, they are weak; if the state is rich, they are licentious, and consequently there will be parasites and parasites will bring weakness. Therefore, the poor should be benefited with rewards, so that they become rich, and the rich should be injured by punishments, so that they become poor. The important thing in undertaking the administration of a state is to make the rich poor and the poor rich. If that is effected, the state will be strong. . . . [p. 210]

The Calculation of Land

If the ruler controls the handles of fame and profit, so as to be able to acquire success and fame, it is due to numerical calculations. A sage examines the weights, in order to control the handle of the scales; he examines the numerical calculations in order to direct the people. Numbers provide the true method for directing the people. Numbers provide the true method of ministers and rulers and an essential of the state. . . . [p. 218]

Making Orders Strict

The six parasites are: rites and music, odes and history, cultivation and goodness, filial devotion and brotherly love, sincerity and trustworthiness, uprightness and integrity, humaneness and rightness, criticism of the army and being ashamed of fighting. . . .[1] [p. 256]

In applying punishments, light offenses should be punished heavily; if light offenses do not appear, heavy offenses will not come. This is said to be abolishing penalties by means of penalties, and if penalties are abolished, affairs will succeed. If crimes are serious and penalties light, penalties will appear and trouble will arise. This is said to be bringing about penalties by means of penalties, and such a state will surely be dismembered.

The sage ruler understands what is essential in affairs and so, in the governing of the people, there is that which is most essential. Therefore in administering rewards and punishments he relies on uniformity. Humaneness is extending the heart. The sage ruler, by his governing of men, is certain to win their hearts; consequently he is able to exert strength. Strength produces force; force produces prestige; prestige produces virtue. Virtue has its origin in strength. The sage ruler alone possesses it, and therefore he is able to transmit humaneness and rightness to all-under-Heaven. . . . [pp. 258–259]

Rewards and Punishments

Punishments should know no degree or grade, but from ministers of state and generals down to great officers and ordinary folk, whoever does not obey the king's commands, violates the interdicts of the state, or rebels against the statutes fixed by the ruler should be guilty of death and should not be pardoned. Merit acquired in the past should not cause a decrease in the punishment for demerit later, nor should good behavior in the past cause any derogation of the law for wrong done later. If loyal ministers and filial sons do wrong, they should be judged according to the full measure of their guilt, and if among the officials who have to maintain the law and to uphold an office, there are those who do not carry out the king's law, they are guilty of death and should not be pardoned, but their punishment should be extended to their family for three generations. Colleagues who, knowing their offense, inform their superiors will themselves escape punishment. In neither high nor low offices should there be automatic hereditary succession to the office, rank, lands, or emoluments of officials. Therefore I say that if there are severe penalties that extend to the whole family, people will not dare to try [how far they can go], and as they dare not try, no punishments will be necessary. . . . [pp. 278–279]

---

1. There is obviously a textual problem here: the "six parasites" actually involve sixteen items. Despite the problem of numbering, the list is significant and suggestive.

The Cultivation of the Right Standard

The principle on which ministers serve their ruler is dependent, in most cases, on what the ruler likes. If the ruler likes law, then the ministers will make law their principle in serving; if the ruler likes words, then the ministers will make words their principle in serving. If the ruler likes law, then upright scholars will come to the front, but if he likes words, then ministers, full of praise for some and blame for others, will be at his side. If public and private interests are clearly distinguished, then even small-minded men do not hate men of worth, nor do worthless men envy those of merit. . . . [p. 263]

But nowadays, among rulers and ministers of a disorderly world each, on a small scale, appropriates the profits of his own state, and each exercises his own office for his private benefit. This is why the states are in a perilous position. For the relation between public and private interests is what determines existence or ruin.

However, if models and measures are abolished and private appraisal is favored, then bad ministers will let their standards be influenced by money in order to obtain emoluments, and officials of various ranks will, in a stealthy and hidden manner, make extortions from the people. The saying runs: "Many wood-worms and the wood snaps, a large fissure and the wall collapses." So if ministers of state vie with each other in selfishness and do not heed the people, then inferiors are estranged from superiors. When this happens, there is a fissure in the state. . . . [pp. 264–265]

Weakening the People

A weak people means a strong state and a strong state means a weak people. Therefore, a state that has the right way is concerned with weakening the people. If they are simple they become strong, and if they are licentious they become weak. Being weak, they are law-abiding; being licentious, they let their ambition go too far; being weak, they are serviceable, but if they let their ambition go too far, they will become strong. . . . [p. 303]

Attention to Law

Those people who form parties with others do not need us for obtaining success, and, if superiors pull one way with the people, then the latter will turn their backs on the ruler's position and will turn toward private connections. When this is the case, the prince will be weak and his ministers strong, and if the ruler does not understand this, then if the state is not annexed by the feudal lords, it will be robbed by the people. [p. 323]

[*Shangzi* (SBCK), chs. 1–5 — trans. adapted from Duyvendak, *Lord Shang*, pp. 167–323]

THE *HAN FEIZI*

Han Fei (d. 233 B.C.E.) was said to have been a student of Xunzi but turned away from the latter's emphasis on Confucian self-cultivation and practice of rites to become a synthesizer of several strains of Daoist and Legalist thought. This synthesis involved a Daoist-type mystique of the ruler, now envisioned as presiding over a perfectly defined system of laws and institutions, using techniques of statecraft developed by another Legalist thinker, Shen Buhai (d. 337 B.C.E.). For a time Han Fei enjoyed the favor of the Qin state, but he eventually met a violent death through the machinations of the prime minister of the Qin, Li Si (d. 208 B.C.E.), a former fellow student under Xunzi. A quarter century later, Li Si himself met a similar fate.

Although traditionally Han Fei, like Shang Yang before him, was classed as a Legalist (*fajia*), some modern scholars have preferred to call both of them "realists," because of their seeming practicality and ruthlessness in concentrating on power factors in government. It is ironic then that these prime spokesmen for Legalist "realism," should have shown such an idealistic faith in the rational uses of power yet in the end suffered a quixotic martyrdom — both of them meeting untimely deaths as the result of power struggles from which they could not extricate themselves.

Chapter 49: The Five Vermin

There was a farmer of Song who tilled the land, and in his field was a stump. One day a rabbit, racing across the field, bumped into the stump, broke its neck, and died. Thereupon the farmer laid aside his plow and took up watch beside the stump, hoping that he would get another rabbit in the same way. But he got no more rabbits, and instead became the laughingstock of Song. Those who think they can take the ways of the ancient kings and use them to govern the people of today all belong in the category of stump-watchers! . . . [p. 97]

When Yao ruled the world, he left the thatch of his roof untrimmed, and the raw timber of his beams was left unplaned. He ate coarse millet and a soup of greens, wore deerskin in the winter days and rough fiber robes in summer. Even a lowly gatekeeper was no worse clothed and provided for than he. When Yu ruled the world, he took plow and spade in hand to lead his people, working until there was no more down on his thighs or hair on his shins. Even the toil of a slave taken prisoner in the wars was no bitterer than his. Therefore those men in ancient times who abdicated and relinquished the rule of the world were, in a manner of speaking, merely forsaking the life of a gatekeeper and escaping from the toil of a slave. Therefore they thought little of handing over the rule of the world to someone else. Nowadays, however, the magistrate of a district dies and his sons and grandsons are able to go riding about in carriages for generations after. Therefore people prize such offices. In the matter of relinquishing things, people thought nothing of stepping down from the position of Son of Heaven in ancient times, yet they are very reluctant to give up the post of district magistrate today; this is because of the difference in the actual benefits received. . . . [pp. 97–98]

When men lightly relinquish the position of Son of Heaven, it is not because they are high-minded but because the advantages of the post are slight; when men strive for sinecures in the government, it is not because they are base but because the power they will acquire is great.

When the sage rules, he takes into consideration the quantity of things and deliberates on scarcity and plenty. Though his punishments may be light, this is not due to his compassion; though his penalties may be severe, this is not because he is cruel; he simply follows the custom appropriate to the time. Circumstances change according to the age, and ways of dealing with them change with the circumstances. . . . [pp. 98–99]

Past and present have different customs; new and old adopt different measures. To try to use the ways of a generous and lenient government to rule the people of a critical age is like trying to drive a runaway horse without using reins or whip. This is the misfortune that ignorance invites.

Now the Confucians and the Mohists all praise the ancient kings for their universal love of the world, saying that they looked after the people as parents look after a beloved child. And how do they prove this contention? They say, "Whenever the minister of justice administered some punishment, the ruler would purposely cancel all musical performances; and whenever the ruler learned that the death sentence had been passed on someone, he would shed tears." For this reason they praise the ancient kings.

Now if ruler and subject must become like father and son before there can be order, then we must suppose that there is no such thing as an unruly father or son. Among human affections none takes priority over the love of parents for their children. But though all parents may show love for their children, the children are not always well behaved. . . . And if such love cannot prevent children from becoming unruly, then how can it bring the people to order? . . .

Humaneness may make one shed tears and be reluctant to apply penalties, but law makes it clear that such penalties must be applied. The ancient kings allowed law to be supreme and did not give in to their tearful longings. Hence it is obvious that humaneness cannot be used to achieve order in the state. . . . [pp. 101–102]

Now here is a young man of bad character. His parents rail at him, but he does not reform; the neighbors scold, but he is unmoved; his teachers instruct him, but he refuses to change his ways. Thus, although three fine influences are brought to bear on him — the love of his parents, the efforts of the neighbors, the wisdom of his teachers — yet he remains unmoved and refuses to change so much as a hair on his shin. But let the district magistrate send out the government soldiers to enforce the law and search for evildoers, and then he is filled with terror, reforms his conduct, and changes his ways. Thus the love of parents is not enough to make children learn what is right, but must be backed up by the strict penalties of the local officials; for people by nature grow proud on love, but they listen to authority. . . .

The best rewards are those that are generous and predictable, so that the people may profit by them. The best penalties are those that are severe and inescapable, so that the people will fear them. The best laws are those that are uniform and inflexible, so that the people can understand them. . . . [pp. 103–104]

Those who practice humaneness and rightness should not be praised, for to praise them is to cast aspersion on military achievements; men of literary accomplishment should not be employed in the government, for to employ them is to bring confusion to the law. In the state of Chu there was a man named Honest Gong. When his father stole a sheep, he reported the theft to the authorities. But the local magistrate, considering that the man was honest in the service of his sovereign but a villain to his own father, replied, "Put him to death!" and the man was accordingly sentenced and executed.[2] Thus we see that a man who is an honest subject of his sovereign may be an infamous son to his father.

There was a man of Lu who accompanied his sovereign to war. Three times he went into battle, and three times he ran away. When Confucius asked him the reason, he replied, "I have an aged father, and if I should die, there would be no one to take care of him." Confucius, considering the man filial, recommended him and had him promoted to a post in the government.[3] Thus we see that a man who is a filial son to his father may be a traitorous subject to his lord.

The magistrate of Chu executed a man, and as a result the felonies of the state were never reported to the authorities; Confucius rewarded a man, and as a result the people of Lu thought nothing of surrendering or running away in battle. Since the interests of superior and inferior are as disparate as all this, it is hopeless for the ruler to praise the actions of the private individual and at the same time try to ensure blessing to the state's altars of the soil and grain.

In ancient times when Cang Jie created the system of writing, he used the character for "private" to express the idea of self-centeredness, and combined the elements for "private" and "opposed to" to form the character for "public."

---

2. Cf. *Analects* 13:18 in ch. 3.

3. This story about Confucius is not recorded anywhere else and evidently is fabricated out of Confucius's teaching on filial piety.

The fact that public and private are mutually opposed was already well under-stood at the time of Cang Jie. To regard the two as being identical in interest is a disaster that comes from lack of consideration. . . . [pp. 105–106]

The world calls worthy those whose conduct is marked by integrity and good faith, and wise those whose words are subtle and mysterious. But even the wisest man has difficulty understanding words that are subtle and mysterious. Now if you want to set up laws for the masses and you try to base them on doctrines that even the wisest men have difficulty in understanding, how can the common people comprehend them? . . . Now in administering your rule and dealing with the people, if you do not speak in terms that any man or woman can plainly understand, but long to apply the doctrines of the wise men, then you will defeat your own efforts at rule. Subtle and mysterious words are no business of the people.

If people regard those who act with integrity and good faith as worthy, it must be because they value men who have no deceit, and they value men of no deceit because they themselves have no means to protect themselves from deceit. The common people in selecting their friends, for example, have no wealth by which to win others over, and no authority by which to intimidate others. For that reason they seek for men who are without deceit to be their friends. But the ruler occupies a position whereby he may impose his will upon others, and he has the whole wealth of the nation at his disposal; he may dispense lavish rewards and severe penalties and, by wielding these two handles, may illuminate all things through his wise policies. In that case, even traitorous ministers like Tian Chang and Zihan would not dare to deceive him. Why should he have to wait for men who are by nature not deceitful?

Hardly ten men of true integrity and good faith can be found today, and yet the offices of the state number in the hundreds. If they must be filled by men of integrity and good faith, then there will never be enough men to go around; and if the offices are left unfilled, then those whose business it is to govern will dwindle in numbers while disorderly men increase. Therefore the way of the enlightened ruler is to unify the laws instead of seeking for wise men, to lay down firm policies instead of longing for men of good faith. Hence his laws never fail him, and there is no felony or deceit among his officials. . . . [pp. 108–109]

Now the people of the state all discuss good government, and everyone has a copy of the works on law by Shang Yang and Guan Zhong in his house, and yet the state gets poorer and poorer, for though many people talk about farming, very few put their hands to a plow. The people of the state all dis-cuss military affairs, and everyone has a copy of the works of Sun Wu and Wu Qi in his house,[4] and yet the armies grow weaker and weaker, for though

---

4. See pp. 213–23.

many people talk about war, few buckle on armor. Therefore an enlightened ruler will make use of men's strength but will not heed their words, will reward their accomplishments but will prohibit useless activities. Then the people will be willing to exert themselves to the point of death in the service of their sovereign.

Farming requires a lot of hard work, but people will do it because they say, "This way we can get rich." War is a dangerous undertaking, but people will take part in it because they say, "This way we can become eminent." Now if men who devote themselves to literature or study the art of persuasive speaking are able to get the fruits of wealth without the hard work of the farmer and can gain the advantages of eminence without the danger of battle, then who will not take up such pursuits? So for every man who works with his hands there will be a hundred devoting themselves to the pursuit of wisdom. If those who pursue wisdom are numerous, the laws will be defeated, and if those who labor with their hands are few, the state will grow poor. Hence the age will become disordered.

Therefore, in the state of an enlightened ruler there are no books written on bamboo slips; law supplies the only instruction. There are no sermons on the former kings; the officials serve as the only teachers. There are no fierce feuds of private swordsmen; cutting off the heads of the enemy is the only deed of valor. Hence, when the people of such a state make a speech, they say nothing that is in contradiction to the law; when they act, it is in some way that will bring useful results; and when they do brave deeds, they do them in the army. Therefore, in times of peace the state is rich, and in times of trouble its armies are strong. . . . [pp. 110–111]

These are the customs of a disordered state: Its scholars praise the ways of the former kings and imitate their humaneness and rightness, put on a fair appearance and speak in elegant phrases, thus casting doubt upon the laws of the time and causing the ruler to be of two minds. Its speechmakers propound false schemes and borrow influence from abroad, furthering their private interests and forgetting the welfare of the state's altars of the soil and grain. Its swordsmen gather bands of followers about them and perform deeds of honor, making a fine name for themselves and violating the prohibitions of the five government bureaus. Those of its people who are worried about military service flock to the gates of private individuals and pour out their wealth in bribes to influential men who will plead for them, in this way escaping the hardship of battle. Its merchants and artisans spend their time making articles of no practical use and gathering stores of luxury goods, accumulating riches, waiting for the best time to sell, and exploiting the farmers.

These five groups are the vermin of the state. If the rulers do not wipe out such vermin, and in their place encourage men of integrity and public spirit, then they should not be surprised, when they look about the area within the four seas, to see states perish and ruling houses wane and die. . . . [pp. 116–117]

Chapter 50: Eminence in Learning

In the present age, the Confucians and the Mohists are well known for their learning. The Confucians pay the highest honor to Confucius, the Mohists to Mo Di. . . . Since the death of its founder, the Confucian school has split into eight factions, and the Mohist school into three. Their doctrines and practices are different or even contradictory, and yet each claims to represent the true teaching of Confucius and Mozi. But since we cannot call Confucius and Mozi back to life, who is to decide which of the present versions of the doctrine is the right one?

Confucius and Mozi both followed the ways of Yao and Shun,[5] and though their practices differed, each claimed to be following the real Yao and Shun. But since we cannot call Yao and Shun back to life, who is to decide whether it is the Confucians or the Mohists who are telling the truth? . . . [p. 118]

He who claims to be sure of something for which there is no evidence is a fool, and he who acts on the basis of what cannot be proved is an impostor. Hence it is clear that those who claim to follow the ancient kings and to be able to describe with certainty the ways of Yao and Shun must be either fools or impostors. The learning of fools and impostors, doctrines that are motley and contradictory — such things as these the enlightened ruler will never accept. . . . Because the ruler gives equal ear to the learning of fools and impostors and the wranglings of the motley and contradictory schools, the gentlemen of the world follow no fixed policy in their words and no constant code of action in their behavior. . . . If equal ear is given to motley doctrines, false codes of behavior, and contradictory assertions, how can there be anything but chaos? . . . [pp. 119–120]

When the scholars of today discuss good government, many of them say, "Give land to the poor and the destitute, so that those who have no means of livelihood may be provided for." Now, if men start out with equal opportunities and yet there are a few who, without the help of unusually good harvests or outside income, are able to keep themselves well supplied, it must be due either to hard work or to frugal living. If men start out with equal opportunities and yet there are a few who, without having suffered from some calamity like famine or sickness, still sink into poverty and destitution, it must be due either to laziness or to extravagant living. The lazy and extravagant grow poor; the diligent and frugal get rich. Now if the ruler levies money from the rich in order to give alms to the poor, he is robbing the diligent and frugal and indulging the lazy and extravagant. If he expects by such a means to induce the people

---

5. Judging from the *Analects*, Confucius himself had little to say about the sage rulers Yao and Shun, and the few references to them may be later insertions in the text. But Confucian scholars of late Zhou times paid great honor to Yao and Shun and compiled the "Canon of Yao," the first section of the *Classic of Documents*, as a record of their lives.

to work industriously and spend with caution, he will be disappointed. . . . [pp. 120–121]

Then there are other men who collect books, study rhetoric, gather bands of disciples, and devote themselves to literature, learning, and debate. The rulers of the time are sure to treat them with respect, saying, "It is the way of the former kings to honor worthy men." The farmers are the ones who must pay taxes to the officials, and yet the ruler patronizes scholars — thus the farmer's taxes grow heavier and heavier, while the scholars enjoy increasing reward. If the ruler hopes, in spite of this, that the people will work industriously and spend little time talking, he will be disappointed. . . . [pp. 121–122]

Moreover, when the ruler listens to a scholar, if he approves of his words, he should give them official dissemination and appoint the man to a post; but if he disapproves of his words, he should dismiss the man and put a stop to his teaching. Now, though the ruler may approve of some doctrine, he does not give it official dissemination, and though he may disapprove of some doctrine, he does not put a stop to it. Not to use what you approve of and not to suppress what you disapprove of — this is the way to confusion and ruin. . . . [pp. 122–123]

When a sage rules the state, he does not depend on people's doing good of themselves; he sees to it that they are not allowed to do what is bad. If he depends on people's doing good of themselves, then within his borders he can count fewer than ten instances of success. But if he sees to it that they are not allowed to do what is bad, then the whole state can be brought to a uniform level of order. Those who rule must employ measures that will be effective with the majority and discard those that will be effective with only a few. Therefore they devote themselves not to virtue but to law. . . . [p. 125]

And even if, without depending upon rewards and punishments, there were a man who became good of himself, the enlightened ruler would not prize him. Why? Because the laws of the state must not be ignored, and it is more than one man who must be governed. Therefore a ruler who understands policy does not pursue fortuitous goodness but follows the way of certain success. . . . [p. 126]

When the Confucians of the present time counsel rulers, they do not praise those measures that will bring order today, but talk only of the achievements of the men who brought order in the past. They do not investigate matters of bureaucratic system or law, or examine the realities of villainy and evil, but spend all their time telling tales of the distant past and praising the achievements of the former kings. . . . No ruler with proper standards will tolerate them. Therefore the enlightened ruler works with facts and discards useless theories. He does not talk about deeds of humaneness and rightness, and he does not listen to the words of scholars.

Nowadays, those who do not understand how to govern invariably say, "You must win the hearts of the people!" If you could assure good government merely by winning the hearts of the people, then there would be no need for [wise ministers] like Yi Yin and Guan Zhong[6] — you could simply listen to what the people say. The reason you cannot rely on the wisdom of the people is that they have the minds of little children. If the child's head is not shaved, its sores will spread; and if its boil is not lanced, it will become sicker than ever. But when it is having its head shaved or its boil lanced, someone must hold it while the loving mother performs the operation, and it yells and screams incessantly, for it does not understand that the little pain it suffers now will bring great benefit later.

Now, the ruler presses the people to till the land and open up new pastures so as to increase their means of livelihood, and yet they consider him harsh; he draws up a penal code and makes the punishments more severe in order to put a stop to evil, and yet the people consider him stern. He levies taxes in cash and grain in order to fill the coffers and granaries so that there will be food for the starving and funds for the army, and yet the people consider him avaricious. He makes certain that everyone within his borders understands warfare and sees to it that there are no private exemptions from military service; he unites the strength of the state and fights fiercely in order to take its enemies captive, and yet the people consider him violent. These four types of undertaking all ensure order and safety to the state, and yet the people do not have sense enough to rejoice in them. [pp. 127–129]

[Han Feizi (SBCK), chs. 49, 50 — Watson, Han Fei Tzu, pp. 97–129]

LI SI: LEGALIST THEORIES IN PRACTICE

The feudal state of Qin, utilizing Legalist practices of strong centralization of power, regimentation of its people, and aggressive warfare, had built itself up to a position of formidable strength in the late years of the Zhou dynasty. Finally, under the vigorous leadership of King Cheng, it succeeded in swallowing up the last of its rivals and uniting all of China under its rule. In 221 B.C.E. King Cheng assumed the title of Qin Shihuangdi, the First Exalted Emperor of the Qin.

He had been aided in his efforts toward unification by a group of astute and ruthless statesmen identified with Legalist doctrines, the most important of whom was Li Si, who became prime minister of the new empire. Thus, for the first time, one of the schools of classical thought had its teachings adopted as the official doctrine of a regime ruling all of China.

At Li Si's urging the First Emperor carried out a series of sweeping changes

---

6. Yi Yin was a sage minister to King Tang, the founder of the Shang dynasty, and Guan Zhong was an adviser to King Huan of Qi in the seventh century B.C.E.

and innovations that, in the course of a few years, radically affected the entire structure of Chinese life and society. One of these was the complete abolition of all feudal ranks and privileges and the disarmament of all private individuals. The entire area of China was brought under the direct control of the central court through an administrative system of prefectures and counties. With this unification of the nation came measures for the standardization of weights, measures, and writing script, the destruction of all feudal barriers between districts, and the construction of better roads and communications. Wars were undertaken to subdue neighboring peoples and expand the borders of the nation, great masses of people were forcibly moved to new areas for purposes of defense or resettlement, and labor gangs were set to work constructing the Great Wall out of smaller defensive walls of the old feudal states.

The First Emperor of the Qin was a man of extraordinary vision and demonic energy. He worked tirelessly to build up the power and prestige of his regime, directing campaigns, constructing defenses, erecting magnificent palaces for himself and his court, and traveling on extensive tours of inspection throughout his realm. With the aid of Li Si and a few other trusted advisers he managed to carry out his drastic measures and hold down the ever-growing threat of revolt among his subjects. Never before had China been so vast and powerful.

For a while it seemed that Legalism as a theory of government had achieved incontrovertible success. But with the death of this dictatorial emperor the weakness in the Legalist system became apparent. The emperor had ruled from behind the scenes, remaining aloof from his people and ministers. This placed enormous power in the hands of a few trusted officials and eunuchs who were allowed access to him. On his death a struggle for power broke out. Li Si and the powerful eunuch Zhao Gao, by concealing the death of the emperor and forging orders in his name, succeeded in destroying their rivals and seizing actual control of the government. The Second Emperor became a helpless puppet, cut off in the depths of the palace from all contact with or information about the outside world. Then Zhao Gao turned on Li Si and destroyed him and his family, using against him the very Legalist methods that Li Si had employed. Popular revolts broke out all over the nation as the people grew increasingly restless under the burden of taxation and oppression. But all news of the seriousness of the situation was kept from the court by officials who had learned to fear the consequences of speaking out. The government was paralyzed by the force of its own autocratic laws. In the end the Second Emperor was forced to commit suicide, Zhao Gao was murdered, and the last ruler of the Qin submitted meekly to the leader of a popular revolt. In 207, less than fifteen years after its glorious establishment, the new dynasty had come to a violent and ignoble end.

The Qin, though short-lived, had a profound effect upon the course of Chinese history. The measures for unification, standardization, and centralization of power, coercive though they were, destroyed for all time the old enfeoffment system and gave to the Chinese people a new sense of unity and identity. The destruction of the old feudal states, the shifts of population, and the wars and uprisings that accompanied the downfall of the dynasty, wiped out the old aristocracy of Zhou times and opened the way for new leaders and new families to rise to power. Nevertheless, the spectacular failure of the Legalists to stamp out rival schools of thought, to suppress criticism by police control, and to rule the people by exacting laws and harsh penalties, discredited Legalist policies for centuries to come. Later regimes might in fact make use of Legalist ideas and methods in their administrations, but never again did they dare openly to espouse the hated philosophy of the Qin. The First Emperor and his advisers became the symbols of evil and oppression in Chinese history, and the dynasty an example to all later rulers of what happens when the people are exploited and oppressed to the breaking point, when force and tyranny replace humaneness and rightness as the guiding principles of government.

MEMORIAL ON ANNEXATION OF FEUDAL STATES

The foregoing view of the First Emperor and Li Si is reflected in the following memorials as recorded by Sima Qian, the foremost historian of early China. That Sima Qian's record represents a Han view of the Qin past is significant.

He who waits on others misses his opportunities, while a man aiming at great achievements takes advantage of a critical juncture and relentlessly follows it through. Why is it that during all the years that Duke Mu of Qin (659–621 B.C.E.) was overlord (*ba*) among the feudal princes, he did not try to annex the Six States to the east? It was because the feudal lords were still numerous and the power of the imperial Zhou had not yet decayed. Hence, as the Five Overlords succeeded one another, each in turn upheld the House of Zhou. But since the time of Duke Xiao of Qin (361–338 B.C.E.) the House of Zhou has been declining, the feudal states have been annexing one another, and east of the pass there remain only Six States.

Through military victories, the state of Qin has, in the time of the last six kings, brought the feudal lords into submission. And by now the feudal states yield obeisance to Qin as if they were its commanderies and prefectures. Now, with the might of Qin and the virtues of Your Highness, at one stroke, like sweeping off the dust from a kitchen stove, the feudal lords can be annihilated, imperial rule can be established, and unification of the world can be brought about. This is the one moment in ten thousand ages. If Your Highness allows it to slip away and does not press the advantage in haste, the feudal lords will revive their strength and organize themselves into an anti-Qin alliance. Then no one, even though he possess the virtues of the Yellow Emperor, would be able to annex their territories.

[*Shiji* (BNB) 87:2a–b — BW]

MEMORIAL ON THE ABOLITION OF THE ENFEOFFMENT SYSTEM

Numerous were the sons, younger brothers, and other members of the royal family that were enfeoffed by King Wen and King Wu at the founding of the Zhou dynasty. But as time passed, these relatives became estranged and alienated one from another; they attacked each other as if they were enemies. Eventually the feudal lords started wars and sent punitive expeditions against one another, and the king could do nothing to stop them. Now, owing to the divine intelligence of Your Majesty, all the land within the seas is unified and it has been divided into commanderies and prefectures. The royal princes and the meritorious ministers have been granted titles and bountiful rewards from the government treasury,[7] and it has proved sufficient. When the government institutions have been thus changed and there has been no contrary opinion in the empire, it is evidently the way to keep peace and quiet. To institute an enfeoffed nobility again would not be advantageous.

[*Shiji* (BNB) 6:12b — BW]

MEMORIAL ON THE BURNING OF BOOKS

Among the most infamous acts of the First Exalted Emperor of the Qin were the "burning of books," ordered in 213 B.C.E., and the "execution of scholars," ordered in 212. The first was an effort to achieve thought control through destroying all literature except the *Classic of Changes*, the royal archives of the Qin house, and books on technical subjects, such as medicine, agriculture, and forestry. The measure was aimed particularly at the *Classic of Documents* and the *Classic of Odes*. The execution of some 460 scholars in the following year[8] was an attempt to eliminate opposition to the emperor by ruthlessly destroying all potentially "subversive" elements in his entourage. The two measures taken together suggest something of the habit of mind of the First Emperor, as he was influenced by advisers like Li Si, but, again, it is significant that the following document comes down to us from the ensuing Han period.

In earlier times the empire disintegrated and fell into disorder, and no one was capable of unifying it. Thereupon the various feudal lords rose to power. In their discourses they all praised the past in order to disparage the present and embellished empty words to confuse the truth. Everyone cherished his own favorite school of learning and criticized what had been instituted by the authorities. But at present Your Majesty possesses a unified empire, has regulated

---

7. That is, instead of being granted noble titles and income from a fief, they have received honorary ranks and salaries paid out of taxes.

8. Traditionally referred to as "the burial of the scholars," on the view that the scholars were actually buried alive, though it is not certain that they met their end in this way.

the distinctions of black and white, and has firmly established for yourself a position of sole supremacy. And yet these independent schools, joining with each other, criticize the codes of laws and instructions. Hearing of the promulgation of a decree, they criticize it, each from the standpoint of his own school. At home they disapprove of it in their hearts; going out they criticize it in the thoroughfare. They seek a reputation by discrediting their sovereign; they appear superior by expressing contrary views, and they lead the lowly multitude in the spreading of slander. If such license is not prohibited, the sovereign power will decline above and partisan factions will form below. It would be well to prohibit this.

Your servant suggests that all books in the imperial archives, save the memoirs of Qin, be burned. All persons in the empire, except members of the Academy of Learned Scholars, in possession of the *Classic of Odes*, the *Classic of Documents*, and discourses of the hundred philosophers should take them to the local governors and have them indiscriminately burned. Those who dare to talk to each other about the *Odes* and *Documents* should be executed and their bodies exposed in the marketplace. Anyone referring to the past to criticize the present should, together with all members of his family, be put to death. Officials who fail to report cases that have come under their attention are equally guilty.[9] After thirty days from the time of issuing the decree, those who have not destroyed their books are to be branded and sent to build the Great Wall. Books not to be destroyed will be those on medicine and pharmacy, divination by the turtle and milfoil, and agriculture and arboriculture. People wishing to pursue learning should take the officials as their teachers.

[*Shiji* (BNB) 87:6b–7a — BW]

MEMORIAL ON EXERCISING HEAVY CENSURE

The worthy ruler should be one able to fulfill his kingly duties and employ the technique of censure.[10] Visited with censure, the ministers dare not but exert their ability to the utmost in devotion to their ruler. When the relative positions between minister and ruler are thus defined unmistakably, and the relative duties between superior and inferior are made clear, then none in the empire,

---

9. The passage from the beginning of the paragraph to this point has been inserted from the fuller account given in the *Records of the Grand Historian (Shiji)* 6:23b.

10. The Chinese term rendered as "censure" here may be more literally translated as "inspection and punishment." To relieve the awkwardness from the repeated use of this cumbersome expression, we have adopted "censure" as a more convenient, though less exact, equivalent throughout the memorial.

whether worthy or unworthy, will dare do otherwise than exert his strength and fulfill his duties in devotion to the ruler. Thus the ruler will by himself control the empire and will not be controlled by anyone. Then he can enjoy himself to the utmost. How can a talented and intelligent ruler afford not to pay attention to this point?

Hence, Shen Buhai[11] has said, "To possess the empire and yet not be able to indulge one's own desires is called making shackles out of the empire." The reason is that a ruler who is unable to employ censure must instead labor himself for the welfare of the people as did Yao and Yu. Thus it may be said that he makes shackles for himself. Now, if a ruler will not practice the intelligent methods of Shen Buhai and Han Feizi, or apply the system of censure in order to utilize the empire for his own pleasure, but on the contrary purposelessly tortures his body and wastes his mind in devotion to the people — then he becomes the slave of the common people instead of the domesticator of the empire. And what honor is there in that? When I can make others devote themselves to me, then I am honorable and they are humble; when I have to devote myself to others, then I am humble and they are honorable. Therefore he who devotes himself to others is humble, and he to whom others devote themselves is honorable. From antiquity to the present, it has never been otherwise. When men of old considered anyone respectable and virtuous, it was because he was honorable; when they considered anyone despicable and unworthy, it was because he was humble. Now, if we should exalt Yao and Yu because they devoted themselves to the empire, then we would have missed entirely the reason for considering men respectable and virtuous. This may indeed be called a great misapprehension. Is it not fitting then to speak of it as one's shackles? It is a fault resulting from the failure to exercise censure.

Hence, Han Feizi has said, "The affectionate mother has spoiled children, but the stern household has no overbearing servants."[12] And the purpose for saying so is to make certain that punishments are applied.

Hence, according to the laws of Lord Shang [Shang Yang], there was corporal punishment for the scattering of ashes in the streets. Now, the scattering of ashes is a small offense, whereas corporal punishment is a heavy penalty. Only the intelligent ruler is capable of applying heavy censure against a light offense. If a light offense is censured heavily, one can imagine what will be done against a serious offense! Thus the people will not dare to violate the laws. . . .

The fact that intelligent rulers and sage kings were able for a long time to

---

11. A Legalist philosopher, d. 337 B.C.E.
12. *Han Feizi*, ch. 50. Watson, *Han Fei Tzu*, p. 125.

occupy the exalted position, hold great power, and monopolize the benefits of the empire is due to nothing other than their being able, on their own responsibility, to exercise censure without neglect and to apply severe punishments without fail. It was for this reason that none in the empire dared to be rebellious. If, now, a ruler does not busy himself with what prevents rebellion, but instead engages in the same practices by which the affectionate mother spoils her children, indeed he has not understood the principles of the sages. When one fails to practice the statecraft of the sages, what else does he do except make himself the slave of the empire? Is this not a pity? . . .

The intelligent ruler is one able . . . to exercise alone the craft of the ruler, whereby he keeps his obedient ministers under control and his clear laws in effect. Therefore his person becomes exalted and his power great. All talented rulers should be able to oppose the world and suppress established usage, destroying what they hate and establishing what they desire. Thus they may occupy a position of honor and power while they live and receive posthumous titles that bespeak their ability and intelligence after they die. So, the intelligent ruler acts on his decisions by himself, and none of the authority lies with his ministers. . . . Stopping the avenues of hearing and sight, he sees and hears inwardly by himself. Then from without he cannot be moved by the deeds of humane and righteous men . . . from within he cannot be carried away by arguments of remonstrance and disputation. Therefore he is able to act according to his heart's desire, and no one dares oppose him.

Thus only may a ruler be said to have succeeded in understanding the craft of Shen Buhai and Han Feizi, and in practicing the laws of Lord Shang. I have never heard of the empire falling into disorder while these laws were practiced and this craft understood. Hence, it is said that the way of the king is simple and easily mastered, yet only the intelligent ruler is able to carry it out.

Thus only may the exercise of censure be said to be real. [When the exercise of censure is real], the ministers will be without depravity. When the ministers are without depravity, the empire will be at peace. When the empire is at peace, its ruler will be venerated and exalted. When the ruler is venerated and exalted, the exercise of censure will be without fail. When the exercise of censure is without fail, what is sought for will be obtained. When what is sought for is obtained, the state will be wealthy. When the state is wealthy, its ruler's pleasures will be abundant. Therefore, when the craft of exercising censure is instituted, then all that the ruler desires is forthcoming. The ministers and people will be so busy trying to remedy their faults that they will have no time to scheme for trouble.

Thus is the way of the emperor made complete, and thus may the ruler be said really to understand the craft between ruler and subject. Though Shen Buhai and Han Feizi were to return to life, they would have nothing to add.

[From *Shiji* (BNB) 87:15a–18a — BW]

THE MILITARY TEXTS: THE *SUNZI*

War brings change. And endemic warfare in the fifth, fourth, and third centuries B.C.E. fundamentally altered Chinese tradition. Not only were all of the central states consumed by Qin, but as battles increased in size, severity, and consequence, the lives of peasant, townsperson, and functionary were forced into new patterns. State power was centralized and extended, conscripting farmers for violent acts far from home. Huge armies demanded a multitude of standardized weapons, elaborate transportation systems, and the effective extraction and management of wealth. Ruthless warfare brought ruin or reward. In these processes social values changed profoundly.

According to the idealized code of warfare of Shang and Western Zhou times, combat was viewed as an aristocratic affair, governed by complex protocols that may be aptly compared to the chivalry of European knighthood. Battle was to be between individuals, on horseback in Europe, in chariots in China. Honor required fair treatment of one's enemy, and insult to honor required vengeance. Oaths of men and nations were sealed in blood.

Remnants of these values could still be discerned in the Spring and Autumn period (771–479). The state of Song, seat of the deposed Shang kings, was weak. Yet in 638 its duke felt compelled to fight a much stronger state. When the duke's forces were outnumbered at the battle, his minister of war urged him to attack the enemy while they were still fording a river and again before they had drawn up ranks after crossing. The duke twice refused; he was wounded, his army routed. In defense the *Zuozhuan* put these words into his mouth: "The noble person (*junzi*) does not inflict a second wound. He does not capture those with graying hair. Of old, when campaigning one did not obstruct those in a defile. Though I am but the remnant of a destroyed state, I will not drum to attack when they have not drawn up ranks" (Duke Xi, 22d year). In the duke's idealized world winning was only one good, which competed with considerations such as fair combat or respect for age. Such considerations served to constrain warfare's destructive potential — thus a wound ended its victim's combat status, not his life. Momentary accidents of terrain were ignored so that higher values might prevail.

In a chivalric world of interstate negotiations, the duke's sense of honor might once have possessed considerable functionality. Now, however, such honor was "but the remnant of a destroyed state." Instead of supporting this moribund value system, his minister of war retorted, "My lord does not know battle. If the mighty enemy is in a defile or with his ranks not drawn up, this is Heaven assisting us. Drumming to attack when they're obstructed — is this really not permissible?" Whether his invocation of Heaven was cynical or devout, the minister's message is clear: warfare is not about virtue, it is about taking advantage of fleeting opportunities. By the middle of the Warring States period, when huge, recurrent battles engulfed the populace in unprecedented acts of destruction, warfare was about creating those conditions of advantage by any means, even those conventionally considered immoral. The *Sunzi* puts it bluntly: "The military is a way (*dao*) of deception." And this text so drains the terms *Heaven* and *Earth* of their religious content that one modern English translator simply renders them "weather" and "terrain."

In this Warring States world no political or social thinker could ignore the military. Indeed, nearly every master whose thought is presented in this volume was intensely concerned with military affairs. Confucius frequently referred to them.[13] The Mohists were in demand for their skills in siege defense. Xunzi devoted his fifteenth chapter, "Debating Military Affairs," to the Confucian way in warfare. Among the administrators retrospectively known as Legalists, Lord Shang and Han Feizi, discussed in the first part of this chapter, wrote extensively on it.

Most masters (*zi*) were political thinkers. Some were moralists, some simply administrators, but their texts treated military matters as an aspect of governance. In contrast is a set of texts that may have included matters of administration but always began from a military perspective. Instead of asking the question "How does one establish order in all-under-Heaven?," they focused on questions of strategy, tactics, military organization, logistics, training, and the ruler's relationship with the army. The *Zuozhuan* quotes two lost texts of this sort, and about half a dozen survive from the Warring States period. The best known of them is the *Sunzi*.

According to his biography in the *Records of the Grand Historian*, Sunzi, or Master Sun, was a contemporary of Confucius who served the state of Wu in its battles with rival states in the late Spring and Autumn period. There is, however, no historical evidence for this patriarch of East Asian strategy in any records before the third century B.C.E., and the text that bears his name was probably compiled from oral traditions in the second half of the fourth century B.C.E. The *Sunzi* is famous for certain strategic epigrams, such as "The military is a way (*dao*) of deception" (ch. 1). In isolation these epigrams encourage a stereotyped vision of the text, one much maligned by later Confucian moralists. Taken in context, however, such epigrams can introduce us step by step to the *Sunzi*'s complex thought.

"One hundred victories in one hundred battles is not skillful. Subduing the other's military without battle is skillful" (ch. 3). Warfare is destructive, of life, property, and value systems. Whether one's goal is conquest or defense, it is generally preferable to win without expending resources. This does not mean, of course, that the *Sunzi* is pacifist, or reluctant to engage. It does, however, imply the next epigram: "What is meant by skilled is to be victorious over the

---

13. See *Analects* 12:7, 13:9, 13:29, 13:30, and 16:1 in ch. 3.

easily defeated" (ch. 4). Great generals of the past were not those who charged uphill against overwhelming odds. On the contrary, they chose to fight when they knew in advance that they could easily win — thus they were "victorious over those who were already defeated." For "the victorious military is first victorious and after that does battle."

How is this done? "Knowing the other and knowing oneself, in one hundred battles no danger" (ch. 3). The general wins through knowledge, not prowess. Sun Bin, reputed grandson of Sunzi, is the best exemplar of this. Punished by having his legs chopped off at the knees, he was unable even to walk to the battlefield — yet he was still revered as a legendary strategist.

For the *Sunzi* knowledge must comprehend everything pertinent to war — terrain, morale, logistics, spies, weather, economics, psychology, and so on. These factors are related to each other in discernible yet shifting ways. Their relationship is discussed as the term *shi*, which refers both to the power inherent in a particular arrangement of elements and to its developmental tendency — what we might discern when we look at a chessboard and notice its present power configuration as well as its potential to change in definite directions. The *Sunzi* compares the power of *shi* to rocks atop a mountain. At rest, they are a form of potential energy. When released, they cascade down with overwhelming natural force. "Thus the *shi* of one skilled at setting people to battle is like rolling round rocks from a mountain one thousand *ren* high" (ch. 5). The good general can both recognize and create *shi*. But configurations always change, and once enacted, a strategy loses its power of surprise. Thus, "do not repeat the means of victory, but respond to form from the inexhaustible" (ch. 6).

Deception and strategic mutability lead to a particular kind of indirect approach in which the general ideally achieves victory without either expending his own resources or utterly destroying those of the enemy. The essence of this approach lies first in comprehensively conceiving the elements that constitute warfare and then identifying an action that is easy to accomplish (because it engenders no opposition) and effective (because it fundamentally rearranges the configuration of forces to the general's advantage).

The intellectual world of the Warring States period was characterized not only by bitter debate but also by the broad sharing of ideas; through both of these means the *Sunzi* is conceptually related to many of its contemporaries. One of its more unexpected kinships is with the *Laozi*, which also eschews conventional morality, emphasizes reversal, and views all things in terms of their relationships. The *Laozi* abhors violence. Yet it also says:

> If you would weaken it,
> You must cause it to be strengthened. . . .
> If you would take from it,
> You must give to it. [ch. 36]

It also employs a pair of terms that are prominent in the *Sunzi*, "the orthodox" and "the extraordinary":

> Rule the state by the orthodox.
> Employ soldiers by the extraordinary.
> Seize the empire by not acting (*wushi*). [ch. 57][14]

The *Sunzi* has been the most influential strategy text in East Asia. Its earliest surviving commentary comes from the hand of the great general Cao Cao (155–220 C.E.), who participated in the overthrow of the Han dynasty in the early third century. Canonized as the first of the *Seven Military Classics* (*Wujing qishu*) in early Song times, it is read today in the military academies of the People's Republic, the Republic of China, Japan, and the United States. Translations can even be found in the economics section of many American bookstores.

The rhetorical form of the *Sunzi* reflects its recent emergence from the oral tradition. Each of its thirteen fascicles consists of a series of short sections, strung together around a loosely shared topic, rather than a set of closely reasoned essays. On this level as well, it resembles the *Laozi*. Our translation attempts to reproduce the choppy nature of the original, rather than presenting ideas as if they formed naturally into the paragraphs of contemporary English style.

SELECTIONS FROM THE *SUNZI*

Fundamental Definitions

These are the opening passages of the *Sunzi*, which give the text's response to and redefinition of certain key terms in Warring States period discourse. Note that "the five" consist of Heaven, Earth, and humanity within an envelope of the Way (*dao*) and methods (or models or laws, *fa*). The *Sunzi* does not usually provide definitions of terms, instead recommending actions and approaches. The passages immediately below, then, are probably the latest stratum of the text, added by an editor to provide an orientation to the whole.

The military is a great matter of the state. It is the ground of life and death, the Way (*dao*) of survival or extinction. One cannot but investigate it. Thus base it in the five. Compare by means of the appraisals, and so seek out its nature.

---

14. A somewhat different translation of this passage is found in ch. 5.

The first is the way (*dao*), the second is Heaven, the third is Earth, the fourth is the general, the fifth is method.

The Way is what orders the people to have the same purpose as their superior. Thus they can die with him, live with him, and not harbor deceit.

Heaven is yin and yang, cold and hot, the order of the seasons. Going with it, going against it — this is military victory.

Earth is high and low, broad and narrow, far and near, steep and level, death and life.

The general is wisdom, trustworthiness, courage, and strictness.

Method is ordering divisions, the way of ranking, and principal supply. [ch. 1]

Deception and Reversal

The *Sunzi* has been consistently reviled by Confucians for advocating deception. Xunzi, for example, in the debate on military matters that occupies the fifteenth chapter of his writings, declares, "The army of a humane man cannot be deceived." As we shall see, however, the *Sunzi* is concerned not with mere trickery but with working with the binary nature of experiential categories.

The conclusion of this section notes that deception is entirely situation-oriented: it depends for its effectiveness on the accurate reading of present conditions, which by their nature cannot be entirely foreseen.

The military is a way (*dao*) of deception.
  Thus when able, manifest inability. When active, manifest inactivity.
  When near, manifest as far. When far, manifest as near.
  When he seeks advantage, lure him.
  When he is in chaos, take him.
  When he is substantial, prepare against him.
  When he is strong, avoid him.
  Attack where he is unprepared. Emerge where he does not expect.
  These are the victories of the military lineage. They cannot be transmitted in advance. [ch. 1]

On Victory

In general, the method of employing the military —
  Taking a state whole is superior. Destroying it is inferior to this.
  Taking a division whole is superior. Destroying it is inferior to this.
  Taking a battalion whole is superior. Destroying it is inferior to this.
  Taking a company whole is superior. Destroying it is inferior to this.
  Taking a squad whole is superior. Destroying it is inferior to this.

Therefore, one hundred victories in one hundred battles is not skillful. Subduing the other's military without battle is skillful.

Thus the superior military cuts down strategy. Its inferior cuts down alliances. Its inferior cuts down the military. The worst attacks cities.

Knowing victory has five aspects.

Knowing when one can and cannot do battle is victory.

Discerning the use of the many and the few is victory.

Superior and inferior desiring the same is victory.

Using preparation to await the unprepared is victory.

The general being capable and the ruler not interfering is victory.

These five are a way (*dao*) of knowing victory.

Thus it is said —

> Knowing the other and knowing oneself,
> In one hundred battles no danger.
> Not knowing the other and knowing oneself,
> One victory for one defeat.
> Not knowing the other and not knowing oneself,
> In every battle certain danger. [ch. 3]

In the past the skillful first made themselves invincible to await the enemy's vincibility.

Invincibility lies in oneself. Vincibility lies in the enemy.

Thus the skilled can make themselves invincible. They cannot cause the enemy's vincibility. Thus it is said, "Victory can be known but cannot be made."

Invincibility is defense. Vincibility is attack.

Defend and one has a surplus. Attack and one is insufficient.

One skilled at defense hides below the nine earths and moves above the nine heavens. Thus one can preserve oneself and be all-victorious.

In seeing victory, not going beyond what everyone knows is not skilled.

Victory in battle that all-under-Heaven calls skilled is not skilled.

Thus lifting the down of an autumn leaf does not make great strength. Seeing the sun and the moon does not make a clear eye. Hearing thunder does not make a keen ear.

What is meant by skilled is to be victorious over the easily defeated. Thus the battles of the skilled are without extraordinary victory, without reputation for wisdom, and without merit for courage.

Thus one's victories are without error. Being without error, what one arranges is necessarily victorious, since one is victorious over the already defeated.

One skilled at battle takes a stand in the ground of no-defeat and so does not lose the enemy's defeat.

Therefore, the victorious military is first victorious and after that does battle. The defeated military first does battle and after that seeks victory. [ch. 4]

The Orthodox and the Extraordinary

This is the most famous pair of terms in the *Sunzi*. The orthodox, or *zheng*, refers to military action that is conventionally correct — for example, that one should not fight with one's back to water, as that leaves no route for retreat. It is military operations by the book, and as such it constitutes an indispensable part of any military action. But to obtain victory the *Sunzi* advocates "the extraordinary" — or, literally, "the strange" (*qi*) — that which the enemy does not expect. From the interplay of these two elements emerges an unending series of strategies.

Note that what is at first extraordinary immediately loses its surprise value. Eventually it may even turn into orthodoxy. Thus in certain circumstances it may be more extraordinary to do that which is normally considered orthodox. What is most striking about the pair, then, is that the label *extraordinary* or *orthodox* is applied to strategies not according to some assessment of their intrinsic nature but rather in light of the enemy's expectations. In this sense strategy is a matter of perception.

This long selection, which probably contains two or more passages that were originally separate, also introduces the term *shi*. In other contemporary military texts *shi* simply indicates the advantage that can be found within the configuration of a situation — the power of taking the right place. In the Warring States administrative texts later grouped under the heading "Legalism," *shi* comes to mean the power that the ruler has by virtue of sitting on the throne — in other words, the authority of his position. It is thus relational but static. In the *Sunzi*, however, this power also has a dynamic aspect. It is something that one develops or cultivates and then releases at the right moment. Here the central images of *shi* are the crossbow that has been drawn and rocks that are poised to roll down a mile-high mountain. This aspect of *shi* is best rendered "potential energy." However, since no English word captures both the term's static sense of a configuration of power and its dynamic sense of potential energy, we have left it untranslated.

In general when in battle:
Use the orthodox to engage. Use the extraordinary to attain victory.

Thus one skilled at giving rise to the extraordinary is as boundless as Heaven and Earth, as inexhaustible as the Yellow River and the ocean.

Ending and beginning again, like the sun and moon. Dying and then being born, like the four seasons.

Musical pitches do not exceed five, yet all their variations cannot be heard. Colors do not exceed five, yet all their variations cannot be seen. Tastes do not exceed five, yet all their variations cannot be tasted. The *shi* of battle do not exceed the extraordinary and the orthodox, yet all their variations cannot be exhausted.

The extraordinary and orthodox circle and give birth to each other, like a circle without beginning. Who is able to exhaust it?

The rush of water, to the point of tossing rocks about: this is *shi*. The strike of a hawk at the killing snap: this is the node.

Therefore, one skilled at battle: his *shi* is steep, his node is short.

Shi is like drawing the crossbow. The node is like pulling the trigger. [ch. 5]

Order

These lines from the end of chapter 5 demonstrate how the *Sunzi* brings together materials that are only loosely related to each other. Among other things, the passages assembled here address the common military problem of chaos, cowardice, and weakness. Normally one wishes to create their opposites — order, bravery, and strength — but to attempt to do so, the text suggests, merely continues a slide around the continuum from negative to positive and back to negative — since "chaos is born from order." Instead, the *Sunzi* recommends stepping out of this polarity and using impersonal forces such as *shi* that will bring about the desired behavior on the soldiers' part. In this instance no attempt is made to discipline human beings or improve their nature.

The subsequent section makes a more precise recommendation: place your troops in an environmental configuration where their natural responses will be what you want, where it will be a matter of "rolling round rocks from a mountain one thousand *ren* high."

Pwun-pwun, huat-huat. The fight is chaotic, yet one is not subject to chaos.

Hun-hun, dun-dun. One's form is round, and one cannot be defeated.

Chaos is born from order. Cowardice is born from bravery. Weakness is born from strength.

Order and chaos are a matter of counting. Bravery and cowardice are a matter of *shi*. Strength and weakness are a matter of form.

One skilled at moving the enemy forms and the enemy must pursue, offers and the enemy must take.

One moves them by this and awaits them with troops.

Thus one skilled at battle seeks it in *shi* and not in people. Thus one can dispense with people and use *shi*.

One who uses *shi* sets people to battle as if rolling trees and rocks. As for the nature of trees and rocks: When still, they are at rest. When agitated, they move. When square, they stop. When round, they go.

Thus the *shi* of one skilled at setting people to battle is like rolling round rocks from a mountain one thousand *ren* high. This is *shi*. [ch. 5]

Form and Formlessness

Beginning with a loose collection of materials, this section then turns to the complex question of *form* (*xing*), a term whose meaning ranges from the most concrete issues of military drill to the most abstract sense of formlessness. Like water, the skillful general has no predetermined form. Thus he can transform endlessly, spiritlike. He may even act like the cosmos itself.

One who takes position first at the battleground and awaits the enemy is at ease. One who takes position later at the battleground and hastens to do battle is at labor.

Thus one skilled at battle summons others and is not summoned by them.

How one can make the enemy arrive of their own accord is through benefit. How one can prevent the enemy from arriving is through harm.

Thus one can make the enemy labor when at ease and starve them when full. It is a matter of emerging where they must hasten.

To go a thousand *li* without fear is to go through unpeopled ground.

To attack and surely take it is to attack where they do not defend. To defend and surely hold firm, defend where they will surely attack.

Thus with one skilled at attack the enemy does not know where to defend. With one skilled at defense the enemy does not know where to attack.

Subtle! Subtle! To the point of formlessness. Spiritlike! Spiritlike! To the point of soundlessness. Thus, he can act as the enemy's fate star.[15]

The ultimate in giving form to the military is to arrive at formlessness. When one is formless, deep spies cannot catch a glimpse and the wise cannot strategize.

Rely on form to bring about victory over the multitude, and the multitude cannot understand. People all know the form by which I am victorious, but no one knows how I determine form.

Do not repeat the means of victory, but respond to form from the inexhaustible.

Now, the form of the military is like water. Water in its movement avoids the high and hastens to the low. The military in its victory avoids the solid and strikes the empty.

Thus water determines its movement in accordance with the earth. The military determines victory in accordance with the enemy.

The military is without fixed *shi* and without constant form.

To be able to transform with the enemy is what is meant by spiritlike.

Of the Five Phases, none is the lasting victor. Of the four seasons none

---

15. A pair of stars in the constellation *xu* (β Aquarii) that were thought to determine the time of one's death.

has constant rank. Days shorten and lengthen. The moon waxes and wanes. [ch. 6]

Invading Enemy Territory

This passage provides a final example of how the general relies on *shi* — the dynamic configuration of things — to attain the result he seeks. Here his troops are deep in enemy territory, fearing for their lives. He does not attempt to alter their state of mind but rather uses it to make them invincible.

In general, the way (*dao*) of being an invader:
    Enter deeply and one is concentrated. The defenders do not subdue one. Plunder rich countryside. The army has enough to eat.
        Carefully nourish and do not work them.
        Consolidate *qi* and accumulate strength.
        Move the army and appraise one's strategies.
        Be unfathomable.
    Throw them where they cannot leave. Facing death they will not be routed. Officers and men facing death, how could one not gain their utmost strength?
        When military officers are sinking, they do not fear.
        Where they cannot leave, they stand firm.
        When they enter deep, they hold tightly.
        Where they cannot leave, they fight.
    Therefore, they are
        Unregulated yet disciplined,
        Unsought yet obtained,
        Without covenant yet in kinship,
        Without orders yet trusting.
    Prohibit omens, remove doubts, and even death seems no disaster.
    My officers do not have surplus wealth. It is not that they hate goods. They do not have surplus deaths. It is not that they hate longevity.
    On the day that orders are issued, the tears of seated officers moisten their lapels, the tears of those reclining cross their cheeks. Throw them where they cannot leave — it is the bravery of Zhuan Zhu and Cao Mo.[16]
    Thus one skilled at employing the military may be compared to the *shuairan*. The *shuairan* is a snake of Mount Heng. Strike its head and the tail arrives. Strike its tail and the head arrives. Attack its midsection and both head and tail arrive.
    Dare one ask, "Can one then make them like the *shuairan*?"

---

16. Assassin-retainers whose biographies are preserved in ch. 86 of the *Records of the Grand Historian* (*Shiji*). Cao Mo is elsewhere referred to as Cao Gui.

I reply, "One can. The people of Yue and the people of Wu hate each other. When they are in the same boat crossing the river, they help each other like the left and right hand."

Therefore, tying horses together and burying wheels is not enough to rely on.

Make bravery uniform. This is a way (*dao*) of governance. Attain both hard and soft. This is a principle of earth.

Thus one skilled at employing the military takes them by the hand as if leading a single person. They have no alternative. [ch. 11]

[Yang, *Sunzi huijian*, pp. 1–9, 12–15, 33–35, 45–55, 62–76, 84–89, 161–169 — KS]

PART 2

The Making of a Classical Culture

Chapter 8

THE HAN REACTION TO QIN ABSOLUTISM

Though China witnessed periods of imperial splendor under several dynasties, the Qin (221–207 B.C.E.) and Han (202 B.C.E.–220 C.E.) clearly represent the original "imperial age," because in these years the basic pattern for succeeding empires was laid out. The rule of the Qin was short-lived but marked a great turning point in Chinese history. For the first time the country was brought under a single unified administration, a centralized state wielding unprecedented power, controlling vast resources, and displaying a magnificence that inspired both awe and dread among its subjects. Achieved after years of steady, systematic conquest, this empire nevertheless proved an unexpected graveyard for the grandiose ambitions of its masters.

Yet when the Qin suddenly collapsed, it left to the House of Han an important legacy: the idea of empire and the governmental structure to embody it. For almost four centuries under the Han the implications of this great fact were to work their way out in all aspects of Chinese life, not least in the intellectual sphere. It is with this long period of consolidation and coordination that we shall be chiefly concerned here. In several fundamental respects it shaped the intellectual and institutional traditions of China until modern times, and not of China only but of much of East Asia as well.

The downfall of the Qin, more dramatic and sudden even than its rise, had a profound effect upon the thinking of the Chinese. It proved to their satisfaction that terror and strength alone could never rule the world. But the men who wrested from the Qin the vast empire it had created were not bent simply on restoring the old order of things.

The aristocratic families of the older feudal states of Zhou, which had bitterly resisted the expansion of Qin, had been seriously weakened by the steps the conqueror later took to prevent them from again threatening his power. The opposition that eventually proved fatal to the Qin dynasty, therefore, came not from the ranks of the old aristocracy but from the common people. Chen She, who led the first major revolt against Qin rule, was a day laborer in the fields. Liu Ji, the man who finally set up the Han dynasty after destroying both the Qin and rival rebel factions, was likewise of humble origin, as were most of his comrades who fought with him to victory.

As commoners under the Qin, these men knew firsthand the suffering that its harsh rule had brought to the people. They were quick to abolish its more offensive laws and institutions, while leaving intact much of the rest of its elaborate machinery of government. Under their leadership the new regime of the Han was marked by plebeian heartiness and vigor, simplicity and frugality in government, and abhorrence of the Legalist doctrines of the hated Qin.

The early years of the Han were marked by a long, slow struggle to recover for the empire the advantages of the harsh unification effected by the Qin and to establish them firmly in the pattern of Chinese society. The Qin had abolished the enfeoffment system in one sweeping stroke, yet it arose again among the followers and family of the founder of the Han, whose successors had to set about quietly and patiently whittling away at feudal rights and holdings until they were finally and for all time reduced to an empty formality. The great web of central government, held together by the terror of Qin's laws and the personal power of its First Emperor, had quickly disintegrated with the fall of the dynasty. The Han worked gradually to build it up again, unifying, organizing, and standardizing the vast area brought under its control. This effort at standardization extended even to the systematizing of thought in which, again, the Han succeeded in accomplishing, by gradual and peaceful means, what the violent proscriptions of the Qin had failed to secure.

JIA YI: "THE FAULTS OF QIN"

The following excerpt is from the celebrated essay "The Faults of Qin" ("Guo Qin lun"), by the Han poet and statesman Jia Yi (201–168? B.C.E.). Jia Yi, employing the florid style popular at this time, reviews the history of Qin and analyzes the causes of its precipitous downfall. Note, however, that he finds fault not with the Qin state itself but primarily with the failings of the founder of the empire and his heir, the Second Emperor, who squandered the magnificent achievements of their forebears.

Duke Xiao of Qin, sequestered in the natural stronghold of Yaohan and based in the land of Yongzhou,[1] with his ministers in proper array, eyed the House of Zhou with the thought of rolling up the empire like a mat, enveloping the entire universe, pocketing all within the Four Seas, and swallowing up everything in all Eight Directions. At the time he was counseled by Lord Shang,[2] who aided him in establishing laws, encouraging agriculture and weaving, preparing the tools of war for defense and offense, and negotiating alliances far and near so that the other feudal lords fell into strife with one another. Thus the Qin effortlessly acquired the territories just to the east of the upper reaches of the Yellow River.

After the death of Duke Xiao, King Huiwen, King Wu, and King Zhaoxiang inherited the legacy and continued his policies, acquiring Hanzhong in the south, Ba and Shu in the west, fertile lands in the east, and other strategic areas in the north. . . .

[Later] when the First Emperor ascended [the throne] he flourished and furthered the accomplishments of the six generations before him. Brandishing his long whip, he drove the world before him; destroying the feudal lords, he swallowed up the domains of the two Zhou dynasties. He reached the pinnacle of power and ordered all in the Six Directions, whipping the rest of the world into submission and thus spreading his might through the Four Seas. . . . He then abolished the ways of ancient sage kings and put to the torch the writings of the Hundred Schools in an attempt to keep the people in ignorance.[3] He demolished the walls of major cities and put to death men of fame and talent,[4] collected all the arms of the realm at Xianyang and had the spears and arrowheads melted down to form twelve huge statues in human form — all with the aim of weakening his people. Then he . . . posted capable generals and expert bowmen at important passes and placed trusted officials and well-trained soldiers in strategic array to challenge all who passed. With the empire thus pacified, the First Emperor believed that, with the capital secure within the pass and prosperous cities stretching for ten thousand *li*, he had indeed created an imperial structure to be enjoyed by his royal descendants for ten thousand generations to come.

Even after the death of the First Emperor, his reputation continued to sway the people. Chen She was a man who grew up in humble circumstances in a hut with broken pots for windows and ropes as door hinges and was a mere hired field hand and roving conscript of mediocre talent. He could neither

---

1. Yaohan refers to the mountain pass linking Mount Yao and the Hangu Pass in present-day He'nan, near Tongguan in Shaanxi province. Yongzhou was one of nine provinces occupied by the Qin, consisting of most of present-day Shaanxi and portions of Gansu and Qinghai.

2. See ch. 7, pp. 193–98.

3. See ch. 7, pp. 209–210.

4. See ch. 7, p. 210.

equal the worth of Confucius and Mozi nor match the wealth of Tao Zhu or Yi Dun, yet, even stumbling as he did amidst the ranks of common soldiers and shuffling through the fields, he called forth a tired motley crowd and led a mob of several hundred to turn upon the Qin. Cutting down trees to make weapons, and hoisting their flags on garden poles, they had the whole world come to them like gathering clouds, with people bringing their own food and following them like shadows. These men of courage from the East rose together, and in the end they defeated and extinguished the House of Qin.

Actually, the Qin empire was by no means small and weak, having always been secure within the pass in Yongzhou. Moreover, Chen She's position was far below the level of respect commanded by the rulers of Qi, Chu, Yan, Zhao, Han, Wei, Song, Wei, and Zhongshan. His weapons made of farm implements and thorny tree branches were no match in battle against spears and halberds, his roving conscripts in no way compared to the armies of the nine states. In matters of strategy and tactics, and other military arts, Chen was no match for the men of the past. . . . Qin, from a tiny base, had become a great power, ruling the land and receiving homage from all quarters for a hundred-odd years. Yet after they had unified the land and secured themselves within the pass, a single common rustic could nevertheless challenge this empire and cause its ancestral temples to topple and its ruler to die at the hand of others, a laughingstock in the eyes of all. Why? Because the ruler lacked humaneness and rightness; because preserving power differs fundamentally from seizing power.

. . . Had the Second Emperor been even a mediocre ruler who knew how to employ loyal and capable persons, so that together they would care for the ills of the world and reform the ways of the previous emperor, even as he mourned; had he divided the land and appointed deserving officials, thus setting up proper rulers in proper states so that propriety governed the land; had he emptied the prisons and reduced harsh punishments, abolished group and family responsibilities for crimes and thus enabled people to return to their home areas; had he only reduced taxation and statutes to alleviate oppression, curtailed sumptuary laws, and, after all the above had been done, had he lightened punishments, thus enabling people under heaven to renew themselves and change their ways so as to conduct their lives properly, each respecting himself; had he indeed fulfilled the wishes of the multitudes and bestowed high virtue on them, he would have certainly brought peace and quiet to the world. Within the Four Seas, all would have been content with their lot, only fearing further change. Even if an occasional mean or calculating person had appeared, no desire to oppose the ruler would have been aroused, and unscrupulous officials would have had no excuse to give play to their ambitions. The villainy of violence and deceit would have been eliminated. . . .

During that time, the world saw many men of prescience and far-reaching vision. The reason for their not showing deep loyalty by helping to correct evils [at court] lay in the Qin's excesses in proscribing contrary opinions. Often before upright words could even be uttered, the body had met death. Thoughtful people of the empire would only listen and incline their ears, standing with one foot on the other, not daring to offer their services while keeping their mouths shut in silence. The three sovereigns lost the proper way while loyal officials offered no remonstrance and advisers no plans. With the realm in chaos and unworthy officials not reporting troubles to their superiors, was this not a tragedy?

[Xinshu, "Guo Qin lun" (SBCK 1:1a–8b) — DWYK]

THE REBELLION OF CHEN SHE AND WU GUANG

This description of the beginning of the first major revolt against the Qin dynasty is taken from the biographies of its leaders, Chen She and Wu Guang, in the *Records of the Grand Historian (Shiji)* and the *History of the Former Han (Hanshu)*. It illustrates how the severity of the Qin laws and institutions drove its people to such desperation that revolt became the only hope of survival.

When Chen She was young he was one day working in the fields with the other hired men. Suddenly he stopped his plowing and went and stood on a hillock, wearing a look of profound discontent. After a long while he announced: "If I become rich and famous, I will not forget the rest of you!"

The other farm hands laughed and answered, "You are nothing but a hired laborer. How could you ever become rich and famous?"

Chen She gave a great sigh. "Oh, well," he said, "how could you little sparrows be expected to understand the ambitions of a swan!"

During the first year of the Second Emperor of Qin (209 B.C.E.), in the seventh month, an order came for a force of nine hundred men from the poor side of the town to be sent to garrison Yuyang. Chen She and Wu Guang were among those whose turn it was to go, and they were appointed heads of the levy of men. When the group had gone as far as Daze County, they encountered such heavy rain that the road became impassable. It was apparent that the men would be unable to reach the appointed place, an offense punishable by death. Chen She and Wu Guang accordingly began to plot together. "As things stand, we face death whether we stay or run away," they said, "while if we were to start a revolt we would likewise face death. Since we must die in any case, would it not be better to die fighting for the sake of a state?" . . .

Wu Guang had always been kind to others and many of the soldiers would do anything for him. When the officer in command was drunk, Wu Guang made a point of openly announcing several times that he was going to run away. In this way Wu Guang hoped to arouse the commander's anger, get him to punish him, and so stir up the men's ire and resentment. As Wu Guang had expected, the commander began to beat him, when the commander's sword slipped out of its scabbard. Wu Guang sprang up, seized the sword, and killed the commander. Chen She rushed to his assistance, and they proceeded to kill the other two commanding officers as well. Then they called together all the men of the group and announced: "Because of the rain we encountered, we cannot reach our rendezvous on time. And anyone who misses a rendezvous has his head cut off! Even if you should somehow escape with your heads, six or seven out of every ten of you are bound to die in the course of garrison duty. Now, my brave fellows, if you are unwilling to die, we have nothing more to say. But if you would risk death, then let us risk it for the sake of fame and glory! Kings and nobles, generals and ministers — such men are made, not born!" The men of the garrison all replied, "We'll do whatever you say!"

[From *Shiji* (BNB) 48:1a–3a — BW]

THE RISE OF LIU BANG, FOUNDER OF THE HAN

Liu Bang, like Chen She, was a man of humble birth who formed a small band of adventurers and opposed Qin rule. When his forces grew to a sizable army, he entered into an agreement with other rebel groups that the one who first reached the capital area of Qin, Guanzhong or the land "within the Pass," should become its ruler. In 207 B.C.E. Liu Bang succeeded in fighting his way to the capital city of Xianyang, and the Qin dynasty came to an end. At this time he issued his famous three-article code (ten characters in Chinese) to replace the elaborate legal code of Qin. Though when the dynasty got on its feet a more elaborate set of laws had to be worked out, this three-article code has often been held up as an example of the simplicity and leniency of early Han government. The translations are from the biography of Liu Bang, the "Annals of Emperor Gaozu" (his posthumous title) in the *Records of the Grand Historian*. Liu Bang's various titles have been omitted for the sake of clarity.

In the tenth month of the first year of Han (November–December 207 B.C.E.) Liu Bang finally succeeded in reaching Bashang [near the capital] ahead of the other leaders. Ziying, the king of Qin, came in a plain carriage drawn by white horses, wearing a rope about his neck,[5] and surrendered the imperial seals and credentials by the side of Chi Road. Some of the generals asked that the king of Qin be executed, but Liu Bang replied: " . . . To kill a man who has already surrendered would only bring bad luck!" With this he turned the king of Qin over to the care of his officials. Then he proceeded west and entered Xianyang.

---

5. White is the color of mourning, while the rope indicated total submission. Ziying had succeeded the second emperor as ruler of Qin, but because of the wobbly state of his empire he had ventured only to call himself king, not emperor.

. . . He sealed up the storehouses containing Qin's treasures and wealth and returned to camp at Bashang. There he summoned all the distinguished and powerful men of the districts and addressed them, saying, "Gentlemen, for a long time you have suffered beneath the harsh laws of Qin. Those who criticized the government were wiped out along with their families; those who gathered to talk in private were executed in the public market. I and the other nobles have made an agreement that he who first enters the Pass shall rule over the area within. Accordingly, I am now king of this territory within the Pass. I hereby promise you a code of laws consisting of three articles only: he who kills anyone shall suffer death; he who wounds another or steals shall be punished according to the gravity of the offense; for the rest I hereby abolish all laws of Qin. Let the officials and people remain undisturbed as before. I have come only to save you from further harm, not to exploit or tyrannize over you. Therefore do not be afraid! The reason I have returned to Bashang is simply to wait for the other leaders so that when they arrive we may settle the agreement."

He sent men to go with the Qin officials and publish this proclamation in the district towns and villages. The people of Qin were overjoyed and hastened with cattle, sheep, wine, and food to present to the soldiers. But Liu Bang declined all such gifts, saying, "There is plenty of grain in the granaries. I do not wish to be a burden to the people." With this the people were more joyful than ever and their only fear was that Liu Bang would not become king of Qin.

[From *Shiji* (*BNB*) 8:15a–16b — BW]

LIU BANG BECOMES THE FIRST EMPEROR OF THE HAN DYNASTY

To ensure the loyalty of his comrades and supporters, Liu Bang was obliged to hand out titles and fiefs to them as his conquests advanced. In 202 B.C.E., when his final success seemed assured, they in turn urged him to assume the old Qin title of Exalted Emperor, arguing that if he failed to do so their own titles would lack authority. Like Caesar he modestly declined three times before accepting.

In the first month [of 202 B.C.E.] the various nobles and generals all joined in begging Liu Bang to take the title of Exalted Emperor (*huangdi*), but he replied, "I have heard that the position of emperor may go only to a worthy man. It cannot be claimed by empty words and vain talk. I do not dare to accept the position of emperor."

His followers all replied, "Our great king has risen from the humblest beginnings to punish the wicked and violent and bring peace to all within the four seas. To those who have achieved merit he has accordingly parceled out land and enfeoffed them as kings and marquises. If our king does not assume the supreme title, then all our titles as well will be called into doubt. On pain of death we urge our request!"

Liu Bang declined three times and then, seeing that he could do no more, said, "If you, my lords, all consider it a good thing, then it must be to the good of the country." On the day *jiawu* [February 28, 202 B.C.E.] he assumed the position of Exalted Emperor on the north banks of the Si River.

[From *Shiji* (*BNB*) 8:28b — BW]

Chapter 9

SYNCRETIC VISIONS OF STATE, SOCIETY, AND COSMOS

During the period of intense conflict in the late fourth and third centuries B.C.E., one independent kingdom after another fell to the overwhelming military power of the Qin state, which, as we have seen, conquered all others and unified China under a single emperor in 221 B.C.E. This was a chaotic period for everyone, including the intellectuals who scrambled for patronage at the various local courts and attempted to develop philosophies that would be effective in combating tyranny and governing the state.

In this period we see the rise of highly politicized syncretisms, founded on the cosmological ideas of many thinkers and on the self-cultivation theories of the *Laozi* and *Zhuangzi* and that extended them, often in a quite specific manner, to the problems of government. Sometimes called "Huang-Lao," after the Yellow Emperor and Laozi, these new doctrines integrated relevant ideas from several philosophical lineages, such as the Confucian, Mohist, and Legalist, and synthesized them within a Daoist framework. By the first part of the Han dynasty, this syncretic form became so dominant that the famous historian Sima Tan believed that it defined the essence of Daoism. It even received imperial sanction for several decades until the ascent to power of Emperor Wu in 141 B.C.E.

We include in this chapter selections from a number of texts that span more than a century from about 250 B.C.E. Two of these texts, the *Springs and Autumns of Mr. Lü (Lüshi chunqiu)* (241 B.C.E.) and the *Huainanzi* (139 B.C.E.), can be dated with some certainty. The others — the *Huang-Lao Silk Manuscripts*, the *Guanzi*, the syncretist sections of the *Zhuangzi*, and the *Inner Canon of the Yellow Emperor* (*Huangdi neijing*) — are of more uncertain date. Sima Tan's "Discourse on the Six Lineages" must have been written in the latter part of the second century B.C.E. between the presentation of the *Huainanzi* to Emperor Wu and Sima Tan's death in 110 B.C.E.

Taken individually, these texts represent the work of many authors who did not belong to a single philosophical lineage. Taken together, they exhibit so many striking similarities in philosophical outlook that they can fairly be viewed as representing stages of syncretism, influenced in varying degrees by the *Laozi* and *Zhuangzi*, that were a dominant intellectual influence in this period and beyond.

Perhaps the predominant theme in these texts is that of the spiritual self-perfection of the ruler. Human society must be governed by an individual who has attained profound integration through techniques of "inner cultivation" and who has gained the gnostic vision of the unifying power of the Way that enables him to govern effectively. Living in a holistic universe governed by resonances between macrocosm and microcosm, a universe of which human societies were perceived to be integral parts, subject to its laws, such a sage king perceived these fundamental patterns of Heaven and Earth and established a government based upon them. This governing framework having been constructed, the sage king would be able to govern through nonaction, that is, without interfering with natural processes. By delegating responsibilities to his subordinates and cultivating clarity of mind he could respond spontaneously and harmoniously to any situation that arose.

THE THEORETICAL BASIS OF THE IMPERIAL INSTITUTION

The Springs and Autumns of Mr. Lü (Lüshi chunqiu)

The Han dynasty for the first time built an apparatus of government on a firm foundation of ritual, capable of governing, from a single center of power, a domain immensely larger than any Chinese ruler had administered before. The basic doctrines that justified this new order asserted that it reflected the eternal and regular order of the cosmos, the Dao. This sweeping claim wiped away the need to justify enactments one by one. The form of government was supremely natural; any recalcitrance or opposition was by definition unnatural, and bound to fail. Just as direction emanated from government to people, the emperor drew spiritual power from his special relationship to the cosmos and with it vivified his large administration. The gulf between emperor and the officials who carried out his orders had to be as absolute as that between government and commoners.

None of these ideas originated in the Han. Some developed gradually, but the *Springs and Autumns of Mr. Lü (Lüshi chunqiu)*, completed by 241 B.C.E., pulled them all together.

Lü Buwei, after whom the text is named, was not a typical intellectual. His official biography explains that he began as "a big merchant of Yangdi who traveled back and forth, buying cheap and selling dear, until his family had stored up a thousand in gold." But he used his wealth to become councilor-in-chief of Qin and the greatest patron of learning in his time. According to a persistent rumor, he was the natural father of the First Emperor. Whether or not that was true, the latter, as a young prince, treated him as a second father.

His book is clearly meant to guide the ruler who would eventually unify China. The part from which this translation is drawn was completed in 241 B.C.E. The essays in it were written by a variety of Lü's protégés; what part he played is unknown. The book reflects most of the intellectual currents of its time. It draws heavily on the arcane beliefs that later came to be called Huang-Lao and to varying extents on practically every other philosophic tradition of its time, but scantily on Legalist writings. Despite this eclecticism, its views and recommendations are with few exceptions consistent.

If Lü hoped that his young monarch would accept this guidance, one can only say that he failed. The man who was to become the First Emperor soon discharged him, sent him into exile, and disregarded almost every idea in the book except for its approval of "righteous" military conquest. When the conquest was over, the new regime, which relied on coercive statist doctrines, quickly fell apart. With its long-lived successor, the Han, Lü's treatise came into its own. As the Han created a new order capable of earning a mandate from the elite, the *Springs and Autumns of Mr. Lü* greatly influenced the other thinkers included in this section.

The book is oriented toward control of a large state with an active officialdom whose knowledge and capacities make up for the ruler's inevitable limits and who, unlike him, must be subject to restraint and correction. The good social order is patterned on Nature. The state's dynamism is that of Nature's cyclic processes. The demarcation of sky and earth, moral and hierarchic as much as spatial, dictates the separation of ruler and officials. The monarch's responsibility is self-cultivation, which puts him in touch with the order of Heaven-and-Earth. His commands must be obeyed. At the same time, his mystical link to the cosmic flow is essential to overcome his own arbitrariness and selfishness. Administration is not his business, but that of the bureaucrats. He is unable to act except through them. Their inner lives, unlike that of the monarch, are of no concern to Lü so long as they are upright and keep within the strict limits of their posts. These restrictions separate officials from each other as surely as from the sovereign.

It would be a mistake to read this document simply as justifying the ruler's domination. That is certainly part of the story, but, as the rest of the book makes even more clear, this ideology binds the ruler as much as it does his civil service.

Just as his ministers cannot infringe on his sovereignty, the ruler cannot interfere in their management. Unlike the sage ruler of the more or less contemporary *Han Feizi*, who monopolizes and wields the power to reward and punish, so that his government becomes the mere instrument of his personal authority, Lü Buwei's sage never lets the details of government distract him from self-cultivation. As one chapter puts it:

> [The monarch] who has attained the Way is bound to be quiescent. Because he is quiescent, he is unknowing; his knowing is like unknowing. Thus we can speak of the Way of the Ruler. Thus it is said that the desires that arise within him cannot get out. We say they are locked in. The desires that arise from outside him cannot get in. We say they are closed out. . . . He has a water-level, but he does not level with it. He has a carpenter's line, but he does not draw perpendiculars with it. His is the greatest quiescence in the natural order; he is not only serene but tranquil. Because of that he can provide the standard for all-under-Heaven.[1]

THE ROUND WAY

The following excerpt is perhaps the most eloquent expression in Chinese — among a great many — of the notion that the state is a microcosm, a miniature replica of the universe. This is a great document of natural philosophy, but its aim — to justify a political hierarchy that separates ruler and officials — is obvious. Much Han writing on conceptions of Nature lies in the same tradition and is equally political in intent. In this sense scientific theory and political theory were invented in tandem. Like the rest of the book, this excerpt also surrounds the emperor himself with arcana, drawn here from a lost *Book of the Yellow Lord*.

The opening of this chapter explains why one speaks of the Way of Heaven as round and that of Earth as square, but its argument is tailored to its own themes. This contrast was a familiar one in the third century B.C.E. It probably originated in the astronomer's difference between measuring locations in the sky in degrees radiating from the North Pole and those on the Earth in linear distances north and south, east and west. But it also came to stand for the overarching magnanimity of Heaven in distinction to the boundedness of Earth. Heaven and round became the yang in relation to the yin of Earth and squareness. By calling on these yin-yang correspondences Lü implies that ruler and subordinates are inherently complementary, not antagonistic, opposites. Yang is creative, yin receptive, and neither can be realized except by interaction with the other.

But as this symbolism separated Heaven and Earth, they were reunited by the mediation of man, above all of the emperor. When a later book writes of the sage

---

1. *Lüshi chunqiu*, Ian 5:2, p. 1049.

emperor as "bearing the round on his head and treading on the square, holding to the measuring-rod and sleeping with the surveyor's cord,"[2] it is invoking ritualistic images of symmetry and order.

The Way of Heaven is round; the way of Earth is square. The sage kings took this as their model, basing on it [the distinction between] above and below. How do we explain the roundness of Heaven? The essential *qi* alternately moves up and down,[3] completing a cycle and beginning again, delayed by nothing; that is why we speak of the way of Heaven as round. How do we explain the squareness of Earth? The ten thousand things are distinct in category and shape. Each has its separate responsibility [as an official does], and cannot carry out that of another; that is why one speaks of the way of Earth as square. When the ruler grasps the round and his ministers keep to the square, so that round and square are not interchanged, his state prospers.

Day and night make up a cycle; this is the Round Way. The threading of the moon through its twenty-eight lodges, so that Horn and Axletree are connected; this is the Round Way.[4] As the essences [of yin and yang] move through the four seasons, alternately upward and downward, they encounter each other; this is the Round Way.[5] Something stirs and burgeons; burgeoning, it is born; born, it grows; growing, it matures; mature, it declines; declining, it dies; dead, it becomes latent [preceding another birth]; this is the Round Way.

The *qi*, as clouds, moves westward, always in motion, not slackening winter or summer. The streams flow eastward, never stopping night or day. What is above never dries up; what is below never fills; the smaller makes up the larger; the heavy makes up the light. That is the Round Way.[6]

The [*Book of the*] *Yellow Lord* says, "The Lord [of Heaven (*Tian*)] does not abide in a single place. If he had such a place he would have no place," by which it means he never stumbles. That is the Round Way.[7]

Human beings have nine orifices. If [the *qi*] abides in a single one, eight will be depleted. If eight are depleted for a very long time, the body will die. If

---

2. *Wenzi zuan yi* in *Ershier zi*, 29 a–b.

3. This refers to the movements of the energies that correspond to the seasons. See the next paragraph.

4. In the customary enumeration of the lunar lodges — the twenty-eight divisions of the solar, lunar, and planetary paths — Horn (roughly, Virgo) is the first and Axletree (roughly, Corvus) the last. Thus the motion of the moon ties the succession of lodges, and of the constellations they organize, into a cycle.

5. The sentence may also refer to the heavenly bodies considered as pure *qi*.

6. The customary explanation of this riddle is that what is above and smaller is the streams; what is below and larger is the sea; what is heavy is water; and what is light is clouds. Here one suspects that what is above is the clouds.

7. The reference is possibly to the cyclic tours of gods through the universe, which play an important role in astrology and other kinds of divination.

while acknowledging someone we listen, our acknowledgment may falter. If while listening we look, we may stop listening. This refers to concentrating on one thing. In doing so one does not want to stagnate, for stagnation results in failure. That is the Round Way.

The One is most exalted of all. No one knows its source. No one knows its incipient form (*duan*). No one knows its beginning. No one knows its end. Still the myriad things take it as their progenitor. The sage kings took it as their model in order to perfect their natures, to settle their vital forces, and to form their commands.

A command issues from the ruler's mouth. Those in official positions receive it and carry it out, never resting day and night. It moves unimpeded all the way down. It permeates the people's hearts and propagates to the four quarters [of the realm]. Completing the circle, it reverts to the place of the ruler. That is the Round Way. As the command goes round,[8] it makes possible what is impossible[9] and makes good what is not good, so that nothing impedes it. That nothing impedes it is because the Way of the ruler penetrates. Thus the command is what the ruler makes his life, and what determines his moral character and security.

People have a body with four limbs. Their ability to control it depends on their awareness when it responds to something. If they are not aware of its response, they are unable to control their body with its four limbs. The same is true of one's ministers. If there is a command and they do not respond to it, one will no longer be able to control them. To have them and not control them is worse than not having them. The ruler is one who must control what he does not own. This was true even of Shun, Yu, Tang, and Wu.[10]

When the Former Kings appointed high officials, they insisted that they be upright [literally, "square and correct"], in order to keep their responsibilities definite, so that [the ruler] would not be obstructed by those below. Yao and Shun were worthy rulers. They took worthies as their successors, for they were unwilling to bestow [the kingdom] on their own sons and grandsons. Still, in appointing high officials, they insisted that they be upright.[11] Nowadays the rulers of men insist merely that the succession not be lost, so that they can bestow [the kingdom] on their own sons and grandsons. When they appoint high officials they cannot demand that they be upright, for their own selfish

---

8. Here *ling yuan* literally means "the order rounds." But in this context it also implies "as the order accords with the Round Way." *Yuan* also can mean "complete" or "perfect," further enriching the implication.

9. The text at the same time means "makes the impermissible permissible."

10. Exemplary rulers from legendary prehistory to the beginning of the Zhou dynasty.

11. This sentence is ambiguous, but presumably it means that even exemplary rulers, although not as dependent on their ministers as weaker monarchs would be, insisted on moral probity in their officials.

desires have thrown [the state] into chaos. Why is that so? Because their desires extend so much further than their awareness.

Now [in music] the Five Modes always stimulate a response in each other, because their differences are precise. Each of the five keeps to its place, for the modes are attuned and balanced, and cannot conflict. That is why they are always receptive to each other.

The appointment of officials by a worthy ruler is similar to this. When each of the hundred officials[12] keeps to his responsibilities and puts his own affairs in order to await [the judgment of] the ruler, the ruler will not fail to be secure. Governed in this way, no state will fail to benefit. Forestalled in this way, no disaster will have a way to happen.

[*Lüshi chunqiu jiao shi* 3:5, pp. 171–173 — NS]

The Huang-Lao Silk Manuscripts (Huang-Lao boshu)

During the first six decades of the Han dynasty, a philosophy called Huang-Lao, named after the mythical Yellow Emperor Huangdi and the sage Laozi, was the predominant influence at the imperial court. It seems to have completely disappeared, however, after the ascendancy of Confucianism under Emperor Wu (r. 141–87 B.C.E.) beginning in 136 B.C.E. Known from terse references in historical writings, it was said to advocate a central government controlled by a ruler who had achieved profound states of tranquillity and who governed by taking no intentional action (*wuwei*), concepts found in the *Daodejing*.[13] It was said to be the product of a master-disciple lineage that reached back for more than a century before the Han dynasty began, but scholars were unable to identify any extant texts as having come from this lineage.

The situation changed dramatically in 1973 with the announcement of the discovery of a major cache of texts at a tomb excavation near the village of Mawangdui, close to the present-day city of Changsha in Hunan province. Among the silk scrolls unearthed at this tomb, which had been closed in 168 B.C.E., were two manuscripts of the *Daodejing* and four texts of varying lengths that were attached to one of them. The four became quite controversial when Chinese scholars initially identified them as the *Huangdi sijing* (*Four Canons of the Yellow Emperor*), lost for almost two thousand years. Amid the flurry of scholarship generated by this discovery, questions were raised about the precise identification of these texts with this lost work. Because of these questions we shall refer to them as the *Huang-Lao Silk Manuscripts* (*Huang-Lao boshu*). Many scholars have taken these works as the first concrete textual evidence of the long-lost Huang-Lao lineage.

---

12. I.e., "all officials."
13. See ch. 5.

The four texts, titled *Normative Standards* (*Jingfa*), *Sixteen Canons* (*Shiliu jing*), *Collected Sayings* (*Cheng*), and *The Source That Is the Way* (*Daoyuan*), are of widely varying lengths: the first contains 5,000 characters divided among nine distinct essays, while the last is a complete essay a mere 464 characters in length. Here we translate and analyze three essays from the first text and the last in its entirety.

There is as yet no scholarly consensus on the date and compilation of these four texts. Various theories place them anywhere from the beginning of the fifth century to the beginning of the second century B.C.E. and argue for both single and multiple authorship. Many scholars see the texts as related to one another, but some do not. Given the historical information and internal textual data, one would not go wrong in thinking of these texts as compilations that were written down between the middle of the third century and 200 B.C.E.

The philosophy found in the texts, particularly the two that follow, can best be described as a syncretism that is grounded in a cosmology of the Way and an ethos of self-cultivation and that fully embraces relevant concepts from the Daoists, Mohists, Legalists, Terminologists,[14] and Naturalists.[15] The predominant concern is how to establish an effective and just government, one that enables the mutual flourishing of ruler and subjects. *Normative Standards*, in particular, calls for this to be done by an enlightened sage king who has cultivated a profound tranquillity that enables him to see clearly the fundamental patterns that underlie, in a parallel fashion, both the cosmos and all the numerous endeavors of human beings. Humans are not only an integral part of the cosmos, and hence subject to its laws, but also constitute changing microcosmic homologies to the macrocosmic whole. Therefore, human behavior and all human endeavors must be carefully aligned with the greater standards and patterns of Heaven and Earth. To do this is to live life and organize society and its government according to the "Heavenly Correspondences." To fail to do this is to invite disaster — the spontaneous response of a cosmos out of balance because of inharmonious human activity.

BOOK 1: *NORMATIVE STANDARDS* (*JINGFA*), PART 1

The first selection is an essay titled "The Standards of the Way," which begins *Normative Standards*. It speaks of the Way as the ultimate source of all things within the cosmos but focuses on the standards it generates that serve as models for human behavior at both the societal and the individual levels. In order to act in harmony with this Way (and hence to succeed in every undertaking), the ruler must know its relevant

---

14. The Terminologists (School of Names) (*ming jiao*) were concerned with the correspondence of names and reality.

15. Or the yin-yang school.

standards in a particular situation and set his state on the right course by bringing his behavior and that of his people in line with these cosmic patterns. Of particular importance is the establishment of the definitive names for things that spontaneously manifest themselves to those with a purified and lucid mind, weights and measures to evaluate things, titles and performance expectations for government officials, and general standards of human behavior that do not violate the seasonal patterns (e.g., planting in the spring, not the fall). The sage king is able to do this because of the attainment of a profound level of self-cultivation that confers the ability to "look at and know," that is, spontaneously and accurately to assess the details and underlying pattern of any situation that presents itself.

The Standards of the Way (*Daofa*)[16]

I

The Way generates standards. Standards serve as marking cords to demarcate success and failure and are what clarify the crooked and the straight.[17]

Therefore, those who hold fast to the Way generate standards and do not to dare to violate them; having established standards, they do not dare to discard them.

[Missing graph] Only after you are able to serve as your own marking cord, will you look at and know all-under-Heaven and not be deluded.[18]

II

Empty and Formless:
Its core is impenetrably dark.
It is where all living things are generated.

---

16. We have divided an originally unbroken text into a number of topically derived sections in order to facilitate comprehensibility. In some cases the Chinese characters (or graphs) in these manuscripts, on fragile silk, are illegible or missing, but they have been tentatively restored by the team of scholars who compiled this edition, based on educated guesses about the likely meaning or on comparison with other texts. Instances in which such conjectural restoration has been made by the translators rather than by the Chinese editorial team are noted here.

17. The marking cord is an early Chinese chalk line that was used to mark a straight line. Unlike the level or plumb line, each of which can mark only a horizontal or a vertical line, the marking cord can mark a straight line at any angle.

18. To "look at and know" (*jian zhi*) is a characteristic phrase of *Normative Standards*. It denotes a direct knowledge attained the instant one perceives a thing, situation, or endeavor. It is contrasted with "to look into and know" (*shen zhi*), a phrase found in the fifth and eighth sections of *Normative Standards*. This is reflective knowledge that is attained after sifting through information and analyzing its underlying patterns. The contrast between the two is perhaps best understood as the difference between intuitive and rational apprehension of phenomena.

With life there are obstructions:
Call one desire;
Call one not knowing sufficiency.
With life there is inevitably movement,
With movement there are obstructions:
Call one untimeliness;
Call one being timely but [missing graph].
With movement there are endeavors,
With endeavors there are obstructions:
Call one deviance;
Call one failing to evaluate [an endeavor], not knowing what purpose it
    serves.
Endeavors inevitably involve speech,
With speech there are obstructions:
Call one not being trustworthy;
Call one not knowing to stand in awe of others;
Call one self-deception;
Call one empty boasting, taking insufficiency as surfeit.
Therefore, living things alike emerge from the impenetrably dark.
Some die because of it; some live because of it.
Some fail because of it; some succeed because of it.
Misfortune and good fortune share the same Way,
But no one knows where they are generated.

III

The Way to look at and know
Is simply to be empty and to have nothing.

When you are empty and have nothing, even if an autumn hair comes into
view, it will inevitably have its own form and name.[19] When forms and names
are established, then distinctions [such as] black and white are already there.[20]

Therefore, when those who hold fast to the Way observe all-under-Heaven:

---

19. The inherent form and name of a thing will be obvious when the sage does not impose
preexisting categories upon it. The autumn hair is a common metaphor in early Chinese philosophical texts for something that is extremely fine because the hair grown by animals in the fall
was said to be this way.

20. Sages who empty their minds of everything can directly perceive the inherent identity
and shape of each thing and of each human endeavor and instantly know the appropriate name
that corresponds to this form. Once these are established for the sage, life is extremely clear-cut
and unambiguous, literally "black and white."

> They cling to nothing.
> They settle in nothing.
> They do nothing.
> They are partial to nothing.

This is why, when endeavors occur in all-under-Heaven, there is no longer anything that does not manifest [to these sages] its own form and name, appraisal and rank.[21] Once form and name have been established, and appraisal and rank have been set up, there will be no way to flee the traces [of one's actions] or to conceal one's being on the right course.

IV

Those who are unbiased are lucid; the completely lucid are efficacious.
Those who are completely on the right course are tranquil; the completely
    tranquil are sagely.
Those who are impartial are wise; the completely wise are the norms of all-
    under-Heaven.

When there are endeavors in the world, [the sages] evaluate them with the weight and balance of the steelyard and align them with the Heavenly Correspondences, so that they inevitably give them a skillful assessment.[22] Endeavors are like growing trees and are as numerous as stored grains of millet. But when the peck (*dou*) and stone (*dun*) measures have been provided, and the foot (*chih*) and inch (*cun*) measures have been laid out, there will be no way to flee their numinous [insight] (*shen*). Therefore it is said: "Once rules and measures have been provided, [sages] order and regulate them."

> Detached and then rejoined,
> Absent and then present:
> Who understands their numinous [insight]?

---

21. While "form and name" refer to important epistemological categories in the objective world in general, they are also applied to setting up a government bureaucracy. In this sense they can be thought of as "title and performance." A bureaucrat must perform the duties assigned to his position; otherwise there will be chaos. Every so often the ruler must assess the performance of the officials and, when this is done, assign suitable ranks based on this appraisal. This is what is meant by "appraisal and rank." The historian Sima Tan apparently provides us with a general account of such an audience between rulers and ministers. See pp. 280–82.

22. The steelyard is a kind of balance with a short arm on one side on which things to be weighed are suspended and a long, graduated arm on the other side along which a weight is moved. It works like the scale found in many modern physicians' offices. The statement is metaphorical; it advocates evaluating endeavors with a balanced and unbiased mind.

> Dead and then reborn,
> Taking misfortune as good fortune:
> Who understands their ultimate limits?

They follow endeavors back to the Formless.
Therefore they understand where misfortune and good fortune are generated.

V

The Way of responding to transformations is to balance them out fairly and nothing more. When unimportant and important have not been evaluated, this is called "losing the Way."

> Heaven and Earth have their constant regularities;
> All people have their constant endeavors;
> The noble and base have their constant positions;
> Shepherding the ministers has its constant Way;
> Employing the people has its constant measures.

The constant regularities of Heaven and Earth are the four seasons, darkness and light, engendering and killing, the yielding and the firm.
The constant endeavors of all people are that men farm and women weave.
The constant positions of the noble and base are that worthy and unworthy do not interfere with one another.
The constant way of shepherding the ministers is to employ the capable and not exceed their strengths.
The constant measures of employing the people are to discard the partial and establish the unbiased.

If you alter these constants and exceed these measures, anomalies will trample one another. But when the anomalous and the correct have their set positions, names [and forms][23] will not depart from them.

> In all cases,
> Whether endeavors be small or great
> Things make a lodging place for themselves.
> Whether deviating or complying, dying or living,

---

23. This is our conjectural restoration of a missing graph.

Things make a name for themselves.
When names and forms have been established
Things will set themselves on the right course.

Therefore only those who can hold fast to the Way are able to clarify the reversing tendency of Heaven above, comprehend the differing responsibilities of ruler and minister in the middle, and secretly scrutinize where all living things end and begin without acting as their master.

Therefore only after you are able to become completely unadorned, completely purified, and can flow into the Formless, can you apply this to set all-under-Heaven on the right course.[24]

[*Mawangdui Hanmu boshu*, pp. 43–44]

NORMATIVE STANDARDS (*JINGFA*), PART 5

The two sections of this essay that are translated here deal with concrete examples of the kind of cosmic patterns and their human parallels spoken of in a more general fashion above. They also give a more detailed presentation of what it means to comply with or deviate from these underlying patterns and the consequences of the latter — which are dire indeed. A good example of the syncretism of these sources can be seen in the four measures that are the main focus of the essay. Rigid hierarchy between ruler and officials is also found in Legalist texts; honoring the worthy was initially a Mohist tenet; timely activity in line with cosmic patterns is one of the dominating themes of the Naturalists.

The Four Measures (*Sidu*)

I

When ruler and ministers change places,
We call this deviant.
When the worthy and the unworthy are established on a par,
We call this chaotic.
When activity and tranquillity are not timely,
We call this deviant.
When generating and killing do not correspond [to cosmic patterns],
We call this cruel.

---

24. This conclusion for the entire essay recapitulates the central message that only the sage who has cultivated himself to the point of temporarily dissolving his ego into the great formless Dao is able, upon his return from this condition, to set the world on its proper course by applying his transformed and totally selfless consciousness to the task.

With deviance, you lose the foundation.
With chaos, you lose the organization.
With deviance, you lose the Heavenly [correspondences].
With cruelty, you lose human beings.

When you lose the foundation, there will be [missing graph].
When you lose the organization there is encroachment [by one person on the
    responsibilities of another].
When you lose the Heavenly, there will be famine.
When you lose human beings, there will be enmity.

The cycles and motions [of Heavenly bodies]:
Heaven makes these its Norms.
The Way of Heaven is not distant:
One enters it and stays,
One emerges from it and returns.

When ruler and ministers are in their corresponding positions,
We call this quiescence.
When worthy and unworthy are in their corresponding positions,
We call this being on the right course.
When activity and quiescence align with [the patterns of] Heaven and Earth,
We call this civility (*wen*).
When punishments and (prohibitions)[25] are seasonally corresponding,
We call this martiality (*wu*).

With quiescence there is security.
With being on the right course there is order.
With civility there is lucidity.
With martiality there is strength.
With security you attain the foundation.
With order you attain [the allegiance of] human beings.
With lucidity you attain the Heavenly.
With strength you act majestically.

When you align with Heaven and Earth,
When you unite with the minds of the people,
When you establish civility and martiality on a par:
The name for this is "identifying with what is above."

---

25. Here we conjecturally restore an illegible graph to *jin* (prohibitions), following Chen
Guying, *Huangdi sijing jinzhu jinyi*, p. 156.

Look into and know[26] these Four Measures;[27]
With them you can stabilize all-under-Heaven
And you can make a single state secure.

Note in the following section the belief that the criteria by which we judge things in the human world come from a variety of sources, of which none is more important than Heaven and Earth. Because human beings are an integral part of the cosmos, we are subject to its patterns and influences. Consequently, we must use these patterns as criteria for determining our own behavior. If we succeed in this, human society forms microcosmic parallels to these macrocosmic patterns and in this way perfectly aligns itself with Heaven and Earth. This is the meaning of the triadic alignment of Heaven, Earth, and the human that preoccupied Chinese philosophers of the third century B.C.E.

II[28]

The inside of a compass is said to be round.
The inside of a carpenter's square is said to be square.
The underside of a hanging scale is said to be level.
The [surface of] the water level is said to be even.
[The center mark of a marking cord is said to be straight.][29]
The measures of feet and inches are said to be small, great, short, and long.
The balance of a steelyard is said to be where light and heavy do not err.
The quantities of a peck and a stone are said to be where the few and the
    many have their measure.
These eight measures are the norms of utility.

The periodic movements of the sun, moon, stars, and planets,
The limits of the four seasons,
The [sequential] positions of activity and quiescence,
The [relative] locations of inner and outer:
These are the Norms of Heaven.

That high and low do not obscure their forms;
That beautiful and ugly do not conceal their true characters:
These are the Norms of Earth.

---

26. To "look into and know" (*shen zhi*) is contrasted with to "look at and know" (*jian zhi*) from the first essay, "The Standards of the Way." It represents reflective knowledge, while the latter represents intuitive knowledge.

27. As given above, quiescence, being on the right course, civility, and martiality.

28. This passage begins from page 51, line 14 of the Wenwu edition.

29. This missing measure is conjecturally restored by the editors of the Wenwu edition from a parallel list in ch. 4 of the *Mozi*. By restoring this measure at this point, we end the list with a total of eight.

That ruler and minister do not lose their [relative] positions,
That scholars do not lose their places [in government],
To employ the capable and not exceed their strengths,
To discard the partial and establish the unbiased:
These are the Norms of human beings.

Beauty and ugliness have their names,
Deviation and compliance have their forms,
The genuine and the false have their reality.
The king, without bias, grasps (these),[30]
And with them sets all-under-Heaven on the right course.

III

Adapting to the seasons of Heaven,
To attack when Heaven is destroying:
We call this "martiality."

If you wield the martial sword
And then use civility to follow in its wake,
Then you will achieve success.

The one who uses two parts civility
And one part martiality
Is the king.

[*Mawangdui Hanmu boshu*, pp. 51–52]

NORMATIVE STANDARDS (*JINGFA*), PART 8

This essay continues the theme of the consequences of complying with or deviating from the normative patterns of the cosmos. Of particular concern here is the balance of civility, the state-building and people-nurturing activities that the ruler undertakes during the appropriate seasons, and martiality, the aggressive expeditions against unjust states that the ruler conducts only during the winter months when Heaven is also taking life.

A Synopsis of Discourses (*Lun yue*)

I

To begin in civility and end in martiality: this is the Way of Heaven and
    Earth.

---

30. Conjectural restoration of missing graph, following Chen Guying, *Huangdi sijing jinzhu jinyi*, p. 169.

The four seasons have their limits: these are the patterns of Heaven and
  Earth.
The sun, moon, stars, and planets all have their numerical regularities: these
  are the sequences of Heaven and Earth.
To bring achievements to completion in three seasons; to punish by death in
  one season: this is the Way of Heaven and Earth.

The four seasons are timely and stable; they do not err, they do not waver;
they always have standards and rules. [The four seasons]:[31] as one is established,
another is abandoned; when one springs to life, another dies away. The four
seasons rule successively; at the winter solstice their cycle begins anew.

II

The patterns of human endeavors are such that [the distinction between]
  deviation from and compliance with [Heavenly norms] must be guarded.
If human achievements exceed Heaven, therefore there is the punishment of
  death.[32]
If human achievements do not reach up to Heaven, then you will recede and
  have no reputation.[33]
If human achievements are united with Heaven, then your reputation will
  greatly develop.

The patterns of human endeavors are such that:
If you comply [with Heavenly norms], you will live,
If you pattern yourself on them, you will succeed,
If you deviate from them, you will die,
If you mistake them, [then you will have no] reputation.[34]

If you defy the Way of Heaven, your state will have no ruler. In a rulerless
state, deviation and compliance attack one another. If your foundation is attacked and your achievements are destroyed, chaos will arise and the state will
be lost.

If you act as if you attained the Heavenly [norms], you will lose your territory
and your rulership.

---

31. We propose *si shi ye* (the four seasons) as a conjectural restoration of three missing graphs.

32. An example of this might be continuing a punitive expedition past the limit that ends the
winter season into the springtime, when all should be occupied with planting and generating
life.

33. An example of this might be failing to take full advantage of the season of planting and
therefore not having enough to feed your people.

34. We accept this conjectural restoration of the two missing graphs as *ze wu* (then, no) by
Chen Guying, *Huangdi sijing jinzhu jinyi*, pp. 225–226.

If you do not comply with the regularities of Heaven, you will not moderate the strength of the people and you will circle around repeatedly without achieving anything. You nourish the dying and attack the living. The name for this is "total deviation." If you are not executed by another human being, you will inevitably receive the punishment of Heaven.

If deviance is moderated when it first springs to life, and you are careful about your transgression and correct it before heaven punishes you, then, contrary to expectations, you can ward off Heaven's punishments.

III

Therefore, when those who hold fast to the Way observe all-under-Heaven, they inevitably look into and observe how human endeavors begin to arise, and they look into their forms and names. When form and name are determined, deviation and compliance will have their respective positions, death and life will have their respective distinctions, and preservation and loss, prosperity and decline will have their respective places. Only then do you align them with the Constant Way of Heaven and Earth and thereby determine the locations of misfortune and fortune, death and life, survival and destruction, and prosperity and decline.

For this reason, whatever you initiate will not lose sight of this basic pattern and when you assess all-under-Heaven you will not omit any plan.

Therefore, to be able to establish the Son of Heaven, set up the Three Dukes, and have all-under-Heaven be transformed by them: this is called Possessing the Way.

[*Mawangdui Hanmu boshu*, p. 57]

BOOK 4: *THE SOURCE THAT IS THE WAY (DAOYUAN)*[35]

This complete text is a philosophical paean in praise of the unfathomable Way that is the source from which all living things emerge. It explores the manner in which it has pervaded all existence as its imperceptible yet palpable guiding power from the very origins of the cosmos. We also find in these verses a description of those few sages who have been able to merge with this Way and use it to guide the creation and evolution of human societies. This text most certainly echoes various verses on the Way and the sage from the *Daodejing*, but unlike the latter, it is a more sustained presentation. It bears a strong resemblance to the opening section of the first essay of

---

35. *Mawangdui Hanmu boshu*, pp. 87–88. Like many short Chinese texts of this era, this one was not originally divided into sections. We have created sections in the text wherever a new topic begins in order to facilitate its use.

the *Huainanzi*[36] which is, not coincidentally, titled "The Original Way" ("*Yuandao*"). As the last of the four *Huang-Lao Silk Manuscripts*, it strongly affirms their connection with major sources of early Daoist thought.

I

From the beginning when there was constantly nothing
It has been deeply merged with Vast Emptiness.
Empty and merged as one.
Constantly One and nothing more.

Murky and indistinct,
It has never been bright or dark.
Numinous and subtle, it fills everywhere.
Pure and tranquil, it is not visible.

From of old it has never relied on anything.
None of the myriad things has it relied on.
From of old it has been without form.
Vast and unfathomable, it has no name.

Heaven is not able to cover it.
Earth is not able to support it.
By means of it the small become small.
By means of it the great become great.

It fills the land within the Four Seas
And embraces whatever lies beyond.
When in the yin, it does not decay;
When in the yang, it does not scorch.
A unifying measure, it does not alter.
It can reach even insects and worms.

Birds attain it and fly.
Fish attain it and swim.
Beasts attain it and run.
When all living things attain it they are generated.
When all human endeavors attain it they thereby succeed.

Human beings all rely on it, yet none knows its name.
Human beings all make use of it, yet none sees its form.

---

36. See pp. 270–71.

"The One" is its byname (*hao*),
Emptiness is its abode.
Doing nothing is its simple practice,
Harmony is its manifestation.

II

For these reasons, this exalted Way is:
So lofty it cannot be discerned;
So deep it cannot be fathomed;
So brilliant we cannot give it a name;
So vast we cannot give it a form.

Solitary and without peer
No living thing can command it.

Heaven and Earth, yin and yang,
The four seasons, the sun and the moon,
The stars and the planets, the clouds and the air,
Various kinds of crawling insects, wriggling worms, and growing plants:
All draw life from it, yet the Way is not decreased by them;
All return to it, yet the Way is not increased by them.

Firm and strong, yet it does not dominate;
Soft and weak, yet it cannot be transformed.
It is what the purified and subtle cannot reach;
What the normative and ultimate cannot surpass.

III

Therefore, only Sages are able to discern it in the Formless,
And hear it in the Soundless.
After knowing the reality of its emptiness,
They can become totally empty,
And then be absorbed in the purest essence of Heaven-and-Earth.
Absorbed and merged without any gaps,
Pervasive and united without filling it up.

Fully to acquiesce to this Way:
This is called "being able to be purified."
The lucid are inherently able to discern the ultimate.
They know what others are unable to know,
And acquiesce to what others are unable to attain.
This is called "discerning the normative and knowing the ultimate."

IV

If sage kings make use of this,
All-under-Heaven will acquiesce.

Devoid of likes and dislikes,
If the one above makes use of this, [the ones below will respond,][37]
And the people will not be confused and deluded.
If the one above is empty, the ones below will be tranquil,
And the Way will actualize the right course.

One who is truly able to be without desires
Can give commands to the people.
If the one above truly acts without striving
Then all living things will be completely at peace.

V

Allot them their proper roles
And all the people will not contend.
Assign them their proper names
And all living things will be naturally stable.

Do not be encouraged when there is order;
Do not be inattentive when there is disorder.
Be broad and vast: do not work for it and you will achieve it.
Be deep and subtle: do not search for it and you will attain it.

If you can become unified and do not transform:
You will attain the foundation of the Way
And by grasping the few you will know the many;
You will attain the essentials of human endeavors
And by steering the right course you will set the anomalous upon it.

This final verse speaks of two complementary acts. The first is observing how the Way has manifested itself throughout the origin and evolution of the cosmos and of the human beings and societies that developed in it. The second is seeking deep within the Way to a point before the cosmos originated and thereby grasping why it operates as it does.

---

37. Two missing graphs. We suggest their conjectural restoration as *xia ying* (below will respond) based on parallelism and meaning.

Once you know great antiquity
Afterward you (can)[38] become purified and lucid.

Embrace the Way; hold fast to it as your measure
And all-under-Heaven can be unified.

Observe it from great antiquity,
And you will fully [see] how it operates.
Search for it in what is prior to nothingness,
And you will grasp why it operates.

[*Mawangdui Hanmu boshu*, pp. 43–44, 51–52, 57, 87–88 — HR, SQ]

The Guanzi

TECHNIQUES OF THE MIND, I (*XINSHU, SHANG*)

The *Guanzi*, a collection of essays mainly devoted to social and political philosophy (see chapter 7), is traditionally ascribed to the statesman Guan Zhong, who lived in the seventh century B.C.E. The text actually originated in the state of Qi in the mid-fourth century B.C.E. and was augmented for some two centuries or more, probably reaching final form early in the first century B.C.E. While it later came to be known as a Legalist work, it was initially classified as "Daoist" in the bibliographical section of the *History of the Former Han*. It does contain several short essays that deal with the familiar Daoist themes of the Way, emptiness, and their application to political thought through the self-cultivation of the enlightened ruler. One of these essays is "Techniques of the Mind, I" ("*Xinshu, shang*").

"Techniques of the Mind, I" is devoted to demonstrating how its prescribed methods of self-cultivation, limiting lusts and desires, emptying the mind of thoughts and precedents, and developing a profound tranquillity give the ruler the means to respond spontaneously and harmoniously to any situation that may arise. It is divided into two parts, the first a series of authoritative statements mostly in rhymed verse and the second a line-by-line commentary on these verses. While there is no scholarly consensus, the prevailing opinion is that the first part dates from the mid-third century B.C.E. (and is thus roughly contemporary with the *Springs and Autumns of Mr. Lü* (*Lüshi chunqiu*) and that the second is an early Han work from about 180 B.C.E.

The first selection here elaborates upon the theme of a universe with precise homologies between its different levels that we have seen in the *Springs and Autumns of Mr. Lü*. Here the parallel is between the cultivation by the enlightened ruler of "nonpurposive action" or "doing nothing" (*wuwei*) and his governing of the state,

---

38. Reading *neng* (to be able to) in the lacuna, a conjectural restoration based on parallelism. See Chen Guying, *Huangdi sijing jinzhu jinyi*, p. 484.

which is also a manifestation of *wuwei*. The ruler does not interfere with the officials in the governing of the state, just as the mind does not interfere with the spontaneous functioning of the perceptual organs.

The second selection presents the sages' unique ability to perceive clearly the forms of all living things and the patterns and shapes of all human situations and to fashion well-defined names and appropriate categories of behavior for each and every one of them. The sages can do this because they have developed the ability to respond (*ying*) spontaneously to all things and situations and to adapt (*yin*) to them without asserting their own individual viewpoint. These are two cardinal qualities of the Daoist sage in two of the later syncretic sources included here, the *Huainanzi* and Sima Tan's discourse on the lineages.[39]

The third selection is a continuation of the second. It speaks of the intricate relationship between the inner cultivation of tranquillity in rulers and the development of a facility at governing. It refers to this cultivation of a balance between inner quality and outer virtue as the "Way of stillness and adaptation" (*jingyin zhi Dao*), a catchphrase that finds striking parallels in the syncretist *Zhuangzi*'s "in stillness a sage, in motion a king" (*jing er sheng, dong er wang*)[40] and "inner sageliness and outer kingliness" (*neisheng, waiwang*).[41]

The fourth selection places the cultivation of the ruler in a cosmic context and defines a number of key terms associated with the establishment of good order in human society. Among the terms so defined are the notions of "rightness" (*yi*) and "laws" (*fa*). The way in which they are defined provides an excellent example of the syncretic use of ideas from other intellectual traditions redefined and reorganized within a cosmology of the Way.

I

[STATEMENT]

The position of the mind in the body
[Is analogous to][42] the position of the ruler [in the state].
The functioning of the nine apertures
[Is analogous to] the responsibilities of the officials.

> When the mind keeps to its Way,
> The nine apertures will comply with their inherent
> guiding principles.[43]

---

39. See pp. 268–73 and 278–82.
40. *Zhuangzi*, ch. 13.
41. Ibid., ch. 33.
42. Textual emendations are taken from Xu, Wen, and Guo, *Guanzi jijiao*, pp. 633–649.
43. This means that the sense organs will function properly and spontaneously if the mind

> When lusts and desires fill the mind to overflowing,
> The eyes do not see colors, the ears do not hear sounds.
> When the one above departs from the Way,[44]
> The ones below will lose sight of their tasks.

Therefore we say, "The techniques of the mind are to take no action and yet control the apertures."[45] [13:1a]

[COMMENT]

The position of the mind in the body
[Is analogous to] the position of the ruler [in the state].
The functioning of the nine apertures
[Is analogous to] the responsibilities of the officials.

The eyes and ears are the organs of seeing and hearing. When the mind does not interfere with the tasks of seeing and hearing, the organs will be able to keep to their duties.

When the mind has desires, things pass by and the eyes do not see them; sounds are there but the ears do not hear them. Therefore [the statement] says:

> When the one above departs from the Way,
> The ones below will lose sight of their tasks.

Therefore [the statement] calls the mind "ruler." [13:2a–b]

II

[STATEMENT]

Things inherently have forms; forms inherently have names.
Persons who match names [and forms] — call them sages.

---

does not interfere with them. This occurs because each has an inherent pattern of activity that derives from its individual characteristics and its relation to the whole body. In translating texts of this period, the term *li* — which we will encounter again in later texts as "principle" — is more often translated as "patterns" or "inherent patterns." In English, however, "patterns" may have a stronger determinative force than does *li*. If a pattern is understood as a regular form or order (e.g., a behavioral pattern), this might suggest that things or activities must conform to it exactly, with little room for individual variation. By contrast, *li* admits of freedom within structure; the *li* guide the spontaneous responses that develop from the natures of things.

44. Deleting *gu yue* (therefore it says) at the start of the sentence, following many scholars.

45. Moving this sentence here following Guo Moruo from a position in the Comment section (just before the final line), to which it was erroneously displaced.

Therefore, one must know the unspoken word and the
    nonacting deed.[46]
Only then will one know how the Way sorts things out.
Though they have distinct forms and different conditions,[47]
[Sages] do not have different inherent guiding principles
    from all other living things.[48]
Therefore, they can become the origin of all-under-Heaven.[49]
[13:1b–2a]

[COMMENT]

Things inherently have forms; forms inherently have names.

This says that names[50] must not exceed realities and that realities must not amplify names. Describe forms using forms; with the form, pay attention to the name.[51] Scrutinize words; correct names. Therefore [the statement] says that [one who does this] is a sage.

The unspoken words [of the sage] are [spontaneously] responsive. To be responsive is to take others just as they are. Take control of their names; pay attention to how they develop.[52] This is the Way to be responsive.[53]

The Way of doing nothing is to adapt to [other things]. Adapting means that nothing is added to them and nothing is subtracted from them. To make the name by adapting to the form, this is the technique of adaptation.[54] Names are what the sage makes use of to sort out all living things.

Most people find their foothold in being strong, strive to be good, promote their talents, and act according to precedent.[55] Sages have none of this. They

---

46. Adding *zhi yan* (word) after *bu yan* (unspoken), following Wang Niansun.

47. Emending *zhi* (grasp) to *shi* (condition), the reading in all other major editions.

48. Deleting *bu* (not) as an erroneous insertion, following Wang Niansun. Although sages behave differently from the multitude, because they are human they share the same inherent guidelines that ultimately emerge from the Way. The main difference is that sages have cultivated themselves and are able to comply with their inherent guidelines; the multitude cannot do this.

49. Adding *shi* (origin or beginning), as in all other major editions.

50. Inserting *ming* (names) after *yan* (says), following many scholars.

51. Reading *gu* (tolerate) as an error for *gu* (describe), following Guo Moruo.

52. Deleting *ying* (respond) as an erroneous insertion, following Wang Yinzhi.

53. Reading *zhi* (it, of, this) as *zi* (this), following many scholars.

54. Responsiveness refers to the sage's ability spontaneously to perceive things "just as they are" and, without any forethought, to react to them in a completely appropriate and harmonious manner. Adaptation refers to the sage's ability to go along with other things and not force them into a predetermined mold. These are cardinal qualities of the Daoist sage in this text and other related ones that some believe are part of the Huang-Lao tradition.

55. Reading *wei* (not yet) as an error for *ju* (to promote or raise up), following Guo Moruo.

have none of this and so they are different from other beings. They are different and so they are empty. Emptiness is the source of all living things. Therefore [the statement] says:

They can become the origin of all-under-Heaven. [13:4a]

III

[STATEMENT]

Most people can be executed because they dislike death.
They can be harmed because they like profit.
But noble persons are neither enticed by likes
Nor oppressed by dislikes.
Calm and tranquil, they take no action,
And they discard wisdom and precedent.
Their responses are not contrived.
Their movements are not chosen.
The mistake lies in intervening directly oneself.
The fault lies in altering and transforming things.
Therefore the ruler who has the Way:
At rest, seems to be without knowledge,
In response to things, seems to fit together with them.
This is the Way of stillness and adaptation.
[13:2a]

[COMMENT]

Most people are so burdened by their dislikes that they lose sight of what they like. They are so enticed by what they like that they forget what they dislike. This is not the Way. Therefore [the statement] says:

[They are] neither enticed by likes,
Nor oppressed by dislikes.

[Noble persons'] dislikes do not lose sight of their inherent guiding principles. Their desires do not exceed what is essential to them. Therefore [the statement] says:

Noble persons, calm and tranquil, take no action
And discard wisdom and precedent.

Therefore this says that they are empty and unadorned.

> Their responses are not contrived,
> Their movements are not chosen.

This says that they are adaptable. To be adaptable is to relinquish the self and take other things as standards. To respond only when stimulated is not something you contrive to do. To move according to inherent guiding principles is not something you [deliberately] choose to do.

> The mistake lies in intervening directly oneself.
> The fault lies in altering and transforming things.

To intervene directly oneself is to not be empty. One is not empty and so one bumps up against other things. One alters and transforms things and so one artificially generates them. One artificially generates them and so there is chaos. Therefore the Way values adaptation. Adaptation is to adapt to the talents [of others]. This speaks of how they employ others.

> Noble persons at rest seem to be without knowledge.

This speaks of their being perfectly empty.

> In response to things, they seem to fit together with them.

This speaks of their conforming to the seasons. It is like the shadow's imaging the shape, the echo's responding to the sound. Therefore when things arrive, they immediately respond. When things pass by, they just let them go. This says that they return to being empty.[56] [13:4a–b]

IV

[STATEMENT]

> What is empty and Formless, we call the Way.[57]
> What transforms and nurtures the myriad things,
>   we call Inner Power.

---

56. The sages' cultivation of an inner stillness that is empty of egotistical thoughts and desires is the basis for their ability to respond spontaneously to all things that arise and to adapt perfectly to any situation that develops.

57. Emending *wu* (nothing) to *er* (and), following Wang Niansun.

What is involved in the interactions between ruler and official, father and son, and among all human beings, we call rightness (*yi*).

That there are levels of ascending and descending, bowing and ceding, honoring and humbling, and that there is the reality of familiarity and distance — this we call rites (*li*).[58]

That things both small and great are subjected to a uniform way of execution and extermination, prohibition and punishment — this we call laws (*fa*). [13:1b][59]

[COMMENT]

The Way of Heaven is empty and formless.[60] Empty and so it does not bend; formless and so there is nothing to oppose it. There is nothing to oppose it.[61] Therefore it flows everywhere through all living things and it does not alter.

Inner Power is the lodging place of the Way. Things attain it and are thereby born. The living attain it and thereby understand the vital essence of the Way.[62] Therefore "Inner Power" is to attain. "To attain" means to attain the means by which things are so.[63]

It is what does not act that is called the Way. It is what lodges [the Way], that is called Inner Power. Therefore, there is no gap between the Way and Inner Power. Therefore to speak of them is not to separate them. That there is no gap between them addresses how Inner Power lodges the Way.[64]

"Rightness" means that each [person] keeps to what is suitable (*yi*). "Rites" are what adapt to the genuine feelings of human beings, go along with the inherent guiding principles (*li*) of what is right for them, and then create limitations and embellishments. Therefore, "rites" means "to have inherent guiding principles." Inherent principles are what clarify [interpersonal] distinctions in order to illustrate the meaning of rightness. Therefore, rites are derived from rightness; rightness is derived from inherent principles; and inherent principles are derived from the Way.[65]

Laws are the means by which [all people of] the same generation are made to conform.[66] Therefore execution and extermination, prohibition and punishment, are used to unify them. Therefore human endeavors are supervised by

---

58. Emending *zhi* (possessive particle) to *you* (there is, there are), following Ding Shihan.

59. Emending *wei* (not yet) to *da* (great), following Guo Moruo.

60. Reading *qi* (its) as *er* (and), following Xu Weiyu.

61. Emending *wei* (position) to *di* (oppose), following Wang Yinzhi.

62. Deleting *zhi* (knowledge), following Zhang Wenhu.

63. Following the word order suggested by Guo Moruo.

64. Restoring *wu* (no) before *jian* (gap) and deleting *li* (guideline), following Wang Yinzi.

65. Emending *yin* (adapt) to *qu* (derive) based on parallels in the previous sentences. Also emending *yi* (suitable) to Dao (Way), following Guo Moruo.

66. Emending *qu* (derive) to *shi* (generation), following Yu Yue.

laws; laws are derived from political authority (*quan*); and political authority is derived from the Way. [3a–b]

[*Guanzi* (SBCK) 13:1a–4a — HR]

The Syncretist Chapters of the Zhuangzi

The seven "inner chapters" of the *Zhuangzi* were transmitted — probably among the followers of their putative author, Zhuang Zhou — for almost two centuries into the early Han dynasty, when a number of chapters were added to the core text, including a final group advocating a syncretism similar to the other sources in this chapter. The following excerpt is taken from the "Way of Heaven" ("*Tiandao*") chapter in this last group. It presents the image of the Daoist sage king who has cultivated quiescence and emptiness to such a degree that he remains unperturbed amidst strife and able to respond spontaneously and harmoniously to any situation that arises. The phrase used to describe him is "in stillness a sage, in motion a king," and it parallels the more famous description found in the final chapter of the text, "inner sageliness, outer kingliness" (*neisheng, waiwang*). Such a ruler is so attuned to the greater powers of Heaven and Earth that he models his society on their hierarchical and sequential patterns.

THE WAY OF HEAVEN (*TIANDAO*)

The Way of Heaven as it circuits is not clogged by precedents, and so the myriad things come to full growth. The Way of the Emperor as it circuits is not clogged by precedents, and so the whole world pays allegiance to him. The Way of the Sage as it circuits is not clogged by precedents, and so all within the four seas submit to him.

The man who, being clear about Heaven and versed in sagehood, has an understanding that ranges in the six directions and is open through the four seasons, by the Power which is in emperor or king — in his own spontaneous actions, as though he were unseeing he never ceases to be still. When the sage is still, it is not that he is still because he says, "It is good to be still"; he is still because none among the myriad things is sufficient to disturb his heart. If water is still, its clarity lights up the hairs of beard and eyebrows, its evenness is plumb with the carpenter's level: the greatest of craftsmen take their standard from it. If mere water clarifies when it is still, how much more the stillness of the quintessential-and-daemonic, the heart of the sage! It is the reflector of Heaven and Earth, the mirror of the myriad things.

Emptiness and stillness, calm and indifference, quiescence, doing nothing, are the even level of Heaven and Earth, the utmost reach of the Way and the Power; therefore emperor, king or sage finds rest in them. At rest he empties, emptying he is filled, and what fills him sorts itself out. Emptying he is still, in stillness he is moved, and when he moves he succeeds. In stillness he does nothing; and if he does nothing, those charged with affairs are put to the test. If he does nothing he is serene; and in whoever is serene, cares and misfortunes cannot settle, his years will be long.

Emptiness and stillness, calm and indifference, quiescence, doing nothing, are at the root of the myriad things. To be clear about these when you sit facing south is to be the kind of lord that Yao was; to be clear about these when you stand facing north is to be the kind of minister that Shun was. To have these as your resources in high estate is the Power that is in emperor, king, Son of Heaven; to have these as your resources in low estate is the Way of the obscure sage, the untitled king. Use these to settle in retirement or wander at leisure, and the hermits of river, sea, mountain, and forest submit to you. Use these to come forward and act in order to bring comfort to the age, and your achievement is great and name illustrious, and the empire is united. In stillness a sage, in motion a king, you do nothing yet are exalted, you are simple and unpolished yet no one in the empire is able to rival your glory. . . .

The Power that is in emperor or king has Heaven and Earth for its ancestors, the Way and the Power as its masters, doing nothing as its norm. Doing *nothing*, one has more than enough to be employer of the entire empire; doing *something*, one is inadequate for more than to be employed by the empire. That is why the men of old valued doing nothing. If as well as the man above the men below did nothing, the men below would share the Power in the man above; and if the men below share the Power in the man above, they do not minister. If as well as the men below the man above did something, the man above would share the Way of the men below; and if the man above shares the Way of the men below, he is not sovereign. The man above must do nothing and be employer of the empire, the men below must do something and be employed by the empire; this is the irreplaceable Way.

Therefore those who of old reigned over the empire, though wise enough to encompass Heaven and Earth would not do their own thinking, though discriminating enough to comprehend the myriad things would not do their own explaining, though able enough for all the work within the four seas would not do their own enacting. Heaven does not give birth, but the myriad things are transformed; earth does not rear, but the myriad things are nurtured; emperors and kings do nothing, but the world's work is done.

[*Zhuangzi*, 13; adapted from Graham, *Chuang Tzu*, pp. 259–261]

THE WORLD OF THOUGHT (*TIANXIA*)

The following selection is drawn from the final chapter of the *Zhuangzi*, known as "The World of Thought" ("*Tianxia*"). This is, again, a later addition to the text, reflecting syncretic tendencies of the Qin-Han period. It assumes, like most early Chinese thinkers, including Zhuangzi, that the Way existed in its fullness and wholeness in primordial antiquity but later somehow became fragmented. In the lofty perspective of this chapter, each of the schools of late Zhou thought is seen as serving its own distinct, relative function but not as embracing the whole. The author includes characterizations of leading thinkers (among them Confucians, Mohists, Legalists, Daoists, and Logicians), the succinct descriptions of which became famous for their aptness in distilling the essence of each school. The excerpt that follows focuses on characterizations of the Mohists and the Daoists — and, most tellingly, of Zhuangzi himself.

To make Heaven his source, Virtue his root, and the Way his Gate, revealing himself through change and transformation — one who does this is called a sage.

To make humaneness his standard of kindness, rightness his model of reason, rites his guide to conduct, and music his source of harmony, serene in mercy and humaneness — one who does this is called a gentleman.

To employ laws to determine functions, names to indicate rank, comparisons to discover actual performance, investigations to arrive at decisions, checking them off, one, two, three, four, and in this way to assign the hundred officials to their ranks; to keep a constant eye on administrative affairs; to give first thought to food and clothing; to keep in mind the need to produce and grow, shepherd, and store away; to provide for the old and the weak, the orphan and the widow, so that all are properly nourished — these are the principles whereby the people are ordered.[67]

How thorough were the men of ancient times! — companions of holiness and enlightenment, pure as Heaven and Earth, caretakers of the ten thousand things, harmonizers of the world, their bounty extended to the hundred clans. They had a clear understanding of basic policies and paid attention even to petty regulations — in the six avenues and the four frontiers, in what was great or small, coarse or fine, there was no place they did not move.

The wisdom that was embodied in their policies and regulations is in many cases still reflected in the old laws and records of the historians, handed down over the ages. As to that which is recorded in the *Classic of Odes* and *Classic of Documents*, the *Rites* and the "Music," there are many gentlemen of Zou and Lu,[68] scholars of sash and official rank, who have an understanding of it. The *Classic of Odes* describes aspirations; the *Classic of Documents* describes

---

67. Judging from the terminology, the "sage" represents the Daoist ideal, the "gentleman" represents the Confucian ideal, and what follows, the Legalist ideal of government by laws and bureaucratic control. But the writer may also intend these concepts of government to represent different levels in one great, eclectic concept of ideal government.

68. Zou and Lu were the native states of Mencius and Confucius, respectively.

events; the *Rites* speaks of conduct; the "Music" speaks of harmony; the *Classic of Changes* describes the yin and yang; the *Spring and Autumn Annals* describes titles and functions.

These various policies are scattered throughout the world and are propounded in the Middle Kingdom, the scholars of the hundred schools from time to time taking up one or the other in their praises and preachings. But the world is in great disorder, the worthies and sages lack clarity of vision, and the Way and its Power are no longer One. So the world too often seizes on one of its aspects, examines it, and pronounces it good. . . . The various skills of the hundred schools all have their strong points, and at times each may be of use. But none is wholly sufficient, none is universal. The scholar cramped in one corner of learning tries to judge the beauty of Heaven and Earth, to pry into the principles of the ten thousand things, to scrutinize the perfection of the ancients, but seldom is he able to encompass the true beauty of Heaven and Earth, to describe the true face of holy brightness. Therefore the Way that is sagely within and kingly without has fallen into darkness and is no longer clearly perceived, has become shrouded and no longer shines forth. The men of the world all follow their own desires and make these their "doctrine." How sad! — the hundred schools going on and on instead of turning back, fated never to join again. The scholars of later ages have unfortunately never perceived the purity of Heaven and Earth, the great body of the ancients, and "the art of the Way" in time comes to be rent and torn apart by the world.

To teach no extravagance to later ages, to leave the ten thousand things unadorned, to shun any glorification of rules and regulations, instead applying ink and measuring line to the correction of one's own conduct, thus aiding the world in time of crisis — there were those in ancient times who believed that the "art of the Way" lay in these things. Mo Di (Mozi) and Qin Guli[69] heard of their views and delighted in them, but they followed them to excess and were too assiduous in applying them to themselves.

Mozi wrote a piece "Against Music" and another titled "Moderation in Expenditure," declaring there was to be no singing in life, no mourning in death. With a boundless love and a desire to ensure universal benefit, he condemned warfare, and there was no place in his teachings for anger. Again, he was fond of learning and broad in knowledge, and in this respect did not differ from others. His views, however, were not always in accordance with those of the former kings, for he denounced the rites and music of antiquity. . . .

Men want to sing and he says, "No singing!"; they want to wail and he says, "No wailing!" — one wonders if he is in fact human at all. A life that is all toil, a death shoddily disposed of — it is a way that goes too much against us. To make men anxious, to make them sorrowful — such practices are hard to carry out, and I fear they cannot be regarded as the Way of the Sage. They are contrary

---

69. A leading disciple of Mozi.

to the hearts of the world, and the world cannot endure them. Though Mozi himself may be capable of such endurance, how can the rest of the world do likewise? Departing so far from the ways of the world, they must be far removed indeed from those of the true king. . . .

Mo Di and Qin Guli were all right in their ideas but wrong in their practices, with the result that the Mohists of later ages have felt obliged to subject themselves to hardship "till there is no down left on their calves, no hair on their shins" — their only thought being to outdo one another. Such efforts represent the height of confusion, the lowest degree of order. Nevertheless, Mozi was one who had a true love for the world. He failed to achieve all he aimed for, yet, wasted and worn with exhaustion, he never ceased trying. He was indeed a gentleman of ability! . . .

To regard the source as pure and the things that emerge from it as coarse, to look upon accumulation as insufficiency; dwelling alone, peaceful and placid, in spiritual brightness — there were those in ancient times who believed that "the art of the Way" lay in these things. The Barrier Keeper Yin[70] and Lao Dan (Laozi) heard of their views and delighted in them. They expounded them in terms of constant nonbeing and headed their doctrine with the concept of the Great Unity. Gentle weakness and humble self-effacement are its outer marks; emptiness, void, and the noninjury of the ten thousand things are its essence. . . .

Lao Dan said, "Know the male but cling to the female; become the ravine of the world. Know the pure but cling to dishonor; become the valley of the world."[71] Others all grasp what is in front; he alone grasped what is behind. He said, "Take to yourself the filth of the world." Others all grasp what is full; he alone grasped what is empty. He never stored away — therefore he had more than enough; he had heaps and heaps of more than enough! In his movement he was easygoing and did not wear himself out. Dwelling in inaction, he scoffed at skill. Others all seek good fortune; he alone kept himself whole by becoming twisted. He said, "Let us somehow or other avoid incurring blame!" He took profundity to be the root and frugality to be the guideline. He said, "What is brittle will be broken, what is sharp will be blunted." He was always generous and permissive with things and inflicted no pain on others — this may be called the highest achievement.

The Barrier Keeper Yin and Lao Dan — with their breadth and stature, they were indeed the True Men of old!

Blank, boundless, and without form; transforming, changing, never constant: are we dead? are we alive? do we stand side by side with Heaven and Earth?

---

70. Legend has it that when Laozi was leaving China he was asked by Barrier Keeper Yin for some written exposition of his teachings and produced the *Daodejing* as a result.

71. Cf. *Daodejing* 28.

do we move in the company of spiritual brightness? absentminded, where are we going? forgetful, where are we headed for? The ten thousand things ranged all around us, not one of them is worthy to be singled out as our destination — there were those in ancient times who believed that the "art of the Way" lay in these things. Zhuang Zhou (Zhuangzi) heard of their views and delighted in them. He expounded them in odd and outlandish terms, in brash and bombastic language, in unbound and unbordered phrases, abandoning himself to the times without partisanship, not looking at things from one angle only. He believed that the world is drowned in turbidness and that it was impossible to address it in sober language. . . . So he used "goblet words" to pour out endless changes, "repeated words" to give a ring of truth, and "imputed words" to impart greater breadth. He came and went alone with the pure spirit of Heaven and Earth, yet he did not view the ten thousand things with arrogant eyes. He did not scold over "right" and "wrong" but lived with the age and its vulgarity. Though his writings are a string of queer beads and baubles, they roll and rattle and do no one any harm. Though his words seem to be at sixes and sevens, yet among the sham and waggery there are things worth observing, for they are crammed with truths that never come to an end.

Above he wandered with the Creator; below he made friends with those who have gotten outside of life and death, who know nothing of beginning or end. As for the Source, his grasp of it was broad, expansive, and penetrating; profound, liberal, and unimpeded. As for the Ancestor, he may be said to have tuned and accommodated himself to it and to have risen on it to the greatest heights. Nevertheless, in responding to change and expounding on the world of things, he set forth principles that will never cease to be valid, an approach that can never be shuffled off. Veiled and arcane, he is one who has never been completely comprehended.

[*Zhuangzi*, ch. 33; adapted from Watson, *Chuang Tzu*, pp. 362–367, 371–374]

The Huainanzi *on Rulership*

The *Huainanzi* is a work of twenty-one essays that was composed by a group of scholars and adepts working at the court of Liu An, first king of Huainan, under the king's direction. Presented by Liu to his nephew, the powerful Han emperor Wu, on a court visit in 139 B.C.E., this work was intended to be a compendium of all the knowledge the Daoist sage ruler needed in order to govern effectively. Thus its topics run a wide gamut from cosmology and astrology to inner cultivation, government, and political thought. At the time it was presented to Emperor Wu, the emperor was on the verge of sanctioning the exclusive teaching of five Confucian classics in place of the Huang-Lao texts that had been influential at the imperial court during the previous four decades. Some scholars therefore see it as the last attempt of Huang-Lao enthusiasts to head off this move to Confucianism. Others do not see it as a Huang-Lao text. Whatever the case, the major themes addressed in the *Huainanzi* bear such a close resemblance to those included in the overview of Daoism by the famous Han historian Sima Tan that one might almost be led to conclude that he had this text in mind when he wrote it.

Because of the length and diversity of the *Huainanzi*, it is impossible to represent here all its many topics and literary styles. Instead we focus on the nature and practice of sage rulership, the overriding theme of the entire work. Here one finds many philosophical and terminological parallels with other sources included in this chapter. Sage rulers, according to the *Huainanzi* authors, clear their minds of all passions and prejudices through the cultivation of quiescence (*jing*) and can therefore, in an unbiased fashion, respond spontaneously and harmoniously to any situation that arises. They adapt policies and practices to the seasons, comply with the inherent patterns (*li*) of the cosmos, and act effortlessly by doing nothing (*wuwei*). One philosophical innovation of the *Huainanzi* is its assertion that the innate nature of human beings (*xing*) has a metaphysical dimension that this nature serves as the basis for the sage ruler's inner cultivation.

HUAINANZI 9, THE TECHNIQUES OF RULERSHIP (*ZHUSHU*)

The techniques of the ruler are to
Keep to endeavors that take no action
And practice the teaching that contains no words.
Clear and quiescent, he does not act,
Once he acts, he is not agitated.[72]
Adapting and complying, he entrusts his subordinates.
Holding them to account, he does not labor.

Therefore, although his mind knows the principles, he permits the imperial
   tutors to explain the Way to him.[73]
Although his mouth is able to speak, he permits his diplomats to announce
   the ceremonial words.
Although his feet are able to walk, he permits his ministers to lead the way.
Although his ears are able to hear, he permits his administrators to propose
   their own strategies.[74]

Therefore, in his deliberations he has no oversights;
In his conduct there is nothing excessive.[75]
His words are cultured and elegant;

---

72. Reading *du* (standard) as *dong* (to act), after Wang Shumin. Lau, *Concordance*, p. 67.

73. Reading *dao* (to guide) as *Dao* (the Way), after the *Qunshu zhiyao*. Lau, *Concordance*, p. 67.

74. Reading *jian* (to admonish) as *mou* (strategy), the variant given in the Kao You commentary. Lau, *Concordance*, p. 67.

75. Reading *mou* (strategy) as *ju* (conduct) after Wang Niansun. Lau, *Concordance*, p. 67.

His actions are models of exemplary behavior for all-under-Heaven.
In advancing and retreating he responds to the seasons;
In activity and quiescence he complies with inherent principles.
He is not made to like or dislike things by their being ugly or beautiful;
He is not made angry or pleased by rewards and punishments.
Because he allows each name and each category to determine itself, his
endeavors proceed spontaneously.[76]
This is because none of his actions comes from a fixed self.

HUAINANZI 1, THE ORIGINAL WAY (YUAN DAO)[77]

Therefore, those who penetrate the Way return to purity and quiescence.
Those who look deeply into things end in doing nothing.
If you nourish your innate nature through calmness
And stabilize your numen through stillness,
You will enter the Gateway of Heaven.

What I call "Heaven" is that which is pure and unmixed, unhewn and
simple, innate and direct, dazzling and radiant, and which has never even
begun to become adulterated.
What I call "human" is that which is led astray by wisdom and precedent, is
clever and deceitful, and which gets on in the world by having dealings
with the common.
Therefore that an ox has cloven hooves and horns on its head and a horse has
a mane and uncloven hooves is Heavenly [natural].
To put a bridle in a horse's mouth and to pierce an ox's nose is human
[artifice].
To comply with Heaven is to wander freely with the Way.
To follow humans is to have dealings with the common.

The reason one can't discuss largeness with a fish who lives in a well is
because it is confined in a narrow space.
The reason one can't discuss the cold with a summer insect is because its life
is restricted to one season.
The reason one can't discuss the perfect Way with a clever scholar is because
he is confined to the common and bound up in what he's been taught.

Therefore the sage does not allow the human to becloud the Heavenly,
And does not allow desires to disrupt his true responses (qing).

---

76. Reading you (similar to) as you (go along with, proceed) after Wang Shumin. Lau, Concordance, p. 67.

77. Lau, Concordance, p. 4.

Without planning he hits the mark;
Without speaking he is trusted.
Without deliberating he attains,
Without acting he succeeds,
His vital essence is absorbed into the spiritual storehouse,
And he is a companion of the Creative Force (the Way).

HUAINANZI 14, INQUIRING WORDS (QUANYAN)

Zhan He said:[78]
"I have never heard of the ruler's [inner] person (*shen*) being well ordered
    and the state being chaotic.
I have never heard of the ruler's [inner] person being chaotic and the state
    being well-ordered."
When a carpenter's square is not set aright, you cannot use it to make
    squares.
When a compass is not set aright, you cannot use it to make circles.
The [inner] person is the square and compass of all endeavors.
I have never heard of one whose self was crooked being able to set other
    people aright.

When you get to the source of the Decree of Heaven,[79]
Master the techniques of the mind,
Make likes and dislikes comply with inherent patterns,
And accord with your true responses and innate nature,
Then the way to govern is comprehended.
When you get to the source of the Decree of Heaven, then you are not
    deluded by bad or good fortune.
When you master the techniques of the mind, then you are not led astray by
    pleasure and anger.[80]
When you make likes and dislikes comply with inherent patterns, then you
    do not crave what is useless.
When you accord with your true responses and innate nature, then desires do
    not exceed their appropriate limits.

---

78. Zhan He is the late Warring States Daoist teacher who appears in *Han Feizi* 20 and *Liezi* 5. The eminent Chinese scholar Ch'ien Mu identified him with the Zhanzi in *Zhuangzi*, chapter 28, gave his dates as 350–270 B.C.E., and suggested that he was perhaps the first Huang-Lao teacher. See Ch'ien, *Hsien Ch'in chu-tzu hsin-nien*, pp. 223–226, 448.

79. *Tianming*, elsewhere in this volume translated as the Mandate of Heaven or "what Heaven ordains."

80. Reading *wang* (to forget) as *wang* (to be led astray) after the Daoist Canon edition. Lau, *Concordance*, p. 133.

When you are not deluded by bad or good fortune, then in activity and
quiescence you will comply with inherent patterns.
When you are not led astray by pleasure and anger, then rewards and
punishments will not affect you.
When you do not crave what is useless, then you will not allow desires to
interfere with your innate nature.[81]
When desires do not exceed their limits, then you understand what is
sufficient to nourish your innate nature.
Of these four [principles]:
Do not seek them externally,
Do not borrow them from others;
Return to the self and they will be attained.

The following selection has been described as resembling a Daoist version of the *Great
Learning*, a major Confucian text translated in chapter 10.

The foundation of governing lies is making the people content.[82]
The foundation of making the people content lies in giving them sufficient
use [of their time for farming].
The foundation of giving them sufficient use lies in not stealing their time
[for state endeavors].
The foundation of not stealing their time lies in restricting the state's
endeavors.
The foundation of restricting the state's endeavors lies in limiting the desires
[of the ruler].
The foundation of limiting the desires [of the ruler] lies in his returning to
his innate nature.
The foundation of returning to one's innate nature lies in removing what fills
the mind.
When one removes what fills the mind, one is empty.
When one is empty, one experiences equanimity.
Equanimity is the simplicity of the Way.
Emptiness is the abode of the Way.

Those who are able to possess all-under-Heaven certainly do not neglect their
states.

---

81. Deleting *yong* (utility), after Wang Niansun. Lau, *Concordance*, p. 133.
82. Deleting *wu* (to endeavor), after Lau, *Concordance*, p. 133.

Those who are able to possess their states certainly do not lose their families.
Those who are able to master their families certainly do not neglect their
inner person.
Those who are able to cultivate their inner person certainly do not forget
their mind.
Those who are able to reach the source of their mind certainly do not impair
their innate nature.
Those who are able to keep their innate nature whole certainly are not
deluded about the Tao.
Therefore Guang Chengzi said:[83]

> "Diligently guard what is within you;
> Fully prevent it from being externalized.
> Too much knowledge is harmful.
> Do not look! Do not listen!
> Embrace the numen by being quiet
> And the body will set itself aright."

There has never been anyone who was able to understand it in others
without first attaining it within himself.
Therefore the *Classic of Changes (Yijing)* says: "Tie it up in a bag. No blame.
No praise."[84]

[Lau, *Concordance*, 4, 67, 133 — HR]

THE MEDICAL MICROCOSM

The new universal order of the Han was configured as a microcosm, a small
model of Nature. As such it was aligned with another miniature counterpart of
Nature, namely, the human body. Thus, the ruler should regulate his officers
just as an individual must control his limbs if he is to live a normal life. Han
thinkers often speak of the healthy body as in harmony with Nature, opening
itself to illness if it does not maintain that concord.

Medicine gradually separated from philosophy between the third and first
centuries B.C.E. as physicians worked out detailed and comprehensive doctrines
to put in order their experience of the body, health, and illness, and to pass on
their understanding to their pupils. Three books that carry the main title *Inner*

---

83. Guang Chengzi is the master who taught techniques of inner cultivation to the Yellow
Emperor in *Zhuangzi* 11, where this saying appears almost verbatim.

84. *Yijing, kun* hexagram, line text for six in the fourth place.

Canon of the Yellow Emperor — namely, the *Basic Questions* (*Huangdi neijing suwen*), its companion, the *Divine Pivot* (*Huangdi neijing ling shu*), and an overlapping compilation, the *Grand Basis* (*Huangdi neijing taisu*) — are the main surviving documents of several great medical syntheses of the Han period.[85]

The Han medical masters greatly elaborated the idea of cosmos and body as interacting organisms. This was, of course, not the only way to make sense of human suffering and healing, but it seemed a desirable one because by the first century the parallel had already become a staple of philosophers. We find it in many important writings, and, as political ideology, it was one of the consequential ideas of its time.

We can see a reflection of the latter in the form of the *Inner Canon*. Four fifths of the chapters (*pian*) in the two books are in the form of a dialogue between the Yellow Emperor and one of his ministers. In all except a few, the Yellow Emperor is asking the questions one would expect of a disciple when he is being prepared to receive a text from his teacher. The minister is at the same time a master initiating his disciple and a sage adviser counseling his sovereign. This form reflects that of the Huang-Lao texts associated with the Yellow Emperor that were so influential in earlier Han thought. Like the others, it mirrors the political ideals of the elite in its master image of the emperor as a man of knowledge concerned not with running a government but with embodying the link between the cosmic order and the individual. This image is so pervasive that in a passage on the correspondence of acupuncture points to compass points and yin-yang orientations, the body described is that of "the sage enthroned facing south," that is, the emperor.[86]

This may seem an odd affiliation between politics, philosophy, and medicine, but such clear-cut modern distinctions are of little use in making sense of ancient culture. In the last three centuries B.C.E., as we have seen, there was no boundary between philosophy and political thought. The physicians were defining their own domain of learning out of general philosophy, but at the same time they were contributing to it. Among other things, the *Divine Pivot* and the *Basic Questions* set out what may be the first theory that fully integrates the two major concepts of Chinese abstract reasoning: yin/yang, and the Five

---

85. The current versions of the first two were edited in 762 C.E. and further revised in the eleventh century; the third was compiled between 666 and 683 C.E. The content of all three is close to early quotations of the Han *Inner Canon*, but the arrangement is different. No one of the three is consistently more reliable than the others. The original *Inner Canon* assembled writings of several medical traditions, the earliest of which may have been first set down in the third century. There is thus a great deal of inconsistency, which can be resolved only by examining the constituent writings individually.

86. *Suwen* 6:2; *Taisu* 5:13.

Phases (*wuxing*).[87] To form an overview of Han thought about Nature, society, and humanity, the *Inner Canon* is essential reading.

The correspondences outlined below may seem too unsystematic and too much based on verbal reasoning to be scientific. That judgment is anachronistic; no early medical theory of any civilization can measure up to twentieth-century physical, chemical, and biological criteria. The Chinese authors were not trying for plain expression using the simple and unambiguous concepts that became the norm nearly two thousand years later. Their goals were, rather, the richest possible structures of symbols and meaning that could order all medical experience without moving away from language that any educated person could understand. This made multiple meanings for a single concept desirable, as the final question-and-answer section in this selection explains.[88] By the only criteria that are of any use for early medicine — namely, the ability of theory to encompass phenomena, its connections to wider ranges of thought, and its openness to new data — the *Inner Canon* can be compared with any writing of its time on medicine, or, for that matter, on natural philosophy, anywhere.

THE *DIVINE PIVOT*[89]

The Yellow Emperor inquired of Bogao, "I would like to hear how the limbs and joints of the body correspond to sky and earth."

Bogao replied, "The sky is round, the earth rectangular;[90] the heads of human beings are round and their feet rectangular to correspond. In the sky there are the sun and moon; human beings have two eyes. On earth there are the nine provinces; human beings have nine orifices.[91] In the sky there are wind and rain; human beings have their joy and anger. In the sky there are thunder and lightning; human beings have their sounds and speech. In the sky there

---

87. This judgment depends on uncertain dating of the two books and of other writings. If, as some scholars believe, the *Inner Canon* is from the first century C.E., priority would go to Yang Xiong's *Supreme Mystery* (*Taixuan*) (4? B.C.E.). The approach of the latter is very different.

88. In the *Grand Basis* 5:11–12, the wording is different, but the idea of multiple dimensions of meaning is the same. There is no way to be certain which version is closer to that of the Han.

89. Probably first century B.C.E. The version in the *Divine Pivot* (*Ling shu*) has been collated with the partial text in the *Grand Basis* (*Huangdi neijing taisu*, 666–683 C.E., 5:1–12), which corresponds to the translation from "in the sky there are yin and yang" to the end. Parallels in the *Basic Questions* (*Huangdi neijing suwen*) have also been consulted. For the *Taisu*, the photographic reproduction in *Tōyō igaku zempon sōsho*, vols. 1–3, was used, and for *Suwen* and *Ling shu*, the *Huangdi neijing zhangju suoyin* edition.

90. It is clear from some of the correspondences that follow that "sky" is used, as often happens, to stand for "sky and earth," or Nature generally.

91. The nine provinces are a legendary system often mentioned in cosmology. The orifices are ears, eyes, mouth, nostrils, and the urethral and anal openings.

are the four seasons; human beings have their four extremities. In the sky there are the Five Sounds; human beings have their five yin visceral systems.[92] In the sky there are the Six Pitches; human beings have their six yang visceral systems. In the sky there are winter and summer; human beings have their chills and fevers. In the sky there are the ten-day 'weeks'; human beings have ten fingers on their hands. In the sky there are the twelve double-hours; human beings have ten toes on their feet, and the stalk and the hanging ones complete the correspondence.[93] Women lack these two members, so they are able to carry the human form [of the fetus]. In the sky there are yin and yang; human beings are husband and wife.

"In the year there are 365 days; human beings have 365 joints. On the earth there are high mountains; human beings have shoulders and knees. On the earth there are deep valleys; human beings have armpits and hollows in back of their knees.[94] On the earth there are twelve cardinal watercourses; human beings have twelve cardinal circulation tracts.[95] In the earth there are veins of water; human beings have defensive *qi*.[96] In the earth there are wild grasses; human beings have body hair. On the earth there are daylight and darkness; human beings have their [times for] lying down and getting up. In the sky there are stars set out in constellations; human beings have their teeth. On the earth there are little hills; human beings have their minor joints. On the earth there are boulders on the mountains; human beings have their prominent bones. On the earth there are groves and forests; human beings have their sinews.[97] On the earth there are towns and villages in which people gather; human beings have their bulges of [thickened] flesh. In the year there are twelve months; human beings have their twelve major joints. On the earth there are seasons when no vegetation grows; some human beings are childless. These are the correspondences between human beings and sky and earth. . . ."

---

92. The Five Sounds are the musical modes. In the Han there are various counts of the systems of bodily functions associated with the viscera; this one refers to the yin systems, which like the Five Sounds correspond numerologically to the Five Phases. The next sentence cites their yang counterparts.

93. I.e., the penis and testicles.

94. The basis of these associations is prominent convex shapes for the yang features and concavities for the yin.

95. This set of correspondences is greatly elaborated in *Taisu*, 5:25–40, with a parallel passage in *Ling shu* 12.

96. Defensive *qi* (*weiqi*) flows round the perimeter of the body and protects it from invasion. *Taisu*, p. 3, instead of "veins of water" (*zhuanmai*), has two characters, the first of which is only partly legible; the compound may be "the *qi* of rain" (*yuqi*).

97. The sinews (*jin, jinmo*) are the muscles, ligaments, and other fibrous tissues that operate the locomotive system of the body. This association refers to their gathered fibers.

The Yellow Emperor asked, "I have heard that Heaven is yang and Earth yin, that the sun is yang and the moon yin. How is this matched in human beings?"

Qibo said, "From the waist up is Heaven; from the waist down is Earth; thus Heaven is yang and Earth yin. The twelve cardinal circulation tracts connected with the feet correspond to the twelve months. The moon is engendered from water. Thus what is below is yin. The ten fingers of the hand correspond to the ten days of the week. The sun is engendered from fire. Thus what is above is yang."[98]

The Yellow Emperor said, "How are they matched in the circulation vessels?"

Qibo said, "The third [astronomical month], the first civil month, engenders yang, and is in charge of the immature yang [circulation vessel] of the left foot.[99] The eighth [astronomical month], the sixth civil month, is in charge of the immature yang [circulation vessel] of the right foot. . . ." [The enumeration continues for the twelve months and the twelve circulation branches connected with the feet.]

"The first day [of the ten-day week] is in charge of the immature yang vessels of the left hand. The sixth day is in charge of the immature yang vessels of the right hand." [The enumeration continues for the ten days and ten of the twelve circulation branches connected with the hands. Qibo then itemizes the subdivisions of yin and yang and warns against using acupuncture on the circulation branches in which human *qi* is concentrated in each season.]

The Yellow Emperor said, "According to the Five Phases, the eastern quarter, the first two of the ten stems [used to count days in the week], and the phase Wood rule over spring. Spring [is associated with] the color of the blue sky and governs the liver functions. The liver functions are those of the attenuated yin tracts connected with the feet. But now you claim that the first stem [corresponds to] the immature yang tract connected with the left hand, which does not tally with these regular relationships. Why is that?"

---

98. In ancient China days were grouped into tens to determine days of rest for civil servants. The point of this reply is that yin, water, and the moon correspond, and are complementary to yang, fire, and the sun.

99. Though this varied from state to state, in the Zhou system the first lunar month was the one that contained the winter solstice. New Year's Day thus fell at the end of November or in December. The Qin and its successors, with some minor divergences, called the solstitial month the eleventh, which put the civil new year in late January or February, as is still the case. But astronomers continued to use the Zhou standard, just as in the time of Copernicus astronomers were still using the ancient Egyptian calendar. A given astronomical month fell two months earlier than the civil month with the same number. *Zhu*, "is in charge of," connotes bureaucratic responsibility. This "authority" determines in which circulation branch the vital substances concentrate at a given time, an important datum in therapy.

Qibo said, "These are the yin and yang [correspondences] of Heaven and Earth, not the sequential changes of the four seasons and the Five Phases. Now yin and yang are names without physical form [i.e., abstractions, not concrete things]. 'They can be enumerated ten ways, separated a hundred ways, distributed a thousand ways, deduced a myriad ways' refers to this."[100]

[From *Huangdi neijing ling shu* 71:2, 41 — NS]

A SYNCRETIST PERSPECTIVE ON THE SIX SCHOOLS

Records of the Grand Historian, completed by Sima Qian in about 100 B.C.E., contains a seminal essay on early Chinese thought written by his father, Sima Tan, who began the compilation of this text. In it he provides a brief assessment of each of six early philosophical traditions and attaches to them the suffix of *jia* (family), which has been taken to mean "school" but which is probably closer to the notion of "lineage." Sometimes in the West *jia* has been translated by the suffix -*ism* — hence, "Confucianism," Daoism," "Legalism," and so on. These terms refer, however, not to monolithic schools but to evolving traditions of practice and philosophy handed down by lineages of masters and disciples.

Sima Tan was a follower of Huang-Lao thought, and he assesses the relative merits of the five other lineages in order to establish the superiority of his own. In the process he provides a picture of how this major early Han intellectual tradition conceived of itself. The essay also clearly demonstrates that early Han Daoism was thoroughly syncretic in nature and adopted elements from other schools.

"ON THE SIX LINEAGES OF THOUGHT," BY SIMA TAN

Sima Qian's Introduction

The Grand Historian [Sima Tan] studied astronomy with Tang Du, received instruction in the *Classic of Changes* from Yang He, and mastered Daoist discourse under Master Huang. The Grand Historian held office from the Jianyuan to the Yuanfeng periods (between 140 and 110 B.C.E.). Because he sympathized with scholars who did not understand his purpose and teachers who were confused about it, he discoursed on the essential tenets of the six lineages and stated the following:

---

100. Quotation from an unidentified book. The *Inner Canon* often quotes its predecessors, and sometimes names them. The main point of Qibo's reply is that because yin and yang and the Five Phases are concepts, they can be interpreted on many levels. In this instance, Qibo claims he had been talking about their spatial meanings in the circulation system, not their meanings in time sequences. He reminds his monarch that the two need not correspond in detail.

Sima Tan's Lecture

The *Great Commentary* to the *Classic of Changes* says: "All-under-Heaven share the same goal, yet there are a hundred ways of thinking about it; they return to the same home, yet follow different pathways there." The Naturalists (*yin yang jia*), Confucians, Mohists, Terminologists (*ming jia*), Legalists, and Daoists all strive to create order [in the world]. It is just that, in the different routes they follow and in what they say, some are more perceptive than others.

I once observed that the techniques of the Naturalists magnify the importance of omens and proliferate avoidances and taboos, causing people to feel constrained and to fear many things. Nonetheless, one cannot fault the way they set out in order the grand compliances of the four seasons.

The Confucians are erudite yet lack the essentials. They labor much yet achieve little. This is why their doctrines are difficult to follow completely. Nonetheless, one cannot detract from the way they set out in order the various rituals between ruler and minister and father and son and enumerate the various distinctions between husband and wife and elder and younger.

The Mohists are frugal and difficult to follow. This is why it is not possible fully to conform to their doctrines. Nonetheless, one cannot disregard the way they strengthen the foundation [agriculture] and economize expenditures.

The Legalists are harsh and lacking in compassion. Nonetheless, one cannot improve upon the way they rectify the distinctions between ruler and minister and superior and subordinate.

The Terminologists cause people to be strict [with words], yet they outdo themselves and lose sight of the truth. Nonetheless, one cannot disregard the way they rectify names and their realities.

The Daoists enable the numinous essence within people to be concentrated and unified. They move in unison with the Formless and provide adequately for all living things. In deriving their techniques, they follow the grand compliances of the Naturalists, select the best of the Confucians and Mohists, and extract the essentials of the Terminologists and Legalists. They shift [their policies] in accordance with the seasons and respond to the transformations of things. In establishing customs and promulgating policies, they do nothing unsuitable. Their tenets are concise and easy to grasp; their policies are few but their achievements are many.

The Confucians are not like this. They maintain that the ruler is the exemplar for all-under-Heaven. For them, the ruler guides and the officials harmonize with him; the ruler initiates and the officials follow. Proceeding in this manner, the ruler labors hard and the officials sit idle.

The essentials of the Great Way are simply a matter of discarding strength and avarice and casting aside perception and intellect. One relinquishes these and relies on the techniques [of self-cultivation]. When the numen (*shen*, "spirit") is used excessively it becomes depleted; when the physical form labors excessively it becomes worn out. It is unheard of for one whose physical form and numen are agitated and disturbed to hope to attain the longevity of Heaven and Earth.

Sima Tan's Self-Commentary

According to the Naturalists, the four seasons, eight positions, twelve limits, and the twenty-four seasonal nodes each have their instructions and commands.[101] Those who comply with them will flourish; those who defy them, if their own person does not perish, will lose [their states]. Yet it does not necessarily have to be this way. Therefore I said, "They cause people to feel constrained and to fear many things." In the spring, living things are generated, in the summer they mature, in the autumn they are harvested, in the winter they are stored away: this is the Great Norm of Heaven's Way. If you do not comply with it, then you lack the means to become the guiding basis for all-under-Heaven. Therefore I said, "One cannot fault the way they prioritize the grand compliances of the four seasons."

The Confucians take the Six Arts as their standards. The scriptures and commentaries on the Six Arts are innumerable. Successive generations have not been able to master their scholarship, while the present generation is not able to penetrate their rituals. Therefore I said, they "are erudite yet lack the essentials; they labor much yet achieve little." Yet even the hundred lineages cannot modify how they enumerate the various rituals between ruler and minister and father and son and how they prioritize the distinctions between husband and wife and elder and younger.

The Mohists indeed esteem the Way of Yao and Shun. When they speak of their virtuous conduct they say: "The ancestral altar should be three and one half feet high. It should have three earthen steps and should have a thatched roof that is not trimmed and should use rafters that are not cut. Food should be presented in square earthenware vessels and should be sipped using earthenware utensils and should consist of coarse millet and a soup of assorted greens. In the summer one should wear clothes made of linen and in the winter one should wear garments made of deer[skin]." In their funerals they insist on a coffin of only three inches in thickness and raise their voices in mourning tones that do not exhaust their feelings of grief. In their teachings about the rites of mourning, they insist that all people follow these practices. By making all-under-Heaven follow these methods, they lose the distinction between hon-

---

101. The eight positions refer to the eight directions of the compass. Each is correlated with the seasons. The twelve limits are the chronograms, the annual change in position of the planet Jupiter as it moves through the sky. Along with the seasons and the seasonal nodes, all have specific actions the ruler and the people should take on any given day of the year in order to maintain the proper harmony in both the human microcosm and the universal macrocosm.

orable and humble. Generations differ and times change, so one's policies and undertakings do not necessarily remain the same. This is why I said they "are frugal and difficult to obey." In essence because they claim to "strengthen the foundation and economize expenditures," theirs is a way by which people can provide enough for their families. This is what Mozi excelled in; even a hundred lineages cannot disregard it.

The Legalists do not distinguish between close and distant relations and do not differentiate between noble and base. All are one before the law. They therefore destroy the compassion that comes from cherishing one's close relations and honoring the honorable. While one can implement their schemes for a single season, they cannot be used for longer than that. Therefore I said they "are harsh and lacking in compassion." Nonetheless, even the hundred lineages cannot improve upon the way they honor the ruler and humble the ministers and the way they distinguish official duties so that they do not overstep one another.

The Terminologists chase around in circles over petty details and cause people to be unable to return to their basic meaning. They become obsessed with names, yet they lose sight of the genuine basis of human beings. Therefore I said they "cause people to be strict [with words], yet they outdo themselves and lose sight of the truth." However, their methods of selecting names and demanding a corresponding reality and of the three [tests to determine a minister's merit] and the five [tests to determine a minister's faults] do not err and cannot be ignored.

The Daoists do nothing, but they also say that nothing is left undone. Their substance is easy to practice, but their words are difficult to understand. Their techniques take emptiness and nothingness as the foundation and adaptation and compliance as the application. They have no set limits, no regular forms, and so are able to penetrate to the genuine basis of living things. Because they neither anticipate things nor linger over them, they are able to become the masters of all living things.[102]

They have methods that are no methods:

They take adapting to the seasons as their practice.

They have limits that are no limits:

They adapt to things by harmonizing with them.

Therefore they say:

The sage is not clever:

The seasonal alternations are what the sage preserves.[103]

Emptiness is the constant in the Way.

---

102. Daoists are not supposed to worry over things to come nor become obsessed with what has happened. For Sima Tan they remain constantly in the present moment, responding fully and harmoniously to whatever arises.

103. These two lines are found in the second section ("Observations") of the second book of the *Huang-Lao boshu, Sixteen Canons.* See *Mawangdui Hanmu boshu,* p. 63, line 1.

Adaptation is the guiding principle of the ruler.

When the various ministers arrive together [for an audience], the ruler makes each clarify himself. When their accomplishments have matched their appraisal, the ruler calls this scrupulous. When their accomplishments have not matched their appraisal, the ruler calls this deceptive. When deceptive speech is not heard, traitors do not arise, the worthy and worthless will differentiate themselves, and white and black will then take shape.[104] Among those whom one desires to employ, what endeavor will not succeed? This is, then, how the ruler unites with the Great Way, obscure and dark, illuminates all-under-Heaven, and reverts to the Nameless.

What gives life to all human beings is the numen (spirit), and what they rely upon is the body. When the numen is used excessively it becomes depleted; when the body toils excessively it wears out. When the body and numen separate we die; when we die we cannot return to life; what separates cannot return to how it was. Therefore the sage attaches great importance to this. From this we observe that the numen is the foundation of life, and the physical form is the vessel of life. How could anyone say, "I possess the means to rule all-under-Heaven" without first stabilizing the numen?

[*Shiji* (BNB) 130:3a–6b — HR, SQ]

---

104. When the ruler keeps a close check on how his officials are living up to their responsibilities, he creates clear categories of performance, evaluation, and response. Doing so differentiates the worthy from the unworthy and nips sedition in the bud, so to speak. This is the practical benefit of the clearly distinguished categories of "name" and "form."

Chapter 10

THE IMPERIAL ORDER AND HAN SYNTHESES

With the expanding horizons of the Han empire came a broadening of intellectual interest in questions of cosmology and the natural order, accompanied by a conviction of the sort expressed in the *Mean* (22) that the person who is perfectly sincere can "assist in the transforming and nourishing powers of Heaven and Earth; being able to assist in the transforming and nourishing powers of Heaven and Earth, he can form a triad with Heaven and Earth."[1]

This concept that Heaven, Earth, and humankind can form a triad is basic in Han thought. It was first of all the duty of human beings to observe and comprehend the order presided over by Heaven in both a religious and a physical sense. Equally strong is the conviction, hardly to be wondered at in an agricultural society, that human beings, and especially the government, must attend to concerns of the earth, particularly to matters of irrigation, land usage, and flood control. Han thinkers stressed, as had Mencius earlier, that economic welfare is the basis of popular morality. The scholar or sage might deliberately choose to remain poor if riches could be his only by resorting to unworthy means. The masses, however, could not be expected to adhere to such a high standard. They naturally desire material well-being. If it cannot be acquired by just means, they will seek it by any means available. If a poor man steals, it is

---

1. See pp. 333–39.

because he is unable to make a living honestly. Therefore the course of profit and the course of virtue must be made identical, so that the people's needs can be met by proper means. Accordingly, the ruler bears a responsibility to provide for both the material welfare and the moral instruction of the people, thereby "transforming" them and enabling them to form a harmonious triad with Heaven and Earth.

Confucianism talks a great deal about this duty of the government to transform or bring to completion the nature of the people — in other words, to civilize them. The first step in the process is to provide peace and prosperity. The second step is moral training or education, done mainly through rites (which include everything from the most solemn religious ceremonies to the simplest daily courtesies), music (instrumental music, song, and mimic dance), and literature. Rites and music can be appreciated, and even learned to some extent, by all men, but literate discourse, being a long and difficult study, can be mastered only by the intelligent and the leisured. The final product of such study is the sage, whose learning is confirmed in the most refined moral sense. Ideally, he should become emperor, but in practice, since the Confucians generally eschewed any struggle for power, the dynastic principle of hereditary rulership was accepted, and the sage or scholar was expected to take up a position as adviser to the emperor or participant in government service, working through the established machinery of government, which has total responsibility for the economic, social, and spiritual welfare of the empire.

During the Han period the social conscience of the Confucians, and their scholarly qualifications, brought them in increasing numbers into the new officialdom that replaced the feudal aristocracy of Zhou times. Reconciling themselves to the new imperial system and its bureaucratic structures, they succeeded in having a state college and system of competitive examinations set up, which, at least in normal times, assured a dominant position for scholars in the civil bureaucracy.

GUIDELINES FOR HAN RULERS

The passage from the Qin to the Han was not just an ordinary dynastic change but a political and intellectual transition that involved a redefining of imperial polity and ideology, a settlement that lasted for two thousand years. Whereas the Qin accomplished the truly revolutionary change from relatively loose "feudal" arrangements of power to tightly centralized bureaucratic rule, the Han, which inherited this unified empire, faced the task of finding sanctions for it other than those that derived from brute force. The early emperors of the Han sought and listened to a number of advisers and scholars, whose memorials have come down to us as essays in political thought that bridge the classical world of thought with the real world of a unified empire. The joining of moral knowledge with practical governance, a combination that Confucius himself had envisaged and, but for the lack of a listening prince, might have achieved, is the result of early Han intellectual and ideological achievements by a number of dazzling talents.

The following selections are from two early Han figures, Lu Jia (?–170 B.C.E.) and Jia Yi (201–168? B.C.E.). The former advised the dynasty's founder, Liu Bang, later known by the title Han Gaozu (or High Ancestor of the Han, r. 206–195 B.C.E.), while the latter counseled Emperor Wen (r. 180–157 B.C.E.). Lu Jia advised on how the Qin failed and the Han could benefit from that lesson. Jia Yi, after experiencing some twenty years of ruthless court politics surrounding Han Gaozu's widow, the Empress Lü, which saw a return to "feudal" practices of enfeoffing the princes, advised Emperor Wen on imperial dignity, strength, and moral scope. Both scholars addressed central questions concerning the nature of power and authority and involved themselves in critiques of its use and abuse. In so doing, they not only helped define Han Confucianism but stood in a line of Confucian tradition that, out of its humane concern with moral issues, was to show a capacity for regeneration, growth, and expansion over the course of centuries to come.

LU JIA: THE NATURAL ORDER AND THE HUMAN ORDER

The following selections from Lu Jia come from the first two chapters of his *New Discourses* (*Xinyu*), a work of twelve chapters responding to Han Gaozu's charge to offer a discourse on "why the Qin failed and the Han succeeded, and also on the merits of rulers throughout history." The first two chapters, "Foundation of Dao" ("Daoji") and "Handling Affairs" ("Shushi"), laid down the basis of the work, which, with uncanny logic, handled questions of personal cultivation in the even-numbered chapters and those of selecting talents in the odd-numbered ones. Both cosmological and practical aspects of imperial rule can be found in these passages. Note especially the holistic view of the human and natural orders.

Tradition has it that Heaven gives birth to the myriad things to be nurtured by Earth and brought to completion by sages. When our deeds and virtues accord with Heaven and Earth, the practice of the Way emerges.

Therefore it is also understood how the sun and the moon are displayed, the stars arrayed, the four seasons set in order, yin and yang regulated, energies distributed, and the nature of things put in tune, the Five Phases (*wuxing*) set in proper order, with growth during spring, flourishing during summer, harvest in autumn, and hibernation in winter. Yang gives forth thunder and lightning, while yin forms frost and snow, nurturing all living beings as they wax and wane. Winds and rain moisten living things, and the sun parches them; the seasons modulate [living things], and the killing frost reduces them. The stars show their various locations, and the north polar star points out directions to them. The six directions [*liuhe*] envelop them, and the moral precepts give them warp and woof. Disasters and change alter them, and propitious signs inform their life; life and death keep them in motion, and patterns and order awaken them.

Thus, what is in Heaven can be discerned; what is on Earth can be measured. What is in the material world can be ordered; what is in the human world can be contemplated. . . . [The Earth] maintains all things and sustains the species. It establishes all living beings, keeping their essences while exhibiting their forms. In establishing all living forms, it does not go against the seasons or the nature of things, and it conceals neither their feelings nor deceptions.

For these reasons, those who know Heaven raise their heads and observe the patterns of Heaven, and those who know Earth bend their heads and study the principles of Earth. All species that walk and breathe, those that fly and crawl, those on land or on sea, and deep-rooted plants with leafy crowns, all will be peaceful of mind and calm of nature; all will be brought to completion when Heaven and Earth interact, and the vital energies (*qi*) resonate with each other.

The former sage [Fu Xi] thus raised his head and observed the patterns of Heaven and looked down and studied the principles of Earth, charting the cosmos[2] and setting the human way. Thus enlightened, the people came to know filiality between parent and child, rightness between ruler and minister, the proprieties of husband and wife,[3] and the order between elder and younger. Henceforth the offices of state were established and the kingly way arose. . . .

When the people only feared the laws, they could not know rites and rightness. Thus the middle sages [Emperor Wen of Zhou and the Duke of Zhou] set up various levels of schools (*xu* and *xiang*) and academies (*piyong*),[4] so as to rectify the principles governing superior and inferior and make manifest rites between parent and child, as well as bonds between ruler and minister. This way, the strong would not oppress the weak, the many would not victimize the one, while greed and avarice would be replaced by pure and refined conduct.

When rites and rightness were not practiced and regulations and disciplines were not maintained, succeeding generations became weak and decadent. Thus the later sage [Confucius] defined the Five Classics[5] and taught the Six

---

2. Literally, *qian* and *kun*. Legend has it that Fu Xi, having observed Heaven and Earth, devised the Eight Trigrams, of which *qian* and *kun* were the two most important diagrams. *Qian* represents Heaven and all yang-related things, and *kun* represents earth and all yin-related things. See pp. 318–22.

3. Literally, the separate functions of husband and wife.

4. *Xu* were village schools; *xiang* were local schools; *piyong* were high academies established by kings.

5. Lu Jia was the first to refer to the Five Classics as consisting of the *Classic of Odes*, the

Arts,[6] following the principles of Heaven and Earth, all the while exhaustively pursuing the minutest ways of things and events. Studying human sentiments and establishing the basis, he ordered interpersonal relationships. Basing himself on the principles of Heaven and Earth, he edited and revised the classics to be passed on to future generations, benefiting even the world of birds and beasts. All of these he did to correct decay and disorder. So that the Heavenly and human [orders] would be one, so that the original Way would be fully manifest, so that the wise would maximize their minds, and the handy extend their skills, the sage harmonized all with the sounds of flute and strings and established music for bells, drums, and dance. This way he curbed extravagance, rectified customs, and extended true culture.

Later generations became self-indulgent and wicked, made still worse by the music of the states of Zheng and Wei.[7] The people forsook what is basic[8] and pursued what is secondary.[9] Proceeding from various intentions, they indulged in unnecessary ornamentation, adding excessive glue and lacquer, and mixing unusual and strange colors, all with the purpose of pleasing the senses and satisfying the artisan's penchant for craftiness.

Donkeys and mules, camels, rhinoceroses and elephants, along with tortoiseshells, amber and coral, kingfisher feathers, pearls and jades, are all found either on mountains or in water. They are found in their habitats, pure and clear, damp and moistened as the case may be. . . . They await their usefulness and their nature being turned into useful implements. Thus it is said that the sage brought them to fulfillment. He could in these circumstances manage all creatures and understand their changes, control their base nature, and display their humanity (*ren*) and rightness (*yi*).

Those sages were able to be grand and magnanimous, liberal and broadminded, prudent and precise, being at peace far and near, attracting and caring for all states under Heaven. Thus sages embrace humaneness and dispense rightness, exercise meticulous care in judgment, and gauge Heaven and Earth. . . . Hence, when the sage becomes the ruler of the world, all worthy men are able to attain meritorious deeds. Emperor Tang thus promoted [his counselor] Yi Yin, and Zhou [Xibo] employed Lü Wang [Lü Shang, also Taigong Wang].[10]

Classic of Documents, the Classic of Rites (at first referring to the *Yili*, later replaced by the *Liji*), the *Classic of Changes*, and the *Spring and Autumn Annals*.

6. There are two versions of the Six Arts: as the Six Classics, with that of Music added to the above five; and as the six arts or skills of ritual observance, musical performance, archery, charioteering, calligraphy, and mathematics. Ordinarily, the reference is to the first meaning, but here it refers to the second, as it would be redundant following the mention of the Five Classics.

7. Two states known for their licentious music.

8. I.e., agriculture.

9. I.e., commerce.

10. Elderly Taigong Wang was discovered while fishing on the Wei River by King Wen of

The sagely deed accorded with Heaven and Earth, and sagely virtue meshed with the yin-yang principle. They obeyed Heaven and eradicated evil, overcame violence and eliminated disaster. They nurtured vital energy and nourished the myriad things. They illuminated all with knowledge and gave sight, hearing from and looking into all directions. As a result the upright prevailed and debauchery ceased. Such good and bad qualities cannot flourish together. Follow the original principles and nip [bad] things in the bud.

Now actions that do not combine humaneness and rightness are doomed to failure; structures that forsake a firm foundation for a high perch are certain to topple. Thus the sage uses the classics and the arts to prevent disorder, as the craftsman uses the plumb line to correct crookedness. One who is rich in virtue has far-flung influence; one who is ample in brute strength may be merely overbearing. Duke Huan of Qi claimed hegemony through virtue, while the Second Emperor of the Qin perished through his fondness for penal codes.

Cruel deeds therefore accumulate grievance, and manifest virtue promotes merit. . . . By the same token, those who maintain the country with humaneness are themselves secure, and those who aid the sovereign are not in jeopardy. The sovereign rules over a good government with humaneness; the ministers conduct orderly affairs in keeping with rightness. The people of the realm respect each other through humaneness, and the officials of the court discourse with each other on the basis of rightness. . . . The yang energy is born of humaneness, and the yin rhythm is set by rightness. The "call of the deer"[11] is humane in its thoughtfulness for companionship; the "call of the osprey"[12] is correct in its expression of propriety. The *Spring and Autumn Annals* makes denunciations and condemnations in the name of humaneness and rightness, and the *Odes* uses humaneness and rightness to preserve or discard. Heaven and Earth are harmonized by humaneness; the Eight Trigrams are interrelated through rightness. The *Documents* traces the nine family relationships through humaneness. Between sovereign and ministers, loyalty is governed by rightness. The *Rites* tells of ritual decorum governed by humaneness and of music informed by humaneness.

Humaneness is the standard for the Way, and rightness is the learning for sages. Those who learn humaneness and rightness are enlightened; those who lack them are confused, and those who deny them are destined to perish.

Talents being already possessed and displayed, it is rightness that establishes

---

Zhou. His role as counselor to King Wen was traditionally regarded as pivotal to the rise of the Zhou dynasty.

11. A reference to Ode 161 in the *Classic of Odes*. The deer, when foraging for grass and feed, will call for their companions to come and share the food. The sound of the deer is thus taken to express humaneness or fellow-feeling.

12. A reference to Ode 1 in the *Classic of Odes*. The osprey were reportedly often seen in pairs of female and male and were known for their distinct mating calls.

merit. Among marching troops, it is humaneness that brings firmness and right exertion that ensures strength. In regulating one's energy and nurturing one's nature, the humane person enjoys longevity. In rating talents and judging virtues, the one who is right observes proper conduct. Sovereign men praise each other in light of rightness, while petty persons cheat one another with profit in mind. The stupid will use strength in mutual discord, while the worthy will use rightness in mutual accord. The *Guliang Commentary to the Spring and Autumn Annals* states, "Humaneness is there to regulate family relations; rightness is there to benefit parents and elders. If for ten thousand ages there were no disorder, it would be because of the rule of humaneness and rightness."

[Lu Jia, *Xinyu*, "Daoji" (*Zhongguo zixue mingzhu jicheng*) 1:189–198 — DWYK]

Be Current and Relevant

Those skilled in speaking of antiquity see its reflection in the present, and those skilled in speaking of distant affairs measure them against those close by. Thus a commentator on events will proclaim the merits of the Five Emperors in light of the experiences of his own times and cite the failures of Jie and Zhou[13] as an admonition to themselves. When this is done, one's virtue matches the sun and moon, and one's deeds equal the spirits. In reaching the high and the far, approaching the deep and the unseen, one hears what is unspoken and perceives what is without form. The world cannot see his signs or know his feelings. Cultivating the messages of the Five Classics and discerning true morality from the specious, one's intent is [made known] while one's person is not seen.

The ordinary world tends to treasure what is passed down through the ages and to slight the accomplishments of the present, to make light of what is seen but to relish what is only heard about. Therefore it is often deceived by appearances and loses the essential meanings of things. The sage does not prize what is rare, whereas ordinary people despise the commonplace. The five grains nurture life, yet they often are left to waste. Pearls and jade are useless, yet they are treasured to adorn bodies. The sage does not value pearls and jade as much as he treasures his own self. Thus Emperor Shun left gold behind in the mountains and Yu cast away pearls and jade in the water marshes. This way the sages curbed greed and avarice and put an end to extravagance.

The Way is never far from us, so there is no need to go to remote antiquity to find it. One needs only to discern essential and consequential matters. The *Spring and Autumn Annals* does not mention the Five Emperors and the Three Rulers[14] but narrates the minor accomplishments of Duke Huan of Qi and

---

13. Traditionally viewed as tyrants of the Xia and Shang dynasties, respectively.

14. According to Sima Qian in his *Records of the Grand Historian* (see ch. 12), the five emperors were the Yellow Emperor, Zhuan Xu, Ku, Yao, and Shun; the three rulers were Yu of Xia, Tang of Shang, and Wu of Zhou.

Duke Wen of Jin and describes the political conduct of the twelve dukes of Lu. From their deeds, the standards of success and failure are obvious. What need is there to go back to the Three Rulers? By the same token, the deeds of the ancients are similar to those of the present. Those who accomplish things do not deviate from morality, just as the tuners of stringed instruments do not stray from the standards of pitch. The Way of Heaven regulates the four seasons, and the Way of humans regulates the five cardinal relationships. The Duke of Zhou shared the same felicitous auspices with Emperors Yao and Shun, and the Second Emperor of the Qin the same calamitous fate with Jie and Zhou.

King Wen[15] originated among the Eastern barbarians, and King Yu came from the Western tribes. They lived in different times and different places, but their laws were uniform and their standards similar. . . . Writings need not originate only from Confucian teachings, and prescriptions need not be written by Bian Que.[16] One needs only to comply with goodness and adapt oneself to the ways of the world.

Thus while nature abides with humankind, vital force (*qi*) reaches Heaven. Whether the matter be minute or huge, by learning here below we may penetrate to what is above.[17] . . . Those who are concerned with the branches must mind the roots; those who want to see proper images in the mirror must first correct their own countenance. When the roots are nurtured, the branches and leaves flourish; when one's intentions and vital force are in balance, the Way is unswerving.[18] Thus those who seek the distant must not lose sight of the near; those concerned about their image must not neglect their true faces. When those on high are understanding, those below will be honest; when the king is wise, his ministers will be loyal. Those who seek things from afar often lose sight of the present; and those whose eyes are fixed only on the road often head toward a dead end. . . . Alas, those who wish to advance cannot overlook difficulties at hand, and those who make plans must not fail to demonstrate full loyalty. When penal codes are enacted, virtue dissipates; when deceit prevails, loyalty perishes. The *Classic of Odes* says: "By a change of one's heart, the myriad states may be nurtured."[19] When wholeheartedness transforms all-under-Heaven, the myriad states are at peace. So it was said!

[From *Xinyu*, "Shushi" (*Zhongguo zixue mingzhu jicheng* ed.) 2:199–206 — DWYK]

JIA YI: THE PRIMACY OF THE PEOPLE (*MINBEN*)

Jia Yi's contributions to early Han thought are in the elegance, range, and pertinence of his ideas. His major work, the *New Writings* (*Xinshu*), is composed of three kinds

---

15. This should read "Emperor Shun."
16. The most famous doctor of antiquity.
17. Alludes to *Analects* 14:37. See ch. 3.
18. Alludes to *Daodejing* 4. See ch. 5, where the phrase is differently translated.
19. Ode 191.

of materials: his seminal writings, his advice at the court of Emperor Wen, and his counsels to Prince Liang in Changsha, where he served as assistant grand tutor before dying there at the age of thirty-three. This material is organized into fifty-eight chapters ranging over fifty subjects, including how to handle princes, manage vassals, centralize royal authority, exercise powers of coinage, employ the right talents, interpret yin-yang and the Five Phases (*wuxing*) in the moral and social makeup of the prince, provide prenatal care of the royal heir, and, of course, analyze the faults of Qin ("Guo Qin lun").[20] Some questions have been raised concerning the authenticity of portions of the work, but the influence of its main ideas remains, especially his emphasis on the importance of the people even in an imperial order.

As we have seen, Jia Yi found fault not with the entire Qin house but with the lack of humaneness of its emperors, and especially the moral degeneracy of the Second Emperor. Thus Jia Yi carried on in the vein of Lu Jia, indicating for Han rulers the pitfalls that might beset their own rule upon the achievement of empire.

It is said that in government, the people are in every way the root (base) [*ben*].[21] For the state, the ruler, and the officials, the people constitute the root. Thus the security of the state or its endangerment depends on them [the people]; the prestige of the ruler or his disgrace depends on them; and the honor of the officials or their debasement is contingent on them. This is what is meant by saying the people are in every way the root. Then again, it is said that in government, the people constitute in every way the mandate. For the state, the ruler, and the officials all depend on the people for their mandate. The life or death of the state depend on the people, the vision or blindness of the ruler depends on them, and whether officials are respected or not depends on them. This is why the people are in every way the mandate. . . .

Still further it is said that the people are the power on which the state, the ruler, and the officials all depend for their power. If victory is won, it is because the people want to be victorious; if an attack succeeds, it is because the people want it so; if defense succeeds, it is because the people want to survive. . . . If the people are fearful of the enemy, they will surely retreat and defeat will surely come. Disaster and fortune, as we see, are determined not in Heaven but by the officers (*shi*) and the people. . . .

Good deeds will in the end bring good fortune, and bad deeds will inevitably bring misfortune. Those who are blessed by Heaven need not thank Heaven, and those who suffer from natural disasters need not blame Heaven, for it is all one's own doing. . . . Heaven will present good fortune to the virtuous and

---

20. As seen in ch. 8.

21. *Ben-mo* is a dichotomy expressing Chinese estimations of value, priority, or sequence. Thus *ben* (originally the root or trunk of the tree) is the base or fundamental value, and *mo* (the branches of the tree) is the subordinate means or secondary, often nonessential, value. The former is associated here with the honest occupations of ploughing and weaving and the latter with business activities that are thought to distort human nature through utilitarian calculations.

disaster to those who deprive the people. Even the lowest of people should not be slighted, and the most foolish among them should not be taken advantage of. Thus, throughout history, those who oppose the people sooner or later are defeated by the people. . . . How can anyone think of behaving with arrogance and self-deception? The enlightened ruler and the noble person will vie to practice good when they perceive it, and they will treat evil like an enemy if they hear of it. . . .

Punishments and rewards must be meted out with caution. Lest the innocent be killed, it is better to be lenient toward the guilty. Thus, in matters of guilt, if doubt exists, it is better to forgive; and in matters of merit, if there is uncertainty, it is better to confer the reward. . . . To forgive in the case of a questionable crime is to be humane; to confer a reward in the case of questionable merit is to be credible. Take heed, take heed!

. . . The ruler is honorable only because the officers and people honor him. This is true honor. The ruler prospers only because the people are pleased to cause him to do so. This is true prosperity. The honor of the ruler comes from endowing his people with fortune; in turn the people honor him. The wealth of the ruler comes from enriching the people, who then are pleased to support him. This is why when the honor and prosperity of the ruler extend through only a few generations and then decline, the people exclaim, "Why does the Way of the ruler decline so quickly?" In the case of the unscrupulous and tyrannical ruler who brings disaster upon himself, the people say, "Why does Heaven take so long to kill him?"

Thus the people are the root of [dynastic] longevity, never to be taken lightly. . . . Moreover, the people have great strength and cannot be opposed. Oh, be warned, in any opposition to the people, the people will win.

[Xinshu, "Dazheng" (SBCK) 9:541–549 —DWYK]

DONG ZHONGSHU

When the Han dynasty established an imperial system of government that was to persist until 1911, Confucian scholars of that day, among them Dong Zhongshu (195?–105? B.C.E.), articulated a vision of an omnipotent but disciplined sovereign, who sought to align the population with the norms of Heaven and Earth, based on the advice and counsel of scholar-officials versed in the classical traditions of antiquity. This ideal of the ruler as high priest and fount of wisdom contained within it basic patterns and tensions that came to define the relationship between the state and intellectual, center and periphery, power and authority, and politics and culture for centuries to come.

Confucian scholars were deeply engaged in the politics of their day. They sought to gain political power by influencing the policies and practices emanating from the emperor based on their textual interpretations. At the same time, they endeavored to maintain an independent and critical voice based on the authority and prestige they derived from their mastery of the Confucian texts. To what extent would cultural endeavors restrain politics or be restrained by them? To what extent would other centers of regional power rival or reinforce the emperor's court in either literary prowess or military power? These unresolved tensions reemerged in every dynasty to follow. Moreover, some scholars would argue that, even after the abolition of imperial government in 1911 and the Communist revolution of 1949, many of these issues continue to shape the political culture of contemporary China.

Like his predecessors Lu Jia and Jia Yi, Dong Zhongshu sought to develop a rationale and a model of rulership appropriate to the new circumstances of the unified state. He vied for political influence and competed for literary patronage with devotees of esoteric learning and popular lore as diverse as the different areas over which the Han rulers now claimed sovereignty. Chief among them were the followers of Huang-Lao (the Yellow Emperor and Laozi),[22] whose techniques and texts were favored by Emperor Jing (r. 157–141 B.C.E.), and the doctors, diviners, and magicians known collectively as *fangshi* (masters of technical methods or technicians), who bedazzled his successor, Emperor Wu (r. 141–87 B.C.E.) with their elixirs of immortality. The confluence of local cultural traditions at the Han court also gave rise to the cross-fertilization of philosophical ideas, cosmological principles, and political techniques among advocates of these various traditions. As they evolved in the pluralistic intellectual atmosphere, shifting political alliances, and changing imperial patronage of the Former Han, traditions — master-disciple lineages centering on a text or corpus of texts that transmitted a set of doctrines and techniques — were neither impermeable nor immune to other intellectual trends at court. Thus Dong Zhongshu's contributions to the Han ideal of rulership involved both the rejection and the absorption of ideas, principles, and techniques from other traditions. Nor were they unaffected by the personalities and proclivities of the successive Han emperors, empresses, and empress dowagers whose varying receptivity toward Confucian scholars often determined the critical difference between Confucian principle and practice.

Relying on two attitudes that characterized the Confucian scholar, a respect for the past and a veneration for the writings of Confucius, Dong hoped to reform imperial sovereignty by re-creating both history and text. Following his predecessors Lu Jia, whom Emperor Gao commissioned to write the *Xinyu* (*New Discourses*), and Jia Yi, who composed the famous essay "Guo Qin lun" ("The Faults of Qin")[23] during the reign of Emperor Wen (r. 180–157 B.C.E.), he also sought to discredit the Qin dynasty. The demonic character of the

---

22. See ch. 9.
23. See ch. 8.

dynasty was a prominent theme in his writings and came to define traditional historiography for centuries to follow. This interpretation of the Qin provided an intellectual rationale for discrediting the political and religious framework of imperial sovereignty that had developed under the earlier regime.

It was through his interpretations of the Confucian texts that Dong delineated his program for renewed kingship. This was particularly true of the *Spring and Autumn Annals* (*Chunqiu*) and the accompanying *Gongyang Commentary* (*Gongyang zhuan*), Dong Zhongshu's special focus of inquiry. He believed the *Spring and Autumn Annals* could resolve Qin excesses and endeavored to explicate how and why the text was relevant, indeed indispensable, to the creation of an alternative social, political, and religious culture for the Han. Consequently, Dong Zhongshu and his disciples read into the *Spring and Autumn Annals* a particular vision of history and ascribed to the text new modes of legal, ritual, and cosmological authority that were relevant to their reformist goals. His persuasive interpretations, among other factors, enabled Dong Zhongshu and other reformist scholars under Emperor Wu to end state support for the teaching of non-Confucian texts and to establish a text-based ideology represented in the first Confucian canon. Thenceforth, the Confucian canon played a prominent role in the doctrinal and political life of the traditional state. The designation in 136 B.C.E. of official posts known as the "Erudites of the Five Classics" and the establishment in 124 B.C.E. of the Imperial College, where these texts were taught as a basic prerequisite for training in the polity, were the institutional expressions of this canonization.

Here, too, the Han legacy was complex. For while Dong and other Confucian scholars sought to break with the past and discredit the political and cultural excesses of the preceding Qin dynasty, they also drew upon a number of pre-Qin ideals. Though scholars like Dong Zhongshu sought exclusive imperial patronage for the Confucian canon, their interpretations of these texts were influenced by the diverse techniques and doctrines represented at the central court and at competing centers of literary patronage across the empire.

Although traditionally ascribed to Dong Zhongshu, the *Luxuriant Gems of the Spring and Autumn Annals* (*Chunqiu fanlu*) is most likely the product of an anonymous compiler who lived sometime between the third and sixth centuries. The received text preserves authentic writings as well as other materials not authored by Dong Zhongshu. Like many other philosophical works from China's classical period, the text is best understood as an anthology: a collection of materials authored by Dong Zhongshu and records of his doctrinal expositions to different audiences in diverse venues. But it also contains other writings, probably by his disciples and critics. Indeed, the authentic materials provide a retrospective view of Dong's thought as it evolved throughout his long political career, while those by his disciples shed light on their activities during the later years of the Han dynasty. Those composed by his critics indicate the contested areas of Han discourse. The translations that follow from the *Luxuriant Gems of the Spring and Autumn Annals* represent what are generally accepted to be the original teachings of this Han master. The final selection is from "Deciding Court Cases According to the *Spring and Autumn Annals*," another work of Dong's.

Luxuriant Gems of the Spring and Autumn Annals
(Chunqiu Fanlu)

DERIVING POLITICAL NORMS FROM MICROCOSMIC AND MACROCOSMIC MODELS

Like other intellectuals of the late Warring States and Han periods, Dong sought to legitimate his views of government based on natural models derived, on the one hand, from the macrocosm of Heaven and Earth and, on the other, from the microcosm of the human body. In the first essay, Dong correlates the conduct of the ruler with Heaven and that of the minister with Earth. In the second essay, he correlates techniques to regulate and nourish the body with those meant to order and vitalize the state. These forms of correlative thought had already appeared by the third century B.C.E. in the *Springs and Autumns of Mr. Lü* (*Lüshi chunqiu*) and were no doubt popularized by followers of the Yellow Emperor and Laozi in the early centuries of the Han.[24] As the next two essays demonstrate, they also represent important aspects of Dong Zhongshu's thought. Thus, while striving to secure exclusive patronage for the Confucian canon, Dong endeavored to synthesize many intellectual trends that had historically stood beyond the purview of the Confucian tradition.

THE CONDUCT OF HEAVEN AND EARTH

The conduct of Heaven and Earth is beautiful. For this reason Heaven holds its place high and sends down its manifestations; conceals its form and reveals its light; arranges the stars and accumulates vital essence; relies on yin and yang and sends down frost and dew. Heaven holds a high position and so is honored. It sends down its manifestations and so is humane. It conceals its form and so is numinous. It reveals its light and so is brilliant. It orders and arranges the stars and so there is mutual succession. It accumulates vital essence and so endures. It relies on yin and yang and so completes the year. It sends down frost and dew and so brings life and death.

The norms of the people's ruler are derived from and modeled on Heaven. Therefore he values ranks and so is honored. He subjugates other states and so is humane. He resides in a hidden place and does not reveal his form and so is numinous. He appoints the worthy and employs the capable, observes and listens to the four corners of his realm, and so is brilliant. He confers office according to capability, distinguishing the worthy and stupid, and so there is

---

24. For similar themes, see the selections from the *Zuozhuan* (ch. 6) and the *Guanzi*, *Huang-Lao boshu*, and *Huainanzi* (ch. 9).

mutual succession. He induces worthy men to draw near and establishes them as his legs and arms and so endures. He investigates the true nature of the ministers' achievements, ranks and orders them as the worst and the best, and so completes his age. He promotes those who possess merit and demotes those who lack merit and so rewards and punishes.

For this reason Heaven clings to the Way and acts as the master of all living things. The ruler maintains constant norms and acts as the master of a single state. Heaven must be resolute. The ruler must be firm. When Heaven is not resolute, the arrayed stars become chaotic in their orbits. When the ruler is not firm, evil ministers become chaotic in their offices. When stars become chaotic, they stray from Heaven.[25] When ministers become chaotic, they stray from their ruler. Therefore Heaven strives to stabilize its vital force (*qi*), while the ruler strives to stabilize his government. Only when resolute and firm will the Way of yang[26] regulate and order others.

Earth humbles its position and sends up its vital energy; exposes its forms and manifests its true feelings; receives the dead and offers up the living; completes its tasks and confers its merit [on Heaven]. Earth humbles its position and so serves Heaven. It sends up its vital energy and so nourishes yang. It exposes its forms and so is loyal. It manifests its true feelings and so is trustworthy. It receives the dead and so hides away the end of life. It offers up the living and so enhances Heaven's brilliance. It completes its tasks and so enhances Heaven's transformations. It confers its merit on Heaven and so achieves rightness. . . .

The norms of the people's ministers are derived from and modeled on Earth. Therefore from morning to evening they advance and retreat, taking up various tasks and responding to various inquiries, and so serve the honored [ruler]. They provide food and drink, attend to him in sickness and illness, and so provide nourishment [to the ruler]. They entrust and sacrifice their lives and serve without thoughts of usurpation and so are loyal. They expose their ignorance, manifest their true feelings, do not gloss over their mistakes, and so are trustworthy. They maintain proper conduct even when facing death, do not covet life, and so relieve others in distress. They promote and praise his goodness, and so enhance [the ruler's] brilliance. They follow his orders, proclaim his grace, assist and complete him, and so enhance his transforming influence. When achievements are completed and tasks are finished, they confer their virtue upon the ruler and so achieve rightness.

For this reason Earth manifests its principles and acts as the mother of all living things. The minister manifests his duties and acts as the counselor of a single state. The mother must be trustworthy. The counselor must be loyal.

---

25. Literally, "to stray from Heaven" means that the stars will fall from the sky. Heaven also signifies the physical sky.

26. The Way of yang is synonymous with the Way of Heaven and the way of the ruler.

When the mother is untrustworthy, grasses and trees suffer injury at their roots. When the counselor is disloyal, treacherous ministers endanger the ruler. When the roots suffer injury, trees and grasses lose their branches and leaves. When the ruler is endangered, the ruler loses his state. Therefore Earth strives to expose its actions while the minister strives to manifest his true feelings.

[*Chunqiu fanlu yizheng* 17:9b–12b — SQ]

COMPREHENDING THE STATE AS THE BODY

The purest vital force (*qi*) is vital essence.

The purest men are worthies.

Those who regulate their bodies consider the accumulation of vital essence to be a treasure.

Those who regulate the state consider the accumulation of worthy men to be the Way.

The body takes the mind-and-heart as the foundation.

The state takes the ruler as the master.

When vital essence accumulates at the foundation, the blood and vital force support one another.

When worthy men accumulate around their master, superiors and inferiors order one another.

When the blood and vital force support one another, the body is free from pain.

When superiors and inferiors order one another, the numerous offices each achieve their proper place.

Only when the body is free from pain can it achieve tranquillity.

Only when the numerous offices each obtain their proper place can the state achieve security.

Those who desire to accumulate vital essence must empty their minds-and-hearts and still their bodies.

Those who desire to accumulate worthy men must humble their persons.

Where the form is still and the mind-and-heart empty, vital essence collects.

Where there are humble and self-effacing rulers, humane and worthy men serve.

Therefore, those who regulate their bodies endeavor to maintain emptiness and stillness, and thereby accumulate vital essence.

Those who regulate the state endeavor fully to develop their humility, and thereby accumulate worthy and competent men.

Those able to accumulate vital essence achieve enlightenment and longevity.

Those able to accumulate worthy men widely extend their virtue and their states achieve ultimate peace.

[*Chunqiu fanlu yizheng* 7:4b–5a — SQ]

THE RESPONSIBILITIES OF RULERSHIP

In the following essays Dong Zhongshu outlines the responsibilities of rulership. We see Dong synthesizing Daoist ideals that emphasized the quietude and passivity of the ruler with the more active orientation of the Confucian ideal. These essays also ex-emplify the tensions implicit in Dong's vision of imperial rulership. While he strove to limit and restrain the powers of the emperor by subordinating him to Heaven, he also endeavored to sanction and amplify the ruler's revered position as a "cosmic pivot" responsible for aligning the three realms of Heaven, Earth, and humanity.

ESTABLISHING THE PRIMAL NUMEN[27]

Section 1[28]

He who rules the people is the basis of the state. Issuing edicts and initiating undertakings, he is the pivot of all living things. The pivot of all living things, he is the source of honor and dishonor. If he errs by a millimeter, a team of horses cannot retrieve him. This is why he who acts as the people's ruler is attentive toward the fundamental, careful of the beginning, respectful of the small, and cautious of the subtle. His will resembles [the stillness of] dead embers, while his form resembles [the emptiness of] abandoned clothing. He calms his vital essence and nourishes his numen.[29] He is quiet and nonactive. He stills his body and does not cast a shadow; he silences his voice and does not emit a sound. With an empty mind-and-heart he lowers himself to associate with his officers. He contemplates what lies in the future and observes what has past. He deliberates with his numerous worthies to seek out the opinions of the majority of his people.[30] He knows their hearts and understands their senti-

---

27. The term *shen*, translated here as "numen," is translated elsewhere in this volume as "spirit."

28. Traditional commentators generally divide this chapter into two sections. However, this chapter may comprise material from no fewer than six different essays, combined here because of their common theme. These divisions are noted in the translation below.

29. *Vital essence (jing)* and *numen (shen)* are important technical terms in a number of essays dating from the fourth to the second centuries B.C.E. that appear in such works as the *Lüshi chunqiu, Guanzi,* and *Huainanzi* and are devoted to nourishing the vital energy. The vital essence is the purest and most concentrated vital force (*qi*). The numen is the finest portion of the vital force. Seated in the cardiac system, it governs the vital processes, is responsible for all conscious-ness and mental activity, and, like the vital essence, is the object of Daoist self-cultivation.

30. The Qing scholar Su Yu cites the following relevant passage from the "Ruler and Subject" ("Jun Chen") chapter of the *Guanzi*:

> If the people are divided and the ruler heeds them he is a fool. If the people are united and the ruler heeds them he is a sage. Even if he possesses the virtue of a Tang or Wu, he repeatedly cleaves to the opinions of the marketplace. This is why an enlightened ruler follows the hearts of the people, finds security in their sentiments, and proceeds from a

ments. He investigates their likes and dislikes to verify whether they are loyal or treacherous. He examines their past activities to verify their present dispositions. He reckons to what extent their accomplishments are derived from former worthies.[31] He dispels their grievances and observes the causes of their disputes. He separates their factions and clans and observes the men they esteem. He relies upon his position to order his people and employs [correct] words to establish their reputations. As days pile up and time accumulates, what effort will not reach fruition? It is possible to rely on the internal to verify the external. It is possible to rely on the insignificant to verify the significant. The ruler must know the true substance of things. This is called "eliminating obstructions."

Section 2

He who rules the people is the foundation of the state. Now in administering the state, nothing is more important for transforming [the people] than reverence for the foundation. If the foundation is revered, the ruler will transform [the people] as if a spirit. If the foundation is not revered, the ruler will lack the means to unite the people. If he lacks the means to unite the people, even if he institutes strict punishments and heavy penalties, the people will not submit. This is called "throwing away the state." Is there a greater disaster than this? What do I mean by the foundation? Heaven, Earth, and humankind are the foundation of all living things. Heaven engenders all living things, Earth nourishes them, and humankind completes them. With filial and brotherly love, Heaven engenders them; with food and clothing, Earth nourishes them; and with rites and music, humankind completes them. These three assist one another just as the hands and feet join to complete the body. None can be dispensed with because without filial and brotherly love, people lack the means to live; without food and clothing, people lack the means to be nourished; and without rites and music, people lack the means to become complete. If all three

---

consensus of people's opinions. This is why his orders issue forth, and they are not defied. His punishments are established, but they are not applied. The former kings were skilled at uniting [literally, "forming one body"] with their people. Thus the ruler relied on the state to preserve the state and the people to preserve the people. Hence the people would not easily commit wrongs. Even if a state possesses an enlightened ruler, beyond one hundred paces one listens but does not hear him. Within the walls and battlements [of the ruler's city], one searches but does not see him. Yet he possesses a reputation of being an enlightened ruler because he is skilled at employing his ministers and his ministers are skilled at rendering their loyalty." [*Guanzi* 6:11b–12a]

31. Generally speaking, the ruler must determine to what extent his officials have preserved the Way of the former kings. More narrowly, he must consider whether his officials are reaping the legacies of those who have preceded them or whether their accomplishments are due to their own efforts.

are lost, people become like deer, each person following his own desires and each family practicing its own customs. Fathers will not be able to order their sons, and rulers will not be able to order their ministers. Although possessing inner and outer walls, [the ruler's city] will become known as "an empty settlement." Under such circumstances, the ruler will lie down with a clod of earth for his pillow. Although no one endangers him, he will naturally be endangered; although no one destroys him, he will naturally be destroyed. This is called "spontaneous punishment." When it arrives, even if he is hidden in a stone vault or barricaded in a narrow pass, the ruler will not be able to avoid "spontaneous punishment."

One who is an enlightened master and worthy ruler believes such things. For this reason he respectfully and carefully attends to the three foundations. He reverently enacts the suburban sacrifice, dutifully serves his ancestors, manifests filial and brotherly love, encourages filial conduct, and serves the foundation of Heaven in this way. He takes up the plough handle to till the soil, plucks the mulberry leaves and nourishes the silkworms, reclaims the wilds, plants grain, opens new lands to provide sufficient food and clothing, and serves the foundation of Earth in this way. He establishes academies and schools in towns and villages to teach filial piety, brotherly love, reverence, and humility, enlightens [the people] with education, moves [them] with rites and music, and serves the foundation of humanity in this way.

If these three foundations are all served, the people will resemble sons and brothers who do not dare usurp authority, while the ruler will resemble fathers and mothers. He will not rely on favors to demonstrate his love for his people nor severe measures to prompt them to act. Even if he lives in the wilds without a roof over head, he will consider that this surpasses living in a palace. Under such circumstances, the ruler will lie down upon a peaceful pillow. Although no one assists him, he will naturally be powerful; although no one pacifies his state, peace will naturally come. This is called "spontaneous reward." When "spontaneous reward" befalls him, although he might relinquish the throne and leave the state, the people will take up their children on their backs and follow him as the ruler, so that he too will be unable to leave them. Therefore when the ruler relies on virtue to administer the state, it is sweeter than honey or sugar and firmer than glue or lacquer. This is why sages and worthies exert themselves to revere the foundation and do not dare depart from it.

[*Chunqiu fanlu yizheng* 6:11a–16a — SQ]

THE WAY OF THE KING PENETRATES THREE[32]

In ancient times those who created writing took three horizontal lines and connected them through the center to designate the king. The three horizontal

---

32. "Three" refers to Heaven, Earth, and humankind.

lines represent Heaven, Earth, and humankind while the vertical line that connects them through the center represents comprehending the Way.[33] As for the one who appropriates the mean of Heaven, Earth, and humankind and takes this as the thread that joins and connects them, if it is not one who acts as a king then who can be equal to this [task]? Therefore one who acts as king is no more than Heaven's agent. He models himself on Heaven's seasons and brings them to completion. He models himself on Heaven's commands and causes the people to obey them. He models himself on Heaven's numerical categories and initiates affairs. He models himself on Heaven's Way and sends forth his standards. He models himself on Heaven's will and always returns to humaneness. The beauty of humaneness is found in Heaven. Heaven is humaneness. Heaven shelters and nourishes the myriad things. It transforms and generates them. It nourishes and completes them. Heaven's affairs and achievements are endless. They end and begin again, and all that Heaven raises up it returns to serve humankind. If you examine Heaven's will you will surely see that Heaven's humaneness is inexhaustible and limitless.

Since human beings receive their lives from Heaven, accordingly they appropriate Heaven's humaneness and are thereby humane. For this reason they possess reverence toward Heaven for receiving life; affection for their fathers, older brothers, sons, and younger brothers; minds-and-hearts that are loyal, trustworthy, and caring; actions that are right (*yi*) and yielding; and regulations that distinguish right from wrong and deviance from compliance. Their cultural refinement and inner principles are brilliant and abundant. Their knowledge is broad and deep. Only the way of humankind can join with Heaven. Heaven constantly takes loving and benefiting as its intent and takes nourishing and completing as its task. Spring, autumn, winter, and summer are all Heaven's agents. The king likewise constantly takes loving and benefiting all-under-Heaven as his intent and takes bringing peace and joy to an age as his task. Love, hate, happiness, and anger are all the king's agents. And yet, the master's love, hate, happiness, and anger are tantamount to Heaven's spring, summer, autumn, and winter, which, possessing warmth, coolness, cold, and heat, thereby develop, transform, and complete their tasks. When Heaven sends forth these four, if they are timely then the yearly harvest is good; if they are untimely then the yearly harvest is bad. When the people's master sends forth these four, if they are right then the age is ordered; if they are not right then the age is disordered. For this reason an orderly age and a fine year partake of the same destiny, while a chaotic age and a destructive year partake of the same destiny. From this we see that the principles of humankind correspond to the Way of Heaven.

[*Chunqiu fanlu yizheng* 11:9a–12a — SQ]

---

33. The Chinese character for *king* (*wang* 王) is written with three horizontal lines connected by a vertical line.

DEFINING HUMAN NATURE

During the Han, as in earlier periods, scholars continued to discuss and debate the qualities inherent in human nature. Effecting a compromise between the theories identified with Mencius and Xunzi, Dong Zhongshu argued that human nature possessed the potential to become good, but it could not do so without the transforming influence of the ruler's instruction. In the essay that follows, we find one of the clearest expressions of the paternalism that characterized later Confucian political theory. This ideal, which held that the people are dependent upon the ruler for their moral guidance, greatly expanded both the authority and the responsibility of the ruler.

AN IN-DEPTH EXAMINATION OF NAMES AND DESIGNATIONS

Names are generated by realities. Devoid of their corresponding realities, they cannot be considered names. Names are the means by which the sage authenticates things. The term *name* (*ming*) means "reality" (*zhen*). Whenever you encounter incomprehensible things, if you always return to its reality, then darkness will turn back to light. If you desire to discover the crooked and the straight, nothing compares to stretching out the measuring line. If you desire to discover the true and the false, nothing compares to making use of names. Names reveal the true and the false as a measuring line reveals crooked and straight. Investigate names and actualities, observe whether they depart from or coincide with one another; then there will be no mutual deception concerning the disposition of what is true and what is false. The present generation is ignorant about human nature. Theorists differ from one another. Why don't they simply try returning to the term *nature* (*xing*)? Does not the term *nature* mean "inborn" (*sheng*)?[34] If it means what is inborn, then the spontaneous endowments that one possesses at birth are termed "nature." Nature is the basic substance. If we investigate the basic substance of nature by applying the term *good*, will that be correct? If not, how can we still say that the basic substance is good? The term *nature* cannot be separated from the basic substance. If it is separated from the basic substance by as much as a hair's width, then it has already ceased to be nature. This must be understood.

The *Spring and Autumn Annals* examines the inner principle of things and rectifies their names. It names things according to their reality and does not err as much as "the tip of an autumn hair." Therefore when the *Spring and Autumn Annals* discussed "falling meteorites," it mentioned the term *five* after the meteorites, and when it discussed "fishhawks flying backward," it mentioned the term *six* before the fishhawks.[35] The sage Confucius was this cautious concern-

---

34. This had been the claim of Gaozi, the philosophical antagonist of Mencius. See above, ch. 6, *Mencius* 6A:3.

35. According to the *Spring and Autumn Annals*, in the sixteenth year of Duke Xi (642) five

ing the rectification of names. "The noble person does not take speech lightly."[36] His statements about the five meteorites and six fishhawks are good illustrations of this.

It is the mind-and-heart that weakens the various evils within and does not allow them to find expression without. Therefore the mind-and-heart is termed "weak" (*ren*). If human beings are endowed with a vital force devoid of evil, then what would the mind-and-heart need to weaken? I take *mind-and-heart* as a name that comprehends what a person genuinely is. What a person genuinely is includes both greed and humaneness. The vital forces of humaneness and greed coexist in one's person.

The term *person* (*shen*) is derived from Heaven (*tian*). Heaven has its dual operations of yin and yang, and one's person has its dual nature of greed and humanity. Heaven sometimes restricts yin. Likewise, a person sometimes weakens the emotions and desires, becoming one with the Way of Heaven. This is why when yin functions it cannot interfere with the spring and summer, and the full moon is always overwhelmed by sunlight, so that at one moment it is full and at another it is not. If Heaven restricts yin in this way, how can a person not reduce his desires and suppress his emotions to respond to Heaven?

What Heaven restricts, one's person restricts. Therefore it is said that one's person resembles Heaven. To restrict what Heaven restricts is not to restrict Heaven. We must acknowledge that if our Heavenly natures do not receive education, ultimately they will not be able to weaken the emotions and desires. If we examine the actuality and thereby consider the term [*nature*], how can nature be like this [that is, good] when it has not undergone education? Therefore the nature is like the rice stalk, and goodness is like rice. Rice emerges from within the stalk, but not all of the stalk becomes rice. Likewise, goodness emerges from within the nature, but not all of the nature becomes good. Both goodness and rice are representative of the ways in which human beings continue Heaven's activities but complete them beyond the sphere of Heaven's activities. They do not lie within the sphere of Heaven's activities. Heaven's activities extend to a certain point and stop. What stops within the sphere of Heaven's activities is termed the Heavenly nature. What stops beyond the sphere of Heaven's activities is termed human affairs. Human affairs lie beyond the nature, but the nature cannot help but be transformed by them.

The term *people* (*min*) is derived from the term *sleep* (*mian*). If nature is already good at birth, why employ the term *sleep* to designate "people"? Take the case of meteorites. If they were not supported in place, they would be rolling

---

meteorites fell over the state of Sung, and six fishhawks were observed to fly backward over the capital. According to the *Gongyang Commentary*, the number five was specified *after* the reference to the meteorites because the meteorites were sighted first and their number determined later. In the case of the fishhawks, the number of birds was stated first because the six birds were observed first and their identification as fishhawks followed later.

36. *Analects* 13:1.

about wildly. How could this be good? The nature resembles the eyes. In sleep they are shut and there is darkness. They must wait for awakening before they can see. Before they are awakened we can say that they possess the basic substance of sight, but we cannot say that they see. Now the nature of all people possesses a basic substance, but it has not yet been awakened, just as those with closed eyes await awakening. It must be educated before it can become good. Before it is awakened, we can say that it possesses a basic substance that is good, but we cannot yet say that it is good. It is the same as the case of the eyes being shut and becoming awakened. If we examine this with a calm mind-and-heart, the point can be seen. When the nature "sleeps," it is not yet awakened, and it belongs to the sphere of Heaven's activities. We give it a designation that is modeled after Heaven's sphere of activity and call those in such a state "people" (*min*). The term *people* (*min*) certainly resembles the term *sleep* (*mian*).

If you follow names and designations to penetrate their inner principles, you will apprehend them. Thus rectify names and designations according to Heaven and Earth. Heaven and Earth generate what we designate nature and emotions. Both nature and emotions are the same in a state of sleep. Emotions are part of the nature. If we say that the nature is already good, what can we say about emotions [which are the source of evil]? Therefore the sage never said that the nature is good because it would have violated the term. A person possesses the nature and emotions just as Heaven possesses yang and yin. To mention the basic substance of a human being without mentioning the emotions resembles mentioning the yang of Heaven without mentioning the yin. Such fruitless discussions will never be accepted. What we call the nature refers neither to the highest type of person nor to the lowest, but to the average. The nature of a person is like a silk cocoon or an egg. An egg must be hatched to become a chicken; a silk cocoon must be unraveled to make silk, and the nature must be educated to become good. This is called "authenticating Heaven." Since Heaven has generated the people's nature, which possesses the basic substance of goodness but which is not yet capable of goodness, it sets up the king to make it good. This is Heaven's intent. The people receive from Heaven a nature that is yet capable of goodness, and they turn to the king to receive the education that will complete their nature. It is the duty of the king to obey Heaven's intent and to complete the people's nature. Now those who investigate the true character of the basic substance and claim that the people's nature is already good, negate Heaven's intent and disregard the duty of the king. If the nature of all people were already good, then what duty would the king fulfill when he received Heaven's mandate [to rule]? To establish names incorrectly and consequently abandon one's solemn duty and violate the Mandate of Heaven is not to use any word in an exemplary way.

In using terms the *Spring and Autumn Annals* approaches a thing from its external aspect if its internal aspect depends on the external aspect [for its full meaning]. Now the nature of all people depends on education, which is external, before it becomes good. Therefore goodness corresponds to education and does not correspond to the nature. If you equate it with the nature, then there will be many violations and terms will not be refined. Having completed these achievements on your own, you will negate the worthies and sages. The highly respected people of our time mistakenly propagate such a theory, but it is not the technique by which terms are used in the *Spring and Autumn Annals*. Unexemplary words and unfounded doctrines are avoided by the noble person. Why utter them?

[*Chunqiu fanlu* (SBCK) 10:1a–14a; adapted by SQ from Chan,
Source Book, pp. 273–279]

INTERPRETING OMENS

Like his predecessors in the late Warring States and early Han periods, Dong Zhongshu articulated both anthropomorphic and naturalistic explanations of omens. When he attributed anomalies to Heaven's conscious intent, as in the excerpt below, he depicted an omnipotent power that spoke through omens to awaken rulers who strayed from Heaven's Way, so they would realign themselves with Heaven's norms. In his naturalistic explanations, Dong wrote that the ruler disrupted the natural processes when he did not follow Heaven's norms by generating what he called "deviant energy." Since humans and Heaven share the vital energy of the cosmos, activities in the human realm "stimulate" phenomena in other parts of the universe, which "respond" according to the yin or yang categories to which they belong. Yet they did not simply operate spontaneously, as the Daoists claimed. Dong believed Heaven ultimately brought these operations into effect. Han theories of omens and portents helped establish a Heaven-centered mode of political criticism, providing opportunities for officials to censure the emperor and predict the fall of unworthy rulers and dynasties.

HUMANENESS MUST PRECEDE WISDOM

According to a rough classification, when things in Heaven and Earth undergo abnormal changes they are called "anomalies." Lesser ones are called "portents." Portents always appear first and are followed by anomalies. Portents are Heaven's warnings; anomalies are Heaven's threats. If Heaven warns [the ruler] and he does not acknowledge [these warnings], then Heaven sends anomalies to awe him. The Ode says: "We tremble at the awe and fearfulness of Heaven."[37] It perhaps is referring to this.

The source of all portents and anomalies lies in faults that exist within the state. When faults have just begun to germinate, Heaven sends forth fearful portents to warn and inform the ruler of these faults. If after being warned and

---

37. Ode 272.

informed, the ruler fails to recognize the cause of these portents, then strange anomalies appear to frighten him. If after being frightened he still fails to recognize the cause of his fear, only then do misfortunes and calamities overtake him. From this we can see that Heaven's intent is humane and does not desire to entrap a person.

If one examines these portents and anomalies carefully, one will observe Heaven's intent. Heaven's intent desires certain things and does not desire other things. As for those things that Heaven desires and does not desire, if one examines oneself, one will surely find such warnings within oneself. If one observes affairs around oneself, one will surely find verification [of these warnings] in the state. Thus Heaven's intent is manifested in these portents and anomalies. Stand in awe of them but do not despise them; consider that Heaven desires to save us from error and from doing wrong. Therefore Heaven relies on these means [portents and anomalies] to warn us. . . .

According to the standards of the *Spring and Autumn Annals*, when the ruler of a state altered the ancient ways, departing from the norms, and Heaven responded with portents, these states were designated "fortunate states." . . . When Heaven did not send down portents and Earth did not bring forth calamities, King Zhuang of Chu prayed to the mountains and rivers, saying, "Is Heaven about to destroy me? It does not announce my faults or criticize my crimes." From this we see that the portents of Heaven are a response to human transgressions and anomalies are clearly to be feared. This is how Heaven hopes to save a state that has transgressed. This alone is what the *Spring and Autumn Annals* takes to be fortunate [in portents]. This is why King Zhuang of Chu prayed and asked [Heaven to cause portents to appear]. If a sagely ruler or worthy lord delights in receiving the reproofs of his loyal ministers, then how much more should he delight in receiving the warnings of Heaven.

[*Chunqiu fanlu yizheng* 8:23b–25b — adapted by SQ from BW]

SELF-CULTIVATION

Dong Zhongshu believed that Confucius composed the *Spring and Autumn Annals* to set out a standard of rightness for all-under-Heaven. He held that each one of Confucius' Six Teachings excelled at developing a particular virtue, while, taken together, they provided the basis for ordering all aspects of human existence. According to Dong, the *Spring and Autumn Annals* rectified right and wrong and therefore excelled in ordering humaneness. The text embodied cosmic norms presented in light of the dynamic circumstances of human rule and the changing contexts of human relationships. The historical events that filled its pages, judged praiseworthy or blameworthy by Confucius, provided positive standards to be emulated and negative models to be avoided. The text possessed the power to transform the empire because it embodied a code of ethics to be followed by the ruler and the scholar-officials who served him.

STANDARDS OF HUMANENESS AND RIGHTNESS

What the *Spring and Autumn Annals* regulates are others and the self. The means by which it regulates others and the self are humaneness and rightness. With humaneness it brings peace and security to others, and with rightness it rectifies the self. Therefore the term *humaneness* (*ren*) refers to "others" (*ren*), while the term *rightness* (*yi*) refers to the "self" (*wo*). Utter the terms and see the distinction. The fact that humaneness refers to others and rightness refers to the self must be examined, but most people do not examine it. On the contrary, they employ humaneness to indulge themselves while they employ rightness to make demands of others. They pervert their proper application and defy their principles. Rarely are the two terms not confused. Therefore although no one desires disorder, disorder often arises. Generally speaking, it is because people are ignorant of the distinction between the other and the self, and they do not examine where humaneness and rightness properly apply. For this reason the *Spring and Autumn Annals* established standards (*fa*) of humaneness and rightness.[38] The standard of humaneness lies in loving others and not in loving the self. The standard of rightness lies in rectifying the self and not in rectifying others. If one does not rectify the self, even if one can rectify others, the *Spring and Autumn Annals* will not grant that this is rightness. If one does not love others, even if one is full of self-love, the *Spring and Autumn Annals* will not grant that this is humaneness. In earlier ages Duke Ling of Jin murdered his chief cook to improve his food and drink. He shot arrows at his ministers to amuse himself. He certainly was filled with self-love, but the *Spring and Autumn Annals* did not judge him to be a virtuous person because he did not love others. If you do not sincerely love others, extending your love from the people on down to the birds, beasts, and insects, so that there is nothing that is not an object of your love, then how can your love be sufficient to be called humaneness? *Humaneness* is the term that designates loving others. . . .

As for the definition of love, one who is a king extends love to the four tribes; one who is a hegemon extends it to the enfeoffed lords; one who secures his state extends it only to those within his territory; one who is endangered extends it only to his neighbors; and one who is ruined extends it only to his solitary person. One who loves only himself may be established in the position of Son of Heaven or Enfeoffed Lord, but being a solitary person he will lack the assistance of his ministers and his people. If the situation comes to this, although no one ruins him, he will ruin himself. [For example,] the *Spring and Autumn Annals* does not say that the state of Liang was attacked but, rather, that Liang destroyed itself. For, in fact, the love of the ruler extended only to his own

---

38. It is difficult to employ a single English term to capture the many connotations of the term *fa* used here. The *fa* of humaneness and rightness are at once standards of perfection, models of emulation, and methods of becoming humane and right.

person. Thus I say that humaneness is to love others, not to love the self. This is a standard of the *Spring and Autumn Annals*.

Rightness does not refer to rectifying others but to rectifying the self. Even a reckless ruler living in a chaotic age desires to rectify others. How can this be called rightness! In previous ages King Ling of Chu punished the traitors of Chen and Cai. Duke Huan of Qi seized upon the crimes of Yuan Taotu. Both were certainly able to rectify others, but the *Spring and Autumn Annals* did not praise them. It did not consider them to be right because they had not rectified their own persons and hastened to benefit themselves. Ge Lu was able to rectify the difficulties in Chu and Cai, but the *Spring and Autumn Annals* did not praise him for his rightness because he had not rectified his own person. Lu Zi was not able to rectify a single feudal lord, yet the *Spring and Autumn Annals* granted that he was right because he had rectified his person. Thus I say that rightness means rectifying the self, not rectifying others. This is a standard of the *Spring and Autumn Annals*. If one has not rectified one's self and seeks to rectify others, or if one has rectified one's self but condemns others, such a person will not be accepted by others because that person has defied their inner principles. How could this be called rightness!

Rightness designates what is appropriate to the self. Only after what is appropriate relates to the self can one be called right. Thus the expression *rightness* combines the self (*wo*) and appropriate (*yi*) into one term. From this, one can grasp that rightness is for the purpose of designating the self. Thus I say that one who acts and achieves rightness is said to have achieved it by oneself (*zide*). One who acts and negates rightness is said to have lost it by oneself (*zishi*). A person who is fond of rightness is said to [possess] self-love. A person who is not fond of rightness is said to lack self-love. Having considered these things, the meanings of rightness and the self are clarified. Thus rightness and humaneness differ. Humaneness refers to what moves away from the self; rightness refers to what moves toward the self. Humaneness refers to what is distant; rightness refers to what is close. Love toward others is called humaneness, while appropriateness in the self is called rightness. Humaneness presides over others; rightness presides over the self. Thus I say that *humaneness (ren)* refers to others (*ren*) and *rightness (yi)* to the self (*wo*). This is what I mean. The noble person seeks out the distinction between humaneness and rightness and thereby regulates the other and the self. Then the noble person distinguishes the internal and external and clarifies cases of conformity and deviation. Therefore the noble person is ordered within by returning to proper principles to rectify the self and by relying upon the rites to encourage good fortune. The noble person is ordered without by extending kindness to broaden his sphere of operation and by liberalizing the regulations to embrace the multitudes. . . .

The *Spring and Autumn Annals* criticizes the ruler's faults and pities the people's hardships. When there were small evils beyond the state of Lu the *Spring and Autumn Annals* did not record them, but when they occurred within the person of the ruler the *Spring and Autumn Annals* recorded them and condemned them. In general, when it mentions such matters, it employs humaneness to regulate others and rightness to regulate the self; it is generous with criticisms of the self but sparing of them toward others. This is what is meant. In fact, the *Analects* has already revealed this principle, but no one has examined it. It states, "The noble person criticizes his own evils but does not criticize others' evils."[39] If you don't criticize others' evils, isn't this the most generous kind of humaneness? To criticize one's own evil, isn't this the perfection of rightness? How does this differ from the expression "humanity enriches others; rightness enriches the self"? Thus one who refers to one's own evil is said to be truthful, while one who refers to the evil in others is said to be deceitful. One who seeks such things in the self is said to be generous, while one who seeks such things in others is said to be stingy. One who finds fault with oneself in order to become perfect is said to be enlightened, while one who blames others for the sake of perfection is said to be deluded. Therefore the ruler who relies upon orders regulating the self to regulate others is not broadminded, while the ruler who relies upon orders regulating others to order the self is not respectful in carrying forth propriety. If the ruler is not respectful in carrying forth propriety, his actions will be impeded, and the people will not respect him. If the ruler is not broadminded, his generosity will be impeded, and the people will not cherish him. If they do not feel affection for the ruler, they will not trust him. If they do not revere the ruler, they will not respect him. If the ruler defies these two principles of government and carries them forth in a biased way he will be condemned by the people below. Is it possible not to deliberate on the proper place of humaneness and rightness?

[*Chunqiu fanlu yizheng* 8:16a–22a — SQ]

THE ISSUE OF MORAL AUTONOMY

Unlike Confucius, Mencius, or Xunzi, who served rulers of several of the contending feudal states of the late Zhou period, Dong Zhongshu served two powerful rulers of a unified Han empire. By contrast with his predecessors, Dong has sometimes been seen as rationalizing this enormous imperial power. Note, however, that in the preceding selections, Dong reveals a deep concern to impress upon the ruler both the extent of his power and its inevitable limitations. Playing as he does a crucial role in a highly interactive universe, the ruler must realize that he is both answerable to Heaven and responsible for the people.

Our final selection — along with considerable evidence from Dong's biography — suggests that Dong was not so much celebrating the imperial institution as he was

---

39. *Analects* 12:21.

seeking to reform it. Perhaps his most enduring contribution to an evolving Confucian tradition was to read into the *Spring and Autumn Annals* a model of sovereignty that, on the one hand, rejected the ruler's absolute and arbitrary exercise of power, his use of violence, and his primary reliance on impersonal laws and, on the other, emphasized his indebtedness to Heaven, his use of moral persuasion, and his reliance on the transforming influences of ritual and education. Dong also sought to enhance the powers of the scholar-official in various ways. His interpretations reflected a critical spirit and a sense of moral autonomy that would inspire many generations of Confucian scholar-officials in later times to challenge, reform, and renew the imperial Chinese state.

Of particular importance to Dong in his reformist thinking was the fundamental Confucian concept of humaneness. Once, when confronted with a choice between humaneness and the duties involved in the five relationships — between ruler and subject, parent and child, husband and wife, elder and younger brother, friend and friend — Dong was unequivocal in choosing humaneness. "Faced with [an opportunity to practice] humaneness," he said, "do not yield to your commander." Here he was paraphrasing the *Analects* of Confucius,[40] yet the implications of this choice in the Han context were rather different, as the following passage from Dong's *Deciding Court Cases According to the* Spring and Autumn Annals suggests.

A prince was hunting and captured a fawn. He ordered his minister to take up the fawn and return with it. On the way home, the minister noticed that the fawn's mother was following him and whining. He was moved to release the fawn. [Upon discovering this] the ruler was angered. The [minister's] crime was under discussion and had not yet been determined when the ruler fell ill. Fearing that he would die, the ruler wished to entrust his young son [to someone's care]. He recalled the minister and exclaimed: "How humane is the minister! He encountered a fawn and treated it with compassion, how much more is this the case with regard to other human beings." He released the minister and entrusted his son to him. What opinion should be upheld? Dong Zhongshu stated: "The noble man does not take young animals or eggs. The minister did not protest when ordered to take the fawn home. This would have been contrary to rightness. Nevertheless, in the midst of carrying out his orders, he was moved by the fawn's mother and demonstrated his compassion. Although he disregarded his ruler's order, it is possible that he be transferred."[41]

[*Chunqiu jueshi* 31:1b — SQ]

---

40. Ibid. 15:36.

41. The harsher punishment usually associated with the crime of disregarding the ruler's command is reduced because of the minister's humaneness.

THE CODIFYING OF THE CONFUCIAN CANON

STATE ORTHODOXY

Gaozu, the founder of the Han, a commoner with no pretensions to learning, ridiculed pompous Confucian scholars, but he did not hesitate to make use of them and follow their advice when it helped his designs. Above all, he honestly accorded with the Confucian teaching that the emperor should act on the advice of his ministers, setting an important precedent that did much to check despotism among his successors. Still, the influence of Confucianism was by no means exclusive. Some of Gaozu's successors favored Huang-Lao ideas or other schools of thought, and it was not until the time of Emperor Wu that Confucians secured substantial imperial patronage for their teachings.

The single man most responsible, as an influential adviser in the court, for furthering the cause of Confucian orthodoxy was Dong Zhongshu, whose ideas have been discussed above. In his career as teacher and government official during the reign of Emperor Wu, he formulated doctrines and brought about the establishment of institutions that had a profound influence on later ages. It was his conviction that the Han should take constructive measures to change what remained of the old order inherited from the Qin. His recommendations to the emperor were presented in a series of answers to questions on government policy posed by the emperor himself. One of these advocated rejecting all but the Five Confucian Classics as the teaching of the state:

> The great principle of unity of the *Spring and Autumn Annals* is a constant warp binding Heaven and Earth, a moral law pervading past and present. But the teachers of today have different doctrines, and men expound diverse theories; the various schools of philosophy differ in their ways, and their principles do not agree. Thus the ruler has no means by which to achieve unity, the laws and institutions undergo frequent changes, and the people do not know what to honor. Your unworthy servant considers that whatever is not encompassed by the Six Disciplines and the arts of Confucius should be suppressed and not allowed to continue further, and evil and vain theories be stamped out. Only then will unity be achieved, the laws be made clear, and the people know what to follow.[42]

Emperor Wu eventually followed this suggestion, removing official support from the other teachings and endorsing Confucianism. Thus he promoted a unification of thought that the violent proscriptions of Qin had sought but failed to produce.

---

42. *Hanshu* 56:21a.

STATE UNIVERSITY

Closely connected with this plan to give official support to Confucianism was Dong Zhongshu's suggestion to establish a government college for the training of officials in which Confucian ideas would be taught. He wrote:

> Among the things paramount for the upbringing of scholars, none is more important than a state college. A college is intimately related to the fostering of virtuous scholars and is the foundation of education. . . . Your servant desires Your Majesty to erect a college and appoint illustrious teachers for it, for the upbringing of the empire's scholars.[43]

In 124 B.C.E., by imperial order, a college was established near the capital in which government-appointed teachers gave instruction to students selected and sent to the capital by provincial authorities. The course of study was normally one year, and upon graduation all those shown to be capable were given positions in the bureaucracy. By the end of the first century B.C.E. there were some three thousand students enrolled in the college, and in the Latter Han the number grew to more than thirty thousand. Thus the bureaucracy became filled with men trained in the official Confucian learning.

CIVIL SERVICE

As early as the reign of the first Han emperor, the government had sent out requests asking the provincial officials to recommend capable scholars and men of ability to serve the government. This idea, old in Confucian tradition, gradually increased in power and effectiveness. Dong Zhongshu himself was selected for an official career after having written outstanding answers, quoted above, to the examination questions set by the emperor. It was consistent with his plans for the shaping of a Confucian bureaucracy that he should exert his influence to encourage and develop what would later grow into the famous examination system. Thus he recommended that the emperor have

> the marquises, governors of commanderies, and officials of two thousand piculs salary all select those of worth among the officials and common people and once a year send to the capital two men each who will be housed there and taken care of. . . . In this way all will do their best in

---

43. Ibid. 56:12b–13a.

seeking out men of worth, and scholars of the empire can be obtained, given official posts, and used in the government.[44]

THE RIVALRY BETWEEN LEGALISM AND CONFUCIANISM

In spite of these measures taken under his rule, Emperor Wu himself was far from a model Confucian ruler. His system of harsh and detailed laws, heavy taxes, extensive military expeditions, and government monopolies embodied specifically Legalist measures. He disregarded the precedent set by the founder of the dynasty, acting on his own initiative and often ignoring the counsel of his ministers. In private life he devoted much time and expense to pursuing the elixir of immortality, attempting to communicate with the spirits of the dead, and other occult practices. So averse was he to any criticism of his measures that under his reign an official was executed on the charge of "disapproval in the heart," based on the evidence of a reported "subtle wry twist of his lips" when a new law was being discussed.[45] Nothing could be further from the Confucian insistence upon outspoken criticism and discussion of all administrative practices as the sacred duty of ministers and scholars.

Though a process of reform began during the reign of Emperor Wu's great-grandson, Emperor Xuan (r. 74–49 B.C.E.), Legalist attitudes persisted. When once reproached by the crown prince for his departure from Confucian principles, Emperor Xuan replied angrily:

> The House of Han has its own institutions and laws based on a combination of the ways of the overlords and the sage kings. How could we rely solely upon moral instruction and the governmental system of the Zhou? The common lot of Confucians do not understand what is appropriate to the times but applaud everything ancient and criticize the present. They cause people to confuse names and realities so that they do not know what to abide by. How should they be entrusted with responsibility?[46]

It was not until the reign of Emperor Xuan's son, Emperor Yuan (r. 49–33 B.C.E.), that a ruler more fully in accord with Confucian ideals for the first time occupied the throne. Unfortunately, by this time the influence of the emperor's maternal relatives and the eunuchs had become so strong that the emperor,

---

44. Ibid. 56:9b.
45. *Shiji* (BNB) 30:13b–14a.
46. *Hanshu* 9:1b.

though well meaning, was largely ineffectual, and the decay of the dynasty was clearly foreshadowed.

THE CONFUCIAN CANON

During the course of the Han dynasty, as Confucianism came to hold a dominant position as the official teaching of the Chinese state, the classic literature of this school came to be compiled into a canon of works known today as the Confucian Classics. As we have already seen, most of the Confucian Classics had their origins in the Zhou period. But it was during the Han that they were recovered and compiled in the form in which they would be transmitted to later generations.

If Han thought seems to show less diversity and originality than the "Hundred Schools" of the late Zhou, its accomplishments lay more in the impressive labors of editing and annotating the ancient literature, the systematization of earlier ideas, and the compilation of great works of history and lexicography. The compilation of the classics was chiefly done by Confucian literati who, with hard toil and devoted scholarship, set about repairing the damage wrought by Qin's burning of the books and the fire and destruction that had razed the old Qin capital during the troubled days of the founding of the new dynasty.

The books of this age were in the form of bamboo slips, inscribed in lampblack ink with a line of characters and bound together with cord or thongs. It may easily be imagined how, when the thongs had rotted and the slips became jumbled or lost, a work could be damaged or rendered almost unintelligible. Thus, though copies of many of the ancient books ordered destroyed by the Qin were found still to exist, a different task was involved in editing them, reconciling varying versions, and establishing a trustworthy text.

As might be expected, however, the scholars often could not agree upon authoritative texts, and so there existed side by side slightly different versions of the classical works, each with its own traditions, masters, and disciples. Some of these versions, reported by legend to have been found sealed in the wall of Confucius' home, came to be known as Old Text versions, so called because they were written in part not in the style of characters adopted by the Qin and used by the Han but in an archaic orthography used during the Zhou. Others, called New Texts, were identified with Dong Zhongshu and his followers, who made use of yin-yang theories in the interpretation of omens and portents. Another group of private scholars who adhered to the Old Texts was led by men from the area of Confucius' own state of Lu — one of the most famous, Kong Anguo (156?–74? B.C.E.), being himself a direct descendant of the sage. The first important official patron of the Old Texts was Liu Xin (46 B.C.E.–23 C.E.), an outstanding scholar whose reputation has suffered because of his association

with Wang Mang whose short-lived Xin ("New") dynasty (9–23 C.E.) marked
an interregnum between the Former Han and the Latter Han dynasties.[47] Emperor Guangwu (r. 25–57 C.E.), who restored the Han after Wang's execution,
lent his support to the New Texts, abolishing the study of the Old Texts that
had been established at the end of the Former Han. Despite this, the Old Texts
gained acceptance from some important thinkers and scholars of the Latter
Han. Much later, in the late nineteenth and early twentieth centuries, differences between these two textual traditions became construed as subjects of great
political and scholastic controversy, but there is little evidence that these issues
figured prominently in the Han itself.

To promote the unification and systematization of thought that he strove for,
Emperor Wu in 136 B.C.E. had set up an imperial commission for the recovery
of classical texts. With Confucianism established as state doctrine, imperial
support of this work of recovering and editing the ancient literature increased.
In 53 B.C.E., Emperor Xuan called a conference of scholars to discuss varying
interpretations of the classics, with the emperor himself attending and acting
as final judge in the controversies. The conference continued for two years, and
the results were published to form the official interpretation, though varying
interpretations were not actually proscribed.

Some years later, during the reign of Emperor Cheng (r. 33–7 B.C.E.), a still
more ambitious program was undertaken. Under the directorship of Liu Xiang
(79–8 B.C.E.), a court official and eminent scholar, a group of scholars set to
work collecting copies of all the existing literature of the day. For each work a
copy of the table of sections and an abstract of its contents was made. When
Liu Xiang died, his work was continued by his son, Liu Xin, who presented to
the throne a bibliography in seven sections listing all the important books in
the imperial library. This bibliography was incorporated into the *History of the
Former Han Dynasty*, forming an invaluable aid to the study of ancient China
and its literature.

Something of the situation that prevailed and the task confronting the scholars in bringing order to it may be judged from the following comments of the
historian Ban Gu:

> From the time when Emperor Wu set up Erudites of the Five Classics
> and appointed students for them, established competitive examinations,
> and encouraged men to study for official positions, until the era Yuanshi
> (1–5 C.E.) was a period of over one hundred years. During this time the
> teachers of classical studies increased like the branches and leaves of a
> spreading tree. The explanations of one classic ran to over a million words

---

47. See ch. 11.

and the number of professors grew to more than a thousand, for this was the way to official position and profit.[48]

Scholars of ancient times while farming and taking care of their families were able to complete their study of one classic in three years because as they went through the text they concentrated only upon the general meaning. Thus they spent little time and reaped great benefit. By the time they were thirty they had mastered all Five Classics. In later times when the classics and their commentaries had already become diverse and contradictory, the scholars of wide learning forgot the advice of Confucius to "hear much and put aside the points of which you are in doubt."[49] They worked to twist the meaning of passages in order to avoid difficulties of interpretation and with glib phrases and contrived theories destroyed the integrity of the text. Explanations of five characters of the text ran to twenty or thirty thousand words. In time this situation became so bad that a youth who spent all his time on one classic could not speak with authority on it until his head had grown gray. Scholars rested complacently upon what they had learned and attacked anything unfamiliar, so that in the end they condemned themselves to sterility. This is the great danger of scholarship.[50]

It is no wonder that, after the troubled times of Wang Mang, a council of scholars was again held, modeled on that held under Emperor Xuan. The results, combined with those of the former council, were compiled and published in a work known as *Discourses in the White Tiger Hall* (*Bohu tong*), representing an official interpretation of the Confucian Classics and Confucian teachings.

Thus the classics were established as the basis for all Confucian learning, and, in turn, for entrance into official position. With minor exceptions, this is the canon as it was known in later ages and as it has come down to us.

By the end of the Han, silk scrolls had largely replaced bamboo slips as writing material for books, and in 105 C.E. the invention of paper was officially recorded. But Han scholars, with the chaos wreaked on the ancient texts by Qin's laws and the disorders of the early Han and Wang Mang's time still vivid in their minds, trusted to none of these media for the preservation of their sacred books. Toward the end of the dynasty, by imperial order, the complete texts of the Five Classics and the Confucian *Analects* were engraved on stone tablets and set up at the imperial college, a monument to the scholarly labors of the Han Confucians.

---

48. *Hanshu* 88:25a–b.
49. *Analects* 2:18.
50. *Hanshu* 30:12b–13a.

In addition to the canonical works included in this chapter, there was another "classic," not formally installed in the Confucian canon but with virtually that status as a standard text of female instruction: Ban Zhao's *Admonitions for Women*. The sister of the famous historian Ban Gu, Ban Zhao (48?–116? C.E.) upheld the scholarly tradition of her family and was honored at the Han court for her learning. On account of its enduring importance, her *Admonitions for Women* was later included in the Four Books for Women, selections from which are found in the section on "Women's Education" in chapter 23.

THE ESTABLISHMENT OF CONFUCIANISM

Much speculation has been devoted to the question of why Confucianism, of the major schools of thought that flourished in Zhou times and continued into the early Han, should have triumphed over its rivals and attained a position of sole authority. Some writers have suggested that Confucianism supplies a philosophical basis for the divine right of the emperor, and for this reason was enthusiastically supported by the Han rulers. Confucian thought is indeed based upon the concept of a hierarchically ordered society, but one based on merit. Thus it so hedges the ruler's power about with moral restrictions and qualifications that strong-minded emperors such as Emperor Wu, while a patron of the Confucians, often resisted them and acted quite contrary to their tenets in practice. Confucianism, in its political thought, is more the philosophy of scholar-officials than that of the ruler. It insists on the right to criticize and restrain the exercise of absolute power. In this endeavor it makes full use of the appeal to tradition (of which it, as the guardian and interpreter of the ancient texts, is the arbiter), curbing imperial extravagance by a reminder of the simple life of old; insisting upon the importance of ministers and counselors in government; making scholastic achievement and dedication to public service, not noble birth, the requisite for entrance into officialdom; and even reserving to itself the right to judge whether a ruler is morally fit to hold the throne. The literati, moreover, as the men capable of handling records, regulations, edicts, and the other necessary papers of highly organized central government, were indispensable to any ruler. As a famous Confucian pointed out to the founder of the Han, though he might have won the empire on horseback, he assuredly could not rule it from horseback.

Finally, the Confucians were the teachers and guardians of the ancient literature, originally not exclusively Confucian but embracing the best in China's literary heritage — a mass of writings that included ideas borrowed from different schools and philosophies and absorbed to some extent into Confucianism. As an official canon it remained somewhat limited in its effect, without an extensive state school system or agencies of ideological enforcement to back it up. Yet once established as the state teaching, with the examination system and the imperial college to ensure its continuance, it became almost a fixture of the imperial system itself.

THE FORMATION OF THE *CLASSIC OF CHANGES (YIJING)*

Much of the *Classic of Changes* (*Yijing*) derives from the Zhou period, and traditionally it, with its later overlay of Confucian interpretation, ranked as the primordial source of traditional wisdom and first of the Confucian classics. Known also as the *Changes of Zhou* (*Zhouyi*), it was originally a divination manual, which later gradually acquired the status of a wisdom book. We include a discussion of this important work here because, while parts of the text derived from earlier sources, it was during the Han period that the *Changes* acquired this reputation and assumed its canonical form.

The *Classic of Changes* consists of sixty-four hexagrams (*gua*) and related texts. The hexagrams are formed by combinations of six unbroken (yang —) and/or broken (yin – –) lines (*yao*), arranged one atop the other in vertical sequence. Though many questions surround the origin of the hexagrams, it was traditionally believed that they were developed by King Wen of Zhou out of the eight primary trigrams invented by the legendary culture hero and sage Fu Xi:

☰ ☱ ☲ ☳ ☴ ☵ ☶ ☷

For one consulting the *Changes* as a divination manual, the relevant hexagrams were originally identified through a process of numerical manipulation of divining sticks — milfoil (*Achillea millefolium*) or yarrow stalks — and, later, by the casting of coins. In early times this process apparently resembled the kind of divination that had been practiced in the Shang period; over time, however, divination changed from a method of consulting and influencing ancestors — the "powerful dead" — to a method of penetrating moments of the cosmic process to learn how the Way is configured, what direction it takes at such moments, and what one's own place is — and should be — in the scheme of things. By developing the capacity to anticipate and accord with change, one could avert wrong decisions, avoid failure, escape misfortune, and, on the other hand, make right decisions, achieve success, and garner good fortune.

Each hexagram is accompanied by (1) a hexagram name (*guaming*), (2) a hexagram statement (*guaci*) or "Judgment" (*tuan*), and (3) line statements (*yaoci*) for each of the six lines. Again, the traditional Chinese belief was that King Wen composed the hexagram statements or Judgments, the line statements having been the contribution of the Duke of Zhou. The hexagram names suggest crucial life situations — for example, Birth Throes (3), Viewing (20), Suppression of the Light (36), Abundance (55). The line statements have a sequential or associational organization based on the general topic given in the Judgment; each states a specific, differentiated instance or variation of the topic, which in complete line statements (many statements seem to be fragments) is followed by a charge or injunction — that one should take some action or refrain from it — and a final determination — often "misfortune," or "good fortune." The hexagrams, hexagram statements or Judgments, and line statements, while no longer ascribed to sagely authorship, are still generally recognized as the oldest parts of the *Changes*, going back perhaps as far as the latter part of the ninth century B.C.E. and constituting the first layer in the text.

Another layer consists of two parts: (1) commentaries on the hexagram statements or Judgments called Commentaries on the Judgments (*Tuanzhuan*) and (2) commentaries on the abstract meanings or "Images" (*xiang*) of the Judgments and the line statements called Commentaries on the Images (*Xiangzhuan*). The Judgments have "Great Images" (*daxiang*) — the abstract meanings of hexagrams as whole entities — and the line statements have "Little Images" (*xiaoxiang*) — the abstract meanings of individual lines. These commentaries are the first of the exegetical materials in the *Changes* traditionally attributed to Confucius.

The traditional format of the *Changes* divides the Commentaries on the Judgments (*Tuanzhuan*) and the Commentaries on the Images (*Xiangzhuan*) each into two sections; they thus form the first four of the "Ten Wings" (*Shiyi*) of the exegetical material included in the classic. Although all of the Ten Wings were traditionally attributed to Confucius, scholarly opinion in the twentieth century has tended to the view that individual Wings actually date from different periods. The dating of these Wings has been a matter of debate, but some appear to be as late as the third or early second centuries B.C.E.

Of the Ten Wings, the most philosophically influential have been the sixth and seventh, formed by the two sections of the *Great Commentary* (*Dazhuan*), otherwise known as the *Commentary on the Appended Phrases* (*Xici zhuan*). This commentary contains two kinds of material: one deals with the nature and meaning of the *Changes* in general, and the other is concerned with the meaning of the Judgments and line statements of individual hexagrams. We include here a selection from this important commentary.

THE *COMMENTARY ON THE APPENDED PHRASES*, PART 1

The *Great Commentary* (*Dazhuan*), or the *Commentary on the Appended Phrases* (*Xici zhuan*), seems to consist of fragments of two different texts, one a general essay or group of essays dealing with the nature and meaning of the *Changes* in general and the other a collection of specific remarks about the Judgments and line statements of various individual hexagrams. As the *Changes* is supposed to be a "paradigm of Heaven and Earth," the *Commentary on the Appended Phrases* has a great deal to say about the universal order that underlies the myriad phenomena and about the sage, who allows his understanding to be shaped and nurtured by the *Changes* and thus stays attuned to this order. The sage becomes a model for all humankind and the leader of the good, harmonious society. The universe may be mysterious, but, thanks to the *Changes* and to the sages who first created it and who forever after employ it as guide, its mysteries can be plumbed, the secrets of good fortune and misfortune can be known, and human beings, as individuals and in society, can learn how to live in accordance with the cosmic and moral Way.

The following passages from the *Commentary on the Appended Phrases*, presenting an overall interpretation and context for the *Changes*, were often referred to in later literature. (The numbering of the passages has been added.)

1. As Heaven is high and noble and Earth is low and humble, so it is that *qian* [pure yang, Hexagram 1] and *kun* [pure yin, Hexagram 2] are defined. The high and the low being thereby set out, the exalted and the mean have their places accordingly. There are norms for action and repose, which are determined by whether hardness or softness is involved. Those with regular tendencies gather according to kind, and things divide up according to group; so it is that good fortune and misfortune occur. In Heaven this process creates images, and on Earth it creates physical forms; this is how change and transformation manifest themselves. In consequence of all this, as hard and soft stroke each other, the Eight Trigrams activate each other. It [the Way] arouses things with claps of thunder, moistens them with wind and rain. Sun and moon go through their cycles, so now it is cold, now hot. The Way of *qian* forms the male; the Way of *kun* forms the female. *Qian* has mastery over the great beginning of things, and *kun* acts to bring things to completion. *Qian* through ease provides mastery over things, and *kun* through simplicity provides capability. As the former is easy, it is easy to know, and as the latter is simple, it is easy to follow. If one is easy to know, he will have kindred spirits; and if one is easy to follow, he will have meritorious accomplishments. Once one has kindred spirits, he can endure, and once one has meritorious accomplishments, he can grow great. Being able to endure is inherent in a worthy man's virtue, and being able to grow great is inherent in the enterprise of the worthy man. It is through such ease and simplicity that the principles of the world obtain. As the principles of the world obtain in this way, they form positions here between them [Heaven and Earth].

2. The sages set down the hexagrams and observed the images. They appended phrases to the lines in order to clarify whether they signify good fortune or misfortune and let the hard and the soft lines displace each other so that change and transformation could appear. Therefore, good fortune and misfortune involve images of success or failure. Regret and remorse involve images

of sorrow and worry. Change and transformation involve images of advance and withdrawal. The strong and the weak provide images of day and night. The respective functions of the six hexagram lines embody the Way of the Three Ultimates [Heaven, Earth, and the human]. Therefore, what allows the noble person to find himself anywhere and yet remain secure are the sequences presented by the *Changes*. What he ponders with delight are the phrases appended to the lines. Therefore, once the noble person finds himself in a situation, he observes its image and ponders the phrases involved, and once he takes action, he observes the change [of the lines] and ponders the prognostications involved. This is why, since Heaven helps him, "it is auspicious" and "nothing will fail to be advantageous." . . .

4. The *Changes* is a paradigm of Heaven and Earth, and so it shows how one can fill in and pull together the Way of Heaven and Earth. Looking up, we use it [the *Changes*] to examine the configurations of Heaven, and, looking down, we use it to examine the patterns of Earth. Thus we understand the reasons underlying what is hidden and what is clear. We trace things back to their origins, then turn back to their ends. Thus we understand the axiom of life and death. With the consolidation of material force into essence, a person comes into being, but with the dissipation of one's spirit, change comes about. It is due to this that we understand the true state of gods and spirits. As [a sage] resembles Heaven and Earth, he does not go against them. As his knowledge is complete in respect to the myriad things, and as his Way brings help to all under Heaven, he commits no transgression. Such a one extends himself in all directions yet does not allow himself to be swept away. As he rejoices in Heaven and understands its decrees, he will be free from anxiety. As he is content in his land and is genuine about humaneness, he can be loving. He perfectly emulates the transformations of Heaven and Earth and so does not transgress them. He follows every twist and turn of the myriad things and so deals with them without omission. He has a thorough grasp of the Way of day-and-night and so is knowing. Thus, the numinous (*shen*)[51] is not restricted to place, and change is without substance.

5. The reciprocal process of yin and yang is called the Way. That which allows the Way to continue to operate is human goodness (*shan*), and that which allows it to bring things to completion is human nature (*xing*). The humane see it and call it humaneness, and the wise (*zhi*) see it and call it wisdom. It functions for the common folk on a daily basis, yet they are unaware of it. This is why the Way of the noble person is a rare thing! It is manifested in humaneness and hidden within its functioning. It arouses the myriad things but does not share the anxieties of the sages. As replete virtue and great enterprise, the

---

51. Translated elsewhere in this volume as "spiritual."

Way is indeed perfect! It is because the Way exists in such rich abundance that we refer to it as "great enterprise." It is because the Way brings renewal day after day that we refer to it here as "replete virtue." In its capacity to produce and reproduce, we call it "change." When it forms images, we call it *qian*. When it duplicates patterns, we call it *kun*. The means to know the future through the mastery of numbers is referred to as "prognostication," and to keep in step freely with change is referred to as "the way one should act." What the yin and the yang do not allow us to plumb we call "the numinous" (*shen*). . . .

8. The sages had the means to perceive the mysteries of the world and, drawing comparisons for them with analogous things, made images out of those things that seemed appropriate. This is why these are called "images." The sages had the means to perceive the activities taking place in the world and, observing how things come together and go smoothly, they thus enacted statutes and rituals accordingly. They appended phrases to the hexagram lines in order to judge the good and bad fortune involved. This is why these are called the line phrases. These line phrases speak to the most mysterious things in the world, and yet one may not feel aversion toward them; they speak to the things in the world that are most fraught with activity, and yet one may not feel confused about them. One should speak only after having drawn the appropriate comparisons [as offered in the *Changes*] and act only after having discussed what is involved. It is through such comparisons and by such discussions that one becomes successful with the way change and transformation operate. . . .

10. In the *Changes* there are four things that pertain to the Way of the sages. In speaking we regard its phrases as the supreme guide; in acting we regard its changes as the supreme guide; in fashioning implements we regard its images as the supreme guide; and in divining by cracking shell and bone or by the use of stalks we regard its prognostications as the supreme guide. This is why when the noble person would act in a certain way or would try to do something, he addresses his doubts to the *Changes* in terms of words. The charge that it receives comes back to him like an echo, with no distance or concealment to it. In consequence, one knows of things to come. . . .

12. That which transforms things and regulates them is called change. By extending this to practical action one may be said to achieve complete success. To take up this [the Way of change] and integrate it into the lives of the common folk of the world is called the great task of life. . . . To plumb the mysteries of the world to the utmost is dependent on the hexagrams; to drum up people to action all over the world is dependent on the phrases; to transform things and regulate them is dependent on change; to start things going and carry them out is dependent on the free flow of change; to be aware of the numinous and bring it to light is dependent on the men involved; to accomplish things while remaining silent and to be trusted without speaking is something intrinsic to virtuous conduct.

[*Yijing, Xici zhuan*, Part 1, *Shisanjing zhushu* — RJL]

THE *COMMENTARY ON THE APPENDED PHRASES,* PART 2

1. Thanks to constancy, the Way of Heaven and Earth reveals itself. Thanks to constancy, the Way of the sun and the moon makes them bright. All the activity that takes place in the world, thanks to constancy, is the expression of the One. *Qian* being unyielding shows us how easy it is; *kun* being yielding shows us how simple it is. The lines reproduce how particular things act, and the images provide likenesses of particular things. As the lines and images move within the hexagrams, so do good fortune and misfortune appear outside them. Meritorious undertakings are revealed in change, and the innate tendencies of the sages are revealed in the attached phrases. The great virtue of Heaven and Earth is called "generation." The great treasure of the sage is called his "position." The means by which such a one preserves this position we call "humaneness"; the means by which he gathers people to him we call "resources." The regulation of resources, the rectification of pronouncements, and his preventing the people from doing wrong we call "rightness." . . .

5. The Master said, "To understand incipience, is this not a matter of the numinous! The noble person is not fawning toward what is above and is not contemptuous of what is below. Is this not to understand incipience! As for incipience itself, it is the infinitesimally small beginning of action, the point at which the precognition of good fortune can occur. The noble person acts upon something as soon as he becomes aware of its incipience and does not wait for the day to run its course. . . ." The Master said, "The noble person acts only after he has made his person secure, speaks only after he has calmed his mind-and-heart, makes requests only after making his relationships firm. The noble person cultivates these three matters and so succeeds completely. If one acts from a position of precariousness, the people will not join in; if one speaks out of anxiety, the people will not respond; if one has not established relationships and yet makes requests, then the people will not join with him. Since no one will join in with him, those who would harm him will surely draw near. . . ."

6. The *Changes* both makes evident what has already happened and scrutinizes what is yet to come; thus subtlety comes to light, revealing what is hidden. The hexagrams are elucidated in such a way that they suit their names. These elucidations, in their differentiation of things and rectification of language, form decisive phrases. Thus they are perfect and complete. The way they are named involves insignificant things, but the analogies so derived concern matters of great importance. The meanings are far-reaching and the phrasing elegant. The language twists and turns but hits the mark. The things and events dealt with are obviously set forth, but hidden implications are involved. One uses the concept of the two to assist the common folk in the way they behave and to clarify the retribution and reward involved with failure and success. . . .

8. As a book, the *Changes* is something that cannot be kept at a distance. As a manifestation of the Way, the *Changes* involves frequent shifts. Change and action never stand still but keep flowing all through the six vacancies. Rising and falling without any consistency, the hard and the soft lines change one into the other, something for which it is impossible to make definitive laws, since they are doing nothing but keeping pace with change. One uses the *Changes* as the standard to determine whether one should go forth or withdraw. The hexagrams make one feel caution about being abroad or staying in. They also cast light on calamities as well as the incidents that underlie them. Let it not be there as a teacher or guardian but rather as if it were one's parents who had drawn near! At first one follows their phrases and then appraises their prescriptions. After that one will find that the hexagrams do contain a constant law. . . .

9. As a book, the *Changes* takes the plumbing of beginnings and the summing up of endings as its material. The way the six lines mix in together is due to the fact that they are nothing other than momentary things. The phrases attached to the first lines draw comparisons with things, about which the ending ones formulate conclusions. As for complicated matters, the calculation of the virtues and the determination of the rights and wrongs involved could not be complete without the middle lines. Ah! If one actually were to sum up the chances for survival or destruction and good fortune or bad in this way, he could, even without stirring, understand what they will be! One who has such understanding has but to look at the hexagram Judgments to have his thought cover more than half of what is involved! . . .

12. *Qian* is the strongest thing in the entire world, so it should always be easy to put its virtue into practice. Thus one knows whether or not there is going to be danger. *Kun* is the most compliant thing in the entire world, so it should always be simple to put its virtue into practice. Thus one knows whether or not there are going to be obstacles. The one is able to delight minds-and-hearts, and the other is able to refine the concerns of the various lords. The Way of change is what determines all the good fortune and misfortune that take place in the world; it is that which allows the world to realize all its unceasing and untiring efforts. Therefore, as speech and deed are subject to change and transformation, auspicious endeavors result in blessings, matters rendered into images provide understanding of concrete things, and the practice of divination allows one to know the future. Heaven and Earth established the positions of things, and the sages fully realized the potential inherent in them. Whether consulting with men or consulting with spirits, they allowed the ordinary folk to share in these resources. . . .

Change and action speak to us in terms of the expression "advantageous." Good fortune and misfortune shift from one to the other in accordance with the innate tendencies involved. Therefore it is when the covetous and the hateful make their attacks that good fortune and misfortune are produced. It is when the distant and the contiguous try to seize each other that regret and remorse are produced. It is when true innate tendencies and spurious countertendencies work their influence that advantage and harm are produced. For all the tendencies inherent in change, whenever the contiguous do not serve each other's interests, this is termed misfortune. Even when something might have caused harm [but did not], this is still an occasion for remorse and regret. The words of someone who is about to revolt have a sense of shame about them; the words of someone who entertains doubts in his innermost mind tend to prevaricate; the words of a good person are few; the words of an impatient and impetuous person are many; the words of someone who tries to slander good people tend to vacillate; and the words of someone who has neglected his duty or lost his integrity tend to be devious.

[*Yijing, Xici zhuan*, Part 2, *Shisanjing zhushu* — RJL]

HEAVEN, EARTH, AND THE HUMAN IN THE *CLASSIC OF FILIALITY (XIAOJING)*

Filial piety was an age-old concept and practice even before Confucius' time, but only toward the end of the Zhou period did it become the subject of a "classic" text emerging from the school of Confucius' disciple Zengzi, in what purported to be a dialogue between him and the Master. Its main point is that filiality, as the generic source of all virtue, serves as the basis of public morality, maintains the spiritual continuity between the living and the dead, and links together the creative powers of Heaven, Earth, and the Human order.

Some differentiation in the practice of filiality is recognized in separate sections addressed to the Son of Heaven, the enfeoffed nobility, the great officers, scholar-officials, and common people. While thus envisioning a structured, hierarchical society, the creators of the text also stress the universality of the filial relationship as the common moral denominator among people of all classes. Moreover, it co-implicates authority and responsibility, underscoring the ruler's responsibility to the people and the ministers' duty of forthright remonstration to keep the ruler from going astray — also a duty of the son to remonstrate with his father to keep him from wrong. Both illustrate the basic Confucian principle of reciprocity or mutual response.

As a text emerging from the family school of Confucius in the Han period, the *Classic of Filiality* maintained quasi-canonical status down into the twentieth century. The Tang emperor Xuanzong recognized it as one of the "Thirteen Classics." Versions of varying length, organization, and commentary fueled scholarly controversy down through the centuries. Zhu Xi, who had doubts about the text (though not about the importance of filiality) did not include it among the Four Books and Five Classics in the core of the Neo-Confucian curriculum. Still, this did not keep the *Classic of*

Filiality from enjoying wide popularity throughout premodern East Asia. It became especially influential in Japanese thought of the Tokugawa period (1603–1868) and figured prominently in nationalistic ideologies of late nineteenth- and early twentieth-century Japan. Questions of authenticity did not impede its being widely accepted as a classic statement not only of the virtue of filial piety but of the Confucian values of self-preservation, reciprocity, reverence, moderation, diligence, service to others, and moral remonstration.

Though the text is in the classic dialogue form, missing here is the spirit of inquiry and personal give-and-take characteristic of the *Analects* and *Mencius*. Instead the tone, as in the first section, is didactic and authoritative, with Zengzi no more than a passive foil to the Master.

THE *CLASSIC OF FILIALITY (XIAOJING)*

1. Introduction to Basic Principles

Confucius was at leisure, with Zengzi in attendance. He asked Zengzi, "Do you know by what surpassing virtue and essential way the early kings kept the world in order, the people in harmony both with their relatives and at large, and all, both high and low, uncomplaining?" Zengzi, rising from his seat, said, "Unenlightened as I am, how could I know that?" Confucius said, "Filiality is the root of virtue and the wellspring of instruction. Take your seat and I shall explain.

"Our body, skin, and hair are all received from our parents; we dare not injure them. This is the first priority in filial duty. To establish oneself in the world and practice the Way; to uphold one's good name for posterity and give glory to one's father and mother — this is the completion of filial duty. Thus filiality begins with service to parents, continues in service to the ruler, and ends with establishing oneself in the world [and becoming an exemplary person].

"As it is said in the *Daya* [of the *Classic of Odes*]: 'Forget not your forebears; cultivate the virtue received from them.' "[52]

The following sections typically end with a similar, memorable quotation from the Classic of Odes *or the* Classic of Documents, *which for brevity's sake we delete from this abridgement.*

2. The Son of Heaven

The Master said, "Loving one's parents, one dare not hate others. Revering one's parents, one dare not be contemptuous of others. When his love and

---

52. Ode 235.

reverence are perfected in service to parents, [the ruler's] moral influence is shed on all the people and his good example shines in all directions. . . ."

Deleted here are similar maxims for the conduct of the enfeoffed nobility and high officers. Observance of these is a filial duty, but the conduct itself relates to the office, not to filiality.

5. Scholar-Officials (*Shi*)

As one serves one's father, one serves one's mother, drawing on the same love. As one serves one's father, one serves one's prince, drawing on the same reverence. The mother draws upon one's love, the prince on one's reverence. Therefore, if one serves one's prince with the filiality one shows to one's father, it becomes the virtue of fidelity (loyalty). If one serves one's superiors with brotherly submission it becomes the virtue of obedience. Never failing in fidelity and obedience, this is how one serves superiors. Thus one may preserve one's rank and office and continue one's family sacrifices. This is the filiality of the scholar-official. . . .

6. Commoners

In keeping with Heaven's seasons and Earth's resources, by one's industry and frugality one supports one's father and mother. This is the filiality of the common people.

From the Son of Heaven down to the common people, if filiality is not followed from beginning to end, disaster is sure to follow.

In some editions the previous paragraph is a separate section titled "Equality of Filiality." This means that although filial duties are differentiated according to particular stations, the filial obligation is shared by all — a common human denominator and the genetic basis of all moral relations.

7. The Three Powers [Heaven, Earth, and the Human]

The Master said, "Filiality is the ordering principle of Heaven, the rightness of the Earth, and the norm of human conduct. This ordering of Heaven and Earth is what people should follow; illumined by the brightness of Heaven and benefited by the resources of the Earth, all-under-Heaven are thus harmonized. This is how the teachings [of the sage king] succeed without being stringent, and his rule achieves order without being severe. The early kings, seeing that instruction could transform the people, gave them an example of outspreading love so that people did not neglect their kin; promulgated virtue and rightness, which the people willingly emulated in practice; set an example of respect and deference, by which the people became non-contentious; led them by rites and music, by which the people became harmonious; distinguished between good and evil, whereby the people knew what was forbidden. . . ."

8. Governing by Filiality

The Master said, "The reason the illustrious kings of old governed all-under-Heaven by filiality was that, not daring to neglect the ministers even of small states (much less their own enfeoffed nobility), they sought to engender in the myriad states an eagerness to serve [sacrifice to] their predecessors. Heads of states, not daring to abuse widows and widowers (much less scholar-officials and commoners), instilled in all an eagerness to serve the princely ancestors. Heads of families, not daring to mistreat servants and concubines (much less their own wives and children), instilled in all an eagerness to serve their parents. Living, they were at peace; in death, content. Thus with all-under-Heaven at peace, no calamities occurred, no disasters or disorders arose. This is why the illustrious kings governed through filiality. . . ."

9. The Governance of the Sages

The Master said, ". . . In the virtue (*de*) of the sage is there anything that can surpass filiality? . . . The Way of parent and child is rooted in the Heavenly moral nature and engenders the [relation of] rightness between prince and minister. Parents give one life; no bond could be greater. . . . Therefore not to love one's parents but to love others is to act against one's moral nature (*de*). Not to respect one's parents but to respect others is to violate the ritual order. . . ."

12. The Essential Way, Further Expounded

The Master said, "For teaching people love and affection, nothing is better than filiality. For teaching people ritual restraint, nothing is better than fraternal love. For transforming manners and customs, nothing is better than music. For stability [of the throne] above and order [among the people] below, nothing is better than the rites. And ritual decorum [accordance with the rites] is essentially reverence. . . ."

15. Remonstrance

Zengzi said, "I have heard your instructions concerning affection and loving respect, comforting one's parents, and upholding one's good name. May I presume to ask, if a child follows all of his parents' commands, can this be called filiality?"

The Master replied, "What kind of talk is this! What kind of talk is this! Of old the Son of Heaven had seven counselors, so that even if he himself lost the Way, he still would not lose his sway over all-under-Heaven. . . . If a father had even one son to remonstrate with him, he still would not fall into evil ways. In the face of whatever is not right, the son cannot but remonstrate with his father, and the minister cannot but remonstrate with his prince. If it is not right, remonstrate! . . ."

18. Mourning One's Parents

The following passage is marked by the characteristic Confucian qualities of balance and moderation in all things, and of care of one's own body as the primary filial obligation to one's parents.

The Master said, "In mourning for his parents, the filial child weeps but does not wail, performs the rites without affectation, speaks without adorning his words, does without splendid raiment, hears music without taking any joy in it, and eats without relish — all these are feelings natural to one who grieves. After three days one again takes food, in order to show people that death should not be allowed to harm life and that destruction [of one's body] should not lead to the destruction of [another] life. These are how the sages regulated things. . . ."

[*Songke Xiaojing* 5–31; Kurihara, *Kōkyō*, 67–335 — dB]

THE *RECORD OF RITES (LIJI)* AND THE RITUAL TRADITION

Rites were at the heart of early Confucian thought and practice, as will have been evident in the selections from the *Analects* and *Xunzi* especially.[53] Rites represented a connection between the Confucian tradition and the earliest Chinese religious practices known to us, so that within the tradition was preserved something very ancient, together with a keen and appreciative consciousness of its antiquity. At the same time, ritual practice and the understanding of the purpose and significance of ritual also evolved over time along with the evolution of Confucianism itself. Among the noteworthy developments were a heightened sense of the moral significance of the rites and of their educative and disciplinary value within the life of an individual as well as in the life of the state and the empire. In fact, it was characteristic of the adherents of the tradition known as *ru* — the ritualists — to believe that it was through rites that individuals were best able to cultivate themselves, to exert positive influence

---

53. See ch. 3 and ch. 6.

over others, and ultimately to bring order to the family, the state, and the world at large.

Here we offer a selection from two of the most important Confucian ritual texts, the *Great Learning* and the *Mean*. These two texts were chapters of a classic known as the *Record of Rites* (*Liji*), a work compiled at the end of the first century B.C.E. and the beginning of the first century C.E. on the basis of materials that were in many cases considerably older. Though the interest and importance of these works were noted already during the Han period, they were preserved for many centuries simply as part of this much larger compilation. In the Song period (960–1279) they would receive fresh attention when Zhu Xi (1130–1200), one of the leading scholars of the Song dynasty, selected them from the *Record of Rites*, assigning them an independent status, alongside the *Analects* and the *Mencius*, as two of the Four Books. From that time on these four — the *Great Learning*, the *Mean*, the *Analects*, and the *Mencius* — became the most important and formative texts deriving from the classical Confucian tradition and, as we shall see, a focus and point of reference for much of the tradition that would develop from the twelfth through the seventeenth centuries and that has been identified as Neo-Confucian.

THE *GREAT LEARNING* (*DAXUE*)

For all its brevity, the *Great Learning* is one of the most seminal works in the Chinese tradition. Its Chinese title, *Daxue*, is usually understood to mean education for the adult, or higher education; its central theme is self-cultivation. Most famous in the *Great Learning* is the catena — known in Chinese as the "eight items" — setting forth a series of links connecting intellectual and moral cultivation on the part of the individual with the establishment of harmony in the family, order in the state, and peace in the world. The *Great Learning* has been variously attributed to Confucius' grandson Zisi (483? – 402? B.C.E.), to Confucius' disciple Zengzi, and to one of his pupils. Some scholars, however, have dated it as late as the Former Han period (ca. 200 B.C.E.).

The Text

The Way of the Great Learning lies in illuminating luminous virtue, treating the people with affection, and resting in perfect goodness. Knowing where to rest, one is able to be settled; having become settled, one is able to become tranquil; having become tranquil, one is able to be at peace; being at peace, one is able to reflect; through reflection one is able to attain understanding.

Things have their roots and their branches; affairs have their ends and their beginnings. Knowing what to put first and what to put last, one comes near to the Way.

Those in antiquity who wished to illuminate luminous virtue throughout the world would first govern their states; wishing to govern their states, they would first bring order to their families; wishing to bring order to their families, they would first cultivate their own persons; wishing to cultivate their own persons, they would first rectify their minds; wishing to rectify their minds, they would first make their thoughts sincere; wishing to make their thoughts sincere, they would first extend their knowledge. The extension of knowledge lies in the investigation of things.

It is only when things are investigated that knowledge is extended; when knowledge is extended that thoughts become sincere; when thoughts become sincere that the mind is rectified; when the mind is rectified that the person is cultivated; when the person is cultivated that order is brought to the family; when order is brought to the family that the state is well governed; when the state is well governed that peace is brought to the world.

From the Son of Heaven to ordinary people, all, without exception, should regard cultivating the person as the root. It can never happen that the root is disordered and the branches are ordered. It should never be that what is significant is regarded lightly and what is insignificant is regarded with gravity. This is called knowing the root; this is called the perfection of knowledge.

From the Commentary to the Text

Chapter 6: What is meant by "making one's thoughts sincere" is this: One allows no self-deception, just as when one hates a hateful smell or loves a lovely color. This is called being content within oneself, and this is why the noble person must be watchful over himself in solitude. The petty person, when living alone, is quite without restraint in doing what is not good. As soon as he sees a noble person he moves to dissemble, concealing what is not good and making a display of what is good. The other sees right through him, as if seeing his lungs and liver. Of what use is his dissembling? This is a case of what is truly within being manifested without, and this is why the noble person must be watchful over himself in solitude. . . .

Chapter 7: What is meant by "cultivating the person depends upon correcting the mind" is this: Whenever one is influenced by anger and resentment, the mind will not attain correctness; whenever one is influenced by fear and dread, the mind will not attain correctness; whenever one is influenced by enjoyment and pleasure, the mind will not attain correctness; whenever one is influenced by sorrow and distress, the mind will not attain correctness. When the mind is not present, one looks but does not see; one listens but does not hear; one eats without knowing the flavors. This is what it means to say that "cultivating the person depends upon correcting the mind."

Chapter 8: What is meant by "bringing order to one's family depends on the cultivation of one's person" is this: A person is biased by the objects of his affection and love, biased by the objects of his derision and hate, biased by the objects of his awe and reverence, biased by the objects of his pity and compassion, and biased by the objects of his contempt and scorn. This is why there are so few in the world who, being fond of something, are yet aware of its faults and who, disliking something, are yet aware of its merits. Thus the adage has it that "a person never knows his son's faults, nor does he realize the fullness of the growing grain." This is what is meant by saying that unless one's person be cultivated, one cannot regulate the family.

Chapter 9: What is meant by "governing the state requires that one first bring order to one's family" is this: No one who is unable to teach his own family will be able to teach others. Therefore the ruler, without going beyond his own family, brings to completion his teachings throughout the state: filial devotion, which is the way to serve a ruler; brotherliness, which is the way to serve elders; and kindness, which is the way to treat the multitude. . . .

As the humaneness of one family evokes humaneness in an entire state, and the courtesy of one family evokes courtesy in an entire state, so covetousness and cruelty on the part of one man will bring chaos to the entire state.[54] Thus are the springs of action.[55] This is what is meant by the saying that "through one word an enterprise may be ruined; through one man a state may be brought to order." Yao and Shun ruled the empire with humaneness, and the people followed them. Jie and Zhou ruled the empire through violence, and the people followed them. If what one orders for others runs counter to what one loves oneself, the people will not follow. Thus, only after the ruler possesses merits in himself may he seek to find them in others, and only when he himself is free from faults may he condemn them in others. It can never happen that one who does not harbor reciprocity within himself will be able to instruct others. This is why "governing the state depends on regulating the family."

Chapter 10: What is meant by "bringing peace to the world depends on governing the state" is this: When those above treat the old as the old should be treated, filial devotion will be evoked among the people. When those above treat elders as elders should be treated, brotherliness will be evoked among the people. When those above treat the orphaned with compassion, the people will not do otherwise. Therefore the ruler has the Way of the measuring square.

What one dislikes in those above, let him not employ in the treatment of those below; what one dislikes in those below, let him not employ in serving those above. What one dislikes in those who go before, let him not employ in leading those who follow; what one dislikes in those who follow, let him not employ in following those who go before. What he dislikes in those on his right, let him not bestow on those on his left. What he dislikes in those on his left,

---

54. While potentially true of all families, this refers primarily to the ruling house and the ruler himself.

55. In the translation of Wing-tsit Chan, "Such is the subtle, incipient activating force of things."

let him not bestow on those on his right. This is called the Way of the measuring square. . . .

Therefore the ruler is watchful first over his virtue. Having virtue, he will have the people; having the people, he will have the land; having the land, he will have its wealth; having its wealth, he will have its resources for expenditure.

Virtue is the root; wealth, the branch. But if the ruler regards the root as inconsequential, and the branch as consequential, he will contend with the people and teach them to plunder. Therefore by gathering wealth one causes the people to be dispersed, and by dispersing wealth, one causes the people to be gathered. Therefore words that are ill-spoken will come back to one for ill; and gain that is ill-gotten will depart in like manner.

It says in the "Announcement of Kang": "The Mandate of Heaven is not constant."[56] By following the Way of goodness, one gets it; by not being good, one loses it. . . .

To love what other people hate or to hate what other people love is to go against human nature. Calamities will surely be visited upon one who does so. Therefore the ruler has a great Way to follow, which he must attain through loyalty and integrity and which he will lose through pride and extravagance. In the production of wealth there is also a great Way. Let the producers be many and the consumers few. Let there be energy in production and economy in expenditure. Then the wealth will be always sufficient. One who is humane employs his wealth to enlarge himself, while one who is inhumane employs his self to enlarge his wealth.

Never has it happened that the one above loves humaneness while those below do not love rightness. Nor has it happened that where the people love rightness, their work has not been brought to completion, nor that the wealth gathered in treasuries and granaries has ceased to exist.

[*Liji zhengyi* 60:1a–b, 4b–6b — IB]

THE *MEAN* (*ZHONGYONG*)

The Chinese title of the essay, *Zhongyong*, is composed of the elements "centrality" or "equilibrium" (*zhong*) and "normality" (*yong*). The translation of these two words as the *Mean* suggests the fundamental moral idea of moderation, balance, and suitableness. But in this essay the concept is much deeper, denoting a basic norm of human action that, if comprehended and complied with, will bring human beings into harmony with the whole universe.

Another important concept in the *Mean* is that of *cheng* — sincerity or truth. Sincerity involves the moral integrity that enables an individual to become a fully devel-

---

56. "The Announcement of Kang" in the *Classic of History*; Legge, *The Chinese Classics*, 3:397.

oped person. One is to be "genuine" with others but also "genuinely" oneself, a true human being. But the *Mean* also seeks to relate what is most essential and real in human beings to the underlying reality or truth of the universe. Human virtue does not exist or act in a sphere all its own, an "ethical" sphere that might be understood to be distinct from the metaphysical order. Rather, sincerity puts us in touch with ourselves, with our fellow human beings, and with the universe as a whole. The moral order and the cosmic order are one, and, through ethical cultivation, the individual not only achieves human perfection but also becomes part of a unity with Heaven and Earth. In this way sincerity, as an active and dynamic force, works for the realization not only of human beings but also of all things. The *Mean*, in other words, expresses in psychological and metaphysical terms the same progression from the individual self to world order and unity that the *Great Learning* expresses in social and political terms.

The *Mean* has traditionally been ascribed to Zisi, the grandson of Confucius. Though some scholars have suggested that it may actually be a combination of two or more texts dating in part as late as the Qin or early Han, there is also support in recent scholarship for the view that the text does indeed have much earlier origins.

1. What Heaven has endowed is called the nature. Following the nature is called the Way. Cultivating the Way is called instruction.

The Way cannot be departed from for so much as an instant. If it were possible to depart from it, it would not be the Way. Therefore the noble person is cautious and watchful about what is unseen and fearful and apprehensive about what is unheard. There is nothing more visible than what is hidden, nothing more apparent than what is minute. Therefore the noble person is watchful over himself while alone.

Before pleasure, anger, sorrow, and joy have arisen, this is called centrality. After they have arisen and have attained their appropriate degree, this is called harmony. Equilibrium is the great root of the world, and harmony is the pervasive Way of the world. Once centrality and harmony are realized, Heaven and Earth take their proper places and all living things are nourished.

2. Confucius said, "The noble person exemplifies the Mean; the inferior person contravenes the Mean. The noble person exemplifies the Mean by being a noble person and constantly holding to centrality; the small person contravenes the Mean by being a small person, devoid of caution and restraint."

3. The Master said, "Perfect indeed is the Mean! For a long time there have been few people who have had the capacity for it."

4. The Master said, "I know why it is that the Way is not practiced: the knowing go beyond it, while the ignorant do not come up to it. I know why it is that the Way is not understood: the worthy go beyond it, while the unworthy do not come up to it. There is no one who does not eat and drink, but there are few who are able to discriminate flavors. . . .

12. "The Way of the noble person is far-reaching, yet hidden. Ordinary men and women, however ignorant, know something of it, yet in its furthest reaches,

there is that which even a sage does not know. Ordinary men and women, however unworthy, are able to practice it, yet in its furthest reaches, there is that which even a sage is unable to put into practice. For all of the greatness of Heaven and Earth, people still find cause for dissatisfaction. Therefore if the noble person speaks of its greatness, there is nothing in the world capable of bearing it up, while if he speaks of its smallness, there is nothing in the world capable of breaking it down. The Ode says,

> The hawk flies up to Heaven
> The fish leaps in the deep.[57]

"This speaks of how it is seen above and below. The Way of the noble person originates among ordinary men and women, and, at its furthest reaches, is displayed brightly in Heaven and Earth."

13. The Master said, "The Way is not far from human beings. If a human being takes as the Way something that distances him from others, it cannot be the Way. The Ode says,

> In hewing an ax handle,
> In hewing an ax handle,
> The pattern is not far off.[58]

"One grasps one ax handle in order to hew another; it is looking askance at it that makes it appear as if it were distant. Therefore, in governing human beings, the noble person uses human beings as a model, and when they are changed, he stops. In practicing loyalty and reciprocity one will not deviate far from the Way. What you do not want to have done to yourself, do not do to others. The way of the noble person involves four things, and as yet I[59] have been incapable of even one of them. I have been unable to serve my father as I would have my son serve me; I have been unable to serve my ruler as I would have a minister serve me; I have been unable to serve my elder brother as I would have my younger brother serve me; I have been unable to be first in treating my friend as I would have the friend treat me. If in his practice of these ordinary virtues and in his care in ordinary speech there is anything deficient, he dare not fail to exert himself, and if there is anything in excess, he dare not indulge it. His words accord with his actions; his actions accord with his words. Is it not just complete sincerity that marks the noble person?"

14. The noble person acts in accordance with his position and does not desire what goes beyond it. When his situation entails wealth and honor, he acts in a

---

57. Ode 239.
58. Ode 158.
59. Confucius is still the speaker and refers here to himself.

way consistent with wealth and honor. When his situation entails poverty and lowliness, he acts in a way consistent with poverty and lowliness. When he is among the Yi and the Di[60] he acts in ways appropriate to the Yi and the Di. When he is in a situation of difficulty and distress, he acts in ways appropriate to difficulty and distress. There is no circumstance in which the noble person is not himself. When he is in a superior position, he does not look down on his inferiors; when he is in an inferior position he does not seek to ingratiate himself with his superiors. Rectifying himself, seeking nothing from others, he is free from resentment. Above, he finds no fault with Heaven; below, he bears no grudge against men. Therefore the noble person remains quiet, awaiting destiny;[61] the small person follows dangerous ways, anticipating good fortune. The Master said, "In archery there is something that resembles the Way of the noble person: when one misses the center of the target, one turns back and seeks the cause within oneself."

20. Duke Ai asked about government. The Master said, "The government of Wen and Wu is set forth in the historical records on wood tablets. Given the man,[62] the government will flourish; without the man, the government will perish. Men must be active in matters of government, just as the earth is active in making things grow: the government is a growing reed. Therefore the conduct of government depends on having the man, one obtains the man through one's own person,[63] one cultivates one's person through the Way, and one cultivates the Way through humaneness. Humaneness is what it means to be human, and being affectionate toward one's kin is the greatest part of it. Rightness is doing what is right, and honoring the worthy is the greatest part of it. The diminishing degree of affection due to one's kin[64] and the different gradations of honor owed to the worthy are born of ritual. When those below do not gain the confidence of the one above, the people cannot be governed. Therefore the noble person cannot but cultivate his person. As he thinks about cultivating his person, he cannot but serve his parents. As he thinks about serving his parents, he cannot but know other human beings. As he thinks about knowing other human beings, he cannot but know Heaven.

"The universal Way of the world involves five relations, and practicing it involves three virtues. The five are the relations between ruler and minister,

---

60. Tribes in the east and the north, respectively.

61. The Chinese term is *ming*, meaning what is ordained or endowed by Heaven (or, in other contexts, the Mandate of Heaven). It is the same word used in the opening line of the *Mean*, which refers to the nature as that which is *endowed* by Heaven.

62. Here, and in the rest of the passage, this is understood to refer to the *right* man or men to rule.

63. Or personality.

64. This refers to a diminishing level of affection owed to those whose degree of relationship to oneself is more and more remote.

between parent and child, between husband and wife, between older and younger brother, and among friends. These five are the universal way of the world. The three — knowledge, humaneness, and courage — are the universal virtues of the world. And the means by which they are practiced is oneness. Some are born with knowledge of them; some attain knowledge of them through learning; and some acquire knowledge of them through painful exertion. But the knowledge having been achieved, it comes to the same thing. Some practice them with a sense of peace; some practice them out of a sense of their efficacy; some practice them through strenuous exertion. But the effort having been completed, it comes to the same thing."

The Master said, "To be fond of learning is to be near to knowledge; to practice diligently is to be near to humaneness; to know shame is to be near to courage. One who knows these three knows how to cultivate his person; one who knows how to cultivate his person knows how to govern men; and one who knows how to govern men knows how to govern the states and families of the world. All those who govern the states and families have nine standards to follow: cultivating one's person; honoring the worthy, displaying affection to one's kin; respecting the great ministers; identifying with the whole company of officers; treating the common people as one's children; being hospitable to the hundred artisans;[65] showing kindness to travelers from afar; and cherishing the several lords. When one cultivates one's person, the Way is set forth; when one honors the worthy, one is kept from error; when one is affectionate to one's kin, uncles and younger brothers are not resentful; when one respects the great ministers, one is not deluded; when one identifies with the whole company of officers, they amply reciprocate one's courtesy; when one treats the common people as one's children, the people encourage one another; when one is hospitable to the hundred artisans, the resources one has to utilize are sufficient; when one shows kindness to travellers from afar, they come to him from all directions; when one cherishes the several lords, the world holds him in awe.

"Regulating and purifying oneself, being fully attentive to one's dress, and making no movement contrary to propriety — this is the way to cultivate one's person. Removing slanderers, keeping away from seduction, making light of wealth, paying honor to virtue — this is the way to encourage the worthy. According them positions of honor, offering them generous emoluments, sharing their likes and dislikes — this is the way to encourage affection among one's kin. Providing a full complement of officials to assume responsibility and discharge commissions — this is the way to encourage the great ministers. Maintaining loyalty and good faith and making their emoluments generous — this is the way to encourage the men of service. Employing them only at the proper time and being sparing in one's exactions — this is the way to encourage the people.

---

65. This refers to all of the different kinds of artisans.

Holding daily inspections and monthly examinations, and matching their rations to their achievements — this is the way to encourage the hundred artisans. Escorting them when they depart and welcoming them when they arrive, responding with commendation for the good and kindness toward the incompetent — this is the way to show kindness to travelers from afar. Sustaining families whose line of succession has been broken, restoring states that have been destroyed, bringing order out of chaos, supporting those in danger, allowing them timely reception at court, sending them away with generous gifts, and welcoming them with modest offerings — this is the way to cherish the various lords. All those who carry out the government of the world and its states and families have these nine standards. The means by which they are practiced is oneness." . . .

Sincerity is Heaven's Way; achieving sincerity is the human Way. One who is sincere attains centrality without striving, apprehends without thinking. One who naturally and easily is centered in the Way is a sage. One who attains sincerity chooses what is good and holds to it firmly. This involves broad learning, extensive inquiry, careful thought, clear discrimination, and earnest practice. When there is anything one has not studied, or has studied but been unable to understand, one will not give up. If there is anything one has not inquired into, or has inquired into but not understood, one will not give up. If there is something one has not thought about, or has thought about but not understood, one will not give up. If there is anything one has not discriminated, or has discriminated but not been clear about, one will not give up. If there is anything one has not practiced, or has practiced but without being earnest, one does not give up. What another person can do through a single effort, one will accomplish in a hundred, and what another person can do in ten efforts, one will accomplish in a thousand. If one can follow this way, though ignorant, one will surely become intelligent; though weak, one will surely become strong.

21. Intelligence that comes from sincerity is called the nature; sincerity that comes from intelligence is called instruction. Given sincerity, one will be intelligent, and given intelligence, one will be sincere.

22. Only that one in the world who is most perfectly sincere is able to give full development to his nature. Being able to give full development to his nature, he is able to give full development to the nature of other human beings and, being able to give full development to the nature of other human beings, he is able to give full development to the natures of other living things. Being able to give full development to the natures of other living things, he can assist in the transforming and nourishing powers of Heaven and Earth; being able to assist in the transforming and nourishing powers of Heaven and Earth, he can form a triad with Heaven and Earth.

25. Sincerity is completing oneself; the Way is to be followed for oneself. Sincerity is the end and the beginning of living things; without sincerity there is nothing. Therefore the noble person regards sincerity as precious. Sincerity

is not only completing oneself but is also the means for completing other living things. Completing oneself is humaneness; completing other living things is understanding. These are the virtues of the nature and the way of uniting inner and outer. Therefore whenever one employs them one is right.

26. Therefore perfect sincerity is unceasing. Being unceasing, it is long-lasting; lasting long, it becomes manifest. Being manifest, it is far-reaching; reaching far, it becomes broad and deep. Being broad and deep, it becomes lofty and bright. Because it is broad and deep, it is able to contain living things; because it is lofty and bright, it is able to embrace living things. Far-reaching and long-lasting, it is able to complete living things. Broad and deep, it is the counterpart of Earth; lofty and bright, it is the counterpart of Heaven. Far-reaching and long-lasting, it is limitless. In that it is like this, it is manifest even when it is invisible; it transforms even when it is unmoving; it brings to completion without action. The Way of Heaven and Earth can be fully expressed in one sentence: these things being without doubleness, their giving birth to living things is unfathomable. The Way of Heaven and Earth is broad, deep, lofty, bright, far-reaching, and long-lasting.

[*Liji zhengyi* 52:1a–2b, 10a–12b; 53:1a–3b — IB]

THE MEANING OF SACRIFICES (*JIYI*)

This chapter of the *Record of Rites* affords a moving insight into the psychology of the most fundamental of all ritual performances — the sacrifice for departed parents.

1. Rites should not be frequently repeated. Such frequency is indicative of importunateness, and importunateness is inconsistent with reverence. Nor should they be at distant intervals. Such infrequency is indicative of indifference; and indifference leads to forgetting them altogether. Therefore the noble person, in harmony with the course of Heaven, offers the sacrifices of spring and autumn. When he treads on the dew that has descended as hoarfrost he cannot help a feeling of sadness, which arises in his mind and cannot be ascribed to the cold. In the spring when he treads on the ground, wet with the rains and dews that have fallen heavily, he cannot avoid being moved by a feeling as if he were seeing his departed friends. We meet the approach of our friends with music and escort them away with sadness. Hence at the sacrifice in spring we use music, but not at the sacrifice in autumn.

2. The most complete vigil is carried on inwardly, while a less intense vigil is maintained externally. During the days of such vigil, the mourner thinks of his departed, how and where they sat, how they smiled and spoke, what were their aims and views, what they delighted in, and what things they desired and enjoyed. On the third day of such exercise he will see those for whom it is employed.

3. On the day of sacrifice, when he enters the apartment [of the temple] he will seem to see [the deceased] in the place [where his spirit-tablet] is. After he has moved about and is leaving at the door, he will seem to be arrested by hearing the sound of his movements and will sigh as he seems to hear the sound of his sighing.

4. Thus the filial piety taught by the ancient kings required that the eyes of the son should not forget the looks [of his parents], nor his ears their voices; and he should retain the memory of their aims, likings, and wishes. As he gave full play to his love, they seemed to live again; and to his reverence, they seemed to stand out, so unforgotten by him. How could his sacrifices be without the accompaniment of reverence?

5. The noble person, while [his parents] are still alive, reverently nourishes them; and when they are dead, he reverently sacrifices to them; his thought is how to the end of life not to disgrace them. The saying that the noble person mourns all his life for his parents has reference to the recurrence of the day of their death. That he does not do his ordinary work on that day does not mean that it would be unpropitious to do so; it means that on that day his thoughts are occupied with them, and he does not dare to occupy himself as on other days with his private and personal affairs.

6. It is only the sage who can sacrifice to God (Di), and the filial son who can sacrifice to his parents. To sacrifice (xiang) means to face toward one's direction (xiang). One establishes one's direction, and then one can offer his sacrifice. Hence the filial son approaches the personator of the departed without having occasion to blush; the ruler leads the victim forward, while his wife puts down the bowls; the ruler presents the offerings to the personator, while his wife sets forth the various dishes; the ministers and the great officers assist the ruler; those acknowledged as their wives assist his wife. How well sustained is their reverence! How complete is the expression of their loyal devotion! How earnest is their wish that the departed should enjoy the service!

7. King Wen,[66] in sacrificing, served the dead as if he were serving the living. He thought of the dead as if he did not wish to live [any longer himself]. On the recurrence of their death-day, he was sad; in calling his father by the name elsewhere forbidden,[67] he looked as if he saw him. So sincere was he in sacrificing that he looked as if he saw the things that his father loved, and the pleased expression on his face — such was King Wen! The Ode says:

> Light dawns without my having slept,
> Being so full of thoughts of two people.[68]

---

66. Founder of the Zhou dynasty.

67. A son would have been enjoined from speaking the personal name of his father during the father's lifetime.

68. Ode 196. The "two people" to whom the speaker refers are his parents.

This is King Wen's poem.[69] On the day after the sacrifice his joy and sorrow were blended together. He could not but rejoice for the opportunity of offering the sacrifice; and when it was over, he could not but be sad.

8. At the autumnal sacrifice, when Zhongni[70] advanced, bearing the offerings, his general appearance was indicative of simple sincerity, but his steps were short and oft repeated. When the sacrifice was over, Zigong questioned him, saying, "The Master said that sacrifice should be marked by dignity and intense absorption; now how is it that in the Master's sacrificing there is no such dignity and absorption?" The Master said, "Dignity is in the demeanor of one who is distant.[71] Absorption is in the demeanor of one who turns within.[72] What does the demeanor associated with distance or with turning within have to do with communicating with the spiritual intelligences? How should such dignity and absorption be seen in my sacrifice? [At the sacrifices of the king and rulers] there is the return of the personator to his apartment and the offering of food to him there; there are the performances of the music and the setting forth of the stands with the victims on them; there is the ordering of the various ceremonies and the music; and there is the complete array of the officers for all the services. When the noble person is given over to dignity and absorption, what profound communion can there be? Should words be understood only in one way? Each saying has its own appropriate application."

9. When a filial son is about to sacrifice, he is anxious that all preparations should be made beforehand. When the time arrives, everything necessary should be complete, and he undertakes it with a mind that is empty within.[73]

10. The temple and its apartments having been repaired, the walls and roof having been put in order, and all things having been provided, husband and wife, after vigil and fasting, bathe their heads and persons and array themselves in full dress. As they come in with the things that they carry — grave, grave! rapt, rapt! — it is as if they could not bear them, as if they would lose them. Is not theirs the highest filial reverence? They set forth the stands with the victims on them, arrange all the ceremonies and music, and provide the officers for the various ministries who aid in sustaining and bringing in the things.

11. Thus he declares his intention and wish, through profound communion, to communicate with the spiritual intelligences, so that they might receive the offering, so that they might receive it! This is the intention of the filial child.

12. The filial son expresses the utmost earnestness, and still remains earnest; expresses the utmost trustworthiness, and still remains trustworthy; expresses the

---

69. Not that it was written by King Wen, but that it applies to him.

70. I.e., Confucius.

71. I.e., distantly connected to the one to whom the sacrifice is directed.

72. Suggesting self-consciousness and concern on the part of the one sacrificing lest he should make any mistake.

73. *Xu zhong* — the sense is that the mind is free of all preoccupation.

utmost reverence, and still remains reverent. He fulfills the rituals without excess or deficiency. In advancing, as in retiring, he is reverent — as if he were hearing his parents' commands, or as if they were directing him.

14. A filial son, cherishing a deep love, will have a harmonious air; having a harmonious air, he will have a look of pleasure; having a look of pleasure, his demeanor will be mild and compliant. A filial son will move as if he were carrying jade, as if he were bearing a vessel. Grave, grave! rapt, rapt! — as if he could not bear them, as if he would lose them. A severe gravity and austere manner are not proper to the service of parents: this is the way of the mature man.

20. The rites observed by all-under-Heaven bring about a return to the beginning. They reach spiritual beings, effect harmonious use [of all resources], promote rightness, and encourage humility. Because they bring about a return to the beginning, there is honor for the source. Because they reach spiritual beings, there is respect for superiors. Because they effect harmonious use of things, regulations are established [for the well-being of] the people. Because they promote rightness there is no conflict between high and low. Because they encourage humility occasions of strife are eliminated. Let these five things be united through the rites for the regulation of all-under-heaven, and, though there may be those who are extravagant and perverse and are not kept in order, they will be few.

[*Liji zhengyi* 47:1a–7b — adapted by IB from Legge, *Li ki*]

THE EVOLUTION OF RITES (*LIYUN*)

The Age of Grand Commonalty and the Rise of Dynastic Rule

The following passage from the *Record of Rites*, one of the most celebrated in Confucian literature, has been traditionally taken as representing Confucius' highest ideal in the social order, the age of Grand Commonalty (*Datong*), in which the world was shared by all the people (*tianxia wei gong*). This ideal has been of special importance in modern China, and the latter motto was often inscribed on public buildings and monuments, such as the tomb of the Nationalist leader Sun Yat-sen. Following the age of Grand Commonalty came the rise of dynastic rule.

This excerpt depicts a primordial ideal state ordered by the spontaneous workings of natural human sentiments in a shared cooperative community — a loving society such as had been identified with the beneficent rule of Emperor Yao in the first chapter of the *Classic of Documents* (*Shujing*). This stage is succeeded by a less perfect human order in which people pursue their own selfish interests and can only be restrained by leaders who civilize them by adopting institutions of government, ritual, and moral instruction. The heroic figures here are Confucian sage kings and worthy ministers who make the best of a less than ideal situation but who are also identified as founders and rulers of dynasties — in this respect not unlike the Han. Thus, responding to time and change, Confucian ideals are adjusted to realistic, historical circumstances.

Once Confucius was taking part in the winter sacrifice. After the ceremony was over, he went for a stroll along the top of the city gate and sighed mournfully. He sighed for the state of Lu.

His disciple Yan Yan [Ziyou], who was by his side, asked, "Why should the noble person sigh?"

Confucius replied, "The practice of the Great Way, the illustrious men of the Three Dynasties — these I shall never know in person. And yet they inspire my ambition! When the Great Way was practiced, the world was shared by all alike. The worthy and the able were promoted to office and men practiced good faith and lived in affection. Therefore they did not regard as parents only their own parents, or as sons only their own sons. The aged found a fitting close to their lives, the robust their proper employment; the young were provided with an upbringing, and the widow and widower, the orphaned and the sick, with proper care. Men had their tasks and women their hearths. They hated to see goods lying about in waste, yet they did not hoard them for themselves; they disliked the thought that their energies were not fully used, yet they used them not for private ends. Therefore all evil plotting was prevented and thieves and rebels did not arise, so that people could leave their outer gates unbolted. This was the age of Grand Commonalty.

"Now the Great Way has become hid and the world is the possession of private families. Each regards as parents only his own parents, as sons only his own sons; goods and labor are employed for selfish ends. Hereditary offices and titles are granted by ritual law while walls and moats must provide security. Ritual and rightness are used to regulate the relationship between ruler and subject, to ensure affection between father and son, peace between brothers and harmony between husband and wife, to set up social institutions, organize the farms and villages, honor the brave and wise, and bring merit to the individual. Therefore intrigue and plotting come about and men take up arms. Emperor Yu, Kings Tang, Wen, Wu, Cheng, and the Duke of Zhou achieved eminence for this reason: that all six rulers were constantly attentive to ritual, made manifest their rightness, and acted in complete faith. They exposed error, made humanity their law and humility their practice, showing the people wherein they should constantly abide. If there were any who did not abide by these principles, they were dismissed from their positions and regarded by the multitude as dangerous. This is the period of Lesser Prosperity."

[*Liji zhengyi* 21:1a–3a — BW]

THE "RECORD OF MUSIC" ("*YUEJI*")

Human Desires and the Rites

The Confucian rites recognize both the affective nature of man and the need for powerful human emotions to be directed into life-sustaining channels and life-ornamenting expression. The following passage describes how human desires arise in the natural course of things but need to be guided by civilized norms embodied in the rites.

What the ancient kings intended in instituting rites and music was not to satisfy fully the desires of the mouth and the stomach, the ears and the eyes, but to teach people to moderate their likes and dislikes and return to the proper human Way (*rendao*). Human beings are tranquil at birth; this is their nature as given by Heaven. As they are influenced by external things they become active; this is the nature as prompted by desire. With things arriving, and knowledge increasing, likes and dislikes take form in them. When these are not regulated from within, and knowledge misleads from without, they cannot return to themselves, and the principle of Heaven in them is extinguished.

Now the circumstances in which human beings are influenced by things are limitless. If their likes and dislikes are not regulated, then, as things come to them, human beings are transformed into things. For human beings to be transformed into things means that the principle of Heaven is extinguished and they are reduced to human desires, thus being given in their minds-and-hearts to deviance and deceit and in their conduct to dissoluteness and disorder. Then the strong coerce the weak; the many oppress the few; the knowing deceive the unknowing; the bold abuse the timid; the ill are not nurtured; the old and the young, the orphaned and the solitary are neglected: such is the way of great chaos. Therefore the ancient kings, in instituting the rites and music, regulated them according to human behavior. . . .

Rites were to regulate the people's minds; music was to harmonize the people's voices; government was to promote their performance; punishments were to protect them. When these four — rites, music, laws, and punishments — were made universal, the kingly Way was complete.

[*Liji zhengyi* 37:5a–6b — IB]

BAN GU: *DISCOURSES IN THE WHITE TIGER HALL*

The *Discourses in the White Tiger Hall* (*Bohu tong*), from which this excerpt is taken, is a record by the historian Ban Gu (32–92 C.E.) of discussions on the classics and on Confucian themes held at the court of the Han Emperor Zhang (r. 75–88 C.E.) in 79 C.E. It is typical of the process by which Confucianism became codified through state patronage of classical scholarship linked to public morality. The formula of the "Three Mainstays" (the relationship of ruler/minister, parent/child, husband/wife), though mentioned by Dong Zhongshu, is not found in the Confucian classics, and in giving primacy to state over family loyalties, it stands in some contrast to the Five Moral Relations enunciated in *Mencius* and the *Mean*, wherein the parent/child relation takes priority over ruler/minister. Presumably the Han imperial view of cosmic hierarchy, with the ruler in the center, is at work here.

In late imperial China official interpretations of the Three Mainstays (sometimes less literally rendered as the "Three Bonds," *San'gang*), tended to stress subordination of inferiors to superiors in a manner that buttressed hierarchical authority rather than emphasizing the complementarity of human relations. Yet in the *Discourses in the White Tiger Hall* there is a clear reaffirmation of the Confucian emphasis on complementarity, on the heavy moral responsibilities of the ruler, on the minister's duty to remonstrate with the ruler lest he go wrong (or leave his service if this is unavailing), and on the son's duty to remonstrate with his father, as well as the wife's to admonish her husband ("because they form one body and share glory and shame together").[74] The *Classic of Filiality* is often quoted to the same effect. Moreover, these positions would be reiterated in the Song by the leading Neo-Confucian thinker, Zhu Xi. Nevertheless, in modern times the view of the Three Mainstays as enforcing a traditional authoritarianism was so strong that twentieth-century critics of Confucianism often singled out the "Three Bonds" for special attack.

The Three Mainstays

Here *mainstays* (the main ropes of a net) and lesser *ties* (threads) represent the social network and moral fabric that sustain the human order.

What are the Three Mainstays? They are [the relations] of ruler and minister, parent and child, and husband and wife. The six [lesser] ties are those that link the father's brothers, elder and younger brothers, kinsmen, mother's brothers, teachers and elders, and friends. Thus the ruler is the mainstay of the minister, the parent the mainstay of the child, the husband the mainstay of the wife. . . .

What is meant by "mainstays" (*gang*) and "ties" (*ji*)? *Gang* means *zhang*, to extend or lengthen; *ji* means *li*, to order or regulate. The greater ones constitute the mainstays; the lesser ones the ties; thereby the higher and lower are linked and ordered, and the Way of humankind is regulated. All men cherish the instinct for the Five Constant Virtues and possess a loving mind-and-heart, which are developed through the network [of human moral relations], just as a net has mainstays and ties, spreading out into [the fine mesh of] a myriad minor ties.

Why is it that, though ruler and minister, parent and child, husband and wife are altogether six people, they are referred to as the "Three Mainstays"? [Because] the alternation of yin and yang constitutes one Way. The yang completes itself by obtaining the yin; the yin finds order in the yang; the firm and

---

74. *Bohu tong delun* 4:10a.

soft complement each other. Therefore, together, the six people make up Three Mainstays.

The Three Mainstays model themselves on [the triad] of Heaven, Earth, and the human. The Six Ties model themselves on the six directions [the four quarters of east, west, north, and south and above and below]. Ruler and minister model themselves on Heaven, as in the going and coming of the sun and moon, following the workings of Heaven. Parent and child model themselves on Earth, as with the revolving of the Five Phases mutually to produce one another. Husband and wife model themselves on the human, as with the combination of the Six Directions, and yin and yang, to effect human propagation. . . .

What do *jun* (prince, ruler) and *chen* (minister) mean? *Jun* means *qun*, "to gather," as the hearts of the people are attracted [to the ruler]. *Chen* means "solid and firm" (*jian*), as the minister strengthens his will to serve. What do *fu* (parent, father) and *zi* (child, son) mean? *Fu* means *ju*, "a square rule"; the parent teaches the child through [setting] rules and norms. Therefore the *Classic of Filiality* says: "If a father has a remonstrating son it will keep him from falling into wrongdoing." What do husband and wife mean? *Fu* (husband) means "to support," providing support [for his wife] in accordance with the Way. *Fu* (wife) means *fu* "to submit," to submit in accordance with the rites. . . . The commentary [on the *Yili*] says: "Husband and wife, though distinguishable, are united."[75]

[Ban Gu, *Bohu tong de lun*, 7:15a–16a; cf. Tjan, *Po-hu t'ung*, pp. 467, 559–561 — dB]

HAN VIEWS OF THE UNIVERSAL ORDER

THE CREATION OF THE UNIVERSE

FROM THE *HUAINANZI*

The following account of the creation is taken from the *Huainanzi*. Though mainly Daoist in conception, it was adopted by Han Confucians to round out their cosmology, as seen in the previous selection, from the *Discourses in the White Tiger Hall*. This same account of the creation was also taken over by the Japanese and prefaced to their native mythology in the *Nihongi*.

Before Heaven and Earth had taken form all was vague and amorphous. Therefore it was called the Great Beginning. The Great Beginning produced emptiness, and emptiness produced the universe. The universe produced material-

---

75. *Yili zhushu*, "Sang fu."

force,[76] which had limits. That which was clear and light drifted up to become Heaven, while that which was heavy and turbid solidified to become Earth. It was very easy for the pure, fine material to come together but extremely difficult for the heavy, turbid material to solidify. Therefore Heaven was completed first and Earth assumed shape after. The combined essences of Heaven and Earth became the yin and yang; the concentrated essences of the yin and yang became the four seasons; and the scattered essences of the four seasons became the myriad creatures of the world. After a long time the hot force of the accumulated yang produced fire, and the essence of the fire force became the sun; the cold force of the accumulated yin became water, and the essence of the water force became the moon. The essence of the excess force of the sun and moon became the stars, while Earth received water and soil. [3:1a]

When Heaven and Earth were joined in emptiness and all was unwrought simplicity, then, without having been created, things came into being. This was the Great Oneness. All things issued from this Oneness, but all became different, being divided into various species of fish, birds, and beasts. . . . Therefore while a thing moves it is called living, and when it dies it is said to be exhausted. All are creatures. They are not the uncreated creator of things, for the creator of things is not among things. If we examine the Great Beginning of antiquity we find that man was born out of nothing to assume form as something. Having form, he is governed by things. But he who can return to that from which he was born and become as though formless is called a "true man." The true man is one who has never become separated from the Great Oneness. [14:1a]

[From *Huainanzi* (SBCK) 3:1a, 14:1a — BW]

THE FIVE PHASES

Similar in concept to the yin-yang theory is that of the Five Phases or Agents (*wuxing*) of fire, water, earth, wood, and metal. The Five Phases were quantitative aspects of *qi*, which dominate or control processes in time or configurations in space in a fixed succession. For example, the Five Phases were thought to correlate spatially with the four directions plus the center and to correlate temporally with cyclical signs known as the ten heavenly stems and the twelve earthly branches,[77] as well as with the four seasons and twelve months.

---

76. The word *qi*, translated in our readings as "vital force" or "material-force," in order to emphasize its dynamic character, plays an important part in Chinese cosmological and metaphysical thought. At times it means the spirit or breath of life in living creatures, at other times the air or ether filling the sky and surrounding the universe. In some contexts it denotes the basic substance of all creation.

77. See "The Concept and Marking of Time," pp. 351–52.

A Table of Correspondences for the Five-Phases System

The Five Phases

Five Phases or Agents	Wood	Fire	Earth	Metal	Water
Correspondence					
Seasons	Spring	Summer		Autumn	Winter
Divine Rulers	Tai Hao	Yan Di	Yellow Emperor	Shao Hao	Zhuan Xu
Attendant Spirits	Gou Mang	Zhu Yong	Hou Tu	Ru Shou	Xuan Ming
Sacrifices	inner door	hearth	inner court	outer court	well
Animals	sheep	fowl	ox	dog	pig
Grains	wheat	beans	paniceled millet	hemp	millet
Organs	spleen	lungs	heart	liver	kidneys
Numbers	eight	seven	five	nine	six
Stems	*jia/yi*	*bing/ding*	*mou/ji*	*geng/xin*	*ren/gui*
Colors	green	red	yellow	white	black
Five Tones	*jue*	*zhi*	*gong*	*shang*	*yu*
Tastes	sour	bitter	sweet	acrid	salty
Smells	goatish	burning	fragrant	rank	rotten
Directions	East	South	center	West	North
Creatures	scaly	feathered	naked	hairy	shell-covered
Beasts of the directions	Green Dragon	Scarlet Bird	Yellow Dragon	White Tiger	Black Tortoise
Virtues	humaneness	wisdom	trust	rightness	ritual decorum
Planets	Jupiter	Mars	Saturn	Venus	Mercury
Officers	Minister of Agriculture	Minister of War	Minister of Works	Minister of Interior	Minister of Justice

Over time various theories were evolved to explain the cyclical relation among the Five Phases, the two most prominent among them being two major cycles of conquest and generation. According to the "conquest" series, fire is overcome by water, water by earth, earth by wood, and wood by metal, producing the series: fire — water — earth — wood — metal. The conquest cycle, with its correlated colors and dynasties, was the dominant court ideology of the Qin and Former Han dynasties until Wang Mang[78] replaced the Han with his

---

78. See pp. 314–15 and ch. 12.

Xin (or New) dynasty in 9 C.E. At this point the scholars Liu Xiang and Liu Xin, who were influential in laying an ideological foundation for Wang Mang's rule, proposed that the "generation" cycle of the Five Phases should replace the "conquest" cycle as the cosmological foundation for the imperial succession. The essentially Confucian idea of a "generation" cycle was based on the idea that the moral intention of Heaven was to prefer birth and nurturing and to dislike punishment and conquest. According to this "generation" cycle, wood produces fire, fire produces earth, earth produces metal, and metal produces water, yielding the series: wood — fire — earth — metal — water.

It is fairly obvious how the mode or element of wood should be assigned to the season of spring, associated with the color green and the direction east. In like manner fire is assigned to summer, its color red and direction south; metal to autumn, its color white and direction west; and water to winter, its color black and direction north. However, since there are Five Phases, proceeding, according to the "generation" cycle, in the order in which they produce or "beget" each other, but only four seasons, earth, with the color yellow, was commonly assigned to the transitions between seasons, aiding the other elements in their governance.

In another version, deriving from the *Huainanzi*, a fifth season, the "middle of summer" (*jixia*), was devised to fill out the correspondences.

The correspondences derived by analogy according to this system are innumerable. One influential version deriving from the *Record of Rites* (*Liji*) and the *Huainanzi*, illustrates how all facets of the divine and natural worlds could be classified according to these Five Phases. These correspondences are shown here in diagram form.

THE RECONSTRUCTION OF CHINESE HISTORY

Important also is the application of this theory to history and the succession of dynasties. As each season is ruled by a phase or agent, so, it was believed, each dynasty ruled by virtue of a phase that it honored by adopting the color of that phase in its vestments and flags, and by similar ritual observances. The First Emperor of the Qin, for instance, believing that his dynasty ruled by the virtue or power of water, adopted black as his official color and even changed the name of the Yellow River to "Water of Power" (Deshui).

Because the Qin had claimed to rule by the power of water, it was urged by some scholars early in the Han that the Han dynasty should adopt earth, with the color yellow, as its phase, to signify that the Han had conquered the Qin, since, according to the "conquest" theory, earth conquers water. According to tradition, Heaven had sent appropriate signs and omens to past dynasties, such as earthworms (earth), knife blades (metal), red birds (fire), etc., to indicate which element the dynasty should adopt. Thus the reported appearance during the time of Emperor Wen of a yellow dragon was cited by supporters of this theory as additional evidence. Though other interpretations were offered, the Former Han adopted this idea and honored earth as its patron phase.

Toward the end of the Former Han, however, there was, as we have noted above, a shift to the "generation" theory advanced by Liu Xiang and Liu Xin. Using this idea newly applied to the interpretation of history, Liu Xin and his school proceeded to reconstruct a history of past ages that would conform to the theory, assigning a ruling element to each ancient dynasty and inserting "intercalary reigns" of the element water where necessary to make it consistent. One of the innovations of this system was the assertion that the Han dynasty ruled not by the power of earth but by that of fire. A second innovation was the extension of history back beyond the legendary Yellow Emperor, who had been the starting point of Chinese history for earlier writers like Zou Yan (305?–240? B.C.E.) and Sima Qian (145?–86? B.C.E.).[79] It is difficult to say exactly when each step of this new theory was set forth or accepted, but it was substantially completed by the time of Wang Mang, who made use of it in justifying his assumption of the throne. The final system thus worked out as follows:

Phase	Ruler or Dynasty	Phase	Ruler or Dynasty
Wood	Fu Xi, Tai Hao	(Water)	Di Zhi
(Water)	Gong Gong [Intercalary or illegitimate reigns]	Fire	Emperor Yao
		Earth	Emperor Shun
Fire	The Fire Emperor, Shen Nong	Metal	Emperor Yu, Xia dynasty
Earth	The Yellow Emperor	Water	Shang dynasty
Metal	Shao Hao, Metallic Heaven	Wood	Zhou dynasty
Water	Zhuan Xu	(Water)	Qin dynasty
Wood	Di Ku	Fire	Han dynasty

Obviously the next dynasty to follow the Han should rule by the phase earth. It is not surprising, therefore, that, as Wang Mang rose to power, it was discovered that according to a certain ancient text, he was a descendant of the Yellow Emperor and thus was fitted to found a new dynasty under the phase of earth.

Though with the downfall of Wang Mang many of his innovations and the doubtful texts used to support them were swept away, this account of the ancient past of China continued to be accepted. It is recorded in the *History of the Former Han Dynasty* (*Hanshu*) by Ban Gu[80], who said he was following Liu Xin, and it was generally accepted in China as historical fact until recent times. Thus, using a preconceived philosophical doctrine of historical evolution, the

---

79. See ch. 12.
80. *Hanshu* 21B.

Chinese, with the best intentions and their customary love of order and system in all things, proceeded to rearrange and tailor their ancient legends and records to fit into a neat pattern that should be both immediately comprehensible in its past and infallibly predictable in its future development.

THE CONCEPT AND MARKING OF TIME

The Chinese conception of history, as we have seen above, was cyclical. This is only natural, since history is no more than a counterpart in the human sphere of the similar cycles of Heaven and Earth, those of the planets and the seasons. For this reason Chinese historians, unlike their Japanese, Jewish, or Christian counterparts — but like the Greek philosophers — never attempted to assign a temporal beginning or end to the history of the world or the state. Since time is itself a series of cycles based upon the motions of the planets, it may be conceived as extending indefinitely into the past and future for as long as the planets themselves exist.

Dates in Chinese history are customarily recorded in terms of the years of the reigning monarch. But by Han times there was already in use an additional system of cyclical signs for designating years, days, and hours. The origin of these signs, one a set of ten known as the "ten heavenly stems," another of twelve called the "twelve earthly branches," remains today a mystery, though it is apparent that they are very ancient. It is probable that the ten stems were originally designations for the ten days of the ancient ten-day week, the twelve branches designations for the months. These signs and their associations are listed below:

Five Phases	Ten Stems	Twelve Branches	Beasts	Directions	Hours
wood	jia	zi	rat	N	11 P.M.–1 A.M.
	yi	chou	ox	NNE	1–3
fire	bing	yin	tiger	ENE	3–5
	ding	mao	hare	E	5–7
earth	mou	chen	dragon	ESE	7–9
	ji	si	snake	SSE	9–11
metal	geng	wu	horse	S	11 A.M.–1 P.M.
	xin	wei	sheep	SSW	1–3
water	ren	shen	monkey	WSW	3–5
	gui	you	cock	W	5–7
		xu	dog	WNW	7–9
		hai	boar	NNW	9–11

Sometime during the Zhou dynasty these two sets of signs were combined to form a cycle of sixty binomial terms used to designate a cycle of sixty days.

Thus in the *Springs and Autumns of Mr. Lü (Lüshi chunqiu)* we read that the first two days of spring are *jia* and *yi* (A and B), which means that the first term in the binomial designations of the first two days of the sixty-day cycle beginning in spring will be these two signs, *jia* and *yi*. The season of spring being seventy-two days long, the designations for the first two days of summer will be *bing* and *ding* (C and D), the cycle of ten stems having revolved seven times plus two. In this way the ten stems that designate the first and second days of each season came to be associated with the Five Phases, which, as we have seen, correspond to the seasons.

Again, this cycle of sixty binomial terms (A-I, B-II, etc.) was used to designate cycles of sixty years. The twelve branches, as indicated above, were used to designate thirty-degree divisions of the circle of the horizon. Observing the position of Jupiter in the sky for each year of its twelve-year cycle, the Chinese then employed the sign designating that portion of the sky for the year and combined these with the ten stems to form designations for a sexagenary cycle. This they used to reckon dates independent of the reigns of emperors. Finally, the twelve branches were used to designate twelve two-hour periods making up the day.

At least by Han times these twelve branches had become associated with twelve beasts, as indicated in the table on p. 351. Because of this, the twelve hours of the day and the years of the sexagenary cycle were each associated with one of these beasts. This system of marking time was adopted by other countries in contact with China. Based on these various associations with the Five Phases and twelve beasts, a great deal of lore concerning lucky and unlucky times grew up about the various cycles. Yet, as we have seen, their basis is rational. They provided the Chinese with a convenient method of reckoning time as useful as Western time divisions, which replaced them only as a part of a thoroughgoing process of Westernization in the modern period.

Chapter 11

THE ECONOMIC ORDER

Han moralists and philosophers, far from ignoring the mundane problems of the human struggle for livelihood, placed great stress on the material needs of the people. The importance of economic thought in the Han derives both from this basic recognition of the "facts of life" and from the appearance in Han times of acute agrarian crises such as have plagued China down through the centuries. The solutions proposed to these crises, as well as the actual measures taken by the government in the Han, tended to set a pattern for later times.

The wars and uprisings that marked the fall of the Qin led to extreme suffering and poverty among the people. Needed to effect a recovery, as the Han quickly realized, was a period of peace and security with a minimum of government expenditure and interference to allow the people to recoup their livelihood. Gaozu, the founder of the Han, therefore relaxed the harsh laws of Qin, reduced the land tax, which under the Qin was said to have been as high as two-thirds of the total produce, and kept court expenditures at a minimum. This policy of frugality and laissez-faire was continued more or less consistently by his successors during the early Han, with the result that the population increased and the nation recovered with remarkable success.

The government did, however, attempt to take steps to control the amassing of large fortunes by industrialists and traders. Gaozu passed sumptuary laws against merchants who had grown rich during the troubled times accompanying the founding of the dynasty, laws designed to turn people from trade — a subsidiary or "branch" activity — back to the fundamental occupation of farming. Though these laws were later relaxed, it was still forbidden for traders or their descendants to hold public office, thus preventing their rise in the social scale. This struggle to keep people in the more productive but less remunerative farming activities from seeking their fortunes in trade and manufacturing continued throughout the Han. A rite was instituted (or, according to some scholars, revived from ancient times) in which the emperor personally performed a ceremonial act of plowing to encourage his people and emphasize the importance of agriculture.

EDICT OF EMPEROR WEN ON THE PRIMACY OF AGRICULTURE (163 B.C.E.)

During the time of Emperor Wen (r. 180–157 B.C.E.), the government granted commutation of penalties or honorary court ranks in exchange for gifts of grain, thus making grain a commodity of enhanced value. This policy met with considerable success, and by the time of Emperor Wu (r. 141–87 B.C.E.), we are told, the government granaries were filled, the government had sufficient funds, and the people lived in ease and plenty. The following states the concerns that gave rise to Wen's policy.

For the past several years there have been no good harvests, and our people have suffered the calamities of flood, drought, and pestilence. We are deeply grieved by this, but being ignorant and unenlightened, we have been unable to discover where the blame lies. We have considered whether our administration has been guilty of some error or our actions of some fault. Have we failed to follow the Way of Heaven or to obtain the benefits of Earth? Have we caused disharmony in human affairs or neglected the gods that they do not accept our offerings? What has brought on these things? Have the provisions for our officials been too lavish or have we indulged in too many unprofitable affairs? Why is the food of the people so scarce? When the fields are surveyed, they have not decreased, and when the people are counted they have not grown in number, so that the amount of land for each person is the same as before or even greater. And yet there is a drastic shortage of food. Where does the blame lie? Is it that too many people pursue secondary activities to the detriment of agriculture? Is it that too much grain is used to make wine or too many domestic animals are being raised? I have been unable to attain a proper balance between important and unimportant affairs. Let this matter be debated by the chancellor, the nobles, the high officials, and learned doctors. Let all exhaust their efforts and ponder deeply whether there is some way to aid the people. Let nothing be concealed from us!

[From *Hanshu* (BNB) 4:15a–b — BW]

CHAO CUO: MEMORIAL ON THE ENCOURAGEMENT OF AGRICULTURE

The following memorial, by the eminent Han statesman Chao Cuo, being dated 178 B.C.E., cannot be a reply to the emperor's plea above, but it was one of a number of suggestions designed to alleviate the conditions of which he complains. The emperor approved Chao's suggestion, with the result that grain became plentiful and the government granaries were filled.

The reason people never suffered from cold or famine under the rule of the sage kings was not that these kings were capable of plowing to provide food or spinning to make clothes for them. It was that they opened up for the people the way to wealth. Therefore although emperors Yao and Yu encountered nine years of flood and King Tang seven years of drought, there were no derelicts or starving within the kingdom, because provisions had been stored up in plenty and all precaution taken beforehand.

Now all within the seas are united. The plenitude of land and people is not inferior to that of Tang and Yu, and in addition we have not suffered from natural calamities of flood or drought for several years. Why then are the stores of supplies so inferior? Because the land has benefits that have been overlooked and the people have untapped energies. There is still land suitable for growing grain that has not been brought under cultivation, resources of hills and lakes that have not been exploited, and vagrants who have not yet returned to agricultural pursuits. When the people are in poverty, then crime and evil-doing are born. Poverty is bred of insufficiency that is caused by lack of agriculture. If men do not farm, they will not be tied to the land; and if they are not tied to the land, they will desert their villages, neglect their families, and become like birds and beasts. Then although there be high walls and deep moats, strict laws and severe punishments, they still cannot be held in check.

When one is cold he does not demand the most comfortable and warmest garments; when one is starving he does not wait for the tastiest morsels. When a man is plagued by hunger and cold he has no regard for modesty or shame. It is the nature of man that if he does not eat twice a day he will starve, and if in the course of a year he cuts himself no new clothes he will freeze. When the belly is famished and gets no food, when the skin is chilled and has no clothing to cover it, then even the most compassionate father cannot provide for his own child. How then can the ruler keep the allegiance of his people? An enlightened ruler, realizing this, will encourage his people in agriculture and sericulture, lighten the poll tax and other levies, increase his store of supplies and fill his granaries in preparation for flood and drought. Thereby he can keep and care for his people. The people may then be led by the ruler, for they will follow after profit in any direction like water flowing downward.

Now pearls, jewels, gold, and silver can neither allay hunger nor keep out the cold, and yet the people all hold them dear because these are things used by the ruler. They are light and easy to store, and one who holds them in his grasp may roam the world and never fear hunger or cold. They cause ministers lightly to turn their backs upon their lords and the people easily to leave their villages; they provide an incentive for thieves and a light form of wealth for fugitives.

Grains and fibers, on the other hand, are produced from the land, nurtured through the seasons, and harvested with labor; they cannot be gotten in a day. Several measures of grain or cloth are too heavy for an average man to carry and so provide no reward for crime or evil. Yet if people go without them for one day they will face hunger and cold. Therefore an enlightened ruler esteems the five grains and despises gold and jewels.

At present in a farming family of five not fewer than two are required to perform labor service [for the state], while those who are left to work the farm are given no more than one hundred *mu* of land, the yield of which is not over one hundred *piculs*. . . . No matter how diligently they work nor what hardships they suffer, they still must face the calamities of flood and drought, emergency government measures, inordinate tax levies, and taxes collected out of season. Orders issued in the morning are changed before nightfall. Faced with such levies, the people must sell what they have at half price in order to pay, and those who have nothing must take money offered at 100 percent interest. Thus they are forced to sell their fields and houses, vend their children and grandchildren, to pay their debts.

Among the traders and merchants, on the other hand, the larger ones hoard goods and exact 100 percent profit, while the smaller ones sit lined up in the markets selling their wares. Those who deal in luxury goods daily disport themselves in the cities and market towns; taking advantage of the ruler's wants, they are able to sell at double price. Thus though their men neither plow nor weed, though their women neither tend silkworms nor spin, yet their clothes are brightly patterned and colored, and they eat only choice grain and meat. They have none of the hardships of the farmer, yet their grain is ten to one hundredfold. With their wealth they may consort with nobles, and their power exceeds the authority of government officials. They use their profits to overthrow others. Over a thousand miles they wander at ease, their caps and cart covers filling the roads. They ride in fine carriages and drive fat horses, tread in silken shoes and trail white silk behind them. Thus it is that merchants encroach upon the farmers, and the farmers are driven from their homes and become vagrants.

At present, although the laws degrade the merchants, the merchants have become wealthy and honored, and although they honor the farmers, the farmers have grown poor and lowly. Thus what common practice honors the ruler degrades, and what the officials scorn the law exalts. With ruler and ruled thus at variance and their desires in conflict, it is impossible to hope that the nation will become rich and the law be upheld.

Under the present circumstances there is nothing more urgently needed than to make the people devote themselves to agriculture. To accomplish this one must enhance the value of grain. This may be done by making it possible for the people to use grain to obtain rewards and avoid punishments. If an order is sent out that all who send grain to the government shall obtain honorary rank or pardon from crimes, then wealthy men will acquire rank, the farmers will have money, and grain will circulate freely. If men can afford to present grain in exchange for ranks, they must have a surplus. If this surplus is acquired for the use of the ruler, then the poll tax on the poor can be reduced. This is what is known as reducing the surplus to supply the deficiency. . . . Ranks are something that the ruler may dispense at will: he has only to speak and there is no end to them. Grain is something grown on the land by the people and its supply is continuous. All men greatly desire to obtain high ranks and avoid penalties. If all are allowed to present grain for supplying the frontiers and thereby obtain rank or commutation of penalties, then in no more than three years there will be plenty of grain for the border areas.

[From *Hanshu* (BNB) 24A:9b–13a — BW]

DONG ZHONGSHU: MEMORIAL ON LAND REFORM

In the latter years of his life the famous Confucian Dong Zhongshu[1] submitted a memorial to Emperor Wu advising limitation of land and slave ownership and other measures to relieve the rapidly developing agrarian crisis. Because of opposition from wealthy families and powerful officials, his suggestions and similar ones made later were never put into effect. It is noteworthy that Dong, while proclaiming the ancient "well-field" system of equal ownership as the ideal, did not go so far as to advocate its restoration. Not until Wang Mang came to power was this drastic step attempted to return to the ideal enshrined in Confucian tradition.

In ancient times the people were not taxed over one-tenth of their produce, a demand that they could easily meet. They were required to give no more than three days of labor a year, which they could easily spare. The people had wealth enough to take care of the aged and look after their parents, serve their superiors and pay their taxes, and support their wives and loved ones. Therefore they took delight in obeying their rulers.

But the Qin changed all this. It used the methods of Shang Yang (Legalism), altered the imperial institutions, did away with the well-field system, and allowed the people to buy and sell land. The rich bought up great connecting tracts of ground, and the poor were left without enough land to stick the point

---

1. See ch. 10.

of an awl into. In addition, the rich had sole control of the resources of rivers and lakes and the riches of hills and forests. Their profligacy overstepped all restrictions and they outdid each other in extravagance. In the cities they commanded as much respect as the rulers, and in the villages their wealth equaled that of the nobles. How could the common people escape oppression? . . . In addition, labor services were increased until they were thirty times those of ancient days, while taxes on fields and population and profits from salt and iron increased to twenty times those of old. Those who worked the land of the rich had to give half their crops in rent. Therefore the poor were forced to wear clothing fit only for cattle and horses and eat the food of dogs and swine. On top of this, harsh and greedy officials punished and executed them indiscriminately until the people, grieved and deprived of their livelihood, fled to the hills or turned to a life of banditry. Condemned men half filled the roads, and tens of thousands were imprisoned each year.

Since the Han began it has followed the ways of the Qin without change. Although it would be difficult to restore at once the ancient well-field system, it is proper that present usage be brought somewhat closer to the old ways. Ownership of land should be limited so that those who do not have enough may be relieved and the road to unlimited encroachment blocked. The rights to salt and iron should revert to the people. Slavery and the right to execute servants on one's own authority should be abolished. Poll taxes and other levies should be reduced and labor services lightened so that the people will be less pressed. Only then can they be well governed.

[From *Hanshu* (*BNB*) 24A:14b–15b — BW]

STATE CONTROL OF COMMERCE
AND INDUSTRY

Ban Gu, principal author of the *History of the Former Han Dynasty*, saw the reign of Emperor Wu as the turning point from prosperity to eventual ruin of the dynasty. Though economic life recovered considerably after Wu's reign, the historian designated this period as the beginning of policies and trends that led to the downfall of the Han.

The non-Chinese tribes bordering China on the north and west had constituted a constant menace to the empire, frequently invading and pillaging as far as the capital itself. Emperor Wu set out upon a series of military conquests that extended Chinese hegemony far out to the northwest, placing the empire for the first time in close contact with the states of Central and Western Asia and indirectly with Rome. Following these conquests, he undertook vast programs of colonization of the newly acquired areas, as well as extensive canal and road building, repairing of dikes, and other government projects. Famous and glorious as these military conquests and other undertakings were, they may well have undermined the economic health of the nation. Because of the frugality of his predecessors and the prosperity of the empire, Wu was able to embark upon his grandiose plans. But he soon found it necessary to secure new revenues to sustain them.

The means that he took to acquire the needed funds were not really in the nature of a state-planned economy to benefit the nation as a whole, though this was claimed for them; they were merely attempts to fill the imperial coffers at any cost. He continued the campaign begun by his predecessors to deprive the remaining feudal lords of their power and wealth, penalizing them for all manner of offenses and confiscating their wealth in land. He sold honorary titles, military ranks, and government offices in such profusion that the official hierarchy was reduced to chaos. He set about to crush individual traders and industrialists and transfer their lucrative enterprises to government control. High taxes were levied upon the rich and a system of spies set up so that at any suspicion of attempted evasion, their entire estates were confiscated.

Perhaps most famous and widely discussed of his fiscal measures was the setting up of government monopolies in iron, salt, liquor, and coinage of money, as well as offices to engage in government trading. The iron and salt industries had formerly been the source of great wealth to private individuals or feudal lords who controlled them. By making them government monopolies the emperor sought to divert these profits to the imperial treasury. Moreover, he set up, under a bureau of "Equalization and Standardization," a system of government marketing offices that bought up goods at low prices or collected taxes in produce and sold them in other areas or, at other times, at an advantageous price. Though it was claimed that this measure, like the salt and iron monopolies, was designed to protect the people from exploitation by unscrupulous private traders, its main function was to secure government revenues. These measures were successful in supplying the government treasuries, but along with the forced conscription and heavy labor services imposed upon the people, they reduced the nation to poverty and brought extreme popular resentment.

Emperor Wu, though professing support of Confucian ideals, was, in fact, by establishing such government monopolies and speculation, using traditional Legalist methods such as the Qin had followed. Moreover, to ensure the success of his ventures, he appointed competent industrialists and financial experts to administer the government monopolies, pursuing Legalist policies.

In 81 B.C.E., shortly after the death of Emperor Wu, a debate was called at court between these Legalist officials, headed by the Lord Grand Secretary, and a group of Confucian literati representing opinions of the opposition. A record of this famous debate, the *Debate on Salt and Iron (Yantie lun)*, shows clearly the struggle of the Confucian scholars to reverse the policies of the Legalists installed by Emperor Wu.

THE *DEBATE ON SALT AND IRON*

In this debate the government argued that its fiscal policies were necessary to maintain defensive warfare against the Xiongnu tribes (probably Huns) who threatened the empire; that the government by its disinterested control of vital industries was protecting the people from private exploitation; and, finally, that the trade opened up by the western expansion had brought to the empire heretofore unknown goods and luxuries such as horses, camels, furs, rugs, precious stones, exotic fruits, and so on.

To these arguments the Confucian literati stolidly replied that the Chinese had no business in the barbarian lands of Central Asia, that China should make peace with its neighbors and be content to remain safely within its traditional boundaries. In reply to the second argument, they pointed to the fact that corruption and maladministration in the government system of monopolies were forcing the people to use inferior products or at times to do without them entirely. The government, they claimed, was in actuality entering into competition with the people (private enterprise) in trade, an area outside its proper sphere of activity. On the question of increased foreign trade, they noted that the furs, precious stones, and exotic fruits bought with silk produced at great labor by the common people found their way only to the houses of the rich and noble. The debate was a lively affair, the government constantly taunting the scholars with their poverty, which, though claimed as evidence of their frugality and moral probity, was alleged by their critics to be proof of their incompetence in worldly affairs. The scholars replied that the government's pursuit of increased revenue was not, as claimed, serving the public interest but instead set a bad example of profiting at the people's expense, thereby undermining public morality by putting "profit" ahead of what was right. Many of these arguments were couched in terms of the doctrines of Mencius on governing through humaneness and rightness, maintaining the well-field system of equal landholding, and providing schools to educate the people.

The literati had some immediate success, but the government monopolies were not all abolished because of the need for revenue, and many of the same economic problems persisted.

In the sixth year of the era Shiyuan [81 B.C.E.], an imperial edict was issued directing the chancellor and the imperial secretaries to confer with the worthies and literati who had been recommended to the government and to inquire into the grievances and hardships of the people.

The literati responded: We have heard that the way to govern men is to prevent evil and error at their source, to broaden the beginnings of morality, to discourage secondary occupations, and open the way for the exercise of humaneness and rightness. Never should material profit appear as a motive of government. Only then can moral instruction succeed and the customs of the people be reformed. But now in the provinces the salt, iron, and liquor monopolies, and the system of equitable marketing have been established to compete with the people for profit, dispelling rustic generosity and teaching the people greed. Therefore those who pursue primary occupations [farming] have grown few and those following secondary occupations [trading] numerous. As artifice increases, basic simplicity declines; and as the secondary occupations flourish, those that are primary suffer. When the secondary is practiced the people grow decadent, but when the primary is practiced they are simple and sincere. When the people are sincere then there will be sufficient wealth and goods, but when they become extravagant then famine and cold will follow. We recommend that the salt, iron, and liquor monopolies and the system of equitable marketing be abolished so that primary pursuits may be advanced and secondary ones suppressed. This will have the advantage of increasing the profitableness of agriculture.

His Lordship [the Imperial Secretary Sang Hongyang] replied: The Xiongnu have frequently revolted against our sovereignty and pillaged our borders. If we are to defend ourselves, then it means the hardships of war for the soldiers of China, but if we do not defend ourselves properly, then their incursions cannot be stopped. The former emperor [Wu] took pity upon the people of the border areas who for so long had suffered disaster and hardship and had been carried off as captives. Therefore he set up defense stations, established a system of warning beacons, and garrisoned the outlying areas to ensure their protection. But the resources of these areas were insufficient, and so he established the salt, iron, and liquor monopolies and the system of equitable marketing in order to raise more funds for expenditures at the borders. Now our critics, who desire that these measures be abolished, would empty the treasuries and deplete the funds used for defense. They would have the men who are defending our passes and patrolling our walls suffer hunger and cold. How else can we provide for them? Abolition of these measures is not expedient! [sec. 1, 1:1a–2a]

His Lordship stated: In former times the peers residing in the provinces sent in their respective products as tribute, but there was much confusion and trouble in transporting them and the goods were often of such poor quality that they were not worth the cost of transportation. For this reason transportation offices have been set up in each district to handle delivery and shipping and to facilitate the presentation of tribute from outlying areas. Therefore the system is called "equitable marketing." Warehouses have been opened in the capital for the storing of goods, buying when prices are low and selling when they are high. Thereby the government suffers no loss and the merchants cannot speculate for profit. Therefore this is called the "balanced level" [stabilization]. With the balanced level the people are protected from unemployment, and with equitable marketing the burden of labor service is equalized. Thus these measures are designed to ensure an equal distribution of goods and to benefit the people and are not intended to open the way to profit or provide the people with a ladder to crime.

The literati replied: In ancient times taxes and levies took from the people what they were skilled in producing and did not demand what they were poor at. Thus the husbandmen sent in their harvests and the weaving women their goods. Nowadays the government disregards what people have and requires of them what they have not, so that they are forced to sell their goods at a cheap price in order to meet the demands from above. . . . The farmers suffer double hardships and the weaving women are taxed twice. We have not seen that this kind of marketing is "equitable." The government officials go about recklessly opening closed doors and buying everything at will so they can corner all the goods. With goods cornered prices soar, and when prices soar the merchants make their own deals for profit. The officials wink at powerful racketeers, and the rich merchants hoard commodities and wait for an emergency. With slick merchants and corrupt officials buying cheap and selling dear we have not seen that your level is "balanced." The system of equitable marketing of ancient times was designed to equalize the burden of labor upon the people and facilitate the transporting of tribute. It did not mean dealing in all kinds of commodities for the sake of profit. [sec. 1:5a–b]

The Literati Attack Legalist Philosophy

The literati spoke: He who is good with a chisel can shape a round hole without difficulty; he who is good at laying foundations can build to a great height without danger of collapse. The statesman Yi Yin made the ways of Yao and Shun the foundation of the Yin dynasty, and its heirs succeeded to the throne for a hundred generations without break. But Shang Yang made heavy penalties and harsh laws the foundation of the Qin state and with the Second Emperor it was destroyed. Not satisfied with the severity of the laws, he instituted the system of mutual responsibility, made it a crime to criticize the government, and increased corporal punishments until the people were so terrified they did not know where to put their hands and feet. Not content with the manifold taxes and levies, he prohibited the people from using the resources of forests and rivers and made a hundredfold profit on the storage of commodities, while the people were given no chance to voice the slightest objection. Such worship of profit and slight of what is right, such exaltation of power and achievement, lent, it is true, to expansion of land and acquisition of territory. Yet it was like pouring more water upon people who are already suffering from flood and only increasing their distress. You see how Shang Yang opened the way to imperial rule for the Qin, but you fail to see how he also opened for the Qin the road to ruin! [sec. 7, 2:2b–3a]

Confucian Literati Ridiculed

His Excellency spoke: . . . Now we have with us over sixty worthy men and literati who cherish the ways of the Six Confucian Arts, fleet in thought and exhaustive in argument. It is proper, gentlemen, that you should pour forth your light and dispel our ignorance. And yet you put all your faith in the past and turn your backs upon the present, tell us of antiquity and give no thought to the state of the times. Perhaps we are not capable of recognizing true scholars. Yet do you really presume with your fancy phrases and attacks upon men of ability to pervert the truth in this manner? [sec. 10, 2:10a–b]

See them [the Confucians] now present us with nothingness and consider it substance, with emptiness and call it plenty! In their coarse gowns and worn shoes they walk gravely along, sunk in meditation as though they had lost something. These are not men who can do great deeds and win fame. They do not even rise above the vulgar masses.

> [From *Yantie lun*, sec. 1, 1:1a–5b; sec. 7, 2:2b–3a; sec. 10, 2:10a–b;
> sec. 19, 4:10b — BW]

THE REFORMS OF WANG MANG

Though a brief period of prosperity followed the relaxation of Emperor Wu's fiscal policies, the economic health of the nation gradually worsened. Corruption spread through the government from top to bottom. In spite of frequent recommendations for the limitation of land and slave ownership, land and wealth became concentrated in the hands of large official or merchant families. As the peasants were deprived of their land or lost it because of natural disasters, they went into slavery or formed bands of robbers. Government-maintained dikes and waterworks fell into disrepair, increasing the menace of flood and drought. It was when conditions had reached a critical stage that Wang Mang managed to seize power and attempted to remedy the situation by a series of sweeping reforms.

WANG MANG: EDICT ON LAND REFORM

In 9 C.E. Wang Mang ordered the establishment of an equal landholding system based on the ancient "well-field" ideal. This involved the nationalization of all land, abolition of private landholding and prohibition of the sale of land or slaves. The attempt proved a failure and was repealed three years later. Subsequent proposals for solution of the land problem, which was a chronic difficulty in later dynasties, tended to follow along the lines suggested by these Han reformers, i.e., either simple limitation on landholding or outright nationalization and redistribution. Note how Wang Mang's edict follows the wording of Dong Zhongshu's memorial above.

The ancients set up cottages and wells with eight families to a "well-unit" (900 *mu*). One husband and wife cultivated one hundred *mu* of land, remitting one-tenth of the produce as tax. Thus the state enjoyed plenty, the people were rich, and the sound of hymns of praise arose in the land. This was the way of Yao and Shun, and it was followed and continued by the Three Dynasties. But the Qin was without principle and increased the levies and taxes for its own use, exhausting the strength of the people with its inordinate desires. It destroyed the institutions of the sages and abolished the well-field system. Consequently there arose those who encroached upon the lands of the farmers, avaricious and vile men, the strongest of them measuring their fields in the thousands, while the weak were left without enough land to stick the point of an awl into. In addition they set up markets for slaves where people were penned up like cattle and horses. In handling common people and servants they usurped the right to punish even by death. Villainous and tyrannical men, with profit as their sole concern, went so far as to kidnap and sell men and their wives and children, profaning the will of Heaven, destroying human relationships, and perverting the principle that man is the noblest creation of Heaven and Earth. . . .

The House of Han lightened the tax on land to one-thirtieth of the produce. However, there were taxes for commutation of military service, which even the aged and ill had to pay. In addition, the powerful and rich families oppressed the people, allotting lands for cultivation to sharecroppers and plundering them by high rents for borrowed lands. Thus, though in name the tax was one-thirtieth, actually it amounted to one-half. Though father and son, husband and wife, year in and year out plowed and weeded, yet the produce left to them was not enough to support life. Therefore the rich, whose very horses and dogs had a surplus of meal and grain, grew arrogant and perpetrated evil deeds, while the poor, without even the dregs of grain to satisfy themselves with, were reduced to despair and turned to a life of crime. Both sank into wickedness, and punishments had to be used and could not be set aside.

Formerly, when I occupied the position of regent, it was my intention to nationalize all land and apportion it into "well-units" according to the population. At that time the empire enjoyed the portentous blessing of the double-headed grain, but because of the unfortunate occurrence of rebellions and banditry, I was forced temporarily to abandon my plans.

Now at this time let the term be altered and the land throughout the empire be designated "king's fields" and slaves be called "private retainers." Neither land nor slaves are to be bought or sold. Those families whose adult males do not number eight, but whose fields amount to more than one "well-unit," shall divide the surplus lands among their near relatives of the nine generations and the people of their townships and boroughs. Thus those who are without lands shall justly receive them according to this system. Anyone who shall dare to criticize the well-field system of the sages, or seek in defiance of the law to delude the populace, shall be cast out beyond the four borders to face demons and evil spirits.

[From *Hanshu* (BNB) 99B:9a–10a — BW]

Some modern historians have attempted to see in Wang's reforms a sincere attempt to alleviate the sufferings of the people, while others regard them to be, like Emperor Wu's policies, merely plans for securing increased government revenues. Whatever Wang's real motivation, his reforms did not succeed.

Wang Mang revived all the monopolies of Emperor Wu on coinage, salt, iron, liquor, and natural resources; he also restored the system of government marketing. As formerly, this had the same effect: it forced up the prices of necessary commodities, lowered the quality, deprived many people of their livelihood, and imposed an additional tax burden upon the population. In addition he imposed taxes on artisans and professional men, forced the officials to take reductions in salary during bad years, and demanded voluntary contributions of four-fifths of their salary to support military expenses made necessary by a foreign policy that put him at war with the border tribes. In a series of rapid changes, he issued a profusion of new coins, withdrew old ones from circulation, and threw the currency into such chaos that people lost all confidence in it and secretly traded with old Han money. So great was the number of persons convicted of violating this rash of new laws and reforms that it soon became impossible to carry out sentences upon them all and efforts at punishment of offenders had to be abandoned.

The furious activity of Wang's brief reign served to antagonize all classes of society, and his purported attempts to revive ancient practices cost him the backing of the Confucian bureaucracy that had earlier supported him. Without the confidence of his officials, his measures foundered on the administrative level because of noncooperation and corruption. He tried vainly to carry on alone, working day and night to handle all administrative matters personally. But as Ban Gu relates in the *Hanshu*, nothing availed to allay the disaffection:

> The people could not turn a hand without violating some prohibition.
> . . . The rich had no means to protect themselves and the poor no way
> to stay alive. They rose up and became thieves and bandits, infesting the
> hills and marshes, and the officials, being unable to seize them, contrived
> on the contrary to hide their presence so that they grew more prevalent
> day by day. . . . Famine and pestilence raged and people ate each other
> so that before Wang Mang was finally punished half the population of
> the empire had perished. . . . [In 25 c.e.] the founder of the Eastern Han
> received the Mandate of Heaven and, washing away their vexations and
> hardships, together with all people of the empire made a "new begin-
> ning."[2]

---

2. *Hanshu* 24B:25a–b. The Eastern Han is also known as the Latter Han.

This "new beginning" carried the Han dynasty until its final fall in 220 C.E. Decimation of the population and the thorough shaking up of the social order accompanying the fall of Wang Mang served to alleviate the economic crisis of the empire and give it a new lease on life. The period that followed was one of relative peace and cultural attainment. Yet the same economic problems that marked the history of the Former Han repeated themselves with ineluctable persistence. Court intrigue, official corruption, the concentration of land in the hands of wealthy families, and the displacement of the people from their fields, which turned them to banditry — all of this bred warlordism and antidynastic revolution. The reign of Wang Mang, which itself involved a prolongation and aggravation of the agrarian crisis of the Former Han, had precipitated a peasant revolt known as the Red Eyebrows, originating in the eastern province of Shandong. The Latter Han fell victim to a similar revolt, which began, under Daoist influence, in Sichuan, led by a group known as the Yellow Turbans. This cycle of agrarian crisis and decay of the central government, climaxed by peasant revolts originating in the hinterland, formed a recurring pattern in later Chinese history.

Chapter 12

THE GREAT HAN HISTORIANS

The intellectual and literary glory of the Han found its highest expression in two great histories of the period, the *Records of the Grand Historian (Shiji)* and the *History of the Former Han (Hanshu)*. Few works outside the classics themselves have been so much admired, studied, and often in part committed to memory by the Chinese. They set the pattern for all later Chinese histories, establishing a precedent that was responsible for giving to the Chinese the most complete and unbroken record of their past possessed by any people.

From very early times the Chinese seem to have possessed an extraordinary love and respect for history. According to tradition, even the earliest dynasties had their official historians, who were closely associated with astronomical affairs and divination. They were also responsible for acting as mentors to the rulers, instructing them in the lessons of the past, and recording their deeds for the judgment of posterity. Confucianism, with its humanistic emphasis, did much to encourage and develop this sense of history and feeling for the past. Two of the five Confucian Classics, the *Classic of Documents* and the *Spring and Autumn Annals*, traditionally believed to have been compiled and edited by Confucius, are historical works, and the appeal to past example has always been among the principle techniques of Confucian instruction and argumentation.

The *History of the Former Han Dynasty* says of these two historical classics: "The *Classic of Documents* broadens one's information and is the practice of wisdom; the *Spring and Autumn Annals* passes moral judgments on events and is the symbol of trustworthiness."[1]

The function of history, as seen in this statement, is twofold: to impart tradition and to provide edifying moral examples as embodied in the classics. These two traditions, one recording the words and deeds of history, the other illustrating moral principles through historical incidents, run through all Chinese historiography. In practice, the former tradition has dominated. The common method of the Chinese historian has been to transmit verbatim as nearly as possible what his sources tell him, adding only such background and connecting narrative as may be necessary. For example, the historian does not tell us that the emperor issued an edict to such and such an effect but reproduces the edict whole or in part so that we may read what he said for ourselves. Since the Chinese historian was often working in an official capacity, he had access to government files of memorials, edicts, court decisions, and other papers that made such a procedure possible. His own job, then, became one of selecting the most pertinent documents and arranging them in a way best calculated to demonstrate the cause and effect of events. If in addition he wished to inject his own personal opinion, he usually marked it clearly by some conventional literary device so that the reader could readily distinguish it.

The tradition of the *Spring and Autumn Annals*, the didactic function of history, was by no means forgotten. Only a sage might dare actually to record moral judgments in his writing, as Confucius was supposed to have done in the *Spring and Autumn Annals*. But all literate people were expected to study the histories of the past carefully and thoughtfully to deduce for themselves the moral lessons embodied there, to descry the pattern hidden beneath the succession of recorded events. For, like all the rest of creation, history was thought to manifest an underlying order and process. Han scholars, influenced by yin-yang and Five Phases theories, conceived of history as a cyclical succession of eras proceeding in a fixed order. Not only this succession but all of history was a manifestation of the universal process of birth, growth, decay, and rebirth, constantly coming to realization in the course of human events. Thus, for the Confucian scholar, the proper study of humankind is human life as revealed in the pages of history.

THE RECORDS OF THE GRAND HISTORIAN

During the Zhou, numerous chronicles and works of history were compiled by the various states and schools of philosophy. But not until the Han, when the Chinese acquired a new sense of cultural unity, was there any evidence of an

---

1. *Hanshu* 30:12b.

attempt to produce a comprehensive history of the entire past. The *Records of the Grand Historian* (*Shiji*) was begun by Sima Tan (d. 110 B.C.E.), Grand Historian under Emperor Wu, and carried on and brought to completion by his son, Sima Qian (145?–86? B.C.E.), who succeeded to his father's position. Comprising 130 chapters, it covers the history of the Chinese people from the Yellow Emperor to the time of the historians.

Sima Qian divided his material into five sections: "Basic Annals," "Chronological Tables," "Treatises," "Hereditary Houses," and "Memoirs." This arrangement, with various modifications, has been followed by almost all later official historians. In later histories the section called "Basic Annals" might better be referred to as "Imperial Annals," since it deals only with acts of the officially reigning emperors. Sima Qian, however, did not so confine himself but included here the account of Xiang Yu, who, though not officially emperor, in actuality ruled the country for a time. The "Chronological Tables" needs little explanation, being tables of dates for important events. The "Treatises," one of the most valuable parts of the work, comprises essays devoted to the history and description of important institutional matters and topical subjects. Below are listed the eight Treatises of the *Shiji* together with those of the *Hanshu* that were based upon *Shiji* material.

Shiji Treatises	*Hanshu Treatises*
Rites	The Calendar
Music	Rites and Music
The Pitch Pipes	Punishments and Laws
The Calendar	Food and Money (Economics)
Astronomy	State Sacrifices
Sacrifices of Feng and Shan[2]	Astronomy
The Yellow River and Canals	Five Phases (Portents)
Balance of Commerce (Economics)	Geography
	Land Drainage
	Literature

"Hereditary Houses," being largely accounts of feudal families, was not usually included after the abolition of the enfeoffment system. The "Memoirs" section was generally devoted to the lives of famous persons — military leaders, politicians, philosophers, and so on. Some chapters deal with particular groups such as famous assassins, upright officials, tyrannical officials, wandering knights, imperial favorites, and merchants. Others treat non-Chinese lands and people,

---

2. The Feng and Shan were sacrifices of the greatest solemnity, performed by the emperor at the sacred Mount Tai and addressed to Heaven and Earth respectively.

including those of Korea, southeast China, and Ferghana. The concluding chapter is the biography of the historians themselves.

SIMA QIAN: THE SACRED DUTY OF THE HISTORIAN

The following excerpt from the autobiography of Sima Qian relates the words of Sima Tan to his son as he lay dying.

The Grand Historian [Sima Tan] grasped my hand and said, weeping, "Our ancestors were Grand Historians for the House of Zhou. From the most ancient times they were eminent and renowned when in the days of Yu and Xia they were in charge of astronomical affairs. In later ages our family declined. Will this tradition end with me? If you in turn become Grand Historian, you must continue the work of our ancestors. . . . When you become Grand Historian, you must not forget what I have desired to expound and write. Now, filial piety begins with the serving of your parents; next, you must serve your sovereign; and, finally, you must make something of yourself, that your name may go down through the ages to the glory of your father and mother. This is the most important part of filial piety. Everyone praises the Duke of Zhou, saying that he was able to expound in word and song the virtues of King Wen and King Wu, publishing abroad the odes of Zhou and Shao; he set forth the thoughts and ideals of Taiwang and Wang Ji, extending his words back to King Liu and paying honor to Hou Ji [ancestors of the Zhou dynasty]. After the reigns of Yu and Li the way of the ancient kings fell into disuse and rites and music declined. Confucius revived the old ways and restored what had been abandoned, expounding the *Odes* and *Documents* and making the *Spring and Autumn Annals*. From that time until today men of learning have taken these as their models. It has now been over four hundred years since the capture of the unicorn [481 B.C.E.]. The various feudal states have merged together, and the old records and chronicles have become scattered and lost. Now the House of Han has arisen and all the world is united under one rule. I have been Grand Historian, and yet I have failed to make a record of all the enlightened rulers and wise lords, the faithful ministers and gentlemen who were ready to die for duty. I am fearful that the historical material will be neglected and lost. You must remember and think of this!"

I bowed my head and wept, saying, "I, your son, am ignorant and unworthy, but I shall endeavor to set forth in full the reports of antiquity that have come down from our ancestors. I dare not be remiss!" . . . [130:8a–b]

[Now] I have sought out and gathered together the ancient traditions of the empire that were scattered and lost. Of the great deeds of kings I have searched the beginnings and examined the ends; I have seen their times of prosperity and observed their decline. Of the affairs that I have discussed and examined,

I have made a general survey of the Three Dynasties and a record of the Qin and Han, extending back as far as Xian Yuan [the Yellow Emperor] and, coming down to the present, set forth in twelve Basic Annals. After this had been put in order and completed, because there were differences in chronology for the same periods and the dates were not always clear, I made the ten Chronological Tables. Of the changes of rites and music, the improvements and revisions of the pitch pipes and calendar, military power, mountains and rivers, spirits and gods, the relationships between Heaven and the human, the economic practices handed down and changed age by age, I have made the eight Treatises. As the twenty-eight constellations revolve about the North Star, as the thirty spokes of a wheel come together at the hub, revolving endlessly without stop, so the ministers, assisting like arms and legs, faithful and trustworthy, in true moral spirit serve their lord and ruler: of them I made the thirty Hereditary Houses. Upholding duty, masterful and sure, not allowing themselves to miss their opportunities, they made a name for themselves in the world: of such men I made the seventy Memoirs. In all 130 chapters, 526,500 words, this is the book of the Grand Historian, compiled in order to repair omissions and amplify the Six Disciplines. It is the work of one family, designed to supplement the various interpretations of the Six Classics and to put into order the miscellaneous sayings of the hundred schools. [30b–32a]

[From *Shiji* (BNB) 130:8a–b, 30b–32a — BW]

In 98 B.C.E., because he dared to speak out in defense of a military leader whom Emperor Wu and the rest of the court believed had disgraced himself, Sima Qian was condemned to suffer the punishment of castration. The following excerpt is from a famous letter that the historian wrote to a friend relating the circumstances of his disgrace and explaining why it was he chose to suffer the ignominy of castration rather than commit suicide. He consoles himself with the memory of the great men of the past who, in the midst of misfortune, produced writings that have guaranteed their everlasting fame, as he believes his history will do for him.

My father had no great deeds that entitled him to receive territories or privileges from the emperor. He dealt with affairs of astronomy and the calendar, which are close to divination and the worship of the spirits. He was kept for the sport and amusement of the emperor, treated the same as the musicians and jesters, and made light of by the vulgar men of his day. If I fell before the law and were executed, it would make no more difference to most people than one hair off nine oxen, for I was nothing but a mere ant to them. The world would not rank me among those men who were able to die for their ideals, but would believe simply that my wisdom was exhausted and my crime great, that I had been unable to escape penalty and in the end had gone to my death. Why? Because all my past actions had brought this on me, they would say.

A man has only one death. That death may be as weighty as Mount Tai, or it may be as light as a goose feather. It all depends upon the way he uses it. . . . It is the nature of every man to love life and hate death, to think of his relatives and look after his wife and children. Only when a man is moved by higher principles is this not so. Then there are things that he must do. . . . The brave man does not always die for honor, while even the coward may fulfill his duty. Each takes a different way to exert himself. Though I might be weak and cowardly and seek shamefully to prolong my life, yet I know full well the difference between what ought to be followed and what rejected. How could I bring myself to sink into the shame of ropes and bonds? If even the lowest slave and scullery maid can bear to commit suicide, why should not one like myself be able to do what has to be done? But the reason I have not refused to bear these ills and have continued to live, dwelling among this filth, is that I grieve that I have things in my heart that I have not been able to express fully, and I am shamed to think that after I am gone my writings will not be known to posterity.

Too numerous to record are the men of ancient times who were rich and noble and whose names have yet vanished away. It is only those who were masterful and sure, the truly extraordinary men, who are still remembered. When the Earl of the West was imprisoned at Youli, he expanded the *Changes*; Confucius was in distress and he made the *Spring and Autumn Annals*; Qu Yuan was banished and he composed his poem "Encountering Sorrow"; after Zuo Qiu lost his sight he composed the *Narratives of the States*; when Sunzi had had his feet amputated he set forth the *Art of War*; Lü Buwei was banished to Shu but his *Lülan* (*Lüshi chunqiu*) has been handed down through the ages; while Han Feizi was held prisoner in Qin he wrote "The Difficulties of Disputation" and "The Sorrow of Standing Alone"; most of the three hundred poems of the *Book of Odes* were written when the sages poured forth their anger and dissatisfaction. All these men had a rankling in their hearts, for they were not able to accomplish what they wished. Therefore they wrote of past affairs in order to pass on their thoughts to future generations. . . .

I too have ventured not to be modest but have entrusted myself to my useless writings. I have gathered up and brought together the old traditions of the world that were scattered and lost. I have examined the deeds and events of the past and investigated the principles behind their success and failure, their rise and decay, in 130 chapters. I wished to examine into all that concerns Heaven and the human, to penetrate the changes of the past and present, completing all as the work of one family. But before I had finished my rough manuscript, I met with this calamity. It is because I regretted that it had not been completed that I submitted to the extreme penalty without rancor. When I have truly completed this work, I shall deposit it in some safe place. If it may be handed down to men who will appreciate it and penetrate to the villages and great cities, then, though I should suffer a thousand mutilations, what regret would I have?

[From *Hanshu* (BNB) 62:17b–21b — BW]

THE WRITING OF THE FIRST DYNASTIC HISTORY

The historical labors of Sima Qian were admirably carried on by Ban Biao (3–54 C.E.) and his son Ban Gu (32–92 C.E.), principal authors of the *History of the Former Han Dynasty* [*Hanshu*]. The following extracts are from the biographies of Ban Biao and Ban Gu in the *History of the Latter Han Dynasty*. It was apparently Ban Biao's intention only to continue the writing of history from the point at which Sima Qian had stopped. But Ban Gu conceived the idea of one unified work covering the entire Former Han period. His *Hanshu*, covering the complete span of one dynasty, has been the model for all the later "dynastic histories" compiled to cover every reigning house from Ban Gu's time down to the founding of the Republic in 1911.

It is noteworthy that Ban Gu's daughters carried on the scholarly traditions of their family, and his sister Ban Zhao (48?–116? C.E.), recognized at court for her scholarship, wrote the *Admonitions for Women* excerpted in chapter 23.

Ban Biao had great talent and was fond of writing, devoting himself solely to histories and chronicles. At the time of Emperor Wu, Sima Qian wrote the *Records of the Grand Historian* [*Shiji*], but for the period from the Taichu era [104–101 B.C.E.] on, the volumes were lacking or had never been written. Men of later years who were interested in such things had made various attempts to continue the former work and add material on recent times, but for the most part the results were common and tasteless and completely unworthy to act as a continuation of Sima Qian's work. Biao then took up this work, continuing and selecting material from earlier histories and supplementing it with various traditions, and composed a "Supplementary Chronicle" in several tens of chapters. [40A:2b–3a]

Ban Gu took the continuation of the former history that Ban Biao had written and, since it was incomplete, immersed himself in study and shaped its ideas, intending to bring it to completion. At this time, however, someone sent a letter to Emperor Xianzong informing him that Ban Gu was privately revising and writing a dynastic history. An order was issued to the prefecture for Gu's arrest, and he was bound and placed in prison in the capital and all his personal books were seized. Formerly there had been a man of Fufeng, one Su Lang, who had been thrown into prison for deceitfully expounding charts and prophecies and had died there. Gu's younger brother, Chao, fearing that in the prefectural inquiry Gu would not be able to make his case clear, hastened to the capital and sent a request to the emperor for an audience. There he explained in detail what Gu's intentions were in writing his work, and the prefecture also sent Gu's book. Emperor Xianzong was amazed at it and summoned Gu to the Department for the Editing of Books, where he was appointed one of the official historiographers of the Lantai. . . . The emperor charged him to complete the former history. . . . He selected material from earlier sources and gathered together oral traditions to complete his *History of the Former Han Dynasty*, beginning with Emperor Gaozu (r. 202–195 B.C.E.) and ending with the execution of Wang Mang (23 C.E.), some twelve generations, a period of 230 years. He ordered all events, imbued them with the spirit of the Five Classics, and penetrated into all things above and below, completing season-by-season "Annals," "Chronological Tables," "Treatises," and "Memoirs," one hundred chapters in all. From the time when Gu first received the imperial appointment during the Yongping era (58–75 C.E.), when he was immersed in study and gathering ideas, until the Jianchu era (76–83 C.E.), when his work was finally completed, was a period of over twenty years. His own age greatly honored his work and among men of learning there were none who did not read and praise it.

[From *Hou Hanshu* (BNB) 40A:2b–3a, 11b–12b — BW]

PART 3

Later Daoism and Mahāyāna Buddhism in China

Chapter 13

LEARNING OF THE MYSTERIOUS

For almost four centuries after the disintegration of the Han dynasty, China was to be without that unity and stability that had seemed for the previous four centuries to be one of its chief characteristics. Instead, during the period of the Three Kingdoms and the Northern and Southern dynasties (220–589 C.E.), China's division into numerous contending states and subjection to successive ruling houses brought her perilously close to a loss of cultural identity — or so it appeared to many who lived during these troubled times. Owing to the prevailing disunity and disruption, the situation was hardly favorable to the kind of scholarly enterprise that the imperial court had once encouraged; at the same time Confucianism was deprived of its importance as a state cult. The textual study of the classics that had absorbed many of the best minds during the Han shifted to a different plane now that classical scholarship served no vital function for state or society. It was under such circumstances that intellectual interest in Daoism revived and a foreign religion, Buddhism, first gained a foothold among both the masses and the educated class.

The "Learning of the Mysterious," or *xuanxue*, was a many-sided movement that found expression in the spheres of metaphysics, religion, literature, and aesthetics. It can be described as a revival of Daoism in the sense that it centered on the study of the *Laozi* or *Daodejing*,[1] the *Zhuangzi*,[2] and the *Classic of Changes*[3] — the first two being core texts of the Daoist tradition, the third having become during the Han period a classic revered by Confucians and Daoists alike. The term *xuan* — meaning deep, dark, abstruse, profound, or mysterious — is very old, being found on oracle-bone inscriptions. But for those steeped in Daoist tradition, *xuan* would specifically have recalled the first chapter of the *Laozi*, which, in its closing lines, evokes a reality recognized as "mysterious (*xuan*) and still more mysterious, the gateway of all subtleties!"[4]

Among the major contributors to the Learning of the Mysterious were Wang Bi (226–249 C.E.) and He Yan (d. 249 C.E.), both admirers of the *Laozi* and authors of early commentaries on that text, and Guo Xiang (d. 312 C.E.), author of what is still the most famous commentary on the *Zhuangzi*.[5] Probing the metaphysical depths of Daoism, these commentators shared a common search for the source of unity or oneness in a world in which any semblance of unity had disappeared from the political and social realm. Yet their philosophical explorations went far beyond elaboration of the earlier Daoist tradition, and the spirit in which these explorations were carried on was anything but detached. In a climate that was conducive to escapism and abandonment of the public sphere — and that demonstrably prompted just such a response on the part of some of their contemporaries — all three of these leading figures of *xuanxue* were involved in government and served in official positions. Committed to the value of active involvement in the world, they may be said to have reinterpreted Daoism in the light of the social and moral philosophy of Confucianism. Thus, while the Learning of the Mysterious was philosophically innovative, it did not entail a complete redirection of Chinese thought. In spite of Confucianism's decline as the basis of the bureaucratic institution, its ideals and values would remain important, and in this period, as in so many others in Chinese history, there was a strong tendency toward syncretism.

WANG BI

Wang Bi's philosophical accomplishments were remarkable, particularly when we consider the fact that he lived in such troubled times and died at the early age of twenty-four. In some respects his underlying concerns resembled those of his predecessors in the Han period. Like Dong Zhongshu, for example, Wang devoted himself to the

---

1. See ch. 5.
2. Ibid.
3. See ch. 10.
4. See ch. 5.
5. This commentary is sometimes known as the Xiang-Guo commentary because parts of it are thought to have been written by Xiang Xiu in the mid-third century.

relation between ontology and ethics — that is, to the connections between how things ultimately are and how virtue is to be attained. But, perhaps in part because unity in the political sphere was now so obviously lacking and an imperial government was no longer a fixed point of reference, Wang's approach was characterized by greater philosophical openness and subtlety. His legacy to later Chinese thought would include new ways of conceptualizing the nature of reality and the criteria for human action, along with a new philosophical vocabulary for articulating this complex understanding.

Wang wrote extensive commentaries on the *Classic of Changes* and the *Laozi*, as well as a partial commentary on the *Analects* called *Resolving Uncertainties in the Analects* [*Lunyu shiyi*]. His *General Remarks on the* Changes of the Zhou (*Zhouyi lüeli*) is a seven-part introduction to his commentary on the *Changes* that explains in detail how he read the classic. In it, his interests range from the pragmatics of realpolitik to the metaphysics of the Way, from strategies of living to the meaning of life. Excerpts from two of the seven sections of this work follow.

In the first, Wang's emphasis is on the fundamental concept of *li* or principle. *Li* was a term that had been used in the earlier Chinese tradition to refer to the patterns in natural things — the markings in jade, for example, or the grain in wood. Here we find Wang Bi using it to designate the order to be discovered in the universe and the processes of nature. In the second selection Wang discusses the way human beings apprehend reality through images and words but come to recognize that a true appreciation of reality transcends both of these "snares."

GENERAL REMARKS ON THE CHANGES OF THE ZHOU

Principle

CLARIFYING THE JUDGMENTS (*MING TUAN*)

What is a Judgment?[6] It discusses the body or substance of a hexagram as a whole and clarifies what the controlling principle is from which it evolves. The many cannot govern the many; that which governs the many is the most solitary [the One]. Activity cannot govern activity; that which controls all activity that occurs in the world, thanks to constancy, is the One. Therefore, for all the many to manage to exist, their controlling principle must reach back to the One, and for all activities to manage to function, their source cannot but be the One.

No thing ever behaves haphazardly but necessarily follows its own principle. To unite things there is a fundamental regulator; to integrate them there is a primordial generator. Therefore things are complex but not chaotic, multitudinous but not confused. This is why when the six lines of a hexagram inter-

---

6. For an explanation of the nature of the "Judgments" on the hexagrams of the *Classic of Changes*, see ch. 10.

mingle, one can pick out one of them and use it to clarify what is happening, and as the hard and the soft supersede one another, one can establish which one is the master and use it to determine how they are ordered. This is why for mixed matters the calculation of the virtues and the determination of the rights and wrongs involved could never be complete without the middle lines. This is why if one examines things from the point of view of totality, even though things are multitudinous, one knows that it is possible to deal with them by holding fast to the One, and if one views them from the point of view of the fundamental, even though the concepts involved are immense in number and scope, one knows that it is possible to cover them all with a single name. . . .

Now, although past and present differ and armies and states then and now appear dissimilar, the way these central principles function is such that nothing can ever stray far from them. Although kinds and gradations of things exist in infinite variety, there is a chief controlling principle that inheres in all of them. Of things we esteem in a Judgment, it is this that is the most significant. [*Zhouyi lüeli*, 591–592]

Images, Words, and Understanding

CLARIFYING THE IMAGES (*MING XIANG*)

Images are the means to express ideas. Words [i.e., the texts] are the means to explain the images. To yield up ideas completely there is nothing better than the images, and to yield up the meaning of the images there is nothing better than words. The words are generated by the images; thus one can ponder the words and so observe what the images are. The images are generated by ideas; thus one can ponder the images and so observe what the ideas are. The ideas are yielded up completely by the images, and the images are made explicit by the words. Thus, since the words are the means to explain the images, once one gets the images, he forgets the words, and, since the images are the means to allow us to concentrate on the ideas, once one gets the ideas, he forgets the images. Similarly, "the rabbit snare exists for the sake of the rabbit — once one gets the rabbit, he forgets the snare; and the fish trap exists for the sake of fish — once one gets the fish he forgets the trap."[7] If this is so, then the words are snares for the images, and the images are traps for the ideas.

Therefore someone who stays fixed on the words will not be one to get the images, and someone who stays fixed on the images will not be one to get the ideas. The images are generated by the ideas, but if one stays fixed on the images themselves, then what he stays fixed on will not be images as we mean them here. The words are generated by the images, but if one stays fixed on the words

---

7. A quotation from the *Zhuangzi* (HYISIS ed.), 75/26/48.

themselves, then what he stays fixed on will not be words as we mean them here. If this is so, then someone who forgets the images will be one to get the ideas, and someone who forgets the words will be one to get the images. Getting the ideas is in fact a matter of forgetting the images, and getting the images is in fact a matter of forgetting the words. Thus, although the images were established in order to yield up ideas completely, as images they may be forgotten.

[*Zhouyi lüeli*, 609–610 (*Wang Bi ji jiaoshi* ed.) — RJL]

GENERAL REMARKS ON THE SUBTLE AND PROFOUND MEANING OF THE LAOZI

Wang also wrote a similar work on the *Laozi*, which became detached from the textual recension of Wang's commentary on the *Laozi*, perhaps as early as the sixth century C.E., and was preserved only in an obscure corner of the great compendium of Daoist texts, the Daoist Canon (*Daozang*), where it was ignored and largely lost to the tradition. Since its discovery there in the 1950s, despite some doubts raised concerning its authorship, most modern scholars have accepted it as Wang's long-lost introduction to the *Laozi*. The excerpt included here corresponds to the first third of the work.

In Wang's commentary on the *Laozi* he explains issues and concepts in terms of a new analytical vocabulary, using *ti* (substance), *benti* (original substance/pure being), *yong* (function), *shi* (origin or beginning), *ziran* (nature, the natural), *li* (principle), *wu* (nothingness), and *you* (what exists), among other terms. This set of analytical terms, rich in philosophical significance, provided much of the vocabulary of later Chinese thought, and in this sense Wang's influence can be traced in the later history of Chinese Buddhism as well as in the later evolution of Confucianism in a very broad trend of thought known as Neo-Confucianism that began in the tenth century and continued to evolve into the eighteenth. Noteworthy in the passage that follows is the fact that the key concept of *wu* (literally, "nothingness") is not *nonexistence* but *pure being* that transcends forms and images and, precisely because it is indeterminate and unbound, can accomplish everything.

Nothingness, Being, and the Way

The way things come into existence and efficacy (*gong*) comes about is that things arise from the formless (*wuxing*) and efficacy emanates from the nameless (*wuming*). The formless and the nameless [the Way] is the progenitor of the myriad things.[8] It is neither warm nor cool and makes neither the note *gong*

---

8. Cf. Wang Bi's commentary to *Laozi* 1: "All things that exist have their origin in nothingness (*wu*). Thus, it is when things do not yet have forms and still lack names that the origin of the myriad things occurs. Once they have forms and possess names, it [the Way] causes them to grow, nourishes them, gives them different shapes, and brings them to mature physical existence

nor the note *shang* [i.e., is not subject to the sense of touch or hearing]. You might listen for It, but it is impossible to get a sense of Its sound; you might look for It, but it is impossible to get a sense of Its appearance; you might try to realize what It is like, but it is impossible to get It in terms of understanding; or you might taste It, but it is impossible to get It in terms of flavor. Thus, try to conceive of It as a thing, and It will have a thoroughly nebulous existence; try to capture It as an image, and It will be utterly formless; try to hear It as tonality, and It will greet you as inaudible sound; try to experience It as flavor, and It will have an indistinguishable taste. Thus, It is capable of serving as the progenitor and master of things in all their different categories, of covering and permeating everything in Heaven and Earth, so that nothing is allowed to escape the warp of Its weave. If It were warm, It could not be cold; if It were the note *gong*, It could not be the note *shang*. If It had a form, It would necessarily possess the means of being distinguished from other things; if It made a sound, It would necessarily belong somewhere among other sounds.

Thus, an image that takes an actual form is not the Great Image; a note that makes an actual sound is not the Great Note.[9] However, if the four [basic] images[10] did not take actual forms, the Great Image would have no way to become manifested, and if the five notes did not make actual sounds, the Great Note would have no way to get expressed. The four basic images may take forms, but things are not at all made subject to them, so through them the Great Image is manifested. The five notes may make sounds, but our human hearts [i.e., sensibilities] are not at all made to conform to them, so through them the Great Note is expressed. Thus, if one holds fast to the Great Image, the whole world will come to him,[11] and if one uses the Great Note, folkways and customs will undergo moral transformation. When the formless is manifested, although the whole world might come, this coming is impossible to explain, and when the inaudible sound is expressed, although folkways and customs undergo moral transformation, this transformation is impossible to analyze. Heaven may have produced the five things [metal, wood, water, fire, earth], but it is *nothingness* (*wu*) that brings about their utility.[12] The Sage [Confucius] may have promulgated the five teachings [i.e., concerning the five human relationships], but it is those who *do not speak* (*bu yan*) who bring

---

[cf. *Laozi* 51]; as such, it is then their Mother. In other words, it is when the Way is in its formless and nameless aspect that it begins to give existence to the myriad things."

9. Cf. *Laozi* 41: "The Great Note is an inaudible sound; the Great Image is formless."

10. See *Commentary on the Appended Phrases*, Part 1, 11: "Therefore, in Change there is the Great Ultimate. This is what generates the two modes [yin and yang]. The two basic modes generate the four basic images, and the four basic images generate the eight trigrams." The four basic images consist of (1) two yang lines, (2) a yin and a yang line, (3) two yin lines, and (4) a yang and a yin line.

11. Cf. *Laozi* 35: "Hold fast to the Great Image, and the whole world will come."

12. Cf. *Laozi* 11: "Thirty spokes share one hub. It is exactly there where the nothing (*wu*) exists that the function of the cart inheres." For an alternative translation, see ch. 5.

about moral transformation.[13] Therefore, "the Way that can be spoken of is not the constant Way; the name that can be named is not the constant name."[14] The mother of the five things is neither hot nor cold, neither soft nor hard. The mother of the five teachings is neither bright nor dark, neither kind nor cruel. Although past and present differ and folkways and customs change with time, this [the Way] never changes. It is what the *Laozi* means when it says, "From antiquity up to now, Its name has never been absent."[15] If Heaven did not operate this way, things would not come into existence, and if government did not operate this way, efficacy would not come about. Thus, as the past and the present are interchangeable and endings and beginnings are identical, by holding fast to the Way of old one can control what happens in the present, and by taking evidence from the present, one can understand how things began in the past.[16] This is what the [*Laozi*] means by the "constant" (*chang*). It has neither a bright nor a dark appearance, neither a warm nor a cool image, so "to know the constant is called enlightenment (*ming*)."[17] When a thing comes into existence or when efficacy comes about, it never happens but that it comes forth from this [the constant Way]. Thus, [the *Laozi* says:] "In It observe the father of all things (*zhongfu*)."[18]

If you could hurry by running with the speed of lightning, it would still not be fast enough to get there and back in a single instant. If you could travel by riding the wind, it would still not be fast enough to arrive in a single breath. Being good at making quick progress lies in not hurrying, and being good at reaching goals lies in not forcing one's way.[19] Thus, even the most replete [Way], as long as it can still be expressed in words, would never have the capacity to govern Heaven and Earth, and the greatest thing that can possibly have form would never be large enough to house the myriad things. This is why no sighing in admiration of It could ever completely express how beautiful It is, and no singing of Its praises could ever tell how great is Its size. No name for It could ever match what It is, and no comparison for It could ever deal with Its absolute wholeness. A name necessarily involves how one thing is distinct from other things, and a comparison necessarily involves how [the tenor of] one thing depends upon [the vehicle of] another. Making distinctions, any name would result in exclusion; being dependent, any comparison would fall short of the

---

13. Cf. *Laozi* 2: "Thus the sage conducts affairs by doing nothing (*wu wei*) and furthers teachings without speaking (*bu yan*)."

14. *Laozi* 1.

15. *Laozi* 21.

16. Cf. *Laozi* 14.

17. Cf. *Laozi* 16.

18. *Laozi* 21. The text also permits a different reading: "So we call it [the constant Way] the Father of all things."

19. Cf. *Commentary on the Appended Phrases*, Part 1, 10: "It is the numinous (*shen*) alone that thus allows one to make quick progress without hurrying and reach goals without forcing one's way."

absolute. As it cannot be perfectly inclusive, any name for It would deviate greatly from the truth; as it cannot be absolute, any comparison for It would fail to designate what It really is. This can be clarified by further elaboration.

The term *Way* is derived from the fact that It is that on which the myriad things make their way. The term *xuan* (the mysterious) is derived from the fact that It emerges from the secret and the dark. The term *shen* (the deep) is derived from the fact that you might try to plumb to the bottom of It but can never reach that far. The term *great* (*da*) is derived from the fact that you might try to fill It all in or pull It all together but can never ultimately do so.[20] The term *yuan* (the far-reaching) is derived from the fact that It stretches on so far that you can never reach the end of It. The term the *subtle* (*wei*) is derived from the fact that It is so elusive and inconspicuous that you can never see It. Since this is so, although each of the words *Way, mysterious, deep, great, far-reaching,* and *subtle* possesses something of Its meaning, none of them can express all of what It is. Thus, something that can never be entirely filled in or all pulled together certainly cannot be termed *tiny*, and something that is so subtle and marvelous that it has no form certainly cannot be termed *great*. This is why sections [of the *Laozi*] say: "One might write It with the character Way"[21] or "might call It *xuan* [the mysterious],"[22] but one does not give It a name. Given what It is, those who speak of It do violence to Its constancy; those who give It a name separate themselves from Its truth; those who try to force It ruin Its nature; and those who try to hold on to It do violence to Its source.[23] Thus, as the sage does not allow words to become his master, he does not do violence to Its constancy; as he does not confuse names for It with Its constancy, he does not separate himself from Its truth; as he does not think that the forcing of It should be the means to carry out affairs, he does not ruin Its nature; as he does not hold on to It as a means of control, he does not do violence to Its source.[24]

Since all this is so, those who wish to debate the text of the *Laozi* and make it a form of exegesis will do violence to its aims, and those who wish to use names and make it responsible for them will distort its meaning. The supreme objective of the *Laozi* is to discuss the source of the Great Beginning of all things in order to clarify the nature of the natural (*ziran*) and to expound upon the ultimate meaning of the secret and the dark in order to alleviate the confusion of those trapped in the net of deception.

[*Laozi weizhi lilüe* (*Wang Bi ji jiaoshi* ed.) 195–196 — RJL]

---

20. Cf. *Commentary on the Appended Phrases*, Part 1, 4: "[The *Changes*] shows how one can fill in and pull together the Way of Heaven and Earth" — that is, as if patching fabric and pulling together seams fill in the missing parts in one's understanding of the Way.

21. *Laozi* 25.

22. *Laozi* 1.

23. Cf. *Laozi* 29.

24. Cf. *Laozi* 64.

THE SAGE

Wang Bi is known not only for such searching discussions of principle, being and nothingness, naturalness, and the relation of symbols and language to reality, but for a new view of the sage. A famous passage from a biography of Wang by He Shao found in the *Chronicles of the Three Kingdoms* purports to recount a conversation between Wang Bi and the official Pei Hui:

At the time when Pei Hui was serving as Director of the Ministry of Personnel, Wang Bi, who then had not yet been capped,[25] went to pay him a visit. As soon as Pei saw him he knew that this was an extraordinary person, and so he asked him, "Nothing (*wu*) is, in truth, what the myriad things depend on for existence, yet the Sage (Confucius) was unwilling to talk about it, while Master Lao expounded upon it endlessly. Why is that?" Wang Bi replied, "The Sage embodied nothing (*wu*), so he also knew that it could not be explained in words. Thus he did not talk about it. Master Lao, by contrast, operated on the level of being (*you*). This is why he constantly discussed nothingness; he had to, for what he said about it always fell short."

There is a metaphysical statement here — a further indication of Wang Bi's idea of the relation between being and nothingness — and also a statement about the personality of the sage and his sphere of action. The statement attributed to Wang suggests that, for him, the personality of the sage is such that he does not withdraw from the world, nor does he just talk or hold certain views. Rather, he exemplifies a certain bearing toward the world; his sphere of action is the ordinary world of human experience.

Another lively issue in the period from the third to the fifth centuries was whether or not a sage experienced ordinary human emotions, and on this matter Wang Bi and his contemporary He Yan evidently disagreed. An indication of what Wang thought about the capacity of the sage for responsiveness and sensitivity is also recorded by Wang's biographer He Shao, who summarized the disagreement between He Yan and Wang as follows:

It was He Yan's opinion that the sage is free of pleasure, anger, sadness, or happiness, and his discussion of this issue was meticulously argued. People such as Zhong Hui (225–264) transmitted what he had to say, but Wang Bi took a different position from them and thought that what makes the sage superior to people in general is his intelligence (*shenming*) and that what makes him the same as people in general is his having the five emotions.[26] It is because his intelligence is superior that he can embody gentleness and amiability and, in

---

25. That is, he had not yet reached the age of majority at twenty *sui* by the Chinese way of counting years of age or nineteen years by Western reckoning.

26. Happiness, anger, sadness, pleasure, and desire.

so doing, identify with nothingness (*wu*). It is because he is the same as other people in having the five emotions that he is unable to respond to things free from either sadness or pleasure. Nevertheless, the emotions of the sage are such that he may respond to things but without becoming attached to them. Nowadays because the sage is considered free of such attachment, one immediately thinks it can be said that he no longer responds to things. How very often this error occurs!

> [*Wei zhi* (*Chronicles of Wei*), in *Sanguo zhi* (*Chronicles of the Three Kingdoms*) (*Wang Bi ji jiaoshi* ed.) 2:639–644 —RJL]

GUO XIANG: COMMENTARY ON THE *ZHUANGZI*

In the commentary on the *Zhuangzi* by Guo Xiang (who was probably building on the work of the mid-third-century commentator Xiang Xiu), a positive note is struck in the emphasis on naturalness and spontaneity in both the internal and the external life. Guo Xiang returns to Zhuangzi's themes of naturalness and spontaneity, self-transformation, and contentment; in Guo's view, however, the sage moves in the realm of human affairs as well as in the transcendental world.

Nature (*Tian*), the Natural (*Ziran*), and Nothingness (*Wu*)

The universe (*tiandi*) is a general name for the myriad things. The universe attains its reality through the myriad things, and the myriad things take the natural as their norm. Being natural means to exist spontaneously without having to take any [deliberate] action. Therefore the great *peng* bird can soar high, and the quail can fly low; the cedrela can live for a long time, and the mushroom for a short time. All are capable of doing so not because of their taking any action but because of their being natural. [sec. 1; 1:5a]

The music of nature is not an entity existing outside of things. The different apertures, the pipes and flutes and the like, in combination with all living beings, together constitute nature. Since nothingness is nothing, it cannot produce being. Before being itself is produced, it cannot produce other beings. Then by whom are things produced? They spontaneously produce themselves, that is all. This does not mean that there is an "I" that produces them. The "I" cannot produce things, and things cannot produce the "I." The "I" exists of itself, and because it is self-existent, we call it natural. Everything is what it is by nature, not through taking any action. Therefore [Zhuangzi] speaks in terms of nature. The term *nature*[27] is used to explain that things are what they are spontaneously, and not to mean the blue sky. But someone says that the music of nature makes all things serve or obey it. Now, nature cannot even possess

---

27. Elsewhere the word *tian* is translated as "Heaven."

itself. How can it possess things? Nature is the general name for all things. [sec. 2; 1:11b]

Everything is natural and does not know why it is so. The more things differ in corporeal form, the more they are alike in being natural. . . . Heaven and Earth and all things change and transform into something new every day and so proceed with time. What causes them? They do so spontaneously, that is all. . . . What we call things are all that they are by themselves, that is all; they did not cause each other to become so. Let us leave them alone and principle (*li*) will be perfectly realized. [sec. 2; 1:12a–b]

Not only is it impossible for nothing to be transformed into something, it is also impossible for something to become nothing. Therefore, although something that exists as a thing may undergo a thousand changes and ten thousand transformations, it cannot ever be transformed into nothing, and because it cannot ever become nothing, nothingness must, from antiquity, always have existed. . . . What came into existence before there were things? If I say yin and yang came first, then, since yin and yang are themselves things, what came before them? Suppose I say the natural (*ziran*) came first? But the natural is only things being themselves. Suppose I say perfect Dao came first? But perfect Dao is perfect nothingness. Since it is nothingness, how can it come before anything else? Then what came before it? There must be another thing, and so on, endlessly. We must understand that things are what they are spontaneously and are not caused by something else. [sec. 22; 7:29a–b]

Self-Transformation and "Taking No Action" (*Wuwei*, Doing Nothing)

If we insist on the conditions under which things develop and search for the cause thereof, such search and insistence will never end, until we come to something that is unconditioned, and then the principles of self-transformation will become clear. . . . There are people who say that the penumbra is conditioned by the shadow, the shadow by the body, and the body by the Creator. But let us ask whether there is a Creator or not? If not, how can it create things? If there is, it is incapable of materializing all the forms. Therefore before we can talk about creation, we must understand the fact that all things materialize by themselves. If we go through the entire realm of existence, we shall see that there is nothing, not even the penumbra, that does not transform itself beyond the phenomenal world. Hence everything creates itself without the direction of any Creator. Since things create themselves they are unconditioned. This is the norm of the universe. [sec. 2; 1:25a]

He who can cause the empire to be governed is one who does no governing. Therefore Yao governed by not governing; it was not because of his governing that his empire was governed. Now [the recluse] Xuyou only realized that since the empire was well governed he should not replace Yao. He thought it was Yao who did the actual governing. Consequently he said to Yao, "You govern the empire." He should have forgotten such words and investigated into the conditions [that made the empire already well governed and at peace]. Someone may say, "It was Yao who actually governed and put the empire in good order, but it was Xuyou who enabled Yao to do so by refusing to govern himself." This is a great mistake. Yao was an adequate example of governing by not governing and acting by not acting. Why should we have to resort to Xuyou? Are we to insist that a man fold his arms and sit in silence in the middle of some mountain forest before we will say he is taking no action? This is why the words of Zhuangzi and Laozi are rejected by responsible officials. This is why responsible officials insist on remaining in the realm of action without feeling any regret. [sec. 1; 1:5b]

Taking no action does not mean folding one's arms and closing one's mouth. If we simply let everything act by itself, it will be contented with its nature and destiny. [sec. 11; 4:15b]

In the cutting of a tree the workman takes no action; the only action he takes is in plying the ax. In the actual managing of affairs the ruler takes no action; the only action he takes is in employing his ministers. If the ministers can manage affairs, the ruler can employ ministers, the ax can cut the tree, and the workman can use the ax, each corresponding to his capacity, then the principles of nature (*tianli*) will operate of themselves, not because someone takes action. If the ruler does the work of his ministers, he will no longer be the ruler, and if the ministers control the ruler's employment, they will no longer be ministers. Therefore when each attends to his own responsibility, both ruler and ruled will be contented and the principle of taking no action will be attained. [sec. 13; 5:13b]

Contentment

If one is contented wherever he goes, he will be at ease wherever he may be. Even life and death cannot affect him, much less flood or fire. The perfect man is not besieged by calamities, not because he escapes from them but because he advances the principles of things and goes forward and naturally comes into union with good fortune. [sec. 1; 1:7b]

Sorrow and joy are the results of losses and gains. A cultivated person (*shi*) who profoundly penetrates all things and is in harmony with their transformations is at peace at all times and at home in all circumstances. Being intuitively united with creation, where could I be and not be myself? Where do gain or loss, life or death, come in? Therefore, if one lets what one has received from nature take its own course, there will be no place for sorrow or joy. [sec. 3; 2:3b]

Allow the foot to walk according to its capacity, and let the hand grasp according to its strength. Listen to what the ear hears and see what the eye sees. In knowing, stop at what cannot be known. In acting, stop at what cannot be done. Employ [the faculties] as they would use themselves. Do things that would be done by themselves. Be unrestrained within your nature, but do not attempt the least thing outside of your lot. This is the easiest way of taking no [unnatural] action. There has never been a case of taking no action and yet of one's nature and destiny not being preserved, nor have I ever heard of any principle according to which the preservation of nature and destiny is not a blessing. [sec. 4; 2:15a]

The expert driver utilizes the natural capacity of horses to its limit. To use the capacity to its limit lies in letting it take its own course. If forced to run at a rapid pace, with the expectation that they can exceed their capacity, horses will be unable to bear it and many will die. On the other hand, if both worn-out and thoroughbred horses are allowed to use their proper strength and to adapt their pace to their given lot, even if they travel to the borders of the country, their nature will be fully preserved. But there are those who, upon hearing the doctrine of allowing the nature of horses to take its own course, will say, "Then set the horses free and do not ride on them;" and there are those who, upon hearing the doctrine of taking no action, will immediately say, "It is better to lie down than to walk." Why do they go off like this and fail to return? In so doing they end up far from Zhuangzi and miss his point. [sec. 9; 4:6b]

Society and Rulership

In adapting Daoist nonassertion or "doing nothing" (*wuwei*) to Confucian principles, Guo Xiang, like many of his contemporaries, recognized such values as humaneness and rightness but stressed the need to adapt them to changing times and circumstances. This raised questions similar to those encountered in the adaptation later of Buddhist doctrines to Chinese social and political practice. Did a laissez-faire Daoist "nonassertion" (*wuwei*) and "naturalness" or spontaneity (*ziran*), really accord with Confucian conceptions of constant human values, or did they not lend themselves readily to an amoral pragmatism, so that in contrast to the morally prudent and carefully measured response to change in the *Yijing*, we now get an amoral expediency and opportunism? Note that Guo Xiang has little to say about the organization and conduct of government but only dwells on how the sage king conducts himself, i.e., how one rules.

Although the sage is in the midst of government, his mind seems to be in the mountain forest. . . . His abode is in the myriad things, but this does not mean that he does not wander freely. [sec. 1; 1:6b; 1:8a]

Man in society cannot get away from his fellow beings. The changes in society vary from generation to generation according to different standards. Only those who have no minds of their own and do not use their own judgment can adapt themselves to changes and not be burdened by them. [sec. 4; 2:4a]

When a thousand people gather together with no one as their leader, they will be either unruly or disorganized. Therefore when there are many virtuous people, there should not be many rulers, but when there is no virtuous person, there cannot but be a ruler. This is the Way of Heaven and man and the most proper thing to do. [sec. 4; 2:9a]

When the king does not make himself useful in the various offices, the various officials will manage their own affairs. Those with clear vision will do the seeing, those with sharp ears will do the listening, those with knowledge will do the planning, and those with strength will provide protection. What need is there to take any action? Only profound silence, that is all. [sec. 4; 2:13b]

Events that took place in the past have disappeared with the past. Some may be transmitted to us [in writing], but can this make the past exist in the present? The past is not in the present, and the events of the present are soon changed. Therefore only when one abandons learning, lets one's nature take its own course, and changes with the times, can one be perfect. [sec. 13; 5:18b–19a]

Humaneness and rightness are principles of human nature. Human nature undergoes changes and is different past and present. If one takes a temporary abode in a thing and then moves on, one will intuit [the reality of things]. If, however, one stops and is confined to one place, one will develop prejudices. Prejudices will result in hypocrisy, and hypocrisy will result in many reproaches. [sec. 14; 5:24a]

The ceremonies of ancient kings were intended to meet the needs of the time. When the time has past and the ceremonies are still not cast away, they will become an evil influence to the people and serve to hasten the start of affectations and imitation. [sec. 14; 5:22b]

[*Commentary on the Zhuangzi* (SBBY) — adapted from WTC by IB]

XI KANG: ON THE ABSENCE OF PREDETERMINATION

From the third to the sixth centuries it was fashionable for men of literary and philosophical interests to gather in small coteries and engage in what the Chinese call *qingtan*, or "pure conversation" — conversation that is highly witty, refined, and concerned with philosophical matters transcending the concerns and conventions of the mundane world. Many of the literati were members of such groups, as were many eminent Buddhist monks. The most famous of these groups was the Seven Sages of the Bamboo Grove, which included Ruan Ji, Xi Kang, and Xiang Xiu. For many years these friends met in the bamboo groves to the north of Luoyang, the capital of the state of Wei, and behaved with utter disregard for social and intellectual convention. They engaged in philosophical discussion inspired by naturalness (*ziran*) and freedom from traditional norms (*wuming*). The following excerpt is from the writings of one of this famous group, Xi Kang (232–262).

A gentleman is so called because he is not fixed in his mind as to what is right and wrong, but acts without violating the Way. How is this? He whose vital force is tranquil and whose spirit is absolutely peaceful and pure does not occupy his mind with attachments. And he whose physical faculties are clear and whose mental faculties are enlightened does not allow his feelings to be bound by desires. Since his mind is not occupied with attachments, he is able to transcend the established doctrines of social relations and let nature take its own course. And since his feelings are not bound by desires, he is able to discern what is noble and what is lowly and be in harmony with the feelings of people and things. Because he is in harmony with the feelings of people, he does not violate the Great Way, and because he transcends social ranks and lets his mind take its own course he is not predetermined about what is right and what is wrong. Therefore when we talk about the gentleman, absence of predetermination is the point of fundamental importance and harmony with things is the point of excellence. When we talk about the inferior man, we consider his concealment of feelings as wrong and his violation of the Way as a defect.

[*Shisilun*, in *Xi Zhongsan ji* 6:1a–b — WTC]

Chapter 14

DAOIST RELIGION

The historical development of Daoism in the first half of the Han dynasty was marked by its influence on political syncretism via the Huang-Lao movement, named after Laozi and the Yellow Emperor, Huangdi. At the same time, the search for immortality and the cult of the immortals spread to all levels of society. The influence of Huang-Lao teachings at court had reached a high point just before the reign of Emperor Wu (r. 141–87 B.C.E.), declining sharply as a result of his decision to confer official patronage on the teaching of five Confucian classics, effectively installing Confucianism as the state ideology.[1] The emperor's personal interest in immortality and various occult arts, meanwhile, continued to be celebrated in fiction and mythology.

With the gradual decline of the dynasty's political fortunes, during the reign of Wang Mang and under the Latter Han, apocalyptic prophecy came to the foreground. The *Great Peace Scripture* (*Taiping jing*) is said to have been presented to the Han court amidst millenarian expectations of the imminent collapse of the world order, to be followed by the survival of an elect people under a reign of good government and great peace. The popular Yellow Turban uprising in 182 C.E. and the simultaneous establishment of an autonomous theocratic state by a group known as the Heavenly Masters in Sichuan pursued visions that may have been similar.

---

1. See chs. 9 and 10.

The Heavenly Masters movement founded by Zhang Daoling constitutes the earliest form of Daoist liturgical organization for which a relatively detailed record is available. The authority vested in Zhang Daoling, the putative founder, and his successors by means of a covenant with the Newly Appeared Lord Lao (Laozi deified) has with few interruptions been the mainstay of the Daoist ordination system throughout China to this day. After his arrival in Sichuan from eastern China, Zhang Daoling appears to have founded his movement in opposition to existing shamanistic practices among the peoples of the southwest, some of which were nevertheless partly incorporated. In the same way, the Heavenly Masters and other Daoist movements provided a liturgical superstructure for a variety of local cults and indigenous religious practices throughout its history. The introduction of Buddhism to China around the same time supplied to popular religion new forms and practices. Much of the subsequent textual tradition of Daoism shows distinct traces of Buddhist influence, especially in the areas of morality, eschatology, and iconography.

The most important medieval additions to the Daoist textual canon were provided by the Shangqing and Lingbao revelations of the fourth and fifth centuries, subsequently systematized by Tao Hongjing (456–536) and Lu Xiujing (406–477), respectively. The Shangqing corpus of inspired scriptures and cosmological and hagiographic revelations from the Maoshan area in southern Jiangsu province incorporated elements of ancient shamanistic traditions of southeast China. Shamanistic ritual seems indeed to have been at the origin of these texts, which in turn developed meditative and visionary techniques, while their ecstatic poetry and inspired calligraphy exercised a major influence on Chinese art and letters. The Lingbao revelations served essentially to create links between the Daoist canon and the transmitted public liturgy. For the most part inspired by Buddhism, they included new hymns using "Brahman" psalmody in pseudo-Sanskrit language, and such practices as scriptural recitation with circumambulation. The fifth century also saw the first compilation of Daoist scripture into a canon structured according to Three Caverns or Receptacles (*Sandong*), formed around the Shangqing, Lingbao, and Sanhuang corpora.

However, the rapport of Daoism with local cults worked as a deterrent to full centralization and ecclesiastical organization. In the fifth and sixth centuries apocalyptic cults produced new scriptures, which were eventually also incorporated into the canon. The *Divine Incantations Scripture* introduced below is but one example. The Tang dynasty, a high point of both the Chinese schools of Buddhism and of Daoism as the official imperial cult, generated a wealth of Daoist scholastic and literary texts and works related to ritual, meditative, and physiological practices. The bulk of Tang Daoist scriptures, meanwhile, was composed in plain imitation of popular Buddhist *sūtras*. The most prominent systematizer and creative author of this period was the scholar and court Daoist Du Guangting (850–933), whose life straddled the end of the Tang (618–906) and the beginning of the Five Dynasties (907–960).

The Song (960–1279) once again stands out as a period of revelation. The modern Taoist canon contains many scriptures and liturgical manuals of numerous new schools that sprang up in this period. In the face of the growing threat of foreign invasions, Northern Song (960–1126) rulers also increasingly turned to Daoism as a religion of state. The present chapter ends with an account of the summons of the Quanzhen[2] Daoist Qiu Changchun by the Mongol conqueror Chinggis (Genghis) Khan seeking in Daoism, as with Buddhism, a key for controlling the Chinese populations administered under his Central Asian empire.

THE *LIVES OF THE IMMORTALS*

The *Lives of the Immortals* (*Liexian zhuan*),[3] is traditionally attributed to Liu Xiang (79–8 B.C.E.), but probably dates to the Latter Han period. The unknown compiler may have fashioned the title after Liu's collection of biographies of virtuous women, the *Lienü zhuan*. Quoted in other works as early as the second century C.E., the *Lives* constitutes a major reflection, if not a part, of the numerous Han cults devoted to immortals. A parallel record of some of these cults has survived in the form of contemporary inscriptions. The sample below describes the apotheosis of the Zhou prince Wangzi Qiao, followed by his ascension and the installation of the first places of worship in his honor. The liturgical date of the event, the seventh day of the seventh lunar month, was significant to Daoists as a day particularly favorable for transcendental communication. The popularity of the cult of Wangzi Qiao in Han times is well attested, e.g., in the Former Han Chu–style[4] poem "Far-off Journey" ("Yuanyou") and the stele inscription "*Wangzi Qiao bei*," composed by the chief clerk Bian Qian to mark an imperially sponsored ritual in 165 C.E.

Wangzi Qiao was the heir apparent, named Jin, of King Ling of the Zhou (r. 571–545 B.C.E.). An adept at imitating the song of the phoenix on a reed-pipe organ, he wandered between the Yin and Luo rivers [in Henan]. The Daoist master Lord Fuqu introduced him to Mount Songgao [Songshan, He'nan]. When thirty years later he was being sought out on the mountain, he met with Bo Liang and said to him, "Tell my family to expect me on the seventh

---

2. Quanzhen is one of the principal movements of modern Daoism, founded under the Jurchen Jin (1115–1260) dynasty by Wang Zhe (1112–1170). Not a sect, nor really a separate school of thought, it drew (and still draws) on the main scriptural and liturgical traditions of earlier Daoism, proposing new and more rigorous ways of practicing these. Widely appreciated for its literary productions, especially in poetry and drama, it emphasized asceticism, morality, and inner alchemy.

3. For a critical edition and complete, annotated translation, see Kaltenmark, *Le Lie-sien tchouan*.

4. Poetry of the southern state of Chu, epitomized in the anthology known as the *Chuci* or *Songs of Chu*.

day of the seventh month on the peak of Mount Goushi [in the Songshan range]." On the appointed day he did indeed alight on the mountain peak, riding a white crane. They saw him from afar but were unable to reach him. He raised his hand to take leave of the men of his time. A few days later he disappeared. Thereupon shrines were erected beneath Mount Goushi and on top of Songgao.

[*Liexian zhuan* (DZ) 138,[5] no. 294 — FV]

COMMANDMENTS OF LORD LAO

The *One Hundred and Eighty Commandments Pronounced by the Lord Lao* (*Laojun shuo yibaibashi jie*, third century C.E.?) is, as the title indicates, a set of rules for Daoists. In this case the rules are intended as a guide for the life of the Libationers (*jijiu*), the leaders of Daoist communities in the early middle ages. The preface indicates that Lord Lao, or the Old Lord (that is, the divine form of Laozi), revealed these rules in ancient times to the immortal Gan Ji, the legendary founder of Taiping Daoism. Although this is no more than a pious legend, it is a fact that the set of rules is one of the oldest texts on communal Daoism that have come down to us. This can be seen from the evidence that it served as the model for another set of rules that was written toward the end of the fourth century C.E. Internal evidence suggests that it originated in the peasant society sometime during the Latter Han or the Three Kingdoms (220–280) periods. Many of the rules are about the necessity of maintaining a frugal life and about the protection of the natural environment. Others are directed against the ancient sacrificial practices, against divination, against politics, warfare, court intrigues, etc. Here follow some of the rules; the number given at the end of each of them indicates its place in the sequence of the 180 commandments.

Do not retain numerous servants or concubines. (1)
Do not commit adultery. (2)
Do not steal. (3)
Do not injure or kill any living being. (4)
Do not unjustly accept from other people anything worth more than one copper coin. (5)
Do not throw edibles into the fire. (6)
Do not keep any pigs or sheep. (7)
Do not write notes addressed to others in cursive script. (11)
Do not write frequent letters. (12)
Do not practice abortion. (13)

---

5. In these source references the first number given refers to the fascicle number in the *Zhengtong Daozang* and the second to the number in Kristofer Schipper, *Concordance du Tao-tsang: titres des ouvrages.*

Do not burn fields or mountain forests. (14)

Do not seek knowledge of military or political matters, nor practice divination to determine what is auspicious or not. (16)

Do not cut trees without good reason. (18)

Do not wantonly pick herbs or flowers. (19)

Do not frequent the emperor or his officials; do not engage in marital or other family relationships with them. (20)

Do not eat alone. (26)

Do not buy or sell slaves. (27)

Do not speak about the private matters of others. (32)

Do not throw anything poisonous into sources, lakes, rivers, or seas. (36)

Do not commit suicide. (39)

Do not dig out the nests and hiding places of insects in winter. (95)

Do not wantonly climb trees to rob birds' nests of their eggs, nor break them. (97)

Do not deceive elderly people. (102)

Do not urinate on plants or in water that people may drink. (116)

Do not stand guarantee for transactions involving the sale of land or slaves. (123)

Do not proffer ugly or harsh sounds; always remain gently smiling. (126)

Do not seek to obtain books with secret stratagems, nor read them. (128)

If people scold you, listen with diffidence; never answer. (167)

[*Taishang Laojun jinglü* (DZ) 562, no. 786, 2a–12b — KS]

REGULATIONS FOR PETITIONING

This excerpt is from an anonymous book, *Regulations of the Dark Capital* (*Xuandu lüwen*), which exemplifies the elaborate code of regulations that governed Taoist communities. It probably reflects the rules of the earliest stable Daoist community in Sichuan in the second century. It appears to have been compiled shortly after 500 to reconcile the practices of movements of the time with those of the early Heavenly Masters.

The *Regulations* clearly reflects the conviction that the community of initiated believers was not merely subject to the bureaucracy of the gods, but, unlike masters or priests of the popular religion, the Daoist masters were part of this bureaucracy. They had the power to petition, but they were as bound by the rigid rules as mundane officials were by those of the government, and as subject to penalties for minor infractions of ritual and form. Because immortality (as officials in the bureaucracy of the gods) was what Daoism offered its initiates, the penalties often took the form of subtracting units of life span. What made a good believer was not a private inner state but behavior and attitudes that met the needs of the community.

Regulation: From his meditation chamber in Loyang the Heavenly Master followed the immortals westward to Shu, to the Chi and Cheng mountains. Since "people were corrupt and unclean and it was a disorderly and unsettled age," the Heavenly Master scaled the Pillar of Heaven and strode across the celestial threshold in order to produce for the first time the Way of the Authoritative Covenant of Orthodox Unity [i.e., the Way of the Heavenly Masters]. Hoping to purify and enlighten the cosmos and mankind, to punish the unrighteous, and to nurture all living things, he established twenty-four parishes. For each parish he established male and female officers, a total of twenty-four [per parish]. He made use of the grace of the Dark Origin, opening the way to reform in later generations, so that all [believers] will repent of their errors and be ranked as Realized Immortals.

Offerings may be submitted to the celestial offices three times a month, to repent of sins, reform conduct, cut oneself off from undesirable companions, and escape calamities, diseases, and hazards. Each month three petitions may be submitted.

Regulation: When an officiant enters the parish temple to present a petition, he must conduct himself formally. Wearing formal Daoist vestments, he is to sit quietly and visualize in meditation the vital *qi* (energy or vital force) of the Five Directions [east, south, west, north, center] and the Inspector of Merits, officials, and soldiers within his own body. In order of their hierarchic positions, they reverently come to him, wait on him, and surround him [i.e., in his meditation he becomes the center of the configuration]. When one enters the parish temple and submits a petition, one stops outward thoughts and concentrates, calling up the gods from one's memory.

Regulation: A petition to the celestial offices is not to be presented in the parish temple on sexagenary day 5 or 35.[6] Pollution, according to the law, does not extend beyond the last day of the month, but one may still not submit a petition on the first of the [next] month. The uninitiated may not, when polluted, visit the parish temple and have an audience with the Master in charge. When this regulation is violated, [the priest's] allotted life span will be reduced by a year, for the crime will revert to him.

[Note in text: According to the regulations, each violation will be assessed by the Director of Errors and the Director of Investigations.]

Regulation: Those who enter the temple to present petitions must do so with upright carriage and quickened step. During the rites they are to keep to their

---

6. The Chinese marked time by pairing one by one the members of a cycle of ten denary "stem" characters with one of twelve duodenary "branch" characters in succession to form 60 possible unique day designations (similar to I-A, II-B, . . . X-J, I-K, II-L, III-A, and on to X-L, after which the cycle of pairings began again with another I-A.

places without men and women intermingling, looking idly about, speaking falsely, or moving too quickly or too slowly. Violators in positions of authority will be reduced one grade in rank. Those who cannot be demoted will be fined three ounces (liang) of jade and six hundred days of life.

Regulation: The ordained may not in an undisciplined fashion submit a petition on behalf of a perverse person. A perverse person is defined as one who is disrespectful or lewd; one who takes goods forcibly; one who is wicked and does not embody the Dao; one who does not act filially toward his parents or masters; one who does not act in accordance with obligation toward his rulers and elders, female [as well as male]; one who does not reverently uphold the morality of the Dao; one who is disrespectful toward the gods; one who steals or harms another, or acts treacherously; one who vilifies the worthy or slanders another as a result of envy; one who turns his back upon his parents; one who rebels against his master; or one who is uncompliant and will not do good. Until a full year has elapsed [since one of these infractions], one may not submit a petition for such a person. [An officiant] who does so will be punished by a deduction of five years from his allotted life span. Then, upon his death, he will be handed over to the Earl of the River (Hebo) for banishment. Furthermore, he will be fined eight ounces of jade and demoted two ranks.

Regulation: Petitions are to be phrased in simple rather than polished language. They may be clumsy but not artful; simple but not flowery; truthful and not false; straightforward and not convoluted; precise but not vexatious; weak (delicate) but not corrupt; pure and unsullied; straightforward but disciplined; compendious but sincere. Such petitions will move Heaven and Earth and arouse the sympathy of the spirits and gods. They will be forwarded to the celestial offices, and a response will come immediately. Violations will be prosecuted by the Director of Wrongs. Parish officials and under-officials will be held responsible.

Regulation: Petitions to cure illness shall be delivered with the officiant facing the Gate of the Spirits (northeast). Petitions seeking longevity should be delivered facing the Gate of Heaven (northwest). Petitions seeking monetary gain or worldly honor should be delivered facing the Gate of Earth. Petitions seeking to end disputes or annul curses should be delivered facing the Gate of the Human. Those to control the movements of tigers should be delivered facing in the tiger direction (slightly north of east) and those to control the movements of snakes facing in the snake direction (slightly east of south). This supplements one's spiritual powers with those of the cosmic meridians and secures great good fortune.

Regulation: To present a petition seeking wealth and honor, use the "celestial granary day," sexagenary day 25. To ask for rank, use the "celestial storehouse day." Don't use "self-punishing" days, duodenary days 7, 10, 12, or 5. In the duodenary terrestrial branch cycle, 3 punishes 6, 11 punishes 8, 1 punishes 4, 9 punishes 3, 4 punishes 1, and 6 punishes 9. Violations will incur 50 days of illness.[7]

Regulation: A request to petition for relief with respect to judgments enacted by the purgatorial authorities against one's deceased ancestors or with respect to sickness, calamity, or bad luck enacted as a sentence on account of one's own transgressions, must be made to one's parish. If one is far from one's master, one is permitted to proceed as the law permits. Petitions will not reach the celestial offices unless they are submitted by one's own master, a grade-A libationer, or an officer directly responsible for one's household or parish. Libationers below grades A through D must petition upward. Those responsible are [defined as] parish officials who lead three hundred or more households and those holding appointment as disease officer for three or more households.

[*Xuandu lüwen* (DZ) 78, no. 188, pp. 15–16 — NS]

THE MASTER WHO EMBRACES SIMPLICITY

The title of this work, *Baopuzi,* is the pen name of its author, Ge Hong (283–343). The Inner Chapters, the *Baopuzi neipian,* completed in 320 C.E., a sample of which is translated below,[8] deals with Daoist subjects, especially immortality and alchemy; the separate Outer Chapters, *waipian,* represent Ge's Confucian writings. The author was the descendant of a family long settled in the South, which had distinguished itself through both court service and initiation into Daoist arcana. Ge Hong himself declined official appointment by the Eastern Jin court, installed at Jianye (modern Nanjing) in 317, but was granted a title of nobility and land. His writings inform us that he devoted considerable energies to the unsuccessful pursuit of alchemical experiments and other methods of immortality. The following excerpt, from "Disquisition Regarding Immortality" (*Lun Xian*), forms part of a lengthy rejoinder to rationalist objections to the possibility of immortality.

As a rule, what exists will perish and what ends has a beginning. This is indeed a general principle. Yet there are differences and discrepancies, and what holds true for one does not hold true for another. The categories of transformation being legion, deviations from the norm are boundless. Things remain the same,

---

7. The choice of proper days could be specified not only by place in the sexagenary cycle, as explained in note 6, above, but also by the duodenary or denary character included in the pair of symbols that marks each day. Specifying a duodenary day, as the text does here, includes the five pairs that contain it out of each 60. The meaning of "punish" (*xing*) in early medieval China is not clear, but it is one of a number of technical terms for unfavorable astrological relationships.

8. For a complete translation, see James R. Ware, *Alchemy, Medicine, and Religion in the China of* A.D. *320: The Nei P'ien of Ko Hung (Pao-p'u tzu).*

while circumstances change. Though the trunk is like unto itself, the branches are diverse. There can be no single standard. Those who affirm that what begins must end are indeed numerous. However, confounding and equalizing things do not amount to establishing a universal principle.

It is said that in summer there must be growth, yet that is when shepherd's purse and wheat dry up. It is said that in winter there must be decline, yet that is when bamboo and cypresses grow luxuriant. It is said that what begins must end, yet Heaven and Earth are inexhaustible. It is said that what is born must die, yet tortoises and cranes enjoy longevity. The fullness of the yang principle ought to bring the heat of summer, yet summer weather is not necessarily without cool days. The zenith of yin corresponds to the cold season, yet a severe winter is not necessarily without warm spells. The hundred rivers discharge to the east, yet there is also the mighty flow of those that run north. The *kun* principle [i.e., Earth] is complete stillness, yet sometimes [the Earth] quakes and collapses. The nature of water is pure and cold, but there are hot springs in Wengu valley. The essence of fire is intense heat, but there are cold flames on Xiaoqiu isle. Heavy things should sink, yet in the South Sea there is a mountain of floating stone. Light objects ought to float, but feathers sink in the Zangke river. The infinitely varied categories cannot be judged summarily. This has always been so.

Among the most spiritual of living creatures, none surpasses human beings. Beings of a noble nature should all be uniformly of the same kind. Yet they are sagacious and stupid, perverse and righteous, handsome and ugly, tall and short, clear and turbid, chaste and lascivious, calm and hurried, slow and quick. The differences in the outcomes of their choices and in the objects of their desires are as great as those between Heaven and Earth, as opposite as ice and glowing coals. Why marvel only at the strangeness of the transcendents who do not die like ordinary people?

[*Baopuzi neipian jiaoshi*, pp. 12–13 — FV]

THE DOCTRINE OF THE THREE HEAVENS

This short treatise, the title of which means literally *An Initiate's Explanation of the Three Heavens* (*Santian neijie jing*), was written during the Liu Song dynasty (420–478) by an otherwise unknown Daoist named Xu. It presents a concise outline of the doctrines of Six Dynasties Daoism and offers valuable insights into the way the Dao was perceived at the time when Buddhism was expanding its influence not only in the North but also in the South. The approach of this text is fundamentally ecumenical, considering Buddhism as a true faith, while at the same time making a clear distinction between Chinese and foreign. That the ideas of the author were commonly shared by the Daoist initiates of his time is borne out by many other sources, yet nowhere else have they been put forward with such clarity.

The Dao originally sprang from what had nothing before it, from that infinite misty [Chaos] in which there was nothing that caused it to be. From that void something whole was produced spontaneously and through transformation: the Great Being of the Way and its Power, which was born before the Original *qi*-energy. This is the Venerable in the center of the Dao, and thus it is called "the Great Being of the Way and Power." From it are derived all the True Beings as they are addressed in our petitions today to the [Heavens] of Greatest Purity: "Their Highnesses the Limitless Great Dao of the Supreme Three Heavens of the Mysterious Origin of Greatest Purity, the Most High Old Lord, the Most High Great Being, the Ancestral Sovereigns of Heaven, the Nine Ancient Lords of the Capital of the Immortals, the Great Beings of the Nine *qi*-energies, etc., [ending with] the hundred and thousand energy layers of the Dao, [which produce] the Twelve Hundred [Cosmic] Officials."[9] After this, in the midst of obscure darkness appeared the Empty Cavern, and in the midst of the Empty Cavern appeared the Great Non-Being, and this Great Non-Being transformed and became the *qi*-energy of mystery, principle, and beginning. These three *qi*-energies mingled in chaotic coalescence and through transformation produced the Jade Maiden of Dark Mystery. When the Jade Maiden was born, the chaotic *qi*-energy coalesced again and through transformation produced Laozi. He was born through the left armpit of the Jade Maiden of Dark Mystery.[10] At his birth his hair was [already] white, and thus he was called Laozi (the Old Infant). Laozi is Laojun (the Old Lord). Through transformation he achieved the *qi*-energy [creating] Heaven, Earth, and humankind. . . . The Old Lord disseminated the [three] *qi*-energies of mystery, principle, and beginning. . . . The *qi*-energy of mystery, clear and limpid, rose and created Heaven; the *qi*-energy of beginning, dense and turbid, coalesced and descended to form the Earth; the *qi*-energy of principle, being light and subtle, streamed forth and became water. Sun and moon, stars and constellations then were expanded and scattered [through the sky]. The Old Lord then harmonized the [different] *qi*-energies and transformed them into nine countries, in which he placed nine human beings: three men and six women. At the time of Fu Xi and Nüwa, each of these adopted family and personal names. Thereupon [the Old Lord] produced three Dao, in order to instruct the Heavenly people [i.e., the elect]: in China (the Middle Kingdom) the *qi*-energy of yang being pure and correct, he made (the people) venerate the Great Dao of Non-Assertion [i.e., ancient Daoism]; in the lands of the foreigners with their eighty-one regions, where the *qi*-energy of yin predominates, he made the people venerate the Dao of Buddha with its severe rules and commandments in order to counter the yin-energy. In the lands

---

9. This is, as the text indicates, the ritual address of the Dao in its multiple One-ness, as used in the written prayers (*zhang*) in Taoist liturgy.

10. In contrast to the Buddha, who was born through the right armpit of Queen Maya.

of Chu and Yue, where yin and yang *qi*-energies are weak, he made the people venerate the Great Dao of the Pure Covenant. At that time, the reign of the Six Heavens[11] flourished.

The text continues by describing the repeated manifestations of Laozi as the teacher of kings in each major period of the history of ancient China. At last, during the Zhou, he was incarnated again, becoming first Mother Li (Mother Plumtree) and her "old child," who lived in her womb and there recited scriptures during eighty-one years. Born again through her left armpit, he lived in China until the time of King You. Then, observing the growing decadence of the dynasty, he "let down his hair and raved like a madman; he took leave of the Zhou and departed." Next follows the well-known story of his journey through the mountain pass and transmission of the *Daodejing*, here coupled with another book, the *Middle Scripture of the Laozi* (*Laozi zhongjing*). Finally he departed with Yin Xi, the guardian of the pass, for the western regions, where he was reincarnated as the Buddha, "and from these times on, Buddhism [which had already existed before] flourished again." However, in later times, decline and corruption set in. Buddhism, which originally was meant for non-Chinese, was introduced into the Middle Kingdom, and the Three Ways became confused:

The more things went wrong in the world of men, the more the *qi*-energy of Heaven became greatly troubled. When Heaven's *qi*-energy had become troubled and impure, the people lost their Fundamental Truth. Thereupon, in the years of Emperor Shun of the Han dynasty (r. 125–144 C.E.), the Most High (Laojun) chose a personal emissary in order to rectify the reign of the Six Heavens, to separate the true from the false and to reveal the *qi*-energy of the Highest Three Heavens. Thus, in the first year of the Han'an period, [the cyclical year being] *renwu* (142 C.E.), on the first day of the fifth moon, Laojun met with Zhang Daoling, the Daoist, in the cave of the Quting mountain in the district of Shu . . . and appointed him Master of the Three Heavens, of the One Correct *qi*-energy of Peace of the Great Mysterious Capital.

[DZ 876, no. 1205 — KS]

PRONOUNCEMENTS OF THE PERFECTED

The *Pronouncements of the Perfected* (*Zhen Gao*) is a vast and multifaceted collection of poetry and prose of the fourth century C.E. The texts, thought to have been divinely inspired, were originally "dictated" (*gao*) by Daoist "true beings," or the Perfected (*zhen*), to the highly literate medium and shaman Yang Xi (fl. 364–370), hence the title of the collection. Yang Xi lived in Jiankang (present-day Nanjing) as a servant in

---

11. The Six Heavens are those of the gods of ancient times, to be superseded by the pure gods of the Three Heavens in the new era heralded by the second coming of Laozi.

the large, aristocratic household of the Xu family. Most texts received by Yang Xi were intended for the patriarch of the family, Xu Mi, and his sons. They were first transmitted inside the Xu family and later collected by several eminent Daoists. The present edition was made by the great Daoist scholar Tao Hongjing (456–536). Tao painstakingly authenticated, collated, and annotated all the autograph fragments he could find. His edition of the *Zhen Gao*, published in 499, stands out as an early monument of text-critical scholarship.

The *Zhen Gao* is a unique source for our understanding of the ancient shamanistic Daoism of Southern China. The texts — especially the poems — show a distinct relationship to earlier shaman-inspired literature such as certain cantos found in the *Chuci* anthology.[12] As in these earlier works, the spiritual quest for a divine lover who is at the same time a redeemer is a central theme in the ecstatic poetry of the *Zhen Gao*. The Daoist adepts — male and female — exchange love poems with their immortal counterparts, in celebration of their ecstatic union.

Owing to its exceptional literary value, the belief in its supernatural origins, and other qualities such as the celebrated but now lost calligraphy of Yang Xi, the *Zhen Gao* has been very influential in medieval Chinese literature. The works of many of China's greatest poets, including Li Bo, Wang Wei, Bo Juyi, and Li Shangyin, were influenced by it.

Song of An, the True Consort of Ninefold Florescence

(dictated to Yang Xi)

My chariot has departed from the realm of Western Flowers,
Wandering between the worlds of impermanence and transcendence.
I now look at the summits of the Five Marchmounts,
Then again I bathe myself in the Milky Way.
Leaving my chariot behind, I search for an empty vessel,
In all this I am full of passionate feelings,
Who like a mustard grain can suddenly grow to cover ten thousand acres!
In the center stands Mount Sumeru:
There is no difference between large and small.
The same cause stands at the root of what is far and near;
You come from the impermanent world of phenomena,
But I love you as a transcendent being!

[*Zhen Gao* 3:4a]

---

12. The *Chuci*, or *Songs of Chu*, is a collection of poems from the ancient state of Chu, written between the third century B.C.E. and the second century C.E. and compiled in the mid-second century.

Exhortation by the Lady of Purple Tenuity

Ascending to the summit of Mount Xiling,
I roam freely in the realms in which there is neither circle nor square.
Vast empty spaces, beyond symbols and numbers,
Where Being and Non-Being spontaneously fuse in obscurity.
Sublime! Oh harmony of virtuality and sound!
With winged steps, I pace the Ultimate Void,
Meandering traces, wanton as waves,
The sounds of the bells carried away on the wind.
You who practice inward meditation in the Belvedere of the Seven Ways,
You will be able to obtain total oblivion.
Why force ourselves to continue exchanging poems,
Relying on these messages in the writing of the world?
Free of the passions of the heart, awakening will come spontaneously,
In silence, you will surely attain the highest level!

[*Zhen Gao* 2:16b; DZ 637–649, no. 1016 —KS]

THE *FIVE SENTIMENTS OF GRATITUDE*

The *Five Sentiments*, from the *Dongxuan lingbao wugan wen*, is an exercise in contrition written by the Lingbao patriarch Lu Xiujing (406–477) for his disciples. This exhortation was intended to be meditated upon in preparation for the Mud and Charcoal Retreat, a severe rite of repentance for the remission of sins that were believed to be the cause of disease and premature death. The anxiety expressed in Lu's stirring sermon with regard to the felicity and salvation of one's deceased parents reflects an important development in fifth-century Daoism. The radical separation of the realms of the living and the dead in the earlier Heavenly Masters dispensation of the Latter Han period (second century C.E.) had imposed restrictions on ancestral sacrifices. Meanwhile, however, Daoists, like their Buddhist counterparts, had found ritual means to accommodate the pervasive need in Chinese society to extend filial devotion beyond the grave. As the terminology in the selection that follows suggests, Daoist ritual had indeed adopted some of the ethical categories and imagery of Buddhist karmic belief regarding the salvation of both practitioners and their ancestors.

First Sentiment: Father and mother engendered me and gave me life, nourished me and nurtured me. Coming and going, they cradled me in their arms, soothed and comforted me, caressed and tended me. They damaged their health with anxiety and wore themselves out with worry. When I was unwell or fell ill, they were distressed and preoccupied on my account, their hearts burning as if on fire. Apprehensive day and night, they forgot their food[13] and

---

13. Emending *wangshi* for *wangjin*, "mindless of expense."

gave up their sleep; with growing agitation, they became emaciated. Shedding ceaseless tears they yearned for my growth and development. Enabled to become as I am now, I am mindful of their great, their immeasurable kindness. I sincerely vow to repay the boundless beneficence of my parents!

Second Sentiment: Father and mother provided for my education in adolescence and arranged for my marriage. They accumulated property and acquired the foundations of my livelihood. When it came to wanting more for me, they did not notice their greed. Contending with others engenders envy and avarice, which lead to transgressions and misdemeanors. In disobedience against Heaven and Earth, they caused injury to men and creatures. Without, they broke the king's law, and, within, offended against the rites of the nether world. They incurred increasing sanctions to the point of forfeiting their lives. And I am at the origin of it all, having invited this misfortune. Now they have fallen into the Three Paths (of retribution) encountering numerous hardships. They are subjected to the Tree of Swords and fall upon the Mountain of Knives; they walk the Fire of Flames, hot as a boiling cauldron, and are submerged in the Night of Darkness, cold as icy frost. Suspended in the flogging cage, their thousand pains and ten thousand sufferings are unbearable under the rod. Vexed and distraught, and ever hard-pressed to endure it, they hope for release but are unable to deliver themselves by their own effort. Thinking of this, I collapse and choke, my liver and heart break down in confusion, and my whole body trembles. My body and soul confounded and oblivious, I prostrate myself and with mud and coal beg for mercy.

Third Sentiment: In the whole world, noble and lowly, men and women, all alike receive a human body, and the burdens of the body and mouth. All alive prize the five flavors in food and five-colored silks in clothing. Even when already satisfied and warm, they can no longer restrain themselves. They use clothing and precious objects recklessly and delight in dissipation and the pursuit of schemes. Never feeling satiety, they harm the spirit and hurt the body, mindless that their vitality is already withering, their bodies decrepit. A lifetime of handling things, and to what use in the end? The orphaned soul dies alone and fully undergoes all its sufferings. Truly benighted, the world does not understand this! Once the excess wealth is distributed, it becomes the bane of posterity, engendering treachery and giving rise to thievery. Disputed by children and grandchildren, the strong grasp much, while the weak obtain little. Giving and taking, loss and gain increase their mutual rancor. If they take their plaints to the tribunal, they suffer chastisement and execution; if they appeal to spirits and demons, they incur occult calamities. The kinship with one's closest is contrived to create mutual enmity. Esteem for one's natural kin is discarded like dirt. [Under these conditions even the natural] love between brothers becomes war to the knife. The body perishes and the family is destroyed. Such feuds proceed from cupidity and extravagance. Altogether they sink and go under forever. Either they have not yet seen the light or, if they have understood, they are incapable of renunciation. The departed were thus, as those to come shall be again. They are content to accept this as the norm, without regret. I understand this is wrong and therefore turn my back on the world. Taking leave of my Six Kin and putting aside all cares and ambitions, I seek the Dao and strive for life, accumulate learning, and work for my salvation. If I can attain some usefulness, I shall first repay the kindness of my parents, who raised and nurtured me day after day. If I now obtain the divine elixir with which to rescue them from submersion, may they ascend the Dharma Bridge and cross over to the distant shore. Leaping with joy, the five emotions exalted, my heart soars and my spirit wanders. Suddenly I become oblivious of my four limbs. Unconscious, I abandon myself and take refuge in the Three Treasures. I pour out my possessions and make everything over to the dharma, fearing only that it will not suffice and that I have not yet relinquished all avarice. I wish that my father and mother shall ascend to the Hall of Felicity, forever escape the Eight Hardships, and never again suffer distress. May my small sincerity afford them sustenance.

Fourth Sentiment: All the Venerables on High, the great Sages, and the Perfected brought forth this great civilization and issued the wonderful dharma to deliver us from the Three Paths (of retribution) and save us from the Five Ways (of reincarnation). Once the calamitous grievances of myriads of generations of great-grandfathers and grandfathers through the accumulated *kalpas* are resolved, the souls of the departed are relieved and rise up to the Hall of Felicity. The elect of karmic causation all at once receive their recompense. My body attains the Way, and felicity is bestowed on succeeding generations. This rare grace occurs once in ten thousand *kalpas*. I shall faithfully carry out the ritual with all my heart and utmost devotion, and resolve to be remiss in nothing.

Fifth Sentiment: If I obtain this blessing, it will not happen without reason. Causation illumines salvation. It is the kindness of my teacher that caused me to see. My veneration for him knows no bounds, exceeding Heaven and Earth. Therefore, each day we carry out the rites I pray with utmost sincerity, hoping that I may possess some small merit with which to repay his benevolence. Even as I suffer bodily hardship and physical fatigue, I shall not dare spare myself.

[DZ 1004, no. 1278 — FV]

THE DIVINE INCANTATIONS SCRIPTURE

Every Daoist movement believed in the imminent end of the world, or at least of the great part of the human community that had not undertaken worship of the Way. *The Divine Incantations Scripture (Taishang dongyuan shenzhou jing)* is the oldest book that details the coming apocalypse. It emerged from a reform movement inside the

Heavenly Masters during the exceptionally chaotic political turmoil of the Jin dynasty (265–419). The earliest parts of the book, almost certainly written at the beginning of the fifth century, refer to events in the Jin dynasty between 380 and 400. The book is composed of several accumulated strata; in the early tenth century, it was supplemented, edited, and printed by Du Guangting.

In the original Heavenly Masters tradition, the faithful reached salvation through a series of initiations, which gave them "registers" (*lu*) that enrolled them among the immortals. But this book offers a new route to transcendence. The book itself (like a Buddhist text such as the *Heart Sūtra*) becomes not only the message but the all-powerful talisman that guarantees life amidst all too prevalent death.

For Daoists, of course, the gods of popular religion are subordinates of the true divinities — the Way and its emanations — about which "the vulgar" know nothing. The gods are, in a word, merely the officials of the celestial bureaucracy. Like yamen runners,[14] they can make trouble as well as enforce order. This text is typical in playing on that ambiguity. The same gods who are sent to punish the unbelievers are the ones who restore peace and normalcy; the Way gives the orders. The overall motion of the section is from dire threat to deliverance.

The Dao says: Sexagenary year 21 is about to arrive. The flood is not far off. Now, epidemic demons are killing people. The world abounds in vice and lacks goodness. The people do not recognize the truth. The Three Caverns (*Sandong*)[15] revelations have been spreading for a long time, but the people are benighted and fail to seek out and accept them. They bring suffering on themselves. What can be done? The people are to be pitied. I will now send eight units of palace guards to annihilate the epidemic ghosts and dispatch an order to banish [the epidemic ghosts]. Let Daoist priests convert people and make them accept the Three Caverns revelations.

The Dao says: From now on, for those who accept this *Divine Incantations Scripture*, thirty thousand celestial elite troops will protect you. Convert all the unenlightened day by day on behalf of all the living. If the unenlightened persist in their confusion and ridicule people who do good, Heaven will send epidemic ghosts to kill these people. Souls of such people will enter the three evil paths of rebirth, with no prospect of egress.

The Dao says: In sexagenary years 18 and 19, eighty million great ghosts will come to annihilate bad people. As for those with forked tongues, those who slander the law of the Dao, those who refer to their masters by their taboo-

---

14. I.e., low-ranking assistants of local officials.

15. The Three Caverns (*Sandong*) are the three traditions of divine revelation that came together to produce the body of Taoist scriptures. The text writes further on of the "divine protectors of the Three Caverns," gods dedicated to enforcing the prescriptions of the sacred writings. For a detailed discussion, see Ōfuchi Ninji, "The Formation of the Taoist Canon," in *Facets of Taoism*, ed. Holmes Welch and Anna Seidel, pp. 257–265.

names, those who dispute the scriptures, those who have no faith in the Three Caverns revelations, and those who are unwilling to accept the Dao, the great ghost king will come and annihilate all of them.

The Dao says: From now on, if there is a place where Daoist priests obediently follow the Three Caverns revelations, practice the Dao, and teach the people, I will send a multitude of ninety billion great soldiers to come all at once and protect you. If there is one ghost that won't leave, the divine protectors of the ten regions will come down immediately to arrest it.

The Dao says: From now on, wherever there are Daoist priests who recite this scripture, Heaven will order four hundred ninety thousand divine protectors of the Three Caverns, eight hundred thousand divine protectors from the six-fold heaven and ninety billion from the thirty-six-fold heaven to come and in unison kill those epidemic ghosts. Heaven will allow those among the living who are ill and those with official entanglements to obtain release.

Illnesses will lighten or remit. A pleasant disposition will be brought about in all the gods, and there will be household felicity. Within and without, god of the locality and god of the stove will be made clearly distinguishable [i.e., will not intrude upon one another's responsibilities]. They will not act against the rules and make trouble for the living. Those ghosts that do not belong to the household cult will be exiled forever to other places. If there are ghost troops who disobey my orders and do not depart, each and every one will be executed by the demon kings, without lenience. Take heed! The sages do not speak empty words.

The Dao says: In this *Divine Incantation Scripture* there are the names of the demon kings of the thirty-six-fold heaven as well as of seven billion minor kings. Wherever a Daoist priest recites this scripture, the demon king of the thirty-six-fold heaven, Ju Penzi, and seventy-two minor kings will come together and offer submission. Thus, in the cases of those who can recognize the impending end of the world age, accept this scripture, and make offerings in their households, no evil ghost will be able to come in an undisciplined way. Why? Because all the demon kings send divine protectors to guard this scripture. One hundred billion Celestial Men, Jade Women,[16] and immortals also come to guard it. Ghost troops will not dare come against the rules, either in front of you or behind your back.

The Dao says: From now on, if, wherever the scriptures are recited, there are evil ghosts or vicious spirits who still dare to perpetrate bad deeds and intentionally confront the living and [even] practitioners, eight billion ghost kings and demon kings take an oath to have their [own] heads cut off three times and split into thirty thousand pieces [since they will have permitted a breach of discipline].

---

16. Celestial Men and Jade Women are low-ranking members of the bureaucracy of immortals.

A demon king says: From now on, if there is a Daoist priest who heals illness, recites the scripture, and brings on prosperity, then I will allow everything he does to find fulfillment, all his wishes to be granted, and every plan to have its fruition. If I go back on my oath, I, your disciple Jumin, will suffer dismemberment ten thousand times.

The Dao says: From now on, the Three Caverns revelations will be disseminated far and wide. The Realized Ones [i.e., adepts] will accept it and the unenlightened [who need it] still more. Henceforth, ghost troops will help those who accept the Three Caverns revelations. Every action will reach completion and all that is done will be harmonious. The great demon kings will protect them. You Daoists must assiduously convert the unenlightened. If a master who has received the Three Caverns scriptures[17] journeys to save people when there is acute illness, and a Daoist priest recites the *Divine Incantations Scripture*, the demon kings of the threefold heaven will summon the lesser kings to shore up the disciple's power.

The Dao says: When Daoist priests receive the *Divine Incantations Scripture* they may not receive other scriptures at the same time. They must receive and practice this book separately. Why is this? Because there is so much divine power of the great demon kings in this scripture. It must not be received or copied alongside the others. It should also be stored in a separate case. When traveling, if you carry it on your person, the multitudes of ghosts can't come near. Those performing the communal rituals may also use its countless invocatory rites.

The Dao says: In this *Divine Incantations Scripture* are the names of all the demon kings. Therefore the Most Exalted considers it especially important. Where the scripture is recited, evil ghosts will not dare approach the living. Those that are not ghosts of ancestors will not approach them in violation of the rules. The great spirits of inside and outside, spirits infesting dwellings and tombs, spirits of the living and dead, and male and female spooks are henceforth banished ten thousand *li* away. If you do not obey this order you will be truncated ten thousand times, with no leniency.

The Dao says: In the world there are eighty thousand drowned people. The ghosts are about three feet high. They move about in immense groups. They kill people in water. Those who do not believe in the Dao will not be protected by good spirits and will also drown there. Furthermore, there are nine hundred eighty thousand kinds of water illness. There are thirty-two black illnesses, white illnesses, red illnesses, virid illnesses, and yellow illnesses that cannot be cured. There are ninety-six varieties of sudden death. All these happen to criminals and to the worldly who do not follow the law of Dao and who plunge the country

---

17. It is impossible to be sure whether "Three Caverns scriptures" refers to a particular set of scriptures (or even a Three Caverns scripture not elsewhere recorded) or to Daoist scriptures in general.

into disorder. This is because when bad people are unwilling all their lives to consider what is good, Heaven sends divine guardians with ten thousand illnesses to annihilate them. From now on, wherever a Daoist offers his meritorious good works and carries out communal rituals to save the people, you demon kings are to help this master of the law. I order you to ensure that when he treats illness the patients recover. If they do not recover, the head of the demon king Gao Linzi is to be broken into ninety pieces.

[DZ 170–173, no. 335, pp. 2–4 — NS]

ENCOUNTERS WITH IMMORTALS

The *Shenxian ganyu zhuan* by Du Guangting, from which the following text is taken, was completed about 904 C.E. It represents the genre of Daoist hagiography that emphasizes the esoteric transmission — of texts, formulae, sacred objects, rituals, and so on — that takes place when human beings enter into contact with the realm of the immortals. The sample translated here concerns a legendary explication of the abstruse military scripture the *Secret Talisman of the Yellow Emperor* (*Huangdi yinfu*),[18] a matter of some interest to the author, who was himself a commentator on that scripture. Although Du Guangting's commentary does not survive, it is clear that the present tale, by asserting the scripture's antiquity and authenticity, served to shore up its uncertain textual history in late Tang times.

Such doubts as the present story aimed to dispel would later prompt the Neo-Confucian author Zhu Xi (1130–1200) to attribute the *Secret Talisman* to Li Quan, the hero of this piece. An author of military treatises under the reign of Xuanzong (r. 713–756), Li certainly was responsible for an earlier commentary on the scripture, inspired by the revelation described here. His prophetic teacher can be identified from other sources as the Daoist immortal, the Old Woman of Lishan (*Lishan Laomu*). Her injunctions concerning the transmission of the sacred text reflect the Tang ordination system in which each degree of initiation was associated with the transmission of a determined set of canonical scriptures.

Li Quan, surnamed Master Daguan, lived at Mount Shaoshi [in the Songshan range in Dengfeng county, Henan province]. An adept in the Way of the Immortals, he regularly roamed the great mountains, searching widely for esoteric methods and skills. When he came to Tiger Mouth Cliff at Songshan, he found a copy of the *Secret Talisman of the Yellow Emperor* (*Huangdi yinfu*) there. The white silk scroll with vermilion script on a black lacquered roller was enclosed in a jade casket inscribed with the words "Secreted in the famed mountains by the Supreme Purity Daoist master Kou Qianzhi (364–448), on the seventh day of the seventh month of the second year Zhenjun under the Great Wei dynasty

---

18. *Daozang* 27, no. 31.

(441), for transmission to fellow devotees." The copy was in a state of decay. After Quan had copied it out and recited it several thousand times he still did not understand its meaning.

Upon entering Qin (Shaanxi) and arriving at the foot of Mount Li (in Lintong county), he encountered an old woman. She wore a topknot, letting half her hair hang down. Clad in tattered clothes and leaning on a staff, she had the extraordinary air of a spiritual being. On the side of the road, he saw a burning tree in flames. Thereupon the old woman mumbled to herself: "Wood begets Fire; when calamity arises, it must needs prevail." Quan was startled and asked, "These words are from the *Secret Talisman of the Yellow Emperor*, Part One. How did the old lady come to be able to pronounce them?" The old woman said, "I already received the talisman six cycles of the three monads' sexagesimal periods ago [i.e., in the mists of antiquity]. And where did the young man get it from?" Quan prostrated himself and after repeated reverences fully related how he had obtained it. The old lady said, "Young man, your cheekbones connect with your parietal bones; your wheel of fate joins a prominent forehead. Your vitality is undiminished, you have a detached disposition and a virtuous nature, and you are interested in esoteric methods; your spirit is brave and you love wisdom; truly, you are meant to be my disciple! At forty-five, however, there shall be great misfortune." Thereupon she produced a paper charm in vermilion script that was attached to the end of her staff. She bade Quan kneel and swallow it, saying, "May Heaven and Earth protect you!" Then, sitting on a rock, she proceeded to explain the meaning of the *Secret Talisman* to Quan:

"This talisman comprises three hundred characters in all. One hundred expound the Way; one hundred expound Methods; and one hundred expound Stratagems. Section one contains the Way of the immortals and of embracing the One;[19] the middle section, methods for making the nation prosper and bringing peace to the people; and the final section, stratagems for strengthening one's arms and winning victory in battle. They each foster discernment within and correspond to human concerns without. When it comes to contemplating deeply perceived truth, the Yellow Court and Eight Effulgences[20] do not measure up to it in subtlety; as for inquiring into matters of quintessential importance, scripture, tradition, philosophy, and history are unequal to it as literature; and in exercising skillful perspicacity, Sun, Wu, Han, and Bo[21] are inferior to its ingenuity. Only gentlemen possessing the Way may be apprised of it. Thus

---

19. Embracing the One: the Way of the Sages; see *Daodejing* 22 in ch. 5.

20. *Huangting bajing*: essential teachings of the Maoshan lineage of self-cultivation based on the Shangqing revelations. The *Taiping guangji* anthology emends the expression to "*Huangting neijing*," referring to the Inner Effulgences, the Maoshan version of the *Book of the Yellow Court*.

21. I.e., the famous strategists Sun Wu (sixth century B.C.E.) and Wu Qi (440–381 B.C.E.) and generals Han Xin (d. 196 B.C.E.), and Bo Qi (d. 257 B.C.E.) of the Warring States and Former Han periods.

if a perfected man uses it, he obtains its Way; if a superior man uses it, he obtains its methods; and if the common people use it, they meet with disaster. Each has a different degree of understanding. To transmit it to fellow devotees, one must celebrate a pure retreat before bestowing it. The holder of the book is the master; he who does not [yet] possess it, the disciple. It is not admissible to value wealth and influence while disregarding the poor and the humble. Offenders have their life span cut by twenty years. Recite the scripture seven times on your Personal Destiny day.[22] This will benefit your intelligence and increase your longevity. On the seventh day of the seventh month of each year write out one copy and secrete it in the cliff side of a great mountain. That will earn you another increase [in longevity]."

A long time had passed. The old woman said, "It is already the hour of *bu* (3–5 P.M.). I have some wheat meal that we shall eat together." She drew a gourd from her sleeve and told Quan to fetch water from the valley. Once it was filled with water, the gourd suddenly grew heavy, weighing more than a hundred pounds. As Quan did not have the strength to hold it, it sank into the spring. When he returned, the old woman had already disappeared. All that remained were several *sheng* of wheat meal. Quan served as deputy military governor of Jiangling (Hubei) and as vice president of the Censorate. A master of military strategy, he compiled the *Secret Classic of Taibo* (*Taibo yinjing*) in ten scrolls. An accomplished statesman, he also wrote the *Zhongtai zhi* (*Record of Zhongtai*) in ten scrolls. As a result of having been ostracized by [the faction of Chief Minister] Li Linfu (d. 752), he did not rise to a prominent position. In the end he entered the great mountains in search of the Way. After that, his whereabouts were unknown.

[DZ 328, no. 592 — FV]

THE WESTERN JOURNEY OF THE PERFECTED CHANGCHUN

This account of the travels of the Quanzhen patriarch Qiu Changchun in Central Asia, titled *Changchun zhenren xiyouji*, is the work of Li Zhichang (1193–1256). The historic journey, which took place in 1221–1224 in response to a summons by Chinggis (Genghis) Khan, led Qiu from Peking to the vicinity of Kabul. There a series of audiences and discussions took place during which Qiu expounded Quanzhen doctrine in reply to the ruler's inquiries. The following excerpts describe episodes from the journey and the exchanges between Qiu Changchun and the Khan.

[Yelü Tuhua] bore a Command addressed "from the emperor Chinggis to the adept, Master Qiu." This document praised the Dao of the Master above that

---

22. One's birthday—each day, according to the sexagenary cycle of days, being associated with a tutelary divinity.

of the Three Philosophers (Laozi, Liezi, and Zhuangzi) and declared that his merits were recognized in the remotest corners of the earth. Further on, the Emperor said, "Now that your cloud-girt chariot has issued from the realm of the immortals, the cranes that draw it will carry you pleasantly through the realms of India. Bodhidharma, when he came to the East, by spiritual communication revealed the imprint on his heart; Laozi, when he traveled to the West, perfected his Dao by converting the Central Asians. The way before you, both by land and water, is indeed long; but I trust that the comforts I shall provide will make it seem not long. This reply to your letter will show you my anxiety on your behalf. Having learned that you passed safely through the severe heat of autumn, I will not now trouble you with further friendly messages." Such was the respect with which the emperor addressed him! . . . [p. 60]

The journey began on the eighth day of the second month (March 3) in excellent weather. His Daoist friends accompanied him to the western outskirts of the town and there standing at his horse's head they asked him, weeping, when they might expect to see him back from this immense journey upon which he was setting out. At first he would say no more than that if their hearts remained firmly set upon the Dao, they would surely see him again. But when, with tears in their eyes, they begged him to be more specific, he told them that the goings and stopping of Man were determined elsewhere than on earth. "Moreover," he said, "traveling thus into strange lands I cannot yet tell whether their Dao will harmonize with mine or not." But the people said, "Master, we cannot believe that you do not know these things. We beseech you to foretell them to us." He saw that there was nothing for it but to tell them, and twice he said distinctly, "I shall return in three years." . . . [pp. 61–62]

On the eighteenth day of the eleventh month (December 3, 1221) after crossing a great river, we reached the northern outskirts of the mighty city of Samarkand. The Civil Governor his Highness I-la,[23] together with the Mongol and local authorities, came to meet us outside the town. They brought wine and set up a great number of tents. Here we brought our wagons to a stop. The envoy Liu Wen, who had not been able to get far owing to the road being blocked, now said to the Master when seated with him, "I have just learned that it is at present impossible to cross the great river,[24] which lies a thousand *li* ahead of us, as native bandits have destroyed the boats and bridge. Moreover, it is now the middle of winter. Would it not be better, my father and master, if your meeting with the Great Khan took place in the spring?" The Master agreed. . . . [p. 92]

After four more days of traveling we reached the Khan's camp. He sent his high officer, He-la-bo-de, to meet us. This was on the fifth day of the fourth

---

23. Yeh-lü (I-la) A-hai.
24. The Amu Darya.

month. When arrangements had been made for the Master's lodging, he at once presented himself to the emperor, who expressed his gratitude, saying, "Other rulers summoned you, but you would not go to them. And now you have come ten thousand *li* to see me. I take this as a high compliment."

The Master replied, "That I, a hermit of the mountains, should come at your Majesty's bidding was the will of Heaven." Chinggis was delighted, begged him to be seated and ordered food to be served. Then he asked him, "Adept, what medicine of long life have you brought me from afar?" The Master replied, "I have means of protecting life, but no elixir that will prolong it." The emperor was pleased with his candor and had two tents for the Master and his disciple set up to the east of his own. . . . [pp. 100–101]

The Master's words were translated into Mongol by A-hai. The emperor was delighted with his doctrine and on the nineteenth, when there was a bright night, sent for him again. On this occasion too he was much pleased by what he heard and sent for the Master to come to his tent once more on the twenty-third (October 29). He was here treated with the same regard as before and the emperor listened to him with evident satisfaction. He ordered that the Master's words should be recorded and especially that they should be written down in Chinese characters, that they might be preserved from oblivion. To those present he said, "You have heard the holy Immortal discourse three times upon the art of nurturing the vital spirit. His words have sunk deeply into my heart. I rely upon you to repeat what you have heard." During the remainder of the Imperial Progress to the east, the Master constantly discoursed to the emperor concerning the mysteries of Dao. [p. 113]

> [*Changchun zhenren xiyouji*, DZ 1056, no. 1429; trans. Waley,
> *Travels of an Alchemist*, pp. 60–62, 92, 100–101, 113]

Chapter 15

THE INTRODUCTION OF BUDDHISM

The coming of Buddhism to China was an event of far-reaching importance in the development of Chinese thought and culture and of Buddhism itself. After a long and difficult period of assimilation, this new teaching managed to establish itself as a major system of thought, contributing greatly to the enrichment of Chinese philosophy, and also as a major system of religious practice, which had an enduring influence on Chinese popular religion. Indeed, it came to be spoken of along with the native traditions, Confucianism and Daoism, as one of the Three Teachings or Three Religions, thus achieving a status of virtual equality with these beliefs.

By the time Buddhism reached China (according to official tradition, in the first century C.E.), it had already undergone several centuries of development in regard to both its philosophical doctrines and its religious practices. This is not the place to attempt a summation of that historical development, but a brief statement of the major principles and concepts of Buddhism in India is essential to understanding the forms it took in China.

BASIC TEACHINGS OF BUDDHISM

The fundamental truths on which Buddhism is founded are not metaphysical or theological but, rather, psychological. Basic is the doctrine of the "Four

Noble Truths": (1) all life is inevitably sorrowful, (2) sorrow is due to craving, (3) sorrow can only be stopped by the stopping of craving, and (4) this can be done by a course of carefully disciplined conduct, culminating in the life of concentration and meditation led by the Buddhist monk. These four truths, which are the common property of all schools of Buddhist thought, are part of the true Doctrine (Sanskrit, *dharma*), which reflects the fundamental law of the universe.[1]

All things are composite, and, as a corollary of this, all things are transient, for the composition of all aggregates is liable to change with time. Moreover, being essentially transient, they have no eternal Self or soul, no abiding individuality. And, as we have seen, they are inevitably liable to sorrow. This threefold characterization of the nature of the world and all that it contains — sorrowful, transient, and soulless — is frequently repeated in Buddhist literature; without fully grasping its truth no being has any chance of salvation, for until one thoroughly understands the three characteristics of the world one will inevitably crave for permanence in one form or another, and as this cannot, by the nature of things, be obtained, one will suffer, and probably make others suffer also.

All things in the universe may also be classified into five components or are composed of a mixture of them: form and matter (*rūpa*), sensations (*vedanā*), perceptions (*saṃjñā*), psychic dispositions or constructions (*saṃskāra*), and consciousness or conscious thought (*vijñāna*).

The first consists of the objects of sense and various other elements of less importance. Sensations are the actual feelings arising as a result of the exercise of the six senses (mind being the sixth) upon sense-objects, and perceptions are the cognitions of such sensations. The psychic constructions include all the various psychological emotions, propensities, faculties, and conditions of the individual, while the fifth component, conscious thought, arises from the interplay of the other psychic constituents. The individual is made up of a combination of the five components, which are never the same from one moment to the next, and therefore the individual's whole being is in a state of constant flux.

The process by which life continues and one thing leads to another is explained by the Chain of Causation or Dependent Origination. The root cause of the process of birth and death and rebirth is ignorance, the fundamental illusion that individuality and permanence exist, when, in fact, they do not. Hence there arise in the organism various psychic phenomena, including desire, followed by an attempt to appropriate things to itself — this is typified es-

---

1. The word *dharma* as employed in Buddhism is untranslatable in English. Besides meaning "Law" or "Doctrine" it also represents phenomena in general, as well as the qualities and characteristics of phenomena.

pecially by sexual craving and sexual intercourse, which are the actual causes of the next links in the chain, which concludes with old age or death, only to be repeated again and again indefinitely. Rebirth takes place, therefore, according to laws of karma, which do not essentially differ from those of Hinduism, though they are explained rather differently.

As we have seen, no permanent entity transmigrates from body to body, and all things, including the individual, are in a state of constant flux. But each act, word, or thought leaves its traces on the collection of the five constituents that make up the phenomenal individual, and their character alters correspondingly. This process goes on throughout life, and when the material and immaterial parts of the being are separated in death, the immaterial constituents, which make up what in other systems would be called soul, carry over the consequential effects of the deeds of the past life and obtain another form in one of the ten realms of existence: namely, those of hell dwellers, hungry ghosts, animals, human beings, *asuras* (or spirits), heavenly beings, *śrāvakas* (or direct disciples of Buddha), *pratyeka-buddhas*,[2] bodhisattvas, or buddhas. Thus there is no permanent soul, but nevertheless room is found for the doctrine of transmigration. Though Buddhism rejects the existence of the soul, this makes little difference in practice, and the more popular literature of Buddhism, such as the *Birth Stories* (*Jātaka*), takes for granted the existence of a quasi-soul, at least, which endures indefinitely.

The process of rebirth can be stopped only by achieving *nirvāṇa*, first by adopting right views about the nature of existence, then by a carefully controlled system of conduct, and finally by concentration and meditation. The state of *nirvāṇa* cannot be described, but it can be hinted at or suggested metaphorically. The word literally means "blowing out," as of a lamp. In *nirvāṇa* all idea of an individual personality or ego ceases to exist and there is nothing to be reborn: as far as the individual is concerned *nirvāṇa* is annihilation. But it was not generally thought of by the early Buddhists in such negative terms. It was rather conceived of as a transcendent state, beyond the possibility of full comprehension by the ordinary being enmeshed in the illusion of selfhood but not fundamentally different from the state of supreme bliss as described in other non-theistic Indian systems.

These are the doctrines of the Theravāda or Hīnayāna school, and with few variations, they would be assented to by all other schools of Buddhism. But when Mahāyāna Buddhism arose in India, claiming to offer salvation for all, it styled itself *Mahāyāna*, the Greater Vehicle to salvation, as opposed to the older Buddhism, which it referred to disparagingly as *Hīnayāna*, or the Lesser Vehicle. The Mahāyāna scriptures also claimed to represent the final doctrines of the Buddha, revealed only to his most spiritually advanced followers, while the

---

2. Private buddhas who have attained enlightenment for themselves.

earlier doctrines were merely preliminary ones. Though Mahāyāna Buddhism, with its pantheon of heavenly buddhas and bodhisattvas and its idealistic metaphysics, was strikingly different in many respects from the Theravāda, it can be viewed as the development into finished systems of tendencies that had existed long before.

A tendency to revere the Buddha as a god had probably existed in his own lifetime. In Indian religion, divinity is not something completely transcendent, or far exalted above all mortal things, as it is for the Jew, Christian, or Muslim; neither is it something concentrated in a single unique omnipotent and omniscient personality. In Indian religions godhead manifests itself in so many forms as to be almost, if not quite, ubiquitous, and every great sage or religious teacher is looked on as a special manifestation of divinity, in some sense a god in human form. How much more divine was the Buddha, to whom even the great god Brahma himself did reverence, and who, in meditation, could far transcend the comparatively tawdry and transient heavens where the great gods dwelt, enter the world of formlessness, and pass thence to the ineffable *nirvāṇa* itself! From the Buddhist point of view, even the highest of the gods was liable to error, for Brahma imagined himself to be the creator, when in fact the world came into existence as a result of natural causes. The Buddha, on the other hand, was omniscient.

Yet, according to theory, the Buddha had passed completely away from the universe, had ceased in any sense to be a person, and no longer affected the world in any way. But the formula of the "Three Treasures" or "Jewels" — "I take refuge in the Buddha, the *dharma*, and the *saṅgha*" — became the Buddhist profession of faith very early and was used by monk and layman alike. Taken literally, the first clause was virtually meaningless, for it was impossible to take refuge in a being who had ceased to exist as such. Nevertheless, the Buddha was worshiped from very early times, and he is said to have himself declared that all who had faith in him and devotion to him would obtain rebirth in paradise.

A further development that encouraged the tendency to theism was the growth of interest in the bodhisattva. This term, meaning literally "Being of Wisdom," was first used in the sense of a previous incarnation of the Buddha. For many lives before his final birth as Siddhārtha Gautama, the Bodhisattva did mighty deeds of compassion and self-sacrifice, as he gradually perfected himself in wisdom and virtue. Stories of the Bodhisattva, known as *Birth Stories* (*Jātaka*) and often adapted from popular legends and fables, were very popular with lay Buddhists, and numerous illustrations of them occur in early Buddhist art.

It is probable that even in the lifetime of the Buddha it was thought that he was only the last of a series of earlier buddhas. Later, perhaps through Zoroastrian influence, it came to be believed that other Buddhas were yet to come, and interest developed in Maitreya, the future Buddha, whose coming was said to have been prophesied by the historical Buddha and who, in years to come, would purify the world with his teaching. But if Maitreya was yet to come, the chain of being that would ultimately lead to his birth (or, in the terminology of other sects, his soul) must be already in existence. Somewhere in the universe, the being later to become Maitreya Buddha was already active for good. And if this one, how many more? Logically, the world must be full of bodhisattvas, all striving for the welfare of other beings.

The next step up in the development of the new form of Buddhism was the changing of the goal at which the believer aimed. According to Buddhist teaching there are three types of perfected beings — Buddhas, who perceived the truth for themselves and taught it to others; *pratyeka*-buddhas, "private Buddhas," who perceived it but kept it to themselves and did not teach it; and *arhats*, "worthies," who learned it from others but fully realized it for themselves. According to earlier schools, the earnest believer should aspire to become an *arhat*, a perfected being for whom there was no rebirth, who already enjoyed *nirvāṇa* and who would finally enter that state after death, all vestiges of his personality dissolved. The road to *nirvāṇa* was a hard one and could only be covered in many lives of virtue and self-sacrifice; even so, the goal began to be looked on as selfish. Surely a bodhisattva, after achieving such exalted compassion and altruism, and after reaching such a degree of perfection that he could render inestimable help to other striving beings, would not pass as quickly as possible to *nirvāṇa*, where he could be of no further use, but would deliberately choose to remain in the world, using his spiritual power to help others, until all had found salvation. Passages of Mahāyāna scriptures describing the self-sacrifice of the bodhisattva for the welfare of all things living are among the most passionately altruistic in the world's religious literature.

The replacement of the ideal of the *arhat* by that of the bodhisattva is the basic distinction between the old sects and the new Mahāyāna. Faith in the bodhisattvas and the help they afforded was thought to carry many beings along the road to bliss, while the older schools, which did not accept the bodhisattva ideal, could save only a few patient and strenuous souls.

The next stage in the evolution of the theology of the new Buddhism was the doctrine of the "Three Bodies" (*Trikāya*). If the true ideal was that of the bodhisattva, why did not Siddhārtha Gautama remain one, instead of becoming a Buddha and selfishly passing to *nirvāṇa*? This paradox was answered by a theory of docetic type, which, again, probably had its origin in popular ideas prevalent among lay Buddhists at a very early period. Gautama was not in fact an ordinary man, but the manifestation of a great spiritual being. The Buddha had three bodies — the Body of Essence (*Dharmakāya*), the Body of Bliss (*Sambhogakāya*), and the Body of Transformation (*Nirmāṇakāya*). It was the Body of Transformation that lived on earth as Siddhārtha Gautama, an emanation of the Body of Bliss, which dwelled forever in the Heavens as a sort of supreme god. But the Body of Bliss was in turn the emanation of the Body of Essence, the ultimate Buddha, who pervaded and underlay the whole universe. Subtle philosophies and metaphysical systems were developed parallel with these theological ideas, and the Body of Essence was identified with *nirvāṇa*. It was in fact the World Soul, the Brahman of the Upaniṣads in a new form. In the fully developed Mahāyānist cosmology there were many Bodies of Bliss, all of them emanations of the single Body of Essence, but the heavenly Buddha chiefly concerned with our world was *Amitābha* (Immeasurable Radiance), who dwelt in *Sukhāvatī*, the "Happy Land" (or "Pure Land," as it was known to the Chinese), the Paradise of the West. With him was associated the earthly Gautama Buddha and a very potent and compassionate bodhisattva, Avalokiteśvara (the Lord Who Looks Down).

The older Buddhism and the newer flourished side by side in India during the early centuries of the Christian era, and we read of Buddhist monasteries in which some of the monks were Mahāyānist and some Hīnayānist. But, in general, the Buddhists of northwestern India were either Mahāyānists or members of Hīnayāna sects much affected by Mahāyānist ideas. The more austere forms of Hīnayāna seem to have been strongest in parts of western and southern India, and in Sri Lanka. It was from northwestern India, under the rule of the great Kushāna empire (first to third centuries C.E.) that Buddhism spread throughout Central Asia to China; since it emanated from the northwest, it was chiefly of the Mahāyāna or near-Mahāyāna type.

THE COMING OF BUDDHISM TO CHINA

As Buddhism spread from its homeland, it became the harbinger of civilization in many of the areas that it penetrated. Many of them had no system of writing before the advent of the new religion. One of the most notable exceptions to this statement, however, was China. By the time Buddhism was introduced, China boasted a civilization that was already very old, a classic canon, time-hallowed traditions, and the conviction that its society was the only truly civilized society in the world. Thus, while Buddhism was the vehicle for the introduction into Central Asia of many arts of civilization, the Buddhist missionaries found in China a country that possessed these things in an already highly developed state. Buddhism was obliged to compete with indigenous philosophical and religious systems to win the hearts of the Chinese, and the Chinese, for their own part, were hindered in their understanding of Buddhist philosophy by preconceptions based on indigenous philosophical systems.

No one can say when or in what fashion the Chinese first came into contact with Buddhism. It is to be presumed, from conjecture, and from what sparse documentation there is, that this contact was with Buddhist icons worshiped by Central Asians coming into China. The Chinese of the time adopted the Buddha into their scheme of things as a demigod on the order of their own mythical Yellow Emperor and the philosopher Laozi, who was believed to have attained immortality. But the dawn of history for Chinese Buddhism came with the rendition of Buddhist sacred texts into the Chinese language.

The Chinese were particularly desirous of knowing whether Buddhism could add to their knowledge of elixirs and practices that would contribute to longevity, levitation, and other superhuman achievements. As it happened, Buddhism (like many other Indian religions) prescribed a precise set of practices, varying from school to school, which was believed to enhance the intuitive faculties. The early Buddhist missionaries found that the scriptures containing these prescriptions were what the Chinese wanted most to read, and so they proceeded to translate them. This was the beginning of Buddhist literature in China.

As time went on, and as the interest of China's intellectuals veered toward metaphysical speculation, it became fashionable to seek in Buddhism those sublime truths that persons so inclined were seeking in some of China's own canonized classics. When, in 317 C.E., non-Chinese peoples forced the Chinese court out of North China, an educated elite was displaced to the south. A refined and sophisticated culture developed among them, with the dominant trend in southern Buddhism being toward abstruse philosophical discussion in salons that brought together the cream of secular society and the best wits from the great metropolitan monasteries. An often facile interpretation of Buddhism in terms of Daoism and the Learning of the Mysterious[3] prevailed, and Buddhism's Indian origins were somewhat effaced.

There were contrary trends, however. In the first place, not a few monks, in both North and South China, were earnestly concerned with the true meaning of Buddhism and of Buddhist salvation. The Chinese aversion to foreign languages being what it was, these persons showed their zeal principally in seeking out capable translators or in participating in translation projects themselves. Also, simultaneously with the philosophical salons and the great translation projects a trend developed, more pronounced in the north than in the south, toward a practical and devotional Buddhism, which consisted of an emphasis on contemplative practices as well as on adoration and good works. Temples and statuary were soon erected all over China.

The selections that follow are intended to illustrate the general character of Buddhism in this early period and some of the problems encountered in gaining acceptance for it among the Chinese.

MOUZI: *DISPOSING OF ERROR*

Though the date and authorship of this work are not known, the general tone of the composition leads one to suspect that the work was written at a time when Buddhism had gained a sufficient foothold to cause many Chinese to fear its influence and to

---

3. See ch. 13.

attempt to strike back. While the counterattack against Buddhism in the north took the form of official persecution or curtailment, under the Southern Dynasties (317–589 C.E.) it usually took the form of polemics. *Disposing of Error*, or *Lihuo lun*, as it is known in Chinese, appears to be an apologia for Buddhism, written in answer to such polemical writings.

The form of the work is conversational — an exchange between Mouzi and a questioner (or questioners) bent on criticizing Buddhist ideas and practices from a distinctively Chinese perspective. The author — Mouzi himself or a recorder of his words — takes the stand that it is possible to be a good Chinese and a good Buddhist at the same time, that there is no fundamental conflict between the two ways of life, and that the great truths preached by Buddhism are preached, if in somewhat different language, by Confucianism and Daoism as well.

Why Is Buddhism Not Mentioned in the Chinese Classics?

The questioner said, "If the way of the Buddha is the greatest and most venerable of ways, why did Yao, Shun, the Duke of Zhou, and Confucius not practice it? In the Seven Classics[4] one sees no mention of it. You, sir, are fond of the *Classic of Odes* and *Classic of Documents*, and you take pleasure in the *Rites* and "Music." Why, then, do you love the way of the Buddha and rejoice in outlandish arts? Can they exceed the Classics and commentaries and beautify the accomplishments of the sages? Permit me the liberty, sir, of advising you to reject them."

Mouzi said, "All written works need not necessarily be the words of Confucius, and all medicine does not necessarily consist of the formulae of Bian Que.[5] What accords with rightness is to be followed, what heals the sick is good. The gentleman-scholar draws widely on all forms of good and thereby benefits his character. Zigong[6] said, 'Did the Master have a permanent teacher?'[7] Yao served Yin Shou; Shun served Wucheng; the Duke of Zhou learned from Lü Wang; and Confucius learned from Laozi. And none of these teachers is mentioned in the Seven Classics. Although these four teachers were sages, to compare them to the Buddha would be like comparing a white deer to a unicorn,[8] or a swallow to a phoenix. Yao, Shun, the Duke of Zhou, and Confucius learned even from such teachers as these. How much less, then, may one reject the Buddha, whose distinguishing marks are extraordinary and whose superhuman

---

4. There are several different lists of the Seven Classics. One found in the *History of the Latter Han* includes the *Odes, Documents, Rites,* "Music," *Changes, Spring and Autumn Annals,* and the *Analects* of Confucius.

5. The most famous physician of antiquity.

6. A prominent disciple of Confucius.

7. *Analects* 19:22.

8. *Qilin*, a mythical beast like the unicorn, but not actually one-horned.

powers know no bounds! How may one reject him and refuse to learn from him? The records and teachings of the Five Classics do not contain everything. Even if the Buddha is not mentioned in them, what occasion is there for suspicion?"

Why Do Buddhist Monks Do Injury to Their Bodies?

One of the greatest obstacles confronting early Chinese Buddhism was the aversion of Chinese society to the shaving of the head, which was required of all members of the Buddhist clergy. The Confucians held that the body is the gift of one's parents and that to harm it is to be disrespectful toward them.

The questioner said, "The *Classic of Filiality* says, 'Our body, limbs, hair, and skin are all received from our fathers and mothers. We dare not injure them.' When Zengzi was about to die, he bared his hands and feet.[9] But now the monks shave their heads. How this violates the sayings of the sages and is out of keeping with the way of the filial!" . . .

Mouzi said . . . "Confucius has said, 'There are those with whom one can pursue the Way . . . but with whom one cannot weigh [decisions].'[10] This is what is meant by doing what is best at the time. Furthermore, the *Classic of Filiality* says, 'The early kings ruled by surpassing virtue and the essential Way.' Taibo cut his hair short and tattooed his body, thus following of his own accord the customs of Wu and Yue and going against the spirit of the 'body, limbs, hair, and skin' passage.[11] And yet Confucius praised him, saying that his might well be called the ultimate virtue."[12]

Why Do Monks Not Marry?

Another of the great obstacles confronting the early Chinese Buddhist church was clerical celibacy. One of the most important features of indigenous Chinese religion is devotion to ancestors. If there are no descendants to make the offerings, then there will be no sacrifices. To this is added the natural desire for progeny. Traditionally, there could be no greater calamity for a Chinese than childlessness.

---

9. To show he had preserved them intact from all harm. *Analects* 8:3.

10. *Analects* 9:29. The full quotation is "There are those with whom one can learn but with whom one cannot pursue the Way; there are those with whom one can pursue the Way but with whom one cannot take one's stand; there are those with whom one can take one's stand but with whom one cannot weigh [decisions]."

11. Uncle of King Wen of the Zhou who retired to the barbarian land of Wu and cut his hair and tattooed his body in barbarian fashion, thus yielding his claim to the throne to King Wen.

12. *Analects* 8:1.

The questioner said, "Now of felicities there is none greater than the continuation of one's line, of unfilial conduct there is none worse than childlessness. The monks forsake wife and children, reject property and wealth. Some do not marry all their lives. How opposed this conduct is to felicity and filiality!" . . .

Mouzi said . . . "Wives, children, and property are the luxuries of the world, but simple living and doing nothing (*wuwei*) are the wonders of the Way. Laozi has said, 'Of reputation and life, which is dearer? Of life and property, which is worth more?'[13] . . . Xu You and Chaofu dwelt in a tree. Boyi and Shuqi starved in Shouyang, but Confucius praised their worth, saying, 'They sought to act in accordance with humanity and they succeeded in acting so.'[14] One does not hear of their being ill-spoken of because they were childless and propertyless. The monk practices the Way and substitutes that for the pleasures of disporting himself in the world. He accumulates goodness and wisdom in exchange for the joys of wife and children."

Death and Rebirth

Chinese ancestor worship was premised on the belief that the souls of the deceased, if not fed, would suffer. Rationalistic Confucianism, while taking over and canonizing much of Chinese tradition, including the ancestral sacrifices, was skeptical about the existence of spirits and an afterlife apart from the continuance of family life.

The Buddhists, though denying the existence of an immortal soul, accepted transmigration, and the early Chinese understood this to imply a belief in an individual soul that passed from one body to another until the attainment of enlightenment. The following passage must be understood in the light of these conflicting and confusing interpretations.

The questioner said, "The Buddhists say that after a man dies he will be reborn. I do not believe in the truth of these words. . . ."

Mouzi said . . . "The spirit never perishes. Only the body decays. The body is like the roots and leaves of the five grains. When the roots and leaves come forth they inevitably die. But do the seeds and kernels perish? Only the body of one who has achieved the Way perishes." . . .

Someone said, "If one follows the Way one dies. If one does not follow the Way one dies. What difference is there?"

Mouzi said, "You are the sort of person who, having had not a single day of goodness, yet seeks a lifetime of fame. If one has the Way, even if one dies, one's soul goes to an abode of happiness. If one does not have the Way, when one is dead one's soul suffers misfortune."

---

13. *Daodejing* 44.
14. *Analects* 7:14.

Why Should a Chinese Allow Himself to Be Influenced by Indian Ways?

This was one of the objections most frequently raised by Confucians and Daoists once Buddhism had acquired a foothold on Chinese soil. The Chinese apologists for Buddhism answered this objection in a variety of ways. Here we see one of the arguments they used.

The questioner said, "Confucius said, 'The barbarians with a ruler are not so good as the Chinese without one.'[15] Mencius criticized Chen Xiang for rejecting his own education to adopt the ways of [the foreign teacher] Xu Xing, saying, 'I have heard of using what is Chinese to change what is barbarian, but I have never heard of using what is barbarian to change what is Chinese.'[16] You, sir, at the age of twenty learned the Way of Yao, Shun, Confucius, and the Duke of Zhou. But now you have rejected them and instead have taken up the arts of the barbarians. Is this not a great error?"

Mouzi said . . . "What Confucius said was meant to rectify the way of the world, and what Mencius said was meant to deplore one-sidedness. Of old, when Confucius was thinking of taking residence among the nine barbarian nations, he said, 'If a noble person dwells in their midst, what rudeness can there be among them?'[17] . . . The commentary says, 'The north polar star is in the center of Heaven and to the north of man.'[18] From this one can see that the land of China is not necessarily situated under the center of Heaven. According to the Buddhist scriptures, above, below, and all around, all beings containing blood belong to the Buddha-clan. Therefore I revere and study these scriptures. Why should I reject the Way of Yao, Shun, Confucius, and the Duke of Zhou? Gold and jade do not harm each other, crystal and amber do not cheapen each other. You say that another is in error when it is you yourself who err."

Does Buddhism Have No Recipe for Immortality?

Within the movement broadly known as Daoism there were several tendencies, one the quest for immortality, another an attitude of superiority to questions of life and death. The first Chinese who took to Buddhism did so out of a desire to achieve superhuman qualities, among them immortality. The questioner is disappointed to learn that Buddhism does not provide this after all. Mouzi counters by saying that even in Daoism, if properly understood, there is no seeking after immortality.

---

15. *Analects* 3:5.
16. *Mencius* 3A:4.
17. *Analects* 9:13.
18. It is not clear what commentary is quoted here.

The questioner said, "The Daoists say that Yao, Shun, the Duke of Zhou, and Confucius and his seventy-two disciples did not die, but became immortals. The Buddhists say that men must all die, and that none can escape. What does this mean?"

Mouzi said, "Talk of immortality is superstitious and unfounded; it is not the word of the sages. Laozi said, 'Even Heaven and Earth cannot last forever. How much less can human beings!'[19] Confucius said, 'The wise man leaves the world, but humaneness and filial piety last forever.' I have looked into the six arts and examined the commentaries and records. According to them, Yao died; Shun had his [place of burial at] Mount Cangwu; Yu has his tomb on Kuaiji; Boyi and Shuqi have their grave in Shouyang. King Wen died before he could chastise [the tyrant] Zhou; King Wu died without waiting for [his son] King Cheng to grow up. . . . And, of Yan Yuan, the Master said, 'Unfortunately, he was short-lived,'[20] likening him to a bud that never bloomed.[21] All of these things are clearly recorded in the Classics: they are the absolute words of the sages. I make the Classics and the commentaries my authority and find my proof in the world of men. To speak of immortality, is this not a great error?"

[From *Hongming ji*, *TD*, no. 2102:1–7 — adapted from LH by IB]

HUIYUAN: A MONK DOES NOT BOW DOWN BEFORE A KING

When an Indian entered the Buddhist clergy, he left his clan, his caste, and all his worldly possessions. As one standing outside of ordinary society, he from then on paid no outward signs of veneration to secular potentates. In China, too, early Buddhist clerics, though they knelt in their religious ceremonies, displayed no signs of respect to laymen in positions of authority, not even to the emperor.

At first this constituted no great problem, since only the most eminent monks were ever likely to meet the emperor, and these were usually foreigners who were not expected to follow full Chinese etiquette. When native Chinese came to constitute the majority of Buddhist clerics, however, the problem became more serious. The question was brought under discussion at court during the Eastern Jin period, but no settlement was reached until 402 C.E. At that time the high minister Huan Xuan (369–404), who had temporarily usurped the throne, referred the problem to one of the outstanding monks of the day, Huiyuan (334–417), for a recommendation. Huiyuan replied with a letter stating that, though Buddhist laymen, like other laymen, were obliged by the customary etiquette to acknowledge their loyalty and respect for their sovereign, the Buddhist clergy, who by the nature of their life and aims were far removed from ordinary men, could not be expected to go through the outward signs

---

19. *Daodejing* 23.
20. *Analects* 11:6.
21. *Analects* 9:21.

of obeisance. Huan Xuan accepted Huiyuan's argument and decreed that monks need not bow before the emperor. Shortly after this, Huiyuan composed a treatise titled "A Monk Does Not Bow Down Before a King" ("Shamen bu jing wang zhe lun"), stating his argument in greater detail.

Buddhism in the Household

If one examines the broad essentials of the teachings of the Buddha, one will see that they distinguish between those who leave the household life and those who remain in it. . . . Those who revere the Buddhist laws but remain in their homes are subjects who are obedient to the transforming powers [of temporal rulers]. Their feelings have not changed from the customary, and their course of conduct conforms to the secular world. Therefore this way of life includes the affection of natural kinship and the proprieties of obedience to authority. Decorum and reverence have their basis herein, and thus they form the basis of the doctrine. That on which they are based has its merit in the past. Thus, on the basis of intimacy it teaches love and causes the people to appreciate natural kindness; on the basis of austerity it teaches veneration and causes the people to understand natural respect. . . . Thus obedience is made the common rule, and the natural way is not changed. . . .

Hence one may not benefit by [the ruler's] virtue and neglect propriety, bask in his kindness and cast aside due respect. Therefore they who rejoice in the way of Śākya invariably first serve their parents and respect their lords. They who change their way of life and throw away their hair ornaments must always await [their parents'] command, then act accordingly. If their lords and parents have doubts, then they retire, inquire of their wishes, and wait until [the lords and parents] are enlightened. This, then, is how the teaching of Buddha honors life-giving and assists kingly transformation in the way of government.

Buddhism Outside the Household

This second part sets forth the core of Huiyuan's argument as to why the monk should not make a display of respect for worldly potentates. The monk, so the argument goes, is not a disrespectful, much less an impious, person, but he stands completely outside of the framework of lay life; hence he should not abide by its regulations insofar as merely polite accomplishments are concerned.

He who has left the household life is a lodger beyond the earthly [secular] world, and his ways are cut off from those of other beings. The doctrine by which he lives enables him to understand that woes and impediments come from having a body, and that by not maintaining the body one terminates woe. . . .

If the termination of woe does not depend on the maintenance of the body, then he does not treasure the benefits that foster life. This is something in which the principle runs counter to physical form and the Way is opposed to common practice. Such men as these commence the fulfillment of their vows with the putting away of ornaments of the head [shaving the head] and realize the achievement of their ideal with the changing of their garb. . . . Since they have changed their way of life, their garb and distinguishing marks cannot conform to the secular pattern. . . . Afar they reach to the ford of the Three Vehicles,[22] broadly they open up the Way of Heaven and the human. If but one of them be allowed to fulfill his virtue, then the Way spreads to the six relations and beneficence flows out to the whole world. Although they do not occupy the positions of kings and princes, yet, fully in harmony with the imperial ultimate, they let the people be. Therefore, though inwardly they may run counter to the gravity of natural relationships, yet they do not violate filial piety; though out-wardly they lack respect in serving the sovereign, yet they do not lose hold of reverence.

He Who Seeks the First Principle Is Not Obedient to Change

In general, those who reside within the limits [of ordinary existence] receive life from the Great Change. . . . Life is fettered by physical form, and life depends upon change. When there is change and the feelings react, then the spirit is barred from its source and the intellect is blinded to its own illumina-tion. If one is thus shut up as in a hard shell, then what is preserved is only the self, and what is traversed is only the state of flux. Thereupon the bridle of the spirit loses its driver, and the road to rebirth is reopened daily. One pursues lust in the long stream of time; is one thus affected only once? Therefore he who returns to the source and seeks the First Principle does not encumber his spirit with life. He who breaks out of the grimy shell does not encumber his life with feelings. If one does not encumber one's spirit with life, then one's spirit can be made subtle. The subtle spirit transcending sense-objects — this is what is meant by *nirvāṇa*. The name *nirvāṇa*, can it possibly be an empty appellation? I beg leave to extend this argument and so to prove its truth. Heaven and Earth, though they are great because they give life to living beings, cannot cause a living being not to die. Kings and princes, though they have the power of preserving existence, cannot cause a preserved creature to be without woe. Therefore in our previous discussion we have said, "[He who has left the house-hold life] understands that woes and impediments come from having a body

---

22. That is, postponing enlightenment in order to bring others closer to salvation, attaining enlightenment by personal exertions in an age in which there is no Buddha, and attaining enlightenment by hearing the Buddha's preaching. These three are associated with the bodhi-sattva, the *pratyeka* or "private buddha," and the *śrāvaka* or "voice-hearer," respectively.

and that by not maintaining the body one terminates woe. He knows that continued life comes from undergoing change, and by not obeying this change he seeks the First Principle." Herein lay our meaning, herein lay our meaning. This is why the monk refuses homage to the Lord of the Myriad Chariots [i.e., the emperor] and keeps his own works sublime, why he is not ranked with kings or princes and yet basks in their kindness.

[From *Hongming ji, TD* 52, no. 2102:29–32 — LH]

ADMONITIONS OF THE *FANWANG SŪTRA*

The following admonitions represent the basic moral code to which many Mahāyāna monks in China subscribed when they took the bodhisattva vows or precepts. From what now appears to be an apocryphal text, never canonically sanctioned, these admonitions purport to come from the mouth of the Buddha. In effect they constitute a substantial reduction and modification of the disciplinary code for monks in the earlier, so-called Hīnayāna or Smaller Vehicle (seen as "smaller" because it was more restrictive, difficult to practice, and thus limited in its practicability for all). Here the unlimited expedient or adaptive means available through the later, Greater Vehicle enable it to overcome some of the Chinese objections to the Hīnayāna cited in the preceding Mouzi text.

Note in these admonitions the strong invocation of filiality as a basis for Buddhist discipline. This adaptation to the more life-affirming, family orientation of Confucianism contrasts with the earlier characterization of the Buddhist religious vocation as "leaving the family" (*chujia*). As a major concession to Chinese values, this new view of Buddhism as fulfilling the ends of filial piety became a marked feature of East Asian Buddhism in general.

Later even this simplified code was further minimized in the two main schools of Chinese Buddhist practice, Pure Land and Chan, which emphasized means other than adherence to the traditional disciplinary code for the attainment of salvation.

At that time, the Buddha Śākyamuni, seated under the Bo tree after having attained supreme enlightenment, first set up the Precepts (*Prātimokṣa*): to be filial to one's parents, teacher[s], members of the Buddhist community, and the Three Treasures. Filial obedience is the way by which one attains the Way. Filial piety is called the "admonitions"; it is also called the "prohibitions." Then the Buddha emanated infinite light from his mouth.

At that time, trillions of participants in the assembly, including all the bodhisattvas, eighteen Brahmin kings, the kings of the six heavens in the realm of desires, and sixteen great kings, etc., all joined their palms in front of their chests and listened to the Buddha reciting the Mahāyāna Admonitions of all the Buddhas.

The Buddha told all the bodhisattvas: "I now recite by myself every fortnight, the Admonitions of the Law. All of you bodhisattvas — bodhisattvas who have just aspired [for supreme enlightenment] — should also recite them; bodhisatt-vas who are in the ten stages of directional decision, the ten stages of the well-nourished heart, the ten stages of "diamond heart," and bodhisattvas who are in the ten stages before attaining Buddhahood, should also recite them. This is why the light of the Admonitions issues forth from my mouth. It has some conditions that make it possible, and it is not without a cause; hence the man-ifestation as light. [Yet] the light is neither green, nor yellow, nor red, nor white, nor black. It is neither material nor mental. It is neither being nor nonbeing. It is not causation. It is the source of all Buddhas and the root of all bodhisattva deeds. It is the root of all sons of the Buddha in this assembly. Therefore, all sons of the Buddha should receive it and hold to it. You should read, recite, and master it.

"All sons of the Buddha, listen carefully: those who wish to receive the Admonitions, be they kings, princes, ministers, prime ministers, monks, nuns, eighteen Brahmin kings, the six kings of Heaven's realm of desire, or sixteen great kings, commoners . . . male prostitutes, female prostitutes, male servants, female servants, the eight classes of supernatural beings, guardians, animals, even illusory beings, as long as they understand the language of the master [who gives the Admonitions], they are all able to receive the Admonitions and thereby be called 'most pure ones.' "

The Buddha proclaimed to all the sons of the Buddha, saying, "There are ten major precepts. Anyone who has received the Bodhisattva Admonitions and yet does not recite them is not a bodhisattva, nor is one the seed of a Buddha. I also recite them. All the [past] bodhisattvas have learned, all the [future] bodhisattvas will learn, and all the [present] bodhisattvas are learning them. Now that I have explained briefly the nature of the Bodhisattva Precepts, you should learn them and follow them with respect."

1. The Buddha said: "Sons of the Buddha, in the case of killing or urging others to kill; killing for expediency or condoning others who kill; or rejoicing at seeing others kill, or killing by means of a spell — whatever the causes of killing, the condition of killing, the method of killing, or the action of killing — the killing of any living being should not be done intentionally. A bodhisattva should always give rise to a heart of compassion, a heart of filial piety, using all expedient means to save all sentient beings. If, on the contrary, one kills living beings as one pleases, one commits an unpardonable offense for a bodhisattva."

2. "In the case of a son of the Buddha stealing, urging others to steal, stealing for expediency, or stealing by means of spells — whatever the cause of stealing, the condition of stealing, the method of stealing, and the action of stealing — even things owned by gods and spirits — and whatever the goods — even a nee-dle or a blade of grass — there should be no intentional stealing. A bodhisattva should give rise to the heart of filiality of the Buddha-nature, a heart of com-

passion, always helping all people to achieve felicity and happiness. If, on the contrary, one goes so far as to steal the property of others, one commits a most unpardonable offense for a bodhisattva."

3. "In the case of a son of the Buddha committing fornication, urging others to commit fornication, or committing fornication with any woman — there should be no intentional fornication, no matter what the cause, condition, method, or act of fornication, whether with female animals, female deities, or female spirits, or any such sexual misconduct. A bodhisattva should give rise to the heart of filiality, bring all sentient beings to salvation, and offer them pure truth. If, on the contrary, one commits any kind of fornication, whether with animals, one's own mother, sisters, and relatives, showing no compassion or restraint, one commits an unpardonable offense for a bodhisattva."

4. "In the case of a son of the Buddha lying, urging others to lie, or lying for expediency — whatever the cause . . . condition . . . method . . . or the act of lying — even if one says one sees something without actually seeing it, or says one did not see something when one has seen it — a bodhisattva should always give rise to correct speech and [help] all sentient beings to give rise to correct speech and correct views. If, on the contrary, one prompts sentient beings to evil speech or evil views, one commits a most unpardonable offense for a bodhisattva."

5. "In the case of a son of the Buddha dealing in alcoholic liquors, or urging others to deal in them — whatever the cause . . . the condition . . . the method . . . or the act of dealing in alcohol — one should do nothing of that kind. Alcoholic liquors are a cause and condition that give rise to wrongdoing, whereas a bodhisattva should give rise to the clear and thorough wisdom of all sentient beings. If, on the contrary, one causes confusion in the minds-and-hearts of all sentient beings, one commits an unpardonable offense for a bodhisattva."

6. "In the case of a son of the Buddha criticizing the transgressions of a bodhisattva who has renounced the world, a bodhisattva who is a householder, a *bhikṣu* monk or a *bhikṣuṇī* nun, or of someone urging others to criticize such people — whatever the cause . . . condition . . . method . . . or act of criticizing — or when a bodhisattva hears an evil person of a non-Buddhist sect or an evil person who is either a *śrāvaka* or a *pratyeka*-buddha criticizing any Buddhist's violations of law or discipline, if, instead of motivating such an evil person to adopt a positive Mahāyāna mind, the bodhisattva rather lends himself to such criticism, it is a transgression of the Buddha's law and a most unpardonable offense."

7. "In the case of a son of the Buddha himself praising or blaming others, or telling others to do so — whatever the cause . . . the condition . . . the method . . . or act of blaming — whereas the bodhisattva should take upon himself the blame or shame that attaches to all other living beings, whether for evil deeds to oneself or great deeds of others, if, instead, he praises his own merits and

conceals others' good deeds, or lets others take the blame, it is a most unpardonable offense for a bodhisattva."

Similar formulations are given for three other offenses — stinginess, anger, and slander against the Three Treasures — which, with the preceding items, make up the ten major vices. These are then followed by a detailing of forty-eight minor violations or vices to be avoided by the bodhisattva, such as disrespect to one's master, drinking liquor, eating meat, eating five forbidden spices, and so on.

[*Fanwang jing, TD* 24, no. 1484:1004–1005 — THT]

Chapter 16

SCHOOLS OF BUDDHIST DOCTRINE

Doctrinal Buddhism developed in China at least three hundred years after Buddhism's presence was first noted there in the first century. It arose not as a result of violent schisms or protestant revolts but as an outgrowth of tendencies already manifest in the earlier period of Buddhist thought.

THE GENERAL CHARACTER OF DOCTRINAL BUDDHISM

The division of Chinese Buddhism into discrete schools had its origins in the tendency to concentrate on the study of one particular scripture or group of scriptures, as containing the most essential truths of the religion. The Chinese knew almost nothing of the splintering of Buddhism into sects in India and Central Asia. They did not know to what extent the scriptures themselves were sectarian writings, nor did they properly understand the sectarian motivation that lay behind the selection by the various missionaries of the scriptural texts they translated. For them, any Buddhist text translated into Chinese was the word of the Buddha. And since all of the Buddha's pronouncements had to be true, it was necessary to find some way to reconcile the frequently glaring inconsistencies found in the scriptures. A suggestion on how to deal with this problem was furnished to them by the Mahāyāna scriptures themselves.

By the time of the emergence of the Mahāyāna, the so-called Hīnayāna scriptures had already been canonized, and anyone calling himself a Buddhist regarded them as the word of the Buddha. The Mahāyānists composed their own scriptures as they went along, and they found themselves obliged to justify their scriptures as the good coin of Buddhism to a religious community accustomed to reading religious writings of a vastly different tone. To deny the validity of the firmly entrenched Hīnayāna canon was impossible, and the Mahāyānists resorted to a more subtle device. They said that the Hīnayāna was not untrue but was merely a preparatory doctrine, preached by the Buddha to disciples whose minds were not yet receptive to the ultimate truth. When he had prepared them with the provisional doctrine, he then revealed to them his final truth. Thus the Hīnayāna and the Mahāyāna alike were the word of the Buddha, but the full significance of the former became apparent only with the later revelation.

The difficulty here, as far as the Chinese were concerned, was the fact that while the Hīnayāna scriptures, having been canonized by a series of ecclesiastical councils, were more or less homogeneous, the Mahāyāna scriptures had never been canonized or coordinated, and they frequently contradicted not only the Hīnayāna sacred writings but each other as well. To deal with this, the first distinct schools in Chinese Buddhism either concentrated on one scripture or set of scriptures in preference to all others or catalogued the entire canon in such a way as to make one particular scripture appear to contain the Buddha's ultimate teaching. The great Tiantai and Huayan schools did both.

Their doctrines, however, were of a kind that could never have much popular appeal. In addition, the religious practices prescribed by them for the attainment of salvation could be performed only by monks whose whole lives were devoted to religion. On both accounts these schools tended to be limited to the few who had the leisure and training that were required for the study and practice of such sophisticated teachings. Among the great masses of people, therefore, it was not doctrine of this type but rather salvationism of the type represented by the Pure Land school[1] that prevailed.

Furthermore, the view that all scriptures represented the word of the Buddha tended to blur, even for the learned, the doctrinal differences that might have distinguished one sect from another. In the latter half of the Tang dynasty, from about 750 to about 900, one frequently encounters an eminent Chinese monk going about from one center to another studying the precepts of all the schools, as if anything short of mastery of all of them was an imperfect knowledge of Buddhism. Some Chinese monks are claimed as patriarchs by as many as three or four different schools. Thus was confirmed in Chinese Buddhism a strong tendency toward syncretism, which had long been a feature of Chinese thought.

---

1. See ch. 17.

SCHOOLS OF CHINESE
BUDDHIST PHILOSOPHY

From the readings in chapter 15 it will be apparent that some of the most fundamental concepts of Buddhism were comprehended and assimilated by the Chinese with the greatest of difficulty, if at all. Moreover, as one takes up the writings of Buddhist philosophers, one is conscious of having entered another world — not just different from one's own but different even from the Chinese traditions that preceded it. For one thing, one is dealing with metaphysical and psychological questions to which earlier Chinese writers had given less attention than they had to the problems of the individual in society. Yet not only are these questions in their very nature extremely complex and elusive, but also, as discussed by Chinese writers, they presupposed some familiarity with a vast body of Buddhist doctrine from India possessed only by those who had some education (always a small minority in traditional China) and who had dedicated themselves to the pursuit of the religious life, most often in monasteries. Their audience was neither "the general public," nor the "congregation," nor anything resembling the general membership of a creedal church.

Buddhist philosophy first began to flourish in the fourth century C.E., when it was interpreted largely in Daoist terms, on the basis of which "six schools and seven branches" were formed, including Daoan's theory of Original Nonbeing or the Originally Undifferentiated; the same theory as modified by Fashen; Zhi Daolin's theory of Matter-as-Such; and Fawen's theory of No Mind or the Emptiness of Mind. These were simply the teachings of individual thinkers, not of sectarian leaders. As important Indian texts were introduced and translated, as Indian masters arrived, and as Chinese Buddhist scholars finally developed their own systems, differences in opinion appeared and schools came into being. In their zeal to defend their ideas, certain schools of thought denounced others as heretical and established a lineage to earlier masters in order to claim for themselves the authority of tradition. Yet as far as the ordinary Buddhist was concerned, these differences were academic.

Altogether there were ten principal schools, traditionally divided into two main categories, schools of Being and schools of Nonbeing, depending on whether they affirmed or denied the self-nature of the *dharmas* (here "elements of existence") and the ego. There was also the Disciplinary school, based on the Vinaya section of the Buddhist canon. Its doctrine was elaborated and completed by Daoxuan (596–667) in the South Mountain. The discipline for which it was known included 250 "prohibitive precepts" for monks and 348 for nuns. Nevertheless, this school hardly existed as an independent sect in China, and its precepts were largely superseded by the Ten Admonitions presented in chapter 15.

None of these schools exerted much influence or lasted very long. The same may be said of two Mahāyāna schools, the Three-Treatise or Emptiness school and the Consciousness-Only school. The concepts of Emptiness and of the Mind, however, were accepted as basic presuppositions of the remaining schools, and thus were important to what followed.

The common Chinese saying "The Tiantai and Huayan schools for doctrine; the Meditation and Pure Land schools for practice" accurately describes both the strong influence of these schools in particular and the syncretic nature of Chinese Buddhism in general. Of these, the Tiantai did not exist at all in India and the Pure Land, Huayan, and Meditation schools, while traceable to India, developed along characteristically Chinese lines, which enabled them to persist throughout Chinese history.

The remaining Mahāyāna school, the Esoteric school (*Zhenyan*, true word), believed that the universe consists of the "three mysteries" of action, speech, and thought. All phenomena represented by these categories of action, speech, and thought are manifestations of a cosmo-theism centered on the Great Sun Buddha. Through secret language, "mystical verse," "true words," and so on, the quintessential truth of the Buddha can be communicated to human beings. This doctrine was transmitted to China by several Indian monks and attained a considerable vogue in the eighth century but lost its separate identity thereafter. Its influence as a distinct school was felt mostly in Tibet and Japan, while in China its practice became widely diffused into indigenous popular religion.

THE THREE-TREATISE SCHOOL

The Three-Treatise (*Sanlun*) school is the Chinese representative of the Indian Mādhyamika (Middle Doctrine) school of Nāgārjuna (ca. 100–200 C.E.). It was introduced into China by a half-Indian missionary named Kumārajīva (344–413), who translated into Chinese three Indian works systematizing the Middle Doctrine. Two of these by the Mādhyamika school taught that the phenomenal world has only a qualified reality, as opposed to those who maintained the ultimate reality of the chain of events or elements that make up the phenomenal being or object. According to the Mādhyamika view, a monk with defective eyesight may imagine that he sees flies in his begging bowl, and they have full reality for the perceiver. Though the flies are not real, the illusion of flies is. The Mādhyamika philosophers tried to prove that all our experience of the phenomenal world is like that of the shortsighted monk, that all beings labor under the constant illusion of perceiving things as real, whereas in fact they are only "empty." This pervasive Emptiness or Void (*Śūnyatā*) is the only true reality; hence the Mādhyamikas were sometimes also called *Śūnyavādins* (exponents of the doctrine of Emptiness). Although the phenomenal world is true pragmatically, and therefore has qualified reality for practical purposes, the whole chain of existence is seen as composed only of a series of transitory events, and these, being impermanent, cannot have reality in themselves. Emptiness, on the other hand, never changes. It is absolute truth and absolute being — in fact, it is the same as *nirvāṇa* and the Body of Essence, or *Dharma*-Body, of the Buddha.

Nāgārjuna's system, however, went farther than this. Nothing in the phenomenal world has full being, and all is ultimately unreal. Therefore every rational theory about the world is a theory about something unreal evolved by an unreal thinker with unreal thoughts. Yet, by the same process of reasoning, even the arguments of the Mādhyamika school in favor of the ultimate reality of Emptiness are unreal, and this argument against the Mādhyamika position is itself unreal, and so on in an infinite regression. Every logical argument can be reduced to absurdity by a process such as this.

The effect of Mādhyamika nihilism was not what might be expected. Skeptical philosophies in the West, such as that of existentialism, are generally strongly flavored with pessimism. The Mādhyamikas, however, were not pessimists. If the phenomenal world was ultimately unreal, Emptiness was real, for though every logical proof of its existence was vitiated by the flaw of unreality, it could be experienced in meditation with a directness and certainty that the phenomenal world did not possess. The ultimate Emptiness was here and now, everywhere and all-embracing, and there was, in fact, no difference between the great Emptiness and the phenomenal world (*saṁsāra*). Thus all beings were already participants in the Emptiness that was *nirvāṇa*; they were already Buddha if only they would realize it. This aspect of Mādhyamika philosophy was especially congenial to Chinese Buddhists, nurtured in the doctrine of the Dao, and it had much influence on the development of the special forms of Chinese and Japanese Buddhism, which often show a frank acceptance of the beauty of the world, and especially of the beauty of nature, as a vision of *nirvāṇa* here and now.

For an understanding of this doctrine as it is discussed in Chinese texts, familiarity with certain technical terms is necessary. One is the concept of *common truth* and *higher truth*. From the standpoint of common or worldly truth, i.e., relatively or pragmatically, *dharmas* are said to exist. From the standpoint of higher truth, they are seen to be transitory and lacking in any substantiality or self-nature. Emptiness or the Void alone represents the changeless Reality. The dialectical process by which this ultimate truth is reached is known as the "Middle Path of Eightfold Negations," which systematically denies all antithetical assertions regarding things: "There is no production, no extinction, no annihilation, no permanence, no unity, no diversity, no coming in, no going out." Production, extinction, and so on are shown to be unreal by the use of the "Four Points of Argument" — that is, by refuting any concept of being, of nonbeing, of both being and nonbeing, and of neither being nor nonbeing. The belief in any of the four is an extreme and must be transcended by a higher synthesis through the dialectic method until the Ultimate Void is arrived at, which is the Absolute Middle.

The Middle Way was greatly elaborated and systematized by Jizang (540–623), who had a Parthian father and a Chinese mother. Jizang made the Three Treatises the center of his system of thought, and his influence extended to the eighth century. However, as a school it rapidly declined after the ninth century, while its method was assimilated into other teachings.

A large number of Jizang's writings survive, consisting principally of commentaries on Mahāyāna scriptures and treatises, and containing one of the earliest overall attempts at a systematization of Mahāyāna doctrine.

JIZANG: *THE PROFOUND MEANING OF THE THREE TREATISES*

Having set forth his interpretation of the Three Treatises in detailed commentaries to each of them, Jizang arranges topically what he considers to be the essential doctrine of the treatises as a whole.

Of those who misunderstand the Twofold Truth[2] there are, in all, three kinds of men. First are the Abhidharmists, who insist upon the existence of a definite substance, who err in [taking as ultimate what is in fact no more than] dependent existence [that is, a thing coming into existence depending on causes and conditions] and who therefore lose [the true meaning of] Common Truth. They also do not know that dependent existence, just as it is, has no existence, and thus they also lose [the true meaning] of the One True Emptiness. Second are those who learn the Great Vehicle and who are called Men of the Extensive and Broad Way. They adhere to a belief in Emptiness and fail to recognize dependent existence, hence they lose the [true meaning of] Common Truth. Having adhered to the misunderstood Emptiness, they err with regard to the true Emptiness, and thus also lose the [true meaning of] Higher Truth. Third are those in this very age who, though knowing of the Twofold Truth, in some cases say that it is one substance, in some cases say that it is two substances. These theories are both untenable, hence they lose the [true meaning of both] Higher and Common Truth.

Question: "Higher and Common Truths are one substance." What error is there in this?

Answer: If Higher and Common Truths are one and the same in being true,

---

2. The Common Truth — that *dharmas* have a relative or dependent existence — and the Higher Truth — that they are ultimately unreal and that Emptiness or Voidness alone constitutes changeless reality.

then Higher Truth is true and Common Truth is also true. If Higher Truth and Common Truth are one and the same in being common, then Common Truth is common and Higher Truth is also common. If Higher Truth is true and Common Truth is not true, then Common Truth and Higher Truth are different. If Common Truth is common and Higher Truth is not common, then Higher Truth and Common Truth are different. Therefore both ways are blocked, and the two cannot be one.

Question: If it is an error to regard the two as one substance, then it should be blameless to regard them as different.

Answer: The scriptures say, "Matter in and of itself is void; void in and of itself is matter." If you say that each has its own substance, then their mutual (shared) identity is destroyed. If they have mutual identity, then duality of substance cannot be established. Therefore there is no latitude [for argument] in any direction, and conflicting theories are all exhausted.

Mahāyāna Truth is beyond all predication. It is neither one nor many, neither permanent nor impermanent. In other words, it is above all forms of differentiation or, as its adherents might say, it transcends both difference and identity. In order to make this point clear, the Three Treatises doctrine teaches that each thesis that may be proposed concerning the nature of Truth must be negated by its antithesis, the whole process advancing step by step until total negation has been achieved. Thus the idea of being, representing Common Truth, is negated by that of nonbeing, representing Higher Truth. In turn, the idea of nonbeing, now having become the Common Truth of a new pair, is negated by the idea of neither being nor nonbeing, and so forth, until everything that may be predicated about Truth has been negated.

Objection: If there is neither affirmation nor negation, then there is also neither wrong nor right. Why, then, in the beginning section do you call it the"refutation of wrong" and the "demonstration of right"?

Answer: That there are negation and affirmation, we consider "wrong." That there is neither affirmation nor negation, we call "right." It is for this reason that we have explained it in this section in terms of the "Refutation of Wrong" and the "Demonstration of Right."

Objection: Once there are a wrong to be refuted and a right to be demonstrated, then the mind is exercising a choice. How can one say then that it "leans [depends] on nothing"?

Answer: In order to put an end to wrong, we force ourselves to speak of "right." Once wrong has been ended, then neither does right remain. Therefore the mind has nothing to which it adheres [or on which it depends].

Objection: If wrong and right are both obliterated, is this not surely a [positive] view of Emptiness?

Answer: The *Treatise on Right Views* says:

The Great Sage preached the Law of Emptiness
In order to separate [human beings] from all [positive] views.
If one still has the view that there "is" Emptiness,
Such a person even the Buddhas cannot transform. . . .

Question: Why does the scripture set up the Twofold Truth?

Answer: There are two reasons. First it wishes to demonstrate that the Law of Buddha is the Middle Way. Since there is a Common Truth, there is no [heresy of] annihilation [that is, the view that things have no existence whatever]. Because of the Supreme Truth there is no [heresy of] eternity [that is, the view that things have enduring, changeless existence]. This is why it establishes the Twofold Truth. Further, the two wisdoms are the father and mother of the *Dharma*-Body of the Buddhas of the three ages [past, present, and future]. By reason of the Supreme Truth, true wisdom is produced. By reason of the Common Truth, [the use of] expedient devices [to save all sentient beings] comes into being. When true wisdom and expedient wisdom are both present, then one has the Buddhas of the ten directions and the three ages. For this reason the Twofold Truth is established.

Again, to know the Supreme Truth is to benefit oneself; to know the Common Truth is to be able to benefit others; to know both truths simultaneously is to be able to benefit all equally. Therefore the Twofold Truth is established. Also, it is because there is Twofold Truth that the Buddha's words are all true. By virtue of the Common Truth, when he preaches the doctrine based on existence, that is true. By virtue of the Supreme Truth, when he preaches the doctrine based on Emptiness, that is true. In addition, the law of Buddha becomes gradually more profound. First he preaches the Common Truth of cause and effect to convert people. Then he preaches the Supreme Truth for them. Also, for the purpose of achieving perfection and achieving the Way he preaches the Supreme Truth to those who possess wisdom and the Common Truth to those who do not. Furthermore, had he not first preached the Common Truth of cause and effect, but preached right away the Supreme Truth, he would have given rise to the heresy of annihilation. For these reasons he preaches both aspects of the Twofold Truth.

[From *Sanlun xuanyi*, TD 45, no. 1852:1–11 — LH]

THE SCHOOL OF CONSCIOUSNESS-ONLY

The school of Consciousness-Only (*Weishi*) corresponds to the Vijñānavāda or Yogācāra school of Indian Buddhism, which, together with the Doctrine of the Middle Way, represented the two main branches of Mahāyāna philosophy. Its great teachers in India were Asaṅga (fourth century C.E.) and Vasubandhu, of about the same period. When Asaṅga's works were translated into Chinese in the sixth century C.E., the school was first known as the Shelun, but eventually it was absorbed into the school of the great Chinese monk, translator, and philosopher Xuanzang (599–664). The latter's school was also known as the *Dharma*-Character (*Faxiang*) school, after one of the characteristic features of its teaching, as explained below.

The seventh-century pilgrimage of Xuanzang to the Western regions in search of the true teachings of Buddhism is one of the great sagas of Chinese history and literature. After a long and arduous journey, he reached the great centers of Buddhist learning in India and Central Asia, where he studied for many years and engaged in debate with the great philosophers of the time. Upon returning home, he devoted himself to the monumental task of translating no fewer than seventy-five basic Buddhist texts into Chinese. Among his most significant accomplishments were the selecting, summarizing, translating, and systematizing of the works of ten great idealists, especially Dharmapāla, in his *Establishment of the Consciousness-Only System* (*Cheng weishi lun, Vijñapti-mātratā-siddhi*).

The Yogācāra or Vijñānavāda school was one of pure idealism, and may be compared to the system of Bishop Berkeley (1685–1753). The whole universe exists only in the mind of the perceiver. The fact of illusion, as in the case of the flies in the bowl of the shortsighted monk, or the experience of dreams, was adduced as evidence to show that all normal human experience was of the same type. It is possible for the monk in meditation to raise before his eyes visions of every kind, which have quite as much vividness and semblance of truth as have ordinary perceptions, yet he knows that they have no objective reality. Perception therefore is no proof of the independent existence of any entity, and all perceptions may be explained as projections of the percipient mind. Vijñānavāda, like some Western idealist systems, found its chief logical difficulty in explaining the continuity and apparent regularity of the majority of our sense impressions, and in accounting for the fact that the impressions of most people who are looking at the same time in the same direction seem to cohere in a remarkably consistent manner. Bishop Berkeley, to escape this dilemma, postulated a transcendent mind in which all phenomena were thoughts. The Vijñānavādins attributed the regularity and coherence of sense impressions to an underlying storehouse of perceptions (*ālaya-vijñāna*), evolving from the accumulation of traces of earlier sense impressions. These are active and produce impressions similar to themselves, according to a regular pattern, as seeds produce plants. Each being possesses one of these stores of perceptions, and beings that are generically alike will produce similar perceptions from their stores at the same time. By this conception, which bristles with logical difficulties and is one of the most difficult in all Indian philosophy, the Vijñānavādins managed to avoid the logical conclusion of idealism in solipsism. They admitted the existence of at least one entity independent of human thought — a pure and integral being without characteristics, about which nothing could truly be predicated because it was without predicates. This was called Thusness or Suchness (*Tathatā*) and corresponded to the Emptiness or Void of the Mādhyamikas, and to the Brahman of Vedānta. Though the terminology is different, the metaphysics of Mahāyāna Buddhism has much in common with the doctrines of some of the Upaniṣads and of Śaṅkara.

For the Consciousness-Only school, salvation was to be obtained by exhausting the store of consciousness until it became pure being itself, identical with the Thusness that was the only truly existent entity in the universe. The chief means of doing this, for those who had already reached a certain stage of spiritual development, was yogic praxis. Adepts of this school were taught to conjure up visions, so that, by realizing that visions and pragmatically real perceptions had the same vividness and subjective reality, they might become completely convinced of the total subjectivity of all phenomena. Thus the meditating monk would imagine himself a mighty god, leading an army of lesser gods against Māra, the spirit of the world and the flesh.

Whereas the other schools treated the mind as one *dharma*, here it is divided into eight consciousnesses. According to this doctrine, the external world is produced when the *ālaya* or storehouse consciousness, which is in constant flux, is influenced ("perfumed") by "seeds" or effects of good and evil deeds. As such, the phenomenal world is one of appearance or specific characters. It is from this that the school is called the *Faxiang* or *Dharma*-Character school. But in the final analysis everything is consciousness only, whence comes the other common name for this school.

The school began to decline in China in the ninth century and gradually disappeared. In the twentieth century, however, a new interest was shown in this philosophy by Chinese scholars, and some Buddhists even made an effort to revive it.

The following selection is taken from the *Cheng weishi lun*, the most important philosophical work of the school, to give an idea of its central concept of consciousness as the only reality.

XUANZANG: *CONFIRMATION OF THE CONSCIOUSNESS-ONLY SYSTEM*

The verse [by Vasubandhu] says:

First of all, the storehouse [*ālaya*] consciousness,
Which brings into fruition the seeds [effects of good and evil deeds].
[In its state of pure consciousness] it is not conscious of its clinging and
    impressions.
In both its objective and subjective functions it is always associated with
    touch,
Volition, feeling, sensation, thought, and cognition.

But it is always indifferent to its associations. . . .

The verse says:

The second transformation
Is called the mind-consciousness
Which, while it depends on that transformation, in turn conditions it.
It has the nature and character of intellection.
It is always accompanied by the four evil defilements,
Namely, self-delusion, self-view,
Self-conceit and self-love,
And by touch, etc. [volition, feeling, sensation, thought and cognition]. . . .

The Treatise says:
   Spontaneously this mind perpetually conditions the storehouse consciousness and corresponds to the four basic defilements. What are the four? They
are self-delusion, self-view, and also self-conceit and self-love. These are the
four different names. Self-delusion means ignorance, lack of understanding of
the character of the self, and being unenlightened about the principle of the
non-self. Therefore it is called self-delusion. Self-view means clinging to the
view that the self exists, erroneously imagining to be the self certain dharmas
that are not the self. Therefore it is called self-view. Self-conceit means pride.
On the strength of what is clung to as the self, it causes the mind to feel superior
and lofty. It is therefore called self-conceit.

The verse says:

Based on the root-consciousness [*ālaya*]
The five consciousnesses [of the senses] manifest themselves in accordance
   with the conditioning factors.
Sometimes [the senses manifest themselves] together and sometimes not,
Just as waves [manifest themselves] depending on water conditions.
The sense-center consciousness always arises and manifests itself,
Except when born in the realm of the absence of thought,
In the state of unconsciousness, in the two forms of concentration,
In sleep, and in that state where the spirit is depressed or absent.

The Treatise says:
   The root consciousness is the storehouse consciousness because it is the root
from which all pure and impure consciousnesses grow. . . . By "conditioning
factors" are meant the mental activities, the sense organs, and sense objects. It
means that the five consciousnesses are dependent internally upon the root
consciousness and externally follow the combination of the conditions of the
mental activities, the five sense organs, and sense objects. They [the senses]

manifest themselves together and sometimes separately. This is so because the external conditions may come to be combined suddenly or gradually. . . .

The verse says:

> Thus the various consciousnesses are but transformations.
> That which discriminates and that which is discriminated
> Are, because of this, both unreal.
> For this reason, everything is mind only.
> [From the *Cheng weishi lun, TD* 31, no. 1585:7, 10, 19, 26, 37, 38 — WTC]

THE LOTUS SCHOOL: THE TIANTAI SYNTHESIS

From the philosophical standpoint, and in terms of its influence on other schools in China, Korea, and Japan, the Lotus or Tiantai teaching is of major importance. Moreover, it has distinctively Chinese features. Though its basic scripture is the *Lotus of the Wonderful Law* (*Saddharmapuṇḍarīka Sūtra*), a work from North India or Central Asia, the school is founded upon the interpretation given this text by the great Chinese monk Zhiyi (538–597), and its other name indicates its place of geographical origin, the Tiantai (Heavenly Terrace) Mountain of Zhejiang province, where Zhiyi taught.

For this Grand Master of the Tiantai, the *Lotus*, one of the most popular of Mahāyāna *sūtras*, was not primarily a philosophical text but a guide to religious salvation through practice. Zhiyi lectured for years on its written text, minutely examining every detail of language and subtlety of meaning and giving special attention to the methods of religious practice embodied in the *Lotus*. His deliberations were recorded by his pupil Guanding and have come down to us as the "Three Great Works" of the school, namely, the *Words and Phrases of the Lotus* (*Fahua wenju*), the *Profound Meaning of the Lotus* (*Fahua xuanyi*), and the *Great Calming and Contemplation* (*Mohe zhiguan*).

In Zhiyi's time, Buddhist thought in South China was distinctly philosophical in character, while in the north Buddhists were developing a religion of faith and discipline. Himself a product of the southern Chinese gentry, but with a northerner, Huisi (514–577), as his teacher, Zhiyi came to the conclusion that the contemplative and philosophical approaches to religion were like the two wings of a bird. Consequently, the Tiantai school is characterized by a strong philosophical content and at the same time an even stronger emphasis on meditative practice.

The Tiantai doctrine centers around the principle of the Perfectly Harmonious Threefold Truth: (1) all things or *dharmas* are empty because they are produced through causes and conditions and therefore have no self-nature, but (2) they do have tentative or provisional existence, and (3) being both Empty and Tentative is the nature of *dharmas* and is the Mean. These three — Emptiness, Tentativeness, and the Mean — involve one another so that one is three and three are one, the conditional thus being correlated with the unconditional.

Furthermore, within this threefold scheme of Emptiness, Tentativeness, and the Mean an additional distinction may be made among ten realms of existence — those of the hell dwellers, hungry ghosts, animals, human beings, *asuras* (spirits), heavenly beings, *śrāvakas* ("voice-hearers" or direct disciples of the Buddha), *pratyeka*-buddhas ("private" buddhas or buddhas-for-themselves), bodhisattvas, and Buddhas.

Each of these ten realms shares the characteristics of the others, thus making one hundred realms. Each of these in turn is characterized by ten thusnesses or such-likenesses through which the true state is manifested in phenomena, namely, such-like character, such-like nature, such-like substance, such-like power, such-like activity, such-like causes, such-like conditions, such-like effects, such-like retributions, and such-like beginning-and-end-ultimately-alike. This makes one thousand realms of existence. In turn, each realm consists of the three divisions of living beings, of space, and of the aggregates that constitute *dharmas*, thus making a total of three thousand realms of existence, representing experienced reality in all its diversity.

These realms are so interwoven and interpenetrated that they may be considered "immanent in a single instant of thought." This does not mean that they are produced by the thought of man or Buddha, as taught in some Mahāyāna schools, but rather that in every thought-moment, all the possible worlds are involved. Accordingly, the great emphasis in this school is on calming and contemplation as a means of perceiving the ultimate truth embodied in such a thought-moment. In short, this teaching is crystallized in the celebrated saying that "Every color or fragrance is none other than the Middle Path." Every *dharma* is thus an embodiment of the real essence of the Ultimate Emptiness, or True Thusness. It follows that all beings have the Buddha-nature in them and can be saved. This is the great message of the *Lotus*, as explained by Zhiyi.

The school claims that the *Lotus* offers the most complete doctrine among all the Buddhist teachings. It classifies the teachings of the Buddha into five periods. The first four, represented by the literature of various schools, are regarded as provisional or tentative, whereas the teaching contained in the *Lotus* is considered final. Thus a qualified truth is seen in the teachings of other schools, which in certain respects are mutually contradictory, while the *Lotus* is seen as fulfilling and reconciling them in a final synthesis. It is an attempt to replace the Three Vehicles[3] by One Vehicle. In its all-inclusiveness, then, the

---

3. Those of the *pratyeka*-buddhas, who attain to their personal enlightenment by their own exertions; the *śrāvakas*, who attain to their own salvation by hearing the Buddha's teaching; and the bodhisattvas, who postpone their translation into final *nirvāṇa* for the sake of helping all beings to be saved.

Tiantai points again to the doctrine of universal salvation, the outstanding characteristic of the Mahāyāna movement.

EXCERPTS FROM THE *LOTUS SŪTRA*

The *Lotus Sūtra* is by far the most popular and influential of Mahāyāna scriptures in East Asia. It claims to represent the culmination of Śākyamuni Buddha's teaching before his decease and final translation into *nirvāṇa*. The excerpts given here, taken from Kumārajīva's translation into Chinese of 406 C.E., illustrate the following main doctrines of the text: (1) the fulfillment of successive stages in the Buddha's teaching in the One Great Vehicle; (2) the principle of accommodation or expedient means and the parables used for this comprehension; (3) the revelation of Śākyamuni, the human Buddha, as identical with the ageless Eternal Buddha; (4) the *Lotus Sūtra* itself as embodying the Buddha's truth; (5) the salvation of women as personified by the Dragon King's daughter; and (6) the personification of infinite expedient means in the popular Bodhisattva of Compassion or Goddess of Mercy, Guanyin (Perceiver of the World's Sounds).

This is what I heard:

At one time the Buddha was in Rājagṛha, staying on Mount Gṛdhrakūṭa. Accompanying him were a multitude of leading monks numbering twelve thousand persons. All were *arhats* whose outflows had come to an end, who had no more earthly desires, who had attained what was to their advantage and had put an end to the bonds of existence, and whose minds had achieved a state of freedom. . . .

There were bodhisattvas and *mahāsattvas*, eighty thousand of them, none of them ever regressing in their search for supreme perfect enlightenment. All had gained *dhāraṇīs*, delighted in preaching, were eloquent, and turned the wheel of the Law that knows no regression. They had made offerings to immeasurable hundreds and thousands of Buddhas, in the presence of various Buddhas had planted numerous roots of virtue, had been constantly praised by the Buddhas, had trained themselves in compassion, were good at entering the Buddha wisdom, and had fully penetrated the great wisdom and reached the farther shore. Their fame had spread throughout immeasurable worlds and they were able to save countless hundreds of thousands of living beings. . . .

At that time the Buddha emitted a ray of light from the tuft of white hair between his eyebrows, one of his characteristic features, lighting up eighteen thousand worlds in the eastern direction. There was no place that the light did not penetrate, reaching downward as far as the Avīci hell and upward to the Akaniṣṭha heaven. . . .

At that time Bodhisattva Maitreya had this thought: Now the World-Honored One has manifested these miraculous signs. But what is the cause of these auspicious portents? . . .

At that time Bodhisattva Maitreya wished to settle his doubts concerning the matter. And in addition he could see what was in the minds of the four kinds of believers, the monks, nuns, laymen, and laywomen, as well as the heavenly beings, dragons, spirits, and the others who made up the assembly. So he questioned Mañjuśrī, saying, "What is the cause of these auspicious portents, these signs of transcendental powers, this emitting of a great beam of brightness that illumines the eighteen thousand lands in the eastern direction so we can see all the adornments of the Buddha worlds there?" . . .

The Buddha Preaches the One Great Vehicle

At that time Mañjuśrī said to the bodhisattva and *mahāsattva* Maitreya and the other great men, "Good men, I suppose that the Buddha, the World-Honored One, wishes now to expound the great Law." . . .

At that time the World-Honored One calmly arose from his *samādhi* and addressed Śāriputra, saying, "The wisdom of the Buddhas is infinitely profound and immeasurable. The door to this wisdom is difficult to understand and difficult to enter. . . .

"Śāriputra, ever since I attained Buddhahood I have through various causes and various similes widely expounded my teachings and have used countless expedient means to guide living beings and cause them to renounce their attachments. Why is this? Because the Thus-Come One is fully possessed of both expedient means and the perfection of wisdom. . . .

"Śāriputra, to sum it up: the Buddha has fully realized the Law that is limitless, boundless, never attained before. . . .

"Śāriputra, the Buddhas preach the Law in accordance with what is appropriate, but the meaning is difficult to understand. Why is this? Because we employ countless expedient means, discussing causes and conditions and using words of simile and parable to expound the teachings. This Law is not something that can be understood through pondering or analysis. Only those who are Buddhas can understand it. . . .

"Śāriputra, I know that living beings have various desires, attachments that are deeply implanted in their minds. Taking cognizance of this basic nature of theirs, I will therefore use various causes and conditions, words of simile and parable, and the power of expedient means and expound the Law for them. Śāriputra, I do this so that all of them may attain the one Buddha vehicle and wisdom embracing all species. . . .

"Śāriputra, if any of my disciples should claim to be an *arhat* or a *pratyeka*-buddha and yet does not heed or understand that the Buddhas, the Thus-Come Ones, simply teach and convert the bodhisattvas, then he is no disciple of mine; he is no *arhat* or *pratyeka*-buddha.

"Again, Śāriputra, if there should be monks or nuns who claim that they have already attained the status of *arhat*, that this is their last incarnation, that they have reached the final *nirvāṇa*, and that therefore they have no further intention of seeking supreme perfect enlightenment, then you should understand that such as these are all persons of overbearing arrogance. Why do I say this? Because if there are monks who have truly attained the status of *arhat*, then it would be unthinkable that they should fail to believe this Law. . . . There is no other vehicle, there is only the one Buddha vehicle." . . .

The Parable of the Burning House

"Moreover, Śāriputra, I too will now make use of similes and parables to further clarify this doctrine. For through similes and parables those who are wise can obtain understanding.

"Śāriputra, suppose that in a certain town in a certain country there was a very rich man. He was far along in years, and his wealth was beyond measure. He had many fields, houses, and menservants. His own house was big and rambling, but it had only one gate. A great many people — a hundred, two hundred, perhaps as many as five hundred — lived in the house. The halls and rooms were old and decaying, the walls crumbling, the pillars rotten at their base, and the beams and rafters crooked and aslant.

"At that time a fire suddenly broke out on all sides, spreading through the rooms of the house. The sons of the rich man — ten, twenty, perhaps thirty — were inside the house. When the rich man saw the huge flames leaping up on every side, he was greatly alarmed and fearful and thought to himself, 'I can escape to safety through the flaming gate, but my sons are inside the burning house enjoying themselves and playing games, unaware, unknowing, without alarm or fear. The fire is closing in on them, suffering and pain threaten them, yet their minds have no sense of loathing or peril and they do not think of trying to escape!'

"Śāriputra, this rich man thought to himself, 'I have strength in my body and arms. I can wrap them in a robe or place them on a bench and carry them out of the house.' And then again he thought, 'This house has only one gate, and moreover it is narrow and small.

"'My sons are very young, they have no understanding, and they love their games, being so engrossed in them that they are likely to be burned in the fire. I must explain to them why I am fearful and alarmed. The house is already in flames, and I must get them out quickly and not let them be burned up in the fire!'

"Having thought in this way, he followed his plan and called to all his sons, saying, 'You must come out at once!' But though the father was moved by pity and gave good words of instruction, the sons were absorbed in their games and unwilling to heed him. They had no alarm, no fright, and in the end no mind to leave the house. Moreover, they did not understand what the fire was, what the house was, what danger was. They merely raced about this way and that in play and looked at their father without heeding him.

"At that time the rich man had this thought: 'The house is already in flames from this huge fire. If I and my sons do not get out at once, we are certain to be burned. I must now invent some expedient means that will make it possible for the children to escape harm.'

"The father understood his sons and knew what various toys and curious objects each child customarily liked and what would delight them. And so he said to them, 'The kind of playthings you like are rare and hard to find. If you do not take them when you can, you will surely regret it later. For example, things like these goat-carts, deer-carts, and ox-carts. They are outside the gate now where you can play with them. So you must come out of this burning house at once. Then whatever ones you want, I will give them all to you!'

"At that time, when the sons heard their father telling them about these rare playthings, because such things were just what they had wanted, each felt emboldened in heart and, pushing and shoving one another, they all came wildly dashing out of the burning house.

"At this time the rich man, seeing that his sons had gotten out safely and all were seated on the open ground at the crossroads and were no longer in danger, was greatly relieved and his mind danced for joy. At that time each of the sons said to his father, 'The playthings you promised us earlier, the goat-carts and deer-carts and ox-carts — please give them to us now!'

"Śāriputra, at that time the rich man gave to each of his sons a large carriage of uniform size and quality. The carriages were tall and spacious and adorned with numerous jewels. A railing ran all around them and bells hung from all four sides. A canopy was stretched over the top, which was also decorated with an assortment of precious jewels. Ropes of jewels twined around, a fringe of flowers hung down, and layers of cushions were spread inside, on which were placed vermilion pillows. Each carriage was drawn by a white ox, pure and clean in hide, handsome in form and of great strength, capable of pulling the carriage smoothly and properly at a pace fast as the wind. In addition, there were many grooms and servants to attend and guard the carriage.

"What was the reason for this? This rich man's wealth was limitless, and he had many kinds of storehouses that were all filled and overflowing. And he thought to himself, 'There is no end to my possessions. It would not be right if I were to give my sons small carriages of inferior make. These little boys are all my sons and I love them without partiality. I have countless numbers of large carriages adorned with seven kinds of gems. I should be fair-minded and give one to each of my sons. I should not show any discrimination. Why? Because even if I distributed these possessions of mine to every person in the whole country I would still not exhaust them, much less could I do so by giving them to my sons!'

"At that time each of the sons mounted his large carriage, gaining something he had never had before, something he had originally never expected. Śāriputra, what do you think of this? When this rich man impartially handed out to his sons these big carriages adorned with rare jewels, was he guilty of falsehood or not?

"Śāriputra said, 'No, World-Honored One. This rich man simply made it possible for his sons to escape the peril of fire and preserve their lives. He did not commit a falsehood. Why do I say this? Because if they were able to preserve their lives, then they had already obtained a plaything of sorts. And how much more so when, through an expedient means, they are rescued from that burning house.'" . . .

The Impoverished Son

At that time, the men of lifelong wisdom . . . gazing up in reverence at the face of the Honored One, said to the Buddha, "We stand at the head of the monks and are all of us old and decrepit. We believed that we had already attained *nirvāṇa* and that we were incapable of doing more, and so we never sought to attain supreme perfect enlightenment. . . .

"When we heard of this supreme perfect enlightenment, which the Buddha uses to teach and convert the bodhisattvas, our minds were not filled with any thought of joy or approval. But now in the presence of the Buddha we have heard this voice-hearer receive a prophecy that he will attain supreme perfect enlightenment, and our minds are greatly delighted. . . .

"World-Honored One, we would be pleased now to employ a parable to make clear our meaning. Suppose there was a man, still young in years, who abandoned his father, ran away, and lived for a long time in another land, for perhaps ten, twenty, or even fifty years. As he grew older, he found himself increasingly poor and in want. He hurried about in every direction, seeking for clothing and food, wandering farther and farther afield until by chance he turned his steps in the direction of his homeland.

"The father meanwhile had been searching for his son without success and had taken up residence in a certain city. The father's household was very wealthy, with immeasurable riches and treasures. . . .

"At this time the impoverished son wandered from village to village, passing through various lands and towns, till at last he came to the city where his father was residing. The father thought constantly of his son. . . . 'If I could find my son and entrust my wealth and possessions to him, then I could feel contented and easy in mind and would have no more worries.'

"World-Honored One, at that time the impoverished son drifted from one kind of employment to another until he came by chance to his father's house. He stood by the side of the gate, gazing far off at his father, who was seated on a lion throne, his legs supported by a jeweled footrest, while Brahmans, noblemen, and householders, uniformly deferential, surrounded him. . . .

"When the impoverished son saw how great was his father's power and authority, he was filled with fear and awe and regretted he had ever come to such a place. Secretly he thought to himself, 'This must be some king, or one who is equal to a king. This is not the sort of place where I can hire out my labor and gain a living. It would be better to go to some poor village where, if I work hard, I will find a place and can easily earn food and clothing. . . .' Having thought in this way, he raced from the spot.

"At that time the rich old man, seated on his lion throne, spied his son and recognized him immediately. . . .

"Thereupon he dispatched a bystander to go after the son as quickly as possible and bring him back. At that time the messenger raced swiftly after the son and laid hold of him. The impoverished son, alarmed and fearful, cried out in an angry voice, 'I have done nothing wrong! Why am I being seized?' But the messenger held on to him more tightly than ever and forcibly dragged him back. . . .

"The father, observing this from a distance, spoke to the messenger, saying, 'I have no need of this man. Don't force him to come here, but sprinkle cold water on his face so he will regain his senses. Then say nothing more to him!'

"Why did he do that? Because the father knew that his son was of humble outlook and ambition, and that his own rich and eminent position would be difficult for the son to accept. He knew very well that this was his son, but as a form of expedient means he refrained from saying to anyone, 'This is my son.' . . .

"At that time the rich man, hoping to entice his son back again, decided to employ expedient means and send two men as secret messengers, men who were lean and haggard and had no imposing appearance. 'Go seek out that poor man and approach him casually. Tell him you know a place where he can earn twice the regular wage. If he agrees to the arrangement, then bring him here and put him to work. If he asks what sort of work he will be put to, say that he will be employed to clear away excrement, and that the two of you will be working with him.' . . .

"Later he spoke to his son again, saying, 'Now then, young man! You must keep on at this work and not leave me anymore. I will increase your wages. . . . I have an old servant I can lend you when you need him. You may set your mind at ease. I will be like a father to you, so have no more worries. . . . From now on you will be like my own son.' And the rich man proceeded to select a name and assign it to the man as though he were his child.

"At this time the impoverished son, though he was delighted at such treatment, still thought of himself as a person of humble station who was in the employ of another. Therefore the rich man kept him clearing away excrement for the next twenty years. By the end of this time, the son felt that he was understood and trusted, and he could come and go at ease, but he continued to live in the same place as before. . . .

"After some time had passed, the father perceived that his son was bit by bit becoming more self-assured and magnanimous in outlook, that he was determined to accomplish great things and despised his former low opinion of himself. Realizing that his own end was approaching, he ordered his son to arrange a meeting with his relatives and the king of the country, the high ministers, and the noblemen and householders. When they were all gathered together, he proceeded to make this announcement: 'Gentlemen, you should know that this is my son, who was born to me. In such-and-such a city he abandoned me and ran away, and for over fifty years he wandered about suffering hardship. . . . Now everything that belongs to me, all my wealth and possessions, shall belong entirely to this son of mine. Matters of outlay and income that have occurred in the past this son of mine is familiar with.'

"World-Honored One, when the impoverished son heard these words of his father, he was filled with great joy, having gained what he had never had before, and he thought to himself, 'I originally had no mind to covet or seek such things. Yet now these stores of treasures have come of their own accord!'

"World-Honored One, this old man with his great riches is none other than the Thus-Come One, and we are all like the Buddha's sons. The Thus-Come One constantly tells us that we are his sons. But because of the three sufferings, World-Honored One, in the midst of birth and death we undergo burning anxieties, delusions, and ignorance, delighting in and clinging to lesser doctrines. But today the World-Honored One causes us to ponder carefully, to cast aside such doctrines, the filth of frivolous debate." . . .

The Emergence of the Treasure Tower

At that time in the Buddha's presence there was a tower adorned with the seven treasures, five hundred *yojanas* in height and two hundred and fifty *yojanas* in width and depth, that rose up out of the earth and stood suspended in the air. Various kinds of precious objects adorned it. . . .

At that time a loud voice issued from the treasure tower, speaking words of praise: "Excellent, excellent! Śākyamuni, World-Honored One, that you can take the great wisdom of equality, a Law to instruct the bodhisattvas, guarded and kept in mind by the Buddhas, the *Lotus Sūtra of the Wonderful Law*, and preach it for the sake of the great assembly!" . . .

At that time there was a bodhisattva and *mahāsattva* named Great Joy of Preaching, who . . . said to the Buddha, "World-Honored One, for what reason has this treasure tower risen up out of the earth? And why does this voice issue from its midst?"

At that time the Buddha said, "Bodhisattva Great Joy of Preaching, in the treasure tower is the complete body of a Thus-Come One. Long ago, an immeasurable thousand, ten thousand, million *asaṅkhyeyas* of worlds to the east, in a land called Treasure Purity, there was a Buddha named Many Treasures. When this Buddha was originally carrying out the bodhisattva way, he made a great vow, saying, 'If, after I have become a Buddha and entered extinction, in the lands in the ten directions there is any place where the *Lotus Sūtra* is preached, then my funerary tower, in order that I may listen to the *sūtra*, will come forth and appear in that spot to testify to the *sūtra* and praise its excellence.'"...

The Unity and Diversity of Buddhahood

At that time Śākyamuni Buddha saw the Buddhas that were his emanations all assembled, each sitting on a lion seat, and heard all these Buddhas say that they wished to participate in the opening of the treasure tower. . . .

Śākyamuni Buddha with the fingers of his right hand then opened the door of the tower of seven treasures. A loud sound issued from it, like the sound of a lock and crossbar being removed from a great city gate, and at once all the members of the assembly caught sight of Many Treasures Thus-Come One seated on a lion seat inside the treasure tower, his body whole and unimpaired, sitting as though engaged in meditation. And they heard him say, "Excellent, excellent, Śākyamuni Buddha! You have preached this *Lotus Sūtra* in a spirited manner. I have come here in order that I may hear this *sūtra*."

At that time the four kinds of believers, observing the Buddha who had passed into extinction immeasurable thousands, ten thousands, millions of *kalpas* in the past speaking in this way, marveled at what they had never known before and took the masses of heavenly jeweled flowers and scattered them over Many Treasures Buddha and Śākyamuni Buddha.

At that time Many Treasures Buddha offered half of his seat in the treasure tower to Śākyamuni Buddha, saying, "Śākyamuni Buddha, sit here!" Śākyamuni Buddha at once entered the tower and took half of the seat, seating himself in cross-legged position.

At that time the members of the great assembly, seeing the two Thus-Come Ones seated cross-legged on the lion seat in the tower of seven treasures, all thought to themselves, "These Buddhas are seated high up and far away! If only the Thus-Come Ones would employ their transcendental powers to enable all of us to join them there in the air!"

Immediately Śākyamuni Buddha used his transcendental powers to lift all the members of the great assembly up into the air. And in a loud voice he addressed all the four kinds of believers, saying, "Who is capable of broadly preaching the *Lotus Sūtra of the Wonderful Law* in this *sahā* world? Now is the time to do so, for before long the Thus-Come One will enter *nirvāṇa*. The Buddha wishes to entrust this *Lotus Sūtra of the Wonderful Law* to someone so that it may be preserved." . . .

The Daughter of the Dragon King

Bodhisattva Wisdom Accumulated questioned Mañjuśrī, saying, "This *sūtra* is very profound, subtle, and wonderful, a treasure among *sūtras*, a rarity in the world. Are there perhaps any living beings who, by earnestly and diligently practicing this *sūtra*, have been able to attain Buddhahood quickly?"

Mañjuśrī replied, "There is the daughter of the dragon king Sāgara, who has just turned eight. Her wisdom has keen roots, and she is good at understanding the root activities and deeds of living beings. She has mastered the *dhāraṇīs*, has been able to accept and embrace all the storehouse of profound secrets preached by the Buddhas, has entered deep into meditation, thoroughly grasped the doctrines, and in the space of an instant conceived the desire for *bodhi* and reached the level of no regression. Her eloquence knows no hindrance, and she thinks of living beings with compassion as though they were her own children. She is fully endowed with blessings, and when it comes to conceiving in mind and expounding by mouth, she is subtle, wonderful, comprehensive, and great. Kind, compassionate, benevolent, yielding, she is gentle and refined in will, capable of attaining *bodhi*." . . .

At that time Śāriputra said to the dragon girl, "You suppose that in this short time you have been able to attain the unsurpassed way. But this is difficult to believe. Why? Because a woman's body is soiled and defiled, not a vessel for the Law. How could you attain the unsurpassed *bodhi*? The road to Buddhahood is long and far-stretching. Only after one has spent immeasurable *kalpas* pursuing austerities, accumulating deeds, practicing all kinds of *pāramitās*, can one finally achieve success. Moreover, a woman is subject to the five obstacles. First, she cannot become a Brahma heavenly king. Second, she cannot become the king Śakra. Third, she cannot become a devil king. Fourth, she cannot become a wheel-turning sage king. Fifth, she cannot become a Buddha. How then could a woman like you be able to attain Buddhahood so quickly?"

At that time the dragon girl had a precious jewel worth as much as the thousand-millionfold world, which she presented to the Buddha. The Buddha immediately accepted it. The dragon girl said to Bodhisattva Wisdom Accumulated and to the venerable one, Śāriputra, "I presented the precious jewel and the World-Honored One accepted it — was that not quickly done?"

They replied, "Very quickly!"

The girl said, "Employ your supernatural powers and watch me attain Buddhahood. It will be even quicker than that!"

At that time the members of the assembly all saw the dragon girl in the space of an instant change into a man and carry out all the practices of a bodhisattva, immediately proceeding to the Spotless World of the south, taking a seat on a jeweled lotus, and attaining impartial and correct enlightenment. With the thirty-two features and the eighty characteristics, he expounded the wonderful Law for all living beings everywhere in the ten directions. . . .

The Bodhisattva Perceiver of the World's Sounds (Guanyin)

The following brief extracts are from chapter 25 of the *Lotus*, which became separately known and widely recited as the "Guanyin Sūtra." Note that whatever the expedient means or transformations employed by Guanyin (also popularly known as the Bodhisattva of Mercy), the primary function of the bodhisattva is to enlighten deluded, suffering beings. Under this aspect, Guanyin is portrayed iconographically as carrying the lamp of enlightenment.

At that time the bodhisattva Inexhaustible Intent immediately rose from his seat, bared his right shoulder, pressed his palms together, and, facing the Buddha, spoke these words: "World-Honored One, this Bodhisattva Perceiver of the World's Sounds — why is he called Perceiver of the World's Sounds?"

The Buddha said to Bodhisattva Inexhaustible Intent, "Good man, suppose there are immeasurable hundreds, thousands, ten thousands, millions of living beings who are undergoing various trials and suffering. If they hear of this bodhisattva Perceiver of the World's Sounds and single-mindedly call his name, then at once he will perceive the sound of their voices and they will all gain deliverance from their trials. . . .

"If there should be living beings beset by numerous lusts and cravings, let them think with constant reverence of Bodhisattva Perceiver of the World's Sounds, and then they can shed their desires. If they have great wrath and ire, let them think with constant reverence of Bodhisattva Perceiver of the World's Sounds, and then they can shed their ire. If they have great ignorance and stupidity, let them think with constant reverence of Bodhisattva Perceiver of the World's Sounds, and they can rid themselves of stupidity. . . .

"If they need a monk, a nun, a layman believer, or a laywoman believer to be saved, immediately he becomes a monk, a nun, a layman believer, or a laywoman believer and preaches the Law for them. . . .

"If they need a heavenly being, a dragon, a *yakṣa*, a *gandharva*, an *asura*, a *garuḍa*, a *kinnara*, a *mahoraga*, a human, or a nonhuman being to be saved, immediately he becomes all of these and preaches the Law for them. . . .

"Inexhaustible Intent, this Bodhisattva Perceiver of the World's Sounds has succeeded in acquiring benefits such as these and, taking on a variety of different forms, goes about among the lands saving living beings. . . ."

[From Watson, *The Lotus Sutra*, 3–6, 23–24, 31–32, 56–58, 80–86, 170–176, 186–188, 298–304; translation based on the *Myōhō-renge-kyō narabi ni kaiketsu*]

GUANDING: ON THE FIVE PERIODS OF THE BUDDHA'S TEACHING

During the late Northern and Southern Dynasties period (420–589) the practice of "classification of the teachings" (*panjiao*) became a principal means by which Buddhist exegetes sought to deal with the overwhelming diversity of scriptures and teachings that poured into China between the second and sixth centuries. Motivated by the desire to explain the comprehensive design of the Buddha's preachings as well as the most effective path to salvation, this classification of the teachings played a seminal role in reshaping Indian motifs of Buddhist thought and practice into a distinctive Sinitic Buddhist tradition.

The selection that follows provides an outline of the five periods or flavors (*wu shi/ wu wei* — the core of the Tiantai scheme of doctrinal classification). It is taken from the *Guanxin lun shu*, a commentary on Zhiyi's short *Treatise on the Contemplation of the Mind* (*Guanxin lun*) compiled by his disciple Guanding. This system, derived from the *Nirvāṇa Sūtra* but supported by parables from the *Lotus*, organizes the Buddha's preaching career into five basic periods, which unfold one upon the other, leading the Buddha's assembly of followers progressively to the highest and purest expression of the Buddha's vision. That vision is the unadulterated preaching of the perfect teaching in the *Lotus Sūtra*, wherein he reveals both the pedagogic strategy and the ultimate purpose of his teaching career. Note that throughout his discussion of the five periods, Guanding refers repeatedly to the parable of the impoverished son in the *Lotus Sūtra* and to a classification of Four Teachings used in guiding beings of different spiritual capacities, namely, (1) the "*Tripiṭaka* teaching," attracting them to the attainment of *arhat*hood and extinction in *nirvāṇa*; (2) the "shared teaching," involving an elementary and one-sided understanding of Emptiness; (3) the "separate teaching," aimed at reaching Buddhahood by intermediate stages involving both the empty and the provisional; and (4) the "perfect or rounded teaching," as the direct and full realization of the Middle Truth or Mean, combining all polarities of empty and provisional, *nirvāṇa* and *saṃsāra*.

When the Buddha first attained the way on the *bodhi*-seat of perfect quiescence, he conceived the desire to test [beings of the transmigratory world] with the [perfect] *Dharma* of the Great [Vehicle].[4] However, animate beings did not have the capacity [for it] and were unreceptive to training by the Great [Vehicle]. Hence, in the chapter on Belief and Understanding [of the *Lotus Sūtra*], [the Buddha] illustrates [this situation] by saying, "The rich old man, seated on his lion throne, spied his [long-lost] son and recognized him immediately. Thereupon he dispatched a bystander to go after the son as quickly as possible and bring him back. At that time the messenger raced swiftly after the son and laid hold of him. . . . The impoverished son, alarmed and fearful, cried out in an angry voice, 'I have done nothing wrong! Why am I being seized?' But the messenger held on to him more tightly than ever and forcibly dragged him back.". . .

In the Expedient Means chapter of the *Lotus Sūtra* [the Buddha says], "If I were to force my teaching on sentient beings, they would persecute the *Dharma* and thereby fall into evil destinies of rebirth." Thus he says, "I would rather speedily enter *nirvāṇa* and not preach the *Dharma*." This, then, is the meaning of [the simile] likening everything that the Buddha produced to the [tasteless]

---

4. I.e., the teaching of the *Flower Garden Sūtra* (the *Huayan jing* or *Avataṃsaka Sūtra*), which the Buddha allegedly preached on the *bodhi*-seat during the first three weeks after his enlightenment.

flavor of plain milk.[5] Calling to mind the powers of expediency employed by Buddhas of the past, the Buddha thought to himself, "I now will do as they have done and bring sentient beings to salvation through expedient means."[6] Thereupon he set off for Vārāṇasī, where he preached the doctrine of the arising and cessation [of *saṃsāra*] and the elimination of the four bases of delusion. It is with this idea in mind that [the Belief and Understanding chapter of the *Lotus Sūtra*] says, "[The rich father] dispatched two more attendants to pursue his son and bring him back." For "twenty years" [the son, unaware of his heritage, labored to] expel the excrement of the intellectual and affective delusions. This [period] corresponds to the transformation of raw milk into *cream*, which represents the shift from the ordinary unenlightened state to the sainthood [of the Hīnayāna].

Next comes the [period when the Buddha] preached the expanded or *Vaipulya* [discourses], drawing on the expedient devices of the three [*Tripiṭaka*, shared, and separate] teachings to advocate [eventual] submission to the perfect [teaching]. Thus, in the *Vimalakīrti* [*Sūtra*], the two separate and perfect teachings are used to humble the ten great [*arhat*] disciples [of the Buddha], and the perfect [teaching] is employed to repudiate the approach that progresses through distinct [stages] and is adhered to by bodhisattvas of one-sided practice. In this way they are led gradually to submit [to the perfect teaching].

Previously, people responded to the Buddha's expounding of the Great [Vehicle] with revilement and disbelief, making it impossible for [the Buddha] even to preach it. At this juncture, when persons who had already obtained the saintly path of the two vehicles heard him preach the Great [Vehicle], they harmed themselves and destroyed their karmic propensity [for the Mahāyāna by slandering it]. Thus, with a voice that reverberated through the great chiliocosm, [the Buddha] praised the wondrous *Dharma* [of the Mahāyāna] as something difficult to conceive. [Consequently] even those who had not yet achieved enlightenment no longer gave rise to disparagement. With this idea in mind, [the Belief and Understanding chapter of the *Lotus*] states, "By the end of this time the son felt that he was understood and trusted, and he could come and go at ease, but he still lived in the crude hut as before." Moreover, "he was unable to cease thinking of himself as mean and lowly." This represents the transformation of cream into *butter curds*, which corresponds to the preaching of the *Vaipulya* or expanded teaching that followed in the wake of the *Tripiṭaka* teaching.

Next comes [the period in which the Buddha] preached the Wisdom (*Prajñā*) *sūtras*. The Buddha expounded the Perfection of Wisdom (*Prajñā-*

<hr>

5. That is to say, ordinary sentient beings derived no benefit from the Buddha's initial preaching of the perfect middle truth of the Mahāyāna, responding to it as though "deaf and dumb."

6. From the Expedient Means chapter of the *Lotus*; Watson, *The Lotus Sutra*, p. 44.

pāramitā) *sūtras* for the bodhisattvas, drawing on the expedients of the two shared and separate teachings in an effort to advocate [eventual] submission to the perfect [teaching]. The Belief and Understanding chapter [of the *Lotus*] says, "The father perceived that his son was bit by bit becoming more self-assured and magnanimous in outlook," and "he ordered him to take over the family affairs." Hence it says in the verses [of the chapter] that "the Buddha charged us to preach the *pāramitā* on behalf of the bodhisattvas," and yet, "we never thought of appropriating for ourselves even a single meal." This represents the transformation of raw butter curds into *melted butter*. It corresponds to the preaching of the Wisdom [*sūtras*] that came after the expanded (*Vaipulya*) [period].

After the Wisdom [period] comes the preaching of the perfect teaching of the *Lotus Sūtra*. In the [Expedient Means chapter of the *Lotus*] *Sūtra* [the Buddha] says, "I will straightaway cast aside [all] expedients and preach only the unexcelled way." This [refers to] none other than the expounding of the present contemplation of the perfect [teaching], in which one contemplates the mind of a single instant of thought as being identical with the Thus-Come One's jeweled trove of the middle way and the Buddha's wisdom of permanence, pleasure, selfhood, and purity. Thus the [Expedient Means chapter of the *Lotus*] *Sūtra* says, "[A Buddha] comes forth into the world for one great reason alone." The Buddha replies, "[It is] to cause sentient beings to open the door to Buddha Wisdom," as well as reveal, awaken to, and enter [this wisdom]. With this idea in mind, it says in the chapter on Belief and Understanding, "The father, realizing that his end was approaching, gathered his relatives and said, 'I am your father; you are my son. All of my wealth and property I entrust to you.'"[This corresponds to the transformation of melted butter into the finest *essence of ghee*], which represents the preaching of the perfect teaching of the *Lotus* [*Sūtra*] that comes in the wake of the Wisdom [*sūtras*].

Thus one should realize that the other three teachings are all expedients for this marvelous contemplation of the perfect teaching, [devised for the purpose of] subduing and readying people to receive this wondrous contemplation. Also one should know that the perfect contemplation is both arcane and wondrous. How could the other three teachings possibly compare with it?

[*Guanxin lun shu*, TD 46, no. 1921:599–600 — DS]

HUISI: *THE METHOD OF CALMING AND CONTEMPLATION IN THE MAHĀYĀNA*

The Mind is the same as the Mind of Pure Self, Nature, True Thusness, Buddha-Nature, Dharma-Body, Tathāgata-Store, Realm of Law, and Dharma-Nature.

Question: Why is [the Mind] called True Thusness?

Answer: All *dharmas* depend on this Mind for their being and take Mind as their substance. Viewed in this way, all *dharmas* are illusory and imaginary and their being is really nonbeing. Contrasted with these unreal *dharmas*, the Mind is called True.

Furthermore, although the *dharmas* have no real being because they are caused by illusion and imagination, they have the appearance[7] of being created and annihilated. . . . Because of the power, from time immemorial, of ignorance and imagination to influence it, the substance of the Mind is affected by this influence and manifests itself. These unreal appearances have no substance; they are but the Pure Mind. Hence it is said that [substance and appearance] are not different. . . .

The substance of the Pure Mind, although it possesses the two functions of purity and being defiled, does not have the character of distinction between the two; all is everywhere the same and undifferentiated. It is only because of the illusory manifestations caused by the power of influence that differences appear.

But these illusory appearances are created and annihilated, whereas the substance of the Pure Mind is eternal, without coming into or going out of existence, and it endures forever without change. Hence it is said that [substance and appearance] are not one.

Question: When the *Tathāgata*-store possesses innumerable *dharmas*, does it have the character of differentiation or not?

Answer: The substance of the store is everywhere the same and undifferentiated and, in fact, has no character of differentiation. In this respect it is the *Tathāgata*-store of Emptiness. However, because this substance of the *Tathāgata*-store also has mysterious functions, it possesses all *dharma* natures to the fullest extent, including their differentiations. In this respect, it is the *Tathāgata*-Store of Non-Emptiness, that is, the difference in the realm of no-difference.

What does this mean? I am not saying that it is like a lump of clay possessing many particles of dirt. Why? The clay is false, whereas the particles of dirt are real. Therefore each particle has its own distinctive material. But since they are combined to form the clay, this possesses the distinctive characteristic of involving many particles. But the *Tathāgata*-store is different from this. Why? Because the *Tathāgata*-store is the True Law; it is perfect harmony without duality. Therefore the *Tathāgata*-store, in its totality, is the nature of a single hair-pore of a single being, and at the same time the nature of all hair-pores of that being. And as in the case of the hair-pore, so in that of the nature of every *dharma* in the world.

Therefore it is said in the scripture: "In each particle of dirt, all the Buddha lands in the ten directions are revealed," and again, "All the Three Worlds and

---

7. The Chinese word *xiang* is a key term in Buddhist philosophy, with a wide range of meanings, including "specific character or characteristic," "appearance," "phenomenon." In general, it is translated here as "character[istic]" when contrasted with a universal nature, and as "appearance" or "phenomenon" when contrasted with ultimate reality.

all periods in time can be understood in an instant of thought. . . . Again, "The past is the future, and the future is the present." This means that the three times involve one another.

By calming is meant to know that all *dharmas*, originally having no self-nature of their own, are never created nor annihilated by themselves but come into being because they are caused by illusions and imagination, and exist without real existence. In those created *dharmas*, their existence is really non-existence. They are only the One Mind, whose substance admits of no differentiation. Those who hold this view can stop the flow of false ideas. This is called calming (or stopping).

By contemplation is meant that although we know that [things] are originally not created and at present not annihilated, nevertheless they were caused to arise out of the Mind's nature and hence are not without a worldly function of an illusory and imaginative nature. They are like illusions and dreams; they [seem to] exist but really do not. This is therefore contemplation.

As to the function of calming and contemplation: It means that because of the accomplishment of calming, the Pure Mind is merged through Principle with the Nature, which is without duality and is harmoniously united with all beings as a body of one single character. Thereupon the Three Treasures [the Buddha, the Law, and the Order] are combined without being three, and the Two Levels of Truth are fused without being two. How calm, still, and pure! How deep, stable, and quiet! How pure and clear the inner silence! It functions without the appearance of functioning, and acts without the appearance of acting. It is so because all *dharmas* are originally the same everywhere without differentiation, and the nature of the Mind is but *dharma*. This is the substance of the most profound *Dharma*-nature.

It also means that because of the accomplishment of contemplation, the substance of the Pure Mind and the functioning of the objective world are manifested without obstacle, spontaneously producing the capabilities of all pure and impure things. . . . Again, owing to the accomplishment of calming, one's mind is the same everywhere and one no longer dwells within the cycle of life and death; yet owing to the accomplishment of contemplation, one's attitudes and functions are results of causation and one does not enter *nirvāṇa*. Moreover, owing to the accomplishment of calming, one dwells in the great *nirvāṇa*, and yet, owing to the attainment of contemplation, one remains in the realm of life and death.

[From *Dacheng zhiguan famen*, TD 46, no. 1924:642–661 — LH]

ZHIYI: *THE GREAT CALMING AND CONTEMPLATION*

The *Mohe zhiguan*, from which this portion is quoted, is a manual of religious practice — specifically, of the methods of gaining religious intuition.

The name "ten *dharma*-spheres" applies in each case to the aggregates, objects of perception, and spheres. Their realities are different from one another. The three lowest states of existence are the aggregates, objects of perception, and spheres of tainted evil.[8] The next three states of existence are the aggregates, objects of perception, and spheres of tainted good. The Two Vehicles are taintless aggregates, objects of perception, and spheres. The bodhisattva is both tainted and taintless aggregates, objects of perception, and spheres. The Buddha is neither tainted nor taintless aggregates, objects of perception, and spheres. . . .

Now one Mind comprises ten *dharma*-spheres, but each *dharma*-sphere also comprises ten *dharma*-spheres, giving a hundred *dharma*-spheres. One sphere comprises thirty kinds of worlds, hence a hundred *dharma*-spheres comprise three thousand kinds of worlds. These three thousand are contained in a fleeting moment of thought. Where there is no Mind, that is the end of the matter; if Mind comes into being to the slightest degree whatsoever, it immediately contains the three thousand. One may say neither that the one Mind is prior and all *dharmas* posterior nor that all *dharmas* are prior and the one Mind posterior. For example, the eight characters [of matter][9] change things. If the thing were prior to the characters, the thing would undergo no change. If the characters were prior to the thing, it would also undergo no change. Thus neither priority nor posteriority is possible. One can only discuss the thing in terms of its changing characters or the characters in terms of the changing thing. Now the Mind is also thus. If one derives all *dharmas* from the one Mind, this is a vertical relationship. If the Mind all at once contains all *dharmas*, this is a horizontal relationship. Neither vertical nor horizontal will do. All one can say is that the Mind is all *dharmas* and that all *dharmas* are the Mind. Therefore the relationship is neither vertical nor horizontal, neither the same nor different. It is obscure, subtle, and profound in the extreme. Knowledge cannot know it, nor can words speak it. Herein lies the reason for its being called "the realm of the inconceivable."

[From *Mohe zhiguan*, TD 46, no. 1911:52, 54 — LH]

---

8. The objects of perception are those of the six senses, while the spheres are the six sensory organs, the six senses, and the objects of perception. "Tainted" means giving rise to a process that will maintain existence in the world. Such are the six lowest states of existence. The *śrāvaka* and *pratyeka*-buddha, on the other hand, extricate themselves from the world. The bodhisattva does so eventually, but remains in the world for a time. The Buddha, of course, is above all forms of differentiation.

9. The primary and secondary characteristics of coming into being, abiding, changing, and perishing (an Abhidharma doctrine).

ZHIYI: *THE LOTUS SAMĀDHI RITE OF REPENTANCE*

In theory, the meditative system of the ten modes of calming and contemplation aspires to discern the perfect truth of the middle way amidst any and all forms of activity, without imposing any distinction between good and evil or overtly religious and non-religious circumstances. Practically speaking, however, it found its concrete expression in Tiantai monastic life through an institution known as the "four forms of *samādhi*" (*sizhong sanmei*).

The scheme of the four forms of *samādhi* was devised by Zhiyi as a rubric for classifying different Mahāyāna meditative and devotional rites on the basis of the dominant mode of physical activity (i.e., sitting, walking, a mix of both, or indiscriminate). In principle the scheme is open-ended and capable of accommodating any form of religious exercise. Early Tiantai sources, however, indicate that the contents of the four *samādhis* were limited to some half a dozen specific contemplative rites held to be especially effective by Zhiyi and his followers. Each of these rites had its own unique cultic orientation and ritual program. At the same time they shared a number of common structural features, including an emphasis on isolated retreat and intensive cycles of meditation and ritual repentance, all of which was geared to inducing experiences of ecstatic insight, or *samādhi*. As Chinese Buddhist religious sensibilities changed over the succeeding centuries, some cults fell out of favor and new ones were added to the Tiantai ritual repertoire, two of the most important areas of later development being devotion to Amitābha Buddha — the Buddha of the Western Paradise — and the Bodhisattva Guanyin (Avalokiteśvara).

The selections that follow concern the lotus *samādhi* rite of repentance, one rite among the four *samādhis* that has enjoyed constant popularity throughout all periods of Tiantai history. The concept of the lotus *samādhi* derives from the *Lotus Sūtra* and centers around the latter as an object of devotion. The passages in question are taken from Zhiyi's *Lotus Samādhi Rite of Repentance* (*Fahua sanmei chanyi*). As the most detailed of the various early Tiantai manuals on the rites of the four *samādhis*, the *Lotus Samādhi Repentance* served as a model for the production of Tiantai ritual literature in later periods, thereby assuming a textual importance that extended well beyond the cult of the lotus *samādhi* proper.

The Procedure for Entering the Sanctuary and Undertaking the Main Practice

From the time of first entering the sanctuary the practitioner should complete in full [the following] ten procedures: (1) adornment and purification of the sanctuary, (2) purification of the person, (3) offering of the three deeds (or the offering of incense and flowers), (4) invocation of the three jewels, (5) praising of the three jewels, (6) veneration of the Buddhas, (7) confession [and profession of vows], (8) ritual circumambulation, (9) recitation of the *Lotus Sūtra* [while circumambulating], (10) [seated] contemplation of the sphere of the one reality.

When it comes to the cycle of the six daily intervals of worship [to be observed] over the twenty-one-day period, the practitioner must carry out these ten procedures in their entirety during the particular interval in which he first enters the sanctuary. For each of the six intervals thereafter he should omit the procedure for inviting the Buddhas but continue to perform the remaining nine without alteration.

1. RESPLENDENTLY ADORNING AND PURIFYING THE SANCTUARY

In a quiet and untrammeled spot the practitioner should resplendently arrange a single chamber to use as the ritual sanctuary (*daochang*). At a spot apart from it he should set up a place for himself to sit [in meditation], taking care that it is partitioned off from the sanctuary proper. A fine altar-piece should be installed in the sanctuary and on it placed a single copy of the *Lotus Sūtra*. There is no need to enshrine any other images, relics, or scriptures. Only the *Lotus Sūtra* is [to be] placed there, and around it various banners, canopies, and the usual implements of offering are distributed.

At first light in the morning when he is to enter the sanctuary, the practitioner should sweep the floor clean, then sprinkle it with fragrant water and smear the surface with fragrant paste. He should light various lamps containing fragrant oils, scatter all kinds of flowers and powdered aromatics, burn precious incenses, and make offerings to the Three Jewels. All such [preparations] he should attend to personally, striving with all his might to make them as pure and resplendent as possible.

Why is this necessary? If a practitioner solemnly reveres the Three Jewels within his own heart he will surely transcend the three realms. Since one now intends to summon (*fengqing*) and present offerings [to the Three Jewels], how can [such matters] be taken lightly? If you are unwilling to give of your own wealth in offering to the Great Vehicle you will never be able to attract the worthies and move the saints [to descend]. If grave sins are not extinguished, how can *samādhi* possibly appear?

2. CLARIFYING THE PROCEDURE BY WHICH THE PRACTITIONERS PURIFY THEIR PERSONS

Upon first entering the sanctuary the practitioner should bathe with perfumed water and put on a clean set of robes — that is to say, the large [ceremonial] robe and newly dyed [inner] robes. If new robes are not available, he should choose the best among his existing clothing to use as the set of robes for entering the sanctuary. Thereafter, whenever he leaves the sanctuary for unclean places he should take off the purified robes and change into an ordinary set. When his business is finished, he should once again wash himself, don the original purified set of robes, enter the sanctuary, and proceed with the practice.

3. CLARIFYING THE PROCEDURE FOR OFFERING OF THE THREE DEEDS

Upon entering the sanctuary one goes before the altar and, after spreading the *niṣīdana*,[10] with proper decorum takes one's stance slightly off to the side (*zheng-shen yili*). One begins by generating thoughts of loving-kindness toward all living beings, as well as the desire to bring about their deliverance. Next, with solemn heart, one should foster a deep sense of personal contrition and shame. Fixing one's thoughts on the *Tathāgatas*, one imagines that the Three Jewels manifest their forms in the sanctuary [before one], crowding the air in all directions. At this point, taking incense censer in hand, one lights precious incense, scatters different sorts of flowers and, so, performs offerings to the Three Jewels. . . .

Next, one should mentally conjure up the image of a [cloud of] incense and blossoms, which, in an instant of thought, spreads universally to all the Buddha lands of the ten directions. There it produces all manner of exceedingly fine forms, such as myriads of precious jewels that garland and adorn various terraces, multistoried towers, and halls. It produces all kinds of orchestral music, [along with] wondrous melodies, songs, and eulogies. It produces all kinds of [clothing, garlands, and] marvelous aromatic fragrances, such as sandalwood and the incense that sinks in water. It produces arrays of wonderful flavors, including fine delicacies and medicinal potions. It produces all manner of things exquisitely fine to the touch, such as clothing, garlands, flowing springs, and bathing pools. It produces countless wonderful gates to the *dharma*, involving meditative concentration, wisdom, and the pure reality [that is the true character of all things]. Filling the *dharma*-realm (*dharmadhātu*), [the cloud of incense and all its marvels] are used to accomplish the work of the Buddhas, as well as make offerings to the Buddhas of the three times and every aspect of the Three Jewels throughout the ten directions. One should make the wish that the Three Jewels receive it and that it permeates beings everywhere, [subtly influencing] them to make the resolution to [seek] *bodhi*.

Imagining oneself to be standing in person before each of the Buddhas [throughout the universe], one presents identical offerings to all, without the slightest difference between them. Moreover, one should express the following wish: "May living beings of the six destinies and four forms of birth all meld into my offering to the ocean-like *dharmadhātu* and realize that such offering as this is born entirely of the mind and without any self-existent nature. [May their] minds thereby not cling to it."

4. INVITING OR INVOKING THE THREE JEWELS

Having completed the offering of the three deeds, the practitioner should once again burn incense and scatter flowers. With singular and proper mindfulness

---

10. A broad cloth used for sitting or prostration.

he should re-establish the mental visualization of the previous offering and invite the Three Jewels [into the sanctuary]. As to the procedure for summoning the Three Jewels, one should imagine oneself standing directly before [whatever deity] is to be invited, then intone that [deity's] name out loud. Each figure is summoned, one at a time, according to established procedure. One must not allow the mind to become distracted or frivolous. . . .

6. VENERATING THE BUDDHAS, [SAINTS, AND PROTECTING DEITIES] OF THE *LOTUS SŪTRA*

Having finished praising, the practitioner, with proper and dignified decorum, should single-mindedly venerate the Buddhas according to sequence. In this procedure for venerating the Buddhas, one should attentively recollect [as follows] every time a Buddha is saluted: "This Buddha's Body of *Dharma*-essence is [undifferentiated] like empty space but manifests physical form in response to living beings. [Hence it appears here now] to receive my [offerings and] obeisance (*libai*), as though right before my very eyes." The same applies [for salutation] to the rest of the Buddhas as well.

In applying the mind [to visualization] one must never allow it to become confused or distracted. Moreover, when saluting the Buddhas, the practitioner should maintain the awareness that body and mind are empty and quiescent and that no sign [of the act of] salutation is to be found anywhere. At the same time one should realize that, even though this body is insubstantial — like a phantom, it is not without the ability to manifest an image. As such, this body appears before every Buddha throughout the *dharmadhātu* and one [touches] one's head [to their feet] in obeisance.

7. THE PROCEDURE FOR CONFESSING THE SIX SENSE FACULTIES, AS WELL AS IMPLORING [THE BUDDHAS TO PREACH], SYMPATHETIC CELEBRATION [OF THE MERITS OF OTHERS], DEDICATION OF MERITS [TO THE ENLIGHTENMENT OF ALL BEINGS], AND MAKING OF VOWS[11]

Having finished venerating the Buddhas, the practitioner assumes a proper and dignified stance before the altar, burns incense, scatters flowers, and, fixing his thoughts on the Three Jewels, [imagines that they] fill the air [about him]. Thereupon, the Bodhisattva Universal Worthy (Samantabhadra) appears, as though right before one's very eyes — riding a white elephant with six tusks,

---

11. The five elements of the famous Tiantai formula of the fivefold penance (*wu hui*): (1) confession (*chanhui*); (2) solicitation of the Buddhas (to remain in the world and turn the wheel of *dharma*) (*quanqing*); (3) sympathetic rejoicing in the merits and wholesome deeds of others (*suixi*); (4) transference or dedication of merits toward the Buddhahood of all beings (*huixiang*); and (5) making of vows (*fayuan*).

[resplendently bedecked with] countless ornaments, and surrounded by a [vast] retinue of attendants. With single mind and single will one performs the procedure for confession on behalf of beings everywhere. Evoking a keen sense of contrition and shame, one confesses all the evil deeds (*karma*) — from unfathomable *kalpas* of the past up through the present existence — that oneself and sentient beings as a whole have perpetrated through the six senses. Severing once and for all any thought of continuing [to commit evil deeds], one [resolves], henceforth until the end of time, never to create evil *karma* [like this] again.

Why must one do this? Because, even though actions may be empty by nature, the retribution [that attends action] is not effaced. A person who knows emptiness does not even [invest in] doing good, let alone commit evil deeds. Anyone who would pursue evil without restraint is certain to be under the influence of inverted [views]. [When one acts under the influence of depravity], one will reap an equally deluded result. Thus, for the very reason that he knows [things to be] empty, the practitioner fosters a deep sense of shame, burns incense, scatters flowers, reveals [his sins], and repents. . . .

8. CLARIFYING THE PROCEDURE FOR RITUAL CIRCUMAMBULATION

The procedure for reciting the *sūtra* is explained in detail [in the next section] below. Not only must the practitioner maintain full awareness that the voice reciting the *sūtra* is by nature empty, he must also know that body and mind [are insubstantial], like a cloud or shadow. Whether picking the foot up or putting the foot down, one's mind [should be] free of all grasping and not dwell on any aspect of walking. At the same time, one should realize that this body [is able to] manifest its form throughout the ten directions. Filling the entire *dharmadhātu*, there is no place where it does not appear and [simultaneously] circumambulate the Buddhas.

In this manner one performs from three, to seven, twenty-one, forty-nine, or one hundred rounds of circumambulation. There is no pre-set number. One should decide the amount for oneself. When one wishes to bring the circumambulation to an end, he or she should go back and recite the names of the Three Jewels as before. Lighting incense, with full mindfulness one then intones the accompanying hymn [of praise]. When the hymn is finished, one returns to the original spot where veneration of the Buddhas [was performed] and takes refuge in the Three Jewels.

9. CLARIFYING THE PROCEDURE FOR RECITATION OF THE *SŪTRA*

As to the proper technique for reciting the *sūtra*, the lines of the text should be made perfectly distinct and the sound [of their words] enunciated clearly, their pace being neither too lax nor too rushed. One should fix one's attention on the given passage from the *sūtra* and allow no errors, just as though the written text itself were at hand. Then, with quieted mind, one should understand the nature of the voice to be like an echo in an empty valley. Yet, even though one finds the sound of the voice to be inapprehensible, the mind successively illumines the meaning of every line. Speaking each word with perfect clarity, [the practitioner] imagines (*yun*) this sound of *dharma* to spread throughout the *dharmadhātu*. There it [spontaneously] produces offerings to the Three Jewels and provides for [the needs of] sentient beings everywhere, causing them to enter the realm of the single reality of the Great Vehicle.

[Zhiyi, *Fahua sanmei chanyi*, TD 46, no. 1941:949–54, *passim* —DS]

ZHIYI ON THE CONCEPT OF RITUAL REPENTANCE

In Tiantai literature, the ritual meditations of the four forms of *samādhi* (including the lotus *samādhi* repentance) are often referred to as repentance practices. The reason for this lies primarily in their blending of meditative contemplation with ritual worship and confession before the Buddhas, together with the belief that this orchestration is particularly effective for removing karmic impediments and manifesting the innate wisdom of the middle way. The following selection is taken from Zhiyi's *Elucidation of the Sequential Approach of the Perfection of Dhyāna* (as the text is known for short); its discussion of the three forms of repentance represents one of Zhiyi's most thorough discussions of the nature of evil *karma* and its removal, revered to this day as one of the key statements of Tiantai ritual theory.

The polar tension between the world of *karma* and moral retribution, on the one hand, and, on the other, the ultimate emptiness of doer and deed represents a longstanding ethical problem in the Buddhist tradition. Cast in the language of indigenous Chinese categories such as principle (*li*) and its actualization or practice (*shi*), this tension became a focal point for later Neo-Confucian charges that the Buddhist tradition was flawed by a "one-sided" preoccupation with principle in its transcendent aspect, a preoccupation that hindered Buddhists from fully appreciating the manifest presence of principle in the particulate relations of everyday existence.

The explanation of repentance [that follows] consists of two basic points: first comes the explanation of [what it means to] engender a mind of repentance. Second is the explanation of the different methods of repentance proper.

First, what do we mean by a "mind of repentance"? If a person by nature does not engage in evil, there will be no sin to repent. But when practitioners are unable to keep the precepts firmly, or else break the precepts when confronted with evil circumstances, because the precepts have been violated, their moral integrity (*śīla*) will not be pure and *samādhi* will not arise. It makes no difference whether the infraction is a grave or a minor one. [Such a person] is like a soiled robe that, because of the grime, will not accept dye. It is therefore necessary to repent. Through repentance the different grades of precept will be purified, and *samādhi* can be manifested just as the dirty robe can be dyed once it is washed clean. Practitioners should reflect on themselves in this way. If they are not pure in [their observance of] the precepts, they should by all means repent.

As for the term *chanhui* (repentance), *chan* means to confess [one's sins] to the Three Jewels and all living beings. *Hui* means to feel ashamed and [desire to] reform and seek forgiveness for one's transgressions, thinking, "If this sin of mine can be extinguished, I would rather die than commit such a painful deed as this again." . . .

Then again, *chan* means not to conceal [anything] outwardly; and *hui*, to remonstrate inwardly with oneself in one's heart. Or, *chan* means to know that sin is evil; and *hui*, to fear its retribution. . . . If one can grasp the fact that *dharmas* (the constituents of existence) are unreal, forever put an end to evil *karma*, and cultivate the path of goodness, then this is known as "repentance." . . .

Now we will clarify the [different] methods of repentance. There are many such approaches [set forth in] the Buddhist teachings. But, when we consider their essentials, they do not go beyond three basic forms: one is repentance involving the observance of a fixed regimen of action (*zuofa chanhui*). This form relies on the Vinaya codes to explain repentance. A second is repentance involving the discernment of a sign, which relies on methods of meditative concentration to define repentance. A third is the repentance of nonarising. This relies on methods of [liberative] wisdom to explain repentance. In concept these three forms of repentance are common to both the [Hīnayāna] *Tripiṭaka* and the Mahāyāna [*sūtras*]. In terms of relative degree of emphasis, however, the first method is primarily a Hīnayāna form of repentance. The other two are for the most part Mahāyāna methods of repentance.

First comes the explanation of repentance involving a fixed regimen [of action]. Doing good actions will reverse evil actions. Hence we refer to [doing good] as [a form of] repentance. It is just as in the Vinaya, where one relies exclusively on this approach to eliminate sins. On what basis do I make this claim? When one confesses [violations] of the second [of the seven] categories [of infraction], an assembly of twenty monks prescribes the particular *karma* [or "regimen of action"] for removing the sin, such as dwelling apart and submitting to the will [of the monastic community]. When [the particular] regimen of action has been completed, [the infraction] is declared "eliminated." This [approach] gives no consideration to the perception of different signs or [changes in] demeanor. Nor does it take into account [the presence of] wisdom and the contemplation of emptiness. Thus one should realize that it is simply a [form of] repentance that involves observance of a fixed regimen of action. [The term] *karma* itself may be translated as "fixed regimen of action."

The same applies for the remaining three categories of infraction [that follow the second category]: all of them [involve observance of] fixed regimens of action. This matter is easy to understand, its basic concept being explained in detail in the Vinaya codes. However, [the Vinaya] has never taught a procedure for repenting the four grave infractions [of taking life, unchastity, theft, and falsehood]. . . .

Second is repentance involving the discernment of signs. [According to this approach], the aspirant selects a rite of repentance from the [Buddhist] *sūtras*, concentrates his mind, applies his will, and, in a serene and quiet mind, [comes to] perceive various types of sign. According to the explanations found in the bodhisattva precepts, anyone wishing to repent the ten grave [evils] must perceive an auspicious sign, which serves as an indication [that the sin has been] eradicated. [For example,] if the Buddha comes and massages the crown of one's head, or one sees various auspicious omens, such as flowers [in the air] and beams of radiant light, then sins have been successfully eliminated. If such a sign does not appear, one's efforts to repent have been to no avail.

Among the *dhāraṇī* rites of the Mahāyāna *Vaipulya* [scriptures],[12] there are many examples of this sort of repentance involving the discernment of signs. The [*sūtras* of the Hīnayāna] *Tripiṭaka* and *Āgamas* also describe repentance rites that involve the discernment of signs, including meditative visualization of the hell realms, venomous serpents, the white [tuft of] hair of the Buddha and so forth. When visualization of the mark is successful [and its desired meditative sign manifests], sins are said to be eliminated. Since all of these are performed within the context of a mind concentrated [in *samādhi*], repentance involving the discernment of signs is usually taught in conjunction with methods for cultivating meditative concentration. . . .

Signs [indicating that sins have been eliminated] do not go beyond four basic types: (1) seeing signs in a dream; (2) hearing voices in the air or seeing unusual signs and auspicious spiritual omens while performing ritual circumambulation (*xingdao*); (3) seeing signs of [past] good and evil [deeds] or observance and violation of the precepts while one is sitting [in meditation]; and (4) signs indicating such things as the internal realization of various Buddhist teachings (lit., *Dharma*-gates) or the manifestation of the mind of the Way (*daoxin*). . . .

False and genuine are difficult to distinguish, and one must not take [any of these signs] as definitive. Should a sign appear, a competent master will recognize it. The matter must be settled in person. It cannot be determined on the basis of a written text. Thus, when a practitioner first takes up [the practice of] repentance, he must approach a good spiritual friend who is capable of differentiating between genuine and false [experiences].

---

12. I.e., rites involving the use of magical incantations and/or invocation of specific Buddhas and bodhisattvas. Most of the rites of the Tiantai four *samādhis* fall in this category.

Moreover, when signs appear, they often do so abruptly. Since it is difficult enough to determine whether [a sign] is genuine or false, if you should [go on to] chase after written texts with the aim of seeking [some special interpretation] of it, you will more than likely fall prey to [the demonic] *māras*.

By "apprehension of a sign" we simply mean that one applies the mind to the ritual cycle. When one's efforts mature, signs appear, and one uses these to evaluate [the state of one's practice]. One thereby knows whether sins have been eliminated or not. This is not to say, [however,] that your mind should harbor [thoughts of] this sign or event during the course of the practice itself, thereby giving rise to attachment [to it]. If you apply the mind in this fashion, you are sure to invite a lot of demonic influence.

Third is the explanation of repentance involving the contemplation of [the ultimate truth of] nonarising. As it says in the verses (*gāthās*) of the *Sūtra on the Contemplation of the Bodhisattva Universal Worthy*, "The ocean of all the karmic obstructions is born entirely from deluded thinking. Should you wish to repent, seat yourself in proper [meditative] posture and fix your mind on ultimate reality. The multitude of sins are like frost and dew: the sun of wisdom can dissipate them [instantly]."[13] Thus, with a heart of utmost sincerity, confess [and repent] the sins of the six sense faculties.

Whenever a practitioner intends to undertake this great repentance, he should generate a heart of great compassion, take pity on all [living beings], and deeply penetrate to the source of sin itself. What does this mean? All things are originally empty and quiescent. Blessedness itself does not exist; how much the less does sin? Yet because of their lack of skill in contemplation [of this truth], sentient beings deludedly cling to existence, thereby giving rise to ignorance, craving, and anger. Because of these three poisons, they commit boundless and limitless sins of every description. All of this arises from a single instant of incomprehension [deep] within the mind. If one wishes to eliminate [these evils], one should simply turn back and discern whence this mind itself arises. . . .

In this respect, one should realize that "great repentance" refers to profound contemplation of [the ultimate truth of] nonarising. Among the repentances, this form is the most honored and most sublime. . . .

If one applies the mind as described, in thought after instant of thought evil *karma* will automatically be extinguished with each successive moment of thought. But if one wants to know that sinful obstructions to the way have [themselves] been transformed, one must persevere [in this practice] without cease. Signs will again spontaneously appear, and upon experiencing these one will be able to know [whether sinful obstacles have been eliminated]. They are similar to the good dreams, numinal omens, manifestations of meditative concentration and wisdom, and other such signs explained previously in the [re-

---

13. *Guanpuxian pusa xingfa jing*, TD 277:9:393b.

pentance involving] the discernment of signs. From this it should be sufficiently clear.

Then again, if the practitioner's contemplation of the mind is in direct accord with the principle [of ultimate reality], this in itself is a sign that sins are eliminated. There is no need to trouble oneself with seeking after anything else. Thus it says in the *Sūtra on the Contemplation of the Bodhisattva Universal Worthy*, "If you can bring the mind into mutual accord with this wisdom of emptiness, you should realize that it is possible to extinguish incalculable billions of aeons of grave sins of cyclic birth and death, all in a single instant of thought." This [passage] verifies it. When one [eventually] achieves the wisdom that comes with [realization of] the forbearance of the nonarising [of the *dharmas*], the source of sin will thereupon be completely exhausted.

[Zhiyi, *Shichan poluomi cidi famen*, TD 46, no. 1916:485–86 — DS]

THE FLOWER GARLAND (HUAYAN) SCHOOL

The basic scripture of the Flower Garland (*Huayan*) school is the *Flower Garland Sūtra* (*Huayan jing*), a lengthy work describing an enormously grand vision of the universe. The language of the *sūtra* is mythic and extravagant, so much so that it has acquired a reputation for being abstruse and impossible to comprehend. Widely regarded in the Mahāyāna tradition as being the first sermon preached by the Buddha, revealing the full content of his enlightenment, the *sūtra* was said to be too profound and lofty for human understanding. Thereafter, making concessions to human limitations, the Buddha preached other *sūtras* that were easier to understand.

Despite its reputation for complexity, the *Flower Garland Sūtra* teaches tenets similar to those developed in other schools, and contributes to a doctrinal common ground for Mahāyāna Buddhism in general. The terms *interdependence, interpenetration, simultaneous co-arising*, and *nonduality* express this basic notion of how the diverse elements of the universe are interdependent and interrelated with each other. This is not to say that everything is identical; quite to the contrary, the Huayan vision affirms diversity and attempts to explain an inherent and simultaneous interrelatedness of each thing with all things, and all things with each thing, without loss of individual identities.

The patriarchs of the Huayan school often enjoyed the patronage of rulers. Dushun (557–640), the founder of the school, was held in high esteem by Emperor Wen (r. 589–605) of the Sui dynasty; and Fazang (643–712), the third patriarch and great systematizer of Huayan teachings, was honored several times by Empress Wu (r. 684–704) of the Tang,[14] who supported a new Chinese translation of the *Flower Garland Sūtra* by Śikṣānanda.

---

14. Actually, Empress Wu assumed the title of "Emperor" (the only woman in Chinese history

The last section of the *Sūtra* tells of the pilgrimage of Sudhana, a youth who visits a wide variety of people, each of whom teaches him something about the Flower Garland universe. Maitreya welcomed Sudhana by showing him the great tower of Vairocana, the central Buddha of the *sūtra*. The tower was a place in which the interrelatedness of the universe could be seen, and is described in the following excerpt taken from Śikṣānanda's translation.

In the Huayan view, a Buddhist state (*foguo*) would be one which lent itself to the support of this universal spiritual communion. However, as a universal principle underlying a universal state, the mutual fusion and permeability of all things, while acting as a solvent of all local loyalties and cultural particularism, also left questions as to the solid ground on which one might erect any social or political structure or ethic.

The Tower of Vairocana

This is the place where all the buddhas live peacefully. This is the dwelling place where a single aeon permeates all aeons, and all aeons permeate one aeon without loss of any of their own characteristics. This is the dwelling place where one land permeates all lands, and all lands permeate one land without loss of any of their own characteristics. This is the dwelling place where one sentient being permeates all sentient beings, and all sentient beings permeate one sentient being without loss of any of their own characteristics. This is the dwelling place where one buddha permeates all buddhas, and all buddhas permeate one buddha without loss of their own characteristics. This is the dwelling place where in a single moment of thought everything about the past, present, and future can be known. This is the dwelling place where in a single moment of thought one can travel to all countries. This is the dwelling place where all sentient beings manifest all of their prior lives. This is the dwelling place of concern for the benefit of everyone in the world. This is the dwelling place of those who can go everywhere. This is the dwelling place of those who are detached from the world and yet constantly remain there to teach other people.

[*Huayan jing, TD* 10, no. 279:423 — GT]

Indra's Net

One of the most memorable metaphors in Huayan literature is that of Indra's Net, which describes a vision of all things in an interrelationship with each other without being blended into a single homogeneous entity. This characteristic metaphor is found

---

to have done so) and adopted the dynastic name of Zhou, rather than Tang, during her ascendancy.

at the end of *Calming and Contemplation in the Five Teachings of Huayan*, a work often, though perhaps inaccurately, attributed to Dushun.

The jeweled net of Śakra is also called Indra's Net, and is made up of jewels. The jewels are shiny and reflect each other successively, their images permeating each other over and over. In a single jewel they all appear at the same time, and this can be seen in each and every jewel. There is really no coming or going.

Now if we turn to the southwest direction and pick up one of the jewels to examine it, we will see that this one jewel can immediately reflect the images of all of the other jewels. Each of the other jewels will do the same. Each jewel will simultaneously reflect the images of all the jewels in this manner, as will all of the other jewels. The images are repeated and multiplied in each other in a manner that is unbounded. Within the boundaries of a single jewel are contained the unbounded repetition and profusion of the images of all the jewels. The reflections are exceedingly clear and are completely unhindered.

If you sit in one jewel, you will at that instant be sitting repeatedly in all of the other jewels in all directions. Why is this? It is because one jewel contains all the other jewels. Since all the jewels are contained in this one jewel, you are sitting at that moment in all the jewels. The converse that all are in one follows the same line of reasoning. Through one jewel you enter all jewels without having to leave that one jewel, and in all jewels you enter one jewel without having to rise from your seat in the one jewel.

Question: You say that through one jewel entry is made into all jewels, but how can all jewels be entered without leaving that one jewel?

Answer: It is precisely because you do not leave that one jewel that you are able to enter into all jewels. If you leave that one jewel and try to enter all the other jewels, you will not be able to enter them all. Why is this? It is because there are no jewels that can be separated from this one jewel.

Question: If there are no jewels apart from this one jewel, then does this net not consist of only one jewel? Why do you say it is made of many jewels connected together?

Answer: It is precisely because there is only this one jewel to begin with that many can be connected to form the net. Why is this? It is because it is from this one jewel alone that the net can be made. If you take away this one jewel, then there will be no net.

Question: If there is only one jewel, then how can you speak of it as being connected to form the net?

Answer: This one jewel consists of the connections of many jewels to form the net. Why is this? It is because one is an aspect of the whole, and it is formed by containing the many. Without the existence of one, all cannot exist; therefore this net is formed from this one jewel. Along this line of reasoning you should be able to understand how everything enters one thing.

[*Huayan wujiao zhiguan*, TD 45, no. 1867:513 — GT]

Fazang: Indra's Net and the Tower of Vairocana

Like Dushun, Fazang sets his explanation of the Huayan universe in the context of meditation. The explanation is less of a logical argument and more of an attempt to describe the meditative vision of the grand interrelatedness of all things. Known for his systematic thinking, Fazang here explains Indra's Net by recurring to Sudhana's visit to the tower of Vairocana.

In the meditation on Indra's Net, the principal master and the subordinate retainers are manifestations of each other. We can speak of this by thinking of the self as the master and regarding others as retainers; or by thinking of one thing as the master and all other things as retainers, or by taking one body as the master and all other bodies as retainers. As soon as one thing is designated master, both the master and retainers are equally brought together in relationships that multiply without end. This indicates that the nature of things lies in multiple relationships reflecting each other unendingly in all things. This is true also of the unending relationships between wisdom and compassion.

This is much like the young man Sudhana, who left the Jeta Grove and gradually made his way south until he stood before the great tower of Vairocana's magnificent splendor. He gathered his thoughts for a few moments and then said to Maitreya, "I ask you, great sage, to open the gates of the great tower and let me in." Maitreya snapped his fingers and the door opened. Sudhana entered and the doors closed as they were before. Inside this tower he saw hundreds of thousands of other towers. And in each one of these hundreds of thousands of towers there were further hundreds of thousands of towers. In front of each one of these towers was Maitreya Bodhisattva, and in front of each Maitreya Bodhisattva was Sudhana. Each Sudhana stood with his palms joined together before Maitreya Bodhisattva. This manifests the multiple interrelationships in the *dharma* universe and is like the unending connections in Indra's Net. This also makes clear that Sudhana had a sudden, ultimate insight into the *dharma* universe as a result of his practice according to the principles of the Flower Garland *dharma* universe. Thinking of one tower as the master and all the other towers within it as the retainers is the meditation on Indra's Net in which masters and retainers manifest each other. This is also the meditation on the unobstructed interrelatedness of things with all things.

[*Xiu huayan aozhi wangjin huanyuan guan*, TD 45, no. 1876:640 — GT]

The Buddha-Kingdom of the *Flower Garland Sūtra*

A common refrain in Huayan Buddhism is the claim that the perfect realm of the Buddha (*li*) is interfused with the ordinary world (*shi*) without obstruction (*wu ai*), and that earthly rulers should manifest this universal harmony and order by "turning the wheel of the *dharma*" throughout the land. With its vivid descriptions of this unity of all parts within a whole, the *Flower Garland Sūtra* articulated a spiritual ideal that easily resonated with political objectives for unification and stability. In other East Asian countries as well, the Huayan ideal of harmony inspired the building of Bulguk-sa (Temple of the Kingdom of the Buddha), which commemorated the unified rule of the Korean kingdom of Silla; and the establishment of the Great Temple of the East (Tōdaiji) in Nara, which exemplified Emperor Shōmu's (r. 724–749) vision of centralized rule in Japan.

CHAPTER ON THE EXQUISITE ADORNMENTS OF THE RULERS OF THE WORLD

All of the kingdoms in the ten directions
Will become purified and beautiful in a single moment
When rulers turn the wheel of the *dharma*
With the wondrous sounds of their voices
Reaching everywhere throughout their lands
With no place untouched.
The world of the Buddha is without bounds,
And his *dharma* realm inundates everything in an instant.
In every speck of dust the Buddha establishes a place of practice,
Where he enlightens every being and displays spiritual wonders.
The World-Honored One practiced all spiritual disciplines
While coursing through a past of a hundred thousand aeons,
Adorning all of the lands of the buddhas,
And manifesting himself without obstruction, as if in empty space.
The Buddha's divine powers are unbounded,
Filling endless aeons;
No one would tire of constantly watching him
Even for countless ages.
You should observe the realms of the Buddha's power
Purifying and adorning all of the countries in the ten directions.
In all these places he manifests himself in myriad forms,
Never the same from moment to moment.
Observe the Buddha for a hundred thousand countless aeons,
But you will not discern a single hair on his body,
For through the unhindered use of expedient means
It is his radiance that shines on inconceivably numerous worlds.
In past ages the Buddha was in the world
Serving in a boundless ocean of all the buddhas.
All beings therefore came to make offerings to the World-Honored One,
Just as rivers flow to the sea.
The Buddha appears everywhere in the ten directions,
And in the countless lands of every speck of dust

Wherein are infinite realism
The Buddha abides in all, infinitely unbounded.
The Buddha in the past cultivated an ocean
Of unbounded compassion for sentient beings,
Whom he instructed and purified
As they entered life and death.
The Buddha lives in the *dharma* realm complex of truth
Free of forms, signs, and all defilements.
When people contemplate and see his many different bodies,
All their troubles and sufferings disappear.

[*Huayan jing, TD* 10, no. 279:22 — GT]

CHAPTER ON THE TEN DEDICATIONS OF MERIT

Sons of the Buddha, why are bodhisattvas and great sages firm in practicing the root of all good when they dedicate their merits to others? Sons of the Buddha, when these bodhisattvas and great sages are rulers of great countries, their dignity and virtue are widely received, and their fame shakes everything under Heaven. All their enemies obey without coercion; all their orders and official decrees are based on the right law. They hold up a single vast canopy that gives shade in all directions. They travel all over the face of the earth, unobstructed wherever they turn. They tie the silken scarves of nondefilement around their heads and are sovereign in the law. Coming under the influence of their virtue, those who see them submit without having to be penalized or punished. In dealing with all living beings, these rulers use the four embracing laws of charity, loving words, beneficial assistance, and sympathy with others. They provide everything as kings who turn the wheel of the *dharma*.

[*Huayan jing, TD* 10, no. 279:135 — GT]

BUDDHISM'S ASSIMILATION TO
TANG POLITICAL CULTURE

Buddhism's early claim to exist beyond the authority of the state, as asserted by Huiyuan,[15] was radically transformed in Tang China when institutionally it became an arm of the state. The institution of "superintendent of the Buddhist clergy (*saṅgha*)," which first appeared under the Northern Wei in the mid-fifth century, marked the inception of this transformation. The superintendent headed a bureaucracy staffed by lay officials or nominal "monks," charged with oversight of monastic affairs. He was not the head of an autonomous religious

---

15. See ch. 15, pp. 426–29.

organization but rather an appointee of the emperor and given tonsure by the emperor's hand.

The religious rationale for this government-run Buddhism was supplied by the first superintendent Faguo, who justified monks' service of the government by directly identifying the emperor as the Buddha. In contrast to Huiyuan's rigorous defense of clerical independence, Faguo said that "Taizu is enlightened and loves the Way. He is in his very person the Thus-Come One. Monks (*śramaṇas*) must and should pay him all homage. . . . He who propagates the teaching of the Buddha is the lord of men. I am not doing obeisance to the Emperor, I am merely worshiping the Buddha."[16] In response, the anonymous author of the *Perfect Wisdom Sūtra for Humane Kings Who Wish to Protect Their States* saw superintendency as a sure sign of the corruption of Buddhism in the last days or decadent End of the Teaching, saying, "If any of my disciples, *bhikṣu* and *bhikṣuṇī*, accept registration (of monks and nuns) and serve as officials, they are not my disciples."[17]

THE HUMANE KING AS PROTECTOR OF BUDDHISM

As an alternative to Buddhism's serving the state, the *Sūtra for Humane Kings* proposes that the state and Buddhism serve each other. Using the vocabulary of Chinese monarchy, the scripture asserts that "humane" or "benevolent" kings (*renwang*) practice "outer protection" (*waihu*) and that this protection involves the patronage of an independent *saṅgha* who practice the "inner protection" (*neihu*) of the bodhisattva virtue of "forbearance" (*ren*). The pun on the term *ren*[18] is the basis of the scripture and the starting point of all of its commentaries. Thus, according to an early seventh-century *Commentary on the Sūtra for Humane Kings*, the ruler who protects Buddhism thereby protects the state.

Because the humane king (*renwang*) explicates the Teaching and disseminates virtue here below, he is called "humane." Because he has transformed himself, he is called "king." The humane king's ability is to protect (*hu*). What is protected is the state. This is possible because the humane king uses the Teaching to order the state. Now if we consider the Highest Perfect Wisdom (*Prajñāpāramitā*), its ability is to protect. The humane king is he who is protected. Because he uses the Highest Perfect Wisdom, the humane king is tranquil and hidden. Thus, if he uses his ability to propagate the Teaching, the king is able to protect [the state], and it is the Highest Perfect Wisdom that is the [method

---

16. Hurvitz, *Wei Shou*, p. 53.

17. *TD* 8, no. 245:833.

18. *Ren*, meaning "humaneness," and *ren*, meaning "forbearance," are near homophones, but the words are written with different Chinese characters.

of] protection. Moreover, one who is humane is forbearing [*renzhe ren ye*].[19] Hearing of good he is not overjoyed; hearing of bad he is not angry. Because he is able to hold to forbearance in good and bad, therefore he is called forbearing (*ren*).

[TD 33, no. 1705:253 — CO]

Here the scripture's adroit use of language to reorder the relationship between religion and the state is coupled with Mahāyāna teachings of Perfect Wisdom. Amoghavajra's eighth-century recension of the text further accentuates these teachings through the addition of such passages as the following, based on the dialectics of negation.

At that time the World-Honored One said to King Prasenajit, "By what signs do you contemplate the Thus-Come One?" King Prasenajit answered, "I contemplate his body's real signs; [I] contemplate the Buddha thus: without boundaries in front, behind, and in the middle; not residing in the three times and not transcending the three times; not residing in the five aggregates, not transcending the five aggregates; not abiding in the four great elements and not transcending the four great elements; not abiding in the six abodes of sensation and not transcending the six abodes of sensation; not residing in the three realms and not transcending the three realms; residing in no direction, transcending no direction; [neither] illumination [nor] ignorance, and so on. Not one, not different; not this, not that; not pure, not foul; not existent nor nonexistent; without signs of self or signs of another; without name, without signs; without strength, without weakness; without demonstration, without exposition; not magnanimous, not stingy; not prohibited, not transgressed; not forbearing, not hateful; not forward, not remiss; not fixed, not in disarray; not wise, not stupid; not coming, not going; not entering, not leaving; not a field of blessings, not a field of misfortune; without sign, without the lack of sign; not gathering, not dispersing; not great, not small; not seen, not heard; not perceived, not known. The mind, activities, and senses are extinguished, and the path of speech is cut off. It is identical with the edge of reality and equal to the [real] nature of things. I use these signs to contemplate the Thus-Come One."

[TD 8, no. 246:836 — CO]

In the preceding passage the "unboundedness" of the Buddha's body, and the principle of universal emptiness in the Prajñāpāramitā (expressed in the negation of all determinate views) could also be understood in the more affirmative terms of the Huayan philosophy, i.e., the universal tolerance and mutual non-obstruction of all things (expressed as "nothing precludes or bars anything else," shishi wu ai, or, politically, anything goes

---

19. A punning inversion of *Mencius* 7B:16, "To be humane (*ren*) is what it means to be human (*ren*)," recalling also Confucius' pun on "humaneness" (*ren*) and "forbearance" (*ren*) in *Analects* 12:3.

if it serves the purposes of Buddhism. Both formulations underlay the practice of Amoghavajra's Esoteric Buddhism or Mystical Teaching, which was predicated on a view similar to Huayan's "True Emptiness [allows for] Mysterious or Wondrous Manifestations (zhen kong miaoyou)." Thus mystic rites and incantations could play a part in Esoteric Buddhism's consecrating and legitimating of imperial rule.

By the time of Amoghavajra's new recension of the Sūtra for Humane Kings, *Chinese Buddhism was unquestionably an arm of the state. His recension deepened its theological component while softening and transforming objections to the monks' service of the government — a transformation motivated by Amoghavajra's role as saṅgha superintendent and by his Esoteric Buddhist ideology. Thus, he added a long incantation (dhāraṇī) to the text and produced three new commentaries that outlined esoteric rites for invoking the wrathful "Kings of Illumination" (ming wang, Sanskrit vidyārāja) for the defense of the state. In Amoghavajra's new recension of the* Sūtra for Humane Kings, *one of these Kings of Illumination says:*

Because of our original vows we have received the Buddha's spiritual power. If, in all the states of the worlds of the ten directions, there is a place where this scripture is received and held, read, recited, and expounded, then I and the others go there in an instant, to guard and protect the Correct Teaching or to establish the Correct Teaching. We will ensure that these states are devoid of all calamities and difficulties. Swords, troops, and epidemics all will be entirely eliminated.

World-Honored One! I possess a *dhāraṇī* that can afford wondrous protection. It is the speedy gate originally cultivated and practiced by all the Buddhas. Should a person manage to hear this single scripture, all his crimes and obstructions will be completely eliminated. How much more benefit will it produce if it is recited and practiced! By using the august power of the Teaching, one may cause states to be eternally without the host of difficulties. Then, before the Buddha and in unison, they pronounced this *dhāraṇī*:

Namo ratna-trayāya, nama ārya-vairocanāya tathāgatāyarhate samyaksam-buddhāya, nama ārya-samanta-bhadrāya bodhisattvāya mahāsattvāya ma-hākāruṇikāya, tad yathā; jñāna-pradīpe akṣaya-kośe pratibhānavati sarva-buddhāvalokite yoga-pariniṣpanne gambhīra-duravagāhe try-adhva-pariniṣpanne bodhi-citta-saṃjānāni

[844a] sarvābhiṣekābhiṣikte *dharma*-sāgara-sambhūti amogha-śravane mahā-samanta-bhadra-bhūmi-niryāte vyākaraṇa-pariprāptāni sarva-sid-dha-namaskṛte sarva-bodhi-sattva-saṃjānāni bhagavati-buddhamāte araṇe akarane araṇakaraṇe mahā-prajñā-pāramite svāhā!

At that time the World-Honored One heard this pronouncement and praised Jingangshou and the other bodhisattvas, saying, "Excellent! Excellent! If there are those who recite and hold this *dhāraṇī*, I and all the Buddhas of the ten directions will always be supportive and protective [of them], and all of the evil demons and spirits will venerate them like Buddhas and in not a long time they should attain the highest perfect enlightenment."

[TD 8, no. 246:843–844 —CO]

Amoghavajra's new recension of the Sūtra for Humane Kings *was part of a comprehensive relationship between the state and Esoteric Buddhism that flowered in the second half of the eighth century. Under three successive Tang emperors—Xuanzong (r. 713–756), Suzong (r. 756–762), and Daizong (r. 762–779)—Amoghavajra and his disciples developed a new vision of Buddhist-state polity that wedded the idioms of Buddhism to those of Chinese rulership. This new vision was nowhere more apparent than in the correspondence between Amoghavajra and the three emperors whom he served. It was not uncommon for Amoghavajra to address the emperor using the idiom of the loyal minister, while the emperor often addressed Amoghavajra in the Buddhist idiom of a disciple. Some exchanges are a skillful blend of Chinese and Buddhist rhetoric, a blend that indicates the assimilation of Buddhism to Chinese culture and politics. In the following memorial to Suzong, dated 17 March 758, Amoghavajra expressed his appreciation of a gift of incense in a way that simultaneously evokes his role as servant of the ruler and as the cosmocratic protector of the empire.*

The monk Amoghavajra says: Your Majesty gave me rare incense; through your messenger you bestow upon me great favor. I am speechless with delight. . . . I have dedicated my life to the Buddhist cause . . . I have prayed with the strength of the all-embracing [bodhisattva] vow that I would encounter the triumphant appearance of a world-ruler (*Cakravartin*). . . . [During the early part of the rebellion][20] your majesty's noble plans were carried out by you alone, yet the Teaching mysteriously contributed [toward victory]; the gang of bandits was fragmented and destroyed, and the imperial portents have returned to their normative state. . . . In the tenth month you cleansed the palace by setting up an assembly to drive out evil influences; when you rectified your rule by granting official titles, you went up to the altar (*bodhimaṇḍa*) for consecration (*abhiṣeka*). . . . Already you have showered me with gifts. When can I ever repay you? It is proper that I reverently bathe the statues at the appointed times and that I perform the immolation (*homa*) rites at the half moon in order that the thirty-seven divinities [of the Diamond world, *Vajradhātu maṇḍala*] may protect your earth, my brilliant king, and that the sixteen protectors [bodhisattvas of the *Vajradhātu maṇḍala*] might guard your majestic spirit, so that you may live as long as the southern mountain, eternally, without limit.

[TD 52, no. 2120:827–828; trans. adapted from Orlando,
Life of Amoghavajra, pp. 45–49 —CO]

---

20. The Rebellion of An Lushan, which began in 755.

Chapter 17

SCHOOLS OF BUDDHIST PRACTICE

In the preceding chapter, four of the major schools of Buddhist doctrine were presented. Here we introduce two of the most important schools of Buddhist religious practice. The first of them, the Pure Land sect, emphasized salvation by faith and became the most popular form of Buddhism in China. The second, the Meditation sect, though appealing to a more limited following, became the most influential form of Buddhism among artists and intellectuals, as well as monks. Together they may be taken to represent a general reaction against the scriptural and doctrinal approach to religion, but their growing ascendancy in later centuries should not be regarded as the superseding of older schools by newer ones. In fact, both the Pure Land and the Meditation schools existed along with the others, even antedating some, like the Tiantai, and their enduring popularity was only a matter of their surviving better the vicissitudes of religious and social change.

THE PURE LAND SCHOOL

The "Pure Land" (Chinese *Jingtu*; Sanskrit *Sukhāvatī*) is the sphere believed by Mahāyāna Buddhists to be ruled over by the Buddha Amitābha (also known as Amitāyus and Amita). Indian Mahāyānists conceived of the universe as consisting of an infinite number of spheres and as going through an infinite number of cosmic periods. In the present period there is, according to this belief, a sphere called the Pure Land, the beauties and excellences of which are described in the most extravagant terms by certain of the Mahāyāna scriptures. Among its advantages is the fact that it is free of the temptations and defilements (for example, the presence of women, thought to be impure) that characterize the world inhabited by mortals.

A common belief among Mahāyāna Buddhists, and one supported by scripture, was that the earthly dispensation of each Buddha's teaching terminated with his final *nirvāṇa* and was followed by a gradual degeneration of the teaching. The period immediately following the Buddha's demise, known as the era of the True Law or Doctrine, is characterized by the continued vigor of the religion in spite of his absence. That is followed in turn by the era of Reflected Law, in which the outward forms of the religion are maintained but the inner content perishes. Finally comes the era of the Final Degeneration of the Law, in which both form and substance come to nought. The scriptures dealing with the spiritual reign of Śākyamuni differ considerably as to the relative length of the three eras following his entry into *nirvāṇa*. But it was possible for certain Chinese clerics during the Northern and Southern Dynasties period (420–589) to find scriptural justification for their sense that the period in which they themselves were living was the very era of Final Degeneration of the Law that the sacred writings had predicted. The confused state of Buddhist doctrine and the difficulty of any but a few to master it, either in the pursuit of scriptural studies or in the practice of monastic disciplines, helped to convince many clerics and untold numbers of laymen that their only hope of salvation lay in faith — faith in the saving power of the buddhas.

In the *Sūtra of the Buddha of Limitless Life* (*Sukhāvatīvyūha*), one of the principal scriptural bases of Pure Land salvationism, Amita, while yet a bodhisattva under the name Dharmākara, took forty-eight vows that were instrumental in his attainment of buddhahood. The eighteenth of these, which came to be considered the most important, was, "If, O Blessed One, when I have attained enlightenment, whatever beings in other worlds, having conceived a desire for right, perfect enlightenment, and having heard my name, with favorable intent think upon me, if when the time and the moment of death are upon them, I, surrounded by and at the head of my community of mendicants, do not stand before them to keep them from frustration, may I not, on that account, attain to unexcelled, right, perfect enlightenment." Since, according to believers in this scripture, the bodhisattva Dharmākara *did* in fact become a Buddha (Amita), the efficacy of his vows is proved, and anyone who meditates or calls upon his name in good faith will be reborn in his Buddha-world.

Hence the simple invocation or ejaculation of Amita's name (A-*mi-tuo-fo* in Chinese) became the most common of all religious practices in China and the means by which millions sought release from the sufferings of this world. Nor was it simply a sectarian devotion. The meditation upon Amita and his Pure

Land became a widespread practice in the temples and monasteries of other sects as well. In religious painting and sculpture too, Amita, seated on a lotus throne in his Western Paradise and flanked by his attendant bodhisattvas (e.g., Guanyin, the so-called Goddess of Mercy), was a favorite theme.

TANLUAN: *COMMENTARY TO VASUBANDHU'S ESSAY ON REBIRTH*

The work from which portions are presented below is a commentary on the Chinese translation of a short essay, partly in prose and partly in verse, ascribed to Vasubandhu and purporting to set forth the essence of the *Sūtra of the Buddha of Limitless Life* (Sukhāvatīvyūha). The author of the commentary is Tanluan (476–542), a famous patriarch of the Pure Land school.

> Behold the phenomena of yon sphere,
> How they surpass the paths of the three worlds!

The reason that the [Amita] Buddha brings forth the pure merit of these adornments of his sphere is that He sees the phenomena of the three worlds as false, ceaselessly changing in a cycle, and without end, going round like a cankerworm, imprisoned like a silkworm in its own cocoon. Alas for the sentient beings, bound to these three worlds, perverse and impure! He wishes to put the beings in a place that is not false, not ceaselessly changing in a cycle, not without end, that they may find a great, pure place supremely happy. For this reason He brings forth the pure merit of these adornments. What is meant by "perfection"? The meaning is that this purity is incorruptible, that it is incontaminable. It is not like the phenomena of the three worlds, which are both contaminable and corruptible.

Question: Vasubandhu . . . says: "All together with the sentient beings shall go to be reborn in the Happy Land." To which "beings" does this refer?

Answer: If we examine the *Sūtra of the Buddha of Limitless Life*, preached at Rājagṛha city, we see that the Buddha announced to Ānanda: "The Buddhas, the Thus-Come Ones of the ten directions, as numerous as the sands of the Ganges, shall all together praise the incalculable awesome divinity and merit of the Buddha of Limitless Life. Then all of the beings that are, if, hearing his name, they shall with a believing heart rejoice for but a single moment of consciousness and with minds intent on being reborn in His land, shall be immediately enabled to go there and be reborn and stay there without return. There shall be excepted only those who commit the five violations[1] and malign

---

1. Killing father, mother, or an *arhat*; doing harm to the body of the Buddha; introducing disharmony into the monastic community.

the True Law."[2] From this we see that even the commonest of men may go thither to be reborn. . . .

How does one give rise to a prayerful heart? One always prays, with the whole heart single-mindedly thinking of being ultimately reborn in the Happy Land, because one wishes truly to practice *śamatha* [calming]. . . .

Śamatha is rendered *zhi* [calming] in three senses. First, one thinks single-mindedly of Amita Buddha and prays for rebirth in His Land. This Buddha's name and that Land's name can stop all evil. Second, that Happy Land exceeds the path of the three worlds. If a man is born in that Land, he automatically puts an end to the evils of body, speech, and mind. Third, Amita Buddha's power of enlightenment and persistent tenacity can naturally arrest the mind that seeks after lower stages of the Vehicle. These three kinds of cessation arise from Buddha's real merit. Therefore it is said that "one wishes truly to practice *Śamatha*."

How does one observe? With wisdom one observes. With right mindfulness one observes Him, because one wishes truly to practice *vipaśyanā* [contemplation].

Vipaśyanā is translated *guan* [contemplation] in two senses. First, while yet in this world, one conceives a thought and views the merit of the above-mentioned three kinds of adornments. This merit is real, hence the practitioner also gains real merit. "Real merit" is the ability to be reborn with certainty in that Land. Second, once one has achieved rebirth in that Pure Land one immediately sees Amita Buddha. The pure-hearted bodhisattva who has not yet fully perceived is now able to perceive fully the Law Body that is above differences and, together with the pure-hearted bodhisattvas and the bodhisattvas of the uppermost station, to attain fully to the same quiescent equality. Therefore it is said that "one wishes truly to practice *vipaśyanā*." [pp. 835–836]

How does one apply [one's own merit] to and not reject all suffering beings? By ever making the vow to put such application first, in order to obtain a perfect heart of great compassion.

"Application" has two aspects. The first is the going aspect; the second is the returning aspect. What is the "going aspect"? One takes one's own merit and diverts it to all the beings, praying that all together may go to be reborn in Amita Buddha's Happy Land. What is the "returning aspect"? When one has already been reborn in that Land and attained to the perfection of calming and contemplation, and the power of saving others through convenient means, one returns and enters the withered forest of life and death, and teaches all beings to turn together to the Path of the Buddha. [p. 836]

[From *Yuansheng lun zhu*, TD 40, no. 1819:827–36 — LH]

---

2. Probably alludes to the *Wuliang shou jing you-po-ti she* of Vasubandhu, TD40.

DAOCHUO: *COMPENDIUM ON THE HAPPY LAND*

The compendium from which these extracts are taken was compiled by Daochuo (d. 645), a monk who was particularly devoted to the recitation of the Buddha's name and became one of the great patriarchs of Pure Land Buddhism.

A Teaching Appropriate to the Times

If a particular teaching is appropriate to the times and suits the capacity of the particular individual, then it is easy to practice and easy to become enlightened. But if capacity, teaching, and age are out of harmony, then practice will be laborious and realization difficult to achieve. Thus the *Sūtra on Mindfulness of the True Dharma* says, "Practitioners in single-minded pursuit of the Path should carefully evaluate the situation at hand and the expedient means appropriate to it."[3] If the occasion is not right and there is no proper expedient, then it will be tantamount to failure and is not what we call benefit. . . .

Therefore the *Sūtra of the Bodhisattva Candragarbha* (*Daji yuezang jing*) says, "In the first five hundred years after I, the Buddha, have entered final extinction (*parinirvāṇa*), my followers will be able to achieve firm stability [in the Way] through the cultivation of wisdom (*prajñā*). During the second five hundred years they will become established in the Way [primarily] through the practice of *samādhi* [meditative concentration]. In the third five hundred years academic learning, reading, and recitation [of scripture] will be on a firm foundation. During the fourth five hundred years they will become established in the faith through the building of reliquaries [*stūpa*] and monasteries, as well as the cultivation of merits and repentance [of sins]. In the fifth five hundred years the pure *Dharma* will enter [final] eclipse, and there will appear considerable controversy and strife. Beings will be able to establish themselves through only the most meager deeds of virtue."[4]

Furthermore that same *sūtra* says, "When the Buddhas come forth in the world they have four types of *Dharma* by which they save living beings. What are the four? The first is preaching by word the twelve classes of scripture. This is known as delivering beings through the giving of the *Dharma*. The second is [the thirty-two major] marks and [eighty minor] excellent qualities as well as the infinite radiance possessed by all Buddhas. If beings can simply fix their minds on and discern these features they will all receive benefit. This is known as delivering beings through the activity of the body. Third, [the Buddhas] are endowed with all manner of supernatural powers and modes through which to

---

3. *Zhengfa nian[chu] jing* (TD 17, no. 721).

4. *Sūtra of the Bodhisattva Candragarbha from the Mahāsaṃnipāta [Collection]* (*Dajijing, Yuezang fen*) (TD 13, no. 397:363a-b).

manifest themselves that arise as a function of their infinite merits. This amounts to saving beings through supernatural powers. Fourth, the Buddha *Tathāgatas* have an infinite number of names: some are common epithets, some specific names. If beings fix their minds on and invoke (*chengnian*) these names, without fail they will eliminate impediments [to the Path], gain great benefit, and all be reborn in the presence of the Buddhas. This is known as delivering sentient beings through name."[5]

We calculate that sentient beings of the present age are in the period of the fourth five hundred years after the Buddha departed from the world. It is precisely the period to which repentance, cultivation of merits, and invocation of the Buddha's name are most suited. [As it states in the *Sūtra on the Contemplation of the Buddha of Limitless Life*], "If you invoke the name of Amitābha Buddha for even a single instant you will be able to expel sins accumulated over eighty million aeons [*kalpas*] of lifetimes."[6] If just one instant [of recitation has such power], how much more must it hold true for those who practice constant recollection and recitation (*nian*)! Indeed, this is a person who is constantly repenting.

[*Anle ji*, TD 47, no. 1958:4 —DS]

The Difficult Path and the Easy Path

Dwelling in the realm of the burning house, I harbor fear in my breast and look to the Three Vehicles. Yet . . . even if I should manage to return to the true and correct path [of the Mahāyāna] after following the [less difficult] course of the two vehicles, my progress would still be convoluted and roundabout. I could aspire directly to the One Great Cart [of the Buddha Vehicle]. But even though it may be one single path, I fear that my progress may still be steep and long, for I am yet at a stage of practice where I may easily backslide. Indeed, if one's meritorious powers are not yet sufficiently established it is very difficult to make steady progress [on one's own].

For this reason the Bodhisattva Nāgārjuna said, "There are two paths by which one may seek the stage of non-retrogression [in one's advance to Buddhahood]. One is by a path that is hard to tread; the other a path that is easy to tread."[7]

Now, the "difficult path" refers to the fact that it is difficult to seek the stage

---

5. *Ibid.*, TD 13, no. 397.

6. *Sūtra on the Contemplation of the Buddha of Limitless Life* (*Guan wuliangshou fo jing*) (TD 12, no. 366:346a).

7. *Avaivartika*, or "non-retrogression," refers to the stage on the bodhisattva path at which the bodhisattva is assured of future Buddhahood and is sufficiently established in wisdom and merits as to be beyond the danger of "falling back" into deluded paths.

of non-retrogression in an age when there is no Buddha present and the world is afflicted with the five turbidities. Actually the difficulties are quite numerous, but in essence we reduce them to five. What are they? The first is the fact that notions of relative good espoused by heterodox teachers intermingle with and confuse the bodhisattva teachings. Second is the fact that the aims of self-benefit espoused by the *śrāvakas* impede [development of] great kindness and compassion. Third is the fact that evil people who have no regard for others do their utmost to destroy the virtues of others. Fourth is the fact that goals falsely esteemed as good by gods and humans undermine the practice of the *brahma-carin* (i.e., renunciation and celibacy). Fifth is the fact that people advocate reliance only on self-power (*zili*) and so lack sustainment through other-power (*tali*). . . . Because it is analogous to traveling overland on foot, it is called "the path that is difficult to traverse."

The expression "path that is easy to traverse" refers to the vow to be reborn in the Pure Land through recourse to faith in the Buddha [Amitābha]. One puts forth the great determination [to achieve Buddhahood], establishes merits, and undertakes various practices. Then, through the power of the Buddha Amitābha's original vow one is born in the Pure Land. Sustained by the Buddha's power one enters the ranks of those properly assured [of Buddhahood], which is itself none other than the stage of non-retrogression. Because it is likened to traveling by boat down a river, it is called "the path that is easy to traverse."

[*Anle ji, TD* 47, no. 1958:8–11 — DS]

A Doctrinal Justification of the Pure Land Practice

Question: According to the holy doctrine of the Great Vehicle, if the bodhisattva evinces toward the beings a loving view or great compassion, he should immediately resist it. Now the bodhisattva encourages all beings to be reborn in the Pure Land. Is this not a combining with love, a grasping at character? Or does he escape defiling attachments [in spite of this]?

Answer: The efficacy of the *dharmas* practiced by the bodhisattva is of two kinds. Which are they? One is perception of the understanding of Emptiness and Perfect Wisdom. The second is full possession of great compassion. In the case of the former, by virtue of his practice of the understanding of Emptiness and Perfect Wisdom, though he may enter into the cycles of life and death of the six stages of existence, he is not fettered by their grime or contamination. In the case of the latter, by virtue of his compassionate mindfulness of the beings, he does not dwell in nirvāṇa. The bodhisattva, though he dwells in the midst of the Twofold Truth, is ever able subtly to reject existence and non-existence, to strike the mean in his acceptances and rejections, and not to run counter to the principles of the Great Way. . . . [p. 8]

Question: There are some who say: "The realm of purity which one contemplates is restricted to the inner mind. The Pure Land is all pervasive; the mind, if pure, is identical with it. Outside of the Mind there are no *dharmas*. What need is there to enter the West[ern Paradise]?"

Answer: Only the Pure Land of the *dharma*-nature dwells in principle in empty all-pervasion and is in substance unrestricted. This is the birth of no-birth, into which superior gentlemen[8] may enter. . . . There are the middle and lower classes [of bodhisattvas], who are not yet able to overcome the world of characters, and who must rely on the circumstance of faith in the Buddha to seek rebirth in the Pure Land. Though they reach that Land, they still dwell in a Land of characters. It is also said, "If one envelops conditions and follows the origin,[9] this is what is meant by 'no *dharmas* outside the Mind.' But if one distinguishes the Twofold Truth to clarify the doctrine, then the Pure Land does not conflict with the existence of *dharmas* outside the Mind."

Question: There are some who say that one vows to be reborn in this filthy land in order to convert the beings by one's teaching and that one does not vow to go to the Pure Land to be reborn. How is this?

Answer: Of such persons also there is a certain group. Why? If the body resides in or beyond [the state from which there is] no backsliding, in order to convert the sundry evil beings it may dwell in contamination without becoming contaminated or encounter evil without being affected by it, just as the swan and the duck may enter the water but the water cannot wet them. Such persons as these can dwell in filth and extricate the beings from their suffering. But if the person is in truth an ordinary man, I only fear that his own conduct is not yet established, and that if he encounters suffering he will immediately change. He who wishes to save him will perish together with him. For example, if one forces a chicken into the water, how can one not get wet? [p. 9]

Question: There are some who say: "Within the Pure Land there are only enjoyable things. Much pleasure in clinging to enjoyment hinders and destroys the practice of the Way. Why should one vow to go thither and be reborn?"

Answer: Since it is called "Pure Land," it means that there are no impurities in it. If one speaks of "clinging to enjoyment," this refers to lust and the afflictions. If so, why call it pure? [p. 9]

Question: The *Sūtra of the Buddha of Limitless Life* says, "If the beings of the ten directions shall with intense belief and desire for as much as ten moments wish to be reborn in my Land, and if then they should not be reborn there, may I never attain enlightenment." Now there are men in the world who hear this holy teaching and who in their present life never arouse their minds to it but wait until the end approaches and then wish to practice such contemplation. What do you say of such cases?

---

8. That is, the bodhisattvas of the upper stages.
9. Rising above conditioned things to seek the Absolute.

Answer: . . . Everyone should arouse his faith and first conquer his own thoughts, so that through the accumulated practice it will become his nature and the roots of goodness become firm. As the Buddha proclaimed to the great king, if men accumulate good conduct, at death they will have no evil thoughts, just as, when a tree is first bent in a certain direction, when it falls it will follow that bent. . . . Everyone should form a bond with three or five comrades to enlighten one another. When life's end faces them, they should enlighten one another, recite Amita Buddha's name to one another, and pray for rebirth in Paradise in such a way that voice succeeds upon voice until the ten moments of thought are completed. It is as, when a wax seal has been impressed in clay, after the wax has been destroyed, the imprint remains. When this life is cut off, one is reborn immediately in the Comfortable and Pleasant Land. At that time one enters completely into the cluster of right contemplation. What more is there to worry about? Everyone should weigh this great blessing. Why should one not conquer one's own thoughts ahead of time?

[*Anle ji, TD* 47, no. 1958:8–11 —LH]

SHANDAO: THE PARABLE OF THE WHITE PATH

Shandao (613–681), a disciple of Daochuo, is another of the great patriarchs of the Pure Land faith. He is known especially for his *Guanjing shu*, a commentary on the *Amitāyur-dhyāna Sūtra*, in which appears this famous parable vividly delineating the existential crisis of man and his need for faith.

And to all those who wish to be reborn in the Pure Land, I now tell a parable for the sake of those who would practice the True Way, as a protection for their faith and a defense against the danger of heretical views. What is it? It is like a man who desires to travel a hundred thousand *li* to the West. Suddenly in the midst of his route he sees two rivers. One is a river of fire stretching south. The other is a river of water stretching north. Each of the two rivers is a hundred steps across and unfathomably deep. They stretch without end to the north and south. Right between the fire and water, however, is a white path barely four or five inches wide. Spanning the east and west banks, it is one hundred steps long. The waves of water surge and splash against the path on one side, while the flames of fire scorch it on the other. Ceaselessly, the fire and water come and go.

The man is out in the middle of a wasteland and none of his kind are to be seen. A horde of vicious ruffians and wild beasts see him there alone and vie with one another in rushing to kill him. Fearing death, he runs straightway to the west and then sees these great rivers. Praying, he says to himself: "To the north and south I see no end to these rivers. Between them I see a white path, which is extremely narrow. Although the two banks are not far apart, how am

I to traverse from one to the other? Doubtless today I shall surely die. If I seek to turn back, the horde of vicious ruffians and wild beasts will come at me. If I run to the north or south, evil beasts and poisonous vermin will race toward me. If I seek to make my way to the west, I fear that I may fall into these rivers."

Thereupon he is seized with an inexpressible terror. He thinks to himself: "Turn back now and I die. Stay and I die. Go forward and I die. Since death must be faced in any case, I would rather follow this path before me and go ahead. With this path I can surely make it across." Just as he thinks this, he hears someone from the east bank call out and encourage him: "Friend, just follow this path resolutely and there will be no danger of death. To stay here is to die." And on the west bank there is someone calling out, "Come straight ahead, single-mindedly and with fixed purpose. I can protect you. Never fear falling into the fire or water!"

At the urging of the one and the calling of the other, the man straightens himself up in body and mind and resolves to go forward on this path, without any lingering doubts or hesitations. Hardly has he gone a step or two when from the east bank the horde of vicious ruffians calls out to him: "Friend, come back! That way is perilous and you will never get across. Without a doubt you are bound to die. None of us means to harm you." Though he hears them calling, the man still does not look back but single-mindedly and straightway proceeds on the path. In no time he is at the west bank, far from all troubles forever. He is greeted by his good friend, and there is no end of joy.

That is the parable and this is the meaning of it: what we speak of as the "east bank" is comparable to this world, a house in flames. What we speak of as the "west bank" is symbolic of the precious land of highest bliss. The ruffians, wild beasts, and seeming friends are comparable to the Six Sense Organs, Six Consciousnesses, Six Dusts, Five Components, and Four Elements [that constitute the "self"]. The lonely wasteland is the following of bad companions and not meeting with those who are truly good and wise. The two rivers of fire and water are comparable to human greed and affection, like water, and anger and hatred, like fire. The white path in the center, four or five inches wide, is comparable to the pure aspiration for rebirth in the Pure Land, which arises in the midst of the passions of greed and anger. Greed and anger are powerful, and thus are likened to fire and water; the good mind is infinitesimal and thus is likened to a white path [of a few inches in width]. The waves inundating the path are comparable to the constant arising of affectionate thoughts in the mind, which stain and pollute the good mind. And the flames that scorch the path are comparable to thoughts of anger and hatred, which burn up the treasures of *dharma* and virtue. The man proceeding on the path toward the west is comparable to one who directs all of his actions and practices toward the West[ern Paradise]. The hearing of voices from the east bank encouraging and exhorting him to pursue the path straight to the west, is like Śākyamuni Buddha, who has already disappeared from the sight of men but whose teachings may still be pursued and are therefore likened to "voices." The calling out of the ruffians after he has taken a few steps is comparable to those of different teachings and practices and of evil views who wantonly spread their ideas to lead people astray and create disturbances, thus falling themselves into sin and losing their way. To speak of someone calling from the west bank is comparable to the vow of Amitābha. Reaching the west bank, being greeted by the good friend, and rejoicing there, are comparable to all those beings sunk long in the sea of birth and death, floundering and caught in their own delusions, without any means of deliverance, who accept Śākyamuni's testament directing them to the West and Amitābha's compassionate call, and obeying trustfully the will of the two Buddhas, while paying no heed to the rivers of fire and water, with devout concentration mount the road of Amitābha's promised power and when life is over attain the other Land, where they meet the Buddha and know unending bliss.

[*Guanjing shu*, TD 37, no. 1753: 272–273 — dB]

THE MEDITATION SCHOOL

The Meditation School, called Chan in Chinese from the Sanskrit *dhyāna*, is best known in the West by the Japanese pronunciation, "Zen." As a religious practice, of course, meditation was not peculiar to Chan; it had been a standard fixture in all forms of Buddhism, whether Indian or Chinese, from earliest times. Indian texts on yoga practice and *dhyāna* were among the first works translated into Chinese, and they found an enthusiastic audience among the intelligentsia, many of whom were ardent followers of Daoism. Yet these Indian texts were obscure and at times almost unintelligible; thus the concept of *dhyāna* gradually went through a process of sinicization, whereby it was greatly simplified and altered. Before the emergence of Chan as an independent school, early Buddhist monks had arrived at a variety of interpretations, some highly scholastic and close to the Indian original, and others quite near to the later Chan version.

Little is known of the teaching methods and techniques used in early Chan. Great emphasis was undoubtedly placed on meditation practice as a means of attaining an intuitive realization of the Ultimate Truth or First Principle. In order to achieve this intuitive recognition, all conceptual thinking was to be set aside and external influences rejected. Emphasis was placed chiefly on the ability to meditate successfully. In fact, achievement in meditation was equated with intuitive wisdom.

As Chan developed in China, it came to style itself as "a separate transmission outside the scriptures, not dependent on words and phrases" and to describe its teachings as "transmitted from mind to mind." Here the Master played a dominant role; all practice and study was done under his direction. The monk was completely subservient to his will, and it was the Master who verified the degree of progress a monk had made; it was the Master again who acknowledged the understanding of his disciple and who, in the end, transmitted his teaching to him.

"To see into one's own nature and become Buddha" was the objective of all Chan practitioners, and it was to this end that all study was directed. Different Masters developed various techniques to bring the student to realization and awakening. In addition to meditation over a period of months and years, physical work, initially instituted for the purpose of supporting the community of monks, was stressed and eventually became an integral part of the Chan training program. The most commonly used method of instruction came to be the use of the *gongan* (*kōan* in Japanese). Originally a legal term meaning "public case," it came to refer to the brief stories, primarily questions and answers of an enigmatic or paradoxical nature, with which Chan literature abounds. Most likely the first *gongan* were used in public meetings before an assemblage of monks. On these occasions an encounter dialogue might take place; the Master would put forth a question or statement to which a member of the gathering might reply by stepping forward and offering a response. At another time a monk might step forward, pose his question, hear his answer, and retire to meditate upon its purport. For the more advanced practitioner, going on pilgrimage from one Master to another in order to test and mature one's understanding became standard practice in the school. Gradually these *gongan* came to be collected and written down, and to gain wide circulation. Instead of making *gongan* of their own, later Masters used the stories of famous old monks to teach their own disciples, until eventually a system evolved in which a series of *gongan* formed what might be called a planned program of instruction, in which the student would meditate until he satisfied his Master that he had come to an intuitive understanding of each *gongan*. Frequently these *gongan* could not be answered verbally, which accounts in part for the beatings, shouts, and gestures so often described in the stories. Often the Master would find his disciple's mind so sensitized and receptive, that a scream, a blow of the stick, or a blasphemous word would be the cause of his awakening to the Truth.

Traditionally, Chan traces its origin to Śākyamuni Buddha, who, holding a flower before the assembly, saw Kāśyapa smile and realized that he alone had understood. Thus the True Law was entrusted to Kāśyapa and from him it passed through twenty-eight generations in India until it came to Bodhidharma, a prince of southern India, who is said to have come to China in 520 C.E. and who became the First Patriarch there. From Bodhidharma the Law was passed to succeeding generations until Huineng (638–713), the Sixth Patriarch, inherited the teachings. This is the traditional version of early Chan. But it is so encrusted with legendary accretions that it is almost impossible to know what the true facts are. Recent research has established that a person known as Bodhidharma was indeed in China, but during the years 420–479. An ascetic, his teachings were based on the *Lankāvatāra Sūtra*, and he practiced an exceedingly simplified form of meditation. His disciples, of whom virtually nothing is known, carried on his teachings until they reached Hongren (600–674), the Fifth Patriarch, who resided at Dongshan, the East Mountain. Hongren had a large number of disciples who scattered throughout China, each teaching his own style of Chan. Some of these schools soon faded away; others prospered for a brief period; several of them composed histories, each of which championed its own lineage.

By the third decade of the eighth century two schools had attained a significant prosperity. One, which came to be called Northern Chan, was led by a distinguished Master, Shenxiu (606?–706), who was greatly honored by the Tang court. The other school, known as Southern Chan, claimed Huineng as its founder. Its cause was championed by an obscure monk, Shenhui (684–758), who had studied briefly with Huineng. In 732 Shenhui mounted a platform at his temple north of Loyang and opened a virulent attack on Puji (651–739), the heir of Shenxiu, who enjoyed the strong support of the imperial throne. Claiming his own teacher, Huineng, to be the true heir of the Fifth Patriarch, he condemned the meditation concepts of the Northern School, maintaining that the Southern enlightenment doctrine, which emphasized "absence of thought" and the "identity of meditation (*samādhi*) and intuitive wisdom (*prajñā*)" was the true teaching. His eloquence won the day; Southern Chan was accepted as the official teaching, and its popularity increased, not only in the cities but in outlying areas as well.

During the eighth century numerous Chan teachers, all tracing themselves to Huineng, spread their versions of the meditation doctrines, and many Chan works were composed: histories, treatises, biographies, all of which added to the legends and stories, until in the Song period the traditions concerning the early Masters became codified in very nearly the present form.

During the Tang dynasty all sects of Buddhism enjoyed the lavish patronage of the court and the elite, vast temples were erected and great fortunes amassed by the church. Chan remained aloof, to some extent, from this process, but during this period its temples were not clearly distinguishable from other monastic institutions. Nevertheless, when a persecution of Buddhism was instituted in 845, the anti-Buddhist measures may have wreaked greater havoc in urban areas than in the provinces. This was particularly so in northern China, where the military commanders, who were "barbarians" with little interest and fewer prospects in the Confucian environment of the cities, continued their enthusiastic support of Chan as lay believers. It was in the north that one of the greatest leaders, Yixuan (d. 867) of Linji, propagated his iconoclastic doctrines and individualistic teachings with great success.

The Linji school, established by his followers, came to dominate Chinese Buddhism in the succeeding centuries. During the Tang (618–906) and Five Dynasties (907–960) periods a variety of Chan sects developed, the so-called

Five Schools and Seven Houses, but by the eleventh century the most signifi-cant were the Linji and the Caotong, which claimed Liangjie (807–869) as its founder and had been further developed by Benji (840–901) of Caoshan and other masters. By this time, Chan, which had had a strong lay following, had made significant inroads in elite society, and a considerable number of Chan masters of the Song exercised substantial influence among the intellectual and ruling circles of the capital. Chan, while priding itself on being a transmission that did not depend on words and phrases, continued to produce and see into print a vast body of literature: biographical histories, records of individual mas-ters, poetry, *gongan* collections, prose literature, inscriptions, and other writings. Indeed, Chan has produced the greatest body of literature of any school of Buddhism.

The selections given below include excerpts from a basic Chan work attrib-uted to Huineng; examples of two methods of Chan teaching, the sermon and the encounter dialogue (or question-and-answer session); a selection from a collection of *gongan* with detailed commentary; and materials related to temple discipline and the conduct of monks.

THE PLATFORM SŪTRA OF THE SIXTH PATRIARCH

This brief work is said to represent a collection of a number of sermons and the autobiography of Huineng (638–713), as purportedly transcribed by an obscure disci-ple, Fahai. Recent scholarship attributes the work to a monk of the same name but of an unrelated school who, around the year 780, determined to write a record of Hui-neng, recognized by this time throughout Chan as the legitimate Sixth Patriarch. Our text, which was discovered in the Dunhuang caves in northwest China, is corrupt and contains numerous errors; it is probably a copy made by a semiliterate scribe. The continued popularity of this work in China, however, is attested to by the great number of versions that have appeared over the centuries. The traditional version, current today, which was printed some five hundred years after the present text, is greatly revised and expanded and is almost twice the size of the original.

Following are autobiographical passages and others that reflect the thought after-ward developed by later Chan masters. Deleted, however, is a prefatory passage pur-porting to describe the precise circumstances in which the Sixth Patriarch's sermon was recorded. It is typical of Chan accounts that retrospectively conjure up an aura of historical verisimilitude for what is essentially a mythmaking process, serving in the absence of any other criteria of public certification or doctrinal orthodoxy to support claims to a legitimate lineage inheritance. (The section numbers follow those estab-lished by D. T. Suzuki in his edition of the Dunhuang text.)

2. The Master Huineng said, "Good friends, purify your minds and concen-trate on the *Dharma* of the Great Perfection of Wisdom."

The Master stopped speaking and quieted his own mind. Then after a good while he said, "Good friends, listen quietly. Although my father was originally an official at Fanyang, he was dismissed from his post and banished as a commoner to Xinzhou in Lingnan. While I was still a child my father died, and my mother and I, a solitary child, moved to Nanhai. We suffered extreme poverty, and here I sold firewood in the marketplace. By chance a certain man bought some firewood and then took me with him to the lodging house for officials. He took the firewood and left. Having received my money and turning toward the front gate, I happened to see another man who was reciting the *Diamond Sūtra*.

"I asked him, 'Where do you come from that you have brought this *sūtra* with you?'

"He answered, 'I have made obeisance to the Fifth Patriarch Hongren at the East Mountain, Fengmu shan, in Huangmei *xian* in Qizhou. At present there are over a thousand disciples there. While I was there I heard the Master encourage the lay followers, saying that if they recited just the one volume, the *Diamond Sūtra*, they could see into their own natures and with direct apprehension become buddhas.'

"Hearing what he said, I realized that I was predestined to have heard him. Then I took leave of my mother and went to Fengmu shan in Huangmei and made obeisance to the Fifth Patriarch, the monk Hongren.

3. "The monk Hongren asked me, 'Where are you from that you come to this mountain to make obeisance to me? Just what is it that you are looking for from me?'

"I replied, 'I am from Lingnan, a commoner from Xinzhou. I have come this long distance only to make obeisance to you. I am seeking no particular thing, but only the Buddhadharma.'

"The Master then reproved me, saying, 'If you're from Lingnan, then you're a barbarian. How can you become a Buddha?'

"I replied, 'Although people from the south and people from the north differ, there is no north and south in Buddha nature. Although my barbarian's body and your body are not the same, what difference is there in our Buddha nature?'

"The Master wished to continue the discussion with me; however, seeing that there were other people nearby, he said no more. Then he sent me to work together with the assembly. Later a lay disciple had me go to the threshing room, where I spent over eight months treading the pestle.

4. "Unexpectedly one day the Fifth Patriarch called all his disciples to come, and when they had assembled, he said, 'Let me preach to you. For people in this world birth and death are vital matters. You disciples make offering all day long and seek only the field of blessings, but you do not seek to escape from the bitter sea of birth and death. Your own self-nature obscures the gateway to blessings; how can you be saved? All of you return to your rooms and look into yourselves. Men of wisdom will of themselves grasp the original nature of their

prajñā intuition. Each of you write a verse and bring it to me. I will read your verses and if there is one who has awakened to the cardinal meaning, I will give him the robe and the *Dharma* and make him the Sixth Patriarch. Hurry, hurry!'

5. "The disciples received his instructions and returned each to his own room. They talked it over among themselves, saying, 'There's no point in our purifying our minds and making efforts to compose a verse to present to the priest. Shenxiu, the head monk, is our teacher. After he obtains the *Dharma* we can rely on him, so let's not compose verses.' They all then gave up trying and did not have the courage to present a verse.

"At that time there was a three-sectioned corridor in front of the Master's hall. On the walls were to be painted pictures of stories from the *Lankāvatāra Sūtra*, together with a picture in commemoration of the Fifth Patriarch transmitting the robe and *Dharma* in order to disseminate them to later generations. The artist, Lu Zhen, had examined the walls and was to start work the next day.

6. "The head monk, Shenxiu, thought, 'The others won't present a mind-verse; how can the Fifth Patriarch estimate the degree of understanding within my mind? If I offer my mind-verse to the Fifth Patriarch with the intention of gaining patriarchship, then it cannot be justified. Then it would be like a common man usurping the saintly position. But if I don't offer my mind, then I cannot learn the *Dharma*.' For a long time he thought about it and was very much perplexed.

"At midnight, without letting anyone see him, he went to write his mind-verse on the central section of the south corridor wall, hoping to gain the *Dharma*. 'If the Fifth Patriarch sees my verse [tomorrow and is pleased with it, then I shall come forward and say that I wrote it. If he tells me that it is not worthwhile, then I will know that][10] there is a weighty obstacle in my past karma, that I cannot gain the *Dharma* and shall have to give it up. The honorable patriarch's intention is difficult to fathom.'

"Then the head monk, Shenxiu, at midnight, holding a candle, wrote a verse on the wall of the central section of the south corridor, without anyone else knowing about it. The verse read:

> The body is the *bodhi* tree,
> The mind is like a clear mirror.
> At all times we must strive to polish it,
> And must not let the dust collect.

7. "After he had finished writing this verse, the head monk, Shenxiu, returned to his room and lay down. No one had seen him.

---

10. There is a gap in the Dunhuang text at this point. The missing passage has been supplied from the Northern Song version (*Kōshōji* text).

"At dawn the Fifth Patriarch called the painter Lu to draw illustrations from the *Laṅkāvatāra Sūtra* on the south corridor. The Fifth Patriarch suddenly saw this verse and, having read it, said to the painter, 'I will give you thirty thousand cash. You have come a long distance to do this arduous work, but I have decided not to have the pictures painted after all. It is said in the *Diamond Sūtra*, "All forms everywhere are unreal and false." It would be best to leave this verse here and to have the deluded ones recite it. If they practice in accordance with it, they will not fall into the three evil ways. Those who practice by it will gain great benefit.'

"The Master then called all his disciples to come, and burned incense before the verse. The disciples came in to see and were all filled with admiration.

"[The Fifth Patriarch said], 'You should all recite this verse so that you will be able to see into your own natures.[11] With this practice you will not fall [into the three evil ways].'

"The disciples all recited it and, feeling great admiration, cried out, 'How excellent!'

"The Fifth Patriarch then called the head monk, Shenxiu, inside the hall and asked, 'Did you write this verse or not? If you wrote it, you are qualified to attain my *Dharma*.'[12]

"The head monk, Shenxiu, said, 'I am ashamed to say that I actually did write the verse, but I do not dare to seek the patriarchship. I beg you to be so compassionate as to tell me whether I have even a small amount of wisdom and discernment of the cardinal meaning or not.'

"The Fifth Patriarch said, 'This verse you wrote shows that you still have not reached true understanding. You have merely reached the front of the gate but have yet to be able to enter it. If common people practice according to your verse they will not fall. But in seeking the ultimate enlightenment (*bodhi*) one will not succeed with such an understanding. You must enter the gate and see your own original nature. Go and think about it for a day or two and then make another verse and present it to me. If you have been able to enter the gate and see your own original nature, then I will give you the robe and the *Dharma*.' The head monk, Shenxiu, left, but after several days he was still unable to write a verse.

8. "One day an acolyte passed by the threshing room reciting this verse. As soon as I heard it I knew that the person who had written it had yet to know his own nature and to discern the cardinal meaning. I asked the boy, 'What's the name of the verse you were reciting just now?'

"The boy answered me, saying, 'Don't you know? The Master said that birth

---

11. This statement contradicts the story as it later develops. It represents, probably, an interpolation in the text.

12. A further contradiction; the text is corrupt here.

and death are vital matters, and he told his disciples each to write a verse if they wanted to inherit the robe and the *Dharma*, and to bring it for him to see. He who was awakened to the cardinal meaning would be given the robe and the *Dharma* and be made the Sixth Patriarch. There is a head monk by the name of Shenxiu who happened to write a verse on formlessness on the wall of the south corridor. The Fifth Patriarch had all the disciples read the verse, [saying] that those who awakened to it would see into their own self-natures and that those who practiced according to it would attain emancipation.'

"I said, 'I've been treading the pestle for eight months but haven't been to the hall yet. I beg you to take me to the south corridor so that I can see the verse and make obeisance to it. I also want to recite it so that I can establish a causation for my next birth and be born in a Buddhaland.'

"The boy took me to the south corridor and I made obeisance before the verse. Because I was uneducated I asked someone to read it to me. As soon as I had heard it I understood the cardinal meaning. I made a verse and asked someone who was able to write to put it on the wall of the west corridor, so that I might offer my own original mind. If you do not know the original mind, studying the *Dharma* is to no avail. If you know the mind and see its true nature, you then awaken to the cardinal meaning.[13] My verse said:

> The *bodhi* tree is originally not a tree,
> The mirror also has no stand.
> Buddha-nature is always clean and pure;
> Where is there room for dust?

> Another verse said:
> The mind is the *bodhi* tree,
> The body is the mirror stand.
> The mirror is originally clean and pure;
> Where can it be stained by dust?

"The followers in the temple were all amazed when they saw my verse. Then I returned to the threshing room. The Fifth Patriarch realized that I had a splendid understanding of the cardinal meaning. Being afraid lest the assembly know this, he said to them, 'This is still not complete attainment.'

9. "At midnight the Fifth Patriarch called me into the hall and expounded the *Diamond Sūtra* to me. Hearing it but once, I was immediately awakened, and that night I received the *Dharma*. None of the others knew anything about it. Then he transmitted to me the *Dharma* of Sudden Enlightenment and the robe, saying, 'I make you the Sixth Patriarch. The robe is the proof and is to

---

13. These two sentences are out of context and represent a later interpolation.

be handed down from generation to generation. My *Dharma* must be transmitted from mind to mind. You must make people awaken to themselves.'

"The Fifth Patriarch told me, 'From ancient times the transmission of the *Dharma* has been as tenuous as a dangling thread. If you stay here, there are people who will kill you. You must leave at once.'

10. "I set out at midnight with the robe and the *Dharma*. The Fifth Patriarch saw me off as far as Jiujiang Station. I was instantly enlightened. The Fifth Patriarch instructed me, 'Leave, work hard, take the *Dharma* with you to the south. For three years do not spread the teaching or else calamity will befall the *Dharma*. Later, work to convert people; you must guide deluded persons well. If you are able to awaken another's mind, he will be no different from me.'[14] After completing my leave-taking I set out for the south.

11. "After about two months I reached Dayuling. Unknown to me, several hundred men were following behind, wishing to try to kill me and to steal my robe and *Dharma*. By the time I had gone halfway up the mountain they had all turned back. But there was one monk of the family name of Zhen, whose personal name was Huiming. Formerly he had been a general of the third rank, and he was by nature and conduct coarse and evil. Reaching the top of the mountain, he caught up with me and threatened me. I handed over the *dharma*-robe, but he did not dare to take it.

"[He said], 'I have come this long distance just to seek the *Dharma*. I have no need for the robe.' Then, on top of the mountain, I transmitted the *Dharma* to Huiming, who when he heard it was at once enlightened. I then ordered him to return to the north and to convert people there.

13. "Good friends, my teaching of the *Dharma* takes meditation and wisdom as its basis. Never under any circumstances say that meditation and wisdom are different; they are one unity, not two things. Meditation itself is the substance of wisdom; wisdom itself is the function of meditation. Just when there is meditation, then wisdom exists in meditation. Good friends, this means that meditation and wisdom are alike. Students, be careful not to say that meditation first gives rise to wisdom, or that wisdom first gives rise to meditation, or that meditation and wisdom are different from each other. To hold this view implies that things have duality, and if good is spoken while the mind is not good, meditation and wisdom will not be alike. If mind and speech are both good, then the internal and the external are the same and meditation and wisdom are identical. The practice of self-awakening does not lie in verbal arguments. If you argue which comes first, meditation or wisdom, you are deluded people. You won't be able to settle the argument and instead will attach to objective things and will never escape from the four states of phenomena.[15]

---

14. Following the Northern Song text.
15. Birth, being, change, and death.

14. "The *samādhi* of oneness is direct mind at all times, walking, staying, sitting, and lying. The *Vimalakīrti Sūtra* says, 'Direct mind is the place of practice; direct mind is the Pure Land.'[16] Do not with a dishonest mind speak of the directness of the *Dharma*. If while speaking of the *samādhi* of oneness, you fail to practice direct mind, you will not be disciples of the Buddha. Just practicing direct mind only, and in all things having no attachments whatsoever, is called the *samādhi* of oneness. The deluded man clings to the characteristics of things, adheres to the *samādhi* of oneness, [thinks] that the direct mind is sitting without moving and casting aside delusions without letting things arise in the mind. This he considers to be the *samādhi* of oneness. This kind of practice is the same as insentiency and is the cause of an obstruction to the Dao. Dao must be something that circulates freely; why should he impede it? If the mind does not abide in things, the Dao circulates freely; if the mind abides in things, it becomes entangled. If sitting in meditation without moving is good, why did Vimalakīrti scold Śāriputra for sitting in meditation in the forest?[17]

"Good friends, some people[18] teach men to sit viewing the mind and viewing purity, not moving and not activating [the mind], and to this they devote their efforts. Deluded people do not realize that this is wrong, attach to this doctrine, and become confused. There are many such people. Those who instruct in this way are from the outset greatly mistaken.

17. "Good friends, in this teaching of mine, from ancient times up to the present, all have set up no-thought as the main doctrine, non-form as the substance, and non-abiding as the basis. Non-form is to be separated from form even when associated with form. No-thought is not to think even when involved in thought. Non-abiding is the original nature of man.

"Successive thoughts do not stop; prior thoughts, present thoughts, and future thoughts follow one after the other without cessation. If one instant of thought is cut off, the *Dharma* body separates from the physical body, and in the midst of successive thoughts there will be no place for attachment to anything. If one instant of thought attaches, then successive thoughts attach; this is known as being fettered. If in all things successive thoughts do not attach, then you are unfettered. Therefore, non-abiding is made the basis.

"Good friends, being outwardly separated from all forms, this is non-form. When you are separated from form, the substance of your nature is pure. Therefore, non-form is made the substance.

"To be unstained in all environments is called no-thought. If on the basis of your own thoughts you separate from environment, then in regard to things

---

16. *Jingming jing*, another name for the *Vimalakīrti Sūtra* (TD 14, no. 475:537-57). The quotation here does not appear as such in the *sūtra*; the first five characters are from the *Pusa pin* (p. 542c); the second from the *Foguo pin* (p. 538b).

17. Reference is to a passage in the *Vimalakīrti Sūtra*.

18. Practitioners of Northern Zen.

thoughts are not produced. If you stop thinking of the myriad of things and cast aside all thoughts, as soon as one instant of thought is cut off you will be reborn in another realm. Students, take care! If you do not stop notions of the *Dharma*, it will be bad enough that you yourselves are in error, but how much worse if you encourage others in these mistakes. The deluded man, however, does not himself see and slanders the teachings of the *sūtras*. Therefore, no-thought is established as a doctrine. Because man in his delusion has thoughts in relation to his environment, heterodox ideas stemming from these thoughts arise, and passions and false views are produced from them. Therefore, this teaching has established no-thought as a doctrine.

"Men of the world, separate yourselves from views; do not activate thoughts. If there were no thinking, then no-thought would have no place to exist. 'No' is the 'no' of what? 'Thought' means 'thinking' of what? 'No' is the separation from the dualism that produces the passions. 'Thought' means thinking of the original nature of True Reality. True Reality is the substance of thoughts; thoughts are the function of True Reality. If you give rise to thoughts from your self-nature then, although you see, hear, perceive, and know, you are not stained by the manifold environments, and are always free. The *Vimalakīrti Sūtra* says, 'Externally, while distinguishing well all the forms of the various *dharmas*; internally, he stands firm within the First Principle.'[19]

18. "Good friends, in this teaching from the outset sitting in meditation does not concern the mind nor does it concern purity; we do not talk of constancy. If someone speaks of 'viewing the mind,' [then I would say] that the 'mind' is of itself delusion and, as delusions are just like fantasies, there is nothing to be seen. If someone speaks of 'viewing purity,' [then I would say] that man's nature is of itself pure, but because of false thoughts, True Reality is obscured. If you exclude delusions, then the original nature reveals its purity. If you activate your mind to view purity without realizing that your own nature is originally pure, delusions of purity will be produced. Since this delusion has no place to exist, then you know that whatever you see is nothing but delusion. Purity has no form, but nonetheless, some people try to postulate the form of purity and consider this to be Chan practice. People who hold this view obstruct their own original natures and end up by being bound by purity. One who practices constancy does not see the faults of people everywhere. This is the constancy of self-nature. The deluded man, however, even if he doesn't move his own body, will talk of the good and bad of others the moment he opens his mouth and thus behave in opposition to the Way. Therefore, both 'viewing the mind' and 'viewing purity' will cause an obstruction to Way."

35. The Prefect[20] bowed deeply and asked, "I notice that some monks and laymen always invoke the Buddha Amitābha and desire to be reborn in the

---

19. *Vimalakīrti Sūtra* (TD 14, no. 475:537).
20. Wei Qu, a government official, of whom little is known.

West. I beg of you to explain whether one can be born there or not, and thus resolve my doubts."

The Master said, "Prefect, listen and I shall explain things for you. At Śrāvastī the World-Honored One preached of the Western Land in order to convert people, and it is clearly stated in the *sūtra*, '[The Western Land] is not far.'[21] It was only for the sake of people of inferior capacity that the Buddha spoke of nearness; to speak of farness is only for those of superior attainments. Although in man there are naturally two types, in the *Dharma* there is no inequality. In delusion and awakening there is a difference, as may be seen in slowness and fastness of understanding. The deluded person concentrates on Buddha and wishes to be born in the other land; the awakened person makes pure his own mind. Therefore the Buddha said, 'In accordance with the purity of the mind the Buddha land is pure.'[22]

"Prefect, people of the East [China], just by making the mind pure, are without crime; people of the West [the Pure Land of the West], if their minds are not pure, are guilty of a crime. The deluded person wishes to be born in the East or West; [for the enlightened person] any land is just the same. If only the mind has no impurity, the Western Land is not far. If the mind gives rise to impurities, even though you invoke the Buddha and seek to be reborn [in the West], it will be difficult to reach there. If you eliminate the ten evils,[23] you will proceed ten thousand *li*; if you do away with the eight improper practices,[24] you will pass across eight thousand *li*. But if you practice direct mind, you will arrive there in an instant.

"Prefect, practice only the ten virtues.[25] Why should you seek rebirth [in the Western Land]? If you do not cut off the ten evils, what Buddha can you ask to come welcome you? If you awaken to the sudden *Dharma* of birthlessness, you will see the Western Land in an instant. If you do not awaken to the Sudden Teaching of Mahāyāna, even if you concentrate on the Buddha and seek to be reborn, the road will be long. How can you hope to reach there?"

The Sixth Patriarch said, "I will move the Western Land in an instant and present it to you right before your eyes. Does the Prefect wish to see it or not?"

The Prefect bowed deeply. "If you can see it here, why should I be reborn there? I ask you in your compassion to make the Western Land appear for my sake. It would be most wonderful."

The Master said, "There is no doubt that the Western Land can be seen

---

21. Quotation from the *Sūtra of the Contemplation of the Buddha of Limitless Life*.

22. Quotation from the *Vimalakīrti Sūtra*.

23. Killing, stealing, adultery, lying, double-tonguedness, coarse language, filthy language, covetousness, anger, perverted views.

24. The eight delusions and attachments that arise in opposition to the true form of the various *dharmas*: birth, destruction, oneness, differentiation, past, future, permanence, and cessation.

25. The opposite of the ten evils, above.

here in China. Now let us disperse." The assembly was amazed and did not know what to do. . . .

42. There was another priest by the name of Fada, who had been reciting the *Lotus Sūtra* continuously for seven years, but his mind was still deluded and he did not know where the True *Dharma* lay. [Going to Mount Caoqi, he bowed and asked],[26] "I have doubts about the *Sūtra*, and because the Master's wisdom is great, I beg of him to resolve my doubts."

The Master said, "Fada, you are very proficient in the *Dharma*, but your mind is not proficient. You may have no doubts insofar as the *sūtras* are concerned [but your mind itself doubts].[27] You are searching for the True *Dharma* with falsehood in your mind. If your own mind were correct and fixed, you would be a man who has taken the *Sūtra* to himself. All my life I have not known written words, but if you bring me a copy of the *Lotus Sūtra* and read a section of it to me, upon hearing it, I shall understand it at once."

Fada brought the *Lotus Sūtra* and read a section to the Master. Hearing it, the Sixth Patriarch understood the Buddha's meaning and then discoursed on the *Lotus Sūtra* for the sake of Fada.

The Sixth Patriarch said, "Fada, the *Lotus Sūtra* does not say anything more than is needed. Throughout all its seven volumes it gives parables and tales about causation. The *Tathāgata*'s preaching of the Three Vehicles was only because of the dullness of people in the world. The words of the *Sūtra* clearly state that there is only one vehicle of Buddhism, and that there is no other vehicle."

The Master said, "Fada, listen to the one Buddha vehicle, and do not seek two vehicles, or your nature will be deluded. Where in the *sūtra* do we find this one Buddha vehicle? Let me explain to you. The *Sūtra* says,[28] 'The various Buddhas and World-Honored One appeared in this world because of the one great causal event.' How do you understand this *Dharma*? How do you practice this *Dharma*? Listen and I shall explain to you.

"The mind has nothing to do with thinking because its fundamental source is empty. To discard false views, this is the great causal event. If within and without you are not deluded, then you are apart from duality. If on the outside you are deluded, you attach to form; if on the inside you are deluded, you attach to emptiness. If within form you are apart from form and within emptiness you are separated from emptiness, then within and without you are not deluded. If you awaken to this *Dharma*, in one instant of thought your mind will open and you will go forth in the world. What is it that the mind opens? It opens Buddha's wisdom, and the Buddha means enlightenment. Divided

---

26. Lacuna in text, restored from Northern Song edition.
27. A further lacuna, restored from Northern Song edition.
28. The *Lotus Sūtra* (TD 9, no. 262:7a).

there are four gates: the opening of the wisdom of enlightenment, the instruction of the wisdom of enlightenment, the awakening of the wisdom of enlightenment, and the entering into the wisdom of enlightenment. This is called opening, instructing, awakening, and entering.[29] Entering from one place,[30] this is the wisdom of enlightenment, and [with this] you see into your own nature; then you succeed in transcending the world." . . .

The Master said, "Fada, this is the one-vehicle *Dharma* of the *Lotus Sūtra*. Later on in the *Sūtra* the Buddha's teaching is divided into three [vehicles] in order to benefit the deluded. Depend only on the one Buddha vehicle."

The Master said, "If you practice with the mind, you turn the *Lotus*; if you do not practice with the mind, you are turned by the *Lotus*. If your mind is correct, you will turn the *Lotus*; if your mind is incorrect, you will be turned by the *Lotus*. If the wisdom of the Buddha is opened, it will turn the *Lotus*; if the 'wisdom' of sentient beings is opened, it will be turned by the *Lotus*."

The Master said, "If you practice the *Dharma* with great effort, this then is turning the *Sūtra*."

Fada, upon hearing this, at once gained great enlightenment and broke into tears. "Master," he said, "indeed up to now I have not turned the *Lotus*, but for seven years I have been turned by it. From now on I shall turn the *Lotus*, and in consecutive thoughts practice the practice of the Buddha."

The Master said, "The very practice of Buddha, this is Buddha."

Among the audience at that time there was none who was not enlightened.

[From the photographic reproductions of the Dunhuang manuscript; section numbers as in D. T. Suzuki ed. — PY]

LINJI YIXUAN: "SEEING INTO ONE'S OWN NATURE"

This sermon by Yixuan (d. 867), known more commonly as Linji, the name of the small temple in which he served, is contained in his *Recorded Sayings*. It represents a portion of a much longer address, delivered before an assembly of monks and laymen, and is one of the most famous sermons in the Linji school of Chan. Nowhere, perhaps, do we find a more forceful expression of the doctrine of seeing into one's own nature and awakening to Buddhahood.

The Master addressed the assembly: "Followers of the Way, the Law of the Buddha has no room for elaborate activity; it is only everyday life with nothing to do. Evacuate, pass your water, put on your clothes, eat your food; if you are tired, lie down. The fool will laugh, but the wise man will understand. A man

---

29. Paraphrase of a passage in the *Lotus Sūtra* (TD 9, no. 262:7a).

30. Unclear, but reference may be to "the place where the True *Dharma* lay," mentioned at the beginning of this section.

of old has said, 'Those who practice meditation seeking things on the outside are all imbeciles.' If you make yourself master in all circumstances, any place you stand will be the true one. In whatever environment you find yourself you cannot be changed. You encounter evil influences; yet even the five violations[31] that lead to the nethermost hell will of themselves form the great sea of deliverance. Students today do not know the Law; they are like half-blind sheep who gobble up anything that comes close to their noses. They cannot distinguish between slave and master, guest and host. People such as these enter the Way with deluded minds and become involved in confused and crowded places. One cannot call them true monks who have left their homes; they are really nothing but laymen.

"Monks who have left their homes must be aware of what true understanding is. They must distinguish buddha and demon, true and false, sacred and profane. If they are aware in this way, then they can be called true monks who have left their homes. If they cannot distinguish buddha and demon, it is as if they had left one ordinary home only to enter another. Such people are called common karma-creating beings; they cannot yet be called true monks who have left their homes. Suppose one had a single buddha-demon, indistinguishable in one body, like milk and water mixed together. It is only the King of Geese who can drink the milk and leave the water. Followers of the Way, with a clear eye destroy both buddha and demon. If you love the sacred and hate the profane you will continue floating and sinking in the sea of birth and death."

Someone asked, "What is this buddha-demon?"

The Master said, "A single moment of doubt on your part is the buddha-demon. Once you realize that all things are not produced, the mind, too, is like an illusion, and without a single speck of dust, it is at all times pure. This is the Buddha. Moreover, buddha and demon are the two states, purity and impurity. In my view there is no Buddha, no sentient being, no past, no present; whatever you gain you gain, and there is no need to spend time. There is nothing to practice, nothing to prove, nothing to obtain, nothing to lose; at all times there is no other thing. And even if there were something else, I say that it would be nothing but a dream and an illusion. Everything I've been talking about just comes to this.

"Followers of the Way, that person [you] who is standing before me, resolute and clear, listening to my sermon, gets bogged down nowhere. He penetrates in all directions and throughout the three worlds is everywhere free. Although he enters into the differentiations of all things, he cannot be changed. Within one moment he penetrates the Dharma world. When he meets a Buddha he preaches to that Buddha, when he meets a patriarch he preaches to that patri-

---

31. Killing father, mother, or *arhat*; doing harm to the body of the Buddha; introducing disharmony into the monastic community.

arch, when he meets a hungry ghost he preaches to that ghost. In any land he travels, although he devotes himself to the conversion of sentient beings, he never for a moment is apart [from his understanding]. All places are pure, and his light penetrates in all directions, and all things are the One.

"Followers of the Way, the resolute man must know right now that from the outset there is nothing to do. But because your faith is insufficient, from moment to moment you rush about seeking; you throw away your heads and then go looking for them[32] and are yourselves unable to stop. Even the Perfect Immediate Bodhisattva,[33] when he makes his appearance in the *Dharma* world, looks to the Pure Land, despises the profane, and seeks the sacred. Those such as he have yet to forget both taking and throwing away; their minds are still involved with uncleanliness and purity. This is not the view of the Chan sect. At once everything is the present; indeed, there is no time. Even what I have been preaching to you is no more than medicine used temporarily to cure a disease. There is no such thing as a fixed principle. If you understand this you are a true monk who has left his home, able to enjoy ten thousand gold coins a day.

"Followers of the Way, do not go about haphazardly accepting the sanction of any old master, saying, 'I understand Chan, I understand the Way!' Even though your eloquence be like a rushing torrent, it will be nothing but hell-producing karma. If you are a true student of the Way you will not look to the faults of the world, but will single-mindedly seek true understanding. Once you have achieved this true understanding and made it clear, then for the first time everything will have been completed."

Someone asked, "What is true understanding?"

The Master said, "You enter the profane, enter the sacred, enter impurity, enter purity, enter the various Buddha worlds, enter the palace of Maitreya, enter the world of Vairocana, and everywhere all these worlds appear they are established, exist, decay, and perish into nothingness. The Buddha appeared in this world, turned the Wheel of the Law, and later entered *nirvāṇa*, but his past and future cannot be seen. Thus, seeking his birth and death is to no avail. Therefore, entering the world of no birth and no destruction and traveling about it everywhere, you enter the world of the Lotus-treasury, see the emptiness of all things, and know that all things are unreal. It is only the man who listens to the Law and is not conditioned by anything who is the mother of all Buddhas. Therefore, the Buddha was produced from the non-conditioned. If you awaken to this non-conditioned, Buddha is then something that need not be attained. Once you are aware of this, this is then true understanding.

---

32. Reference is apparently to the story of Yajñadatta from the *Śūraṅgama Sūtra*. Yajñadatta, on seeing his head in a mirror, thought he had lost it.

33. The highest bodhisattva rank.

"Students do not understand, attach to words and phrases, and because they are blocked by terms such as *sacred* and *profane*, their eye of wisdom is obscured and they cannot gain awakening. Things like the twelve divisions of the teachings are but obvious explanations. Students do not know this and thus base their understanding on such things. Because they depend on them, they fall into cause and effect and are unable to escape birth and death in the three worlds. If you wish to attain freedom in moving through the world of birth and death, then know the man who right now is listening to the Law. He is without shape, without characteristics, without root, without basis, yet always brisk and lively. There is no trace of the activity of all his many devices. If you try to find him, he is far away; if you seek him, he goes against you. Given a name, this is mystery.

"Followers of the Way, do not acknowledge this dreamlike illusory world, for sooner or later death will come. Just what is it that you are seeking in this world that you think will give you emancipation? Go out into the world and, seeking only the barest minimum of food, make do with it; spend your time in the shabbiest garments and go to visit a good teacher. Do not heedlessly seek after pleasure. Time is precious and things change with each moment. In their grosser aspects they are subject to the four elements, earth, water, fire, and wind; in their more detailed aspects they are subject to the incessant oppression of the four states, birth, existence, change, and death. Followers of the Way, come to know the states of the four kinds of non-form and keep yourselves from being swayed by environment."

Someone asked, "What are the states of the four kinds of non-form?"

The Master said, "With a single instant of doubt in your mind, the element earth comes and impedes you; with a single instant of love in your mind, water comes and drowns you; with a single instant of anger in your mind, fire comes and burns you; with a single instant of joy in your mind, wind comes and shakes you. If you understand this well, you will not be swayed by the things around you, and everywhere you will be able to take advantage of your environment. You may rise in the east and set in the west, rise in the south and set in the north, rise in the center and set on the borders, rise on the borders and set in the center.[34] You may walk on water as if it were land and walk on land as if it were water. Why is this so? It is because you have realized that the four elements are nothing but a dream and an illusion.

"Followers of the Way, you who are listening to the Law right now, it is not the four elements that govern you but you who can make use of these elements. If you understand this well, then whether you go or you stay you will be free. To my way of thinking there is nothing to be despised. You may say you love

---

34. An allusion to the six different kinds of shakings of the universe when the Buddha entered into the *samādhi* of "joyful wandering."

the sacred, but sacred is nothing but a name. Students turn to Mount Wutai and seek Mañjuśrī there. They are mistaken from the start. There is no Mañjuśrī on Mount Wutai. Do you want to know Mañjuśrī? He is our own activity right now, at all times unchanging, constant without a single moment of doubt — this is the living Mañjuśrī. The brilliance of one instant of non-differentiation on your part — this on all occasions and in all places is the true Samantabhadra. The one instant of thought in which you or yourself unfetter your bonds and are emancipated wherever you go — this is becoming one with Avalokiteśvara. Together these three are both hosts and companions, and when they appear they appear together and at the same time. The one is at once the three and the three are at once the one. If you understand this, then for the first time you will be qualified to read the *sūtras*."

The Master addressed the assembly: "Students today must have faith in themselves and must not seek things on the outside. Don't take what someone else had said and on the basis of it make judgments on what is false and what is true. Even if they be [the sayings of] patriarchs and buddhas, they are no more than written traces. Some people fasten on to some phrase of the past or, fixing on something with both an obvious and a hidden meaning, allow doubts to arise and, then, staggering in surprise, rush madly about asking questions, and end up completely confused.

"Resolute fellows, do not spend your days in idle talk, arguing with a one-track mind about landowner and thief, good and bad, sundry pleasures and alms-giving. Here I make no distinction between monk and layman. Just let anyone at all come and I will discern him at once. No matter from where he comes, any words he may have to say will be nothing but a dream and an illusion.

"On the other hand, when I see a person who has reached a state of understanding, I see the mysterious principle of the many buddhas, the state of the buddhas cannot of itself proclaim: 'I am the state of the buddhas.' The follower of the Way, dependent on nothing, comes forth himself, resplendent in the state of his understanding. If someone comes forward and asks me about seeking the Buddha, I meet him on the basis of the state of purity. If someone comes forward and asks me about the bodhisattva, I meet him on the basis of the state of compassion. If someone comes forward and asks me about *bodhi*, I meet him on the basis of the state of purity and mystery. If someone comes forward and asks me about *nirvāṇa*, I meet him on the basis of the state of calmness and quiet. Although there are countless differentiations in the states, men themselves are not different. Therefore it is said: 'The form appears in accordance with the thing, just as the moon in the water.'[35]

"Followers of the Way, if you wish to attain what is truly so you must be

35. Quotation from the *Sūtra of the Golden Light* (*Jin guangming jing*, TD 16, no. 663).

resolute, and then for the first time you can attain it. If you vacillate you will gain nothing. A cracked jar won't do for storing ghee. A person of great capacity is not deluded by other men. If he makes himself master in all circumstances, then any place he stands will be the true one. No matter who comes along, do not accept anything [that he says]. An instant of doubt on your part and a demon will steal into your mind, just as doubt on the part of even a bodhisattva will give an opening to the demon of birth and death. Just stop your thoughts and do not seek things on the outside! Penetrate whatever comes before you! Have faith in your own activity right now; there is no other thing. An instant of thought in your mind produces the Three Worlds, and circumstances serve to obscure the environment and turn it into the Six Dusts.[36] What are you lacking in your immediate functioning at this very moment? In one instant you enter into purity, enter into defilement, enter the palace of Maitreya, enter the three-faceted world,[37] and everywhere you travel you see that all things are nothing but empty names."

[From *Linji Huizhao chanshi yulu*, TD 47, no. 1985:498–499 — PY]

ANECDOTES OF MASTER CAOSHAN

Benji (840–901), more commonly known as Caoshan, the name of the mountain on which he lived, was one of the many Tang Chan Masters whose sayings and stories were recorded by his disciples and preserved over the years in manuscript or in printed books. Stories of these Masters were gathered together in the great Song compilation *Jingde chuandeng lu* (*Jingde Era Record of the Transmission of the Lamp*) (1004). Caoshan is generally associated with the Caotong sect (Sōtō in Japanese), and one theory holds that the name of the sect is derived from a combination of the names of the mountains on which he and his teacher, Dongshan, lived. It is more likely, however, that the *Cao* of *Caotong* stems from *Caoqi*, the name of the temple at which Huineng, the Sixth Patriarch, served. Caoshan's line became extinct in the eleventh century, and it was not until the Ming period that his *Recorded Sayings* appeared in a collection of works by famous monks and not until 1741 that they first were published as an independent work — and this in Japan. The text, other than the brief biographical information, contains short paradoxical stories concerning the Master, which supposedly indicate the depth of his understanding of Chan. In later centuries stories such as these came to be used as "public cases" (*gongan*), subjects for meditation by Chan students. Unsolvable by ordinary rational thinking, they require that the practitioner abandon his usual thought processes in order to arrive at a solution acceptable to his mentor. Our text is drawn from volume 17 of *The Transmission of the Lamp*.

---

36. Sight, sound, smell, taste, thought, and idea.
37. Reference is to a passage in the *Flower Garland Sūtra* (*Huayan jing*, TD 9, no. 278).

Biography of Caoshan

The Master Benji of Mount Cao in Fuzhou was a native of Putian in Quan-zhou. His family name was Huang. While young he was interested in Confu-cianism, but at nineteen he left his home to become a monk, entering the temple at Mount Lingshi in Futang *xian* in Fuzhou where, at twenty-five, he took the precepts. In the early years of the Xiantong era (860–872), the Chan sect flourished greatly, and just at this time the Master [Liang]jie (807–869) was in charge of the monastery at Dongshan. Benji went there to request in-struction of him.

Dongshan asked, "What's your name, monk?"

"Benji."

Dongshan said, "Say something more."

"I won't."

"Why not?"

"My name is not Benji."

Dongshan was much impressed with his potential, allowed him entry to his quarters, and in secret gave sanction to his understanding. After staying there for several years, he took his leave of Dongshan.

Dongshan asked, "Where are you going?"

Benji answered, "I'm going to a changeless place."

Dongshan said, "If there's a changeless place you won't be going there."

Benji replied, "Going is also changeless."

Then he said good-bye and left, wandering about and doing as he pleased. At first he was asked to stay at Mount Cao in Fuzhou, and later he lived at Mount Heyu. At both places students flocked to him in great numbers.

The Master said, "You tell me! Where have all the people in Hongzhou gone?"

Someone asked, "Do the eye and the eyebrow know each other?"

The Master said, "No, they don't."

"Why not?" he asked.

The Master said, "Because they are in the same place."

"In that case they can't be told apart," he said.

The Master replied, "Yet the eyebrow is not the eye."

"What about the eye?" he asked.

The Master said, "It goes straight to the point."

"What about the eyebrow?" he asked.

The Master said, "I have my doubts."

"Why do you have doubts?" he asked.

The Master said, "If I didn't have doubts then it would go straight to the point." . . .

Jingqing asked, "What is the principle of pure emptiness when the time comes that the body no longer exists?"

The Master said, "The principle is just like this. What about things then?"

Jingqing said, "Like principle as it is; also like things as they are."

The Master said, "It's all right to trick me, but what are you going to do about the eyes of all the sages?"

Jingqing said, "If the eyes of the sages don't exist, how is it possible to tell that it's not like this?"

The Master said, "Officially a needle is not allowed through, but horses and carriages enter by the back door."

Yunwen asked, "If a person who doesn't change himself should come, would you receive him?"

The Master said, "I haven't got time to waste with such business." . . .

Someone asked, "The patriarch Lu sat facing the wall. What was he trying to show?"

The Master covered his ears with his hands. . . .

Someone asked, "I've heard that the teachings [in the *Nirvāṇa Sūtra*] say, 'The great sea does not harbor a corpse.' What is the 'sea'?"

The Master said, "It includes the whole universe."

He asked, "Then why doesn't it harbor a corpse?"

The Master said, "It doesn't let one whose breath has been cut off stay."

The man asked, "Since it includes the whole universe, why doesn't it let one whose breath has been cut off stay?"

The Master said, "In the whole universe there is no virtue; if the breath is cut off, there is virtue."

He asked, "Is there anything more?"

The Master said, "You can say there is or there isn't, but what are you going to do about the dragon king who holds the sword?"

Someone asked, "With what sort of understanding should one be equipped to cope satisfactorily with the cross-examinations of others?"

The Master said, "Don't use words and phrases."

"Then what are you going to cross-examine about?"

The Master said, "Even the sword and ax cannot pierce it through!"

He said, "What a fine cross-examination! But aren't there people who don't agree?"

The Master said, "There are."

"Who?" he asked.

The Master said, "Me."

Someone asked, "Without words how can things be expressed?"

The Master said, "Don't express them here."

"Where can they be expressed?" he asked.

The Master said, "Last night at midnight I lost three coins by my bed." . . .

The Master asked a monk, "What are you doing?"

"I'm sweeping," he replied.

The Master asked, "Are you sweeping in front of the Buddha image or behind it?"

"Both at the same time," the monk answered.

The Master said, "Bring me my sandals." . . .

Someone asked, "How should I take charge [of it] all day long?"

The Master said, "When passing through a village where there's an epidemic, don't let even a single drop of water touch you."

Someone asked, "Who is he in this country who is putting his hand to the hilt of his sword?"

"Me!" said the Master.

"Whom are you trying to kill?" he asked.

The Master said, "Everyone in the world."

He said, "What are you going to do about yourself?"

The Master said, "Who can do anything about me?"

"Why don't you kill yourself?" he asked.

"No place to lay hold of," the Master said.

Someone asked, "What about: 'When the ox drinks water and the five horses do not neigh?'"[38]

The Master said, "I can abstain from harmful foods." On another occasion he answered the same question with: "I've just come out of mourning."

Someone asked, "What sort of people are those who are always sinking in the sea of birth and death?"

The Master said, "The second month."

He asked, "Do they try to escape?"

The Master said, "Even if they try to escape there is still no way out."

He asked, "If they do escape, what sort of people would receive them?"

The Master said, "Prisoners in cangues."

A monk brought up the story: "Yueshan (751–834) asked a monk, 'How old are you?' The monk said, 'Seventy-two.' Yueshan asked, 'Is this seventy-two years?' When the monk said, 'Yes,' Yueshan hit him. What does this story mean?"

The Master said, "The first arrow may not be so bad, but the second one pierced the man deeply."

---

38. The ox is the mind; the horses are the five sense organs.

The monk asked, "Was there any way to escape the stick?"

The Master said, "When the king's edict is in force all the feudal lords yield the way."

Someone asked, "What is the essential meaning of Buddhism?"

The Master said, "[Countless dead bodies] fill all the chasms and valleys."[39]

Someone asked, "What do you think about: 'The moment discrimination arises, one becomes confused and loses one's mind?' "[40]

The Master said, "Kill, kill!"

A monk brought up the story: "Someone asked Xiangyan, 'What is the Way?' and Xiangyan answered, 'A dragon's song from a withered tree.' This person then said, 'I don't understand,' and Xiangyan replied, 'An eye in the skull.' The same person later asked Shishuang, 'What is a dragon's song from a withered tree?,' and Shishuang replied, 'There's still some consciousness remaining.' "

The Master then responded with a verse:

"A dragon's song from a withered tree — this is truly seeing the Way.
No consciousness in the skull — now for the first time the eye is clear.
Yet when joy and consciousness are exhausted, they still do not completely
    disappear;
How can that person distinguish purity amidst the turbid?"

The monk then asked the Master: "What about 'a dragon's song from a withered tree'?"

The Master said, "The blood vessel is not cut off."

The monk asked, "What about 'an eye in the skull'?"

The Master said, "It can't be completely dried up."

The monk asked, "I don't know whether there is somebody who can hear?"

The Master said, "In the great earth there is not a single person who has not heard."

The monk said, "Then what kind of phrase is 'a dragon's song from a withered tree'?"

The Master said, "I don't know what phrase this is, but [I do know that] all who hear are doomed."

Although the Master furthered the development of those of superior capacity, he did not leave any pattern by which he could be traced. After he was examined

---

39. The extinction of humankind.

40. Quotation from the "Inscription on Trust in the Mind" (*Xinxin ming*, TD 48, no. 2010) by the Third Chan Patriarch Sengcan.

by Dongshan's Five Ranks[41] [and passed it], he was esteemed as an authority throughout the Chan world. At one time Mr. Jing of Hongshou repeatedly urged him [to preach in public], but he declined. In return he copied a verse on the secluded life in the mountains composed by the Master Damei (752–839) and sent it to him. One night in late summer of the first year Tianfu (901) he asked a senior monk, "What's the date today?"

The monk answered, "The fifteenth day of the sixth month."

The Master said, "I've spent my whole life going on pilgrimages [from one Chan temple to another], but every place I came to I limited my meditation sessions to the ninety days." Next day, at the hour of the dragon, he passed away.

He was sixty-two years of age and had been a monk for thirty-seven years. His disciples erected a pagoda for him and installed his bones within it. The Imperial Court bestowed on him the posthumous title "Yuansheng dashi" and on his pagoda the name "Fuyuan."

[From *Jingde chuandeng lu*, TD 51, no. 2076:336–337 — PY]

YUANWU: *BLUE CLIFF RECORDS*

The *Blue Cliff Records* (*Biyanlu*) is a celebrated collection of one hundred lectures by the Chan Master Yuanwu Keqin (1063–1135) on the subject of a similarly renowned collection of one hundred *gongan* (*kōan*) with commentary in verse originally compiled by Xuedou Zhongxian (980–1052). Yuanwu's lectures were recorded by his disciples and published in 1128. The book enjoyed immediate success and widespread use; however, the Chan Master Dahui Zonggao (1089–1163) took exception to this. Fearing that the work was too facile an aid to Chan students and might serve as an impediment to the progress of their own efforts, he collected and destroyed all copies he could find. Not until 1317 was a copy discovered and republished.

Yuanwu first states the *gongan*, interspersing it with his own brief remarks or comments (enclosed in parentheses in the following translation). He next provides a fairly lengthy commentary on the *gongan*. This is followed by Xuedou's original comments in verse, here again interspersed with Yuanwu's own comments. The text then concludes with a long commentary on the verse itself.

This work attained great popularity in both China and Japan and was printed numerous times. There are two principal recensions with slight textual variations, and the order in which the *gongan* are given differs with the recension. The *gongan* translated below is number 83 (67 in another version).

---

41. A dialectic doctrine, devised by Dongshan and perfected by Caoshan, in explanation of the identity of the relative and the Absolute. It is greatly influenced by the *Classic of Changes*.

[*Gongan*] Yunmen addressed the assembled monks: "The old buddhas communed with the pillars;[42] what dimension of activity is this?" (three thousand miles away; no connection; all scattered). Yunmen supplied the answer himself (when a person dies in the house to the east those in the house to the west offer condolences; a completed entity cannot be grasped). "When clouds gather on the southern mountains (nothing can be seen in Heaven and Earth; even a sword can't cut through). Rain falls on the northern mountains" (not a single drop of rain can fall; half to the south of the river, half to the north).

[Commentary] The great Master Yunmen produced some eighty good teachers. Seventeen years after he passed away his tomb was opened; his body was majestic in its dignity, just as it had been when he died. His breadth of vision was bright and clear; his method of instruction direct and to the point. His instructions, alternative answers, and replies made in place of others were immediate, lofty, and acute. This very *gongan* is like the fleeting spark that flies from a stone when it is struck, like a momentary flash of lightning, swift and ungraspable as the appearance and disappearance of spirits and demons. The keeper of the library, Qing, has asked, "Are there stories such as these in the vast treasury of the canonical writings?" People of today, on the basis of intellectual understanding, think, "The Buddha is teacher to the three worlds,[43] compassionate father of the four forms of birth."[44] Why should the old buddhas commune with pillars? If you understand things in this way you will never arrive at a solution. Some call out, saying that it is preaching from the midst of nothingness. They are totally unaware that the words of the masters of our school cut off consciousness, cut off conceptual thinking, cut off birth and death, cut off phenomenal existence. If you reason and calculate in the slightest degree your hands and feet are bound.

You tell me. What did old Yunmen mean? If you merely make the mind and the environment a single oneness, then good and evil, right and wrong, cannot move you. You will gain by saying yes: you will gain by saying no; you will gain with capacity or without. Each beat of the tune accords with the rule. My former teacher Wuzu[45] said, "Even Yunmen was at the outset cowardly. Had it been me, I would have told others, 'The eighth (*ālaya*) consciousness.'"

He also said, "The old buddhas and the communing with pillars, which consciousness is this?" All at once he wrapped it up right before your eyes. A monk asked, "What's the point? I don't get it." Yunmen said, "One waistband

---

42. These pillars are frequently mentioned by Chan masters, but it is unclear as to just what they represent. Presumably they were not an integral architectural feature of the building, but stood apart either inside or outside the building. Recent scholarship has suggested that the term *communed* has sexual connotations: that the old buddhas had congress with the pillars.

43. The worlds of desire, form, and non-form.

44. Egg, womb, moisture, and transformation.

45. Wuzu Fayan (1024–1104).

for thirty cash."[46] Yunmen has the eyes to determine Heaven and Earth; already people do not understand. Later he said, in the place of others, "If clouds gather on the southern mountains, rain falls on the northern mountains." Later, for the sake of students to come, he opened up a path [to enlightenment].

This is why Xuedou holds up the place where Heaven and Earth are settled so that people may see. But if you give rise in the least bit to measuring and comparing, you lose any connection and miss the opportunity right before your eyes. Just base yourself on Yunmen's essential teachings and make clear his keen activity.

Therefore the verse says:

Clouds on the southern mountains (nothing to see on heaven and earth; even a knife cannot cut through).
Rain on the northern mountains (not a single drop of rain can fall; half to the south of the river, half to the north).

The Twenty-eight Indian Patriarchs and the Six Chinese Patriarchs see each other (no matter where you look you can't see; an extraneous person is involved; a lantern hanging on the pillar).

In Silla[47] they have already gone to the lecture hall (rising in the east, setting in the west; the store to the east pays no attention to the profits of the store to the west; from where does he get this news?).

In Tang China they have yet to beat the drum [that signals the call to the lecture hall] (half an hour late; come, give me back my *gongan*; the one that went ahead did not reach his goal; the one that went last went past it).

Happiness amidst suffering (whom would you inform of this?)

Suffering amidst happiness (a double *gongan*; who would bring this up?; suffering is suffering, happiness is happiness; coming with two heads and three faces).[48]

Who says gold is like excrement? (discern it with the eye with which you are endowed; just try to brush it off and look. My oh my? What a pity? but just tell me: is it the old buddhas or the pillars?).

[Commentary] "Clouds on the southern mountains, rain on the northern mountains." Xuedou measures his head to buy a hat, watches the wind to adjust his sails. Facing the sword blade, he comments on this *gongan* for you. "The Twenty-eight Indian Patriarchs and the Six Chinese Patriarchs" all see it. Don't

---

46. One scholar has suggested that this might refer to the payment for a prostitute.

47. An early Korean kingdom.

48. Confusing people by saying one thing at one time and something else at another time and never revealing the essential aspect.

misunderstand. It is just "the old buddhas commune with pillars" set to verse. What activity is this?

Later [Xuedou] opens up the way and destroys the complications to reveal Yunmen's meaning. "In Silla they have already gone to the lecture hall; in Tang China they have yet to beat the drum." Xuedou turns to where the thunder sounds and the stars fly and says, "Happiness amidst suffering, suffering amidst happiness." It is as though Xuedou made a small pile of rare jewels and left them here. For this reason he added at the end the phrase "Who says gold is like excrement?" This phrase is from the poem "Traveling the Road Is Difficult," by Chanyue,[49] which Xuedou cites here.

Chanyue wrote:

> People cannot gauge the mountain's height or the ocean's depth.
> Past and present, even more green and blue.
> Do not associate with the frivolous and trivial,
> Low-lying land can produce nothing but brambles.
> Who says gold is like excrement?
> News of Zhang Er and Chen Yu[50] has been cut off.
> Traveling the road is difficult, see for yourself!

Isn't the land broad and aren't the people few? The arhats of Yunju [look with disdain on those passing on the road below].

[*TD* 48, no. 2003:208–209 — PY]

THE LEGEND OF BAIZHANG, "FOUNDER" OF CHAN MONASTIC DISCIPLINE

A theme commonly found in modern as well as traditional writings on the history of Chan Buddhism is the idea that during the Tang dynasty (618–906) the Chan school developed a unique, independent system of monastic training that allowed it to exist apart from the mainstream of Chinese Buddhist institutions. According to the traditional account, this development was instigated by the Chan master Baizhang Huaihai (a.k.a. Dazhi, 720–814), who is credited with founding the first Chan monastery and authoring the first Chan monastic rules (known generically as "rules of purity" [*qinggui*]).

In point of fact, there is scant historical evidence to support the traditional account of the founding of a Chan institution in the Tang by Baizhang or anyone else. Tang

---

49. Chanyue is a title given to the celebrated poet and Chan Master Deyin Guanxiu (832–912).

50. Zhang Er (d. 202 B.C.E.) and Chen Yu (d. 204 B.C.E.) were staunch friends during the wars surrounding the fall of the Qin and the establishment of the Han dynasties, but ended up as bitter enemies.

accounts, including biographies and epigraphs memorializing Baizhang written closest
to his lifetime, say nothing about independent Chan monasteries or rules. The first
Chan monasteries on record actually appeared in the early decades of the Song dynasty
(960–1279), when the imperial court decreed that the abbacies of certain large state
monasteries were to be reserved for members of the Chan lineage. Shortly thereafter,
the abbacies of other state monasteries similar in organization and operation were
reserved for eminent monks in the Tiantai lineage, and others, in the thirteenth century, to members of the Nanshan Vinaya lineage.

The oldest depiction of Baizhang as the inventor of a Chan system of monastic
discipline is found in a brief text known as the *Regulations of the Chan School* (*Chanmen guishi*), which first appeared in the late tenth century — just the time when major
Buddhist monasteries were beginning to be designated as Chan abbacy establishments.
The text circulated widely from the Song onward in several different redactions, was
frequently quoted in other works, and became the basis for a cult of the "founder"
Baizhang that was centered in the patriarch halls (shrines to ancient patriarchs in the
lineage and former abbots) of Chan monasteries. Its account of Baizhang's role thus
became widely accepted and its historicity went unquestioned down to modern times.

Although the *Regulations of the Chan School* is often said to represent "Baizhang's
rules," or the oldest extant set of Chan rules, the text is actually not a set of monastic
rules as such. It speaks in a voice that is historical and descriptive, not the imperative,
prescriptive voice ("you must/must not do such-and-such") that is characteristic of the
genre of texts known as "rules of purity." The oldest extant set of monastic rules
associated with the Chan school is actually the *Rules of Purity for Chan Monasteries*
(*Chanyuan qinggui*)[51] a work compiled in 1103.

The *Regulations of the Chan School* implies that the main features of monastery
organization and training it describes were invented by Baizhang and unique to Chan
institutions. Those features include: the key role played by the abbot as a spiritual
teacher and object of veneration; communal life in a *saṅgha* hall, where the monks
ate, slept, and sat in meditation; the establishment of separate administrative offices
that ran the monastery and thus enabled the *saṅgha* hall monks to concentrate on
spiritual training, communal manual labor, and procedures for expelling troublemak-
ers and rule breakers. It is true that Chan monasteries in the Song and later were
organized along these lines, but so too were the large state-sanctioned monasteries
where monks in the Tiantai or Vinaya lineages served as abbots. The monastic discipline described in the *Regulations*, moreover, had precedents in earlier, non-Chan
monastic rules.

In light of the apparent falsity of its historical claims, the *Regulations of the Chan*

---

51. Editions of the *Chanyuan qinggui* (*Zennen shingi*) may be found in ZZ 2:16.5; *Sōtōshū
zensho, Shingi*, pp. 867–934; *Kanazawa bunkoshi zensho*, Zenseki hen: for a critical edition and
annotated Japanese translation, see Kagamishima Genryū, Satō Tetsugen and Kosaka Kiyū, eds.
and trans., *Yakuchū zennen shingi* (Tokyo: Sōtōshū Shūmuchō, 1972).

School is best interpreted today as a piece of religious mythology. By singling out features of monastic discipline that were in fact the common heritage of Chinese Buddhists at large and suggesting that they had been invented by the Chan patriarch Baizhang, the text articulated an idealized vision of monastic practice that Chan could claim as its own. It thus provided a justification for the unprecedented and essentially arbitrary designation of existing Buddhist establishments as Chan monasteries. At the same time, the installation of an image of the "founder" Baizhang in the patriarch halls of monasteries recently converted to Chan obscured the true history of their founding.

REGULATIONS OF THE CHAN SCHOOL (*CHANMEN GUISHI*)

The following translation of the *Regulations of the Chan School* is based primarily on the redaction of the text appended to the biography of Baizhang in the *Jingde Era Record of the Transmission of the Lamp* (*Jingde chuandeng lu*), completed in 1004. It follows other redactions and pericopes of the text,[52] at some points where the *Record of the Transmission of the Lamp* is in error. Passages in the translation that are indented represent interlinear comments found in the text. These were added by one or more redactors subsequent to the work of the original author(s). The longest of these notes speaks to the problem of how the supposedly "wordless" Chan could deal with problems of organization and discipline without committing itself to words. Since the recording of "public cases" (*gongan*) and disciplinary rules arose together with the "organizing" of the tradition in the Song period, both reflect the compromise by which "wordless" Chan produced a great body of literature, while radical purists like Dahui railed against such perversions.

From the origination of the Chan lineage with Shaoshi [the first patriarch Bodhidharma] up until Caoqi [the Sixth Patriarch Huineng] and after, members of the lineage resided in Vinaya monasteries.[53] Even when they had separate cloisters, they did not yet follow independent regulations pertaining to preaching the *dharma* and the appointment of abbots.

Chan Master Baizhang Dazhi was always filled with regret on account of this. He said, "It is my desire that the way of the patriarchs be widely propagated.

---

52. Other redactions and pericopes of the *Chanmen guishi* are found in: the *Song gaoseng zhuan* (TD 50, no. 2061:770–771), written in 988; the *Da Song sengshi lüe* (TD 54, no. 2126:240), written by Zanning (919–1001); the *Shishi yaolan* (TD 54, no. 2127:301), compiled in 1019; the *Chanyuan qinggui* (ZZ 2:16.5:465–469), written in 1103; the *Fozu lidai tongzai* (TD 49, no. 2036:619), compiled in 1333; and the *Chixiu Baizhang qinggui* (TD 48, no. 2025:1157–1158), completed in 1343.

53. "Vinaya monastery" here means a monastery regulated by the Buddhist monastic rules translated from Indic languages.

If we wish to escape destruction in the future, why should we regard the teachings of the various *Āgamas* (*A-ji-mo*) as practices to be followed?"

Formerly this Sanskrit term was transliterated as A-han. *The new way of saying it is* A-shi-mo. *It means the Hīnayāna teachings.*

Someone said, "The *Yujia shidi lun* and the *Pusa yingluo benye jing* are texts containing the Mahāyāna precepts. Why not follow them?" Baizhang said, "What we hold as essential is not bound up in the Mahāyāna or Hīnayāna, nor is it completely different from them. We should select judiciously from a broad range [of earlier rules], arrange them into a set of regulations, and adopt them as our norms." Thereupon he conceived the idea of establishing a Chan monastery separately.

A spiritually perceptive and morally praiseworthy person was to be named as abbot, just as in India, where spiritually advanced senior monks were called Subhūti. When serving as chief instructor, the abbot was to occupy "ten-foot-square" quarters. It was to be a room like Vimalakīrti's,[54] not a private residence.

A buddha hall was not built, and only a dharma hall erected. That was because the current abbot, representing the buddhas and patriarchs in his very person, was to be regarded as the "honored one."[55]

Those belonging to the assembly of trainees, regardless of their numbers or status, all had to enter the *saṅgha* hall, where they were placed in rows in accordance with their seniority.

Platforms were constructed in the *saṅgha* hall, and a robe rack provided, where the trainees hung up their monkish implements.

When reclining, they had to place their pillows on the edge of the platform and sleep on their right sides in the auspicious posture.[56]

In order to sit in meditation for a long time, they took only a brief rest and then got up again. Thus they maintained the proper deportment at all four times [when standing, walking, sitting, or lying down].

The exception was entering the abbot's room to request instruction, which was left up to the diligence of the trainees. Neither seniors nor juniors were bound by any set of rules in this regard.

The great assembly of the entire monastery convened in the morning and gathered in the evening when the abbot entered the *dharma* hall and mounted the lecture seat. The monastery officers and assembly of followers stood in ranks

---

54. Vimalakīrti, the protagonist of a famous Buddhist *sūtra* by that name, was a lay bodhisattva who magically received and debated a huge audience of sages in his room despite the fact that it was only "ten-feet square" (*fangzhang*).

55. The "honored one" (*benzun*) is the central image on the altar in a buddha hall.

56. The posture in which the Buddha entered *nirvāṇa*.

at the sides and listened. Questions and answers between guests and host stimulated the raising of essential points of doctrine, which showed how to dwell in accordance with the dharma.

Meals,[57] in accordance with what was proper, were served only twice a day and were distributed equally to all. Thus temperance was maintained and the joint revolving of the [wheels of] *dharma* and food was manifested.

The rule for the practice of communal labor was for seniors and juniors to do equal work.

Ten administrative departments were established. These were called offices. Each had one person as chief who supervised a number of other persons in managing [the office's] affairs.

> The person in charge of rice was listed as the "rice steward," the person in charge of the vegetable side dishes was listed as the "vegetable steward," and so on.

If there was anyone who falsely assumed a title and impersonated [a properly ordained monk], thereby sullying the pure assembly, or otherwise caused clamor and disturbance, the rector controlled the situation by revoking his status of registration and ordering his expulsion from the monastery. Tranquillity in the pure assembly was highly valued.

If the offender had committed a serious offense, he was beaten with his staff. His robe, bowl, and other monkish implements were burned in front of the community, and he was thereby expelled [from the order of Buddhist monks]. He was then thrown out of the monastery through a side gate, as a sign of his disgrace.

If we examine this particular rule in detail, it may be seen to have four benefits. First, it prevents contamination of the pure assembly and produces respectfulness and faithfulness.

> If a person's three modes of action [bodily, verbal, and mental] are not good, he should not be permitted to dwell together with the community. Those who, according to the Vinaya, would be chastised with the "pure punishment" (*brahmadaṇḍa*) [of never being spoken to by other Buddhists] should simply be expelled from the monastery. Only when the pure assembly is pacified will respectfulness and faithfulness be produced.

Second, it prevents damage to the *saṅgha* and accords with the Buddha's regulations.

---

57. Literally, "the forenoon meal and morning congee."

The punishment must be carried out when it is appropriate. If an offender is allowed to keep his monkish robes it will be cause for regret later.

Third, it prevents disturbing the civil authorities and avoids litigation. And fourth, it prevents a leaking [of the community's internal problems] to the outside, while guarding the morality of the lineage.

When [monks] gather from the four directions and dwell together, who can discriminate between the saintly ones and the worldly? Even when the *Tathāgata* was in the world, there was the "gang of six" [bad monks who were guilty of various transgressions]. How, then, could we possibly achieve the complete absence of bad ones in the present age of the counterfeit and defunct *dharma*? If there is but one monk with transgressions, people are quick to generalize and ridicule the entire *saṅgha*. Although they do not really know how most monks behave, the injury is great when they form a low opinion of the assembly and slander the *dharma*. In the Chan school, if we are to have little or no interference [from the civil authorities], we should follow Baizhang's guidelines for monasteries in weighing matters and making distinctions. Of course, rules are made to restrain the licentious, not for the sake of the virtuous. But it is better to have regulations and no offenses than to have offenses and no teachings. Consider how great the benefits were of Chan master Baizhang's protection of the *dharma*!

The Chan school's independent practice followed from Baizhang's initiative. At present I have briefly summarized the essential points and proclaimed them for all future generations of practitioners, so that they will not be forgetful of our patriarch [Baizhang]. His rules should be implemented in this monastery.

[*TD* 51, no. 2076:250–251 — TGF]

ZONGZE: PRINCIPLES OF SEATED MEDITATION (ZUOCHAN)

This guide to seated meditation, the earliest such in the Chan tradition, is found in the *Chanyuan Code* (*Chanyuan qinggui*) compiled by Changlu Zongze[58] in 1103. It was probably circulated as an independent work both before and after its inclusion in the *Code*, but it has been generally assumed that Zongze was its author. By the twelfth century differences of opinion with regard to the method and goal of meditation had

---

58. For an account of Zongze and his teachings on meditation, see Carl Bielefeldt, *Dōgen's Manuals of Zen Meditation*, ch. 3 (pp. 55-77).

already appeared, leading to the rise of various Chan "houses," chief among which were Linji (Japanese, Rinzai) and Caotong (Japanese, Sōtō). The present text, however, is remarkable for its lack of any sectarian bias or partisan stance. Moreover, it cites with approval earlier meditation manuals outside of the Chan tradition, such as the *Small Calming and Contemplation* (*Xiao zhiguan*) written by the Tiantai master Zhiyi (538–597). This is not surprising, for Zongze was an early promoter of the joint practice of Chan and Pure Land, showing his openness and tolerance of traditions other than Chan. Indeed for this very reason the Japanese Sōtō master Dōgen (1200–1253) criticized Zongze as too liberal, even though his own manuals of Zen meditation were heavily indebted to this work and sometimes copy it verbatim.

The bodhisattva who studies *prajñā* should first arouse the thought of great compassion, make the extensive vows, and then carefully cultivate *samādhi*. Vowing to save sentient beings, he should not seek liberation for himself alone.

Then cast aside all involvements and discontinue all affairs. Make body and mind one, with no division between action and rest. Regulate food and drink, so that you take neither too much nor too little; adjust sleep, so that you neither deprive nor indulge yourself.

When you sit in meditation, spread a thick mat in a quiet place. Loosen your robe and belt, and assume a proper demeanor. Then sit in the full cross-legged position. First place your right foot on your left thigh; then place your left foot on your right thigh. Or you may sit in the half cross-legged position: simply rest your left foot on your right foot.

Next, place your right hand on your left foot, and your left hand on your right palm. Press the tips of your thumbs together. Slowly raise your torso and stretch it forward. Swing to the left and right; then straighten your body and sit erect. Do not lean to the left or right, forward or backward.

Keep your hips, back, neck, and head in line, making your posture like a *stūpa*. But do not strain your body upward too far, lest it make your breathing forced and unsettled. Your ears should be in line with your shoulders, and your nose in line with your navel. Press your tongue against the front of your palate and close your lips and teeth. The eyes should remain slightly open in order to prevent drowsiness. If you attain *samādhi* [with eyes open], it will be the most powerful. In ancient times, there were monks eminent in the practice of meditation who always sat with their eyes open. More recently, the Chan master Fayun Yuantong criticized those who sit in meditation with their eyes closed, likening [their practice] to the ghost cave of the Black Mountain. Surely this has a deep meaning, known to those who have mastered [meditation practice].

Once you have settled your posture and regulated your breathing, you should relax your abdomen. Do not think of any good or evil whatsoever. Whenever a thought occurs, be aware of it; as soon as you are aware of it, it will vanish. If you remain for a long period forgetful of objects, you will naturally become unified. This is the essential art of seated meditation [*zuochan*]. Honestly speaking, seated meditation is the *dharma* gate of ease and joy. If there are many people who become ill [from its practice], it is because they do not take proper care.

If you grasp the point of this [practice], the four elements [of the body] will become light and at ease, the spirit will be fresh and sharp, thoughts will be correct and clear; the flavor of the *dharma* will sustain the spirit, and you will be calm, pure, and joyful. One who has already achieved clarification [of the truth] may be likened to the dragon gaining the water or the tiger taking to the mountains. And even one who has not yet achieved it, by letting the wind fan the flame, will not have to make much effort. Just assent to it; you will not be deceived. Nevertheless, as the path gets higher, demons flourish, and agreeable and disagreeable experiences are manifold. Yet if you just keep right thought present, none of them can obstruct you. The *Śūraṅgama Sūtra*, Tiantai's (Zhiyi, 538–597) *Calming and Contemplation* (*Zhiguan*), and Guifeng's (Guifeng Zongmi, 780–841) *Principles of Cultivation and Realization* (*Xiuzheng yi*) give detailed explications of these demonic occurrences, and those who would be prepared in advance for the unforeseen should be familiar with them.

When you come out of *samādhi*, move slowly and arise calmly; do not be hasty or rough. After you have left *samādhi*, always employ appropriate means to protect and maintain the power of *samādhi*, as though you were protecting an infant. Then your *samādhi* power will easily develop. This one teaching of meditation is our most urgent business. If you do not practice meditation and enter *dhyāna*, then when it comes down to it, you will be completely at a loss. Therefore, to seek the pearl, we should still the waves; if we disturb the water, it will be hard to get. When the water of meditation is clear, the pearl of the mind will appear of itself. Therefore, the *Perfect Enlightenment Sūtra* says, "Unimpeded, immaculate wisdom always arises dependent on meditation." The *Lotus Sūtra* says, "In a quiet place, he practices the control of the mind, abiding motionless like Mount Sumeru."

Thus, transcending the profane and surpassing the holy are always contingent on the condition of *dhyāna*; shedding [this body] while seated and fleeing [this life] while standing are necessarily dependent on the power of *samādhi*.

Even if one devotes himself to the practice his entire life, he may still not be in time; how then could one who procrastinates possibly overcome karma? Therefore, one of the ancients has said, "Without the power of *samādhi*, you will meekly cower at death's door." Shutting your eyes, you will end your life in vain; and just as you are, you will drift [in *saṃsāra*].

Friends in Chan, go over this text again and again. Benefiting others as well as ourselves, let us together achieve full enlightenment.

[From Zongze's *Chanyuan qinggui*, 8:460–461 — translation adapted from Bielefeldt, *Dōgen's Manuals of Zen Meditation*, 175–187]

THE CHANYUAN MONASTIC CODE *(CHÜN-FANG YÜ)*

This list of questions for monks to test the depth of their religious understanding is found in the *Chanyuan Code* cited earlier. We do not know if it was to be read aloud in an assembly, as was the *Prātimokṣa* at the semimonthly ceremony, in which case, as each question was asked aloud, the members of the congregation might have reflected on their own moral purity and spiritual maturity. There is no evidence, however, that this was actually done. More probably the text served instead for either classroom instruction or individual study and review, as a comprehensive outline of the key areas of moral and spiritual cultivation. The list of questions is also known to have been circulated as an independent book, separate from the *Chanyuan Code*, in order to facilitate its wider use.

The 120 questions cover a wide range of topics, which for purposes of discussion, may be divided into five areas: (1) morality common to Confucianism and Buddhism—filial piety, loyalty, respect, kindness, humility, and other virtues; (2) Buddhist precepts stressed in the *Vinaya*, particularly those of nonharming; (3) Mahāyāna ideals such as the six perfections and thought for enlightenment; (4) technical knowledge of Buddhist doctrine and philosophy, heavily Tiantai and Huayan; and (5) Chan, primarily knowledge of public cases [*gongan*]. Aside from these categories, Zongze asks learners to seek out good teachers, not to exploit their disciples, not to use their position to oppress others, to obey the law of the land, to make commitments to the Buddhist way of life, and to be diligent in the Buddhist practice of burning incense, worship, and cultivation. Warnings against befriending officials and criticism of the desire for fame and profit reflect concerns frequently expressed by contemporary Chan leaders. Finally, the call to treat "barbarians" the same as Chinese, although based in Mahāyāna universalism, bears the mark of Zongze's own forceful way of thinking.

One Hundred and Twenty Questions

1. Do you respect the Buddha, the *Dharma*, and the *Saṅgha*?
2. Do you try to seek out good teachers?
3. Have you given rise to the thought for enlightenment?
4. Do you have faith that you can enter into Buddhahood?
5. Have you exhausted the feelings for the past and the present?
6. Are you securely settled without relapsing?
7. Can you stand on the edge of a cliff of a thousand feet without flinching?
8. Do you understand clearly the meaning of purifications and prohibitions?
9. Are your body and mind relaxed and tranquil?
10. Do you always delight in sitting meditation?
11. Have you become as pure and clear as the sky?
12. Have you attained the state of "one in all, all in one"?

13. Can you be unmoved confronting any circumstances?
14. Has *prajñā* [wisdom] appeared in front of you?
15. Can you cut off language and words?
16. Can you extinguish activities of the mind?
17. Can you regard any form you see as mind?
18. Can you regard any sound you hear as nature?
19. Can you be like Bodhidharma facing the wall?
20. Can you be like Master Longya hiding his body?[59]
21. Can you be like the Bodhisattva of One Thousand Arms and Eyes?
22. Do you understand the meaning of "old buddhas communing with the pillars"?[60]
23. Do you have no difficulties with the ultimate Way?
24. Can you raise up the mountain like level ground?[61]
25. Have you met Bodhidharma without realizing it?[62]
26. "As a resident within the retreat, can you be oblivious of events happening outside the retreat?"[63]
27. "When clouds gather on the southern mountain, will rain fall on the northern mountain?"[64]
28. Are you as fierce and energetic [in meditation] as a lion?
29. Do you teach others with compassion?
30. Can you sacrifice your body in order to protect the *Dharma*?
31. Is your mind illumined by ancient teachings?
32. Is your spirit calmed by the three contemplations of the empty, the Mean, and the unreal?
33. Can you freely go in and out of *samādhi*?
34. Has the "Universal Door" [Guanyin] been manifested to you?
35. Have you studied deeply the "six qualities" (*liu xiang*)?[65]
36. Have you understood thoroughly the "ten mysteries" (*shixuan*)?[66]

---

59. Probably a *gongan*, but not yet identified.

60. This *gongan* is no. 83 in the *Blue Cliff Records* (*Biyanlu*) and no. 31 in Hongzhi Zhengjue's (1090–1157) *Record of Natural Ease* (*Congronglu*). "Yunmen spoke to his disciples and said, 'The old buddhas communed with the pillars; what dimension of activity is this?' He supplied the answer himself, saying, 'When clouds gather on the southern mountains, rain falls on the northern mountains.'" See above, *Blue Cliff Records* section, pp. 514–17.

61. An unidentified *gongan*.

62. Ibid.

63. A *gongan* used by Song monks. For instance, a monk asked this *gongan* when he was with Xiatang Huiyuan (1102–1176).

64. See question 22 and the accompanying note.

65. The six qualities refer to generalness, specialness, similarity, diversity, integration, and disintegration. This is a basic concept in Huayan Buddhism.

66. The Huayan master Fazang (see ch. 16) explains another basic Huayan concept, the ten mysteries: (1) simultaneous completeness; (2) pure and mixed attributes of various storehouses;

37. Have you harmonized the perfect causations for the "six stages" [of the Bodhisattva career]?[67]

38. Have you attained the ocean of fruition of the "ten bodies" of the Buddha (*shishen guohai*)?[68]

39. Do you have the faith of Mañjuśrī?

40. Can you follow the example of Samantabhadra [of returning to work for the sentient beings after his enlightenment]?

41. Is your deportment dignified?

42. Is your speech correct?

43. Does your word accord with your thought?

44. Do you praise yourself but denigrate others?

45. Can you step back to let others advance?

46. Do you make known others' merits?

47. Can you refrain from speaking about others' mistakes?

48. Can you refrain from showing a dislike for difficult questions?

49. Can you not be fond of jests and jokes?

50. Do you always take delight in silence?

51. Can you be without self-deception even in a dark room?

52. Can you be as firm as a mountain in managing the community?

53. Do you always practice humility?

54. Are you peaceful and without argument?

55. Are you fair in handling affairs?

56. Are you glad to hear flattering words?

57. Do you not dislike to hear true words?

58. Can you bear suffering with patience and fortitude?

59. Can you endure harsh scolding?

60. Can you subdue thoughts of pleasure?

61. Can you stop butting into others' affairs?

62. Can you refrain from laziness and neglect in your religious practice?

63. Can you refrain from appropriating public property?

---

(3) mutual compatibility between the dissimilarities between the one and the many; (4) mutual freedom among things; (5) hidden-and-displayed correlation; (6) peaceful compatibility of the minute and abstruse; (7) the realm of Indra's net; (8) relying on phenomenal things in order to elucidate things; (9) the variable formation of the ten ages in sections; and (10) excellent achievement according to the evolutions of mind only.

67. The six stages of Bodhisattva development, according to the *Flower Garland Sūtra* (*Huayan jing*).

68. The ten perfect bodies of a Buddha are (1) bodhi-body in possession of complete enlightenment; (2) vow-body, i.e., the vow to be born in and from the Tuṣita Heaven; (3) *Nirmāṇakāya*; (4) Buddha who still occupies his relics or what he has left behind on earth and thus upholds the *Dharma*; (5) *Sambhogakāya*; (6) power-body embracing all with his heart of mercy; (7) at-will body, appearing according to wish or need; (8) *samādhi*-body or body of blessed virtue; (9) wisdom-body, whose nature embraces all wisdom, and (10) *Dharmakāya*.

64. Can you refrain from using money and things of others?
65. Can you refrain from keeping gold, silk, and jewels?
66. Can you refrain from hoarding books, paintings, and antiques?
67. Can you refrain from borrowing from others?
68. Do you realize that, even though you do not practice sericulture, you nevertheless have clothes to wear?
69. Do you realize that, even though you do not farm, you nevertheless have food to eat?
70. Do you realize that, even though you do not fight in war, you nevertheless live in safety?
71. Can you be satisfied with your upkeep?
72. Can you moderate your eating and drinking?
73. Are you tireless in giving offerings?
74. Can you be without greed in receiving offerings?
75. Can you do without extra robes and begging bowls?
76. Do you give *dharma* talks without thought of profit?
77. Do you not seek others' admiration?
78. Do you not exploit your disciples?
79. Can you be without desire for fame?
80. Can you stay away from royalty and officials?
81. Can you refrain from oppressing others because of your position?
82. Can you refrain from interesting yourself in official affairs?
83. Do you fear and obey the law of the land?
84. Can you refrain from engaging in fortune-telling?
85. Can you refrain from becoming intimate with women?
86. Can you refrain from jealousy of the worthy and the able?
87. Can you refrain from envy of those who are superior to you?
88. Can you refrain from despising the poor and lowly?
89. Can you protect the minds of others [from distraction or temptation]?
90. Can you refrain from bothering and harming sentient beings?
91. Can you always carry out "releasing life" [saving the lives of animals, birds, etc.]?
92. Do you always think of protecting the living?
93. Do you respect the old and treat the young with kindness?
94. Do you take care of the sick?
95. Do you feel pity for those who are in prison?
96. Do you help the hungry and the cold?
97. Do you stay away from military battles?
98. Do you regard Chinese and barbarians the same way?
99. Have you repaid the kindness of the sovereign and officials?
100. Have you returned the kindness of your parents who bore you and nourished you?
101. Have you thanked your teachers and friends for their instruction?

102. Do you remember the kindness of patrons who provide your livelihood?
103. Do you cherish the aid your relatives and friends have rendered to you?
104. Do you notice the kindness with which the servants work for you?
105. Do you think about the protection provided by *nāgas* and *devas*?
106. Are you aware of your indebtedness to soldiers who guard the state?
107. Do you feel sorry for the decay of *devas*?
108. Do you feel pity for the eight distresses[69] found among human beings?
109. Do you feel sad over the fighting among the *asuras*?
110. Do you lament the loneliness of the hungry ghosts?
111. Do you mourn the ignorance of animals?
112. Do you grieve for the beings in hell?
113. Do you treat the enemy the same way as loved ones?
114. Do you respect everyone as you respect the Buddha?
115. Do you love everyone as you love your parents?
116. Do you vow to save all sentient beings without exception?
117. Do you examine yourself at the three times [morning, noon, and evening]?
118. Have you finished doing what you were born to do?
119. Have you obtained great liberation?
120. Have you realized the great *nirvāṇa*?

[*Chanyuan qinggui* 8:461–462 — CFY]

BUDDHIST RITUALS AND DEVOTIONAL PRACTICES

ZHONGFENG MINGBEN: *ADMONITION ON FILIALITY*

Ever since Buddhism was introduced into China, Buddhist monks have had to defend themselves against the charge of unfiliality because they had to leave the life of the householder and observe the precept of celibacy. This short essay by the Yuan Chan master Zhongfeng Mingben (1263–1323) is a well-known example of this genre of writing.

Mingben at first plays on the homophones of *xiao*, which can mean either filiality or imitation. Filiality is essentially imitation. Since our parents nurture and love us, we in turn should nurture and love them. But to nurture one's parents' physical body and to practice "love with form" is the filiality appropriate for a householder, while a monk shows his filial piety by nurturing the parents' *dharma*-nature and by practice

---

69. These are birth, age, sickness, death, parting with what one loves, meeting with what one hates, unattained aims, and all the ills of the five *skandhas*.

of "formless love." The former, mundane type of filiality has a time limit, for we can love and serve our parents this way only when they are alive, whereas by leading a pure and disciplined life, by serious and sustained effort at meditation, and finally by achieving enlightenment, a monk can fulfill the requirements of filiality on the basis of the Buddhist principle of the "transference of merit," by which a son applies the merits of a sanctified life to benefit his parents spiritually, whether they are alive or dead.

All parents of this world nurture and love their children. Therefore sages and worthies teach us to be filial to our parents. Filiality (*xiao*) means imitating (*xiao*). Children imitate parental nurturing and repay their parents with nurturing. Children imitate parental love and repay their parents with love. Therefore, filiality cannot be exceeded by nurturing, but it reaches its utmost with love. However, there are two ways of nurturing and two ways of love. To serve parents with grain and meat and to clothe them with fur and linen is to nourish their physical bodies. To discipline oneself with purity and restraint and to cultivate blessedness and goodness for them is to nourish their *dharma*-nature. The nourishment of their physical bodies follows human relationships, but the nourishment of their *dharma*-nature conforms to heavenly principle. Even sages and worthies cannot perform both. That is because there is a difference between being a householder and being a monk. If one is a householder but fails to nourish the physical bodies of his parents, he is unfilial. If one is a monk but fails to nourish the *dharma*-nature of his parents, he is also unfilial. This is what I mean by the two ways of filiality.

To inquire after one's parents morning and evening and dare not leave them for any length of time is what I call love with form (*youxing zhi ai*). To engage in the effort of meditation whether walking or sitting, to vow to realize the Way within the span of this life, and, with this, to repay the kindness of parents is what I call formless love (*wuxing zhi ai*). Love with form is near and intimate, but love without form is distant and inaccessible. But if a person feels no love, he cannot even reach the near, not to mention the distant and inaccessible. One cannot fulfill both the easy and the difficult types of love. This is because there is a difference between remaining in the world and leaving the world. To remain in the world but not to carry out the love with form is unfilial. To leave the world but not to carry out the formless love is also unfilial. This is why I say that there are two ways of love.

Furthermore, the mundane type of nurturing and love has a time limit, but the otherworldly type of nurturing and love has no time limit. Why does the former have a time limit? Because we can only love our parents when they are alive. When they die, this love vanishes. Why does the latter have no time limit? Because my mind of studying the Way is not altered by the existence or death of my parents. Parents are the great foundation of my physical form. Yet is my physical form something I only have in this life? From innumerable *kalpas* until now, I have transmigrated in the three realms [of desire, form, and form-lessness] and have received forms as numberless as the grains of sand. The so-called foundation of physical form fills the universe and pervades the cosmos. All that I see and hear could be the basis of my previous existences. There is no way to take account of my parents' labors and sufferings. That I should fail to repay their kindness may cause my parents to fall into other realms of rebirth and suffer the pain of transmigration. Thus the Way is no other than filial piety, and filial piety is no other than the Way. When a person does not know how to be filial but says that he wants to study the Way, that is like seeking water while turning his back on it.

If someone is unable to practice this but is only able to nourish the parents' physical bodies and to love them with form, can we call this filial piety? I would say this is the filial piety of a householder. The reason we monks cannot engage in worldly filial piety is because we have entered the gate of emptiness and silence and have put on the monastic robe. We may try to emulate the other-worldly filial piety of the Great Sage of the Snowy Mountain [Śākyamuni]. Suppose we should make a mistake in one single thought; we would then lose both benefits [of the worldly and otherworldly filial love]. This is the height of unfiliality.

[*Tianmu Mingben Chanshi zalu*, ZZ 2:27.4:366 — CFY]

MIRACLES OF GUANYIN

Guanshiyin, or more familiarly Guanyin (Sanskrit Avalokiteśvara) Bodhisattva is one of the most important and beloved Buddhist divinities in China. Among the many scriptures glorifying Guanyin, the best known is the *Lotus Sūtra* (see chapter 16), in which the chapter called "Pumen" (Universal Gate) centers around Guanyin's salvific powers. Soon after one of the earliest translations of this *sūtra* by Zhu Fahu in 286, miracle stories about people who invoked the bodhisattva's name began to appear.

The selections below report miracles of the Northern and Southern Dynasties period (420–589) that resulted either from invoking the name of the bodhisattva or chanting the *Guanyin Sūtra*.

THE REAL PRESENCE

Gao Xun of Rongyang was arrested at the age of fifty for murder. He was locked up in a dungeon and had resigned himself to death. Another prisoner, however, urged that they together strive to concentrate on Guanyin. Xun answered, "My crime is extremely heavy and I have made up my mind to die. How could I possibly be saved?" His fellow prisoner instructed him, saying he should begin by making a mental oath: he would abandon evil and do good, and he would concentrate his thoughts on Guanyin without a single lapse. If he received pardon and release, he vowed, he would erect a five-story pagoda, would abandon himself to service [on behalf of the *sangha*], and would make donations to the *sangha*.

Then he applied his mind for a week, after which time his shackles fell loose. The warden was startled and afraid. He told Xun: "If the Buddha and the gods are indeed taking pity on you, then let them stop your execution." On the day of his execution, the blade of the [executioner's] sword broke. A written memorial was then sent up [to higher officials], and as a result Xun was pardoned.

During the Song period [there lived] one Gu Mai, a native of Wu commandery [in modern Jiangsu], who was very careful in his observance of the *Dharma*. He served as a military adjutant. In the nineteenth year of the Yuanjia period [442] he was returning from the capital [at Jiankang] to Guangling [upriver, in Jiangsu] when, after setting out [by boat] from the city wall, he encountered an adverse current due to a strong northerly wind. Before the wind had subsided, the boatmen attempted to proceed. When they reached the middle of the river they found that the waves were mighty and their boat was the only one to have left shore. Fearing disaster and without any other recourse, Gu recited the *Guanyin Sūtra*. When he had completed more than ten recitations the wind gradually subsided and the waves also died down. Furthermore, in midstream they could smell a strange and persistent fragrance. Gu quietly rejoiced in his heart and kept up his reciting until they reached safe harbor.

During the Yuanjia era [424–453] of the Song dynasty there occurred a devastating fire within the outer wall of the city of Wuxing [in modern Zhejiang province]. The dwellings of the commoners who lived in that area were all consumed; but there was one home that, although made of thatch and located in the heart of the fire area, alone remained standing. When the governor, Wang Shaozhi, went out to inspect the fire damage, he was startled by this and sent someone to investigate. As it happened, the house in question belonged to a functionary employed by [Wang's] commandery. This functionary, it turned out, did not usually perform Buddhist observances, but he had always heard about Guanyin. When the fire drew close, he grew earnest [in his devotion] and soon, on account of his [having attained] a perfect mind, was able to avoid it.

[From Campany, "The Real Presence," *History of Religions*, vol. 32, no. 3]

GUANYIN AND CUTTING ONE'S BODY (*GEGU*)

The practice of cutting out a piece of one's flesh to feed an ailing parent has a long history in China, attested by both medical texts and dynastic histories. As an act of filial devotion it was often celebrated in commemorative essays and poems, portrayed in popular art, and sometimes even given official commendation. However, many leading Confucians condemned this practice, considering it a violation of the true filial obligation to respect the body as a legacy from one's forebears and preserve it intact.

In late imperial China people sometimes resorted to this practice in hopes of saving a dying parent, cooking the flesh from one's thigh or inner organs to make a nourishing broth. To help those who had difficulty doing this, the aid of Guanyin was often invoked. The following stories illustrate how Buddhist compassion, as embodied by Guanyin, thus became associated in popular religion with the practice of filial piety in what, from a Confucian point of view, was an extreme and unorthodox form.

Filial son Peng Youyuan of the Ming was a native of Yiyang, Huguang. He had the habit of chanting scriptures of Guanyin, the Three Officials, and other deities in the hope of prolonging his parents' life. Once his father was very ill, and he cut off a piece of flesh from his arm to cure him. The father recovered and lived for more than ten years after that. In the autumn of 1636 his mother became too ill to get up from her bed. Yuan was worried day and night. One night he dreamt of Guanyin telling him that the mother's life span had come to an end, but if she ate human liver she could survive. When he woke up the next morning, the mother told him that she would like to have some sheep liver. Realizing the significance of his dream, he knelt down and thanked Guanyin tearfully. In the night he saw Guanyin come to him surrounded by many saints carrying banners. He woke up with a start and was drenched all over with perspiration. After bathing and worshiping, he took up the knife and aimed at the place where his liver and lung were located. Blood gushed out after one cut. The rib cage was exposed after the second cut. After the third and fourth cuts, there was a resounding sound and after the sixth cut, the heart leapt out. Following the heart he groped for the lung and after the lung he found the liver. By then he nearly fainted because of the extreme pain. After a moment's rest, he called his wife and told her to cook the liver quickly [the text is not clear if it is the whole liver or a piece of it] to serve his mother. Not knowing what it really was, the mother ate it happily and soon became well. People from near and far came to know the story and were all greatly moved. Because his wounds did not heal and his lung could still be seen, some people prayed to gods for help. They dreamt of Guanyin, who told them, "It is not difficult to heal the wound, but because few people are filial in this degenerate age, I let the lung hang out for a hundred days so that everyone can view it." The above was recorded by Wang Wennan, a second-degree holder.

[*Guanyin jingzhou linggan huiyao*, 424 —CFY]

Xie Fenlan was extremely filial by nature, and she had worshiped Guanyin all her life. One day an old nun took out some pills from her sleeve and gave them to her, saying, "These pills can cure injuries resulting from the knife." Fenlan took them and forgot about it. The following year her mother-in-law became seriously ill, and no doctor could help her. She prayed to Heaven and asked for help. She then secretly stole into her room and cut flesh from her thigh in order to cook a soup for her mother-in-law. The wound became unbearably painful, and she suddenly remembered the pills from before. So she asked her maid to get them and apply them to her wound. As soon as they were applied, new flesh began to grow and it looked as if the thigh had never been cut. The old nun must have been the "Great Being" [Guanyin], and filial piety must indeed have moved the divinity.

[*Gujin tushu jicheng* 398:10b — CFY]

MIRACLES ABOUT WHITE-ROBED GUANYIN AS GIVER OF CHILDREN

Guanyin began to assume feminine characteristics by the tenth century. The sexual transformation became complete by the sixteenth century, and Jesuit missionaries could thus nickname her the Goddess of Mercy. In the development of the cult of Guanyin in China, the bodhisattva appeared in several forms. Among them, the White-robed (*Baiyi*) Guanyin is the one most familiar to her devotees.

White-robed Guanyin began to appear in sculpture, paintings, poetry, founding myths of monasteries, miracle tales, and pilgrims' visions from the tenth century on. She wears a long, flowing white cape, whose hood sometimes covers her head and even her arms and hands. Some scholars have traced her to Tantric female deities such as White Tārā or Pāṇḍaravāsinī, the consort of Avalokiteśvara and one of the chief deities of the World of Womb Treasury Maṇḍala. Others have identified her as a typical subject of paintings, symbolizing the serenity and wisdom of Chan meditative states.

The origins of this deity, however, may well lie with a group of indigenous scriptures that portray her primarily as a fertility goddess able to grant sons, protect pregnant women, and assure safe childbirth. One indigenous scripture, titled *The Dhāraṇī Sūtra of the Five Mudrās of the Great Compassionate White-robed One* (*Baiyi Dabei wuyinxin tuoluoni jing*), enjoyed particular popularity among the Chinese people who hoped to have sons in late imperial China.

Literati in the sixteenth century appear to have actively promoted the cult of the White-robed Guanyin. Yuan Huang (1533–1606), a literatus who promoted morality books (see chapter 24) still did not have a son by the time he was forty. He started to chant this scripture and, in 1580, became the father of a son. When he compiled a collection of texts to help people in obtaining heirs, titled *True Instructions for Praying for an Heir* (*Jisi chenjuan*), he put this text at the very beginning. Copies of this scripture were printed and distributed free of charge by donors who wanted to bear witness to White-robed Guanyin's efficacy and promote her cult. They ranged from members of the royal family, literati-officials, and merchants, on down to obscure men and women. In all cases the donors provided accounts of miracles that had happened either to others or to themselves.

Ding Xian of Yibin, Nanyang [in present Honan province] was fifty years old and had no son. So he decided to print this *sūtra* and distribute it for free. He also had a thousand catties of iron melted down in the South Garden of the city to make an image of Guanyin, which was then gilded. It stood over six feet.

At the same time, in order to seek for a son, Xing Jian, the Grand Commandant, had a shrine dedicated to the White-robed Guanyin erected in the northern part of the city. So the image was moved there to be worshiped. The local official set aside several thousand acres of good farmland to provide for the shrine's upkeep so that people could continue to offer incense in future generations.

Not long after this, Ding dreamt one night of a woman who presented him with a white carp. On the next morning a son was born wrapped in a white placenta. That was the fourth day of the twelfth month, 1583. Earlier, when the image was moved to the White-robed Guanyin Shrine, the gardener had a dream in which the bodhisattva appeared to him looking rather unhappy. When he told Ding about his dream, Ding had another image cast looking exactly like the first one in the South Garden. He invited a monk of repute to stay in the temple to take care of it. Subsequently, Ding dreamt of an old man wearing a white gown who came to visit him. The day after he had this dream, while he was relating it to his friend, a man suddenly came to the house seeking to sell the woodblocks of this *sūtra*. Ding bought them and printed a thousand copies for distribution. He also hired a skilled painter to paint several hundred paintings of the White-robed Guanyin to give to the faithful as gifts. In the fourth month of 1586, he had another son. By then, Xing Jian, the Grand Commandant, also had a son and a daughter born to him and his wife.

[*Baiyi Dabei wuyinxin tuoluoni jing* — CFY]

THE SOUTHERN MOUNT WUTAI AS A PILGRIMAGE CENTER

The Southern Mount Wutai (*Nanwutaishan*), a five-peaked mountain situated on the southern side of Mount Zhongnan, is some fifty *li* to the south of Changan (modern Xian). Yinguang (1861–1940), a Pure Land master and great devotee of Guanyin who was familiar with the place as a pilgrimage site, wrote a history of it using material recorded on a stele written by monk Puming of Taibai shan and erected in 1271. The following is a translation of the stele.

During the Renshou era (601–604) of the Sui, a poisonous dragon lived in the mountain. Relying upon his paranormal powers, he assumed the form of an immortal [*yuren*, "feathered man"] and came to Changan to sell drugs made of cinnabar. He fooled the ignorant, saying that whoever took his drug would be able to ascend to Heaven in broad daylight right away. Many people took his bait. They all ended up in the dragon's lair and became his food. But the people were deluded and did not wake up to the truth. The Great Being used the power of the compassionate vow and appeared in the form of a monk. Gathering grasses and building a hut on the top of the mountain, he tamed the evil power with his wondrous wisdom. The wind of purity swept away heated vexation. Wherever the thought of compassion spread, poisonous ether disappeared. The dragon obtained release in clarity and coolness (*qingliang*) and stayed in his cave peacefully. The residents were no longer endangered. The news of the monk's efficacy reached the court, which decreed that a monastery should be built for him. Local gentry admired him, and some managed to extricate themselves from the net of attachment and, shaving off their hair, entered the Way. The Great Being liked to stay among the rocks. Monkeys and wild animals would sit around him. Birds in the forests would not cry, as if they were listening to his *dharma* talk. They would disperse only after a very long time. Unfortunately, the very next year after the monastery was erected, on the nineteenth day of the sixth month, he suddenly entered *nirvāṇa*. A strange fragrance filled the room. The sky became overcast. Birds and animals cried piteously, and the mountain forests changed color. Members of the *saṅgha* reported the sad news to the court, and eunuchs were dispatched to offer incense. At the time of cremation Heaven and Earth darkened. But suddenly, in one instant, the whole area turned into a silver realm. Music resounded in the sky; the mountain shook; auspicious clouds flew by; and the air was filled with a strange fragrance. A golden bridge suddenly appeared above the Eastern Peak. A host of heavenly beings stood on the bridge, carrying banners and scattering golden flowers which, however, did not touch the ground. Finally, on top of the Southern Terrace, brilliant jewels of a hundred varieties filled a space whose breadth and height could not be measured. A glimmer of a dignified form in royal ease could be discerned. His compassionate face was grave and beautiful. Wearing a suit studded with coins and covered with necklaces, he moved in the wind and looked at everyone with bright illumination. At that time, there were more than a thousand people, both monks and lay people, who witnessed the true form of the bodhisattva. They were overwhelmed with emotion and realized that the monk was a manifestation of Guanyin. The fragrance lingered for several months. Mr. Gao, the Left Executive Assistant of the Department of Ministries, wrote a memorial about this to the emperor, who read it and offered praise. The bones of the monk were gathered together and housed in a *stūpa*. The emperor bestowed a plaque naming it the Temple of Guanyin Terrace (*Guanyintai si*) and gave the monks a hundred square *li* of land for their sustenance. Every year the emperor sent messengers who came as pilgrims to make offerings and celebrate the ordination of the new monks. . . . Whenever there was drought, supplicants would come here to pray for rain. The prayer was always answered without fail. Such happenings have been recorded in the documents kept by the district and provincial offices. Pilgrims come in the month of the festival of Clear and Bright (*Qingming*) as well as the death anniversary of the monk in the summer. Holding the young and helping the old, pilgrims would come from a hundred miles away. Defying danger and carrying offerings, they would crowd the roads leading to the temple for more than a month without a break.

[*Putuoluojia xinzhi*, 18–20 — CFY]

PART 4

The Confucian Revival and Neo-Confucianism

Chapter 18

SOCIAL LIFE AND POLITICAL CULTURE
IN THE TANG

The Tang (618–906) is known for the vitality and vibrancy of its culture—the dynamic and cosmopolitan cultural life of the capital city of Changan, a flourishing trade and cultural contact with Western Asia, the evolution of distinctively Chinese forms of Buddhism, the proliferation of Buddhist sculpture and painting, the early development of the short story and the fictional imagination, an unprecedented and dazzling efflorescence in the art of poetry. In government too there were remarkable developments that had a profound effect not only on Tang political culture but also on the course of later Chinese civilization—the revival of the civil service examination system as a basis for recruiting an effective bureaucracy based on the principle of merit, a far-reaching land reform designed to equalize landholding, the establishment of an administrative structure of the central government that would endure, with minor modifications, down to the twentieth century.

The Tang is also known for its vigorous empire-building—a familiar pattern seen under the Qin, the Han, and the Sui (589–617) dynasties—in which there was expansion in the early years of the dynasty, followed by contraction in later periods as the burdens of war took their toll. Early in the reign of the Tang emperor Taizong (r. 627–649) Chinese forces succeeded against the Turks in Central Asia and brought Tibet under Chinese control, while in subsequent reigns Chinese influence was established in Korea and in part of Vietnam. By the end of the seventh century China was the largest empire and the most powerful state in the world.

This empire was maintained until well into the eighth century, when several developments, including intense pressure from non-Chinese peoples in the north and northwest and the dynasty's loss of control of its own military organization, brought about irreversible changes in the Tang world. These developments are epitomized in the Rebellion of An Lushan of 755, which brought warfare, devastation, and famine into the Tang heartland.

THE ROLE OF CONFUCIANISM IN THE TANG

If today Chinese civilization seems almost synonymous with Confucian culture, we need to be reminded of the long centuries during which Buddhism and Daoism exerted a powerful and formative influence. For nearly eight centuries, from the fall of the Han (220 C.E.) to the rise of the Song (960), Chinese culture was so closely identified with Buddhism that neighbors like the Japanese and the Koreans embraced the one with the other and thought of great Tang China, the cynosure of the civilized world, as perhaps more of a "Buddha-land" than the "land of Confucius." The famed centers of learning to which pilgrims came from afar were the great Buddhist temples, where some of the best Chinese minds were engaged in teaching and developing new schools of Buddhist philosophy. The great works of art and architecture, which impressed these same visitors with the splendor of China, were most often monuments to the Buddha. Until the close of this period few among the Confucians could dispute the preeminence of the Buddhist philosophers or slow the progress of the Daoist church, officially supported by the Tang imperial house.

Indeed, it may be said that during this period, though there were Confucian scholars, there were virtually no Confucians — that is, persons who adhered to the teachings of Confucius as a distinct doctrine that set them apart from others. The sense of orthodoxy came later and mostly to an educated elite. People followed Confucius in the home or in the office, but this did not prevent them, high or low, from turning to Buddhism or Daoism to find satisfaction of their spiritual needs.

Still, it is significant that, if Confucianism could not contend with its rivals in the religious sphere, neither were they able to displace it in the social or political sphere. Though in an attenuated and not very dynamic form, Confucianism remained the accepted code of ethics and the basis of the educational system. The family and the imperial bureaucracy kept Confucian teachings alive during these times until their validity and relevance to a wider sphere of thought could be reasserted by more vigorous minds. Even a patron of Buddhism like Emperor Wu of the Liang dynasty (464–549) saw to it that his sons studied the Five Classics, the *Analects*, and the *Classic of Filiality*.

The chief means by which Confucian teachings were perpetuated were the civil service examination system and the schools serving it. Revived by the Sui, based on a Han model, and continued under the Tang dynasty, this system became more highly organized and efficiently administered than ever before, and the basic subjects were still the Confucian classics. (Because the imperial house claimed descent from Laozi, there was also one type of examination based on a knowledge of Daoist texts.) Buddhists might from time to time win a monarch's favor, eliciting contributions to religious establishments or securing his participation in their special rites. Individual monks, too, might occasionally rise high in the government ranks. Buddhism itself, however, both as a philosophy and as a religion, sought to transcend politics and offered nothing in the way of either a political program or a set of basic principles that might have been incorporated into the examination system. Therefore the vast majority of those whose education conformed to the requirements of the civil service system, the great avenue to worldly success in China, submitted to a curriculum in which the position of the Confucian classics remained unchallenged. To many this study of the classics served only as a method for achieving a degree of mastery over the language. To others it provided also a treasury of historical lore and prudential maxims that might be drawn upon in the business of government.

The nature of Confucian scholarship in the Tang dynasty reflected the function that it served for the bureaucracy. Carrying on in the manner of the Han classicists, learned men devoted themselves to the kind of textual annotation and exegesis that would provide more definitive editions of the Confucian canon used in the examinations. From the scholarly point of view this work was important, and yet we find in it evidence more of painstaking study than creative thought. In the actual conduct of state affairs, however, we may see quite readily how Confucianism continued to influence thinking on the vital political and economic issues of the day.

The vast problems with which the Han had had to wrestle confronted the Tang as well, and the latter showed itself capable of strong action on a grand scale. At the inception of the dynasty, for instance, it embarked on a program of land nationalization and redistribution, upon which was based the whole system of taxation and military organization, the two most vital operations of the state. So impressive was this system that both the Japanese and the Koreans copied it almost to the last detail.

HOUSE INSTRUCTIONS OF MR. YAN (*YANSHI JIAXUN*)

Following are extracts from the prime extant example of a genre of family instruction perennially important not only in China but elsewhere in East Asia down into the nineteenth century. Yan Zhitui (531–591) was from a leading family of scholar-officials known for their public service and literary accomplishments. In times of great military and political turmoil before the reunification of China under the Sui, Yan experienced hardships and poverty but served four successive, brief dynasties (with foreigners among them) while sustaining his family's commitment to Chinese cultural traditions. His life and work illustrate a more general long-term pattern in Chinese history: the persistence of Confucian social and scholarly values through periods dominated by foreign rulers, as well as by Buddhist or Daoist religious influences.

Yan's *Instructions* cover such matters as the conduct of family relations, social customs, the importance of education, dedication to high moral and cultural standards (rather than rank and wealth), proper bureaucratic practice, and various scholarly matters of concern to the literati. Predominantly Confucian in tone and subject matter, the *Instructions* are noteworthy also in this age of strong Buddhist influence for one chapter expressing respect for Buddhism, based on its doctrines of moral retribution, affirmation of a moral and spiritual order beyond the sensate and sensible, and respect for life, as shown in the nonkilling of living beings.

Preface

Of books written by sages and worthies that teach men to be sincere and filial, to be careful in speech and circumspect in conduct, and to take one's proper place in society and be concerned for one's reputation, there are more than enough already. Since the Wei and Jin periods prudential writings have reiterated principles and repeated practices as if adding room upon room [to the household] or piling bed upon bed. In doing the same now myself, I do not presume to prescribe rules for others or set a pattern for the world, but only to order my own household and give guidance to my own posterity. . . .

The habits and teaching of our family have always been regular and punctilious. In my childhood I received good instruction from my parents. With my two elder brothers I went to greet our parents each morning and evening to ask in winter whether they were warm and in summer whether they were cool; we walked steadily with regular steps, talked calmly with good manners, and moved about with as much dignity and reverence as if we were visiting the awe-inspiring rulers at court. They gave us good advice, asked about our particular interests, criticized our defects and encouraged our good points — always zealous and sincere. When I was just nine years old, my father died. The family members were divided and scattered, every one of us living in dire straits. I was brought up by my loving brothers; we went through hardships and difficulties. They were kind but not exacting; their guidance and advice to me were not strict. Though I read the ritual texts, and was somewhat fond of composition, I tended to be influenced by common practices; I was uncontrolled in feelings, careless in speech, and slovenly in dress. When about eighteen or nineteen years old I learned to refine my conduct a little, but these bad habits had become second nature, and it was difficult to get rid of them entirely. After my thirtieth year gross faults were few, but still I have to be careful always, for in every instance my words are at odds with my mind, and my emotions struggle with my nature. Each evening I am conscious of the faults committed that morning, and today I regret the errors of yesterday. How pitiful that the lack of instruction has brought me to this condition! I would recall the experiences of my youth long ago, for they are engraved on my flesh and bone; these are not merely the admonitions of ancient books, but what has passed before my eyes and reached my ears. Therefore I leave these twenty chapters to serve as a warning to you boys.

Instructing Children

Those of the highest intelligence will develop without being taught; those of great stupidity, even if taught, will amount to nothing; those of medium ability will be ignorant unless taught. The ancient sage kings had rules for prenatal training. Women when pregnant for three months moved from their living quarters to a detached palace where they would not see unwholesome sights nor hear reckless words, and where the tone of music and the flavor of food were controlled by the rules of decorum [rites]. These rules were written on jade tablets and kept in a golden box. After the child was born, imperial tutors firmly made clear filial piety, humaneness, the rites, and rightness to guide and train him.

The common people are indulgent and are unable to do this. But as soon as a baby can recognize facial expressions and understand approval and disapproval, training should be begun so that he will do what he is told to do and stop when so ordered. After a few years of this, punishment with the bamboo can be minimized, as parental strictness and dignity mingled with parental love will lead the boys and girls to a feeling of respect and caution and give rise to filial piety. I have noticed about me that where there is merely love without training this result is never achieved. Children eat, drink, speak, and act as they please. Instead of needed prohibitions they receive praise; instead of urgent reprimands they receive smiles. Even when children are old enough to learn, such treatment is still regarded as the proper method. Only after the child has formed proud and arrogant habits do they try to control him. But one may whip the child to death and he will still not be respectful, while the growing anger of the parents only increases his resentment. After he grows up, such a child becomes at last nothing but a scoundrel. Confucius was right in saying, "What is acquired in infancy is like original nature; what has been formed into habits is equal to instinct."[1] A common proverb says, "Train a wife from her first arrival; teach a son in his infancy." How true such sayings are!

Generally parents' inability to instruct their own children comes not from

---

1. Not in any of the Confucian classics but quoted by Jia Yi (201–168? B.C.E.) in *Jiazi xinshu* (*SBBY*) 5:3b and also in Jia Yi's biography in *Hanshu* 48.

any inclination just to let them fall into evil ways but only from parents' being unable to endure the children's looks [of unhappiness] from repeated scoldings, or to bear beating them, lest it do damage to the children's physical being. We should, however, take illness by way of illustration: how can we not use drugs, medicines, acupuncture, or cautery to cure it? Should we then view strictness of reproof and punishment as a form of cruelty to one's own kith and kin? Truly there is no other way to deal with it. . . .

As for maintaining proper respect between father and son, one cannot allow too much familiarity; in the love among kin, one cannot tolerate impoliteness. If there is impoliteness, then parental solicitude is not matched by filial respect; if there is too much familiarity, it gives rise to indifference and rudeness.

Someone has asked why Chen Kang [a disciple of Confucius] was pleased to hear that gentlemen kept their distance from their sons, and the answer is that this was indeed the case; gentlemen did not personally teach their children [because, as Yan goes on to show, there are passages in the classics of a sexual kind, which it would not be proper for a father to teach his sons.] . . .

In the love of parents for children, it is rare that one succeeds in treating them equally. From antiquity to the present there are many cases of this failing. It is only natural to love those who are wise and talented, but those who are wayward and dull also deserve sympathy. Partiality in treatment, even when done out of generous motives, turns out badly. . . .

Brothers

After the appearance of humankind, there followed the conjugal relationship; the conjugal relationship was followed by the parental; the parental was followed by the fraternal. Within the family, these three are the intimate relationships. The other degrees of kinship all develop out of these three. Therefore among human relationships one cannot but take these [three] most seriously. . . .

When brothers are at odds with each other, then sons and nephews will not love each other, and this in turn will lead to the cousins drifting apart, resulting finally in their servants treating one another as enemies. When this happens then strangers can step on their faces and trample upon their breasts and there will be no one to come to their aid. There are men who are able to make friends with distinguished men of the empire, winning their affection, and yet are unable to show proper respect toward their own elder brothers. How strange that they should succeed with the many and fail with the few! There are others who are able to command troops in the thousands and inspire such loyalty in them that they will die willingly for them and yet are unable to show kindness toward their own younger brothers. How strange that they should succeed with strangers and fail with their own flesh and blood! . . .

Family Governance

Beneficial influences are transmitted from superiors to inferiors and bequeathed by earlier to later generations. So if a father is not loving, the son will not be filial; if an elder brother is not friendly, the younger will not be respectful; if a husband is not just, the wife will not be obedient. When a father is kind but the son refractory, when an elder brother is friendly but the younger arrogant, when a husband is just but a wife overbearing, then indeed they are the bad people of the world; they must be controlled by punishments; teaching and guidance will not change them. If rod and wrath are not used in family discipline, the faults of the son will immediately appear. If punishments are not properly awarded, the people will not know how to act. The use of clemency and severity in governing a family is the same as in a state.

Confucius said, "Extravagance leads to insubordination, and parsimony to meanness. It is better to be mean than to be insubordinate."[2] Again he said, "Though a man has abilities as admirable as those of the Duke of Zhou, yet if he be proud or niggardly, those other things are really not worth being looked at."[3] That is to say, a man may be thrifty but should not be stingy. Thrift means being frugal and economic in carrying out the rites; stinginess means showing no pity for those in poverty and urgent need. Nowadays those who would give alms are extravagant, but in being thrifty are stingy. It would be proper to give alms without extravagance and be thrifty without being stingy. . . .

A wife in presiding over household supplies should use wine, food, and clothing only as the rites specify. Just as in the state, where women are not allowed to participate in setting policies, so in the family, they should not be permitted to assume responsibility for affairs. If they are wise, talented, and versed in the ancient and modern writings, they ought to help their husbands by supplementing the latter's deficiency. No hen should herald the dawn lest misfortune follow. . . .

The burden of daughters on the family is heavy indeed. Yet how else can Heaven give life to the teeming people and ancestors pass on their bodily existence to posterity? Many people today dislike having daughters and mistreat their own flesh and blood. How can they be like this and still hope for Heaven's blessing? . . .

It is common for women to dote on a son-in-law and to maltreat a daughter-in-law. Doting on a son-in-law gives rise to hatred from brothers; maltreating a daughter-in-law brings on slander from sisters. Thus when these women, whether they act or remain silent, draw criticism from the members of the family, it is the mother who is the real cause of it. . . .

---

2. *Analects* 7:35.
3. *Analects* 8:11.

A simple marriage arrangement irrespective of social position was the established rule of our ancestor Qing Hou.[4] Nowadays there are those who sell their daughters for money or buy a woman with a payment of silk. They compare the rank of fathers and grandfathers, and calculate in ounces and drams, demanding more and offering less, just as if bargaining in the market. Under such conditions a boorish son-in-law might appear in the family or an arrogant woman assume power in the household. Coveting honor and seeking for gain, on the contrary, incur shame and disgrace; how can one not be careful?

[*Yanshi jiaxun jijie* 19–64; trans. adapted and revised from Teng, *Family Instructions*, 1–20, and Lau, "Advice," 94–98 —AD]

THE GREAT TANG CODE

One of the great achievements of the Tang dynasty was its legal system, especially the criminal code (*Tanglü*), which, supplemented by civil statutes and regulations, became the basis for later dynastic codes not only in China but elsewhere in East Asia. The *Code* synthesizes the Legalist tradition, centered on the state, and Confucian traditions, focused more on family relations and conflict resolution in the local community. Both traditions are mediated in forms characteristic of Han dynasty thought and practice. Important among these is the holistic view expressed earlier by the Han Confucian scholar Dong Zhongshu, who saw the human and natural orders as so intimately linked that actions in the former have an effect on the latter. Prime responsibility for linkage between the two falls on the emperor and his ministers, whose actions can exert either a beneficial or a harmful influence on both the human and the natural orders. Preserving overall balance is the key. An offense is regarded as a disruption of society that requires compensatory, corrective action by the ruler if the natural balance and harmony are to be restored.

To this end the *Code* embodies a blend of Legalist concern for universality, consistency, impartiality, and inexorability in the application of the law, along with a Confucian disposition to take into account particular statuses, qualitative (hierarchical) distinctions, and degrees of personal relationship. Reference is made to earlier law codes as well as to the Confucian ritual classics, but little overt credit is given to the Legalists.

Overall, the *Code* reflects an attempt by a centralized, bureaucratic, dynastic state (not the decentralized "feudal" state idealized by the Confucians) to assert its authority and protect its power over all of China. Yet the effective limits of that authority are acknowledged by the *Code*'s heavy reinforcement of Confu-

---

4. Qing Hou was the posthumous name of Yan Zhitui's ninth-generation ancestor. His name was Yan Han.

cian ritual practice by which social order would normally be maintained through the family system, without recourse to law or the intervention of state power. Law was only the last resort after other, more consensual mechanisms failed.

ZHANGSUN WUJI: THE TANG CODE

Although the names of several early Tang officials are associated with the *Code*, the preface and major portions are attributed to the brother-in-law of Tang Taizong, Zhangsun Wuji (?–659), one of the most powerful statesmen of his time.

The scope of the *Code* and its primary orientation to the dynastic state rather than to society are indicated by the contents of its twelve main divisions [books], namely (1) General Principles, (2) Imperial Guard and Prohibitions, (3) Administrative Regulations, (4) Household and Marriage, (5) Public Stables and Granaries, (6) Unauthorized Levies, (7) Violence and Robberies, (8) Assaults and Accusations, (9) Fraud and Counterfeiting, (10) Miscellaneous Articles, (11) Arrest and Flight, and (12) Judgment and Imprisonment.

Under these headings there are 502 articles, and each article has several parts: the basic text, commentary, subcommentary, and, sometimes, queries and questions. Excerpts are given below from the Preface and Article 6.

Preface

In the beginning, the three powers[5] were established, and only then were the myriad forms divided. Among the creatures endowed with *qi* and possessing consciousness, human beings may be considered the chief.[6] Never was a prime minister installed without the agreement of the masses, nor were penal laws promulgated except in accord with the moral teachings concerning government.

There were those, however, whose passions were unrestrained and who acted stupidly, those whose knowledge declined and who offended criminally. If great, then they disrupted the entire world and, if small, they violated the standards for their own group. Thus it would be unheard of not to establish controls for such persons. Hence the statement "Punishments are used to stop punishments and killing is used to stop killing."[7] Punishments may not be discarded in a

---

5. In this context the three powers represent Heaven, Earth, and the human. See the selection from the *Commentary on the Appended Phrases, Classic of Changes,* in ch. 10.

6. "The Great Declaration," *Classic of Documents*; Legge, *The Chinese Classics,* 3:283.

7. "The Counsels of the Great Yu," *Classic of Documents*; Legge, *The Chinese Classics,* 3:58. Here Yu is quoted as saying to Gao Yao, his minister of crime: "Through punishment there may come to be no punishments, but the people accord with the Mean."

country; chastisements may not be dispensed with within a home.[8] Depending upon whether the times are virtuous or unprincipled, the use of punishments is great or small.[9]

Thereupon the knotting of cords to record events was inaugurated, and the overflowing channels of watercourse were dredged out. The light punishments of the early rulers were brightly awesome, their great rules of ritual decorum were exaltedly respectful.[10] The *Classic of Changes* states: "Heaven hung images in the sky . . . and the sages regarded these as meaningful signs."[11] They observed the thunder and lightning and so created awe-inspiring punishments;[12] they saw the autumn frost and so had stern executions.[13] They warned those who had not yet offended and so guarded against what had not yet occurred; they laid out the fetters used to bind criminals but maintained their widespread love. Thus the sage kings used these things only when there was no other recourse.

In antiquity, for the greatest punishment, armor and weapons were used, followed by axes. For the middle punishments, knife and saw were used, followed by auger and chisel. For the smallest punishments, the whip and stick were used.[14] Their origin is indeed ancient. . . .

Coming to the time of Yao and Shun, their influence was pervasive, so that offenses were few. They discussed the punishments in order to fix the penalties and had pictures drawn illustrating them in order to shame the people.[15] The articles and sections of their laws, even though numerous, were simple and concise. The period was long ago, however, and we cannot know those laws in detail. In the time of Yao and Shun, the officer who maintained order was called the *shi*. Gao Yao held this office.[16] The general outline of their laws has been preserved and is often in good part visible. This is what the *Treatise on Customs* speaks of when it states: "Gao Yao advised Shun in making the statutes."[17]

---

8. Based on *Hanshu* (BNB) 23:8b; Hulsewé, *Han Law*, 1: 329, and *Lüshi chunqiu* 7:4a; both insist on the necessity of punishment.

9. "The Prince of Lü on Punishments," *Classic of Documents*; Legge, *The Chinese Classics*, 3:607.

10. A similar phrase appears in *Hanshu* (BNB) 23:1b; Hulsewé, *Han Law*, 32:1.

11. *Commentary on the Appended Phrases, Classic of Changes*, Part 1; Lynn, *The Classic of Changes*, p. 66.

12. Hexagram 21, "Shihe" ("Bite Together"), *Classic of Changes*; Lynn, *The Classic of Changes*, p. 267.

13. The commentator here quotes an otherwise unknown apocryphal work on the *Spring and Autumn Annals*, the *Chunqiu fu*. "Frost is the sign of punishment."

14. A similar phrase is found in *Hanshu* (BNB) 23:2a; Hulsewé, *Han Law*, 1:322; see also *Sui shu* (BNB) 25:1b; Balazs, *Traité juridique*, p. 29.

15. This refers to displaying pictures of the punishments on the palace gates on the first day of the new year, which is described in "Dasikou," *Zhouli*; Biot, 2:314.

16. "Canon of Shun," *Classic of Documents*; Legge, *The Chinese Classics*, 3:44–45.

17. *Fengsu tongyi*, p. 101.

A statute is similar to a measure or a model. The *Classic of Changes* states: "The regulation of resources, the rectification of pronouncements, and his [the sage's] preventing the people from doing wrong we call 'rightness.'"[18] Therefore the lawmaker must measure the gravity of offenses; he institutes statutes in accordance with rightness. The *Great Commentary* on the *Classic of Documents* speaks of vast Heaven's great statute.[19] The commentary explains: "We receive Heaven's great law (*fa*). Law is also statute (*lü*)."[20] Hence the use of the term *statute*.

Formerly the sages made treatises that we call classics. The words of the scholars who transmitted these treatises we call commentaries. Such are Zuo Qiuming's and Zixia's commentaries on the *Spring and Autumn Annals* and the *Record of Rites*, respectively.[21] Coming down to recent times, scholars have combined the classics with the commentaries and have explained them, calling these later commentaries *yishu*, "explaining the meaning."

Article 6: The Ten Abominations

The following illustrates, in an abridged form, the contents of a single article of the *Code*. Some of the articles from numbers 160 to 174 refer to the particular land, tax, and labor service systems adopted in the early Tang but no longer viable in the late Tang.

Subcommentary: The ten abominations (*shie*) are the most serious of those offenses that come within the five punishments. They injure traditional norms and destroy ceremony. They are specially placed near the head of this chapter [14b] in order to serve as a clear warning. The number of extreme abominations being classified as ten is the reason why they are called the ten abominations. . . .

Article: The first is called plotting rebellion (*moufan*).

Subcommentary: The *Gongyang Commentary* states: "The ruler or parent has no harborers [of plots]. If he does have such harborers, he must put them to death."[22] This means that if there are those who harbor rebellious hearts that would harm the ruler or father, he must then put them to death. The *Zuo Commentary* (*Zuozhuan*) states: "When the seasons of Heaven are reversed, we have calamities . . . when the virtues of men are reversed, we have disorders."[23]

---

18. *Commentary on the Appended Phrases, Classic of Changes*, Part 2; Lynn, *The Classic of Changes*, p. 77.

19. *Shangshu dazhuan* (SBCK) 3:3a.

20. Ibid.

21. Zuo Qiuming is supposed to have been a contemporary of Confucius and author of the *Zuozhuan*; Zixia was one of Confucius' disciples.

22. *Gongyang zhuan*, Zhuang 32.

23. *Zuozhuan*, Xuan 15; Legge, *The Chinese Classics*, 5:328.

The king occupies the most honorable position and receives Heaven's precious decrees. Like Heaven and Earth,[24] he acts to shelter and support, thus serving as the father and mother of the masses. As his children, as his subjects, they must be loyal and filial. Should they dare to cherish wickedness and have rebellious hearts, however, they will run counter to Heaven's constancy and violate human principle. Therefore this is called plotting rebellion.

Commentary: Plotting rebellion means to plot to endanger the Altars of Soil and Grain [*sheji*, that is, the ruler and the state that he rules].

Subcommentary: *She* is the spirit of the five colors of soil [corresponding to the Five Phases]. *Ji* is the regulator of the fields, which uses the spirits' earthly virtue to control the harvest.[25] The ruler is the lord of these spirits of agriculture. The food that they ensure is as Heaven to the people. When their lord is in peace, these spirits are at rest. When the spirits are in repose, the seasons give a plentiful harvest.

However, ministers and subjects may plot and scheme to rebel against traditional norms and have minds that would discard their ruler. If the ruler's position is endangered, what will the spirits rely upon? Not daring to make direct allusion to the honored name of the ruler, we therefore use the phrase "Altars of Soil and Grain" to designate him. The *Rites of Zhou* states: "On the left the Temple of the Ancestors, on the right the Altar of the Soil."[26] These are what the ruler honors.

Article: The second is called plotting great sedition (*mou dani*).

Subcommentary: This type of person breaks laws and destroys order, is against traditional norms, and goes contrary to virtue. There can be no greater sedition. Therefore it is called great sedition.

Commentary: Plotting great sedition means to plot to destroy the ancestral temples, tombs, or palaces of the reigning house.

Subcommentary: There are persons who "offend against Heaven,"[27] "who do not know where to stop,"[28] and who secretly think of letting loose their hatred. Planning recklessness, they conceive evil thoughts and plot destruction of the ancestral temples, tombs, or palaces of the reigning house. . . .

Article: The third is called plotting treason (*mou pan*).

Subcommentary: The kindness of father and mother is like "great Heaven, illimitable."[29] "Entering into the inheritance of our ancestors,"[30] we may not

---

24. A paraphrase of the *Mean* in the *Record of Rites*. See ch. 10.

25. Apparently a garbled version of "The Single Victim at the Border Sacrifices" ("Jiao tesheng"), *Record of Rites*; Legge, *Li ki*, 1:425.

26. "Jiangren," *Zhouli*, p. 643; Biot, 2:556. The same idea is expressed in "The Meaning of Sacrifices," ("Jiyi"), *Record of Rites*; Legge, *Li ki*, 2:235.

27. *Analects* 3:13; Legge, *The Chinese Classics*, 1:159. "He who offends against Heaven has none to whom he can pray."

28. *Zuozhuan*, Wen 18; Legge, *The Chinese Classics*, 5:283.

29. Ode 202.

30. Ode 189.

be frivolous. Let one's heart be like the *xiao* bird or the *jing* beast,[31] and then love and respect both cease. Those whose relationship is within the five degrees of mourning are the closest of kin. For them to kill each other is the extreme abomination and the utmost in rebellion, destroying and casting aside human principles. Therefore this is called contumacy.

Commentary: Contumacy means to beat or plot to kill [without actually killing] one's paternal grandparents or parents; or to kill one's paternal uncles or their wives, or one's elder brothers or sisters, or one's maternal grandparents, or one's husband, or one's husband's paternal grandparents, or his parents. . . .

Article: The fifth is called depravity (*budao*).

Subcommentary: This article describes those who are cruel and malicious and who turn their backs on morality. Therefore it is called depravity.

Commentary: Depravity means to kill three members of a single household (*jia*) who have not committed a capital crime, or to dismember someone. . . .

Commentary: The offense also includes the making or keeping of poison (*gu*) or sorcery.

Subcommentary: This means to prepare the poison oneself, or to keep it, or to give it to others in order to harm people. But if the preparation of the poison has not yet been completed, this offense does not come under the ten abominations. As to sorcery, there are a great many methods, not all of which can be described. All, however, comprise evil customs and secret practices that are illegal and whose intent is to cause the victim pain and death.

Article: The sixth is called great irreverence (*da bujing*).

Subcommentary: Rites are the root of reverence; reverence is the expression of rites. Therefore, "The Evolution of Rites" [chapter of the *Record of Rites*] states: "Rites are the great instrument of the ruler. It is by them that he resolves what is doubtful and brings to light what is abstruse . . . examines institutions and regulations, and distinguishes humaneness and rightness."[32] The responsibility of those who offend against ritual is great and their hearts lack reverence and respect. Therefore it is called great irreverence. . . .

Commentary: Great irreverence means to steal the objects of the great sacrifices to the spirits or the carriage or possessions of the emperor.

Article: The seventh is called lack of filiality (*buxiao*).

Subcommentary: Serving one's parents well is called filiality. Disobeying them is called lack of filiality.

Commentary: This has reference to accusing to the court or cursing one's paternal grandparents or parents. . . .

Article: The ninth is called what is not right (*buyi*).

---

31. The earliest Chinese dictionary, the *Shuowen jiezi*, describes the *xiao* as an unfilial bird that eats its mother, coupling it with the *jing*, an unfilial beast that eats its father (p. 2645). *Weishu* (BNB) 59:28b speaks of "turning one's back on mercy and forgetting rightness, having a heart like the *xiao* bird and the *jing* beast."

32. "Evolution of Rites," ("Liyun"), *Record of Rites*; Legge, *Li Ki*, 1:375.

Subcommentary: Rites (ritual decorum) honor rightness. This section originally did not include blood relatives because, basically, rightness is exercised only toward associates. It is concerned with turning one's back on rightness and violating humaneness. . . . Therefore it is called "what is not right."

Commentary: [This] means to kill one's department head, prefect, or magistrate, or the teacher from whom one has received one's education. . . .

Article: The tenth is called incest (*neiluan*).

Subcommentary: The *Zuo Commentary* (*Zuozhuan*) states: "The woman has her husband's house; the man has his wife's chamber; and there must be no defilement on either side."[33] If this is changed, then there is incest. If one behaves like the birds and beasts[34] and introduces licentious associates into one's family, the rules of morality are confused. Therefore this is called incest.

Commentary: This section includes having illicit sexual intercourse (*jian*) with relatives who are of the fourth degree of mourning or closer. . . .

Book 4: The Household and Marriage

Following is a listing, by title only, of the 46 articles that comprise the fourth division or book (Articles 150–195 out of a total of 502).

150. Omitting to File a Household Register
151. Village Headmen Who Do Not Know That a Household Register Has Not Been Filed or That Household Members Have Been Left Off of It
152. Prefects and County Magistrates Who Do Not Know That a Household Register Has Not Been Filed or That Household Members Have Been Left Off of It
153. Village Headmen or Officials Who Erroneously Do Not File a Household Register or Who Leave Household Members Off of It
154. Unauthorized Ordainment as a Buddhist or Daoist Priest
155. Sons and Grandsons in the Male Line Are Not Permitted to Have a Separate Household Register
156. Having a Child During the Period of Mourning for Parents
157. Adopted Sons Who Reject Their Adoptive Parents
158. Violation of the Law in Taking a Wife
159. Adoption of a General Bondsman as a Son or Grandson
160. Manumission of a Personal Retainer as a Commoner

---

33. *Zuozhuan*, Huan 18; Legge, *The Chinese Classics*, 5:69–70.

34. This refers to the passage in "The Rules of Propriety" ("Qu li"), *Record of Rites*; Legge, *Li ki*, 1:64, where it is stated that animals have no morality; the stag and his male offspring both couple with the same doe.

161. Falsely Combining Households
162. Family Members of a Lower Generation or of the Same Generation but Younger than Other Family Members Who Improperly Make Use of Family Goods
163. Sale of Personal Share Land
164. Possession of More than the Permitted Amount of Land
165. Illegal Cultivation of Public or Private Land
166. Wrongfully Laying Claim to or Selling Public or Private Land
167. Officials Who Encroach Upon Private Land
168. Illegal Cultivation of Other Persons' Grave Plots
169. Drought, Flood, Frost, or Hail Within an Area
170. Land Classified as Uncultivatable Land or Waste Land Within an Area
171. Village Headmen's Allocation of Land and Plots for Mulberry Trees
172. Not Allowing Rightful Exemption from Taxes and Labor Services
173. Violation of the Law in Assessment of Taxes and Labor Services
174. Violation of the Time Limit in Remitting Articles for Taxes
175. Betrothal of a Daughter and Announcement of the Marriage Contract
176. Wrongful Substitution by the Bride's Family in a Marriage
177. Taking a Second Wife
178. Making the Wife a Concubine
179. Marriage During the Period of Mourning for Parents or Husband
180. Marriage While Parents Are in Prison
181. Acting as a Master of the Marriage During the Period of Mourning for Parents
182. Marriage by Those of the Same Surname
183. Taking a Wife Within the Sixth Degree of Mourning
184. Remarriage of a Widow While Mourning Her Husband
185. Marrying a Runaway Wife
186. Marriage of Officials with Women Within Their Area of Jurisdiction
187. Marrying Another Man's Wife by Consent
188. Family Members of a Higher Generation or of the Same Generation but Older than Other Family Members Making Engagements to Marry for Relatives of a Lower Generation or of the Same Generation but Younger than Themselves
189. Divorcing a Wife Who Has Not Given Any of the Seven Causes for Repudiation
190. Divorce
191. Slaves Who Take Commoners as Wives
192. General Bondsmen Are Not Permitted to Marry Commoners
193. Marriages that Violate the *Code*
194. Divorce and Correction of Status in Marriages that Violate the *Code*
195. Violation of the *Code* in Giving and Taking in Marriage

[Adapted from Johnson, *The T'ang Code*, pp. 49–82, 278–280]

DEBATES ON TAXES AND ENFEOFFMENT
IN THE TANG

By the middle of the Tang dynasty the system of equalized landholding adopted by its founder had seriously deteriorated. The virtual abolition of private property and resale of land had been a formative feature of the early Tang system; in the latter part of the eighth century, these practices, though not legally sanctioned, steadily increased. As a direct result the tax system, which had been predicated upon the old scheme of land tenure, became more difficult to administer, more susceptible to evasion, and therefore less productive of revenue for the state. Finally, in 780, a new method of taxation was adopted on the recommendation of the statesman Yang Yan (727–781).

Besides greatly simplifying tax collection, Yang's Twice-a-Year Tax introduced for the first time the systematic budgeting of government income and expenditures. First the expenses of local and central governments were estimated; then each region was assessed its quota of the needed funds, prorated according to local conditions. This also meant adopting money for the first time as the basis for levying taxes. All other forms of taxation were abolished, and this alone collected in two installments during the early summer and late fall.

Despite the success of his reform program and the fact that his Twice-a-Year Tax system was to endure for centuries, Yang Yan suffered a sudden reversal of fortune and, in a manner characteristic of the insecurity of high office in China, was banished the following year and forced to commit suicide.

YANG YAN: MEMORIAL PROPOSING THE TWICE-A-YEAR TAX

The following are excerpts from the *New History of the Tang Dynasty*, describing the conditions that Yang sought to remedy and the solution proposed, which was to remain in effect down into the Ming dynasty, almost eight centuries. The opening passage describes the failings of the earlier system and then continues with Yang's proposal.

Very little of the tax revenue that should have gone to the emperor was actually presented. Altogether there were several hundred kinds of taxation: those that had been formally abolished were never dropped, and those that duplicated others were never eliminated. Old and new taxes piled up, and there seemed to be no limit to them. The people drained the last drop of their blood and marrow; they sold their loved ones. . . . Rich people with many able-bodied adults in their families sought to obtain exemption from labor services by having them become officials, students, Buddhist monks, and Daoist priests. The poor had nothing they could get into [to obtain such an exemption] and continued to be registered as able-bodied adults liable to labor service. The upper class had their taxes forgiven, while the lower class had their taxes increased. Thereupon the empire was ruined and in distress, and the people wandered around like vagrants. Fewer than four or five out of a hundred lived in their own villages and stayed on their own land.

Yang Yan was concerned over these evils and petitioned the throne to establish the Twice-a-Year Tax in order to unify the tax system.

"The way to handle all government expenses and tax collections is first to calculate the amount needed and then to allocate the tax among the people. Thus the income of the state would be governed according to its expenses. All households should be registered in their places of actual residence, without regard to whether they are native households or non-native. All persons should be graded according to their wealth, without regard to whether they are fully adult or only half adult.[35] Those who do not have a permanent residence and do business as traveling merchants should be taxed in whatever prefecture or subprefecture they are located at the rate of one-thirtieth [of their capital holdings]. It is estimated that the amount taken from them will be the same as that paid by those having fixed domicile, so that they could not expect to gain from chance avoidance of the tax. The tax paid by residents should be collected twice a year, during the summer and autumn. All practices that cause annoyance to the people should be corrected. The separate land and labor tax, and all miscellaneous labor services, should be abolished, and yet the count of the able-bodied adults should still be kept. The tax on land acreage should be based upon the amount of land cultivated in the fourteenth year of Dali [779], and the tax should be collected equally. The summer tax should be collected no later than the sixth month, and the autumn tax no later than the eleventh month. At the end of the year, local officials should be promoted or demoted according to the increase or decrease in the number of households and tax receipts. Everything should be under the control of the President of the Board of Revenue and the Commissioner of Funds."

The emperor approved of this policy, and officials in the capital and the various provinces were informed of it. There were some who questioned and opposed the measure, considering that the old system of land and labor taxes had been in operation for several hundred years and that a change should not be made precipitously. The emperor did not listen to them, however, and eventually the empire enjoyed the benefits of the measure.

[*Xin Tangshu* 145:13a–14a — TTC, dB]

---

35. According to the earlier system of census registration, persons aged sixteen or more were classified as "half adult" (*zhong*), and those twenty-one or older were classified as adult (*ding*). After 744, the ages were raised to eighteen and twenty-two, respectively. *New History of the Tang Dynasty* (*Xin Tang shu*), 51:2a, 6a.

LU ZHI: AGAINST THE TWICE-A-YEAR TAX

Lu Zhi (754–805), a close adviser to the Emperor Dezong at the end of the eighth century, possessed rare qualifications as a scholar-official, being admired for both his moral integrity and his literary gifts. Eventually he suffered banishment for speaking out against a favorite of the emperor and was not recalled to court until just before his death.

Initially supportive of Yang Yan's Twice-a-Year Tax, Lu later wrote three memorials critical of its defects. Composed in the classic essay style for which he became famous, these memorials may also be considered classic statements of the dominant conservative strain in Confucian political thought, as opposed to the type of Confucian reformism that advocated strong action by the state to solve economic and fiscal crises. Characteristic of this conservative view are a concern for economy in government and simplicity of administration and a resistance to sudden, drastic changes in time-tested practices. These attitudes are based on two fundamental principles of Confucian teaching: that governmental actions should be intended primarily to benefit the people, not simply the state; and that they should be equitable to all in their application. Lu Zhi finds himself, however, in the typical dilemma of the moderate conservative in regard to drastic reforms already put into effect: to abolish them altogether would likewise involve great dislocation and confusion. Therefore he asks only to remedy the most flagrant defects of the new system, rather than demanding its outright repeal.

According to the established law of the dynasty, there were three kinds of taxes. The first was known as the land tax; the second, cloth contribution; the third, labor service. This threefold tax system followed the example of former sages and took into consideration the advantages and disadvantages of the tax measures of previous dynasties. . . . As a means of making life secure, it made for permanence of domicile without restrictive legislation; as a means of imposing labor service, it became possible to know the population without a vexatious census; as a means of government, it enabled the rulers to carry out their duties without complex and exacting laws; as a means of taxation, it produced enough for those above [the government] without impoverishing those below [the people]. . . .

But as a result of the barbarian uprisings in the later years of the Tianbao period (742–756), utter confusion reigned in our land and untold suffering came upon our people; the registers and administrative divisions became outmoded because of the shift in population and the tax laws vitiated because of the ever-growing demands of the armies. At the beginning of the Jianzhong period (780–783) there was an attempt at reform. The government realized the necessity of rectifying the evils, but the measures it introduced were not based upon sound principles. It realized the wisdom of simplification, but the methods it adopted were not founded on realities. . . .

Now, without trying first to bring order to the times that are at fault, changes have been made in laws that are free from blame. The traditional measures of cloth contribution and labor service were swept aside and the new scheme of the Twice-a-Year Tax introduced. Being faulty in conception and careless in detail, the new tax scheme has only exhausted the people and made their lot worse every day. . . . To achieve this [reform] proper steps should have been taken to take away from those above in order to give to those below, to cut expenses in order to save wealth, to discourage extravagance and greed in order to reverse the trend toward corruption, to eliminate unnecessary outlays in order to relieve the people of heavy exactions. But instead, the provinces have been subjected to great hardship because of the irksome examination of the registers and tax rolls necessary to determine the highest annual tax rate during the Dali period (766–780), which the Twice-a-Year Tax must use as a base. This is in effect the adoption of an unconstitutional expedient as fixed law and the incorporation of oppressive exactions of doubtful origin as regular features of the tax scheme. This amounts to making the extraction of money from the people the primary objective of government; one can hardly say that it is consistent with concern for the people. . . .

Now surely wealth can be produced only by human labor. Skill and industry lead to wealth and plenty, ineptitude and laziness to want and deficiency. It is for this reason that the ancient sage kings made the able-bodied male the tax unit when they instituted the tax system. They did not demand from a man more than his just portion; nor did they let him escape with less. They did not increase a man's taxes because he worked hard at his crops, nor did they lighten them because he abandoned his tillage. Thus people were encouraged to sow as much as they could. They did not add to a man's taxes because he lived in settled productivity, nor did they exempt a man from his cloth contribution because he wandered about without an established home. Thus stability was achieved. They did not exact more labor from a man because of his industry, nor did they accept less from a man because of his laziness. Thus diligence was encouraged. Only by such ways as these can the people be happy in their abode and willingly contribute their best. . . .

The Twice-a-Year Tax works on a different principle. It is based upon property only and not on the able-bodied male. This means that the more property one has, the more one has to pay, and the less property, the less tax. The system entirely fails to take into account the diverse natures of various types of property. . . . But under the Twice-a-Year system, these diverse types of property are all converted into so many strings of money, and it surprises no one that the system should work inequities and encourage evasion. For under this system those who range over the land and traffic in commerce are often able to escape their share of the tax burden, while those who devote themselves to the basic vocation [of agriculture] and establish fixed homes are constantly harassed by ever-increasing demands. This amounts to tempting the people to circumvent the law and forcing them to shirk their just share of labor. It is inevitable that productivity should decline and morals deteriorate, depression come to the villages and towns, and a decrease result in the tax collections.

Furthermore, in drawing up the scheme no effort was made to achieve an equal distribution of the tax burden. The provinces and districts were merely ordered to levy the new taxes according to the old rate. It was not realized that because of the long military campaigns conditions were far from being the same in the different localities. Not only was the nature of the demands made upon a place different from that made upon another, but there was also great disparity in the ability of the administrators. Thus the tax burden varies greatly from place to place, just as opinions differ among the respective commissioners.

In introducing new regulations, existing inequities should have been recognized and changes made wherever necessary; but instead, the officials were more interested in collecting as much in taxes as they could and were loath to eliminate anything. The actual resources and capacities of the various administrative districts were not given any weight at all; the old rate was the only thing that mattered. Thus the new law had the effect of causing ever heavier migrations away from regions where the rate was high and toward regions where the rate was low. The result was that in the former regions the burden became heavier because the quota had to be shared by fewer people than before, while in the latter regions the burden became even lighter because the quota could be distributed among more people. In this way the situation tends to become more and more inequitable.

Next Lu Zhi lists specific abuses that have brought great hardship to the people. One of these is the inflexibility of the new system, which allows no tax reduction or exemption to meet local emergencies. Another is that, despite the attempt to combine all taxes into this one, additional levies have been superimposed on the Twice-a-Year Tax. Further, there is the loss suffered by the people in having to exchange their goods or produce at low rates of commutation for cash in the payment of taxes. Another hidden form of taxation is the special gifts from each locality to the emperor, which, though nominally sent by officials, are actually paid for by the people. There is also the inequity resulting from shifts in population, not reported by local governors, which leave a reduced number of taxpayers to meet the fixed quotas.

Lu Zhi recommends the following relief measures: (1) Unwise and unnecessary expenses should be eliminated, and excessive ones should be reduced. More specifically, the surtax of 20 percent must be abolished and emergency levies lifted as soon as the emergency passes. This would bring relief to the extent of 20 or 30 percent. (2) Aside from the traditional requirements, no presents should be accepted from the provinces. Not only would this plan bring direct relief, it would also eliminate many attending abuses inflicted on the people by unscrupulous officials. This would bring relief to the extent of another 40 to 50 percent. (3) Conversion of tax money units into cloth should be made on the basis of the monthly average price of the respective localities. Since the cloth is inspected by the receiving officials, they should be held responsible for any serious loss due to the poor quality of the cloth, instead of making the people pay again. This would bring relief to the extent of still another 20 or 30 percent.

Lu Zhi then makes two positive proposals. The first is a more accurate determination of the number of households in the various provinces, to be carried out by the provincial Twice-a-Year Tax officials in consultation with the Ministry of Revenue. The second is a classification of the prefectures into two categories after a careful consideration of their respective resources and the drawing up of an appropriate tax schedule for each. Thus, without repealing the Twice-a-Year Tax law, it would be possible to bring about a certain degree of fairness and justice in the distribution of the tax burden and to make tax collection more effective and evasion less attractive.

[From *Lu Xuangong zouyi* (GXJC), pp. 90–93 — TTC, dB]

LIU ZONGYUAN: "ESSAY ON ENFEOFFMENT"

In the declining years of the Tang the dynasty was forced to yield much of its authority to provincial warlords and border commanderies. Some writers argued in favor of confirming this de facto decentralization by reviving the classic enfeoffment system of the Zhou dynasty. Others called for a reassertion of central control.

Probably the most memorable contribution to the debate, from a literary point of view, was an essay by Liu Zongyuan (773–819), a noted poet, litterateur, and sometime official identified with a group of scholar-officials at court who were strong, but in the end unsuccessful, proponents of central authority. Briefly, Liu's argument against a revival of the enfeoffment system runs as follows:

The enfeoffment system of the Zhou was a creation not of the sage kings but of inexorable historical forces. Far from representing an ideal form of government, the system allowed the enfeoffed lords to pursue their own interests at the expense of the people and the emperor. Nor did it ensure long years of Zhou rule, as the proponents of the enfeoffment system claim. Indeed, during the Warring States period the Zhou kings had no real power but held only an empty title.

The Han, by contrast, held the throne much longer because they weakened and then destroyed the "feudal" institutions provisionally set up in the early years of the dynasty, confirming instead the prefectural system first set up by the Qin. This system served the interests of both the people and the ruler so long as the latter enforced policies that ensured peace and stability, since it had been the people's desire for peace and stability that led to the founding of the state in the first place.

In the beginning, men lived among the myriad other creatures. Brush and trees grew in thickets; wild deer and boar roamed in herds over the land. Men could use neither their hands nor their teeth for fighting, nor had they hair or feathers, and so they were unable to nourish and protect themselves. To use a phrase of Xun Qing's, [i.e., Xunzi's] it was necessary to depend on other things put to artificial use.[36]

Quarrels were bound to arise over these other things. Unable to put a stop to these quarrels, men had to seek out someone who was able to differentiate between right and wrong, and follow his commands. Large numbers were certain to go and do obeisance to an intelligent and enlightened person. If they failed to change after he had told them the right way, he had to inflict pain on them so that they would understand fear. Through this process, princes and chiefs, as well as punishments and laws, came into being. Thus, everyone in a locality would gather together and form a group. But, since there were other, separate groups, the quarrels between them naturally became greater than before, and when they became greater, men with weapons and men with moral authority appeared. When this happened, the heads of local groups went to a man of greater moral authority and followed his commands, so that their subordinates might have peace. And so there arose the order of feudal lords. But then the quarrels became greater still, and so the feudal lords went and followed the commands of those whose moral authority was greater, so that their fiefs might have peace. And so there appeared regional chiefs and leaders. But then the quarrels became greater still, and the regional chiefs and leaders went and followed the commands of one whose moral authority was greater yet, so that the people might have peace. And so it was that all-under-Heaven came together and was unified.

Hence, at first there were village heads, and later district officials appeared. There were district officials, and later enfeoffed lords appeared. There were enfeoffed lords, and later regional chiefs and leaders appeared. There were regional chiefs and leaders, and later the Son of Heaven appeared. From the Son of Heaven down to the village heads, when those who had been humane toward the people died, their heirs would be entreated to succeed them, and would be supported and venerated by the people. Thus the enfeoffment system did not result from the intentions of the sages, but from the conditions of the times. . . .

The events of the time of Yao, Shun, Yu, and Tang are remote, but when we come down to the Zhou, there are many more details. When Zhou gained control of all-under-Heaven, the land was divided and apportioned, the five ranks were established, and the vassal lords were enfeoffed. They were spread far and wide over the land, like the stars in the skies, or like the spokes of a wheel, all converging toward the hub. They came to the court in spring and autumn, on special occasions, and at times gathered there together. They were dispersed over the land to guard the land and shield the towns.

---

36. See ch. 6.

But in the time of King Yi [ninth century], injury was done to the rituals, and damage was done to the dignity of the king, for he descended from the audience hall to meet the feudal lords. Later, King Xuan [ninth and eighth centuries], although he possessed the character to achieve a restoration and to return to ancient ways, and the authority to conduct campaigns in the south and expeditions to the north, was unable to determine the successor to the Duke of Lu. The power of the Zhou kings gradually subsided, so that by the times of kings You and Li [eighth century], the house of Zhou had to move eastward, and the king became merely an equal of the feudal lords.

. . . Depravity spread over the empire; no one thought of treating kings as kings. I say that life had vanished from the Zhou kingdom for a long time, and that the Zhou kings retained only the empty title of superior among the feudal lords. Did the fault not lie in the might of the feudal lords? Had they not become like a tail too big for the dog to wag? And so the empire was divided into twelve parts, then consolidated into seven states, as authority fell to the hands of former servants, and the Zhou kingdom was finally annihilated by the kingdom of Qin, the last of the feudal lords to be enfeoffed by the Zhou kings. The causes of the destruction of the Zhou lay precisely here, in the enfeoffment system.

When Qin gained control of the empire, the feudatories were divided into commanderies and prefectures, and the vassal lords were removed and replaced by administrators and prefects. Qin occupied the strategic spots of the empire, its capital [at Xianyang] overawed the whole land, and control of the whole empire came into its grasp. This was sound and correct. But, within a few years, the empire was thrown into turmoil. There were reasons for this: repeated impressment of thousands of men, cruel enforcement of strict punishments, and draining the people of goods and wealth. Thus it was that a band of conscript laborers, shouldering hoes and long poles, marching to the borders of the empire, looked at each other in consternation, made a pact together, and, rising up with a great shout, soon became a multitude.

At that time there were rebellious people, but no rebellious officials; below, the people were enraged, but above, the officials were only afraid. All over the empire men joined together and rose in unison, slaughtering the administrators and coercing the prefects. The fault lay in the people's rage [against the ruler], not in the failure of the prefectural system.

When Han gained control of the empire, the errors of Qin were corrected. Following the Zhou system, the land within the seas was carved up, the kin of the emperor were appointed kings, and meritorious officials were enfeoffed. . . .

Originally, when the feudal system was restored by Gaozu, the empire was divided equally between [centralized] commanderies and [dispersed] kingdoms. At this time, there were rebellious kingdoms but no rebellious commanderies. This once again illustrates the soundness of the Qin system [reaffirmed by the Han], and whoever succeeds the Han on the imperial throne shall find this true for hundreds of generations.

When Tang rose to power, the prefectural system was instituted, and prefects and magistrates were appointed. All this was entirely appropriate. Nevertheless, clever and unscrupulous men later appeared, and cruelly ravaged large areas of the empire. The fault lay not in the prefectural system but in the military commanderies. At that time, there were rebellious generals, but no rebellious prefectures. The prefectural system definitely should not be abolished.

Some say, "Under the enfeoffment system vassals are sure to treat the land as their own property and the people as their own children, to adapt themselves to the local customs in amending the laws and thereby govern and transform the people with ease. On the other hand, prefects and magistrates are lax in their duties and think only of [bureaucratic] advancement and promotion. How can they govern well?"

I disagree. The facts in the case of Zhou are surely clear enough to see. The feudal lords were arrogant, greedy for wealth, and devoted to warfare. In general, many states were in turmoil, while few were stable and well ordered. The captain of the feudal lords was unable to make changes in the administrations of the feudal lords, and the Son of Heaven was unable to remove his vassals. Not one in a hundred treated the land as his own and the people as his children. The fault was in the system, not in the administration of it. Such are the facts in the case of Zhou.

The facts in the case of Qin are also surely clear enough to see. There was a system to govern the people, but no authority was delegated to the commanderies and prefectures. There were ministers capable of governing, but the administrators and prefects were given no leeway. The commanderies and prefectures were not permitted to amend the ordinances of the central government, and the administrators and prefects were not permitted to govern [on their own]. [Yet] cruel punishments and hard impressment inflamed the masses. The fault was in the running of the system, not in the system itself. Such are the facts in the case of Qin.

When Han rose to power, the ordinances of the Son of Heaven were enforced in the commanderies but not in the kingdoms. The Son of Heaven controlled the administrators and prefects but not the vassal kings. . . . Until their misdeeds were exposed, the feudal lords sought personal gain unscrupulously, and snatched wealth rapaciously, relying on their might to intimidate and oppress the people. And nothing could be done about it. Meanwhile, in the commanderies and prefectures, peace and order prevailed. . . . How is this to be explained? The Han emperors . . . were able to appoint, or to reinstate, able officials. . . . Offenses were punished and abilities rewarded. An official who was appointed in the morning but acted improperly was discharged that very evening. . . .

Suppose that Han had placed all of the cities and towns under vassals and kings. Even if the feudal lords had abused the people, the emperor could have done nothing but grieve for them. . . . The feudal lords might have been reprimanded and exhorted to reform, but after listening respectfully, they would have returned to their fiefs and completely disregarded it all. . . . Was not depriving the feudal lords of all their lands and transferring them away from them, thereby safeguarding the people, the perfect solution? Such are the facts in the case of Han.

At present the country is administered entirely by the prefectural system, under the jurisdiction of prefects and magistrates. This unquestionably is not to be changed. If the army is firmly controlled, and local officials carefully selected, then there will be peaceful rule.

Some also say, "Xia, Shang, Zhou, and Han used the enfeoffment system and endured a long time. Qin used the prefectural system and came to a sudden end." This shows no understanding at all of the principles of government. In succeeding Han, Wei still set up feudal lands and ranks. In succeeding Wei, Jin carried on without alterations. These two dynasties rapidly disappeared. They did not remain on the throne for long. Now, having rectified the system, the house of Tang has ruled for two hundred years and has consolidated itself. What connections does this have with feudal lords?

Some also believe "the founders of Shang and Zhou were sage kings. They did not abolish the feudal system, hence there should be no further discussion of the subject." This is not true at all. Shang and Zhou did not abolish it because they were unable to do so. . . . Neither Tang nor Wu was able to do anything about it. . . . There was no deep concern for the public weal involved at all. Rather, they used others' strength for their own purposes and used others to protect the throne for their sons and grandsons. Qin, by abolishing the enfeoffment system, insofar as the system of administration was concerned showed deep concern for the public weal. [True,] the Qin emperor was motivated by selfish desires and did this to enhance his own personal authority, in order to subject everyone to himself. Nevertheless, concern for the public weal originated with the Qin.

It is a fixed principle of the world that the ruler gains the allegiance of the people by bringing peace and stability. He causes wise men to hold high posts and unworthy men to hold low places and thereby brings peace and stability. [Yet] under the enfeoffment system, government is hereditary. Under hereditary government, will those in high posts really be wise and those in low places really be unworthy? If not, then there is no way of knowing whether the people will be well governed or not. . . . How could the system of the sages be intended to bring about such a situation? And so I say the enfeoffment system was not the intention of the sages. It was brought about by the conditions of the times.

[*Liu Hedong ji* 3:44–48 —JMG]

In some respects the foregoing presents itself as a realistic analysis in historical terms, not an ideal or moralistic prescription — thus Liu's acceptance of the long-term benefits of the system established by the Qin. But when he deals with the prefectural system, his arguments wander some distance from a description of historical reality and lead off toward an idealization of what the prefectural system should be. Liu tends to look at the worst side of conditions during the Zhou and the best side of conditions in the Han. His concept that both the emperor and the people are interested in peace, that their fundamental interests coincide, is similar in form to those arguments in favor of the feudal system that emphasized the identity of interests of the local feudal lords and the people in their domains. Liu gives no reasons to support his assumption that an emperor will not behave as selfishly as feudal vassals had — that, unlike the feudal lords, the emperor will see his own interests as intimately bound up with the desires of the people for peace and act accordingly. Indeed, Liu's argument is that the emperor *must* realize this, not that all emperors ruling through the prefectural system have in practice realized it and lived up to what Liu demands of them.

Nor does Liu explain why his arguments against hereditary office holding do not apply to the office of emperor. In his description of the origins of the state, Liu says that in the earliest times the position of the Son of Heaven, like those of all other officials, was in some sense subject to the approval of the people. Thereafter, he forgets this. Liu first argues that a unified empire was necessary to ensure peace. Then he assumes throughout that the unified empire and emperor will continue to follow policies that ensure peace. Having demonstrated the logical necessity of an emperor, Liu assumes that in practice the real emperors will live up to the ideal required by his logic.

These logical difficulties did not prevent Liu's essay from achieving a certain fame as having made the case for the necessity and inevitability of centralized rule — the predominant view in later times. Yet Liu's essay also invited counterarguments and different formulations of the problem by other writers, notably Huang Zongxi and Gu Yanwu in the seventeenth century.

[JMG]

LI BO AND DU FU: TWO TANG POETS IN A TROUBLED WORLD

As we have seen, the Tang was one of the high points in the development of Chinese culture, with the century from about 705 to 805 becoming known as the High Tang or the Flourishing Tang. In terms of the span of civilization and of Chinese perceptions of what it means to be civilized, there can be little question that poetry has been highly favored among cultural expressions and that the High Tang was the age that the Chinese people would always look back to as the most flourishing, vigorous, and influential era in the entire poetic tradition.

While this volume is concerned primarily with society and civilization rather than with literature per se, it is important to note that poetry plays a significant role in Chinese public life, often serving as a vehicle for the expression of social and political conscience. This fact is illustrated in the poems of two of the greatest poets of the Tang — Li Bo (701–762) and Du Fu (712–770). The highly iconoclastic Li Bo, prodigious both as a writer and as a drinker, is generally thought to have been devoted to Daoism, while the deeply reflective Du Fu, known as the Sage of Poetry, has been described as the artistic counterpart of Confucius. However different the two may have been as personalities, their poems show how deeply involved they were in the common human life of their time.

Li Bo's poem imagines the suffering entailed by the wars of the early 750s, as the Tang armies began to be decisively defeated at the margins of the empire. The reader will find in it a powerful and unflinching statement about the horrors of war. Du Fu's poem vividly evokes the disparities between the lives of the privileged elite and those of the populace at large at a time just before the momentous Rebellion of An Lushan (755–763). Autobiographical in nature, it affords a poignant insight into the terrible disruption of human life and the touching challenge to the human spirit occasioned by that devastating rebellion.

LI BO: FIGHTING SOUTH OF THE RAMPARTS

Arthur Waley, the translator of this poem, believed that it was very likely written in 751. It was in the summer of that year that the Tang forces sustained major defeats in two far-flung parts of the empire — one at Dali in southwestern Yunnan in the course of a campaign against the Nanzhao kingdom and the other in the Battle of Talas River in northern Turkestan. War here has nothing of the glorious and heroic about it: the poet imagines a terrible carnage and writes in the mode of a lament.

Last year we were fighting at the source of the Sanggan;[37]
This year we are fighting on the Onion River road.[38]
We have washed our swords in the surf of Parthian seas;
We have pastured our horses among the snows of the Tian Shan.[39]
The King's armies have grown gray and old
Fighting ten thousand leagues away from home.
The Huns have no trade but battle and carnage;
They have no fields or ploughlands,
But only wastes where white bones lie among yellow sands.
Where the House of Qin built the great wall that was to keep away the
     Tartars,

---

37. The river that runs west to east through northern Shanxi and Hebei, north of the Great Wall.

38. The Kashgar-darya in Turkestan.

39. The "Heavenly Mountains" in China's northwest.

There, in its turn, the House of Han lit beacons of war.
The beacons are always alight, fighting and marching never stop.
Men die in the field, slashing sword to sword;
The horses of the conquered neigh piteously to Heaven.
Crows and hawks peck for human guts,
Carry them in their beaks and hang them on the branches of withered trees.
Captains and soldiers are smeared on the bushes and grass;
The General schemed in vain.
Know therefore that the sword is a cursed thing
Which the wise man uses only if he must.[40]

> [Adapted from Waley, *Poetry of Li Po*, pp. 34–35]

DU FU: A SONG OF MY CARES
WHEN GOING FROM THE CAPITAL TO FENGXIAN

The following selections are from a long poem in which Du Fu recounts his journey
from the capital to visit his family just before the outbreak of the An Lushan Rebellion.
As he leaves the capital at night, he evokes the darkness, cold, and misery of the lives
of ordinary people—a stunning contrast to the light, warmth, and opulence of the
imperial villa that he passes at dawn. The poem closes with the poet's arrival at Feng-
xian to find that he has not left death behind: it has come to meet him. His heartrending expression of remorse over his failure to protect his family conveys a subtle note
of protest: in rebuking himself he also implicitly rebukes the Tang emperor—the
"father and mother of the people"—for his remoteness from suffering humanity.

> In commoner's robes, a man of Duling,
> As he ages, his ideas fall deeper
> > into naiveté and foolishness,
> And the goals to which he vows himself—
> > simpleminded—
> In the secret heart comparing himself
> > to Hou Ji, Zhou's ancestor,
> > to Jie, the Shang's founder.
> But he may be deceived and instead become
> > a useless vacancy,
> Hair now white and willing
> > to meet long suffering:
> When the coffin lid closes, the matter is done.
> And yet my goals still and forever
> > long for fulfillment. . . .

---

40. Alluding to *Daodejing* 31.

It was year's end; all plants shriveled and fell,
The rushing wind split the high hills,
The avenues of the capital were dark canyons
As the traveler set out at midnight.
His stiffened belt cracked in the harsh frost.
And fingers, stiff and straight, could not tie back the ends.
Then, by dawn's breaking, I passed the Li Mountain Villa,[41]
A royal bed set on towering heights
Where battle flags blocked a cold and empty sky,
Where slopes and valleys were worn smooth
    by the tramp of armies.
There from the hot springs, vapors curled upward
past the clack and clatter of the Household Guard. . . .
Around Vermilion Gates, the reek of meat and wine
Over streets where lie the bones of the frozen dead. . . .

I had lodged my wife off in a different country,
ten mouths to protect from the winds and snow.
Who could go long without looking to them?
I hoped now to share their hunger and thirst.
I came through the gate. I heard a crying out,
my youngest child had died of starvation. . . .

And this thought obsesses me — as a father,
Lack of food resulted in infant death:
I could not have known that even after harvest
Through our poverty there would be such distress.
All my life I've been exempt from taxes,
and my name is not registered for conscription.
Brooding on what I have lived through, if even I
    know such suffering,
the common man must surely be rattled by the winds:
then thoughts silently turn to those who have lost
    all livelihood
and to troops in far garrisons.
Sorrow's source is as huge as South Mountain,
a formless, whirling chaos that the hand cannot grasp.

[Trans. by Stephen Owen, *The Great Age of Chinese Poetry:*
The High T'ang, pp. 195–96]

---

41. This was the Huaqing Palace, the pleasure resort of the Emperor Xuanzong and the imperial consort, Yang Guifei.

HAN YU AND THE CONFUCIAN "WAY"

Han Yu (768–824) is one of the most important figures in the history of Confucianism between the classical Zhou dynasty paragons of the formative period and the Neo-Confucians of the eleventh century. Like Confucius, he was both a reviver and a transmitter of earlier tradition and at the same time an innovative, even iconoclastic, commentator on contemporary issues. His self-stated task was to restore a Confucian social and political order to a society long acclimated to Buddhist and Daoist teachings. His arguments against these teachings in his most famous tract — "Essentials of the Moral Way" — are mostly economic, social, and moral rather than philosophical.

Han Yu had a respectable if stormy career as a Tang civil servant but is best known as a writer of both prose and poetry. He invented and advocated a literary style known as *guwen*, "the literature of antiquity," to give voice to his program for Confucian revival. Like this program, *guwen* traces its origins to the language of the Zhou dynasty Confucian classics, and Han Yu posited *guwen* as an alternative to the highly rigid "parallel prose" style that had links to the Buddhist culture of the Six Dynasties. All the texts by Han Yu in this section were written in *guwen*, an eclectic and supple style that in the eleventh century became the literary standard for Neo-Confucianism.

Like all true Confucians, Han Yu was a practical man of action who wanted his Confucian program put into contemporary practice. The political aspect of that program was support for a strong, centralized monarchy. In his "Poem on the Sagacious Virtue of Primal Harmony," written in 807, Han Yu expressed his hope that the new Emperor Xianzong (r. 806–820) would unify the Tang state and act as a model Confucian sovereign. Han Yu put great emotional commitment behind Xianzong's effort to restore Tang unity, and in 817 he personally participated in the campaigns against the independent military governors. But his realization that the emperor was more interested in the benefits of political unity than in serving as a Confucian model sparked in 819 the Memorial on the Bone of the Buddha, a text that betrayed his outrage and frustration over the obstacles that blocked realization of his Confucian program and earned him exile to southern China.

Yet Han Yu's opposition to Buddhism was not inflexible: he saw value in several practical aspects of Buddhism, especially Buddhist teaching practice that encouraged direct learning sessions between master and disciple. His "Discourse on Teachers," although it does not mention the Buddhist prototype, was probably written to adapt the Buddhist example to Confucian practice and to provide a Confucian justification and pedigree for this type of teaching. Han Yu himself imitated such teaching methods, taking large numbers of students into his own household for personal instruction in the classics and composition.

ESSENTIALS OF THE MORAL WAY

Han Yu's "Essentials of the Moral Way" ("Yuandao") is among the most important texts in the history of Chinese thought. It is nothing less than an attempt to define the distinguishing characteristics of Chinese civilization. In other words, it states the case for civilization versus countercultural conceptions of the Way. The first two sections are prologue: Han Yu defines terms and explains the historical trends that have led to the demise of Confucian teachings in his day. The third and fourth sections present the economic argument against Buddhist and Daoist monasticism: monks (the new fifth and sixth classes of society) are nonproductive and exist on the labor of others, thus creating economic and social dislocation.

The fifth section, with its opening quotation from the *Great Learning* (see chapter 10), is the crux of the text. Confucian spirituality, unlike that of the Buddhists and Daoists, links the private, moral life of the individual with the public welfare of the state. In antiquity a personal unity of thought and action made possible the political and social unity of the state. The sages of antiquity achieved this unity and laid the foundations of Chinese civilization. This new conception of sagehood as spiritual wisdom expressed through political action was to form the intellectual basis for the spiritual and political world of Neo-Confucianism.

1. To love largely[42] is called humaneness (*ren*); to act according to what should be done is called rightness (*yi*). To proceed from these principles is called the moral Way (*dao*); to be sufficient unto oneself without relying on externals is called inner power (*de*). The first two, *ren* and *yi*, are fixed concepts; but the latter two, *dao* and *de*, are relative terms. Thus there is the Way (*dao*) of the superior man and the way of the petty man; and inner power (*de*) can work either for good or for evil.[43]

Laozi belittled humaneness and rightness; he disparaged and spoke ill of them. Yet his view was limited. Just because one sits in a well and says the sky is small does not mean the sky is really small. For Laozi humaneness meant a small kindness and rightness meant a petty favor, so it was natural that he belittled them. Therefore, the moral way and the inner power that he spoke of and put into practice are not the same as what I mean by the Way and its Power.

---

42. Han Yu's choice of the expression *bo ai* (lit., "to love largely, amply") sets his idea apart from the Mohist concept of *jian ai* ("universal love"). Consideration of the semantic range of the two graphs (*bo*, "vast, large, ample" versus *jian*, "combine, unite") suggests that for Han Yu *bo ai* emphasizes the idea of love given generously yet always to known individuals with specific social relationships to the donor. It thus allows for particularity and heterogeneity, while avoiding the Mohist implication of an indiscriminate, homogenized love addressed to humankind in general.

43. *De*, often translated in this volume as "virtue," is rendered here as "inner power" to accommodate Han Yu's sense of it as a power that can work for good or ill.

Whenever I use these terms, they encompass both humaneness and rightness —
which is the common interpretation of the whole world. Laozi's use divorces
humaneness and rightness from the Way and from inner power; and this is the
private interpretation of only one man.[44]

2. After the traditions of the Zhou dynasty declined and Confucius passed
away, there was the burning of the books in Qin and the rise of Daoism in the
Han and of Buddhism in the Jin, Wei, Liang, and Sui dynasties. During these
times those who spoke of humaneness and rightness, of the Way and its power,
were either followers of Yang Zhu or Mozi, Laozi or Buddha. To adopt one of
these, one had to reject the others; so when believers took these men as their
masters and followed them, they despised and defamed Confucius. And those
of later ages who might wish to hear of the teachings on humaneness and
rightness, the Way and its power, had no one to listen to.

The followers of Laozi and Buddha both maintained that Confucius had
been a disciple of their masters. And the followers of Confucius grew so accustomed to hearing these theories that they began to enjoy such calumnies and
belittled themselves, acknowledging that the Master himself had indeed taken
Laozi or the Buddha as his master. They not only said such things but also
recorded them in their books. Those of later ages who might have wished to
hear of the teachings on humaneness and rightness, the Way and its power,
had no one from whom to seek them. How great has become men's fondness
for the fantastic! They do not inquire into fundamentals or essentials but wish
only to hear of the fantastic.

3. In antiquity there were four classes of subjects; now there are six. In
antiquity only one class were teachers; now there are three. For each farmer
there are six people that consume his produce. For each craftsman six use his
products. For each merchant, there are six people who must live off his profits.
Under such conditions, is it any wonder the people are impoverished and driven
to brigandage?

In ancient times men confronted many dangers. But sages arose who taught
them the way to live and to grow together. They served as rulers and as teachers.
They drove out reptiles and wild beasts and had the people settle the central
lands. The people were cold, and they clothed them; hungry, and they fed
them. Because the people dwelt in trees and fell to the ground, dwelt in caves
and became ill, the sages built houses for them.

They fashioned crafts so the people could provide themselves with implements. They made trade to link together those who had and those who had not

---

44. This attack against Laozi is directed against *Daodejing* 18: "When the great Way declined, / There were humaneness and rightness" and 38: "Therefore after the Way was lost there
was virtue, / After virtue was lost there was humaneness, / After humaneness was lost there was
rightness, / And after rightness was lost there was ritual propriety." See ch. 5.

and medicine to save them from premature death. They taught the people to bury and make sacrifices [to the dead] to enlarge their sense of gratitude and love. They gave rites to set order and precedence, music to vent melancholy, government to direct idleness, and punishments to weed out intransigence. When the people cheated each other, the sages invented tallies and seals, weights and measures to make them honest. When they attacked each other, they fashioned walls and towns, armor and weapons for them to defend themselves. So when dangers came, they prepared the people; and when calamity arose, they defended people.

But now the Daoists maintain:

> Till the sages are dead,
> theft will not end . . .
> so break the measures, smash the scales,
> and the people will not contend.[45]

These are thoughtless remarks indeed, for humankind would have died out long ago if there had been no sages in antiquity. Men have neither feathers nor fur, neither scales nor shells to ward off heat and cold, neither talons nor fangs to fight for food.

4. And so for this reason, the ruler is the one who issues commands. His ministers effect their ruler's commands and transmit them to the people. The people produce grains and rice, hemp and silk, make implements and exchange commodities in order to serve their superiors. If the ruler issues no commands, then he loses his reason for being ruler. If the ministers do not effect their ruler's commands and transmit them to the people, if the people do not produce grains and rice, hemp and silk, make implements and exchange commodities in order to serve their superiors, they are punished.

But now the Buddhist doctrine maintains that one must reject the relationship between ruler and minister, do away with father and son and forbid the Way that enables us to live and to grow together — all this in order to seek what they call purity and *nirvāṇa*. It is fortunate for them that these doctrines emerged after the Xia, Shang, and Zhou dynasties and so were not discredited by the ancient sages and by Confucius. It is equally unfortunate for us that they did not emerge before that time and so could have been corrected by the same sage.

The titles of emperor and of king are different, yet they are sages for the same reason. To wear linen in summer and fur in winter, to drink when thirsty and to eat when hungry — in both cases the concern is different, yet the logic

---

45. Han Yu here excerpts two couplets from a long passage in *Zhuangzi*, ch. 10; trans. Watson, pp. 109 ff.

is the same. But now the Daoists advocate "doing nothing" as in high antiquity. Such is akin to criticizing a man who wears furs in winter by asserting that it is easier to make linen, or akin to criticizing a man who eats when he is hungry by asserting that it is easier to take a drink.

5. According to a traditional text, "Those in antiquity who wished to illuminate luminous virtue throughout the world would first govern their states; wishing to govern their states, they would first bring order to their families; wishing to bring order to their families, they would first cultivate their own persons; wishing to cultivate their own persons, they would first rectify their minds; wishing to rectify their minds, they would first make their thoughts sincere."[46] And so what the ancients called rectifying the mind and making thoughts sincere were things they actually put into practice.

Yet today those who would rectify their minds do so by rejecting the empire and the state and by abrogating the natural principles of human relations: although they are sons, they do not regard their fathers as fathers. Although ministers, they do not regard their ruler as ruler. Although subjects, they do not attend to their duties.

When Confucius wrote the *Spring and Autumn Annals*, if the enfeoffed lords followed the usage of the barbarians, he treated them as barbarians. If they progressed to the level of the central states, then he treated them as central states. The classic says: "The barbarians with their rulers are not the equal of all Xia without them."[47] The Ode says: "The Rong and Di barbarians, them he withstood; Jing and Shu, those he repressed."[48]

Yet today we elevate barbarian practices and place them above the teachings of our former kings. How long will it be before we ourselves have all become barbarians?

6. What is the teaching of the former kings? To love largely is called a sense of humaneness; to act according to what should be done is called rightness. To proceed from these principles is called the moral Way; to be sufficient unto oneself without relying on externals is called inner power. Its texts are the *Odes*, the *Documents*, the *Changes*, and the *Spring and Autumn Annals*. Its methods are the rites, music, chastisement, and government. Its classes of people are scholars, peasants, craftsmen, and merchants. Its social relationships are ruler and minister, father and son, teacher and pupil, guest and host, older and younger brother, husband and wife. Its dress is hemp and silk; its dwellings are houses; its foods are rice and grains, fruits and vegetables, fish and meat. Its ways are easy to explain; its teachings are easy to execute.

---

46. The quotation is from the *Great Learning*. See ch. 10.
47. *Analects* 3:5.
48. Ode 300.

And so

Take it unto yourself; find ease and happiness
use it with others; be loving and fair
take it to your own mind; find peace, quietness
use it for empire and state; find it works everywhere

And so

in life they held to human feeling
and in death fulfilled their obligations,
so the spirits of Heaven came to their altars
and the manes of mortals received their libations.

7. What Way is this? It is what I call the Way, not what the Daoists and Buddhists have called the Way. Yao passed it on to Shun, Shun to Yu, Yu to Tang, Tang to King Wen, King Wu, and the Duke of Zhou; then these passed it on to Confucius, who passed it on to Mencius. But after the death of Mencius it was not passed on. Xunzi and Yang Xiong

Excerpted it but not its essence,
Discussed it but not in detail.
Before the Duke of Zhou
Our sages were kings,
And things got done.
After the Duke of Zhou
Our sages were subjects
And long theory won.

This being so, what can be done? Block them or nothing will flow; stop them or nothing will move. Make humans of these people, burn their books, make homes of their dwellings, make clear the way of the former kings to guide them, and "the widowers, the widows, the orphans, the childless, and the diseased all shall have care." This can be done.[49]

[*Changli xiansheng wenji* (SBCK) 11:1a–3b —CH]

---

49. This final quotation is from "Evolution of Rites," *Record of Rites* (trans. in ch. 10), where Confucius characterizes the utopian age of Grand Commonalty (*Datong*) as one where even persons without family were cared for. The quotation implies that "this can be done" by following the "great moral Way" that Han Yu has outlined in his text. There may also be a more subtle implication. Buddhist monasteries managed most charitable works in the Tang and provided economic subsistence to those left without resources by the established social order. Han Yu argues that realization of the "Grand Commonalty" of ancient times will reform this social order so as to provide for the welfare of these people.

POEM ON THE SAGACIOUS VIRTUE OF PRIMAL HARMONY

Support for a centralized political state can be seen as a plausible extension of the Confucian emphasis on family unity and hierarchy: a vision of the family writ large, with the emperor acting as father to the state. But during the Tang, the 755 rebellion of An Lushan destroyed all reality of a centralized state and ushered in a period of regional autonomy during which separatist military governors maintained their independence from the crown. Soon after his ascension, Emperor Xianzong moved to crush the power of these separatist forces and to restore the primacy of centralized power under his monarchy. Han Yu's career as writer and Confucian thinker peaked during this time of "primal harmony," the reign-title for the entire period of Xianzong's rule. Han Yu's enthusiastic support for Xianzong's military campaigns against the separatists is an important part of his own larger program of Confucian restoration. No text better articulates Han Yu's practical and contemporary commitment to the centralized political state than his "Poem on the Sagacious Virtue of Primal Harmony," a text he placed at the beginning of his collected works and a poem unique in the history of Chinese literature.

After a short preamble (2:1–20) that describes the suppression of the minor separatist Yang Huilin in Shanxi province (Xia), the bulk of the poem recounts the capture and execution of Liu Pi, military governor of Sichuan province (Shu) on December 12, 806 (2:21–146) and the subsequent performance by Emperor Xianzong of the new year rites on February 11, 807 (2:147–202). The poem concludes with a paean to the emperor's wisdom, frugality, justice, and filiality (2:203–254).

Some traditional Chinese critics objected to the poem because its narrative and heroic, even epic qualities are far from the lyric core of Tang poetry. But Han Yu's style, as his own preface and conclusion (2:251–254) make clear, is a conscious imitation of the heroic and martial qualities of the *Classic of Documents* and the *Classic of Odes*, and his poem is laced with quotations, adaptations, and echoes of these earlier classics. As Xianzong would restore the body politic, so Han Yu would restore the body of literature to its origins in the Confucian classics. Other critics objected to the mention of Liu Pi's cannibalism and the inclusion of the grizzly details of his execution. Yet these passages are crucial to the contrast between the villainy of Liu Pi and the "sagacious virtue" of Xianzong. Han Yu emphasizes many times the emperor's concern that military action not harm the common people, and the poem carefully balances the supposed martial (*wu*) and the civil (*wen*) virtues of Xianzong. The poem presents Han Yu's idealized vision of the Confucian sovereign, "for a myriad years and for eons . . . father and mother to all."

Preface

Your servant, Yu, bowing his head in repeated obeisance, makes bold to observe that Your Majesty, our August Thearch,[50] since ascending the throne has executed or exiled traitorous retainers, thus cleansing the court of deceit and treachery. In the provinces you beheaded Yang Huilin and Liu Pi and recovered Xia and Shu. In the east you suppressed the long-standing rebellions in Jing and Xu. All in the land tremble, and none dares oppose you. You have sacrificed to Heaven and made report in the ancestral temple, so the divine spirits have been well pleased, and wind and rain, darkness and light, have followed in the proper order. A period of Great Tranquillity has come to pass in this age.

Your servant, benefiting from your most gracious favor, has daily stood with the host of retainers at the foot of the Hall of Purple Sovereignty and gazed on the brightness of the imperial visage. Since it is my responsibility to instruct the sons of the state in our classic texts, I have deemed it appropriate to compose as a model for them a poem in praise of your consummate virtue. I have not dared to use the poor quality of my writing as an excuse not to exert myself to the fullest on this work. I have taken antiquity as my model and composed in four-word lines "Poem on the Sagacious Virtue of Primal Harmony," which, complete in 1,023 characters, constitutes a true factual record that illumines in detail the Son of Heaven's divine sagacity in civil and military matters, such that it may serve as an exhortation to the common people and be passed on as an example for all time. The poem is as follows:

> When our August Thearch mounted the dais,
> Nothing in nature refused to comply:
> the sun was called, and the sun shone forth;
> the rains were called, and the rains came down.
> But when it was still in his primal year,
> a brigand arose in the town of Xia
> and intended there to tumble the State
> and tread again the recent paths of war.
> And the August Thearch responded, "Lo,
> this will indeed affect us, for trusting   10
> their remoteness have they dared to rebel.
> We cannot allow this!" So he declared,
> and out marched the armies — ten brigades —
> five-thousand men to chastise the rebels.
> The troops encamped beneath the city walls
> and called out the choice: submit or be destroyed.

---

50. Or "god-ruler."

So the core gave way, and the branches snapped,
for they dared not hold in their unity.
Over the ramparts they tossed their leader's head
and raised by night the flag of surrender.   20
For dangers arising on far frontiers
no place surpassed the land of Shu.
Wei Gao, long governor there, was not dead,
and Liu Pi, on his own, took up command:
full-bloodied were his teeth with human flesh
which loath he was to spit forth from his mouth.
Opening storerooms wide to lure the troops,
he said, "Now take as you please, then stretch taut
your bows, sound forth your drums, and send up word
that it's me you demand for top command."   30
When first this matter came before our Lord,
all those at Court flashed with anger and rage.
But the August Thearch said, "So be it.
I pity the people of that far land,
so if he submits and will hold the peace,
then we grant him the post he desires."
So the order was read aloud at court,
and at early morning emblems of office
left the royal workshops in the capital
and by nightfall had reached his camp in Shu.   40
Pi was delighted and addressed his horde:
"Look you now to arousing our soldiers,
and all of Shu we can have for our own:
there's no need to accept this order here."
Thousands of oxen were roasted on spits
and countless jugs of wine passed round at feasts.
For leggings the best brocade they used,
bandanas were the finest scarlet silk.
Some followed him who feared his violent rage,
others his cajolery enticed;   50
they mustered all, numerous as stalks of grain,
troops that numbered in the tens of thousands.
Off they marched to pillage Eastern Valley
and overrun the high walls of Zizhou.
The August Thearch spoke: "Alas! Alas!
How can we once again indulge this man?"
And so charged the general Gao Zhongwen
to divide the royal army and attack,

"But mind you restrain their surging spirit,
do not lay waste my land and my people."   60
Ten miles a day they marched, encircling slow
the right flank of the enemy. Liu Pi
took council with his cohorts, deciding
to erect a defense at Deer Head Pass.
Gao Zhongwen received the imperial charge,
rules and guides were set for advance and retreat:
be not in battle too eager for kill,
nor yet let swell the number of captives.
Throughout the land the military chiefs
marshaled their troops, made ready their horses,   70
petitioned His Majesty to join the attack,
awaiting orders to move or remain.
The August Thearch responded then, "Lo,
trouble you not, nor make too much concern.
Jing and Bing and Liang, these three areas,
stand as the doors and windows of our land.
Let each send forth a force of three thousand strong:
and pick whatever kind of troops you need."
And so four armies arose together,
and they were grand like the mountain masses.   80
Sometimes they tugged at the horns of the beast,
sometimes they pulled off the spurs of the cock.[51]
In forced marches they covered vast stretches,
but nowhere was resistance encountered.
In the eighth month, the twenty-second day,
Pi abandoned his defenses and fled,
loading on carts his wives and concubines
who clutched in arm their babes and small children.
And Gao Zhongwen entered and occupied
the enemy stronghold on the same day;   90
to pursue and to seize he split up his troops
who searched through fields and cut thickets away.
Liu Pi, at his wits' end, and pressed sore hard,
saw no place around to betake himself;
he gazed at the great River far below

---

51. These metaphors describe the skill of the government forces and the ferocity of the enemy. The lines are probably inspired by a passage in the *Zuozhuan*: "As in the pursuit of a stag, the people of Jin took Qin by the horns, and we took it by the feet" (Legge, *The Chinese Classics*, 5:460).

and although he saw no shore nor island,
he plunged headlong in, as when a pestle
is pitched downward into the mortar's midst.
They pulled him from the river's water,
a cangue went around his neck, his hands were cuffed; 100
his women were strung like pearls on a string,
wailing and crying, begging for mercy.
He was brought as tribute before the throne,
and all was proclaimed within the ancestral shrine.
Led round he was through the city bazaar,
an example for all the world to see.
Then his cangue and shackles were taken off,
his body was stretched between blade and block.
First his children, supple and submissive,
standing stoop-shouldered and naked, were seized   110
and hauled by their heads and dragged by their feet;
their spines were sliced at the waist in a stroke.
Next followed train and retinue;
their corpses were stacked and leaned up in piles.
Then they came at last to Liu Pi himself,
terror-stricken, his sweat flowed down in streams.
The swords flew in a welter of motion,
in an instant he was hacked into mince.
The commanders were richly rewarded,
accorded jade scepters of state and seals   120
of new office, their homes heaped high with silks,
their storerooms brimmed in overflow with grain.
Those fallen in battle were grieved and mourned,
with pensions paid to widows and orphans,
posthumous ranks were conferred, and grave sites
vast and great were marked across the land.
In all the regions affected by war
there was a broad remission of taxes;
decrees were spread and rewards for service
moved with the swiftness of fire spreading.   130
In the whole world between Heaven and Earth
nothing was undisposed to order:
from the districts of Wei, You, Heng, and Qing
(so eastward down to the edge of the sea)
southward to the districts of Xu and Cai
and even till the rude races beyond,
all feared his awesome might; and shamed by his
virtues, they danced for joy in reverence

and cast off armor and weapons of war
to practice with basins of ritual grain.[52]   140
And over a thousand strong, together,
they came to audience at autumn Court.
The August Thearch addressed them thus: "Lo,
my uncles, brothers of both my parents,
be content, each of you, with your stations,
and look well to your lands and your people."
On the opening day of the new year,
he first appeared in the ancestral hall
to perform in person the hundred rites;
climbing high, he made profound obeisance,   150
then gave offer before his father's tomb,
and when he looked up to behold the broad beams,
deep sorrow was seen in the royal visage,
and his tears dropped down on the offering plates.
Retainers who assisted at these rites
shared Our Majesty's woes and his deep grief.
Then on the first *xin* day of the new year,[53]
he sacrificed with oxen at Heaven's
altar, south of the capital, the site
set out with rack of chimes and carillons   160
and a canopy to cover it all;
and it rose high like a mighty boulder.
Their tiger-emblemed bucklers held aloft,
the round altar now prepared and ready,
the guards of Heaven deployed to the four sides,
standards and pennants graceful in the breeze.
Twelve coursers harnessed in form like fish schools
or birds in even flight pulled the royal coach,
which climbed at evening up the round hill
to present the jade disk and sacred urn.   170
Then a multitude of music burst forth,
sonorous sounds that merged in harmony;

---

52. Han Yu describes the supposed submission of the separatist military using the terminology of the early Zhou feudal court. "Basins" were among the ritual utensils used at the ceremonies through which the feudal lords expressed their loyalty to the sovereign. The emperor addresses the military governors as "uncles," again in imitation of early Zhou usage.

53. The suburban sacrifice took place on the first day of the sexagenary cycle made by combining the "ten stems" and the "twelve branches" to contain *xin*, the eighth stem. This dating was ancient (see ch. 10) and seems to have related to the homonymic nature of *xin* and *xin* meaning "new."

and as torches' violet flames suspired,
the exalted *anima* descended.[54]
The stars of Heaven all sat in perfect place,
spread in vast array across the wide sky,
where the sun as Lord, the moon as Queen,
one blazing bright, one soft and lovely.
And the spirits of water vast and broad,
the gods of the mountains amassed and high   180
feasted on the vapors of meat and grain
and brought joy and spread plenty through the land.
Phoenixes, in response to the music,
came dancing, spreading and flapping their wings;
scarlet unicorns and yellow dragons
writhed in joy and coiled in happy union.
The officials and the common people,
from green youngsters to white-headed old men,
trembled and leapt for joy with open mouths
till lost in raptures, choked with happiness.   190
The skies were clear, the earth was at ease, and
spirits rose in dwellings across the land.
The chariot of the Royal Thearch,
returning to the capital at high noon,
traveled to the Vermilion Phoenix Gate
there to issue an Act of Grace for the
empire, that washed clean, that polished smooth,
that wiped away all flaws and defilements.
He entitled the sons of the worthy,
drew forth the sage-like, employed the aged;   200
he nurtured like children the defenseless,
and humaneness and charity rained down.
Divine is our August Thearch and wise,
embracing antiquity and today;
your clearness of sight, keenness of hearing
are fully the equal of Yao and Yu.
You knew at your birth our laws and standards,
and your actions attained to their order;
Heaven has ordained you August Thearch
to be master of all the empire,   210

---

54. The Latin *anima* is used here in an attempt to translate the Chinese *ling*, the vital spirit
of *Haotian shangdi*, which descends from Heaven to receive the sacrifice.

to protect it, to nourish and foster
with no distinction between great and small;
for a myriad years and for eons
who shall dare to proffer opposition?
Frugal is our Thearch and hardworking
(you wash your hands in argil basins);
abjuring splendor and luxury, you
prefer clothing of homespun pongee.
Diligently you warn the four quarters
that extravagance breeds calamity,   220
so Heaven ordained you August Thearch
with surfeit of millet and barley.
There is no cause now for drought or for flood,
no damage or loss from sparrows or rats,
for a myriad years and for eons
there will be prosperity without want.
Just as our August Thearch and true,
you discern clearly the good from the bad;
those who presumed to usurp your power
you have already dispatched or exiled.   230
To a man you have dispelled these traitors,
and none of their companions remain.
Heaven ordained you August Thearch
with grand ministers and great advisers;
you questioned widely and searched far
in order to establish your escort;
for a myriad years and for eons
none shall dare to offend your majesty.
Our August Thearch is most filial,
kind and magnanimous, a good brother;   240
affably and with great sweetness of heart,
you attend the Grand August Dowager.
These virtues you extend to all your clan,
from whence they permeate the nine domains;
Heaven ordained you August Thearch,
to endure as long as shall Heaven itself.
You have brought forth our Great Tranquillity,
which shall prevail without cease forever;
for a myriad years and for eons
you shall be father and mother to all.   250

Your humble servant, Yu, a professor
charged with explicating the classic texts,
has crafted and written this song-poem
to accord with the work of Yin Jifu.[55]
[*Changli xiansheng wenji* (SBCK) 1:5b–9b — CH]

DISCOURSE ON TEACHERS (SHISHUO)

Han Yu had little use for the kind of classical training given as a preparation for the civil service examinations. The tutor who merely taught his pupil the literary tricks needed to satisfy the formal requirements was, to his mind, a far cry from the great teachers of the past who had made Confucianism a teaching to live by. In this essay he argues for a return to the original conception of a teacher and for the necessity of continuing one's education throughout life. So important is this to Han Yu that he believes that considerations of social status and seniority should not stand in the way of the pursuit of true learning.

Students of ancient times all had their teachers, for it is only through the teacher that the Way is transmitted, learning imparted, and doubts dispelled. . . . The man born before me who has truly learned the Way before me I shall follow and make my teacher. The man born after me but who has learned the Way before me I shall also follow and make my teacher. What I seek from my teacher is the Way. What is it to me, then, whether he is older or younger than I? Regardless of high or low station, age or youth, he who has the Way shall be my teacher. . . .

If a man loves his son he selects a teacher to give the boy instruction, and yet he is ashamed to follow a teacher himself. This is folly indeed. The sort of teacher who only gives a child a book and teaches him to punctuate and read it is not what I call a transmitter of the Way and a dispeller of doubts. But at least the child who cannot read goes to a teacher, while the father who is in doubt will not. This is to learn the minor things and neglect the major ones, and I for one fail to see the wisdom of it.

Sorcerers, doctors, musicians, and the various craftsmen are not ashamed to study with teachers. And yet among the families of scholar-officials if you speak of a teacher or a disciple people all gather around and begin to laugh. If you ask them why they laugh, they reply: "These two men are practically the same

---

55. Yin Jifu was a general and poet mentioned in the *Classic of Odes* as the author of a number of poems written to praise Emperor Xuan of the Zhou dynasty. This monarch is traditionally credited with restoring the fortunes of the Zhou dynasty, whose power had fallen after the demise of its founders, by asserting authority over the feudal lords and by repulsing incursions of the non-Chinese tribes. Han Yu intends by this reference an obvious parallel between Emperor Xuan and Emperor Xianzong and between Yin Jifu and himself.

age, and so they must understand the Way equally well." Again, if the teacher is lower in social status than the disciple it is considered shameful to study with him, while if he is a high official it is thought that one studies with him only to curry favor. Alas, it is obvious that in such circumstances the teaching of the Way can never be restored. Sorcerers, doctors, musicians, and craftsmen are not considered the equal of gentlemen, and yet gentlemen these days cannot match them in knowledge. Is this not strange?

A sage has no constant teacher. Confucius acknowledged Tanzi, Chang Hong, Shi Xiang, and Lao Dan as his teachers, although Tanzi and his like were surely not so wise as Confucius.[56] Confucius said, "Walking along with three people, my teacher is sure to be among them. I choose what is good in them and follow it and what is not good and change it."[57] Thus a disciple is not necessarily one who is inferior to his teacher and the teacher one who is wiser than his disciples. It is simply that the teacher has learned the Way before others and devoted himself to the art of instruction.

[From *Changli xiansheng wenji* (SBCK) 12:1b–2b — BW]

MEMORIAL ON THE BONE OF BUDDHA

Your servant begs leave to say that Buddhism is no more than a cult of the barbarian peoples, which spread to China in the time of the Latter Han. It did not exist here in ancient times. . . . When Emperor Gaozu [first emperor of the Tang] received the throne from the House of Sui, he deliberated upon the suppression of Buddhism. But at that time the various officials, being of small worth and knowledge, were unable fully to comprehend the ways of the ancient kings and the exigencies of past and present, and so could not implement the wisdom of the emperor and rescue the age from corruption. Thus the matter came to naught, to your servant's constant regret.

Now Your Majesty, wise in the arts of peace and war, unparalleled in divine glory from countless ages past, upon your accession prohibited men and women from taking Buddhist orders and forbade the erection of temples and monasteries, and your servant believed that at Your Majesty's hand the will of Gaozu would be carried out. Even if the suppression of Buddhism should be as yet impossible, your servant hardly thought that Your Majesty would encourage it and, on the contrary, cause it to spread. Yet now your servant hears that Your Majesty has ordered the community of monks to go to Fengxiang to greet the bone of Buddha, that Your Majesty will ascend a tower to watch as it is brought into the palace, and that the various temples have been commanded to wel-

---

56. From Tanzi he is supposed to have learned the naming of officials; from Chang Hong, music; from Shi Xiang, the lute; from Lao Dan (or Laozi), rites.

57. *Analects* 7:21.

come and worship it in turn. Though your servant is abundantly ignorant, he understands that Your Majesty is not so misled by Buddhism as to honor it thus in hopes of receiving some blessing or reward, but only that, the year being one of plenty and the people joyful, Your Majesty would accord with the hearts of the multitude in setting forth for the officials and citizens of the capital some curious show and toy for their amusement. . . . But the common people are ignorant and dull, easily misled and hard to enlighten, and should they see their emperor do these things they might say that Your Majesty was serving Buddhism with a true heart. "The Son of Heaven is a Great Sage," they would cry, "and yet he reverences and believes with all his heart! How should we, the common people, then begrudge our bodies and our lives?" Then would they set about singeing their heads and scorching their fingers,[58] binding together in groups of ten and a hundred, doffing their common clothes and scattering their money, from morning to evening urging each other on lest one be slow, until old and young alike had abandoned their occupations to follow [Buddhism]. . . . Then will our old ways be corrupted, our customs violated, and the tale will spread to make us the mockery of the world. This is no trifling matter!

Now Buddha was a man of the barbarians who did not speak the language of China and wore clothes of a different fashion. His sayings did not concern the ways of our ancient kings, nor did his manner of dress conform to their laws. He understood neither the duties that bind sovereign and subject nor the affections of father and son. If he were still alive today and came to our court by order of his ruler, Your Majesty might condescend to receive him, but . . . he would then be escorted to the borders of the state, dismissed, and not allowed to delude the masses. How then, when he has long been dead, could his rotten bones, the foul and unlucky remains of his body, be rightly admitted to the palace? Confucius said, "Respect spiritual beings, while keeping at a distance from them."[59] So when the princes of ancient times went to pay their condolences at a funeral within the state, they sent exorcists in advance with peach wands to drive out evil, and only then would they advance. Now without reason Your Majesty has caused this loathsome thing to be brought in and would personally go to view it. No exorcists have been sent ahead, no peach wands employed. The host of officials have not spoken out against this wrong, and the censors have failed to note its impropriety. Your servant is deeply shamed and begs that this bone be given to the proper authorities to be cast into fire and water, that this evil may be rooted out, the world freed from its error, and later generations spared this delusion. Then may all men know how the acts of their wise sovereign transcend the commonplace a thousandfold. Would this not be glorious? Would it not be joyful?

Should the Buddha indeed have supernatural power to send down curses

---

58. Acts symbolic of a person's renunciation of the world upon entering Buddhist orders.
59. *Analects* 6:20.

and calamities, may they fall only upon the person of your servant, who calls upon high Heaven to witness that he does not regret his words. With all gratitude and sincerity your servant presents this memorial for consideration, being filled with respect and awe.

[From *Changli xiansheng wenji* (SBCK) 39:2b–4b — BW]

EMPEROR WUZONG'S EDICT ON THE SUPPRESSION OF BUDDHISM

The subjection of Buddhism and other foreign faiths to severe persecution under the Emperor Wuzong (r. 841–846) owed nothing directly to the fulminations of a Han Yu or to any concerted movement on the part of Confucians. The emperor, desperately seeking the secret of immortality, was under the influence of Daoist priests who urged on him this repression of their rivals. Still, the justification for this move as set forth in the following edict is largely practical, rather than ideological, in nature. The obvious advantages to the state of confiscating Buddhist wealth and secularizing monks and nuns, so that they might serve the state as cultivators liable to land and labor taxes, had been pointed out long before at the inception of the dynasty. The edict itself was merely a last step in the process of suppression that Wuzong had been pursuing for some time.

This process did not result in the complete elimination of Buddhism from China, which would have taken a greater and more sustained effort by Wuzong's successors than it had, but it was a setback for the religion. Organizationally weakened, Buddhism could not maintain its institutional or doctrinal identity as it did in Japan, and it tended to become fused with a welter of popular cults. The edict also served to reassert with awesome finality a basic principle of the Chinese bureaucratic state: that a religion maintained its corporate existence only on sufferance of the state.

Edict of the Eighth Month [845]:

We have heard that up through the Three Dynasties the Buddha was never spoken of. It was only from the Han and Wei on that the religion of idols gradually came to prominence. So in this latter age it has transmitted its strange ways, instilling its infection with every opportunity, spreading like a luxuriant vine, until it has poisoned the customs of our nation; gradually, and before anyone was aware, it beguiled and confounded men's minds so that the multitude have been increasingly led astray. It has spread to the hills and plains of all the nine provinces and through the walls and towers of our two capitals. Each day finds its monks and followers growing more numerous and its temples more lofty. It wears out the strength of the people with constructions of earth and wood, pilfers their wealth for ornaments of gold and precious objects, causes men to abandon their lords and parents for the company of teachers, and severs man and wife with its monastic decrees. In destroying law and injuring mankind, indeed, nothing surpasses this doctrine!

Now if even one man fails to work the fields, someone must go hungry; if one woman does not tend her silkworms, someone will be cold. At present there are an inestimable number of monks and nuns in the empire, each of them waiting for the farmers to feed him and the silkworms to clothe him, while the public temples and private chapels have reached boundless numbers, all with soaring towers and elegant ornamentation sufficient to outshine the imperial palace itself. . . .

Having thoroughly examined all earlier reports and consulted public opinion on all sides, we no longer have the slightest doubt in Our mind that this evil should be eradicated. Loyal ministers of the court and provinces have lent their aid to Our high intentions, submitting most apt proposals that We have found worthy of being put into effect. Presented with an opportunity to suppress this source of age-old evil and fulfill the laws and institutions of the ancient kings, to aid mankind and bring profit to the multitude, how could We forbear to act?

The temples of the empire that have been demolished number more than 4,600; 26,500 monks and nuns have been returned to lay life and enrolled as subject to the Twice-a-Year Tax; more than 40,000 privately established temples have been destroyed, releasing 30 or 40 million *qing* of fertile, top-grade land and 150,000 male and female servants who will become subject to the Twice-a-Year Tax. Monks and nuns have been placed under the jurisdiction of the Director of Aliens to make it perfectly clear that this is a foreign religion. Finally, We have ordered more than 2,000 men of the Nestorian and Mazdean religions to return to lay life and to cease polluting the customs of China.

Alas, what had not been carried out in the past seemed to have been waiting for this opportunity. If Buddhism is completely abolished now, who will say that the action is not timely? Already more than 100,000 idle and unproductive Buddhist followers have been expelled, and countless of their gaudy, useless buildings destroyed. Henceforth We may guide the people in stillness and purity, cherish the principle of doing nothing, order Our government with simplicity and ease, and achieve a unification of customs so that the multitudes of all realms will find their destination in Our august rule.

[*Jiu Tang shu*, 18A:14b–15a — BW]

Chapter 19

THE CONFUCIAN REVIVAL IN THE SONG

As dynasties go in China, the Song (960–1279) was not known for its power and stability. It struggled against great odds to bring back under Chinese rule all the lands once held by the Tang. During the earlier years of the dynasty there was almost constant fighting with "barbarian" tribes in the north and west; during the latter half of the period these invaders held North China, the ancient seat of Chinese civilization, firmly in their grasp until the Mongols swept down to reunify the empire under alien auspices. Even within the Song domains the nation was beset by chronic fiscal, agricultural, and administrative problems such as those that had plagued earlier regimes.

Yet in spite of all this, Chinese society showed remarkable vitality. Commerce was expanding, and with it a more diversified economy developed. Money, especially the new paper currency, was coming into greater use. As a natural concomitant of such growth there was an increase in the number and size of cities, which at this time attained the wealth, culture, and sheer magnificence reported in the accounts attributed to Marco Polo. In the arts of peace, if not in those of war, the Song distinguished itself. Printing, which had been developed during the Tang, for the first time provided the means for more widespread education. Academies, which were centers of higher education, sprang up around the more sizable collections of books, sometimes endowed by grants of land from the state or from private individuals. It was in institutions such as these that the new scholarship, so much an expression of the whole

Song concern for cultural achievement as opposed to military aggrandizement, arose. Whereas for centuries the great Buddhist temples had been the intellectual centers of China, now academies presided over by one or another noted scholar began to attract students in great numbers. Under such circumstances the new scholarship grew and flowered into the new (or Neo-) Confucianism.

As an example of this new type of scholar and teacher, we may cite Hu Yuan (993–1059), who typifies the spirit of the Confucian revival and whose influence was felt among its most prominent leaders. Hu Yuan answered well to the need that Han Yu saw for genuine teachers in the tradition of Confucius and Mencius. He was above all a man who took seriously his duties as a moral preceptor of youth and stressed a close teacher-disciple relationship as essential to education. It was regarded as noteworthy in his time that Hu Yuan "adhered strictly to the traditional concept of the teacher-disciple relationship, treating his students as if they were sons or younger brothers and being trusted and loved by them as if he were their father or elder brother." One of his disciples later explained Hu Yuan's contribution in the following terms to the Emperor Shenzong:

> It is said that the Way has three aspects: substance [or basis, *ti*], function [*yong*], and literary expression [*wen*]. The bond between prince and minister and between father and son, humaneness, rightness, rites, and music — these are the things that do not change through the ages; they are its substance. The *Classics of Odes* and *Documents*, the dynastic histories, the writings of the philosophers — these perpetuate the right example down through the ages; they are its literary expression. To activate this substance and put it into practice throughout the empire, enriching the life of the people and ordering all things to imperial perfection — this is its function.
>
> Our dynasty has not through its successive reigns made substance and function the basis for the selection of officials. Instead we have prized the embellishments of conventional versification, and thus have corrupted the standards of contemporary scholarship. My teacher [Hu Yuan], from the Mingdao through the Baoyuan periods (1032–1040), was greatly distressed over this evil and expounded to his students the teaching that aims at clarifying the substance [of the Way] and carrying out its function. Tirelessly and with undaunted zeal, for more than twenty years he devoted himself wholly to school-teaching, first in the Suzhou region and finally at the Imperial Academy. Those who have come from his school number at least several thousand. The fact that today scholars recognize the basic importance to government and education of the substance and function of the Way of the sages is all due to the efforts of my master.[1]

---

1. *Song Yuan xue'an* 1:17.

This tribute to Hu Yuan suggests several characteristic features of the Confucian revival in the early Song. Hu Yuan is both a traditionalist and a reformer. He is more a moralist than a metaphysician, and his primary interest is in the application of Confucian ethics to the problems of government and everyday life. Hu Yuan is also an independent scholar, one whose success came through years of private study and teaching, and who gained official recognition only late in life. Echoing criticism by late Tang writers of the literary examination system, he condemns it as a perverter of scholarship and as productive of a mediocre officialdom. Finally, in the threefold conception of the Way as substance, function, and literary expression, Hu Yuan adapts the terminology of Neo-Daoist Buddhist philosophy (and also of Tiantai metaphysics) to the exposition of the traditional Confucian Way and suggests the manner in which Confucian thought would be enriched and deepened in the process of encountering Buddhism and Daoism.

According to this view, the classics were to be studied as deposits of enduring truth rather than as antiquarian repositories, and the true aim of classical studies was to bring these enduring principles, valid for any place or time, to bear upon both the conduct of life and the solution of contemporary problems. Conversely, no attempt to solve such problems could hope to succeed unless it was grounded in these enduring principles and undertaken by people dedicated to them. Yet neither classical teaching nor a practical program of reform could be furthered except through the mastery of literature and writing — not the intricacies of form and style with which the literary examinations were concerned but literature as a medium for preserving and communicating the truth in all its forms.

With this in mind we can recognize the many-sided character of the Confucian revival in the Song. The broad current of political reform, culminating in the New Laws (or Measures) of Wang Anshi, and the work of the great Song historians are as much products of this revival as the metaphysical speculations now identified with Neo-Confucianism. Even the work of the great philosopher Zhu Xi (1130–1200) must be appreciated as an expression of the Song spirit in the fields of history and government as well as in classical scholarship and metaphysics. Such breadth and versatility, indeed, were not uncommon in the great intellectual giants of the Song: Wang Anshi, whose reputation as an outstanding writer and classicist in his day has been overshadowed by his fame as a statesman; Sima Guang, his chief political antagonist, who is better known today as one of China's great historians; and Su Dongpo, the celebrated poet and calligrapher, who was also a man of affairs and played a leading part in the political struggles of that memorable era. These men — to name just a few — are all beneficiaries of the creative and widespread energies of the Song revival.

Especially in its emphasis upon the practical application of Confucian principles to the problems of the day, Hu Yuan's teaching points to the fact that political, economic, and social thought was to be as integral a part of the Confucian revival as were classical studies and philosophical inquiry. Hu Yuan himself urged practical measures to improve the people's livelihood, to strengthen military defenses against the barbarian menace, to expand irrigation projects in order to increase agricultural production, and also to promote the study of mathematics and astronomy. In his school Hu Yuan set up two study halls, one for the classics and the other for practical studies, the latter including government, military affairs, water control, and mathematics. Hu warmly praised the special achievement in water conservation of one of his former students. Later this educational model, combining the humanities and practical sciences, was cited in two of Zhu Xi's most influential educational works, his *Elementary Learning* (*Xiaoxue*) and *Reflections on Things at Hand* (*Jinsi lu*). Thus, though Neo-Confucianism was strongly oriented toward the humanities, and less so to the natural or pure sciences, it was by no means averse to specialized, technological studies.

Hu Yuan remained a teacher and did not engage in the politics of the court. At court it was men like Fan Zhongyan and Ouyang Xiu who led the reform movement. The latter, a noted poet and historian, proved himself a mighty champion of Confucian orthodoxy who carried on Han Yu's struggle against the twin evils of Buddhist escapism and literary dilettantism. He insisted that "literary activity just benefits oneself, while political activity can affect the situation around us." In him also the Song school found a vigorous defender of the scholar's right to organize politically for the advancement of common principles. To him, then, we turn for a statement of the need for reform put in its most fundamental terms.

INSTITUTIONAL, EDUCATIONAL, AND MORAL REFORM IN THE SONG

OUYANG XIU: ESSAY ON FUNDAMENTALS (*BENLUN*)

Like Han Yu, Ouyang Xiu (1007–1070) saw China's ills as attributable to the forsaking of Confucian teachings in favor of Buddhism, which had corrupted the whole body politic. Nevertheless, outright suppression of Buddhism, as Han Yu had urged, seemed to Ouyang a futile policy. Only a positive program of fundamental reform would remove the underlying causes for the popularity of Buddhism. This called for a complete renovation of Chinese society, a reform especially of basic institutions to make them conform to the ancient ideal.

This essay was written in the 1040s, during the first blush of Song Confucian reformism. It combined institutional reforms through strong state policies (Part 1) with educational and moral reforms (Part 2). Later, as Ouyang came into strenuous opposition to Wang Anshi's aggressive exercise of state power by the central government, he no longer gave such high priority to central military and fiscal measures and deleted Part 1, which had pressed for them, from the essay. This shift in his thinking corresponds to a similar shift on the part of Neo-Confucians later, when they likewise backed away from strong centralist policies, giving priority instead to educational and moral reform, while focusing more on voluntarism and cooperation under elite leadership in the local community.

The affairs of the empire have their trunks and their branches. The one who governs it puts certain things first and certain things after. . . .

The three kings knew well how to proceed from trunk to branch, knew what to put first and what after, and in doing this they had system and regularity. Among those who have gained the empire after them, who has not wanted to bring peace and govern well? Why is it that the more laborious their concern, the more unsuccessful their government, and that, while trembling lest disorder or defeat should touch them, they go headlong into it? It is because they have not proceeded from trunk to branch, have not known what to put first and what after. Now among the tasks of the present day, which have become a multitude, those to be put first are five. Two of these are known to those in authority, but to three they have given no thought.

To assure expenditures for the empire, nothing comes before revenue. In significance for the safety or endangerment of the empire, nothing comes before soldiers. These are what those in authority know. But even given revenue in abundance, if one takes it without limit and spends it without measure, then those below will be more and more resistant and those above will be more and more wearied. Even given soldiers in force, if one does not know what to use them for, then the soldiers will grow arrogant and breed disaster.

Of all the means for sparing revenue and employing soldiers, none comes before institutions. Once institutions are provided, soldiers are employable and revenue suffices for expenditures. Of all the means for sharing in the preservation of [institutions], none comes before delegating to [the right] men. Thus one equalizes revenues and controls troops, sets up laws to regulate them, delegates the preservation of the laws to the worthy, and honors fame in order to give the worthy incentive [to accept employment]. These five, used in conjunction, are the constant task of anyone who has gained the empire; [these are] what to put first in the present age and what those in charge overlook. . . .

Why is it that though the populace grows ever more multitudinous, the produce of the earth grows ever more extensive, and public expenditure grows ever more zealous, the four barbarians do not submit, China is not honored, and the empire is insecure? It is because these five are not provided.

Allow me to speak of one or two of them. At present the farmer's cultivating may be called laborious. The merchant's taking of resources [profit] from mountain and pond may be called diligent. The emperor's ministers who levy taxes on trade and on the profits of merchants may be called thoroughgoing and precise without omission. Yet when we encounter a single flood or drought, . . . public and private [spheres] throughout the empire are in want. This is [because even] in this age of no crises, the people lack provision for a single year, and the state lacks several years' accumulation. From this one knows that revenue is insufficient.

In former days the disorder of the Five Dynasties[2] (907–960) was extreme. In fifty-three years they changed ruling houses five times and rulers thirteen times, and those who lost their states and were killed were eight. . . . The empire was divided into thirteen or fourteen parts. [Enemies on] four sides surrounded it, even squeezing their way into China. There were also rebellious generals and strong ministers who carved off pieces and occupied them. . . . The situation of the empire became like a broken-down dwelling: fix the main beam, and the corner gives way; repair the rafters, and the ridgepole falls down. Though you prop it up and support it so that it barely survives, how can you also have the leisure to follow a model, compass your circles, square your angles, and make a systematic plan? Thus soldiers were uncontrolled, revenue was unspared, the nation was without laws and regulations; all was helter-skelter.

As of the present day, Song has been Song for eighty years. Outside, usurpation and disorder are pacified, and there is no state [our] equal. Inside, the local garrisons are pared away, and there are no powerful and rebellious ministers. The empire is one. All within the seas is at peace. [We have] not been a state a short time. The empire is not of small extent. . . . Now, having inherited the founding enterprise of the three sages [the first three Song emperors], having acquired the honored name of a lord of ten thousand chariots, and thus having an empire that contains all within the four seas in one household, all paying in for the one above alone to take, one cannot say one lacks wealth. The six-foot soldiers, wielding halberds and bearing armor, strong enough to draw a five-*dan* crossbow or bend a two-*dan* [regular] bow, number a million, for the one above alone to control and direct; one cannot say one lacks troops. Of officials inner and outer, those in active posts are several thousand. . . . With one [civil service] examination every three years, those without office who come forward are more than ten thousand men, those tested at the Board of Rites seven or eight thousand, for the one above alone to select from; one cannot say one lacks worthy men. It has been almost forty years that the people have not seen military conflict. To brandish the military and drive away the barbarian without, to cultivate law and regulation and promote virtuous transformation within, are for the one above alone to do. One cannot say one has no time. . . .

But revenue is insufficient for expenditures above, while there is already ruin below; the soldiers are inadequate to provoke awe without but dare to be arrogant within; the institutions and regulations are not such as could be a model for ten thousand generations but grow daily more numerous and com-

---

2. The period of division that followed the fall of the Tang dynasty.

plicated. All is helter-skelter, much as in the time of the Five Dynasties. It is greatly to be lamented. This is what is called occupying the seat from which it could be accomplished, at the time when it could be accomplished, and with the resources by which to accomplish it; who then would long shrink from doing it? [— RH]

Part 2

Particularly noteworthy in this section of Ouyang's essay is that his brand of Confucian fundamentalism puts such strong emphasis on the rites, reaffirming the importance originally attaching to them in the classical tradition but in this context responding especially to the challenge of Buddhism. Also to be noted is his reiteration in both Part 1 and Part 2 of the courageous prophetic role of the individual scholar in reversing the evil tide and restoring the rites. This heroic moral stance became a defining mark of the Neo-Confucian civil ideal and the self-image of the educated literocratic elite.

The cult of Buddhism has plagued China for more than a thousand years. In every age men with the vision to see through its falseness and the power to do something about it have all sought to drive it out. But though they drove it out, it reappeared in greater force. . . . But is the situation really hopeless, or is it simply that we have not used the proper methods?

When a doctor treats a disease, he tries to ascertain the origin of the sickness and heal the source of the infection. When sickness strikes a man, it takes advantage of the weak spot in his vitality to enter there. For this reason a good doctor does not attack the disease itself but rather seeks to strengthen the patient's vitality, for when vitality has been restored, then the sickness will disappear as a natural consequence. . . .

In the age of Yao, Shun, and the Three Dynasties, kingly rule was practiced, government and the teachings of rites and rightness flourished in the world. At that time, although Buddhism existed, it was unable to penetrate into China. But some two hundred years after the Three Dynasties had fallen into decay, when kingly rule ceased, and rites and rightness were neglected, Buddhism came to China. It is clear, then, that Buddhism took advantage of this time of decay and neglect to come and plague us. . . .

In ancient times the governments of Yao, Shun, and the Three Dynasties set up the well-field system. They made a registry of all subjects, calculated the population, and distributed land to all. Then all men who were capable of farming had land to farm. One-tenth of the produce was taken as tax, while other levies were differentiated in order to discourage indolence and cause all men to devote their full efforts to agriculture and not allow them time for less worthy occupations. . . .

When they were at rest from the work of the fields, they were instructed in rites. Thus for hunting they learned the ceremonies of the spring and autumn hunts, for taking a mate the rites of marriage, for death the rites of funeral and sacrifice, and for banquets and gatherings the rites of the village archery contest. . . .

In this way the rules for supporting the living and bidding farewell to the dead were all made to accord with the desires of the people. They were brightened with ceremonial objects and beautifully ordered so that they were a delight to the people and easy to carry out. They were in harmony with the nature and feelings of the people and imparted a restraint that prevented men from going to excess. Still fearing that this might not be enough, the rulers set up schools for the people to teach and enlighten them, so that from the courts of the emperor down to the smallest hamlet there was no place without its school where keen and intelligent men from among the people were sent to study, to discuss with each other, and to lead and encourage the indolent. Ah, how complete was this system of government of the Three Dynasties! . . .

But when the Zhou declined and the Qin conquered the world, it discarded the methods of the Three Dynasties and the Way of the former kings was cut off. . . . The well-field system was the first to be abolished, and there arose the evils of encroachment and idle landlordism. After this the rites of the spring and autumn hunts, marriage and funeral ceremonials, sacrifice and archery contests, and all the ways by which the people had been instructed, one by one fell into disuse. . . . Then Buddhism, entering at this juncture, trumpeted abroad its grand, fantastic doctrines to lead them, and the people could do no other than follow and believe. . . .

What then can be done? I say there is nothing so effective in overcoming it as practicing what is fundamental. Long ago, in the period of the Warring States, the teachings of Yang Zhu and Mozi were the cause of great confusion. Mencius was grieved at this and devoted himself to preaching humanity and rightness, for when the doctrine of humanity and rightness prevails then the teachings of Yang Zhu and Mozi will be abandoned.[3] In Han times all the schools of philosophy flourished side by side. Dong Zhongshu was concerned at this and retired to devote himself to the practice of Confucianism, for he knew that when the Way of Confucius was made clear the other schools would cease.[4] This is the effect of practicing what is fundamental in order to overcome Buddhism.

These days a tall warrior clad in armor and bearing a spear may surpass in bravery a great army, yet when he sees the Buddha he bows low, and when he hears the doctrines of the Buddha he is sincerely awed and persuaded. Why? Because though he is indeed strong and full of vigor, in his heart he is confused and has nothing to cling to. But when a scholar who is small and frail and

---

3. See ch. 6, *Mencius* 3B:9.
4. See ch. 10.

afraid to advance hears the doctrines of Buddhism his rightness is revealed at once in his countenance, and not only does he not bow and submit, but he longs to rush upon them and destroy them. Why? It is simply because he is enlightened in learning and burns with a belief in rites and rightness, and in his heart he possesses something that can conquer these doctrines. Thus rites and rightness are the fundamental things whereby Buddhism may be defeated. If a single scholar who understands rites and rightness can keep from submitting to these doctrines, then we have but to make the whole world understand rites and rightness and these doctrines will, as a natural consequence, be wiped out. . . .

In ancient times Xunzi held the theory that man's nature is basically evil and wrote an essay to prove it. I used to favor this idea, but now as I see how the men of my day follow Buddhism, I know that Xunzi's theory is gravely mistaken. Man's nature is basically good, and those who follow Buddhism, abandoning their families and discarding their wives or husbands, are actually going much against this basic nature. Buddhism is a corruption that eats into and destroys men, and yet when the people lead each other on to follow it, it is only because they think that Buddhism teaches the way to do good. Alas, if we could but truly awaken our people to see that it is through rites and rightness that they may do good, then would they not lead each other on to follow these?

[From *Ouyang Wenzhong gong ji* (SBCK) 17:1a–4b — RH, BW]

ON PARTIES

As a leading official under the emperors Renzong (r. 1023–1063) and Yingzong (r. 1064–1067), Ouyang Xiu attempted to recruit and bring into the government able men inspired by Confucian ideals and sympathetic to the reforms he envisioned. Such an attempt to rally the serious scholars of the land in support of a new political program necessarily involved forming a group much like a political party, committed to working in a government composed of like-minded individuals.

Chinese political traditions did not allow for such a development, however. Rulers had always looked with suspicion on any political alignment that might bring pressure on the throne or threaten its security. Any organized opposition was likely to be regarded as a "faction" or "clique," bent on serving its own interests rather than those of the state. One of the main objectives of the civil service examination system was to prevent "packing" of offices with representatives of any single group or faction through favoritism in the recruitment of officials.

Thus the political movements inspired by the Confucian revival, insofar as they were assertive and well organized, were likely to stir up contention and become involved in factional struggles. Against such attacks Ouyang Xiu, in a memorial of 1045, sought to justify the existence of groups dedicated to the best interests of the state and its people, and not to the selfish advantage of their own members.

Your servant is aware that from ancient times there have been discussions on the worth of parties. It is only to be hoped that a ruler will distinguish between those of gentlemen and those of inferior men. In general, gentlemen join with other gentlemen in parties because of common principles, while inferior men join with other inferior men for reasons of common profit. This is quite natural. But your servant would contend that, in fact, inferior men have no parties, and that it is only gentlemen who are capable of forming them. Why is this? Inferior men love profit and covet material wealth. When the time seems to offer mutual advantages, they will temporarily band together to form a party, which is, however, essentially false. But when they reach the stage where they are actually competing among themselves for advantage, or when the advantages they have sought fail to materialize and they drift apart, then they turn about and begin to attack each other, and even the fact that a man is a brother or a relative does not spare him. Therefore your servant maintains that such men have no real parties and that those which they form on a temporary basis are essentially false. But this is not true of gentlemen, who abide by the Way and rightness, who practice loyalty and good faith, and care only for honor and integrity. When they employ these qualities in their personal conduct they share a common principle and improve each other, and when they turn them to the use of the state, they unite in common ideals and mutual assistance and from beginning to end act as one. These are the parties of gentlemen. Thus if the ruler will but put aside the false parties of inferior men and make use of the true parties of gentlemen, then the state may be ordered.

[From *Ouyang Wenzhong gong ji* (SBCK) 17:6b–8a — dB]

THE CONFUCIAN PROGRAM OF REFORM

The first steps in the government itself to implement a broad program of reform were taken by the statesman and general Fan Zhongyan (989–1052), who was among those defended by Ouyang Xiu when he submitted his memorial on political parties. Fan was an earnest student of the classics, as well as a man of practical affairs, who became known as a staunch upholder of the Confucian Way and a vigorous opponent of Buddhism. When a young man he adopted for himself the maxim "To be first in worrying about the world's worries and last in enjoying its pleasures,"[5] which expresses his high ideal of public service as a dedicated Confucian. During the reign of Renzong, Fan tried as prime minister to implement a ten-point program including administrative reforms to eliminate entrenched bureaucrats, official favoritism, and nepotism; examina-

---

5. Amusement parks and ball fields in Japan have drawn on this celebrated motto by incorporating it in their names, such as "Later Enjoyment Park" (*Kōraku-en*).

tion reform; equalization of official landholdings to ensure a sufficient income for territorial officials and to lessen the temptation toward bribery and squeeze; land reclamation and dike repair to increase agricultural production and facilitate grain transport; creation of local militia to strengthen national defense; and reduction of the labor service required of the people by the state.

There is nothing startling or revolutionary in this program, but many of the reforms proposed by Fan anticipate changes later made by Wang Anshi that aroused great controversy. To us they represent simply a reorganization of certain governmental activities or practices, and we may fail to appreciate that in a society so dominated by the state and so sensitive to its operations, even administrative changes of this sort could have a deep impact. As it turned out, however, these reforms dealing with education and the examination system had the most significant effect. In his memorial Fan called for the establishment of a national school system through which worthy men could be trained and recruited for the civil service. Though conceived, characteristically enough, more to meet the needs of the government for trained personnel than to make education available to one and all, this system nevertheless represented the first real attempt to provide public school education on a large scale in China. Since nothing on that scale had been set up before, it also represented a departure from the established order as embodied in dynastic tradition and precedent. Fan appealed therefore to an earlier and, from his point of view, more hallowed tradition, justifying the change as a return to the system set forth in the classics as obtaining under the humane rule of the early Zhou kings.

Fan also asked that in the examinations conducted at the capital for the *jinshi* degree (the highest in the regular system of advancement), more importance be attached to an understanding of the classics and of political problems than to the composition of poetry. One of his most revealing proposals was to abolish the pasting of a piece of paper over the candidate's name on an examination paper, a practice that had been designed to ensure impartial judgment by the examiner. The reasoning behind this suggestion follows from the importance that Fan attached in both teaching and politics to a man's personal integrity. It was just as vital to know the candidate's moral character as his literary and intellectual capacities, and character was impossible to judge except from personal knowledge.

Prompted by Fan's memorial, the emperor called for a general discussion of these questions at court. Fan's proposals were supported by Song Qi and others, who spoke out against the evils of the existing system and urged a "return" to the ancient ideal. As a result, a national school system was promulgated by Renzong in 1044, calling for the establishment of a school in each department and district, to be maintained and staffed by the local magistrate. At the same time the civil service system was reformed so that the examinations were divided into three parts, with priority given to problems of history and politics, then to interpretation of the classics, and last of all to composition of poetry. Subsequently, instruction in the Imperial Academy was also revamped by Hu Yuan, who had been brought to court by Fan Zhongyan, to conform to the methods Hu had used in his private academy.

Few of Fan's reforms survived when he fell from power as a result of bitter factional struggles. Nevertheless, the agitation for reform went on among some of the best minds of the age. One of these was Li Gou (1009–1059), a scholar who wrote extensively on the need for Confucians to pay more attention to military matters (advocating primary reliance on a soldier-farmer militia, rather than a large standing army), economy in administration, land redistribution, public granaries, and a more extensive school system. Many of his ideas, especially his strong emphasis on the *Rites of Zhou* as a recipe for achieving the early Song ideal of "Supreme Peace and Order" (*Taiping*), were taken up by the great reformer Wang Anshi. These included the need for administrative efficiency and economy, the orderly management of the court and imperial household, the proper expenditure of state revenues, and equitable collection of taxes — all in practical detail of a kind that Confucian scholars rarely dealt with. The selections that follow are meant to illustrate the types of reform most widely espoused in Confucian circles. To show that this ferment was not confined to persons whose interests and activities were mostly political, but instead pervaded the Song school in general, we have made selections from scholars later identified with Neo-Confucian orthodoxy and better known as philosophers than as officials. They are, moreover, thinkers whose intellectual antecedents are found among the progenitors of the Song school already mentioned (e.g., Hu Yuan) and whose political and scholarly affinities early linked them to Wang Anshi. The first two selections are memorials of the famous Cheng brothers, documents that reveal the breadth and variety of the reforms that were advocated. Following them are excerpts from the writings of the philosopher Zhang Zai and the scholar-official Su Xun, presenting divergent views on a single question: the age-old problem of land distribution.

THE WAY AS THE BASIS FOR GOVERNMENT POLICY

CHENG YI: MEMORIAL TO EMPEROR RENZONG

This memorial was presented in 1050, a few years after the fall of Fan Zhongyan and his allies, when Cheng Yi (1033–1107) was still only seventeen years old. It is prefaced by a long appeal (abbreviated here) for acceptance of the Confucian Way as the basis of government policy. Only a full return to the ideal society of the sage kings will suffice to meet the needs of the day. To imitate the Han and Tang dynasties, great though these were in some respects, would mean succumbing eventually to the same weaknesses that brought them down. This is a recurrent theme of the reformers, who had to overcome widespread skepticism at court that ancient institutions, as well as

Confucian moral precepts, could have any practical application in the very different social circumstances of the Song period. Cheng Yi then describes the prevailing economic and social evils that must be remedied, and like so many other reformers of the time, he concludes that the first step in solving them must be a change in the civil service system, so as to bring into the government men with the ability and the determination to rectify these conditions.

In the Three Dynasties the Way was always followed; after the Qin it declined and did not flourish. Dynasties like the Wei and Jin indeed departed far from it. The Han and Tang achieved a limited prosperity, but in practicing the Way they adulterated it. . . .

In the *Classic of Documents* it says: "The people are the foundation of the nation; when the foundation is solid the nation is at peace."[6] Your servant thinks that the way to make the foundation firm is to pacify the people, and that the way to pacify the people is to see that they have enough food and clothing. Nowadays the people's strength is exhausted and there is not enough food and clothing in the land. When spring cultivation has begun and the seed has been sown, they hold their breath in anxious expectation. If some year their hopes are disappointed, they have to run away [and abandon the land]. In view of these facts, the foundation can hardly be called firm. Your servant considers that Your Majesty is kind and benevolent, loves the people as his children, and certainly cannot bear to see them suffer like this. Your servant suspects that the men around Your Majesty have shielded these things from Your Majesty's discerning sight and prevented you from learning about them.

Now the government frequently has insufficient funds to meet its expenditures. Having an insufficiency, it turns to the fiscal intendants of the various circuits. But where are the fiscal intendants to get the money? They simply have to wring it from the people. Sometimes peace is disturbed in all directions at once, and so troops are called out just when the men should attend to the cultivation of their fields, causing still more grievous harm. As these pressing demands are put upon the people, their blood and fat become exhausted; frequently they are brought to financial ruin and their livelihood is lost, while the members of the family are separated and dispersed. Even ordinary men are pained at the sight of this. Surely Your Majesty, who is like a parent to the people, cannot help but take pity on them! The people have no savings and the government granaries are empty. Your servant observes that from the capital on out to the frontiers of the empire, there is no place that has a reserve sufficient to carry over two years. If suddenly there is a famine for more than one year, such as the one that occurred in the Mingdao period (1032–1033), I do not know how the government is going to deal with it.

The soldiers who do no work and yet must be fed number more than one

---

6. "Songs of the Five Sons," *Classic of Documents*; Legge, *The Chinese Classics*, 3:158.

million. Since there is no means to support them, the people will be heavily taxed. And yet the people have already scattered. If strong enemies seize the opportunity to attack from without, or wicked men aspire to power from within, then we may well be fearful of a situation that is deteriorating and threatens to collapse.

Your servant considers that humaneness is the foundation of the Kingly Way. He observes that the humaneness of Your Majesty is the humaneness of Yao and Shun; and yet the empire has not had good government. This is because Your Majesty has a humane heart but not a humane government. Therefore Mencius says, "Though he may have a humane heart and a reputation for humaneness, one from whom the people receive no benefits will not serve as a model for later generations because he does not practice the Way of the former kings."[7] . . . Good government in the empire depends upon obtaining worthy men; misgovernment in the empire derives from a failure to obtain worthy men. The world does not lack worthy men; the problem is how to find them. . . .

In the selection of scholars for the civil service, though there are many categories under which men may qualify, yet there are only one or two persons who may be considered [under the category of] "wise, virtuous, square, and upright."[8] Instead, what the government obtains are scholars who possess no more than erudition and powerful memory. Those who qualify in [the examination on] understanding of the classics merely specialize in reciting from memory and do not understand their meaning. They are of little use in government. The most prized and sought after is the category of *jinshi*, which involves composition of verse in the *ci* and *fu* form according to the prescribed rules of tone and rhythm. In the *ci* and *fu* there is nothing about the way to govern the empire. Men learn them in order to pass the examination, and after the passage of a sufficient time, they finally attain to the posts of ministers and chancellors. How can they know anything of the bases of education and cultivation found in the Kingly Way? . . .

For two thousand years the Way has not been practiced. Foolish persons of recent times have all declared that times are different and things have changed, so that it can no longer be practiced. This only shows how deep their ignorance is, and yet time and again the rulers of men have been deceived by their talk. . . . But I see that Your Majesty's heart is filled with solicitude for the people; how can any difficulties stand in the way?

[From *Yichuan wenji* (SBBY) 1:14a–16b — dB]

---

7. *Mencius* 4A:1.

8. A title conferred on a limited number of candidates given a special imperial examination which was held at infrequent intervals.

CHENG HAO: TEN MATTERS CALLING FOR REFORM

This memorial, presented by Cheng Yi's elder brother, Cheng Hao (1032–1085), to the Emperor Shenzong (r. 1068–1085), opens with the characteristic assertion that despite the need for adapting institutions to the times, certain underlying principles of Confucianism remain valid even for later dynasties like the Song. He then details ten evils of the day, which require bold action. Some of these are urgent problems from almost any point of view — unequal distribution of land, the need for universal schooling, the expense and ineffectiveness of a professional army, the danger of famine and the need for increased grain storage, and the need for conservation of natural resources.

Prerequisite to any of these, however, is the ruler's recognition of constant human norms that endure from past to present, of the need to adopt the models of the sage kings to present circumstances, and — most important — of how he should consult with Confucian ministers and treat them as close colleagues, so that true learning and supreme political authority would once again be conjoined, as in the ideal days of the Duke of Zhou. This strong assertion of the role of the scholar-official, sharing in and balancing the power of the supreme autocrat, also finds expression in what came to be called the Learning of the Emperors.

Your servant considers that the laws established by the sage kings were all based on human feelings and in keeping with the order of things. In the great reigns of the Two Emperors [Yao and Shun] and Three Kings [founders of the Xia, Shang, and Chou dynasties], how could these laws not but change according to the times and be embodied in systems that suited the conditions obtaining in each? In regard to the underlying basis of government, however, to the teachings by which the people may be shepherded, to the principles that remain forever unalterable in the order of things, and to that upon which the people depend for their very existence — on such points there has been no divergence but rather common agreement among the sages of all times, early or late. Only if the way of sustaining life itself should fail could the laws of the sage kings ever be changed. Therefore in later times those who practiced the Way [of the sage kings] to the fullest achieved perfect order, while those who practiced only a part achieved limited success. This is the clear and manifest lesson of past ages. . . .

But it may be objected that human nature today is no longer the same as in ancient times, and that what has come down to us from the early kings cannot possibly be restored in the present. . . . Now in ancient times all people, from the Son of Heaven down to the commoners, had to have teachers and friends in order to perfect their virtue. Therefore even the sages — Shun, Yu, [King] Wen, and [King] Wu — had those from whom they learned. Nowadays the function of the teacher and preceptor is unfulfilled and the ideal of the "friend-minister" is not made manifest. Therefore the attitude of respect for virtue and enjoyment in doing good has not been developed in the land. There is no difference between the past and the present in this matter. . . .

Heaven created the people and raised up a ruler to govern and to guide them. Things had to be so regulated as to provide them with settled property as the means to a flourishing livelihood. Therefore the boundaries of the land had to be defined correctly, and the well-fields had to be equally distributed — these are the great fundaments of government. The Tang dynasty still maintained a system of land distribution based on the size of the family.[9] Now nothing is left, and there is no such system. The lands of the rich extend on and on, from this prefecture to that subprefecture, and there is nothing to stop them. Day by day the poor scatter and die from starvation, and there are countless persons without sufficient food and clothing. The population grows day by day, and if nothing is done to control the situation, food and clothing will become more and more scarce and more people will scatter and die. This is the key to order and disorder. How can we not devise some way to control it? In this matter, too, there is no difference between past and present.

In ancient times, government and education began with the local villages. The system worked up from [the local units of] *bi, lü, zu, dang, zhou, xiang, can,* and *sui.*[10] Each village and town was linked to the next higher unit and governed by them in sequence. Thus the people were at peace and friendly toward one another. They seldom violated the criminal law, and it was easy to appeal to their sense of shame. This is in accord with the natural bent of human feelings and, therefore, when practiced, it works. In this matter, too, there is no difference between past and present.

Education in local schools was the means by which the ancient kings made clear the moral obligations of human relationships and achieved the ethical transformation of all-under-Heaven. Now true teaching and learning have been abandoned, and there is no moral standard. Civil ceremonies have ceased to be held in the local community, and rites and rightness are not upheld. Appointments to office are not based upon the recommendation of the village communities, and the conduct [of appointees to high office] is not proven by performance. The best talents are not nurtured in the schools, and the abilities of men are mostly wasted. These are matters clearly evident, and there is in them no difference between the past and the present.

In ancient times, government clerks and runners were paid by the state, and there was no distinction between soldiers and farmers. Now the arrogant display of military power has exhausted national resources to the limit. Your servant considers that if the soldiery, with the exception of the Imperial Guards, is not

---

9. Under the equal land system of the early Tang, each adult was entitled to hold thirty *mu* of hereditary land and eighty *mu* on assignment from the state.

10. Units of local administration in ascending order as described in the classic *Rites of Zhou.*

gradually reconverted to a peasant militia, the matter will be of great concern. The services of government clerks and runners have inflicted harm all over the empire; if this system is not changed, a great disaster is inevitable, This is also a truth that is most evident, and there is no difference between the past and the present.

In ancient times, the people had to have [a reserve of] nine years' food supply. A state was not considered a state if it did not have a reserve of at least three years' food. Your servant observes that there are few in the land who grow food and many who consume it. The productivity of the earth is not fully utilized, and human labor is not fully employed. Even the rich and powerful families rarely have a surplus; how much worse off are the poor and weak! If in one locality their luck is bad and crops fail just one year, banditry becomes uncontrollable and the roads are full of the faint and starving. If, then, we should be so unfortunate as to have a disaster affecting an area of two or three thousand square *li*, or bad harvests over a number of years in succession, how is the government going to deal with it? The distress then will be beyond description. How can we say, "But it is a long, long time since anything like that has happened," and on this ground trust to luck in the future? Certainly we should gradually return to the ancient system — with the land distributed equally so as to encourage agriculture and with steps taken by both individuals and the government to store up grain so as to provide against any contingency. In this, too, there is no difference between the past and the present.

In ancient times, the four classes of people each had its settled occupation, and eight or nine out of ten people were farmers. Therefore food and clothing were provided without difficulty, and people were spared suffering and distress. But now in the capital region there are thousands upon thousands of men without settled occupations — idlers and beggars who cannot earn a living. Seeing that they are distressed, toilsome, lonesome, poor, and ill, or resort to guile and craftiness in order to survive and yet usually cannot make a living, what can we expect the consequence to be after this has gone on for days and years? Their poverty being so extreme, unless a sage is able to change things and solve the problem, there will be no way to avoid complete disaster. How can we say, "There is nothing that can be done about it"? This calls for consideration of the ancient [system] in order to reform the present [system], a sharing by those who have much so as to relieve those who possess little, thus enabling them to gain the means of livelihood by which to save their lives. In this, too, there is no difference between the past and the present.

The sages followed Heaven's way of putting things in order through the administration of the six resources.[11] The responsibility for the administration of the six resources was in the hands of the Five Offices. There were fixed

---

11. That is, earth, metal, stone, wood, furs and skins, and plant products.

prohibitions covering the resources of hills, woodlands, and streams. Thus the various things were in abundance and there was no deficiency in the supply. Today the duties of the Five Offices are not performed and the six resources are not controlled. The use of these things is immoderate and the taking of them is not in due time and season. It is not merely that the nature of things has been violated but that the mountains from which forests and woods grow have all been laid bare by indiscriminate cutting and burning. As these depredations still go uncurbed, the fish of the stream and the beasts of the field are cut short in their abundance, and the things of Nature [Heaven] are becoming wasted and exhausted. What then can be done about it? These dire abuses have now reached the extreme, and only by restoring the ancient system of official control over hills and streams, so as to preserve and develop them, can the trend be halted, a change made, and a permanent supply be assured. Here, too, there is no difference between the past and the present.

In ancient times, there were different ranks and distinctions observed in official capping ceremonies, weddings, funerals, sacrifices, carriages, garments, and utensils, and no one dared to exceed what he was entitled to. Therefore expenses were easily met, and people kept their equanimity of mind. Now the system of rites is not maintained in practice, and people compete with each other in ostentation and extravagance. The families of officials are unable to maintain themselves in proper style, whereas members of the merchant class sometimes surpass the ceremonial display of kings and dukes. The system of rites is unable to regulate the human feelings, and the titles and quantities[12] are unable to preserve the distinction between the noble and the mean. Since there have been no fixed distinctions and proportions, people have become crafty, deceitful and grasping; each seeks to gratify his desires and does not stop until they are gratified. But how can there be an end to it? This is the way leading to strife and disorder. How, then, can we not look into the measures of the ancient kings and adapt them to our need? Here, too, there is no difference between the past and the present.

The above ten points are but the primary ones. Your servant discusses these main points merely to provide evidence for his belief that the laws and institutions of the Three Dynasties can definitely be put into practice. As to the detailed plans and procedures for their enactment, it is essential that they conform to the instructions contained in the classics and be applied with due regard for human feelings. These are fixed and definite principles, clearly apparent to all. How can they be compared with vague and impractical theories? May your sage intelligence deign to consider them.

[From *Mingdao wenji* (SBBY) 2:6a–7b; *Song Yuan xue'an* 14:332 — dB]

---

12. As stated in the *Zuozhuan*, there was to be a proportional relation between one's rank and the quantity of goods one might devote to social display within the limits of good form ([SBBY] 9:8b; Legge, *The Chinese Classics*, 5:97).

ZHANG ZAI: LAND EQUALIZATION AND THE ENFEOFFMENT SYSTEM

The philosopher Zhang Zai (1020–1077), an uncle of the Cheng brothers, strongly advocated the adoption of the institutions described in the classical books of rites (especially the *Rites of Zhou*). Zhang long cherished the dream of purchasing some land for himself and his disciples and of dividing it up into well-fields in order to demonstrate the feasibility of restoring the system that the early sage kings had left to posterity. He died without accomplishing his objective.

Note especially the reasons given by Zhang for the superiority of the enfeoffment system and the steps by which he would gradually return to this form of social organization. He is particularly concerned about the problems created by the increasing centralization of government, a trend that many recent historians have pointed to as having been greatly accelerated and intensified in the Song dynasty and after. His solutions, however, are no less simplistic and idealistic than those of Liu Zongyuan (773–819) in the Tang.

If the government of the empire is not based on the well-field system, there will never be peace. The way of Zhou is simply this: to equalize. . . .

The well-field system could be put into effect with the greatest ease. The government only needs to issue an edict and the whole thing can be settled without having to beat a single person. No one would dare to occupy and hold land as his own. Moreover, it should be done in such a manner as to obtain the people's ready compliance and not cause those with much land to lose all their means. In the case, let us say, of a high official holding lands comprising a thousand hamlets, he should be enfeoffed in a state no more than fifty *li* in extent. But for what he possesses in excess of this, he should be assigned jurisdiction as an official[13] over a proportionate area of land, so that he may have its tax income. [In this way] people will not lose their former property.

To achieve good government in the empire the only method is to start with this. The land of the empire should be laid out in squares and apportioned, with each man receiving one square. This is the basis of the people's subsistence. In recent times [i.e., since the Zhou] no provision has been made for the people's means of subsistence, but only for the commandeering of their labor. Contrary to expectation, the exalted position of the Son of Heaven has been used for the monopolizing of everything productive of profit. With the government thinking only of the government, and the people thinking only of themselves, they have not taken each other into consideration. But "when the people have plenty, their prince will not be left alone in want. If the people are in want, their prince cannot alone enjoy plenty."[14]

---

13. Presumably an appointment to terminate at death, and not held by hereditary right, as in the case of his fief. The interpretation of this passage is uncertain.

14. *Analects* 12:9; Legge, *The Chinese Classics*, 1:255.

Zhang proceeds to a detailed discussion of the ancient pattern and how it may be conformed to in the present. Then he returns to the political implications of this system.

In the case of those families that had formerly held much landed property, though their land is turned over to the people, it is not the same as sharecropping or tenancy. Their income may thereby be somewhat reduced, yet they will be made land officials and placed in charge of the people. Once this idea is made clear to them, they will follow along. Even if a few should be unwilling, nevertheless a great majority will be pleased with it and only a minority displeased. Besides, how can you possibly take into consideration the feelings of every single individual?

At first we will merely distribute public land to the people, but after ten or twelve years other measures will have to be taken. To start with, land officials will be appointed [as explained], but later men should be selected for their personal merits. . . . Thus the well-fields may be seen to lead to a restoration of enfeoffment. For this a determination must be made of the merits of those to be enfeoffed, for only if there are persons of great merit and virtue can we set up the enfeoffment system. . . . Now, since we cannot yet propose the adoption of such a system, much the same thing can be accomplished by appointing lifetime local administrators.

The reason an enfeoffment system must be established is that the administration of the empire must be simplified through delegation of power before things can be well managed. If administration is not simplified [through decentralization], then it is impossible to govern well. Therefore the sages were certain to share the management of the empire with other men. It was thus that everything was well administered in their times. . . .

If we adopt an enfeoffment system, and one of the lords proves unworthy, he can still be removed and no harm will come of it. How could it be that with the might of a whole empire we could not discipline the ruler of a small state and keep the lords from conspiring to disturb the peace of the land? Of course, only if the court is powerful can peace and order be preserved in this way.

Still, in more recent times there have been those [e.g., Liu Zongyuan] who declared that for the Qin empire not to have maintained a feudal system was the wisest policy. They have just not understood what the sages had in mind!

[From *Zhangzi quanshu* (GXJC) 4:83–86 — dB]

SU XUN: THE LAND SYSTEM — A DISSENTING VIEW

Su Xun (1009–1066) was the father of two famous scholar-statesmen, one of whom was the poet Su Dongpo. With the backing of Ouyang Xiu, he achieved fame himself as a writer and official without advancing through the regular civil service channels.

Widely admired for both the style and the sense of his essays, Su here takes up the land problem and attempts to refute two widely held theories: that the distress of the peasantry is attributable to excessive taxes and that the well-field system should be restored. The essay opens with a discussion (abridged here) of tax rates under the Zhou dynasty, which were usually considered to represent the norm. Su's essay was later taken to be one of the key position papers in the continuing debate over well-fields.

At the height of the Zhou dynasty the heaviest taxes ran to as much as one part in four, the next heaviest to one part in five, and then on down to rates as low as one part in ten or below. Taxes today, though never as low as one part in ten, likewise do not exceed one part in four or one in five, provided that the local magistrate is not rapacious and grasping. Thus there is not a great difference in the rate of taxation between Zhou times and our own. . . .

During the Zhou dynasty, however, the people of the empire sang, danced, and rejoiced in the benevolence of their rulers, whereas our people are unhappy, as if they were extracting their very muscles and peeling off their very skins to meet the needs of the state. The Zhou tax was so much, and our tax is likewise so much. Why, then, is there such a great difference between the people's sadness today and their happiness then? There must be a reason for this.

During Zhou times, the well-field system was employed. Since the well-field system was abolished, the land no longer belongs to the cultivators, and those who own the land do not cultivate. Those who do cultivate depend for their land upon the rich people. The rich families possess much land and extensive properties; the paths linking their fields run on and on. They call in the migratory workers and assign each a piece of their land to till, whipping and driving them to work and treating them as slaves. Sitting there comfortably, they look around, give commands, and demand services. In the summer the people hoe for them; in the fall they harvest for them. No one disobeys their commands. . . .

Alas, the poor cultivate and yet are not free from hunger. The rich sit with full stomachs and amuse themselves and yet are not free from resentment over taxes. All these evils arise from the abolition of the well-fields. If the well-fields were restored, the poor would have land to till, and not having to share their grain and rice with the rich, they would be free from hunger. The rich, not being allowed to hold so much land, could not hold down the poor. . . . For this reason all the scholars of the empire outdo themselves calling for the restoration of the well-fields. And some people say, "If the land of the rich were taken away and given to those who own no land, the rich would not acquiesce in it, and this would lead to rebellion. But after such a great cataclysm, when the people were decimated and vast lands lay unused, it would be propitious for instituting the well-field system all at once. . . ."

I do not agree with any of this. Now even if all the rich people offered to turn their lands over to the public, asking that they be turned into well-fields, it still could not be done. Why?

Su Xun proceeds to describe in detail the system of land organization, irrigation, and local administration associated with the well-field system as it is set forth in the Rites of Zhou. *He concludes that such an intricate system could never be reproduced under existing conditions.*

When the well-fields are established, [a corresponding system of] ditches and canals [will] have to be provided. . . . This could not be done without filling up all the ravines and valleys, leveling the hills and mountains, destroying the graves, tearing down the houses, removing the cities, and changing the boundaries of the land. Even if it were possible to get possession of all the plains and vast wildernesses and then lay them out according to plan, still we would have to drive all the people of the empire, exhaust all the grain of the empire, and devote all our energy to this alone for several hundred years, without attending to anything else, if we were ever to see all the land of the empire turned into well-fields and provided with ditches and canals. Then it would be necessary to build houses within the well-fields for the people to settle down and live in peace. Alas, this is out of the question. . . .

Now if there were something approximating the well-field [system] that could be adopted, we might still be able to relieve the distress of the people.

At this point Su reviews the proposals made in the Han dynasty for a direct limitation of land ownership and the reasons for their failure.

I want to limit somewhat the amount of land that one is allowed to hold, and yet not restrict immediately those whose land is already in excess of my limit, but only make it so that future generations would not try to occupy land beyond that limit. In short, either the descendants of the rich would be unable to preserve their holdings after several generations and would become poor, while the land held in excess of my limit would be dispersed and come into the possession of others, or else, as the descendants of the rich came along, they would divide up the land into several portions. In this way, the land occupied by the rich would decrease and the surplus land would increase. With surplus land in abundance, the poor would find it easy to acquire land as a basis for their family livelihood. They would not have to render service to others, but each would reap the full fruit of the land himself. Not having to share his produce with others, he would be pleased to contribute taxes to the government. Now just by sitting at court and promulgating the order throughout the empire, without frightening the people, without mobilizing the public, without adopting the well-field system, still all the advantages of the well-fields would be obtained. Even with the well-fields of the Zhou, how could we hope to do better than this?

[From *Jiayouji* (SBCK) 5:7a–9a — dB]

THE NEW LAWS OF WANG ANSHI

The reform movement that marked time after Fan Zhongyan's fall from power reached its greatest heights during the reign of the Emperor Shenzong (r. 1068–1085) under the leadership of Wang Anshi (1021–1086), one of China's most celebrated statesmen. With the sympathetic understanding and patient support of Shenzong, who was widely acclaimed for his conscientiousness as a ruler, Wang embarked on a most ambitious and systematic program of reform, designed to remedy the evils already described in the memorials and essays of his Confucian contemporaries. A brilliant scholar and a vigorous administrator, Wang had close ties both officially and intellectually to the leading figures in the Confucian revival, and he burned with a desire to achieve the restoration of the ancient order that they believed to be the only solution to China's ills. This came out in Wang's first interview with the emperor in 1068, when the latter asked what Wang thought of the famous founder of the Tang dynasty as a model for later rulers. Wang replied: "Your Majesty should take [the sage kings] Yao and Shun as your standard. The principles of Yao and Shun are very easy to put into practice. It is only because scholars of recent times do not really understand them that they think such standards of government are unattainable."

Wang, as a matter of fact, had no thought of completely revamping Chinese society and restoring the institutions described in the classical texts. As the first of the readings to follow makes clear, his aim was rather to adapt the general principles embodied in those institutions to his own situation, making due allowance for vastly changed circumstances. Furthermore, from the manner in which he set about his reforms, we can see that he was no social revolutionary or utopian theorist but, rather, a practical statesman whose first concern was always the interests of the Chinese state and only secondarily the welfare of the Chinese people. Thus his initial reforms were aimed at the reorganization of state finances, with a view to achieving greater economy and budgetary efficiency. And virtually all of the important economic changes later effected by Wang were proposed by a special "brain trust" assigned to the task of fiscal reorganization, with state revenue very much in the forefront of their minds. Nevertheless, it is to the credit of Wang that he saw what few Chinese statesmen or emperors were willing to consider: that in the long run the fiscal interests of the state were bound up with the general economic welfare of the people, and both with the promotion of a dynamic and expanding economy. Therefore, even though he did nothing so drastic as the reorganization of Chinese agriculture into well-fields, his approach was bold and visionary in the sense that he saw the problem of reform as reaching into virtually all spheres of Chinese life; and, though few of his measures were new or highly original, his program taken as a whole was broader in scope and more diversified in character than anything attempted before or after — until Communist rule.

The first of Wang's New Laws (or Measures) (*xinfa*) aimed at achieving greater flexibility and economy in the transportation of tax grain or tribute in kind to the capital. His basic principle was that officials be enabled to resell the goods collected and use funds at their disposal to procure at the most convenient time and place (and with the least transportation cost) the goods required by the government. This was later expanded greatly into a vast state marketing operation that extended to all basic commodities the type of price control and storage system traditionally associated with the "Ever-Normal Granary." In this way the state's assumption of a much more active role in the economy was justified by the common interest of the state and the people in reducing the cost of government and stabilizing prices.

So, too, with the second of Wang's measures, a system of crop loans to provide peasants in the spring with necessary seed, implements, and so on, which would be repaid at harvest time. It was designed, on the one hand, to help the peasant stay out of the clutches of usurers at a difficult time of the year, while on the other hand, it brought revenue to the government through the interest paid on the loans.

Besides the sphere that would be recognized as pertaining to government finance, there were two other activities of the state that vitally affected both the physical well-being of the people and the health of the state. These had to do with the time-honored "right" or "power" of the government to demand from the people both labor service and military service. In the Song, Chinese armies were maintained on a professional basis, with tax revenues providing the means for hiring constabulary and soldiery. To eliminate the great expense of such mercenaries, who were idle much of the time, Wang introduced a militia system whereby each locality would be organized for self-defense and self-policing, with families grouped pyramidally in units of ten, a hundred, and a thousand, taking a regular turn at providing such able-bodied service. This represented not only a system of collective security in each locality but one of collective responsibility as well, the various members of each group being held mutually responsible for the misconduct of any individual. Curiously enough, to achieve the same ends of economy and efficiency in the handling of local government services, Wang used precisely the reverse method. That is, the minor functions of government, which were sometimes menial and often burdensome, had always been performed on an unpaid, draft basis. Wang considered this a system that weighed too heavily on the individuals and households to whom the assignment fell. In place of the draft services, which were essentially a labor tax, he therefore substituted a money tax graduated to "soak the rich," and from the proceeds of that tax men were hired to perform these official services.

The same principle of equalization was applied to the land tax through a new system of land registration and assessment, which was designed to accomplish the same aim as the legendary "well-field" system without any actual redistribution of land or property. This was known as the "square-fields" system, because all taxable land was divided up into units one *li* square, upon which the taxes were graduated in accordance with the value of the land, so that those with less productive land paid proportionately less.

The foregoing examples will serve to indicate the general character and scope of the *New Laws* having an economic importance. In addition, Wang embarked on a fundamental overhauling of the civil service examination system, which in the early Song had come in for much criticism from Confucians who deplored the premium it placed on literary style and memorization of the classics at the expense of a genuine understanding of Confucian principles and their practical application. In place of the traditional forms of composition and memory testing, Wang substituted an essay on the "general meaning" of the classics. This raised problems, however, as to how traditional standards of objectivity and impartiality could be maintained in judging the performance of candidates with respect to the handling of ideas and interpretation. Wang solved this in his own way by promulgating a standard essay form and a revision of the classics with modernized commentary to serve as an authoritative guide for both candidates and judges.

Almost immediately controversy developed over Wang's interpretations of the classics, which were closely bound up with his whole political philosophy and governmental program. Whether or not Wang's policies were truly in keeping with the basic teachings of the Confucian tradition is a question that has been debated right down to modern times. There can be no doubt that the New Laws or systems that he adopted bore a strong resemblance to Legalist-inspired institutions that had vastly augmented the economic power of the state during the reign of Emperor Wu of Han. It is equally evident, however, that the benevolent paternalism ascribed by Confucians to the ancient sage kings could be easily construed, as it was by Wang, to justify a vigorous exercise of state power to promote the general welfare. Wang's memorials are replete with classical precedents for each of the actions he proposes to take. Perhaps nowhere is the close tie between Wang's reforms and classical authority better illustrated than in his use of the *Rites of Zhou*, which he revised under the title *New Interpretation of the Institutes of Zhou* (*Zhouguan xinyi*). For this classical text Wang made the strongest claims in his personal preface:

> When moral principles are applied to the affairs of government . . . the form they take and the use they are put to depend upon laws, but their promotion and execution depend upon individuals. In the worthiness of its individual officials to discharge the duties of office, and in the effectiveness with which its institutions administered the law, no dynasty has surpassed the early Zhou. Likewise, in the suitability of its laws for per-

petuation in later ages, and in the expression given them in literary form, no book is so perfect as the *Institutes of Zhou* (*Zhouguan*).

So effectively did Wang use this book to justify his reforms that his edition of it became one of the most influential and controversial books in all Chinese literature. To deny Wang the support he derived from it, his opponents alleged that the *Institutes of Zhou* was itself a comparatively recent forgery. In later times writers commonly attributed the fall of the Northern Song dynasty to Wang's adoption of this text as a political guide.

Thus Wang's espousal of the *Institutes of Zhou* represents the culmination in the political sphere of the long debate in Confucian circles over the applicability of classical institutions, as described in the books of rites, to conditions obtaining in the Song dynasty. At the same time Wang's effort to reinterpret these texts — to discard the Han and Tang commentaries — and to use a modernized version as the basis for a reformed civil service examination system, stressing the general meaning of the classics instead of a literal knowledge of them, is a concrete expression of the Confucian urge to break with the scholarship of the Han and Tang dynasties, both in the field of classical scholarship and in the form of civil service examinations, in order to return to the essential purity of the classic order. In this respect Wang stands together with the Cheng brothers, Zhu Xi, and a host of other Song scholars in their determination to set aside accepted interpretations and find new meaning in their Confucian inheritance, just as subsequent scholars of a more critical temper would someday reject the Song interpretations and press anew their inquiry into the meaning and validity of the classics.

WANG ANSHI: MEMORIAL TO EMPEROR RENZONG (1058)

This document, sometimes called the Ten Thousand Word Memorial, is famous as Wang's first important declaration of his political views. Those who look to it for a manifesto outlining his later program will be disappointed, for aside from his general philosophy it deals only with the problem of recruiting able officials. Those who recognize, however, that in China any reformer had to wrestle first of all with the intractable bureaucracy will appreciate why Wang, like many other Song reformers, should have given first priority to this question. Subsequent readings, including the protests of Wang's critics, will show that in the final analysis this remained the most crucial issue.

Note how Wang strikes a balance between the importance of laws and systems (the Legalist tendency) and the Confucian view that good government depends ultimately on men of character and ability, unhampered by legalistic restrictions. Observe also his final insistence that the accomplishment of needed reform may justify coercive measures.

Your servant observes that Your Majesty possesses the virtues of reverence and frugality and is endowed with wisdom and sagacity. Rising early in the morning and retiring late in the evening, Your Majesty does not relax for even a single day. Neither music, beautiful women, dogs, horses, sight-seeing, nor any of the other objects of pleasure distract or becloud your intelligence in the least. Your humanity toward men and love of all creatures pervade the land. Moreover, Your Majesty selects those whom the people of the empire would wish to have assisting Your Majesty, entrusts to them the affairs of state, and does not vacillate in the face of [opposition from] slanderous, wicked, traitorous, and cunning officials. Even the solicitude of the Two Emperors and Three Kings did not surpass this. We should expect, therefore, that the needs of every household and man would be filled and that the empire would enjoy a state of perfect order. And yet this result has not been attained. Within the empire the security of the state is a cause for some anxiety, and on our borders there is the constant threat of the barbarians. Day by day the resources of the nation become more depleted and exhausted, while the moral tone and habits of life among the people daily deteriorate. On all sides officials who have the interests of the state at heart are fearful that the peace of the empire may not last. What is the reason for this?

The cause of the distress is that we ignore the law. Now the government is strict in enforcing the law, and its statutes are complete to the last detail. Why then does your servant consider that there is an absence of law? It is because most of the present body of law does not accord with the government of the ancient kings. Mencius says, "Though he may have a humane heart and a reputation for humaneness, one from whom the people receive no benefits will not serve as a model for later generations because he does not practice the Way of the former kings."[15] The application of what Mencius said to our own failure in the present is obvious.

Now our own age is far removed from that of the ancient kings, and the changes and circumstances with which we are confronted are not the same. Even the most ignorant can see that it would be difficult to put into practice every single item in the government of the ancient kings. But when your servant says that our present failures arise from the fact that we do not adopt the governmental system of the ancient kings, he is merely suggesting that we should follow their general intent. Now the Two Emperors were separated from the Three Kings by more than a thousand years. There were periods of order and disorder, and there were periods of prosperity and decay. Each of them likewise encountered different changes and faced different circumstances, and each differed also in the way he set up his government. Yet they never differed as to their underlying aims in the government of the empire, the state, and the family, nor in their sense of the relative importance and priority of things [as set forth

---

15. *Mencius* 4A:1.

in the *Great Learning*, chapter 1]. Therefore, your servant contends that we should follow only their general intent. If we follow their intent, then the changes and reforms introduced by us would not startle the ears and shock the eyes of the people, nor cause them to murmur. And yet our government would be in accord with that of the ancient kings. [1a–2a]

The most urgent need of the present time is to secure capable men. Only when we can produce a large number of capable men in the empire will it be possible to select a sufficient number of persons qualified to serve in the government. And only when we get capable men in the government will there be no difficulty in assessing what may be done, in view of the time and circumstances, and in consideration of the human distress that may be occasioned, gradually to change the decadent laws of the empire in order to approach the ideas of the ancient kings. The empire today is the same as the empire of the ancient kings. There were numerous capable men in their times. Why is there a dearth of such men today? It is because, as has been said, we do not train and cultivate men in the proper way. [3a]

In ancient times, the Son of Heaven and feudal lords had schools ranging from the capital down to the districts and villages. Officers of instruction were widely appointed, but selected with the greatest care. The affairs of the court, rites and music, punishment and correction were all subjects that found a place in the schools. What the students observed and learned were the sayings, the virtuous acts, and the ideas underlying the government of the empire and the states. Men not qualified to govern the empire and the states would not be given an education, while those who could be so used in government never failed to receive an education. This is the way to conduct the training of men. [4a]

What is the way to select officials? The ancient kings selected men only from the local villages and through the local schools. The people were asked to recommend those they considered virtuous and able, sending up their nominations to the court, which investigated each one. Only if the men recommended proved truly virtuous and able would they be appointed to official posts commensurate with their individual virtue and ability. Investigation of them did not mean that a ruler relied only upon his own keenness of sight and hearing or that he took the word of one man alone. . . . Having inquired into his actions and utterances, they then tested him in government affairs. What was meant by "investigation" was just that — to test them in government affairs. . . . [But] it is not possible for the ruler to investigate each case personally, nor can he entrust this matter to any other individual, expecting that in a day or two he could inquire into and test their conduct and abilities and recommend their employment or dismissal. When we have investigated those whose conduct and ability are of the highest level, and have appointed them to high office, we should ask them in turn to select men of the same type, try them out for a time and test them, and then make recommendations to the ruler, whereupon ranks and salaries would be granted to them. This is the way to conduct the selection of officials. [5a–b]

[In ancient times] officials were selected with great care, appointed to posts that suited their qualifications, and kept in office for a reasonable length of time. And once employed, they were given sufficient authority for the discharge of their duties. They were not hampered and bound by one regulation or another but were allowed to carry out their own ideas. It was by this method that Yao and Shun regulated the hundred offices of government and inspired the various officials. [6a–b]

Today, although we have schools in each prefecture and district, they amount to no more than school buildings. There are no officers of instruction and guidance; nothing is done to train and develop human talent. Only in the Imperial Academy are officers of instruction and guidance to be found, and even they are not selected with care. The affairs of the court, rites and music, punishment and correction have no place in the schools, and the students pay no attention to them, considering that rites and music, punishment and correction are the business of officials, not something they ought to know about. What is taught to the students consists merely of textual exegesis [of the classics].

That, however, was not the way men were taught in ancient times. In recent years, teaching has been based on the essays required for the civil service examinations, but this kind of essay cannot be learned without resorting to extensive memorization and strenuous study, upon which students must spend their efforts the whole day long. Such proficiency as they attain is at best of no use in the government of the empire, and at most the empire can make no use of them. . . . [6b–7a]

[Of old] . . . those scholars who had learned the way of the ancient kings and whose behavior and character had won the approval of their village communities were the ones entrusted with the duty of guarding the frontiers and the palace in accordance with their respective abilities. . . . Today this most important responsibility in the empire . . . is given to those corrupt, ruthless, and unreliable men whose ability and behavior are not such that they can maintain themselves in their local villages. . . . But as long as military training is not given, and men of a higher type are not selected for military service, there is no wonder that scholars regard the carrying of weapons as a disgrace and that none of them is able to ride, or shoot, or has any familiarity with military maneuvers. This is because education is not conducted in the proper way. [8a–9b]

In the present system for selecting officials, those who memorize assiduously, recite extensively, and have some knowledge of literary composition are called "splendid talents of extraordinary accomplishment" or "men of virtue, wise, square, and upright." These are the categories from which the ministers of state are chosen. Those whose memories are not so strongly developed and [who] cannot recite so extensively, yet have some knowledge of literary composition and have also studied poetry in the *shi* and *fu* forms, are called "advanced scholars" (*jinshi*). The highest of these are also selected as ministers of state. It can be seen without any question that the skills and knowledge acquired by men in these two categories do not fit them to serve as ministers. . . . [11b]

In addition, candidates are examined in such fields as the Nine Classics, the Five Classics, specialization [in one classic], and the study of law. The court has already become concerned over the uselessness of this type of knowledge and has stressed the need for an understanding of general principles [as set forth in the classics]. . . . When we consider the men selected through "understanding of the classics," however, it is still those who memorize, recite, and have some knowledge of literary composition who are able to pass the examination, while those who can apply them [the classics] to the government of the empire are not always brought in through this kind of selection. [12b]

It has already been made clear that officials are not selected with care, employed in accordance with their competence, and kept in office long enough. But, in addition, when entrusted with office, they are not given sufficient authority to fulfill their duties, but find their hands tied by this law or that regulation so that they are unable to carry out their own ideas. . . . Nevertheless, there has not been a single case in history . . . that shows that it is possible to obtain good government merely by relying on the effectiveness of law without regard to having the right man in power. On the other hand, there has not been a single case in history, from ancient times to the present, that shows that it is possible to obtain good government even with the right man in power if he is bound by one regulation or another in such a way that he cannot carry out his ideas. [14a–b]

Your servant also observes that in former times when the court thought of doing something and introducing some reforms, the advantages and disadvantages were considered carefully at the beginning. But whenever some vulgar opportunist took a dislike to the reform and opposed it, the court stopped short and dared not carry it out. . . . Since it was difficult to set up laws and institutions, and since the men seeking personal advantages were unwilling to accept these measures and comply with them, the ancients who intended to do something had to resort to punishment. Only then could their ideas be carried out. [17a]

Now the early kings, wishing to set up laws and institutions in order to change corrupt customs and obtain capable men, overcame their feeling of reluctance to mete out punishment, for they saw that there was no other way of carrying out their policy. [17b]

[From *Linchuan xiansheng wenji* (*SBCK*) 39:1a–19a — dB]

MEMORIAL ON THE CROP LOANS MEASURE

This memorial submitted to the Emperor Shenzong in 1069 calls for the extension to other parts of China of a system of crop loans already experimented with on a limited basis in Shaanxi province. For this purpose Wang proposes to draw upon the reserves of the government granaries, which he insists would still be able to fulfill their function of stabilizing agricultural prices and storing grain despite the diversion of funds for lending purposes. The memorial is somewhat vague in its wording, and the precise details of the operation of this system are unclear, perhaps because Wang assumed a familiarity with the existing system on the part of those he addressed.

In the second year of Xining (1069), the Commission to Coordinate Fiscal Administration presented a memorial as follows:

The cash and grain stored in the Ever-Normal and the Liberal-Charity granaries of the various circuits, counting roughly in strings of cash and bushels of grain, amount to more than 15 million. Their collection and distribution are not handled properly, however, and therefore we do not derive full benefit from them. Now we propose that the present amount of grain in storage should be sold at a price lower than the market price when the latter is high and that when the market price is low, the grain in the market should be purchased at a rate higher than the market price. We also propose that our reserves be made interchangeable with the proceeds of the land tax and the cash and grain held by the fiscal intendants, so that conversion of cash and grain may be permitted whenever convenient.

With the cash at hand, we propose to follow the example set by the crop loan system in Shaanxi province. Farmers desirous of borrowing money before the harvest should be granted loans, to be repaid at the same time as they pay their tax, half with the summer payment and half with the autumn payment.[16] They are free to repay either in kind or in cash, should they prefer to do so if the price of grain is high at the time of repayment. In the event that disaster strikes, they should be allowed to defer payment until the date when the next harvest payment would be due. In this way not only would we be prepared to meet the distress of famine but since the people would receive loans from the government, it would be impossible for the monopolistic houses[17] to exploit the gap between harvests by charging interest at twice the normal rate.

Under the system of Ever-Normal and Liberal-Charity Granaries, it has been the practice to keep the grain in storage and sell it only when the harvest is poor and the price of grain is high. Those who benefit from this are only the idle people in the cities.

Now we propose to survey the situation in regard to surpluses and shortages in each circuit as a whole, to sell when grain is dear and buy when it is cheap, in order to increase the accumulation in government storage and to stabilize

---

16. Interest of 2 percent per month (24 percent per annum) was to be charged for the loans. Private moneylenders generally charged more.

17. This refers to usurers who seek to monopolize wealth in the form of money, goods, or land, but not to industrial monopolists in the modern sense.

the prices of commodities. This will make it possible for the farmers to go ahead with their work at the proper season, while the monopolists will no longer be able to take advantage of their temporary stringency. All this is proposed in the interests of the people, and the government derives no advantage therefrom. Moreover, it accords with the idea of the ancient kings, who bestowed blessings upon all impartially and promoted whatever was of benefit by way of encouraging the cultivation and accumulation of grain.

This proposal was adopted by the emperor and put into effect first in the limited areas of Hebei, Jingtong, and Huainan, as suggested by the Commission to Coordinate Fiscal Administration. The results obtained were later considered to justify extension of the system to other areas.

[From *Songshi* 176:17b–18b — dB]

CHENG HAO: REMONSTRANCE AGAINST THE NEW LAWS

This memorial by Cheng Hao, who was originally a supporter of Wang Anshi, is directed primarily against the crop loan system. Cheng contends that the system is generally unpopular and that force is required to compel repayment. It is difficult to determine, however, just what segment of the populace Cheng presumes to speak for — the peasantry as a whole or only an influential, articulate minority. There is no evidence of any widespread discontent or violence in opposition to Wang, but it is possible that the administration of the system was quite uneven and that certain areas may have been adversely affected. Though the interest charges were less than those of private moneylenders, at 20 to 24 percent per annum they were substantial enough that an extensive program might be turned by venal officials into a highly lucrative business.

Recently, your servant has presented repeated memorials asking for the abolition of the advancing of crop loans at interest[18] and abolition of the [Economic] Administrators.[19] Day and night [your servant] waits expectantly, and yet Your Majesty still has not acted upon them. . . .

Now whether the state is secure or insecure depends upon the feelings of the people; whether there is order or disorder hinges upon how things are handled at the start. If great numbers of people are opposed, then whatever one may say, one will not be believed; but if all the people are of one accord, then whatever one does will certainly succeed. . . .

Your servant considers that Your Majesty already sees clearly into the heart of the matter and fully realizes what is right and what wrong. The mind of Your

---

18. The text is vague here, referring only to "advance allocations."

19. Administering the various economic activities of the government, such as the Ever-Normal Granaries, the salt and iron monopolies, and so on.

Majesty does not hesitate to make a change; it is only the minister in charge of the government who still persists in his obstinacy. Thus the people's feelings are greatly agitated and public opinion becomes more clamorous. If one insists on carrying these policies out, certain failure awaits them in the end. . . . Rather than pursue one mistaken policy at the expense of a hundred other undertakings, would it not be better to bestow a grand favor and reassure the people's minds by doing away with the disturbances caused by those sent out to enforce these decrees and by manifesting your humanity to the extent of abolishing the interest charged on crop loans? Moreover, when the system of buying and selling grain is put back into effect,[20] our accumulated reserve will expand. The government will then be without fault in its administration, and public opinion will have no cause to be aroused.

[From *Mingdao wenji* (SBBY) 2:4b–5a — dB]

WANG ANSHI: IN DEFENSE OF FIVE MAJOR POLICIES

In this memorial Wang reaffirms the correctness of his principal policies, while conceding that in three cases much will depend on the effectiveness with which the officials concerned administer them.

During the five years that Your Majesty has been on the throne, a great number of changes and reforms have been proposed. Many of them have been set forth in documents, enacted into law, and have produced great benefits. Yet among these measures there are five of the greatest importance, the results of which will only be felt in the course of time and which, nevertheless, have already occasioned a great deal of discussion and debate: (1) the pacification of the Rong [Tangut] barbarians, (2) the crop loans, (3) the local service exemption, (4) the collective security [militia], (5) the marketing controls.

Now the region of Jingtang and the Tiao River [in the northwest] extends more than three thousand *li* and the Rong tribes number two hundred thousand people. They have surrendered their territories and become submissive subjects of the empire. Thus our policy of pacifying the Rong barbarians has proved successful.

In former times the poor people paid interest on loans obtained from powerful persons. Now the poor get loans from the government at a lower rate of interest, and the people are thereby saved from poverty. Thus our policy on agricultural loans has worked in practice.

It is only with regard to the service exemption, the militia, and the marketing controls that a question exists as to whether great benefit or harm may be done.

---

20. That is, when the reserves of the Ever-Normal Granaries are used for price-support operations rather than being committed to the lending program.

If we are able to secure the right type of man to administer these acts, great benefits will be obtained, but if they are administered by the wrong type of man, great harm will be done. Again, if we try to enforce them gradually, great benefits will be obtained, but if they are carried out in too great haste, great harm will be done.

The *Commentary* says, "Things not modeled after the ancient system have never been known to last for a generation." Of these three measures mentioned above, it may be said that they are all modeled after the ancient system. However, one can put the ancient system into practice only when he understands the Way of the ancients. This is what your servant means about great advantages and disadvantages.

The service exemption system is derived from the *Institutes of Zhou* [i.e., the *Rites of Zhou*], in which the *fu, shi, xu,* and *du* are mentioned. They are what the King's System [section of the *Record of Rites*] describes as "the common people who render services to the government."

However, the people of the nine provinces vary in wealth, and the customs of the various regions are not the same. The classifications used in the government registration [for local service] are not satisfactory for all. Now we want to change it forthwith, having officials examine every household so that they will be assessed on an equitable basis and requiring the people to pay for the hiring of men for all kinds of local services, so that the farmers can be released and return to their farms. If, however, we fail to secure the right kind of person for the administration of this measure, the classification of people into five grades [in proportion to their financial status] is bound to be unfair, and the hiring of men to perform services would not be executed in an equitable manner.

The militia act had its origin in the *qiujia*[21] system of the Three Dynasties, which was adopted by Guan Zhong in Qi, Zichan in Zheng, and Lord Shang in Qin, and was proposed by Zhong Zhangtong to the Han ruler. This is not just a recent innovation. For hundreds and thousands of years, however, the people of the empire have been free to live together or to disperse and go in all directions as they chose, not subject to any restriction. Now we want to change it forthwith, organizing the people into units of fives and tens and attaching one village to another. Unlawful activities would thus be kept under observation while humaneness would be manifested to all; the soldiers would be housed in their own homes and ready for any use. If, however, we fail to secure the right kind of person to administer this measure, the people will be alarmed by summonses and frightened by mobilization, and thus the people's confidence will be lost.

---

21. A system under which units of 128 families each provided men and weapons for military service.

The marketing controls originated with the Supervision of the Market in the Zhou dynasty and the Price Stabilization and Equalization System of the Han dynasty. Now with a fund of one million cash we regulate the prices of commodities in order to facilitate the exchange of goods and also lend the people money on which they pay the government an interest of several tens of thousands of cash annually. We are, however, aware of the fact that commodities and money do not circulate very well in the empire. It is feared that officials eager for personal fame and rewards will seek to achieve speedy results within a year's time, and thus the system will be subverted.

Therefore, your servant considers that the above three measures, if administered by the right kind of person and put into effect with due deliberation, will bring great benefits, whereas, if administered by the wrong men and put into effect with too great haste, they may do great harm.

Thus, if we succeed in carrying out the Service Exemption Law, the seasonal agricultural work of the farmers will not be disturbed and the manpower requirements [of the state] will be borne equally by the people. If the Militia Law is carried out, the disturbances caused by bandits will be brought to an end and our military power will be strengthened. If we succeed in carrying out the Marketing Control Law, goods and money will be circulated and the financial needs of the state will be met.

[From *Linchuan xiansheng wenji* (SBCK) 41:4a–5a —dB]

OPPOSITION TO THE NEW LAWS OF WANG ANSHI

SU SHI: MEMORIAL TO EMPEROR SHENZONG

Su Shi (1037–1101), also known by his pen name Su Dongpo, was one of two famous sons of a famous father, Su Xun. An outstanding poet, calligrapher, and painter as well as a public official, Su Shi was initially sympathetic to the aims of Wang Anshi but was subsequently driven from court because of his outspoken opposition to the New Laws. In this eloquent memorial, which suggests something of his famous prose style, Su criticizes especially the new labor service, crop loan, and state marketing systems. Note his complaint that Wang's original proposal concerning the marketing system seemed to have been deliberately vague and seemingly innocuous, as if to hide Wang's real intentions.

What a ruler has to rely upon is only the human heart. Human hearts are to the ruler what roots are to a tree, what oil is to a lamp, water to fish, fields to a farmer, or money to a merchant.

Now Your Majesty knows that the hearts of the people are not happy. Men, whether within the court or outside, whether worthy or unworthy, all say that from the founding of the dynasty to the present, the fiscal administration of the empire has been entrusted solely to the commissioner, assistant commissioners, and the supervisors of the Finance Commission, who for more than one hundred years have left no matter untended. Now, for no cause, another commission has been set up in the name of "Coordinating the Policies of the Three Fiscal Offices."[22] Six or seven young men are made to discuss fiscal policies day and night within the bureau, while more than forty aides are sent out to explore this situation. The vast scale of their initial operations has made people frightened and suspicious; the strangeness of the New Laws adopted has made officials fearful and puzzled. Worthy men seek for an explanation, and failing to get any, cannot relieve their anxiety; small men simply conjecture as to what is going on at court and give voice to slander, saying that Your Majesty, as the master of a hundred thousand chariots [i.e., of a large empire and army] is interested in personal profit and [that] the official in charge of the government administration, as the chancellor of the Son of Heaven, is concerned with controlling wealth. Business is at a standstill and the prices of goods have been rising. . . . [3b–4a]

Now the Commission to Coordinate Fiscal Administration has the reputation of seeking for profit, while the six or seven young men and their forty or more aides are instruments for the pursuit of profit. . . . The man who plunges into the forest with a pack of hunting dogs and then protests, "I am not hunting," would do better to get rid of the hunting dogs, and then the animals will not be so frightened. . . . Therefore your servant considers that in order to expunge the slander, to call forth harmonious feelings, to restore public confidence, and put the nation at rest, nothing better could be done than to abolish the Commission to Coordinate Fiscal Administration. . . . [4b]

Since ancient times men drafted from the households in each district have always had to be used for local services. . . . Now some people have heard that in the region of Zhejiang and Jiangsu, a few prefectures hire men to perform these services, and they want to extend this practice throughout the empire. This is like seeing the dates and chestnuts of Beijing and Shaanxi, or the taro root of Sichuan and then advocating that the five grains be done away with. How could that be made feasible? Besides, they want the proceeds from government factories to be used for the hiring of public storage and transport officers.[23] Although they are expected to render long-term service, they receive meager payment for their labors. Since they receive so little for such long service, from now on they may be expected gradually to fall away and go else-

---

22. The Office of Salt and Iron [Monopolies], the Office of Funds [Disbursements], and the Office of the Census [Revenue].

23. *Yajian* — a type of service involving responsibility for the storage and transportation of public goods or property. Considered extremely burdensome, this responsibility was previously assigned to and rotated among the more well-to-do families, who often tried to evade it.

where. How seriously this will affect the whole basis and functioning of local governments can well be imagined! [7b–8a]

Although in recent years, households in the rural districts have been allowed to hire men [to perform these services], nevertheless, if these hired men ran away, the households still had the responsibility [of replacing them]. Now in addition to the Twice-a-Year Tax, another tax item has been introduced, called the labor charge, which pays for the government's hiring of men. Thus the government has taken upon itself the responsibility for the hiring of men. Since Yang Yan (727–781) in the Tang dynasty abolished the system of [land] taxes in grain, labor taxes [on able-bodied men], and the cloth exaction [on households] and replaced it with the Twice-a-Year Tax,[24] the sum of all taxes collected in the fourteenth year of Dali (779) was used as the basis for determining the rate of the Twice-a-Year Tax. Thus the land, labor, and cloth taxes were all combined in the Twice-a-Year Tax. Yet now, while the Twice-a-Year Tax is kept as before, how can a labor tax again be demanded? When a sage introduces a law, he always takes thousands of generations into consideration. How can we add another item to the regular taxes? [8b–9a]

Households of which a female is head and those with only a single male are the most unfortunate of all-under-Heaven. The first concern of the ancient kings was to show them compassion; and yet now the first concern of Your Majesty is to make them [pay for] local services. These are the households in which the family line will be discontinued when its present members die or those in which the only male is still too young. If several years were allowed the latter, he would become an adult, render service, grow old and die, and have his property confiscated by the government [since there is no one to inherit it]. How can a ruler, so rich as to possess all within the four seas, have the hardness of heart not to take pity on such persons? [9b]

There has long been a prohibition against the practice of crop loans. Now Your Majesty has inaugurated the system and made it a regular practice year after year. Although it is declared that there shall be no compulsion to make people take the loans, nevertheless after several generations, if there should be oppressive rulers and corrupt officials, can Your Majesty guarantee that there will be no compulsion? . . . [10a]

Even if the regulations are strictly enforced and there is really no compulsion, those people and households who would willingly apply for it must be the poor and the families in need, for if they had any surplus of their own, why would they come and do business with the government? But when the [poor] people are whipped and pressed to the extreme, they will run away, and when they have run away, their debts to the government will be apportioned among their neighbors, who are collectively responsible. . . .

---

24. See ch. 18.

Of all such measures the Ever-Normal Granary may be considered the best. It is modest in what it seeks to preserve and yet far-reaching in its effects. Suppose a county of ten thousand households has only one thousand bushels of grain in storage. When the price of grain is high, if the one thousand bushels are put on the market, the prices of goods are kept stable. When the price of goods in the market is kept stable, there is a sufficiency of food in the land. There is no hoarding of grain by some while others beg for food, no pursuing and pressing by the headman of the village to make people pay back their loans. Now if the Ever-Normal Granary is converted to a crop loan fund, and one bushel of grain is lent to each household, then what will be done to relieve the hunger of all those besides the thousand households [so provided for]? Besides, there is always the fear that the government funds of the Ever-Normal Granary will prove insufficient. If all the funds are used up to buy the grain, then none will be left for moneylending; if the fund is held for lending purposes, then very little grain will be bought. Thus we see that the Ever-Normal Granary and the crop loan system are by nature incompatible. . . . [10b–11a]

During the time of Emperor Wu of Han, the financial resources of the nation were exhausted, and the proposal of the merchant Sang Hongyang, to buy commodities when prices were cheap and sell them when prices were dear, was adopted. This was called Equal Distribution.[25] Thereupon business came to a standstill and banditry became widespread. This almost led to revolution. When Emperor Zhao ascended the throne, scholars all rose up in opposition to the theory [of Sang]. He Guang [the chief minister] heeded the desires of the people and granted their request that the system be abandoned. Then all-under-Heaven were reconciled to the throne and no further trouble arose. It is surprising to hear this kind of proposal raised again. When this law was first introduced, it sounded as if very little were involved. They said merely that goods bought cheaply here should be transferred elsewhere when prices were high, using supplies near at hand to ease scarcity afar. But offices and staffs have been set up all over, and a large amount of cash has been appropriated. The big and wealthy merchants have all become suspicious and dare not move. They believe that . . . the government never engages in the exchange of goods without competing with the merchants for profit. . . . Now for the government to buy such and such a commodity, it must first set up offices and staffs, so that the expense for clerical and fiscal services is considerable at the outset. If not of good quality, an item will not be bought; if not paid for in cash, an item cannot be purchased. Therefore the price paid by the government must be higher than that paid by the people. And when the government sells goods, it will still suffer the disadvantages mentioned before. How can the government get the same profit as the merchant? . . . [11a–12a]

---

25. A state marketing system covering all principal commodities. See ch. 11.

The preservation or loss of a state depends upon the depth or shallowness of its virtue, not upon its strength or weakness. . . . When a ruler knows this, he knows what is important and what is not important. Therefore the wise rulers of ancient times did not abandon virtue because the country was weak, nor did they permit social customs to suffer because the country was poor. [12b–13a]

[From *Jingjin Dongpo wenji shilue* (SBCK) 24:1a ff. — dB]

SIMA GUANG: A PETITION TO DO AWAY WITH THE MOST HARMFUL OF THE NEW LAWS

Sima Guang (1019–1086) was one of the giants among the scholar-statesmen of the Confucian revival in the eleventh century. He had already had a long and distinguished career in high office when he left the government in 1070 out of opposition to Wang Anshi's policies and subsequently devoted himself to writing his monumental general history of China. Following the death of Wang's patron, the Emperor Shenzong, Sima Guang served briefly as prime minister before his own death and was responsible for the abolition of many of Wang's reforms.

Your servant sees that the late emperor was sagacious and intelligent, did his utmost to govern well, and sought to employ an able man to assist him in achieving peace and order. This man was entrusted with the administration of government. His advice was acted upon, and his plans were followed. Nothing could ever come between them. . . . Unfortunately the one in whom he placed his trust was a man who largely failed to understand the feelings of men and the principles of things and who could not fulfill the expectations of his sage master. He was self-satisfied and opinionated, considering himself without equal among the men of the past and the present. He did not know how to select what was best in the laws and institutions of the imperial ancestors and to bring together the happiest proposals put forth throughout the empire, so as to guide the imperial intelligence and assist in accomplishing the great task. Instead he often adulterated the traditional regulations with his own ideas, which he termed "the New Laws (or Measures)." Whatever this man wanted to do could neither be held up by the ruler nor changed by the people. Those who agreed with him were given his help in rising to the sky, while those who differed with him were thrown out and cast down into the ditch. All he wanted was to satisfy his own ambitions, without regard to the best interests of the nation. . . .

The crop loans, the local service exemption, the marketing controls, the credit and loan system, and other measures were introduced. They aimed at the accumulation of wealth and pressed the people mercilessly. The distress they caused still makes for difficulties today. . . . Besides, officials who liked to create new schemes that they might take advantage of to advance themselves suggested setting up the collective security militia system (*baojia*), horse-raising system, and the horse-care system[26] as a means of providing for the military establishment. They changed the regulations governing the tea, salt, iron, and other monopolies and increased the taxes on family property, on [buildings] encroaching on the street,[27] on business and so forth, in order to meet military expenses. The result was to cause the people of the nine provinces to lose their livelihood and suffer extreme distress, as if they had been cast into hot water and fire. All this happened because the great body of officials were so eager to advance themselves. They misled the late emperor and saw to it that they themselves derived all the profit from these schemes while the emperor incurred all the resentment. . . .

Your servant has already pointed out that training and inspection of the militia involves a great expenditure of labor and money for both the government and the people, and yet the militia is of no real use in war. To pay money in lieu of local services is easy on the rich and hard on the poor, who must contribute to the support of idlers and vagrants [paid to perform these services]. It results in the peasantry losing their property and being reduced to utter misery, without recourse or appeal. The general commanderies now have absolute control over the army administration, while local civil officials have no authority whatever and no means of coping with emergencies. [47:9b]

The best plan now is to select and keep those New Laws that are of advantage to the people and of benefit to the state, while abolishing all those that are harmful to the people and hurtful to the state. This will let the people of the land know unmistakably that the court loves them with a paternal affection. . . . This worthy achievement will be crowned with glory, and there will be no end to the blessings it bestows. Would this not be splendid?

[From *Wenguo wenzheng Sima gong wenji (SBCK)* 46:5b–9b, 47:9b —dB]

ZHU XI: WANG ANSHI IN RETROSPECT

Though Wang's New Laws were largely abolished by Sima Guang, after the latter's demise political forces representing Wang's point of view recouped their strength and held power much of the time until the ignominious fall of the Northern Song dynasty in 1126. Many of Wang's policies were briefly revived, and some of them—like his public services system, the local security and militia system, and the type of exami-

---

26. These systems were designed to provide horses for the army after the old grazing lands had been occupied by hostile tribes. Under the horse-raising system (*huma*), people bought horses that, when raised, were sold to the government. Under the horse-care system (*baoma*), the government provided the horses or the funds to buy them, and the people were expected to take care of them for the militia. In either case, horses that died had to be replaced at the individual's expense.

27. A tax on roadside stalls, kiosks, etc.

nation essay he introduced into the civil service system — reappeared in later dynasties. Nevertheless, Wang's reputation among later generations of Confucian scholars was generally low, the majority sympathizing with Sima Guang, Su Shi, the Cheng brothers, and others who had condemned Wang for his flagrant disregard of "human feelings" (which should not necessarily be interpreted to mean "public opinion") and especially for his suppression of criticism at court. Zhu Xi (1130–1200), the preeminent philosopher of the Song school whose views became enshrined as orthodox Neo-Confucianism in later dynasties, was a follower of the Cheng brothers. In these excerpts from his recorded conversations, however, he attempts a balanced judgment of Wang Anshi's strengths and weaknesses, trying to rise above the partisan passions stirred up in the great era of reform.

We were discussing Wang Anshi's meeting with Emperor Shenzong. "It was a chance that comes only once in a thousand years," I said. "Unfortunately Wang's ideas and methods were not correct so that in the end everything went to pieces the way it did." Someone asked, "When Wang Anshi started, was he so self-assured about his methods and tactics, or did he become so only later?" I replied, "At first he felt only that something should be done. But later when other people began to attack him, he became obstinate and unyielding. Unless one reads his diary one has no way of understanding the full story. As a matter of fact, he became so overbearing in argument and so contemptuous of everyone around him that men like Wen Lugong [Wen Yanbo] did not dare to utter a word." Someone asked about Sima Guang's actions. I replied,"He saw only that Wang Anshi was wrong, and this led him to go too far in the other direction. When the whole matter first came under discussion, men like Su Dongpo also felt that reforms should be undertaken, but later they all changed their minds completely." [30b–31a]

The implementation of the reforms was actually planned by all the statesmen together. Even Cheng Hao did not consider them to be wrong, for he felt that the time was ripe for a change. Only later, when everyone's feelings had been aroused, did Cheng Hao begin to urge Wang Anshi not to do things that went against human feelings. Finally, when Wang had rejected the advice of everyone else and was using all his power to enforce his policies, the other statesmen began to withdraw. Daofu asked, "If even the man in the street could tell that the implementation of these reforms would be harmful, why was it that Cheng Hao did not consider them wrong?" I replied, "The harm came from the way that Wang put them into practice. If Cheng Hao had been doing it, things would certainly not have ended up in the mess they did." . . . [32a–b]

Renjie remarked that the *baojia* [militia] system that Wang Anshi put into effect in the capital area naturally aroused opposition at the start. But when the gentlemen of the Yuanyou Party abolished it entirely, what they did was to upset completely a system that was already well established. "That is quite true," I replied. [32b]

It was the opinion of the various worthy men of the [opposition] Yuanyou Party[28] that in general everything should go according to established ways. Their idea was to correct the mistakes arising from the changes [made by Wang Anshi] during the Xining and Yuanfeng periods, but they did not realize that they were lapsing into mere standpattism. Since the empire exists, soldiers must be trained, abuses must be corrected, and government affairs must be properly ordered. How could one simply do nothing at all? [33a]

[From *Zhuzi quanshu* 62:30b–33a — dB]

THE LEARNING OF THE EMPERORS
AND THE CLASSICS MAT

The "Classics Mat" is an antique expression for a place where a scholar interpreted the contemporary significance of the classics (or, in Buddhism, a place from which senior monks lectured on the *sūtras*). Much promoted in the neoclassical Confucian revival of the Song, it stood for a privileged space at court wherein a learned Confucian could lecture and discuss with the emperor and his ministers how passages from the classics and histories bore on current issues. Cheng Yi, a leading philosopher in the new School of the Way, sought to make it nearly a full-time educational process for the heir apparent and young emperor Zhezong, thinking to elevate the Classics Mat lecturers into a role of almost constant companions and mentors to the emperor, equal in status to the prime minister. Thus, in a time of increasing centralization of power in the Song, reformist Confucians sought to convert the new importance of the scholar-official class as civil servants into a "constitutional" role at court, granting a certain immunity or freedom of speech to those who might criticize the ruler and his administration and thus balance to some degree the heightened power and authority of the supreme autocrat himself.

"The Learning of the Emperors" is an expression used for the content and method of Classics Mat discussions by which rulers might be educated to their responsibilities, based on the example of sage kings and worthy ministers from high antiquity to the present. It is also the title of a work by the eminent historian Fan Zuyu (1041–1098), an associate of the even more famous historian and statesman Sima Guang, who was, like Fan and others of their prominent contemporaries, a participant in the Classics Mat discussions.

Out of these discussions arose a literary genre recording the historical cases cited by these lecturers, along with the advice that went with them. Thereafter the collected works of leading Neo-Confucians included their Classics Mat lectures and accompanying memorials — scholars including Cheng Yi, Zhu Xi, Zhen Dexiu (1178–1235), and Xu Heng (1209–1281), who were leading proponents of the Neo-Confucian

---

28. Associated with Sima Guang and others.

movement. Indeed, so influential was this advocacy that the institution, lectures, and writings identified with the Classics Mat became fixtures of Neo-Confucian discourse in later dynasties and were especially emphasized at the court of the Korean Yi dynasty.

A basic theme of this "Learning" was that the earliest rulers combined both sage wisdom and political authority, but when these two subsequently became disjoined, worthy rulers modestly relied on wise ministers for guidance, especially with regard to education. Close correlates of the "Learning" were the concepts of the Succession to the Way as the rejoining of humane wisdom and ruling authority and the Message (or Method) of the Mind-and-Heart as the content and practice of the ruler's "rectification of his mind-and-heart." Concomitant with this came the rising importance of the *Great Learning* as the textual basis for this instruction.

FAN ZUYU: *THE LEARNING OF THE EMPERORS*

Fan's work consists of quotations from the classics, histories, and philosophers, characterizing the rule of successive sage kings and emperors and evaluating their successes and failures in relation to the effort each made to learn and get good advice. The earliest of the sages exhibited an innate intelligence that enabled them to learn directly from the observation of the heavens and natural processes. Later sages, including Yao and Shun, had to learn from other human beings. Thus Fan quotes the "Canon of Shun" from the *Classic of Documents*:

"Examining into antiquity [we find] that Emperor Shun . . . was profound, wise, refined, and brilliant. He was completely gentle and courteous, genial and sincere. . . ."[29]

Mencius said, "The great Shun took great [delight in what was good]. He [regarded] virtue as a thing to be shared in common with all people, giving up his own way to follow that of others and taking delight in learning from others to practice what is good. From the time when he plowed and sowed, exercised the potter's art, and was a fisherman, to the time when he became emperor, he was continually learning from others. To take example from others to practice virtue is to help them in the same practice. . . ."[30]

Your subject Zuyu comments: The learning of the emperors is called the *Great Learning* . . .

[There follow the opening lines of the *Great Learning* and the further comment by Fan:] The reason that learned individuals attached importance to the extension of knowledge, to making the intentions sincere, to the rectification of their hearts, to the cultivation of their persons, to the regulation of their

---

29. "Canon of Shun," *Classic of Documents*; Legge, *The Chinese Classics*, 3:29.
30. *Mencius* 2A:8; Legge, *The Chinese Classics*, 2:205.

families, to governing the state well, and to illuminating their bright virtue in the world is because that was the Way of Yao and Shun. "The Learning of the Emperors" is to be found in learning from Yao and Shun. . . .

Yang Xiong said, "Those who follow Yao, Shun, and King Wen all act to rectify the Way."[31] In later generations, the only one who was able to learn from Yao and Shun and reach their level was King Wen. That is why Confucius took Yao and Shun as his ancestors, modeled institutions on [those of] Wen and Wu, and put into practice [the teachings of] the Duke of Zhou. To do anything else is contrary to the Way."

[At the conclusion of the first chapter, dealing with ancient rulers down to the founding of the Zhou, Fan quotes the admonition of the elder statesman the Duke of Zhou to the scion of the Zhou house:]

"From this time forward, you who have succeeded to the throne must imitate [the way King Wen] avoided excess in what he saw, in his recreation, his excursions, his hunting. From the myriads of people you must receive only the correct amount of contribution.[32] . . .

"From this time forward, in establishing government, make no use of artful-tongued men, but [seek out] good officers and let them use all their powers in aiding the government of our empire. Now, [you who are] the accomplished son [of King Wu] and grandson of King Wen, my young son the King, do not err in the matter of litigations. There are the officers and the pastors to attend to them. From this time forth, may you and your successors, in establishing the government, seek to employ men of constant virtue."[33]

Your minister, Zuyu, makes the following comment: The Xia dynasty were Sons of Heaven for seventeen generations, lasting 432 years. The Shang dynasty were Sons of Heaven for thirty-one generations, lasting 629 years. The Zhou dynasty were Sons of Heaven for thirty-six generations, lasting 867 years. Altogether, the three dynasties lasted for 1,928 years. During that time, only the Great Yu, Tang the Completer, Gao Zong, King Wen, King Wu, and King Cheng were rulers who undertook study, looking into the classics and [ancient] records. [That kind of ruler was] rare indeed. . . . Although records differ from one another, and the facts are far from clear, one thing is definite: sagacious rulers were few and ordinary rulers many. This is why the periods of good government were short and the periods of disorder long. . . . Some rulers such as Jie [the last ruler of the] Xia dynasty or Zhou [the last ruler of the] Shang dynasty, could not be urged [toward learning] at all. They brought disorder [to the state], and their lack of virtue was such that they caused a lapse in [the heritage of] their ancestors and the discontinuance of sacrifices to them. When

---

31. Yang Xiong, *Fayan* (SKQS) 3:2a (p.290).

32. "Against Luxurious Ease," *Classic of Documents*; Legge, *The Chinese Classics*, 3:470.

33. "The Establishment of Government" (*Lizheng*), *Classic of Documents*; Legge, *The Chinese Classics*, 3:520.

later generations speak of evil rulers, it is always these two that are held up as the example. Could it be that they were by nature incapable of goodness? No, it was because they did not model themselves after the former kings, did not make wise and worthy men their intimate associates, and did not regard learning as fundamental. . . .

[*Dixue* 1:5a–6a, 12a–14b — MG]

Debate Over Wang Anshi's New Laws

The final section of Fan's *Learning* includes a debate in the reign of Shenzong (1068–1085) during a session of the Classics Mat, in which Sima Guang criticized Wang Anshi's New Laws and Lü Huiqing (1031–1111) defended the reforms. Although for brevity's sake, many of the classical and historical cases cited are not reproduced here, the following excerpts may show how these precedents were invoked on different sides in this policy debate and suggest something of the tenor of the personal confrontations.

On the *gengchen* day of the eleventh month [of 1070], Sima Guang discussed the *Comprehensive Mirror in Aid of Governance*. . . .

[He said,] "The Han emperor Wu (r. 141 B.C.E.–87 B.C.E.) took the advice of Zhang Tang to change the policies of Emperor Gaozu, and, as a result, thieves and bandits were rampant throughout half the world. The Han emperor Xuan (r. 74 B.C.E.–49 B.C.E.) embraced the long-standing policies of Emperor Gaozu but at the same time selected two thousand good and rock-solid [men] to employ in governing the people. As a result, the world was well governed. When the emperor Yuan (r. 49 B.C.E.–33 B.C.E.) first came to the throne he changed the government of Emperor Xuan. Later Counselor-in-Chief [Kuang] Heng sent a memorial to the emperor, saying, 'I humbly and deeply regret that our state has given up its endeavor to bring about prosperity. This gratuitous action will cause great confusion to us now.'

"Now, Your Majesty, looking at the actions of Emperor Xuan and Emperor Yuan, who governed better? Xun Qing [Xunzi] said, 'Good government is achieved by men, not by laws.' Therefore the practice of good government rests in obtaining [good] men; it does not rest in changing laws."

Emperor Shenzong said, "Are not men and laws two sides of the same coin?"

Sima Guang said, "As long as you get [good] men there need be no concern about bad laws. But if you do not get good men, then even if you have good laws, a mistake will have been made in the proper sequence of things. That is, an urgent search for able men comes first and the making of new laws can wait."

[Later Lü Huiqing commented,] "The other day, Sima Guang said that when the laws of Xiao He[34] were preserved, the Han dynasty was well governed,

---

34. Chief minister to the founder of the Han dynasty.

and when those policies were changed, the Han dynasty was ill governed. In my humble opinion, this is not so. . . . If laws are disadvantageous then they must be changed. Why should we sit back and watch corrupt practices and not change them? The statement quoted [earlier by Sima Guang] from the *Classic of Documents* saying, 'It is not wise to wreak havoc with long-standing regulations [of government],' in fact, means that one should not impose changes arbitrarily when it is clearly unwise to do so. It does not mean that none of the past laws should be changed. . . ."

On summoning Sima Guang to court [again], the emperor asked him, "Have you heard the argument by Lü Huiqing? What do you think of it?"

Sima Guang answered, "He is right on some points but wrong on others. . . . Governing a state is just like keeping a house that has some problems: you repair it. You do not take it down without any intention of rebuilding it. To demolish an old house and build a new one, excellent craftsmen and quality materials are needed. Now I am afraid that we lack both. I fear that the house we have cannot shelter our nation from the wind and the rain." . . .

Lü Huiqing said, "Sima Guang serves at court but doesn't have much to do. So whenever he sees anything inappropriate he criticizes it. When one wants to do something but is kept from doing it, one normally withdraws [from service]. Similarly when one has the duty to criticize but is unable to do so, one should withdraw. How can it be any other way?"

Sima Guang said, "In a reply to the last imperial order that encouraged us expositors to express criticism, I immediately memorialized Your Majesty about our successes and failures, including every detail of the newly established regulations. I wonder if Your Majesty has ever had the chance to see it."

The emperor said, "I have seen it."

Sima Guang said, "Of course, I must speak out. If my advice is not heeded, and I do not withdraw, that would indeed be to my discredit. But Lü Huiqing has accused me of wrongdoing and I dare not run away from his accusation."

The emperor said, "All of you exchange views with one another all the time about what is right and what is wrong. How then did it reach the point of such hostility [between you]?"

Wang Gui came in and said, "What Sima Guang said perhaps suggests that some of the reforms our empire has undertaken do more harm than good. And perhaps there have also been some unnecessary changes."

With this, Wang Gui cast a glance at Sima Guang, causing him to step aside. Then Wang Gui presented his reading of the *Records of the Grand Historian*, and Sima Guang discoursed on his *Comprehensive Mirror in Aid of Governance*. After they finished the reading, both stepped down to leave. Then the emperor had them move their seats across the threshold to a place right in front of the throne and asked them to sit down. . . .

The emperor said, "Whenever we make some changes, the whole court is in an uproar. You all say it may not be done, but no one is able to point out the specific shortcoming. What is the matter?"

Wang Gui replied, "I humbly serve Your Majesty outside the court and cannot get full access to what is going on inside the court. I have only overheard some gossip circulating around, but I am not sure of its truth."

The emperor said, "Just say what you have overheard."

Sima Guang said, "I heard that the government was distributing spring "green sprouts" loans to farmers. This is not proper. These days in the country-side the rich take advantage of the poor, who already suffer from an extreme shortage of funds. The rich provide loans with interest, which have to be repaid with corn and wheat at harvest time. The poor then toil all year through heat and cold only to find that their meager income of a few *hu* of grain is taken away by the rich peasants when it has hardly been removed from the threshing ground. These rich families who compile the tax registers are rich because they have power above and below and can threaten severe punishment [to force the peasants to take usurious loans]. So they gradually force the poor into extreme distress and poverty. Now add to that the still more severe demands from the county magistrate and I fear that the poor people will be unable to eke out a living."

Lü Huiqing said, "Sima Guang does not understand this issue. The rich households do take advantage of the poor peasants. But what the district mag-istrate is actually doing now is only to benefit the poor. For example, yesterday the government distributed 'green sprouts' loans to those willing to take them but forced no one to accept a loan if he was unwilling to do so."

Sima Guang said, "The ignorant people are aware of the advantage the loans give them but unaware of the harm the heavy debts may bring them later. . . ."

The emperor asked, "What about buying surplus rice for storage? . . ."

Sima Guang said, "Now the capital has a stock of rice enough to last us seven years, yet the cash reserve is often short. If the government buys large quantities of leftover rice for storage, the cash reserve will be even shorter while more rice will be stored, only to become spoiled. What is the good of this?"

Lü Huiqing said, "If government buys the leftover rice, we will have one million *piculs* of rice for storage so that we can exempt the people of the south-east from the annual one million *piculs* of tribute rice. Instead we will tax them in terms of cash to supply the capital. Then there will be no problem of low cash reserves."

Sima Guang said, "The people in the southeast are short of money but have a surplus of rice. If we force them to pay tribute in cash instead of in rice, taking away what they are very short of but refusing what they have in plenty, the morale of the farmers will be seriously lowered. . . ."

Sima Guang said, "These are just details unworthy of Your Majesty's con-sideration. What you must do is select good people and employ them. When you find some who are meritorious you should reward them, and when you find those who are guilty [of wrongdoing], you should punish them."

The emperor said, "This is so. It is exactly like the passage from the *Classic of Documents* saying that King Wen 'would not himself appear in the various notifications, in litigations, and in precautionary measures of government; there were officers and pastors to attend to these things.' "[35]

Then the emperor went on discussing with these officials until late afternoon the best way to govern the state. Wang Gui and others asked for permission to leave. The emperor ordered that they be served some broth, and then said to Sima Guang, "Please do not be put off by the disturbing things that Lü Huiqing said [about you]."

Sima Guang said, "I wouldn't dare," and left.

[*Dixue* 8:1b–7a — MG]

CHENG YI: LETTER TO THE EMPRESS DOWAGER CONCERNING THE CLASSICS MAT

When Zhezong as a child of twelve acceded to the throne in 1086, the Empress Dowager was the power behind the throne. On being invited to serve as a Classics Mat lecturer, Cheng Yi had doubts about the Classics Mat being used merely as an adornment, whereby the prestige of Confucian scholarship would be lent to a regime that did not actually take Confucian principles seriously. Hence he addressed this letter to the Empress Dowager to emphasize how serious a matter was the education of the young emperor. Although conforming to the polite, self-deprecating conventions of the court, Cheng Yi was quite frank in his criticisms. He insisted, after the manner of Mencius, that he was unprepared to let himself be used improperly but rather meant to be quite forthright in speaking out on matters of principle. On the one hand, it was more important for him to preserve his own integrity than to pursue high office; on the other hand, if he were to serve at all, he should be treated with the proper dignity and respect.

An example of Cheng Yi's strong sense of self-respect is the episode involving his stipend as Classics Mat lecturer. The convention at court was that the lecturer should submit an application for his salary to the Board of Revenue. This Cheng Yi would not do, even though he had to borrow money to live on. When asked about this, he replied that to apply for his salary, as if for a favor, was demeaning, and especially so for the lecturer from the Classics Mat. "The trouble," he said, "is that today scholars and officials are accustomed to begging. They beg at every turn."

In my humble opinion, it is not a common occurrence for a Confucian scholar to have the opportunity to assist the ruler in his learning of the Way (*daoxue*). If I could choose any place I would like to be, no place would be better than this. Although I must decline appointment to the Classics Mat on the grounds that I am not talented enough, my mind to serve the state has nevertheless been aroused. . . .

---

35. "The Establishment of Government," *Classic of Documents*; Legge, *The Chinese Classics*, 3:517.

Looking at antiquity, no one was better able to teach and nourish a young ruler than the Duke of Zhou.[36] What the Duke of Zhou did became the model for ten thousand generations. Your subject hopes that the emperor will extend the vision of the former dynasties, place his trust in the teachings of the sage [Confucius], carry out the way of the ancient kings, avoid following rigidly the advice of his own close entourage, and avoid becoming mired in confusion by popular sentiment.

How could we be misled by what the ancients have recorded about the Duke of Zhou? When "The Establishment of Government" [chapter of the *Classic of Documents*][37] was made, [they quoted] the Duke of Zhou as having begun by speaking about "how few know how to be sufficiently anxious [about those who surround the ruler], from the regular chiefs and continuing through the keepers of the robes.[38] What he reiterated and emphasized throughout the entire chapter was just this one thing. It is also said, "If retainers and ministers are upright, their ruler will be able to be upright."[39] It is also said, "That the ruler is virtuous is due to the minister; that the ruler is not virtuous is [also] due to the minister."[40] . . .

Broadly speaking, a ruler who has received the Mandate of Heaven [to found a dynasty] has a natural endowment that is exceptional. But a careful examination of history shows that the intelligence of most emperors and kings seldom surpasses that of other people. Why is it that rulers endowed with perfect virtue and possessing the Way are so rare? If those who are the emperor's teachers and nurturers have not gotten the Way themselves, then it is only natural that such a situation will occur. . . .

Since your subject has taken office, six officials-in-waiting have lectured from the Classics Mat, but it was observed that the gathered ministers all sat quietly with folded hands, and the lecturer, standing next to the imperial bench, explained a few lines and then withdrew. If things are conducted in such a fashion, even if the emperor were of mature age and accumulated experience, what benefit could he derive from such a lecture? This is completely different from the way the Duke of Zhou taught and nurtured King Cheng! And if the emperor is of a minor age and things are done like this, it shows that those responsible do not know the most fundamental things.

As for the way the ancients reared their children, the reason they instructed

---

36. As regent to King Cheng, the successor to King Wu of the Zhou dynasty.

37. "The Establishment of Government," *Classic of Documents*; Legge, *The Chinese Classics*, 3:508–22. The theme of this work is that good government requires that well-chosen and well-qualified men be placed in the highest positions. It is ultimately the responsibility of the ruler to recognize and appoint such men.

38. "The Establishment of Government," *Classic of Documents*; Legge, *The Chinese Classics*, 3:508–11.

39. "The Charge to Jiong," *Classic of Documents*; Legge, *The Chinese Classics*, 3:586.

40. Ibid.

them in the Elementary Learning as soon as they could eat and speak was that the ancients regarded early preparation [for learning] as the first priority. When people are young, they know how to think but lack direction and a capacity for judgment. This is the time to put before them the best instruction and the best teachers. Although not yet aware [of the significance of what they are learning] they will internalize it and it will become second nature to them. . . .

Recently, the prime minister attends the lectures from the Classics Mat one day out of ten, and even so [his participation] stops at sitting silently and no more. . . . The Classics Mat is a place where questions can be raised and so it should be a place where people are at ease. When Your Majesty is about to begin his studies, his mind and body ought to be at ease so that it will be a pleasant [experience for him]. Now, however, facing the great officials, Your Majesty is made to feel anxious and uncomfortable. Standing nearby, the official historian calls out and perfunctorily writes things down. If Your Majesty wishes to let his thoughts flow, will he be able to? If he desires to speak, will he dare? This profoundly affects learning and must be corrected. . . .

Now, altogether there are five instructional officials (*jiangdu guan*) and four of them hold concurrent appointments. . . . The fact that the lectureship is made a concurrent assignment not only hinders the lecturers [in carrying out the duty of that office] but also shows how little Your Majesty values them. [The result is that] they won't dare to speak out in a way that [frankly] informs the ruler, and instead they will merely echo majority opinion. As for those whose responsibility it is to inform others, if they don't marshal their sincere intentions (*chengyi*) then their influence will not be felt. . . .

Your Majesty has drawn me from out in the fields so that the emperor might read the words of the sage and hear the Way [of the sages]. Could your subject dare not to take what he has learned [in his lifetime] and report on it to the emperor? Your subject humbly suggests that the learning [of the sages] has not been transmitted for a long time. Fortunately, your subject has been able to obtain it from the classics that have been handed down, not because of any [intellectual capacity] of his own but because he took upon himself the responsibility for the Way. Although those who would ridicule this are many, in recent years those who follow the Way have grown more numerous. Now, your subject begs humbly to make use of what he has just spoken about in order to make learning manifest, with the ardent hope that this learning will be transmitted to later generations.

[From *He'nan Chengshi wenji* 6:541–546 — MG]

CHENG YI: MEMORIALS TO THE THRONE ON THE CLASSICS MAT

Shortly before writing to the Empress Dowager, Cheng Yi submitted three short memorials, ostensibly to the young emperor but implicitly even more for the eyes of the dowager, explaining his reluctance to serve as Classics Mat lecturer unless there were mutual understanding on the nature and conditions of this service. Indeed, he asks that this mentorial function be treated on a par with the prime ministership, rather than just as an occasional lectureship.

Your Majesty is of a young age,[41] and your servant humbly suggests that even though your Heaven-endowed nature is sagelike, the way to cultivate it must be perfected, and this consists not in teaching Your Majesty to do this or that, or in remonstrating after an error is made, but in nothing else but cherishing [Heaven's moral endowment], steeping oneself in it, and being transformed by it. If each day Your Majesty were more often surrounded by worthies and gentlemen, and less often by eunuchs and palace women, then Your Majesty's moral disposition would naturally be transformed and your capacity for virtue perfected. I beg that Your Majesty earnestly select scholar-officials (*shi*) who are worthy and virtuous to serve as lecturers. When the lectures are finished, two persons should remain on duty during the day, and one person throughout the night, always prepared [to take] questions. When Your Majesty has a respite from study or enjoys a moment of relaxation, the lecturer should often be summoned to the inner palace, and conversation [between you] should flow in a leisurely way. Your discussions should concern not only the rightness of the Way but also the feelings and conditions of the people and the difficulties of agriculture, so that you will naturally and gradually acquire a broad knowledge and understanding. How can this not be to Your Majesty's great advantage when compared with being [idle] in the private quarters all the time?

Your subject has heard that every other day there is one meeting of the Classics Mat and that after hearing several lines recited and a few words of lecture, Your Majesty, accompanied by the assembled officials and ranks of retainers, solemnly withdraws. This kind of attendance violates the spirit of the lectures. If [the lectures are conducted like this] then will it not be difficult to expect that "assistance and nurturance" will take place? . . .

If Your Majesty spends all your time with personal servants or eunuchs, you will develop an arrogant attitude, but if you spend your time with worthy scholar-officials, then you will develop an attitude of love and kindness. This is the way to nourish and perfect [your] sagely virtue and to bring fortune to the people. There is nothing in the affairs of the world more urgent than this. . . .

[From the second memorial:]
Your subject begs that the emperor select as his personal retainers and palace servants only those who are forty-five years of age or older and who are honest and careful; that the emperor's clothing, implements, and accoutrements all

---

41. Emperor Zhezong was twelve years old at the time this memorial was written.

should be of simple materials; that nothing showy or extravagant should be put before him; that things that require great expense and wastefulness not meet his eyes; and that shallow and vulgar words not enter his ears. Furthermore, your subject begs that ten cabinet officers be appointed to fill the position of the Classics Mat in order to wait upon the emperor at all times. . . .

[From the third memorial:]

Your subject humbly suggests that as the ruler occupies such a lofty and honored position and holds the power to punish and reward, the officials all hold him in great fear and no one dares look him in the eye [and speak his mind]; wherever his commands go they are obeyed and what he desires will be instantly obtained. If such be the emperor's education that he does not know the way to hold rightness in awe, it is quite possible that he will be led astray. Even an average ruler will become boastful or rude; and even a brave and illustrious lord will tend to become self-satisfied and pretentious. This has been a common problem since ancient times; indeed it has been the pivot of peace or disorder. Thus, the Duke of Zhou advised King Cheng, spoke of the virtue of the former kings, and put reverential awe and respectful fear to the fore.[42] Since ancient times, it has never happened that sagely virtue could be achieved by one who failed to respect worthies and stand in awe of his ministers. . . .

Your subject humbly observes that when the Classics Mat is in session, officials and retainers are all seated, and the lecturer alone is made to stand, which is contrary to what was done in the past.[43] Your subject begs that from now on Your Majesty make a point of ordering the lecturer to be seated, not only so as to accord with rightness and principle but also to encourage respect for Confucian scholars and for the importance of the Way.

Your subject believes that it is the intention of Your Majesty to follow precedent, and that Your Majesty considers the Classics Mat merely to be a praiseworthy activity [in which he ought to take part]. Your subject believes that the most important appointments under Heaven [that the emperor makes] are to the post of prime minister (*zaixiang*) and to the Classics Mat: whether there is order or chaos in the world is linked to the prime minister, and the perfecting of the ruler's virtue is the responsibility of the lecturers from the Classics Mat. How, then, can the importance of the Classics Mat lectures be slighted?

[*He'nan Chengshi wenji*, 6:537–539 — MG]

---

42. "The Establishment of Government," *Classic of Documents*; Legge, *The Chinese Classics*, 3:508–522.

43. In the reign of Zhenzong (998–1022) the lecturer was permitted to sit while he lectured. Often the emperor and lecturer sat down together to study books and discuss issues. See *Yuhai* (*Sea of Jade Encyclopedia*) 26:7b, 26:8b.

REGISTERING PUBLIC OPINION IN THE SONG

SU SHI ON PUBLIC DISCOURSE

In this excerpt from his Ten Thousand Word Memorial of 1069, the versatile scholar, poet, and statesman Su Shi expresses his concern that the Censorate[44] and Board of Policy Criticism, which he viewed as channels for conveying popular opinion to the throne, were being subverted, with the effect of fostering the rise of autocratic rule. Since the Song dynasty has generally been thought to have promoted civil government and enlarged the functions of the civil bureaucracy, the question addressed by Su has to do in part with whether the Song dynasty, which exhibited many features of a modern state, also provided for the kind of infrastructure and process identified in the West with "civil society," by which "public opinion" could be brought to bear on the formulations of state policy. The Board of Policy Criticism may not have enjoyed as much autonomy as organs of civil society in the modern West, but it did serve some of the same function as a balancing or countervailing force, and Su deplores any move to weaken it. He has Wang Anshi's alleged dictatorial methods in mind.

Gongyi, the expression translated here as "public opinion," refers to views widely shared concerning the common welfare. It does not necessarily imply participation of the people as a whole in decision making. Thus when scholar-officials like Su speak confidently for "public opinion," it can mean only that they, as responsible members of the leadership elite, think themselves able to read the popular mind and know what is in the common interest, rather than that the people themselves, or individual persons, have the means or the right to articulate their thinking on major issues. Hence Su and Wang Anshi can hold opposing views but speak with equal conviction about what is in the public interest, while Su can insist that consultation is essential in determining a fair outcome.

The ancients established their states in such a way that the inner [the court] and the outer [the provincial] divisions of government moderated each other and that emphasis on each was in balance. But in the Zhou and in the Tang dynasties there was undue weight on the outer, and this evil produced the trouble of larger states threatening the smaller. In the Qin and the Wei (220–

---

44. "Censorate" is the English translation of the Chinese *yushi tai*, literally, the "Terrace of Imperial Scribes." The *yushi tai*, which dates from the Han dynasty, was the major government institution charged with overseeing regulations and enforcing discipline among career civil service officials. It did not deal with censorship per se, but, much like the internal affairs department of a modern police department, monitored against internal corruption and misbehavior. The Board of Policy Criticism (*jianyuan*), on the other hand, was a unique Northern Song institution. Established in 1017 and disbanded about 1082, it was intended to provide oversight, policy options, and even criticism for the emperor himself.

264) there was undue weight on the inner, and this evil produced the disaster of control by autocratic ministers.

The sage plans for decline while still in the midst of prosperity and regularly implements measures to remedy such evils. Tax revenues for our state are centralized in the State Finance Commission; large numbers of troops are concentrated in the capital region. Thus, in historical terms, it would seem that we give undue weight to the inner. Although it is hardly possible for a minor official like myself fully to comprehend the deepest plans and designs of our revered imperial ancestors, when I observe how they deputed authority to the Censorate and the Board of Policy Criticism, then it seems to me this was the ultimate sagelike plan for preventing excess. If we look at the period from the Qin through the Five Dynasties (907–960), several hundred censors were executed, and yet since the founding of our house not once has a censor been punished. Even if one of them received some slight chastisement, their careers immediately resumed. Public petitions were permitted and were not reserved to those with official status; the criticism could touch anyone without regard to high or low. If these criticisms touched the emperor, then the Son of Heaven took notice. If the affair touched the court, then the chief ministers awaited their punishment. Therefore, in the time of Emperor Renzong (r. 1023–1063) there was even the criticism that the chief ministers merely promulgated the policies of the Censorate and Policy Board [so strong were the latter in determining policy].

But there was a deeper meaning to this policy of the founding sages in promoting these agencies, a meaning unappreciated by ordinary people. It was not that their officials were all great worthies, nor that their opinions were always correct. Rather, by the fostering of their zealous spirit and the delegating of great power to them, these agencies were able to nip nefarious officials in the bud and so preserve us from the evil of weight to the inner [overcentralization]. For when such officials have only begun, it is easy for these agencies to root them out; but once established, they cannot be dislodged even by force of arms.

At present, our laws are strict, the court is free of corruption, and there is barely a trace of nefarious officials. One raises a cat to exterminate mice. But if there were no mice at the moment, you would hardly teach a cat not to catch them. One trains a dog to ward off the nefarious. But if there are no nefarious persons around, you would hardly teach a dog not to bark. How can Your Majesty not recall the intentions of the founding ancestors in establishing these offices, and consider them as a defensive strategy that will enable your ancestors to endure for a myriad generations? Among the institutions of the court, none are more important than these agencies.

I remember when I was small the elders saying that the criticisms of the Censorate and the Policy Board always followed the public opinion (*gongyi*) of all-under-Heaven. What public opinion supported, the Censorate supported; what it attacked, the Censorate attacked. But beginning with the reign of Emperor Yingzong (1064–1067), matters came to be decided in accordance with the personal wishes of the sovereign; and, although he made no major errors, there was no clear ritual authority for such a procedure. The people were troubled, and public opinion was against such a trend. The Censorate and Policy Board at that time protested strenuously. At present, discussion of the matter is seething; resentment and hatred are at a pitch. And one well knows what public opinion on the matter is. Yet nothing is done directly and both the center and the provinces are losing hope.

Once those who have arrogated power have been impeached, even the man of mediocre talents can prosper. But once solicitation of public criticism has vanished, then even the greatest hero will be unable to rise. I fear that if this custom becomes established, henceforth government decision making will become totally the province of [the ruler's] private desires. The point will come when the emperor will stand alone, the system will collapse, and anything may happen. Confucius has said, "Is it really possible to work side by side with a mean fellow in the service of a lord? Before he gets what he wants, the mean man worries lest he should not get it. After he has got it, he worries lest he should lose it, and when that happens he will not stop at anything."[45]

[From *Jingjin Dongpo wenji shilüe* (SBCK) 24:17b–19b — CH]

POLITICAL ACTIVITIES OF SONG UNIVERSITY STUDENTS

CHEN DONG: MEMORIAL TO EMPEROR QINZONG DECLINING OFFICIAL APPOINTMENT

Involvement of university students in political activities has a long history in China. The earliest student movement took place in the second century C.E. when university students attacked the eunuchs for their meddling in government affairs. Several hundred students and officials were imprisoned and executed as a result. During the last days of the Northern Song, with the capital under siege by the invading nomads and the court riven by factional struggles, weakening its ability to deal with the invasion, Chen Dong (1086–1127), a university student at the time, led students in six petitions demanding that the court should impeach corrupt officials, reappoint a loyal general (notably Li Gang), and concentrate on military defense against the nomadic Jurchen invaders. After the Song lost to the Jurchen and was forced to relocate its capital to the south (Hangzhou), while still under threat from the north, Chen renewed his demonstrations in front of the palace. Tens of thousands of people joined him in these demonstrations, the memory of which created a legacy that was to last throughout the

---

45. *Analects* 17:15; trans. D. C. Lau, p. 146.

Southern Song and into the early Ming when Ming Taizu banned all interference of university students in politics.

Chen Dong's activities were so influential that Emperor Gaozong of the Southern Song felt the need to get rid of him. Ten months after he first gathered students to kneel in front of the palace, petitioning the emperor, the latter ordered him arrested and executed — at age forty-one. This act only led to further criticism, now joined by government officials. Regretting his action, the emperor then ordered posthumous honors for Chen.

Little attention was paid to Chen Dong and his memorials throughout the later dynasties. His works were first published only in the eighteenth century and became well known only after student activism became more a part of Chinese life in the early part of the twentieth century.

On the thirteenth day of this [second] month, I received an Order from the Department of State Affairs appointing me to the position of Gentleman for Meritorious Achievement with the Advanced Scholar degree but without portfolio. I do not merit such a favor and am writing this for submission to the department, asking them to rescind the order. I joined a group of university students to kneel in front of the palace gate on the twenty-seventh day of the twelfth month last year and petitioned that [Prime Minister] Cai Jing and five other criminals [ministers] be executed. I then went twice to the Public Petitioners Review Office, each on the sixth and thirtieth of the first month, to remind them of what the abdicated emperor [Huizong] had said about the evils of the six criminals. The students again went to kneel in front of the gate on the fifth day of the second month, petitioning that Li Gang should be restored to office and that Li Bangyan should be removed. A total of more than one hundred thousand troops and commoners gathered to support us; the voice of their protest could be heard even beyond the ninth wall of the palace. . . . The reason that we went to kneel at the palace gate certainly was not to seek for any personal benefit [such as this appointment].

I am but a commoner, but have dared to criticize the powerful high officials, placing my life as if hanging on a thread from their cap. . . . We have heard that students have been forced to flee and that several inspectors have been dispatched to arrest the remaining students for execution. We would all have been killed had it not been for Your Majesty's personal intervention.

[Chen Dong, *Shaoyang ji (SKQS)* 2:9a–12b — THCL]

The following excerpt is from Chen Dong's biography.

When he returned to the university after mourning for his father, Chen Dong made up his mind that he should help to bring moral government to the state.

He would often become highly excited when he talked with his learned friends about the leading corrupt official in the government. Everyone was impressed. In the eighth year of Xuanhe (1126), the Jurchens invaded Hebei. Emperor Huizong became tired of his duties and abdicated in favor of his son, who was to become Emperor Qinzong.The second day after his ascendance, the new emperor decreed that officials and commoners alike were welcome to offer their views on national affairs. Chen Dong sighed, "The Imperial University is where the nation cultivates its intelligent young people, there should be someone to respond to the call." He therefore gathered several hundred students in front of the palace gate to submit a memorial criticizing the corrupt officials, [such as] Cai Jing and Wang Fu. They demanded that these officials be removed and punished so as to show the enemy the determination [of the Song government].

The emperor was receptive to their recommendations, but did nothing because other officials came out to defend the two. The Jurchens stepped up their siege of the capital and Chen decided to submit a second memorial, detailing the crimes of Cai and his followers. . . . The court then responded by impeaching them.

In the spring of the following year . . . officials recommended that no counteroffensive be launched against the Jurchens. . . . As a result, the Jurchens again encircled the capital. Chen Dong decided that the time was critical and drafted another memorial that night. In the morning, he led students to kneel in front of the palace to send in the memorial. More than one hundred thousand people, troops and commoners alike, gathered to join the petition. . . .

At first, when Chen Dong and his university compatriots knelt in front of the palace, soldiers and common people began to gather in order to watch and, before long, tens of thousands were on the scene. When told that the memorials were not being delivered to the emperor, the crowd broke the fence in front of the palace, bringing sticks with which to beat the drum in the Office of the Public Petitioners' Drum. . . .

In the first year of the Jingkang reign (1126) . . . Chen Dong was forced out of the university at the instigation of the officials then trusted by the emperor, on the grounds that he had demonstrated against the emperor, the ruler-father. Soon Wang Shiyong tried to forge an imperial edict for the execution of Chen and other petitioners from the university. However, with help from the Prefect of Kaifeng, Nie Shan, they were able to escape, and in fact were reinstated in the university, with a secret order from the emperor himself to Nie Shan, in which the emperor acknowledged the loyal and righteous acts of Chen and his associates. [The rector of the university, Yang Shi, then succeeded in persuading Chen to return to the university.]

[*Shaoyang ji* (SKQS) 6:5b–9a — THCL]

HISTORICAL REFLECTIONS ON GOVERNMENT

CHEN LIANG ON UTILITY

Coming from a family marginally within the literati class of central Zhejiang, Chen Liang (1143–1194) addressed himself to the pressing political and military issues of his day and won a hearing from some of the leading intellectuals of the late twelfth century. Resisting the rising tide of the moralistic and metaphysical Confucianism of his own day, which idealized the sages of antiquity, Chen set forth his ideas as grounded in the thought of Confucius and in the practical policies of heroic emperors and scholar-officials of the Han and Tang dynasties. Combining concerns for virtue and practical utility, he developed a Confucian ethic of results — viewed both by his opponents and by some modern scholars as "utilitarianism."

Chen was obsessed with liberating North China from Jurchen rule and restoring the Song dynasty's control over all of China. Offering concrete military strategies and advocating institutional changes in support of the war effort, he disdained the speculative philosophers of his day who, he said, diverted attention from the basic issue of the country's survival. Even when these moralistic Confucians advocated war, their proposals gave such priority to reforming the personal morality of the emperor that they contributed almost nothing to the war effort.

The direction of Chen Liang's thought on governance is evident in his efforts to delineate the theoretical and practical options historically available to Chinese. He sought a practical middle path between what, to him, were the idealistic extremes of the moralists and the utopian fundamentalists whose institutional schemes were too antiquarian. Although Chen does not cite by name the contemporaries associated with these two groups, his critique of the speculative Confucian philosophers plainly points to the school of the Cheng brothers and Zhu Xi. The institutionalists are less easily identified. On one level, he explicitly belittles as anachronistic and impractical those who follow too closely the classical institutions of the *Rites of Zhou* (for which Wang Anshi, 1021–1086, was famous) or specific classical institutions such as the well-field system (of which Hu Hong, 1105–1161, was the foremost champion).

At the same time, Chen in the mid-1180s praised officials who "regarded the most significant consideration in governing the world to be reality." By this, he meant scholar-officials who, avoiding abstract philosophizing, "examine and compare names and actualities, make rewards dependable and punishments certain, and implement a policy in the morning and see its effect by that evening."[46] The model here for Chen in "comparing names and actualities," as

---

46. *Chen Liang ji* 15:168.

well as in "making rewards dependable and punishments certain," was Emperor Xuan of Han (r. 74–49 B.C.E.). Confucian moralists of Chen's era generally condemned this Han emperor for using the way of the hegemon and the way of the king together. Even Confucian scholars who readily found fault with the way of the hegemon, however, could not dispense with it in practice. Drawing on the historical contribution of the hegemon in antiquity in defending Chinese culture and restoring order in an era of decline, Chen sought to use the Chinese term for *hegemon* as a metaphor for realistic approaches to sociopolitical problems in times of crisis.

As the situation in the Southern Song progressively worsened, Chen warned against the danger of government officials resorting to the Legalist theory of wealth and power. Southern Song officials were already making laws and regulations increasingly stringent. There was a way out: "In joining together the ways of kings and hegemons and in the meeting of affairs and results, there is something that compensates for the deficiency of the [Confucian quest for] kingly governance and transcends [the Legalist search for] wealth and power."[47] Thus, Chen regarded himself as offering a more inclusive and practical approach to problems of governance.

Chen Liang's ideas contributed to Chekiang scholarship on governance and historical studies, a tradition from which advocates of reform in later centuries drew. But the translations in this section are taken from essays that were unknown in later centuries until discovered in the mid-1970s in a rare book printed in the early thirteenth century. The essays on governance and history preserved only in that rare edition enable us to reconstruct a more complete view of his thought as his own contemporaries would have had access to it.

THE WAY OF ORDER AND THE WAY OF INSTITUTIONS, PAST AND PRESENT

In this school essay from the mid-1180s, Chen Liang gave a summary history of different schools of statecraft thought. Confucius had compiled data about governance during the Three Dynasties to produce the classics in order to provide a reference for later generations. Still, even early Confucians had divergent views. The *Great Learning* had simply asserted that the way to rule the state and bring peace to the world was based on rectifying the mind-and-heart and making the intentions sincere. When Confucius' grandson Zisi (492?–431? B.C.E.) added nine sections of commentary to this classical text, he implied that governance was complicated enough to require further explanation. In the final analysis, however, he simply called for being watchful over oneself when alone. Mencius, realizing that kingly governance required specific policies for agriculture and sericulture, detailed everything from the chickens of the peas-

---

47. Ibid. 15:173.

ants to the salary of the officials and the boundaries of the state. Yet, Mencius, too, returned to the simple idea of self-cultivation as the way to bring peace to the world and order to family and social relationships.

According to Chen, after the collapse of the Qin regime's experiment in ruling through penal law, the Han turned to tolerance and generosity rooted in the Way of the Confucians. Confucian scholars came forward with diverse interpretations; others advanced Laozi's theories. Emperor Wen of Han (r. 180–157 B.C.E.) adopted the Daoist policy of quiescence, and thus demonstrated that peace could be brought to the world without relying on Zisi's notion of being watchful over oneself while alone. Still, when it became clear that decadence had not been completely cleansed from the world, Jia Yi (201–168? B.C.E.) attributed this to the failure to establish classical institutions. Emperor Wu of Han (r. 141–87 B.C.E.) then turned to employ Confucians; consequently, culture and writing, rites and music flourished. In the wake of this progress, troubles became more complex, and explanations offered by scholars proliferated. Having arisen from the countryside, Emperor Xuan understood how bureaucrats harmed the people. Ignoring other Confucian theories, he simply examined and compared names and realities, made rewards dependable and punishments certain. The world then became well governed. But kingly administration became adulterated with the methods of the hegemonic way, and rites and music did not flourish. Thus, according to Chen, history demonstrated that it was truly difficult to attain both a well-ordered polity and flourishing culture and rites, not to mention the even greater improbability of recapturing the optimum ideal ascribed to the golden age of the Three Dynasties. Based on this view of history, Chen then turned to criticize the theories of his own era.

In the last one hundred years, theories have simply been contrary [to those of the Han and Tang]. The first group says, "Scholars since the Han period have never heard the Way; therefore, the culture of the world has not been complete, and the principle of the mutual interaction among all things has not been manifest. If one truly obtained the Way, that would be sufficient to achieve interaction with Heaven and Earth and to have resonance between ancient and recent times. Such subtlety of the vital spiritual arts of the mind-and-heart can only be faithfully adopted by a ruler of clear intelligence who has personally experienced it."

A second group says, "To pursue the Way and to preserve it with institutions is essentially one principle. If humaneness is not carried out through administration, there will be substance without function; what is primary and secondary will be confused; and the Way of [joining] Heaven and human beings will be lacking. The well-field system, decentralization through enfeoffment, corporal punishment, and schools provided the means whereby the sages of the Three Dynasties gave functional expression to the vital spiritual arts of their minds-and-hearts. One should conduct extensive research to recover the old institutions of the early kings, unlike later generations who have governed by dealing only with superficial matters."

According to the theories expounded by both groups, the Han and Tang dynasties had nothing to offer and, tracing back to the Three Dynasties, they found the key in compatibility [with Heaven and Earth]. Today's distorting, pedantic scholars of peripheral learning, as well as their petty-minded students, having eavesdropped on these theories and learned them by rote, insult their elders as unworthy of being imitated and belittle the most talented and wise statesmen of an era as "unwittingly leading a befuddled life as if drunk or in a dream." If one pursues this line of thinking, elders and juniors (including the competent and the incompetent) would not be content with their lot, so how could one actually form one body with Heaven, Earth, and the myriad things [as the Cheng-Zhu school proposes]? Therefore, the first theory cannot be utilized.

Antiquity and recent times change in such a way that things lose their appropriateness, so how could one expect to cope with the mandate to rule with only the *Rites of Zhou*? Thus the second theory cannot be used.

[From *Chen Liang ji*, rev. ed., 15:167–169 — HCT]

ON PEOPLE AND LAWS

Chen Liang's 1193 essay "On People and Laws" was written in the departmental examination for the *jinshi* degree. His use of the term *laws* encompasses both regulations and institutions. Chen here tries to establish an alternative approach to a statecraft problem of his day. In contrast to those who condemn dependence on institutional solutions instead of relying on ethical individuals, or to the more institutionally oriented officials who — believing in institutional solutions — decide on ever-increasing rigor in laws and regulations, Chen argues for employing men to administer laws, regulations, and institutions flexibly. This option would allow personnel to adapt to changed circumstances and would not require such strict administrative regulations. Chen Liang sought to distinguish his solution from the usual extremes of relying upon either men or laws, as well as from using both men and laws side by side. His approach was, rather, to use men to manage institutions flexibly enough so that detailed regulation would be unnecessary.

There is an apparent linkage between "using men" and the old decentralized enfeoffment system of the Eastern Zhou (770–256 B.C.E.) on the one hand, and between "using laws and institutions" and the centralized bureaucratic system of the Qin, on the other. Using both men and laws side by side would be a dual system, such as Chen Liang ascribed to the Tang, but it was not an integrated one. Chen's own preference for a fourth choice — "utilizing men to administer laws and institutions" — might appear to be a simple focus on the centrality of personnel issues. If so, he would be merely reiterating a Song theme of finding the right man and giving him discretionary power. Chen here argues for a position that is distinct in some fundamental ways. According to him, the centrality of law was crucial because it served to correct excessive self-interestedness in the human mind-and-heart. Moreover, the centrality of law could not be reversed because of the precedents set by the dynastic founder and because the trend in favor of laws and institutions had become part of the natural order. The weight of laws as "regulations," however, had become overbearing since the mid-eleventh century and needed to be reduced. Officials have implemented increasingly stringent regulations to counter the prevailing self-interestedness among people and officials and to safeguard against favoritism. In Chen's view, these regulations served to hamstring administrators and diminish their ability to act.

The prevailing trends in the world cannot be changed by Heaven, Earth, ghosts, or spirits; the one agent of change is people. Ever since there were Heaven and Earth, people have been ranged between them. Once the Way of people is established, it is impossible not to have laws, regulations, and institutions in the world. Human minds-and-hearts are mostly self-interested, but laws can be used to make them public-minded. This is why the prevailing trend in the world inevitably moves toward laws and institutions. In discussing phenomena in the *Classic of Changes*[48] the sages related them to processes of change and in discussing changes related them to [the actions of] men; they were never one-sided or neglectful of such factors [in the process]. Therefore, the sages in the Three Dynasties always established laws and institutions without any of the shortcomings that attach to reliance on laws and institutions [alone]. The Three Dynasties always made use of people without any of the defects that attach to reliance on the use of people [alone]. They employed people to implement the laws without having to explain it as using people and laws side by side. Ever since the Qin upset the norms of Heaven and Earth, the world began to change. The Han dynasty put its reliance on people, and the Tang opted for utilizing people and laws side by side. Our own [Song] dynasty simply relies on laws and institutions. If the trend of the world is moving toward laws and institutions and we try to redirect it totally toward reliance on people, [our efforts will be in vain because] even Heaven, Earth, ghosts, and spirits would not be able to alter this trend, and people will certainly not be able to change the course of things either.

Besides utilizing people, utilizing laws, and utilizing people and laws side by side, what other course can we take to rectify [things and restore] the long-term order of Heaven and Earth? Even if one had the wisdom of a sage, how could one avoid being sick over this difficulty? I have long pondered the fact that laws certainly cannot be abandoned and personnel also cannot be disregarded. I have heard of using people to administer laws and regulations; I have never heard of letting laws and regulations run by themselves. The establishment of a law or regulation cannot be implemented without people; this is the

---

48. *Commentary on the Appended Phrases*, Part 1, *Classic of Changes*.

correct rule of the world. Once laws and institutions are established, the ruler should be concerned about employing people and apprehensive lest appointment of the wrong personnel would result in the laws not being properly administered. Therefore, if the ruler at the top bears this concern and the subordinates below fulfill their responsibilities, the world can enjoy lasting control with no disorder.

If a ruler becomes distraught over not having the right personnel and relies on regulations alone, it is short-sighted, selfish calculation. Once the regulations for institutions become so detailed and the ruler no longer has concerns that appointment of improper personnel might really be harmful, he will think the regulations are complete and detailed enough so that they can suffice to govern the world, and no one can escape the bounds of his laws and regulations. Thereupon, the ruler feels relieved of any immediate worries, and his subordinates shirk their responsibilities, which is why the affairs of the world become a matter of constant concern. Thus, it is one thing to use people to administer laws and regulations and another to let laws run by themselves.

The laws and regulations of the present day can be described as rigorously detailed. If the world only heeds laws and regulations, the virtuous and intelligent cannot exert any personal influence, but neither can thieves and robbers do whatever they wish; hence, the advantages and disadvantages are almost balanced. If, however, the laws and regulations are very detailed and the empire has already utilized them for a long time, so that everyone has grown accustomed to them, then if one morning, in despair that the virtuous and wise cannot exert any influence, we were to contemplate governing without using laws and regulations, I am afraid that thieves and robbers would be able to do whatever they wished. Our troubles would be worse than those at present. On the other hand, if we allowed the prevailing trend in the world to continue unchecked, it would not be being responsible to the people. Why then would there be any reason for the ruler who bears responsibility for the people to exist, and what would there be for the high officials who share the [ruler's] concerns for the country to do? This is the reason why relying upon laws and regulations has become the standard for our dynasty. Changing the founders' standard is not something that later descendants should do.

Perhaps, as we reflect on this problem, if we started from laws, regulations, and institutions themselves, the way to change would not be delayed. People should administer laws and institutions so that laws and regulations are not left to run by themselves. Now, the bad effects of depending upon laws and regulations come from leaving them to run by themselves. If the motive behind [our dynasty] allowing laws and institutions to run by themselves can be changed, would it then not be possible for the present detailed laws and regulations to be simplified? Isn't there something we could eliminate in the process of getting approval chops in government agencies? In general, if we regard [having] laws as definitive and have proper people to administer them, while dispensing with the idea that laws and regulations can run by themselves, this would be in harmony with Heaven's principle above, satisfy the hearts of the people below, and serve as a policy for adapting to the long-term trend of two hundred years' standing.

Laws are [should be] principles of the public interest. To let laws and regulations run themselves is selfish [expediency]. If we rely upon the principle of the common good and not the selfish [expediency] of allowing laws and regulations to run by themselves, then the day will certainly come when we can finally achieve change that is endless. Who says there is no other way except relying on people, or relying on laws, or using people and laws side by side? If we follow the general [long-term] trend of the world, and obtain the right personnel, we can effect change without losing our balance and composure.

The regulations for recruiting scholars and appointing officials have never been as detailed and as stringent as the ones today. In the beginning when Song Taizu (r. 960–975) had just established institutions, the regulations for pasting over the name [with a piece of paper to prevent the examiners from knowing the identity of the candidate] and recopying the examination essay [before sending it to the graders] were not thoroughly utilized, so the safeguards against favoritism were not altogether tight, and yet most of those with the highest marks on the *jinshi* examinations became famous councilors of the era. The regulations for evaluating officials and seniority were not thoroughly established, and the qualifications for promotion and transfer were not completely set; yet all officials and administrators had demonstrated accomplishments. This is because in recruiting scholars they valued obtaining the right people, and in appointing officials they valued delegating responsibilities. They used public-mindedness to set up laws and used people to manage institutions and regulations. They never ventured to say that laws and regulations could be implemented without proper personnel. Afterward, in order to counteract people's excessive self-interestedness, institutional regulations became daily more detailed; unable to find the proper personnel, we wanted laws and regulations to run by themselves. The regulations for recruiting scholars and appointing officials became unprecedentedly numerous, but the personnel only became more unprincipled. Isn't this the result of our desire to have laws and regulations run by themselves?

Regulations for controlling the military and planning finances have also never been as detailed as at present. In the beginning, when Song Taizu set up institutions, the essential things for soldiers were to follow the strict differentiation of ranks and to become accustomed to riding horseback and obeying orders; however, the restrictive regulations were still for the most part loose and general enough so that people could perform their tasks. The priorities for finances were to have a sufficiency of the essentials but be cautious about expenditures; however, the loopholes were still in most cases more than ample, and this allowed people to exercise their own discretion. This was because in managing the military they valued controlling the enemy, and in planning finances they valued sufficiency for the people. They set up laws in the public interest and used people to manage these laws and regulations. Moreover, they never went so far as to say that institutions could function without proper personnel.

Afterward, in order to counteract the excessive self-interestedness of people, institutional regulations became daily more detailed; unable to find the proper personnel, we wanted institutions to run by themselves. Thus the regulations for managing the military and planning finances have become so detailed and precise that no one can cope with them, and the authority of the implementor has gotten progressively weaker — but hasn't this arisen from our desire to have laws and regulations that run by themselves?

Now, the theories of the [moralistic] Confucian scholars propose that the ancients did not rely on laws in order to govern; while the proposals of the chief ministers and the advice of the councilors suggest that a certain regulation is not yet complete, or that another law is not yet enacted, or that precautions against things have to be taken to the limit, or that prohibitions have to be complete because each person has his own [ulterior] motive. These suggestions [by the councilors] may be convenient for the present but are not in harmony with antiquity. The Confucian scholars are in harmony with antiquity but not helpful in the present. Therefore, the ruler alone is left with worrying about the affairs of state and tediously scrutinizing those who work for him.

My own humble opinion is: the world must have laws, regulations, and institutions, but laws, regulations, and institutions can operate only when proper personnel are appointed. We have made many institutional regulations in order to be able to say to the world that, just on the remote chance that there were no proper personnel, our institutions could still function. What promotes such an attitude, however, is actually selfish [expediency], and this is the reason why corruption in the world is incessant and unending. If those who set up laws and regulations would adopt my viewpoint and change laws and regulations, not only would the day come when we could cure the source of this corruption but also from this day forward the intent [of the sages during the golden ages] of the Three Dynasties in establishing laws and institutions and the original intention of Song Taizu in establishing his laws and institutions would become clearly manifest. Doesn't the *Classic of Odes* say, "Should you not think of your ancestors, and so cultivate your virtues";[49] and "Just because he knows how to do it, therefore . . . it shows in his whole appearance."[50]

[From *Chen Liang ji*, rev. ed., 11:124–126 — HCT]

---

49. Ode 235; trans. B. Karlgren.
50. Ode 214; trans. B. Karlgren.

THE WRITING OF HISTORY

The Song Confucian revival brought with it a heightened interest in history. We have already noted how many of the leading Song figures were engaged in the writing of history — the statesmen Ouyang Xiu and Sima Guang, for instance, and the philosopher Zhu Xi. The breadth of their historical vision reflected the wide range of intellectual inquiry in the Song and found expression in a variety of literary forms and genres. Some of these were new to the Song; others went back to the Tang or earlier.

In the field of historiographical criticism, the Tang led the way. The *Understanding of History* (*Shitong*) of Liu Zhiji (661–721) discusses the origin, development, and relative merits of various forms of historical writing in detail unmatched in the Song, but he was concerned with substance as well as form. His insistence that the historian should employ a tight, disciplined style in which every word counts is just one indication of the seriousness with which he regarded the task of the historian.

Encyclopedias (*leishu*) were both a product of historical inquiry and an aid to it. This type of work, first attempted in the Northern and Southern Dynasties period (fourth to sixth centuries) consisted of compilations of references to given subjects culled from all possible written sources and arranged by topics. They were designed primarily as handy references for students, writers, and government officials. Such encyclopedias, which have continued to be compiled up to the present, have also preserved in quotation parts of many books that have otherwise been lost.

A similar genre was the political encyclopedia as exemplified by the *Comprehensive Institutions* (*Tongdian*) compiled by the Tang dynasty scholar Du You (735–812). This work in two hundred chapters contains historical essays on such subjects as economics, warfare, bureaucratic systems, laws, geography, and so on, tracing each from its beginnings in the dawn of Chinese history down to the time of the writer, for the word *tong* in the title of this and other works excerpted in this section signifies linkage through time. The *Records of the Grand Historian* (*Shiji*) and later histories modeled on it often included essays treating various topics historically, but Du You was the first to undertake such detailed and comprehensive coverage, producing a history centered not on the ups and downs of political power but on the long and unbroken development of institutions.

The basic organization of the encyclopedias was by topics, but there were other ways to write history. Continuing in the tradition of the dynastic histories of combining political chronology and topical treatises was Ouyang Xiu, whose *New History of the Tang Dynasty* and *New History of the Five Dynasties* went beyond the government records that constituted the principal sources for earlier historical works to include works of fiction, belles lettres, and historical anecdotes. An ardent advocate of the prose style known as *guwen* or ancient prose, which had developed in the late Tang, Ouyang employed that style exclusively in his historical writings, even going so far as to rewrite quotations from earlier sources written in a different style. He also followed the tradition associated with the *Spring and Autumn Annals* of conveying moral meanings by the precise use of terminology.

As earlier, the *Annals* was considered the product of Confucius' editing, late in his life, the records of his home state. In the Song context, perhaps in the Chinese context as a whole, it is hard to imagine any more authoritative exemplar for those engaged in historical projects. Yet, just what Confucius had accomplished remained in dispute, and interpretations of the *Annals* again, as during the Han, became vehicles for political thought and controversy, as well as for exploring the purposes of writing history. Wang Anshi even considered the *Annals* worthless.

A champion of the value of history and the dynasty's most important and influential historian was Sima Guang (1019–1086), principal author of a chronological account of 1,362 years preceding the Song, with his own comments on events and principles inserted at various places. Compiled largely under official sponsorship, this work in 294 chapters was presented to the emperor, who conferred on it the title *Comprehensive Mirror in Aid of Governance (Zizhi tongjian)*. As reflected in this title, history remained predominantly political history and was seen as having a political purpose. The image of history as a mirror is an old one in China, where it occurs in the *Classic of Odes*, in the sense that history reflects the past truthfully just as a mirror does not lie, and also in the sense that by looking into it the emperor and his minister could discover truths about themselves and the issues of their own day. These truths could be moral as well as political: the mirror would reveal beauty and ugliness, qualities seen as inherent and not just in the eyes of the beholder.

The *Comprehensive Mirror* inspired some historians to take the story back to the beginning of time and others, most notably Li Tao (1115–1184), to extend it beyond 959. Still others were moved to rework Sima Guang's materials. One such was Yuan Shu (1131–1205), who, distressed at the way material relating to a single subject was broken up by the chronological form, compiled a work called *Topical Treatment of Events in the General Mirror (Tongjian jishi benmo)* that initiated a new genre. Most influential of all was the *Outline and Details of the Comprehensive Mirror (Tongjian gangmu)* planned by the philosopher Zhu Xi (1130–1200) and compiled by his disciples. This work followed the tradition of the *Spring and Autumn Annals* in selecting and reordering the materials in such a way that they would clearly convey the moral lessons of history.

Aside from formal works of history, the Song sense of the past found expression in many areas of intellectual life. There was an efflorescence of scholarly study of classic texts. Among what we may consider historical subgenres was the study of ancient bronzes and their inscriptions begun in the early Song and including among its practitioners Ouyang Xiu, author of the oldest extant work of this kind. Another new, essentially historical, form was the annalistic biography (*nianpu*) providing an account of a person's life year by year. From the very end of the dynasty comes China's first annalistic autobiography (self-written *nianpu*) composed by the Song loyalist Wen Tianxiang (1236–1283), a reminder that historical works were written to connect the present not only with the past but also with the future.

LIU ZHIJI

Both of our selections exemplify the insistence of Liu Zhiji (661–721) that history be an accurate record, which includes accurate value judgments. That the historian should fulfill his mission even if it costs him his life is indicated in the first selection, for the South Historian (an office in the state of Qi) was prepared to lay down his life after three historians had been killed for refusing the ruler's demand that they alter the record. The second selection comes from a chapter titled "Doubts About the Classics." In his quest for accuracy, Liu Zhiji did not shrink from criticizing even Confucius' editing of the *Spring and Autumn Annals*. The personages named in the first selection are all famous historians.

There are three ways for a history official to fulfill his duties. What are they? To celebrate the good, censure the evil, and confront the powerful, as did Dong Hu of Jin[51] or the South Historian of Qi[52]: that is the best. To complete a history and hand down to posterity a great, imperishable work, as did Zuo Qiuming[53] of Lu or Sima Qian of the Han dynasty[54]: that is next best. To impress one's age by one's great talent and broad learning as did Shi Yi in the Zhou and Yi Xiang of Chu: that is the final way. If all three of these are lacking, how can it be done? . . .

When a clear mirror reflects objects, beauty and ugliness are bound to be revealed. Should [the beauty] Mao Qiang have a blemish on her face, the reflection is not stopped. When empty space transmits sound, the clear and the murky are bound to be heard. Should [the singer] Mian Jun hit a false note in his song, the resonance is not halted. Now the history officer holding his tablets also belongs in this category. If he loves someone but understands his ugly

---

51. Grand historian of the feudal state of Jin under Duke Ling; see *Zuozhuan*, Xuan 2; Burton Watson, trans., *Tso chuan*, pp. 78–79.

52. *Zuozhuan*, Xiang 25; Burton Watson, trans., *Tso chuan*, pp. 143–47. This episode appears in an adapted form in ch. 6.

53. Reputedly the author of the *Zuozhuan*.

54. Author of the *Records of the Grand Historian*. See ch. 12.

aspects, hates someone but understands his good points, then good and bad are bound to be recorded. This is a true record.

[*Shitong* (SBCK) 10:6a–b, 14:3a — CS]

DU YOU: PREFACE TO THE SECTION ON "FOOD AND GOODS" OF THE *COMPREHENSIVE INSTITUTIONS*

The *Comprehensive Institutions* (*Tongdian*) of Du You (735–812) reflects mid-Tang concerns over the decay of dynastic institutions, loss of control from the center, and weaknesses in fiscal administration, already shown in the tax proposals of Yang Yan and Lu Zhi in the eighth century.[55] For Du You, any hope for political improvement had to be grounded in sound economic programs. Accordingly, he compiled his *Comprehensive Institutions* to provide a reference base in institutional history for dealing with systemic problems. Thereafter, his encyclopedic work became a model for a whole genre of institutional histories in late imperial China, which served as an important informational resource for later statecraft thinkers. In the following preface, Du explains why he gives the first priority in his work to material factors, as prerequisite to educating the people.

Although I engaged in the study of books from an early age, because I was a dullard by nature, I did not succeed in mastering the arts of number or astrological sciences, nor was I good at literary composition. Thus my *Comprehensive Institutions* actually amounts to no more than a compilation of various records that, if used in dealing with human affairs, might be helpful in governmental administration.

The first priority in ordering things according to the Way lies in transforming the people through education, and the basis of education lies in providing adequate clothing and food.[56] The [*Classic of*] *Changes* says that what attracts people is wealth. The "Grand Model" [chapter of the *Classic of Documents*] lists eight administrative functions, of which the first is food and the second the provision of goods.[57] The *Guanzi* says: "When the storehouse is full, then people can understand rites and good manners; when there is a sufficiency of food and clothing, people can understand the difference between honor and shame."[58] The Master [Confucius] spoke of enriching people first and then educating them.[59] All these sayings express the same idea.

To carry out education one must first establish offices, to establish offices;

---

55. See ch. 18.
56. Based on *Analects* 13:9.
57. "Grand Model," *Classic of Documents*; Legge. *The Chinese Classics*, 3:327.
58. "Shepherding the People," *Guanzi* (GXJC ed.) 1:1.
59. *Analects* 13:9.

one must recruit people with the requisite talents; and to recruit talent one must have an examination system, establish proper rites to rectify popular customs, and have music to harmonize people's minds-and-hearts. These were the methods employed by the early sage kings to establish proper governance.

It is only when there has been a failure in education that one resorts to laws and punishments, to commanderies and prefectures for local administration, and to fortifying the borders against barbarians. Thus "Food and Goods" come first [in this compilation]; official recruitment next; offices next after that; then rites, music, punishments, and local administration, with border defenses last. Anyone who reads this book should keep in mind my reasons for arranging things in this order.

[Du You, *Tongdian* 1:1a, preface —THCL]

SIMA GUANG: HISTORY AS MIRROR

From the Latter Han dynasty it had become the practice to have official historiographers at court taking notes on the emperor's words and actions as he attended to state business. These matters were then written up and preserved in the archives as the *Diaries of Action and Repose* (*Qijuzhu*) to provide source material for later historians. Meanwhile, they impressed on the emperor that everything he said or did would be recorded for posterity. During the Tang it was still the practice to keep the records out of the reach of the imperial glance in order to assure objectivity. This was no longer the case in the Song, but memorialists continued to appeal to emperors to act in a manner that would ensure their posthumous reputation.

The year 642, summer, fourth month. The Emperor Taizong spoke to the Imperial Censor Chu Suiliang, saying, "Since you, Sir, are in charge of the *Diaries of Action and Repose*, may I see what you have written?" Suiliang replied, "The historiographers record the words and deeds of the ruler of men, noting all that is good and bad, in hopes that the ruler will not dare to do evil. But it is unheard of that the ruler himself should see what is written." The emperor said, "If I do something that is not good, do you then also record it?" Suiliang replied, "My office is to wield the brush. How could I dare not record it?" The Gentleman of the Yellow Gate Liu Ji added, "Even if Suiliang failed to record it, everyone else in the empire would" — to which the emperor replied, "True."

[*Zizhi tongjian* 196:642, no. 5; 3:6175 —CS]

Sima Guang's history was centered on emperors, and emperors needed to hear the truth about themselves face-to-face as well as having it recorded for posterity. The emperor in the following anecdote is Taizong, the de facto founder and second emperor of the Tang. Sima Guang's comment is clearly addressed to his own emperor.

The emperor, troubled that many officials were taking bribes, secretly ordered his attendants to test some of them with bribes. When a registrar in the Board of Punishments took a roll of silk and the emperor wanted to have him executed, Minister of the Treasury Bei Zhu remonstrated, "An official taking a bribe should be punished by death, but Your Majesty entrapped this man by sending someone to give it to him. This, I fear, is not 'leading the people by virtue and restraining them by the rules of decorum.' "[60] Delighted, the emperor summoned all officials above the fifth rank and told them, "Bei Zhu was able to contest this case forcefully at court and did not pretend acquiescence. If every matter is handled this way, what cause will there be to worry about misgovernment?"

Your official Guang comments, The ancients had a saying that if the ruler is enlightened, the ministers will be honest. That Bei Zhu was given to flattery under the Sui dynasty but to loyalty under the Tang was not because his personality changed: a ruler who resents hearing of his faults turns loyalty into flattery, but one who is pleased by straight talk turns flattery into loyalty. Thus we know that the ruler is the gnomon [or post for measuring the height of the sun], the minister the shadow. When the gnomon moves, the shadow follows.

[*Zizhi tongjian* 192:626, no. 16; 3:6029 — CS]

Sima Guang has been much criticized for his defense of the "hegemons" (ba), leaders who during the Eastern Zhou were able to prevail for a time but none of whom succeeded in unifying China. Mencius had charged that these rulers, in contrast to genuine worthies, only pretended to virtue [7A:30] but Sima holds that they met the needs of their time. This, however, does not make him a historical relativist, for he stresses that there is only one Way.

Sima dates the following exchange, which he recapitulates as a basis for his own comment on the subject of the king and the hegemon, to 53 B.C.E. during the Former Han dynasty. The speakers are the heir apparent and future emperor Yuan (r. 49–33 B.C.E.) and his father, the reigning emperor, Xuan (r. 74–49 B.C.E.). The heir apparent appeals to his father to employ more Confucian scholars and fewer Legalists in his government.

The heir apparent was soft and humane. He liked scholars but observed that many legal officials employed by the emperor used punishments in order to control subordinates. Once at a banquet he let himself go and said, "Your Majesty relies too heavily on punishments. It would be appropriate to employ scholars." The emperor changed expression. "The House of Han has its own system based on mixing the way of the hegemon and that of the king. How

---

60. *Analects* 2:3.

could we possibly rely solely on moral instruction and employ Zhou governance? Moreover, ordinary scholars do not understand the needs of the day but
like to affirm antiquity and deny the present, causing men to confuse name
and reality so that they don't know what to hold on to. How can they be entrusted with the state?"[61]

Your official Guang comments, There are not different ways for king and
hegemon. Of old when the Three Dynasties flourished and "rites, music, and
punitive expeditions proceeded from the Son of Heaven"[62] [the ruler] was called
"king." When the Son of Heaven became weak and was unable to control the
lords, there appeared among them those who could lead allied states to punish
false states, thereby honoring the royal house: these were called hegemons.
Their conduct in both cases was based on humaneness and founded on rightness. They entrusted the worthy and employed the capable, rewarded the good
and punished the evil, prohibited cruelty and executed the rebellious. Therefore, they differ in the honor or pettiness of their status, in the depth or shallowness of their virtue, in the greatness or insignificance of their achievements,
in the breadth or narrowness of their governmental orders, but they do not
contradict each other like white and black or sweet and bitter.

The reason why the Han could not return to the government of the Three
Dynasties was because the rulers did not do it and not because the way of the
former kings could not again be carried out in later ages. Among scholars there
are superior and petty men. Ordinary scholars truly are not qualified to participate in government. But why could they not have sought for genuine scholars and employed them? Ji, Xie, Gao Yao, Boyi, Yi Yin,[63] the Duke of Zhou,
and Confucius were all great scholars. Had the Han employed men such as
these, the glory of its accomplishments would not have been as limited as it
was.

[*Zizhi tongjian* 27:53 B.C.E., no. 3, 1:880–81 — CS]

SU CHE: THE AUTHORITY OF THE HISTORIAN

The reputation of Su Che (1039–1112) has been overshadowed by that of his brilliant
brother Su Shi, but he was a prolific writer as well as a prominent political figure. His
political writings were much admired, he contributed to classical studies, and he was
the author of a *History of Antiquity* (*Gushi*), dealing with history down to the Qin
unification and highly critical of Sima Qian.

Su Che was a forceful writer with an unusually strong view of the responsibilities

---

61. The difference in outlook between these two Han rulers has already been discussed by
Fan Zuyu. See p. 631.

62. *Analects* 16:2.

63. All exemplary and semi-legendary ministers.

of the official historian and, by extension, of historians in general, but something of his sense of the solemn obligations and the elevated role of the historian as ultimate judge informed the work of many practitioners through the ages.

There are three authorities in the land: Heaven, the sovereign, and the historiographer (*shiguan*). The sages used these three authorities to govern right and wrong in the world and had them assist each other. Now, only the authority of Heaven can bestow long or short life, good fortune or calamity on the people, allow the virtuous to avoid an untimely death and dire poverty, and deny the good fortune of wealth, honor, and long life to the unworthy. But Jici and Yuan Xian,[64] though called worthy in antiquity, yet suffered in a mean alley without clothing or porridge, while Robber Zhi and Zhuang Jiao, who ran wild in the world and made a meal of people's livers, died at home of old age without meeting a violent death. Thus at times there are cases not reached by the authority of Heaven. Therefore the sovereigns applied their authority over rewards and punishments to the cases Heaven did not reach in order to help Heaven achieve order. Yet how could rewards and punishments exhaust the rights and wrongs in the world? Still, fearing that the rewards and punishments of one time will not be clearly visible for myriad generations, the sovereign entrusted this to an official whom he called the historiographer. Now, the authority of the Official Historian is equal to that of Heaven and the sovereign. Generally the three mutually assist each other so that right and wrong in the world will not be lost.

[*Luanzheng ji yingzhao ji* (SBCK) 11:10a–b — CS]

LÜ ZUQIAN: HOW TO STUDY HISTORY

Lü Zuqian (1137–1181), historian, classical scholar, and friend of Zhu Xi, wrote extensively on the *Zuozhuan* but became ill before he could complete his projected history covering the period from the end of the *Spring and Autumn Annals* era to the Song. In the following short essay he makes two important points. The first is that history must be viewed not as a collection of miscellaneous facts but as the continued record of organic growth and change. This was the concept that inspired Lü and others of his time to undertake the writing of giant histories covering all the past.

The second point is that by thinking oneself into the past and weighing the options available at that time a person can exercise a sense of judgment and thus gain in understanding. Here the traditional Confucian teaching that one should place oneself

---

64. Both were disciples of Confucius. Jici was an alternate name of Gongxi Ai, who, in contrast to other disciples of Confucius, never served in office. After Confucius died, Yuan Xian lived as a hermit and was very poor. Entries on the two are found in *Records of the Grand Historian* (*Shiji*), ch. 67.

in the position of another acquires a historical dimension. Furthermore, there is a sense not only that history provides models of conduct but also that the study of history provides opportunities for intellectual growth.

Chen Yingzhong [Chen Guan] once remarked that the *General Mirror* is like Medicine Mountain: anywhere you pick you always are sure of getting something. But though it may be Medicine Mountain, you must know how to select, for if you do not know how to select, you will end up with nothing more than a vast collection of facts crammed into your memory. Hu Qiuzi once asked Liezi why he liked to travel. Liezi replied, "Other men travel in order to see what there is to see, but I travel in order to observe how things change."[65] This might be taken as a rule for observing history. Most people, when they examine history, simply look at periods of order and realize that they are ordered, periods of disorder and recognize their disorder, observe one fact and know no more than that one fact. But is this real observation of history? You should picture yourself actually in the situation, observe which things are profitable and which dangerous, and note the misfortunes and ills of the times. Shut the book and think for yourself. Imagine that you are facing these various facts and then decide what you think ought to be done. If you look at history in this way, then your learning will increase and your understanding will improve. Then you will get real profit from your reading.

[*Lü Donglai wenji (CSJC)* 19:431 — BW]

THE CHENG BROTHERS: CYCLICAL AND LINEAR CHANGE

Interest in history was not limited to scholars engaged in historical projects but was shared widely in the intellectual world. Song scholars generally saw in the past both evidence of the cycles of dynastic change and examples of long-term linear change. The Cheng brothers and, later, Zhu Xi were primarily concerned with philosophical truths unaffected by the ebb and flow of time, but this did not mean that they were insensitive to history. On the contrary, their awareness of change provided the background that set off in high relief the nobility of the enduring values and principles to which they devoted themselves.

The following discussion by one of the Cheng brothers is in response to a query asking why modern people do not live as long as did the ancients. It is consistent with the view that the *qi* (energy, breath) had undergone long-term decline.

The cycle of rise and fall is hard to understand. In terms of generations, the [age of] the Two Emperors and Three Kings was [the time] of rise, and the

---

65. *Liezi*, ch. 4; A. C. Graham, *The Book of Lieh-tzu*, p. 81.

later ages that of decline. In terms of a single age, Kings Wu, Wen, Cheng, and Kang [of the Zhou] were [the time] of rise, Yu, Li, Ping, and Huan that of decline. In terms of a single sovereign,[66] the Kaiyuan reign period (713–741) was [the time of] rise and the Tianbao reign period (742–756) that of decline. In terms of a year, spring and summer are [the time] of rise, fall and winter that of decline. In a month the first ten-day period is rise and the last is decline. In a day the hours *yin* (3–5 A.M.) and *mao* (5–7 A.M.) are rise, *xu* (7–9 P.M.) and *hai* (9–11 A.M.) decline. The same holds for an hour. But in, for example, the hundred years of a human life those before fifty are rise, those after that, decline. Thus there are cases of decline and revival and cases of decline without return.

If we discuss this in terms of the great cycle, the [period of] the Three Royal Houses [Xia, Shang, and Zhou] did not rise to the height of the Five Emperors; the two Han dynasties did not rise to the height of the Three Royal Houses, and, again, those who came later did not rise to the height of the Han. In this process there were some rises and declines — for example, the Three Royal Houses declined and the Han rose; the Han declined and the Wei rose. These are cases of the principle of decline and revival like the moon after its last days being reborn or the passing and return of the seasons.

If we discuss the great cycle of Heaven and Earth in terms of the great substance, then there is the principle of daily decline and diminution. It is as in the hundred years of a human life: even for a baby just born, each day that passes is one day lost [from its life span]. The natural growth of its body and the natural loss in the number of days left to live do not impinge on one another.

[*Er Cheng yishu* (SBBY) 18:14a — CS]

ZHU XI: HISTORY AND PHILOSOPHY IN TANDEM

Zhu Xi, as a student of history and author of the well-considered historical works *Words and Deeds of Eminent Ministers of Eight Courts* (*Bazhao mingchen yanxing*) and *Record of the Origins of the School of the Two Chengs* (*I Luo yuanyuan lu*), did not minimize the importance of history. At the same time that he gave priority to the study of enduring principles in the classics, his thinking about issues of his time was informed by a sense of history.

Zhu Xi's attitude toward history was more nuanced and complex than one would think if one read the following guidelines for the compilation of his *Outline and Details of the Comprehensive Mirror* only as an attempt to contain history in a moral straitjacket. The wide readership of the resulting work suggests that the effort to condense, simplify, and structure the record on the basis of defined criteria served an educational purpose for many.

---

66. I.e., Emperor Xuanzong of the Tang.

The legitimate dynasties are Zhou, Qin, Han, Jin, Sui, and Tang. Feudal states are those that have been enfeoffed by legitimate dynasties. Usurpers are those who usurp the throne, interfere with the legitimate line of succession, and do not transmit their rule to their heirs. The periods in which there is no legitimate line occur between Zhou and Qin, Qin and Han, Han and Jin, Jin and Sui, Sui and Tang, and during the Five Dynasties period.

Rulers of legitimate dynasties: those of Zhou are called "kings," those of Qin, Han, and after are called "emperors." Rulers of feudal states: those of Zhou are referred to by state, feudal rank, and name. Those who unlawfully usurped the title of king are referred to as "so-and-so, the ruler of such-and-such a state"; from the Han on they are referred to as "so-and-so, the king of such-and-such." Those who usurped the title of emperor are referred to as "so-and-so, the lord of such-and-such." Those who revolted and usurped the throne of a legitimate dynasty are referred to by name only.

Ascending the throne, legitimate dynasties: when the Zhou kings passed their rule on to their heirs, write: "his son so-and-so was set up" and note that this person then became king so-and-so. When the succession is by natural heir, write: "so-and-so succeeded to the throne." When someone establishes a state and sets himself up as ruler, write: "so-and-so set himself up as king of such-and-such." If someone else sets him up, write: "so-and-so honored so-and-so with such-and-such a title." When someone usurps a state and begins to style himself emperor, write: "so-and-so (title, family, and personal name) styled himself emperor." When the rule of a state is transferred to a brother of the ruler, this is called "transmission"; when to someone else, it is called "cession."

[*Zhiyuan kaoding tongjian gangmu*, introduction — BW]

In the following conversation Zhu Xi tells a disciple that the study of history requires much preparation, that to turn to history too soon is futile but never to turn to it misses the whole purpose of study.

If people today who have not yet read many books, nor attained an integrated understanding of moral principles, go and read history in order to examine past and present, order and disorder, and to comprehend institutions and statutes, the situation will be like building a pond to irrigate fields. Only if you drain the pond after it is already full can the water flow and nourish the crops in the fields. If the pond holds only a foot of water and you drain it in order to irrigate the fields, it will not only fail to benefit the fields, but the foot of water will also be lost. If someone has already read many books, thoroughly understands moral principles with the details clear in his mind, does not read history, examine past and present, order and disorder, comprehend institutions and statutes, it is like a pond being full and failing to open it to irrigate the fields. But if one who has not read many books, nor attained an integrated understanding of moral principles, impulsively makes reading history his first priority, this is like draining a pond holding a foot of water in order to irrigate a field. It will dry up while you stand and wait.

[*Zhuzi yulei, juan* 11, 1:195 — CS]

ZHENG QIAO: HISTORY AS A CONTINUOUS STREAM

Zheng Qiao's *Comprehensive Treatises* (*Tongzhi*) was divided into annals, chronological tables, treatises, and biographies. Five of the twenty treatises were on topics treated here for the first time as independent categories: family and clan, philology, phonetics, capitals, and flora and insects. The annals and biographies run from antiquity to the end of the Sui, while the other two parts also include the Tang.

In his preface Zheng Qiao (1108–1166) argues vigorously for treating history as a continuous stream, as had Confucius and Sima Qian, and denounces Ban Gu, whose *History of the Former Han Dynasty* (*Qian Han shu*) began the tradition of more-limited dynastic histories, which violated and obscured the grand continuity of the historical landscape.

The many rivers run each a separate course, but all must meet in the sea; only thus may the land be spared the evil of inundation. The myriad states have each their different ways, but all must join in the greater community of our multifarious land; only then may the outlying areas be spared the fears of stagnation. Great is this principle of meeting and joining!

From the time when books were first invented, there have been many who set forth their words, but only Confucius was a sage given full scope by Heaven.[67] Therefore he brought together the *Odes* and *Documents*, the *Rites* and "Music," and joined them by his own hand such that he could standardize the literature of the world. By penetrating the deeds of the two emperors Yao and Shun and the kings of the Three Dynasties, he created one school of philosophy such that he could fully comprehend the evolution of past and present. Thus was his Way brilliant and enlightened, surpassing all the ages before and all ages after him.

After Confucius passed away, the various philosophers of the hundred schools appeared, and, in imitation of the *Analects*, each composed a book setting forth his general principles. But no one undertook to carry on the record of the historical facts of ensuing ages. Then in the Han, around the year 140 and later, Sima Tan and his son Sima Qian appeared. The Sima family had for generations been in charge of documents and records, and they were skilled in compilation and writing. Therefore they were able to understand the inten-

---

67. Based on *Analects* 9:6.

tion of Confucius, to join together the narratives of the *Odes* and *Documents*, the *Zuozhuan*, the *Narratives of the States*, the *Genealogical Origins*, the *Intrigues of the Warring States*, and the *Spring and Autumn Annals of Chu and Han*, covering the ages from the Yellow Emperor and Yao and Shun down to the Qin and Han, and to complete one book. . . .

Zheng Qiao goes on to praise the Records of the Grand Historian (Shiji) *and denounce Ban Gu. In his conclusion he again invokes Confucius.*

Confucius said, "The Yin (Shang) dynasty followed the rites of the Xia; wherein it took from or added to them may be known. The Zhou followed the rites of the Yin; wherein it took from or added to them may be known."[68] This is what is known as the continuity of history. But from the time when Ban Gu wrote the history of only one dynasty, this principle of continuity has been ignored. Thus although one be a sage like Confucius he can never know what was taken away or added in each period. The way of meeting and joining was from this time lost.

[Zheng Qiao, *Tongzhi* 1 — BW]

MA DUANLIN: INSTITUTIONAL HISTORY

In the preface to his *Comprehensive Study of Literary Remains* (*Wenxian tongkao*), Ma Duanlin (1254–?) reiterated the importance of continuity as well as comprehensiveness and the special need to study institutions from a long, multi-dynastic perspective. Clearly, many Song advocates of institutional change had viewed them in historical perspective, and Zheng Qiao too had paid them much attention, but Ma Duanlin's work was the most far-reaching and remains a major source for the study of institutional history. His introduction to this section on the land tax illustrates the scope and methodology of his work. In it he discusses changing historical circumstances as they relate to the perennial issues of land distribution, the well-fields, enfeoffment system, centralization of administration, and so on, as debated by previous writers in the Han, Tang, and Song dynasties.

The rulers of ancient times did not regard all-under-Heaven as their own private possession. Therefore the land of the Son of Heaven was a thousand *li* square, while that of the dukes and marquises was a hundred *li* square. Earls held seventy *li*, barons fifty *li*, and within the area of the king's domain the high ministers and officials were granted lands and villages from which they received emoluments. Each of these held possession of his own land, treated its inhab-

---

68. *Analects* 2:23.

itants as his personal charges, and passed it down to his sons and grandsons to possess. He regarded questions of the fertility and depletion of the land, and the abundance or want of the peasants, as of immediate concern to his own family. He took the trouble to examine and supervise things himself so that there was no room for evildoing or deception. Thus at this time all land was under the jurisdiction of the officials, and the people provided support for the officials. The peasants who received land from the officials lived by their own labor and paid revenue. In their work of supporting their parents and providing for their wives and children, they were all treated with equal kindness, so that there were no people who were excessively rich nor any who were excessively poor. This was the system of the Three Dynasties.

The rulers of the Qin were the first to consider all land as their own possession and to exercise all power by themselves. The men who filled the posts of county magistrates were shifted about frequently so that they came to regard the land of the county where they were posted as no more than a temporary lodging. Thus no matter how virtuous or wise a magistrate might be, it was impossible for him to know fully the true situation in the villages and hamlets he was supervising. The appointments and terms of office of these local magistrates were subject to time limitations, while evil and corrupt practices in connection with the transfer and holding of land multiplied endlessly. Therefore, from the time of Qin and Han on, government officials no longer had the power to grant land, and, as a result, all land eventually became the private possession of the common people. Although there were intervals, such as the Taihe period of the Wei (227–232 C.E.) or the Zhenguan period of the Tang (627–649), when some effort was made to return to the system of the Three Dynasties, it was not long before their reforms became ineffective. This was because without a revival of the enfeoffment of land, it was impossible to restore the well-field system.

Before and during the Three Dynasties, the Son of Heaven could not hold private possession of the country, but the Qin abolished the enfeoffment system and for the first time made the entire country the domain of one man. In the Three Dynasties period and before, the common people could not claim the produce of the land as their private possession, but the Qin abolished the well-field system and first granted people the right to the produce of their land. Therefore, the Qin took away from the feudal lords what it properly ought to have granted and granted the people what it properly ought to have taken from them. But this process has already gone on for such a long time that it would be exceedingly difficult to return to the old ways. If one were to try to revive the enfeoffment system, it would mean dividing and parceling out all the land again, and this would provoke confusion and strife. If one attempted to restore the well-field system, it would mean forcibly seizing people's land and inviting resentment and bitterness. This is why the theories of scholars who recommend such a revival cannot be put in to practice.

The system of taxing the landholdings of the people but putting no restriction upon the size of their holdings began with Shang Yang (d. 338 B.C.E.). The system of taxing people for the land they held but taking no consideration of the number of adult or underage persons[69] began with Yang Yan (727–781). Thus Shang Yang was responsible for abolishing the excellent well-field system of the Three Dynasties, and Yang Yan was responsible for the abandonment of the superior tax system of the early Tang. Scholars have been very critical of the changes made by these two men, but all later administrations have found it necessary to follow their methods. If they attempted to change back to the old ways, they found that, on the contrary, they only ended up in worse difficulty and confusion and both the state and the people suffered. This is because the things appropriate to the past and those appropriate to the present are different. Thus I have devoted the first of my surveys to the land tax, tracing the development of the land tax systems throughout the ages and adding to it a study of water control and of military and government farms, making seven chapters in all.

[*Wenxian tongkao*, author's introduction, 3c–4a — HLC]

---

69. That is, by incorporating the old labor tax, under which such persons were exempt, into the land tax.

Chapter 20

NEO-CONFUCIANISM: THE PHILOSOPHY OF HUMAN NATURE AND THE WAY OF THE SAGE

The Confucian revival in the Song was distinguished by its broad range of interests and intellectual vigor. But among the many fields of learning that it pursued, the philosophy of human nature, buttressed by a new metaphysics, was the one in which it achieved the widest and most enduring influence. Intense intellectual struggles might have been fought over political and social questions, on the outcome of which the very fate of China, threatened by foreign conquest, seemed to depend. Yet the passage of time quickly deprived these debates of their urgency and point, while the philosophical speculations emerging from the academies of the Song eventually won victories at home and abroad of which the statesman and soldier never dreamed.

When we speak of the new Confucian learning that emerged in the Song period as "Neo-Confucianism," we refer primarily to the Learning of the Way as synthesized by Zhu Xi (1130–1200). During the Song it was also known as the Learning of the Sage(s) and the Way to Sagehood, and subsequently as the Learning of Human Nature, of Principle, and of the Mind-and-Heart. Since Zhu Xi's view of it dominated Chinese (and later East Asian) tradition down into the nineteenth century, however, it is essentially his view of the Learning of the Way that we present here — not a fully representative account of Song intellectual history but a capsulized version, a conspectus of key figures and texts as Zhu Xi saw them contributing to the repossession and fuller exposition of the Confucian Way.

As seen by Zhu, this revival exhibited both elements of continuity and discontinuity. He followed Han Yu in depicting the Way as having lapsed after Mencius, and he believed that it had been two thousand years since it had been practiced. In the Song, he credited the Cheng brothers and Zhou Dunyi (at different times and in different connections) with having rediscovered the True Way after China had long been submerged under Daoism, Buddhism, and utilitarianism. Like Confucius, Zhu claimed no originality for himself in achieving a new synthesis but gave credit to key Song predecessors as major contributors to his own version of the Succession to the Way (*daotong*). These thinkers he anthologized in his *Reflections on Things at Hand* (*Jinsi lu*), a collection of Song dynasty writings[1] that he saw as updating Confucian thought (*Jinsi lu* can be read as *Record of Recent Thinking* as well as *Reflections on Things at Hand*). Zhu's anthology quickly became a classic of the Neo-Confucian movement, along with his selection of the "Four Books,"[2] defining for centuries its key issues, doctrines, and players. The present chapter attempts to reproduce that Neo-Confucian story and worldview.

In formulating it, Song Confucians faced fundamental challenges on the philosophical level, paralleling those in the practical order already seen in the last chapter. One was the need for a more coherent and systematic cosmology on which to ground its central conception of human nature as moral, rational, and (following Mencius) fundamentally good. Another need, in defense of the Confucian belief in constant human values, was to meet the challenge of the Buddhist doctrines of impermanence, "Emptiness," and moral relativism. Implicit in these latter doctrines was a profound questioning of the existence of the "self" or "self-nature," which tended to undermine the Confucians' prime concern with the moral person and practical self-cultivation.

In response to these challenges the Neo-Confucians came up with a new doctrine of human nature as integrated with a cosmic infrastructure of principle (*li*) and material-force (*qi*), along with a reaffirmation of the morally responsible and socially responsive self. This culminated in a lofty spirituality of the sage, preserving a stability and serenity of mind even while acting on a social conscience in a troubled world.

Until this time Confucianism had focused on the Way of the sage kings or Way of the noble person as social and political leader. Now, aiming at education for all through universal schooling and a neoclassical curriculum — an aim furthered by the spread of printing and literacy — the Neo-Confucians aspired to a spiritual ideal of sagehood for everyone, achievable by methods of cultivation outlined by Zhou Dunyi, the Cheng brothers, and Zhang Zai, as anthologized in the *Reflections on Things at Hand* (*Jinsi lu*) and explained in Zhu

---

1. Coauthored with Lü Zuqian.
2. The *Great Learning*, the *Mean*, the *Analects*, and the *Mencius*.

Xi's Four Books. Herein one found the Neo-Confucian response to Mahāyāna Buddhism's conception of the universality of the Buddha-nature, as well as the latter's lay ideal of the compassionate bodhisattva.

Given the difficulties — military, political, and economic — in which Southern Song Neo-Confucians found themselves after the fall of Wang Anshi and the loss of the North to non-Chinese conquerors, they had much less confidence than Northern Song reformers in programmatic solutions that depended on the effectiveness of the central state. In these limiting circumstances they looked more to what individuals could do through self-discipline, personal initiative, and voluntary association on the local level. This depended in turn on restraint and unselfish serving of the common good. Thus the sagely ideal was meant to inspire heroic self-sacrifice on the part of all, but especially of the educated leadership class of scholar-officials and, above all, of the ruler. Yet this stress on the rigorous, demanding role of the cultural elite stood in some tension with the realities of life among the less advantaged common people. Much of the subsequent history of Neo-Confucianism involved the working out of such tensions between an elitist ideal and Neo-Confucianism's avowed aim to promote universal education and serve the general welfare.

A philosophy concerned very much with this world, at the center of which is always the human, Neo-Confucianism reasserted in an even more far-reaching manner what Confucius and his followers had always taught — that the human sense of order and value does not leave one alienated from the universe but is precisely what unites one to it. The world of human ethics, of social relations, of history and political endeavor is a real one, an unfolding growth process, and not just a passing dream or nightmare from which men must be awakened to the truth of Emptiness or Nothingness. It is this conviction that gave to Neo-Confucianism its abundant vitality and a degree of universality that recommended it strongly not only to the Chinese but also to many Mongols, Koreans, Japanese, and Vietnamese, who likewise sought assurance that their lives had meaning and value.

ZHOU DUNYI: THE METAPHYSICS AND PRACTICE OF SAGEHOOD

Zhou Dunyi (or Zhou Lianxi, 1017–1073) occupies a position in the Chinese tradition based on a role assigned to him by Zhu Xi (1130–1200). According to one version of the Succession to the Way (*Daotong*) given by Zhu Xi,[3] Zhou was the first true Confucian sage since Mencius (385?–312? B.C.E.) and was a formative influence on Cheng Hao and Cheng Yi, from whom Zhu Xi drew

---

3. Another version credited Cheng Hao with this. See ch. 21, preface to the *Mean*.

significant parts of his system of thought and practice. Thus Zhou Dunyi came to be known as the "founding ancestor" of the Cheng-Zhu school, which dominated Chinese philosophy for more than seven hundred years. His "Explanation of the Diagram of the Supreme Polarity" ("Taijitu shuo"), as interpreted by Zhu, became the accepted foundation of Neo-Confucian cosmology.[4] Along with his other major work, *Penetrating the Classic of Changes* (*Tongshu*), it established the "wings" or appendices to the *Classic of Changes* as basic textual sources of the Neo-Confucian revival of the Song dynasty. And Zhou's short essay "On the Love of the Lotus" ("Ai lian shuo") is still a regular part of the high school curriculum in Taiwan.

Zhou was born to a family of scholar-officials in Hunan province. When he was about fourteen, his father died and he was adopted by his maternal uncle, Zheng Xiang, through whom he later obtained his first government post. Despite the increasing importance of the civil service examination system in determining status in Song society, Zhou never obtained the "Presented Scholar" (*jinshi*) degree. Consequently, while he earned praise for his service in a very active official career, he never rose to a high position.

Zhou's honorific name, Lianxi (Lian Stream), was the one he gave to his study, built in 1062 at the foot of Mount Lu in Jiangxi province; it was named after a stream in Zhou's home village. He was posthumously honored in 1200 as Yuangong (Duke of Yuan) and in 1241 was accorded sacrifices in the official Confucian temple.

During his lifetime, Zhou was not an influential figure in Song political or intellectual life. He had few, if any, formal students other than the Cheng brothers, who studied with him relatively briefly when they were young. He was most remembered by his contemporaries for the quality of his personality and mind. He was known as a warm, humane man who felt a deep kinship with the natural world, a man with penetrating insight into the Way of Heaven, the natural-moral order. To later Confucians he personified the virtue of "authenticity" (*cheng*), the full realization of the innate goodness and wisdom of human nature.

Zhou's connection with the Cheng brothers was the ostensible rationale for his being considered the founder of the Cheng-Zhu school of Neo-Confucianism. Yet that connection was, in fact, slight. Although they later spoke fondly of their short time with him and were personally impressed with him (as were many other contemporaries), the Chengs did not acknowledge any specific philosophical debts to Zhou. Nor are any such debts evident in their teachings. In fact, Zhou's teachings were rather suspect in the eyes of many Song Con-

---

4. For a note on the translation of *taiji* as "Supreme Polarity," see the introduction to the "Taijitu shuo" below.

fucians because of his evident debts to Daoism. This was especially true during the Southern Song (1127–1279), when Confucians increasingly defined themselves in opposition to Buddhism and Daoism. Indeed, Zhou's "Explanation of the Diagram of the Supreme Polarity" attracted considerable interest among Daoists and even made its way into the Daoist Canon (*Daozang*).[5]

Given Zhou's tenuous connection with the Chengs, why did Zhu Xi regard him as the first sage of the Song? The question is significant, for had it not been for Zhu Xi's estimation of him, Zhou's writings would almost certainly not have become as central to the Neo-Confucian tradition as they are. They apparently were not widely known outside the circle of the Chengs and their students until the twelfth century, and today the only extant editions besides those edited by Zhu Xi are the "Taijitu shuo" in the Daoist Canon and the *Tongshu* in another anthology,[6] neither of which is accompanied by a commentary. So it is safe to say that Zhou Dunyi's place in the Chinese tradition is largely a creation of Zhu Xi.[7]

It was the content of Zhou's teachings in relation to Zhu Xi's system of thought and practice that persuaded Zhu to exalt Zhou Dunyi, to ignore his Daoist connections, and to stretch the available data concerning Zhou's affiliation with the Chengs.[8] Zhu was particularly interested in the relationship between the active, functioning mind (*xin*) and its metaphysical substance or nature (*xing*), and in the implications of that relationship for moral self-cultivation. Zhou's writings supported Zhu's position on these issues by integrating the metaphysical, psycho-physical, and ethical dimensions of the mind, chiefly by means of the concepts of "Supreme Polarity" (*taiji*), "authenticity" (*cheng*), and the interpenetration of activity (*dong*) and stillness (*jing*).

Translated below are the complete text of his best-known work, the "Explanation of the Diagram of the Supreme Polarity," and six of the forty short sections of *Penetrating the Classic of Changes* (*Tongshu*). These works stand on their own as foundational texts of the Neo-Confucian tradition and as superb examples of the integration of Confucian ethics and Daoist naturalism.

---

5. *Zhengtong Daozang* (1962 Taibei ed.), case 8, vol. 7.

6. *Zhuru mingdao ji* (*Writings by Various Confucians for Propagating the Dao*), compiled in the 1160s.

7. Nevertheless, Zhu was not the first to consider Zhou as a founder. Hu Hong (Hu Wufeng, 1105–1161) had earlier done so and had written a preface to the *Tongshu*, but his edition of the text itself did not survive. Zhu Xi wrote first drafts of his commentaries on Zhou's works in 1169; they were completed in 1179 and 1187.

8. Zhu Xi used a qualified genealogical model of the Succession to the Way (*daotong*) for its transmission in the Song. But whether he attributed its resumption to Zhou Dunyi or to Cheng Hao, this repossession of the Way came after a break of more than a millennium since Mencius, a view similar to Han Yu's in his essay on the Way (see ch. 18). Thus Zhu asserted no claim to direct or continuous genealogical succession (as in the Daoist priesthood from Zhang Daoling,

EXPLANATION OF THE DIAGRAM OF THE SUPREME POLARITY
(*TAIJITU SHUO*)

Zhou's best-known contribution to the Neo-Confucian tradition was his brief "Explanation of the Diagram of the Supreme Polarity" and the diagram itself. The text has engendered controversy and debate ever since the twelfth century, when Zhu Xi and Lü Zuqian (1137–1181) placed it at the head of their Neo-Confucian anthology, *Reflections on Things at Hand* (*Jinsi lu*), in 1175. It was controversial from a sectarian Confucian standpoint because the diagram explained by the text was attributed to a prominent Daoist master, Chen Tuan (Chen Xiyi, 906–989), and because the key terms of the text had well-known Daoist origins. Scholars to the present day have attempted to interpret what Zhou Dunyi meant by them.

The two key terms, which appear in the opening line, are *wuji* and *taiji*, translated here as "Non-Polar" and "Supreme Polarity."[9] *Wuji* had been used in the classical Daoist texts, *Laozi* (chapter 28), *Zhuangzi* (chapter 6), and *Liezi* (chapter 5). *Wu* is a negation, roughly equivalent to "there is not"; *ji* is literally the ridgepole of a peaked roof and usually means "limit" or "ultimate." So in these early texts *wuji* means "unlimited" or "infinite." But in later Daoist texts it came to denote a state of primordial chaos, prior to the differentiation of yin and yang, and sometimes equivalent to *dao*.

Taiji was found in several classical texts, mostly but not exclusively Daoist. For the Song Neo-Confucians, the *locus classicus* of *taiji* was the *Commentary on the Appended Remarks* (*Xici*), or *Great Treatise* (*Dazhuan*), one of the appendices of the *Classic of Changes* (*Yijing*): "In change there is the Supreme Polarity, which generates the Two Modes [yin and yang]." *Taiji* here is a generative principle of bipolarity.

But the term was much more prominent and nuanced in Daoism than in Confucianism. *Taiji* was the name of one of the Daoist heavens, and thus was prefixed to the names of many Daoist immortals, or divinities, and to the titles of the texts attributed to them. It was sometimes identified with Taiyi, the Supreme One (a Daoist divinity), and with the polestar of the Northern Dipper. It carried connotations of a turning point in a cycle, an end point before a reversal, and a pivot between bipolar

---

the first "Heavenly Master") or "from mind to mind" (as in the patriarchal succession in Chan Buddhism). Zhu was the first to use the term *daotong* for a succession that actually meant a reconstituting or repossessing of the Way.

9. *Taiji* is usually translated as "Supreme Ultimate" and sometimes as "Supreme Pole," but neither of these terms conveys the meaning that both Zhou Dunyi and Zhu Xi seem to have intended. For example, in both texts translated here, Zhou identifies the yin-yang polarity as *taiji*. And Zhu Xi says: "Change is the alternation of yin and yang. *Taiji* is this principle (*li*)" (*Zhouyi benyi* 3:14b, comment on *Commentary on the Appended Phrases* (*Xici*), Part 1, 11.5, quoted below). He also insists that *taiji* is not a thing (hence "Supreme Pole" will not do). Thus, for both Zhou and Zhu, *taiji* is the yin-yang principle of bipolarity, which is the most fundamental ordering principle, the cosmic "first principle." *Wuji* as "Non-Polar" follows from this. Both are also consistent with later Daoist usage of the terms (see below), with which Zhou must certainly have been familiar.

processes. It became a standard part of Daoist cosmogonic schemes, where it usually denoted a stage of chaos later than *wuji*, a stage or state in which yin and yang have differentiated but have not yet become manifest. It thus represented a "complex unity," or the unity of potential multiplicity. In the form of Daoist meditation known as *neidan*, or physiological alchemy, it represented the energetic potential to reverse the normal process of aging by cultivating within one's body the spark of the primordial *qi* (psycho-physical energy), thereby "returning" to the primordial, creative state of chaos from which the cosmos evolved. Chen Tuan's *Taiji* Diagram, when read from the bottom upward, is thought to have been originally a schematic representation of this process of "returning to *wuji*" (*Laozi* 28), the "Non-Polar," undifferentiated state.

Zhou Dunyi ignored the bottom-up reading of the diagram, leaving one or two of its elements unexplained. Focusing on the top-down differentiation of the cosmos from the primordial unity to the "myriad things," he departed from a Daoist interpretation by singling out the human being as the highest manifestation of cosmic creativity, thereby giving the diagram a distinctly Confucian meaning. The enigmatic opening line of his "Explanation" suggests that the Supreme Polarity, the ultimate principle of differentiation, is itself fundamentally undifferentiated (as is stated explicitly a few sentences later). Similarly, both activity and stillness, the first manifestations of polarity, contain the seeds of their opposites.[10]

Chaos was generally frowned upon by Confucians. In bringing this largely Daoist terminology into Confucian discourse, Zhou may have been attempting to show that the Confucian view of humanity's role in the cosmos was not really opposed to the fundamentals of the Daoist worldview, in which human categories and values were thought to alienate human beings from the Dao. In effect, he was co-opting Daoist terminology to show that the Confucian worldview was actually more inclusive than the Daoist: it could accept a primordial chaos while still affirming the reality of the differentiated, phenomenal world. For Zhu Xi and his school, the most important contribution of this text was its integration of metaphysics (*taiji*, which Zhu equated with *li*, the ultimate natural/moral order) and cosmology (yin and yang and the Five Phases).

Non-Polar (*wuji*) and yet Supreme Polarity (*taiji*)![11] The Supreme Polarity in activity generates yang; yet at the limit of activity it is still. In stillness it generates yin; yet at the limit of stillness it is also active. Activity and stillness alternate; each is the basis of the other. In distinguishing yin and yang, the Two Modes are thereby established.

The alternation and combination of yang and yin generate water, fire, wood,

---

10. This is reiterated in *Tongshu*, sec. 16.

11. The line reads simply, "*Wuji er taiji.*" Since *er* can mean "and also," "and yet," or "under these circumstances," the precise meaning of the line is far from clear. Another possible translation would be "The Supreme Polarity that is Non-Polar!" It seems to be an expression of awe and wonder at the paradoxical nature of the ultimate reality.

The Diagram of the Supreme Polarity

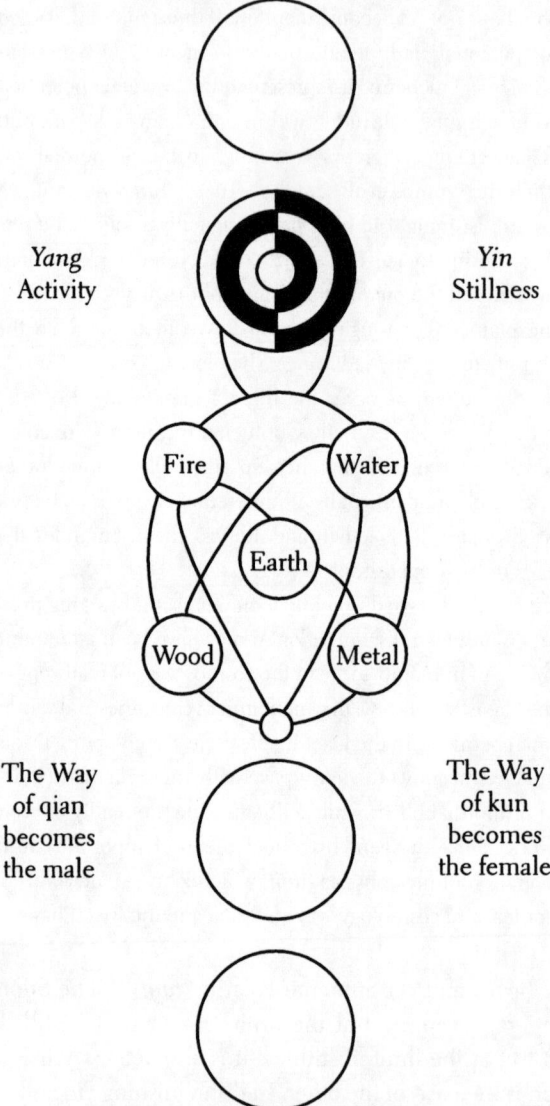

Transformation and generation of the myriad things

metal, and earth. With these Five [Phases of] *qi* harmoniously arranged, the Four Seasons proceed through them. The Five Phases are simply yin and yang; yin and yang are simply the Supreme Polarity; the Supreme Polarity is fundamentally Non-Polar. [Yet] in the generation of the Five Phases, each one has its nature.[12]

---

12. In other words, seen as a whole system, the Five Phases are based on the yin-yang polarity;

The reality of the Non-Polar and the essence of the Two [Modes] and Five [Phases] mysteriously combine and coalesce. "The Way of *qian* becomes the male; the Way of *kun* becomes the female";[13] the two *qi* stimulate each other, transforming and generating the myriad things.[14] The myriad things generate and regenerate, alternating and transforming without end.[15]

Only humans receive the finest and most spiritually efficacious [*qi*]. Once formed, they are born; when spirit (*shen*)[16] is manifested, they have intelligence; when their fivefold natures are stimulated into activity, good and evil are distinguished and the myriad affairs ensue.[17]

The sage settles these [affairs] with centrality, correctness, humaneness, and rightness (the Way of the Sage is simply humaneness, rightness, centrality, and correctness) and emphasizes stillness. (Without desire, [he is] therefore still.)[18] In so doing he establishes the ultimate of humanity. Thus the sage's "virtue equals that of Heaven and Earth; his clarity equals that of the sun and moon; his timeliness equals that of the four seasons; his good fortune and bad fortune equal those of ghosts and spirits."[19] The superior person (*junzi*) cultivates these and has good fortune. The inferior person rejects these and has bad fortune.

Therefore [the *Classic of Changes* says], "Establishing the Way of Heaven, [the sages] speak of yin and yang; establishing the Way of Earth they speak of yielding and firm [hexagram lines]; establishing the Way of Humanity they speak of humaneness and rightness."[20] It also says, "[The sage] investigates be-

---

the yin-yang polarity is the Supreme Polarity; and the Supreme Polarity is fundamentally Non-Polar. However, taken individually as temporal phases, each of the Five Phases has its own nature (as do yin and yang).

13. *Commentary on the Appended Phrases* (*Xici*), Part 1:1, *Classic of Changes* (*Zhouyi benyi* 3:1b). *Qian* and *kun* are the first two hexagrams, symbolizing pure yang and pure yin, or Heaven and Earth, respectively.

14. Paraphrasing the *Tuan* commentary to hexagram 31 (*xian*), *Classic of Changes*: "The two *qi* stimulate and respond in mutual influence, the male going beneath the female. . . . Heaven and Earth are stimulated and the myriad things are transformed and generated" (*Zhouyi benyi* 2:1a–b).

15. Cf. *Commentary of the Appended Phrases* (*Xici*), Part 1, 5.6, "Generation and regeneration are what is meant by *yi* (change)" (*Zhouyi benyi* 3:6a).

16. The word *shen* can refer either to a deity or to the finest form of *qi* (psycho-physical energy), which is capable of penetrating and pervading things and accounts for human intelligence. See *Tongshu*, chs. 3, 4, and 16.

17. The fivefold nature consists of the "Five Constant Virtues": humanity (*ren*), rightness (*yi*), ritual decorum (*li*), wisdom (*zhi*), and trustworthiness (*xin*). They correspond to the Five Phases. For incipient activity and the differentiation of good and evil, see *Tongshu*, sec. 3.

18. The two parenthetical notes are by Zhou; they are taken from *Tongshu*, sec. 6 and sec. 20. The terms "without desire" and "emphasizes stillness" were questionable to many Confucians, who usually preferred to speak of limiting desires (especially selfish desires) but not eliminating them. Both terms had Buddhist as well as Daoist connotations.

19. "Commentary on the Words of the Text" (*Wenyan*), under hexagram 1 (*qian*), *Classic of Changes* (*Zhouyi benyi* 1:8b).

20. "Explaining the Trigrams" (*Shuogua*) 2, *Classic of Changes* (*Zhouyi benyi* 4:1b).

ginnings and follows them to their ends; therefore he understands death and birth."[21] Great indeed is [the *Classic of*] *Changes*! Herein lies its perfection.

["Taijitu" and "Taijitu shuo," in *Zhou Lianxi ji* 1:1b–2b — JA]

PENETRATING THE CLASSIC OF CHANGES (*TONGSHU*)

The *Tongshu*, in forty sections, focuses on the sage as the model of humanity. Here Zhou Dunyi defines sagehood in terms of *authenticity* or *sincerity* (*cheng*), a term found prominently in the classical Confucian text, the *Mean* (*Zhongyong*). To be authentic is to be true to the innate goodness of one's nature; to actualize one's moral potential. Zhou defines authenticity in cosmological terms taken from the appendices to the *Classic of Changes* (*Yijing*). In this way he uses the concept of authenticity to link cosmology and Confucian ethics. There is significant overlap between the *Tongshu* and the "Taijitu shuo," especially in their discussions of activity and stillness as the basic expressions of yang and yin. But the *Tongshu* is less metaphysical; the emphasis here is on the moral psychology of the sage.

1. Being Authentic (*cheng*), Part 1

Being authentic is the foundation of the sage. "Great indeed is the originating [power] of *qian*! The myriad things rely on it for their beginnings."[22] It is the source of being authentic. "The way of *qian* is transformation, with each [thing] receiving its correct nature and endowment."[23] In this way authenticity is established. Being pure and flawless, it is perfectly good. Thus: "The alternation of yin and yang is called the Way. That which issues from it is good. That which fulfills it is human nature."[24] "Origination and development" are the penetration of authenticity; "adaptation and correctness" are the recovery of authenticity.[25] Great indeed is change (*yi*)![26] It is the source of human nature and endowment. [5:2a–3b]

---

21. *Commentary on the Appended Phrases* (Xici), Part 1,4, *Classic of Changes* (*Zhouyi benyi* 3:4a–b).

22. *Tuan* commentary on hexagram 1 (*qian*), *Classic of Changes* (*Zhouyi benyi* 1:3a).

23. Ibid. (*Zhouyi benyi* 1:3b).

24. *Commentary on the Appended Phrases* (Xici), Part 1,5, *Classic of Changes* (*Zhouyi benyi*, 3:5a).

25. "Origination, development, adaptation, and correctness," from the *qian* hexagram text, came to be known as the "Four Virtues (or Powers)" of *qian* (see *Zhouyi benyi*, 1:1a).

26. This sentence is the same as the penultimate sentence of the "Explanation," where *yi* is interpreted as the *Classic of Changes* rather than the process of change (following Zhu Xi's readings). But while the different readings make sense in their contexts, both meanings were probably intended by Zhou in both cases. This would reflect a traditional view (expressed in the *Commentary on the Appended Phrases* of the *Classic of Changes*) that the hexagrams comprising the core of the text are "spiritual things" (*shenwu*); they are manifestations of the cosmic process, not merely symbols of it.

2. Being Authentic, Part 2

Being a sage is nothing more than being authentic. Being authentic is the foundation of the Five Constant [virtues] and the source of the hundred practices. It is imperceptible when [one is] still, and perceptible when [one is] active;[27] perfectly correct [in stillness] and clearly pervading [in activity]. When the Five Constants and hundred practices are not authentic, they are wrong, blocked by depravity and confusion.

Therefore one who is authentic has no [need for] undertakings (*shi*). It is perfectly easy, yet difficult to practice; when one is determined and precise, there is no difficulty with it. Therefore [Confucius said], "If for a single day one can master oneself and return to ritual decorum the whole world will return to humaneness."[28] [5:9a–10a]

3. Authenticity, Incipience, and Virtue

In being authentic there is no deliberate action (*wuwei*). In incipience (*ji*) there is good and evil.[29] As for the [Five Constant] Virtues,[30] loving is called humaneness (*ren*), being right is called rightness (*yi*), being principled (*li*) is called ritual decorum (*li*), being penetrating is called wisdom (*zhi*), and preserving is called trustworthiness (*xin*). One who is by nature like this, at ease like this, is called a sage. One who recovers it and holds on to it is called a worthy. One whose subtle signs of expression are imperceptible, and whose fullness is inexhaustible, is called spiritual (*shen*). [5:11b–12a]

4. The Sage[31]

That which is "completely silent and inactive"[32] is authenticity. That which "penetrates when stimulated"[33] is spirit (*shen*). That which is active but not yet formed, between existing and not existing, is incipient.[34] Authenticity is of the essence (*jing*), and therefore clear. Spirit is responsive, and therefore mysterious.

---

27. "Imperceptible" and "perceptible" are *wu* and *you* — literally, "absent" and "present."

28. *Analects* 12:1, referring to the ruler. See ch. 3.

29. As explained below and in the previous section, the sage is authentically good without deliberate effort. "Incipience" is the first subtle stirring of activity, the first point at which good and evil can meaningfully be differentiated. The "Five Constant Virtues" are the full expression of the innately good nature.

30. See note 17, above.

31. The characteristics described here refer specifically to the *mind* of the sage.

32. *Commentary on the Appended Phrases (Xici)*, part 1,10, *Classic of Changes (Zhouyi benyi* 3:12b).

33. Ibid.

34. I.e., the point at which mental activity has begun but is not yet apparent.

Incipience is subtle, and therefore obscure. One who is authentic, spiritual, and incipient is called a sage.[35] [5:17b–18a]

16. Activity and Stillness

Activity as the absence of stillness and stillness as the absence of activity characterize things (*wu*). Activity that is not [empirically] active and stillness that is not [empirically] still characterize spirit (*shen*). Being active and yet not active, still and yet not still, does not mean that [spirit] is neither active nor still. For while things do not [inter]penetrate (*tong*),[36] spirit subtly [pervades] the myriad things.

The yin of water is based in yang; the yang of fire is based in yin. The Five Phases are yin and yang; yin and yang are the Supreme Polarity.[37] The Four Seasons revolve; the myriad things end and begin [again]. How undifferentiated! How extensive! And how inexhaustible! [5:33b–34b]

20. Learning to Be a Sage

[Someone asked:] "Can Sagehood be learned?" Reply: It can. "Are there essentials (*yao*)?" Reply: There are. "I beg to hear them." Reply: To be unified (*yi*)[38] is essential. To be unified is to have no desire.[39] Without desire one is vacuous when still and direct in activity. Being vacuous when still, one will be clear (*ming*); being clear one will be penetrating (*tong*). Being direct in activity one will be impartial (*gong*); being impartial one will be all-embracing (*pu*). Being clear and penetrating, impartial and all-embracing, one is almost [a sage]. [5:38b]

[*Tongshu*, in *Zhou Lianxi ji* 5:2a–3b, 9a–10a, 11b–12a, 17b–18a, 33b–34b, 38b — JA]

THE NUMERICALLY PATTERNED UNIVERSE IN THE PHILOSOPHY OF SHAO YONG

The thought of Shao Yong (1011–1077) reflects the continuing philosophical integration of diverse intellectual traditions in terms of primary concerns, specific concepts and ideas, and fundamental assumptions. Although Shao was classified as one of the five masters of the Neo-Confucian Learning of the Way

---

35. In other words, the mind of the sage expresses the moral nature; it responds immediately to stimuli; and it is aware of the first stirrings of its activity.

36. I.e., they are limited by their physical forms.

37. There is a nearly identical sentence in the "Explanation," above.

38. I.e., to focus the mind on fundamentals.

39. See Zhou's parenthetical note in the "Explanation," above, p. 675.

(*daoxue*), his philosophical thought put little emphasis on the moral, social, and political interests typically associated with Confucianism. His concerns were of another sort, namely, to elucidate the inherent patterns of nature and the universe and to describe, insofar as possible, the experience of sagely knowledge.

The unusual mix of characteristics that constituted Shao Yong's life and thought has posed numerous difficulties for interpreters. While Shao appears to have accepted Confucian moral, social, and political ideas, his actual references to Confucian thought largely focused on the subject of political history and how it exhibited the same patterns as those of the natural universe. His ideas on philosophical topics, including the nature of knowledge, language, and the enjoyment of life, were closely related to the Daoist view found in *Zhuangzi* and *Laozi*. There are suggestions of Buddhist influence in his thought, particularly in his ideas about sagely perception and knowledge. Dominating Shao's philosophy, his ideas concerning the underlying patterns of nature and the universe derived from an esoteric tradition associated with the *Classic of Changes* and known as the "Learning of Images and Numbers."

Shao's philosophical reputation was based to a great extent on his numerological formulations, his apparent predictive abilities, and his ideas about the sage. Shao was greatly admired as a loyal, Confucian-type dissenter, an eccentric, a teacher and a poet. Although some scholarly questions remain about the authorship of the writings attributed to him, his two major works were *Book of the Supreme Ultimate (or Supreme Polarity) Ordering the World (Huangji jingshi shu)*, a philosophical work, and *Collection of Beating on the Ground at Yichuan (Yichuan jirang ji)*, a collection of poetry.

Shao held that the world was characterized by constant change and that all change occurred according to certain regular patterns. In theoretical terms, the structure of the world consisted of a set of integrated levels of all kinds of things. Given the assumption that everything was composed of *qi* (matter-energy), these levels ranged from the extrasensory level of the ultimate One, in which no "thing" was differentiated, to the various levels of perceived things of ordinary human experience — for example, Heaven (the sky) and Earth, the myriad things, and human beings. Heaven and Earth were the two largest things in human experience, and the activities and changes that occurred in these two realms were linked together according to certain patterns. No matter whether it belonged to human beings, animals, or nature, all activity relied on the set of systematically organized categories that classified all things.

The most important patterns of activity were the binary and quaternary patterns. The binary pattern is illustrated by the pattern of production (*sheng*) and completion (*cheng*), or movement (*gan*) and response (*ying*), otherwise known as resonance. The quaternary pattern is illustrated by the four seasons, four directions, or four classics. In both cases, the two or four aspects were seen as constituting a larger event, which could itself be further expanded by numerical methods. Shao used images of both things and numbers to represent the categories that were associated respectively with Heaven and Earth, or yang (and movement) and yin (and stillness). The four forms of Heaven and the corresponding four of Earth could be symbolized, for instance, either in terms of the eight images of sun, moon, stars, zodiacal space, water, fire, earth, and stone or in terms of numbers (one to eight).

The philosophical significance of the categories was that their systematic relationships were seen as explaining how all kinds of behavior and activity were possible, while the significance of the numbers was to make clear how absolutely regular the patterns of change and the categories of things were. Shao Yong taught people to expand their perspectives, but he held that only a sage truly overcame the limited viewpoint of ordinary people. Only a sage perceived and comprehended things from the viewpoint of the whole and so "reversed" the cosmological process.

ON THE CATEGORIES AND IMAGES OF THE UNIVERSE

Nothing is larger than Heaven and Earth, and yet even they are limited. Yin and yang [qi] complete the greatness of earth. When [the movements of] yin and yang reach their limit, the four seasons are completed. When [the movements of] the hard and the soft reach their limit, the four directions are completed. [5:1a]

Heaven is produced from movement, and Earth is produced from stillness. When one movement and one stillness interact, the Way of Heaven and Earth is fulfilled. At the beginning of movement, yang arises, and at the apogee of movement, yin arises. When one yin and one yang interact, the activities (yong) of Heaven are fulfilled. At the beginning of stillness, the soft arises, and at the apogee of stillness, the hard arises. When one hard and one soft interact, the activities of earth are fulfilled. The larger of movement is called greater yang, and the smaller of movement is called lesser yang. The larger of stillness is called greater yin, and the smaller of stillness is called lesser yin. Greater yang is sun, greater yin is moon, lesser yang is stars, lesser yin is zodiacal space. When sun, moon, stars, and zodiacal space interact, the forms (ti) of heaven are fulfilled. The larger of stillness is called greater rou (soft), the smaller of stillness is called lesser rou. The larger of movement is called greater gang (hard), and the smaller of movement is called lesser gang. Greater rou is water, greater gang is fire, lesser rou is earth, lesser gang is stone. When water, fire, earth, and stone interact, the forms (ti) of earth are fulfilled. [5:1b–2a]

ON HUMAN EXPERIENCE

Therefore, the eye completes the appearances, the ear completes the sounds, the nose completes the odors and the mouth completes the flavors of the myriad things. Is human consciousness (*ling*) of the myriad things indeed not fitting? [5:4a]

The reason that humans are able to be conscious (*ling*) of the myriad things is that their eyes can receive the appearances, their ears can receive the sounds, their noses can receive the odors, and their mouths can receive the flavors of the myriad things. Sounds, appearances, odors, and flavors are the forms (*ti*) of the myriad things. The [functioning of the] eyes, ears, nose, and mouth is the activity (*yong*) of the myriad people.[40] Forms are not limited in activity but change these activities. Activities are not limited in form but transform these forms. When forms and activities intermingle, the way of humans and things is completed. [5:5a]

August Heaven's completion of things and the sage's completion of the people both have the four treasuries. The four treasuries of august Heaven are spring, summer, autumn, and winter, and yin and yang ascend and descend in their midst. The four treasuries of the sages are the *Changes*, *Documents*, *Odes*, and *Annals*, and rites and music succeed and fail in their midst. [5:8b]

Spring, summer, autumn, and winter are the seasons of august Heaven; the *Changes*, *Documents*, *Odes*, and *Annals* are the classics of the sages. When the seasons of Heaven are not deficient, the year is accomplished. When the classics of the sages are not in error, the virtue of the ruler is completed. Heaven has its constant seasons; the sage has his constant classics. [6:8a]

ON BECOMING A SAGE

That which is called perceiving things (*guanwu*) is not observing things with one's eyes. Rather than observing things with one's eyes, one contemplates them with one's mind. And rather than contemplating things with one's mind, one understands them in terms of principle (or pattern, *li*). All the things of the world have their principle, their nature (*xing*), and their endowment (*ming*).[41] The principle can be known after it is thoroughly investigated. The nature can be known after it is completed. The endowment can be known after it is reached. [6:26a]

The capability of a mirror to reflect depends on its not obscuring the forms of the myriad things. Even so, a mirror's capability not to obscure the forms of the myriad things does not measure up to water's capability to unite the forms of the myriad things. Even further, water's capability to unite the forms of the myriad things does not measure up to the sage's capability to unite the sentiments of the myriad things. The sage can unite the sentiments of the myriad things because he can perceive reflectively (*fanguan*). Perceiving reflectively is

---

40. Read *ren* (people), for *wu* (things), following the *SKCS* edition.

41. Three important concepts from the *Classic of Changes*. *Ming* is translated elsewhere as mandate, ordinance, or destiny.

not perceiving things from the viewpoint of the self. Not to perceive things from the viewpoint of the self is to perceive things from the viewpoint of things. If one can perceive things from the viewpoint of things, how can there be a self in between? [6:26b]

From this one knows that the self is also the other, the other is also the self, and the self and the other both are things. This is how [the sage] can use the eyes of the world as his own eyes; there is nothing its eyes do not see. This is how he can use the ears of the world as his own ears; there is nothing its ears do not hear. This is how he can use the mouths of the world as his own mouth; there is nothing its mouths do not say. This is how he can use the minds of the world as his own mind; there is nothing its minds do not think. . . . [The sage's] vision is extremely vast, his hearing is extremely far-reaching, his discussions are extremely lofty, and his joy is extremely grand. He can do things that are vast, distant, lofty, and grand to the utmost, and yet in the midst of it all there is no one doing it. How is he not the most spiritual and most sagely one? [6:27a]

[*Huangji jingshi shu* (SBBY) 5:1a–2a, 4a, 5a, 8b; 6:8a, 26a–27a — AB]

ZHANG ZAI AND THE UNITY
OF ALL CREATION

Zhang Zai (1020–1077), a native of the old capital region, Chang'an (Xi'an, in modern Shaanxi province), was a prominent scholar-official among the reformist protégés of Fan Zhongyan, one whom we have already encountered (Chapter 18) as a proponent of decentralization through a revival of the ancient enfeoffment and well-field systems and as a critic of Wang Anshi. A teacher of other leading Song school figures, including his nephews the Cheng brothers and the historian-statesman Sima Guang, Zhang Zai based his learning, like others of this movement, on the *Classic of Changes* and the *Mean* and came to be identified as the second leading figure in the "Succession to the Way" (*daotong*) as propounded by Zhu Xi.

Zhang's essay titled the "Western Inscription" (from having been inscribed on the west wall of his study), became celebrated as a concise and cogent statement of his ethical philosophy, based on his conception of the unity of all things in their shared psycho-physical substance of *qi* (material-force or matter-energy). According to this view, as further expounded in Zhang's larger work, *Correcting Youthful Ignorance* (*Zhengmeng*), the universe and all phenomena are not illusory products of the mind, or ephemeral manifestations of an all-pervading Emptiness, but productions of the primal life force emerging from the Supreme Ultimate or Polarity [the first principle of the *Changes*]. This primal force is in a constant process of change, understood as an ordered, natural growth process, not as a process of distintegration subject to the law of impermanence or "Emptiness," as in Buddhism, which questions whether anything has enduring value or self-nature. *Qi*, a psycho-physical substance that includes both spirit and matter, manifests itself as a dynamic energy which integrates and consolidates to form all creatures, and then, in the natural course, disintegrates to return to the original undifferentiated state of primal vacuity. The task of human beings is to comprehend the processes of change and harmonize with them, not to try to transcend or overcome them.

THE "WESTERN INSCRIPTION" *("XIMING")*

This essay is one of the most celebrated in all of Neo-Confucian literature, reproduced in all of its canonical anthologies and much discussed by later thinkers. As an eloquent statement of the human ideal in its integral relation to the cosmos, it often served as the basis for a critique of the established order. In it Zhang Zai expounds the ethical implications of his theory that all creation is formed of and united by this single underlying substance. In the terms of family relationships, so poignant and meaningful to Chinese readers, he relates how all human beings, all Heaven and Earth, must be joined together as though creatures of one flesh and blood and ruled, as appropriate to their kinship, by the principle of unselfish and humane love.

Perhaps nowhere else in all Neo-Confucian literature does lofty metaphysical theory combine so effectively with the basic warmth, compassion, and humanism of ancient Confucianism as in this short passage — a combination no less true of the language Zhang Zai uses here. For all its expansive Neo-Confucian idealism and cosmic spirit, this short essay is studded with allusions redolent of classic Confucian tradition.

Heaven is my father and Earth is my mother, and even such a small creature as I finds an intimate place in their midst.

Therefore that which extends throughout the universe I regard as my body and that which directs the universe I consider as my nature.

All people are my brothers and sisters, and all things are my companions.

The great ruler [the emperor] is the eldest son of my parents [Heaven and Earth], and the great ministers are his stewards. Respect the aged — this is the way to treat them as elders should be treated. Show affection toward the orphaned and the weak — this is the way to treat them as the young should be treated. The sage identifies his virtue with that of Heaven and Earth, and the worthy is the best [among the children of Heaven and Earth]. Even those who are tired and infirm, crippled or sick, those who have no brothers or children, wives or husbands, are all my brothers who are in distress and have no one to turn to.

When the time comes, to keep himself from harm — this is the care of a son. To rejoice in Heaven and have no anxiety — this is filiality at its purest.

One who disobeys [the principle of Heaven] violates virtue. One who destroys humanity (*ren*) is a robber. One who promotes evil lacks [moral] capacity. But one who puts his moral nature into practice and brings his physical existence to complete fulfillment can match [Heaven and Earth].

One who knows the principles of transformation will skillfully carry forward the undertakings [of Heaven and Earth], and one who penetrates spirit to the highest degree will skillfully carry out their will.

Do nothing shameful even in the recesses of your own home and thus bring dishonor to it. Preserve the mind and nourish the nature and thus [serve them] with untiring effort.

The great Yu[42] shunned pleasant wine but attended to the protection and support of his parents. Border Warden Ying[43] cared for the young and thus extended his love to his own kind.

Emperor Shun's merit lay in delighting his parents with unceasing effort, and Shensheng's[44] reverence was demonstrated when he awaited punishment without making an attempt to escape.

Zeng Can[45] received his body from his parents and reverently kept it intact throughout life, while [Yin] Boqi[46] vigorously obeyed his father's command.

Wealth, honor, blessing, and benefit are meant for the enrichment of my life, while poverty, humble station, care, and sorrow will be my helpmates to fulfillment.

In life I follow and serve [Heaven and Earth]. In death I will be at peace.

[From *Zhangzi quanshu* 1:1a–6b —WTC]

CORRECTING YOUTHFUL IGNORANCE

Supreme Harmony (Chapter 1)

The Supreme Harmony (*taihe*) is called the Way (*dao*). It embraces the nature that underlies all counterprocesses of floating and sinking, rising and falling, and motion and rest. It is the origin of the process of fusion and intermingling, of overcoming and being overcome, and of expansion and contraction. At the commencement, these processes are incipient, subtle, obscure, easy, and simple, but at the end they are extensive, great, strong, and firm. It is *qian* (Heaven)

---

42. Traditionally believed to have been the founder of the Xia dynasty. The story refers to *Mencius* 4B:20.

43. *Zuozhuan*, Yin 1.

44. Heir apparent of the state of Jin, he committed suicide because he was falsely accused of having murdered his father, Duke Xian (r. 676–651 B.C.E.). "Tan gong," Part 1, *Record of Rites*; Legge, *Li ki*, 1:126–127.

45. Disciple of Confucius known for his filiality.

46. Prince of the ninth century B.C.E. who accepted his father's decision to let the son of a scheming stepmother inherit the throne.

that begins with the knowledge of change and *kun* (Earth) that models itself after simplicity. That which is dispersed, differentiated, and capable of assuming form becomes material-force (*qi*), and that which is pure, penetrating, and not capable of assuming form becomes spirit. Unless the whole universe is in the process of fusion and intermingling like fleeting forces moving in all directions, it may not be called the Supreme Harmony. . . .

The Supreme Vacuity (*taixu*) has no physical form. It is the original substance of material-force. Its integration and disintegration are but objectifications caused by change. Human nature at its source is absolutely tranquil and unaffected by externality. When it is affected by contact with the external world, consciousness and knowledge emerge. Only those who fully develop their nature can unify the state of formlessness and unaffectedness, and the state of objectification and affectedness.

Although material-force in the universe integrates and disintegrates, and attracts and repulses in a hundred ways, nevertheless the principle (*li*) according to which it operates has an order and is unerring. . . .

The Supreme Vacuity of necessity consists of material-force. Material-force of necessity integrates to become the myriad things. Things of necessity disintegrate and return to the Supreme Vacuity. Appearance and disappearance following this cycle are all a matter of necessity. When, in the midst [of this universal operation] the sage fulfills the Way to the utmost and identifies himself [with the universal processes of appearance and disappearance] without partiality, his spirit is preserved in the highest degree. Those[47] who believe in extinction expect departure without returning, and those[48] who cling to everlasting life and are attached to existence expect things not to change. While they differ, they are the same in failing to understand the Way. Whether integrated or disintegrated, it is my body just the same. One is qualified to discuss the nature of man when one realizes that death is not extinction.

When it is understood that Vacuity, Emptiness, is nothing but material-force, then something and nothing, the hidden and the manifest, spirit and external transformation, and human nature and destiny, are all one and not a duality. He who apprehends integration and disintegration, appearance and disappearance, form and absence of form, and can trace them to their source, penetrates the secret of change.

If it is argued that material-force is produced from Vacuity, then because the two are completely different, Vacuity being infinite while material-force is finite, the one being substance and the other function, such an argument would fall into the naturalism of Laozi, who claimed that something comes from nothing and failed to understand the eternal principle of the undifferentiated unity of

---

47. I.e., the Buddhists.
48. I.e., the Taoists.

something and nothing.[49] If it is argued that the countless phenomena are but things perceived in the Supreme Vacuity, then since things and the Vacuity would not be mutually conditioned, since the form and nature of things would be self-contained, and since these, as well as Heaven and human beings, would not be interdependent, such an argument would fall into the doctrine of the Buddha who taught that mountains, rivers, and the whole earth are all subjective illusions. This principle of unity is not understood because ignorant people know superficially that the substance of the nature of things is Vacuity, Emptiness, but do not know that function is based on the Way of Heaven [law of Nature]. Instead, they try to explain the universe with limited human knowledge. Since their undertaking is not thorough, they falsely assert that the universal operation of the principles of Heaven and Earth is but illusory. They do not know the essentials of the hidden and the manifest, and jump to erroneous conclusions. They do not understand that the successive movements of yin and yang over the entire universe penetrate day and night and form the standards of Heaven, Earth, and the human. Consequently they confuse Confucianism with Buddhism and Daoism. When they discuss the problems of the nature [of human beings and things] and their destiny or the Way of Heaven, they either fall into the trap of illusionism or determine that something comes from nothing and regard these doctrines as the summit of philosophical insight, as well as the way to enter into virtue. They do not know how to choose the proper method but instead seek to go too far. Thus they are blinded by one-sided doctrines and fall into extremes.

As the Supreme Vacuity, material-force is extensive and vague. Yet it ascends, descends, and moves in all ways without ever ceasing. . . . Here lies the subtle, incipient activation of reality and unreality, of motion and rest, and the beginning of yin and yang, as well as the elements of strength and weakness. That which floats upward is the yang that is clear, while that which sinks to the bottom is the yin that is turbid. As a result of their contact and influence and of their integration and disintegration, winds and rains, snow and frost, come into being. Whether it be the countless variety of things in their changing configurations or the mountains and rivers in their fixed forms, the dregs of wine or the ashes of fire, there is nothing [in which the principle] is not revealed.

If material-force integrates, its visibility becomes effective and corporeal form appears. If material-force does not integrate, its visibility is not effective and there is no corporeal form. While material-force is integrated, how can one not say that it is only transient? While it is disintegrated, how can one hastily say that it is nothing? For this reason, the sage, having observed and examined

---

49. Or, being and non-being.

above and below, claims only to know the causes of what is hidden and what is manifest but does not claim to know the causes of something and nothing.[50]

The integration and disintegration of material-force is to the Supreme Vacuity as the freezing and melting of ice is to water. If we realize that the Supreme Vacuity is identical with material-force, we know that there is no such thing as nothing. . . .

The Supreme Vacuity is clear. Being clear, it cannot be obstructed. Not being obstructed, it is therefore spirit. The opposite of clearness is turbidity. Turbidity leads to obstruction. And obstruction leads to physical form. When material-force is clear, it penetrates, and when it is turbid, it obstructs. When clearness reaches its limit, there is spirit. When spirit concentrates, it penetrates like the breeze going through the holes [of musical instruments], producing tones and carrying them to great distances. This is the evidence of clearness. As if arriving at the destination without the necessity of going there, penetration reaches the highest degree.

From the Supreme Vacuity, there is Heaven. From the transformation of material-force, there is the Way. In the unity of the Supreme Vacuity and material-force, there is the nature [of human beings and things]. And in the unity of the nature and consciousness, there is the mind. . . .

Material-force moves and flows in all directions and in all manners. Its two elements unite and give rise to the concrete. Thus the manifold diversity of human beings and things is produced. Through the ceaseless succession of the two elements of yin and yang the great meaning of the universe is established. . . .

Spirit is not conditioned by space, and change does not assume any physical form. "The successive movement of yin and yang" [and] "unfathomable is the movement of yin and yang"[51] — these [expressions] describe the Way that penetrates day and night. . . .

No two of the products of creation are alike. From this we know that, however numerous the myriad of things, there is in reality not a single thing without yin and yang. From this we know also that the transformations and changes in the universe come about through nothing other than these two fundamental forces alone. [2:1b–5b]

Enlightenment Resulting from Sincerity (Chapter 6)

Knowledge gained through enlightenment that is the result of sincerity[52] is the innate knowledge of one's moral nature (Heavenly virtue). It is not the small knowledge of what is heard or what is seen. . . . [2:17a]

---

50. Or, being and non-being.
51. *Commentary on the Appended Phrases (Xici)*, Part 1:4–5, *Classic of Changes*.
52. As in the *Mean* 21.

By "sincerity resulting from enlightenment"[53] is meant to develop one's nature fully through the investigation of things to the utmost, and by "enlightenment resulting from sincerity"[54] is meant to investigate things to the utmost through fully developing one's nature.

One's nature is the one source of all things and is not one's own private possession. It is only the great person who is able to know and practice its principle to the utmost. Therefore, when one establishes oneself, one will help others to establish themselves. One will share one's knowledge with all. One will love universally. When one achieves something, one wants others to achieve the same. . . . [2:17b]

Those who understand the higher things return to the Principle of Heaven (*tianli*, Principle of Nature), while those who understand lower things[55] follow human desires. . . . [2:18a]

One who can fully develop his nature can also develop the nature of other people and things. One who can fulfill his destiny can also fulfill the destiny of other people and things,[56] for the nature of all human beings and things follows the Way and the destiny of all human beings and things is decreed by Heaven. I form the substance of all things without overlooking any, and all things form my substance, and I know that they do not overlook anything. Only when one fulfills one's destiny can one bring oneself and things into completion without violating their principle. . . . [2:18b]

If one investigates principle to the utmost and fully develops one's nature, then one's nature will be in accord with the virtue of Heaven and one's destiny will be in accord with the Principle of Heaven (Nature). Only life, death, and longevity and brevity of life are due to material-force and cannot be changed. [2:19b]

Enlarging the Mind (Chapter 7)

When the mind is enlarged, one can enter into all things in the universe [to examine and understand their principle].[57] As long as anything is not yet entered into, there is still something outside the mind. The mind of ordinary people is limited to the narrowness of what is seen and what is heard. The sage, however, fully develops his nature and does not allow what is seen or heard to fetter his

---

53. *Mean* 21.

54. *Mean* 21.

55. *Analects* 14:24.

56. *Mean* 22.

57. In his commentary, Zhu Xi says *tiwu* here means entering into things, unlike the same term in the *Mean* 16, where it means forming one substance with things. Both meanings are possible.

mind. As he views the universe, there is not a single thing in it that is not his own self. [2:21a]

Recorded Sayings

The great benefit of learning is to enable one to transform one's physical nature oneself. Otherwise one will have the defect of studying in order to impress others, in the end will attain no enlightenment, and cannot see the all-embracing depth of the sage. [12:3a]

The mind unites [or commands] human nature and feelings. [14:2a]

[From *Zhangzi quanshu* 2:1b–5b, 17a–b, 18a–b, 19a, 21a; 12:3a; 14:2a
— adapted from WTC]

THE CHENG BROTHERS: PRINCIPLE, HUMAN NATURE, AND THE LEARNING OF THE WAY

With the appearance of the Cheng brothers, Zhang Zai's concept of *qi* as the psycho-physical stuff of all things was joined to the concept of *li* as the inner structure or directive principle of things — something like a genetic coding, identified by the Cheng brothers with the creative life-principle (*shengsheng*) as expressed in the *Changes*. All things were seen by them as compounded of both this directive, normative principle and material-force or ether (*qi*). In humans, this principle was structured as human nature (*xing*), the moral nature (*dexing*) or Heavenly nature (*tianxing*), the perfection of which was humaneness or humanity (*ren*). Moreover, all things and affairs of the Way shared in some manner this genetic, magnetic, growth-principle of the Way. Thus the Chengs taught the "unity of principle and the diversity of its particularizations," in the sense that every existent thing or affair was rooted in a shared physical existence as well as in a moral nature, which, following Mencius, they saw as good.

Human fulfillment could be achieved by a combination of two approaches — investigation of the principles in things and introspection of principles in the mind — but the point was not to pursue separate lines of objective inquiry and judgment but to experience the convergence or unity of principle, rational and moral, in both thought and action. This experience was described in affective terms as "the humanity which forms one body with [i.e., feels for] Heaven-and-Earth and all things" — a holistic experience that allowed for the empathetic recognition of things in both their shared unity and their distinct particularity.

Two methods subserved this aim. One was the study of the classics, in which key principles were expressed. The other was examination of one's mind-and-heart through quiet sitting, the regular contemplative practice of moral reflection in the midst of an active engagement with life and the world. For this they stressed not mental quiescence but reverence and moral seriousness, an atten-tiveness to principle by which they could distinguish desires and intentions that served the common good (*gong*) from those that were selfish or partial (*si*), while acting on the former and eschewing the latter. As guides to this practice, the Chengs recommended the *Great Learning* (*Daxue*) and the *Mean* (*Zhong-yong*).

The Chengs had many followers, but their bold claim to speak authorita-tively for the Way on the basis of strong personal conviction, arising from direct experience of the Way in oneself (*zide*), aroused strong opposition to and official condemnation of their "learning of the Way" (*daoxue*). The Cheng school be-came dispersed, and it is mainly in the form reconstituted by Zhu Xi that this "learning of the Way" survived. Some modern scholars have seen the elder brother, Cheng Hao (1032–1085), as emphasizing the "learning [or school] of the mind," and have identified the younger, Cheng Yi (1033–1107), with the "learning [or school] of principle," but Zhu Xi associated the Chengs together with the study of both mind and principle, and historically they were most often referred to as "the two Chengs."

PRINCIPLE AND THE UNIVERSE

All things under Heaven can be understood by their principle. As there are things, there must be specific principles of their being. [As it is said in the *Classic of Odes*:] "Everything must have its principle."[58] [*Yishu* 18:9a]

Due to the interaction of the two material forces [yin and yang] and the Five Phases, things vary as weak and strong in thousands of ways. What the sage follows, however, is the one principle. People must return to their original nature [which is one with principle]. [6:2b]

The mind of each human being is one with the mind of Heaven and Earth. The principle of each thing is one with the principle of all things. The course of each day is one with the course of a year. [2A:1a]

There is only one principle in the world. You may extend it over the four seas and it is everywhere true. It is the unchangeable principle that "can be laid before Heaven and Earth" and is "tested by the experience of the three kings."[59] Therefore to be serious (reverent, *jing*) is to be serious with this principle. To be humane is to be humane according to this principle. And to be truthful is to be truthful to this principle. [2A:19a]

The Master said: The principle of Heaven generates and regenerates, con-tinuously without ceasing. This is because it takes no conscious action. If it had

---

58. Ode 260.
59. *Mean* 29.

acted by exhausting its knowledge and skill, it could never continue without cease. [*Cuiyan*, 2:4a]

> [From *Er Cheng yishu* 2A:1a, 19a; 6:2b; 18:9a; and *Er Cheng cuiyan* 2:4a]

HUMAN NATURE

The nature cannot be spoken of as internal or external. [*Er Cheng cuiyan* 3:4a]

The mind in itself is originally good. As it expresses itself in thoughts and ideas, it is sometimes evil. When the mind has been aroused, it should be described in terms of feelings, and not as the mind itself. For instance, water is water. But as it flows, some to the east and some to the west, it is called streams and branches. [*Er Cheng yishu* 18:17a]

The nature comes from Heaven, whereas capacity comes from material-force. When material-force is clear, capacity is clear. On the other hand, when material-force is turbid, capacity is turbid. Take, for instance, wood. Whether it is straight or crooked is due to its nature. But whether it can be used as a beam or as a truss is determined by its capacity. Capacity may be good or evil, but the nature [of man and things] is always good. [*Er Cheng yishu* 19:4b]

Human nature is universally good. In cases where there is evil it is because of one's capacity. The nature is the same as principle, and principle is the same whether in the sage emperors Yao and Shun or in the common man in the street. Material-force, which may be either clear or turbid, is the source of capacity. Men endowed with clear material-force are wise, while those endowed with turbid material-force are stupid.

Further Question: Can stupidity be changed?

Answer: Yes. Confucius said, "It is only the most intelligent and the most stupid who cannot be changed."[60] But in principle they can. Only those who ruin themselves and cast themselves away cannot be changed.

Question: Is it due to their capacity that the most stupid ruin and throw themselves away?

Answer: Certainly. But it cannot be said that capacity cannot be changed. Since all have the same basic nature, who cannot be changed? Because they ruin and cast themselves away and are not willing to learn, people are unable to change. In principle, if they were willing to learn, they could change.[61] [*Yishu* 18:7b]

"What is inborn is called the nature."[62] Nature is the same as material-force, and material-force is the same as nature. They are both inborn. In principle, there are both good and evil in the material-force with which human beings

---

60. *Analects* 17:3.

61. The foregoing statement is generally attributed to Cheng Yi.

62. A statement attributed to Mencius's opponent, Gaozi, in *Mencius* 6A:6.

are endowed at birth. However, human beings are not born with these two opposing elements in their nature. Due to the material-force with which human beings are endowed some become good from childhood and others become evil. It is true that human nature is originally good, but it cannot be said that evil is not due to human nature. For what is inborn in human beings is called their nature.

"By nature human beings are tranquil at birth."[63] The state preceding this cannot be discussed. As soon as we talk about human nature, it is already no longer human nature. Actually in our discussion of nature we only speak in terms of [what is described in the *Classic of Changes* as] "What issues from the Way is good." This is what Mencius meant by the original goodness of human nature.

The fact that whatever issues from the Way is good may be compared to the fact that water always flows downward. Water as such is the same in all cases. Yet without any effort on the part of human beings, some water flows onward to the sea without becoming dirty, while some flows only a short distance and already becomes turbid. Some travels a long distance before becoming turbid; some becomes extremely turbid, some only slightly so. But though they differ in being turbid or clear, we cannot say that the turbid water [evil] ceases to be water [nature]. This being the case, human beings must make increasing effort to purify the water, as it were. With diligent and vigorous effort, water will become clear quickly. With slow and lazy effort, water will become clear slowly. When it is clear, it is then the original water. It is not that clearness has been substituted for turbidity, or that turbidity has been taken out and laid in a corner. The original goodness of human nature is like the original clearness of water. It is not true that two distinct and opposing elements of good and evil exist in human nature and that each issues from it."[64] [1:7b–8a]

> [From *Er Cheng cuiyan* 3:4a and *Er Cheng yishu* 1:7b–8a; 18:7b, 17a; 19:4b —
> adapted from WTC]

CHENG HAO'S REPLY TO ZHANG ZAI'S LETTER
ON THE STABILIZING OF HUMAN NATURE

By stabilizing the nature we mean that the nature is stabilized whether it is in a state of activity or in a state of tranquillity. One does not lean forward or backward to accommodate things, nor does one make any distinction of the internal and external. To regard things outside the self as external, and drag oneself to conform to them, is to regard one's nature as divided into the internal and external. If one's nature is conceived to be following external things, then

---

63. "Record of Music," *Record of Rites*.
64. This passage is generally attributed to Cheng Hao.

while it is outside what is it that is within the self? One may indeed have the intention of getting rid of external temptations, but one must realize that human nature itself does not possess the two aspects of internal and external. As long as one holds that things internal and things external form two different bases, how can one hastily speak of stabilizing [human nature]?

The constant principle of Heaven-and-Earth is that their mind is in all things, yet of themselves they have no mind; and the constant principle of the sage is that his feelings are in accord with all creation, yet of himself he has no feelings. Therefore, for the training of the gentleman there is nothing better than to become broad and impartial and to respond spontaneously to all things as they come. . . .

Everyone's nature is obscured in some way, and as a consequence one cannot follow truth. In general, the trouble lies in selfishness and intellectual cleverness. Being selfish, one cannot take purposive action to respond to things, and being intellectually clever, one cannot conceive enlightenment as spontaneous. For a mind that hates external things to seek illumination in a realm where nothing exists is to look for a reflection in the back of a mirror. . . . Instead of looking upon the internal as right and the external as wrong, it is better to forget the distinction. When such a distinction is forgotten, the state of quietness and peace is attained. Peace leads to stability, and stability leads to enlightenment. When one is enlightened, how can the response to things become a burden? The sage is joyous because according to the nature of things before him he should be joyous, and he is angry because according to the nature of things before him he should be angry. Thus the joy and the anger of the sage do not depend on his own mind but on things. Does not the sage in this way respond to things? Why should it be regarded as wrong to follow external things and right to seek what is within? Compare the joy and anger of the selfish and clever person to the correctness of joy and anger of the sage. What a difference! Among human emotions the easiest to arouse but the most difficult to control is anger. But if in time of anger one can immediately forget his anger and look at the right and wrong of the matter according to truth, it will be seen that external temptations need not be hated, and one has gone a long way toward the Way.

[*Mingdao wenji* 3:1a–b — adapted from WTC]

REVERENT SERIOUSNESS AND HUMANITY

Jing, usually understood as "reverence" in classical Confucianism, has, as a basic Neo-Confucian virtue, the sense of moral seriousness and attentiveness.

As to the meaning of the Principle of Heaven: To be sincere is to be sincere to this principle, and to be serious [or reverent] is to be serious about this principle.

It is not that there is something called sincerity or seriousness by itself. [*Yishu* 2A:13b]

For moral cultivation, one must practice seriousness; for the advancement of learning, one must extend his knowledge to the utmost. [18:5b]

Question: What about people who devote all their effort to reverent seriousness in order to straighten the internal life but make no effort to square the external life?

Answer: What one has inside will necessarily be shown outside. Only worry that the internal life is not straightened. If it is straightened, then the external life will necessarily be squared. [18:3a]

If one makes singleness of mind the ruling factor with absolute steadfastness and exercises [what the *Classic of Changes* calls] "reverent seriousness to straighten the internal life,"[65] one will possess great natural power. [15:1a]

Further Question: Is reverent seriousness not tranquillity?

Answer: As soon as you speak of tranquillity, you fall into the doctrine of Buddhism. Only the word "reverent seriousness" (*jing*) should be used but never the word "tranquillity" (*jing*). As soon as you use the word "tranquillity," you imply that seriousness is deliberate forgetting. Mencius said, "Always be doing something, but without fixation, with a mind inclined neither to forget nor to help things grow."[66] "Always be doing something" means that the mind is active. "Neither to forget nor to help things grow" means not to try to force their growth. [18:6b]

Reverent seriousness means unselfishness. As soon as one lacks reverent seriousness, thousands of selfish desires arise to injure one's humanity. [15:9a]

[*Er Cheng yishu* 2A:13b; 15:1a, 9a; 18:3a, 5b, 6b — WTC, dB]

ON UNDERSTANDING THE NATURE OF HUMANITY

This essay by Cheng Hao is one of the most celebrated in Chinese literature.

The student must first of all understand the nature of humanity (*ren*). The humane man forms one body with all things comprehensively. Rightness, decorum, wisdom, and trustworthiness are all [expressions of] humanity. [One's duty] is to understand this principle and preserve humanity with sincerity (*cheng*) and reverent seriousness (*jing*), that is all. There is no need to avoid things or restrict oneself. Nor is there any need for exhaustive search. It is necessary to avoid things when one is mentally negligent, but if one is not negligent, what is the necessity for avoidance? Exhaustive search is necessary

---

65. Hexagram 2 (*kun*, the receptive, Earth).
66. *Mencius* 2A:2. See ch. 6.

when one has not found the truth, but if one preserves humanity long enough, the truth will automatically dawn on him. Why should one have to wait for exhaustive search?

Nothing can be equal to this Way. It is so vast that nothing can adequately explain it. All operations of Heaven-and-Earth are our operations. Mencius said, "All the ten thousand things are complete in me. To turn within to examine oneself and find that one is sincere is a great joy."[67] If one examines oneself but finds oneself to be insincere, there is still an opposition between the two [self and nonself]. Even if we try to identify the self with the nonself, we still do not achieve unity. How can we have joy? The purpose of [Zhang] Zai's "Western Inscription" is to explain fully this reality [of complete unity]. If we preserve humanity with this idea, what more is to be done? [As Mencius said,] "Always be doing something, but without fixation, with a mind inclined neither to forget nor to help things grow."[68] Always be doing something! This is the way to preserve humanity.

As humanity is preserved, the self and the other are then identified. For our innate knowledge of good and our innate ability to do good[69] are part of our original nature and cannot be lost. However, because we have not gotten rid of the mind dominated by old habits, we must preserve and exercise our original mind, and in time old habits will be overcome. This truth is extremely simple; the only danger is that people will not be able to hold to it. But if we practice and enjoy it, there need be no worry of our being unable to hold to it.

[*Er Cheng yishu* 2A:3a–b — adapted from WTC]

On Humaneness

The Master said, The humane person regards Heaven-and-Earth and all things as one body. There is nothing that is not part of one's self. Knowing that, where is the limit [of one's humanity]? If one does not possess [humanity as part of] oneself, one will be thousands of miles away from Heaven-and-Earth and the myriad things. [1:7b]

Essentially speaking, the way of humanity may be expressed in one word, namely, impartiality.[70] However, impartiality is but the principle of humanity; it should not be equated with humanity itself. When a person puts impartiality into practice, that is humaneness. Because of impartiality, one can accommodate both others and oneself.

[*Er Cheng yishu* 15:8b]

---

67. The allusion is to *Mencius* 7A:4, though the quotation is not exact.
68. *Mencius* 2A:2.
69. Alluding to *Mencius* 7A:15.
70. *Gong* (sense of commonality, public-mindedness).

Investigation of Things

To investigate things in order to understand principle to the utmost does not require the investigation of all things in the world. One has only to investigate the principle in one thing or one event exhaustively. For example, when we talk about filiality, we must find out what constitutes filiality. If principle cannot be exhaustively understood in one event, investigate another. One may begin with either the easiest or the most difficult, depending on one's capacity. There are thousands of tracks and paths to the capital, yet one can enter it if he has found just one way. Principle can be exhaustively understood in this way because all things share the same principle. Even the most insignificant of things and events have principle. [15:11a]

Someone asked what the first step was in the art of moral cultivation.

Answer: The first thing is to rectify the heart and make the intentions sincere. Sincerity of intention depends upon the extension of knowledge and the extension of knowledge depends upon the investigation of things. The word *ge* (investigate) means to arrive, as in the saying "The spirits of imperial progenitors have arrived."[71] There is principle in everything, and one must investigate principle to the utmost. There are many ways of doing this. One way is to read about and discuss truth and principles. Another way is to talk about people and events of the past and present and to distinguish which are right and which wrong. Still another way is to handle affairs and settle them in the proper way. All these are ways to investigate the principle of things exhaustively. [18:5b]

To investigate principle to the utmost does not mean that it is necessary to investigate the principle of all things to the utmost or that principle can be understood merely by investigating one particular principle. It means that if one investigates more and more, one will naturally come to understand principle. [2A:22b]

Question: Do observation of things and self-examination mean returning to the self to seek [principles] after principles have been discovered in things?

Answer: You do not have to say that. Things and the self are governed by the same principle. If you understand one, you understand the other, for the truth within and the truth without are identical. In its magnitude it reaches the height of Heaven and the depth of Earth, but in its refinement it constitutes the reason for being of every single thing. The student should appreciate both.

Further Question: In the extension of knowledge, how about seeking first of all in the four sprouts [of pity and compassion, shame and aversion, modesty and compliance, and the sense of right and wrong][72]?

Answer: To seek in our own nature and feelings is indeed to be concerned

---

71. "Yiji," *Classic of Documents*; Legge, *The Chinese Classics*, 3:87.
72. *Mencius* 2A:6. See ch. 6.

with our moral life. But every blade of grass and every tree possesses a principle that should be examined. [18:8b–9a]

If one extends knowledge to the utmost, one will have wisdom. Having wisdom, one can then make choices. [15:1a]

A thing is an event. If the principles underlying all events are investigated to the utmost, there is nothing that cannot be understood. [15:1a]

The investigation of principle to the utmost, the complete development of human nature, and the fulfillment of destiny are one and only one. As principle is exhaustively investigated, our nature is completely developed, and as our nature is completely developed, our destiny is fulfilled. [18:9a]

[*Er Cheng yishu* 2A:22b; 15:1a, 11a; 18:5b, 8b–9a — adapted from WTC]

Criticism of Buddhism and Daoism

Let us take a look at Buddhism from its practice. In deserting his father and leaving his family, the Buddha severed all human relationships. It was merely for himself that he lived alone in the forest. . . . As to their discourse on principle and the nature of things, it is primarily in terms of life and death. Their feelings are based on love of life and fear of death. This is selfishness. [15:5b]

You cannot say that the teachings of the Buddhists are ignorant, for actually they are quite lofty and profound. But, essentially speaking, they can finally be reduced to a pattern of selfishness. Why do we say this? In the world there cannot be birth without death or joy without sorrow. But wherever the Buddhists go, they always want to pervert this truth and preach the elimination of birth and death and the neutralization of joy and sorrow. In the final analysis this is nothing but selfishness. [15:7b]

The Buddhists advocate the renunciation of the family and the world. Fundamentally, the family cannot be renounced. Let us say that it can, however, when the Buddhists refuse to recognize their parents as parents and run away. But how can a person escape from the world? Only when a person no longer stands under Heaven or upon the Earth is he able to forsake the world. [18:10b]

[*Er Cheng yishu* 15:5b, 7b; 18:10b — adapted from WTC]

THE SYNTHESIS OF SONG
NEO-CONFUCIANISM IN ZHU XI

Part of the greatness of Zhu Xi (1130–1200) lay in his remarkable capacity to adapt and enfold in one system of thought the individual contributions of his Song predecessors. For this task he was well equipped by his breadth and subtlety of mind, and by powers of analysis and synthesis that enabled him, while putting ideas together, to articulate each of them with greater clarity and coherence than their originators had done. In this way he defined more precisely such concepts as the Supreme Ultimate (Supreme Pole or Polarity, *taiji*), principle (*li*), material-force (*qi*), human nature (*xing*) and the mind-and-heart (*xin*). Of his predecessors it was Cheng Yi upon whose philosophy he mostly built. Consequently his school of thought is often identified as the Cheng-Zhu school, and the doctrine of principle (*li*) is the most characteristic feature of their common teaching.

Zhu Xi likened principle in things to a seed of grain, each seed having its own particularity but also manifesting generic, organic elements of structure, growth pattern, direction, and functional use, whereby each partakes of both unity (commonality) and diversity. Unlike the analogy of the Buddha-nature to the moon and its innumerable reflections in water (in which the latter are understood to be insubstantial, passing phenomena), principle for Zhu was real both in its substantial unity and in its functional diversity. Hence he called the study of principle in all things, under both aspects, "real," "solid," "substantial" learning (*shixue*).

In humankind this principle is one's moral nature, which is fundamentally good. The human mind, moreover, is in essence one with the mind of the universe, capable of entering into all things and understanding their principles. Zhu Xi believed in human perfectibility, in the overcoming of those limitations or weaknesses that arise from an imbalance in one's psycho-physical endowment. His method was the "investigation of things" as taught in the *Great Learning* — that is, the study of principles, and also self-cultivation to bring one's conduct into conformity with the principles that should govern it.

In this type of self-cultivation, broad learning went hand in hand with moral discipline. The "things" that Zhu Xi had in mind to investigate may be primarily understood as "affairs," including matters of conduct, human relations, political problems, etc. To understand them fully required of the individual both a knowledge of the literature in which such principles are revealed (the classics and histories) and an active ethical culture that could develop to the fullest the virtue of humaneness (*ren*). It is through humaneness that one overcomes all selfishness and partiality, enters into all things in such a way as to identify oneself fully with them, and thus unites oneself with the mind of the universe, which is love and creativity itself. *Ren* is the essence of being human, one's "humanity," but it is also the cosmic principle that produces and embraces all things.

At the same time Zhu spoke of this teaching as "real" or "practical" learning (*shixue*) because it was based in natural human sentiments and could be practiced in daily life through normal intellectual and moral faculties. These were to be developed through what Confucius, and now Zhu Xi, called "learning for one's self" (meaning for one's own self-development and self-fulfillment), a learning Zhu Xi urged on all, ruler and subject alike.

In contrast to Buddhism there is in Zhu Xi a kind of positivism that affirms the reality of things and the validity of objective study. His approach is plainly intellectual, reinforcing the traditional Confucian emphasis upon scholarship. Zhu Xi himself is probably the most stupendous example of such scholarly endeavor in the Chinese tradition. He wrote commentaries on almost all of the Confucian Classics, conceived and supervised the condensation of Sima Guang's monumental history of China, and interested himself in rites, governmental affairs, education, and agriculture. He was a dynamic teacher at the Academy of the White Deer Grotto and kept up an active correspondence on a wide variety of subjects. He had less interest, however, in pursuing his "investigation of things" into the realms of what we would call natural or social science. To the last his humanism manifested itself in a primary concern for human values and ends. The kind of objective investigation that set these aside or avoided the ultimate problems of human life would have seemed to him at best secondary and possibly dangerous. Nevertheless, his philosophy, which stressed the order and intelligibility of things, could in a general way be considered conducive to the growth of science in a larger sense.

Zhu's later influence was felt chiefly through his commentaries on the Four Books — the *Great Learning*, the *Mean*, the *Analects*, and the *Mencius* — which he first canonized as basic texts of the Confucian school. In subsequent dynasties these texts, with Zhu Xi's commentaries, became the basis of the civil service examinations and thus, in effect, the official orthodoxy of the empire from the fourteenth century down to the turn of the twentieth century. Though subsequent thinkers arose to dispute his metaphysics, few failed to share in his essential spirit of intellectual inquiry, which involved focusing upon the Classics and reinterpreting them to meet the needs of their own time. Moreover, in Japan and Korea his writings likewise became accepted as the most complete and authoritative exposition of Confucian teaching. As such, they exerted a significant influence on the entire cultural development of East Asia well into modern times.

PRINCIPLE AND MATERIAL-FORCE

In the universe there has never been any material-force (*qi*) without principle (*li*) or principle without material-force.

Question: Which exists first, principle or material-force?

Answer: Principle has never been separated from material-force. However, principle is above the realm of corporeality, whereas material-force is within the realm of corporeality. Hence when spoken of as being above or within the realm of corporeality, is there not a difference of priority and posteriority? Principle has no corporeal form, but material-force is coarse and contains impurities. [49:1a–b]

Fundamentally, principle and material-force cannot be spoken of as prior or posterior. But if we must trace their origin, we are obliged to say that principle is prior. However, principle is not a separate entity. It exists right in material-force. Without material-force, principle would have nothing to adhere to. Material-force consists of the Five Phases of metal, wood, water, fire, and earth, while principle includes humaneness, rightness, ritual decorum, and wisdom. [49:1b]

Question about the relation between principle and material-force:

Answer: Cheng Yi[73] expressed it very well when he said that principle is one but its manifestations are many. When Heaven, Earth, and the myriad things are spoken of together, there is only one principle. As applied to human beings, however, there is in each individual a particular principle. [49:1b]

Question: What are the evidences that principle is in material-force?

Answer: For example, there is order in the complicated interfusion of yin and yang and the Five Phases. This is [an evidence of] principle [in material-force]. If material-force did not consolidate and integrate, principle would have nothing to attach itself to. [49:2b]

Question: May we say that before Heaven and Earth existed there was first of all principle?

Answer: Before Heaven and Earth existed, there was certainly only principle. As there is this principle, therefore there are Heaven and Earth. If there were no principle, there would also be no Heaven and Earth, no human beings, no things, and, in fact, no containing or sustaining [of things by Heaven and Earth] to speak of. As there is principle, there is therefore material-force, which operates everywhere and nourishes and develops all things.

Question: Is it principle that nourishes and develops all things?

Answer: As there is this principle, therefore there is this material-force operating, nourishing, and developing. Principle itself has neither corporeal form nor body. [49:3a–b]

Question: "The Lord-on-High has conferred even on inferior people a moral sense."[74] "When Heaven intends to confer on a person a great responsibility . . ."[75] "Heaven, to protect the common people, made for them rulers."[76] "Heaven, in the production of things, is sure to be bountiful to them, according to their qualities."[77] "On the good-doer, the Lord-on-High sends down all blessings, and on the evil-doer, He sends down all miseries."[78] "When Heaven is

---

73. Zhu Xi refers to predecessors by honorific titles, which have been converted in the following texts to their ordinary names.

74. "Announcement of Tang," *Classic of Documents*; Legge, *The Chinese Classics*, 3:184–85.

75. *Mencius* 6B:15. "When Heaven intends to confer on a person a great responsibility it first visits his mind and will with suffering, toils his sinews and bones, subjects his body to hunger, exposes him to poverty, and confounds his projects."

76. "Great Declaration," 1, *Classic of Documents*; Legge, *The Chinese Classics*, 3:286.

77. *Mean* 17.

78. "Instruction of Yi," *Classic of Documents*; Legge, *The Chinese Classics*, 3:198.

about to send calamities to the world, it will usually produce abnormal people as a measure of their magnitude."[79] In passages like these, does it mean that there is really a master doing all this up in the blue sky or does it mean that Heaven has no personal consciousness and the passages are merely deductions from principle?

Answer: These passages have the same meaning. It is simply that principle operates this way. [49:4a]

Throughout the universe there are both principle and material-force. Principle refers to the Way, which is above the realm of corporeality and is the source from which all things are produced. Material-force refers to material objects, which are within the realm of corporeality: it is the instrument by which things are produced. Therefore in the production of man and things, they must be endowed with principle before they have their material-force, and they must be endowed with material-force before they have corporeal form. [49:5b]

There is principle before there can be material-force. But it is only when there is material-force that principle finds a place to settle. This is the process by which all things are produced, whether [as] large as Heaven-and-Earth or as small as ants. Fundamentally, principle cannot be interpreted in the sense of existence or nonexistence. Before Heaven-and-Earth came into being, it already was as it is. [49:6a]

The nature of man and things is nothing but principle and cannot be spoken of in terms of integration and disintegration. That which integrates to produce life and disintegrates to produce death is only material-force, and what we call the spirit, the soul (*hunpo*), and consciousness are all effects of material-force. Therefore when material-force is integrated, there are these effects. When it is disintegrated, they are no more. As to principle, fundamentally it does not exist or cease to exist because of such integration or disintegration. As there is a certain principle, there is the material-force corresponding to it, and as this material-force integrates in a particular instance, its principle is also endowed in that instance. [49:8a]

[*Zhuzi quanshu* 49:1a–8a — WTC, dB]

THE SUPREME ULTIMATE (POLARITY)

Question: The Supreme Ultimate (Polarity, *taiji*) is not a thing existing in a chaotic state before the formation of Heaven-and-Earth but a general name for the principles of Heaven-and-Earth and the myriad things. Is that correct?

Answer: The Supreme Ultimate is merely the principle of Heaven-and-Earth

---

79. Source unidentified.

and the myriad things. With respect to the myriad things, there is the Supreme Ultimate in each and every one of them. Before Heaven-and-Earth existed, there was assuredly this principle. It is this principle that through movement generates the yang. It is also this principle that out of tranquillity generates the yin. [49:8b–9a]

Fundamentally, there is only one Supreme Ultimate, yet each of the myriad things has been endowed with it and each in itself possesses the Supreme Ultimate in its entirety. This is similar to the fact that there is only one moon in the sky, but when its light is scattered upon rivers and lakes, it can be seen everywhere. It cannot be said that the moon has been split. [49:10b–11a]

The Supreme Ultimate is not spatially conditioned; it has neither corporeal form nor body. There is no spot where it may be fixed. When it is considered in the state before activity begins, this state is nothing but tranquillity. Now activity, tranquillity, yin and yang are all within the realm of corporeality. However, activity is after all the activity of the Supreme Ultimate and tranquillity is also its tranquillity, although activity and tranquillity themselves are not the Supreme Ultimate. This is why Master Zhou Dunyi only spoke of that state as Non-finite (or Non-Polar) — the unconditioned.

The Supreme Ultimate is simply the principle of the highest good. Each and every person has in him the Supreme Ultimate, and each and every thing has in it the Supreme Ultimate. What Master Zhou called the Supreme Ultimate (or Supreme Polarity) is an appellation for all virtues and the utmost good in Heaven-and-Earth, human beings, and things. [49:11b]

The Supreme Ultimate is similar to the top of a house or the zenith of the sky, beyond which point there is no more. It is the ultimate of principle. Yang is active and yin is tranquil. In these it is not the Supreme Ultimate that acts or remains tranquil. It is simply that there are the principles of activity and tranquillity. Principle is not visible; it becomes visible through yin and yang. Principle attaches itself to yin and yang as a man sits astride a horse. As soon as yin and yang produce the Five Phases, they are confined and fixed by physical nature and are thus differentiated into individual things, each with its nature. But the Supreme Ultimate is in all of them. [49:13a]

[*Zhuzi quanshu* 49:8b–13a — WTC]

HEAVEN-AND-EARTH

In the beginning of the universe there was only material-force, consisting of yin and yang. This force moved and circulated, turning this way and that. As this movement gained speed, a mass of sediment became pressed together and, since there was no outlet for this, it consolidated to form the Earth in the center of the universe. The clear part of material-force formed the sky, the sun and moon, and the stars and zodiacal spaces. It is only on the outside that the encircling movement perpetually goes on. The Earth exists motionless in the center of the system, not at the bottom. [49:19a]

Heaven-and-Earth have no other business but to have the mind to produce things. The material-force of the origination [the Supreme Ultimate, including principle and material-force] revolves and circulates without a moment of rest, doing nothing except creating the myriad things.

Heaven-and-Earth reach all things with this mind. When human beings receive it, it becomes the human mind. When things receive it, it becomes the mind of things [in general]. And when grass, trees, birds, and animals receive it, it becomes the mind of grass, trees, birds, and animals. All of these are simply the one mind of Heaven-and-Earth.

[*Zhuzi quanshu* 49:19a–24b — WTC]

SPIRITUAL BEINGS

Someone asked whether there are spiritual beings.

Answer: How can this matter be quickly explained? Even if it could, would you believe it? You must look into all principles of things and gradually understand, and then this puzzling problem will be solved by itself. When Fan Chi asked about wisdom, Confucius said, "Devote yourself to what must rightly be done for the people; respect spiritual beings, while keeping at a distance from them. This may be called wisdom."[80] Let us understand those things that can be understood. Those that cannot be understood let us set aside. By the time we have thoroughly understood ordinary daily matters, the principles governing spiritual beings will naturally be seen. This is the way to wisdom. When Confucius said, "Before you have learned to serve human beings, how can you serve spirits?"[81] he expressed the same idea. [51:2a]

By spirit is meant the master of the body and the vital force. Human beings are born as a result of the integration of refined material-force. They possess their material-force only in a certain amount, which in time necessarily becomes exhausted. When exhaustion takes place, the heavenly aspect of the soul and the vital force return to Heaven, the body and the earthly aspect of the soul return to Earth, and the person dies. . . . At death material-force necessarily disintegrates. It does not disintegrate completely at once, however. Therefore, in religious sacrifices we have the principle of spiritual influence and response. Whether the material-force [spirit] of ancestors of many generations ago is still there or not cannot be known. Nevertheless, since those who perform the sacrificial rites are their descendants, the material-force [spirit] between them is

---

80. *Analects* 6:20.
81. *Analects* 11:11. See ch. 3.

after all the same. Hence there is the principle by which they can penetrate and respond. But the material-force that has disintegrated cannot again be integrated. According to the Buddhists, a person after death becomes a spirit, and the spirit again becomes a person. If so, then in the universe there should always be the same number of people coming and going, with no need of the creative process of generation and regeneration. This is decidedly absurd. [51:18b–20a]

[*Zhuzi quanshu* 51:2a, 18b–20a — adapted from WTC]

HUMAN NATURE, THE NATURE OF THINGS, AND THEIR DESTINY

[The *Classic of Odes* says], "Heaven produces the teeming multitude in such a way that inherent in every single thing there is the principle for its being."[82] This means that at the very time when a person is born, Heaven has already given him his nature. The nature is nothing but principle. It is called the nature because it is endowed in man. It is not a concrete entity by itself, to be destined as nature, and to exist without beginning and without end. As I once illustrated, destiny or mandate is like an appointment to office by the throne, and the nature is like the office retained by the officer. This is why Cheng Yi said that destiny is what is endowed by Heaven and the nature is what things receive.[83] The reason is very clear. Therefore when ancient sages and virtuous men spoke of the nature and destiny, they always spoke of them in relation to concrete affairs. For example, when they spoke of full development of human nature they meant the complete realization of the moral principles of the three mainstays [or bonds]: [between ruler and minister, father and son, and husband and wife] and the Five Constant Virtues [rightness on the part of the father, love on the part of the mother, brotherliness on the part of the elder brother, respect on the part of the younger brother, and filiality on the part of the child], covering the relationships between the ruler and ministers and between father and son. When they spoke of nourishing our nature, they meant that we should nourish these moral principles so as to keep them from injury.

[*Zhuzi quanshu* 42:2b–5a — adapted from WTC]

THE NATURE AS PRINCIPLE

The Way is identical with the nature of man and things and their nature is identical with the Way. They are one and the same. But we must understand why it is called the nature and why it is called the Way. [42:6a]

After reading some essays by Xun[84] and others on the nature, the Teacher

---

82. Ode 260.
83. *Er Cheng yishu* 18:17a.
84. Huang Xun (1147–1212), a disciple of Zhu Xi.

said: In discussing the nature it is important to know first of all what kind of thing it really is. Cheng Yi put it best when he said that "the nature is the same as principle." Now if we regard it as principle, then surely it has neither physical form nor shadow. It is nothing but this very principle. In human beings, humaneness, rightness, ritual decorum, and wisdom are his nature, but what physical shape or form have they? All they have are the principles of humaneness, rightness, decorum, and wisdom. As they possess these principles, many deeds are carried out, and human beings are able to have the feelings of commiseration, shame, deference and compliance, and of right and wrong. . . . In human beings, the nature is merely humaneness, rightness, decorum, and wisdom. According to Mencius, these four fundamental virtues are rooted in the mind-and-heart. When, for example, he speaks of the mind of commiseration, he attributes feeling to the mind. [42:6b]

Original nature is an all-pervading perfection not contrasted with evil. This is true of what Heaven has endowed in the self. But when it operates in human beings, there is the differentiation of good and evil. When humans act in accord with it, there is goodness. When humans act out of accord with it, there is evil. How can it be said that the good is not the original nature? It is in its operation in human beings that the distinction of good and evil arises, but conduct in accord with the original nature is due to the original nature. If, as they say, there is the original goodness and there is another goodness contrasted with evil, there must be two natures. Now what is received from Heaven is the same nature as that in accordance with which goodness ensues, except that as soon as good appears, evil, by implication, also appears, so that we necessarily speak of good and evil in contrast. But it is not true that there is originally an evil existing out there, waiting for the appearance of good to oppose it. We fall into evil only when our actions are not in accord with the original nature. [42:9b–10a]

In your letter you[85] say that you do not know whence comes human desire. This is a very important question. In my opinion, what is called human desire is the exact opposite of the Principle of Heaven [Nature]. It is permissible to say that human desire exists because of the Principle of Heaven, but it is wrong to say that human desire is the same as the Principle of Heaven, for in its original state the Principle of Heaven is free from human desire. It is from the deviation in the operation of the Principle of Heaven that human desire arises. Cheng Hao says, "Good and evil in the world are both the Principle of Heaven. What is called evil is not originally evil. It becomes evil only because of deviation from the Mean."[86] Your quotation, "Evil must also be interpreted as the nature," expresses the same idea. [42:14b–15a]

[*Zhuzi quanshu* 42:6a–15a — adapted from WTC]

---

85. He Shujing.
86. *Er Cheng yishu* 2A:1b.

HUMAN NATURE AND THE NATURE OF THINGS COMPARED

Ji[87] submitted to the Teacher the following statement concerning a problem about which he was still in doubt: The nature of human beings and the nature of things are in some respects the same and in other respects different. Only after we know wherein they are similar and wherein they are different can we discuss the nature. Now, as the Supreme Ultimate (or Supreme Polarity) begins its activity, the two material-forces [yin and yang] assume corporeal form, and as they assume corporeal form, the myriad transformations of things are produced. Both humans and things have their origin here. This is where they are similar. But the two material-forces and the Five Phases, in their fusion and intermingling, and in their interaction and mutual influence, produce innumerable changes and inequalities. This is where they are different. They are similar in regard to principle but different in respect to material-force. There must be principle, for only then can there be that which constitutes the nature of humans and things. Consequently, what makes them similar cannot make them different. There must be material-force, for only then can there be that which constitutes their corporeal form. Consequently, what makes them different cannot make them similar. Therefore, in your *Questions and Answers on the Great Learning* (*Daxue huowen*), you said, "From the point of view of principle, all things have one source, and of course human beings and things cannot be distinguished as higher and lower creatures. From the point of view of material-force, those that receive it in its perfection and are unimpeded become human, while those that receive it partially and and are obstructed become things. Because of this, they cannot be equal, but some are higher and others are lower."[88] However, while in respect to material-force they are unequal, they both possess it as the stuff of life, and, while in respect to principle they are similar, in receiving it to constitute their nature, humans alone differ from other things. Thus consciousness and movement proceed from material-force, while humaneness, rightness, decorum, and wisdom proceed from principle. Both human beings and things are capable of consciousness and movement, but though things possess humaneness, rightness, decorum, and wisdom, they cannot have them completely. . . .

In your *Collected Commentaries on the Mencius* (*Mengzi jizhu*) you maintain "In respect to material-force, humans and things do not seem to differ in consciousness and movement, but in respect to principle, the endowment of humaneness, rightness, decorum, and wisdom is necessarily imperfect in things."[89] Here you say that man and things are similar in respect to material-

---

87. Chen Ji, a pupil from Fuzhou.
88. *Daxue huowen*, p. 8b.
89. *Mengzi jizhu*, ch. 1, commenting on *Mencius* 6A:3.

force but differ in respect to principle, in order to show that human beings are higher and cannot be equaled by things. In the *Questions and Answers on the Great Learning*, you say that human beings and things are similar in respect to principle but differ in respect to material-force, in order to show that the Supreme Ultimate is not deficient in anything and cannot be interfered with by any individual. . . . Is this correct?

The Teacher commented: In discussing this subject you have been very clear. It happened that last evening a friend talked about this matter, and I briefly explained it to him, but not so systematically as you have done in this statement. [42:27b–29a]

Question: Principle is what is received from Heaven by both human beings and things. Do things without feeling also possess principle?

Answer: They certainly have principle. For example, a ship can go only on water while a cart can go only on land. [42:30a]

[*Zhuzi quanshu* 42:27b–30a — adapted from WTC]

THE PSYCHO-PHYSICAL NATURE

The nature is principle only. But, without the material-force and solid substance of the universe, principle would have nothing in which to inhere. When material-force is received in its clear state, there will be no obscurity or obstruction and principle will express itself freely. If there is obscurity or obstruction, then, in the operation of principle, the Principle of Heaven will dominate if the obstruction is small, and human selfish desire will dominate if the obstruction is great. From this we know that the original nature is perfectly good. However, it will be obstructed if the psycho-physical nature contains impurity. In our discussion of the nature, we must include the psycho-physical nature before the discussion can be complete. [43:2b–3a]

The nature is like water. If it flows in a clean channel, it is clear; if it flows in a dirty channel, it becomes turbid. When the nature is endowed with material substance that is clear and balanced, it will be preserved in its completeness. This is true of human beings. When the nature is endowed with material substance that is turbid and unbalanced, it will be obscured. This is true of animals. Material-force may be clear or turbid. That received by humans is clear and that received by animals is turbid. Humans mostly have clear material-force and hence are different from animals. However, those whose material-force is turbid are not far removed from animals. [43:7a–b]

Someone asked about this inequality in the clearness of the material endowment. The teacher said: Differences in the material endowment are not limited to one kind and are not described only in terms of clearness and turbidity. There are human beings who are so bright that they know everything. Their material-force is clear, but what they do may not all be in accord with principle.

The reason is that their material-force is not pure. There are others who are respectful, generous, loyal, and truthful. Their material-force is pure, but their knowledge is not clear. From this you can deduce the rest. [42:8a]

> [*Zhuzi quanshu* 42:8a, 43:2b–3a, 7a–b, 8a — WTC]

THE MIND-AND-HEART

Here the Chinese word *xin* represents both the mind and the heart, intellect as well as feelings.

The principle of the mind is the Supreme Ultimate. The activity and tranquillity of the mind are the yin and yang. [44:1b]

Question: Is consciousness what it is because of the intelligence of the mind or is it because of the activity of material-force?

Answer: Not material-force alone. Before [material-force] existed, there was already the principle of consciousness. But principle at this stage does not give rise to consciousness. Only when it comes into union with material-force is consciousness possible. Take, for example, the flame of this candle. It is because it has received this rich fat that there is so much light.

Question: Mind is consciousness and the nature is principle. How do the mind and principle pervade each other and become one?

Answer: Without the mind, principle would have nothing in which to inhere. [44:2a]

Question: Mind as an entity embraces all principles. The good that emanates, of course, proceeds from the mind. But the evil that emanates is all due to physical endowment and selfish desires. Does it also proceed from the mind?

Answer: It is certainly not the original substance of the mind, but it also emanates from the mind.

Further Question: Is this what is called the human mind?[90]

Answer: Yes.

In the passage [by Zhang Zai], "When the mind is enlarged, it can enter into all things in the universe,"[91] the expression "enter into" is like saying that humaneness enters into all events and is all-pervasive. It means that the operation of the principle of the mind penetrates all as blood circulates and reaches the entire [body]. If there is a single thing not yet entered, the reaching is not yet complete and there are still things not yet embraced. This shows that the

---

90. The "human mind" is contrasted with the "moral mind," or the mind of the Way, in that the former is in a precarious position and liable to make mistakes, whereas the moral mind follows Heaven's principles. The terms derive from "Counsels of the Great Yu," *Classic of Documents*; Legge, *The Chinese Classics*, 3:61–62.

91. *Zhangzi quanshu* 2:21a. See above, p. 688.

mind still excludes something. For selfishness separates and obstructs, and consequently the external world and the self stand in opposition. This being the case, even those dearest to us may be excluded. "Therefore the mind that excludes is not qualified to be one with the mind of Heaven."[92] [44:12b]

Question: How can the mind by means of moral principle (Dao) penetrate all things without any limit?

Answer: The mind is not like a side door that can be enlarged by force. We must eliminate the obstructions of selfish desires, and then it will be pure and clear and able to know all. When the principles of things and events are investigated to the utmost, comprehension will come as a great release. Zhang Zai said, "Do not allow what is seen or heard to fetter the mind." "When the mind is enlarged, it can enter into all things in the universe." This means that if penetration is achieved through moral principles, there will be comprehension like a great release. If we confine [the mind] to what is heard and what is seen, naturally our understanding will be narrow. [44:13a–b]

Someone asked whether it is true that the Buddhists have a doctrine of observation of the mind.

Answer: The mind is that with which human beings rule their bodies. It is one and not a duality, is subject and not object, and controls the external world instead of being controlled by it. Therefore, if we observe external objects with the mind, their principles will be apprehended. Now, [in the Buddhist view], there is another thing to observe the mind. If this is true, then outside this mind there is another one which is capable of controlling it. But is what we call the mind a unity or a duality? Is it subject or object? Does it control the external world or is it controlled by the external world? We do not need to be taught to see the fallacy of the [Buddhist] doctrine.

Someone may say: In the light of what you have said, how are we to understand such expressions by sages and worthies as "discrimination and oneness of mind"[93] or "hold it fast and you preserve it—let it go and you lose it,"[94] "fully develop one's mind and know one's nature,"[95] "preserve one's mind and nourish one's nature"[96]? . . .

Answer: These expressions [and the Buddhist doctrine] sound similar but are different, just like the difference between seedling and weeds, or between vermilion and purple, and the student should clearly distinguish them. What is meant by the precariousness of the human mind is the budding of human selfish desires, and what is meant by the subtlety of the moral mind is the mysterious depth of the Principle of Heaven. The mind is one; it is simply

---

92. Ibid.
93. "Counsels of the Great Yu," *Classic of Documents*; Legge, *Chinese Classics*, 3:61.
94. *Mencius* 6A:8.
95. *Mencius* 7A:1.
96. *Mencius* 6A:8.

called differently depending on whether or not it is rectified. The meaning of "be discriminating [in regard to the human mind] and be one [with the mind of the Way]" is to abide by what is right and discern what is wrong, and to discard the wrong and restore the right. If we can do this, we shall indeed "hold fast the Mean," and avoid the partiality of too much or too little. . . . "Holding it fast"[97] is another way of saying that we should not allow our conduct during the day to fetter and destroy our innate mind, which is characterized by humaneness and rightness. It does not mean that we should sit in a rigid posture to preserve the obviously idle consciousness and declare that "this is holding it fast and preserving it"! As to the full development of the mind, this is to investigate things and study their principles to the utmost, to arrive at broad penetration, and thus to be able fully to realize the principle embodied in the mind. By "preserving the mind" is meant "seriousness to straighten the internal life and rightness to square the external life,"[98] a way of cultivation similar to what has just been called discrimination, oneness, holding fast, and preserving. Therefore one who has fully developed his mind can know his nature and know Heaven because the reality of the mind is unclouded and he is equipped to search into principle in its natural state. One who has preserved the mind can nourish his nature and serve Heaven because the substance of the mind is not lost and he is equipped to follow principle in its natural state.

[*Zhuzi quanshu* 44:1b–13b, 28a–29b — adapted from WTC]

[Amending Cheng Yi's comment that "the human mind-and-heart is human desires":] The human mind cannot be taken simply as human desires. If the human mind were simply human desires, the sage [Shun] would not have spoken of it as "precarious." To say that it is "precarious" means only that it is in danger of running after human [selfish] desires.

[Quoting Lu Xiangshan:] "If Shun had meant to say that the human mind was entirely evil, then he would have stated that it was no good, so men would shun it. His referring to it instead as "precarious" means that it was unsafe and could not be relied upon [being liable to either good or evil]. When he spoke of the need for discrimination, he sought discriminating judgment so as not to allow the good to become mixed with the bad!"

[Zhu Xi's comment:] This is of course correct.

[*Zhuzi yulei* 78:27a (p. 3193); 62:9a (p. 2363) — dB]

THE MIND, THE NATURE, AND THE FEELINGS

Some time ago I read statements by Hu Wufeng (Hu Hong, 1105–1161) in which he spoke of the mind only in contrast to the nature, leaving the feelings un-

---

97. *Mencius* 6A:8.
98. Hexagram 2 (*kun*), *Classic of Changes.*

accounted for. Later when I read Zhang Zai's doctrine that "the mind unites [or commands] human nature and feelings,"[99] I realized that it was a great contribution. Only then did I find a satisfactory account of the feelings. His doctrine agrees with that of Mencius. In the words of Mencius, "The mind of compassion is the sprout of humaneness."[100] Now humaneness is the nature, and compassion is feeling. In this, the mind can be seen through the feelings. He further said, "Humaneness, rightness, decorum, and wisdom are rooted in the mind."[101] In this, the mind is seen through the nature. For the mind embraces both the nature and the feelings. The nature is substance and feelings are function. [45:3a–b]

The nature is the state before activity begins; the feelings are the state when activity has started; and the mind includes both of these states. For the nature is the mind before it is aroused, while feelings are the mind after it is aroused, as expressed in the saying "The mind unites and commands human nature and feelings." Desire emanates from feelings. The mind is comparable to water; the nature is comparable to the tranquillity of still water; feeling is comparable to the flow of water; and desire is comparable to its waves. Just as there are good and bad waves, so there are good desires, such as "I desire to be humane,"[102] and bad desires that rush out like wild and violent waves. When bad desires are substantial, they will destroy the Principle of Heaven, as water bursts a dam and damages everything. When Mencius said that "feelings enable people to do good,"[103] he meant that the concrete feelings flowing from our nature are originally all good. [45:4a]

Question: Is it correct to suppose that sages never show any anger?

Answer: How can they never show anger? When they ought to be angry, they will show it in their countenances. . . . When one becomes angry at the right time, he will be acting to the proper degree. When the matter is over, anger disappears, and none of it will be retained. [45:14b–15a]

[*Zhuzi quanshu* 45:3a–4a, 14b–15a — adapted from WTC]

HUMANENESS

As discussed here by Zhu Xi, humaneness (*ren*) signifies empathetic attention or love in the widest sense, both as the essential human virtue and as a cosmic force.

Whenever and wherever humaneness flows and operates, rightness will be fully rightness and ritual decorum and wisdom will be fully decorum and wisdom.

---

99. *Zhangzi quanshu* 14:2a. See above, p. 688.
100. *Mencius* 2A:6.
101. *Mencius* 7A:21.
102. *Analects* 7:29.
103. *Mencius* 6A:6.

It is like the ten thousand things being stored and preserved. There is not a moment of cessation in such an operation, for in all of these things there is the spirit of life. Take, for example, such things as seeds of grain or the pits of peach and apricot. When sown, they will grow. They are not dead things. For this reason they are called *ren* [the word *ren* means both "pit" and "humaneness"]. This shows that *ren* implies the spirit of life. [*Zhuzi quanshu* 47:3a]

"When a person puts impartiality [the sense of commonality, *gong*] into practice, that is humaneness."[104] Humaneness is the principle originally inherent in the human mind. If there is impartiality, there is humaneness. If there is partiality, there is no humaneness. But impartiality as such should not be equated with humaneness. It must be put into practice by human beings before it becomes humaneness. Impartiality, empathy, and love are all descriptions of humaneness. Impartiality is antecedent to humaneness; empathy and love are subsequent. This is so because impartiality makes humaneness possible, and humaneness makes love and empathy possible. [*Zhuzi quanshu* 47:19b–20a]

Someone said: The followers of Master Cheng have given many explanations of *ren* (humaneness, humanity). Some say that love is not *ren* and regard the unity of all things and the self as the substance of *ren*. Others maintain that love is not *ren* but explain *ren* in terms of the possession of consciousness by the mind-and-heart. If what you say is correct, are they all wrong?

Answer: From what they call the unity of all things and the self,[105] it can be seen that *ren* involves love for all, but unity is not the reality that makes *ren* a substance. From what they call the mind's possession of consciousness,[106] it can be seen that *ren* includes wisdom, but that is not the real reason why *ren* is so called. If you look up Confucius's answer to [his pupil] Zigong's question about whether conferring extensive benefit on the people and bringing salvation to all [will constitute *ren*][107] and also Master Cheng's statement that *ren* is not to be explained in terms of consciousness,[108] you will see the point. How can you still explain *ren* in these terms?

Furthermore, to talk about *ren* in general terms of the unity of things and the self will lead people to be vague, confused, neglectful, and make no effort to be alert. The bad effect — and there has been — may be to consider other

---

104. *Er Cheng yishu* 15:8b. See above, p. 698.

105. Referring to Yang Guishan (Yang Shi, 1053–1135), in the *Guishan yulu* (*Recorded Conversations of Yang Shi*) (SBCK) 2:28a.

106. This is a reference to Xie Shangcai (Xie Liangcuo, 1050–1103), who described *ren* as consciousness. See *Shangcai yulu* (*Recorded Conversations of Xie Liangcuo*), Part 1, 2a–b. There are overtones here of the discussion in Buddhism of the equation of wisdom (*prajñā*) and meditation (*dhyāna*), and of the equation by some writers of Confucian humaneness with Buddhist compassion. Zhu was concerned lest this reduce substance to function and leave out the directive, normative principle that should guide conscious action.

107. For the answer to Zigong (520?–450? B.C.E.), see *Analects* 6:28 (in ch. 3).

108. *Er Cheng yishu* 24:3a.

things as oneself. To talk about love in specific terms of consciousness will lead people to be nervous, irascible, and devoid of any quality of depth. The bad effect — and there has been — may be to consider desire as principle. In one case, [the mind] forgets [its objective]. In the other [there is artificial effort to] help [it grow].[109] Both are wrong.

[*Zhuzi wenji* 67:21a–b]

Ren is the principle of love, and impartiality [what is shared in common] is the principle of *ren*. Therefore, if there is impartiality, there is *ren*, and if there is *ren*, there is love.

[*Zhuzi quanshu* 47:6b — WTC]

BUDDHISM

[A student] asked how to tell the difference between Confucianism and Buddhism. The Teacher said: Just take the teaching "What Heaven has endowed is called the nature."[110] The Buddhists simply do not understand this and dogmatically say that the nature is empty consciousness. What we Confucians talk about is solid principles, and from our point of view they are wrong. . . .

Take the human mind-and-heart, for example. In it there must be the Five Moral Relations between parent and child, ruler and minister, elder and younger, husband and wife, and friends. When the Buddhists are consistent in action, they show no affection in these relationships, whereas when we Confucians are consistent in action, there is affection between parent and child, rightness between ruler and minister, order between elder and younger, attention to their separate functions between husband and wife, and trust between friends.[111] We Confucians recognize only the moral principles of sincerity and genuineness. Sincerity is the essence of all good deeds. [60:14a]

The difference between the Confucians and the Buddhists in their discourses on the nature is that the Buddhists speak of it as emptiness whereas the Confucians speak of it as solid reality, and whereas the Buddhists talk about what is not, the Confucians talk about what is.

With us Confucians, although the mind is empty (open), principle is solid [practices]. The Buddhists, on the other hand, go straight to their destination of emptiness and void. [60:14b]

The mind is simply for the acquisition of principle. At bottom the Buddhists do not understand this part, namely principle, and look upon consciousness and movement as the nature. Take the cases of seeing, hearing, speaking, and

---

109. Alluding to *Mencius* 2A:2.
110. The opening line of the *Mean* 1.
111. Quoting *Mencius* 3A:4.

appearance. With the sage, in seeing there is the principle of seeing, in hearing there is the principle of hearing, in speaking there is the principle of speaking, in acting there is the principle of acting, and in thinking there is the principle of thinking — what Viscount Ji called clearness [in seeing], distinctness [in hearing], accordance [with reason in speech], respectfulness [in appearance], and penetration and profundity [in thought].[112] The Buddhists recognize only that which can see, hear, speak, think, and move, and consider it to be the nature. Whether the seeing is clear or not, whether the hearing is distinct or not, whether the speech is in accord with reason or not, and whether the thought is penetrating and profound or not, they do not care at all. No matter whether it goes this way or that way, they always accept it as the nature. . . .

Generally speaking, the Buddhists merely see a little bit of the shadow of the mind and the nature in a confused situation and have not been able to see in detail the mind and the nature in their reality and concreteness. That is why they do not see the many moral principles inherent in them. Even if they have made an effort at preserving and nourishing, they can only preserve and nourish the shadow they see. Of course, we cannot say that they see nothing. Nor can we say that they cannot nourish anything. But what they see and nourish is not the reality of the mind or the nature. [60:30a–b]

When thinking is correct, there is the Principle of Heaven. In all operations and functioning, there is none that is not a revelation of the Principle of Heaven. Does it need to wait to have all thoughts cut off before the Principle of Heaven can be revealed? Furthermore, what is this that we call the Principle of Heaven? Are humaneness, rightness, ritual decorum, and wisdom (the four moral qualities natural to human beings) not the Principle of Heaven? Are the Five Moral Relations between parent and child, ruler and minister, old and young, husband and wife, and friends not the Principle of Heaven? [60:31b–32a]

[*Zhuzi quanshu* 60:14a–b, 30a–32a — WTC]

THE UNIVERSAL MIND IN LU JIUYUAN

Even in Zhu Xi's own time his impressive philosophical synthesis, for all its comprehensiveness and clarity, did not win unchallenged acceptance. As Zhu Xi adopted and elaborated the ideas of Cheng Yi by declaring that the mind contains principles, Lu Jiuyuan (Xiangshan 1139–1193), a contemporary of Zhu Xi, went back to Mencius and declared that the mind is principle.

Zhu Xi, in order to explain the presence of ignorance and evil among human beings, who by nature are supposed to be good, had distinguished between the

---

112. "Grand Model," *Classic of Documents*; Legge, *The Chinese Classics*, 3:326–327.

original moral nature of human beings and their actual nature as embodied in material-force; further, he maintained this distinction by differentiating between human nature and the mind, between the Principle of Heaven and human desire, and between the so-called "mind of the Way" or "moral mind" and the "human mind," with the latter precariously poised between principle and human desire. To Lu Jiuyuan, such distinctions only obscured the essential unity that underlies the universe and humankind. "Feelings, human nature, the mind, capacity — these are all the same thing; they just happen to be expressed in different words," he declared.[113] Thus he swept aside all of Zhu Xi's subtle distinctions, declaring that the mind is identical with principle, with nature, and indeed with the universe.

Since the human mind is self-sufficient, all-embracing, and originally good, Lu believed that human beings possess innate knowledge of the good and an innate ability to do good. It was not necessary to investigate the principles of things, which, for Zhu Xi, involved, in part, the study of the external world, and in particular of the classics. Such a course would only distract and divide the mind, cutting it loose from what is fundamental and setting it adrift among nonessentials. For personal cultivation Lu Xiangshan advocated turning to oneself to rediscover what is fundamental and to "reestablish the nobler part of one's nature" — the human moral sense. Zhu Xi thought that his own emphasis was on "following the path of study and inquiry," while Lu's emphasis was on "honoring the moral nature." Lu insisted that only when the moral nature is honored would it make sense to follow the path of study and inquiry.

This became a partisan issue between some followers of Zhu Xi and Lu, while others in the late Song and Yuan tried to minimize the differences and reconcile the two. Lu himself favored learning from direct experience, not book-learning. He sought to set up neither a school nor a standard curriculum, and there was virtually no "Lu school" until Wang Yangming in the sixteenth century directed renewed attention to Lu's teachings. Only later did the two become identified as the "Lu-Wang school."

MIND IS PRINCIPLE

Mencius said, "That wherein human beings differ from the birds and animals is but slight. The multitude of people relinquish it, while the noble person retains it."[114] What is relinquished is the mind. That is why Mencius said that some people "lose their original mind."[115] What is to be preserved is the mind. That is why Mencius said, "the great man is he who does not lose the mind of

---

113. *Xiangshan quanji* 35:10a.
114. *Mencius* 4B:19.
115. *Mencius* 6A:10.

a newborn babe."[116] [What Mencius referred to as] the four sprouts [of pity and compassion, shame and aversion, modesty and compliance, and the sense of right and wrong] are this mind. It is what Heaven has endowed in us. All human beings have this mind, and all minds are endowed with this principle. The mind is principle. [11:5b–6a]

The affairs of the universe are my own affairs; my own affairs are the affairs of the universe. [22:5a]

The human mind is most intelligent, and principle is most clear. All people have this in mind and all minds contain this principle in full. [22:5a]

The four directions and upward and downward constitute the spatial continuum. What has gone by in the past and what is to come in the future constitute the temporal continuum. These continua, or the universe, are my mind, and my mind is the universe. Sages appeared tens of thousands of generations ago. They shared this mind; they shared this principle. Sages will appear tens of thousands of generations to come. They will share this mind; they will share this principle. Over the four seas sages appear. They share this mind; they share this principle. [22:5a]

The mind is one and principle is one. Perfect truth is always a unity; the essential principle is never a duality. The mind and principle can never be separated into two. That is why Confucius said, "In my Way there is one thing that runs throughout,"[117] and Mencius said, "The Way is one and only one."[118] [Quoting Confucius,] Mencius also said, "There are just two ways: being humane and being inhumane."[119] To act in a certain way is humaneness. Not to act in a certain way is the opposite of humaneness. Humaneness is the mind, the principle. "Seek and you will get it"[120] means to get this principle. "Those who are first to know" know this principle, and "those who are first awakened"[121] are awakened to this principle. It is this principle that constitutes love for parents, reverence for elders, and the sense of alarm and commiseration when one sees a child about to fall into a well. It is this principle that makes people ashamed of shameful things and hate what should be hated. It is this principle that enables people to know what is right to be right and what is wrong to be wrong. It is this principle that makes people deferential when deference is due and humble when humility is called for. Reverent seriousness (*jing*) is this principle; rightness is this principle. And what is internal and what is external are all this principle. . . . Mencius said, "What people are able to do without having learned it is innate ability. What they know without having to think

---

116. *Mencius* 4B:12.
117. *Analects* 4:15.
118. *Mencius* 3A:1.
119. *Mencius* 4A:2.
120. *Mencius* 6A:6.
121. *Mencius* 5A:7.

about it is innate knowledge."[122] These are endowed in us by Heaven. "We definitely possess them . . . they are not infused into us from without."[123] Therefore Mencius said, "All the ten thousand things are complete in me. To turn within to examine oneself and find that one is sincere — there is no greater joy than this."[124] [1:3b]

The Teacher said that the myriad things exist luxuriantly in the mind. What permeates the mind and, pouring forth, extends to fill the universe, is nothing but principle. [34:21a]

The Teacher always said that outside of the Way there are no events and outside of events there is no Way. [34:1a]

The theory that principle is due to Heaven whereas desire is due to human beings is, surely not the best doctrine. If principle is due to Heaven and desire due to man, then Heaven and humans must be different. This theory can be traced to Laozi. The "Record of Music" says, "By nature a human being is tranquil at birth. When influenced by external things, he begins to be active, which is desire arising from his nature. As one becomes conscious of things resulting from this impact, one begins to have likes and dislikes. . . . When [as a result of these likes and dislikes] one is unable to return to his original mind, the Principle of Heaven is destroyed."[125] Here is the origin of the theory that principle is from Heaven whereas desire is from humans. And the words of the "Record of Music" are based on the Daoists. If it is said that only tranquility is inborn nature, is activity not inborn nature also? It is said in the *Classic of Documents* that "the human mind is precarious, the mind of the Way is subtle."[126] Most interpreters have explained the human mind [which is liable to make mistakes] as equivalent to human desires and the mind of the Way [which follows moral law] as equivalent to the Principle of Heaven. This interpretation is wrong. The mind is one. How can a human being have two minds? [34:1b]

[*Xiangshan quanshu* 1:3b; 11:5b–6a; 22:5a; 34:1a–b, 21a — WTC]

METHODS OF CULTIVATION

Principle exists in the universe without any obstruction. It is only that you sink from it, hide yourself in darkness as in a trap, and lose all sense of what is high and far beyond. It is imperative that this trap be decisively broken and the confining net be pierced and destroyed. [35:15b–16a]

---

122. *Mencius* 7A:15.

123. *Mencius* 6A:6. Mencius refers here to humaneness, rightness, ritual decorum, and wisdom. In this "quotation," Lu Jiuyuan reverses the order of the two clauses.

124. *Mencius* 7A:4.

125. "Record of Music," *Record of Rites*; Legge, *Li Ki*, 2:96.

126. "Counsels of the Great Yu," *Classic of Documents*; Legge, *The Chinese Classics*, 3:61.

There is concrete principle in the universe. The value of study lies in understanding this principle. If it is understood, concrete behavior and concrete accomplishments will result. [14:1a]

The Way in the universe cannot be augmented or diminished. Neither can it be given or taken away. Human beings must find this out for themselves. [35:3a]

The universe never separates itself from human beings; human beings separate themselves from the universe. [34:5b]

Students of today pay attention only to details and do not search for what is fundamental. Mencius said, "One who has fully developed his mind knows his nature. Knowing his nature, he knows Heaven."[127] There is only one mind. My friend's mind, the mind of the sages thousands of years ago, and the mind of the sages thousands of years to come are all the same. The substance of the mind is infinite. If one can completely develop one's mind, one will become identified with Heaven. To acquire learning is to appreciate this fact. [35:10a]

Establish yourself and respect yourself. Do not follow other people's footsteps nor repeat their words. [35:22a]

When the teacher resided in Xiangshan [Elephant Mountain], he often said to his pupils, "Your hearing is by nature keen and your vision is by nature clear. By natural endowment you are capable of serving your father with filiality and your elder brother with respect. Fundamentally there is nothing wanting in you. There is no need to seek elsewhere. All depends on your establishing yourself." [34:10b]

My learning is different from that of others in the fact that with me every word comes spontaneously. Although I have uttered tens of thousands of words, they are all expressions of what is within me, and nothing more has been added. Recently someone has commented of me that aside from Mencius' one saying, "First establish the greater part of oneself,"[128] I had nothing clever. When I heard this, I said, "Very true, indeed." [34:5a]

Mencius said, "First establish the greater part of yourself, then the smaller part is unable to steal it away." It is because people fail to build up the greater part of themselves that it is stolen away by the smaller part. In consequence they violate principle and become different from Heaven and Earth. [11:1a]

Principle is endowed in me by Heaven, not infused into me from the outside. If one understands that principle is the same as a master and really makes it his master, one cannot be influenced by external things or fooled by perverse doctrines. [1:3a]

Gather your spirit. Be your own master. "All the ten thousand things are complete in me." What is it that is lacking? When I should be compassionate,

---

127. *Mencius* 7A:1.
128. *Mencius* 6A:15.

I am naturally compassionate. When I should be ashamed, liberal, generous, affectionate, tender, or strong and firm, I am naturally so. [35:18a]

The moral principle inherent in the human mind is endowed by Heaven and cannot be wiped out. Those who are clouded by material desires so as to pervert principles and violate rightness have become so because they do not think, that is all. If one can truly return [to one's original mind] and think, one's sense of right and wrong and one's ability to choose between right and wrong will have the qualities of quiet alertness, clear-cut intelligence, and firm conviction. [32:4a]

DIFFERENCES BETWEEN LU JIUYUAN AND ZHU XI

Zhu Xi once wrote to one of his students, saying, "Lu Xiangshan teaches people only the doctrine of 'honoring the moral nature.'[129] Therefore those who have studied under him are mostly concerned with putting their beliefs into practice. But he has neglected to follow the 'path of study and inquiry.'[130] In my teaching is it not true that I have put somewhat more emphasis on following the path of study and inquiry? As a consequence, my pupils often do not approach his in putting beliefs into practice." From this it is clear that Zhu Xi wanted to avoid two defects [failure to honor the moral nature and failure to practice] and combine two merits [following the path of study and inquiry and practicing one's belief]. I do not believe this to be possible. If one does not know how to honor his moral nature, how can he talk about following the path of study and inquiry? [34:4b–5a]

[*Xiangshan quanji* 1:3a; 11:1a; 14:1a; 32:4a; 34:4a–5b,
10b; 35:4a, 10a, 15a–16a, 22a — adapted from WTC]

---

129. *Mean* 27.
130. *Mean* 27.

Chapter 21

ZHU XI'S NEO-CONFUCIAN PROGRAM

Zhu Xi's philosophical views have already been recounted in the preceding chapter. These have long commanded the attention of scholars in East Asia and the West because they represent the most general and abstract formulation of his teachings, even though many of them are found not in purely philosophical treatises or discussions but in texts that Zhu Xi thought addressed practical educational needs. This chapter deals with his more practical concerns, especially with the close connection between his educational and social programs, which were well known to later scholars and many officials throughout East Asia.

The son of a Confucian scholar-official, Zhu Xi was a highly precocious youth who in his teens was attracted to Chan (Zen) Buddhism, while also preparing himself for the civil service examinations. Successful in passing the highest regular examination (*jinshi*) at the age of eighteen, he embarked on a career combining periods of official service with longer periods of teaching and writing. Both were marked by a remarkable consistency of philosophical reflection and practical activity in addressing the problem of the self (brought into fundamental question by Chan Buddhism) and its proper relation to society and the cosmos ("Heaven, Earth, and all things").

Zhu's actual service at court was brief, and much of it was limited to lectures and memorials conveying the most general sort of advice to the emperor. But he also spent considerable time in local administration, dealing with problems of a most mundane sort, including the improvement of agricultural methods, the establishment of charitable granaries, famine relief, community organizations, the administration of justice, and the reform of schools and rehabilitation of local academies. Modern philosophers have paid little attention to these quotidian aspects of Zhu's work, and even historians have tended either to overlook them altogether or to dismiss them as not comparing in importance with the great matters of state administered at the central court. Thus they have remained unaware of the great significance attached to these more political writings by generations of scholar-officials and local elite who had to deal in the provinces with many of the same problems that Zhu did, not only in China but elsewhere in East Asia as well.

In this chapter we give samples of Zhu's recommendations for the community granaries and community compacts. In addition, we focus on a range of social proposals that often became models for others later on. Since these are more readily understandable in terms of Zhu's general educational philosophy, we present first his prefaces to two of the Four Books, the *Great Learning* (*Daxue*) and the *Mean* (*Zhongyong*). Though the *Great Learning*, the *Mean*, and the *Mencius* are commonly identified today with the Confucian Classics, it is not often realized that these three of the Four Books, while drawn from the corpus of classical writings, had no separate canonical status before Zhu Xi (following up an earlier Song development) identified them, together with the *Analects*, as four texts that merited special attention alongside the already recognized "Five [or as they were sometimes counted, Six, Nine, or Thirteen] Classics" (*jing*). It should be added, however, that toward the end of his life, Zhu suffered serious political persecution. One consequence of this persecution was that, though his teachings quickly won wide acceptance among scholars, the canonical status of the Four Books would not be officially certified until some years later.

PREFACE TO THE *GREAT LEARNING BY CHAPTER AND PHRASE*

Zhu Xi's commentary is not just another annotation of a classic text. The suffix "by Chapter and Phrase" actually indicates a significant rearrangement of the text, and Zhu's preface, brief and modest though it may seem, attempts in a concise and systematic way to justify not only the liberties he takes with the text but also its extraction from the original *Record of Rites* and elevation to prime status among the Four Books that he is now canonizing. As the first thing to be read by those educated in the new Neo-Confucian curriculum for the "greater" (i.e., higher) learning, the key doctrines compressed in this short preface were to have a powerful influence on generations of literate East Asians.

Zhu's initial premise is that all learning is predicated on the unity and universality of the human moral nature, the full development of which is a responsibility of the ruler but, even more, a prerequisite to sound government. For this purpose the sage kings of antiquity maintained a universal school system, Zhu says, one that could legitimately be called a public school system, since it was open to all and aimed at the general uplift of humankind, not just the recruitment of an elite into state service. Nor does Zhu Xi mean by this just some form of learning in the home or private tutoring. Rather, he has in mind the physical establishment of schools in every village, providing for all who are capable of it an education that is carefully structured and sequenced in order to bring the individual learning process to its full maturity in the "greater learning."

At this point a question naturally arises: "If the system was so great in ancient times, why didn't it last?" The trouble, says Zhu, lay not with the system but with the failure of later dynasties to implement it. The Way itself did not cease to hold true; only the power to practice it was lost to those, like Confucius, who still understood it but did not rule. Fragments of the original model survived in the *Great Learning*, but their true significance was not appreciated until much later, when the Cheng brothers rediscovered it. Now Zhu Xi, picking up the loose or tangled threads from the Cheng school, is attempting to reconstitute it.

In the end Zhu's justification for presuming to speak for this ideal from the prehistoric past, while disallowing the results of most subsequent historical experience, is based on his prophetic claim that only through such a universal school system and the regeneration of all humankind can society be properly reconstituted. Here Zhu's key expression, appearing first in his preface and commentary (not found in the classics or the writings of the Cheng brothers), is *xiuji zhiren*. This could be read simply as "cultivating self, governing others," referring to two distinct duties of the educated elite, except that Zhu is mindful of the former as a precondition of the latter, as in the *Mean* 20 (see chapter 10). But Zhu's whole argument goes beyond simply the cultivation of leaders ("noble men") to govern others, important though that is for rulers and the leadership (*shi*) class themselves to learn. He implies that universal self-cultivation and self-discipline are indispensable to human governance in general — in other words, that the true "governance of men" is not just the "governing of [some by] others" but an undertaking that involves everyone's assuming responsibility for his own self-discipline and self-governance.

The Book of the *Great Learning* comprises the method by which people were taught in the higher learning of antiquity. When Heaven gives birth to the people, it gives each one, without exception, a nature of humaneness, rightness, ritual decorum, and wisdom. They could not, however, be equal in their physical endowments, and thus they do not all have the capacity to know what that nature consists in or how to preserve it whole. Once someone appears among them who is most intelligent and wise, and able fully to develop his nature, Heaven is sure to commission him as ruler and teacher of the myriad peoples, so that, being governed and instructed, they may be able to recover their original nature. This is how Fu Xi, the Divine Farmer, the Yellow Emperor, and [the sage kings] Yao and Shun succeeded to [the work of] Heaven, establishing the norm [for all to follow], and how they came to set up the post of Minister of Education and the office of Director of Music.

In the flourishing days of the Three Dynasties [Xia, Shang, and Zhou] their institutions were steadily perfected until everyone, from the king's court and feudal capitals down to the smallest lane or alley, had schooling. At the age of eight all children of the king and dukes, on down to the common people, started their elementary learning, in which they were instructed in the [social] disciplines of sprinkling and sweeping, responding to others, and coming forward or withdrawing from [the presence of others] [as recorded in *Analects* 19:12], and in the polite arts of ritual, music, archery, charioteering, writing, and arithmetic. Then at the age of fifteen, starting with the heir apparent and other princes, and down through the legitimate sons of the dukes, chief ministers, grandees, and lower aristocracy to the talented sons of the common people — all started their higher learning, in which they were taught the way of self-cultivation and governance of men through the fathoming of principle and rectifying of the mind. This is also how the distinction was made in the gradations of elementary and higher instruction in schools.

Thus widely were schools established, and thus precisely defined was the art of instruction in the details of its sequence and itemized content! As to the reasons for providing this instruction, they followed naturally from the superabundance of the ruler's personal attention to the practice of virtue and did not need to go beyond the constant norms that govern the people's livelihood and everyday needs. This being the case, there was no one without learning in those times, and as to the learning itself, no one would be without an understanding of what was inherent in his individual nature or what was proper to the performance of his individual duties so that each could exert himself to the fullest extent of his energies. This is why, in the great days of high antiquity, good government prevailed on high and beautiful customs below, to a degree that later ages have not been able to attain.

With the decline of the Zhou, sage and worthy rulers no longer appeared, and the school system was not well maintained. The transformation of the people through education became eclipsed and popular customs deteriorated. At that time the sage Confucius appeared, but being unable to attain the position of ruler-teacher by which to carry out government and education, he could do no more than recite the ways of the sage kings and pass them along, in order to make them known to later generations. Thus, for instance, there were such pieces as the *Ritual Matters* (*Quli*); *Lesser Ceremonials* (*Shaoyi*); *Norms for the Household* (*Neize*) [chapters of the *Record of Rites*] and *Duties of the Disciples* (*Dizi zhi*) [from the *Guanzi*], which were only the remnants and byways of the original elementary learning. There was, however, this piece, the *Great Learning*, which followed up what had been accomplished in elementary learning with a view to setting forth the lucid teaching methods of the higher learning. Thus for outward emulation there would be a model great enough to serve as the highest standard of perfection, and for inner cultivation something detailed enough to spell out in full its sequence and contents.

No doubt, among the three thousand disciples of Confucius, none failed to hear his teachings, but it was only Zengzi who got the essential message and wrote this commentary to expound its meaning. Then, with the death of Mencius, the transmission vanished. This work survived, but few understood it. Thereafter came the vulgar Confucian scholarship [of later times], stressing memorization and literary composition, which took double the exertion of the elementary education but was of no real use, and the quietistic and nihilistic teachings of the deviant doctrines [Buddhism and Daoism], which were loftier even than the higher learning (*Great Learning*) but lacked solid substance. Besides these there were the stratagems of expediency and the tactics and calculations [of the so-called Strategists and Realists], all the other theories aiming at worldly power and success, as well as the teachings of the Hundred Schools and myriad splinter groups that confused the world and misled the people, blocking the way to humaneness and rightness. All these were mixed together in great confusion, so that gentlemen [rulers], alas, could no longer hear the essential teachings of the Great Way, and lesser men were no longer so fortunate as to enjoy the beneficial effects of the ultimate in good government. There were obscuration and obstruction; with the compounding of evils, everything became incurably diseased, until the disorder and destruction reached its extreme in the Five Dynasties [tenth century C.E.].

Yet Heaven's cycle goes on turning, and nothing goes forth without returning [for a new start]. The virtuous power of the Song Dynasty rose up, and both government and education shone with great luster, whereupon the two Cheng masters of He'nan appeared and connected up with the tradition from Mencius [that had been long broken off]. The first truly to recognize and believe in this work, they expounded it to the world and further rearranged the fragmented text so as to bring out its essential message. With that, the method whereby the ancients taught men through the *Great Learning* with the guidance of the classic text of the Sage [Confucius] and the commentary of the Worthy [Zengzi], was once again made brilliantly clear to the world.

Although I am not very clever, it was my good fortune through indirect association [with a teacher among the followers of the Cheng brothers] to hear about this. Considering that the work still suffers some damage and loss, I overlooked my own unworthiness and ineptitude, and went ahead to gather up the fragments, rearrange them, and insert my own ideas here and there to fill in for what was missing and then await the judgment of later gentlemen. Realizing full well how presumptuous this is of me, I know there is no way to escape the blame [for what I have done], but I thought it might not be without some small benefit to our country in educating people and improving customs, and also to scholars as a method of "self-cultivation for the governance of men."

Sixteenth year of Chunxi (1189)
Second month, *jiazi* day (February 20)
Zhu Xi of Xin'an [Anhui]

[*Daxue zhangju*, preface — dB]

THE *GREAT LEARNING BY CHAPTER AND PHRASE*, CHAPTER 1

The expression "by Chapter and Phrase" refers to Zhu Xi's rearrangement of the passages in the original text and his phrase-by-phrase interpretation of it. Zhu explains its antique and broadly suggestive wording in terms of his own philosophy of human nature. "Luminous virtue" is understood here as the moral nature or inherent principle [infrastructure], which in its original state is both radiant and transparent, rather than dark or mysterious, though subject to obscuration in the individual psychophysical condition. The Three Main Guidelines [*San gangling*] involve the clarifying and manifesting of this innate goodness and extending it to others, so that one's self-renewal naturally leads to the renewal of others and thus to the regeneration of all humankind, which brings order to the state and peace to all-under-Heaven.

The following is an abridged translation of the text and commentary.

[COMMENTARY] Master Cheng said, "The *Great Learning* is a surviving work of Confucius, and stands as the gate by which the beginner in learning enters on the path to virtue. Today it is only owing to the preservation of this text that we can see in what sequence the ancients took up the pursuit of learning. The *Analects* and *Mencius* come next. He who pursues learning must start his studies with this, and then he may not go far wrong."

[CLASSIC TEXT] The way of the *Great Learning* lies in clearly manifesting luminous virtue, renewing the people, and resting in the utmost good.

[COMMENTARY] Master Cheng [I] says *qin*, "to be kind," should be *xin*, "to renew."

The *Great Learning* (*Daxue*) is learning to become a great person. "Clearly manifesting" (*ming*) means clarifying. "Luminous virtue" (*mingde*) is what a person gets from Heaven. Open, spiritual, and unobscured, it is replete with all the principles by which one responds to the myriad things and affairs, but being hampered by the physical endowment and obstructed by human [selfish] desires, there are times when it becomes obscured. Nevertheless, the radiance of the original substance [nature] is never lost, and one who pursues learning need only keep to what emerges from it and clarify it, so as to restore it to its original condition.

"To renew" means to reform the old. It means that once one has clearly manifested his own clear and bright virtue, he should extend it to others so that they too can do away with the stain of earlier soiling.

"To rest" means to arrive at this point and stay there. The "utmost good" is the ultimate norm in the principled handling of affairs. It means that by clearly manifesting luminous virtue and renewing the people one should reach the point of the utmost good [in that context] and stay there. Thus one would be sure to have a way to fulfill the ultimate norm of Heaven's principle, without one iota of the selfishness of human desires.

These three together are the mainstays [guiding principles] of the *Great Learning*.

[CLASSIC TEXT] Knowing where to rest [stop], there is stability; with stability, one can have composure; with composure one can be at peace; at peace one can deliberate [reflect], and with reflection one can get there [understand].

[COMMENTARY] . . . "Rest" (*zhi*) means the point at which one should stop, which is where the utmost good resides. Knowing it, one's resolve has firm direction.

"Composure" (*jing*) means for the mind-and-heart to do nothing uncontrolled. "Peace" (*an*) means to be at peace wherever one is [or in whatever one does]. "To reflect [deliberate]" (*lü*) means to be precise in the handling of affairs. "Get there" (*de*) means to get to where one should rest.

[CLASSIC TEXT] Things have their roots and branches. Affairs have a beginning and an end. Knowing [learning] what comes before and what comes after is close to the Way.

[COMMENTARY] Luminous virtue [the moral nature] is the root. Renewing the people is the branch. Knowing where to rest is the beginning; getting there is the end. The priority of root and beginning, the posteriority of branch and ending — this brings together the meaning of the two preceding sections [of the original text].

The following passage discusses the celebrated Eight Items or Steps in the process of self-cultivation and dealing with society. Zhu appreciates them for their specificity and their systematic, sequential order, so much in contrast to the Daoist and Buddhist predilection for the undefined and undetermined.

It is important to recognize the broad connotations of the word zhi, "to know," "to learn," "to understand." Here it refers to the mind's faculty or capacity for knowing, more than to knowledge as "what is known," but both readings are possible, which leaves open the question of how much emphasis is put on cognitive learning and moral evaluation (later an issue for Wang Yangming in the early sixteenth century). In terms of the Cheng-Zhu learning of principle, the investigation of things and extension of know-

ing involve a meeting or matching of the inner, directive principles (infrastructure) in-
herent in both the mind and things and affairs—a qualitative appreciation and em-
pathetic identification with the objects of one's learning experience, not just an objective
grasp of them.

[CLASSIC TEXT] The ancients, wishing clearly to manifest luminous virtue to
all-under-Heaven, first put in order their own states. Wishing to govern their
states, they first regulated their families. Wishing to regulate their families, they
first cultivated [disciplined] their own persons. Wishing to cultivate their persons, they first rectified their minds-and-hearts. Wishing to rectify their minds-
and-hearts, they first made their intentions sincere. Wishing to make their intentions sincere, they first extended their knowing. The extension of knowing
lies in investigating things and affairs.

[COMMENTARY] . . . "Clearly to manifest luminous virtue to all-under-
Heaven" is to provide all persons the wherewithal for clearly manifesting their
luminous virtue. The mind-and-heart is the master of one's person. "To make
sincere" is to make real, to substantiate. "One's intention" is what emerges from
the mind-and-heart. "To substantiate" what emerges from the mind-and-heart
is to try to integrate with the good, free of any self-deception. "Extend" means
to project to the limit [the ultimate]. "Knowing" is like recognizing, to project
our knowing to the limit, hoping that our knowing [capacity] will be fully
employed. "To investigate" is to reach. "Thing" is like "affair." Fathoming the
principles of things and affairs, one hopes always to reach the ultimate point.
   These eight items are the specific items in the *Great [Higher] Learning.*

[CLASSIC TEXT] Things being investigated, knowing can be extended; knowing being extended, the intentions can be made sincere; the intentions being
made sincere, the mind can be rectified; the mind rectified, the person can be
cultivated [self disciplined]; with the self disciplined, the family can be regulated; the family regulated, the state can be governed; the state governed, all-
under-Heaven can be at peace.

[COMMENTARY] . . . "Things being investigated" means unfailingly to reach
the ultimate point in the principles of things-and-affairs. "Knowing being extended" means that the knowing of our minds-and-hearts is fully utilized. Knowing having been fully utilized, one's intention can be substantiated. One's intentions substantiated, the mind-and-heart can be rectified.
   All the items preceding the "cultivating of the person" [disciplining of the
self] have to do with "manifesting luminous virtue" [manifesting the moral
nature]. All that follows "the regulating of the family" has to do with "renewing
the people." Things having been investigated and knowing where to rest, one's

knowledge has "reached" [fulfillment]. All that follows "one's intentions being made sincere" represents the order of priorities in "coming to rest."

[CLASSIC TEXT] From the son of Heaven down to the common people, they all as one take cultivating the person to be the root.

[COMMENTARY] . . . All that precedes "rectifying the mind" is the way to cultivate the person. What follows "regulating the family" is merely the application of this.

[CLASSIC TEXT] How could it be that the root be disturbed and yet have the branch remain undisturbed? Not to favor what has a strong claim on one's attention but rather to favor what has only a light claim — this has never been the case.

[COMMENTARY] The root [trunk] is one's person. What should be favored is the family. These two sections bring together the meaning of the preceding two sections [i.e., self-cultivation as the root in the first series, and the family as primary in the second].

[CONCLUDING NOTE] The foregoing classic text in one chapter is the words of Confucius, related by Zengzi. (Altogether, 205 characters.) The commentary in ten chapters represents the ideas of Zengzi, as recorded by his disciples. In the old version they are in the wrong order. Now, following the text as fixed by Master Cheng, on the basis of further investigation of the text, I have rearranged it as follows:

[Zhu Xi's note] Altogether 1,546 characters. The text of the commentary is drawn at random from classics and commentaries in no particular order. It appears to be unsystematic but nevertheless is logically connected, and there is an underlying, unifying thread. It is most precise and detailed as regards its different levels and successive phases. Take the time to read it carefully, savor its meaning, and in time you should see it. Here we cannot fully explain this.

Editor's note: The next two parts, deleted here, cite classical passages, drawn from later portions of the old text, to illustrate the meaning of the preceding.

[CLASSIC TEXT] The Master said, "As regards hearing a lawsuit, I am like anyone else: Surely it would be better to have no lawsuits at all." Those who are not genuine would not dare to finish their words. A great awe would be struck in people's minds. This is called knowing the root.

[COMMENTARY] "Like anyone else" means no different from others. "Genuine" means solid, substantial. Drawing out Confucius's words, it means the sage would make it so that those who have no solid basis [for what they say] would not dare to finish their empty, groundless words. Once my luminous virtue is clearly manifest, it naturally has an awesome effect on the direction of people's minds, so lawsuits would naturally cease, without their even having to be heard. Considering these words [of Confucius], one can learn the sequence of root and branch.

Editor's note: None of Zhu Xi's interventions into the text of the Great Learning *was more important than the following special note on the "investigation of things and extension of knowing." It suggested that the gradual and progressive "fathoming of principle," as both an intellectual and a moral enterprise, would culminate in a state of mind wherein all sense of opposition between self and others was overcome and one experienced a consciousness of oneness with all things.*

[Zhu Xi's note] The preceding, the fifth chapter of commentary, explained the meaning of "to investigate things and extend one's knowing," which is now lost. (In the old text this chapter, which connected with the following passage, was erroneously placed after the classic text.) I have ventured to take Master Cheng's ideas to supplement it as follows: "The extension of knowing lies in the investigation of things" means that if we wish to extend our knowing, it consists in fathoming the principle of any thing or affair we come into contact with, for the intelligent [spiritual] human mind always has the capacity to know [learn], and the things of this world all have their principles, but if a principle remains unfathomed, one's knowing [learning] is not fully utilized. Hence the initial teaching of the Great Learning insists that the learner, as he comes upon the things of this world, must proceed from principles already known and further fathom them until he reaches the limit. After exerting himself for a long time, he will one day experience a breakthrough to integral comprehension. Then the qualities of all things, whether internal or external, refined or coarse, will all be apprehended and the mind, in its whole substance and great functioning, will all be clearly manifested. This is "things [having been] investigated." This is the utmost of knowing.

Zhu's reference to a sudden "breakthrough to integral comprehension" carried with it a sense of self-realization and self-fulfillment akin to a mystical experience, and it is not surprising that some understood it as an enlightenment similar in certain respects but different in approach from Chan [Zen] Buddhism. Interpretation of this suggestive passage remained highly controversial among later Neo-Confucians. What seems clear is that Zhu Xi thought of this culmination neither as a comprehensive grasp of empirical knowledge (i.e., encyclopedic learning, "knowing everything") nor as a trans-rational, trans-moral gnosis ("knowing nothing"), but rather as a thorough empathetic under-

standing or enlargement of the spirit that overcomes any sense of self and other, inner and outer, subjective and objective.

Self-Watchfulness

The following passage provides the classic basis for the Neo-Confucian practice of self-examination, often abetted by the praxis of quiet-sitting. Many Neo-Confucians set great store by constant self-awareness and rigorous self-discipline, through which one's adherence to the Way would become, so to speak, second nature; that is, one's moral sense would be so heightened and one's conduct so disciplined, that one's response to good and evil would be as natural and immediate as the reactions of one's sense of sight or smell. Thus the moral nature was to be grounded in and integral to the affective nature. Such a view was strongly reinforced by the rigorism of Zhu Xi's message and method of the mind-and-heart (*xinfa*) as propounded in his preface to the *Mean* (the selection following this one).

[CLASSIC TEXT] What is called "making one's intentions sincere" allows for no self-deception, as with one's detesting bad smells and being attracted to things pleasing to the sight. This means satisfying one's self [one's own conscience]. Thus the noble person is watchful over himself when alone.

[COMMENTARY] . . . "Making one's intentions sincere" is the first thing in self-cultivation. . . . "Self-deception" means that, even though one knows the good to be done and the bad to be avoided, yet what issues from the mind-and-heart does not bear this out. . . . If one wishes to cultivate oneself, then, knowing the good to be done and the evil to be avoided, one devotes his efforts to accomplishing this, puts an end to self-deception, and sees to it that his detesting of evil is like his [immediate] detesting of bad odors and his attraction to the good is like his [immediate] attraction to what is pleasing to the sight. Resolving to do so and striving to achieve this, one finds inner satisfaction in it. . . .

[CLASSIC TEXT] The inferior person, when alone, stops at nothing in the evil he will do, but when he sees a noble person, tries to conceal his evil-doing and make a show of doing good. The latter, however, can see through this, as if penetrating to his very innards, so what does it avail? This is called "what is true within becomes manifest without." Thus, the noble person is sure to be watchful over himself when alone.

[COMMENTARY] . . . The inferior person covertly practices evil but outwardly tries to disguise it. It is not that he is unaware of the good to be done and the evil to be avoided, but only that he does not truly exert all his effort to accomplish this. But in the end his desire to conceal his evil-doing will not succeed, nor will his pretense to do good, so what is gained by it? This is why the noble person emphasizes caution and is sure to be scrupulous when alone with himself.

[*Daxue zhangju* 1 — dB]

PREFACE TO THE *MEAN BY CHAPTER AND PHRASE*

Zhu Xi's preface to the *Mean* has an importance among his writings almost equal to that of his preface to the *Great Learning*. Among the reasons for this is, first, that Zhu used this preface to introduce key ideas of his own, which then could be followed up in his commentary; and second, while Zhu himself had said the *Mean* was deep and difficult to understand and therefore should be read only after the other three of the Four Books, as a much shorter work than the *Analects* or the *Mencius*, it was usually printed together with the briefer *Great Learning*, i.e., up front in most editions. Thus given special prominence were two key formulations in his preface not found in the original text: the Message (or Method) of the Mind-and-Heart (*xinfa*) and its transmission through the orthodox tradition or Succession to the Way (*daotong*). Both became often quoted and highly contested issues in later Neo-Confucian discourse.

The Message of the Mind (*xinfa*), also alluded to in the preface to the *Great Learning*, refers to the sixteen-word message coming down from the sage kings Yao and Shun concerning the human mind and the mind of the Way as the key to rulership. Here Zhu correlates it with the discussion of the Way, human nature, and instruction featured in the first chapter of the *Mean*, which was to become the basis of Neo-Confucian mind cultivation. It focused on the conflict in a human mind precariously balanced between selfish and unselfish tendencies — the former identified with what were called "human desires" (customarily used to mean "selfish desires") and the latter with the moral imperatives of the Way implanted in human nature as received from Heaven. A distinction is made between Heaven's principles and human desires in the *Record of Rites*, "Record of Music" (*Yueji*), where "human desires" are identified with various excesses harmful to others, and in the subcommentary with greed and lust, in contrast to the purity of the Heaven-endowed moral nature. The contested ground between them was the natural inclinations, affections, and appetites constitutive of one's individual psycho-physical makeup, which could readily be made to serve the common good [*gong*] when directed by the Mind of the Way and the Principles of Heaven, or else could be turned to selfish ends. The easy susceptibility to abuse of one's legitimate self-interest, one's fallibility, as well as one's proneness to self-deception, found expression for Zhu Xi in the terms of "the human mind is precarious, the mind of the Way is subtle [and difficult to perceive]." Thus careful self-examination was called for, consisting of "refined discrimination" as to what was fair and proper, even what was legitimately self-regarding (e.g., the proper care of one's person), in contrast to what was ulterior and selfish, i.e., prejudicial to others, to the common good and even to one's true selfhood. "Single-mindedness" meant adherence to the unity of principle in a shared humanity (*ren*); "holding to the Mean" referred to a mind properly balanced in this respect, and not given to partiality.

What is highlighted in the second concept, Succession to the Way (*daotong*), is not a continuous tradition, passed on from one master to another (as with the "mind-to-mind" transmission in Chan [Zen]), but the long breaks from the founders of the Zhou to Confucius, and from Mencius to the Cheng brothers, who were at least able to reconstitute the Way, rescuing an all too fragile and misunderstood tradition from near oblivion.[1] Later Zhou Dunyi would be added to Zhu's list of those highly perceptive individuals who were able to grasp the Way, as revealed in fragmentary texts, without receiving direct transmission from a teaching lineage. What is emphasized, then, is the special genius and prophetic insight of a few heroic individuals, who speak with authority concerning a Way that endures as an unchanging ideal because it is rooted in the inherent nature of humankind, even though it has not been practiced for millennia.

Corollary to this is the notion of a split in the Way, surviving after the Duke of Zhou only as a tradition of learning, since it has ceased to be practiced by rulers as a way of government (see Fan Zuyu's *The Learning of the Emperors* in chapter 19). Though this conception draws on ideas of Zhu Xi's predecessors and is a natural evolute from the Learning of the Way, which claimed direct, unmediated authority to speak for the Way, the term *daotong* itself is Zhu Xi's. It became a standard feature of later Neo-Confucian discourse and rhetoric: a prophetic role and stance often claimed for one's teacher or ruler, and sometimes, amidst much avowed self-depreciation, implicitly assumed by the writer himself.

Why was the *Mean* written? Master Zisi wrote it because he was worried lest the transmission of the Learning of the Way (*daoxue*) be lost. When the divine sages of highest antiquity had succeeded to the work of Heaven and established the Supreme Norm [of governance], the transmission of the Succession to the Way (*daotong*) had its inception. As may be discovered from the classics, "hold fast the Mean"[2] is what Yao transmitted to Shun. That "the human mind is precarious" and "the mind of the Way is barely perceptible," that one should be discriminating [with regard to the human mind], be one [with the mind of the Way], and should "hold fast the Mean" is what Shun transmitted to Yu.[3] Yao's one utterance is complete and perfect in itself, but Shun added three more in order to show that Yao's one utterance could only be carried out in this way. . . .

As I have maintained, the mind in its empty spirituality [pure intelligence and consciousness] is one and only one. But if we make a distinction between

---

1. A comparable use of *tong* (or succession) in relation to dynastic legitimacy also allows for legitimate succession to occur with the reconstituting of a unified empire after a long period of disunity. (See ch. 19.)

2. *Analects* 20:1.

3. "Counsels of the Great Yu," *Classic of Documents*; Legge, *The Chinese Classics*, 3:61.

the human mind and the mind of the Way, it is because consciousness differs insofar as it may spring from the self-centeredness of one's individual physical form or may have its source in the correctness of one's innate nature and moral imperative. This being so, the one may be precarious and insecure, while the other may be subtle and barely perceptible. But humans all have physical form, so even the wisest do not lack this human mind; and all have the inborn nature, so even the most stupid do not lack the mind of the Way.

These two [tendencies] are mixed together in the square-inch of the mind-and-heart, and if one does not know how to order them, the precariousness becomes even more precarious, and the barely perceptible becomes even less perceptible, so that the sense of the common good [impartiality] of Heaven's principle [in the mind of the Way] is unable in the end to overcome the selfishness of human desires. "Be discriminating" means to distinguish between the two and not let them be confused. "Be one [with the mind of the Way]" means to preserve the correctness of the original mind and not become separated from it. If one applies oneself to this without any interruption, making sure that the mind of the Way is master of one's self and that the human mind always listens to its commands, then the precariousness and insecurity will yield to peace and security, and what is subtle and barely perceptible will become clearly manifest. Then, whether in action or repose, in whatever one says or does, one will not err by going too far or not far enough.

Yao, Shun, and Yu were great sages among all-under-Heaven, and for them to pass on succession to [rulership of] the world was a major matter for all-under-Heaven. As great sages performing a major undertaking for all-under-Heaven, on such momentous occasions their repeated admonitions still consisted only of these few words. How then could anything more be added to this from among all the principles under Heaven?

Subsequently sage upon sage succeeded one another: Tang the Completer, Wen and Wu as rulers, Gao Yao, Yi Yin, Fu Yue, the Duke of Zhou, and Duke Shao as ministers, received and passed on the succession to the Way. As for our master Confucius, though he did not attain a position of authority, nevertheless his resuming the learning of the past sages and imparting it to later scholars was a contribution even more worthy than that of Yao and Shun. Still, in his own time those who recognized him were only [his disciples] Yan [Hui] and Zeng [Shen], who grasped and passed on his essential meaning.

Then in the next generation after Master Zeng, with Confucius's grandson Zisi [reputed author of the *Mean*], it was far removed in time from the sages, and divergent views had already arisen. Zisi, fearing that the more time passed the greater the danger of losing the truth, traced back these ideas transmitted from Yao and Shun, substantiated them from what he had heard his father and teacher say from day to day, and drawing upon one to explain the other, produced this book for the edification of later scholars. His concern being so deep, his words were thus penetrating; his cogitations being so farsighted, his language was thus carefully chosen. When [in the opening lines of the *Mean*] he spoke about "Heaven's ordinance" [being imparted as human nature] and "following one's nature" [being the Way] he was referring to the mind of the Way [the moral mind]. When he spoke [*Mean* 20] about "choosing the good and holding fast to it" he referred to "being discriminating and being one." And when he spoke [*Mean* 2] about the "noble person's timeliness in holding to the Mean," he was referring to "hold fast the Mean." He came more than a thousand years after the age [of Yao and Shun], but his words, differing in no way from theirs, rather tallied exactly with them! In selecting the writings of the former sages and setting forth main principles, as well as in bringing deep secrets to light, there has never been a work so lucid and thoroughgoing as this.

Thereafter the transmission was resumed by Mencius, who was able to interpret and clarify the meaning of this text [the *Mean*] and succeed to the tradition of the early sages; but upon his demise the tradition was finally lost. . . . Fortunately, however, this text was not lost, and when the Masters Cheng, two brothers, appeared [in the Song] they had something to study in order to pick up the threads of what had not been transmitted for a thousand years, and something to rely on in exposing the speciousness of the seeming truths of Buddhism and Daoism. Though the contribution of Zisi was great, had it not been for the Chengs we would not have grasped his meaning from his words alone. But alas, their explanations also became lost.

[*Zhongyong zhangju*, preface — dB]

Zhu goes on to explain with what difficulty he pieced together and pondered for himself the essential message of the *Mean* from the fragmentary material available to him. He reiterates not only the theme of the precariousness of the Way as transmitted by human hands but also the successive struggles of inspired individuals to recover its true meaning. Thus the Succession to the Way (*daotong*) has the sense of reconstituting and repossessing the Way by a process of almost literally "stitching together" or linking materials from different sources and times to fill out and confirm the message coming down from the sages. In the process of emulating Zisi, Zhu says he has compiled a work, *Questions and Answers on the* Mean (*Zhongyong huowen*), explaining his acceptance of certain interpretations and rejection of others, but now, without claiming to make any original contribution to the orthodox tradition himself, he offers his own understanding of the *Mean*.

THE *MEAN BY CHAPTER AND PHRASE* (*ZHONGYONG ZHANGJU*), CHAPTER 1

[Zhu Xi] *Zhong* means not inclining or leaning to one side; it is an expression for not falling short or going too far. *Yong* (the *Mean*) refers to normality.

Master Cheng says, "Not being one-sided is called centrality (*zhong*); to be unchanging is called normality (*yong*). Centrality is the correct course for all-under-Heaven; normality is the fixed principle for all-under-Heaven." This work contains the Message (or Method) of the Mind-and-Heart (*xinfa*) handed down in the Confucian school. [Confucius's grandson] Zisi, fearing lest errors arise with the passage of time, committed it to writing and passed it on to Mencius.

This book starts with one principle, then extends it to myriad things and affairs, and finally returns to embrace all in one principle again. Opened out, it reaches in every direction; rolled back, it lies wrapped in the subtlest of mysteries. Its savor is inexhaustible, [but] it is all solid learning. One who studies it well, exploring and assimilating it, will find that it serves one well as an inexhaustible resource throughout life.

[CLASSIC TEXT] What Heaven has ordained is called [human] "nature" (*xing*); to follow that nature is called the Way. To cultivate that Way is called "instruction."

[COMMENTARY] An "ordinance" is like a command. The "nature" is principle. Heaven's generating the myriad things through the interaction of yin and yang and the Five Phases, their becoming embodied with psycho-physical force and endowed with principle, is like Heaven's giving a command or commission. Thus human beings, each receiving their endowment of principle, are constituted with the Five Constant Virtues [humaneness, rightness, ritual decorum, wisdom, and trustworthiness], which are one's nature. "To follow" means to accord with. The Way is like a path. Human beings, each following in their daily life and activities what is natural to their own nature, have their own path for what they should do, which is what we call the Way. "Cultivation" involves the making of measured gradations. Although the Way of [the common] human nature is the same for all, their psycho-physical endowments may differ, so there cannot but be differences in going too far or not far enough. The sage takes into account these individual differences in what it may be expected of them to do, and makes appropriate gradations in setting the norms for all-under-Heaven — and this is what is called instruction. Thus we have the different categories [of instruction] under such headings as rites, music, punishments, and administration. What makes a human being human, what makes the *dao* the Way, what makes the sage offer instruction, is originally and fundamentally nothing other than what derives from Heaven and is endowed in ourselves. . . .

[CLASSIC TEXT] The Way cannot be departed from for even an instant. If it could, it would not be the Way. Therefore the noble person is cautious in regard to what may still be invisible and apprehensive about what is yet inaudible.

[COMMENTARY] . . . The Way consists of the principles for the conduct of everyday things and affairs. These are the virtues of the moral nature replete in the mind-and-heart, which everyone possesses and are ever such, so that there can be no departure from them even for an instant. . . . This being the case, noble persons are ever mindful of preserving reverent awe, so that they would never dare to be neglectful of even what is unseen and unheard.[4] Thus they preserve Heaven's principle in their natural condition and are never separated from them even for a moment.

[CLASSIC TEXT] Before the feelings of pleasure, anger, sorrow, and joy are aroused, is called [the state of] centrality. After these are aroused, if they preserve equilibrium (centrality) it is called [the state of] harmony. Harmony is the universal path.

[COMMENTARY] . . . Pleasure, anger, sorrow, and joy are human feelings. In their unaroused state they are human nature. Not being one-sided or partial, they are spoken of as in a state of centrality. If they are aroused and all attain due degree, they represent the correctness of the nature; manifesting no perversity, they are in the state of harmony. The great root and trunk of all is the nature as Heaven's imperative, and the principles of all-under-Heaven derive from this, it being the substance of the Way. Whether in the past or the present, it is the common resource of all, this being the function of the Way. . . .

In conclusion, Zhu Xi sums up the main points of the Mean's *first chapter as follows:*

Zisi relates the ideas that have been handed down to him as the basis of his discourse. First he explains that the Way originally derives from Heaven and cannot be altered. Its substance inheres in the self and cannot be departed from. Next he sets forth the essentials of preserving and nourishing this [substance in the mind] and of practicing self-examination. Finally, he expresses the ultimate achievement of sagely and spiritual persons in the transforming power of their virtue. In this Zisi wishes for the learner to look within and find it [the substance of the Way] in oneself.

[*Zhongyong zhangju* 1:1a–3a — dB]

From the foregoing it may be seen how Zhu Xi explains the Mean *in terms of his philosophy of human nature and principle, focuses attention on rigorous self-examination and interior cultivation of the mind-and-heart, and equates this with the sixteen-word message of the mind (xinfa) coming down from Yao and Shun. While this message and method are the key to proper governance, and have the utmost importance for the ruler and the ruling elite, they are rooted in a human nature shared by all, wherefore the same essential method is applicable to all. Finally, in using the language of Mencius concerning the noble person's "wishing to find the Way in himself," Zhu returns to a*

---

4. See ch. 2, Ode to King Wen, for reference to Heaven's imperative as neither seen nor heard (i.e., intangible but nonetheless real).

main theme of his teaching as a whole: that the ultimate value is found in the self and that all human governance is ultimately grounded in the human moral nature, which is perfected through "learning for one's self." This, in turn, links up with Zhu's emphasis on "self-discipline for the governance of men" in his preface to the Great Learning.

From this close linking of the concepts of learning for one's self (weiji zhi xue), *the sixteen-word Message and method of the Mind-and-Heart* (xinfa), *and the Succession to the Way* (daotong), *they became much discussed and highly controversial elements in subsequent Neo-Confucian discourse.*

PERSONAL PROPOSALS FOR SCHOOLS AND OFFICIAL RECRUITMENT

Written in 1195, Zhu Xi's proposals contain his most important ideas for the reform of education, the examination system, and the Imperial College. While there is a strong emphasis on moral and intellectual self-cultivation, his proposals also aim to have students study what will be practical to society and to test useful knowledge and skills in the examination system. In other words, it has a core in the humanities but allows for some technical specialization. Broadly conceived, these proposals reflect a consistent set of values as well as Zhu's larger vision for a system of general public education, starting in the village and reaching up to the capital, so as to have the same values govern official recruitment as well. The comprehensiveness of Zhu's recommendations, as well as the problems in evaluating virtuous conduct [exemplary performance], would make them difficult to implement wholesale. Nevertheless, in subsequent debates at court, in imperial decrees of the Yuan and Ming, and in general scholarly discourse down into the Qing (in Korea as well as China) the issues raised by Zhu, as well as the language he used, became standard rhetoric, even if actual official practice was often only a pale reflection of, and often contrary to, the views expressed here.

In antiquity the method of selecting officials from the schools began with [schools] in the villages and communities and reached up to [the Imperial College] at the capital. Students were taught moral conduct and the [six] arts (daoyi), and those who were worthy and capable were promoted [to become officials]. There was just one place where students were educated, just one means by which they were made officials, and just one method by which they were selected. Therefore, scholars (shi) had a fixed purpose and suffered no distractions. They made diligent efforts from morning until night and were only concerned about failing in moral cultivation rather than possible failure in attaining office or emoluments. This is what is meant by Confucius's saying "to have few errors in words and few regrets in conduct, one can find emolument [enough] in that"[5] and by Mencius's saying that "[men of antiquity] cultivated

---

5. *Analects* 2:18.

heavenly rank [true nobility] and human rank followed after it."[6] With respect to education in the Three Dynasties [Xia, Shang, Zhou], the applied arts were considered the least important. Nevertheless, they were practical and indispensable. As a systematic process this could help people to cultivate their minds and nourish their life force. Consequently people were able to make progress toward the goal of virtuous conduct. It was for this reason that the ancient system could develop human talents, enrich culture, regulate society's affairs, and bring about great peace. This is not so, however, of the present system. . . .

It has been my view that if one wants to take advantage of the present opportunity to reform the current system so as gradually to restore the ancient order of the Three Kings and improve today's customs, one must implement the proposal Master Mingdao (Cheng Hao) presented in the Xining reign (1068–1077). Then one can significantly rectify the foundation and completely eradicate the ills created by the extreme degradation [of these institutions]. Yet if this is deemed too much [to hope for], the next best alternative is to adopt [the following steps]: to equalize the quotas for successful candidates in each prefecture so as to strengthen students' sense of purpose; to establish moral conduct as a category in the examinations so as to give students a firm foundation; to abolish the composition of *ci* and *fu* poetry in the examinations and instead to test on the classics, masters, histories, and current affairs in separate years so as to make students' learning complete. Moreover, students should be made to base themselves on a definite school of exegesis (*jiafa*) in dealing with the classics, and examiners should see that they follow the correct punctuation of the text, that in their replies students show a thorough understanding of the text, and that they expound the various commentaries one by one before concluding with their own personal views. Moreover, in schools persons of authentic moral character should be chosen diligently to teach and guide students and to attract scholars who are committed to solid learning.

Then, having changed the system, you will have genuine commitment and not a spirit of opportunism, real practical conduct and not just empty words, solid learning and unfailingly useful talent. The foregoing is just an outline; the details follow.

1. The reason for equalizing the prefectural quotas for successful candidates is that students today are anxious about having to compete in the prefectural examination (*xiangzhu*) and run in droves to compete at the Imperial College because in the prefectures there are many students competing, with a small quota for passing, while in the Imperial College there are only a few students competing, with a large quota. In the prefectures, examination is the only route to advancement. By contrast, in the Imperial College there is an additional means of rapid advancement through the selection process in the study chambers. Moreover, the system is subject to manipulation by clever people. . . .

---

6. *Mencius* 6A:16.

The board should [therefore] reduce the number of the quota for passing students in the study chambers of the Imperial College so that this number will not be too far out of line with quotas in the prefectures. Then scholars will be content to stay in their own home regions and will not harbor the intention of running across the country [in order to compete where there is a larger quota].

2. The reason it is necessary to establish moral conduct as an examination category is that virtuous conduct has great importance for humankind. In fact, morality is inherent in human nature and is what is proper to the human Way. It is called virtue [*de*] because it is inherent [*de*] in the mind-and-heart. It is called conduct [*xing*] because it is carried out [*xing*] by the individual person. [Moral conduct] certainly is not an ornament one puts on in order to please others' eyes and ears. If scholars truly make an effort in this, they can not only cultivate their own persons but also extend it to governing others, the state, and all-under-Heaven. Therefore there was no educator in antiquity who did not consider moral conduct as the first priority. . . .

It would be better now to allocate one quarter of the newly established quota in each prefecture to the category of moral conduct. . . . The items of moral conduct to be recommended should be clearly specified (such as knowing the eight kinds of good conduct). Prefects and their deputies should be especially charged with searching for them in accordance with the facts. After the prefectural examinations are held, they should be vouched for by guarantors and dispatched to the province. Governors and their assistants should there examine the affidavits and report them to the ministry. . . .

Then follow details concerning apprenticeship, probationary service, observation, evaluation, promotion, or demotion in various offices, concluding with:

In this way scholars will know the value of solid conduct and will not devote their whole lives to studying empty words.

3. The reason that *shi* and *fu* poetry must be abolished is because empty words should not be taught in the first place, nor can they be the standard for selecting scholars. Of empty words, *shi* and *fu* poetry are particularly bad. The fact that they are entirely useless as far as education and recruitment are concerned is absolutely clear. However, when they were abolished in the Xining reign, there were many who opposed this action, not because they thought it wrong to abolish these kinds of poetry, but because they maintained that making Wang An-shih's commentaries on the classics the standard [in the examinations] was wrong. . . . Today *shi* and *fu* poetry should be abolished without any hesitation. If, considering that there are many people who have been [preparing themselves] by practicing *shi* and *fu* poetry, it is not desirable to abolish them all at once, one could progressively decrease the number of passing candidates over the course of three examinations and abolish them at a time when few people still practice them. In this way the present practice will not be affected too sharply, but these evils can be [gradually] eliminated.

4. The reason it is necessary to examine candidates in the classics, [individual] masters, histories, and current affairs separately over a period of years is because the ancients' pursuit of the higher [great] learning gave prime importance to the investigation of things and extension of knowledge. . . . Hence scholars should be conversant with the affairs of all-under-Heaven, the principles of which are contained in the classics [as a whole]; but each classic has its own point of emphasis and they are not interchangeable. . . . Nor [on the other hand] can they all be mastered at once, so the tendency is to eschew those that are difficult to understand and concentrate on the easy ones. Is it any wonder that there are things and affairs the principles of which are not understood by the candidates?

The learning of the masters originates from the same source as that of the sages. Each master has his strengths and shortcomings. One has to learn from their strengths and evaluate their shortcomings. The histories reflect changes in rise and decline, order and disorder, gain and loss from ancient times to the present. Matters of great importance, such as rituals and music, systems and institutions, astronomy, geography, military strategy, and penal codes, are indispensable in contemporary society and cannot be neglected. Students cannot afford not to study them. But it is impossible to require students to master all of these thoroughly in a short period of time, and it will not do to impose such a demand on them. However, if the books that students must study are divided and tested in different years, then it will not be too difficult to have all scholars master one third or one quarter of the requirements in three years. Therefore, I propose that the [Classic of] Changes, the [Classic of] Documents, and the [Classic of] Odes be considered one subject and be tested in the first and seventh year of the twelve-year cycle. The Rites of Zhou, the Ceremonial Rites (Yili), and the Rites of the Two Dai are to be considered one subject and be tested in the fourth year. The Spring and Autumn Annals and its three commentaries are to be one subject and be tested in the tenth year. (The years of examinations should be the same as for provincial examinations, and there should be two questions about the meaning of each subject.)[7] All examinations on the classics should include the Great Learning, the Analects, the Mean, and the Mencius. (There should be one question about the meaning of each.) Essay questions should consist of four subjects on the masters, which would be tested in different years. (The subject of the masters should include works by thinkers such as Xunzi, Yang Xiong, Wang Chong, Han Feizi, Laozi, and Zhuangzi, as well as those by various schools of the present dynasty. The list should be discussed further and the year in which they are to be tested should be decided. It should

---

7. Here, and in what follows, statements in parentheses are translations of interlinear notes in Zhu Xi's text.

also be permitted that two essay questions be asked in each year that the examinations deal with the histories and the annals.)

The policy questions should include histories and current affairs and be conducted in a similar manner. (With respect to the histories, the *Zuozhuan* (*Zuo Commentary on the Spring and Autumn Annals*), the *Narratives of the States* (*Guoyu*), *Records of the Grand Historian*, and the *Histories of the Former and Latter Han* should constitute one subject. The *History of the Three Kingdoms*, *History of the Jin*, and the *History of the Northern and Southern Dynasties* should constitute one subject. The *New History of the Tang Dynasty*, the *Old History of the Tang Dynasty*, and the *History of the Five Dynasties* should constitute one subject. The *Comprehensive Mirror [for Aid in Government]* should constitute one subject. With respect to current affairs, music, calendrical studies, and geography should constitute one subject. The *Comprehensive Rites* [*Tongli*] and the *New Ceremonials* [*of the Zhenghe Period*] should constitute one subject. The *Art of War* (*Bingfa*)[8] and the *Penal Laws [of the Song] with the Decrees and Ordinances* ([*Song*] *Xingtong chi ling*) constitute one subject. The *Comprehensive Institutions* [*Tongdian*] constitute one subject. They should be tested in different years in the same manner as the classics and the masters are tested. There should be two policy questions.) In consequence of this, there would be no classic that a scholar had not mastered and no history that scholars had not studied. They will all be useful to present-day society.

5. The reason for dealing with the classics according to a particular school's method of exegesis is that while the principles of all-under-Heaven are not external to one's mind, the words of the sages and worthies, which contain profound meanings and require textual analysis, cannot be understood through mere conjecture. Moreover, the ancient institutions and ways of conducting affairs are not something we can now observe. Therefore those who study the classics must first have recourse to what earlier scholars have arrived at and then go on from there. Some might say that these [earlier] views are not without error, but still, one should examine the reasons why they may be correct or incorrect so that one can reflect on them in one's mind and correct any of their errors. . . .

In recent years the habits of scholars have become imprudent and reckless, and students have no focus or goal [in their studies]. Those who purport to deal with the classics no longer bother to read the original texts themselves or the commentaries of earlier scholars. They merely read and imitate essays that have been successful in the examinations in recent years. Then they compose practice essays on a theme selected from the classics and deliberately bend the original meaning of the text to suit their erroneous views. Although they know they distort the meaning of the classics, they care only about the flow of their

---

8. See ch. 7.

prose, not the meaning of the texts. . . . Now the way to rectify the problem is, after considering various interpretations of the classics, to base oneself on a particular school's method (*jiafa*) for interpreting commentaries on the classics. . . .

Zhu proceeds to list several Song authorities on each classic whom one might adopt for this purpose.

The Imperial College in antiquity was created primarily for educating people, and the role it played in selecting scholars for office was secondary. For this reason, scholars who came to the Imperial College were motivated by rightness, not profit. . . . [Deleted here are accounts of subsequent changes.] Since the Xining reign, [however,] the Imperial College has become a place where people strive for fame and profit. As for the instructors, they have been selected solely because of their skill in writing examination essays and winning some fame in the examination halls. . . . If one wishes to get rid of these evils, it is better to follow completely the system instituted by Emperor Renzong (r. 1023–1064): One should select scholars who have moral character and are qualified as teachers and appoint them to be school officials. They should be given long tenure and entrusted with expounding moral teachings to the students. . . .

If these proposals are adopted, one can expect that, with the teachings of the sages illuminated above and customs beautified among the people below, the way of the ancient kings will be restored to its [former] brilliance in the present age, and its beneficial legacy will reach on down to posterity.

[*Zhuzi daquan, Wenji* 69:18a–26a — RGC, dB]

ARTICLES OF THE WHITE DEER GROTTO ACADEMY

As prefect of Nangang, Jiangxi, Zhu Xi led an effort to revive the White Deer Grotto Academy, located at the foot of Mount Lu by the great bend of the Yangtze River, a scenic spot famous as the site of Buddhist temples and Daoist sanctuaries. It is significant that Zhu took a strong interest in both public schools and the "private" (i.e., quasi-independent) academies that were centers of scholarship and ritual for the educated elite in local settings. The latter became important media for the propagation of his teachings.

The articles translated here are a set of stated precepts, posted for all to see as the basis for the conduct of instruction in the academy when it was reopened in 1180. As was typical of Zhu's work, the articles or precepts consist mostly of quotations from the classics or other early writings (unattributed by him, since he assumed that his readers would recognize the source from memory). Zhu Xi's contribution was in putting them together in a definite order and sequence. Particularly to be noted is the balance that Zhu strikes between personal cultivation and social relations, as well as that between moral and intellectual development.

Affection between parent and child;
Rightness between ruler and minister;
Differentiation between husband and wife;
Precedence between elder and younger;
Trust between friends. [*Mencius* 3A:4]

The above are the items of the Five Teachings, that is, the very teachings that Yao and Shun commanded Xie reverently to propagate as Minister of Education. For those who engage in learning, these are all they need to learn. As to the proper procedure for study, there are also five items, as follows:

Study extensively, inquire carefully, ponder thoroughly, sift clearly, and practice earnestly. [*Mean* 20]

The above is the proper sequence for the pursuit of learning. Study, inquiry, pondering, and sifting are for fathoming principle to the utmost. As to earnest practice, there are also essential elements at each stage from personal cultivation to the handling of affairs and dealing with others, as listed separately below:

Be faithful and true to your words and firm and sincere in conduct. [*Analects* 15:5]
Curb your anger and restrain your lust; turn to the good and correct your errors. [*Yijing*, hexagrams 41, 42]
The foregoing are the essentials of personal cultivation.
Be true to moral principles and do not scheme for profit; illuminate [exemplify] the Way and do not calculate the advantages [for oneself]. [Dong Zhongshu, in *Hanshu* 56:12b]
The foregoing are the essentials for handling affairs.
Do not do to others what you would not want them to do to you. [*Analects* 12:2; 15:24]
When in your conduct you are unable to succeed, reflect and look [for the cause] within yourself. [*Mencius* 4A:4]
The foregoing are the essentials for dealing with others.

To these precepts Zhu Xi added a postscript of his own, emphasizing important points that were not explicit in the quoted precepts, namely that learning should be both individual and social, with appropriation by oneself and discussion with others essential to both self-integration and the conduct of affairs. The same approach had been recommended in Zhu's memorials and lectures to the emperor: that he should first form his own opinion of things and then discuss his opinions with others before making up his mind.

I [Zhu] have observed that the sages and worthies of antiquity taught people to pursue learning with one intention only, which is to make students understand the meaning of moral principle through discussion, so that they can cultivate their own persons and then extend it to others. The sages and worthies did not wish them merely to engage in memorizing texts or in composing poetry and essays as a means of gaining fame or seeking office. Students today obviously act contrary [to what the sages and worthies intended]. The methods that the sages and worthies employed in teaching people are all found in the classics. Dedicated scholars should by all means read them frequently, ponder them deeply, and then inquire into them and sift them.

Zhu concludes this note by taking issue with what became a growing trend in the Song: the adopting of school rules (as also monastic rules in Buddhism, see chapter 17), which he considers demeaning to students, who should be mature enough to take responsibility for their own learning and conduct. Ironically, when these precepts were widely circulated in other Neo-Confucian academies of China, Korea, and Japan, despite what Zhu says here, they were often identified as school rules (xuegui).

If one understands the necessity for principles and accepts the need to take responsibility oneself for seeing that they are so, then what need will there be for someone else to set up such contrivances as rules and prohibitions for one to follow? In recent times regulations have been instituted in schools, and students have been treated in a shallow manner. This method of making regulations does not at all conform with the intention of the ancients. Therefore I shall not now try to put them into effect in this lecture hall. Rather, I have specifically selected all the essential principles that the sages and the worthies have used in teaching people how to pursue learning; I have listed them, as above, one by one, and posted them on the crossbar over the gate. You, sirs, discuss them with one another, follow them, and take personal responsibility for their observance. Then in whatever a man should be cautious or careful about in thought, word, or deed, he will certainly be more demanding of himself than he would be the other way [of complying with regulations]. If you do otherwise or even reject what I have said, then the "regulations" others talk about will have to take over and in no way can they be dispensed with. You, sirs, please think this over.

[Zhu, *Wenji* 74:18a, 18b–19a — dB]

PREFACE TO THE *FAMILY RITUALS*

Although the main focus of Zhu Xi's work was the theory and practice of self-cultivation, the defining and shaping of the self always took place in a social context, and the study of rites remained a major concern of his, as it had been earlier for the

Confucius of the *Analects*, in which humaneness and rites were twin themes. Throughout his lifetime, Zhu sustained a strong interest in the classical rites, the critical, historical study of which he recognized as of great importance, as well as in the question, already of concern to predecessors such as the Cheng brothers and Sima Guang, of how these might be adapted to his own times. This reflects Zhu's strong conviction that scholarly study of the ancient rites was not enough; one must somehow put them into practice.

As a practical matter for the local elite, Zhu gave family ritual priority over the royal and state rituals that occupied so much of the Zhou texts. Yet Zhu's preface reveals his keen awareness of how much the circumstances of the Song scholar-official class (*shi*) have changed from those of the ancient Zhou aristocracy; indeed he himself was much too poor to carry on the classic rites. Accordingly, he sought to make them simpler, less costly, and more practical for the average family. Thus he focused on the more common ones: capping (coming of age), weddings, funerals, and ancestral rites. (There was a separate "Pinning Ritual" for girls at the time of their engagement to be married.) Note the absence of a birth rite, while the "capping" remains as a vestige of ancient induction into the leadership class. Subsequently, Zhu's prescriptions became models for the cultural and social elite, adopted widely in premodern East Asia.

Ritual "has fundamental elements and elaborations" [articulated form].[9] From the perspective of how ritual is carried out at home, the fundamental elements are to preserve roles and responsibilities and give substantial form to love and respect; the elaborations are the ceremonies and specifications for capping, weddings, funerals, and ancestral rites. The fundamental elements are the daily courtesies of householders, the things they must not fail to perform for even a single day. The articulated forms serve further to regulate the beginning and ending of human affairs. Even though the forms are only performed at particular times and places, unless one discusses them clearly and practices them until they become familiar, when the need arises one will not be able to do what is right and fitting. Thus one must also daily discuss and practice the forms.

During the three ancient dynasties[10] the classical texts of the rituals were fully adequate, but in the texts that survive today, the regulations on dwellings, utensils, and clothes, and the instructions on matters like coming and going, rising and sitting are no longer suited to our age. Even when contemporary gentlemen (*junzi*) accommodate the changes from antiquity to the present to formulate a temporary system for today, they still may not attain the proper balance, with some parts too detailed and some too sketchy. It can reach the point where they omit the fundamental elements and concentrate on the sec-

---

9. "Rites in the Formation of Character," *Record of Rites* 23:2a; Legge, *Li Ki*, 1:394–395.
10. Xia, Shang, and Zhou, the periods described in the classics.

ondary ones, showing indifference to the substance but concern about the articulated forms. Thus, even committed scholars who are dedicated to the rites may still fail to perform the essential parts. And those who suffer from poverty have the added worry that they will not have the means to fulfill the ritual.

In my ignorance, I have suffered from both [lack of clear guidance and lack of funds], so I once took on the task of reviewing the ancient and recent texts [on ritual]. I started by identifying the major structures that cannot be changed and made minor emendations, my purpose being to put together a manual for one school [of thought]. In general I paid careful attention to roles and responsibilities and gave a high place to love and respect, considering them to be the fundamental elements. As for the situations in which these values are put into practice, I have been sketchy on the details, concentrating on the fundamental substance.

In writing this book I presume to follow Confucius's idea of carrying on what came from our predecessors. I sincerely hope to be able to discuss these matters fully with some like-minded gentlemen and make every effort to put them into practice. That way we might possibly again see the way the ancients "cultivated themselves and regulated their families"[11] and the heart whose "attention to the departed continues until they are far away."[12] Moreover, this book might make a small contribution to the state's effort to transform and lead the people.

[*Zhuzi daquan, Wenji* 75:16b–17a; trans. adapted from Ebrey,
Chu Hsi's Family Rituals, pp. 3–4]

PROPOSAL FOR COMMUNITY GRANARIES

This proposal is typical of many initiatives Zhu took as a government official to encourage local elites to deal with chronic problems more or less on their own. It is also indicative of the fact that, however much private or local initiative might be promoted, the problem remained one of how local groups could do so with the necessary official approval and oversight but without direct government interference. In this respect Zhu envisaged some kind of civil infrastructure, between the private or household level and the state administration (*guan*), that would serve local public functions through relatively autonomous, cooperative, not-for-profit organizations. In the proposal here one should note especially how interest repayment was used initially to build up a reserve for later operation of a system of interest-free loans. Note too that Zhu first demonstrated the practicality of his plan by a fourteen-year pilot program in one area before recommending it for general authorization by the central government.

In connection with other proposals reported in this chapter, Zhu's proposals for community granaries also serve as an expression of his belief (and Mencius' long

---

11. Allusion to "Great Learning," *Record of Rites*; Legge, *Li Ki*, 2:411. See ch. 10.
12. *Analects* 1:9, a statement attributed to Zengzi.

before) that a strong economic (i.e., agricultural) base was needed to sustain any program of educational or cultural uplift. Some of Zhu's followers (Xu Heng in the Yuan and Wu Yubi in the Ming) believed a system of independent scholar-farmers was preferable to having a class of scholar-officials largely dependent on state funds or the ruler's largesse.

Imperial Edict

On the 28th day of the twelfth month, in the eighth year of the Chunxi era (1181), the Secretariat forwarded a memorial to the emperor from the Ministry of Revenue submitted by the Commissioner for Ever-Normal Granaries, Salt, and Iron in the Liangzhe Eastern District, Zhu Xi.

The memorial says:

There is a community granary in Kaiyao village in Chongan county, Jianning superior prefecture. It was founded in the fourth year of the Qiandao era (1168) because of a famine in the village. An appropriation of 600 *tan* of rice from the Ever-Normal Granary of the prefecture was to serve as the seed rice. I was entrusted with the responsibility for working with Liu Ruyu, a local scholar with the honorific title of "Gentleman for Court Service," to use the amount for lending to those in need of support. The rice was appropriated in the winter. The following summer the prefectural office instructed that the rice should continue to be lent out and those who borrowed should then pay back in the winter.

We consulted the prefectural office and decided that the interest should be two *dou* per *dan* of rice borrowed [i.e., 20 percent]. This rate was to be in force for the coming [several] years, although it was agreed that should any borrower have difficulty in repayment, the interest rate could be reduced by a half, or even in full in the case of serious famine.

The granary has been in operation for fourteen years and we have managed to build three warehouses and have accumulated 3,100 *dan* of interest rice after the initial amount of 600 *dan* had been paid back to the prefecture. The amount of the interest rice has been properly reported to the prefecture.

I further suggest that the lending should continue, although the borrowers should no longer have to pay interest. An administrative fee of three *sheng* (i.e., 3 percent) will be collected, and the [retired] officials residing in this village, together with the local literati and myself, will [continue to] manage the granary. During the lending season, we ask that a county official be present to supervise the process.

Because of this granary, the village, comprising an area of about 40 to 50 [square] *li*, has not suffered hunger even in bad years. I believe that this is a method that could be introduced to other areas. Because there is no legal precedent, and no one would take it upon himself to initiate the system on his own, I request that it be instituted in all circuits and prefectures by Imperial decree, and further that should local households wish to establish a granary, the prefectural or county office should allocate a suitable amount of rice from its Ever-Normal Granary and entrust it to the leading household in the area to manage the lending and borrowing. The interest should also be two *dou* of rice. I hope that the village leaders, resident retired officials, and respected local scholars would work with the county magistrate to manage the lending and collecting. Once the interest rice has accumulated to ten times the seed rice, then the seed rice should be returned to the government and the interest rice be used for future lending, at a fee of three *sheng* [but] without interest. If well-to-do families are willing to contribute rice for seed purposes, they should be encouraged to do so. Their contribution should be paid back in a similar manner. Moreover, if certain regions have different customs, they should follow what is convenient for them and devise their own regulations and submit them to the government for recognition. This granary system is designed for creating long-term benefit, and if any village decides that it does not wish to establish a granary, then the government should not apply any pressure or force them to establish it. . . .

The emperor ordered the Ministry of Revenue to consider the memorial and the following is its opinion:

The Secretariat, commenting on the opinion submitted by the Department of Revenue, says:

We think it desirable that this memorial be circulated to the circuits and various supervisory offices and the prefectural and county offices under them. It should be made known that any people wishing to do as the memorial specifies would be assisted to do so. Retired officials — either coming originally from the county or those retired to the county — if they have shown themselves to be morally upright, should be allowed to apply to the prefectural or county offices for establishing such a granary. The local government should then allocate an amount of rice from the government's own "righteous [charitable] granary" to serve as seed rice. The retired officials should work with local elders to manage the granary, while the prefectural and county offices should not intervene or seek to control things.

[*Wenji* 99:17b–19b — THCL]

PROCLAMATION OF INSTRUCTIONS

This proclamation was issued when Zhu was prefect of Zhangzhou in 1190. It is perhaps the most important proclamation that Zhu Xi issued, the most representative of his efforts in popular education, and the most quoted in later times. There is a great consistency in the views on public morality and community life expressed here and those found in the community compact (next selection).

Particularly to be noted are (1) the elements of basic morality in article 1 (later incorporated in the Sacred Edicts of the Ming and Qing dynasties; (2) the emphasis on filiality (despite Zhu's reservations about the *Xiaojing* as a "Classic" of Filiality); and (3) the identifying of the marital relation as prime among all human relationships. It is also noteworthy that, although there is some functional differentiation, most of the injunctions here apply equally to all members of the community, both scholar-officials (*shi*) and common people (*min*).

Following are items of instructions to be observed:

1. Instructions to members of community units (*baowu*) on matters about which they should encourage and remind each other:

All members should encourage and remind each other to be filial to parents, respectful to elders, cordial to clansmen and relatives, and helpful to neighbors. Each should perform his assigned duty and engage in his primary occupation. None should commit vicious acts or thefts, or indulge in drinking or gambling. They should not fight with or sue each other.

If there are filial sons or grandsons, or righteous husbands and virtuous wives, and their deeds are noteworthy, they should be reported. The government, in accordance with provisions of the statutes, will reward them and honor them with banners. Those who do not follow instructions should be reported, examined, and punished in accordance with the law.

2. Injunctions to members of community units on matters of which they should mutually watch and investigate each other:

People should always be alert to save water, prevent fire, investigate thefts and robberies, and prevent infighting.[13] Do not sell salt that is privately produced,[14] or kill plow oxen. They should not gamble with their properties. Nor should they spread or practice demon religion (*mojiao*).[15] People in the same community unit should watch each other. Anyone who is aware of a crime but fails to report it will share in the punishment.

3. Instructions to gentlemen (*shi*) and commoners (*min*):

People should understand that our body originates from our parents and that brothers come from the same source. Thus, we are endowed by nature with a feeling of obligation to parents and brothers, most profound and grave. What makes us love our parents or respect our elder brothers is not forced but comes spontaneously from the original mind-and-heart. And this love is inexhaustible.

Now some people are unfilial to parents and disrespectful to brothers. They often violate their parents' instructions and commands and even fail to provide for them; they easily become angry and fight with their brothers and even refuse

---

13. The people of Zhangzhou were said to be much given to feuding.

14. Trading salt outside the salt monopoly was prohibited.

15. Although *mojiao* sometimes refers to Manichaeanism, it is more likely that the term here means unorthodox, folk religion.

to help them out. They defy Heaven and violate all principles. I deeply lament and feel sorry for them. They should urgently reform their conduct, otherwise they will invite immediate disaster.

4. Instructions to gentlemen and commoners:

It should be understood that the marital relationship between husband and wife is chief among the human moral relationships.[16] The rites and laws regarding betrothal and engagements are very strict. However, the customs of this region include what is called "looking after [someone]," that is, living openly with a woman who is neither a wife nor a concubine. Another is called "elopement," when two people who are not betrothed seduce each other and flee in secrecy. No violating of the rites and breaking of the law is more serious. The offenders should urgently reform so as to avoid punishment.

5. Instructions to gentlemen and commoners:

People should be kind and cordial toward villagers, neighbors, clansmen, and relatives. If sometimes a minor quarrel occurs, both parties should reflect deeply and make every effort to negotiate and reach a reconciliation. They should not lightly bring suit. Even if one is right, one's property will become diminished and one's work and livelihood may be cut off. How much worse is it if one is not right? In that case one cannot avoid imprisonment and punishment. It will end in calamity. All should earnestly take this as a serious warning.[17]

6. Instructions to official households (*guanhu*):

Since these are known as "households of public servants," and they thus differ from the common people, they should be especially content with their status and obey the law. They should devote themselves to "controlling oneself" and benefiting others. Moreover, villagers and neighbors are, in fact, all relatives and friends. How can one rely on his strength to bully the weak, or his wealth to appropriate the property of the poor? Prosperity and decline come in cycles. This calls for deep reflection.

7. Instructions when there has been a death in the family:

There should be timely burial of the dead. It is not permissible to keep the coffin at home or in a temple. If coffins or ashes have been temporarily stored in a temple, they should be buried within one month. Never should one employ Buddhist monks to make offerings to the Buddha, nor engage in extravagant display at funerals. The ceremony should be on a scale in keeping with one's resources. What matters is only that the dead should be returned to the soil soon. Anyone violating this should be flogged a hundred strokes with a heavy rod in accordance with the law. In addition, officials [violating this] should not

---

16. Refers to the *Classic of Changes*, "Providing the Sequence of the Hexagrams" ("Xu gua"): "When there are husband and wife, then there are parent and child. When there are parent and child, then there are ruler and minister"; *Zhouyi zhengyi* (SBBY) 9:7b.

17. Instructions 1, 2, and 5 above contain admonitions that are similar to those in the Lü Family Community Compact, to be discussed in the following section.

be eligible for appointment, nor should scholars be allowed to take the civil examinations. Villagers, relatives, and friends who come to console may assist by making contributions. They should not oblige the family to provide food and drink for them.

8. Instructions to men and women:

They should not establish hermitages on their own under the pretext of engaging in religious practice. If there are such people, they should be expected to marry before long.

9. Restrictions on temples and people:

They are prohibited from holding mixed gatherings of men and women during the day or evening under the pretext of worshiping the Buddha or transmitting the sutras.

10. Restrictions on town and village:

They are prohibited from collecting money or donations, or making and parading figurines under the pretext of averting disasters or gaining good fortune.[18]

With respect to the instructions above, I only wish that everyone understand what is right and be a good person. Everyone should realize that if he does not offend the authorities, there is no reason why he should be subject to punishment. All should earnestly follow these instructions so that peace and harmony will be with them. If anyone does not follow them and dares to be defiant, the law of the state is clear and officials must be impartial [in enforcing the law]. Everyone should deeply reflect on this so he will have no cause for regret later.

[*Wenji* 100:5b–7a, "Quanyu bang" — RGC]

THE LÜ FAMILY COMMUNITY COMPACT, AMENDED AND EMENDED

Although Zhu Xi was remarkable for both his originality and his powers of high-level synthesis, he characteristically expressed himself by editing or commenting on some earlier work — not only the classics but often the work of recent predecessors, as if to build on the prior insights and experience of others who either represented a kind of local, indigenous tradition or have tried to deal with the same problems as he in circumstances not too different from his own. In not a few cases these works would have been lost had it not been for Zhu's initiative in reclaiming and preserving them.

Such is no doubt the case with the Lü Family Community Compact, originally composed by Lü Dajun (1031–1082), in the Northern Song, which represented an attempt by members of the cultural and social elite to lead in the organization of local associations that would embody in contemporary (eleventh century) form some of the communitarian values that Confucians identified with the ancient enfeoffment system.

---

18. In describing this custom, Zhu Xi's disciple Chen Chun said that people dressed earthen figurines like generals and commanders and marched with them in a parade so as to demand money from spectators (*Beixi daquanji* 47:5b).

Reference is made to the same values, attributed to the Cheng brothers, in the "Systems and Institutions" chapter of Zhu's *Reflections on Things at Hand (Jinsi lu)*. The compact emphasized voluntary subscription to certain values and practices that would govern the common life, stressing moral relations, self-help, and cooperative assistance — all basic human needs and values shared by members of the community regardless of status. At the same time, Zhu recognized the importance of leadership in any group endeavor and was particularly concerned to specify the necessary hierarchy of authority, fix the functions and responsibilities attaching thereto, and embody them in community rituals.

Many variations of this basic pattern were attempted later in imperial China and Korea, but while local structures differed, the key elements were those classified under the four headings indicated at the beginning of the compact's text: (1) mutual encouragement of virtue and meritorious deeds; (2) mutual correction of faults; (3) mutual association in rites and customs; and (4) mutual sympathy [aid] in calamities and difficulties. Other provisions specify the leadership, organization, and conduct of meetings of the members, described in precise detail but too extensive to be reported on here.

Although the excerpts included here may not fairly represent it, the compact as a whole expresses Zhu's conviction that education through joint participation in proper rites and community functions is far more effective for achieving social harmony and promoting the general welfare than attempts at forced indoctrination or punitive laws.

Mutual Encouragement of Virtue and Meritorious Deeds

"Virtue" means being sure to act upon seeing the good and being sure to reform upon hearing of faults; to be able to govern oneself; to be able to govern one's family; to be able to serve father and elder brothers; to be able to instruct sons and younger brothers; to be able to manage servants; to be able to serve superiors; to be friendly with relatives and acquaintances; to be able to choose friends; to be able to maintain integrity; to be able to extend kindness; to be able to fulfill a trust; to be able to relieve distress; to be able to correct faults; to be able to plan things for men; to be able to accomplish things for the people; to be able to resolve conflicts; to be able to decide right and wrong; to be able to promote the beneficial and abolish the harmful; to be able to hold office and reinvigorate offices.

"Meritorious deeds" means, at home, serving one's father and elder brothers, instructing one's children and younger brothers, and managing one's wife and concubines. Outside, it means serving one's superiors, entertaining friends, instructing students, and managing servants. As to reading books, overseeing the fields, managing the household, helping creatures, and favoring the practice of rites, music, archery, charioteering, writing, and arithmetic — all are the kinds of things that should be done. To do anything not of that kind is of no benefit.

The foregoing virtuous deeds should be the subjects of individual emulation and mutual encouragement. At meetings of the compact members they should be cited as cause for mutual congratulation, and the names of those performing them should be recorded for the encouragement or admonition of others.

Mutual Correction of Faults

"Faults" means six faults of violating right conduct, four faults of violating the compact, and five faults of unbecoming conduct.

The faults of violating right conduct:

1. Drunken quarreling, gambling, fighting, litigation.

Drunken quarreling means a brawling argument under the influence of wine.

Gambling means gambling for valuables.

Fighting means assaulting and reviling.

Litigation means accusing someone of a crime with the intention of harming him. If [however] it is a case of going so far that someone attacks and injures another and is accused of it, it [litigation] is not to be disallowed.

2. Excessiveness and abnormality in conduct.

The many evils of exceeding and deviating are all included.

3. Irreverent and unyielding conduct.

To be rude to those of virtue or age; to bully men and to impose on people by relying on one's superior strength; to know of a fault and not change; to hear remonstrance and do even worse.

4. Stating what is not true and not being trustworthy. . . .

5. Making up statements of false accusation and slander. . . .

6. Managing things to one's own undue advantage.

The faults of violating the compact:

1. Not mutually encouraging virtue and meritorious deeds.

2. Not mutually correcting faults.

3. Not mutually observing rites and customs.

4. Not mutually expressing sympathy for the distressed.

The faults of unbecoming conduct:

1. Mixing with men not of the right kind.

Not restricting oneself to the general class of people, but mixing with the wicked and loafing with bad actors who do not conform to ordinary humankind. If one consorts with them day and night, that is mixing with those not of one's own kind. If, [however,] one cannot avoid contact with them briefly, it is not to be faulted.

2. Rambling, playing around, and idling.

Rambling means coming and going without reason. It includes visiting people and stopping them from working or from doing what they ought to be doing.

Playing around means sporting and laughing without limit. It includes ridiculing in contempt and possibly such activities as racing horses and hitting balls without betting valuables. Idling means not practicing one's proper occupation or managing family affairs, not keeping one's gate and courtyard in order, and being sloppy.

3. Acting without proper manners.

Advancing and withdrawing rudely. This includes not being respectful, speaking when it is not fitting to speak, and not speaking when it is fitting to speak.

Dressing ostentatiously, not dressing neatly, and going into the street without proper clothing.

4. Not treating pressing matters with due care.

In directing affairs, to be wasteful and forgetful, late in keeping appointments, and careless about urgent matters.

5. Uneconomical expenditures.

Not reckoning the family's resources and exceeding them by extravagant expenditure. Not being able to accept poor circumstances, and not seeking to improve one's condition in a proper manner.

Those who have joined the compact should each examine themselves in regard to the foregoing faults and mutually admonish one another. If the fault is slight, confidential admonition is in order; if it is great, group admonition is called for. If the person charged will not listen, then at a general meeting the head of the compact, so informed, shall try to reason with him and if he agrees to reform, the matter shall simply be recorded in the register, but if he resists, will not submit, and proves incorrigible, all shall agree to his ejection from the compact. . . .

Not included here are the norms for mutual participation in family, community, and seasonal rituals, prescriptions with regard to polite social correspondence, wedding gifts, help with funerals, proper mourning dress, and so on. Seven kinds of calamities calling for mutual aid are indicated, including fire and flood, catching robbers, illness, death, orphanhood, false accusation, and aid to the poor in times of distress. There is a general emphasis on sharing information and offering help to those in need, while setting reasonable standards as to what kind of help one might be expected to give.

Finally the compact concludes with detailed instructions by Zhu Xi on the holding of meetings of the compact members. For brevity's sake we reproduce here the shorter version in the original Lü text:

Every month there shall be a meeting where a meal is served. Once every three months there shall be a gathering where wine and a meal are served. The person in charge each month shall be responsible for covering these expenses. At these meetings, good and bad deeds shall be entered in a register and rewards and penalties administered. Any troublesome matter should be dealt with on the basis of general discussion (*gongyi*).

[*Zhuzi daquan, Wenji* 74:25a–32a —JM, dB]

Chapter 22

IDEOLOGICAL FOUNDATIONS
OF LATE IMPERIAL CHINA

ZHEN DEXIU'S ADVICE TO THE EMPEROR

Five years before his death in 1200, Zhu Xi was officially condemned as a heretic and propagator of false teachings. For several decades thereafter, the official status of his teachings remained unsettled, though true believers never doubted his eventual vindication. Even when he was rehabilitated in the 1230s by the Song court, it was in a manner that did little credit to either Zhu or the court — a series of face-saving maneuvers and empty honors that accomplished little. After making ritual obeisance to the memory of Zhu Xi and other Neo-Confucian patriarchs at the temple of Confucius and passing out gifts and promotions to members of the educational establishment, the Emperor Lizong (r. 1225–1264) went back to the business of enjoying himself in his palace and letting the dynasty run off to its doom. Nothing significant was done to institutionalize Zhu's teaching in the one form essential to the implementation of state orthodoxy: prescribing it for the civil service examinations, which tended also to determine the school curriculum.

In the early and mid-thirteenth century it was the schools (especially the private academies, *shuyuan*) that took up the mission of spreading Zhu Xi's teachings. Scholars and teachers were prepared to act independently of the state, ready to take the initiative and assume responsibility themselves for transmitting the "Learning of the Way" (*daoxue*), and it was their growing success in this regard that made their support important to the state — more important than the state's support for them — and that was the real issue behind the court's belated tributes to Zhu Xi in the late Song. But in the long run, the teaching could be considered fully established in the traditional Chinese sense only if the values espoused by the teachers and schools were also sanctioned by the ruler in the examinations for scholars who would assist in the governing of the empire.

After the official persecutions of the Cheng brothers and Zhu Xi, their followers were left with a strong sense that the authentic Confucian teaching could survive only through the inspired and heroic efforts of those who represented the true "succession to the Way" (daotong) and were prepared to suffer for it. The wounds of partisan struggle, however, proved far from mortal to the School of the Way, as it not only recovered from them but was strengthened by the ordeal and emerged from the stigma of heresy to become the new orthodoxy. In this struggle of the many scholar-teachers who led the way during the early thirteenth century, none was more important than Zhen Dexiu (1178–1235), like Zhu Xi from Fujian, and one teaching generation removed from him.

From a poor literati family, Zhen was left fatherless at the age of fourteen, and his mother had a difficult struggle to continue his education. With the help of a friend in the locality who recognized Zhen's extraordinary talent, he was able to prepare for the civil service examinations, pass them at the provincial level by the age of seventeen, and, in 1199, succeed in the metropolitan examinations for the *jinshi* degree at the age of twenty-one.

By 1208, as a professor (*boshi*) of the Imperial College, he was already making himself known for his courage and outspokenness in challenging the repressive measures against the Cheng-Zhu school. He criticized the monopolization of power that discouraged criticism at court and deplored the defamation of worthy scholars and officials, as well as the perversions of truth that produced a confusion of values and frustrated all attempts to practice the true Way of government.

Nevertheless, Zhen's forthrightness at court, his calls for open discussion of public issues, his vigorous advocacy of strengthening defenses in the north through the development of colonies of farmer-soldiers, and his attacks on evils in the government as a greater danger than external enemies drew upon him the enmity of the prime minister and led to his reassignment in 1215, at his own request, to service in the provinces. By all accounts, his record in successive local assignments was outstanding.

As precepts for his subordinates in Tanzhou, he is said to have offered incorruptibility, humaneness, impartiality, and diligence:

Discipline the self by incorruptibility [refrain from graft].
Pacify the people by humaneness.
Preserve the mind by impartiality.
Perform your duties with diligence.

In 1225 the situation changed at court with the accession of Emperor Lizong. Zhen was invited back to the capital, where he served in the Secretarial Council (*Zhongshu sheng*) and Ministry of Rites, and he was soon engaged in lecturing the emperor on the need "to take the ancient sage kings as his models and mentors" and to "rule in the interests of all, not just of one man and his family." Zhen performed in the capacity of Lecturer from the Classics Mat, a function that had become especially honored in the Song because of the high distinction of the scholar-officials, notably Cheng Yi and Zhu Xi, who had taken on this duty of expounding the meaning and significance of the classics as they related to historical cases and contemporary problems.

After subsequent service in the provinces, Zhen was recalled to court in 1233, and the following year he presented to the throne his monumental work, the *Extended Meaning of the Great Learning* (*Daxue yanyi*), which he had been compiling over the years in his spare time, mainly while in the provinces, as an extension of his lectures from the Classics Mat. The emperor is said to have exclaimed, "This one book of the *Extended Meaning* is sufficient as a guide and model for the ruler."

Among Zhen's voluminous compilations and notably lucid writings are his *Heart Classic* and his so-called *Classic of Governance* (*Zhengjing*), in which are collected his writings on practical problems of local government — but which, for lack of space, we omit here.

PREFACE TO THE *EXTENDED MEANING OF THE GREAT LEARNING*

In the classical context "to extend the meaning" meant "to enlarge on the significance of the Way of humaneness and rightness." For Zhen this was understood as drawing out a classic work's larger significance and contemporary application — in this case, how the *Great Learning*'s method of self-cultivation should be practiced by the ruler in the contemporary dynastic setting. Although it quotes other classics and historical documents that serve as pretexts for Zhen, he adds comments of his own that make this a highly original and incisive commentary on the conduct of the court in his day. Not a few modern writers have failed to appreciate this, dismissing Zhen's *Extended Meaning* out of hand, assuming it to be just another literal, phrase-by-phrase exegesis of the *Great Learning*, which it is not.

Zhen's preface outlines the contents of the larger work. Particularly to be noted is the prime focus on the mind-and-heart of the ruler, reflective of the optimistic Neo-Confucian belief in the power of the human mind and will to master any situation, as well as the responsibility this implies for the ruler to use his position and great power for the benefit of all the people, not just himself.

When your minister first read the *Great Learning*, he became aware that there is an order of importance and sequence of priorities among the investigation of things, the extension of knowledge, making one's intentions sincere, rectifying the mind-and-heart, cultivating the person, regulating the family, ordering the state, and pacifying all-under-Heaven. As I fondly perused its contents I exclaimed to myself, "He who would be a ruler among men cannot fail to study the *Great Learning*. He who would be a minister among men cannot fail to study the *Great Learning*. The ruler who fails to comprehend the *Great Learning* lacks the means to arrive at a clear understanding of the source of governance. The minister who fails to comprehend the *Great Learning* lacks the means to fulfill his duty of correcting the ruler."

Only when one has inquired into the governance of the emperors and kings of antiquity and found that they invariably take the human person as its basis and extend this to all-under-Heaven, can one appreciate that this book represents an essential text in transmitting the mind-and-heart of the hundred sages and is not just the utterance of Confucius alone. After the Three Dynasties this learning of the emperors and kings was lost, and although this text survived it was no more than a brief outline. Where then could one go if he sought to inquire into good government or sought to expound it to the prince? . . .

The great scholar of recent times, Zhu Xi, wrote the *Great Learning by Chapter and Phrase* and *Questions Concerning the Great Learning* in order to analyze and clarify its meaning. At the beginning of the reign of Ningzong (1195–1224), he was called to serve at court and lecture on the classics. Often he presented this text for discussion. He who would govern well, Zhu said, if he examined this work carefully and understood it thoroughly, would find in it a clear and systematic exposition of the emperors' and kings' order of priorities in the conduct of government as well as the basis for conducting his own learning.

Now your minister makes bold to say that he has ventured to give some thought to supplementing this work. Therefore he has taken some passages from the text, amounting to 205 words, and put them in this compilation, prefacing them with the teachings found in the "Canon of Yao" ("Yaodian"), the "Counsels of Gao Yao" ("Gaoyao mo"), and "Instructions of Yi Yin" ("Yixun") [in the *Classic of Documents*], as well as passages from the Ode "Sizhai"[1] and the *jiaren* hexagram of the *Classic of Changes*. From this, one can see that the precepts of the sages [in these classics] do not differ from those of the *Great Learning*. Following these are the views of such later scholars as Zisi, Mencius, Xunzi, Dong Zhongshu, Yang Xiong, and Zhou Dunyi, from which we can see that the theories of later worthies are also in accord with it. (The foregoing represents the emperors' and kings' priorities in governing.)[2]

The learning of Yao, Shun, Yu, Tang, Wen, and Wu was the purest form of

---

1. Ode 240.

2. This and subsequent sentences in parentheses are translations of interlinear notes in Zhen's text.

the Great Learning. The learning of Gaozong of the Shang and King Cheng of the Zhou came close to it. By the Han and Tang dynasties, even in the case of the more worthy rulers it was no longer possible for their learning to avoid contravention of this learning in some ways, but the learning of the emperors Xiao and Yuan of Han and many rulers thereafter was involved either with mere technical contrivances or with philological niceties and could not but fall into serious error. (The foregoing represents the emperors' and kings' pursuit of learning.) . . .

In the learning of the ruler it is necessary to know what is most essential if one is to know where to apply one's efforts. For the ruler what is most essential in the investigation of things and the extension of knowledge is that there should be a clarification of the practice of the Way, that there should be careful discrimination in the judging of human talents, that there should be careful consideration of the forms of rule, and that there should be attention to ascertaining the feelings of the people. . . .

(Judging human talents also consists of four items: the sages' and worthies' methods of observing men; how the emperors and kings got to know men; the techniques by which clever scoundrels usurp the state; and the passions exploited by those who would ensnare the ruler.)

(Ascertaining the state of the people's feelings consists of two items: according with the people's sensibilities and learning the facts of life in the countryside.) . . .

The most essential things in making one's intentions sincere and rectifying the mind-and-heart are exalting reverent awe and restraining wayward desires. . . .

(Restraining wayward desires consists of five items: restraining drunkenness; restraining lewd desires; curbing wasteful amusements; curbing extravagance; the above are preceded by a general discussion concerning the consequences of failure to restrain these four.)

The most essential things in the cultivation of the person are to be careful in word and deed and to maintain a proper demeanor and bearing. . . .

The most essential items in regulating the family are taking the [problem] of wives as a serious matter, being strong in dealing with the inner court, settling the dynastic succession, and providing proper education for the conjugal relatives.

(Taking the problem of wives seriously consists of four items: care in selecting and installing wives; the benefits of listening to sound advice; differentiating legal wives and consorts from others; the error of disestablishing legal consorts.)

(Strictness in dealing with the inner court consists of four items: strict separation of inner and outer courts; curbing the inner court's interference in affairs of state; the blessings of loyal and conscientious admonition on the part of ministers in the inner court [eunuchs]; the misfortune of ministers of the inner court interfering in state affairs.)

(Settling the dynastic succession consists of four items: planning for the installation of the heir apparent should be done in advance; provision for the system of instruction should be planned for; the differentiation between legal wives and concubines should guard against the danger of disestablishing [the heir apparent].)

(Providing proper education for the conjugal relatives consists of two items: the blessings of modest and respectful comportment on the part of the conjugal relatives and the unfortunate consequences of arrogance and overweening ambition on the part of conjugal relatives.)

If these four ways can be followed [corresponding to the four major topics above], then the ordering of the state and pacifying of the world will require nothing more than can be found therein. Under each heading are given the luminous instructions of the sages and worthies, and then historical examples from former times. In these success and failure are clearly mirrored.

[Preface to *Daxue yanyi* 1:1a–3b, 4b — dB]

Concluding note: In addition to the points noted in the preface, the contents of the work especially emphasize the restraint of the ruler's desires. Zhen draws out the sorry record of imperial decadence and debauchery: drinking to the point of debility, sex to the point of exhaustion, extravagant entertainment, wasteful outings and excursions, destructive hunting parties, overexpenditure on luxurious palaces, and so on — all to the mournful accompaniment of warnings from Confucian ministers who go unheeded by irreverent and inattentive sovereigns.

The concluding portions of the *Extended Meaning*, having to do with the emperor's management of his own household, illustrate the dangerous consequences that follow from not limiting the number and power of those kept in the inner palace — especially wives, concubines, and eunuchs — who exploit the weaknesses of the ruler and employ the stratagems that lead to his undoing. The more positive side of these discourses has to do with proper selection of wives for their virtue and wisdom, protecting the rights of legitimate wives, arranging for the legitimate succession and defending it from attempts to subvert it, and providing for the education of the imperial family.

THE CLASSIC OF THE MIND-AND-HEART

Zhen's *Heart Classic* (*Xinjing*) can claim the status of a classic only in the sense that its contents are all quotations from the Confucian classics, with selected commentary by Song masters, conveying the essence of the Neo-Confucian view of the mind-and-heart, in contrast to the Buddhist view contained in the *Heart Sūtra* (also *Xinjing* in Chinese). It starts with a quotation, from Zhu Xi's preface to the *Mean*, of the sixteen-word dictum attributed to the sage kings Shun and Yu, with Zhu's commentary following. It should be noted that the primary audience intended is the ruler and scholar-officials (*shidafu*).

"The mind of man is precarious, the mind of the Way is barely perceptible. Be discriminating, be one [with the mind of the Way.] Hold fast the Mean!"

The mind-and-heart as the empty spirit and consciousness is one and undivided, but there is a difference between the human mind and the mind of the Way [the moral mind], depending on whether it arises from the selfishness that is identified with the physical form or originates in the correctness of the innate moral imperative, in accordance with which consciousnesses differ. The former may be precarious and insecure, the latter so subtle as to be barely perceptible. All men have this physical form and even the most intelligent invariably possess the human mind, while even the most stupid possess the mind of the Way. If these two are mixed in the human heart and we do not know how to control them, the insecure will become even more insecure, the barely perceptible [Way] will become even less perceptible, and the impartiality of Heaven's principle [in the moral nature] will have no way of overcoming the selfishness of human desires.

"Discriminating" means to discriminate between the two and not let them get mixed. "Oneness" means to hold on to the correctness of the original mind and not become separated from it. If one pursues this task without the slightest interruption, making sure that the mind of the Way is always master and the human mind heeds its commands, then what is insecure will become secure, what is barely perceptible will become more manifest, and whether in action or in quiescence one will not err through going too far or not far enough.

[*Xinjing* 1 — dB]

The only words of Zhen Dexiu himself attached to this text are a poem that starts with the lines "The sixteen words transmitted from Shun to Yu / Are the Learning of the Mind-and-Heart for all ages." Before this the "sixteen words" had been identified with the message or method of the mind (*xinfa*) by Cheng Yi, also quoted by Zhu Xi in his commentary on the *Mean*. This equation of the two — the "Message or Method" (*xinfa*) and the "Learning" of the Mind-and-Heart (*xinxue*) — is the basis for the subsequent identification of the two in orthodox Neo-Confucian discourse, long before the Learning or School of the Mind became identified with Wang Yangming in the sixteenth century. It was this orthodox version that became widely propagated by Yi T'oegye in Korea and others in Japan.

What made this synthetic work so important in the early development of Cheng-Zhu thought was its strong insistence on the need to control human selfish desires. As expressed in other writings of Zhen's, we see evidence of this intense moral rigorism — almost a puritanism — that came to be viewed as characteristic of the self-cultivation of the School of the Way. First, in a discussion of the orthodox tradition or Succession to the Way (*Daotong*):

When one has committed oneself to this Way, to what should he then devote his practice of it and apply his effort? If we look to remote antiquity, we can see that in the one expression "reverent seriousness" (*jing*) as passed down through a hundred sages is represented their real method of the mind-and-heart (*xinfa*). The practice of principle in the world takes the Mean as the ultimate standard of correctness and sincerity as the ultimate norm. However, reverent seriousness is that whereby one achieves the Mean, and without it there can be no achieving the Mean. Only if one is reverent can he be sincere, and without reverent seriousness there is no way to achieve sincerity. The violence of the physical passions surpasses that of runaway horses; reverence is like reining them in. The wildness of the feelings is worse than a river in flood; reverent seriousness is like dikes to hold it back. Therefore, for Master Zhou [Dunyi] to speak of "concentrating on quiescence" (*zhujing*) and for Master Cheng to teach "concentrating on oneness" (*zhuyi*) were most apposite to the condition of man. And Master Zhu was careful to reaffirm the same point.

Here "concentrating on" has the meaning of focusing on the unity of principle (humaneness), which links the human mind-and-heart to Heaven-and-Earth and all things.

If one who pursues learning knows to devote effort to this, one will be certain to exercise caution and apprehension in the state of premeditation, and when actively involved with things and affairs, will be certain to approach them in a humble and respectful manner. The active and quiescent states will lead into each other, with no interruption, so that Heavenly virtue may find completion and human [selfish] desires may be overcome.

[Zhen, "Nanxiong zhouxue . . . ji," *Wenji* 26:448–449 — dB]

Then, in an essay titled "Dedication to the Way," Zhen likens the struggle to armed conflict:

If selfish desires are given free rein, principle is obscured by desires, and inhumaneness follows as a matter of course. Thus in the seeking of humaneness what is of first importance is to "conquer the self" (*keji*). . . . What, then, does it mean "to conquer"? It is like attacking and vanquishing in battle: when selfish thoughts first appear and the original mind has not yet been lost, then principle and desire stand opposed to each other, like two armies ranged in battle. If what is straight wins, what is crooked loses. If principle dominates, desires must be subordinate. The violence of armed conflict and the dangers of war are well known to all, but unless one knows the Way he will not be prepared to guard against the danger of selfish desires, which wound more grievously than a double-edged sword and burn more fiercely than the hottest fire. Therefore, if one is dedicated to the Way, he will value nothing more than the seeking of humaneness, and in seeking humaneness he will put nothing before conquering the self.

[Zhen, "Zhidao zishuo," *Wenji* 81:583–584 — dB]

Taken together, these statements and Zhen's *Heart Classic* probably represent a more extreme view of human desires as evil, and a more austere, straitlaced ideal of human conduct than is characteristic of Zhu Xi. In Zhu's writing one can find statements deprecatory of human desires, and there is some ambiguity too in Zhu's treatment of the evil in human beings as arising from obscurations in the psycho-physical makeup of the individual, so that later critics are not without some grounds in asserting that Zhu held a "puritanical" view of the psycho-physical nature as in some sense evil. Nevertheless, it remains true that there is no warrant for this interpretation in Zhu's philosophy as a whole, and there is repeated stress on the goodness of human nature.

To the extent that Zhen's work had a strong influence on the formulation of Neo-Confucian orthodoxy, its original orientation becomes highly relevant to an understanding of its meaning. The human weaknesses that Zhen attacks so vigorously are not at all typical. They are mostly those of rulers and dynasties, and by extension, of the ruling class who assist them, magnified in proportion to the power they hold. Plausibly the educated elite might recognize themselves in such characterizations, and depending on the historical and cultural circumstances, respond to the challenge of such a lofty ideal of service. On the other hand, a morality prescribed for such an elite leadership class would have its own limitations. One might anticipate signs of strain and rejection if it were generalized and prescribed among persons who could not see themselves in the same role or who failed to find in themselves the weaknesses or excesses that had called for such a stern rigorism in the first place.

Before we leave this, then, a word of two is in order about the later history of the *Extended Meaning*. Printed by Zhen in 1229, it was presented in 1234 to Emperor Lizong, who paid much lip service to it and ordered another printing for official distribution. By the late 1250s at least, it was circulating in Mongol-occupied North China. As heir apparent, Khubilai, before the proclamation of the Yuan dynasty in 1260, received in audience the learned scholar Zhao Bi (1220–1276). Impressed by Zhao's scholarship, Khubilai assigned ten Mongol students to study Confucian texts with him and asked Zhao to study the Mongol language so that he could translate the *Extended Meaning* into Mongol.

Successive Yuan monarchs paid even greater tribute to the work. In the reign of Renzong (1312–1321), the emperor made gifts of the work to his ministers and in 1318 had copies of a new printing of selected passages distributed to court officials. Just after the accession of Emperor Yingzong (Shidebala) in 1321, a new translation of the *Extended Meaning* was presented to the throne, and he responded with another encomium of Zhen's work as unsurpassed for its teaching of "ordering the state through self-cultivation" (*xiushen zhiguo*). Under the reign of Emperor Taiding (Yesun Temur), from 1324 to 1327, great importance was given to lectures from the Classics Mat by both Mongol and Chinese scholars, with the *Extended Meaning* serving as one of the basic texts of instruction.

When the founder of the Ming, who lacked formal education, asked his Neo-Confucian adviser, Song Lian (1310–1381), about "the Learning of the Emperors and Kings," Song recommended that he read Zhen's *Extended Meaning*. Later in the Ming, Zhen's *Extended Meaning* was further extended by the massive supplement of the scholar-statesman Qiu Jun (1420–1495) and the importance of both works continued to be recognized in the Chinese and Korean courts of the seventeenth and eighteenth centuries. Thus Zhen's *Extended Meaning* comes close to qualifying as the prime Neo-Confucian classic of imperial governance.

XU HENG AND KHUBILAI KHAN

From 1127 to 1368 much of China and most of its ancient heartland fell under foreign rule by conquest dynasties from the north. A pattern developed of military control by a garrison state superimposed upon an agricultural society still largely managed through somewhat modified civil bureaucratic rule. Religious Daoism and Buddhism continued to thrive on the popular level, as did many forms of popular culture. Confucianism had greater difficulty regaining its political footing in the midst of marked dynastic instability, but in the traditional form of family ethics and rituals, its position was not seriously challenged, and eventually the Jurchen (Jin) and Mongol (Yuan) dynasties recognized the need for Confucian literati to maintain civil services and serve as an interface between the state and those who worked or managed the land.

Initially, however, things were different for adherents of the new Neo-Confucian Learning of the Way. Though Zhu Xi's teaching had spread rapidly in private academies during the late years of the Southern Song (early and mid-thirteenth century), hostilities and border controls tended to insulate the North from this new development. Only with the Mongol conquest of central and south China, largely completed by 1270, did China again become a unified political and cultural sphere, and did Khubilai (r. 1260–1294) establish a formal Chinese dynasty, the Yuan. At that time a leading exponent of Zhu Xi's teachings, who had already made converts among young scholars, set up an Academy of the Supreme Ultimate in Peking and introduced both Mongols and Chinese to Zhu's major works and the new Neo-Confucian curriculum.

One of the most influential of this new generation of scholars, Xu Heng (1209–1281), inspired by the possibility of regenerating society on the basis of Zhu Xi's teachings, was especially moved by what seemed to him the great educational practicability of Zhu's *Elementary Learning* and the moral/social vision of Zhu's Preface and Commentary on the *Great Learning*. He became "committed to the Learning of the Way as his personal responsibility (*yi daoxue ziren*) and was soon recognized as a prime leader among a group of scholarly activists, likewise converts to the Learning of the Way, who dedicated themselves to 'saving the day' or 'rescuing the times' (*jiushi*) by engaging in efforts of practical use in governing the world (*jingshi zhiyong*)." In memorials to Khubilai and debates at court they emphasized the need for basic laws and institutions of a traditional Han type. In the larger Confucian sense these institutions represented a kind of orderly, constitutional government, combining regular and systematic administration (to which the Mongols were generally unaccustomed) with strong education in public morality, especially through a proper school system. Xu Heng's proposals for reform of tax policies and strengthening of agriculture are a case in point, for Xu considered himself a peasant, not a scholar-official set apart from the common people. Indeed, he believed that Confucian scholars should have a dependable livelihood of their own — preferably agriculture or commerce — rather than be dependent on the largesse of the ruler or the outcome of a competitive struggle for office.

In his writings, Xu Heng sought to convey his basic teachings in simple, unadorned language. He did not strive for originality or stylistic effects but only to get the educational message across, to convert and enlist human talents in the service of the Way. As a self-identified farmer-teacher, with the rugged character of the peasant, Xu communicated his message to his imperial "students" and a new generation of scholar-officials with great earnestness. He was deeply dedicated to the teaching of Mongols, firmly convinced that a Neo-Confucian education was the best way to develop their native intelligence as well as to ensure the survival of the tradition. Yet, for all this, he was charged by some later Neo-Confucians with being a collaborationist who compromised the high principles of the Way.

FIVE MEASURES REQUIRED BY THE TIMES

Xu Heng performed the role of mentor to the emperor both through his memorials and his services as adviser and tutor to the heir apparent. His five-point memorial is believed to have been prepared first as lectures from the Classics Mat, the importance of which had been stressed by Cheng Yi and Zhu Xi, and its opening lines adopt the same stance as they did vis-à-vis the ruler — the high seriousness of the minister's role as sharing responsibility for the governance of all-under-Heaven. Thus Xu quotes the words of Confucius and Mencius (the latter having been made canonical in Zhu Xi's Four Books):

Mencius said, "Charging one's ruler with what is difficult is called showing respect for him. Exposing goodness while foreclosing on evil is called being reverent toward him. Saying that he is 'unable to do it' is called stealing from him."[3] And Confucius said, "[A great minister is one who] serves his ruler

---

3. *Mencius* 4A:1. Mencius was here quoting an earlier saying.

according to the Way, and, when he finds he cannot do so, withdraws [from his service]."[4] The larger purpose that your minister cherishes in his heart is nothing less than this. . . .

In both past and present, though the models and regulations on which the state was established varied from dynasty to dynasty, the most essential thing was to win the hearts of all-under-Heaven. To win the hearts of all-under-Heaven is nothing other than to manifest love and an impartial devotion to the common good. If one loves them, the people's hearts become compliant; if one is impartially devoted to the common good, the people's hearts become willing to serve. Compliance and willingness to serve are what makes for good government.

[*Yuan wenlei* 13:1b–2a — dB]

In the body of his memorial, Xu Heng stresses the urgent importance of governmental reform, telling Khubilai that China can be governed only through traditional Han Chinese institutions and methods, not Mongol ones. Much of his advice is organizational, practical, and prudential, having to do with the emperor's exercise of key leadership functions. Toward the end of the memorial, however, Xu dwells particularly on the need for proper management of agriculture and sericulture (which Mongols had little experience of and handled badly), as well as on the need for universal education, which he (like Mencius) sees as the foundation for all political and social order. In so doing, Xu draws on ideas previously set forth by Zhu Xi.

If from the capital districts down to the local districts schools are set up so that, from the imperial princes on high to the sons of the common people below, the young can engage in study; if day by day the great moral relationships of parent and child, ruler and minister, are explained, along with the great Way that begins [in the home] with the [*Elementary Learning*'s] "sweeping up and responding to questions" and extends to the [*Great Learning*'s] pacifying of the world, then after ten years those above will know how to guide those below and those below will know how to serve those above. With those above harmonious and those below cooperative, it would be far better than what you have now.

If you can do these two things [i.e., provide for the people's livelihood and education], a myriad other things can be accomplished. If you cannot do these things, then nothing can be expected from any of the other things you try to do.

This Way is the Way of Yao and Shun. The Way of Yao and Shun fostered life and promoted unselfishness. If you can do these things, they will foster life

---

4. *Analects* 11:23.

and promote unselfishness. Mencius said, "Anything other than the Way of Yao and Shun I would not dare propose to my king."[5]

["Nongsang xuexiao," *Yuan wenlei* 13:16b–18a — dB]

ON *ELEMENTARY LEARNING* AND *GREAT LEARNING*

In the preface to his commentary on the *Great Learning*, Zhu Xi had traced the origins of schools from the days of the sage kings. The commentary itself put before the reader succinct statements of the guiding principles and ideals of Neo-Confucian education. As almost the first things to be seen by anyone studying Zhu Xi's version of the Four Books, these prefaces had a wide impact on those exposed to the new Learning of the Way (*Daoxue*).

Zhu Xi had also emphasized in his *Elementary Learning* (*Xiaoxue*) the primary education that laid the groundwork for the higher education of the *Great Learning*. As a form of basic training that started in the home, it was meant to be practicable in the everyday life of the Chinese. What is extraordinary here is that Xu Heng should have thought this basic approach suited to the education of Mongols also and that the *Elementary Learning* should later have become widely adopted as a basic text in Korea and Japan as well.

The practical value of Zhu's *Elementary Learning* figured crucially in the conversion of Xu from studies of the *Classic of Changes* to Zhu Xi's teaching, and because of Zhu's insistence upon the *Elementary Learning* as the starting point of all learning, we begin with the opening passage to Xu's *General Significance of the Elementary Learning*, which establishes the basis for learning in the early cultivation of the child's body, mind, and heart, following a sequential growth process.

Xu is mindful of the intense struggle in the mind between selfish desires and the moral principles embodied in the constant human relationships. This calls for constant attentiveness to one's own conduct out of respect — indeed, reverence — for oneself and others.

In ancient times "every child, from the sons of the king and the nobility down to the common people, entered elementary school at the age of eight"[6] and was taught the essentials of "sprinkling, sweeping, responding to inquiries and requests, advancing and retiring,"[7] as well as the polite arts of ritual, music, archery, charioteering, reading, writing, and arithmetic. At the age of fifteen, the crown prince and other princes, the sons of nobility and great officers, and the most talented sons of the common people all began [higher education in]

---

5. *Mencius* 2B:2.
6. Quoting Zhu Xi's Preface to the *Great Learning*.
7. Quoting Zhu Xi's Preface to the *Elementary Learning*.

the *Great Learning*, wherein they were instructed in the way of "self-cultivation for the governance of men" through fathoming principle to the utmost and rectifying the mind-and-heart.

The reason for this distinction between the elementary learning and the greater [higher] learning was that, in their younger years, if they did not receive training in the elementary learning, they would have no way of recollecting their lost mind-and-heart or of nurturing their moral nature, and in their older years, if they did not advance to the greater learning, they would have no means of discerning moral issues or taking responsibility for the handling of affairs. Their starting first with elementary learning was intended to establish the base for the greater learning, and advancing to the greater learning was to reap the benefits of the elementary learning.

In the flourishing days of the Three Dynasties all ability and intelligence were developed and the customs of the people enriched by making the most of this Way. But after the first Qin emperor's burning of the books, the classics and records of the sages were no longer complete and there was no way to ascertain the proper sequence by which the ancients carried on their education.

[Xu Heng, "Xiaoxue dayi," *Quanshu* 4:25b — dB]

Xu then recounts the confusion and disarray in later times that fell into the extremes of either "empty nothingness" or crass "utilitarianism," followed by the successive efforts of Han Yu, the Cheng brothers, and Zhu Xi to revive education on the basis of the Great Learning, *and finally by the compilation of the* Elementary Learning *under Zhu's direction. The main divisions of this work are "Setting Up Instruction," "Clarifying Moral Relations," and "Reverencing the Person." Xu sums up the essence of each in turn.*

"Setting Up Instruction" means the method by which the sage kings of the Three Dynasties taught men. The innate mind of man is originally without imperfection, but after birth through the interference of the psycho-physical endowment, the blinding desire for things, and unrestrained selfishness, imperfections arise for the first time. The sages therefore set up instruction to help men nourish the original goodness of their innate minds and eliminate the imperfections that come from selfishness. . . . [26a–b]

What the early kings set up, however, was not simply their own idea. Heaven has its principles, and the early kings followed these principles. Heaven has its Way, and the early kings carried out this Way. Following the natural course of Heaven's imperative, they made it the proper course of human affairs, and that was what was called instruction. . . . [26b]

What, then, is this Way? It is the moral relation between parent and child, prince and minister, husband and wife, elder and younger, friend and friend. Therein lies the Heaven-bestowed moral nature and the Way for man. . . . [26b–27a]

"Clarifying Moral Relations" — "To clarify" means to make manifest. "Moral relations" means moral principles. In the moral nature endowed in human beings by Heaven each has his proper norm, as in the intimate love between parent and child, the [commitment to] rightness between prince and minister, the differentiation between husband and wife, the order of precedence among older and younger, and the relation of trust between friends. These are Heaven's [natural] relations.

In the Three Dynasties when the sage kings established schools to teach all-under-Heaven, it was only to clarify and manifest these relations and nothing else. Men who cannot clarify these human relations cannot bring order into distinctions of noble and base, superior and inferior, important and unimportant, substantial and insubstantial, controlled and uncontrolled. In the worst case parents do not behave as parents, children as children, princes as princes, ministers as ministers, nor do husband and wife, senior and junior, friend and friend fulfill their proper roles. Nor does it stop simply at their being uncontrolled. When it comes to this, disaster and disorder follow upon one another until everything lapses into bestiality. . . . This is why in instruction among the ancients it was obligatory to teach the moral relations and for students to learn the moral relations. . . . [27a–b]

Like Zhu Xi, Xu grounds the process of socialization in the fundamental reality of creative love, centering it in the human person as the offspring of an intimate parent-child relationship as deeply rooted and inviolable as life itself. Here the concept of human personhood avoids the polarization of individual versus society. Thus these constant moral relations subserve not only the needs of the community but also the development of the human personality, as the mind that is to direct this development has acquired its moral sensitivity through the experiencing of loving relations with others.

"Reverencing the Person" — The preface [to this section] cites Confucius' saying [in the *Record of Rites*] "In the noble person there is no irreverence. To reverence the person is the important thing. The person is the branch [outgrowth] of parental love. How can one not reverence it? Not to reverence the person is to do violence to parental love. To do violence to parental love is to do violence to the trunk [of the tree of life]. Harm the trunk and the branch will die."[8]

The sage uttered this as a warning. One who would be a person cannot for a single day depart from reverence. How much more should one reverence one's own person, which is truly the trunk of all things and affairs? Err in this, and all things go awry. How then could one not be reverent?

Reverencing the person consists of four things: skill in directing the mind,

---

8. "Questions of Duke Ai," *Record of Rites*; Legge, *Li Ki*, p. 266.

proper bearing, clothing, and food and drink. If the direction of the mind is correct within and one's outer bearing is correct, then one has achieved the most substantial part of reverencing the person. Clothing and food are meant for the service of the person. If one does not control them according to what is right and regulate them according to the rites, then that which is meant to nourish humankind will, on the contrary, bring humankind harm.

We can distinguish among these by saying that skillful direction of the mind and proper bearing have to do with the cultivation of virtue [the moral nature], while clothing and food and drink have to do with controlling the self (*keji*). Taking them together we can say that they are all essential to the reverencing of the person. Therefore it will not do if, in the conduct of the relations between parent and child, prince and minister, husband and wife, older and younger, friend and friend, there is not this reverencing of the person. That is why the ancients insisted on reverence as the basis for the cultivation of the person.

[Xu Heng, "Xiaoxue dayi," *Quanshu* 4:27b–28a — dB]

STRAIGHT TALK ON THE ESSENTIALS OF THE *GREAT LEARNING* (*ZHISHUO DAXUE YAOLÜE*)

This lecture is believed to have been delivered to either Khubilai Khan or his heir apparent by Xu Heng in his capacity as Lecturer from the Classics Mat. It is in the vernacular, full of earthy expressions and homely illustrations for an audience not highly literate in the classical Chinese tradition. Xu's interpretation of the *Great Learning* is almost entirely based on Zhu Xi's commentary, but the tone and emphasis are different. Conscious that his audience would not be at home with Song philosophy, he presents the message of the *Great Learning* as coming down from Confucius and the sage kings, whose antiquity and longevity attest to the enduring validity and continuity of the teaching. Xu wanted the Mongols to give up their seemingly capricious, nomadic ways for stable dynastic institutions. One such institution was the Directorate of Education, of which Xu was appointed head. Hence, it is the perennial wisdom and systematic method, not the brilliant metaphysical speculations of the Neo-Confucians, that he puts up front in this rather homespun lecture.

What Xu emphasizes in Zhu Xi's message is universal education, based on a philosophy of the perfectibility of human nature, as well as Zhu's defining of the common human relationships as the focus of self-cultivation. However, Xu also brings in elements of Neo-Confucian cosmology in order to emphasize the grounding of the human moral order in the natural order and the integration of self-cultivation with the processes of nature.

The Book of the *Great Learning* is the words of Confucius. At that time Confucius was not employed by the ruler of [his own state of] Lu, so he traveled around the seven states of Qi, Yan, Zhao, Song, Chen, Chu, and Wei. The rulers of those seven states likewise not employing him, Confucius came back to the state of Lu and taught three thousand disciples there. Among them was the disciple called Zengzi, who recorded Confucius' words and compiled the *Great Learning*. . . . [1a]

Note: *The opening phrase of the* Great Learning, *ming ming de, combines several meanings. The initial* ming *means to clarify and thus make manifest. The second* ming *has the sense of both "translucent" and "luminous." De ("virtue") stands for the moral nature. The idea is that by removing obscurations from the mind-and-heart the inherent luminosity of the moral nature can be made clear to all.*

The way of higher education [in the *Great Learning*] consists in manifesting luminous virtue. "Virtue" is the moral nature inherent in all human minds. It is open, spiritual and transparent, but owing to alterations induced by prevailing customs many obscurations arise. What Confucius spoke of as "manifesting luminous virtue" was precisely to teach men of later times to reform these obscurations and teach everyone how to manifest their luminous virtue. In manifesting luminous virtue they came to understand the creative process of Heaven-and-earth, how yin and yang move in alternation and in the process produce the Five Phases of metal, wood, water, fire, and earth, complementing the four seasons of spring, summer, fall, and winter. Spring is associated with wood, summer with fire, fall with metal, winter with water. The four seasons together are associated with earth, and earth lodges in the four seasons, for eighteen days each. Wood correlates with humaneness, fire with ritual decorum, earth with trustworthiness, metal with rightness, and water with wisdom. Husband and wife correlate with yang and yin. Humaneness is the principle of warmth, harmony, compassion, and love by which Heaven-and-earth produce the myriad things. Rightness is the principle whereby, in deciding things and affairs, everything is done in accordance with what is fitting and is not allowed to go too far or exceed the proper level. Ritual decorum is the principle whereby respect is shown in outward form and inner reverence. Wisdom is the principle whereby one distinguishes right and wrong. Trustworthiness is the principle for being truthful and not lying. These five things, though they constitute the [common] moral nature bestowed on human beings by Heaven, are possessed individually by each human being, each of whom receives a different endowment. Those endowments that get much clear material-force (*qi*) are highly refined; those that get much turbid material-force are innately lacking in refinement.

If one takes the bees, which have a leader, they naturally understand the principle of ruler and minister. Tigers, which do not eat their young, naturally understand the principle of parent and child. Wild geese, old and young respectively leading and following in flying formation, naturally recognize the principle of seniority among siblings. The dog, which recognizes his master, naturally accepts the principle of benefaction and obligation [loyalty].

Although later on men found that their moral natures became unclear owing to the obscurations of turbid material-force (*qi*), there were some of great innate intelligence who appeared to instruct the myriad peoples, to be their rulers and teachers, to instruct them in the Way, and to teach them how to discern the humaneness, rightness, ritual decorum, wisdom, and trustworthiness that they originally possessed, rather than let these be obscured. Among them, those capable of lofty conduct such as most men cannot attain, and who are able to do great deeds, should become sages, and those capable of somewhat lesser attainments should become worthies. Thus Confucius spoke of King Tang's writing on his bathtub: "If one day you can renew yourself, do so from day to day. Yea, let there be daily renewal."[9] If one has dirt on his person but washes himself today, tomorrow and every day, his person will become clean. But if one day he does not wash, the dirt will reappear. Similarly, if one reflects in his mind constantly, he will perform well in the daily conduct of business and not make mistakes, but if one day he does not reflect, there is a fear of his making mistakes. This is that "manifesting (clarifying) luminous virtue." Then there is what is spoken of as "renewing the people." The people are the common people. If they are not instructed and do not follow the Way, they are inhumane when humaneness is called for, lacking in rightness when rightness is called for, lacking in ritual decorum when decorum is called for, unwise when wisdom is called for, and untrustworthy when trustworthiness is called for. Their eyes wish only to see what looks good, their ears only to hear what sounds good, their mouths only to eat what tastes good, and their noses wish only to smell fine fragrances. They seek only their own gratification and make up their minds to get the things just cited, without asking whether it is in accordance with principle or not, but simply seizing upon what they like and doing it. Such people, though they have human form, are the same as beasts. When a sage appears, able to manifest his own luminous virtue, he sees such people and teaches them about their Heaven-given humaneness, rightness, ritual decorum, wisdom, and trustworthiness, so that they may reform their past mistakes and renew themselves. This, then, is to "renew the people."

"Resting in the utmost good" means the highest good in any matter. That is to say in one's presence at court, being respectful and conscientious at heart is the utmost good in [fulfilling] the principle of service as an official. In the presence of parents, to be filial and compliant is the utmost good in [fulfilling] the principle of behaving as a child. In the presence of children, to be loving and compassionate is the utmost good in [fulfilling] the principle of behaving as a parent. As a companion to others, being honest and truthful is the utmost good in [fulfilling] the principle of companionship.

---

9. *Great Learning*, Commentary 2.

If one's conduct is exemplary in all these matters, it is "resting in the utmost good."

[From *Luzhai quanshu* 4:1b–4a (pp. 199–205), *Zhishuo Daxue yaolüe* — dB]

Having dealt in the foregoing with the so-called Three Mainstays (or Guiding Principles) in the opening lines of the Great Learning, *Xu goes on to comment in turn on other basic teachings in the first chapter of the text. Among these, his "straightforward explanation" of Zhu Xi's special note on the "investigation of things and extension of knowledge," culminating in a breakthrough to an expanded consciousness, is particularly revealing.*

On the "breakthrough to integral comprehension" (huoran guantong):

[Zhu Xi] After one has made an effort for a long time, one day one will experience a breakthrough to integral comprehension.

[Xu] *Huoran* has the meaning of "breakthrough" or "opening up to enlightenment." When the learner has fully searched out the principles of things and affairs, searching out one matter today and another tomorrow, his successive efforts will culminate one day in a sudden opening [of the mind] to an enlightenment that is thoroughly penetrating.

On the "complete substance and great functioning" (quanti dayong) of one's nature:

[Zhu Xi] When one's knowledge has been extended to all things and affairs, inward and outward, fine and coarse, the complete substance and great functioning of one's mind are totally clarified and made manifest.

[Xu] "Outward" means "external" and refers to principles easy to see; "inward" is "internal" and refers to principles difficult to see. "Fine" refers to the most subtle of principles; "coarse" refers to the coarsest and most apparent of principles. For someone's mind to be full of principles is to have the "complete substance," and for it to respond to all things is the "great functioning." If someone reaches the point of a sudden breakthrough, then in relation to the principles of all things, manifest or hidden, fine or coarse, there is none that is not [empathetically] understood. The complete substance and great functioning of such a mind is without any obscuration whatever.

["Daxue zhijie," *Xu Wenjun gong yishu* 4:14b–15a — dB]

The foregoing provides the essential rationale for the characteristic Neo-Confucian curriculum that became established under the Mongols and later was widely extended throughout East Asia. Its universality is to be understood not only in terms of its extension throughout the land and its diffusion to all classes but also in terms of its essential message, which was the same for all. Self-rectification and mind-culture should be directed toward nourishing the innate goodness of each person's moral nature, and then by extension to developing the moral nature in others through "clarifying their luminous virtue." By helping all to remove the obscurations of their originally pure virtue, it could be made manifest in social and political endeavor of benefit to all humankind.

Though insisting on rigorous control over selfish desires and on vigilant defense against the corrupting influences of heterodox teachings, this doctrine expressed great confidence in the moral and intellectual powers of human beings to deal with such defects. It was basically an optimistic view of the world and humankind, encouraging human beings to believe in their own potential for sagehood or the ruler's potential for becoming a sage king. In this very common sense of the term, *shengdao*, often translated as "Way of the Sages," also meant for Neo-Confucians "Way of Becoming a Sage."

Individual commitment and acceptance of personal responsibility were the starting point for advancement in this Way, unceasing self-discipline the means. But its premise, the underlying unity in principle (*li*) of the human moral nature (*dexing*) was also seen as the basis of an ordered human community. Hence the educational effort implied by a universal school system could look not only to the individual's achievement of sagehood but also to collective fulfillment in a moral and spiritual communion among all humankind — indeed, among all things — provided only that one dealt first with human weakness and fallibility, especially as found in those holding positions of power and influence. This, then, is the essence of the Neo-Confucian political doctrine subsumed under Zhu Xi's motto "self-cultivation [self-discipline] for the governance of men" (*xiuji zhiren*), establishing a moral claim and responsibility especially on the ruler and leadership elite.

In these terms the Neo-Confucian doctrine of human nature (*xingli*) could be seen as the natural successor to the Mahāyāna doctrine of the universal Buddha-nature, which had contributed not a political philosophy but a moral and spiritual formation to accompany the processes of political unification in China, Korea, and Japan seven centuries earlier. Though the prospect of sagehood had meaning primarily for the educated, and sagehood as the embodiment of the new learning of the Song was something of an elitist ideal, the potential in all human beings for the fulfillment of virtue and advancement in the Way was a plausible basis for enlisting everyone, Mongols as well as Chinese, in the new educational program.

THE EXAMINATION DEBATE UNDER KHUBILAI

In their concern for moral self-cultivation, the Neo-Confucian reformers did not neglect consideration of the complex political and intellectual issues of the day. Their record is replete with discussions of such questions. What prompted their reassertion of the moral claims of Confucian humanism was the need to cope with the pragmatic realism on the part of the Mongols and their fiscal technicians, whose main aim was to maximize the conqueror's power and resources.

In the background of the Neo-Confucian discussion of selfish interest versus the commonweal lies the question of the employment of worthy, humane men able to defend the long-term public interest against those who seek only immediate gains for the state. In 1267 a proposal was made by the Hanlin academician Wang E (1190–1273), a leading scholar among the survivors from the Jin and a *jinshi* degree winner in 1224, that the civil service examinations should be reintroduced. Wang cited the precedents of earlier dynasties from the Zhou and Han down through the Liao and Jin, as well as the example of Ögödei's (r. 1229–1241) examinations in 1237. He argued that if such a system were not available, there would be no ladder of advancement for able and ambitious men to follow. In the absence of such they would be easily diverted into less worthy callings, either becoming sub-officials whose expertise had not benefited from a classical training, or attaching themselves to the service of local satraps, or perhaps even using their talents as merchants and artisans rather than as officials at court or in central administration.

When Khubilai sought other opinions on the matter, he may have been surprised to find a difference of opinion between Confucian traditionalists like Wang E, whose education had prepared them for the earlier Song-style examinations, and those committed to the new Learning of the Way, whose views reflected the Neo-Confucian critique of the Song examinations as placing too much emphasis on literary style and memorization and not enough on practical affairs and the cultivation of moral character based on the teachings of the classics. A colleague of Xu Heng's, Dong Wenzhong (d. 1281), expressed it this way to Khubilai, who suspected him of being one of the School of the Way because he was always citing the Four Books:

Your Majesty has often said that those who neglect the study of the classics and do not ponder deeply the Way of Confucius and Mencius, but rather engage in composition of *shi* and *fu* poetry, have no concern for self-cultivation and nothing of benefit to offer the governance of the state. Therefore, scholars throughout the land wish to engage in studies that are solid and practical (*shixue*). What I cite are the works of Confucius and Mencius; I make no claim to knowing about the School of the Way. But some scholars cling to the ways of fallen dynasties [i.e., the Song and Jin] and talk like this to mislead Your Majesty. I fear that this is not in accord with Your Majesty's intention of setting a proper model on high and maintaining self-discipline among those below.

["Shendaobei," by Yao Sui, in Su, *Shilüe* 61:5b–6a — dB]

Another associate of Xu, Yang Gongyi (d. 1294), told Khubilai he should discard the examinations based on *shi* and *fu* poetry and instead employ men recommended by officials for their personal character and understanding of the classics:

These men should then be examined both on their understanding of the larger significance and precise meaning of the Five Classics and Four Books and on their knowledge of history as it relates to contemporary problems. If this is done and they engage in studies of a practical sort (*shixue*), then the whole climate and style of scholarship will be improved, the people's customs will be enhanced, and the state will obtain men of talent who know how to govern.

[Su, *Shilüe* 13:9a — dB]

Hao Jing (1223–1275), also associated with Xu Heng, depreciated literary skills as opposed to moral character in the following terms:

What the world thinks of as Confucian scholarship is only letters. That is what is used for instruction by parents and teachers; it is what scholars occupy themselves with and what official careers are determined by . . . but it does not correspond to what made a scholar a scholar in ancient times. Really letters are only the outer branches of scholarship; it is moral action and virtuous conduct (*dexing*) that constitute the root and core of scholarship.

[*Hao Wenzhong gong ji* 7:8b–9a — dB]

Whether because of this cleavage between old-style Confucians and the rising Neo-Confucians led by Xu Heng, or because of fears held by Mongols and their Central Asian collaborators that they would be at a disadvantage vis-à-vis Chinese competing in exams based on a knowledge of Chinese classics, nothing was actually done to reestablish the civil service examinations at this time. In the meantime, however, Khubilai appointed Xu Heng to the Directorate of Education with authority to implement a new curriculum based on the Four Books, Five Classics, and other texts either prepared by or sanctioned by Zhu Xi, in state schools from the Imperial College down to the prefectural and county level. Although this curriculum had already gained wide acceptance in private academies associated with the spread of Neo-Confucianism, Khubilai's action was a historic first step in establishing it as an official orthodoxy.

Subsequently, two other important steps were taken to implement Zhu Xi's educational program, at least in a qualified manner. After the appointment of Zhang Wenqian (1217–1282) a protégé of Xu, as minister of agriculture, in 1270 he ordered the establishment of village schooling (i.e., below the county level), which would bring education to people in the countryside in the manner recommended by Zhu Xi and Xu Heng. This was in line with Xu's dual emphasis on promoting agriculture and education together, as shown in his five-point memorial of 1266. There is evidence, however, that this measure, as carried out under the Court of Imperial Granaries, actually involved only part-time, off-season instruction for the moral uplift of farmers in local communities and differed from the full-time instruction in classical studies conducted under the Ministry of Rites in state schools (county and above) for prospective recruits in the bureaucracy. Such a bifurcation in schooling was not what Zhu Xi or Xu Heng had had in mind, but it kept alive, at least nominally, the ideal of universal education.

The next and even more historic step was taken in 1313 by another follower of Xu Heng, Cheng Jufu (1249–1318), a southerner who was highly successful in recruiting scholars for the Mongols who represented a generation educated in the new curriculum. He proposed a resumption of the civil service examination on a new basis but claimed the earlier endorsement of Khubilai:

In the matter of examinations Khubilai . . . repeatedly called for its implemen-tation and his successors, Zhengzong and Wuzong, also shared this intention, but as of now nothing has come of it, apparently because of some obstruction-ists. Now the proper method for the recruitment of scholars is through classical studies that fulfill the Way of Self-discipline for the Governance of Men. The composition of *ci* and *fu* poetry is only artful display. Since the Sui and Tang dynasties there has been exclusive emphasis on the *ci* and *fu*. Therefore scholars have become accustomed to superficiality. Now what we propose . . . will emphasize virtuous conduct and an understanding of the classics. If scholars are chosen in this way, they will all be the right kind of men.

[*Yuanshi* 81:2018 — dB]

Thereupon the Mongol emperor Renzong issued an edict drafted by Cheng Jufu:

After our founding emperor settled the world as if by divine power, Emperor Shizu [Khubilai] established organs of government, defined official functions, recruited Confucian scholars of great distinction, sanctioned schools for the training of men's abilities, and proposed examinations as a means of recruiting scholar-officials — thus setting an example of great breadth of vision and fore-sight. . . . Since the Three Dynasties each age has had an examination system with a definite order of priorities. In the recommendation of scholars virtuous conduct should be the first consideration and in the testing of skills proficiency in the classics should come first, with the composition of prose and poetry subordinated to that. The frivolous and fanciful we can do without. Therefore I command the Central Secretariat to deliberate over past and present practice and fix the details of the system.

[*Yuanshi* 81:2018 — dB]

While thus paying lip service to the values espoused by Zhu Xi and Xu Heng, Cheng Jufu in the Central Secretariat set aside the Neo-Confucian preference for advancement through the schools and personal recommendations and made concessions to gain consensus in favor of an examination system that Neo-Confucians had previously criticized. The most important change was the installing of a Neo-Confucian curriculum, featuring the Four Books and Five Classics with commentaries by Zhu Xi or other Neo-Confucians. Tactical concessions included a less demanding examination format and quota provisions in favor of Mongols and Central Asians. The quotas, however, did not outlive Mongol rule, while the new curriculum, similar to Xu Heng's for the schools, survived into the early twentieth century.

In the Yuan period many (though by no means all) adherents of the Learning of the Way regarded the new system as a great triumph. In 1315, the year the new exams began, Cheng Duanli, a noted proponent of Zhu Xi's curriculum, was euphoric:

In the recruitment of scholars virtuous conduct is being put ahead of all else and study of the classics is being given precedence over literary composition. . . . In the interpretation of the classics the views of Master Zhu are the sole authority, uniting as one the philosophy of principle and study for the civil service examination, to the great advantage of scholars committed to the Way [as distinct from opportunistic candidates]. This is something the Han, Tang, and Song never achieved, and the greatest blessing that has come to scholars throughout the ages.

[Cheng Duanli, Preface 1, *Chengshi richeng* 1; *Song Yuan xuean* 87:65 — dB]

Thus Cheng exudes the idealistic expectation that resurrecting the civil service examinations with this new curriculum will at last join the wisdom of Zhu Xi and his practical learning method to an official recruitment process that will transform state and society.

SAGE KING AND SAGE MINISTER: OUYANG XUAN ON KHUBILAI AND XU HENG

The ideal of sagehood in Neo-Confucianism came to one culmination in the Learning of the Emperors and Kings, in which the Way of Governance and the Learning of the Way would be brought together by a sage king and sage minister. From the foregoing accounts of historic developments in the Yuan period, for which the great prestige of both Khubilai and Xu Heng are often invoked, it is not hard to see why they should be eulogized as sage ruler and sage minister by the distinguished scholar Ouyang Xuan (1283–1357).

With his heavenly endowment [Khubilai] resumed the lost teaching of the sage emperors and kings, while Xu Heng, with the gift of heavenly talents, was able to repossess the untransmitted teachings of the sages and worthies, connecting up with the tradition of the Duke of Zhou, Confucius, Zengzi, Zisi, Mencius, and the other noble men who came after them, to become a minister of unparalleled stature in those times. The aspirations of ruler and minister matched perfectly, and all that was enunciated in the emperor's name served to uphold the perfect norm of rulership, set up proper guidelines for the people, resume the lost teaching, and usher in an era of great peace — all as if myriad ages were fulfilled in one day.

[*Guizhai wenji* (SBCK) 9:1a — dB]

This is not the last time that such an ideal blending of rulership and Confucian learning would be proposed or claimed, as aspiring scholars in almost every age attempted to ride the tiger of imperial power. Other Neo-Confucians of the time, like the distinguished scholar Wu Cheng (1248–1333) and the reclusive Liu Yin (1249–1293), disassociated themselves from such concessions as were made by Xu Heng and Cheng Jufu, either declining to serve or withdrawing from office out of higher allegiance to the purity and integrity of the Way. Both images of the Confucian scholar — of collaborationist ministers like Xu and of scholars heroically resisting the pretensions of sage rulers — recur in later history, as we shall see in the case of Fang Xiaoru in the early Ming.

MING FOUNDATIONS OF
LATE IMPERIAL CHINA

It was far from a foregone conclusion that the Yuan dynasty would have the Ming as its successor. Indeed, through many of the seventeen years of civil war (1351–1368), it was not clear that there would be any unifying successor at all, let alone the Ming. For many years, the chances of the future founder, former peasant and outlaw Zhu Yuanzhang (Ming Taizu, r. 1368–1398), appeared slim. Taizu lacked education; his resources were meager, and his geostrategical advantages slight. That he succeeded despite all the initial odds against him owes much to his openness to the advice offered him by some of the leading Confucian thinkers of his time. These men convinced Taizu that an equitable system of requisitions, coupled with the merciless suppression of corruption, would overcome his disadvantage of slender resources. They convinced him he could vanquish his better-placed rivals if his army and bureaucracy were more tightly centralized and disciplined than theirs were. These counsels worked. Yet the builders of the Ming did not consider efficiency and discipline to be simply instrumental. They were ends in themselves, firmly grounded in Confucian ethics. Fiscal efficiency would result when the idea of impartial service of the common good was put into effect. Centralization was the result when everyone understood that to concede powers or to tolerate indiscipline among subordinates was to allow selfish evil to triumph over good. The Ming foundation soon became a national moral crusade. The founders of the Ming firmly believed that they possessed the Mandate of Heaven and that that mandate charged them with the task not just to reunify China politically but also to carry out the ethical remaking of its people in the light of the Confucian ideals of antiquity — taking the sage kings as their model, not the rule by accommodation or expediency of the Han, Tang, and Song.

Acting upon its sense of mission, the Ming dynasty laid much of the institutional and ideological framework for later imperial China. This included the concentration of all legitimate decision-making authority in the hands of the emperor, accomplished by abolishing the prime ministership and imposing centralized controls over the imperial bureaucracy. From the beginning of the Ming it seemed clear that the use of one or another form of the merit principle was the only acceptable way to recruit officials: first, Taizu reinstituted the Yuan examination system in 1370, dropped it, and then resumed it in 1382; it was implemented again under the Yongle emperor (r. 1402–1424) and continuously thereafter. There was also an assumption by the state of an obligation to "nurture" future scholar-officials by providing the students of China with a public school system, together with Confucian instructors and approved Confucian texts, as well as stipends and other personal benefits.

By 1368, Ming Taizu made himself literate enough to start composing what became a very large number of essays, colloquies, commentaries, Confucian moral exhortations, and political and social regulations, all in a peculiarly crabbed style of his own. He defined his own role as both ruler and teacher of China. He strove intensely to reach out directly to everyone in the realm, so as to explain to them in his own words what good behavior was and to warn them of the dire consequences of moral lapses. Although few of Taizu's successors in the Ming could sustain his vision of the good society, many of his ideas and enactments nonetheless remained influential through the Ming and Qing dynasties.

MING TAIZU: *AUGUST MING ANCESTRAL INSTRUCTION*

As a commoner become emperor, Taizu thought of himself as a great communicator, conveying his own brand of imperial populism in slightly different form to different audiences: the common people, scholar-officials, his prospective dynastic successors, and so on. It is especially in his instructions to the last group that he reveals his larger vision of rulership and the dynastic constitution as well as many detailed regulations for the management of the palace and members of the imperial family. Here we present just a few (out of ninety-six in all), including his general preface.

Notice that in Taizu's preface he makes no attempt to ground the lawmaking function, as does the preamble to the Tang Code, in a cosmological theory of correspondences between man and nature, by which the ruler is called upon to redress imbalances between the two arising from human violations of the natural order. Rather he asserts it as the product of his own personal experience of life and the need for the ruler to take personal responsibility for carrying out the Way. Here we can see the danger that lies in the Neo-Confucian conception of the ruler's living up to the responsibilities of a sage king, directly intuiting the Way in his own mind-and-heart.

Preface: I have observed that since ancient times, when states established their laws it was always done by the ruler who first received the mandate. At that time the laws were fixed and the people observed them. Thus was the imperial benevolence and authority extended throughout the realm so that people could enjoy peace and security. This was because at the outset of the founding the ruler endured hardships, saw many men, and became experienced in handling affairs. In comparison with a ruler born and bred deep within the palace, unfamiliar with the world, or a hermit scholar living alone in the mountains or forests considering himself enlightened, how different it was for me. When I was young I was orphaned and poor and grew up amidst warfare. At the age of twenty-four I joined the ranks and was ordered about for three years. Then I gathered together able followers and studied the ways of training soldiers, planning to compete with the warlords. It was trying and worrisome. I was apprehensive and on guard for nearly twenty years until I was able to eliminate the powerful enemies and unite the empire. Of human deceit I have known plenty. Therefore, drawing on what I have seen and done, together with the officials, I have fixed the law of the land. This has eliminated the indulgent rule of the Yuan dynasty and those who defiled the old customs. The warlords were powerful and deceitful. They were hard to govern, but I have governed them. The people, encountering disorder, tried by all manner of evil means to pass through the unrest. They were hard to manage, but I have managed them. Now since the pacification of Wuzhang there was discussion about enacting the *Code* and the *Commandments*. The additions, deletions, and changes have been innumerable. Ten years have passed and we accomplished the task. They were promulgated and gradually the people came to know the prohibitions. In order to teach later generations the *Ancestral Instruction* was also created. It was set up as a family law. It was written in big characters in the Western Corridor and was read day and night to make the text perfect. From start to finish it has been six years. It went through seven drafts and is now done. How difficult! Many shallow scholars affirm the past and decry the present. Evil officials constantly twist words and bend the law. If I had not selected the able from the masses and made decisions resolutely, I would have been confused by them and unable to accomplish anything. Now I have ordered the Hanlin to compile this book and the Minister of Rites to print it and pass it on to eternity. All my progeny may adhere to my orders and not be crafty and confuse the laws that I have fixed forever. Not a single word may be changed. Not only will you not fail to live up to my intentions to pass on the law, but Heaven and Earth and the Ancestors will also bless and protect you without end. Ah! Heed this.

1. It has been more than forty years since I first took up arms. I have personally ordered the affairs of the realm. The good and bad, true and false of human nature have all been experienced by me. Those who were wicked and crafty by nature and committed serious crimes obvious beyond doubt have been singled out for heavier punishment than the law provides with the intention of making people take heed and thus not lightly dare to break the law. However, this is just a provisional measure to punish the wicked; it is not the normal law of the ruler who preserves what has been accomplished [and entrusted to him]. From now on, when my descendants become emperors they shall only enforce the *Code* and the *Grand Pronouncements*. They certainly shall not employ any punishments like tattooing, cutting off the feet, cutting off the nose, and castration. Why is this so? Because the succeeding rulers will be born and raised in the palace; they cannot have a complete knowledge of human nature's good and evil. I fear that in time something untoward will transpire, harming the innocent by mistake. If there are officials who dare to memorialize requesting the use of these punishments, civil and military officials shall immediately submit accusations. The offender shall be put to death by slicing and his whole family executed.

One of Taizu's most famous enactments was his abolition of the prime ministership after the exposure of an alleged plot by the existing prime minister to usurp the throne. Thenceforth all executive power was concentrated in the emperor, assisted by a secretariat, a system that persisted through the late imperial period.

2. From ancient times policy was discussed among the three dukes (*sangong*), and the duties of government were divided among the six ministers, but a prime minister was never established. The Qin began the establishment of a prime minister and fell soon thereafter. The Han, Tang, and Song continued the practice. Although there were some virtuous prime ministers, many of them were evil men who monopolized power and confused administration. Now our dynasty has abolished the prime ministership and established such offices as the five chief commissions, the six ministries, the Censorate, the Office of Transmission, and the Grand Court of Revision to manage the affairs of the realm. They parallel one another and dare not seek to dominate each other. It is the court that provides overall control of government affairs. That is why there is stability. From now on, when my descendants become emperors, they absolutely shall not establish a prime minister. If there are officials who dare to memorialize requesting such establishment, civil and military officials shall immediately submit accusations. The offender shall be put to death by slicing and his whole family executed.

5. Of the rulers in ancient times only dynastic founders, rulers who presided over restorations, or virtuous rulers who maintained the heritage were sincerely concerned about the realm. The commonplace rulers looked to the realm for pleasure. This was the beginning of the end of the dynasty. How is this so? When a ruler first gains the realm it is because Heaven has chosen a man of virtue. As for rulers who maintain the heritage, if they are constantly reverential toward Heaven and take to heart their ancestor's concern for the realm, they can receive Heaven's blessing forever. If they begin to be negligent, disaster will result. Take heed.

[*Huang Ming zuxun*, in *Mingzhao kaiguo wenxian* 3:1579–1591 — EF]

THE MING CODE AND COMMANDMENTS

Taizu's experience of Mongol rule convinced him that it was erratic, arbitrary, and especially lax. What the empire needed was law and order, and Taizu devoted himself tirelessly to the defining and constant redefining of the law, so that everyone would know exactly what was expected. He realized that central control had its limits and that constant education — or indoctrination — was needed. To convey the word he promulgated a great body of legislation, from his *Code* (*lü*) and supplementary commandments (*ling*) to his *Grand Pronouncements* (*Dagao*) and Placard for the Instruction of the People (*Jiaomin bangwen*). The following are selected from several of these genres.

Preface to *The Great Ming Commandments*

Hongwu first year, first month, 18th day [February 6, 1368], an imperial decree was received:

I consider the *Code* and *Commandments* to be devices for ruling the realm. The *Commandments* instruct before the fact, and the *Code* regulates after the fact. In ancient times the laws were extremely simple. In later generations they gradually became numerous to the point where there were some laws no one could understand. How could the people be made to know the meaning of the law and not go against it? Since it is difficult for people to know, that then opens the way to treachery by officials and functionaries and entraps the people in the law. I feel the greatest compassion for them. The *Code* and *Commandments* fixed today will replace multiplicity with simplicity and achieve consistency. The contents will be directly stated so that everyone can easily understand; violations will be prevented. The *Classic of Documents* (*Shujing*) says: "Use punishment so as to do away with punishment."[10] If the whole realm observes the *Commandments* and is not punished by the *Code*, the resultant setting aside of punishments will not be hard to achieve. Be it therefore ordered that they

---

10. "The Counsels of the Great Yu," *Classic of Documents*; Legge, *The Chinese Classics*, 3:58.

shall be promulgated throughout the realm. Let all officials and commoners realize my intent. Respect this.

[*Da Ming ling*, in *Huang Ming zhishu* 1:5a–b — EF]

The Relationship of the Ruler and His Subjects

[from one of Taizu's *Grand Pronouncements*]

If they sincerely wish to repay [the kindness of] the Soil and Grain (*sheji*), the ruler's people, as soon as the ruler has a command, must hasten to the task, rendering service and taxes without failing the responsibility. With this sort of sincerity, enjoying the benefits of Earth and the securing of Heaven's mandate, the favor is repaid. Everyone says, "The ruler nourishes the people." But how does he nourish them? The ruler's clothing and food are all supplied by the people. If clothing and food are all supplied by the people, then how does he nourish the people? The ruler's nourishing of the people is through the five teachings and five punishments. If you did away with the five teachings and the five punishments the people could never have lived. Thus the five teachings nourish the people's peace. These are: between parent and child there must be affection, between ruler and minister rightness, between husband and wife differentiation, between senior and junior precedence, between friends trust. When the five teachings are established, how can there fail to be peace?

[*Yuzhi dagao* 31 — EF]

Rebellion

[from the penal section of the *Great Ming Code*]

Rebellion (that is, plotting against the dynasty) and lèse-majesté (that is, plotting to desecrate imperial ancestral altars, mausoleums, and palaces). All conspirators regardless of whether they are leaders or followers shall be executed by slicing. Their grandfathers, fathers, sons, grandsons, older brothers, younger brothers, and those who live with them regardless of surname differences; sons of paternal uncles and brothers regardless of whether they have the same registration; if they are sixteen years of age or over, regardless of serious or crippling disease, they shall all be executed. Those fifteen or below, mothers, daughters, wives, and concubines, older and younger sisters, sons' wives and concubines, shall be given as slaves to the households of the titular nobility. Their property shall be confiscated by the government. . . . Those who know about the crime but purposely conceal it shall be executed. When an arrest is made, commoners shall be rewarded with civil office; military shall be rewarded with military offices. In addition, all the criminal's property shall be given as their rewards. In the case of an informer, where the officials make the arrest, award shall be made to him of property only. Those who fail to inform shall receive one hundred strokes of the heavy bamboo and life exile at three thousand *li*.

[*Da Ming lü* 277, in *Da Ming lü jijie fulie*, 1301–1302 — EF]

Duties of Officials

[from *The Great Ming Commandments*]

As for officials of all the prefectures, subprefectures, and districts, increasing the population under their jurisdiction and opening up land for farming are the most important duties. Their administrative accomplishments must be thoroughly evaluated by the investigating censors or the provincial surveillance office and the facts reported as a basis for demotion or promotion.

[*Da Ming ling* 5 — EF]

Equal Inheritance

Taizu reaffirmed a cardinal principle of inheritance that throughout Chinese history tended toward the fragmentation of Chinese landholding, in contrast to the passing down of large estates through primogeniture.

A family's property and land are to be divided equally among sons of the wife or others according to their numbers without regard to whether they were born of the wife, a concubine, or a slave; exception is to be made for beneficiaries of the official *yin* privilege [for offspring of meritorious persons], in which case preference shall be given to the eldest son and grandson of the wife. Bastard sons shall get half the portion of a son. . . . In other cases, if there is no other son, an appropriate successor shall be designated heir, to share equally with the bastard sons. If there is no appropriate successor they may inherit the entire amount.

[*Da Ming ling* 22 — EF]

Marriage and Divorce

All marriages shall be arranged by the paternal grandparents or parents. If there are neither paternal grandparents nor parents, another relative shall do the arranging. If after her husband dies the wife remarries and takes her daughter with her, the mother alone shall arrange the daughter's marriage. If the boy or girl dies after an engagement but before the wedding takes place, the gifts need not be returned. If the betrothed boy is a robber or commits crimes punishable by penal servitude, life exile, or relocation, so that the girl's family wishes to break the engagement, the betrothal gifts may be returned. If a betrothed girl commits fornication, once an investigation bears this out, should the boy's family wish to break the engagement, the betrothal gifts must be returned. If after five years for no reason [a betrothed boy] does not marry the girl, or if the husband disappears and does not return for three years, it is permitted to go to the officials to request and receive approval to marry someone else. In such cases, the betrothal gifts need not be returned.

[*Da Ming ling* 23 — EF]

Note: A subsequent article, no. 53, specified: "Marriages among the people must follow the Family Ritual of Master Zhu (i.e., Zhu Xi)."

Even though a wife meets one of the Seven Grounds for being divorced, she may not be discarded lightly if she meets one of the Three Restrictions precluding divorce. Adulteresses are not covered by these limitations.

Seven Grounds for divorce: no sons, lewdness, not serving parents-in-law, talking too much, theft, jealousy, incurable disease.

Three Restrictions on divorce: the wife having done three years' mourning; the family, formerly poor, is now rich [to the wife's credit]; the wife no longer having a family to return to.

[*Da Ming ling* 28 — EF]

EDUCATION AND EXAMINATIONS

As mentioned earlier, Taizu had a use for both education and trained scholars. Thus he was easily persuaded by his advisers to reestablish state school systems and civil service examinations set up by the Mongols. Taizu shared Khubilai's low esteem for literary refinement, while feeling no less a desire than the Mongols for a curriculum and examination system that would promote basic literacy and practical virtue rather than produce pundits. Instead of scrapping the simpler examinations for Mongols, he favored something much like them for the Chinese themselves, settling essentially for a curriculum of the Four Books and Zhu Xi's commentaries.

Ming Taizu's proclamation in 1370 reestablishing the examinations adopts essentially the same stance as Renzong and Cheng Jufu in the Yuan, using much the same language as they. To have some kind of definite system was the traditional practice, the proclamation says, though the system of each earlier dynasty had its own merits and demerits. In the Han, Tang, and Song the trouble lay in overemphasis on literary composition to the neglect of classical study and practical virtue. In the early Yuan the old system was reestablished momentarily, but powerful families and self-seeking individuals quickly exploited it for their own benefit, and worthy men, ashamed to join in such a scramble for office and emoluments, hid themselves in the mountains and forests. Thus when

Taizu proceeds to reinstitute the same system as the one established in the Yuan, he feels no need to acknowledge it. He will see to it personally that men are selected for their practical virtue and understanding of the classics, and he issues a stern warning, at the conclusion of the proclamation, against the pursuit of power and privilege by self-seeking individuals, who will meet with strong condemnation and heavy punishment. Actually, Taizu had second thoughts about the value of the system in turning out men of practical ability, and suspended it for more than ten years, but none of his doubts had to do with the content of the exams, which, after its resumption in 1384, was even more squarely focused on the Four Books and Zhu Xi.

Much later, a leading eighteenth-century historian, Qian Daxin (1728–1804), reviewing this phase in the development of the examination system, found it necessary to point out the significance of what had happened in these formative years. He noted that in the Yuan the Chinese were still expected to answer questions on the Five Classics and that to be examined on just the Four Books, which were much easier to understand, was originally a special concession to the non-Chinese, intended as part of a sequence from the easier to the more difficult and not meant to displace the Five Classics, as became the case in the Ming and Qing. Moreover, since the Four Books with Zhu Xi's commentaries were prime Neo-Confucian texts, this increasing focus on them brought to a new height the Neo-Confucianization of the curriculum.

When it came to schooling, however, the plebeian autocrat Taizu left no doubt that he conceived of it as training and indoctrination—not at all the voluntaristic process of learning for one's self that Zhu Xi had advocated. He provided Ming China with a universal, state-funded Confucian school system, down to the county level. A college in the capital, and schools in each of some thousand prefectural and county seats throughout China, served a student body of some 25,000 licentiates (*shengyuan*). In 1382 the emperor ordered the Ministry of Rites to have the following twelve rules for students cut into stone slabs and to have the slabs placed at the left of the Minglun tang (Hall for Clarifying Human Relationships) in each school. (In 1652, the Qing dynasty did exactly the same thing, although it revised and condensed Taizu's original rules.) Note that the students were forbidden to argue with their teachers, discuss public issues, or serve as lawyers or advocates. They constituted a pool from which the best would eventually be selected by recommendation or examination for salaried positions in the bureaucracy.

THE HORIZONTAL STELE (DISCIPLINARY RULES FOR STUDENTS)

It was no doubt in part because of the repressive atmosphere and routinization of learning that many scholars turned away from state schools and gravitated to the private academies instead, where the air was freer and more stimulating. Taizu's authoritarian views are clearly stated in the following:

[The emperor] ordered the Ministry of Rites to promulgate [the following] twelve regulations on schools:

1. Students are forbidden to present legal suits before the officials, unless the case involves them personally and in some major way.

2. If the students have parents who are doing wrong, they must plead earnestly with them, again and again if need be. They may not simply let their parents incur danger or humiliation.

3. Students are forbidden to exceed their station and recklessly discuss political or military affairs.

4. All students of superior learning and talent who thoroughly understand the fundamentals of rule, and who have reached the age of thirty and wish to become officials, are allowed to present essays on rulership and on the transforming effects of government. The instructors will screen these and report to the local officials the names of those who do especially well. After that, the students may come in person to the capital.

5. The Way of teaching requires that students revere and respect their teachers. Students must listen with sincere minds to their teachers' explanations. They are forbidden to act arrogantly and argue.

6. Teachers must themselves faithfully act like the worthies of former times. They must cleave with utter fidelity to their teachings when they guide the young and ignorant.

7. It is the responsibility of the local officials to monitor the students, encouraging the bright and hardworking ones, and expelling the uncooperative and lazy.

8. Worthy gentlemen who live in the countryside, and who are versed in the principles of administration and can expound upon imperial rule, are permitted to come to the capital and address the court in person.

Note: The remaining four articles are omitted here, as not actually pertaining to education.

[*Ming shilu* 6:2302–2303 — JD]

MING TAIZU: PLACARD FOR THE INSTRUCTION OF THE PEOPLE

This proclamation was promulgated in the last year of Taizu's reign and remained the basis for public guidance in the villages during the Ming (and one key part, article 19, even into the Qing). It was the last of Taizu's many efforts to reach below the county level of state administration and address the people directly. Many of its forty-one articles have to do with the maintenance of public order, village organization, conduct of family and community rituals, agriculture, water conservation, and so on. Its provisions were closely linked to Taizu's *lijia* system of local administration in groups of ten and a hundred households.

Note that the proclamation was issued through what is usually called the Ministry of Revenue (*hubu*). A more literal reading of the title would be "Ministry of Households," but the households referred to are commoners and most often farmers, and the more common rendering is indicative of the state's main interest in them as producers of revenue. It signified that instruction on this lower, local level was of a different order from that of the schools and examinations conducted under the Ministry of Rites at the county and prefectural level with a view to bureaucratic recruitment. Note especially how Taizu celebrates his own achievements, denigrates scholar-officials as often venal, and, while charging them with having corrupted and obstructed his own plans, invites the people to side with him against them.

In order to instruct the people, Minister You Xin and others of the Ministry of Revenue, together with civil and military officials, on the nineteenth day, the third month of the year Hongwu 31 (1398), attended the morning audience at the Fengtian Gate and respectfully received the sacred edict.

In ancient times, rulers represented Heaven and managed human affairs by setting up various offices and delegating the various duties, so as to bring peace to the lives of the people. The worthies and the gentlemen of those times feared lest they not be employed by the rulers. After being employed, they exerted the utmost diligence to serve the rulers, thus bringing glory to their parents, honor to their wives and children, and establishing their reputations throughout the world. How could there have been any lawbreaking conduct? Therefore, the officials were competent for their posts and the people were content in their livelihoods. Since the world has been unified, I have set up the cardinal principles, promulgated laws, and established offices according to ancient rules: in the capital, the six ministries and the Censorate; in the provinces, the provincial administration commissions, the provincial surveillance commissions, prefectures, subprefectures, and districts. Although the titles are different from previous dynasties, the system of government is the same.

However, most of the appointed officials are from among the common people. For some time it has been very difficult to tell whether they were virtuous or wicked. The scholars are not real scholars, and the officials are all cunning ones. They often take bribes and break the law, turn humaneness and rightness upside down and injure the good people, so that the common people bring all of their complaints to the capital. So it has been for years without cease. Now this order is promulgated to declare to the people of the realm that all minor matters involving household and marriage, land, assault and battery, and disputes shall be judged by the elders and the *lijia* of their communities (*li*). Serious matters involving sexual crime, robbery, fraud, or homicide shall be reported to the officials. After this order is promulgated, any officials or functionaries who dare to violate it shall be sentenced to the death penalty. For those commoners who dare to violate it, their entire families shall be banished to the frontiers. These regulations have been declared before. You in the Ministry of Revenue shall once again proclaim them.

[*Jiaomin bangwen*, in *Huang Ming zhishu* 3:1404–1407 — EF]

Article 19

This provision, disarming in its homely simplicity, actually proved the most enduring part of Taizu's proclamation, much of which lapsed with the breakdown of the *lijia* system of local organization. The core of its message of moral instruction, which became known as the "Six Instructions" or "Sacred Edict," is actually taken from an earlier proclamation of Zhu Xi (unacknowledged by Taizu and unnoticed by most modern commentators, but no doubt instigated by advisers familiar with Zhu Xi's works; see chapter 20).

In each village and *li* a bell with a wooden clapper shall be prepared. Old persons, disabled persons unable to function normally, or blind persons shall be selected and guided by children to walk through the *li* holding the bell. If there are no such persons in the *li*, then they shall be selected from other *li*. Let them shout loudly so that everyone can hear, urging people to do good and not violate the law. Their message is: "Be filial to your parents, respect elders and superiors, live in harmony with neighbors, instruct and discipline children and grandchildren, be content with your occupation, commit no wrongful acts." This shall be done six times each month. At the time of the autumn harvest the people of the village and *li* shall give food to the bell carriers in accordance with their ability to pay. If the residents of the village are scattered and remote, each *jia* unit shall prepare a bell, and it will be easy to deliver the message. The style of the bell: it shall be made of copper with a wooden clapper hanging in the middle.

[*Jiao min bangwen* 1419–1420 — EF]

Article 32

This article refers to the establishment of community schools in the Yuan period, then their reestablishment by Taizu early in his reign (acclaimed as a glorious achievement by Taizu's adviser, Song Lian, in language reminiscent of earlier Neo-Confucian rhetoric), and finally abandoned for reasons cited in this article as follows:

In the Yuan dynasty, many village children attended school. In the early years of the Hongwu period (1368–1398) villages everywhere were ordered to establish community schools (*shexue*) to instruct the children in good conduct. Incompetent officials and *lijia* took advantage of this to indulge in corrupt practices. The children of families with adult males obviously had the spare time to attend school, but the officials took bribes and excused them from attending school. Nevertheless, the children of families without adult males, who had no spare time to attend school, were forced to go to school. This caused hardship for the people. Therefore, the community schools were abolished. From now on, the children of the common people, regardless of their location and number, shall be instructed by virtuous persons. The schools shall open early in the tenth month and close at the end of the twelfth month each year. If families with many adult males have enough spare time, they may have their children continually engaged in study. Those officials, functionaries, and *lijia* who dare to interfere with them shall be punished severely.

[Jiao min bangwen 1433–1434 — EF]

Note: This short article has at least three major significances: (1) it marked the effective privatization of schooling on the village level, with the consequence that only children of the well-to-do would engage in regular study that might prepare them for official schools and exams, while most commoners, engaged in agriculture and handicrafts, would get minimal off-season instruction, if any; (2) taken together with article 19, the regular moral instruction came mostly through the ritual recitation of the Six Instructions (Sacred Edict); (3) the effect of the foregoing was to create two different levels of education, one administered through the Ministry of Revenue on the local level and the other by the Ministry of Rites, leading up to official recruitment. Administratively, then, what had once been envisioned by Neo-Confucians as a single system of general education had become bifurcated into two: one below the county level, largely privatized but retaining a ritual of the Six Instructions for public moral uplift, and the other for the elite, oriented toward the civil service. Alongside this, of course, were the private academies, increasingly the focus of serious scholarly study and discussion but largely maintained by local support of the educated elite.

MING TAIZU: *DISCUSSION OF THE THREE TEACHINGS*

Although heavily influenced by his Confucian advisers, Taizu came from a different social background, and as ruler he occasionally escaped the strict confines of Confucianism to make statements about what he felt were larger social issues. In the following essay, the founder chides the Confucians for their skepticism about religion and the supernatural. He places Confucianism alongside Buddhism and what he calls the worship of the immortals (religious Daoism) as but one of "three teachings," all of which are true and all of which are absolutely requisite to the maintenance of good order among all the classes of Chinese society. Confucianism cannot be China's sole teaching, because, as he explained elsewhere, it is too demanding for most people. The masses will respond to moral injunctions only if these are reinforced by a belief in supernatural sanctions. Taizu's is not an intellectual statement. It is the statement of a believer in religion who also believes that religion is good because it has positive social effects. In this, he resembles Mozi.

In effect, though distinct in their origins and emphases, the Three Teachings are reducible to one common purpose and indispensable function: they buttress imperial rule, here identified with the "Way of Heaven."

The ideas propagated through the Three Teachings have been popular since Han times, through the Song, and down to the present. Confucianism stems from Confucius, Buddhism from Śākyamuni, and Daoism from Laozi. However, of these three, it is Laozi who has for many, many years been completely misinterpreted. The plain truth is that Laozi has nothing whatever to do with alchemical or magical technique. What Laozi really focuses on are things indispensable to running the state and family on an everyday basis. Second, it is also an absolute error to make Laozi stand for vacuity and nothingness. Laozi's real concern is with humaneness (*ren*) as manifested by the Three August Ones and the Five Sovereigns [of remotest antiquity], with rectifying oneself on the model of Heaven, and with making all one's acts appropriate through proper timing. Third, Laozi does not supply secrets for meditational trances or levitating into the sky. Laozi's aims in fact parallel those of Confucius.

Laozi's words are simple, but their meaning is profound. People ignore his meaning because they don't understand it. Then worshipers of the immortals and Buddhas appropriate his words for their own purposes. Yet if this is what is meant by the Three Teachings, then there is nothing wrong in calling them Confucianism, stemming from Confucius; Buddhism, stemming from Śākyamuni; and immortalism (*xian*), stemming [not from Laozi, but] from such figures as the Red Pine Master. Thus defined, the Three Teachings contain things that are abstruse and vital [in substance], yet solidly efficacious when put into practice. Anything that benefits humankind when it is put into practice is the Way of Heaven.

People in the past as well as nowadays develop different aims for themselves. People covet life and fear death. There are unintelligent people who think they can find ways to achieve longevity and escape death altogether. There have been emperors who have encouraged [this cult] and rich commoners who have become fervent devotees of it.

[On the other hand,] there have been agnostic people who fail to understand why things are as they are. These people allege that the teachings of the Buddhas and immortals incite the population and endanger the state. There have indeed been special imperial edicts [in times past] ordering the suppression of these teachings. That is why, through time, these teachings have risen and fallen over and over again. The two teachings [of Buddhism and immortalism] have been victimized by devotees of small intelligence as well as by enemies of great ignorance. . . .

There was Han Yu (768–824), who advised his ruler to cease immediately any further dealing with ghosts and spirits and to follow only the administrative precepts of [Confucian] kingly rule. Well! When the ghosts and spirits found out about Han Yu's attitude, they saw to it that [his own nephew Han Xiang] became a devotee of the immortals! This is a great example of how Heaven operates to provide lessons to humankind.

Now if [the teachings of the immortals and Buddhas] really consist in what their extreme devotees claim they consist in [i.e., levitation and personal immortality], then all they mean for humanity is vacuity and nothingness.

And yet, if a ruler who adapts his rule to the times totally rejects those teachings and makes [the immortals and Buddhas] out to be entities that do not exist, then the people will not think they exist either, and then there will be no way to instill the proper fear in people! The fact is that [the teachings of the immortals and Buddhas] have a central place in the administrative precepts of kingly rule.

Among the Three Teachings, there is no problem about the Way of Confucius. It harks back to Yao and Shun and the founders of the Three Dynasties of Antiquity, and to the classical texts upon which generation after generation has relied.

Unfortunately, there has been less appreciation for the more subtle spiritual benefits of Buddhism and immortalism, which covertly bulwark imperial rule and are of unceasing benefit to humankind.

It is well known that under Heaven there is [ultimately] no duality in the Way and that the sages are essentially of one mind. They differ only on the question of personal praxis or participation in public life. In that they deliver real benefits, they are in principle all one. Let it be known to ignorant people that all three teachings are indispensable!

[*Ming Taizu yuzhi wenji* 345–348 — JD, dB]

FANG XIAORU: FINAL ESSAY ON THE LEGITIMATE SUCCESSION OF DYNASTIES

Fang Xiaoru (1357–1402) wrote this essay around 1380, when he was twenty-three years old and was already recognized as a student of exceptional brilliance. In it, he tried to establish himself as the leading spokesman for China's scholar-elite, here mainly with regard to the question whether and to what extent foreign dynasties in China could be regarded as legitimate. At the time he wrote, the Mongol Yuan dynasty was fresh in many people's memories. The *Yuanshi*, the official dynastic history compiled by the Ming in the 1370s, treated the Yuan dynasty as one mandated by Heaven and therefore legitimate. By quoting excerpts from the Confucian classics, Fang sought to prove that the sages of antiquity could never have considered such a dynasty as legitimate. In Fang's view, people who were not culturally Chinese simply could not provide the kind of moral guidance that the realm had to have. He thought that Chinese culture could not be absorbed readily by foreigners; because of its demanding moral strictures, it was something that took many generations to acquire.

Note that everything Fang alleged against barbarians also applied, in his view, to usurpers. In 1402, Fang, by then a high official, refused to submit to a usurper, the Yongle emperor, and for that he was executed, along with many of his kin.

The term "legitimate succession" (*zhengtong*) has its basis in the *Spring and Autumn Annals*. Its teachings are subtle, but in general the main thrust of the

Annals is simply to make clear the roles of ruler and minister (subject), to sharpen the distinction between China and barbarism, and to uphold Heavenly Principle while suppressing human [selfish] desires.

In the Spring and Autumn era (771–479 B.C.E.), the feudal lords were thriving, but the Zhou house was in decline. The Zhou domain was smaller than the domains of [the big feudal states] Qi, Jin, Wu, and Yue. The Zhou armies and grain reserves were about on a par with those of [the smaller states] Lu, Wei, Cao, and Zheng. Yet the Zhou rulers are always called "Heavenly Kings" in the *Annals*. The *Annals* always disparages big states like Qi and Jin whenever they exceeded their station and acted with impropriety. The rulers of Chu and Wu had long styled themselves "kings," yet the *Annals* castigates them. Confucius remarked, "Surely people do not think that the distinctions between ruler and minister, and between China and barbarism can be abandoned!" The [*Gongyang*] commentary says: "The *Annals* make much of abiding in correctness." Also it says: "The king represents unity and succession." This is where the term "legitimate succession" comes from. People in later ages surely should not make up their own ideas about legitimate succession in defiance of the *Annals*.

After the Zhou, the Qin, Han, Jin, Sui, Tang, and Song unified the realm, ruled China, and caused all the barbarians to submit. On those grounds, they certainly belong in the legitimate succession.

The Qin was founded in 221 B.C.E. and it ended in 207 B.C.E. The Sui was founded in 589 and it ended in 617. The Tang began in 618 and ended in 907. The Han began in 202 B.C.E., the Jin in 280 C.E., and the Song in 979. However, the Han split into three in the era 196–219; the Jin lost North China to the barbarians after Emperor Hui (r. 290–306), and the Song evacuated North China in the reign of Gaozong (r. 1127–1162). In the case of these three dynasties, the first had to defend China from usurpers, the second was humiliated by barbarians, and the third went so far as to offer submission to barbarians. Yet, just as in the Zhou, the distinctions between ruler and subject and China and barbarism must continue to be observed [in theory]. So on these grounds, the Han must end in 263 C.E. [and] the Jin in 404, while the Song Mandate of Heaven was extinguished only in 1279. This is the great method of the *Annals*, a Way that will never change.

Yet there are some people who insist on terminating those dynasties at the point where each grew weak and admitting their competitors at that point, in complete disregard of "succession." They admit usurpers because they fail to take into account the right idea from the *Annals*. What makes China precious is that it has the ruler-minister distinction and the teachings of rites and rightness, whereas barbarians do not. Not to observe the ruler-minister distinction is to adopt barbarism, and adopting barbarism is tantamount to becoming animals. . . .

Common notions are formed when people become imbued with something and, over a long time, just accept it without realizing what they have done. For example, in the Song, people thought it strange whenever they saw barbarian costumes or heard barbarian speech. They would have thought it shameful and repugnant to submit to a barbarian ruler, or to become barbarized themselves. However, during the century of Yuan rule, everyone became barbarized in their eating and living habits, in their speech, and in objects of daily use. People raised their sons and grandsons under these conditions. They were acclimated to these things for so long that it all seemed quite appropriate to them. In the Yuan era, everyone would have been shocked and amazed to hear them [Mongol rulers] repudiated on the grounds of barbarism. This is the skewed outlook that was prevalent in that era. It is not an outlook that is in accord with the Way and therefore destined to prevail forever. . . .

If a barbarian ruler is admitted into [the orthodox dynastic succession of] China, how will the limitless greed of the barbarians ever be contained? How can it be guaranteed that the barbarians will not come into China and damage it again? If they do, it will be a great calamity for the people. No benevolent person could bear to have such a thing happen again. . . .

I venture to offer as my own view the idea that there are three kinds of ruler, who, even though they may possess the realm, cannot be admitted into the legitimate succession. They are: usurpers, empresses, and barbarians. Barbarians bring disorder to China's culture. Usurpers and power-seeking empresses bring disorder to the fundamentals of human relations. . . .

What is precious in China is its system of human relations. [China] can partake of the Way of the former kings, thanks to the beauty of its ritual and culture, and the social discriminations it observes through its system of robes and caps. When usurpers or empresses assassinate a ruler and seize his position, human relations are thereby destroyed. How can such people rule the realm? If and when they do, they encourage the realm to disrespect fathers and rulers, which everyone knows [is bad enough].

But what about barbarians? Nephews cohabit with aunts, and sons fight with fathers because [barbarians] do not observe the hierarchical distinctions implicit in human relations and because they lack the finer things like robes and caps, ritual and culture. It is on these grounds that the former kings treated barbarians as though they were animals and did not put them in the same category as the people of China. . . . And if a maid or manservant killed his or her master and seized control of his family, then even the family dog or horse would get upset and bite the offender! They would all react thus because normality had been disordered. These cases are no different from the disordering of normality occasioned by usurpers, power-seeking empresses, or barbarians. Yet our scholar-officials, who are so fond of praising the Way of the former kings, not only find nothing strange [in barbarian rule], they even make excuses for it! That is sad. . . .

The upright men and great Confucians of former times knew that barbarians were unacceptable as leaders. Therefore they would have nothing to do with even so powerful a leader as Fu Jian [r. 352–355], or so outstanding a one as [Yelü] Deguang [r. 926–947]. They knew, based on China's ritual, that power-seeking empresses were also unacceptable as rulers; therefore they would have nothing to do with even so powerful a woman as Empress Lü [r. 188–180 B.C.E.] or so talented a one as Empress Wu [r. 690–705]. And they knew that they could not obey usurpers who seized the position of Son of Heaven, and so they consistently regarded them as bandits. . . .

[Postscript] After I wrote the above, I never showed it to anyone. Everyone who heard something about it ridiculed me, or reviled me behind my back. The only people who agreed with me were my teacher [Song Lian] and Hu Han of Jinhua. Few men in the realm are like them. Most cleave to their prejudices and personal opinions. How can my argument ever gain standing in the world? Song Lian and Hu Han are matchless in the world for their knowledge of the Way. Only men like them can transmit written arguments to posterity; prejudiced men are soon forgotten. If those two worthies have accepted me, then surely there will be some future worthies who will do the same. So my argument has a chance to gain standing after all.

[Xunzhi zhai ji (SBCK) 2:7b–13b — JD]

LIU ZONGZHOU: ON FANG XIAORU

In resisting the usurper Chengzu (the Yongle emperor), Fang Xiaoru, as a leading Confucian statesman at court, not only risked his own life but defied the emperor's threat to exterminate Fang's entire clan to the ninth degree of relationship. Accounts vary concerning the full extent of the emperor's ferocity in punishing Fang, but according to one widely accepted version, when he threatened Fang with the extirpation of his kin to nine degrees of relationship and Fang still defied him, saying even if it were ten he would not submit, the emperor made it ten. For later scholars Fang became a model of heroic Confucian virtue, one whose "loyalty" to the ruler was shown in his fidelity to principle and upholding it to the ruler even at the cost of his own life. Later the seventeenth-century Confucian philosopher Liu Zongzhou, who took his own life rather than serve the Manchus, paid tribute to Fang in the following. As Liu himself notes, other scholars questioned whether such extreme sacrifice was worth it.

The age of the holy sages being long past, calamities and disorders have followed upon each other. Rare are the scholars and officials who regard living people as their responsibility and the way of the prince as their concern. After the fall of the Song, such have become even rarer. Fang Xiaoru was endowed with a unique native talent and generously took upon himself the mission of reviving this culture. . . . He was deeply conscious both of the intention of Heaven above in giving us life and of that which the ancient sages and worthies strove for. He wanted truly to rid the world of floods and droughts and to begin an era like that of the two [sage] emperors, to do away with hegemons and make manifest [the way] of the Three Kings[11] and further promote their virtuous influence in order to contribute to future generations. . . .

But time and destiny were not opportune, and with nine deaths Fang was to accomplish the one right,[12] achieving in this way his universal and historical mission. The support he gave to the moral teaching of the world is evidently that of a true and correct scholar who will be honored for a thousand years.

In his lifetime, Fang was called a reincarnation of Cheng Yi and Zhu Xi. Yet later men pointed to his death as one that erased the serious efforts of a whole lifetime, saying that heroic virtue and the study of philosophy are two different things and that he may have one or the other. . . . Thus the teaching of martyrdom [literally, fulfillment of humanity and choice of rightness][13] becomes a subject forbidden to the world, while treasonous ministers and rebellious sons multiply everywhere under Heaven. How sad!

Some praise Fang's loyalty as perfect but regard as extreme the sacrifice of his ten relations. I reply: Fang only prepared to die once. That his action should force the killing of relations to the tenth degree [of relationship] meant that each member of these clans had to die only once also. There is no place [and no one] under Heaven that does not belong to the prince [i.e., he holds the fate of all mankind]. Are ten clans too many to lose?

In his daily learning, Fang earnestly taught that a minister should be perfectly loyal and a son perfectly filial, basing all on what the conscience already possesses. He led the entire world in this direction for the length of several decades until he almost changed the world's morals. Hence when the day came and he was able to radiate his special brightness, it became impossible to hide its light. This is fitting, since perfect sincerity manifests itself in all our movements. It is not what human strength can reach by itself. If one should say that Fang's was the way of the Mean [i.e., perfect virtue], it would be quite correct.

[Adapted from Ching and Fang, *Records of Ming Scholars*, pp. 49–50]

HU GUANG: MEMORIAL ON THE *GREAT COMPENDIA*

[Memorial accompanying the submission of the *Great Compendium of the Five Classics and Four Books* and the *Great Compendium of Human Nature and Principle* (*Wujing sishu daquan* and *Xingli daquan*)]

Usurper though he was, the Yongle emperor (r. 1402–1424) was as eager as the

---

11. The "Three Kings" refers to the legendary sage kings of antiquity — Yao, Shun, and Yu.

12. Allusion to Fang's tragic death and the execution of all those related to him within ten degrees of kinship.

13. Allusion to the teachings of Confucius and Mencius on the self-sacrifice that may be required by perfect virtue.

founding Emperor Taizu to assume the role of one who could provide moral and intellectual guidance to his realm. Among his many initiatives (military, diplomatic, and cultural) was a plan to provide China with a set of basic Confucian study materials whose orthodoxy was so well established that any questioning of it might be forbidden. The *Great Compendia (Daquan)* gathered in a form convenient for students the fundamental texts of Neo-Confucian metaphysics, plus all acceptably Neo-Confucian study aids and commentaries on the Five Classics and Four Books. Begun early in 1415 under the general editorship of Hu Guang (1370–1418), the project was completed ten months later. The emperor wrote a preface for the *Compendia*, which were then ordered printed for distribution to every government school in the realm. The printing was finished in 1417. These texts and commentaries remained the basis for the civil service examinations for the rest of the Ming dynasty and were accepted as authoritative in Yi dynasty Korea and Tokugawa Japan. Under the Qing, the texts were somewhat revised, but the idea persisted that a government that seeks legitimacy must establish intellectual and moral standards for its subjects.

Readers will recognize the rhetoric of this memorial as familiar to the genre of the Learning of the Emperors and Kings, the Classics Mat and the *Great Learning*. But whereas Cheng Yi, Zhu Xi, and Zhen Dexiu had invoked the role of the sage mentor to admonish the ruler, Hu Guang's encomium of the Yongle emperor (he who had exterminated Fang Xiaoru and his clan so ruthlessly) as almost a divine sage was taken full advantage of by the Yongle emperor, Chengzu. Besides promulgating this canon of official orthodoxy, he compiled a work titled *The Message of the Mind in the Sage's Learning*, in which he presumed to give the definitive word on sagely cultivation. For this the editors of the Complete Library of the Four Treasuries Library catalog later castigated him. Noting the blood spilled in his rise to power, the harshness of his rule, and the many who had suffered unjustly at his hands — all in sharp contrast to the benevolent professions of the work in question — they concluded, "Men of later generations would not be taken in by this hypocrisy."

The Way of the Six Classics is as bright as the sun and stars. It is the warp and woof [that bind] Heaven and Earth together. It ties antiquity and modern times together on the same string. Cast forth, it reaches every point of the compass; gathered in, it stores everything in compact density. When it is applied to the self, the self is cultivated. When it is carried out in the family, the family is regulated. When it is extended to the state, the state is well ordered. When it is conveyed to society at large, society at large becomes pacified.

In any age, people must study and apply the classics exhaustively before the Way can become bright. It has never been possible for anyone to ignore the classics and then order things according to principle. The sages and kings always had recourse to the Way in order to establish their administrations and enlighten humankind at one and the same time. Similarly, the worthy and wise, when they built the foundations, always based themselves in antiquity when they made their great plans. . . .

But then the kingly Way declined, and unorthodox ideas rose up everywhere. After the Qin burning of the books, and the distortions introduced by the Han Confucians, no one could make complete sense of the tangled remains that survived. . . .

Yet even while it proved so very difficult to find the old pathways, people hoped all the more to repossess their heritage. Fortunately, it happens that after a nadir a zenith must follow, and that after darkness there must come light. Thanks to the learning of Zhou Dunyi, the Cheng brothers, Zhang Zai, and Zhu Xi, the Way of [the former kings] Yao, Shun, Yu, and Tang became knowable at last. These men cleared away all the weeds and underbrush and made orthodox learning stand forth in exemplary splendor once again.

Unfortunately, however, the doctrines of these men came several times under assault. If they were championed on some occasions, they were repressed on others. Moreover, for the last several hundred years, no one has been able to gather all their ideas together in a consistent way. It is only now that that task has at last been accomplished. . . .

And now you, our present emperor [Yongle], with your godly and sagelike accomplishments in both military and civil spheres, and with your surpassing intelligence, have rightfully and grandly succeeded to the throne and have continued the great merits [of your father, the founder]. . . . Your tasks were done, and yet you thought there was something still left to do. So you internalized the Way in a sense of humility, and your mind searched high and far, and you came to the great decision to edit the Six Classics, to regenerate from its origins the Way in its orthodox transmission, and to revive "this culture of ours" from its state of decay. . . .

You have read all [the *Compendia*] in the Imperial [Classics Mat] Seminar, and now you wish to make these available to the world at large. You want everyone to take the right road, You want no one to have his studies be deflected into divergent paths. You want everyone to take Confucius, Mencius, the Cheng brothers, and Zhu Xi into his family and household. . . .

I myself have observed that ever since the decline of the Zhou dynasty and the neglect of the Way, the only people who have been deeply concerned to maintain the Way as instruction for the world have been Confucian teachers and gentlemen. Until this moment, there have been no great and activist rulers capable of taking the lead in propagating the Way of the Six Classics, and resuming the line of transmission from the former sages. In this respect your majesty outshines all other rulers and, indeed, transcends everyone else in more than a thousand years.

[*Ming wenheng* 5:13a–14b — JD]

Chapter 23

NEO-CONFUCIAN EDUCATION

The basic pattern of schooling in late imperial China, which developed in response to new needs and challenges in the Song period, became codified in the Yuan (fourteenth century) and was confirmed in the early Ming. As will be seen from the curricular materials in this chapter, the core of this system, widely adopted by local academies, reflected the views of the Cheng-Zhu school of the Learning of the Way, which, with some variations and modifications, remained standard down into the nineteenth century. Although many new trends of thought and scholarship would emerge out of this basic educational system, the core curriculum itself remained stable and proved remarkably durable.

In the formative stage of this process, as we have seen, education had become a major issue in the Northern Song, partly stimulated by the expansion of the civil bureaucracy early in the life of the dynasty and by the demand thus created for persons with the requisite learning and skills. In addition, economic development and diversification, as well as rising affluence and increased leisure for the pursuit of cultural activities, created new opportunities outside of government for educated persons. Prime among these occupations was teaching, as economic expansion and technological advances created a wider popular interest in learning and led to an increase in the number of schools and academies. Over time the growth of local, semiprivate academies outpaced that of public schools. With this development, tensions arose, but not so much from rivalry between public and private endeavors as from either political pressures and literati involvement with them or resistance to state control and the distorting effects of the civil service examinations on education.

Schools, especially local academies (*shuyuan*), centered on teachers and collections of books. Hence the spread of printing was bound to have a significant impact on them, as on cultural activity in general. The effect has been concisely stated in reference to Feng Dao's printing of the Confucian Classics in 953:

> The printing of the Classics was one of the forces that restored Confucian literature and teaching to the place in national and popular regard that it had held before the advent of Buddhism, and a classical renaissance followed that can be compared only to the Renaissance that came in Europe after the rediscovery of its classical literature, and that there too was aided by the invention of printing. . . . Another result of the publication of the Classics was an era of large-scale printing, both public and private, that characterized the whole of the Song dynasty.[1]

A development of such epochal proportions confronted the literati with both new opportunities for the dissemination of knowledge and new problems about how this technological change would affect the learning process. Neo-Confucians became much occupied with the nature and significance of book learning. On a wider scale, the question became which of the traditional teachings would take advantage of the new printing technology. Buddhists earlier had been quick to do so,[2] but Chan Buddhism, the dominant form among artists and intellectuals, had declared its independence of the written word (*buli wenzi*) and was divided on the question, as we have seen in Dahui's opposition to the publication of *gongan* (*kōan*) (chapter 17). Two questions emerged: Which of these teachings would want to reach a larger public through the use of this medium? And how would they adapt teaching methods to it? Even among Neo-Confucians there was not one single answer, but most found themselves compelled to deal with such issues as the relative importance of reading, lecturing, and discussion. "How to read books" was much discussed in the Cheng-Zhu school, and Zhu Xi's "reading method" (*dushufa*) was widely disseminated.

Song Confucians saw Daoism and Buddhism, and especially Chan, as still exerting a powerful influence on people's minds. Syncretists minimized the conflict between the Three Teachings by assigning them respective spheres of influence: Confucianism was identified with governance, Daoism with physical culture, and Buddhism with mental culture. Neo-Confucians tended to reject

---

1. Carter and Goodrich, *Invention of Printing in China*, p. 83.
2. Ibid., pp. 26–28, 38–51, 57–58, 63–65.

such formulae as too facile, on both theoretical and practical grounds. Among the latter was the educational issue: the practical impossibility of mastering three such disparate systems at once and, given the need to choose among them, the primacy of the moral imperative that claimed priority for humane learning and called for new types of scholarship to meet the increasingly complex problems of secular society. At the same time Buddhist spirituality remained a formidable challenge to Neo-Confucians, who felt a need to provide an alternative compatible with secular goals and lay life. Managing all this in one lifetime was for them clearly a matter of identifying educational priorities.

As we have seen in chapter 20, demands for an empire-wide school system were prominent among reform proposals in the eleventh and early twelfth centuries, and at times the state undertook some ambitious programs. But quite apart from the ideological conflicts that arose from the support of state schools by certain parties and opposition to them by others, there were complaints that such schools had become burdened by inefficient administration and high costs; they were also exposed to charges of favoritism, wracked by the intense competition for office through the civil service examinations, and vitiated by the routinization of instruction. Thus questions arose as to what basic values, goals, and functions the schools should serve. Zhu Xi gave expression to this sense of the impersonality of education when he said with regard to conditions in a government school, "Teachers and students regard each other indifferently, like passers-by on the highway. Elders are concerned by the daily decline of customs and the disappearance of scholarly spirit, but they are unable to remedy it."[3]

These questions were only heightened by the emergence in the Southern Song of a literati class less oriented toward service in the central government and more directed toward involvement with local affairs — less with advancement to the top than with public morality and local leadership at ground level. Thus, underlying Zhu Xi's proposals were at least three major concerns: how to provide for competent leadership on both the higher and the lower levels; how to reconcile the need for both broad humanistic education and the increase in professional and technical specialization in the Song; and how to deal with the problems of infrastructure (including costs) in providing expanded education.

In his *Reflections on Things at Hand* (*Jinsi lu*), Zhu cites the views of two of his predecessors on these matters. He notes that Hu Yuan, a model teacher of the Northern Song, allowed in his school for both broad classical learning and specialization in a particular field, such as political economy, military affairs, hydraulic engineering, or mathematics. He also notes the grand plan of Cheng Hao for a universal school system with government support of all teachers and

---

3. Zhu Xi, *Wenji* 80:20b.

students. Zhu then raises a pair of key questions: how feasible is this in terms of cost and where would the resources come from to support it? Having such doubts about the practicability of this ideal, Zhu apparently believed that on the local level schooling would have to be seasonal — available to all but with most students self-supporting, i.e., continuing to be gainfully employed in the fields.[4]

Childhood education was a major interest of Song scholars, and this is reflected in the special attention that Zhu Xi gave to it in his *Elementary Learning* (*Xiaoxue*), which became a major text of the Neo-Confucian educational movement. Since some such training in the home or neighborhood school was presupposed by the more formal studies begun at age eight, we begin the presentation of basic texts here with reference to the *Elementary Learning* and the most famous of all Chinese primers, the *Three Character Classic*. Next comes the centerpiece: the syllabus of Cheng Duanli (1271–1345), including basic texts ancillary to the classic core of that syllabus, followed by excerpts from the *Four Books for Women*, as formulated in the Ming period.

ZHU XI: PREFACE TO THE *ELEMENTARY LEARNING*

Formal schooling was considered to be preceded by the study of certain primers in the home, among them the *Elementary Learning* (*Xiaoxue*) and the *Three Character Classic* (*Sanzijing*). As we have seen in the case of Xu Heng in the Yuan period, the *Elementary Learning* was a most influential text in the early spread of the Neo-Confucian movement. In effect it expressed the fundamentals of its educational philosophy, starting not only "from the cradle" but even with prenatal influences in the womb.

The contents are divided into three main parts: (1) the "Setting Up of Instruction" (i.e., the basic importance of a defined, structured sequence of education); (2) the prime human/moral relations; and (3) the fundamental, as well as ultimate, value of self-respect ("reverencing the self"), i.e., the need to take responsibility for, to define, and to shape one's self in the context of the foregoing environmental factors and relationships. Each section includes quotations from the classics and histories. For this reason, to read it required a fair knowledge of classical Chinese — unlikely to be found among small children. Hence it was actually more a book *about* childhood education than it was suitable reading for beginners. Since the earlier readings on Xu Heng (chapter 20) have already presented his simplified précis of the *Elementary Learning*, we limit ourselves here to translating Zhu Xi's general preface.

In the elementary learning of ancient times, instruction followed the steps of "sprinkling and sweeping, listening and responding, advancing and retiring

---

4. Chan, *Reflections on Things at Hand*, p. 265.

[in the presence of others]," as well as the loving of parents, respecting of elders, honoring of teachers, and being intimate with friends. All of these constituted the basis for cultivating the self, regulating the family, ordering the state, and bringing peace to all-under-Heaven. Thus they were sure to be discussed and put into practice during the learner's younger years; in this way knowledge and discipline would grow together for the full development and transformation of the mind-and-heart, so that there would be no danger of conflict between nature and nurture.

Today, although there is no complete text extant, there are many fragments indicative of this [elementary learning] to be found mixed into other accounts. Still, those who encounter these in their reading, believing that there are too many differences in circumstances between past and present, do not put these into practice. They do not realize that in some things there is no difference between past and present and nothing that should ever keep one from practicing them. Therefore we have collected some of these pieces into a book, so that they may be imparted to the young, to serve as a resource for their study and practice, hoping that it might make some small contribution to the improvement of the mores of our times.

(Zhu) Huian, First day, third month, fourteenth year of Chunxi (1187)
[Uno, Shōgaku, 5–6 — dB]

WANG YINGLIN: THE THREE CHARACTER CLASSIC (SANZI JING)

This "classic" of childhood education has traditionally been attributed to Wang Yinglin (1223–1296), a distinguished scholar, classicist, encyclopedic historian, and versatile exemplar of the broad learning and interest in popular education characteristic of the Zhu Xi school. Although its authorship has been disputed, the other likely candidates are from the same era, the thirteenth century, in which Neo-Confucians were actively spreading their teachings. The opening line, affirming the goodness of human nature, takes a position not established as "orthodox" before Zhu Xi's time.

To most readers or reciters of this most popular of all primers down into the twentieth century, questions of authorship would have been of little concern. The style is remarkable only for its amazing economy, balance, and simplicity, with three characters to a line, and each two-line couplet a statement unto itself. The regular rhythm, the use of common vocabulary and familiar characters, and the smooth flow of the diction all rendered the text highly readable, easy to recite, and most memorable.

If great popularity and durability were not enough to make this a "classic" of demonstrated appeal, it could also be said that the thirteenth century witnessed frequent loose usage of the term jing ("classic") for similar Neo-Confucian reformulations of classic teachings, as we have seen with Zhen Dexiu's Heart Classic and Classic of Governance.

The content, too, qualifies it as classic: it is basic, easily understood Confucian teaching, yet also neoclassical and Neo-Confucian in that its main points — the goodness of human nature, its perfectibility through individual effort at self-cultivation, the importance of learning and education, the priority of the family and essential human/moral relationships, the need to apply oneself to study, and the lessons of history in illustrating these [too numerous for many to be included here] — all are points reemphasized strongly by the Neo-Confucians.

In 1878 H. A. Giles, a leading British sinologue, published a metrical, rhymed translation, the Victorian style and elegance of which appealed to many scholars as conveying the flavor of the original "classic." Much later, in 1910, Giles published a revised version, more literal and prosaic, saying that the early work "passed muster at the time, but will not do now." In view of his disowning of it, we must forgo, regrettably, the majestic cadences of the metrical translation; we have instead followed the later one, with some adaptations to the style and usage of the present volume.

Human beings at birth / Are naturally good.
Their natures are much the same / [But] nurture takes them far apart.
If there is no teaching / The nature will deteriorate;
The right way in teaching / Is to value concentration.
To feed the body and not the mind / Would be the father's fault;
Instruction without discipline / Is sloth on the teacher's part.
If the child does not learn / This is not as it should be;
If he does not learn while young / When old what will he do?
. . .
Of old, Mencius' mother chose a [good] neighborhood / [For her son to grow
    up in], avoiding a cemetery and a market place [but near a
    school] . . .
A jade unwrought serves no useful purpose.
If one does not learn / One cannot know what is right.
For the child to become a man / When he is young [he must]
Attach himself to teachers and friends / Practice rites and ceremonial
    usage. . . .
To behave as the younger toward the older / Is one of the first things to learn.
First comes filial piety, then fraternal love / Next what is seen and heard;
Learn to count and then to read. . . .
The Three Powers are / Heaven, Earth, and the Human.
The Three Luminaries are / Sun, moon, and stars.
The Three Bonds are / Rightness between prince and minister,
Love between parent and child / Harmony between husband and wife. . . .
One speaks of humaneness and rightness / Ritual decorum, wisdom and
    trustworthiness;
These five constants / Admit of no laxity or confusion. . . .
One speaks of joy and anger / Of pity and of fear.
Of love, of hate, and of desire / These are the seven feelings. . . .

Great-great-grandfather, great-grandfather, and grandfather,
Father and self, self and son, son and grandson
From son and grandson / To great-grandson and great-great-grandson,
These are the nine agnates / Constituting the kinship relations. . . .
In the instruction of the young / There should be explanation and
    investigation;
Careful instruction in philology / Clarification of paragraphs and sentences.
One who would learn / Must know where to begin;
The *Elementary Learning* now finished, / One proceeds to the Four Books
In the *Analects'* twenty chapters, / The disciples record [Confucius'] fine
    words.
The *Mencius* / In seven chapters
Explains the Way and virtue; speaks of humaneness and rightness.
The writing of the *Mean* / Was from the pen of Zisi;
Centrality does not lean to one side / Normality is what does not change.
The Composer of the *Great Learning* / Was Master Zeng;
From self-cultivation and regulation of the family / It goes on to ordering the
    state and bringing peace to all-under-Heaven.
With [*The Classic of*] *Filiality* mastered / And the Four Books well digested,
Next the Six Classics / Are there to be read —
The *Odes, Documents, Changes* / The two *Rites* and *Spring and Autumn*
    Annals. . . .
When the classics are understood, / Then read the masters,
Pick out the important points in each / And take note of all the facts.
There are the Five Masters / Xunzi and Yang Xiong
Wen Zhongzi[5] / And Laozi and Zhuangzi.
The classics and masters well understood, next the several histories should be
    read. . . .

There follows a long conspectus of Chinese dynastic histories and the Veritable Records.

Su Laoquan / [Only] at age twenty-seven
First bent his energies / To study the books and records.
Then, already old, / He repented his tardiness.
You little ones / Think of this early in time.
There was Liang Hao who / At the age of eighty-two,
In an interview at the palace / Distinguished himself among scholars.
Though a latecomer / All called him a prodigy.

---

5. Wen Zhongzi was the honorific title of Wang Tong (584–617), and the title was sometimes
applied to the *Zhongshuo*, a work attributed to him. He was a classicist and teacher in the Sui
period, and some of the statesmen who were his students later became prominent in the early
Tang.

Thus you little ones / Should commit yourselves to learning. . . .
Xie Daoyun [famous poetess of the fourth century] / Was able to compose
  verses
Only a girl / Yet bright and sharp of mind.
You boys / Should take this as a challenge. . . .
If you do not study / How can you become a [true] human being. . . .
Learn while young / When grown up put it to practice
Influence the ruler above / Benefit the people below.
Make a name for yourself / Do honor to father and mother
Shed luster on your forebears / Enrich your posterity.
Men bequeath to their children / Coffers of gold.
What I teach the child / Is just this one book.
Diligence has its reward / Play yields no benefit;
Oh, be on your guard / And put forth all your strength.

[Adapted from H. A. Giles, *San Tzu Ching*, 7–150 — dB]

THE STANDARD SCHOOL CURRICULUM

Although government schools in late imperial China generally followed the
civil service examination requirements, a standard curriculum had already become widely accepted in the semiautonomous "private academies" that had
become the main vehicles for the spread of Neo-Confucianism even before the
examinations were resumed in 1313–1315. In fact, the movement to establish a
definite method and pattern for the conduct of education had already begun
in Zhu Xi's school during his lifetime and spread quickly thereafter. It culminated in Cheng Duanli's (1271–1345) widely emulated "Daily Schedule of Study
in the Cheng Family School, Graded According to Age," published in 1315, the
same year the new examinations came into effect.

The significance of these new developments may be seen in the biography
of Cheng Duanli in the *Yuan History*:

At the end of the Song, the Qing-Yuan area [near Ningbo in Eastern
Zhejiang], all followed the school of Lu Xiangshan (Lu Jiuyuan) and the
Zhu Xi school was not carried on. Cheng Duanli by himself took up with
Shi Jing [i.e., Shi Mengqing (1247–1306)] in propagating Zhu Xi's doctrine of "clarifying the substance and applying it in practice" (*mingti
shiyong*). Scholars came to his gate in great numbers. He wrote the "Working Schedule for Study of Books" (*Dushu gongcheng*), which the Directorate of Education then had distributed to officials in the local schools
to serve as a model for students.[6]

---

6. Song Lian et al., *Yuan shi* 90:4343.

Note here the process of conversion from Lu Jiuyuan's (Xiangshan's) teaching to Zhu Xi's, drawing attention to the combination of principle and practice. A later historian had this to say concerning the significance of this development:

> In the late Song the Qing-Yuan area was all of the Lu school, and the Zhu Xi school was not transmitted there. With Shi Mengqing, however, there came a change. Following Yang Jian [1140–1125, disciple of Lu] most of the school went into Chan and pursued a form of learning without the reading of books. Departing from the source, they drifted apart. Thus, what they transmitted from Master Lu was the very thing that made them lose Master Lu. Having studied Cheng's Daily Reading Schedule, [I find that] there is nothing missing from root to branch and there is a sequential order in its method, from which one may proceed.[7]

Here a connection is suggested between the Lu school's lack of a reading method, reflecting Lu's own depreciation of textual study, the school's getting lost in Chan Buddhism, which "did not depend on the written word," and the contrasting growth of the Zhu Xi school linked to its definite program of study and reading.

In the published "Daily Schedule," prefixed to it were the following texts, which were considered preparatory or ancillary to it:

"Articles of the White Deer Grotto"
"School Code of Masters Cheng and Dong"
Zhen Dexiu's "Instructions for Children"
Zhu Xi's Reading Method in "Essentials of Reading"
Several other selected writings of Zhu Xi on aspects of learning and instruction.

The first of these items has been included in chapter 20. Following are translations from the second, third, and fourth, as well as another that is mentioned in the "Daily Schedule" as to be learned by the prospective student before he enters upon formal schooling at age eight: "A Primer of Human Nature and Principle."

SCHOOL CODE OF MASTERS CHENG AND DONG
(CHENG-DONG ER XIANSHENG XUECE)

This code was drawn up by two of Zhu Xi's followers, Cheng Duanmeng (1143–1191) and Dong Zhu (1152–1214), to define practices and procedures in their local school. As noted in chapter 20, Zhu Xi had opposed "school rules" except as a last resort,

---

7. *Song Yuan xuean* 87:54.

preferring to emphasize positive values rather than negative sanctions. This code, though strict, says nothing about punishment, and the editor who published it in 1178, while noting Zhu's distaste for "rules," spoke of it as offering norms to define shared group activities at school, which would complement Zhu Xi's "Articles" setting forth the values that should guide the content of instruction. It was apparently on this basis that Zhu himself gave his approval to the code in 1181 — i.e., as a set of ritual norms for youngsters in a neighborhood school more than as punitive rules for older students. Nevertheless, thereafter, through the Yuan, Ming, and Qing, the "Articles" and "Code" were adopted together in many schools and academies.

All who study here must respect the [formal] occasions [for meeting] on the first and fifteenth days of the month.

On those days, just before dawn, a man on duty for the day takes charge of beating the sounding block. At the first knocking, all rise, wash, and rinse their mouths. They bind their hair and put on clothing. At the second knocking, all put on *shenyi* robes — or else *liangshan* robes[8] — and enter the hall. The teacher leads the pupils before the image of the Former Sage [Confucius]. They bow twice and burn incense. They bow twice again and move back. The teacher stands facing southwest. The eldest of the students leads them to face northeast in order, bow twice to the teacher, and stand supporting him. One of the older students addresses felicitations to the teacher. They again bow twice to the teacher. He enters his room. All the students stand in order in a ring. They bow twice and withdraw, each going to his desk.

Heed the dawn and dusk orders.

On ordinary days the block is struck as before. On the second knocking the students enter the hall and stand in order. As soon as the teacher emerges from his room and takes his place, all fold hands in salutation. They divide in order into two rows. They fold hands [in salutation] to each other and withdraw. When night comes and they are about to go to bed, the block is struck and salutations are made in assembly as in the morning ceremony. For lecture assembly, meal assembly, and tea assembly, the block is also struck as before. For the morning salutations and lecture assembly, *shenyi* robes — or else *liangshan* robes — are worn. Otherwise, plain jackets and gowns.

Maintain a reverent bearing.

Everyone has a regular place. Sit in order according to age. Whenever sitting, hold the body erect. Do not fan the legs out, lean over, cross the legs, or move the feet. Wait for the elders before going to bed. Once in bed do not speak. Do not go to bed during the day.

---

8. Semiformal garments.

Walk and stand erect.

Walk deliberately; stand with hands folded. Give precedence to elders. Do not turn your back on those who should be honored. Do not step on thresholds.[9] Do not stand on one foot or lean to one side.

Look and listen properly.

Do not stare. Do not cock your ear.[10]

Speak carefully.

Be precise and accurate. Do not give assent lightly. Do not exaggerate. Do not jest or be noisy. Do not engage in gossiping about local figures or gabbing about useless topics dear to the vulgar crowd of the marketplace.

Keep a sedate demeanor.

It is necessary to be solemn and serious. Do not be casual or impertinent. Do not be rough and ready or assertive and haughty. Do not be quick to express pleasure or anger.

Keep clothing neat.

Do not wear odd or fancy clothing. Do not let it be dirty, worn, or unkempt. Even while in one's own quarters, do not expose the body or bare the head. Even in the full heat of summer, do not on the spur of the moment take off your shoes and stockings.

Eat and drink temperately.

Do not seek to eat to the full. Do not hanker after rare delicacies. Eat at proper times. Do not be ashamed of poor food. It is not permitted to drink [wine] except at festivals or when so ordered by superiors. When drinking, do not exceed three cups or reach the point of drunkenness.

It is required to report [to the teacher] before going out and after coming back.

Unless summoned by parents or other superiors or ordered by the teacher or on urgent personal business, it is not permitted to leave the school. Report before leaving; present yourself after returning. Go nowhere other than where reported; return without exceeding the time limit.

In study concentrate on one thing at a time.

The mind must be correct and the attitude respectful. Keep track of the number of times [you have read a passage as assigned]. If you have completed the number of times and [have] not yet been able to memorize the passage, you must keep on until it has been memorized. Even if you memorize the passage before completing the number of times, you must fulfill the number of times. Only when one book has been mastered should you read another book. Do not strive to read extensively; do not strive to memorize everything. Do not read books that are not by the sages and worthies. Do not peruse writings that are of no benefit.

---

9. *Analects* 10:4.
10. "Summary of the Rules of Propriety" ("Quli"), *Record of Rites* A:3; Legge, *Li Ki*, 1:76.

Write characters in square style and respectfully.

Do not use the running style. Do not slant [the characters].

Keep desks in good order.

Everything must have its place. Paper and books should not be in disorder. Book boxes and clothing chests must be carefully barred and locked.

Keep halls and rooms clean.

The one on duty for the day, having beaten the block twice as above, sprinkles the hall thoroughly with water, sweeps the dust out with a broom, and wipes the desks with a cloth. Everywhere else the room servants are ordered to sweep and wipe; and wherever else there is litter, they are ordered to sweep it up, no matter what the hour.

Use forms of address appropriate to age.

To a person twice your age, use "elder" (*zhang*). To one ten years senior, use "elder brother" (*xiong*). To one of similar age, use his courtesy name (*zi*). Do not use "you." Use the same forms of address in writing letters.

In receiving visitors, follow a fixed procedure.

Whenever a guest asks to see the teacher, he is seated, and the one on duty for the day beats the block. All the students, dressed as they are, go into the hall, line up in order, and fold their hands in salutation. They stand in attendance on the teacher and his guest and withdraw when the order is given. If the guest wants to see someone among the students, he goes to his place and sees him after seeing the teacher. Do not be intimate with those not of your own kind.

In time that is free after studying, practice the arts that are suitable to the nature.

Playing the lute, shooting arrows, playing pitchpot—each has its conventions and rules. Do not play when it is not the time. Checkerboard games [gambling, *boyi*] are of the common run; one ought not to learn them oneself.

[*Cheng Dong er xiansheng xuece*, Zhengyitang ed., pp. 1–5 —RGC]

ZHEN DEXIU: "INSTRUCTIONS FOR CHILDREN"

In many early academies and in later collections of basic educational texts, this short work of Zhen Dexiu had almost canonical status, along with Zhu Xi's "Articles of the White Deer Grotto Academy" and the "School Code of Masters Cheng and Dong." If one recalls Zhen's stern rigorism [Ch. 22] one may understand how the highly restrained behavior prescribed here and in the School Code above added an element of stiff formality and constraint to the School of the Way, which became a mark of its distinctive behavior. Other Neo-Confucians reacted against this as contrary to the naturalism and spontaneity that the teaching also encouraged. (In this connection one might also recall that Confucians of the Han period were likewise ridiculed for their stiff formalism and overseriousness.)

1. Learning the rites: To be [truly] human, one must know the Way and its principles and the different ritual prescriptions. At home one must serve parents; at the academy one must serve his teacher. They are entitled to equal respect and compliance. Follow their instructions. Listen to what they say; do what they prescribe. Do not be lazy, careless, or presumptuous.

2. Learning to sit: Settle yourself and sit straight; control your hands and feet; do not sit cross-legged or lean on anything; do not lie back or lean down.

3. Learning to walk: Hold your arms in and walk slowly; do not swing your arms or jump about.

4. Learning to stand: Fold your hands and straighten your body; do not lean to one side or slouch over.

5. Learning to speak: Be plain and honest in your speech; do not lie or boast; speak softly and circumspectly; do not yell or shout.

6. Learning to bow [in salute]: Lower the head and bend at the waist; speak without gesticulating; do not be flippant or rude.

7. Learning to recite: Look at the characters with undivided attention; read slowly, short passages at a time; clearly distinguish, character by character; do not look at anything else or let your hands fiddle with anything.

8. Learning to write: Grasp the brush with firm intent; the characters must be balanced, regular, and perfectly clear; there must be no carelessness or messiness.

[*Yangzheng yigui* (SBBY) A:13a–14a — RGC]

ZHU XI'S READING METHOD

Zhu Xi's recommendations for reading, as codified by his followers and known as his reading method (*dushufa*), spread with his other teachings and the publication of his books throughout East Asia. These methods were also summarized in a short piece of Zhu's titled "Essentials of Reading" ("Dushu zhi yao"), found in his *Collected Writings*, and were further discussed in Zhu's *Classified Conversations* (*Yulei*). Indeed, they were even expounded in memorials to the throne. A large portion of the section on methods of self-cultivation in Zhu's *Elementary Learning* is devoted to the matter of reading methods and how they relate to one's inner self-development. Besides being incorporated into the "Daily Schedule of the Cheng Family School," they were included in the official Ming *Great Compendium of Human Nature and Principle* (*Xingli daquan*) and in numerous reformulations of these methods by Zhu Xi's successors. Modern historians of Chinese thought and education have acknowledged the wide influence of his study and reading methods.

Précis of the reading method as recorded by Fu Guang, a disciple of Zhu Xi:

Abide in reverent seriousness and keep to your resolve [to learn].

Make steady progress by following an orderly sequence.

Read carefully and with thoughtful discrimination.
Open your mind-and-heart; let the reading sink in.
Make it part of your own experience and self-examination.
Make an all-out effort to apply yourself in [daily] practice.

[Cheng Duanli, "Chengshi richeng" (CSJC) 1:7 — dB]

How to Read a Book (*Dushufa*)

Zhu Xi's reading method consists of his answers to questions about how to understand the *Analects* and *Mencius*, as well as the different interpretations of them put forward by Song scholars, which he had gathered together before writing his own commentary. Here again, for Zhu learning starts with one's own understanding of something, followed by corroboration from discussion with others, and not by simple reliance on authority.

With respect to Master Cheng's method for reading and interpreting these two texts, I have gathered together the essentials and set them forth at the beginning of the texts. The student should examine these sincerely, inquiring into them deeply and making a real effort [to understand]. Having finished both texts, one can discuss them together.

"What do you mean by real effort?" Answer: Making steady progress by following an orderly sequence; reading carefully and with thoughtful reflection. "What do you mean by 'making steady progress by following an orderly sequence'?" Answer: Speaking in reference to these two texts, it is first to read the *Analects* carefully before going on to the *Mencius*. [Again] speaking of the two, each has its own sequential order with regard to its beginning and end, chapter, section, and sentence structure; these should not be confused. As for "applying one's effort," one should do so according to a definite plan and keep strictly to it. One should ascertain the proper phonetic reading for each character and then the meaning of each phrase. If one has not accomplished the first, one cannot do the latter, and if one is not thorough about these things, one cannot hope to accomplish one's aim. But having made steady progress in an orderly sequence, then one's ideas become well defined and one's principles clear, so that there is no danger of carelessness and superficiality. Thus this is not only the way to read books[11] but the key to proper direction of one's mind-and-heart. This one cannot fail to understand as one takes up the pursuit of learning.

"What about 'reading carefully and with thoughtful reflection'?" Answer: A chapter of the *Analects* consists of no more than a few passages and is easy to learn by heart. Having memorized it, one should reflect upon it quietly at one's leisure and savor it, thus allowing it to sink in to the depths [of one's mind-and-

---

11. Or method of reading books.

heart]. In the *Mencius* each chapter consists of some thousands or hundreds of words, and the discussion goes back and forth, so it would seem to be an endless task, but there is a clear line of argument and its ideas are most clear, so if one keeps on reading and follows the thought, going back and forth over it a thousand times, then what seemed an endless task will begin to look within one's reach.

Generally speaking, in reading through a text, one should recite the words as if they were coming out of one's own mouth. Then, as one continues to give them thoughtful reflection, the ideas will seem to be coming from one's own mind-and-heart. At that point one has truly gotten it [for one's self].

If there is a passage the meaning of which is in doubt, and the various interpretations conflict, then with an open mind and quiet contemplation, while feeling in no hurry to choose between them, first let each saying speak to you on its own; then, following the thought wherever it may go and finding out whether it passes or there is some impediment to it. It will then become apparent what makes sense and what does not, without one's having to consult others' opinions. Moreover, in the case of conflicting interpretations, look to see where the principles lead and consider whether they are so or not so; then what seems so but actually is not, when brought out into the light of public discussion, will not stand up.

[Zhu Xi, *Wenji* 74:14a–15a —dB]

CHENG DUANMENG: A PRIMER OF HUMAN NATURE AND PRINCIPLE

"Primer" here refers to the learning of a basic vocabulary for understanding the teachings and practice of the "Learning of Human Nature and Principle." Since the "Daily Schedule" speaks of this as something to be studied before the age of eight, one must assume that the "learning" was more in the nature of raw memorization and recitation, with a fuller understanding of the concepts to come later. Certainly, for the modern reader it is both a challenge and a puzzle as to how much could be expected of Chinese seven-year-olds!

The work is attributed to Cheng Duanmeng (1143–1191) an associate of Zhu Xi (who gave it his approval) and coauthor of the school rules excerpted above. It is an example of a genre much in vogue in the Song: the lexicon, responding to the spread of printing and literacy, to an increasing awareness of the fluidity of language, changes in meanings, and the consequent need to define one's terms as a prerequisite for orderly, coherent discourse (an awareness also seen in the writings of such Song scholar-officials as Wang Anshi, Chen Qun, and Zhen Dexiu, among others).

Many of the terms included here have more than one connotation in English; hence the bracketed insertions.

Heaven's Principle, all-pervading, imbued in all things—this is called [Heaven's] "ordinance" (*ming*). The endowment received by all human beings, totally good — this is called the "human [moral] nature" (*xing*). Governing one's self, coordinating the nature and feelings — this is called "the mind-and-heart" (*xin*). Acting in response to things, expressing the desires of one's nature — this is called "the feelings." The qualities of one's nature, distinguished as hard and soft, strong and weak, good and evil — these are called "capacities" (*cai*).

The direction of the mind-and-heart, the goal toward which it is impelled and all that follows from this is called "one's resolve" (*zhi*): the spirit of [the power of] wood, in humans the principle of love, expressed in the feeling of commiseration — this is called "humaneness" (*ren*). The spirit of [the power of] metal, in humans the principle of propriety, expressed in feelings of shame and disgust — this is called [the sense of] "rightness" (*yi*). The spirit of fire, in humans the principle of respect expressing itself in the feeling of deference — this is called ritual decorum (*li*); the spirit of water, in humans the principle of differentiation, expressed in the feelings for right and wrong — this is called wisdom (*zhi*).

The normative principles of human relations and of things and affairs — these are called the Way (*Dao*). To act according to the Way, to take it to heart — this is called "virtue" (*de*). To be true and real, without deceit, this is called "sincerity" [genuineness, authenticity, *cheng*]. Never to act contrary to one's word — this is called "trustworthiness" (*xin*). To be true and give wholly of oneself — this is called "fidelity" [loyalty, *zhong*]. To infer from oneself and extend it to others — this is called "empathy" [reciprocity, *shu*]. To have no partiality — this is called "centrality" (*zhong*).

For one's feelings to be expressed in due measure — this is called "harmony" (*he*); to be single-minded without being obstinate — this is called "reverent seriousness" (*jing*); to have no doubleness, from beginning to end — this is called "oneness" [unity, *yi*]. To serve one's parents well — this is called "filiality" (*xiao*). To serve one's elders and older brothers well — this is called "deference to seniority" (*ti*).

Heaven's ordinance, flowing forth as the inherent natural principle, received as the human endowment, replete with the five innate virtues — this is called "Heaven's Principle" (*tianli*). Human nature responding to things and affairs, necessarily with feeling, operating through the senses as the movement of desire — this is called "human desire" (*renyu*). Doing things without selfish intent, in accordance with Heaven's Principle — this is called decorum (*li*). Doing things with selfish intent, as the self-centeredness of the desires — this is called "gain" (*li*).

Wholly pure and without duplicity, as the expression of Heaven's Principle — this is called "goodness" (*shan*). In violation of the Way, as the expression of what is not good — this is called "evil" (*e*). Self and others both illumined [looked out for], large-minded, and without [narrow] selfishness — this is called the sense of commonality [impartiality, *gong*]. Blinded by egotism, unable to manifest great impartiality — this is called selfishness (*si*).

All of these terms and teachings are the distillation of past experience. You little ones! Revere them, take them to heart! Observe these distinctions, deeply ponder their meanings, so as to grow to maturity; and as you encounter them in learning, inquiring, making judgments and fine distinctions, and putting them into exemplary practice, you may with untiring efforts advance to become a person of genuine worth and possibly even a sage!

[*Song Yuan xuean* 69:2279–80 — dB]

CHENG DUANLI: DAILY SCHEDULE OF STUDY IN THE CHENG FAMILY SCHOOL, GRADED ACCORDING TO AGE (*CHENGSHI JIASHU DUSHU FENNIAN RICHENG*)

Following is a much abridged version of the syllabus for the Cheng Family School, published in 1315. It became the model for many family schools and academies in late imperial China and was widely quoted in educational manuals. Even allowing for the abbreviation of many details here, the basic reading list as shown below is itself comparatively simplified in contrast to the extensive curriculum in Zhu Xi's "Personal Proposals," and its later stages are oriented much more toward preparation for the civil service examinations, which were resumed in the same year. No doubt Cheng thought of this simplified version as only a minor concession in order to achieve practical coordination between what was taught in the schools and what could realistically be incorporated into the new examination system. Accompanying notes show that he still subscribed to Zhu Xi's basic aims and expected that more mature scholars would supplement this and continue with Zhu's larger program of liberal learning — as he put it, "solid learning for the sake of one's self." Yet, both in his own time and often in later times, many serious scholars would complain that preparation for the exams came so to dominate men's minds that this larger goal was sadly neglected.

A. Before entering school at age eight
   [Assignment]
   The *Primer of Human Nature and Principle* [as above] (*Xingli zixun*).[12]
   [Method] Read the primer to learn three to five sections daily. . . .
      [Cheng Duanli, "Chengshi richeng" (*CSRC*) 1:1; Meskill, *Academies*, p. 160]

B. Age: Eight to fifteen.
   [Assignments]
   Elementary Learning, plain text. [That is, the text without commentary.]
   The *Great Learning*, classic and [original] commentary, plain text.
   Analects, plain text.
   Mencius, plain text.

---

12. Replacing the Tang period text *Mengqiu* and the *Thousand Character Classic* (*Qianziwen*).

The *Mean*, plain text.

Emended *Classic of Filiality* [as edited by Zhu Xi, who divided the old text into one section that he called the "classic" and fourteen sections called "commentary." He also deleted 223 characters, which he considered to be later additions to the original "classic" section].

Classic of Changes, plain text.

Classic of Documents, plain text.

Classic of Odes, plain text.

Ceremonial Rites (*Yili*) and *Record of Rites* (*Liji*), plain texts.

Rites of Zhou (*Zhouli*), plain text.

Spring and Autumn Annals, the classic and three commentaries, plain text.

[Method] Read each small section one hundred times; recite it one hundred times. Then recite a large section all the way through. Mornings, recite and review the book at the top of the list; evenings, recite and review in continual order the books already read. . . .

C. Age: Fifteen to twenty-two.

[Assignments]

The *Great Learning by Chapter and Phrase*; and Zhu Xi's *Answers to Questions on the Great Learning*

The *Analects* with collected annotations (*Lunyu jizhu*) [by Zhu Xi].

Mencius with collected annotations (*Mengzi jizhu*) [by Zhu Xi].

The *Mean by Chapter and Phrase* (*Zhongyong zhangju*); and [Zhu Xi's] *Answers to Questions on the Mean* (*Zhongyong huowen*).

[Method] Copy and read those portions of Zhu Xi's *Answers to Questions on the Analects* (*Lunyu huowen*) that correspond to the collected annotations.

Copy and read those portions of *Answers to Questions on the Mencius* (*Mengzi huowen*) that correspond to the collected annotations.

Copy and read one's [chosen] classic among the *Classic of Changes, Classic of Documents, Classic of Odes, Record of Rites*, and *Spring and Autumn Annals*.

["Chengshi richeng," 1:1–14; Meskill, pp. 160–161]

[Method] Chart Number 1 may be used.

Chart Number 1. Daily Schedule of Reading the Classics

Student's Name: Date:

Note: Fill in up to amount read each day. Nine days is one cycle.

Daily Schedule

1. First let the student recite books already read at the head of the list, going as far as the book read the previous day for one round.

2. Recitation before the teacher from the books read the previous day.

3. Personal receipt of the book for the day. . . . The characters are counted and the large sections marked out. . . . The large sections are divided into small

sections. . . . Let the student mark off a section in red . . . let him read each small section that has been corrected as to punctuation and pronunciation; and let him explain before the teacher [from the gloss?] the meaning of the faulty texts corrected.

4. Let the student read each small section from the book two hundred times and then recite it one hundred times. When he has completed that, a passage is selected and the student tested on reciting it and its corrections [from the gloss?]. [When he passes] the red marker is to be covered over with black and a following section marked. When a certain number of sections have been completed, let him recite and be tested on a large section all the way through.

5. Passages are selected from the books thought over during the evening and the student tested.

6. Personal elucidation of books already read. Let the student repeat the explanation of the general meaning and be tested on errors.

7. Nights of odd-numbered days: thinking over of books read. Also thinking over of books on the nature and principle.

8. Nights of even-numbered days: reciting in order all the books that have been read regularly during the round. Also reviewing books on the nature and principle.

9. Free day. Copy standard texts, punctuate phrases, and make tone marks on characters [that are capable of being read in more than one tone].

["Chengshi richeng," 1:2–7; Meskill, pp. 162–163]

Age: Fifteen to twenty-two [continued].

[Assignments]

Peruse *The Comprehensive Mirror for Aid in Governance* (*Zizhi tongjian*) [Sima Guang's comprehensive history, taken as a model of historical writing].

[Method] Chart Number 2 may be used. [Deleted here.]

[Assignments] Read Han [Yu's] works. [As a model of style.]

[Method] Chart Number 3 may be used. [Deleted here.]

[Assignment] Next read the *Chuci*, with Zhu Xi's commentary.

["Chengshi richeng," 2:15; Meskill, p. 162]

D. Age: Twenty-two to twenty-five.

Method of learning to write examination essays [using method of Zhen Dexiu]:

Read aloud and peruse recent essays on themes from the classics and the "Answers to questions" for nine days. Write [your own] for one day. Read aloud and peruse recent essays on the meaning of the classics [*jingyi*, i.e., the prescribed form of examination essay] for nine days. Write [your own] for one day. Read aloud and peruse old-style rhyme-prose pieces for nine days. Write [your own] for one day. Read aloud and peruse edicts, proclamations, and memorials for nine days. Write [your own] for one day. Read aloud and peruse problem essays [*ce*] for nine days. Write [your own] for one day.

["Chengshi richeng," 2:22; Meskill, p. 162]

[Method] Chart Number 4. Daily Schedule of Reading and Composition for the Examinations
[Note:] Every day fill in as far as has been done: read, examined, copied, and punctuated.
[Assignments]

Day	Morning	After Dinner	Evening
1–6	Read in order, the Four Books, Classics, commentaries, annotations, and "Answers to questions."	Read compositions of the type of the First Session [in the examinations] and books on the nature and principle, systems, ways of government, and ancient precedents. Go through them and begin again.	Following the forms in the *Sanchang silei pianchao* [Compilation of the four genres in the three exam sessions], mark notable passages with circles and dots and make deletions and cuts.
7–9	Review Classics, *Lisao* and Han [Yu's] works.		
10	Write a paper for the first session.		Revise what you have written.

["Chengshi richeng," 2:40–41; Meskill, p. 164]

Note: From an egalitarian point of view the virtue and success of Cheng Duanli's basic syllabus, coordinated with the examination system, was that it established a process and standard widely available to everyone who could hope to follow this method anywhere in the empire, whatever his personal circumstances. From the point of view of those who were concerned about maintaining high standards of scholarship, leadership, and public responsibility, there remained a question as to how much real "merit" (or mediocrity) attached to this kind of meritocracy, based on such routinization of learning.

WOMEN'S EDUCATION

Education in traditional China was always male-oriented, but women's roles in the households, especially those of the ruling elite and the imperial family, were of such importance that much attention was given to their training for family roles and responsibilities. Moreover, since women played a key role in the early education of the young, it was essential for mothers and their female surrogates (grandmothers, aunts, older sisters) to achieve a mastery of the classical texts and primers that they taught to the young males before the latter went off to school. Often great scholars and historical figures paid tribute, on this account, to the women whose educational influence had been crucial in their lives. Further, in the days when the transmission of classical learning was largely in the custody of particular families, there were spectacular cases of women in those families who ensured the perpetuation of the family tradition when no male was available or capable of carrying on. Thus education for women was strongly abetted by the centrality of the family and requirements of family life.

Women's education achieved a new level of importance with the rise of the Song learning and its Neo-Confucian extensions in the Ming, marked by the great spread of printing, literacy, and schooling. As we have seen, Zhu Xi's simplification and recodification of the classic Confucian canon had much to do with the propagation of the new culture, and it is not surprising that his Four Books (the *Great Learning*, the *Mean*, the *Analects*, and the *Mencius*) became the pretext for a similar compilation in the Ming of the Four Books for Women (*Nü sishu*). These consisted of Ban Zhao's Han period work *Admonitions for Women* (*Nüjie*); two Tang texts, the *Classic of Filiality for Women* (*Nü xiaojing*) and Song Rozhao's *Analects for Women* (*Nü lunyu*); and the Ming Empress Xu's *Instructions for the Inner Quarters* (*Neixun*). Later, during the Kangxi period in the Qing, a certain Wang Xiang substituted an instructional text written by his mother, *A Handy Record of Rules for Women* (*Nüfan jielu*), for the *Nü xiaojing*, and it is his grouping that has come down to us in most editions.

The female authors of these texts, each in her own distinctive way, sought to advise other women on the Confucian Way for women, the *fudao*, or "wifely way." They accept the general assumption in Confucianism that all humans, male and female, operate in a highly contextual world of hierarchical relationships where behavior is dictated by detailed codes of ritual propriety. In addition, they accept the particular roles assigned to women according to the Confucian sense of their position in the cosmic and human orders. Like the earth, which occupies the inferior position below, women are to be subservient, passive, and yielding, while men are to be dominant, active, and strong like the superior force of Heaven. A woman's sphere of activity is the family, the family of her husband, and her duties in marriage are to assist her husband in serving his family in its broadest terms, that is, to honor the family's dead ancestors with periodic sacrifices, to obey and care for the husband's living parents, and to assist in the procreation of new life to keep the family's bloodline going.

Though the authors of these texts take the subservient but central role of women as their starting point, each has different aspects to emphasize and different ways of approaching the reader. The focus of this section will be on the content of these texts and the variety of articulations of the "wifely Way" found in them. Further work needs to be done on such matters as their historical context and readership. Suffice it to say for now that the texts are written in a fairly literary style with frequent allusions to classical texts, which would indicate that they were meant for women of elite, leisured, cultured families. Eventually, however, much of their content did filter down to a broader audience in such popular rhyming primers as the *Elementary Learning for Women* (*Nü xiaoxue*) and the *Three Character Classic for Girls* (*Nüer sanzijing*).

BAN ZHAO: *ADMONITIONS FOR WOMEN* (*NÜJIE*)

This text was written during the Latter Han dynasty, when Confucianism became established state teaching and attempts were made to bring women into the mainstream of the tradition. One of the first such attempts was by the scholar Liu Xiang (79–8 B.C.E.), who compiled the *Biographies of Virtuous Women* (*Lienü zhuan*).[13] Ban Zhao's work represents a second.

Ban Zhao (48?–116? C.E.), author of *Admonitions for Women*, was a highly educated woman, publicly recognized for her scholarship and intellect. She was called to court to tutor the women of the imperial family and also was instrumental in completing the dynastic history of the Former Han, which her brother left unfinished upon his death. Indeed, the volume and variety of her writings are impressive and leave no doubt that she served as the mainstay of her family's tradition of learning. In the preface to her *Admonitions for Women*, excerpts of which follow, she explains the circumstances and her motive for writing them. Other excerpts from the text emphasize wifely virtues but also the need for women to be treated with respect acccording to the rites. Education should not be for males only.

Preface

This lowly one is ignorant and by nature unclever. I was favored because of my ancestry and, relying on the teachings of governess and instructress, at fourteen I clutched dustbasket and broom [as a young wife] in the Cao household. Now more than forty years have passed . . . and at last I am released [from such duties]. . . .

Yet I am anxious for you, [my daughters] who are about to marry and have not been instructed over the course of time nor heard about proper behavior for wives. I dread that you will lose face [when you are living behind] another's gate and bring shame on our lineage. . . . Whenever I think of you like this, I am fearful and anxious and so have written these "Admonitions for Women" in seven sections. . . . Now that it is done, I urge you to study them. . . .

---

13. An English translation of this text is available in Albert O'Hara, *The Position of Women in Early China* (Washington, D.C.: Catholic University Press, 1945).

Humility

On the third day after the birth of a girl, the ancients observed three customs: [first] for three days to place the baby below the bed; [second] to give her a spindle with which to play; and [third] to fast and announce her birth to her ancestors by an offering. Now to lay the baby below the bed plainly indicated that she was lowly and humble and should regard it as a prime duty to submit to others. To give her a spindle with which to play signified that she should accustom herself to labor and consider it a prime duty to be industrious. To announce her birth before her ancestors clearly meant that she ought to esteem it a prime duty to see to the continuation of the ancestral sacrifices.

These three ancient customs epitomize a woman's ordinary way of life and the teachings of the rites and regulations. Let a woman modestly yield to others; let her respect others; let her put others first, herself last. Should she do something good, let her not mention it; should she do something bad, let her not deny it. Let her bear contempt; let her even endure when others speak or do evil to her. Always let her seem to tremble and to fear. [When a woman follows such maxims as these] then she may be said to humble herself before others.

Let a woman retire late to bed, but rise early to her duties; let her not dread tasks by day or by night. Let her not refuse to perform domestic duties whether easy or difficult. That which must be done, let her finish completely, tidily, and systematically. [When a woman follows such rules as these] then she may be said to be industrious.

Let a woman be composed in demeanor and upright in bearing in the service of her husband. Let her live in purity and quietness [of spirit] and keep watch over herself. Let her not love gossip and silly laughter. Let her cleanse, purify, and arrange in order the wine and the food for the offerings to the ancestors. [Observing such principles as these] is what it means to continue the ancestral rites. . . .

Husband and Wife

Note in the following passage that though the wife's role is clearly subordinate, the complementarity and mutual responsibility of the conjugal relationship are stressed; if the wife as the embodiment of softness is to be compliant, the husband as the embodiment of strength is obliged to be self-controlled and not beat his wife. Further, the indispensability of one to the other becomes the ground for Ban Zhao's question: Isn't education as necessary for women as for men?

The Way of husband and wife is intimately connected with yin and yang and relates the individual to gods and ancestors. Truly it confirms the great principle of Heaven and Earth and the great rule of human relationships. Therefore the *Rites* honor the interrelation of man and woman; and in the

Odes the first Ode manifests the principle of marriage. For these reasons the relationship cannot but be an important one.

If a husband be unworthy, then he possesses nothing by which to control his wife. If a wife be unworthy, then she possesses nothing with which to serve her husband. If a husband does not control his wife, then he loses his authority. If a wife does not serve her husband, then right principles [the natural order] are neglected and destroyed. As a matter of fact, in practice these two [the controlling of women by men and the serving of men by women] work out in the same way.

Now examine the gentlemen of the present age. They only know that wives must be controlled and that the husband's authority must be maintained. They therefore teach their boys to read books and [study] histories. But they do not in the least understand how husbands and masters are to be served or how rites and right principles are to be maintained.

Yet only to teach men and not to teach women — is this not ignoring the reciprocal relation between them? According to the *Rites*, book learning begins at the age of eight, and at the age of fifteen one goes off to school. Why, however, should this principle not apply to girls as well as boys?

Respect and Compliance

As yin and yang are not of the same nature, so man and woman differ in behavior. The virtue of yang is firmness; yin is manifested in yielding. Man is honored for strength; a woman is beautiful on account of her gentleness. Hence there arose the common saying, "A man born as a wolf may, it is feared, become a woman; a woman born as a mouse may, it is feared, become a tigress."

Now for self-cultivation there is nothing like respectfulness. To avert harshness there is nothing like compliance. Consequently it can be said that the Way of respect and compliance is for women the most important element in ritual decorum. . . .

[If a wife] does not restrain her contempt for her husband, then it will be followed by scolding and shouting [from him]. [If a husband] does not restrain his anger, then there is certain to be beating [of the wife]. The correct relationship between husband and wife is based upon harmony and intimacy, and [conjugal] love is grounded in proper union. If it comes to blows, how can the proper relationship be preserved? If sharp words are spoken, how can [conjugal] love exist? If love and proper relationship are both destroyed, then husband and wife are parted.

Womanly Behavior

In womanly behavior there are four things [to be considered]: womanly virtue, womanly speech, womanly appearance, and womanly work. . . .

To guard carefully her chastity, to control circumspectly her behavior, in every motion to exhibit modesty, and to model each act on the best usage: this may be called womanly virtue.

To choose her words with care, to avoid vulgar language, to speak at appropriate times, and not to be offensive to others may be called womanly speech.

To wash and scrub dirt and grime, to keep clothes and ornaments fresh and clean, to wash the head and bathe the body regularly, and to keep the person free from disgraceful filth may be called womanly appearance.

With wholehearted devotion to sew and weave, not to love gossip and silly laughter, in cleanliness and order [to prepare] the wine and food for serving guests may be called womanly work.

[*Hou Hanshu*, 84, Chunghua ed., 2786–2789; rev. from Swann, *Pan Chao*, pp. 82–86]

Note that here, even though Ban Zhao preaches submission and dedication to her husband, the husband at least counts. Later, serving the husband himself becomes subordinate to caring for his parents. Also, for all the talk about submission to the husband, Ban Zhao has a greater sense of the complementary nature of marriage than later writers in this genre, who tend to put greater stress on the hierarchical nature of the relationship.

This text later became the prototype of other instructional texts for women, and Ban Zhao became canonized as the archetypal female wisdom figure, so much so that the authors of the two texts we examine next adopt Ban Zhao's voice rather than their own as the principal speaker.

MADAM CHENG: *CLASSIC OF FILIALITY FOR WOMEN (NÜ XIAOJING)*

In the Tang period the two most popular Confucian texts were the *Analects* and the *Classic of Filiality* (*Xiaojing*); thus it is not surprising that the two female authors of instructional texts for women written during this period would draw on these titles for their works, the *Analects for Women* and the *Classic of Filiality for Women*.

The first of these was written by the wife of a Tang official, Chen Miao, whose own family name was Cheng. She presented it to her niece upon her impending marriage to a Tang prince.

The text opens with Ban Zhao sitting at leisure, attended by a group of women. She asks them if they have heard about the greatness of filiality, especially as exemplified by the two wives of Shun, and how its practice by women consists of mastering the *fudao*, or "wifely way." The women confess their ignorance and beg her to instruct them in these matters. In the instructions that follow, the most striking feature is the extraordinary moral influence and leadership role attributed to women in the domestic sphere, particularly with respect to their husbands. Service to a husband goes beyond obedience and deference to him; it includes responsibility for his moral character and the obligation of firm remonstrance lest he go wrong — points already made in the *Classic of Filiality* and the formulas of the *Three Mainstays*.

Her ladyship [Ban Zhao] said, "By studying [the classics] with thoroughness, questioning with deep penetration, and 'hearing much and casting aside the doubtful parts,'[14] one can serve as a standard for others. If you are willing to heed such teachings and incorporate them into your behavior, I will set them forth for you. Now filiality embraces Heaven and Earth and enriches all human relationships. It moves ghosts and spirits and affects birds and animals. 'Show respect according to the dictates of propriety';[15] 'think three times and then act.'[16] Do not relax your efforts, do not harm your goodness. Be affable and gentle, modest and deferential, humane and understanding, filial and affectionate. Then you will have perfectly embodied correct moral behavior and be without blame. . . . [15a–b]

The next several sections, deleted here, discuss the "wifely Way" for the empress, the wives of high officials, the wives of feudal lords, and those of common people — paralleling the original text of the Classic of Filiality. *Also, in parallel to the latter, each set of precepts ends with a quotation from the* Odes, Record of Rites, *or some other classic — also not reproduced here.*

Serving One's Parents-in-Law

In serving her parents-in-law, a woman gives the same respect [to her father-in-law that] she has shown her own father and the same love [to her mother-in-law that] she has shown her own mother. She keeps to this in accord with rightness and holds to it in accord with the rites. At cock-crow, she washes and dresses to start the morning off early. She makes sure her parents-in-law are cool in summer and warm in winter. She settles them in at night and checks on them first thing in the morning.[17] She uses "reverence to straighten the inner life and rightness to square the outer."[18] She establishes an order for the proper household rituals and then carries them out. . . . [17a]

The Three Powers

Referring to men and women as counterparts of and co-respondents to Heaven and Earth.

---

14. *Analects* 2:18.
15. *Analects* 1:13.
16. *Analects* 5:19.
17. "Summary of the Rules of Propriety" ("Quli"), *Record of Rites* A:2; Legge, *Li Ki*, 1:67.
18. *Classic of Changes*, hexagram 2, *kun*.

Guard against idleness, hold fast to ritual decorum, and you will be able to make a successful marriage. Then, by your guiding of him with respect and love, your gentleman [husband] will not forget his sense of filiality to his parents. By your presenting him with a model of virtuous conduct, he will improve his behavior. By your guiding of him with a sense of modesty and deference, he will refrain from being contentious. By your leading him on with rites and music, he will become pleasant and easy to get along with. By your demonstrating the difference between good and evil, he will understand what conduct is not allowable. . . . [17a–b]

Governing Through Filiality

Her ladyship said, "The virtuous women of ancient times used filiality to govern the nine degrees of familial relations. They never dared demean the younger wives; how much more solicitous were they about their sisters-in-law! Therefore, they won the hearts of the whole family, which made it possible for parents-in-law to be well served. In managing the household, they dared not mistreat the chickens and dogs; how much more careful were they about the servants! Therefore, they were able to please all, high and low, which made it possible for husbands to be better served. . . . [17b–18a]

Chaste Behavior

Her ladyship said, "What a woman must take seriously is her person, for it is the source of all her actions. One who is good at cultivating her person[19] will correct her thoughts, keep a careful watch over her motives, hold firmly to moral standards, and not allow one iota of selfishness to entangle her. She commits herself to correctness and composure, not erring even a little bit. She does not allow considerations of life and death to change her resolve, nor let the prospects of living in affluence or poverty affect her commitment to chastity. . . .

The Duty of Remonstrance

Note here how the duty of remonstrance takes precedence over obedience, as it does for the minister vis-à-vis the ruler.

The women said, ". . . We dare to ask whether if we follow all our husbands' commands, we could be called virtuous?"

Her ladyship answered, "What kind of talk is that! What kind of talk is that!

---

19. *Xiushen*, i.e., self-cultivation.

Long ago, King Xuan of Zhou was late rising to attend his court, so his wife threw down her jewels in the public tribunal [to take the blame]. King Xuan because of this started getting up early again. Emperor Cheng of the Han ordered his concubine to ride out with him, but she refused, saying, 'I have heard that in the Three Dynasties, wise rulers took only their worthy officials by their side. I never heard of them taking their concubines.' Because of her, Emperor Cheng changed his manner. . . .

From these cases, we can see that "if the Son of Heaven has ministers to advise him, even if he is neglectful of the Way, he won't lose his empire. If a lord has remonstrating officials, then even if he is neglectful of the Way, he won't lose his state. If a great officer has someone to remonstrate with him, then even if he is neglectful of the Way, he won't lose his home domain. If a scholar has a remonstrating friend, then he can't be parted from his good name. If a father has a remonstrating son, then he won't fall prey to what is against moral standards."[20] If a husband has a remonstrating wife, then he won't fall into evil ways. Therefore, if a husband transgresses against the Way, you must correct him. How could it be that to obey your husband in everything would make you a virtuous person?"

[*Nü xiaojing, xia*, 15a–21b — TK]

SONG RUOZHAO: *ANALECTS FOR WOMEN*

Song Ruozhao, author of the *Analects for Women*, was the second of five daughters of a high Tang official, Song Fen. According to her biography in the *Tang History*, her elder sister, Ruohua, actually wrote the text, but Ruozhao was the one who propagated it. She made it clear that she wished not to marry but rather to dedicate her life to the example of Ban Zhao in the work of instructing women. After an audience with the Emperor Dezong in the late eighth century, she was made a female scholar at court, assigned to instruct the royal princesses.

The importance of this text lies in its specificity of detail in spelling out the basic Confucian way of wifely perfection for those women needing more explicit guidance. By virtue of its practical approach, the *Analects for Women* was widely used and, along with Ban Zhao's *Admonitions for Women*, remained the most popular and influential instructional text for women in premodern times.

Establishing Oneself as a Person

To be a woman, you must first learn how to establish yourself as a person. The way to do this is simply by working hard to establish one's purity and

---

20. The preceding passage is quoted, though not verbatim, from the *Classic of Filiality* (*Xiao-jing*). See ch. 10.

chastity. By purity, one keeps one's self undefiled; by chastity, one preserves one's honor.

When walking, don't turn your head; when talking, don't open your mouth wide; when sitting, don't move your knees; when standing, don't rustle your skirts; when happy, don't exult with loud laughter; when angry, don't raise your voice. The inner and outer quarters are each distinct; the sexes should be segregated. Don't peer over the outer wall or go beyond the outer courtyard. If you have to go outside, cover your face; if you peep outside, conceal yourself as much as possible. Do not be on familiar terms with men outside the family; have nothing to do with women of bad character. Establish your proper self so as to become a [true] human being.

Learning How to Work

To be a woman one must learn the details of women's work. Learn how to weave with hemp and ramie; don't mix fine and rough fibers. Don't run the shuttle of the loom so quickly that you make a mess. When you see the silkworms spinning their cocoons, you must attend to them day and night, picking mulberry leaves to feed them. . . . Learn how to cut out shoes and make socks. Learn how to cut fabric and sew it into garments. Learn how to embroider, mend, and darn. . . .

Do not learn the ways of lazy women who from an early age are silly and shiftless and who have a distaste for women's work. They don't plan ahead in making clothes to fit the needs of each season and hardly ever pick up a needle to sew. . . . Married, they bring shame upon their new family, who go around in ill-fitted, patched, and ragged clothing, so that meeting others they are pointed to as the laughingstock of the neighborhood. . . .

Ritual Decorum: Learning Proper Etiquette

To be a woman one must learn the rules of ritual decorum. When you expect a female guest, carefully clean and arrange the furniture and tea implements. When she arrives, take time to adjust your clothing, and then, with light steps and your hands drawn up in your sleeves, walk slowly to the door and with lowered voice, invite her in. Ask after her health and how her family is doing. Be attentive to what she says. After chatting in a leisurely way, serve the tea. When she leaves, send her off in a proper manner. . . .

If you are invited to someone's house, understand your female duties and help with the preparation of the tea. After having talked for a time, rise to leave. Don't overstay your welcome. If your hostess presses you to stay longer to share a meal, conduct yourself with propriety. Don't drink so much that your face turns red and you get sloppy in the handling of your chopsticks. Take your leave before all the food is gone and before you forget your manners. . . .

Rising Early [to Begin Household Work]

To be a woman one must learn to make it a regular practice, at the fifth watch when the cock crows, to rise and dress. After cleaning your face and teeth, fix your hair and makeup simply. Then go to the kitchen, light the fire, and start the morning meal. Scrub the pots and wash the pans; boil the tea water and cook the gruel. Plan your meals according to the resources of the family and the seasons of the year, making sure that they are fragrant and tasty, served in the appropriate dishes and in the proper manner at the table. If you start early, there is nothing you can't get done in a day!

Do not learn the ways of those lazy women who are thoughtless and do not plan ahead. The sun is already high in the sky before they manage to get themselves out of bed. Then they stagger to the kitchen, disheveled and unwashed, and throw a meal together, long past the hour. What is more, they are overly fond of eating and compete to get the tastiest morsels at each meal. If there is not enough of the best to go around, they steal some to eat later on the sly. Their inconsiderate manners are displayed to all their neighbors, to the humiliation of their parents-in-law. Talked about by everyone, how can they not be overcome with shame!

Serving One's Parents-in-Law

Your father-in-law and mother-in-law are the heads of your husband's family. . . . You must care for them as your own father and mother. Respectfully serve your father-in-law. Do not look at him directly [when he speaks to you], do not follow him around, and do not engage him in conversation. If he has an order for you, listen and obey.

When your mother-in-law is sitting, you should stand. When she gives an order, you should carry it out right away. Rise early in the morning and open up the household, but don't make any noise that would disturb your mother-in-law's sleep. Sweep and mop the floors, wash and rinse the clothes. When your mother-in-law wakes up, present her with her toiletry articles, withdraw while she bathes until she beckons you. Greet her and then withdraw. Prepare tea and broth; set out spoons and chopsticks. As long known, the aged have poor teeth, so you should be especially careful in the preparation of food for them, so that they might enjoy their old age with all sorts of delicacies, cooked in a manner that allows them to be easily chewed and swallowed. At night before retiring, check to see if they are comfortably settled for the night. Bid them good night and then go to bed. . . .

Serving a Husband

Women leave their families to marry, and the husband is the master of the household [they marry into]. . . . The husband is to be firm, the wife soft;

conjugal affections follow from this. While at home, the two of you should treat each other with the formality and reserve of a guest. Listen carefully to and obey whatever your husband tells you. If he does something wrong, gently correct him. Don't be like those women who not only do not correct their husbands but actually lead them into indecent ways. . . . Don't imitate those shrewish wives who love to clash head on with their husbands all the time. Take care of your husband's clothing so that he is never cold in winter, and of his meals so that he never gets thin and sickly from not being fed enough. As a couple, you and your husband share the bitter and the sweet, poverty and riches. In life you share the same bed; in death the same grave. . . .

Instructing Sons and Daughters

Most all families have sons and daughters. As they grow and develop, there should be a definite sequence and order in their education. But the authority/responsibility to instruct them rests solely with the mother. When the sons go out to school, they seek instruction from a teacher who teaches them proper [ritual] form and etiquette, how to chant poetry, how to write essays. . . .

Daughters remain behind in the women's quarters and should not be allowed to go out very often. . . . Teach them sewing, cooking, and etiquette. . . . Don't allow them to be indulged, lest they throw tantrums to get their own way; don't allow them to defy authority, lest they become rude and haughty; don't allow them to sing songs, lest they become dissolute; and don't allow them to go on outings, lest some scandal spoil their good names.

Worthy of derision are those who don't take charge of their responsibility [in this area]. The sons of such women remain illiterate, they poke fun at their elders, they get into fights and drink too much, and they become addicted to singing and dancing. . . . The daughters of such women know nothing about ritual decorum, speak in an overbearing manner, can't distinguish between the honorable and the mean, and don't know how to serve or sew. They bring shame on their honorable relatives and disgrace on their father and mother. Mothers who fail to raise their children correctly are as if they had raised pigs and rats!

Managing the Household

A woman who manages the household should be thrifty and diligent. If she is diligent, the household thrives; if lazy, it declines. If she is thrifty, the household becomes enriched; if extravagant, it becomes impoverished. . . . If your husband has money and rice, store and conserve them. If he has wine or foodstuffs, save and keep them for the use of guests when they come; do not take any to indulge your own desires. Great wealth is a matter of fate and fortune; a little wealth comes from persistent thrift. . . . Thus a couple may be blessed with riches and enjoy life.

Entertaining Guests

Most families have guests. You should have hot water and clean bottles, and keep the table clean and neat, ready for guests. When a guest arrives, serve him tea and then retire to the rear of the hall and await your husband's orders about the meal. . . .

Don't learn the ways of the lazy woman who doesn't attend to household matters anyway, so that when a guest arrives, the place is in a mess and she is unprepared to offer him tea right away. She is so flustered that she loses her head. If her husband asks the guest to stay for a meal, she is annoyed and loses her temper. She has chopsticks but no soup spoons, soy sauce but no vinegar. She scolds and slaps the servants around, to her husband's great chagrin and the guest's embarrassment.

[Nü sishu, Nü lunyu 2:1a–16b — TK]

EMPRESS XU: *INSTRUCTIONS FOR THE INNER QUARTERS (NEIXUN)*

The title of this work is suggestive of the carefully defined and limited sphere of women's allowable activity. The author, however, was no ordinary woman. She was the Empress Xu, wife of the third Ming emperor, Chengzu (or Yongle, r. 1402–1424), and daughter of the famous general Xu Da, who served under the founder of the dynasty. A redoubtable figure in her own right, she is described in the dynastic annals as a strong character, and as such was accorded a place of her own in the *Dictionary of Ming Biography*, which called her "a strong-willed and colorful person, with some of her father's spirit."[21]

At a time when Neo-Confucian teachings were giving a vital impetus to education, Empress Xu became dissatisfied with the conventional literature available for the cultivation of women and aimed to produce a guide of her own, based on the personal instruction she had received from her mother-in-law, the Empress Ma,[22] wife of the dynasty's founder, Ming Taizu. In contrast to the stereotype of the arbitrary and abusive mother-in-law in China, Empress Ma was much admired by the later Empress Xu as a firm but humane and sympathetic mentor.

As a peasant woman married early to Taizu before his rise to power, the future Empress Ma was, like him, largely self-educated and eventually quite well read (not an altogether uncommon thing in traditional China, for many women did overcome the handicap imposed by a lack of formal schooling, just

---

21. Biography by Chou Tao-chi and Ray Huang, in *Dictionary of Ming Biography* (hereafter *DMB*), pp. 566–569.

22. *Mingshi* 128:3784–3788; biography by Chou Tao-chi, in *DMB*, pp. 1023–1026; and biography of Hsü Ta (Xu Da) by Edward L. Farmer, in *DMB*, p. 606.

as Ming Taizu himself did). Moreover, as an empress, with several daughters-in-law under her charge, she conducted regular study groups on the classics for the women of the palace.

Taizu himself, as we have seen, was well known for his despotic rule, his hot temper, his violence and cruelty, his bloody purges, and his suspiciousness and vindictiveness toward any who opposed him or whom he suspected of treason. Yet there are numerous stories about how Empress Ma remonstrated with and restrained him, saving the lives of many who were unjustly accused. Such was the case when Taizu turned against one of his foremost Neo-Confucian advisers, Song Lian (1310–1381),[23] and ordered his execution. Empress Ma defended Song and got his sentence reduced to exile. In another significant case, when Taizu complained about Empress Ma's interference in state affairs, she refused to back off, saying that just as he had responsibilities as Father of the country, so was she as its Mother entitled to be concerned about the welfare of her children. Thus she turned the family/state analogy into one that set paternal and maternal care nearly on a par, with the latter a definite counterweight to the former. Empress Ma died a natural death after many others in the emperor's service had suffered unnatural ones, and she was said to have been deeply mourned by Taizu, who did not replace her as empress (and earlier defended her strongly for not having bound feet).

Empress Ma's view of her larger social responsibilities seems to have taken deep root in the consciousness of Empress Xu and pervades virtually all of the *Instructions for the Inner Quarters*, at each successive stage of which the "inner" or restricted conception of a woman's role gives way to a more expansive one. For anyone with a sensitivity to its Neo-Confucian meanings, the *Neixun* may be recognized as far from a rehash of conventional views covering the place of women in the home. Indeed, the very structure and thematic development of the work are reminiscent of the Neo-Confucian genre of instruction to rulers and noble men as found in Zhu Xi's memorials and lectures to the emperor, his *Reflections on Things at Hand*, *Elementary Learning*, and *Commentary on the Great Learning* and Zhen Dexiu's lectures from the Classics Mat, as well as the latter's monumental *Extended Meaning of the Great Learning*.

The opening portion deals with women's self-cultivation. Yet instead of leading off with a gendered presentation of the strictly defined role of the woman (and most often of the wife in the home), the previous basis established here for any such role-playing or modeling is the making of a human self and the shaping of a human life, based on the Neo-Confucian principle of the shared moral nature in all human beings: "If you do not cultivate your own moral character, then your chances of managing your own family will be slim, how much less of your bringing order into the world" (3:7a). From this, the work goes on to many specific prescriptions on how this cultivation is to be accom-

---

23. *Mingshi* 128:3784–3788; biography by F. W. Mote, in *DMB*, pp. 1225–1231.

plished in the woman's case, paralleling what is set forth for men in Zhu's *Elementary Learning*. Yet the thought that a woman should undertake this with the ultimate goal of "bringing order into the world" suggests how far beyond the confines of the home goes the aspiration for this Neo-Confucian education.

Subsequent chapters cite historical examples of women who played major roles in assisting founders of dynasties and great rulers in governing well (much as Fan Ziyu's *Learning of the Emperors* credits great scholar-mentors in similar roles). The standout case is, of course, Empress Ma. With such models to emulate, it is not too much, says Empress Xu, for women to aspire even to sagehood. Contrary to a widespread view that only men could achieve this goal, Empress Xu argued that all humans, female as well as male, have the same innate Heavenly endowment of a moral nature, which represents the potential for sagehood. It is a gift not just to certain specially favored persons or just to men, but something anyone could hope to achieve through learning — echoing the assertion of Zhou Dunyi in his *Tongshu,* and prominently quoted in Zhu Xi's *Reflections on Things at Hand,* that sagehood can be learned and should be striven for by all.

Altogether, this is a thoroughly Neo-Confucian work. Taking full advantage of literary genres and concepts developed by Song Neo-Confucians and of their doctrines as synthesized by Zhu Xi, it argues the case for women's education and their participation in the *Great Learning*'s social program, which proceeds from self-cultivation to the managing of the family, the ordering of the state, and the bringing of peace to the world. This is not at all to say that, for the Empresses Ma and Xu, the way for women is the same as for men, but that women could and should play a major active role in pursuing Neo-Confucian goals and thereby achieving their own self-fulfillment in some approximation of sagehood.

Finally, it should be emphasized that this woman's "classic" illustrates for us some of the ironies and ambiguities of the Confucian social involvement in general. On the one hand, as one of the Four Books for Women, it has a claim to some of the same canonical status as Zhu Xi's Four Books, and one could take it — in the absence of any serious rivals — as probably the most authoritative statement of a Neo-Confucian education program for women. We know, too, that it had considerable currency in Korea and Japan as well. On the other hand, we recognize it as an ideal prescription that could not at all be taken as a reliable description of conduct prevailing among women. That is not the function of classics and canons; they do not imitate life so much as propose models to emulate; thus there is always a discrepancy or tension between the two.

Preface

As a child, I was well instructed by my parents, reciting such classics as the *Classic of Odes* and the *Classic of Documents* and carrying out the details of women's work. On account of the accumulated goodness and blessings of our ancestors, I by chance was chosen to enter the imperial harem. Morning and night, I served at court. The Empress Ma instructed all the wives of her sons, especially in the area of proper decorum and ritual. I respectfully accepted and tried to carry out her orders. Every day I received instructions from her, respectfully obeyed them, not daring to transgress even one of her rules.

I have respectfully served the present [Yongle] Emperor for thirty-some years. In doing so, I have tried to carry out completely my predecessor's [Empress Ma's] wishes by putting into practice her teachings on governance of the inner palace. . . .

I often read accounts in the histories, searching for virtuous wives and chaste women of the past. Although they are all praised for the greatness of their [innate] moral nature, still none among them has succeeded without having had some instruction. With the ancients, education had to have some method to it. [According to the *Record of Rites*,] boys at the age of eight entered elementary school and girls at ten received instruction from a governess. But no textbooks for elementary learning were passed down until Zhu Xi compiled and edited a text for this level [the *Elementary Learning*]. It is only in the area of elementary education for girls that there still remains no comprehensive text. . . .

There has been a recent increase in publications of female instructions but . . . better than any of these are the words of our illustrious Empress Ma's instructions, which stand above anything written before and which are well worth being passed down to future generations. I listened to them avidly and stored them in my heart. . . .

For a person to master sagehood, nothing is more crucial than nourishing one's moral nature so that one is able to cultivate one's self. Therefore I begin the text with "The Moral Nature" followed by "Cultivation of the Self." . . .

The Moral Nature

Being upright and modest, reserved and quiet, correct and dignified, sincere and honest: these constitute the moral nature of a woman. Being filial and respectful, humane and perspicacious, loving and warm, meek and gentle: these represent the complete development of the moral nature. The moral nature being innate in our endowment, it becomes transformed and fulfilled through practice. It is not something that comes from the outside but is actually rooted in our very selves.

Of old, upright women ordered their feelings and nature based on moral principle (*li*), kept control over the workings of their mind, and honored the Way and its virtue. Therefore they were able to complement their gentlemen [husbands] in fulfilling the teachings of the Way. This is the reason they took humaneness to be their abode, rightness as their path of action, wisdom as their guide, trustworthiness as their defense, and ritual decorum as the embodiment of it. . . .

The accumulation of small faults will mount up to great harm to one's virtue. Therefore a great house will topple over if the foundation is not solid. One's moral nature will have deficiencies if the self is not restrained.

Beautiful jade with no flaws can be made into a precious jewel. An upright woman of pure character can be made the wife of a great family. If you constantly examine your actions to see if they are correct, you can be a model mother. If you are hardworking and frugal without a trace of jealousy, you are fit to be an exemplar for the women's quarters. . . .

Cultivation of the Self

. . . In the Way of the ancients, if the eye looks at evil sights, then one becomes confused inside; if the ear listens to lewd music, one disturbs one's innate virtue; if the mouth utters boastful talk, arrogance takes over the mind. These are all dangers to the self. Therefore, the wife, while at rest, will certainly be correct so as to guard against harm; and when active in household affairs, will show no partialities so that she can fulfill her moral character.

. . . Now if the self is not cultivated, then virtue will not be established. If one's virtue is not established, rarely can one be an influence for good in the family—how much less in the wider world. Therefore the wife is one who follows her husband. The way of husband and wife is the principle of the strong and the weak. In the past, the reason why enlightened monarchs were careful about establishing marriage was that they valued the way of procreation and perpetuation. The prosperity or decline of the family, the rise and fall of the state are intimately linked to this. . . .

Diligence and Hard Work

Laziness and licentiousness are disasters to the self, while diligence and hard work without any letup are morally beneficial to the self. Therefore, farmers labor hard at their crops, scholars at their studies, and women at their work . . .

The *Classic of Odes* says, "A woman shall have nothing to do with public affairs [yet] she discards her silkworms and weaving [for this]."[24] This is a defect that comes from laziness. For persons in low and mean positions, it is easy not to be lazy; it is persons of wealth, in high positions, who find it hard not to be lazy. You must exert yourself with respect to this difficulty. Do not be remiss in your ease.

---

24. Ode 264, reading *she* (to discard) for *xiu* (to abide).

Frugality

. . . The *Zuozhuan* says, "Frugality is the precious jewel of the sage." It also says, "Frugality is the fullness of virtue. Extravagance is the greatest of evils."[25] Each strand of silk comes from the labor of some working woman; each grain of rice comes from the hard work of a farmer. The efforts that went into the final product were not made easily. To use these without some sense of limits is to do violence to what comes from Heaven—there is no greater fault. . . . Now those above lead those below, the inner [quarters of the palace are] a gauge for the outer [world of other women]. Therefore, the empress must value frugality in order to lead the rest of the palace women. The wives of princes all the way down to those of scholars and commoners must honor the value of frugality in running their households. If this happens, then not one person will go cold or starve to death; rites and rightness will flourish; and the change [for the good] in people's behavior will merit being recorded [for posterity].

Returning to the Good

Now the [principal] faults of women are none other than laziness, jealousy, and licentiousness. Laziness leads to arrogance and then filial respect vanishes. Jealousy leads to harsh treatment of others, whereupon cruelty and avarice take over. Licentiousness leads to self-indulgence and then one's chastity is ruined. These three are all impediments to one's virtue and injurious to the self. Even if you have only one of these, you should get rid of it as you would a grub and distance yourself from it as you would from hornets and wasps. If hornets and wasps are not kept at a distance, they will sting you; if grubs are not gotten rid of, they will eat your grain. If you don't correct your faults, they will compromise your virtue.

Looking Up to Virtuous Exemplars [of the Past]

Those who aspire to be sages flourish; those who walk in evil ways perish. . . . If, in taking the ancients as models and trying to emulate them, you equal them, then you can be a sage. Short of this, you can be a worthy; and if you are not this [successful], you still will not have failed to follow what is good.

Pearls and jade are not what is precious [to a woman]; to emulate sageliness is. If your moral character is without any deficiency, you can order well your household. The Ode says, "The high mountain is to be looked up to. The great road is easy to be traveled on."[26] This is what I mean.

[*Nü sishu, Neixun* 3:1a–19b — TK]

---

25. *Zuozhuan*, Duke Zhuang 24; Legge, *The Chinese Classics*, 5:107.
26. Ode 218.

ZHU XI: FUNERARY INSCRIPTION FOR MADAM YOU, LADY OF JIA'NAN

At first glance it appears that Song philosophers were interested only in men. Their most famous writings address issues of education and personal cultivation in the lives of men. Systematic treatment of women is missing from their philosophical treatises. Nevertheless, the Neo-Confucian agenda for social living reached to all aspects of society and thus included clear ideas about the role of women. These ideas are best understood by looking at the one genre of writing in which Zhu Xi and others addressed women exclusively. This genre is "funerary inscriptions" or "tomb inscriptions" (*muzhiming*) for women.

Funerary inscriptions are short biographies of a man or woman written after a person's death that describe in praiseworthy terms events and achievements in the person's life. They consist of two parts: the first is an introductory essay that contains most of the biographical information; the second is a short poem summing up the main points, usually in flowery or archaic language. Whether or not the inscription was visible for later ages outside the tomb, the text of it was preserved by the family and included in the collected works of the man who had written it (as far as we know, all the authors were men). If the author's works were published, these short biographical essays might be widely read by contemporaries and later readers.

During the Song, wealthy families sought to have famous men of letters or high officials write inscriptions for their deceased, hoping thereby to gain prestige and fame for them and their descendants. Such families might pay large sums of money for a prominent statesman to attach his name to such an inscription. Neo-Confucians, however, were especially opposed to accepting recompense for writing inscriptions and to writing inscriptions for people unknown to the author, people whose virtue in life could not be adequately verified. They argued that funerary inscriptions should celebrate only the lives of the worthy, should present a model of virtue to be followed by people in later generations, and should portray an accurate picture of the person's life.

Funerary inscriptions, when written for women, were usually for the principal wife in a household. Zhu Xi wrote seventeen inscriptions for women; from these we get a detailed picture of his ideas about feminine virtue. Foremost among these is a woman's duty to serve her father-in-law and mother-in-law. Filiality was a cardinal virtue for both men and women, but a woman had to transfer her filial devotion from her natal parents to her husband's parents. Service to in-laws entailed taking over all the household chores, to relieve any burden on the older woman, and caring for the couple in sickness and in health. Rituals within the family were strongly promoted by Zhu Xi, and a principal wife had an important role in them.

Closely related to serving her in-laws was a woman's duty to be subservient to her husband. We can conclude from Zhu Xi's inscriptions that he expected women to take on significant responsibilities within the household, but always within the framework of subordination to the men in the family. While praising women for good judgment and a general understanding of Confucian values, he did not believe them to be capable of higher learning and speculative thought, both of which were so important to men.

Since women were to confine themselves to the home, that became their sphere of activity and they were responsible for the smooth working of the household. If a woman became the wife of the eldest son or head of the household, she might become the manager of a large family enterprise. Such a woman might find herself with significant responsibilities for keeping the family budget balanced.

Responsibility for the financial management of the household went beyond personal frugality, which was a virtue urged in nearly all inscriptions for women and helps to explain the Neo-Confucian emphasis on widow chastity. When her husband died, a woman's duties as household manager increased. She was needed more than ever to hold the family together and preserve its economic viability while she nurtured the sons to manhood. Remarriage of widows was common in the Song, but it violated Zhu Xi's ideal of how a family should operate.

Finally, motherhood and childhood education were celebrated and promoted by Zhu Xi and other Neo-Confucians. A woman's education of her children began even while they were in the womb with chanting of the classics and *sūtras* and vigilance over emotion. When the children were small, the mother taught them moral values, polite behavior appropriate to each sex, and in many cases elementary reading and writing (an indication that many women were at least partially literate). As they grew older, she was to find teachers for the boys and supervise their further education. When sons achieved success in the outside world, the mother received full credit. In fact, inscriptions for women often end with lists of children and details of the success of the sons. In the final analysis, the consummation of a woman's virtue was in the visible results it produced in her sons.

This epitaph was written by Zhu Xi for a woman he had not known personally, at the request of a family, one of whose members had studied with the Cheng brothers. The qualities that he extols fit with those honored in the previous readings, especially Ban Zhao's *Admonitions*, twice referred to herein. The important role of women as bearers of culture is evident. After rendering an account of her family, Zhu proceeds as follows:

Madam You was by nature quiet and modest. A cousin of her father, Madam Ruan, on account of her womanly virtue, was a teacher of girls. When Madam You was young, she studied with her. She was taught the *Admonitions for Women* of Ban Zhao, and she mastered the ethical principles therein. When it came to the arts of needlework and writing, she quickly surpassed others in ability without any undue effort. Early in her life, she lost her father. Her mother loved her dearly and married her to the honorable Mr. Huang. In serving her father-in-law and mother-in-law and performing the family sacrifices, she was diligent and reverent and never remiss. Her father-in-law liked having guests. On festivals and holidays, relatives and old friends filled the house. Madam You served them with great care and never relaxed for a minute lest she cause her sisters-in-law to toil in her place. Her mother-in-law was by nature strict. Her sons' wives waited on her by her side, and in twenty years she never gave them leave to be seated. Madam You alone was able to fulfill all her wishes. She presented the washbasin and comb, kept her [mother-in-law] warm in winter and cool in summer, all according to the rules of propriety.[27] When her mother-in-law was sick, she would only take medicine offered by Madam You. When Madam You performed a task, her mother-in-law would point to her as a model for the others.

At the time of her father-in-law's passing, Madam You's husband was poor. The elder and younger brothers looked at each other and planned to sell some land to pay for the funeral. Madam You told them, "Do not destroy the patrimony of your ancestors!" She then withdrew and sold her own private possessions to meet [the expenses of] the occasion. Because of this, Mr. Huang was able to take care of [the funeral] without troubling the rest of the family.

Mr. Huang was honest and guileless, grave and reverent as a person. Madam You assisted him with obedience and firmness. They respected each other like guests and conferred together on all matters. Madam You treated her relations on both sides of the family with humble respect and decorum. She liked to speak of their good points and did not take pleasure in hearing about their faults. When relatives fell into poverty, she would help them out to the best of her ability. Each day she recited the *Admonitions for Women* and other classical texts to admonish herself. She was also a believer in Buddhism. While pregnant, she sat properly in a quiet chamber, burning incense and reading Confucian and Buddhist texts. She did not utter hasty words or give angry looks, saying, "This is how the ancients instructed the child in the womb." Her children were thus born virtuous and talented. [After they were born] her instruction was also excellent. When they were barely able to speak, she took them on her lap and taught them the *Classic of Odes* and the *Classic of Documents*. As they got older, she invited in teachers and selected friends for them. She reiterated their lessons and encouraged them fully. Madam You's cousin [Mr. You Zuo, 1053–1123], the Censor, studied with the Cheng brothers of Henan. His good deeds and honest virtue were admired by other scholars. Madam You often said to her sons, "Look at your uncle. If you follow his example you can become fine gentlemen."

In the year *renzi* of the Shaoxing period (1132), on the twenty-third day of the fourth month, Madam You died of an illness. As she lay on her deathbed,

---

27. "Summary of the Rules of Propriety" ("Quli"), *Record of Rites* A:2; Legge, *Li Ki*, 1:67.

her husband looked at her and wept. Madam You said, "Life and death, meeting and parting [follow each other] like day and night. Why are you so distressed?" She was fifty-six years old at that time.

There follows an account of her two sons, whose successes in the jinshi *examinations and at court were attributed to her teaching. Zhu concludes with the following encomium:*

The Yous of Changping
For generations had virtuous members
Though the world did not know them
The locality gained from their humanity.[28]
As for how literati women ought to be,
Here was a paragon of the inner quarters.
She matched [her husband's] virtue and gave birth to worthy children,
So that blessings and rewards were many.[29]
As court ministers and provincial prefects,
[Her sons] were virtuous and talented.
They were enfeoffed with districts,
And the state thus prospered.
By illustrious order I write
To illumine this tomb.
The stone is cut, the words are carved,
To bequeath the standard to later generations.

[Zhu Xi, *Wenji* (SBCK) 91:13b–15a — BB]

---

28. *Analects* 4:1.
29. *Classic of Changes,* hexagram 2, *kun.*

Chapter 24

SELF AND SOCIETY IN THE MING

With Zhu Xi's curriculum established in most Ming schools and academies (albeit in much-abridged form), as well as in the civil service examination system, it is understandable why the editors of the Complete Library of the Four Treasuries should later have observed that the intellectual and moral formation of educated persons in the Ming was all based on Zhu Xi's version of the Four Books and also why scholarship in the Ming mostly developed along lines already set by Zhu Xi. Much of it was cast in the language, concepts, and structure of the *Great Learning* and Zhu's Commentary: it remained largely within the terms of Zhu Xi's discourse.

Although the pattern of schooling and examination was well established, this by no means prevented the further development of thought by individual teachers and scholars, some of whom maintained their independence of the state by refusing to serve in office, either out of dissatisfaction with the routinized learning of the examination system or out of unwillingness to be associated with the despotic actions of Ming rulers like Taizu and Chengzu. Thus, for all the limiting effects of Ming autocracy and bureaucracy, and contrary to the dominant early twentieth-century Western view (much influenced by Hegel and Marx) that late imperial China was stagnant and wholly unprogressive, there was actually much new intellectual and cultural activity in the Ming, stimulated by economic growth, social change, and the spread of education and literacy, encouraged by both Zhu Xi's works and the populist views of Ming Taizu, who, as we have seen, could be egalitarian and autocratic at once.

The main lines of new thought and scholarship pursued directions already implicit in Zhu Xi's broad view of "solid learning" (*shixue*) — that is, it combined both intense moral/spiritual cultivation and broad intellectual inquiry, ritual practice as well as public service, with the latter understood as service of the "common good" (*gong*) on several levels of society and in education, as well as in office. In this chapter it is not possible to represent all of these diverse trends adequately or to deal with all the tensions that arose among them. With the great expansion of scholarship, however, and the increasing demands for technical specialization (even in the specialized art of writing examination essays!), a prime problem arose for those who still held to the Neo-Confucian ideal of learning for one's self: how could one be heavily engaged with such a complex world and still achieve the self-integration of the sage?

WANG YANGMING

WANG YANGMING'S NEW LEARNING OF THE MIND-AND-HEART

There can be little doubt that among the new trends in the Ming it was the teachings and personal example of Wang Yangming that were to have the most explosive effect. His views on the mind-and-heart — quickly recognized as strikingly new — dynamized the conception of the self, sagehood, and the individual as nothing had before and came to dominate the intellectual scene during the sixteenth century almost as if they represented a new orthodoxy.

Wang Yangming himself thought of these new formulations as fully orthodox because he understood his own mission in the world against the background of Zhu Xi's concept of the repossession of the Way (*daotong*) and the deep sense of personal responsibility for the Way that was characteristic of the great man.

> Whenever I think of people's degeneration and difficulties I pity them and have a pain in my heart. I overlook my own unworthiness and wish to save them by this teaching. And I do not know the limits of my ability. When people see me trying to do this, they join one another in ridiculing, insulting, and cursing me, regarding me as insane. . . . Of course, there are cases when people see their fathers, sons, or brothers falling into a deep abyss and getting drowned. They cry, crawl, go naked and barefooted, stumble, and fall. They hang on to dangerous cliffs and go down to save them. Some gentlemen who see them behave like this . . . consider them insane because they cry, stumble, and fall as they do. Now to stand aside and make no attempt to save the drowning, while mocking those who do, is possible only for strangers who have no natural feelings of kinship, but even then they will be considered to have no sense of pity

and to be no longer human beings. In the case of a father, son, or brother, because of love he will surely feel an ache in his head and a pain in his heart, run desperately until he has lost his breath, and crawl to save them. He will even risk drowning himself. How much less will he worry about whether people believe him or not?[1]

The key, however, to Wang's near revolution in the sage learning that came down to him through the Cheng-Zhu school was his reformulation of the Learning of the Mind-and-Heart, especially as represented by the message and method of the mind-and-heart (*xinfa*), as shown in the following excerpts.

MEMOIR ON THE RECONSTRUCTION OF SHANYIN PREFECTURAL SCHOOL

Notice here how Yangming takes the Cheng-Zhu "method of the mind-and-heart" and concentrates on the original unity of the mind with Heaven-and-Earth and all things, as expressed in the spontaneous affective response to things and affairs.

The sages' learning is the "Learning of the Mind-and-Heart." It is learning that seeks fully to employ the mind-and-heart. What Yao, Shun, and Yu passed on from one to the other was, "The human mind is precarious; the mind of the Way is subtle. Be discriminating, be one [with the mind of the Way]. Hold fast the Mean." The "mind of the Way" refers to what [in the *Mean*] "follows the nature. . . ." It is unmixed with the human, has no sound or smell, and is manifested with the utmost subtlety. It is the source of sincerity. The mind of man is mixed with the human and thus becomes prone to err. It has the potential for unnaturalness and insincerity. When one sees an infant about to fall into a well and feels a compassionate impulse [to rescue it], that is [an instance of] the Way guiding human nature. If that impulse becomes confused by thought of gaining the approbation of parents or a reputation in the community, that is the [self-regarding] human mind. . . .

To be unified is to be one with the mind of the Way; to be discriminating is to be concerned lest the mind of the Way should lose that oneness and possibly become separated from the human mind. Always to be centered on the Mean and to be unceasingly one with the mind of the Way is to "hold fast the Mean." If it is one with the mind of the Way, the mind will always be kept on center, and in its expressed state there will be no disharmony. Thus, following the mind of the Way, its expression in a parent-child relationship is always affectionate; as expressed in the ruler-minister relationship it is always right; as expressed in the relationship of husband-wife, senior-junior, friend and friend,

---

1. Adapted from Chan, *Instructions*, pp. 168–169.

it is always respectful of gender differences, always respectful of precedence, always respectful of fidelity to friends. . . .

Shun had Xie as minister of education see to instruction in these moral relationships and teach people the Universal Way.[2] At that time people were all noble men and could all be entrusted with the responsibilities of noble rank. There was no instruction but this instruction, and no learning but this learning. With the passing of the sages, however, the learning of the mind-and-heart became obscured, human conduct unnaturally strove for fame and profit; those who pursued the learning of textual exegesis, memorization and recitation, and literary embellishments arose together in confusion and profusion. Fragmentation and divisiveness flourished apace. Month by month and year by year, one scholar copied from another, each confirming the other's mistakes. Thus day by day the human mind became more swollen with self-importance and could no longer perceive the subtlety of the mind of the Way. . . .

How then is the learning of the mind-and-heart to be clarified? . . . In this learning there is no distinction between self and other, internal or external; the mind is one with Heaven-and-Earth and all things. Chan [Buddhist] learning, however, arises from self-interest and expediency and cannot avoid division into internal and external. This, then, is the reason for the difference between the two. Today those who pursue the learning of the mind and nature while not treating human relations as external to one or leaving out things and affairs, but who rather concentrate on preserving the mind and make it their business to nourish the nature, certainly represent the learning of discrimination and oneness in the sages' school.

[*Wang Yangming quanshu, Wenlu* 4:215–217 — dB]

QUESTIONS ON THE *GREAT LEARNING*

In this memoir Wang sees the method of "discrimination and oneness" as a means of preserving the mind of the Way, originally and essentially one with Heaven, Earth, and all things. As something already complete within the mind, it requires nothing external to it but only unmixed, unobstructed expression of its human feelings — its natural empathy for all things. There is no place then for principles to be studied as if they were objects of investigation, no room for the nature, as Heaven's Principle in human beings, to be learned or assimilated from outside. All one needs in the learning of the mind is single-minded attention to the unity of the mind and principle, the oneness of humans with Heaven, Earth, and all things. For Wang this is a unity one starts with and expands upon, in contrast to Zhu Xi, who in his note on the investigation of things in the *Great Learning*, speaks of the gradual penetration of principles until finally one achieves a breakthrough to integral comprehension and coalescence.

---

2. "Canon of Shun," *Classic of History*; Legge, *The Chinese Classics* 3:44.

Wang's new interpretation of the Learning of the Mind-and-Heart, along with his revision of the Succession to the Way, immediately preceded his enunciation of the doctrine of innate knowing (*liangzhi*) and was followed in 1527 by his important "Questions on the *Great Learning*" ("Daxuewen"), excerpted below.

As the title implies, this essay deals with central questions in the text of the *Great Learning*. It also presents the starting point and basic premises of Wang's teaching as drawn from both the *Mean* and the *Great Learning*. Zhu Xi had explained the *Great Learning*'s "manifesting luminous virtue" in terms of the original endowments of Heaven's nature (principle) in the mind, to be nourished and cultivated by methodical practice of intellectual inquiry, the refining of value distinctions, and the exercise of moral restraint — lest the human mind, precariously perched between selfish and unselfish desires, should stray from correct principles as represented by the mind of the Way. Wang's alternative view was that "luminous virtue," instead of being a mind of the Way at odds with the human mind, consisted essentially in the cardinal virtue of humaneness, as expressed in a feeling of oneness with Heaven-and-Earth and all things. Cultivation of this virtue, then, should consist essentially of encouraging the free and full expression of that empathetic feeling without the intervention of any ratiocination or calculation involving self/other or subject/object distinctions. In this, Wang placed a prime value on the feeling of love for, or oneness with, all creation and on the natural integrity of the mind, as opposed to a mind divided against itself by the counterposing of the human mind to the mind of the Way (i.e., the nature).

Wang's original given name was Shouren, meaning "to preserve humaneness"; his honorific name, Yangming, means "luminous and clear," which expresses the brilliant, charismatic appeal of both his outgoing, open personality and his simple, direct, inspirational message.

Question: The *Great Learning* was considered by the former scholar [Zhu Xi] as the learning of the great person. I venture to ask why the learning of the great person should consist in "clearly manifesting luminous virtue"?

Answer: The great person regards Heaven, Earth, and the myriad things as one body, the world as one family, and the state as one person. . . . Thus the learning of the great person consists entirely in getting rid of the obscuration of selfish desires by one's own efforts to make manifest one's luminous virtue, so as to restore the condition of forming one body with Heaven, Earth, and the myriad things. . . . To manifest luminous virtue [i.e., the moral nature (*mingde*)] is to bring about the substance of forming one body with Heaven, Earth, and the myriad things, whereas loving the people is to put into universal operation the function of forming one body. Hence manifesting luminous virtue consists in loving the people, and loving the people is the way to manifest luminous virtue.

People fail to realize that the highest good is in their minds and seek it outside. As they believe that everything or every event has its own definite principle, they search for the utmost good in individual things. Consequently, the mind becomes fragmented, isolated, broken into pieces. Mixed and confused, it has no definite direction. Once it is realized that the utmost good is in the mind and does not depend on any search outside, then the mind will have definite direction and there will be no danger of its becoming fragmented, isolated, broken into pieces, mixed, or confused.

Now the original substance of the mind is human nature. Human nature being universally good, the original substance of the mind is correct. How is it that any effort is required to rectify the mind? The reason is that, while the original substance of the mind is originally correct, incorrectness enters when one's thoughts and intentions are in operation. Therefore one who wishes to rectify one's mind must rectify it in connection with the operation of one's thoughts and intention. If, whenever a good thought arises, one really loves it as one loves beautiful colors, and whenever an evil thought arises, one really hates it as one hates bad odors, then one's intention will always be sincere and one's mind can be rectified. . . .

The extension of knowledge is not what later scholars understand as enriching and widening knowledge.[3] It is simply extending one's innate knowing to the utmost. This innate knowing is what Mencius meant when he said, "The sense of right and wrong is common to all human beings."[4] The sense of right and wrong requires no deliberation to know, nor does it depend on learning to function.[5] This is why it is called innate knowing. It is my nature endowed by Heaven, the original substance of my mind, naturally intelligent, shining, clear, and understanding.

Whenever a thought or a wish arises, my mind's faculty of innate knowing itself is always conscious of it. Whether it is good or evil, my mind's innate knowing faculty itself also knows it. It has nothing to do with others. Therefore, although an inferior person may have done all manner of evil, when he sees a superior man he will surely try to disguise this fact, concealing what is evil and displaying what is good in himself.[6] This shows that innate knowing does not permit any self-deception. Now the only way to distinguish good and evil in order to make the intention sincere is to extend to the utmost this innate knowing faculty.

Wang identified the original pure mind with the "utmost good" of the *Great Learning*, regarding it not as a perfection beyond one, to be reached or achieved, but as an inherent perfection within, to be uncovered, released, and extended to others. He says:

As the utmost good emanates and reveals itself, we will consider right as right and wrong as wrong. Things of greater or less importance and situations

---

3. See Zhu Xi's commentary on the *Great Learning*, ch. 20.
4. *Mencius* 2A:6, 6A:6.
5. *Mencius* 7A:15.
6. Paraphrasing the *Great Learning*, ch. 6.

of grave or light character will be responded to as they act upon us. In all our changes and movements, we will stick to no particular point but possess in ourselves the Mean that is perfectly natural. This is the ultimate of the normal nature of man and the principle of things. There can be no consideration of adding to or subtracting anything from it — such a suggestion reveals selfish ideas and shallow cunning and cannot be said to be the utmost good. Naturally, how can anyone who does not watch over himself carefully when alone, and who lacks refined discrimination and unity, attain to such a state of perfection? Later generations fail to realize that the utmost good is inherent in their own minds, but exercise their selfish ideas and cunning and grope for it outside their minds, believing that every event and every object has its own peculiar and definite principle.

In this passage we see how Wang incorporates into his doctrine of the mind the language of the Cheng-Zhu method of the mind — the method of refined discrimination and oneness and holding fast to the Mean — and focuses it on the unity of principle rather than on the diversity of principles in events and things. Thereby he sets a higher priority on primary intuition, or undifferentiated sensibility, than on acquired learning or secondary rational and moral judgments. In the same way, Wang places a prime emphasis on the substantial unity of innate knowing, rather than on the different steps in the *Great Learning*'s method of self-cultivation. He says:

While the specification of tasks can be expressed in terms of a graded sequence of priorities, in substance they constitute a single unity and in reality there is no distinction of a graded sequence to be made; yet, while there is no such distinction to be made, in respect to function (discrimination, *wei-wei*), these cannot be left wanting in the slightest degree. This is why the [*Great Learning*'s] doctrine of investigation, extension, being sincere, and rectifying can be taken as a correct exposition of the transmission from Yao and Shun and as evincing the mind of Confucius.

[*Wang Yangming quanshu, Wenlu* 1:123 — WTC, dB]

PREFACE TO THE *COLLECTED WRITINGS OF LU XIANGSHAN*

Given the Zhu Xi school's dominance in the early Ming and the almost complete disappearance of the school of Lu Xiangshan as a teaching lineage in the thirteenth century, it is understandable that Wang Yangming's early formation was through the Zhu school curriculum described in the previous chapter. Even Wang's new conception of the Learning of the Mind-and-Heart came about through his rethinking of the Way to sagehood through the "investigation of things and extension of knowing," which was both the starting point and the culmination of Zhu's method, especially as formulated in Zhu's special note on this theme.

Yet in Wang's mature thought he has clearly come to a position closer to Lu

Xiangshan than to Zhu. Accordingly, Wang drew new attention to Lu's ideas and promoted the reprinting of Lu's works for the first time since 1212, the following being an excerpt from the preface of that reprinting. He was also influential in having Lu enshrined in the Confucian temple for the first time in 1530. Thereafter the teachings of Lu and Wang became closely associated, though the connection between them was an affinity of certain ideas, not a genetic filiation through a teaching lineage.

The following illustrates how Wang portrays Lu and not Zhu as the true inheritor of the "Succession to the Way."

The sage learning is the learning of the mind-and-heart. As it was handed on from one to another by Yao, Shun, and Yu, it was said, "The human mind is precarious; the mind of the Way is subtle. Be discriminating, be one. Hold fast the Mean." This is the source of the learning of the mind. The "Mean" refers to the mind of the Way. When the mind of the Way, being discriminating and unified, is referred to as "humaneness," it is what we call the "Mean." The learning of Confucius and Mencius, which urged the pursuit of humaneness, carried on the transmission of the sages' discrimination and unity. Nevertheless a prevalent evil at that time was found among those who insisted on seeking this outside the mind. Thus the question arose with Zigong as to whether Confucius's learning consisted in acquiring much cognitive knowledge [Analects 15:2] and whether humaneness consisted in "extensively benefiting and assisting the people" [Analects 6:28]. So Confucius told him about the pervading unity [running through it all] and taught him how to take what is near at hand [in oneself] as a gauge of the feelings of others, which meant having them seek within their own minds.

Despite Mencius' efforts, Wang goes on to explain, the Way of the sage kings declined, and a utilitarian view came to prevail, which identified principle with selfish gain and in effect disconnected it from the moral mind endowed by Heaven. With this "the mind and principle became two separate things and the learning of discrimination and oneness was lost." Scholars occupied themselves with the external pursuit of the principles in things without realizing that there is truly no difference between principle in the mind and principle in things. Likewise the Buddhist and Daoist teachings of emptiness dispensed with the moral constants that should govern human relations, again not realizing that the mind and principle are inseparable and that moral constants cannot be dispensed with.

Finally, in the Song, Zhou Dunyi and the Cheng brothers tried to rediscover the essential meaning of Confucius and Yan Yuan, and with such doctrines as "Non-finite and yet Supreme Ultimate," "stabilizing the mind with humaneness and rightness," "the Mean and correctness," "putting quiescence first," "stability in both action and quiescence," "neither external nor internal," and "neither following nor going forward to meet events,"[7] they came close to the original idea of refined discrimination and unity. "After this," Wang says, "came Lu Xiangshan (Jiuyuan), who, though not the equal of the two Chengs for purity of character and equability of disposition, nevertheless was able, through his simplicity and directness of mind, to connect up with the transmission from Mencius." Indeed, "his insistence that learning must be sought in the mind was unity of mind itself. It is for this reason," says Wang, "that I have adjudged the learning of Xiangshan to be the learning of Mencius."

[*Wang Yangming quanshu, Wenlu* 3:19a —dB]

THE IDENTIFICATION OF MIND AND PRINCIPLE

One basis for Wang's endorsement of Lu's approach to learning is his acceptance of the idea that the mind and principle are not only inseparable (which Zhu Xi himself had said) but identical.

What Zhu Xi meant by the investigation of things is "to investigate the principle in things to the utmost as we come into contact with them." To investigate the principle in things to the utmost, as we come into contact with them means to search in each individual thing for its so-called definite principle. It means further that the principle in each individual thing is to be sought with the mind, thus separating the mind and principle into two. To seek for principle in each individual thing is like looking for the principle of filiality in parents. If the principle of filiality is to be sought in parents, then is it actually in my own mind or is it in the person of my parents? If it is actually in the person of my parents, is it true that as soon as parents pass away the mind will then lack the principle of filiality? When I see a child about to fall into a well [and have a feeling of commiseration], there must be the principle of commiseration. Is this principle of commiseration actually in the person of the child or is it in the innate knowledge of my mind? Perhaps one cannot follow the child into the well [to rescue it]. Perhaps one can rescue it by seizing it with the hand. All this involves principle. Is it really in the person of the child or does it emanate from the innate knowledge in my mind? What is true here is true of all things and events. From this we know the mistake of separating the mind and principle into two.

[*Chuanxilu*, in *Wang Yangming quanshu* (SBBY) 2:4b–5a —WTC]

THE UNITY OF KNOWING AND ACTING

The following is recorded in *Instructions for Practical Living* by Wang's disciple Xu Ai.

---

7. Referring to *Zhuangzi* 6, 3:7b.

I [Xu Ai] did not understand the Teacher's doctrine of the unity of knowing and acting and debated over it back and forth with Huang Zongxian and Gu Weixian without coming to any conclusion. Therefore I took the matter to the Teacher. The Teacher said, "Give an example and let me see." I said, "For example, there are people who know that parents should be served with filiality and elder brothers treated with respect, but they cannot put these things into practice. This shows that knowing and acting are clearly two different things."

The Teacher said, "The knowing and acting you refer to are already separated by selfish desires and are no longer knowing and acting in their original substance. There have never been people who know but do not act. Those who are supposed to know but do not act simply do not yet know. When sages and worthies taught people about knowing and acting, it was precisely because they wanted them to restore this original substance, and not just to have them behave like that and be satisfied."

[*Chuanxilu*, in *Wang Yangming quanshu* (SBBY) 1:3a–b — WTC]

THE COLLOQUY AT THE TIANQUAN BRIDGE

The two points of view represented in this famous colloquy are those that tended to polarize the school of Wang Yangming, one wing emphasizing the importance of moral cultivation and the other, intuitive spontaneity. The latter, with some leanings in the direction of Chan Buddhism, believed that the original reality or inner substance of the mind transcended good and evil and that natural spontaneity rather than conscious moral effort was the characteristic of the sage.

In the ninth month of the sixth year of Jiajing [1527] our Teacher had been called from retirement and appointed to subdue once more the rebellion in Sien and Tianzhou.[8] As he was about to start Ruzhong [Wang Ji] and I [Qian Dehong] discussed learning. He repeated the words of the Teacher's instruction as follows:

"In the original substance of the mind there is no distinction of good and evil.

"When the intentions become active, however, such a distinction exists.

"The function of innate knowing is to know good and evil.

"The investigation [rectification] of things is to do good and remove evil."

I asked, "What do you think this means?"

Ruzhong said, "This is perhaps not the last word [i.e., there is more to it than this]. If we say that in the original substance of the mind there is no distinction between good and evil, then there must be no such distinction in

---

8. Both were counties in Guangxi.

the intentions, in knowing, or in things. If we say that there is a distinction between good and evil in the intentions, then in the final analysis there must also be such a distinction in the substance of the mind."

I said, "The substance of the mind is the nature endowed in us by Heaven, and is originally neither good nor evil. But because we have a mind dominated by habits, we see in our thoughts a distinction between good and evil. The work of investigating things, extending knowledge, making the intentions sincere, rectifying the mind, and cultivating the person is aimed precisely at recovering that original nature and substance. If there were no good or evil to start with, what would be the necessity for such effort?"

That evening we set ourselves down beside the Teacher at the Tianquan Bridge. Each stated his view and asked to be corrected. The Teacher said, "I am going to leave now. I wanted to have you come and talk this matter through. You two gentlemen complement one another very well and should not hold on to one side. Here I deal with two types of people. The man of sharp intelligence apprehends straight from the source. The original substance of the human mind is in fact crystal-clear without any impediment and is the equilibrium before the feelings are aroused. The man of sharp intelligence has already accomplished his task as soon as he apprehends the original substance, penetrating the self, other people, and things internal and things external all at the same time. On the other hand, there are inevitably those whose minds are dominated by habits so that the original substance of the mind is obstructed. I therefore teach them definitely and sincerely to do good and remove evil in their intention and thoughts. When they become expert at the task and the impurities of the mind are completely eliminated, the original substance of the mind will become wholly clear. I adopt Ruzhong's view in dealing with the man of sharp intelligence, and that of Dehong for the second type. If you two gentlemen use your views interchangeably, you will be able to lead all people — of the highest, average, and lowest intelligence — to the truth.

> [*Chuanxilu*, in *Wang Yangming quanshu* (SBBY) 3:30b–31a
> — adapted from Chan, *Instructions*, pp. 243–244]

SOCIAL AND POLITICAL MEASURES OF WANG YANGMING

Although Zhu Xi had by no means been uninvolved with government, Wang Yangming led an even more active life. His career as an official and general, though marked by both great successes and the conflicts and sharp reversals often experienced by conscientious officials, notably exemplified his doctrine of the unity of knowing and acting. For his followers, too, it exemplified the life of a martyred hero-sage. It is understandable that his personal example should have inspired new forms of activism in many directions, which serve as a reminder that Wang's approach, while somewhat more subjective than Zhu Xi's, was primarily directed at stimulating the inner springs of practical moral action, not at encouraging any form of quietism. In fact, Yangming abjured quiet-sitting for this reason.

It is not surprising that among these active concerns were matters already put high on the Neo-Confucian agenda by Zhu Xi: local schooling and community organization. Others included his recommendations for military policy and defense of the northwestern frontiers. The following selections demonstrate particularly the close connection between his thought and his official measures, as well as the continuity of basic ideas from Zhu Xi, along with the distinct emphasis given them by Wang.

FUNDAMENTAL IDEAS ON ELEMENTARY EDUCATION

In April 1518, after leading a successful campaign to subdue rebels in Jiangxi, Wang adopted a policy of pacification through reeducation rather than through reprisals or repression. In this case he reemphasized the need for community schools (as had Zhu Xi) but put even greater stress on voluntarism and the active liberation of human beings' natural capacities. Note especially the appeal to the affective nature of man, rather than to cognitive learning, but note also his view of the practice of rites and music as stimulating, not stultifying, the natural affections.

In education the ancients taught the fundamental principles of human relations. As the habits of memorization, recitation, and the writing of flowery compositions of later generations arose, the teachings of ancient kings disappeared. In educating young boys today, the sole task should be to teach filiality, brotherly respect, loyalty, faithfulness, ritual decorum, rightness, integrity, and the sense of shame. The ways to raise and cultivate them are to lure them into singing so their will will be roused, to direct them to practice etiquette so their demeanor will be dignified, and to urge them to read so their intellectual horizon will be widened. Today, singing songs and practicing etiquette are often regarded as unrelated to present needs. This is the view of small and vulgar people of this degenerate modern age. . . .

Generally speaking, it is the nature of young boys to love to play and to dislike restriction. Like plants beginning to sprout, if they are allowed to grow freely, they will develop smoothly. If twisted and interfered with, they will wither and decline. In teaching young boys today, we must make them lean toward rousing themselves so that they will be happy and cheerful at heart, and then nothing can check their development. . . .

However, in recent generations the teachers of youngsters merely supervise them every day as they recite phrases and sentences and imitate civil service examination papers. They stress restraint and discipline instead of directing their pupils in the practice of the rites. They emphasize cognitive learning instead of nourishing goodness. They beat the pupils with a whip and tie them with ropes, treating them like prisoners. The youngsters look upon their school as a prison and refuse to enter. They regard their teachers as enemies and do not want to see them. They avoid this and conceal that in order to satisfy their desire for play and fun. They pretend, deceive, and cheat in order to indulge in mischief and meanness. They become negligent and inferior, and daily degenerate. Such education drives them to do evil. How can they be expected to do good?

In truth the following is my idea of education. . . . Every day, early in the morning, after the pupils have assembled and bowed, the teachers should ask all of them one by one whether at home they have been negligent and lacked sincerity and earnestness in their desire to love their parents and to respect their elders, whether they have overlooked or failed to carry out any details in caring for their parents in the summer or the winter, whether in walking along the streets their movements and etiquette have been disorderly or careless, and whether in all their words, acts, and thoughts they have been deceitful or depraved, and not loyal, faithful, sincere, and respectful. All boys must answer honestly. If they have made any mistake, they should correct it. If not, they should devote themselves to greater effort. . . .

In singing, let the pupils be tidy in appearance and calm in expression. Let their voices be clear and distinct. Let their rhythm be even and exact. Let them not be hasty or hurried. Let them not be reckless or disorderly. And let them not sound feeble or timid. In time their spirits will be free and their minds will be peaceful. . . .

In the practice of rites, let the pupils be clear in their minds and reverently serious in their thoughts. Let them be careful with details and correct in demeanor. Let them not be negligent or lazy. Let them not be low-spirited or disconcerted. And let them not be uncontrolled or rude. Let them be leisurely but not to the point of being dilatory and be serious but not to the point of being rigid. In time their appearance and behavior will be natural and their moral nature will be firmly established. . . .

In reading, the value does not lie in the amount read but in learning the material well. Reckoning the pupils' natural endowments, if one can handle two hundred words, teach him only one hundred so that he always has surplus energy and strength, and then he will not suffer or feel tired but will have the beauty of being at ease with himself.

[Adapted from Chan, *Instructions*, pp. 182–185]

THE COMMUNITY COMPACT FOR SOUTHERN GANZHOU

In southern Jiangxi and Fujian, where he suppressed bandits and rebels, Wang, instead of following a punitive policy, stressed the need to convert the former disaffected peoples to take up a life as "new citizens." He turned to the model of Zhu Xi's Community Compact as a method of enlisting people's cooperation in the rehabilitation of former outlaws and for appealing to the better side of the latter's nature.

It should be noted that the movement to reform local government and reorganize village life arose with the breakdown of the *lijia* and village elder system instituted by Ming Taizu at the founding of the dynasty. Wang's is just one example among others of Confucian scholar-officials attempting to address these problems in the sixteenth century. It is significant that the compact had become accepted here as somewhat more an instrument of state policy than the kind of voluntary, grassroots organization originally envisaged by the Lü family and Zhu Xi in the Song. Nevertheless, collective, shared responsibility on the part of both "new citizens" and officials — in short, a spirit of mutuality and reciprocity — is a marked feature of Wang's proposal. Note also that in the second paragraph the essentials of public morality are largely defined in the same terms as Zhu Xi's compact, as Taizu had incorporated them in the "Six Instructions" of the village lecture system.

In the past, new citizens have often deserted their own clans, rebelled against their own community, and gone in all directions to do violence. Was this merely because their nature was different and they were criminals? It was also because, on our part, the government did not govern them properly or teach them in the right way, and on your part, all of you, both old and young, did not reach and regulate your families early enough or exert good influence on your fellow villagers regularly enough. You did not put inducement and encouragement into practice and had no sufficient arrangements for cooperation and coordination. . . .

Alas! Nothing can be done to change what has already gone by, but something can still be done in the future. Therefore a community compact is now specially prepared to unite and harmonize all of you. From now on, all of you who enter into this compact should be filial to your parents and respectful to your elders, teach your children, live in harmony with your fellow villagers, help one another when there is death in the family and assist one another in times of difficulty, encourage one another to do good and warn one another not to do evil, stop litigations and rivalry, cultivate faithfulness and promote harmony, and be sure to be good citizens so that together you may establish the custom of humanity and kindness. Alas! Although a man is most stupid, when it comes to criticizing others his mind is quite clear, and although a person is quite intelligent, when it comes to criticizing himself his mind is beclouded. All of you, both old and young, should not remember the former evil deeds of the new citizens and ignore their good deeds. As long as they have a single thought to do good, they are already good people. Do not be proud that you are good citizens and neglect to cultivate your personal life. As long as you have a single thought to do evil, you are already evil people. Whether people are good or evil depends on a single instant of thought. You should think over my words carefully. Don't forget.

Item: Elect from the compact membership an elderly and virtuous person respected by all to be the compact chief and two persons to be assistant chiefs, four persons who are impartial, just, and firm in judgment to be compact directors, four persons who are understanding and discriminating to be compact recorders, four persons who are energetic and scrupulous to be compact executives, and two persons who are well versed in ceremonies to be compact masters of ceremonies. Have three record books. One of these is to record the names of compact members and their daily movements and activities, and is to be in the charge of the compact executives. Of the remaining record books, one is for the purpose of displaying good deeds and the other for the purpose of reporting evil deeds, both to be in the charge of the compact chief.

Item: Each member shall contribute three cents (*fen*) at each banquet meeting to the compact executives, who will provide the food. Do not be extravagant. The point is that there shall be no thirst or hunger, that is all.

Item: The time of meeting shall be the fifteenth of each month. Those who because of illness or other business are unable to attend may send a messenger to inform a compact executive ahead of time. Those who fail to attend without reason will be recorded as having committed an evil deed and, in addition, fined one dollar (*liang*)[9] for the use of the group.

Item: Build a compact hall on level ground. Choose a spacious temple compound and build it there.

Item: To display good deeds, the language used must be clear and decisive, but in reporting mistakes, the language must be indirect and gentle. . . .

Item: . . . After the meal, the compact master of ceremonies shall sound the drum three times, and in a chanting voice announce the issuance of warning. All shall rise. The compact directors shall stand in the middle of the hall and say in a loud voice, "Oh! All members of the compact please listen distinctly to this warning. Who among men has no good in him, and who has no evil in him? Although our good deeds are not known to others, as they accumulate, in time this accumulation of good will no longer remain hidden. If we do evil deeds and do not reform, in time they will accumulate and reach the point where they can no longer be pardoned."

[Adapted from Chan, *Instructions*, pp. 298–306]

THE WANG YANGMING SCHOOL

Wang's disciple Qian Dehong, in a comment on Wang's *Questions*, appropriates to the latter Zhu Xi's concept of the Succession to the Way, asserting that "the teaching of the *Great Learning* had, after Mencius, found no worthy trans-

---

9. 100 *fen*.

mitter for more than a thousand years, but with this exposition in terms of [Wang's] innate knowing (*liangzhi*) it was restored to full clarity of understanding as if one day had encompassed all of time past."[10] Qian thereby advances the claim that Wang's doctrine of innate knowing represents the authentic renewal of the tradition of the Way and succession to the mind of the sages.

This new learning, encapsulated in the doctrine of innate knowing and the "extension of innate knowing," transformed the sage learning from the "learning of past sages" to "the Learning of Sagehood" for all in the present time, rendering it accessible to Everyman to a degree that Zhu Xi's "Learning to Be a Sage" may have aspired to but in ways Zhu had not conceived. Wang thereby ushered in a kind of "popular" movement with a greater potential for the participation of ordinary people in the fulfillment of Neo-Confucian ideals.

It was possible so to popularize the notion of sagehood only because Wang had internalized or subjectivized it. "How can the signs of sagehood be recognized," he asks, and answers, "If one clearly perceives one's own innate knowing, then one recognizes that the signs of sagehood do not exist in the sage but in oneself."[11] And the way to achieve sagehood is not to set up some idealized image far beyond one, as many scholars have done, "seeking to know what they cannot know and do what they cannot do."[12] It is to stop relying on external standards, to become completely identified with the Principle of Heaven within oneself and thus become self-sustaining. This anyone can do with even a modicum of education.

It would be the mission of the Wang Yangming school to take this message far beyond the usual scholarly audience, now that erudition was no longer a prime qualification. Wang's holistic approach — so evident in the doctrine of "humaneness forming one body with Heaven, Earth, and all things" — stressed what was shared and common to all more than what was unique and different in each individual. Indeed, its common character was almost Wang's fundamental article of faith. Individual differences were important for him, but the uniqueness of the individual is not something Wang sets in opposition to common humanity, any more than one would, accepting the doctrine of the "unity of principle and diversity of its particularizations," see these two aspects as antithetical or mutually exclusive.

Wang's confidence in trusting one's own mind as the ultimate authority rests squarely on his faith that all human minds reflect and express a common standard of truth. Thus we recall him saying, "The Way is public and belongs to the whole world, and the doctrine is also public and belongs to the whole world. They are not the private properties of Master Zhu [Xi] or even Confucius. They are open to all and the only proper way to discuss them is to do so openly."[13]

---

10. *Wang Yangming quanshu* 1, *Wenlu* 1:123.
11. *Wang Yangming quanshu* 1, *Chuanxilu* 2:48.
12. Chan, *Instructions*, p. 69.
13. Ibid., p. 164.

There is perhaps no more striking example than this of Wang's basically Confucian — and we might even say Chinese — outlook: for all his emphasis on individual effort and personal intuition of truth, he retains a faith in the fundamental rationality of man; and for all his insistence on discovering right and wrong for oneself, it does not occur to him that there could be any essential conflict between subjective and objective morality, or that genuine introspection could lead to anything other than the affirmation of clear and common moral standards.

Here is the underlying reason why Wang Yangming's teaching could have had such a quickening effect on the thought of those times and such an explosive impact on all levels of Ming society and culture — its tremendous moral dynamism, its enormous confidence in human beings, and its faith that life could be dealt with by opening people up to one another from within.

Wang's strength as a teacher lay in his seemingly deliberate cultivation of ambiguities that could be explored by his own students and clarified by their own experience, as we have seen in the Colloquy at the Tianquan Bridge. Had he not allowed these ambiguities to stand, there might have been far less discussion and debate within his school, less room for individual and regional differentiation, and perhaps no such ranges of opinion as justify making distinctions between right, center, and left tendencies. Nor could we have found so many remarkable personalities, so many striking individuals, among his followers.

WANG JI AND THE FREEDOM OF INNATE KNOWING

Wang Ji (1498–1583), one of Wang Yangming's closest and most devoted followers, was a disciple of great brilliance and promise. After pursuing an official career with modest success, beset by the usual disappointments and frustrations, he left it in order to take up the life of a teacher. For more than forty years he lectured at academies and lecture halls throughout North, East, and South China, attracting large audiences and many students, as well as much criticism for his highly original — and, some said, unorthodox — views. His influence went far beyond his own school. Thus he stands as one of the most important and controversial figures among the large number of able individuals attracted to Wang Yangming's teaching.

In the Colloquy at the Tianquan Bridge, we have seen how Wang Ji emphasized the transcendental freedom of innate knowing and its spontaneous exercise. In this way he leaned toward a mystical view of innate knowing as bridging the sacred and the profane, the divine and the mundane:

The innate knowing of the mind-and-heart partakes of the holy, the sagely. It is the spirituality of the nature, supremely empty and divine, utmost nothingness and transforming power. Requiring neither study nor deliberation, as the Heavenly it is what comes naturally. At the lowest level it can be readily understood by even ignorant men and women; in its highest reaches it goes beyond the comprehension of even sages and worthies, so that they liken it to the sun or moon shining in the heavens. . . . It can match Heaven-and-Earth, span the four seasons, reach down to a thousand generations. It is active cultivation and ready enlightenment. Gotten for oneself, it owes nothing to externals, while the key to it lies in no more than a fleeting moment of thought.

[*Wang Longxi quanji* 1:32b — dB]

At times Wang Ji describes the practice of innate knowing in terms redolent of popular theisms and even strikingly reminiscent of devotional religions that teach "living in the presence of God." The commitment to the Way of the sages is no less a holy vocation for being directed to self-knowledge and calling for faith or trust in one's self. "The commitment to self-knowledge means to do without selfish calculation, premeditation, or disputation, and just to stand in the sight of the Lord-on-High to the end of one's days." Elsewhere, in terms recalling the *Classic of Odes'* "facing [the spirits] of Heaven [and Earth],"[14] he specifically endorses this kind of religiosity as preferable to a slavish adherence to sacred texts: "If we can always face the Lord-on-High, then we need have no dependence on books."[15]

Wang Ji's spiritual message reached out to religious currents in East Asia during the sixteenth and seventeenth centuries. Wang Ji influenced the thought of Nakae Tōju (1608–1648), the so-called founder of the Wang Yangming school in Japan, who blended the Neo-Confucian philosophy of mind with a Shinto devotionalism. Other Neo-Confucian activists in late Tokugawa Japan, who combined a kind of religious messianism with the cult of the heroic individual, were also inspired by Wang Ji. Moreover, there was an atmosphere of religious revival in the spread of the Wang Yangming movement itself in sixteenth-century China.

This poses a question as to whether a movement of thought like the Wang Yangming school, which stimulated many new currents of moral reform and religious syncretism, had the potential for outgrowing or breaking down some of Neo-Confucianism's elitist character as a product of the scholar-official class. Could the religious impulse in Wang Ji have led to an evangelism and communitarianism that would extend his radical individualism in the direction of social equality or an egalitarian program? It is a question best addressed in connection with Wang Gen, to whom we turn next.

---

14. Ode 266. See the entry on this ode in Morohashi, *Dai Kanwa jiten,* 7457–10.
15. *Wang Yangming quanji yulu* 1:25b.

WANG GEN: THE COMMON MAN AS SAGE

Among the influential followers of Wang Yangming was Wang Gen (1483–1541), who carried forward most vigorously the idea of the common man as sage. He began life as the son of a salt maker and never sought or attained the status of a Confucian scholar-official. A man of tremendous energy and vitality, he seemed to draw strength and self-confidence as if through a taproot striking deep into the soil of China.

After only five years of instruction at the village school, economic necessity forced him, at the age of eleven, to leave it and assist his father in the family business. Later, on repeated business trips to Shandong province, he carried copies of the Four Books and the *Classic of Filiality* in his sleeve and discussed them with anyone he could find who might aid his understanding. His determination to become a sage was aroused, it is said, when he visited the shrine of Confucius at Qufu and realized that the immortal sage himself had been, after all, just a man.

By the age of twenty-one Gen had become established as an independent salt dealer and prospered enough that he could devote more time to self-study. He developed the practice of shutting himself up in a room for quiet-sitting, meditating in silence day and night for long periods of time. His spiritual awakening followed a dream in which he saw the heavens falling and people fleeing in panic. Answering their cries for help, he stood forth, pushed up the heavens, and restored order among the heavenly bodies. People were overjoyed and thanked him profusely. When Gen awoke, bathed in perspiration, he suddenly had his enlightenment, described in terms of an experience of being united with all things through his humanity (*ren*) and of finding the universe within himself.

From this experience arose Wang Gen's sense of mission, a vocation to become a teacher to humankind. But since he had had little formal education, his approach to learning was quite rudimentary, emphasizing personal spirituality and activity as opposed to scholarly study. The classics, he said (in language similar to Lu Xiangshan in the Song), were to be used simply to document one's own experience.

Not long before he met Wang Yangming, Wang Gen's reading of *Mencius* and his reflections on the true meaning of sagehood in one's daily life produced a startling thought. Referring to *Mencius* 6B:2, he said, "Can one speak the words of [the sage king] Yao, and perform the actions of Yao, and yet not wear the clothing of Yao?"[16] Whereupon, following some prescriptions found in the *Record of Rites*, he made himself a long cotton gown, a special hat and girdle to wear, and a ceremonial tablet to carry around with him. Above his door he

---

16. A permutation of the original Mencian saying.

inscribed the declaration "My teaching comes down through [the sages] Fu Xi, Shennong, the Yellow Emperor, Yao, Shun, the Great Yu, Kings Tang, Wen, and Wu, the Duke of Zhou, and Confucius. To anyone who earnestly seeks it, whether he be young or old, high or low, wise or ignorant, I shall pass it on." Many people laughed at this, but some were moved by Wang Gen's sense of active concern to make the ancient Way live in the present and, ignoring the ridicule of others, they took up the cause.

After meeting Yangming and becoming his disciple, Gen found that his active disposition still made him restless to carry the true Way to all human beings. He returned home, built himself a cart like the one Confucius was said to have used when he traveled to the courts of feudal princes, and went off to Peking. There his dress, his cart, and his somewhat piglike appearance attracted much attention, and great crowds came to hear him. Many people became convinced of his deep sincerity and were drawn to his ideas. In ruling circles, however, he was looked on either as a joke or as a potential troublemaker. Later he seems to have settled down to a less spectacular role while Yangming remained alive, but thereafter he resumed an active life as a teacher in his own school and had wide influence.

Wang Gen was not a social revolutionary, but his efforts, following up the implications of Zhu Xi's and Wang Yangming's teachings, probably did more to reach a larger public audience than anyone since Xu Heng in the Yuan had done. The Ming founder, it is true, had tried to promote universal schooling, but the close link between schooling and official recruitment tended to vitiate this effort by orienting education too much toward entry into the governing elite, while Wang Gen explicitly disavowed and personally renounced any such intention, emphasizing instead general education for the ordinary man. In this respect, he may well stand as the preeminent example of a Neo-Confucian who, spurning political power, believed that the main action lay in bringing the benefits of education to every man.

THE HUAINAN INVESTIGATION OF THINGS

Before visiting Wang Yangming, Wang Gen had described his own teaching as "the investigation of things," but he recognized that his interpretation of it was similar to Yangming's "innate knowing." The similarity lies in the fact that "investigation of things" means for both essentially the "rectification of affairs." In other words, the starting point of all self-cultivation as formulated in the *Great Learning* should be an understanding of things, matters, actions, and events, so that these conform to one's own sense of right and wrong, shame and deference, etc., and thus become "rectified." In particular Wang Gen stressed the self as the active center of things. In his view self and society were one continuum, with the self as the trunk or base and society as the branch or superstructure (not unlike Xu Heng's version of the *Elementary Learning*).

The following is a typical expression of what became known as the "Huainan [method of] the investigation of things," so called because Huainan is the classical name for Wang Gen's home region. It rests on two cardinal Confucian principles: that reciprocity is the basis of all social relations and that higher forms of social organization depend on the self-cultivation of individuals in the lower forms and, ultimately, on the individual himself.

When the *Classic of Changes* speaks of the preservation of the state being dependent on the security of the individual it is speaking to the "gentleman" who is a member of the ruling class, if not the ruler himself. Wang Gen, however, is actualizing the theoretical potential in this principle, and broadening its significance to include the common individual as well as the traditional Confucian "gentleman" or "noble person."

If in one's conduct of life there is any shortcoming, one should look for the fault within oneself. To reflect on oneself is the fundamental method for the rectification of things. Therefore, the desire to regulate the family, order the state, and pacify the world [as in the *Great Learning*], rests upon making the self secure (*anshen*). The *Classic of Changes* says, "If the self is secure, then the empire and state can be preserved."[17] But if the self is not secure, the root is not established.

To make the self secure, one must love and respect the self, and one who does this cannot but love and respect others. If I can love and respect others, others will love and respect me. If a family can practice love and self-respect, then the family will be regulated. If a state can practice love and self-respect, then the state will be regulated, and if all-under-Heaven can practice love and self-respect, then all under Heaven will be at peace. Therefore, if others do not love me, I should realize that it is not particularly because of others' inhumanity but because of my own, and if others do not respect me, it is not particularly that others are disrespectful but that I am.

["Wang Gen zhuan," *Mingru xuean* 32:69–70 — dB]

CLEAR WISDOM AND SELF-PRESERVATION

Wang Gen's brief essay titled "Clear Wisdom and Self-preservation" ("Mingzhe baoshen lun"),[18] from which the following passage is drawn, is expressed in a simple style and somewhat repetitive argumentation, which reflect both his own homespun character and his desire to communicate to the simplest people.

---

17. *Classic of Changes, Commentary on the Appended Phrases,* part 2; Lynn, *Classic of Changes,* p. 83.

18. The title of Wang's essay involves an allusion to Ode 260, which speaks of a minister who has "clear wisdom" and "preserves his person."

Clear wisdom is innate knowing. To clarify wisdom and preserve the self is innate knowing and innate ability. It is what is called "to know without deliberating and to know how without learning how."[19] All men possess these faculties. The sage and I are the same. Those who know how to preserve the self will love the self like a treasure. If I can love the self, I cannot but love other people; if I can love other people, they will surely love me; and if they love me, my self will be preserved. . . . If I respect my self, I dare not but respect other people; if I respect other people, they will surely respect me; and if they respect me, my self is preserved. If I respect my self, I dare not be rude to other people; if I am not rude to others, they will not be rude to me; and if they are not rude to me, then my self is preserved. . . . This is humaneness! This is the Way whereby all things become one body!

If by this means I regulate the family, then I can love the whole family; and if I love that family, they will love me; and if they love me, my self is preserved. If by this means I rule a state, I can love the whole state; if I love that state, the state will love me; and if the state loves me, my self is preserved. Only when my self is preserved can I preserve the state. If by this means I pacify all-under-Heaven, I can love all-under-Heaven; and if I can love all-under-Heaven, then all who have blood and breath cannot but respect their kin, and if they all respect their kin, then my self is preserved. Only if my self is preserved can I preserve all-under-Heaven. This is humaneness! This is [the Mean's] unceasing sincerity! This is [Confucius's] Way that threads through all things!

The reason men cannot fulfill it is because of the partiality that arises from their physical endowment and material desires, and this is also what makes them differ from the sage. Only when they differ from the sage do they need education. What kind of education? Education in clear wisdom and self-preservation — that is all.

If I only know how to preserve my self and do not know to love other men, then I will surely seek only to satisfy my self, pursue my own selfish gain, and harm others, whereupon they will retaliate and my self can no longer be preserved. . . . If I only know how to love others and do not know how to love my self, then it will come to my body being cooked alive or the flesh being sliced off my own thighs, or to throwing away my life and killing my self, and then my self cannot be preserved. And if my self cannot be preserved, with what shall I preserve my prince and father?

["Mingzhe baoshen lun," Wang Xinzhai yiji 1:12b–13a — dB]

When Wang Gen speaks of "my body being cooked alive or the flesh being sliced off my own thighs" and "throwing away my life" he is alluding not only to violence done to one by others but to extravagant gestures of self-sacrifice and protests against a highly

---

19. Mencius 7A:15.

idealized view of the self that called for heroic self-denial and an almost religious dedication to one's ruler or parents, so contrary to the natural human instinct for self-preservation.[20]

THE ENJOYMENT OF LEARNING

This ode expresses the natural spontaneity and creative power of the Way manifesting itself through the individual, but a Way that also serves the needs of human beings. Wang Gen's activism is alive with the spontaneous joy of the Dao and finds that joy in learning. Thus his paean to the enjoyment of learning":

> The human heart naturally enjoys itself
> But one binds oneself by selfish desires.
> When a selfish desire makes its appearance,
> Innate knowing is still self-conscious,
> And once there is consciousness of it, the selfish
>   desire forthwith disappears,
> So that the heart returns to its former joy.
> Joy is the enjoyment of this learning:
> Learning is to learn this joy.
> Without this joy it is not true learning;
> Without this learning it is not true joy.
> Enjoy and then learn,
> Learn and then enjoy.
> To enjoy is to learn, to learn is to enjoy.
> Ah! among the joys of this world what compares to
>   learning!
> What learning in the world compares to this joy!
>   [*Wang Xinzhai yiji* 2:9b–10a — dB]

Wang Gen was not the first Chinese thinker to find joy in life. This is a common theme among his predecessors, from Confucius and Zhuangzi down through the Song masters to Wang Yangming. But he may be the first to express such rapturous joy in learning of a kind that is available to all and not just the secret delight of the scholar. Wang Gen's joy arises from the fact that learning is so simple and easy. It does not require any erudition or intellectual exertion; it is the operation of ordinary intelligence in everyday life, which should be effortless. Joy is spontaneous when one does

---

20. The *Zhuangzi* refers to a loyal minister cutting off his flesh to feed his sovereign. In the *New Tang History* and *History of the Song* there are examples of filial sons slicing flesh from their thighs to make medicine for their parents. Cf. Chan, *Instructions*, pp. 107–108, n. 44. See also Ming Buddhist examples of such self-sacrifice in ch. 17. Of course, this was contrary to the prime Confucian filial obligation to preserve one's body intact and was criticized by orthodox scholars.

not rely on one's own strength, but lets nature, innate knowing, the Way be manifested freely through the self.

THE TAIZHOU SCHOOL AS A POPULAR MOVEMENT

From Wang Gen's teachings and personal example his school (named Taizhou, for his hometown) drew remarkable vitality and was able to exert a wide influence on sixteenth-century China. His school was unusual in claiming such a large number of commoners, including among its adherents a woodcutter, a potter, a stonemason, an agricultural laborer, salt makers, clerks, and merchants.

Such a development could not have come about simply through the force of Wang Gen's ideas alone, or even those of the Wang Yangming school as a whole. Other factors contributed. Economic affluence had prepared the ground by raising the general level of subsistence and enabling more people to participate in the cultural life of the society. In the Song and Ming, the spread of high culture is shown in the existence of literary societies, which sponsored the writing and printing of poetry in the classical *shi* form by merchants and artisans. The reverse process is seen in the adoption by the literati of forms (not wholly legitimated), which developed in the marketplaces and amusement centers — especially the popular drama and fiction that grew out of popular storytelling.

In the Taizhou school itself personal relationships crossed traditional class lines, intellectual associations crossed political lines, and educational work crossed religious lines. While the penetration of the movement to the lower levels of society is significant, as contrasted to the type of individuality cultivated almost entirely within the upper class of the Song period, its broad extension to all levels of society and to many areas of life is of more fundamental importance than its class character. This is of importance not only for society but for the role of Confucianism in it. For with its primary engagement in popular education, and what might be called its proselytizing evangelism, in the Taizhou school Confucianism for the first time became heavily involved in the sphere traditionally occupied by popular religion.

The intellectual historian Huang Zongxi, no admirer of the Taizhou school as a whole, said that owing to the activities of Wang Gen and Wang Ji, the teachings of Wang Yangming "spread like the wind over all the land." True to his self-declared mission as a teacher to the world, Gen traveled widely and stirred up discussion wherever he went. On his homemade touring cart he had written that he would "travel to the mountains and forests in order to meet recluses and into the towns and villages in order to mix with ignorant commoners." One of these uneducated commoners, the potter Han Zhen, after his "conversion" and a period of study with Wang Gen's brother, took up the mission of spreading the new gospel among ordinary folk and developed a large following among peasants, artisans, and merchants. After the fall harvest he would gather people together for lectures and discussion. When he had finished in one town he moved on to another. A regular feature of these gatherings was group singing: "With some chanting and others responding, their voices resounded like waves over the countryside." The atmosphere of a religious revival prevailed, and Han Zhen personally exemplified a kind of religious dedication to the cause. At these meetings, when the talk turned toward partisan politics and personalities, he would ask, "With life so short, how can you spend time gossiping?" And when the discussion became too pedantically involved with the niceties of classical scholarship, he would ask if those so engaged thought they were on a scholarly lecture platform.

Considering the Confucian rationalists' diffidence toward (if not aversion to) popular religion and the often poor communication between high and low cultures, this populist movement had great potential significance for bridging the gap, even though Wang Gen thought of it primarily as a force for the moral regeneration of all humanity and not necessarily for greater participation of the common people in a new political process.

LI ZHI: ARCH-INDIVIDUALIST

The tide of individualistic thought in the late Ming reached its height with Li Zhi (1527–1602), who has been both condemned and acclaimed as the greatest heretic and iconoclast in China's history. He is in any case one of the most brilliant and complex figures in Chinese thought and literature.

As a radical individualist who disavowed any school ties, Li does not fit exactly under the heading of the Wang Yangming school, but he did admire Yangming and was much influenced by several of the latter's followers, notably Wang Ji, so he serves as an example — and a particularly striking one — of new trends in that movement, especially the independent, critical temper generated by Wang's doctrine of innate knowing, which in the pursuit of learning for one's self led to a profound questioning of sagehood as both an elite and a popular ideal.

Li was born and raised in the port city of Quanzhou, Fujian province, which in earlier times had been a center of foreign trade, with a somewhat cosmopolitan character. Li's forebears had been active in this trade. The commercial atmosphere of Quanzhou is vividly recalled in Li's writing by his frequent use of the language of the marketplace and by his aggressive, hard-driving mentality. But Quanzhou's foreign trade had been largely cut off by the Ming seclusion policy; what survived was mostly illicit or severely regulated — trade of a kind that had the nefarious connotations of smuggling, the black market, official collusion, and squeeze. Its spirit could hardly have been that of the self-confident bourgeois, the expansive builder of a new world.

Li received a classical Confucian training but, as he said later, he was a skeptic from his youth, repelled by anything or anyone — Confucian, Buddhist, or Daoist — identified with an organized creed. He felt a great revulsion, too, against the kind of mechanical learning required for the examinations to enter an official career, and though he managed to overcome his scruples and pass the provincial examinations in 1552, he did not go on to the higher examinations at the capital. Such an attitude on Li's part fits into a recognizable pattern of alienation among members of the educated class in Ming and Qing China, typified by the sensitive, highly intelligent child of a well-to-do family on the decline, who feels a fundamental conflict between the integrity of the sagely ideal and what one must do to succeed in the world and discharge one's family responsibilities. Something of the same conflict, however, was widely felt in the sixteenth and seventeenth centuries by scholars of varying background and temperament.

After his qualifying examination Li spent almost thirty years in the status of an official, going from one routine assignment to another. Though a somewhat frustrating life, marked by frequent conflict with his superiors, it was not without considerable leisure, in which he could pursue his own studies. A profound spiritual unrest was at work within him, however. As he put it, he yearned to "hear the Way," borrowing the phrase from Confucius: "Hearing the Way in the morning, one could die content in the evening."[21] In other words, he was searching for something worth living and dying for.

Thus through five years at the Board of Rites in Peking, Li's mind was little occupied with official duties but rather was "sunk deep in the Way." In the course of these years, he formed close associations with members of the Wang Yangming school, who introduced him to the teachings of Wang Yangming, Wang Ji, and the Taizhou school. He had a strong aversion, however, to the lecture meetings promoted by that school for "learning by discussion" and did not take part in them. Later, drawn to a life of independent study and contemplation, he resigned from official service and took up residence in a Buddhist temple, sending his wife and children home to Fujian. When a few years later he took the Buddhist tonsure, it signified as much as anything else his determination to make a complete break with family cares and social obligations.

Li gave many different reasons for his decision to shave off his hair and become a monk, some of them perhaps only half serious and some apparently dubious rationalizations. The most plausible was simply that he wished to escape the control of others and achieve a degree of personal freedom not possible for the layman. There can be no doubt of his serious interest in Buddhism, but he was as individualistic in this respect as in all others. In fact, his desire "to be an individual" (*cheng yige ren*) is given by Li as intimately involved in his decision to become a "monk." Officially he was not a licensed monk, nor did

21. *Analects* 4:8.

he keep the monastic discipline. Instead he pursued even more intensively scholarly interests quite unusual for a monk.

Two years after becoming a "monk," in 1590, he published his *Fenshu* (*A Book to Burn*), the title of which acknowledged the dangerousness of its contents. It was a collection of letters, essays, prefaces, and poems expressing his repudiation of conventional morality, his belief in the essential identity of the Three Teachings, and his nonconforming views on history, literature, and a wide range of other subjects. He expected the book to be condemned as heresy and it was. But despite attacks upon it and mounting pressure against him, Li persisted in his course. He became even freer in his conduct and, though the charges of social and sexual misconduct made against him are undoubtedly exaggerated, he did not hesitate to relieve his intense scholarly efforts with pleasant diversions in and out of the temple. After the publication in 1600 of *Cangshu* (*A Book to Be Hidden Away*), which challenged many long-accepted Confucian views of history, a mob incited by local authorities burned down his residence at the temple, and he spent the remaining few years of his life taking refuge in the home of friend after friend in different places. Finally, in 1602, a memorial at the court in Peking charged him with a long list of offenses, and an edict was issued ordering his arrest and the burning of his books. In prison in Peking he made his last protest, committing suicide by slashing his throat.

THE CHILDLIKE MIND-AND-HEART

Basic assumptions for Li Zhi are, first, the cardinal Neo-Confucian doctrine of the essential goodness of the human mind and second, Wang Yangming's view that the manifesting of this inherent virtue comes through the direct, uninhibited expression of "good [innate, intuitive] knowing." Li contrasted this natural innocence and spontaneity to the glib professions of sagely morality all around him. These seemed to him the hypocritical mouthings of "scholars" whose learning and "virtue" were quite conventional, secondhand, and pretentious — uninformed by the searching self-scrutiny ("self-watchfulness") so emphasized in the *Great Learning* and the *Mean*.

The childlike mind, he says, is originally pure, but it can be lost if received opinions come in through the senses and are allowed to dominate it. The greatest harm results when moral doctrines are imposed upon it, and the mind loses its capacity to judge for itself. This comes mainly from reading books and learning "moral principles."

Once people's minds have been given over to received opinions and moral principles, what they have to say is all about these things, and not what would naturally come from their childlike minds. No matter how clever the words, what have they to do with oneself? What else can there be but phony men speaking phony words, doing phony things, writing phony writings? Once the men become phonies, everything becomes phony. Thereafter, if one speaks phony talk to the phonies, the phonies are pleased; if one does phony things as the phonies do, the phonies are pleased; and if one discourses with the phonies through phony writings, the phonies are pleased. Everything is phony, and everyone is pleased.

[*Fenshu* 3:97 — dB]

PHONY SAGES

In Li's scathing attacks on these "hypocrites" one can see what has become of the grand humanitarian slogans of Wang Yangming and Wang Gen among the "lecturers" who propagated their teachings.

If there is something to be gained by it and they want to take charge of public affairs, then the "lecturers" will cite the saying that "all things are one body" [and it is their duty to serve humankind]; if they stand to lose by it, however, and they wish to avoid blame and censure, then they invoke the saying "The clearest wisdom is self-preservation"[22] [in order to withdraw from threatening danger].

[Or again:] In ordinary times when there is peace, they only know how to bow and salute one another, or else they sit the day long in an upright posture [practicing quiet-sitting] like a clay image, thinking that if they can suppress all stray thoughts they will become sages and worthies. The more cunning among them participate in the meetings to discuss innate knowledge, secretly hoping to gain some recognition and win high office. But when a crisis comes, they look at each other pale and speechless, try to shift the blame to one another and save themselves on the pretext that "the clearest wisdom is self-preservation." Consequently, if the state employs only this type of scholar, when an emergency arises it has no one of any use in the situation.

Of their activities as teachers, he says the "lecturers" gather crowds of followers and take in students:

to enhance their own name and fame and make themselves rich and honored, not realizing that Confucius never sought wealth or honors or to surround himself with disciples. . . . But the teachers of today — one day out of office and their disciples abandon them; one day without funds and their followers scatter.

[*Xufenshu* 3:94; *Fenshu* 4:159, 2:61 — dB]

Again and again Li mocks the moralistic pretensions of those who preach the Way but have "their hearts set on high office and the acquisition of wealth." He compares them

---

22. Alluding to Ode 260.

with a type of literary man whom he considers equally "phony" — the so-called mountain-men (shanren) *who affect the independence and eccentricity of artists and poets who live alone in the midst of nature:*

Those who consider themselves sages today are no different from the mountain men — it is all a matter of luck. If it is a man's luck that he can compose poetry he calls himself a "mountain man"; it if is not and he cannot compose poetry and become a mountain man, he calls himself a "sage." If it is a man's luck that he can lecture on "innate knowledge," he calls himself a "sage," but if it is not and he is unable to lecture on innate knowledge, he gives up being a sage and calls himself a "mountain man." They turn around and reverse themselves in order to deceive the world and secure their own gain. They call themselves "mountain men," but their hearts are those of the merchants. Their lips are full of the Way and virtue, but their ambition is to become "thieves of virtue."[23]

Those who call themselves "mountain men," if considered as merchants, would not be worth one copper cash and without the protection of high officials would be despised among men. And how do I know that I am any better? Who knows but that I too have the heart of a merchant and have put on Buddhist robes just to deceive people and make use of the name?

[*Fenshu* 2:46 — dB]

That scholar-officials are worse than merchants and no better than cheats is a constant refrain in Li's writing. Outwardly they are sages, inwardly merchants. But the merchants in their business dealings could never compete with the scholar-officials, who are masters in the business of selling out dynasties, sacrificing rulers on the altar of the sage, and then carrying their heads into the marketplace.

At times, however, Li could turn the same sharp-edged criticism on himself, acknowledging that he was little better than they in these respects:

People all think Confucius a sage and so do I. They all think Laozi and Buddha are heretics and so do I. But people don't really know what sagehood and heterodoxy are. They have just heard so much about them from their parents and teachers. Nor do their parents and teachers really know what sagehood and heterodoxy are; they just believe what they hear from the scholars and elders. And the scholars and elders don't know either, except that Confucius said something about these things. But his saying "Sagehood — of that I am not capable,"[24] they take as just an expression of modesty, and when he spoke of "studying strange teachings [as] harmful"[25] they interpret this as referring to Daoism and Buddhism.

---

23. *Analects* 17:13.
24. As quoted in *Mencius* 2A:2.
25. *Analects* 2:16.

The scholars and elders have memorized these things and embroidered on them; parents and teachers have preserved and recited them, and children have blindly accepted them. . . . So today, though men have eyes, they do not use them. And what then about me? Do I dare use my eyes? I too follow the crowd and regard him [Confucius] as a sage . . . I too follow the crowd in doing him honor at Zhifoyuan.

[*Xufenshu* 4:102 — dB]

Moreover, if he was thus severe in his judgment of contemporary literati who mouthed the fashionable slogans of Wang Yangming's school, he said of himself:

His nature was narrow, his manner arrogant, his speech coarse, his mind mad, his conduct rash and imprudent. He did not mix much with others but in personal contacts could be warm and friendly. Toward others he was critical of their faults and little impressed with their good points: those he did not like he would have nothing to do with except to wish them ill to his dying day.

[*Fenshu* 3:130 — dB]

PURSUING ZHU XI'S "LEARNING FOR ONE'S SELF"

Li Zhi, even more than Wang Yangming, stresses the radically individual nature of learning. "Each human being Heaven gives birth to," he says, "has his own individual function and he does not need to learn this from Confucius. If he did need to learn this from Confucius, how then, in all the ages before Confucius, could anyone have achieved their full humanity?" Indeed, even Confucius had not taught people to study Confucius but only to look within themselves.

Confucius never taught people to study Confucius. If he had taught them to study Confucius, why is it that when Yan Yuan asked about humaneness, Confucius answered that one achieves humaneness in and through one's self, not through others? Why is it that Confucius said, "In ancient times learning was for one's self [not for the sake of others]," and said, "The noble person seeks it in himself"? Because it was from the self, his followers did not need to ask Confucius about humaneness. Because it was for one's self, his teaching of others was based on his own self-study. This is learning that does without either self or others [i.e., as a preconceived dichotomy].

Because it is selfless, it starts with overcoming [a false sense of] self; because it is without [regard to the self's impressing] others, its teaching aims only at motivating others.

[*Fenshu* 1:17 — dB]

The reason learning cannot be for the sake of others, or to gain their acceptance, is that while all humans have common elementary needs, every human being differs in his individual constitution and capacities, and one cannot serve as a model for others, nor can the view of one be taken as the standard for others. "What others consider right and wrong can never serve as a standard for me. Never from the start have I taken as right and wrong for myself what the world thinks right and wrong."

Learning for one's self consists essentially of allowing no self-deception, and this is true for all — common person and sage.

The sage is no different from others; it is just a matter of not deceiving oneself. The sages' ordering of the state and pacifying of the world are no different from this; it is just a matter of extending this principle of having no self-deception. Thus to have no self-deception is essential and to make the intentions sincere is fundamental. How important it is not to deceive oneself in what one learns from "solitary knowing"! How is it then that in the end humans cannot help deceiving themselves in the matter of self-knowledge? It comes from not knowing that this is the true reality of knowing. Thus when the *Great Learning* speaks of making the intentions sincere, it makes extending one's knowledge [learning] the precondition. Extending one's knowledge: that says it all.

[*Daogulu* A:35a — dB]

THE LEGITIMACY OF BEING SELF-INTERESTED

Having no self-deception, and being thoroughly honest with oneself, meant for Li Zhi recognizing the basic, legitimate self-interestedness in man, rather than pretending to a lofty disinterestedness. Here he takes issue with those hypocrites who profess a great unselfishness while rationalizing ulterior motives, not openly acknowledging their natural self-regarding interests. He is at particular pains to debunk the idea in Buddhism and Neo-Confucianism of the sage or bodhisattva as "having no mind [of his own (*wuxin*)]":

The learning of the sage does nothing and yet all is accomplished (*wuwei er cheng*). But those who talk about "doing nothing" today only speak of "not minding" [lit., "having no mind," *wuxin*]. However, once you start talking about the mind-and-heart, how can you speak about "having no mind"? And when you start talking about "doing," how can you "do something" without having a mind [to do it]? If a peasant did not "mind" [what he was about], his fields would surely go to weeds. If the artisan did not mind [what he was about], his tools would surely get ruined. If the scholar did not mind [what he was about], his task would certainly be left undone. How is it possible "not to mind"?

Some explain this "not minding" as meaning not that one literally has "no mind" but that one has no selfish mind or intentions. Now "self-interest" is "man's minding." Man must be self-interested if his mind is to be made known. If he were not self-interested, there would be no mind. It is like tending a field; there must first be some self-interest to obtain the autumn's harvest before one would go to the "effort of working the field." Or like the husbandman, there must first be the self-interest to gain by "storing things up" before one will go to the effort of husbandry. Or like the scholar, there must first be the desire for self-advancement before one will undertake to prepare for examinations.

Thus an officer who had no thought of gaining the emoluments of office would not be responsive to an invitation to serve. If he were to have no high rank, no amount of exhortation could persuade a man to come forth and serve. And even in the case of a sage like Confucius, if there were no office of minister of justice by which he shared in the business of governing, he certainly would not have found even a day of service in the state of Lu tolerable. This is a natural principle, to which practice must conform. One cannot just engage in airy talk and groundless speculation. . . .

Confucius said, "The humane person first faces the difficulties and only later thinks of the rewards."[26] He speaks of facing the difficulties first, after which one could expect some reward. He does not say there should be no seeking for reward at all, nothing aimed at, and all done thoughtlessly and without any consideration.

Thus if you wish to be true to moral principle, there must be some thought of gain. If there is no thought of gain, there can be no "being true." If the Way is to be made manifest, one's own success must thereby be accomplished. If there is no consideration of one's own success, how can the Way ever be made manifest? Now if someone says that in the learning of the Sage there is no self-interestedness, and thus no such aim could be allowed, how could anyone aim to achieve sagehood?

[*Cangshu* 32:544 — dB]

In the foregoing Li challenges the Neo-Confucian concept of lofty impartiality and self-sacrificing devotion to the common good (gong) as the ideal quality of the noble man. Instead, for the sage, noble man, or commoner the public interest or common good should be identified with:

. . . the desire for goods, for sexual satisfaction, for study, for personal advancement, for the accumulation of wealth; the seeking out of the proper geomantic factors (*fengshui*) that will bring blessings to their children — all the things that are productive and sustain life in the world, everything that is loved and practiced in common by the people, and what they know and say in common.

In this Li finds a new basis for human relations — not the moral constants of Mencius, Zhu Xi, and Wang Yangming:

---

26. *Analects* 6:20.

To wear clothing and eat food — these are the principles of human relations. Without them there are no human relations. . . . The scholar should learn only what is real and unreal in respect to these relations and not impose other principles of human relations on top of them.

The essential thing in social relations is to let people satisfy their own desires, to let them find their own natural place in the world.

People have always found their own natural place [when left alone]. If they do not it is only because they are harassed by those who are greedy and aggressive and harmed by humanitarians (*renzhe*). The humanitarians worry about everyone finding his place in the world, and so they have virtue and rites to correct people's minds, and the state with its punishments to fetter their limbs. Then people begin to lose their place in a big way!

[*Fenshu* 1:37 — dB]

Most of the physical needs and appetites referred to above had been recognized as legitimate human concerns by earlier Confucians, including Zhu Xi and Wang Yangming. Indeed, it had been the perennial concern of the Confucian noble man to see that such needs of the common man were met, while, in doing so, he demanded much more of himself than that. (As Fan Zhongyan had put it, one should "be first in worrying about the world's worries and last in enjoying its pleasures.") What is at issue here, then, is how to reconcile an elite conception of noblesse oblige and self-denying service with the new popular doctrine of the common man as sage. As Wang Yangming's teachings spread, proclaiming that the streets were full of sages, self-fulfillment was being redefined to accord more with the realities of everyday life and less with the aspirations (to Li, mere pretensions) of a moral elite. In Li, Neo-Confucian naturalness was assuming a down-to-earth, fleshy, even brash character with more of a premium put on the free expression of natural feelings and less on the restraints of reverent seriousness and straitlaced morality enjoined upon the ruler and leadership elite by the early Learning of the Way.

It is not surprising that Li Zhi stands out as a brilliant, if mordant, critic of his own contemporaries — a unique but idiosyncratic and lonely figure — rather than as the progenitor of an organized movement for social change. As we have seen, he resisted all kinds of organization, had no desire to found a school, and was unlikely to shoulder the responsibilities of leadership. His political philosophy was a kind of Confucian laissez-faire (*wuwei*) just as apt to leave power in the hands of autocrats as to struggle for its restructuring or redistribution. Thus Li's importance remains as a social and literary critic, whose sharp satirization of the establishment, drawing on some of the most authentic values in Neo-Confucianism, challenged the educated elite to a searching reexamination of traditional attitudes and institutions that would mark much of seventeenth-century Chinese thought and literature.

LUO QINSHUN AND THE PHILOSOPHY OF *QI*

While much of the story of sixteenth-century Chinese thought can be told in terms of the charismatic figure of Wang Yangming and the creative innovation and popular appeal of his school, Wang's was not the only compelling voice to be heard in the mid-Ming period. Serious alternative views were espoused as well, some of them by thinkers associated with the Cheng-Zhu school and some as philosophically innovative as Wang's, if less susceptible to popularization.

Luo Qinshun (1465–1547) was a leading figure in the Cheng-Zhu school of the mid-Ming, a contemporary of Wang's, and one of his most effective and influential philosophical opponents. Like Wang, and at similar personal peril, Luo served in high official positions in the Ming government, including that of director of studies at the Imperial University in Nanking and as a minister in the Ministry of Personnel in Nanking and Peking. Also like Wang, Luo was actively involved in public life and concerned with practical issues of governance, land distribution, education, and the management of economic and military affairs. And he too regarded as fundamental the enduring Neo-Confucian idea that an ultimate goal of human life is "forming one body with Heaven, Earth, and all things."

Where Wang and Luo diverged most crucially was in their assessments of how such a goal of identification of the individual with all living things should be understood and how it could be realized — a disagreement over the nature of knowledge. Whereas Wang, developing his idea of "the extension of innate knowledge," came to redefine all significant knowledge as *moral* knowledge, dependent upon the creative projection of the individual's own moral mind, Luo, following the Cheng brothers and Zhu Xi, continued to insist on the importance of the acquisition of intellectual knowledge of the "external" world and on a carefully preserved balance between intellectual and moral cultivation.

While regarding himself as among the heirs of the Cheng-Zhu tradition of the Song, and retaining several of the most defining commitments of his predecessors, Lo was not merely rehearsing or recasting their views. He was at pains to explain that, as one who honored and trusted his predecessors, he was duty-bound to confront certain unresolved problems in their thought. For all of his devotion to the Neo-Confucian tradition and his conception of learning as a cumulative and ongoing enterprise, he was also a creative thinker who set forth metaphysical, psychological, and epistemological positions that were both new and, arguably, modern.

Among the innovative aspects of Luo's thought are his rejection of the Song dualism of principle (*li*) and material-force (*qi*) and development of a philo-

sophical monism of *qi*, applied in an innovative metaphysics and in a philosophical psychology that rejected the Song dualism of a "nature ordained by
Heaven" and a "physical nature," comprehending the nature as one and affirming the importance of both the emotions and sense knowledge. Rigorous in his
epistemology, Luo reassessed earlier views of the nature of knowledge and emphasized an intellectual understanding of the dynamic processes and concrete
realities of the actual world of human experience. In some of these positions,
he and Wang actually came close together, though in the end their differences
over the nature of knowledge proved to be so profound that they found themselves personally respectful but philosophically irreconcilable.

Wang Yangming, as we have seen, is best known for his *Instructions for
Practical Living (Chuanxilu)*, a collection of highly personal and often intimate
conversations between Wang and his disciples and letters written to them and
others on a variety of subjects, but focusing on individual problems of self-
cultivation. The importance of the master-disciple relationship and the shared
experience of life that it involved is apparent throughout. Luo Qinshun's major
work, *Knowledge Painfully Acquired (Kunzhiji)*, is, by contrast, a work of the
study, clearly composed in solitude. The tone is reflective; the choice of language is precise; issues are sharply defined. Luo is revealed in this collection
of reading notes as a scholar of formidable erudition, given to meticulous accuracy in his textual research and rigorous development of his philosophical
views. The reader will note in the selections that follow Luo's thorough grounding in classical as well as Neo-Confucian sources, a sign of a conscious participation in a cumulative and ongoing philosophical undertaking that is often
associated with the tradition known as Cheng-Zhu "orthodoxy."

MONISM OF *QI*

Luo Qinshun was among the first of the Ming thinkers to put forward the argument
that all reality, both physical and phenomenal, is *qi*, which is dynamic and constantly
in process. The regularity that can be observed in an endless process of recurrence is
li or principle. Luo explicitly rejected Zhu Xi's view that *li* represents a causal or
determinative power distinct from *qi*, as expressed in Zhu's statement that "*li* attaches
to *qi* and thus operates." *Li* is simply the pattern to be observed in the natural process
rather than its origin or final cause. With *qi* being the fundamental reality of the
universe, *li* is a designation (*ming*) for the "unregulated regularity" or spontaneous
order to be discovered in *qi*. It is not, in itself, a "thing" (*wu*). It cannot be understood
as ontologically prior to *qi*, or as superior to it, or as allied with *qi* but nonetheless
metaphysically distinct from it. As energy, *qi* is originally one; as order or regularity, *li*
is also one in the sense that it recurs in all the processes of nature.

When Confucius, in compiling the *Classic of Changes*, began with the words
"probing principle to the utmost" (*qiong li*), what, in fact, did he mean

by "principle" (*li*)? That which penetrates Heaven and Earth and connects past and present is nothing other than material-force (*qi*), which is unitary. This material-force, while originally one, revolves through endless cycles of movement and tranquillity, going and coming, opening and closing, rising and falling. Having become increasingly obscure, it then becomes manifest; having become manifest, it once again reverts to obscurity. It produces the warmth and coolness and the cold and heat of the four seasons, the birth, growth, gathering in, and storing of all living things, the constant moral relations of the people's daily life, the victory and defeat, gain and loss in human affairs. And amid all of this prolific variety and phenomenal diversity there is a detailed order and an elaborate coherence that cannot ultimately be disturbed, and that is so even without our knowing why it is so. This is what is called principle. Principle is not a separate entity that depends on material-force in order to exist or that "attaches to material force in order to operate."[27]

The phrase "there is in the changes the Supreme Ultimate"[28] has led some to suspect that there is a single entity that acts as a controlling power amid the transformations of yin and yang. But this is not the case. "Change" is a collective name for the two primary forces, the four secondary forms, and the eight trigrams. "The Supreme Ultimate" is a collective name for all principles taken together. To say that "there is in the changes the Supreme Ultimate" means that manifold diversity takes its origin from a single source.[29] This is then extended to the process of "production and reproduction"[30] to clarify that the dispersal of the single source produces manifold diversity. This is certainly the working of nature, its unregulated regularity, and not something that can be sought in the tangible realm.

It was only the elder Master Cheng [Cheng Hao] who described this most incisively. The views of the younger Master Cheng [Cheng Yi] and Master Zhu [Zhu Xi] seem to have been slightly different, and inasmuch as their theories all coexist, one must try to find a way to reconcile them and recover the ultimate unity.

[*Kunzhiji* 1, no. 11; Bloom, *Knowledge*, pp. 58–59 —IB]

Li is only the *li* of *qi*. It must be observed in the phenomenon of revolving and turning of *qi*. Departing is followed by returning, and returning is followed by departing: this is the phenomenon of revolving and turning. And in the fact

---

27. An explicit rejection of the language used by Zhu Xi in his statement (*Zhuzi quanshu* 49:4b): "Principle attaches to material-force and thus operates."

28. *Classic of Changes, Commentary on the Appended Phrases*, Part 1; Lynn, *Classic of Changes*, p. 65.

29. *Mencius* 3A:5.

30. *Classic of Changes, Commentary on the Appended Phrases*, Part 1; Lynn, *Classic of Changes*, p. 54.

that departure must be followed by return, and return must be followed by departure, there is that which is so even without our knowing why it is so. It is as if there were a single entity acting as a regulating power within things and causing them to be as they are.[31] This is what we designate as *li* and what is referred to in the statement "There is in the changes the Supreme Ultimate."[32] If one gains a clear understanding of the phenomenon of revolving and turning, one will find that everything conforms to it.

Master Cheng said, "Within Heaven and Earth there is only the process of action and reaction. What else is there?"[33] Now, given the reaction of going, there is the action of coming, and given the action of coming, there is the reaction of going. Action and reaction follow in endless succession, and there is nowhere that principle does not pertain. It is the same in Heaven [or Nature, *tian*] and in humans. Because the Way of Heaven is what is common to all, action and reaction are constant and unerring. As the human emotions cannot be free of the encumbrance of selfish desires, action and reaction may be inconstant and liable to error.

What acts and reacts is *qi*, while the fact that a particular action involves a particular reaction without there being the slightest possibility of error is *li*. . . . The so-called "correct principle which is central and straight"[34] does not allow for an instant's deviation. It is what Heaven has ordained and also what constitutes the nature of human beings and things. I have therefore said that *li* must be identified as an aspect of *qi*, and yet to identify *qi* as *li* would be incorrect.

[*Kunzhiji xu* 3, no. 40; Bloom, *Knowledge*, pp. 173–174 —IB]

HUMAN NATURE

In Luo's opinion there was another respect in which Cheng Yi and Zhu Xi had failed to "recover the ultimate unity," and that was in their view of human nature. Following the lead of Zhang Zai (1020–1077), they had accepted a distinction between an original human nature or Heaven-ordained nature and the physical nature. The original nature, which was associated with the Principle of Heaven (or Nature) and the Mind of the Way (*dao*), was pure and perfectly good; the physical nature, which was bound up with the individual's allotment of *qi*, was to one degree or another tainted by dint of its materiality. The object of personal cultivation, in this view, was to refine away the impurity of the physical nature so that the full goodness of the original nature could

---

31. It should be noted that Luo says, "*as if there were* a single entity acting as a regulating power." In the preceding passage he has explicitly denied that this is *actually* the case.

32. *Classic of Changes, Commentary on the Appended Phrases*, Part 1; Lynn, *Classic of Changes*, p. 65.

33. Cheng Yi in *Yishu* 15:7b.

34. Alludes to a statement of Cheng Hao's in *Yishu* 11:11a.

be more fully expressed. In line with his monism of *qi*, Luo Qinshun rejected the notion of two natures, insisting that it was without either classical precedent or philosophical justification. Note that in the following discussion Luo confronts the same challenge faced by his predecessors — that of explaining the relation between unity and diversity — how it happens that, if the nature is a shared endowment from Heaven, human capacities are nonetheless so varied. The nature, he says, is one, but it is differently expressed in the context of phenomenal diversity.

In the Six Classics discussion of the mind began with Emperor Shun.[35] Discussion of the nature began with Tang the Accomplished.[36] The four sentences uttered by Shun did not include the term "nature," though the idea of the nature was definitely implied. It was Tang who first clearly mentioned it, saying, "The High God has bestowed on the common people a moral sense through which they have the potential of a constant nature. To cause them tranquilly to pursue the course that it would indicate is the work of the sovereign."[37]

Confucius spoke of it in greater detail, saying, "The succession of yin and yang is called the Way. That which furthers it is good. That which brings it to completion is the nature. The humane perceive it and call it humane. The wise perceive it and call it wise. The people use it day by day and are not aware of it. Therefore the way of the noble person is rare."[38] He also said, "By nature close together. . ."[39] Zisi transmitted the idea, saying, "What Heaven has ordained is called the nature. Following one's nature is called the Way."[40] Mencius followed in this tradition and said, "The nature is good."[41] The sages and worthies of antiquity always discussed the nature in just such terms.

From Gaozi[42] on there were none with utmost clarity of vision. They all made pronouncements on the basis of mere imagination, and the more pronouncements were made, the fewer were in conformity with the teachings of the sages and worthies. At last there was no one who could finally achieve unity. Then in the Song there emerged Cheng, Zhang, and Zhu, who were the first to use different terms to explain what was the nature endowed by Heaven and what was the physical nature. They formulated their theories with reference to

---

35. This refers to the statement of Shun in the "Counsels of the Great Yu" in the *Classic of Documents*: "The human mind is precarious. The mind of Dao is subtle. Be discriminating, be one. Hold fast to the Mean." Legge, *The Chinese Classics*, 3:61–62.

36. This refers to the *Classic of Documents*, "Announcement of Tang;" Legge, *The Chinese Classics*, 3:185.

37. Translation adapted from Legge, *The Chinese Classics*, 3:185.

38. *Classic of Changes, Commentary on the Appended Phrases*, Part 1; Lynn, *Classic of Changes*, p. 53.

39. *Analects* 17:2.

40. *Mean* 1:1.

41. *Mencius* 3A:1, 6A:6.

42. The philosophical antagonist of Mencius in *Mencius* 6A.

Confucius and Mencius and verified them in terms of human emotions, so that they were in this respect complete. But to a single nature they applied two names. Although [Cheng Yi] said, "It is wrong to regard [the nature and *qi*] as two,"[43] he was not yet able to see them as one. In the end the doubts of scholars were not resolved, so that right down to the present their endless debates are carried on in the world. How can one blame them?

Day and night I was immersed in this, seeking intently to achieve personal realization. I had devoted years to it when suddenly one day it seemed to me that the whole of it had become transparently clear. I submit that the subtle truth of the nature (*xing*) and endowment (*ming*) is summarized in the formulation "Principle is one; its particularizations are diverse."[44] This is simple and yet complete, concise and yet utterly penetrating.

This [oneness of principle and diversity of its particularizations] owes nothing to compulsion or to contrivance, and by its nature it is utterly insusceptible to change. At the inception of life, when they are first endowed with *qi*, the principle of human beings and things is just one. After having attained physical form, their particularizations are diverse. That their particularizations are diverse is nothing but natural principle, for the oneness of their principle always exists within diverse particularizations. This is the explanation for the subtle truth of the nature and endowment. In terms of its oneness, "every human being can become a Yao or a Shun,"[45] and in terms of diversity, "only the very wisest and the very dullest do not change."[46]

[*Kunzhiji* 1, no. 14; Bloom, *Knowledge*, pp. 63–65 — IB]

DESIRES AND FEELINGS

One of the corollaries of Luo's denial of the notion of two natures, an original nature and a physical nature, was his rejection of the idea, basic to the psychological thought of most of the Song Neo-Confucians, that there was a fundamental antagonism between the Principle of Heaven (or Nature) and human desires. Selfish desires had often been thought to arise from the physical nature, to be counter to the original nature, and to demand either eradication or fairly rigorous curtailment. Human desires, in Luo's view, are, like the emotions, signs and expressions of human nature. They are natural and in conformity with principle. What requires control and regulation is the extremity of "selfishness" per se, the lack of awareness that one is fundamentally like others and has the same dispositions and needs.

---

43. *Yishu* 6:2a.
44. A statement of Cheng Yi's found in *Yichuan wenji* 5:12b, in *Er Cheng yishu*.
45. *Mencius* 6B:2.
46. *Analects* 17:3.

The desire, love, and hate spoken of in the "Record of Music,"[47] together with the pleasure, sorrow, anger, and joy mentioned in the *Mean*,[48] are collectively termed the seven emotions. Their principles in each case are rooted in the nature. Among the seven emotions, desire is relatively important. Heaven [or Nature] produces people with desires. By following their desires people find pleasure. From the flouting of them they feel anger. In fulfilling them they feel joy. And in finding them thwarted they know sorrow. Therefore the "Record of Music" speaks only of "the desires arising from the nature."[49] The desires cannot be spoken of as evil. They may be good or evil depending solely on whether they are regulated.

[*Kunzhiji* 1, no. 17; Bloom, *Knowledge*, p. 68 — IB]

THE NATURE OF KNOWLEDGE

The epistemological corollary of Luo's monism of *qi* and his revised attitude toward human nature is seen in his assertion of the validity of sense knowledge and sense experience. Sense knowledge had been devalued by some Song Neo-Confucians, including Zhang Zai and Cheng Yi, who assigned a higher value to knowledge attained through the moral nature, a mode of apprehension more akin to the experience of enlightenment than to ordinary sense perception. Luo does not accept the notion that there are modes of knowing independent of and superior to "the knowledge of seeing and hearing," which, for him, are the primary modes of apprehending the world. The genuine epistemological issue is the care and discernment with which the senses are employed.

At the same time that Luo was asserting the primacy of sense knowledge, he was also strongly reaffirming the central teaching of the Cheng-Zhu school — the "investigation of things" and the "plumbing of principle." In fact, the whole enterprise of *gewu* assumed even greater significance in light of Luo's emphasis on sense experience, his commitment to objectivity, and his resolute opposition to the radical reinterpretation of *gewu* by Wang Yangming. As we have seen, Wang, in redefining *ge* as "correcting" or "rectifying," rather than as "investigating" or "penetrating," was seeking to make *gewu* entirely a moral affair. Luo's response comes through clearly in a letter he wrote to Wang Yangming in the summer of 1520:

During the summer of last year a friend showed me the *Instructions for Practical Living*,[50] which I promptly read. All that I had heard about was con-

---

47. "Record of Music," *Record of Rites*; Legge, *Li Ki*, 2:96.
48. *Mean* 1:4.
49. "Record of Music," *Record of Rites*; Legge, *Li Ki*, 2:96.
50. Luo refers to Part 1 of the *Instructions*, which includes Wang's sayings and conversations from the period up to 1518.

tained in it, along with many other things I had not heard about before. What good fortune it is now to receive two more works from you.[51] Yet in that I am not clever, I have repeatedly examined these texts without having been able to grasp their central meaning. Thus the doubts that I had heretofore have accumulated and cannot be resolved. In the profound hope that your gracious willingness to instruct me will not be wasted, I dare to set forth one or two points, anticipating that in your great generosity you will make allowances for my indiscretion.

Careful study of [your reasons for wanting to] return to the old text of the *Great Learning* indicates that you consider that when a person engages in study, he ought to seek only within himself, whereas according to the theory of the investigation of things of the Cheng-Zhu school, one cannot avoid seeking outside the self. You contend that the intention of the sage was contrary to this, and so you have omitted Master Zhu's division [of the text of the *Great Learning*] into chapters and deleted the amended commentary that he added. . . .

It is my humble opinion that in the teaching of the Confucian school learning and action should assist each other. There is the clear teaching that one should be broadly versed in learning.[52] When Yan Yuan praised the "skillful leading" of Confucius, he said, "He broadened me with learning."[53] Is learning really internal or external? . . .

If one insists that learning does not depend upon seeking outside the self and that only introspection and self-examination are fundamental, then why wouldn't the words [of the *Great Learning* concerning] "rectifying the mind" and "making the intentions sincere" be completely sufficient? Why would it be necessary to burden the student at the beginning with the task of "investigating things"? Yet this passage does exist in the text of the classic, and one is bound to respect and believe it. Since you had to find a way to deal with this, you followed the text but interpreted it to mean that *wu* [i.e., a "thing"] is the functioning of the intentions and *ge* is "to rectify." "It is to rectify what is incorrect so as to return to correctness."[54] By interpreting the text in this way[55] you meant to make it internal rather than external and thus to achieve internal consistency. You have also applied this interpretation, saying, for example, that

---

51. Wang had sent Luo "The Old Text of the *Great Learning*" ("Guben Daxue"), in which he challenged Zhu Xi's views on the *Great Learning*, and "Zhu Xi's Final Conclusions Arrived at Late in Life" ("Zhuzi wannian dinglun"), in which he argued that Zhu by the end of his life had arrived at views similar to Wang's own.

52. *Analects* 6:25.

53. *Analects* 9:10.

54. *Wang Wencheng gong quanshu* 1:41a, *Chuanxilu*; Chan, *Instructions*, p. 55. Philip J. Ivanhoe suggests that a longer quotation, beginning with "*wu* is the 'functioning of the intentions'," may have come from the now lost "Guben daxue."

55. I.e., *ge* and *wu*, which Luo preferred to interpret, as had Zhu Xi, as involving the intellectual endeavor of investigating things.

when the intentions function in serving one's parents, then one investigates the matter of serving one's parents so as to return to correctness and become completely identified with the Principle of Heaven.

But even before you have gotten to the word "knowledge," your view has become convoluted, distorted, and difficult to understand. Let us investigate on the basis of your interpretation of [the word ge as] "rectify." If at the beginning of the Great Learning one could rectify what is incorrect in every event and thing and return to a state of correctness, thus becoming completely identified with the Principle of Heaven, then the mind would already be rectified and the intentions would already be made sincere. Wouldn't it be repetitious, redundant, and pointless to continue toward the goal of making the intentions sincere and rectifying the mind?

"Great is qian, to which all things owe their beginning."[56] "Fine is kun, to which all things owe their growth."[57] What is there in this body that I possess and in the myriad things as they are that does not derive from qian and kun? Their principle is in every case the principle of qian and kun. From my standpoint, external things are definitely "things." From the standpoint of principle, I too am a "thing," altogether merged in the unity of all being. Where, then, is the distinction of internal and external?

What is of value in the investigation of things is precisely one's desire to perceive the unity of principle in all of its diverse particularizations.[58] Only when there is neither subject nor object, neither deficiency nor surplus, and one has truly achieved unity and convergence, does one speak of knowledge being complete. This is also called knowing where to rest.[59] A great foundation can then be established, and the universal Way can then be practiced.[60] One proceeds from making [the intentions] sincere and [the mind] correct to governing [the state] and establishing peace [in the world], so that one can achieve an all-pervading unity[61] in which nothing is left behind.

[Kunzhiji fulu, ch. 5; Bloom, Knowledge, pp. 175–178 — IB]

In another letter, written in the winter of 1528, Luo returned to the same theme of the investigation of things. At the time this letter was written, Wang Yangming was on his way home from his last campaign in Guangxi. He was to die a few weeks later on January 10, 1529, before the letter from his respected adversary could be delivered.

---

56. Classic of Changes, qian hexagram, 1:4a; Lynn, Classic of Changes, p. 129.

57. Classic of Changes, kun hexagram, 1:13b; Lynn, Classic of Changes, p. 143.

58. A reference to Cheng Yi's statement in Yichuan wenji 5:12b.

59. Great Learning 2.

60. Mean 1:4.

61. An allusion to Analects 4:15, where Confucius is recorded to have said, "My doctrine is that of an all-pervading unity" (or "has one thread running through it").

[You have said that] a thing (*wu*) is "the functioning of the intentions" (*yi zhi yong*) and that "to investigate" (*ge*) means "to rectify" (*zheng*). . . . In an earlier letter you graciously bestowed, you said, "To investigate things is to investigate the things of the mind, the things of the intentions, and the things of knowledge. To rectify the mind is to rectify the mind of things. To make the intentions sincere is to make the intentions of things sincere. To extend knowledge is to extend the knowledge of things."[62] Never since the *Great Learning* has been in existence has this interpretation been offered. . . .

When you speak of investigating the things of the mind, the things of the intentions, and the things of knowledge, this assumes three "things." But when you speak of rectifying the mind of things, making sincere the intentions of things, and extending the knowledge of things, you assume that there is just one "thing." On the view that there are three "things," Master Cheng's definition of "the investigation of things" is still intelligible,[63] whereas your definition of "the investigation of things" is not. On the view that there is only one "thing," then what, after all, is this "thing"? If you insist on considering it as "the functioning of the intentions," then no manner of ingenious manipulation will ultimately yield a solution that is intelligible. This is the first of the points concerning which I can only be skeptical.

Furthermore, you have said that "when the intentions are directed toward serving parents, then serving parents is a 'thing,' and when the intentions are directed toward serving the emperor, then serving the emperor is a 'thing.'" In cases of this kind your explanation may be said to be adequate. But there are other examples, such as the exclamation [of Confucius] on the river bank in the *Analects*,[64] or the hawk flying and the fish leaping in the *Mean*.[65] These are instances of vital pronouncements by the sage and worthy[66] concerning the human situation.[67] A student who has not been able to understand their significance cannot be said to know what it is to learn. Were I to suppose that the meaning is that my intentions are directed to the flowing of the stream, the flying of the hawk, or the leaping of the fish, how would I "rectify what is incorrect so as to return to correctness"? This is the second point concerning which I can only be skeptical.

Moreover, you said in a letter that had to do with learning that "the innate

---

62. "Letter in Reply to Vice-Minister Lo Zheng'an" ("Da Luo Zheng'an shaozai shu"), in *Wang Wencheng gong quanshu* 2:61a. Translation adapted from Chan, *Instructions*, p. 161.

63. Both Cheng Hao and Cheng Yi defined the *ge* in *gewu* as "to reach" or "to arrive." This was discussed by Wang in his "Letter in Reply to Gu Dongqiao" ("Da Gu Dongqiao shu"), in *Wang Wencheng gong quanshu* 2b–29b; Chan, *Instructions*, pp. 91–124.

64. *Analects* 9:16.

65. *Mean* 12:3, quoting Ode 239.

66. I.e., Confucius and Zisi.

67. *Er Cheng yishu* 3:1a.

good knowing (*liangzhi*) of my mind is the same as the Principle of Heaven. When the Principle of Heaven in the innate good knowing of my mind is extended to all events and things, all events and things will attain their principle. To extend the innate good knowing of my mind is the extension of knowledge, and to enable all things to attain their principle is the investigation of things."[68] If we accept your interpretation, the *Great Learning* should have said, "The investigation of things lies in the extension of knowledge," rather than having said, "The extension of knowledge lies in the investigation of things." It should have said, "When knowledge is complete, then things are investigated," rather than having said, "When things are investigated, knowledge is complete." You had already spoken of "investigating carefully the Principle of Heaven that is in the mind and thereby extending the innate good knowing inherent in it."[69] You also said, "It is precisely in extending the innate good knowing of the mind that one investigates carefully the Principle of Heaven that is inherent in the mind."[70] Then are the Principle of Heaven and innate good knowing one thing? Or are they not? Thus as far as investigating and extending are concerned, which is prior to the other? This is the third point concerning which I can only be skeptical.

[*Kunzhiji fulu*, ch. 5; Bloom, *Knowledge*, pp. 186–188 — IB]

This debate did not end with Wang's death or with Luo's but had echoes and reverberations down into the seventeenth and eighteenth centuries and even after. While the issue, as framed by Luo, may appear on the surface of it to have to do primarily with fidelity to a classical text and a logic employed in the interpretation of that text, it was actually much larger than that. Moral goodness, he thought, followed from an awareness of the objective reality of principle that unites the self with others, and such an awareness depended on a process of "investigating things" that was in the first instance directed toward knowing events and things in the objective world in their concrete particularity. His larger concern was with the need for an encompassing view that would omit from consideration nothing in the human or natural sphere, so that their relatedness could ultimately be comprehended.

CHEN JIAN AND HIS *THOROUGH* CRITIQUE

No less influential than Luo's refutation of Wang Yangming was the critique advanced somewhat later by Chen Jian (1497–1567), whose *Thorough Critique of Obscurations to Learning (Xuepou tongbian)* came to be viewed as perhaps the most vigorous and thoroughgoing defense of Cheng-Zhu orthodoxy. It is

---

68. "Letter in Reply to Gu Dongqiao"; translation adapted from Chan, *Instructions*, p. 99.
69. *Wang Wencheng gong quanshu* 2:13a. Translation adapted from Chan, *Instructions*, p. 103.
70. Ibid. 2:17a; *Instructions*, p. 108.

particularly noteworthy for its sharp response to Wang Yangming's espousal of Lu Xiangshan. In the process of indicting Lu and Wang together as collaborators in a vast conspiracy to betray Confucianism, Chen repeatedly stigmatized them as "outward Confucians and covert Buddhists."

From a family of scholar-officials in Guangdong, Chen Jian had passed the provincial examinations but never succeeded at the metropolitan level. After serving in relatively minor educational posts, he retired early, in 1544, to a life of study, teaching, and writing. This gave him the leisure in which to complete the documentation of his case against the enshrinement of Lu Xiangshan in 1530. (Chen himself claimed to have devoted ten years to this task of documentation and took extraordinary pains in identifying his sources.) Chen was in fact a prodigious scholar, whose contributions to the study of Ming history would eventually gain him considerable recognition, though in his own dynasty, as in the succeeding Qing, there were attempts at official suppression of his works on account of his outspoken opinions on politically sensitive matters. Thus Chen, at some remove from the center of power, was disposed to be critical of those in high places who failed to uphold Confucian norms for which he, as an educational official and serious scholar, felt responsible.

It is obvious from the timing and contents of the work, as well as from Chen's stated intentions, that it was originally provoked by the official canonization of Lu Xiangshan, as well as by Wang Yangming's writings concerning Zhu Xi's views in relation to Lu — especially the claim that Zhu, though differing with Lu earlier, had largely come to agreement with him later in life. In those circumstances Lu himself, even more than Wang Yangming, became the prime focus of Chen's critique. Indeed, given the widespread popularity and official favor enjoyed by the Wang Yangming school at this time, it is understandable how Chen would feel not only that he was resisting a surging tide but also that a trend of such magnitude — for himself so threatening to education — could have come about only in consequence of a much longer, and more deep-seated, process of subversion, reaching all the way back to the introduction of Buddhism.

If Chen's work thus took on a beleaguered and somewhat paranoid tone, Chen's scholarly capabilities were nevertheless up to the task of documenting a highly plausible case for his views.

Chen's main argument runs as follows:

1. The writings of Lu Xiangshan, Wang Yangming, and other Yuan and Ming thinkers ("ostensible Confucians but covert Buddhists") show unmistakable influences of Chan Buddhism, which has led to the confusing and obscuring of Zhu Xi's teachings. He says, "There is nothing greater under Heaven than scholarship, and no greater calamity for scholarship than the obscuring of truth." The failure to make clear distinctions leads to confusion of issues and to the blurring of Zhu Xi's teachings vis-à-vis those of Lu Xiangshan. Here a basic difference between the two that Chen says must be recognized is that

Lu's self-cultivation aimed at a "nourishing of the spirit," emphasizing an emptiness and quiescence that derived from Daoism and Buddhism, whereas Zhu Xi aimed at scholarly study and discursive analysis, emphasizing concrete facts, things, and affairs. In contrast to Lu's "nourishing of the spirit," according to Chen, stands the true Confucian aim of "nourishing principle." He quotes Hu Juren (1434–1484), an early Ming adherent of the Cheng-Zhu school, who criticized the Buddhists by saying: "Confucians nourish the Way and principles; the Buddhists and Daoists nourish the spirit."

2. Chen's counterposing of Zhu's nourishing of "scholarship" to Lu's "nourishing of spirit" does not mean that Chen is prepared to yield to Lu the domain of spirituality. On the contrary, a correct spiritual cultivation of "reverent seriousness" is prerequisite to scholarly pursuits, along with the "nourishing of principle" in the mind. In fact, according to Chen, Zhu Xi's method represents the true cultivation of the mind as opposed to Lu's cultivation of spirit, which does not recognize the constancy of principle in the mind.

3. Chen devotes much attention to clarifying the role of "quiescence" and "quiet-sitting" in Confucian cultivation. These, he acknowledges, were accepted by the early Song masters, but only on condition that they be used for the nourishing of principle and control of selfish desires, not to gain some mindless, aesthetic, or mystical experience.

4. Underlying erroneous views concerning spirit and principle, quiescence and quiet-sitting, is Lu's (and Wang's) identification of the mind with a value-free consciousness, at the expense of moral principle. Zhu Xi had insisted that "principle in the mind" (roughly "conscience") should guide consciousness. Blurring of the distinction between principle (the Mind of the Way) and consciousness (the human mind) would leave the latter and human desires uncontrolled. "It is all right to say that the mind of the humane person is conscious, but not that consciousness itself is humaneness."

DIAGRAM OF THE MIND

Diagrammatically, Chen represented the mind (as Zhu Xi had in his preface to the *Mean*) as an "empty, spiritual consciousness," to be guided by the Mind of the Way. By collapsing mind and principle, and relying on direct intuition of an undifferentiated consciousness, Lu and Wang, according to Chen, took this consciousness (function) to be "the nature," setting aside Zhu's view of the moral mind or Mind of the Way as the nature (substance) of the mind.

In the Counsels of Yu it says: "The human mind is precarious; the mind of the Way is subtle."

Master Zhang [Zai] says: "Combining the nature and consciousness, there is what we call the mind."

In my own humble opinion: The nature is the mind of the Way.

The Mind

— [Coordinating] —

Humaneness, Rightness, Ritual Decorum and Wisdom (*ren yi li zhi*)	Empty, spiritual consciousness
The moral nature (*dexing*)	Spirituality (*jingshen*)
Moral principles (*yili*)	Psycho-physical endowment (*qibing*)
The Mind of the Way (*daoxin*)	The human mind (*renxin*)

The consciousness [alone] is [simply] the human mind. As an explanation of the mind, the above is right on target.

Further on, Chen quotes Zhu Xi:

"What we Confucians cultivate is humaneness, rightness, ritual decorum, and wisdom. What Chan Buddhists cultivate is simply consciousness. They only recognize the human mind, not the Mind of the Way."

The key to the distinction between Confucianism and Buddhism is just this. As I have already explained, the Learning of the Sages and Worthies is the Learning of the Mind-and-Heart. Chan learning and Lu's learning also call themselves the "learning of the mind-and-heart"; what they do not realize is that, although it is the same term "mind," there is a difference in what is meant by "mind." With the tabular presentation of the mind above, one can distinguish quite clearly the similarities and differences. Thus Confucius and Mencius both speak of mind in terms of humaneness and rightness. The Chan Buddhists speak of mind in terms of consciousness.

[*Xuepou tongbian* 163–164 — dB]

In conclusion it may be added that Chen's views, as more fully expressed in his *Thorough Critique of Obscurations to Learning*, were frequently cited in subsequent Neo-Confucian discourse. The leading seventeenth-century scholar Gu Yanwu (see volume 2, chapter 25) spoke highly of the efforts of both Luo Qinshun and Chen Jian in refuting Wang Yangming. He said that Luo's *Knowledge Painfully Acquired* and Chen's *Thorough Critique* "stood like immovable rocks of integrity in the face of the onrushing current [of Wang Yangming's thought] in those days."[71]

THE PRACTICAL LEARNING OF LÜ KUN

The late Ming witnessed a wide variety of intellectual developments, some stimulated by the challenge of Wang Yangming's philosophy, others reacting against it, and still others following through on the more practical side of Con-

---

71. Gu, *Record of Daily Knowing (Rizhilu)* 18:431.

fucian and Neo-Confucian teaching. Lü Kun (1536–1618), a scholar-official of broad practical experience known for his integrity and forthrightness, spoke for a growing impatience in the late Ming with philosophical disputation ("empty talk") concerning the mind and human nature. In his refusal to be identified with any one doctrinal school (he insisted, "I am just me"), Lü, though less radical than Li Zhi, nevertheless typified the independent and individualistic spirit increasingly evident in late Ming thought.

Well reputed for his effectiveness as an administrator and outspokenness as a minister, Lü pictured himself as a "doctor to the people," approaching the problems of his society empirically and pragmatically, looking for practical solutions rather than adhering to bookish rules or established ways. Much concerned with education, like Zhu Xi and Wang Yangming before him, Lü reflected the growing populism of the Ming period in his efforts to spread learning beyond the elite to the common people and women. He promoted community schools on the local level, while commending literacy among women and emphasizing their moral equality and autonomy. To make his points he often wrote in the colloquial language, using popular rhyme schemes reset to simple tunes and colorful anecdotes. None of this was wholly unprecedented or unique to Lü, but he did it so well that his work was much used. His guidelines for local administration, published under the title "Records of Practical Administration" ("Shizheng lu"), became a model for administrative practice in the following Qing dynasty. His enduring fame is shown by the installation of his tablet in the Confucian temple (1826) and the respect with which his work was regarded by eighteenth- and nineteenth-century Japanese Confucian scholars.

RESTORATION OF COMMUNITY SCHOOLS

The "restoration" called for here evokes the early advocacy of such schools by Zhu Xi, attempts in the fourteenth century under the Yuan dynasty to establish elementary schools, as well as the Ming founder's initial adoption and subsequent abolition of them in favor of private schools. Revival of the idea became a feature of sixteenth-century reform efforts (along with the community compacts advocated by Wang Yangming) to deal with the crisis in local governance after the decline of the early Ming *lijia* system of local administration. In this essay Lü's comments on the deterioration of education on the local level point to chronic ills: neglect of general, public education in official schools by teachers who emphasize only literary skills useful in civil service examinations, with a consequent aversion to this kind of study by a farming population, which sees in it no tangible benefit to compensate for the loss of able-bodied young men from work in the fields.

Rising affluence facilitated efforts at improving the schools, but Lü's aims went beyond providing opportunities for the well-to-do; indeed, his methods were adapted to the needs of the disadvantaged: in his view teachers need not be members of the educated elite; the curriculum need not meet the most exacting standards; texts should be adjusted to the level of the students' own experience, while simplicity and clarity should be emphasized over refinement of writing style.

In Lü's approach two points should be especially noted: in a way reminiscent of Wang Yangming's community compact, he emphasizes that learning should appeal to the emotions, especially through group singing, and also be directed at general moral uplift, not preparation for the civil service examinations. Chen Hongmou (see volume 2, chapter 27) gave Lü special credit for these features when in the eighteenth century he included this essay in an anthology of educational texts.

Regarding the restoration of community schools for the nurturing of uneducated children, nothing is more urgent for realization of the kingly way than to educate the people, and, for the nourishing of uprightness, nothing should take precedence over training for the very young.

[As things stand] today it is long since proper schooling has been carried out, and one cannot expect much from official teachers; one can only do something about the matter of community schools. If officials have a mind to pay attention to contemporary education, can something not be done? Therefore I have summarized the essential points as follows:

— Ever since true education has deteriorated, the whole world has ceased to understand what book learning is all about. For more than two thousand years it has been misconceived, and right down to the present: what teachers have told their disciples and fathers have transmitted to their sons is only that they should come out first in the (*jinshi*) examinations as a stepping-stone to wealth and rank. Today, in selecting teachers for the community [schools], one should pick twenty or so scholars (*shi*) who are more than forty years old, whose pure hearts are intact, and whose purpose is upright — no matter whether they have already attended [state] schools or not. The official in charge should have them assemble at the Confucian Temple and give them daily grain rations. Instruction should begin with explanations of the *Elementary Learning* (*Xiaoxue*) and the *Classic of Filiality* (*Xiaojing*), as well as the study of characters and keys to pronunciation. After a year, if the students' recognition [of characters] is almost correct, their pronunciations accurate, the meaning of the texts roughly understood, and their explications are also correct, then the official in charge should pay a visit to the school to examine them and select the ones who are worthy of teaching others. Looking into where there are community schools, he should assign [the newly trained teachers] accordingly.

— The community schools should be set up at each of the four gates in large cities and at a single location in towns of more than two hundred households. The head of each *jia*-unit[72] should investigate how many [male] children in

---

72. A *jia* usually consisted of one hundred households.

that *jia* fall between the ages of eight and sixteen *sui*[73] and report it to the head of the community compact (*yuezheng*).[74] Excepting those who can pay tuition, the head should list the names of those whose means are limited or are in dire straits and report them to the officials. Establishing a site [for the community school], the official should [provide] the community [school] teacher with a stipend of grain — twenty *piculs* (*dan*) to be generous, or twelve *piculs* at the very least, the amount to be differentiated on the basis of the learning and effectiveness [of the teacher].

— The best thing in the world is for young people to study — whether [they do so] for the lofty goals of achieving a reputation and accomplishing great deeds or for the modest aim of recognizing characters and understanding their meanings. There are some unenlightened parents who do not teach their sons to read; the sons end up becoming evil men, with depraved minds-and-hearts and untamed natures; they turn into thieves and break the laws — all because of this [failure in education]. Have you ever seen anyone who understands principles and recognizes characters willing to become a thief?

The official in charge should proclaim to the common people: Hereafter, students of an age to study are to be sent to community schools; even if they are poor and needed for work at home, they must attend school after the tenth month [harvest] and only return to their homes after the third month [for planting]. If after three years, their talents prove to be such that nothing more can be expected of them, then have them return to their usual occupations.

— In school, because distinctions between seniors and juniors come fore-most, students should be ranked according to age. With the exception of rela-tives, who have their own appellations, juniors will call their seniors "elder brother" and seniors will call their juniors by their given names. The younger [boys] should walk on the right [of the older boys], sit below them, stand up whenever their elders stand, and disperse whenever their elders disperse. They are forbidden: (1) to form play groups; (2) to curse one another; (3) to spoil brushes, ink, and books belonging to others; (4) to incite others to do mischief; and (5) to rely on their position to oppress others. Anyone who transgresses these five prohibitions will be punished by having to study twice as much. . . .

There follow other recommendations for personal conduct similar to those cited in the Cheng-Dong School Code in chapter 23.

— Whenever expounding on texts, one should instruct the children to apply [the contents] to their own personal experience [by asking]: "Are these words

---

73. The Chinese measured years of life in *sui* and reckoned a child to be one *sui* at birth.

74. Lü Kun had combined two methods recommended by Zhu Xi for organizing local society, the *baojia* (for mutual surveillance) and the *xiangyue* (community compact) into one system, the *xiangjia*.

relevant to you? Can you learn from this passage or not?" One should also tell a couple of stories that provide models and warnings, so as to enlighten [the children]. If on some later day the [children] should commit transgressions, then reprimand them by using the stories already told to them, so that they might be improved in body and mind.

— Every day, whenever one encounters children feeling tired and lazy, chant one stanza of *shi* poetry. Select old and new [poems] that are very simple, that are trenchant, to the point, emotionally stirring, and germane, to be assembled into a book; have [the students] chant them, and give them explanations and require that the students learn them — such ancient poems as those in the *Classic of Odes* regarding parents[75] . . . brothers . . . male-female relations . . . husbands and wives . . . secondary wives and concubines . . . friends . . . children . . . the poverty of the people . . . instruction in the rites (*li*) . . . the teaching of rightness (*yi*) . . . warnings against slander . . . the way to frugality . . . ancestral sacrifices . . . taking pleasure in the worthies, and on down to the *yuefu*[76] and ancient-style poems from the Han and Wei dynasties on, and recent popular proverbs for the edification of the people — anything that deals with moral obligations and principles, the Way and rightness, body and mind. Sing one stanza each day. As for those who practice new tunes or provocative and seductive words: punish them as soon as they are found out.

— Those who have just entered the community schools, from the age of eight [*sui*] on, should first read the *Three Character Classic*[77] in order to practice identifying what they see and hear; *The Hundred Surnames*, which facilitates the knowledge of everyday things; and the *Thousand Character Essay*, which also contains moral principles. . . .

There follow detailed instructions on calligraphy, reading method, care in the handling of books, writing compositions, and so on.

— In studying, diligence is most important. Whether living nearby or far away, the children should all arrive at school at the crack of dawn. After reciting their texts from memory, they should study new texts. After eating, let them outside for a while to run freely for one or two quarters of an hour, after which they should read, write compositions, make copies, and then read some more. After lunch, let them again go outside to run about for one or two quarters of an hour and then study further. After sundown, divide them into rows facing

---

75. The text gives examples from the *Odes* for each type that follows.

76. "Music bureau" poems, originally associated with folksongs collected by this Han-dynasty agency to convey to the ruler the sentiments of the common people, but also including literary works designed to be set to music.

77. See ch. 23.

one another. Take out one correct essay and one blemished essay, and then explain the corrections. After that, school should be dismissed. Because the young have weak stomachs, [the students] should not immediately use their mental energies after [the evening] meal, lest they get indigestion.

— The community schools should not take out students to greet and send off officials. Every time I [the governor] go out on tour, I see children several *sui* in age expediently donning caps [i.e., before they have reached sixteen, the age to be capped]. Young and inexperienced children must be strictly taught, but the teachers of the community schools, using as a pretext that no one is supplying them [with funds], become lazy and take off. If the officials are so careless, merely responding with meaningless paperwork, keeping up a facade, and leaving it to parents to instruct their children — how is this the way to fulfill a high official responsibility? . . .

— Community schools are not intended for the preparation of examination candidates. Their entire purpose is to set straight the habits of the young. If the curriculum fails to call for the practice of virtuous deeds and [instead] emphasizes the acquisition of literary skills, then the community school teachers, even if learned men, should be dismissed.

— Recently community schools have not stressed the instruction of the young. Although community schools have been set up, one hears only about the fields [endowed] for the community schools; meanwhile, bad characters, decked out as licentiates, beg for support only to ensure their own survival, without caring whether they have students or not, or whether the students are given any instruction or not. Even though such licentiates reside in official housing and receive stipends under false pretenses, the officials in charge, as if living intoxicated in a dream, fail to pay any attention [to such abuses]. In cases where community schooling has lapsed and there is no remediation, or where community schools exist but they only harbor empty vessels [i.e., the fraudulent licentiates], the officials should be dismissed for having failed in their duties.

[*Shizheng lu* 3:7a–12b — JHS]

FRUGALITY AND FAMINE RELIEF

This public proclamation, which Lü Kun appended to a piece on storing grain, uses several techniques to reach an audience with limited education: it is written in a simple colloquial style, uses memorable, heartrending anecdotes to arouse the listener to action, and encourages voluntary efforts through the promise of specific rewards. Underlying it all is the principle of self-reliance. Unless people make an effort to help themselves, no amount of official handouts will suffice to meet the need.

Because harvest yields are affected by uncontrollable natural factors, it is important that grain be stored for use in bad years. During the late Ming, moreover, as peasants were increasingly drawn into a market economy and engaged in the production of handicrafts, the threat of economic instability was added to natural disasters. Further, as Lü commented elsewhere, there had been a breakdown in the close relationship between peasants and paternalistic landlords, to whom peasants might once have turned for help in bad times.

In the final passage we detect again the close connection in Lü Kun's mind between the community compact and the community granary (as earlier with the community school), a trio of cooperative institutions favored by Zhu Xi to which late Ming local officials turned when they sought ways to reorganize and stabilize rural society. This is just one of many proposals of late Ming scholars to adapt and revitalize Zhu Xi's plan for the Community Compact.

There is one thing in the world that is most important, which I will tell you common people (*baixing*) about. Nowadays you people who make your living on the land may take in two to three hundred *piculs* of grain (*dan*) in one year, which you spend wastefully on clothes, food, and other things, so that it lasts just one year. The next year, you take in just fifty or one hundred *piculs*, which, spent thriftily, is still sufficient for that year. Think about it: during that [latter] time you carefully held on to your money, you did not lack food or clothes, and your other needs were met. It's just that you could not put on a show of prosperity.

If that [earlier] time when you took in two or three hundred *piculs*, you had been willing to put aside one half in a granary or cellar to guard against bad years, then it would have been as though you had harvested only fifty or a hundred fewer *piculs* that year; what would be wrong with that?

As for the poor fellow who wants to save — how can he do it? If one indeed values survival, then there is a poor man's way to calculate. When you are poor you still cannot get by eating less than two meals a day. Yet once you may have bought a jug of wine and a catty of meat to eat, or when someone dragged you before the officials in a lawsuit, you may have spent one or two hundred coins (*qian*). Or there was a time when you spent three to five hundred coins at a [religious] meeting, offered incense, or contributed to building a temple. I urge you: if one day you might consume food worth ten cash (*wen*), then eat only nine cash worth; you will not die of starvation. By putting away one cash a day, you can save 360 cash in one year, so that when grain prices fall, you can buy up two *piculs* of grain to be stored. Enduring this for three years, you can save five or six *piculs* of grain and also raise chickens and pigs, or store bran and vegetables, or work for others so as to feed yourself and also get some cash wages. Whether it is a lot or a little, it will add up over time, and it goes without saying that over ten years you will never experience hunger or cold.

Think of the successive droughts in 1581 and 1582. Whenever those conditions come up for discussion, everyone weeps. Outside the city walls of Pingjing and Guyuan, thirty to fifty [burial] pits were dug, every one of which was completely filled. There was a daughter from a wealthy household whose parents had starved to death. She put straw twists in her hair and went out in the streets to sell herself; when a young man, an outsider, flirted with her, she was so ashamed that she banged her head and died. There was a young wife from an eminent household who, seeing that her husband was about to die of starvation, sold off all her clothes, keeping only a slip to cover her body; she also cut off her hair and went out on the streets, shouting "for sale" — but there were no buyers. Her husband died of starvation. The officials commissioned someone to drag [his corpse] to the mass grave-pit. This young wife, letting out a scream, threw herself into the pit. . . . She said, "My husband is already dead. How could I bear to eat my fill in this world?" She wailed for three days and nights and then died.

Throughout the entire subprefecture and from the city to the court several tens of thousands of men and women were affected [by the famine], half of them people unaccustomed to any hardship. Women and children alike were involved: exhausted by starvation and lacking any strength, [the women] would take shelter in a temple, beguile their children to fall asleep, and then, in the fifth watch, they would run away. There were some [children] who would wake up and [try to] follow, weeping: they were then tied up with sashes to trees. Some even were poisoned to death — [it is enough to make one] weep with grief. How could people be driven to such cruelty, having no way out? . . .

In 1586 on the road to Handan [Hebei] there was a woman carrying three young children. Along the way, she became tired from carrying them and found it difficult to walk any further. Her husband urged the wife to abandon the children, but she wept with grief, unable to bear the thought. The husband, driven by desperation, charged ahead for several tens of *li*; but unable to bear [the thought], he went back. At a glance he saw that his wife and three children had hanged themselves on a tree. Crying piteously, the husband too hanged himself. . . .

Think of how in normal times you uselessly built shrines, or set up idols and paintings with images of the spirits, carried out some [religious] sacrifices, and burned up some prayer money. What spirit has helped you [in return]? Think of how in those good years at harvest time you engaged in reckless spending, hating only restraint. You wore fine clothes and were scornful if they were ugly; you had music played and were scornful if it wasn't sufficiently pleasing; you had a fondness for wine and meat and were scornful if they weren't good enough. Had you put aside what had been left over in [those] normal times to be used at this time — how could it come to the point that you might have to eat elm bark and grass roots and perhaps even die of starvation? There is a popular saying: "Getting something out of father is not as easy as getting it from mother; getting something out of mother is not as good as having it yourself." I only hope that you people who alternately smack your lips [with delight] and then rub your stomachs [in hunger], now rich and now poor — in addition to paying your grain taxes and filling labor obligations — would rather consume a little less and be frugal, and would rather have simple food and coarse clothing, so that through good times and bad, you will put away a little money for surviving emergencies. Rather than being a ghost [of someone] who died of hunger during a bad year, it is better to be a [live] person enduring [a little] hunger in good years — like the rat that robs various grains to be stored away in a hole in preparation for times of dearth, or the magpie that uses its beak to store seeds away in trees to guard against hunger in winter months. Have you ever seen any birds or rats die of starvation during bad harvests? That human beings should indeed fall short of birds and rats in their planning for survival — alas, how sad! . . .

In the community compact (*xiangyue*), we should start a "poor fellows' club" for those who are willing. To those indigent fellows who save the most I will distribute extra rewards. During bad harvests, if you save one *picul* of grain, the officials will give you three additional pecks as aid. To those who accumulate three hundred cash, the officials will give one hundred additional [cash]. If a family has saved no cash or grain, then it will be granted no aid. For those common people who have saved one half, the officials will help out further, so you can make it through to the harvest; but if you are empty-handed and are given three to five pecks of grain or one or two coins, you will starve to death in the end [anyway]. It's better to save the lives of those who have [put aside] one half [of what they need]. I am first explaining this to you so that when the time comes you will have no cause to regret.

[*Shizheng lu* 2:16a–21a — JHS]

MUSIC IN THE HOME

In response to his mother's sudden blindness, Lü Kun broke a rule laid down by his father and followed by many of his peers — namely, that entertainers should not be allowed in the home for fear that they might subvert domestic morality. Here, as in many other instances, he trusted his emotional responses to personal experiences as a guide to formulating policies. Though straitlaced in many respects, he believed that expression of the emotions, especially through music, was conducive to moral health — a view shared by followers of the Wang Yangming school at this time.

In the eighth month of 1547, my mother became blind from an eye ailment. She suddenly opened her eyes and [tried to] look around, but could see nothing, whereupon she knocked her head against the wall, screamed, and refused to eat for three days. . . . I did not know what to do. So I summoned blind female musicians to amuse her, and after five days she gradually began to eat. When one singer had exhausted her repertory, I replaced her with another. . . .

My late father had often cautioned that women in the sundry professions [such as go-betweens and storytellers] should not be allowed inside the gates. But from this time on I bent the rules, and the emotions of women and children were in no way suppressed. As a result virtuous and filial old women and servant girls could also live out their days. . . .

Someone said, "Women from all over should not be allowed into the inner chambers; the sounds of string instruments and songs [music] should not be heard in the women's quarters." [To this] I say, "This is [said] in defense of the household. How dare I say it is incorrect?" [But] the [true] gentlemen of old did not dispense with music even during the three-year period of mourning. . . . When Confucius listened to music, it delighted him; and [his disciple] Zilu in Wucheng used music in his pursuit of the Way. . . .[78]

Now, music is conducive to harmony. How are the strings and winds imbued with meaning? The sounds follow along and the tunes change, while depravity and uprightness rely on them to move men. If the music is popular but the songs played are elegant and refined, then the music will benefit the spirit. If the music is ancient but the songs broadcast are lascivious, then it will be enough to create confusion and disorder. . . . These fellows who feign high culture and correctness but are actually dissolute, summoning entertainers and singing lewd songs, and thus wreaking havoc with family rules — they ought to chastise themselves. If they do not set their hearts straight but blame only the music, then the world, not understanding music and becoming ever more dissolute — how can it be worthy of the Way? Yet they blame it on the music being depraved! [Therefore] I have written this explanation of music in the home.

[*Quweizhai wenji* 7:65a–67b; in *Lüzi yishu*, 1827 ed. — JHS]

EDUCATION FOR WOMEN

Lü Kun was a persistent and resourceful champion of education for women, upholding a high standard of traditional morality but using unconventional, vernacular means of instruction with a strong appeal to the emotions. Without education, women easily fell prey to vice; with it, they could set a good example for his contemporaries, men as well as women, who paid lip service to high-sounding ideals but hypocritically violated or compromised them.

Two compilations illustrate his method. *Models for the Inner Quarters* (*Guifan*) gives examples of virtuous women, many of which were drawn from the Han dynasty work, *Biographies of Virtuous Women* (*Lienü zhuan*), with pictorial illustrations for each anecdote, simplified texts, and explanations of difficult characters and their pronunciations. Lü also added commentaries, sometimes applauding women who used their own judgment in adapting traditional principles to actual life situations and

---

78. *Analects* 17:4.

calling into question reports of extreme self-sacrifice that in fact violate Confucian respect for life and a reasonable concern for self-preservation.

The other type of compilation, *Admonitions for the Inner Quarters* (*Guijie*), illustrates the typical failings of women (e.g., Unfilial Women, Dissolute Women, Talkative Women) who have not been properly educated. Here, however, *properly* means *effectively*, in terms that ordinary women, on any level of society, could understand and be moved by. This was in an age that saw the rapid spread of literacy and vernacular literature.

Introduction to *Admonitions for the Inner Quarters*

Half of the prosperity of a family depends on its women. But so far these [women] have been left uneducated, and thus become accustomed to undisciplined arrogant ways. Those in literati households may sometimes be instructed in poetry and history, but the wives of small farmers, laborers, and peddlers, and the girls in hamlets and remote valleys never, from childhood to old age, hear one edifying word. [Without this] all talk of high principles and discussions of fine literature are, even when a thousand words are spent, utterly useless.

When laid up on sick leave, I occasionally pondered how easily women fall into misconduct, and therefore I composed several verses [to the tune of] "Gazing to the South of the River." For the musical meter and word pattern I used the rural dialect of the Liang and Song dynasties and even went along with errors in language, never substituting [classical] literary expressions for colloquial ones, so that [the songs] would be easy on the ears and penetrate the mind-and-heart. And I had old women musicians who, being blind, begged by singing, spread [the tunes] to the inner quarters, so that when offenders heard [them], their hair would stand on end and their faces would cringe. Might not sprouts of remorsefulness thus arise in their hearts?

"Guijieyin" from *Lüzi sizhong* (*heke*); in *Lüzi yishu*, 1827 ed. — JHS]

Preface to *Models for the Inner Quarters*

The early kings valued the instruction of women. Therefore women had female teachers, who would explicate the sayings of old and cite examples from ancient worthies so that [the women] would carefully adhere to the principle of "thrice obeying" (*sancong*) [i.e., to obey one's father when young, one's husband when married, and one's son when old] and to revere the four virtues [i.e., proper behavior, speech, demeanor, and employment] so as to bring glory on their husbands and not bring down shame on their parents. With the decline of education today, women in the inner quarters have really ceased to be governed by rites and laws. Those born in villages are accustomed to hearing coarse words and those [born] in rich households have loose, proud, and extravagant natures. Their heads are covered with gold and pearls and their entire bodies with fine silks. They affect lightheartedness in behavior and cleverness in speech, but they mouth no beneficial words and perform no good deeds. Their parents- and sisters-in-law will not be able to pass on reputations for worthiness or filiality, and neighbors and relatives will hear only of their obstinacy — all because they are uneducated.

At the high end are those [women] who wield their writing brushes and aspire to [develop] their talents in *sao* poetry so as to brag that they are superb scholars. At the low end are those who strum vulgar [tunes] on their stringed instruments and sing lascivious words, almost like prostitutes — all because of the spread of depraved instruction. If in its myriad forms, education for the women's quarters is like this, then how might the governance of the inner [quarters] be rectified?

Various books for the instruction of women have been prepared by the ancients. But being numerous, they are difficult to master; being abstruse, they are difficult to understand; being diverse, their quality cannot be clearly differentiated; and being dull and flavorless, they cannot move others to feel awe. . . . Alas, [moral sentiments of] filiality, prudence, chastity, and martyrdom [in choosing death over remarrying] are inherent in one's Heaven-given nature. To have a fine reputation that lasts for generations, one need not be literate, but it is rare that someone who learns to recite orally [accounts about] those with fine lasting reputations, fails to follow their good example.

[“Guifan xu,” from *Quweizhai wenji* 3:14a–b; in *Lüzi yishu*, 1827 ed. — JHS]

Following are two of Lü's comments on how virtuous women could show good judgment in adapting traditional precepts to difficult dilemmas.

Of Miss Han, at the end of the Yuan dynasty, who disguised herself as a boy when captured by soldiers, then lived among the troops for seven years without being found out, and was eventually redeemed by an uncle and betrothed, at which point it was learned that she was a woman, Lü comments:

With a noble spirit she kept her chastity intact: that was the deed of a courageous person. With wisdom she preserved her life and person: that was the deed of a wise person. The dead have no way of manifesting these [qualities]. In opting for rightness one need not sacrifice one's life. How indeed could the sages have valued death [more than life]? Someone like Miss Han acted expediently but did not fail to be upright.

Of Boji (fl. 600 B.C.E.), who insisted on adhering to the proper rituals in the matter of her betrothal and later chose to burn to death rather than commit the impropriety of leaving her residence unaccompanied by her governess, Lü commented that her behavior regarding her engagement was correct, but

On the night her house was on fire, there were other women to chaperone her — sufficient to make her intentions clear — and the rite for managing emergency situations surely allows for this. Nevertheless, Boji waited for her governess before she would go out — this was being excessively scrupulous. Then when her matron came but not the governess, she still would not go out and so died in the fire. This is keeping to ritual decorum too strictly. In a thousand years one will find only one such person. The true gentleman will grieve over her determination, but he will also regret her lack of understanding about the expediency [discretion] that is necessary in changing circumstances.

> ["Guifan xu," from *Quweizhai wenji* 2:33b–34a, 3:81a–82a; in *Lüzi yishu*, 1827 ed. — JHS]

MORALITY BOOKS

In the sixteenth century the spread of Wang Yangming's thought gave a further stimulus to education among the lower classes and contributed to the increased demand for popular morality books (*shanshu*). This type of book, which had made its appearance in the Song period, became much more popular in the Yuan and Ming. Together with the encyclopedias for daily use, the morality books served a wide public, especially in the late Ming. By calling them "popular" we mean that these books served not only the lower levels of society but all types and classes of people, irrespective of social status, gender, economic position, and religious affiliation. In fact, so basic was their appeal to the common denominator in ethical thought that they were read and used even by some scholars identified with the main schools of learning.

The underlying idea of the morality books is that virtue is rewarded and vice punished. Besides identifying good deeds and their rewards, as well as bad deeds and their retributions, the morality books give homely tales drawn from the popular consciousness and imagination to illustrate them. Probably the best-known representative of this type is the *Treatise of the Most Exalted One on Moral Retribution (Taishang ganying pian)*, which was published for the first time in the Southern Song period and republished often thereafter. Much of its content was Confucian — that is, it represented Confucianism as practiced among the common people, supplemented and supported by religious notions drawn from Daoism and Buddhism.

THE *TREATISE OF THE MOST EXALTED ONE ON MORAL RETRIBUTION*

This popular treatise was sometimes considered the work of Laozi, but it is probably a work of the twelfth century, authorship still uncertain. Millions of copies of this work, and of the *Silent Way of Recompense*, which follows here, have been distributed over the years by individuals and organizations of goodwill. They are standard texts in most popular cults and would probably be found in any rural village that possessed even a few books.

The Most Exalted One said, "Calamities and blessings do not come through any [fixed] gate; it is man himself that invites them." The reward of good and evil is like the shadow accompanying the body. Accordingly, there are in Heaven and Earth spiritual beings who record a man's evil deeds and, depending upon the lightness or gravity of his transgressions, reduce his term of life by units of three days. As units are taken away, his health becomes poor, and his spirit becomes wasted. He will often meet with sorrow and misery, and all other men will hate him. Punishments and calamities will pursue him; good luck and joy will shun him; evil stars will harm him. When the allotted units are exhausted, he will die.

Furthermore, there are the Three Ministers of the Northern Constellation residing above a man's head. They register his crimes and misconduct and take away from his term of life periods of three hundred or three days. There are also the Three Worm-Spirits residing inside man's body. Whenever the fifty-seventh day [of the sixty-day cycle, the day characterized by severity and change] comes around, they ascend to the court of Heaven and report man's misconduct and transgressions. On the last day of the month, the Kitchen God does the same. When a man's transgressions are great, three hundred days are taken away from his term of life. When they are small, three days are taken away. Great and small transgressions number in the hundreds. Those who seek long life on earth must first of all avoid them.

Go forward if your deed follows the Way (*dao*) but withdraw if it violates it. Do not tread evil paths. Do nothing shameful even in the recesses of your own house. Accumulate virtue and amass merits. Have a compassionate heart toward all creatures. Be loyal to your sovereign, filial to your parents, friendly to your younger brothers, and brotherly to your older brothers. Rectify yourself and so transform others. Be compassionate to orphans and sympathetic to widows. Respect the old and cherish the young. Even insects, grass, and trees you must not hurt. How much more should you grieve at the misfortune of others and rejoice in their good fortune! Assist those in need and save those in danger. Regard others' gain as your own gain and their loss as your own loss. Do not publicize their shortcomings nor boast of your own superiorities. Stop evil and promote good. Yield much but take little. Accept humiliation without complaint and favor with a sense of apprehension. Bestow kindness and seek no recompense. Give without regret.

He who is good is respected by all men. The way of Heaven helps him, happiness and wealth follow him, all evil things shun him, and spiritual beings protect him. Whatever he does will succeed. He may even hope to become an immortal.

He who seeks to become an immortal of Heaven should perform 1,200 good deeds. He who seeks to become an immortal of earth should perform 300.

But if he acts contrary to rightness or behaves improperly . . . [Here follows a long list of misconduct and crimes to be avoided, concluding with:] if he is insatiably covetous and greedy or takes oaths and swears to seek vindication; if he loves liquor and becomes rude and disorderly or is angry and quarrelsome with his relatives; if as a husband he is not faithful and good, or if as a wife she is not gentle and obedient; if the husband is not in harmony with his wife; if the wife is not respectful to her husband; if he is always fond of boasting and bragging; if she constantly acts out her jealousy and envy; if he behaves immorally toward his wife and children; if she behaves improperly toward her parents-in-law; if he treats with slight and disrespect the spirits of his ancestors or disobeys the commands of his superiors; if he occupies himself with what is not beneficial to others or cherishes a disloyal heart; if he curses himself and others or is partial in his love and hatred; if he steps over the well or hearth [which should be taken seriously because water and fire are indispensable to life] or leaps over food [served on the floor] or a person [lying on a floor mat]; if he kills babies or brings about abortion or does many actions of secret depravity; if he sings or dances on the last day of the month or year [when the ends should be sent off with sorrow] or bawls out or gets angry on the first day of the year or the month [when the beginning should be welcomed with joy]; if he weeps, spits, or urinates when facing north [the direction of the North Star and the emperor] or chants and laughs facing the hearth [which should be treated solemnly because the family depends on it for food]; and, moreover, if he lights incense with hearth fire [a sign of disrespect] or uses dirty fuel to cook food; if he shows his naked body when rising at night or executes punishment on the eight festivals of the year; if he spits at a shooting star or points at a rainbow; if he suddenly points to the three luminaries or gazes long at the sun and the moon; if in the spring months [when things are growing] he burns the thickets in hunting or angrily reviles others when he faces north; if without reason he kills tortoises or snakes [which are honored along with the Northern Constellation], if he commits these or similar crimes, the Arbiter of Human Destiny will, according to their lightness or gravity, take away from the culprit's term of life periods of three hundred or three days. When these units are exhausted, he will die. If at death there remains guilt unpunished, the evil luck will be transferred to his posterity.

Moreover, if one wrongly seizes another's property, his wife, children, and other members of his family are to be held responsible, the expiation to be proportionate up to punishment by death. If they do not die, there will be disasters from water, fire, thieves, loss of property, illness, quarrels, and the like to compensate for the wrong seizure.

Further, he who kills men unjustly puts a weapon into the hands of others who will turn on him and kill him. He who seizes property unrighteously is like one who relieves hunger with spoiled food or quenches thirst with poisoned wine. He will be full for the time being, but death will inevitably follow. If good thoughts arise in one's mind, even though the good deeds may not be performed, spirits of good fortune attend one. If evil thoughts arise in one's mind, even though the evil is not performed, the spirits of misfortune descend on him.

If one has already done an evil deed but later repents of his own accord and corrects his way, refrains from doing any evil, and earnestly practices many good deeds, in time he will surely obtain good fortune. This is what is called changing calamities into blessings.

Therefore the man of good fortune speaks good, sees good, and does good. Every day he performs three good deeds. At the end of three years Heaven will send down blessings on him. Why not make an effort to do good?

[*Taishang ganying pian*, DZ 834–839, no. 1167. — WTC]

THE *SILENT WAY OF RECOMPENSE* (*YINZHIWEN*)

The general purport of the text (popularly attributed to the Daoist deity Wenchang) is to encourage people to practice good deeds in secret. The "silent way" means that one should not look for others' approbation when carrying out good deeds. In fact, the implication of the "silent way" is that only good deeds done in secret accrue full merit. The concept of "hidden virtue" (another term for the "silent way") became an important feature of later morality books.

The Lord says, For seventeen generations I have been incarnated as a high official, and I have never oppressed the people or my subordinates. I have saved people from misfortune, helped people in need, shown pity to orphans, and forgiven people's mistakes. I have extensively practiced the Silent Way of Recompense and have penetrated Heaven above. If you can set your minds on things as I have set mine, Heaven will surely bestow blessings upon you. Therefore, I pronounce these instructions to humankind, saying . . .

Whoever wants to expand his field of happiness, let him rely on the ground of his mind-and-heart.

Do good work at all times and practice in secret meritorious deeds of all kinds.

Benefit living creatures and human beings. Cultivate goodness and happiness.

Be honest and straight and, on behalf of Heaven, promote moral reform. Be compassionate and merciful and, for the sake of the country, save the people.

Be loyal to your ruler and filial to your parents.

Be respectful toward elders and truthful to friends.

Obey the purity [of Daoism] and worship the Northern Constellation; or revere the scriptures and recite the holy name of the Buddha.

Repay the four kindnesses [done to us by Heaven, Earth, the sovereign, and parents]. Extensively practice the three religions.

Help people in distress as you would help a fish in a dried-up rut. Free people from danger as you would free a sparrow from a fine net.

Be compassionate to orphans and kind to widows. Respect the aged and have pity on the poor.

Collect food and clothing and relieve those who are hungry and cold along the road. Give away coffins lest the dead of the poor be exposed.

If your own family is well provided for, extend a helping hand to your relatives. If the harvest fails, relieve and help your neighbors and friends.

Let measures and scales be accurate, and do not give less in selling or take more in buying. Treat your servants with generosity and consideration; why should you be severe in condemnation and harsh in your demands?

Write and publish holy scriptures and tracts. Build and repair temples and shrines.

Distribute medicine to alleviate the suffering of the sick. Offer tea and water to relieve the distress of the thirsty.

Buy captive creatures and set them free, or hold fast to vegetarianism and abstain from taking life.

Whenever taking a step, always watch for ants and insects. Prohibit the building of fires outside [lest insects be killed] and do not set mountain woods or forests ablaze.

Light lanterns at night to illuminate where people walk. Build riverboats to ferry people across.

Do not go into the mountain to catch birds in nets, nor to the water to poison fish and shrimps.

Do not butcher the ox that plows the field. Do not throw away paper with writing on it.

Do not scheme for others' property. Do not envy others' skill or ability.

Do not violate people's wives or daughters. Do not stir up litigation among others.

Do not injure others' reputation or interest. Do not destroy people's marriages.

Do not, on account of personal enmity, create disharmony between brothers.

Do not, for a small profit, cause father and son to quarrel.

Do not misuse your power to disgrace the good and the law-abiding. Do not presume upon your wealth to oppress the poor and needy.

Be close to and friendly with the good; this will improve your moral character in body and mind. Keep at a distance from the wicked; this will prevent imminent danger.

Always conceal people's vices but proclaim their virtue. Do not say "yes" with your mouth and "no" in your heart.

Cut brambles and thorns that obstruct the road. Remove bricks and stones that lie in the path.

Put in good condition roads that have been rough for several hundred years. Build bridges over which thousands and tens of thousands of people may travel.

Leave behind your moral instructions to correct people's faults. Donate money to bring to completion the good deeds of others.

Follow the Principle of Heaven in your work. Obey the dictates of the human heart in your words.

[Admire the ancient sages so much that you] see them while eating soup or looking at the wall. [Be so clear in conscience that] when you sleep alone, you are not ashamed before your bedding, and when you walk alone, you are not ashamed before your own shadow.

Refrain from doing any evil, but earnestly do all good deeds.

Then there will never be any influence of evil stars upon you, but you will always be protected by good and auspicious spirits.

Immediate rewards will come to your own person, and later rewards will reach your posterity.

A hundred blessings will come as if drawn by horses, and a thousand fortunes will gather about you like clouds.

Do not all these things come through the Silent Way of Recompense?

[*Yinzhiwen guangyi*, Zhou Mengyan ed. — WTC]

LEDGERS OF MERIT AND DEMERIT

From the *Treatise of the Most Exalted One on Moral Retribution* it may be seen that rewards and punishments were thought to be dispensed by a supreme being. This idea had its ground in the ancient belief that Heaven presides over the moral order, rewarding the good and punishing the wicked. But instead of relying on the belief that everything is dependent on the favor of a god, the morality books are based on the idea that one can control one's own destiny by achieving virtue and eschewing vice. One can judge the value of his own actions and be assured of an appropriate reward.

Such is the idea underlying the morality books known as Ledgers of Merit and Demerit (*Gongguoge*). According to this system, the value of human deeds could be calculated with so many credits or merits attached to each good deed and so many debits or demerits for the evil deeds. Using the point system provided in the ledgers, each individual could evaluate his deeds one by one, add the merits and demerits, and then strike the balance for himself. The greater the balance of merits, the greater the reward he might expect, and vice versa. A conscientious person would go through this process each day and also calculate how he stood at the end of each month and each year. In general, one sought to build up as large a balance of merits as possible and certain extraordinarily virtuous actions could count heavily in erasing an accumulation of demerits. Mechanical though the system was, however, it was based fundamentally on the idea that the individual did the evaluating for himself and, as Mencius had urged, took charge of his own fate.

THE *LEDGER OF MERIT AND DEMERIT OF THE TAIWEI IMMORTAL*

The Ledgers of Merit and Demerit appeared first in the Song period. Of them, the *Ledger of Merit and Demerit of the Taiwei Immortal* is the earliest one still extant and served as a model for later morality books. It is attributed to a Daoist named Youxuan Zi, who stated in the preface, dated 1171, that the ledger was a divine revelation made through him by the Taiwei Immortal. The importance of this ledger can be seen from the fact that the ledger popularized by Yuan Huang (1533–1606) and the *Synthetic Compilation of Ledgers of Merit and Demerit* in the seventeenth century all owe their format and contents to it. The following is an excerpt from this ledger.

Conduct that Results in Merit:
Saving someone from the death penalty: for one person, one hundred points of merit
Commuting someone's death sentence: for one person, fifty points of merit
Exempting someone from imprisonment: one person, forty points of merit
Reducing someone's term of imprisonment: one person, thirty points of merit
If the judgment is made in accordance with the law, [any act of clemency] is without merit. If the clemency is directed toward one's maid or servant, one gains the same merit.
Saving the life of a domestic animal: one animal, ten points of merit
Saving the life of a nondomestic animal: one animal, eight points of merit
Saving the life of an insect, moth, or watery creature: one creature, one point of merit
Giving assistance to the widowed, the orphaned, or the poor: for every one hundred coins spent, one gains one point of merit. For every one thousand coins spent, one gains ten points of merit.
Printing scriptures: for every one hundred coins spent, one gains ten points of merit.
Remonstrating with people not to fight: one person, one point of merit
Recommending intelligent, capable, and virtuous people to office: one person, ten points of merit
Praising someone's good deed: one instance, one point of merit
Not telling about someone's bad deed: one instance, one point of merit

Conduct that Results in Demerit:
Provoking someone into a fight: one person, one point of demerit
Not recommending a capable person to office: one point of demerit

Not seeking teaching from worthy people: one point of demerit

Not providing assistance to the poor: one point of demerit. Furthermore, to humiliate them: for every person [whom one mistreats], three points of demerit

Killing an animal for food: six points of demerit. Buying meat and eating it: three points of demerit

[*Daozang* 186 — RGC]

YUAN HUANG'S LEDGER

The most flourishing days of the ledgers of merit and demerit came in the late Ming through the activity of Yuan Huang (1533–1606), a compiler and publisher of popular encyclopedias and manuals for civil service candidates. He was a man of extraordinary energy and ability, and his own personal experience had much to do with his belief in the individual's capacity to determine his own fortune. A fortune-teller had predicted that Yuan would become an official but fail to achieve the highest degree, would have no children, and would die at the age of fifty-three. On the strength of the favorable indication in the first part of this prophecy, Yuan took and passed the prefectural and provincial examinations. He remained, however, quite fatalistic about his future in regard to the other matters involved, until in 1569 a Buddhist monk recommended that he practice the system of merits and demerits. The accumulation of virtuous acts would overcome the dire prophecy. Taking this advice and acting on it, he was eventually blessed with a son, passed the *jinshi* examination in 1585, and became an official of some importance, first as a magistrate and then in the Board of War. Even his later dismissal from the official rolls on false charges did not shake Yuan's conviction that success could be achieved through the system of merits and demerits.

It may be seen from this account that Yuan practiced the system in the same eclectic atmosphere that had surrounded the morality books from the beginning, namely, the popular acceptance of Confucian, Daoist, and Buddhist ideas as blending harmoniously together. In these respects Yuan Huang reflected a well-established tradition of popular syncretism. The sixteenth century was a period in which the Combined Practice of the Three Teachings and the Unity of the Three Teachings were especially popular notions, and Yuan's many writings were influential in popularizing these ideas still further. But the main point of Yuan's teaching was his positive belief in the individual's ability to "establish his own destiny" (*liming*), or carve out his own fortune in life. This idea, originally from Mencius, had come to Yuan from the teaching of Wang Gen: "Though they say that our destiny lies with Heaven, what creates that destiny [i.e., the means by which it is brought about] lies within ourselves." Yuan had also studied under Wang Ji. Responding to this influence, Yuan Huang took the Ledgers of Merit and Demerit, originally a system of

Daoist popular morality, and made them serve as a concrete method whereby practical application could be given to the idea of "establishing one's own destiny."

Drawing thus upon the religious syncretism of the common people and the popular character of the Wang Yangming school, Yuan Huang was able to formulate a philosophy and way of life that combined strong moral effort and self-discipline with a simple religious faith. Through his own example as well as his numerous publications, Yuan also related his system closely to the worldly aspirations of the people, particularly to the prevalent ambition to rise to official rank through the examination system. But Yuan's method was applicable to all walks of life, and one of the great values of his and other morality books to the student of Chinese history and thought is the way in which these books reflect social change in the sixteenth and seventeenth centuries, precisely because they were concerned with the daily lives of the common people.

Conduct for which one gains one hundred points of merit:
   Saving a person's life
   Ensuring the fidelity of a woman
   Preventing someone from drowning a child or aborting a baby
Conduct for which one gains fifty points of merit:
   Maintaining the family lineage
   Adopting an orphan
   Burying a corpse no one cares for
   Preventing a person from abandoning a village [because of famine]
Conduct for which one gains thirty points of merit:
   Remonstrating with an evildoer to change his way
   Rectifying an injustice
Conduct for which one gains ten points of merit:
   Recommending a virtuous person for office
   Eliminating something harmful to the people
Conduct for which one gains five points of merit:
   Remonstrating with a litigant to withdraw a lawsuit
   Saving the life of a domestic animal
Conduct for which one gains one point of merit:
   Praising someone's good deed
   Not joining in someone's bad deed
   Remonstrating with someone from doing evil
   Curing someone's illness
   Providing a meal to a hungry person
   Burying a dead domestic animal
   Saving the life of an insect or watery creature
For every one hundred coins one spends on the following, one gains 1 point of
   merit:

Constructing a road or bridge; digging a waterway or well to benefit people; repairing or installing a sacred image, temple, shrine, or other sacred place for worship; giving assistance to the poor; donating tea, medicine, clothes, coffins, and so on

Conduct that contributes to demerits is listed in terms generally opposite [to the meritorious deeds above].

[*Yinzhilu*, pp. 175–178 — RGC]

MORALITY BOOKS AND SOCIAL CHANGE

If the morality books were to be applicable to the daily life of the people, they had to adapt to the increasing specialization of functions among the common people and they also had to take into account the effects of a spreading money economy in the Ming. As a result, we find that virtuous conduct comes to be defined both in general terms, in regard to those actions appropriate for all persons in all circumstances, and in more specific terms, for those actions appropriate to particular occupations. Further, the attempt is made to distinguish between virtuous acts that do not involve any monetary expenditure and those that do.

In the Song, Confucian thought affirmed the basic principle that any person might become a sage but tended at the same time to be highly conscious of distinctions between good persons and bad, high and low, rich and poor. Any person might prove himself by rising to the top, but there was a clear hierarchical order through which he had to ascend. And though the conditions for achieving Confucian fulfillment were the same for all, insofar as education and learning were involved, it was accepted that the lower orders of society would have more difficulty obtaining the necessary books or schooling. In other words, there was as yet no conscious inclination to question traditional notions of social structure or to ask whether or not traditional concepts were appropriate to the existing reality. An evidence of this is the persistence of the ancient habit of describing society in terms of the traditional four classes: scholar-officials, peasants, artisans, and merchants. These classifications were conceived primarily from the administrative point of view. They were the categories under which the government dealt with, regulated, and taxed the people.

In the late Song period there was already an embryonic recognition that morality appropriate for the common people had to take into account their actual statuses and functions. This arose out of the close relationship between the early morality books and popular religions, especially the popular forms of Buddhism, like the Pure Land faith, that were concerned with the salvation of souls, without distinction as to wealth or rank. Thus the morality books contained popular lectures on religious salvation directed at "ordinary people" (*fanmin*) and at "ignorant men and women" (*yufu yufu*). But popularization in religion also involved recognition of the greater specialization of function among the common people than among the ruling elite. Thus we find people classified according to such categories as subordinate office helpers, physicians, monks, women, rich men, household slaves, farmers and peasants, dealers and merchants, craftsmen, fishermen, and wine sellers.

A SYNTHETIC COMPILATION OF LEDGERS OF MERIT AND DEMERIT

As the emphasis shifted in the Ming from religious salvation in the afterworld to a person's conduct in this world, there was more attention to the actual circumstances in which meritorious deeds would be performed. To some extent the traditional nomenclature is still used in a rather general and imprecise way, but in the classification of good and bad deeds there is a definite trend toward more realistic and specific social differentiation.

It was in the very nature of traditional Confucian morality that general ethical principles should be given specific interpretation and application through prescribed acts of ritual decorum, which also allowed for a certain degree of social differentiation. While it had been a basic principle of the ritual that it should not exceed what was appropriate to the social and economic circumstances of the persons involved, in religious rituals and funeral ceremonies the lower classes felt a strong compulsion to demonstrate their virtue or faith by sparing no expense in honoring the gods, the buddhas, or their departed parents. In the Ming period, moreover, rising economic prosperity, commercialization, and the spread of a money economy only intensified the strain on the common person trying to find some standard for what constituted proper conduct in these regards.

In the morality books we see an attempt to ease this strain by making a distinction between good deeds that do and do not involve any expense to the performer. That is, while many of the meritorious works recommended are those that offer ordinary people some standards in regard to the performance of traditional Confucian ceremonials that involve some material outlay, many others are specifically identified as works that do not require the performer to spend money. The *Meritorious Deeds at No Cost* is particularly designed to meet the latter need.

The rationale for this, however, is already expressed in Yuan Huang's *Establishing One's Own Destiny (Liming pian)*, as we see in the following:

The virtue of modesty (*qianxu*) is essential for poor scholars and those seeking to enter the civil service without much means. Poor scholars cannot hope to achieve merit [and thus succeed in the examinations] through works that involve the expenditure of money, but the essential thing in the achieving of merit is the attitude of mind. Modesty, which is an attitude of mind, does not require any expense.

[*Liming pian*, 23a — dB]

This emphasis on the attitude or quality of mind shows the influence on Yuan Huang of Wang Yangming's thought. As he attempts to practice "the establishing of one's own destiny" through the practical method of the Ledgers of Merit and Demerit, he tries to establish a more interiorized morality in place of a purely materialistic standard.

In general this view of the Ledgers of Merit and Demerit was to allow for good deeds that involved either some expense or no expense, as in the following excerpt from a seventeenth-century text:

Aid your relatives, teachers, or friends, if they are in need of clothing, food, or money for ceremonies such as marriages and funerals.

Save good people from enmities or calamities [arising from financial troubles?].

Save people from falling into servile status [through debt or crime] and becoming separated from their families.

Help the poor, widowers, widows, and orphans of your own locality.

Help travelers who have fallen into trouble to return to their home locality.

Help the poor with the expense of marriage and funeral ceremonies.

Help those seriously ill to get medical treatment.

Pay taxes in full for the indigent.

Give money and goods to beggars, the disabled, the crippled, and the aged.

Have compassion on poor people who are forced to turn to begging and give them some employment.

Establish endowed schools and educate the people.

Establish a foundling hospital to care for foundlings.

Establish a charitable estate [for one's clan?].

Donate a public cemetery for the poor who have no burial place.

Establish old people's homes and institutions to provide for their security at your own expense.

Take in dependent, disabled, and crippled persons and give them money and goods.

In case of famine provide free kitchens and rice gruel for the poor.

When there is a plague, establish free medical facilities and give medicine to the poor.

In summer provide mosquito nets and tea to the poor.

In winter give bedding to the poor.

Provide burial for those who die without relatives.

Repair roads, set up benches and rest houses in the shade, and build ferryboats.

Print and publish morality books; distribute them to others so as to lead them toward the good.

Print good medical prescriptions and give them to others to rescue them from disease.

Aid in the repair of temples and shrines that have long been dilapidated.

Buy, save, and release living creatures.

In the Ledgers of Merit and Demerit such good deeds as the above were valued in terms of the expense involved for the performer. For instance, expense amounting to one hundred copper cash counted as one merit point. This was in accordance with the system earlier developed in connection with these ledgers when they were first used in the Daoist religion and employed in the Ledger of Yuan Huang given above. A Synthetic Compilation *explains this aspect of the system as follows:*

Generally speaking, the expense of one hundred copper cash counts as one meritorious deed. If the same good deed is performed by a poor person, the number of merits increases in proportion to the degree of poverty. In the case of a really poor man, even if he incurs an expense of no more than five or ten coppers, it is counted as equal to one hundred coppers spent by the rich.

[*Huizuan gongguoge*, Daoguang ed., 8:25a–26b — ST, dB]

MERITORIOUS DEEDS AT NO COST

This seventeenth-century work incorporates two principles: it provides for meritorious deeds at no cost, and it differentiates them according to functional categories, as follows:

1. Local gentry (*xiangshen*), i.e., officials residing in their home locality)
2. Candidates for officialdom (*shiren*), including educated persons who have not attained office and may be serving as teachers, tutors, and so on
3. Agriculturalists (*nongjia*)
4. Craftsmen (*baigong*)
5. Merchants and dealers (*shanggu*)
6. Physicians and pharmacists (*yijia*)
7. Subordinate office workers [of humble status] (*gongmen*)
8. Women (*funü*)
9. Soldiers (*shizu*)
10. Buddhist and Taoist monks (*sengdao*)
11. Household slaves and servants (*pubi gongyi*)
12. People in general (*dazhong*)

In the foregoing the term *local gentry* (*xiangshen*) represents members of the official class (i.e., persons having official rank and status) who are residing at home and have social responsibilities in their own locality even though they are not charged with administrative duties there. In other words, the present work does not presume to prescribe for them in the political sphere or to discuss their official functions, but deals only with their social responsibilities in their home community.

The term *scholars* (*shiren*) represents those engaged in the different stages of preparation for the civil service examinations. As persons with some education and as candidates for the bureaucracy, they stand higher than the common people although they do not qualify as officials. Many of them served in educational capacities, and the meritorious works recommended for them emphasize that role.

Agriculturalists (*nongjia*) include those directly engaged in farming, whether landowners or peasants, but not absentee landlords. Similarly, the term *craftsmen* (*baigong*) means those actually engaged in the production of handicrafts, whether independent or employed, but would not apply to nonworking owners of factories. Absentee landlords or factory owners would be thought of as coming under either the first two classifications or the general group at the end.

Under each of these classifications the work lists good deeds involving no cost with a comparatively high degree of specificity, though in certain cases the context of the original recommendations is no longer so clear that we can always be sure of the exact meaning. In order to provide some idea as to the type of meritorious deeds included, we present here the listings under the first, second, third, and fifth classifications. It is to be expected that a certain amount of duplication will be encountered. The same is also true to some extent within the specialized classifications because their ways of life were different in many respects, although not necessarily in all. Among the categories left out here is *people in general*; it is far longer than the others and repeats many items in earlier ones. Its very length and comprehensiveness is a reminder, however, that attention to particular functions and statuses was balanced by concern for the human commonality.

1. Local Gentry

Take the lead in charitable donations.

Rectify your own conduct and transform the common people.

Make a sincere effort to inform the authorities of what would be beneficial to the people of your locality.

Make every effort to dissuade the local authorities from doing what would be detrimental to the people of your locality.

If people have suffered a grave injustice, expose and correct it.

Settle disputes among your neighbors fairly.

When villagers commit misdeeds, admonish them boldly and persuade them to desist.

Do not let yourself be blinded by emotion and personal prejudice.

Be tolerant of the mistakes of others.

Be willing to listen to that which is displeasing to your ears.

Do not make remarks about women's sexiness.

Do not harbor resentment when you are censured.

Protect virtuous people.

Hold up for public admiration women who are faithful to their husbands and children who are obedient to their parents.

Restrain those who are stubborn and unfilial.

Prevent plotting and intrigue.

Endeavor to improve manners and customs.

Encourage fair and open discussion.

Prevent your household slaves and servants from causing trouble by relying on your influence.

Try not to arouse the resentment of others by showing partiality to the younger members of your own family.

Do not provoke incidents that result in harm or loss to others.

Do not be arrogant, on account of your own power and wealth, toward relatives who are poor or of low status.

Persuade others not to seek gain through oppression or honors through intrigue.

Do not encroach on others' lands and dispossess them.

Do not scheme to buy up others' property.

Do not mix debased silver with good.

Do not ignore your own relatives and treat others as if they were your kin.

Influence other families to cherish good deeds.

Do not officiously take charge of the affairs of those outside your own household.

Do not disport yourself with lewd friends.

Do not look for pretexts to injure others.

Do not allow yourself to be overcome by personal feelings and therefore treat others unjustly.

Do not let your feelings of pleasure and displeasure influence others or suggest to them how they can benefit themselves.

Restrain others from arranging lewd theater performances.

Do not scheme to seize geomantic advantages (*fengshui*) for yourself or deceitfully deprive others of them.

Instruct your children, grandchildren, and nephews to be humane and compassionate toward all and to avoid anger and self-indulgence.

Do not deceive or oppress younger brothers or cousins.

Do not force others off the road by dropping stones in dangerous places.

Do not scheme to deprive others of some advantage in order to suit your own convenience.

Encourage others to read and study without minding the difficulties.

Urge others to esteem charity and disdain personal gain.

Do not underestimate the value of others [or underpay them].

Do not let what you hear from servants and slaves cause you to turn against relatives and friends.

Persuade others to settle lawsuits through conciliation.

Try to settle complaints and grievances among others.

Do not force others to lend you their property.

Do not force others to enter into deals on credit.

Curb the strong and protect the weak.

Show respect to the aged and compassion for the poor.

Do not keep too many concubines.

Do not keep catamites.

Do not marry off household slaves to wicked men or cripples for your own selfish gain.

Choose a favorable time for marrying off household slaves.

Do not force "good" people to become base [i.e., lose their freedom].

2. Scholars

Be loyal to the emperor and filial to your parents.

Honor your elder brothers and be faithful to your friends.

Establish yourself in life by cleaving to honor and fidelity.

Instruct the common people in the virtues of loyalty and filial piety.

Respect the writings of sages and worthies.

Be wholehearted in inspiring your students to study.

Show respect to paper on which characters are written.

Try to improve your speech and behavior.

Teach your students also to be mindful of their speech and behavior.

Do not neglect your studies without reason.

Do not despise others or regard them as unworthy of your instruction.

Be patient in educating the younger members of poor families.

If you find yourself with smart boys, teach them sincerity, and with children of the rich and noble, teach them decorum and duty.

Exhort and admonish the ignorant by lecturing to them on the provisions of the community compact and the public laws.

Do not speak or write thoughtlessly of what concerns the women's quarters.

Do not expose the private affairs of others or harbor evil suspicions about them.

Do not write or post notices that defame other people.

Do not write petitions or accusations to higher authorities.

Do not write bills of divorce or separation.

Do not let your feelings blind you in defending your friends and relatives.

Do not incite gangs (*bang*) to raid others' homes and knock them down.

Do not encourage the spread of immoral and lewd novels [by writing, reprinting, expanding, and so on].

Do not call other people names or compose songs making fun of them.

Publish morality books in which are compiled things that are useful and beneficial to all.

Do not attack or vilify commoners; do not oppress ignorant villagers.

Do not deceive the ignorant by marking texts in such a way as to overawe and mislead them.

Do not show contempt for fellow students by boasting of your own abilities.

Do not ridicule other people's handwriting.

Do not destroy or lose the books of others. . . .

To those of some understanding explain the teachings of the Cheng-Zhu school; to the uneducated give books on moral retribution.

Make others desist from unfiliality toward their parents or unkindness toward relatives and friends.

Educate the ignorant to show respect to their ancestors and live in harmony with their families. . . .

3. Agriculturalists

Do not miss the proper times for farmwork.

Have regard for [the lives of] insects.

When fertilizing the fields, do not harm living creatures.

Do not obstruct or cut off paths. Fill up holes that might give trouble to passersby.

Do not instigate landlords to buy up lands.

Do not steal and sell your master's grain in connivance with his servants.

Do not damage crops in your neighbors' fields by leaving animals to roam at large, relying on your landlord's power and influence to protect you.

Do not encroach [on others' property] beyond the boundaries of your own fields and watercourses, thinking to ingratiate yourself with your landlord.

Do not disturb others' graves or interfere with the geomantic advantages of others.

In plowing, do not infringe on graves or make them hard to find.

Do not suggest to your master that he willfully cut off watercourses and extort payments from neighbors.

Do not take your landlord's seed crop for your own benefit.

Do not damage the crops in neighboring fields out of envy because they are so flourishing.

Do not instigate your landlord to take revenge on a neighbor on the pretext that the neighbor's animals have damaged your crops.

Do not through negligence in your work do damage to the fields of others.

Do not become lazy and cease being conscientious because you think your landlord does not provide enough food and wine or fails to pay you enough.

Fill up holes in graves.

Take good care of others' carts and tools.

Do not kill mules and cattle, pigs and sheep, even if they eat your crops.

Keep carts and cattle from trampling down others' crops.

Do not desecrate the gods of the soil by plowing or hoeing the land or irrigating or spreading manure on days of abstention [*wu*, i.e., the fifth day of each ten-day cycle, which is the first of two days identified with wood in the Five-Phases cycle].

5. Dealers and Merchants

Do not deceive ignorant villagers when fixing the price of goods.

Do not raise the price of fuel and rice too high.

When the poor buy rice, do not give them short measure.

Sell only genuine articles.

Do not use short measure when selling and long measure when buying.

Do not deceitfully serve unclean dishes or leftover food to customers who are unaware of the fact.

Do not dispossess or deprive others of their business by devious means.

Do not envy the prosperity of others' business and speak ill of them wherever you go.

Be fair in your dealings.

Treat the young and the aged on the same terms as the able-bodied.

When people come in the middle of the night with an urgent need to buy something, do not refuse them on the ground that it is too cold [for you to get up and serve them].

Pawnshops should lend money at low interest.

Give fair value when you exchange silver for copper coins. Especially when changing money for the poor, be generous to them.

When a debtor owes you a small sum but is short of money, have mercy and forget about the difference. Do not bring him to bankruptcy and hatred by refusing to come to terms.

When the poor want to buy such things as mosquito nets, wadded clothing, and quilts, have pity on them and reduce the price. Do not refuse to come to terms.

[Sakai, "Educational Works," pp. 352–361 — dB]

THE DONGLIN ACADEMY

The Donglin Academy has long been seen as of major historical importance in the late Ming and a focal point of controversy, for at least four main reasons. First, it represented a reaction, morally conservative and politically reformist, against libertarian tendencies in the Wang Yangming school identified particularly with Wang Ji and Li Zhi. Second, although it was heir to Neo-Confucian teachings concerning the philosophy of human nature, it emphasized practice more than theory, and especially socially relevant action. Third, though it represented a mainline consensus on certain basic principles, which could be called neo-orthodox, it included scholars of diverse views and encouraged the "discussion of learning" or "discursive learning" (*jiangxue*), which to some meant active, open intellectual and political discussion, but by others later was dismissed as empty, airy speculation or partisan polemics. Fourth, the academy represented a notable trend in the late Ming toward the formation of voluntary associations — social, cultural, and religious — that in the modern West might be identified with civil society or a public sphere.

The Donglin Academy was organized at Wuxi in the lower Yangtze Valley, as a private (i.e., unofficial) center for the discussion of philosophical questions. Its principal founder, Gu Xiancheng (1550–1612), had turned to this type of activity after being forced out of the government for his outspoken criticism of those in power around the throne. Other participants in the discussions of the academy were identified, like Gu, with the so-called Righteous Circles at court, considered the champions of legality and official integrity in the government. Nevertheless, the purpose of their discussions was not primarily to exert some kind of public pressure upon their political enemies. Rather, as convinced Confucians, they believed that their efforts should first be directed toward intellectual weaknesses that had corrupted the educated class and undermined public life. Their aim was nothing less than the aim of Confucius himself — the moral regeneration of the ruling class. In this respect, then, they thought of themselves not as breaking new ground or departing from tradition but as returning to the original spirit of Confucianism. Gu and other leading members of the group still regarded Zhu Xi as the soundest exponent of this tradition, and in fact the stated aims of the school were based on the stated principles of Zhu Xi's own academy. Others were more strongly influenced by the philosophy of Wang Yangming. While thus differing in their philosophical approach, however, they agreed in reaffirming the fundamentally ethical character of Confucianism and in condemning the more extreme wing of the Wang Yangming school, which leaned in the direction of Chan Buddhism.

The tendency of this latter group, as we have seen, was to interpret Wang's doctrine of innate knowledge as meaning that the original mind of man was endowed with a transcendental perfection, beyond all relative notions of good and evil. To manifest this perfection, man need only rid himself of arbitrary or conventional conceptions of morality, and respond freely to the promptings of this innate, originally pure mind. "Naturalness" and "spontaneity" were the ideals of this group. Conscious moral effort they considered at best a preparatory method for those who still were fettered by ordinary habits of mind.

Initially what the exponents of this liberal point of view appear to have been driving at, following Wang's own revolt against Confucian formalism and scholasticism, was the destruction not of morality but of all rigid moralism, prudishness, and hypocrisy. The genuine moral virtues, they assumed, would manifest themselves naturally and without conscious effort. Increasingly, however, the moral subjectivism implicit in this teaching led to a repudiation of traditional Confucian values. In Li Zhi (1527–1602), for example, it brought open contempt for Confucian authority and scoffing at the profession of civic virtue and family obligations as hypocritical. Li's adoption of Buddhist garb was only an overt expression of the trend in this group toward an easy syncretism of Buddhism, Daoism, and Confucianism, proclaiming the "three religions to be one." For that reason this tendency won the appellation "Wildcat Chan school."

Gu Xiancheng and his colleagues saw in this kind of freethinking the abandonment of the moral struggle that Confucius had put forward as the highest destiny of man. To it they attributed the moral laxity at court, the readiness of many officials to cooperate with corrupt ministers and powerful eunuchs, and the prevailing fuzziness about right and wrong. Against such opportunism, dignified by the appearance of broadmindedness and spontaneity, the Donglin upheld the human moral nature, the importance of fixed principles, the necessity for moral effort. The perfection of the sage, the Donglin insisted, could be found only in striving. To attain it, the "gentleman" or "noble man" of Confucius had to be strengthened by moral training to withstand hardship and temptation. Seeking the true Mean in conduct and character, one had to distinguish it from compromise. One must be prepared to endure disfavor and resist accommodation to evil. With this as their aim, the Donglin leaders returned to the traditional function of the Confucian school: the inculcation of virtue (especially the civic virtues) and a sense of social responsibility. As a corollary to this they emphasized study of the classics — and sound scholarship in general — to counteract the anti-intellectualism of the Wildcat Chan school. Thus Donglin reformism in politics was based on a strong conservatism in morals and philosophy.

To its reformist struggle the Donglin brought all the fervor and intensity that characterized the bitter battles being waged at court. By their outspoken criticism of those in power, these men risked flogging, official degradation, and perhaps torture and death in the dungeons of the eunuch's secret police. To them the moral issues discussed were of more than pedantic interest — they were matters of life and death. In 1625–1626 the Donglin Academy itself and several affiliated institutions were in fact suppressed by the all-powerful eunuch, Wei Zhongxian, on the ground that they served as centers of factional opposition.

Though it was a policy of the Donglin to discuss political questions "outside of school," the distinction was actually difficult to draw. Many of the issues discussed centered upon personalities in the government, and the Donglin group engaged more in what was called "the judging of other men's characters" than in what we would consider the discussion of public issues or the advancement of a concrete political program. The political battles in which they took part, though they rocked the empire in the early decades of the seventeenth century, are of interest today only as episodes in a struggle over such questions as succession to the throne or the propriety of remaining in office instead of retiring to mourn the death of a parent. This is not to say that the Donglin and its allies were unconcerned with policy, but only that sometimes the political utterance of the Donglin was marked more by righteous indignation than by depth or breadth of analysis. It remained for its heirs in the next generation, scholars like Huang Zongxi and Gu Yanwu, less directly involved in partisan battles, to extend the discussion further into the broader ranges of institutional history.

GU XIANCHENG: COMPACT FOR MEETINGS OF THE DONGLIN ACADEMY

This charter, prepared in 1604 by Gu Xiancheng and subscribed to by several leading scholars, served as an open invitation to meetings, the philosophical and procedural basis for which was set forth in the form of a voluntary compact or agreement. Its main point is to reaffirm the rational, moral nature of man, the value of study and intellectual inquiry, and the need for practical action to reform human society.

In form, the charter combines features of Zhu Xi's "Articles of the White Deer Grotto Academy," with procedural and ritual provisions similar to Zhu Xi's version of the community compact. Like Zhu Xi's works, too, it draws heavily on earlier texts and precedents, while Gu's important contributions are offered ostensibly as subcommentary.

The centerpiece is Zhu Xi's "Articles," which Gu extols for its clarity and logical sequence. This is preceded by quotations from the *Analects*, the *Great Learning*, and the *Mean*, and others from *Mencius* emphasizing the goodness of human nature and man's capacity for sagehood. Following Zhu's "Articles" and postscript, Gu proceeds with a lengthy discussion of Four Essentials, Two Misconceptions, Nine Benefits, and Nine Detriments, which point up the contemporary significance of the basic principles. They are presented here in abridged form.

Four Essentials

1. Know what is fundamental.

What then is fundamental? What is fundamental is one's nature. One learns in order fully to develop one's nature. Developing one's nature starts with recognizing one's nature. If this is not recognized, one can hardly talk about fully developing one's nature, and if one's nature is not to be developed, one can hardly talk about learning. In my estimation, Zhu Xi's "Articles of the White Deer Grotto Academy" is the [true] learning of one's nature, which one cannot fail to ponder with care. Thus the intimate affection between parent and child, rightness between ruler and minister, differentiation between husband and wife, the order of priority between older and younger, trustworthiness between friends, as well as what in fact makes each of these what it is, what indeed is to be studied, inquired into, reflected upon, evaluated, and performed [as in the *Mean* and Zhu Xi's "Articles"] — all of these must be pondered with care. In the cultivation of one's self, can one's speech of itself be true and trustworthy [without careful judgment being exercised], can one's conduct of itself be reverential and exemplary [without careful judgment being exercised], can indignation restrain itself, can desires be controlled of themselves, good deeds be accomplished of themselves, evil deeds be reformed of themselves? In the management of affairs, is there such a thing as questions of right and wrong, merit and profit, being decided of themselves spontaneously [without reflection]; in dealings with others is there such a thing as not doing to others what one does not want for oneself, or being able to reflect upon oneself without having to consider these carefully? [4b–5a]

There follows a lengthy discussion of the erroneous view that "the substance of the mind [the nature] is beyond good and evil" — the first of Wang Yangming's Four Dicta from the Colloquy at the Tianquan Bridge — which Gu identifies with Buddhism and Daoism and earlier with Gaozi's view of human nature as neither good nor evil. This view, he says, subverts the practice of the moral and intellectual virtues encouraged by Confucius, Mencius, and Zhu Xi.

2. Establish a firm resolve.

What does it mean to speak of "firm resolve"? Firm resolve sets the direction the mind-and-heart goes in. It is what a person's whole life spirit converges on, what a person's whole life undertaking is rooted in, what one needs in order to stand on one's own feet. As Master Zhou [Dunyi] says, "The sage aspires to Heaven, the worthy aspires to sagehood, the scholar-official aspires to be worthy." . . . Master Zhang [Zai] says, "Establish one's mind-and-heart for the sake of Heaven and Earth; establish one's mission in life for the sake of the welfare of humankind; follow the sages in carrying on the oft-lapsed tradition for the sake of bringing peace to ten thousand generations. . . ." Scholars who would succeed to the mission inherited from the Song masters find that it all lies in this. Therefore it is essential for the gentleman to establish a firm resolve. [9b–10a]

3. Revere the Classics.

In this section, not translated here, Gu argues for the importance of studying the Six Classics expounded by Confucius and the Four Books as commented on by Zhu Xi. These embody the constant and unvarying Way, which is to be made a part of oneself by careful reading of texts and assimilating of them to one's own experience, rather than following the self-delusory view of Lu Xiangshan, who claimed that the classics are no more than footnotes to oneself.

4. Examine one's motives.

What does it mean to speak of examining one's motives? It is the distinguishing of sincerity and insincerity in the most minute sign of the incipient spring of one's actions. What has its source in the mind-and-heart is bound to show itself in one's person, and what has its source in one's person must become evident to others. Let there be no mistake! . . . Therefore it is essential for the gentleman to examine his motives at their very source.

Two Misconceptions

Against those, including Li Zhi, who ridiculed the practice of "learning by discussion" or "philosophical discussion" at the Donglin Academy:

Those who ridicule such discussion say it is too vague and impractical, and those who decry it say it is too far-fetched and not to be relied on. As far as I am concerned, one's moral obligations are to be strictly honored; one's actions must be worthy of respect; one's anger must be kept under control; one's desires must be checked; good deeds must be practiced and faults corrected; what is fitting should be rightly done; the Way must be made clearly manifest; what it is improper to desire should not be done; what should not be done should be a cause for self-reflection. This is what should be learned by those engaged in learning; this is what should be discussed by those taking part in discussions. These are all things that should be adhered to and never departed from in the ordinary course of daily life and conduct. How can they be called vague and impractical? These all lie within the common knowledge and ability of ordinary men and women. How can they be considered far-fetched? About this there should be no misconceptions!

[Gu Xiancheng, *Donglin huiyue* 1, in *Donglin shuyuan zhi* 17:4b–12a — dB]

The other of the two misconceptions is a confusion between the practice and the content of the discussions. The shallowness or hypocrisy of what is said by some, Gu argues, does not invalidate the practice of holding such open discussions.

Nine Benefits

For brevity's sake, the benefits of such discussions may be summarized as:

1. They promote the fundamental aim of learning to become a sage or worthy.
2. They make moral instruction available to all comers.
3. The solemnity of the proceedings lifts the mind to higher things.
4. An atmosphere suffused with moral instruction and ritual practice has a quiet, transforming influence on the self.
5. A collegial atmosphere of teachers and students is supportive of self-cultivation.
6. The collective experience and wisdom of a large gathering helps to broaden one's horizons and solve one's problems.

7. In such a setting one can get a new perspective on one's past and future life.
8. The ritual observances in the Confucian shrine inspire one to emulate the sages and worthies enshrined therein.
9. The meetings encourage one to keep one's mind set on the primary values of the Way rather than on ephemeral fame and fortune. [12b–14b]

Nine Detriments [i.e., detrimental to self and the conduct of meetings]

In summary:

1. Improper intimacies
2. Factionalism
3. Exploiting public meetings for private ends
4. Criticism of authorities for one's own ulterior purposes
5. Discussion of mysterious, extraordinary, and unorthodox things
6. Minimizing one's own faults and resisting correction
7. Discussing the faults of others in such a way as to embarrass them publicly
8. Bickering in discussions
9. Uncritical acceptance of opinions and rumors. [15a–b]

Procedural Rules for Donglin Meetings

Details are given here for the rituals, protocols, and formalities that should govern the proceedings, which are open to all but show special respect for seniority and for guests. Major meetings are held annually in fall or spring; minor meetings monthly in favorable seasons. Leading scholars preside in turn. The following excerpts explain the conduct of philosophical discussion at meetings:

For every meeting someone is to be chosen to make the main presentation on a chapter in the Four Books. If someone has a question, let him ask it; if one wants further discussion of a point, let it be discussed. During the meeting, let all listen with an open ("empty") mind. Even if one has a point to make, let him wait a little. After the lecture is over, one may in turn ask permission to speak, without disturbing the proceedings.

After prolonged sitting at the meetings, some verses from classic odes [*shi*] should be sung as a way of relaxing and restoring one's spirits. All should sing in unison and deeply savor the melody and meaning. After repeated singing, the mind-and-heart and voice become blended together, one's whole spirit enters into the singing, and the whole experience leaves a deep, lasting impression.

[18a–19a; trans. adapted from Busch, "Tung-lin," p. 38 — dB]

The first stipulation above, focusing the discussion on the Cheng-Zhu Four Books, marks this as a Neo-Confucian, neo-orthodox movement. The last provision under-

scores the importance attached to engaging the spirit and emotions, as well as the intellect and moral sense, in these scholarly meetings. Thus the Donglin Academy continued the strong tradition of Neo-Confucian academies as religious, liturgical, and social centers for the educated classes.

LIU ZONGZHOU ON LIFE AND DEATH

Liu Zongzhou (1578–1645), who had close affinities with the Donglin school, was a leading thinker of the late Ming and the teacher of the eminent scholar and political theorist, Huang Zongxi, whom we will meet in chapter 25 (vol. 2). Though differing in some respects from the Donglin academicians, Liu shared their commitment to the Zhu Xi tradition of learning, their concerns with the moral regeneration of the ruling class, and their courage in speaking out against misgovernment. Like several of his contemporaries, he was unafraid to speak out against the notorious eunuch Wei Zhongxian in the 1620s or, as president of the Censorate,[79] to memorialize in favor of dynastic reform in the early 1640s. His criticisms offended the emperor, leading to Liu's dismissal from office. But, though he had personal experience of the failings of Ming despotism, Liu remained loyal to the Ming cause following the fall of Peking to the invading Manchus in 1644, and when he was reappointed to the Censorate in the Ming government after its retreat to Nanking, he continued his demands for reform. When Nanking fell in turn, and it was clear that the dynasty could not be revived, Liu demonstrated the depth of his convictions about service and sacrifice, committing suicide by fasting for twenty-one days. Liu represents a consummate example of courage, moral scrupulousness, and a typically Confucian kind of loyalty — a loyalty more to principle than to persons. We conclude this volume with his brief but moving "Teaching on Life and Death," which may recall his tribute to Fang Xiaoru (earlier in this chapter) and reevoke the affirmative spirit found in the "Western Inscription" composed centuries earlier by Zhang Zai, though, in this seventeenth-century context, the affirmation seems to be asserted against a sense of darkness and crisis.

TEACHING ON LIFE AND DEATH (*SHENGSI SHUO*)

When they do not clearly understand the learning of the Sages, students often give rise to views based on the physical vessel [the body]. They see that, for the

---

79. The Censorate (*yushi tai*, lit., the "terrace or pavilion of imperial scribes") was, as Charles Hucker describes it, "an agency in the top echelon of the central government [from Han through Ming]. . . with the paramount and characteristic responsibility of maintaining disciplinary surveillance over the whole of officialdom, checking records and auditing accounts in government offices, accepting public complaints and impeaching officials who in their private or public lives violated the law or otherwise conducted themselves improperly." (Hucker, *Official Titles*, p. 593, no. 8184.)

body, the affair of life and death is the greatest of all, and they place the myriad things of Heaven and Earth on the outside of the barrier. They have already cut off the seeds of the constantly reborn living potential of this mind, and so in their work [of self-cultivation] they concentrate on reaching the road of birthlessness, so that all that remains undestroyed is an awareness that is still active. This enables them to become humans again. However, if they follow this way, they cannot escape the cycle of coveting life and fearing death.

Our Confucian learning takes forming one body with Heaven and Earth and the myriad things as the great body. The starting point of Heaven, Earth, and the myriad things is our own starting point, and the end point of Heaven, Earth, and the myriad things is our own end point. From beginning to end, from end to beginning, the cycle never ends. This is our teaching on life and death.

Actually, life and death are commonplace things. Master Cheng Hao said, "If a person can let go of this self and view all things within Heaven and Earth, great and small, in the same way—what joy this would be!"[80] I say that the teaching on life and death ought to be placed between Heaven and Earth, and great and small are all seen as equal. To realize this is at last the learning of fully fathoming the true principle, fully realizing our true nature, and thoroughly extending to Heaven's command. If we merely hold to the life and death of a single life-span in order to know life and death, then, knowing that life ends, we only know the life of coveting life, and knowing the finality of death, we only know the death of fearing death.

Someone asked: "So then, is it unnecessary to know the life and death of a single life-span?"

[The teacher] said, "How can we not know them? This is what Confucius meant when he said, 'If you hear of the Way in the morning, it is all right to die that evening.'[81] What is the hearing of the Way? . . . If there are no arising and no demise, then there are naturally no birth and no death.' " He also said, "If you exhaust the path of speech and silence, then you can exhaust the path of going away and coming back. If you exhaust the path of going away and coming back, then you can exhaust the path of birth and death. Birth and death are not great matters;[82] speech and silence and going away and coming back are not small matters. For those engaged in learning, the barrier of birth and death is often hard to pass through. If you acquire a penetrating understanding of this point, Heaven, Earth, and the myriad things are none other than this. And this at last is 'hearing of the Way.' "

["Shengsi shuo," in *Liuzi quanji* 2:378–81 — TWM]

---

80. Liu appears to have slightly adapted a statement by Cheng Hao in *Er Cheng yishu* (SBBY ed.) 2A:15b in *Er Cheng quanshu*.

81. *Analects* 4:8.

82. Buddhists were told to be constantly mindful of the "great matter" of life and death.

GLOSSARY OF KEY TERMS

Following are key Chinese terms appearing in this volume, with renderings in order of (1) *pinyin* romanization; (2) alternate Wade- Giles romanization (if any); (3) the Chinese character; (4) standard or preferred English translation herein; (5) variant translations used in particular contexts (the Chinese character often connotes several such meanings at once).

ben/pen 本	root, trunk, base; (adj.) primary, fundamental, essential (often in combination with *mo*, branch, secondary, etc. [see *mo*])
benxin/pen-hsin 本心	original or essential mind/heart
chen/ch'en 臣	minister, subject
cheng/ch'eng 誠	sincerity, genuineness, integrity, authenticity
dao/tao 道	the Way, way, path
de/te 德	virtue, moral force, inner power
fa 法	law, system, measure, method (in Buddhism: law, doctrine, phenomenon)
fengjian/feng-chien 封建	enfeoffment, feudal
gewu/ko-wu 格物	investigation of things, rectification of affairs
gong/kung 公	common good, shared, public, fair to all
guo/kuo 國	state, dynastic state, nation
jian ai/chien-ai 兼愛	embracing love, universal love
jing/ching 敬	reverence, reverent seriousness

jing/ching 經 — classic (Confucianism); scripture (Daoism); *sūtra* (Buddhism)

jun/chün 君 — ruler, prince

junzi/chün-tzu 君子 — noble person, gentleman, superior person

li 禮 — rites, ritual decorum

li 理 — principle, order, directive or guiding principle, numen, coding, infrastructure

li 利 — gain, profit, advantage, resources

liang zhi/chih 良知 — innate or good knowledge/knowing

ming ming de/te 明明德 — to clarify or manifest luminous virtue

mingde/ming-te 明德 — luminous virtue, clear virtue, the moral nature

mo 末 — branch, outgrowth; (adj.) secondary, derivative, degenerate

qi/ch'i 氣 — vital force, vital energy, material-force, ether; (adj.) psycho-physical

qing/ch'ing 情 — emotion, feeling

ren/jen 仁 — humaneness (as practical virtue); humanity (as perfection of all virtue); co-humanity (as shared virtue)

ren/jen 人 — humankind, human being, person, man

renyu/jen-yü 人欲 — human desires; selfish desires (i.e., when conflicting with the common good, especially in rulers and those entrusted with responsibility for others)

ru/ju 儒 — Confucian school or scholar

sangang/san-kang 三岡 — Three Mainstays or Three Bonds

sangangling/san-kang-ling 三岡領 — Three Main Guidelines

shen 神 — spirit, deity, numen, *anima*; (adj.) spiritual, numinous

shen 身 — self, person, body

shi/shih 事 — thing, affair, matter, fact, event, instantiation

shi/shih 實 — substantial, real, solid, practical

shi/shih 士 — scholar-official, literatus, man of service

shu 恕 — reciprocity, mutuality, empathy

si/ssu 私 — private or self-interest (as complementary to common good [*gong*]); selfishness (when in conflict with common or public good)

taiji/t'ai-chi 太極 — Supreme Ultimate, Pole, or Norm; Supreme Polarity

ti/t'i 體 — substance, body, essence

tian/t'ien 天 — Heaven, celestial; (adj.) natural

tianming/t'ien-ming 天命 — Heaven's Mandate, ordination, ordinance, charge, decree

tianxia /t'ien-hsia 天下 — All under Heaven, everyone, the world, realm

tiyong/t'i-yung 體用 — substance/function

wen 文	culture, civil, writing, literature, pattern, decoration
wu 無	nothing, nothingness, absence
wuji/wu chi 無極	non-finite, nonpolar, indeterminate
wuwei/wu-wei 無為	doing nothing, nonassertion, taking no deliberate action
wuxing 五行	Five Phases
xiao/hsiao 孝	filiality, filial piety or devotion
xin/hsin 心	mind-and-heart, mind, heart
xin/hsin 信	trustworthiness, trust, faith
xing/hsing 性	human nature, *the* nature (not Nature)
xiu/hsiu 修	cultivation, discipline
xiushen/hsiu shen 修身	self-cultivation, self-discipline, cultivation of one's person
xu/hsü 虛	empty, void, open, receptive
xue/hsüeh 學	learning, study, school
yi/i 義	rightness, concept, meaning; (adj.) righteous, moral
yi/i 意	intention, thought
yong/yung 用	function, use, operation
yu/yü 欲	desire, appetite
zhengxin/cheng-hsin 正心	correcting or rectifying the mind-and-heart
zhi/chih 知	know, learn; knowledge, knowing
zhi/chih 智	wisdom
zhi/chih 止	stop, rest (Buddhism: calming, cessation)
zhi/chih 治	order, governance, peaceful rule
zhi/chih 志	will, resolve, commitment, set one's heart on
zhizhi/chih-chih 致知	the extension of knowledge or of one's capacity to know (knowing)
ziran/tzu-jan 自然	naturally, so-of-itself, self-, auto-

BIBLIOGRAPHY

Titles of collections that appear repeatedly in the list are abbreviated as follows:

BNB *Bonaben ershisi shi*. 820 *ce*. Shanghai: Commercial Press, 1930–1937.

CSJC *Congshu jicheng*. 1,384 titles in 2,000 vols. Shanghai: Commercial Press, 1935–1937.

DZ *[Zhengtong] Daozang*. 1,120 vols. Taipei: Yiwen yinshu guan, 1962.

GXJC *Guoxue jiben congshu*. Shanghai: Commercial Press, 1932?–1939?

HYISIS Harvard-Yenching Institute Sinological Index Series.

SBBY *Sibu beiyao*. 537 titles in 1,372 *ce*. Shanghai: Zhonghua shuju, 1927–1935.

SBCK *Sibu congkan*. 1st ser. 323 titles in 2,102 *ce*. Shanghai: Commercial Press, 1920–1922, reprint 1929. 3d ser. Shanghai: Commercial Press, 1935.

SKQS *[Wenyuan ge] Siku quanshu*. 1,500 vols. Taibei: Taiwan shangwu yinshu guan, 1983–1986.

TD *Taishō [shinshū] daizōkyō*. Ed. Takakusu Junjirō and Watanabe Kaigyoku. 85 vols. Tokyo: Taishō issai-kyō kankō-kai, 1914–1922.

ZZ *[Dai-Nihon] zoku zōkyō*. 750 vols. Kyoto: Zōkyō shoin, 1905–1912.

ZZMJ *Zhongguo zixue mingzhu jicheng*. Taibei: 1977.

Analects (Lunyu). In Ruan Yuan, *Shisan jing zhushu*, or Legge, *The Chinese Classics*, vol. 1.

Anleji. See Daochuo.

Baiyi Guanyin wuxinyin tuoluoni jing. Text collated from various Ming editions in the Rare Book Collection of Buddhist Artifacts and Library, Fayuan Si, Beijing.

Balazs, Stephan [Étienne], trans. *Le Traité juridique du Souei chou*. Leiden: E. J. Brill, 1954.

Ban Gu. *Hanshu*. BNB ed.

Ban Zhao. *Nüjie*. See *Nü sishu*.

Beixi daquan yi. See Chen Chun.

Baopuzi neipian jiaoshi. See Ge Hong.

Bielefeldt, Carl. *Dōgen's Manuals of Zen Meditation*. Berkeley and Los Angeles: University of California Press, 1988.

Biot, Edouard. *Le Tcheou li* (*Rites des Tcheou*). 2 vols. Paris: Imprimerie Nationale, 1851.

Biyan lu. See Yuanwu Keqin.

Bloom, Irene, ed. and trans. *Knowledge Painfully Acquired: The K'un chih chi by Lo Ch'in-shun*. New York: Columbia University Press, 1987.

Bohu tongde lun. Hanwei congshu ed. Shanghai: Hanfen lou, 1925.

Book of Odes, The. Ed. and trans. B. Karlgren. Stockholm: Museum of Far Eastern Antiquities, 1950.

Brooks, E. Bruce and A. Taeko Brooks. *The Original Analects*. New York: Columbia University Press, 1998.

Busch, Heinrich. "The Tung-lin Shu-yüan and Its Political and Philosophical Significance." *Monumenta Serica* 14 (1949–1955). Tokyo: SVD Research Institute, 1955.

Butuo shanzhi. 1924. 18–20.

Campany, Robert F. "The Real Presence." *History of Religions* 32, no. 3 (February 1993): 233-72.

Cangshu. See Li Zhi.

Carter, Thomas, and L. Carrington Goodrich. *The Invention of Printing in China and Its Spread Westward*. New York: Ronald Press, 1955.

Chan, Hok-lam, and Wm. Theodore de Bary, eds. *Yüan Thought: Chinese Thought and Religion Under the Mongols*. New York: Columbia University Press, 1982.

Chan men guishi. Appended to biography of Baizhang. *Jingde chuandeng lu*. TD 51, no. 2076.

Chan, Wing-tsit, ed. and trans. *Instructions for Practical Living and Other Neo Confucian Writings by Wang Yang-ming*. New York: Columbia University Press, 1963.

——. *Reflections on Things at Hand The Neo-Confucian Anthology Compiled by Chu Hsi and Lü Tsu-ch'ien*. New York: Columbia University Press, 1967.

——. *Source Book in Chinese Philosophy*. Princeton: Princeton University Press, 1963.

Changchun zhenren xiyouji. DZ 1056, no. 1429.

Changli xiansheng wenji. See Han Yu

Chanyuan qinggui. See Zongze.

Chen Chun. *Beixi daquan ji*. Xiyin xuan ed., 1840.

Chen Dong. *Shitong*. SBCK ed.

Chen Hongmou. *Yangzheng yigui*. SBBY ed.

Chen Jian. *Xuepou tongbian*. Reprint. Taibei: Guangwen, 1971.

Chen Liang ji. See Chen Liang.

Chen Liang. *Chen Liangji*. Rev. ed. Beijing: Zhonghua shuju, 1981.

Cheng Duanli. *Chengshi richeng*. CSJC ed.

Cheng Duanmeng and Dong Zhu. *Cheng-Dong er xiansheng xuece*. CJSC ed.

Cheng Hao. *Mingdao wenji*. SBBY ed.

Cheng Hao and Cheng Yi. *Er Cheng cuiyan*. In *Er Cheng quanshu*. SBBY ed.

——. *Er Cheng quanshu*. SBBY ed.

——. *Er Cheng yishu*. In *Er Cheng quanshu*. SBBY ed.

Cheng Yi. *Henan Chengshi wenji*. In *Er Cheng ji*. Beijing: Zhonghua shuju, 1981.

Cheng-Dong er xiansheng xuece. See Cheng Duanmeng.

Chengshi richeng. See Cheng Duanli.

Chengweishi lun. TD 31, no. 1585.

Ch'ien Mu. *Xian Qin zhuzi xinian.* 2d ed. Hong Kong: Hong Kong University Press, 1956.

Ching, Julia, and Chaoying Fang, ed. and trans. Huang Tsung-hsi. *The Records of Ming Scholars.* Honolulu: University of Hawaii Press, 1987.

Chunqiu fanlu yizheng. See Dong Zhongshu.

Couvreur, Seraphim. *"Li ki" ou Memoires sur les bienséances et les cérémonies.* 2 vols. Ho kien fou, Imprimerie de la Mission Catholique, 1913.

Da Minglü jijie fulie. Vol. 4. Copy of Ming Wanli ed. Taibei: Xuesheng shuju, 1970.

Dacheng zhiguan fa men. TD 46, no. 1924.

Daochuo. *Anleji,* in *TD* 47, no. 1958.

Daogulu. See Li Zhi.

de Bary, Wm. Theodore, ed. *Self and Society in Ming Thought.* New York: Columbia University Press, 1970.

—— ed. and trans. *Waiting for the Dawn: A Plan for the Prince — Huang Tsung-hsi's Ming-i tai-fang lu.* New York: Columbia University Press, 1993.

de Bary, Wm. Theodore, and John Chaffee, eds. *Neo-Confucian Education: The Formative Stage.* New York: Columbia University Press, 1989.

Dictionary of Ming Biography. Ed. L. Carrington Goodrich and Chaoying Fang. New York: Columbia University Press, 1976.

Dixue. See Fan Ziyu.

Dōgen. *See* Bielefeldt.

Dong Zhongshu. *Chunqiu fanlu yizheng.* With commentary by Lu Yu and preface by Wang Xianqian. 1914. Reprint. Taibei: Heluo tushu chubanshe, 1974.

Dong Zhong shu. *Chunqiu jueshi,* in Ma Guohan, comp. *Yuhan shanfang ji yishu,* vol. 31. Changsha: Lang Huan guan ed., 1883.

Dongxian lingbao wugan wen. DZ 1004, no. 1278.

Du Guangting. *Shenxian ganyu zhuan. DZ* 328, no. 592.

Du You. *Tongdian.* Shitong ed. Shanghai: Commercial Press, 1935–1936.

Dubs, Homer H., ed. and trans. *The Works of Hsüntze.* London: Probsthain, 1928.

Duyvendak, J. J. L., ed. and trans. *The Book of Lord Shang.* London: Probsthain, 1928.

Ebrey, Patricia B., ed. and trans. *Chu Hsi's Family Rituals.* Princeton: Princeton University Press, 1991.

Eno, Robert. *The Confucian Creation of Heaven.* Albany: SUNY Press, 1990.

Er Cheng cuiyan. See Cheng Hao and Cheng Yi.

Er Cheng quanshu. See Cheng Hao and Cheng Yi.

Er Cheng yishu. See Cheng Hao and Cheng Yi.

Fahua xuanyi. TD 33, no. 1716.

Fan Zuyu. *Dixue. SKQS* ed.

Fanwang jing. TD 24, no. 1484.

Fengsu tongyi. Beijing: Centre franco-chinois d'études sinologiques, 1943.

Fenshu. See Li Zhi.

Fung Yu-lan. A *History of Chinese Philosophy.* Vol. 2. Trans. Derk Bodde. Princeton: Princeton University Press, 1953.

Ge Hong. *Baopuzi neipian jiaoshi.* Ed. Wang Ming. Beijing: Zhonghua shuju, 1980.

Giles, Herbert. *San-tzu ching.* 2d ed. rev. 1910. Reprint. Taibei: Literature House, 1964.

———. *The San Tzu Ching and the Ch'ien Tzu Wen*. Shanghai: A. H. De Carvalho, 1873.

Goodrich, L. Carrington, and Chaoying Fang, eds. *Dictionary of Ming Biography*. New York: Columbia University Press, 1976.

Graham, A. C., ed. and trans. *Chuang-tzu: The Seven Inner Chapters and Other Writings from the Book Chuang-tzu*. London: George Allen and Unwin, 1981. Excerpts reprinted here with the permission of the literary estate of A. C. Graham and of Dawn and Der Pao Graham.

———, trans. *The Book of Lieh-tzu: A Classic of the Tao*. New York: Columbia University Press, 1990.

Great Learning (Daxue). *Liji*. SBBY ed. Legge, *The Chinese Classics*, vol. 1.

Gu Duanwen gong yishu. See Gu Xiancheng.

Gu Xiancheng. *Gu Duanwen gong yishu*. Guangxu 3 (1877). Reprint of Wanli zongzi Library edition.

Gu Yanwu. *Jiugulu*. *Xingsu caotang jinshi congshu* ed. 1888.

———. *Rizhilu*. SBBY ed.

———. *Tinglin shiwen ji*. SBBY ed.

Guanxin lun shu. TD 46, no. 1921.

Guanyin jingzhou linggan huiyao. Tianjin, 1934.

Guanzi. GXJC ed. Shanghai: Commercial Press, 1934.

Guanzi jijiao. See Xu Weiyu.

Guizhai wenji. See Ouyang Xuan.

Guo Moruo, ed., and Hu Houxuan, ed. in chief. *Jiaguwen heji*. 13 vols. N.p.: Zhonghua shuju, 1978–1982.

Guo Xiang. *Commentary on Zhuangzi*. In *Nanhua zhenjing*, SBCK ed.

Han Feizi. SBCK ed.

Han Yu. *Changli xiansheng wenji*. SBCK ed.

Handlin, Joanna F. *Action in Late Ming Thought: The Reorientation of Lü K'un and Other Scholar-Officials*. Berkeley and Los Angeles: University of California Press, 1983.

Hanshu. See Ban Gu.

Hao Jing. *Hao wenzhong gong ji*. In *Qiankun zhengqi ji*, 1848 ed.

Hao wenzhong gong ji. See Hao Jing.

Henan Chengshi wenji. See Cheng Yi.

Hongming ji. TD 52, no. 2102.

Hou Han shu. BNB ed.

Hou Han shu. Beijing: Zhonghua shuju, 1966.

Huainanzi. Ed. D. C. Lau. Chinese University of Hong Kong, Institute of Chinese Studies, Ancient Chinese Text Concordance Series. Hong Kong: Commercial Press, 1992.

Huang Ming zhishu. 6 vols. Taibei: Chengwen, 1969.

Huang Qing jingshi wen pian. He Changling, ed. Original ed. 1826; reprinted, 3 vols. Taibei: Guofeng chubanshe, 1963.

Huang Zongxi. *Mingyi daifang lu*. In de Bary, *Waiting for the Dawn*.

———. *Mingru xuean*. Wanyu wenku ed. Taibei: Commercial Press, 1965.

Huangdi sijing jinzhu jinyi. Chen Guying, ed. Taibei: Commerical Press, 1995.

Huangji jingshi shu. See Shao Yong.

Huayan jing. TD 10, no. 279.

Huayan wujiao zhiguan. TD 45, no. 1867.

Hucker, Charles O. *A Dictionary of Official Titles in Imperial China.* Stanford: Stanford University Press, 1985.

Huian Zhu wengong xiansheng wenji. See Zhu Xi.

Huizuan Gongguoge. Daoguang ed.

Hulsewé, A. F. P. *Remnants of Han Law.* Vol. 1, *Sinica Leidensia* 9. Leiden: E. J. Brill, 1955.

Jia I. *Xinshu.* 10 *juan. SBCK* ed.; also *ZZMJ* ed. Reprint of Wang Tingjian ed. Taibei, 1977.

Jiayouji. See Su Xun.

Jingde chuandeng lu. TD 51, no. 2076.

Jingjin Dongbo wenji shilue. See Su Shi.

Jiu Tangshu. BNB ed.

Jiugulu. See Gu Yanwu.

Johnson, Wallace, ed. and trans. *The T'ang Code,* Vol. 1. Princeton: Princeton University Press, 1979.

Kaltenmark, Max. *Le Lie-sien tchouan (Traduit et annoté).* Beijing, 1953. Rev. ed. Paris: Collège de France, 1987.

Karlgren, B., ed. and trans. *The Book of Odes.* Stockholm: Museum of Far Eastern Antiquities, 1950.

Kinugawa, T., ed. *Collected Studies in Sung History. Dedicated to Prof. James T. C. Liu.* Kyoto: Dōyūsha, 1989.

Knoblock, John, ed. and trans. *Xunzi: A Translation and Study of the Complete Works.* 3 vols. Stanford: Stanford University Press, 1988-94.

Kurihara Keisuke. *Kōkyō.* Tokyo: Meiji shoin, 1986.

Laozi. SBBY ed.

Laozi weizhi lilüe. See Wang Bi.

Lau, D. C., trans. "Advice to My Sons," by Yen Chih-t'ui. *Renditions* 1 (1973): 94–98, and "Yen's Family Instructions." *Renditions* 33 (1990): 58–62.

———, ed. *A Concordance to the Huai-nan Tzu.* Chinese University of Hong Kong, Institute of Chinese Studies, Ancient Chinese Text Concordance Series. Hong Kong: Commercial Press, 1992.

———, ed. *A Concordance to the Lüshi chunqiu.* Chinese University of Hong Kong ICS Ancient Chinese Text Concordance Series. Hong Kong: Commercial Press, 1994.

Legge, James. *The Chinese Classics.* 5 vols. Oxford: Clarendon Press, 1893–1895. Reprint. Hong Kong: Hong Kong University Press, 1979.

———. *Li Ki (Li-chi). Book of Rites.* 2 vols. New York: University Books, 1967. Reprint of Oxford 1885 Sacred Books of the East ed.

Li Zhi. *Cangshu.* Beijing: Zhonghua shuju, 1959.

———. *Daogulu.* Ming ed. Preface dated 1599. Collection of Yoshikawa Kojirō.

———. *Fenshu.* Beijing: Zhonghua shuju, 1961.

———. *Xu Fenshu.* Beijing: Zhonghua shuju, 1959.

Li Zhichang. *See Changchun zhenren xiyouji.*

Liexian zhuan. See Liu Xiang.

Liji. 20 *juan. SBBY* ed.

Liji. In Ruan Yuan, *Shisan jing zhushu.* Reprint. Taibei: Yiwen yinshu guan, 1958.

Liming pian. See Yuan Huang.

Linchuan xiansheng wenji. See Wang Anshi.

Linji Huizhao chanshi yulu. TD 47, no. 1985.

Liu Hedong ji. See Liu Zongyuan.

Liu Xiang (attrib.). *Liexian zhuan.* DZ 138, no. 294.

Liu Zhiji. *Shitong.* SBCK ed.

Liu Zongyuan. *Liu Hedong ji.* Shanghai: Zhonghua shuju, 1960.

Liu Zongzhou. *Liuzi quanshu,* vol. 2, ed. Dai Lianzhang, Wu Guang, and Zhong Cai-jun. Taibei: Zhongyang yenjiu yuan, Zhongguo wenzhe yanjiusuo, 1996.

Liuzi quanshu. See Liu Zongzhou.

Lotus Sūtra. See Miaofa lianhua jing; Watson, Burton. *The Lotus Sūtra.*

Lu Jia. *Xinyu.* 1592 ed., collated by Fan Dachong. Reprint. ZZMJ ed. Taibei, 1977.

Lu Xiangshan. *Xiangshan quanji.* SBBY ed.

Lu Xuangong zouyi. See Lu Zhi.

Lu Zhi. *Lu xuangong zouyi.* GXJC ed.

Lunyu. In Ruan Yuan, *Shisan jing zhushu;* Legge, *The Chinese Classics,* vol. 1.

Luo Qinshun. *Knowledge Painfully Acquired—The K'un-chih chi by Lo Ch'in-shun.* Ed. and trans. Irene Bloom. New York: Columbia University Press, 1976.

Luzhai quanshu. See Xu Heng.

Luanzheng yingzhao ji. See Su Che.

Lü Buwei. *See Lüshi Chunqiu.*

Lü Donglai wenji. See Lü Zuqian.

Lü Family Community Compact. See Lüshi xiangyue.

Lü Kun. *Lüzi sizhong* (*heke*). In *Lüzi yishu.*

——. *Lüzi yishu.* 1827.

——. *Quweizhai wenji.* In *Lüzi yishu.*

——. *Shizheng lu.* In *Lüzi yishu.*

Lü Zuqian. *Lü Donglai wenji.* CSJC ed.

Lüshi chunqiu jiao shi. Ed. Chen Qiyou. Shanghai: Xuelin chubanshe, 1984.

Lüshi xiangyue. In *Zhuzi daquan,* SBBY ed.

Lüzi sizhong. See Lü Kun.

Lüzi yishu. See Lü Kun.

Lynn, Richard John, ed. and trans. *The Classic of Changes—A New Translation of the I Ching as Interpreted by Wang Bi.* New York: Columbia University Press, 1994.

Ma Duanlin. *Wenxian tongkao. Shitong* ed. Shanghai: Commercial Press, 1936.

Makita, Tairyō. *Rikuchō koitsu Kanzeon ōkenki no kenkyū.* Kyoto: Hyōrakuji Shōten, 1970.

Makra, Mary Lelia, trans. *The Hsiao Ching.* New York: St. John's University Press, 1961.

Mather, Richard B., ed. and trans. *A New Account of Tales of the World (Shih-shuo hsin-yü).* Minneapolis: University of Minnesota Press, 1976.

Mawangdui Hanmu boshu. Beijing: Wenwu chubanshe, 1980.

[The] *Mean (Zhongyong).* In Ruan Yuan, *Shisan jing zhushu,* or Legge, *The Chinese Classics,* vol. 1.

Mean (Zhongyong). Liji, SBBY ed.

Mencius (Mengzi). In Ruan Yuan, *Shisan jing zhushu,* or Legge, *The Chinese Classics,* vol. 2.

Mengzi. See Mencius

Meskill, John. *Academies in Ming China.* Tucson: University of Arizona Press, 1982.

Miaofa lianhua jing (Lotus Sūtra), *TD* 9, no. 262.

Ming shilu. Photographic reprint of Kiangsu Library ed. Nanking, 1940.

Ming Taizu yuzhi wenji. N.d. Reprint. Taibei: Xuesheng shuju, 1965.

Ming wenheng. SKQS ed.

———. Cheng Mingzheng, comp. N.d. Reprint. Taibei: Guangwen, 1971

Mingdao wenji. See Cheng Hao

Mingru Wang Xinzhai xiansheng yiji. See Wang Gen.

Mingru xuean. See Huang Zongxi.

Mingyi daifang lu. See Huang Zongxi.

Mingzhao kaiguo wenxian. N.d. Reprint. 4 vols. Taibei: Xuesheng shuju, 1966.

Mohe zhiguan. TD 46, no. 1911.

Mozi jiangu. ed. Sun Yirang. Shanghai: Zhonghua shuju, 1954.

Mozi. 16 *juan. SBBY* ed.

Mozi. SBCK ed.

Myōhō-renge-kyō narabi ni kaiketsu. Tokyo: Soka Gakkai, 1961.

Nüjie. See Ban Zhao.

Nü lunyu. See Song Ruozhao.

Nü sishu. 1854 Japanese ed. Preserved in the Naikaku Bunko, Tokyo.

Orlando, Raffaello. "A Study of Chinese Documents Concerning the Life of the Tantric Buddhist Patriarch Amoghavajra (A.D. 705–774)." Ph.D. diss., Princeton University, 1981.

Ouyang wenzhong gong ji. See Oiyang Xiu.

Ouyang Xiu. *Ouyang wenzhong gong ji. SBCK* ed.

———. *Xin Tang shu.* In *[Jinding] ershisi shi,* Hanfenlou reprint of the Palace ed. of 1739. Shanghai, 1916.

Ouyang Xuan. *Guizhai wenji. SBCK* ed.

Owen, Stephen. *The Great Age of Chinese Poetry*: The High T'ang. New Haven: Yale University Press, 1981.

Platform Sutra of the Sixth Patriarch. Ed. and trans. Philip B. Yampolsky. New York: Columbia University Press, 1963.

Platform Sūtra of the Sixth Patriarch. From the photographic reproductions of the Dunhuang manuscript housed in the Stein Collection (S5475) at the British Museum. Section numbers as in the D. T. Suzuki ed.

Putuoluojia xinzhi (A New Gazetteer of Potalaka), 12 *juan,* comp. Wang Hengyan, 1924. Reprinted in *Zhongguo fosi shizhi huikan* (Compendium of Monastic Gazetteers of China), 1st collection, Vol. 10. Taiwan: Mingwen, 1980.

Quweizhai wenji. See Lü Kun

Rickett, W. Allyn. *Guanzi.* Vol. 1. Princeton: Princeton University Press, 1985.

Rizhi lu. See Gu Yanwu.

Sakai Tadao. "Confucianism and Popular Educational Works." In Wm. Theodore de Bary, ed., *Self and Society in Ming Thought,* pp. 331-66.

Sanlun xuanyi. TD 45, no. 1852.

Santian neijie jing. DZ 876, no. 1205.

Schipper, Kristofer. *Concordance du Tao-tsang*: titres des ouvrages. Paris: École Française d'Extrême Orient, 1975.

Schirokauer, Conrad. "The Authority of the Historian: A Sung View." In Kinugawa,

Collected Studies in Sung History, Dedicated to Professor James T.C. Liu. Kyōtō: Dōyōsha, 1989.

Shandao. *Guanjing shu.* TD 37, no. 1753.

Shang Yang. *The Book of Lord Shang.* Ed. and trans. J. J. L. Duyvendak. London: Probsthain, 1928.

———. *Shangzi.* SBCK ed.

Shangshu dazhuan. SBCK ed.

Shangzi. See Shang Yang.

Shao Yong. *Huangji jingshi shu.* SBBY ed.

Shenxian ganyu zhuan. See Du Guangting.

Shiji. See Sima Qian.

Shijing. Xuesheng guoxue congshu ed. Shanghai: Commercial Press, 1926. *See also* Karlgren, *The Book of Odes,* and Legge, *The Chinese Classics,* vol. 4.

Shisan jing zhushu. Nan Chang fuxue ed. Reprint. Taibei: Yiwen yinshu guan, n.d.

Shisi lun (by Xi Kang), in *Xi Zhongsan ji.* SBBY ed.

Shitong. See Chen Dong.

Shiwu wushi. See Xu Heng.

Shizheng lu. See Lü Kun.

Shujing. "Jin teng," in Legge, *The Chinese Classics,* vol. 3.

Shujing (Shangshu jinguwen zhusu). GXJC ed. See also Legge, *The Chinese Classics,* vol. 3.

Shuowen jiezi gulin. Ed. Ding Fubao. Taibei: Xinxing shuju, 1960.

Sima Guang. *Zizhi tong jian.* 4 vols. Beijing: Zhonghua shuju, 1956.

———. *Wenguo wenzheng gong wenji.* SBCK ed.

Sima Qian. *Shiji.* BNB ed.

Smith, Joanna Handlin. *See* Handlin.

Song Lian et al., eds. *Yuan shi.* Beijing: Zhonghua shuju, 1976.

Song Ruozhao. *Nü Lunyu. See Nü sishu.*

Song shi. Hanfen lou reprint of Palace ed. of 1739. Shanghai, 1916.

Song Yuan xuean. Comp. Huang Zongxi and Quan Zuwang. Beijing: Zhonghua shuju, 1986.

Songke xiaojing. Tianjin: Tianjin shi guji shudian, 1987.

Su Che. *Luanzheng ji yingzhao ji.* SBCK ed. Selection adapted from Schirokauer, "The Authority of the Historian."

Su Xun. *Jiayou ji.* SBCK ed.

———. *Xunzhichai ji.* SBCK ed.

Sunzi huijian. Ed. Yang Bingan. Henan: Zhongzhou guji chubanshe, 1986.

Swann, Nancy Lee. *Pan Chao: Foremost Woman Scholar of China.* New York: Century, 1932.

Taishang dongyuan shenzhou jing. DZ 170–173, no. 335.

Taishang ganying pian. DZ 834–839, no. 1167.

Taishang Laojun jinglü. DZ 562, no. 786.

Taiwei xianjun gongguo ge. DZ 78, no. 186.

Tanluan. *Yuanshenglun zhu.* TD 40, no. 1819.

Teng Ssu-yü. *Family Instructions for the Yen Clan,* by Yen Chih-t'ui. Leiden: Brill, 1968.

Tinglin shiwen ji. See Gu Yanwu.

Tjan Tjoe Som, trans. *Po-hu t'ung: The Comprehensive Discussions in the White Tiger Hall.* Leiden: Brill, 1952.

Tongdian. See Du You.

Tongjian gangmu. See Zhu Xi.

Tunnan. See Zhongguo shehui kexueyuan kaogu yanjiusuo.

Uno Seiichi. *Shōgaku.* Tokyo: Meiji shoin, 1965.

Vimalikīrti Sûtra. See Weimojie suo shuo jing.

Waley, Arthur, ed. and trans. *The Poetry and Career of Li Po.* London: George Allen and Unwin; New York: Macmillan, 1958.

Waley, Arthur. *The Travels of an Alchemist.* London: G. Routledge, 1931.

Wang Anshi. *Linchuan xiansheng wenji. SBCK* ed.

Wang Bi. *Laozi weizhi lilüe.* In *Wang Bi ji jiaoshi.* 2 vols. Ed. Lou Yulie. Beijing: Zhoughua shuju, 1980.

Wang Gen. *Mingru Wang Xinzhai xiansheng yiji.* Beijing, 1911.

Wang Ji. *Wang Longxi quanji.* 1822 ed.

Wang Longxi quanji. See Wang Ji.

Wang Yangming. *Wang Yangming quanji.* Shanghai: Datong Book Co., 1935.

———. *Wang Yangming quanshu.* Taibei: Zhengzhong shuju, 1953.

Wang Yangming quanji. See Wang Yangming.

Wang Yangming quanshu. See Wang Yangming.

Wangsheng lun zhu. TD 40, no. 1819.

Ware, James R. *Alchemy, Medicine and Religion in the China of A.D. 320: the Nei-p'ien of Ko Hung (Pao p'utzu).* New York: Dover Publications, 1981.

Watson, Burton, ed. and trans. *Chuang Tzu: Complete Writings.* New York: Columbia University Press, 1963.

———, ed. and trans. *The Columbia Book of Chinese Poetry: From Earliest Times to the Thirteenth Century.* New York: Columbia University Press, 1984.

———, ed. and trans. *The Lotus Sutra.* New York: Columbia University Press, 1993.

———, trans. *The Tso chuan: Selections from China's Oldest Narrative History.* New York: Columbia University Press, 1989.

Weimojie suo shuo jing (Vimalakīrti Sūtra). TD 14, no. 475.

Welch, Holmes and Anna Seidel. *Facets of Taoism.* New Haven: Yale University Press, 1979.

Wenguo wenzheng gong wenji. See Sima Guang.

Wenzi zuan yi in Ershier zi. Comp. Du Daojian. Zhejiang shuju keben.

Wenxian tongkao. See Ma Duanlin.

Wilhelm, R. *The I Ching or Book of Changes.* Trans. Cary Baynes. New York: Pantheon Books, 1950.

Xi Kang. *Shisi lun.* In *Xi Zhongsan ji, SBBY* ed.

Xiangshan quanji. See Lu Xiangshan.

Xiaoxue. See Zhu Xi.

Xinshu. See Jia Yi.

Xinyu. See Lu Jia.

Xiu huayan aozhi wangjin huanyuan guan. TD 45, no. 1876.

Xu fenshu. See Li Zhi.

Xu Heng. *Luzhai quanshu.* In *Kinsei kanseki sōkan,* vol. 5. Kyoto: Chūbun shuppansha, 1974.

———. *Shiwu wushi.* In Su Tianjue, *Yuan wenlei, SKQS* ed.

———. *Xu wenzhong gong yishu.* In *Tang shi jingguan congshu.* Preface dated Qianlong 53 (1788).

Xu Wei-yü, Wen Yiduo, and Guo Moruo. *Guanzi jijiao*. Beijing: Zhonghua shuju, 1955.

Xu wenzhong gong yishu. *See* Xu Heng.

Xuandu lüwen. DZ 78, no. 188.

Xuepou tongbian. *See* Chen Jian.

Xunzhizhai ji. *See* Su Xun.

Xunzi. HYISIS, supplement 22. Reprint. Taipei: Chinese Materials and Research Aids Service Center, 1966.

Xunzi: A Translation and Study of the Complete Works, 3 vols. Ed. and trans. John Knoblock. Stanford: Stanford University Press, 1988–1994.

Xunzi. The Works of Hsüntze. Ed. and trans. Homer H. Dubs. London: Probsthain, 1928.

Yan Zhitui. *Yanshi jiaxun jijie*. Shanghai: Guji chubanshe, 1980.

Yangzheng yigui. *See* Chen Hongmou.

Yanshi jiaxun jijie. *See* Yan Zhitui.

Yantie lun. SBCK ed.

Yijing. In Ruan Yuan, *Shisan jing zhushu*. Reprint. Taibei: Yiwen yinshu guan, 1955.

Yinzhi wen guangyi. Ed. Zhou Mengyan. Yangzhou cangjing yuan ed. 1881.

Yiquan wenji. *See* Shao Yong.

Yishu. *See* Er Cheng Yishu.

Yü, Chün-fang. "Ch'an Education in the Sung: Ideals and Procedures." In de Bary and Chaffee, *Neo-Confucian Education*, pp. 101–104.

Yuan [Guochao] wenlei. Comp. Su Tianjue. SKQS ed.

Yuan [Guozhao] mingchen shi lüe. 1335. Reprint. Beijing: Zhonghua Shuju, 1962.

Yuan Huang. *Liming pian*. 1607 Wanli ed. in the Naikaku Bunko, Tokyo.

Yuan shi. *See* Song Lian.

Yuansheng lun zhu. *See* Tan Luan.

Yuanwu Keqin. *Biyan lu*. TD 58, no. 2003.

Zhang Boxing, comp. *Zhengyitang quanshu*. *Baibu congshu jicheng* ed.

Zhang Zai. *Zhangzi quanshu*. SBBY ed.

Zhangzi quanshu. *See* Zhang Zai.

Zhen Dexiu. *Daxue yanyi*. Ming ed. 1556. National Central Library, Taibei.

———. *Xinjing*. Ming ed. National Central Library, Taibei.

———. *Xishan wenji*. GXJS ed. Taibei: Commercial Press, 1968.

Zhengyitang quanshu, comp. Zhang Boxing. *Baibu congshu jicheng* ed.

Zheng Qiao. *Tongzhi*. Shitong ed. Shanghai: Commercial Press, 1935–1936.

Zheng Shi. *Nü Xiaojing*. Guangxu period ed. Durant Library, University of California, Berkeley.

Zhengao. DZ 637–640, no. 1016.

Zhengyitang quanshu. *See* Zhang Boxing.

Zhiyi. *Fahua sanmei chanyi*. TD 46, no. 1941.

———. *Shichan boluomi cidi*. TD 46, no. 1916.

———. *Zalu*. ZZ 2:27.4. Trans. Chün-fang Yü, "Chung-feng Ming-pen and Ch'an Buddhism in the Yüan." In Chan and de Bary, *Yüan Thought*, pp. 459–460.

Zhongfeng Mingben. *Chanyuan qinggui*. ZZ 2:16.5.

Zhongguo shehui kexueyuan kaogu yanjiusuo. *Xiaotun nandi jiagu*. 2 vols. Shanghai: Zhonghua Shuju, 1980, 1983.

Zhongyong. *See* Mean.

Zhongyong zhangju. See Zhu Xi.

Zhou Dunyi. *Zhou Lianxi ji.* In Zhang Boxing, comp. *Zhengyi tang quanshu.* Baibu congshu jicheng ed.

Zhou Lianxiji. See Zhou Dunyi.

Zhouyi benyi. See Zhu Xi.

Zhouyi lüeli. In *Wang Biji jiaoshi.*

Zhu Xi. *Daxue zhangju.* In *Sishu jizhu, ZZMJ* ed.

———. *Huian Zhu wengong xiansheng wenji.* SKQS ed.

———. *Tongjian gangmu.* 1697. Reprint. Xiwuxuan, 1882.

———. *Zhongyong zhangju.* In *Sishu jizhu, Zhonguo zixue mingju jicheng* ed. Taibei, 1978.

———. *Zhouyi benyi.* 1177. Reprint. Taibei: Hualian, 1978.

———. *Zhuzi daquan (Zhuzi wenji).* SBBY ed.

———. *Zhuzi quanshu.* 1714 ed.

———. *Zhuzi wenji.* In *Zhuzi daquan,* SBBY ed.

———. *Zhuzi yulei.* Beijing: Zhonghua shuju, 1986.

———. *Zhuzi yulei.* Zhengzhong ed. Taibei, 1970.

Zhu Xi, ed. *Xiaoxue.* In bilingual Chinese/Japanese edition of Uno Seichi, ed. and trans., *Shōgaku.* Tokyo: Meiji shoin, 1965.

Zhuangzi. *Chuang Tzu: The Inner Chapters.* Ed. and trans. A. C. Graham. London: George Allen and Unwin, 1981. Excerpts reprinted here with the permission of the literary estate of A. C. Graham and of Dawn and Der Pao Graham.

Zhuangzi. *Chuang Tzu: Complete Writings.* Ed. and trans. Burton Watson. New York: Columbia University Press, 1963.

Zhuangzi. HYISIS, supplement no. 20

Zhuangzi. SBBY ed.

Zhuangzi. SBCK ed.

Zhuzi daquan. See Zhu Xi.

Zhuzi quanshu. See Zhu Xi.

Zhuzi wenji. See Zhu Xi.

Zhuzi yulei. See Zhu Xi.

Zizhi tongjian. See Sima Guang.

Zongze. *Chanyuan qinggui.* Trans. adapted from Bielefeldt, *Dōgen's Manuals of Zen Meditation,* pp. 175–187.

PINYIN TO WADE-GILES ROMANIZATION CHART

Pinyin	Wade-Giles	Pinyin	Wade-Giles	Pinyin	Wade-Giles	Pinyin	Wade-Giles
a	a	cou	ts'ou	gu	ku	kong	k'ung
ai	ai	cu	ts'u	gua	kua	kou	k'ou
an	an	cuan	ts'uan	guai	kuai	ku	k'u
ang	ang	cui	ts'ui	guan	kuan	kua	k'ua
ao	ao	cun	ts'un	guang	kuang	kuai	k'uai
		cuo	ts'o	gui	kuei	kuan	k'uan
				gun	kun	kuang	k'uang
ba	pa			guo	kuo	kui	k'uei
bai	pai	da	ta			kun	k'un
ban	pan	dai	tai			kuo	k'uo
bang	pang	dan	tan	ha	ha		
bao	pao	dang	tang	hai	hai		
bei	pei	dao	tao	han	han	la	la
ben	pen	de	te	hang	hang	lai	lai
beng	peng	deng	teng	hao	hao	lan	lan
bi	pi	di	ti	he	ho	lang	lang
bian	pien	dian	tien	hei	hei	lao	lao
biao	piao	diao	tiao	hen	hen	le	le
bie	pieh	die	tieh	heng	heng	lei	lei
bin	pin	ding	ting	hong	hung	leng	leng
bing	ping	diu	tiu	hou	hou	li	li
bo	po	dong	tung	hu	hu	lia	lia
bou	pou	dou	tou	hua	hua	lian	lien
bu	pu	du	tu	huai	huai	liang	liang
		duan	tuan	huan	huan	liao	liao
ca	ts'a	dui	tui	huang	huang	lie	lieh
cai	ts'ai	dun	tun	hui	hui	lin	lin
can	ts'an	duo	to	hun	hun	ling	ling
cang	ts'ang			huo	huo	liu	liu
cao	ts'ao	e	o			long	lung
ce	ts'e	en	en	ji	chi	lou	lou
cen	ts'en	er	erh	jia	chia	lu	lu
ceng	ts'eng			jian	chien	lü	lü
cha	ch'a	fa	fa	jiang	chiang	luan	luan
chai	ch'ai	fan	fan	jiao	chiao	lüan	lüan
chan	ch'an	fang	fang	jie	chieh	lüe	lüeh
chang	ch'ang	fei	fei	jin	chin	lun	lun
chao	ch'ao	fen	fen	jing	ching	luo	lo
che	ch'e	feng	feng	jiong	chiung		
chen	ch'en	fo	fo	jiu	chiu	ma	ma
cheng	ch'eng	fou	fou	ju	chü	mai	mai
chi	ch'ih	fu	fu	juan	chüan	man	man
chong	ch'ung			jue	chüeh	mang	mang
chou	ch'ou	ga	ka	jun	chün	mao	mao
chu	ch'u	gai	kai			mei	mei
chua	ch'ua	gan	kan	ka	k'a	men	men
chuai	ch'uai	gang	kang	kai	k'ai	meng	meng
chuan	ch'uan	gao	kao	kan	k'an	mi	mi
chuang	ch'uang	ge	ke	kang	k'ang	mian	mien
chui	ch'ui	gei	kei	kao	k'ao	miao	miao
chun	ch'un	gen	ken	ke	k'o	mie	mieh
chuo	ch'o	geng	keng	kei	k'ei	min	min
ci	tz'u	gong	kung	ken	k'en	ming	ming
cong	ts'ung	gou	kou	keng	k'eng	miu	miu

Pinyin to Wade-Giles Romanization Chart

Pinyin	Wade-Giles	Pinyin	Wade-Giles	Pinyin	Wade-Giles	Pinyin	Wade-Giles
mo	mo	qie	ch'ieh	song	sung	ya	ya
mou	mou	qin	ch'in	sou	sou	yai	yai
mu	mu	qing	ch'ing	su	su	yan	yen
		qiong	ch'iung	suan	suan	yang	yang
na	na	qiu	ch'iu	sui	sui	yao	yao
nai	nai	qu	ch'ü	sun	sun	ye	yeh
nan	nan	quan	ch'üan	suo	so	yi	i
nang	nang	que	ch'üeh			yin	yin
nao	nao	qun	ch'ün	ta	t'a	ying	ying
nei	nei			tai	t'ai	yong	yung
nen	nen	ran	jan	tan	t'an	you	yu
neng	neng	rang	jang	tang	t'ang	yu	yü
ni	ni	rao	jao	tao	t'ao	yuan	yüan
nian	nien	re	je	te	t'e	yue	yüeh
niang	niang	ren	jen	teng	t'eng	yun	yün
niao	niao	reng	jeng	ti	t'i		
nie	nieh	ri	jih	tian	t'ien	za	tsa
nin	nin	rong	jung	tiao	t'iao	zai	tsai
ning	ning	rou	jou	tie	t'ieh	zan	tsan
niu	niu	ru	ju	ting	t'ing	zang	tsang
nong	nung	ruan	juan	tong	t'ung	zao	tsao
nou	nou	rui	jui	tou	t'ou	ze	tse
nu	nu	run	jun	tu	t'u	zei	tsei
nü	nü	ruo	jo	tuan	t'uan	zen	tsen
nuan	nuan			tui	t'ui	zeng	tseng
nüe	nüeh	sa	sa	tun	t'un	zha	cha
nuo	no	sai	sai	tuo	t'o	zhai	chai
		san	san			zhan	chan
ou	ou	sang	sang	wa	wa	zhang	chang
		sao	sao	wai	wai	zhao	chao
pa	p'a	se	se	wan	wan	zhe	che
pai	p'ai	sen	sen	wang	wang	zhen	chen
pan	p'an	seng	seng	wei	wei	zheng	cheng
pang	p'ang	sha	sha	wen	wen	zhi	chih
pao	p'ao	shai	shai	weng	weng	zhong	chung
pei	p'ei	shan	shan	wo	wo	zhou	chou
pen	p'en	shang	shang	wu	wu	zhu	chu
peng	p'eng	shao	shao			zhua	chua
pi	p'i	she	she	xi	hsi	zhuai	chuai
pian	p'ien	shen	shen	xia	hsia	zhuan	chuan
piao	p'iao	sheng	sheng	xian	hsien	zhuang	chuang
pie	p'ieh	shi	shih	xiang	hsiang	zhui	chui
pin	p'in	shou	shou	xiao	hsiao	zhun	chun
ping	p'ing	shu	shu	xie	hsieh	zhuo	cho
po	p'o	shua	shua	xin	hsin	zi	tzu
pou	p'ou	shuai	shuai	xing	hsing	zong	tsung
pu	p'u	shuan	shuan	xiong	hsiung	zou	tsou
		shuang	shuang	xiu	hsiu	zu	tsu
qi	ch'i	shui	shui	xu	hsü	zuan	tsuan
qia	ch'ia	shun	shun	xuan	hsüan	zui	tsui
qian	ch'ien	shuo	shuo	xue	hsüeh	zun	tsun
qiang	ch'iang	si	ssu	xun	hsün	zuo	tso
qiao	ch'iao						

Source: From *People's Republic of China: Aministrative Atlas* (Washington, D.C.: Central Intelligence Agency, 1975), pp. 46–47.

INDEX

Translated selections from the Chinese sources are indicated by italic page numbers.

Huang Zongxi, 864, 919, 923

Huangdi neijing. See Inner Canon of the Yellow Emperor

Huangdi sijing. See Four Canons of the Yellow Emperor

Huangji jingshi shu. See Book of the Supreme Ultimate Ordering the World

Huangming zixun. See August Ming Ancestral Instruction

Huayan Buddhism. *See* Flower Garland school

Hui Shi, 99 n22, 100

Huineng, 494

Huiyuan, 477

Huisi, 444

Human desire (*renyu*). *See* Desires

Human mind and mind of the Way, 715, 764–765; Zhu Xi's Preface to the *Mean* on, 734; *Mean* and, 736; *Heart Classic* on, 760–761; Wang Yangming and, 842, 845; Luo Qinshun on, 877–879; Chen Jian on, 886, 887. *See also Classic of the Mind-and-Heart*; Wang Yangming; Zhen Dexiu

Human nature (*xing*): Mencius on, 129, 147, 148–150, 155, 158; *Xunzi* on, 179–183; Dong Zhongshu on, 302–305; *Mean* on, 334, 338, 731, 734; Zhang Zai on, 688; Cheng Hao and Cheng Yi on, 691–692, 693; Zhu Xi on, 704–707, 710–711, 721–722; Xu Heng on, 771, 774; Wang Yangming on, 846; Luo Qinshun on, 875. See also *Cheng Hao's Reply to Zhang Zai's Letter on the Stabilizing of Human Nature*; "Human Nature is Evil"; *Mencius*; *Primer on Human Nature and Principle*

"Human Nature is Evil" (*Xunzi*), 179–183: goodness and conscious activity in, 179, 180, 181; feelings and desires in, 179; ritual and rightness in, 180; teachers in, 180; Mencius and, 180–181; nature and conscious activity in, 180; human nature and emotions in, 181; common man, humaneness, and rightness in, 183

Humane government (*Mencius*), 119, 120–123, 139

Humane king (*Sūtra for Humane Kings*): state and Buddhism in, 477; definition of, 478; non-obstruction of all things and, 478; Buddhism as arm of the state and, 479; Buddhist esoteric teaching and, 479; Amoghavajra on, 479–480

Humaneness (*ren*): Confucius and, 43, 53, 55; filiality, fraternality and, in *Analects*, 45; being human and, in *Analects*, 48; devotion to, in *Analects*, 48–49; Confucius' disciples and, 49; Yan Hui and, 50; success and, in *Analects*, 50; mountains and, in *Analects*, 50; nearness of, in *Analects*, 52; ritual and, in *Analects*, 55; qualities of, in *Analects*, 55, 57, 61–62, 63; speech and, in *Analects*, 55; love and, in *Analects*, 56; Guan Zhong and, in *Analects*, 58; governance and, in *Analects*, 60; teachers and, in *Analects*, 60; *Laozi* on, 81, 84, 84–85, 87; *Zhuangzi* on, 110–111; profit and, in *Mencius*, 116–117; governance and, in *Mencius*, 119, 123, 130, 137, 138; working of, in *Mencius*, 121; "extending" of, in *Mencius*, 122; sprout of, in *Mencius*, 129; deviant teachings and, in *Mencius*, 136; nature of, in *Mencius*, 148; mind of pity and commiseration and, in *Mencius*, 149; mind as, in *Mencius*, 152; nobility of Heaven as, in *Mencius*, 153; inhumaneness and, in *Mencius*, 154; "ripeness" and, in *Mencius*, 154; reciprocity and, in *Mencius*, 156; affection and, in *Mencius*, 156; Xunzi on, 183; *Han Feizi* on, 200, 201; Dong Zhongshu on, 301, 305, 306–309; family and state and, in *Great Learning*, 332; *Mean* on, 337; Han Yu, 569–570; self-cultivation and, in Zhu Xi, 698; Zhu Xi on empathetic attention and, 711–713; unity with all things and, in Wang Gen, 859. *See also On Humaneness*; *On Understanding the Nature of Humanity*

Humaneness and rightness: *Zhuangzi* on,

110–111; *Mencius* on, 114–115; sage and, in *Xunzi*, 183; governance and, in Lu Jia, 289; Dong Zhongshu on, 307–308; Guo Xiang on, 389–390; Han Yu on, 572

"Hundred Schools of Thought," 64, 229, 724

Hundun (Primal Whole, "Chaos"): *Zhuangzi* on, 111; *"Explanation of the Diagram of the Supreme Polarity"* and, 673

Huoran guantong. *See* "Breakthrough to integral comprehension"

"Identification of meditation and intuitive wisdom" (Chan), 493

"Identification With the Superior" (Mozi), 68–69

Ignorance (Buddhism), 416

"Illuminating luminous virtue" (*Great Learning*), 330. *See also* "Manifesting luminous virtue"

Immortality, search for, 293, 392. *See also* *"Disquisition Regarding Immortality"*

Imperial College (Han), 294

In Defense of Five Major Policies (Wang Anshi), 619–621: Tangut "barbarians" in, 619; crop loans in, 619; service exemption in, 620; militia in, 620; marketing controls in, 621

"In the World of Men" (*Zhuangzi*): "fasting of the mind" in, 106; sense perception and knowledge in, 106; virtue of uselessness in, 107

Incest, Tang Code on, 552

Indra's Net (Dushun), 473

Indra's Net and the Tower of Vairocana (Fazang), 474

Innate knowing (*liangzhi*) (Wang Yangming): 845, 860; extension of knowledge and, 846; unity of principle and, 847; good and evil and, 850; Wang Ji and, 857, 858; Wang Gen and, 860, 863; Li Zhi and, 865, 867

Innate knowledge, Lu Jiuyuan on, 715. *See also* Innate knowing

Inner Canon of the Yellow Emperor (*Huangdi neijing*), 275–278. *See also* Medicine

"Inner sageliness, outer kingliness" (*neisheng, waiwang*) (Zhuangzi), 257, 263, 264

"Inquiring Words" (*Quanyan*)(*Huainanzi*), 271–273: techniques of the mind and rulership in, 271; foundations of governing in, 272

Institutional history: Du You on, 655–656; Ma Duanlin on, 664–666

"Instructions for Children" (Zhen Dexiu), 812

Instructions for Practical Living (*Chuanxilu*) (Wang Yangming), 842–843, 850-851, 852-853, 854–855

Instructions for the Inner Quarters (*Neixun*) (Empress Xu), 833–836: Empress Ma and, 831–832, 834; Neo-Confucian educational content of, 832–833; women and sagehood in, 833, 834; Korea, Japan and, 833; Moral Nature, 834–835; Cultivation of the Self, 835; Diligence and Hard Work, 835–836; Frugality, 836; Returning to the Good, 836; Looking Up to Virtuous Exemplars, 836. *See also* Education, women's

Intuitive wisdom (*prajñā*), 493. *See also* Identification of meditation and intuitive wisdom

Investigation of principle: human fulfillment and, in the Cheng brothers, 689–690

Investigation of things and extension of knowledge (*gewu zhizhi*): original text of *Great Learning* on, 331; enlarging the mind and, in Zhang Zai, 687–688; Cheng brothers on, 696–697; Zhu Xi's thought and, 698–699; Cheng-Zhu learning of principle and, 726–727; Zhu Xi's special note on, in *Great Learning*, 729; "breakthrough to integral comprehension" and, 729–730; Wang Yangming on, 846; unity of mind and principle and, in Wang

TRANSLATIONS FROM THE ASIAN CLASSICS

Reflections on Things at Hand: The Neo-Confucian Anthology, comp. Chu Hsi and Lü
  Tsu-ch'ien, tr. Wing-tsit Chan 1967
The Platform Sutra of the Sixth Patriarch, tr. Philip B. Yampolsky. Also in paperback ed.
  1967
Essays in Idleness: The Tsurezuregusa of Kenkō, tr. Donald Keene. Also in paperback ed.
  1967
The Pillow Book of Sei Shōnagon, tr. Ivan Morris, 2 vols. 1967
Two Plays of Ancient India: The Little Clay Cart and the Minister's Seal, tr. J. A. B. van
  Buitenen 1968
The Complete Works of Chuang Tzu, tr. Burton Watson 1968
The Romance of the Western Chamber (Hsi Hsiang chi), tr. S. I. Hsiung. Also in paperback
  ed. 1968
The Manyōshū, Nippon Gakujutsu Shinkōkai edition. Paperback ed. only. 1969
Records of the Historian: Chapters from the Shih chi of Ssu-ma Ch'ien, tr. Burton Watson.
  Paperback ed. only. 1969
Cold Mountain: 100 Poems by the T'ang Poet Han-shan, tr. Burton Watson. Also in
  paperback ed. 1970
Twenty Plays of the Nō Theatre, ed. Donald Keene. Also in paperback ed. 1970
Chūshingura: The Treasury of Loyal Retainers, tr. Donald Keene. Also in paperback ed.
  1971; rev. ed. 1997
The Zen Master Hakuin: Selected Writings, tr. Philip B. Yampolsky 1971
Chinese Rhyme-Prose: Poems in the Fu Form from the Han and Six Dynasties Periods, tr.
  Burton Watson. Also in paperback ed. 1971
Kūkai: Major Works, tr. Yoshito S. Hakeda. Also in paperback ed. 1972
The Old Man Who Does as He Pleases: Selections from the Poetry and Prose of Lu Yu,
  tr. Burton Watson 1973
The Lion's Roar of Queen Śrīmālā, tr. Alex and Hideko Wayman 1974
Courtier and Commoner in Ancient China: Selections from the History of the Former Han
  by Pan Ku, tr. Burton Watson. Also in paperback ed. 1974
Japanese Literature in Chinese, vol. 1: Poetry and Prose in Chinese by Japanese Writers
  of the Early Period, tr. Burton Watson 1975
Japanese Literature in Chinese, vol. 2: Poetry and Prose in Chinese by Japanese Writers
  of the Later Period, tr. Burton Watson 1976
Scripture of the Lotus Blossom of the Fine Dharma, tr. Leon Hurvitz. Also in paperback
  ed. 1976
Love Song of the Dark Lord: Jayadeva's Gītagovinda, tr. Barbara Stoler Miller. Also in
  paperback ed. Cloth ed. includes critical text of the Sanskrit. 1977; rev. ed. 1997
Ryōkan: Zen Monk-Poet of Japan, tr. Burton Watson 1977
Calming the Mind and Discerning the Real: From the Lam rim chen mo of Tson-kha-pa,
  tr. Alex Wayman 1978
The Hermit and the Love-Thief: Sanskrit Poems of Bhartrihari and Bilhaṇa, tr. Barbara
  Stoler Miller 1978
The Lute: Kao Ming's P'i-p'a chi, tr. Jean Mulligan. Also in paperback ed. 1980
A Chronicle of Gods and Sovereigns: Jinnō Shōtōki of Kitabatake Chikafusa, tr. H. Paul
  Varley 1980
Among the Flowers: The Hua-chien chi, tr. Lois Fusek 1982
Grass Hill: Poems and Prose by the Japanese Monk Gensei, tr. Burton Watson 1983

Doctors, Diviners, and Magicians of Ancient China: Biographies of Fang-shih, tr. Kenneth J. DeWoskin. Also in paperback ed. 1983

Theater of Memory: The Plays of Kālidāsa, ed. Barbara Stoler Miller. Also in paperback ed. 1984

The Columbia Book of Chinese Poetry: From Early Times to the Thirteenth Century, ed. and tr. Burton Watson. Also in paperback ed. 1984

Poems of Love and War: From the Eight Anthologies and the Ten Long Poems of Classical Tamil, tr. A. K. Ramanujan. Also in paperback ed. 1985

The Bhagavad Gita: Krishna's Counsel in Time of War, tr. Barbara Stoler Miller 1986

The Columbia Book of Later Chinese Poetry, ed. and tr. Jonathan Chaves. Also in paperback ed. 1986

The Tso Chuan: Selections from China's Oldest Narrative History, tr. Burton Watson 1989

Waiting for the Wind: Thirty-six Poets of Japan's Late Medieval Age, tr. Steven Carter 1989

Selected Writings of Nichiren, ed. Philip B. Yampolsky 1990

Saigyō, Poems of a Mountain Home, tr. Burton Watson 1990

The Book of Lieh Tzu: A Classic of the Tao, tr. A. C. Graham. Morningside ed. 1990

The Tale of an Anklet: An Epic of South India--The Cilappatikāram of Iḷaṇkō Aṭikaḷ, tr. R. Parthasarathy 1993

Waiting for the Dawn: A Plan for the Prince, tr. and introduction by Wm. Theodore de Bary 1993

Yoshitsune and the Thousand Cherry Trees: A Masterpiece of the Eighteenth-Century Japanese Puppet Theater, tr., annotated, and with introduction by Stanleigh H. Jones, Jr. 1993

The Lotus Sutra, tr. Burton Watson. Also in paperback ed. 1993

The Classic of Changes: A New Translation of the I Ching as Interpreted by Wang Bi, tr. Richard John Lynn 1994

Beyond Spring: Tz'u Poems of the Sung Dynasty, tr. Julie Landau 1994

The Columbia Anthology of Traditional Chinese Literature, ed. Victor H. Mair 1994

Scenes for Mandarins: The Elite Theater of the Ming, tr. Cyril Birch 1995

Letters of Nichiren, ed. Philip B. Yampolsky; tr. Burton Watson et al. 1996

Unforgotten Dreams: Poems by the Zen Monk Shōtetsu, tr. Steven D. Carter 1997

The Vimalakirti Sutra, tr. Burton Watson 1997

Japanese and Chinese Poems to Sing: The Wakan rōei shū, tr. J. Thomas Rimer and Jonathan Chaves 1997

A Tower for the Summer Heat, Li Yu, tr. Patrick Hanan 1998

The Classic of the Way and Virtue: A New Translation of the Tao-te ching of Laozi as Interpreted by Wang Bi, tr. Richard John Lynn 1999

The Four Hundred Songs of War and Wisdom: An Anthology of Poems from Classical Tamil, The Puṟanāṉūṟu, eds. and trans. George L. Hart and Hank Heifetz 1999

Original Tao: Inward Training (Nei-yeh) and the Foundations of Taoist Mysticism, Harold D. Roth 1999

MODERN ASIAN LITERATURE SERIES

Modern Japanese Drama: An Anthology, ed. and tr. Ted. Takaya. Also in paperback ed. 1979

Mask and Sword: Two Plays for the Contemporary Japanese Theater, by Yamazaki Masakazu, tr. J. Thomas Rimer 1980

Yokomitsu Riichi, Modernist, Dennis Keene 1980

Nepali Visions, Nepali Dreams: The Poetry of Laxmiprasad Devkota, tr. David Rubin 1980

Literature of the Hundred Flowers, vol. 1: *Criticism and Polemics*, ed. Hualing Nieh 1981

Literature of the Hundred Flowers, vol. 2: *Poetry and Fiction*, ed. Hualing Nieh 1981

Modern Chinese Stories and Novellas, 1919–1949, ed. Joseph S. M. Lau, C. T. Hsia, and Leo Ou-fan Lee. Also in paperback ed. 1984

A View by the Sea, by Yasuoka Shōtarō, tr. Kären Wigen Lewis 1984

Other Worlds: Arishima Takeo and the Bounds of Modern Japanese Fiction, by Paul Anderer 1984

Selected Poems of Sō Chŏngju, tr. with introduction by David R. McCann 1989

The Sting of Life: Four Contemporary Japanese Novelists, by Van C. Gessel 1989

Stories of Osaka Life, by Oda Sakunosuke, tr. Burton Watson 1990

The Bodhisattva, or Samantabhadra, by Ishikawa Jun, tr. with introduction by William Jefferson Tyler 1990

The Travels of Lao Ts'an, by Liu T'ieh-yün, tr. Harold Shadick. Morningside ed. 1990

Three Plays by Kōbō Abe, tr. with introduction by Donald Keene 1993

The Columbia Anthology of Modern Chinese Literature, ed. Joseph S. M. Lau and Howard Goldblatt 1995

Modern Japanese Tanka, ed. and tr. by Makoto Ueda 1996

Masaoka Shiki: Selected Poems, ed. and tr. by Burton Watson 1997

Writing Women in Modern China: An Anthology of Women's Literature from the Early Twentieth Century, ed. and tr. by Amy D. Dooling and Kristina M. Torgeson 1998

STUDIES IN ASIAN CULTURE

The Ōnin War: History of Its Origins and Background, with a Selective Translation of the Chronicle of Ōnin, by H. Paul Varley 1967

Chinese Government in Ming Times: Seven Studies, ed. Charles O. Hucker 1969

The Actors' Analects (Yakusha Rongo), ed. and tr. by Charles J. Dunn and Bungō Torigoe 1969

Self and Society in Ming Thought, by Wm. Theodore de Bary and the Conference on Ming Thought. Also in paperback ed. 1970

A History of Islamic Philosophy, by Majid Fakhry, 2d ed. 1983

Phantasies of a Love Thief: The Caurapañatcāśikā Attributed to Bilhaṇa, by Barbara Stoler Miller 1971

Iqbal: Poet-Philosopher of Pakistan, ed. Hafeez Malik 1971

The Golden Tradition: An Anthology of Urdu Poetry, ed. and tr. Ahmed Ali. Also in paperback ed. 1973

Conquerors and Confucians: Aspects of Political Change in Late Yüan China, by John W. Dardess 1973

The Unfolding of Neo-Confucianism, by Wm. Theodore de Bary and the Conference on Seventeenth-Century Chinese Thought. Also in paperback ed. 1975

To Acquire Wisdom: The Way of Wang Yang-ming, by Julia Ching 1976

Gods, Priests, and Warriors: The Bhṛgus of the Mahābhārata, by Robert P. Goldman 1977

Mei Yao-ch'en and the Development of Early Sung Poetry, by Jonathan Chaves 1976

The Legend of Semimaru, Blind Musician of Japan, by Susan Matisoff 1977

Sir Sayyid Ahmad Khan and Muslim Modernization in India and Pakistan, by Hafeez Malik 1980

The Khilafat Movement: Religious Symbolism and Political Mobilization in India, by Gail Minault 1982

The World of K'ung Shang-jen: A Man of Letters in Early Ch'ing China, by Richard Strassberg 1983

The Lotus Boat: The Origins of Chinese Tz'u Poetry in T'ang Popular Culture, by Marsha L. Wagner 1984

Expressions of Self in Chinese Literature, ed. Robert E. Hegel and Richard C. Hessney 1985

Songs for the Bride: Women's Voices and Wedding Rites of Rural India, by W. G. Archer; eds. Barbara Stoler Miller and Mildred Archer 1986

A Heritage of Kings: One Man's Monarchy in the Confucian World, by JaHyun Kim Haboush 1988

COMPANIONS TO ASIAN STUDIES

Approaches to the Oriental Classics, ed. Wm. Theodore de Bary 1959

Early Chinese Literature, by Burton Watson. Also in paperback ed. 1962

Approaches to Asian Civilizations, eds. Wm. Theodore de Bary and Ainslie T. Embree 1964

The Classic Chinese Novel: A Critical Introduction, by C. T. Hsia. Also in paperback ed. 1968

Chinese Lyricism: Shih Poetry from the Second to the Twelfth Century, tr. Burton Watson. Also in paperback ed. 1971

A Syllabus of Indian Civilization, by Leonard A. Gordon and Barbara Stoler Miller 1971

Twentieth-Century Chinese Stories, ed. C. T. Hsia and Joseph S. M. Lau. Also in paperback ed. 1971

A Syllabus of Chinese Civilization, by J. Mason Gentzler, 2d ed. 1972

A Syllabus of Japanese Civilization, by H. Paul Varley, 2d ed. 1972

An Introduction to Chinese Civilization, ed. John Meskill, with the assistance of J. Mason Gentzler 1973

An Introduction to Japanese Civilization, ed. Arthur E. Tiedemann 1974

Ukifune: Love in the Tale of Genji, ed. Andrew Pekarik 1982

The Pleasures of Japanese Literature, by Donald Keene 1988

A Guide to Oriental Classics, eds. Wm. Theodore de Bary and Ainslie T. Embree; 3d edition ed. Amy Vladeck Heinrich, 2 vols. 1989

INTRODUCTION TO ASIAN CIVILIZATIONS

Wm. Theodore de Bary, General Editor
Sources of Japanese Tradition, 1958; paperback ed., 2 vols., 1964
Sources of Indian Tradition, 1958; paperback ed., 2 vols., 1964; 2d ed., 2 vols., 1988
Sources of Chinese Tradition, 1960; paperback ed., 2 vols., 1964
Sources of Korean Tradition, ed. Peter H. Lee and Wm. Theodore de Bary; paperback ed., vol. 1, 1997

NEO-CONFUCIAN STUDIES

Instructions for Practical Living and Other Neo-Confucian Writings by Wang Yang-ming, tr. Wing-tsit Chan 1963
Reflections on Things at Hand: The Neo-Confucian Anthology, comp. Chu Hsi and Lü Tsu-ch'ien, tr. Wing-tsit Chan 1967
Self and Society in Ming Thought, by Wm. Theodore de Bary and the Conference on Ming Thought. Also in paperback ed. 1970
The Unfolding of Neo-Confucianism, by Wm. Theodore de Bary and the Conference on Seventeenth-Century Chinese Thought. Also in paperback ed. 1975
Principle and Practicality: Essays in Neo-Confucianism and Practical Learning, eds. Wm. Theodore de Bary and Irene Bloom. Also in paperback ed. 1979
The Syncretic Religion of Lin Chao-en, by Judith A. Berling 1980
The Renewal of Buddhism in China: Chu-hung and the Late Ming Synthesis, by Chün-fang Yü 1981
Neo-Confucian Orthodoxy and the Learning of the Mind-and-Heart, by Wm. Theodore de Bary 1981
Yüan Thought: Chinese Thought and Religion Under the Mongols, eds. Hok-lam Chan and Wm. Theodore de Bary 1982
The Liberal Tradition in China, by Wm. Theodore de Bary 1983
The Development and Decline of Chinese Cosmology, by John B. Henderson 1984
The Rise of Neo-Confucianism in Korea, by Wm. Theodore de Bary and JaHyun Kim Haboush 1985
Chiao Hung and the Restructuring of Neo-Confucianism in Late Ming, by Edward T. Ch'ien 1985
Neo-Confucian Terms Explained: Pei-hsi tzu-i, by Ch'en Ch'un, ed. and trans. Wing-tsit Chan 1986
Knowledge Painfully Acquired: K'un-chih chi, by Lo Ch'in-shun, ed. and trans. Irene Bloom 1987
To Become a Sage: The Ten Diagrams on Sage Learning, by Yi T'oegye, ed. and trans. Michael C. Kalton 1988
The Message of the Mind in Neo-Confucian Thought, by Wm. Theodore de Bary 1989